Bertolt Brecht

Baal grew up within the whiteness of the womb
With the sky already large and pale and calm
Naked, young, endlessly marvellous
And Baal loved it when he came to us.

Bertolt Brecht, 'Hymn of Baal the Great'

As the thinking man was overtaken by a great storm,
he was sitting in a big car and took up a lot of space.
The first thing he did was to get out of his car. The
second was to take off his jacket. The third was to
lie down on the ground. Thus reduced to his smallest
magnitude he withstood the storm.

Bertolt Brecht, *Stories of Herr Keuner*

Bertolt Brecht

A Literary Life

Stephen Parker

BLOOMSBURY

LONDON • NEW DELHI • NEW YORK • SYDNEY

Stephen Parker is Henry Simon Professor of German at the University of Manchester and was Leverhulme Research Fellow, 2009–12. His publications include *Sinn und Form: The Anatomy of a Literary Journal*, with Matthew Philpotts (2009), *The Modern Restoration: Re-thinking German Literature 1930–1960*, with Peter Davies and Matthew Philpotts (2004), and *Peter Huchel: A Literary Life in 20th-Century Germany* (1998). He contributed to *Brecht on Art and Politics* (2003).

Bloomsbury Methuen Drama

An imprint of Bloomsbury Publishing Plc

50 Bedford Square	1385 Broadway
London	New York
WC1B 3DP	NY 10018
UK	USA

www.bloomsbury.com

Bloomsbury is a registered trade mark of Bloomsbury Publishing Plc

First published 2014

© Stephen Parker, 2014

British Library Cataloguing-in-Publication Data
A catalogue record for this book is available from the British Library.

ISBN: HB: 978-1-4081-5562-2
ePub: 978-1-4081-5564-6
ePDF: 978-1-4081-5563-9

Library of Congress Cataloging-in-Publication Data
A catalog record for this book is available from the Library of Congress.

Typeset by Fakenham Prepress Solutions, Fakenham, Norfolk NR21 8NN
Printed and bound in India

Contents

Acknowledgements

The material base for a study of Bertolt Brecht's life and work, already remarkably rich, has been transformed since the end of the Cold War. Alongside the publication of the 30-volume *Berliner und Frankfurter Ausgabe*, Werner Hecht has compiled a vast chronicle of Brecht's life and Jan Knopf has edited a five-volume Brecht handbook, with authoritative contributions from a team of leading scholars. The biographies of the women with whom Brecht had long-term working and sexual relationships – principally Sabine Kebir on Helene Weigel, Elisabeth Hauptmann and Ruth Berlau, Hartmut Reiber on Margarete Steffin – have greatly enriched our understanding. Among other recent works, Erdmut Wizisla's account of Brecht's relationship with Walter Benjamin – made available in English by Nicholas Jacobs's Libris – and Jürgen Hillesheim's study of the young Brecht's aesthetics stand out, as do Ronald Speirs's essays in the *Brecht Yearbook* and John White's study of Brecht's dramatic theory. I have benefited greatly from this formidable body of scholarship and from the opportunity to read the manuscript of one of the latest additions to it, David Barnett's history of the Berliner Ensemble. David has kindly allowed me to cite archival material not yet in the public sphere

The two archives in Germany dedicated to Brecht's life and work, the Bertolt Brecht Archive in Berlin and the Bertolt Brecht Research Centre in Augsburg, have been indispensable. At the latter, I have enjoyed the support and advice of Helmut Gier and Jürgen Hillesheim, at the former of Erdmut Wizisla and his staff, particularly Dorothee Aders, Iliane Thiemann, Anett Schubotz and Helgrid Streidt. I have also drawn upon archival material from the following: Akademie der Künste, Berlin; Bundesarchiv, Berlin; and Deutsches Literaturarchiv, Marbach am Neckar. I should like to thank the staff from these institutions for their help.

Brecht in English has long been synonymous with Bloomsbury's extensive list in its Methuen Drama imprint, which was developed with great energy and scholarly innovation over many years under the founding general editor, John Willett. I am delighted that, thanks to the present general editor Tom Kuhn and Bloomsbury's Senior Commissioning Editor Mark Dudgeon, this first English-language biography of Brecht in two decades is appearing with Methuen Drama. I have, of course, used Methuen's translations whenever possible. Where translations are not available, I have used my own except for Sabine Berendse and Paul Clements's excellent, forthcoming translation of the conversations which Sabine's father Hans Bunge conducted with Brecht's friend Hanns Eisler. Mark Dudgeon has been a superb editor, mediating relations with the Brecht Estate and providing judicious advice at all stages in the project's development. I have been extremely fortunate, too, with my principal readers, Henry Phillips, Ronald Speirs, Peter Thomson and Tom Kuhn. Their enormous acumen and experience relating not only to Brecht but to literary and theatre studies in general have not only added a great deal of specialist knowledge but have helped me to navigate some difficult terrain. I am hugely indebted to Henry, Ron, Peter and Tom. This is not an official biography. However, I should like to thank Brecht's daughter, Barbara Brecht-Schall, for reading the manuscript, giving advice and, together with the Suhrkamp Verlag, granting permission for the use of quotations. Others have kindly commented on drafts: David Barnett, Sabine Berendse, Steve Giles, Matthew Philpotts, my son Fred and my daughter Cara, who has also supplied the index and helped in the selection of photographs, Nick Foulds, Steve Hall, Geoff Carter and, from the perspective of a medical practitioner, Dave Gilbert. Wolfgang Frühwald, Martin Durrell, Ritchie Robertson, Ian Kershaw, Hans Ulrich Gumbrecht and John White gave strong support and encouragement at the outset. A particular delight was seeing Brecht's house of exile in Svendborg, Denmark, beautifully restored by the town council, which one of its trustees, Joergen Lehrmann Madsen, kindly showed me round.

The Brecht Archive kindly supplied photographs. I should like to thank the following rights holders for granting permission to use photographs: ullstein bild – Zander & Labisch for photograph 10; Chris Drinkwater for 11; the Brecht Archive for 1–9, 12–17, 20, 22, 24 and 25; Hilda Hoffmann for 18, 19 and 21; and, Suhrkamp Verlag for 23 and 26. Quotations are reprinted by permission of the publisher from Walter Benjamin, *Selected Writings*, Cambridge, Mass: The Belknap Press of Harvard University Press, Copyright 1999 and 2002 by the President and Fellows of Harvard College, as follows: volume 2, 1927–34, translated by Rodney Livingstone, and Others, edited by Michael W. Jennings, Howard Eiland and Gary Smith, pp. 784–6 and p. 789; and, volume 3, 1935–8, translated by Edmund Jepcott, Howard Eiland, and Others, edited by Howard Eiland and Michael W. Jennings, p. 337.

This study could not have been written without the Major Research Fellowship which the Leverhulme Trust awarded me in 2009–12. I should like to thank Leverhulme for its generous support and the University of Manchester for enabling me to complete the work without interruption by drawing on accumulated study leave. Maj-Britt and Victor, Cara and Fred, have had the pleasure of listening to my ideas as they have developed. This book is dedicated to my mother, Mary, and my late father, Bob.

Stephen Parker, Manchester
June 2013

Introduction

The cataclysmic events which twice engulfed Europe and much of the planet in war and mass suffering during the dark times of the early to mid-twentieth century still cast an ominous shadow upon our world. Meanwhile, in the theatres of war the killing goes on. That would not have surprised the subject of this study, Bertolt Brecht (1898–1956), a trenchant opponent of war, whose play *Mother Courage and her Children* (1939) presents the deeply contradictory motivations informing human behaviour at the fault line of barbarism and civilisation. That great work has its place within a vast body of writing, principally drama and poetry, which reveals a rare artistic sensibility, capable of assimilating the most shockingly gross human actions and of presenting them with cool, analytical precision. Writing to his son Stefan during US exile from Nazi Germany, Brecht reflected that the First World War had been the seminal experience for his generation, demanding the adoption of an 'INSENSITIVITY (indestructibility, resilience) which greatly pre-occupied us when we were young'.[1] Brecht explained that he and his friends had

> treated the subject of insensitivity, coming out of a great war, quite personally. How could one become insensitive? The difficulty, not immediately apparent, was that society, awakening in us the wish to be insensitive, simultaneously made productivity (not only in the artistic sphere) dependent on sensitivity, i.e. the productive person had to pay the price of vulnerability.

Out of that predicament shared with a generation damaged by war, in the 1920s Brecht created works notorious for their aggressive, amoral cynicism which have come to define our image of the young Brecht. Surprisingly for an artist of such iconic standing, the sensitivity and vulnerability which Brecht and his friends felt compelled to cover with a skein of insensitivity have received much less attention. Brecht's own evolving attitude towards the self, which assumed ever more self-effacing, impersonal forms, obscured the issue, as did the ideological prism through which critics generally viewed Brecht following his espousal of Marxism amidst the contested belief systems of the twentieth century. As a result, our understanding of Brecht as the artist which beyond all things he supremely was has remained strikingly impoverished.

The life story was a favourite Brechtian mode of dramatic enquiry. Conceived in that spirit, this study aims to achieve a fresh understanding of Brecht's life and work by considering the ramifications of his letter to his son, exploring an artistic sensibility simultaneously sensitive and inured to sensitivity. That paradox is of a piece with the complexity, idiosyncrasy and sheer contrariness which critics have generally recognised in Brecht. As a young man he coined for himself the term 'melancholeric', capturing a play of extremes between Saturnine brooding and exuberant excess.[2] Similarly, his friend Caspar Neher drew him as Hydratopyranthropos, The Water-Fire-Man, who embodied the most contradictory elements possible. In his work, Brecht aspired to parabolic clarity, only to undercut it with ironic inversion and sarcastic provocation. Asceticism and hedonism were co-present, as were arrant recklessness and the obsessive control of feelings. Peter Thomson remarks that Brecht was a man who 'combined timorousness and combativeness as few people have'.[3] Untangling the mass of contradictions is a task suited to literary biography, a mode of enquiry alternating between empathy for its subject and critical distance. Max Frisch adumbrates the direction which this study must then take: 'Only in a poem, that is to say under artistic control, was there permitted what Brecht otherwise isolated through humour and gesture: feelings'.[4]

Thanks to an extraordinarily rich material base, not least Brecht's own early writings and the memoirs of contemporaries, we can probe his beginnings in the Bavaria of the Wilhelmine Empire. Part One of the study, Lyrical Awakening, explores the sensibility of the young Brecht before the cataclysm of August 1914. A picture emerges of a sickly, hypersensitive child, isolated from his peer group and pre-occupied by illness and poetry, through which he quickly learned to give shape to confused feelings in quite particular ways. Initially, writing was a refuge but in adolescence it became a means of asserting himself, as through poetry and song he transformed his idiosyncratic talent into magnetic attraction. Against the backcloth of war, Brecht and his friends created a youthful counter-culture of extraordinary artistic vitality, producing remarkable incarnations of instinct and pleasure in the manner of their heroes, Frank Wedekind and Nietzsche's Zarathustra.

The songwriter and dramatist Wedekind was Brecht's idol in his quest for dramatic greatness, which is charted in Part Two, Dramatic Iconoclast. Brecht's emblematic creation of the late 1910s is the monstrous hedonist Baal, a glorious riposte to the suffocating pressures of school and war. Brecht's eponymous lyrical drama would resist his every effort to reduce the 'gloriously hulking body' of Baal's earthy, biophysical materialism to a manageable artistic form.[5] When it was finally staged, it split the audience between adulation and revulsion, heralding the tumultuous scenes which invariably surrounded Brecht productions. At odds with a society emerging from war morally and financially bankrupt, in the years until the mid–1920s Brecht created powerful, lyrical dramas about the intense struggle for survival, while he pursued the amazingly chaotic tangle of his own relationships.

Why Brecht then shifted his artistic position so radically and what the underlying continuities in his behaviour were are cardinal questions in Brecht scholarship, which this study will attempt to answer. As the 1920s progressed, Brecht expounded his dramatic practice in ever more distinctive terms as Epic Theatre, demanding that the audience's intellectual response to events override emotional reactions and adopting patterns of thought and behaviour more readily associated with the biography of an intellectual. In the cerebral, sceptical and self-effacing revolutionary Herr Keuner, Brecht created the model of the intellectual he might be, whose task it was to teach hedonists like Baal how to channel their energies to socially useful ends. The Baal-Keuner opposition symbolises the quarrel which Brecht conducted with himself for the rest of his life, as he struggled to correct the creature of instinct. However, whatever method of annihilation was chosen, the earth-bound hedonist could never be eradicated.

As Part Three, Marxist Heretic, shows, when Brecht espoused Marxism-Leninism at the end of the 1920s in the struggle against rising Fascism, his biophysical materialism remained a potent force, colouring his dramatic and poetic precepts and intuitions. As Steve Giles has indicated, this set him at odds with proponents of a Communist orthodoxy focused irreducibly upon socio-economic laws and upon developing a commensurate theory of literature.[6] The early years of Brecht's exile from Nazi Germany in Denmark, when the Moscow show trials grossly undermined his commitment to the anti-Fascist Popular Front, entailed an extreme test of the stateless émigré's resilience and resourcefulness, hitherto poorly understood, as Brecht's Muscovite allies moved against the great contrarian. In 1938 Brecht represented his predicament covertly in *Life of Galileo*, his most personal work since *Baal* and crucial to our understanding of Brecht's struggle with a reactionary Soviet Union under Stalin. Brecht found himself forced to abandon an unsustainable Leninism and to adopt a survivalist strategy drawn from Taoist thought. In the magnificently drawn Galileo Galilei, who embodies reason and appetite, Brecht charts the psychological disintegration of the hugely ambitious, relentlessly innovative intellectual, whose pleasure in expanding the horizons of knowledge cannot be tolerated in a reactionary age.

Galileo pays the price for survival, like Brecht's other dramatic creations from those dark times, which are discussed in Part Four, Chastened Survivor. Forced to take refuge in the USA from a Europe brutalised by Fascist expansionism, Brecht then endured singularly meagre years in his art. With the defeat of Fascism, Brecht returned to a continent ravaged by war and genocide, armed with his great body of work from the exile years, simultaneously a warning against Fascism and an exhortation to usher in a new age of humane values. An ailing Brecht regarded his new theatre as a forum for the discussion of what society might look like in that new age and found a place to conduct his experiment with the Berliner Ensemble in East Berlin. That will be the setting for the momentous struggles of the Contentious Master in Part Five with opponents from both the East and the West of a divided Germany. The renewed efforts of orthodox Communists to correct the heretic culminated in hugely pressured and protracted exchanges around the uprising of 17 June 1953, from which Brecht, quite improbably, emerged victorious, a little like a traditional hero. In his final years Brecht had the pleasure of seeing his life's work heralded as the theatre of the future, initiating the Brechtian transformation of world theatre. In the decades following his death, Brecht's stellar reputation was assured, not only in the theatre but also in the poetic sphere. He remains today an iconic artist, one of the world's most frequently performed dramatists, whose literary life offers us an extraordinary story.

Prelude

Eugen Brecht* Goes out to Play

The children from the streets around Augsburg's Bleichstrasse had a strange playmate for their games of Cowboys and Indians.[1] It was not just that the delicate, impeccably spoken Eugen Brecht was a weakling and a bag of nerves. What was really unsettling about this oddball was that his head wouldn't stop shaking and he pulled scary faces.[2] And he wouldn't play like the others: he always had to be the Chief. But he would calm down when he began to recite his Wild West stories, Karl May's tales about Old Shatterhand and Winnetou.† He knew them off by heart. Then he'd hand out his scrawlings and tell everybody to act out their parts, or else they had to listen while he read out his rhymes and asked if they liked them.

Some of the children – Karolina Dietz was one – were amazed at what he could come out with. One day little Anton Niederhofer was blubbing away because he'd filled his pants. In a flash, Eugen called out: 'Anthony of Padua shits merrily over the wada rah'! It was nonsense, it was cruel, and it was fun. Eugen knew from church that poor Anton calling for help with his pants full sort of reminded you of calling for St Anthony's help when you'd lost something.‡ Anton certainly had lost something. But some of the other children, mainly boys like Georg Eberle, were less than impressed with Eugen: 'He always wanted to be the boss and order you about'. They just wanted to have fun, not be some weirdo's play-thing. So they had their fun: 'We often beat him'.

One day, the tribe from Klauckestrasse – some of the children were so poor they had no shoes – captured this rich boy's brightly coloured wigwam. It was a real wigwam, a present from his family in the USA. The Chief fetched his father, Papyrus,§ who marched straight into the enemy camp and re-captured the booty. Protected by Papyrus, the Chief let fly a torrent of abuse at his tormentors. You'd never heard the likes of it. But the following evening, when the Chief was fetching Papyrus's beer from the pub, the tribe from Klauckestrasse gave him a real beating.

---

* Brecht was christened Eugen Berthold Friedrich Brecht and was called Eugen until 1916, from which point he insisted on being called Bert and, from 1922, Bertolt.
† Generations of readers have enjoyed Karl May's (1842–1912) tales of adventure in the Wild West. In German alone, sales of his books have reached some 100 million, with translations in thirty-three languages.
‡ Eugen, a member of the congregation at the Protestant Barefoot Church – originally a foundation of Barefoot, that is to say, Franciscan monks – had picked up that the Franciscan Anthony of Padua was the saint to be invoked when things got lost.
§ The Brecht boys called their father, Berthold, Papyrus because he worked at the Haindl paper mill.

Part One

Lyrical Awakening

The Brechts 1898–1903

A mother's bond with her first-born son

From the day he was born on the 10 February 1898 Eugen Berthold Friedrich Brecht was Sophie Brecht's *Sorgenkind*, her problem child. Sophie saw so much of herself in Eugen, she nearly smothered him with her love. She always said that if one of them caught something, the other one was bound to get it. It was that sort of bond. She tried to teach him that keeping clean helped you not catch things in the first place, but that was always a hopeless struggle. Sophie's husband Berthold had nothing but scorn and contempt for illness. That's how Walter Brecht – Sophie and Berthold's younger son – remembered his father: 'Because he opposed illness as something alien and hostile he was hard with himself. He never complained'.[1] Woe betide anyone who did.

As the mistress of the Brecht household, Sophie was an elegant lady, but all along she had been a sickly, dreamy soul.[2] When she was young they had called her a melancholic but no one really understood her complaints. It would be much the same with Eugen. In 1919, a year before her death aged just forty-nine, he would write that she had been thirty years in the dying. And he knew all along that he would have a short life. She always told him that if they placed their faith in God, He would protect them. Sophie lived her faith in that deeply felt, unostentatious way that was typical of Württemberg's Protestant rural poor, surrounded by an alien Catholic world. Her mother Friederike Brezing had taught her children all manner of biblical stories and songs to keep the ravages of the world at bay. So Sophie sang songs and recited stories to her Genele, little Eugen, at the dingy flat they rented, Auf dem Rain 7, at the bottom of the hill between two of the Lech canals in Augsburg's old town.

In the workshop downstairs the tool grinder was on the go all day: it was bedlam. Sophie tried to rise above the din by singing her favourite hymn, Julie von Hausmann's celebration of Psalm 73.23–4 with its comforting message that poor, weak souls like Sophie and Genele would be delivered to the Father:

O take my hand, dear Father, and lead Thou me,
Till at my journey's ending I dwell with Thee.
Alone I cannot wander one single day,
So do Thou guide my footsteps on life's rough way.

It was not long before they moved to a quieter flat nearby at Bei den sieben Kindeln 1.

Sophie filled her child's ears with her stories from the Bible and with the songs and poems that she loved. She had a beautiful, illustrated edition of the works of the Austrian Romantic Nikolaus Lenau, which her brother Eugen had given her. With its cult of *Weltschmerz*, Lenau's poetry captured her sadness about the sufferings of this life. Sophie had a notebook in which she recorded such thoughts. She copied down the words of another Romantic, Jean Paul: 'If you've felt pain just once, you can understand the suffering of all others'.[3] Suffering, melancholy and love were what moved her; and her faith sustained her. Everyone thought that her interest in literature and the arts, even philosophy, made her a very cultivated lady, perfect to bring up her needy child.

Sophie had an album with her favourite verses in it and she wrote down poems in her notebook too:

If you love, can you forget?
If you forget, have you loved?
Well, love means 'do not forget' –
And forgetting: You have never loved![4]

She had known a number of young men in the towns where she'd lived before she got married, Cannstadt and Esslingen, then Augsburg. She always looked the part, well turned out thanks to her training as a seamstress when she had learnt to knit and to use a sewing machine. Unschooled and sentimental in her taste, Sophie dreamt the same dreams as countless young women. She was inspired to write verses like

The springtime of the year
Blossoms once in May –
Only once in life does love ...
True love is from the heart

True love burns hot.
O how good for those
Who don't know love!!!![5]

She noted down the names and addresses of her beaux. There was a Frank, another one was Wilhelm Klinger from Esslingen. She was quite taken by a Hermann, maybe the same Hermann her sister Amalia married.

A mixed marriage

Amalia Brezing found her beau in the handsome Hermann Reitter, an engineer at the Haindl paper mill in Augsburg. When Sophie moved to the city in 1893 she lived with Hermann and Amalia for a while. Her future husband Berthold Brecht was also a newcomer. Born two years before her in 1869, he had a similar provincial Alemannic background. Sophie and Berthold were among the millions who joined the mass migration from the countryside to the rapidly expanding cities, the powerhouses of Germany's burgeoning economic and industrial might. In his theatrical revolution of the 1920s, their son would proclaim that the migration heralded the dawn of a new urban age, dominated by ruthless entrepreneurs who wielded huge power over their workers through the manipulation of awesome technological and financial instruments.

Berthold had come to Augsburg from a sales job in Stuttgart but his family was from Achern, one of those pretty little Catholic towns in the Black Forest where his father Stephan had a lithography workshop. Berthold understood that whatever traditional craftsmen like his father had to offer, in the new mass market sales were essential to the paper and print industry. At the Haindl paper mill he started at the bottom as a sales assistant. He and Hermann Reitter became friends, and Hermann invited Berthold to his house to meet his wife and her sister, Sophie. Berthold and Sophie married in 1897. Eugen arrived promptly nine months later.

Sophie was awe-struck by her first-born, who rapidly evolved into an extravagantly gifted child. Walter would put it like this: 'What through her had come into the world and grown before her eyes seemed to be a miracle – an intimately close being, who would, however, quite unexpectedly move away from her'.[6] As a small child, Eugen imbibed her popular romantic sentimentality. But from adolescence – by now calling himself Bert Brecht – he would delight in confounding that taste with a cult of cold amorality which scandalised his mother and the many people who thought like her. Famously, in his poem 'Of poor B.B.' Brecht coupled the coldness of his being with the Alemannic countryside out of which his mother had borne him:

I, Bertolt Brecht, came out of the black forests.
My mother carried me into the cities as I lay
Inside her body. And the coldness of the forests
Will be inside me till my dying day.[7]

The bond between mother and son was broken for the first time in the summer of 1900 when Eugen was sent to breathe Württemberg's Protestant air out in the sticks at Pfullingen with Sophie's parents, Josef and Friederike Brezing. Sophie was expecting her second child. Station master Josef Brezing was an old curmudgeon but Grandma Brezing knew how to calm the anxious Eugen with her stories and songs. Then the boy's father Berthold sent his Genele a postcard, telling him that a nice little brother had just arrived.[8] Eugen would never be so sure about Walter. But from then on, everybody, family and friends, old and new, had to send Eugen cards wherever they went.

For a small boy, Eugen Brecht accumulated rather a lot of postcards. The cards he sent have not survived but it is clear from those surviving cards which he received that he was quite soon firing off a good number of his own, engaging his first circle of correspondents. When Eugen went to stay with his grandparents in Achern, his mother, her parents and Hans Eberle, a neighbour from Bleichstrasse, regularly sent him cards. Back in Augsburg, he shared New Year's greetings with his Achern friends Luisa and Karl and with his American cousins the Wurzlers from Brooklyn. Berthold Brecht sent his boys cards from his business trips, sometimes from nearby places like Reutlingen, Karlsruhe and Strasbourg, more often from places further afield like Berlin, Hamburg, Zwickau and Düsseldorf. Eugen began to correspond with some of his mother's female friends from Cannstadt days. Franziska Nallerer was one. She sent him a card from Stuttgart in April 1906 and at New Year she thanked him for his nice letter.[9] They were still exchanging cards in 1910. The boy's collection of picture postcards can be viewed today at the Bertolt Brecht Archive in Berlin.

Sophie and Berthold Brecht's horizons were very different from those of their country-living parents as they established themselves with their family in Augsburg. Augsburg was one of Germany's oldest and grandest cities, which owed its foundation to the Romans. For centuries it enjoyed the status of a free imperial city with its own municipal law. Augsburg achieved world renown around 1600 as the seat of the Fuggers, Europe's greatest bankers, the financiers of popes and emperors. The city's magnificent architecture, statues and many public monuments are from that opulent age: the cathedral in the north; the Perlach Tower and the town hall in the centre; and St Ulrich's Minster to the south. The Holy Roman emperors made Augsburg a seat of the Reichstag. During the reign of Maximilian I and Charles V two Reichstag decrees guaranteed Augsburg's prominent place in history: in 1530 the Augsburg Confession laid the foundation for the Articles of Faith of the Lutheran Church; and in 1555 the Religious Peace brought the Lutheran Church official recognition. These decrees, which cemented the new age of Protestantism, promoted an atmosphere of religious tolerance in a city – at that time Germany's largest – which was predominantly Catholic but had a large Protestant minority. However, the Thirty Years' War between the two faiths devastated Augsburg, as it did much of continental Europe. A population of some 45,000 in 1630 had shrunk by the end of the war in 1648 to just 16,000. The city would never regain its former glory. In Napoleon's reforms of the early nineteenth century it was incorporated into Bavaria, losing its status as a free imperial city. Despite the transformative power of new money in the boom decades following German unification in 1870–1 when Augsburg became an important industrial centre, military and higher civil service values continued to hold sway in this socially conservative South German city.

Once the young family was together in September 1900 in their new flat at Bleichstrasse 2 in the unfashionable Klaucke neighbourhood close to the workers from the Haindl mill, Berthold engaged servants – first Fanny, in 1906 Afra Unverdorben and in October 1908 Marie Miller – to help Sophie look after the boys and the household. Never robust at the best of times, Sophie had been left struggling with illness after Walter's birth and often had to stay in bed. The proud mistress of the Brecht household began her steady decline, which ended with cancer. In her family's eyes, from now on her life was a single, excruciatingly drawn-out act of self-renunciation. Over the next twenty years she gave what was left to her children – while the distance between her and her husband grew.

However, Sophie re-built her Protestant world in Augsburg. Her parents moved to the city to be close to their two daughters, creating an extended family of Brezings, Reitters and Brechts. Like the Brechts, the Reitters had two boys, Fritz and Richard. Grandma Brezing had the boys eating out of her hand with her stories from the Bible. They sat open-mouthed as she spun her brilliant tales while she knitted, infusing her words with life. If it had been raining for a number of days, she reminded them that during the Flood it had not stopped: was it ever going to stop this time? Enthralled, the boys would bombard her with questions and she would reply with the moral of the story.

In his memoir of his early life in Augsburg with his elder brother, Walter Brecht cannot, despite his best efforts, conceal the fault lines in his parents' relationship. Walter describes his beloved, long-suffering mother as the central figure in the household. An excellent cook, she strongly supported her boys in their schooling and their Protestant upbringing. Walter was at a loss to understand his father's attitude towards his mother. While he felt that his father must surely love her, there was no evidence of that whatsoever and, for no apparent reason, his father would fly into a rage with her or the boys. Tenderness was quite alien to Berthold Brecht. In marked contrast to Walter, by adolescence Eugen viewed things with the uncompromising starkness which would become familiar from his scathing satires of domestic life. He told a friend: 'My mother's an intruder. She's the rebellious Protestant in the family'.[10] She was, as Brecht's cousin Fanny put it, a strong-willed woman.[11] Less plausibly, Fanny Brecht also described the Brechts' marriage as a good one. Sophie Brecht's relationship with her husband became a bleak, unloving struggle to her death.

A female's assertion of religious difference within a family was, indeed, in the eyes of many tantamount to rebellion. In 1897 Sophie had insisted on marrying Berthold in a Protestant service and then on having her two boys baptised at the Protestant Barefoot Church, bringing them up within the strong Protestant community of the Barefooters, a world quite separate from the one that her businessman husband – in fact the lone Catholic in the nuclear family – inhabited. Berthold Brecht, of course, demanded respect for his authority as the head of the household in that patriarchal South German society. In 1902, he acquired the right of residence in Augsburg and in 1911 the rights of a Bürger, with them the right to vote. Berthold Brecht was hugely impressive to anyone who met him: sharp and nimble, he was completely on top of his business and was the life and soul of any party, quite without airs and graces. Having started at the bottom, Berthold ended right at the top as the boss of the mighty Haindl paper mill. Paper production and printing books were its business. For his boys, he was Papyrus.

During Berthold Brecht's time the Haindl mill became the biggest and best in Europe, employing 300 workers. It's still up there today, part of a Finnish-led, multi-national corporation. Berthold was a Catholic in a Catholic family business whose mixed marriage did not block his steep rise. His professional skills, together with his shrewdness, energy and gregarious, winning manner, were huge assets to Haindl, not to mention the ruthless aggression which he could on occasion deploy. He took responsibility for administering the four houses that belonged to the Haindls on Bleichstrasse in return for the free use of the large, first-floor flat at number two with its two attic spaces. With his appointment to the senior management position of Prokurist in 1901, he was empowered to set up and sign off deals for raw materials and markets on the company's behalf. He lived the life of the successful, industrious businessman, working long hours at the office and taking frequent business trips as far afield as Paris and Hamburg. And Berthold Brecht knew how to make his money grow: by 1906 he had accumulated enough to invest 15,000 marks in the re-construction of

Augsburg's Mühlberger print works.[12] He reached the pinnacle of his career when he was appointed managing director of Haindl in 1917.

Berthold shared with many compatriots the new nationalist pride cultivated in the Wilhelmine Empire, in which Prussia was pre-eminent. In January 1871 Germany's aristocratic elite had celebrated German unification with much ostentation in Versailles's Hall of Mirrors, Bismarck and his followers rubbing in the defeat of France in 1870 in the Franco-Prussian War. The business-oriented German middle classes generally believed that they could reconcile their patriotism with a progressive liberalism. In truth, they did not remotely understand what they were letting themselves in for. After the blustering Kaiser Wilhelm II acceded to the throne in 1890, their support for his imperialist ambitions and brinkmanship would become ever more strident, drowning out residues of liberalism, while Germany established itself as a major power at breakneck speed. But what a price there was to pay. The whole enterprise would be exposed as folly in the extreme when in 1918 Kaiser Wilhelm's House of Hohenzollern collapsed amidst the bitter recriminations following defeat in the First World War. Germany was *de facto* bankrupt and politically rudderless. Like so many patriotic Germans, Berthold Brecht saw his world fall apart. The punitive settlement in the Treaty of Versailles – an act of revenge for the humiliation of France in 1870–1 – compounded the misery. It ascribed sole responsibility for the war to Germany, reduced German sovereign territory, required huge reparations and stripped Germany of its colonies, making a mockery of Wilhelm's boast of a German 'place in the sun'. An abject Germany was embarked on a path which led to the cataclysm of Hitler's Third Reich. However, unlike many compatriots, Berthold Brecht was neither a petty bourgeois nor a reactionary. While he had nothing but scorn for the Spartacus revolutions in Berlin, Munich – and Augsburg – in 1918–19, he would not join in the call for the extreme Right to take power, nor would he do so in 1933.

For Berthold Brecht, family life was less straightforward than business or even arguably politics. His social liberalism generally counted as one of his strengths but when conversation with his friends, gathered around their Stammtisch at Café Kernstock, turned to religion he would mutter darkly: 'Everyone can take that as they will'.[13] His sombre mood spoke volumes. Things had not worked out. Why did Sophie never stay with Berthold's parents on the few occasions when she visited his family in Achern? For Walter, his grandma Karoline Brecht understood that a lady like Sophie would need to stay not in the modest Brecht household but in a fine residence like Wilhelmshöhe just outside Achern. But Sophie Brecht was no princess: she was railwayman Brezing's daughter. Berthold Brecht no doubt formed his own views. Maybe he should have thought that bit harder when he met those other Brezings. Amalia was hardly the sharpest, not to mention Sophie's brother Eugen. Eugen Brezing was a wastrel who had married a wastrel, alcoholics both of them.[14] Yet Berthold Brecht had agreed to give his first-born that man's name. It was said in the family that Eugen Brezing displayed a propensity to epilepsy.[15] His son Max Hermann was not only born an epileptic with his mind impaired but was an orphan by the age of six who, from May 1908, had to be cared for by Amalia.[16]

Berthold Brecht's anger sometimes got the better of him. His children heard him shouting at their mother that the reason for her abysmal health was crystal-clear:

the Brezings were so stingy that they hadn't even given their children decent food.[17] It was true that a railwayman didn't make much money, and Josef Brezing owned nothing. But Josef and Friederike Brezing had that typical Protestant attitude: you're never doing better than when you're doing without. To them, thrift was everything. Growing up in Achern had hardly meant living in the lap of luxury for Berthold but his parents knew how to enjoy what they had, even if they also knew how to look after their money. Berthold the self-made businessman terrorised his wife, showing her exactly what it meant to look after every penny. On Saturdays after dinner he made her account for every last item of household expenditure.[18] She noted her outgoings in her little book but Berthold knew all the accounting tricks and would never let her get away with all those things hidden away under 'miscellaneous'. That amount was always far too big so he came at her with question after question and would not let go until she finally had no answer. Then, as Walter recalls, he slammed his fist down on the table and she fled in tears.

Berthold's deep frustration was plain with a wife who spent half her life in bed with her ailments and the rest of the time in sanatoriums, her stays paid for with his hard-earned money. For Berthold, there was a simple way to overcome illness: allow it no place in your life. But it would not be long before Sophie and Eugen were spending their summer at his expense in one spa after another. Improbable as it might sound, in childhood Brecht became a *habitué* of the sanatorium life that in modern German literature is more readily associated with Franz Kafka and Thomas Mann. A summer holiday for Eugen and Walter in 1905 would mean joining Sophie at her cure in Bad Rain near Oberstaufen. Brecht's earliest extant piece of writing is on a postcard his father sent to Sophie at Bad Rain on 20 June 1905 when the boy wrote, unremarkably: 'Dear Mummy, best wishes to you from your Eugen'.[19] Berthold Brecht joined his wife and sons there for three days. The two boys and the servant Afra Unverdorben accompanied Sophie for a four-week stay at Oberstaufen the following summer. When Sophie was alone she would write picture postcards to Eugen and Walter back home in Augsburg from her current residence: Bad Rain, Oberstaufen or Oberdachstetten, where she spent three months in 1904. She wrote things like: 'You're not allowed to do anything at all here apart from rest and eat and drink milk. I've not put on weight this week but I've learnt to eat'.[20] Like her elder son Eugen, she would never have a real appetite. He would follow her, struggling against weight loss and the threat of illness.

Berthold spent quite a lot of his free time away from Bleichstrasse. The few surviving books bearing his signature reflect his interests: he was a committee member of the Augsburg male voice choir and of the local angling club. The choir enjoyed high social standing, its membership drawn from Augsburg's great and good. In 1911 Siegfried Wagner accepted their invitation to conduct the final chorale in their production of his father's *Mastersingers of Nuremberg*. After committee meetings Berthold would stay on with his friends at Café Kernstock to play cards. He and Franz Xaver Schirmböck, a close friend from the choir, rented a stretch of water with angling rights, and Berthold would spend weekends away with Franz Xaver, fishing or walking in the foothills of the Alps. Berthold Brecht and Franz Xaver Schirmböck would remain close friends for the rest of their lives.

Walter Brecht could only reason that his father's attitude towards his wife stemmed from the conflicting demands of his professional and domestic lives: 'Without doubt he was filled with love for her. However, the sober behaviour required in everyday life stood in his way'.[21] Even the loyal Walter concedes that with their father 'some things remained concealed'. As we shall see, Walter knew a bit more than he was letting on. In 1910 the family would discover just what Berthold was concealing in a scandal that rocked the family but was then buried. In the years that Sophie had left until her death in 1920 she struggled from operation to operation and Berthold learned to be gentler with her. But for him the fact remained that he had been left with an invalid for the wife who had borne his children.

Rather than moving to one of Augsburg's middle-class districts, the Brechts stayed at Bleichstrasse 2 amongst the Haindl workers in the Colony, as the four Haindl houses were known. In those days it was not unusual for factory owners and senior managers to live nearby. In 'Augsburg', a poem written in exile from Germany in 1939, Brecht recalled the houses looking 'white in the dusk' one spring evening:

The workmen are sitting
At the dark tables in the yard.
They talk of the yellow peril.
A few little girls go for beer
Although the brass bell of the Ursuline convent has already rung.
In shirtsleeves their fathers lean over the window sills.
Their neighbours wrap the peach trees on the house walls
In little white rags against the night frost.[22]

The 'whiteness' framing the poem alludes to the fact that Bleichstrasse took its name from the bleaching grounds which during the Middle Ages existed on that spot by the city moat. In his verse Brecht made much play of the adjective 'bleich' with its meaning of deathly pale, most memorably in the symbol of the pale German mother which he invoked in his verse. It is not difficult to see the memory of his mother behind that symbol, but the name of the street was also bound up with his memory of his own sickliness in that place.

When the officer's son Hanns Otto Münsterer first visited his friend's home in 1917 he was 'appalled at the total absence of any kind of individuality. The house where the Brechts lived, with its walled, concrete yard, compounded the overall impression of aridity and lovelessness'.[23] The interior was no less drab than the house itself. The Brechts were quite affluent but they did not indulge in the trappings of a middle-class lifestyle. Berthold was always careful with his money and Sophie's whole upbringing had emphasised the renunciation of material goods as a prime virtue. They possessed a few books and fed Eugen's hunger for them but certainly never aspired to compile a library, that symbol of the educated middle classes. The Brechts were, however, musical and had a piano in the living room. A centrepiece of family life was a music box encased in walnut. 'Silent Night' was a favourite at Christmas and popular songs like Eugen's favourite 'La Paloma' the rest of the year. However, pride of place in the living room went to Sophie's sewing machine. Set on a pedestal near the window, it showed Frau Brecht as the seamstress she had been. She could look out on to the street below as she made clothes for her boys: harlequin costumes with frilly shirts for the photographer's shot of them with their cousins; and the sailor suits which Eugen and Walter found ridiculous. But all his life Brecht prized hand-made clothes; silk was his favourite material.

At the rear of the house, beyond the yard there were shrubs to the north, including a peach tree which Berthold Brecht planted and tended in a corner away from the wind. Brecht would employ the motif of the cultivation of fruit trees repeatedly in his writing to signify peaceful and productive interaction between man and nature. To the east behind a wash house there was a grassed area with three chestnut trees. The plot was enclosed by a fence and a hedge, through which the children could see nuns working in the vegetable garden of the Ursuline Franciscan Convent of St Anna. For Münsterer, the broader setting of the house, looking on to the beautiful old town, provided some compensation for its drabness:

> It was actually one of the most pleasant in this sorry company: to the south it had a clear view over the old avenue of chestnut trees and the city moat, which lay in the shadow of the old city fortifications, their dark red stone swathed in ivy. There were swans here and punt parties on spring nights, singing, paper lanterns and girls; above them reared the proud silhouette of the Fünfgrat tower and, further on, the 'Dahinab [Down there] steps' wound their precipitous way up to the old town – so-called because Luther is said to have been helped in his flight from the Reichstag with those very words. And all that – the water, walls and white candelabra of the blossoming trees beamed across at the poor drab corner house.[24]

Eugen and the other children pillaged the trees and shrubs for spears, whips and bows and arrows in the running battles between the tribes of Bleichstrasse and Klauckestrasse. In a fine passage in the autobiographical *Conversations among Refugees*, Brecht evoked fragmentary memories of those early years, of school and of home life, of playing out and of being told how to behave:

> Snowball fights. Bread and butter. Hans Pschierer. Mummy's headaches. Too late for meals. School lessons. School books. Rubbers. Quarter-of-an-hour break. Shaking down chestnuts. The butcher's dog at the corner. Respectable children don't go barefoot. A pen-knife is worth more than three whipping tops. Marbles. Hooping. Roller skate. Spanish cane. Breaking windows. Wasn't me. Having to eat sauerkraut is healthy. Father must have his rest. Going to bed. Otto is a worry for his mummy. One doesn't say shit. When one shakes hands, one looks people in the eye.[25]

While Berthold and Sophie set the household rules, the servant girls looked after the Brecht boys much of the time, first Fanny, then Afra and after her Marie. They lived somewhere between the parents and the children, worked virtually round the clock for a pittance and hardly ever went out. They took the boys to school, in winter on a sledge, though Eugen insisted on getting off and walking the last part of the way. Walter Brecht recalls Marie – nicknamed Black Marie because of her thick black hair – with particular affection. While in Walter's view she was devoted to them in a quite selfless way, in *Conversations amongst Refugees* Brecht recalled that she and the boys greatly enjoyed a game in which she hid small objects like a rubber about her person. However, Walter stupidly told their mother about it and she banned the game, telling the boys that Black Marie was not as virtuous as they had thought. Berthold Brecht told his friends at Café Kernstock about his boys' very different temperaments: 'Eugen's a dreamer and always brooding, whereas Walter's a lot more fun and more realistic'.[26] Walter was more like his father: he became a second Papyrus, matching his father's career in the paper industry. Although less obviously his father's son, Eugen would find his own way in that industry: he learnt to read very early and was in no time consuming books voraciously. He was soon past asking for toys for Christmas and begged for more and more things to read.

Walter never had it easy with his elder brother, who harboured intense feelings of sibling rivalry. In fact, Eugen came within a whisker of beating his little brother's brains out: 'Once, when I was still very small and was asleep in my bed, Daddy came in just as Eugen had grabbed the coal shovel and was about to strike a blow to kill a fly on my cheek'.[27] That was just the beginning: 'Eugen made pretty ruthless use of the rights of the elder brother'. He would steal the best food off Walter's plate and bossed Walter around whatever they were doing, looking after their pets or playing out. He once jumped on Walter's new trike, a Christmas present, rode off and smashed it up. He showed off the superior co-ordination and strength of the older boy when they played hopscotch and roller-skating, and learned to ride a two-wheeler bike. He took violin lessons for a while and tried the piano too. In Walter's eyes, Eugen was a good ice skater and a good swimmer, though presently things would change dramatically for Eugen. Others would come to see him quite differently.

Church, School, Sickness 1903–12

God, Kaiser and Fatherland

With Sophie Brecht already confined to bed for lengthy periods, Eugen was sent to kindergarten early, in January 1903. The kindergarten at the Barefoot Church was the obvious choice, close to the Barefoot Primary School where he would next go. As at home, biblical stories were a staple: the story of Christ's Passion captivated the boy whose intelligence was there for everyone to see. The other children were in awe of his wonderful memory: he could repeat word for word the stories that the teacher had told them days before. It was not hard for him: he was only doing as he did with his mother and grandmother.

Kindergarten was a gentle foretaste of the thirteen years of religious education which Eugen received from the Barefoot clergy at church and at school. He joined the Barefoot Primary, a church rather than a state school, in September 1904. After two years there, he attended the 'Stadtpflegeranger' Primary for two more years. His encounter with the organs of the church and state within the school system began promisingly enough, though in time things would go badly wrong. It was not just that Religion enjoyed particular prominence in the curriculum: in Bavaria the clergy delivered all religious education in schools within a system that bound together church and state in the propagation of spiritual and secular dogma.[1] Eugen's teachers of Religion, Pastors Detzer and Krausser, together with their fellow pastors, remained key figures in the boy's religious education for Confirmation at the Barefoot Church and in his years at the Gymnasium, or grammar school, until he was nineteen.

In the fervently nationalist mood, the dogma was moulded into a chauvinist trinity of God, Kaiser and Fatherland, which prefigured the xenophobic Protestant war theology to which he would be exposed in August 1914. Eugen Brecht's primary education fostered his patriotic and Christian upbringing as a loyal subject of the Kaiser, a deeply formative experience for a writer who, after his rejection of this value system, wrestled throughout his life with the paradoxes of theological and secular systems of thought. Indeed, Brecht's later espousal of atheism and Marxism, not to mention his brilliant mock Lutheran tone, can only be properly understood against the background of his deeply religious upbringing.

More so than the other three 'Rs' – Reading, Writing and Arithmetic – Religion had a dominant position in the curriculum. In their four years of primary education and the first four of their secondary school years, the children did not actually read the Bible itself but specially devised works, which lent pedagogic sharpness to the matter at hand. The standard material was a hymn book, Luther's shorter catechism and two books of Protestant biblical history. The clergy inculcated all this material and associated moral guidance with dogmatic certainty, treating it as a body of indisputable facts. In time-honoured fashion, they made the children learn huge chunks of the stuff off by heart so that they could be sure that the young had made the Christian faith their own. Eugen was outstanding at this. The catechisms, stories, and hymns stayed with him, a vast resource that gave structure to his imagination for uses that never ceased to challenge the dogmatic certainty with which it had been inculcated, even though, as Brecht himself later acknowledged, he could be 'a bit doctrinaire' too.[2]

The strong emphasis on Religion coloured the rest of the curriculum at the Barefoot Primary. The school day began with hymns and prayers at assembly. Singing lessons were an opportunity to practise Christian chorales, together with folk songs and patriotic pieces. Like the other states in the new Reich, Bavaria was keen to celebrate the great national victory over France in 1870 and other heroic struggles in the history of the previously fragmented German nation, particularly the Wars of Liberation in 1813–15, which had freed the German states from Napoleonic rule. Songs like Theodor Körner's 'Call to Arms' were great favourites: 'Cleanse the soil, / Your German land, with your blood'. Buttressed by his father's nationalism and his mother's fervent Protestantism, the boy's exposure to this jingoism was not very different from the experience of millions of other children across pre-war Europe.

Eugen Brecht appeared the perfect pupil. He was docile and obedient, easy for his teachers to deal with, and he received almost uniformly excellent marks. His contemporaries remember his rather passive, quiescent attitude. The boy tended to adopt this manner when he was merely part of things beyond his control. Later, the only word that he could muster for his four years of primary education was: boredom. Yet in the hands of Pastors Detzer and Krausser, the story of Christ's Passion became something wholly different from the story-telling of his earliest years, and all the more captivating. The child assimilated his teachers' message that death was part of a Christian sacrificial mission in the national cause. *Dulce et decorum est pro patria mori*![5] However, the sickly Eugen now unexpectedly became acquainted with death from quite a different perspective, death as life's ultimate mystery, in a terrifying encounter which would shape his life to come.

Living with a storm within

Before Berthold joined his boys with their mother for their summer holiday at the sanatorium in Oberstaufen, he sent them some of his own verse, pieced together from popular tropes:

Through grove and vale we roved.

---

[5]   In English Horace's dictum reads: 'It is sweet and fitting to die for one's country'.

I wish you'd come along.
But you're still too young
You must grow really strong.
And when you're big and if you're good,
With me you can go a-roving.[3]

Growing was no straightforward matter for Eugen Brecht. In August 1905, he was sick again. His aunt Marie and her daughter Fanny sent him a card from Hamburg, wishing him a speedy recovery. Other female relatives and family friends added their voices: Aunt Anna led a group of five who signed a card for him in November 1905 during an outing to Hohenasperg.[4] The Brecht boys had the usual rashes and children's complaints like mumps and whooping cough.[5] They managed to avoid scarlet fever and diphtheria but had endless sore throats. Without antibiotics, a sore throat could be quite a different proposition from today: bacterial infections could come back time and again. No one knew then that Eugen – unlike Walter but like thousands of other children – was susceptible to complications from untreated bacterial pharyngitis or 'strep throat'.[6]

The symptoms which he now developed and which recurred in adolescence and adulthood are consistent with the contraction of rheumatic fever, a syndrome affecting the joints, the brain, the heart and the skin, when the immune system reacts badly to streptococcal infection, triggered by strep throat. In the early 1900s rheumatic fever was not understood at all well. In his time, the Brechts' family doctor, Georg Müller, would have seen plenty of sickly, nervous children with rheumatism, some of them with weak hearts. There were plenty of traditional remedies for inflammation and rheumatic complaints: bay leaf, healing earth, hay flowers and arnica. Dr Müller could assure his patients that, like so many things, the inflammation would settle with rest. If you took to your bed it would pass and all would be well. But it wasn't, of course. Left untreated, strep throat and rheumatic fever could produce very nasty complications, with repeat attacks. The boy's body became a battleground. As he would later write, it was as if the storm outside his window which was lashing the trees was raging inside him, threatening to overwhelm him.[7] The anxiety that he might lose control of his limbs would never leave him. A macabre sense of the naked physicality of Death's assault upon the body would colour his writing, reminiscent of the late-Medieval and Renaissance art of Bosch and Brueghel, which Brecht so admired.

During childhood and through to adolescence, Eugen Brecht spent lengthy periods of time taking the waters with his mother in South German sanatoriums, a long way from his friends and the things other children do. He was diagnosed with an enlarged heart, which, he later said he had been told, had come from him over-reaching himself while riding his bike and swimming. That diagnosis, together with a somewhat later diagnosis of 'cardiac shock', was what he retained whenever as an adult he told the story of his childhood condition. In 1922, he wrote to the critic Herbert Ihering that his heart complaint had been triggered by 'all kinds of sport', while in 1944 he noted in his journal that his heart 'had been somewhat enlarged by swimming and cycling'.[8] He joked to Ihering, with the ironic understatement which he used to mask the distress he had experienced, that his heart condition had given him an 'insight into the secrets of metaphysics'. It had, indeed. He became pre-occupied with understanding life in the light of death and developed a life-long fear that he might be buried alive.[9] Aware that something quite serious had happened to him as a child, throughout his life he remained anxious both to understand his condition and to deflect such thoughts with ploys to create ironic distance.

We have a much better understanding of his condition today. We can now say that the recurrent bacterial infection caused carditis, an inflammation of the heart. And in time that escalated into chronic heart failure. The heart valves become vulnerable; sure enough, his aortic valve became damaged. The enlargement of the heart was, in fact, an associated complication, the heart over-extending itself as it struggled to compensate for its weakness. The later diagnosis of cardiac shock was essentially the same phenomenon. After the heart has become enlarged in childhood, in some cases sufferers have no symptoms for years. Chronic heart failure, sometimes fatal in children, can settle somewhat in middle years.

Eugen Brecht had all the symptoms of heart failure: arrhythmia, or heart palpitations, dyspnoea, or breathlessness, and poor circulation. You get a chill and feel tired, dizzy and confused. It's a bit like the flu. As an adolescent Brecht would be forbidden any physical exertions and would later be encouraged to adopt dietary and hydrotherapeutic regimes, as well as to take to his bed whenever the symptoms threatened. In his middle years of greatest strength Brecht generally managed to keep his condition in check, though a person so driven as he was could never wholly comply with the prescribed regimes. The flu-like symptoms, complicated by other complaints, came and went all his life. Sometimes they escalated into fevers and, as he grew older, the complications got nastier. The anxieties and confusions surrounding his physical condition left him already as a child highly sensitive to any threats to his body, real or perceived.

Throughout his childhood in that Age of Nervousness, doctors told Eugen Brecht that he was a nervous child. In a way, that was all too obviously true: you only had to look at him to see that. 'Nerves' could account for the boy's grimace and for his loss of control of his limbs. If you chose to see things that way, his heart problem could be put down to nerves, too. In adolescence it was. They told him that if he was strong he would get better. However, his 'nerves' came from a neurological disorder that we understand much better nowadays. His auto-immune system's bad reaction to the streptococci interfered with the basal ganglia, the part of the brain which controls motor movements. It was this that caused the boy's random movements in a condition called Sydenham's chorea.[10] Sufferers may just experience a little difficulty walking or a slight grimace. But they can also be incapacitated if those random movements get out of control. Throughout his life, at times of stress Brecht would struggle to control erratic movements of his limbs, particularly his head and his hands.

And Sydenham's chorea is not just about physical debility. Sufferers' behaviour can become quite unstable, both depressive and excitable, often on the verge of spinning out of control. The condition may settle after a year or so, or come and go for several years, leaving its mark on the sufferer. That is not to say that the origin of Brecht's genius lies in disease. Eugen Brecht was already displaying his extravagant intelligence before his illness. At the same time, what Ronald Speirs identifies as the adolescent's pre-occupation with 'extreme and contrary responses to life', with boredom and transience, with melancholy and nervous excitability, characteristic of the young Brecht's singular sensibility, is consistent with this condition as he struggled with the clash of physical and psychological extremes.[11] In later life, Brecht would devise behavioural techniques to control his propensity to such extremes. However, none of his doctors properly appreciated the suffering he had experienced. Even though it is impossible retrospectively to measure these things with any precision, knowledge of his childhood illnesses provides greater insight into the erratic force of the young Brecht's dazzling, chameleon-like personality, into his extraordinary, intense creativity as well as into the Saturnine, self-destructive tendencies which close friends like Caspar Neher and Walter Benjamin saw in him.

As a child, Eugen Brecht dreaded the night. He was assailed by the storm that raged within and without, which triggered morbid thoughts. The terrifying example of his epileptic cousin Max Hermann was never far away. Eugen could only fall asleep if a night-light was burning on the bedside table.[12] He later captured his dread of the night in the lines

When it was dark and the light could not reach me
I cried out in the night like a helpless creature
And the light did not reach me.

Since then I've known that in the dark
The light will not reach me.
But I always cry out when it doesn't come
Like a helpless creature.[13]

He knew that once he'd fallen asleep, fear could take hold of him and, as he wrote in his earliest surviving diary, heart palpitations, too. Then he would wake up shaking in a cold sweat with his heart pounding: 'During the night I had terrible heart palpitations at first, then the beat became quite gentle and fast. Daddy stayed by my bed for a long time. I was afraid. Awfully afraid. The night went on forever!'.[14] It could take hours for him to calm down while his mother and father took it in turns to sit by his bed, comforting him. And he knew what a wreck he would be in the morning. It was not just the inevitable headache and the catarrh; the storm raged within him.

Playing out during the day, Eugen Brecht cut a strange figure, seemingly not so very different from Max Hermann: his head shook as he recited his verses and his Karl May stories for the other children. Eugen had read all May's books before the others had even started on them. In 1909 Berthold Brecht would take his elder son to hear May speak.[15] After his encounters with death, Eugen came to understand what May's Wild West stories were really about: the white man's total annihilation of the Indians. Then there were the stories from the Bible: blood-curdling tales of God's wrath and of violent death! Christ nailed to the cross! And the resurrection! Christ died to save us all! But God was so spiteful! Was God evil? In Walter's eyes, Sophie Brecht was the only one who remotely understood her son. Eugen would later tell her that he felt his 'otherness' to be the 'unmistakable, manifest sign of his being'.[16] She looked on, concerned at the distance which was opening up between him and others. Yet the boy came to understand that what others took to be his abject weakness he could turn into an extraordinary, triumphant strength. When Brecht's parents later gave their fifteen-year-old son the diaries of the dramatist Friedrich Hebbel, the boy alighted upon the question: 'Can someone actually make himself out of what he lacks?'. In the margin he wrote with resounding confidence: 'Yes, a poet!'.[17] In adolescence he would learn to celebrate his singularity: 'And just like my mother they all said: / He's a different sort, he's a different sort / He's a completely different sort from us'.[18] That singularity would become a powerful magnet, an irresistible force attracting others to him.

Playing with other children was very important to Eugen Brecht. He didn't particularly like them for their own sake; rather it helped him to overcome his isolation and to prove what he could do. He had no interest in random, unstructured play, in being part of a group for its own sake or in games of pure chance without any skill factor. They were just a waste of time. Hugely competitive, he was the world's worst loser at indoor games of skill like cards and halma, a game in which you have to get all your counters across the board to occupy your opponent's camp. But even when he won at cards or halma, after a while he would go off, bored. Without the prospect of decisively influencing a group's activity, he would withdraw into his own world.

Games of strategy were Eugen Brecht's thing. Chess became a life-long passion, captured in those famous photographs of Brecht in Danish exile playing with Walter Benjamin in Brecht's garden by the Svendborg Sound. As a child, he played with his father and their neighbour Hans Eberle, and with two of his earliest friends, Rudolf Hartmann from nearby Müllerstrasse and the club-footed Georg Pfanzelt from Klauckestrasse. The summer house in Hartmann's garden was a favourite venue, as was the Brechts' living room. Pfanzelt, who was five years older, was Orge. Because of his girlish looks Hartmann was Mädchen or Mädi. And Eugen was Bidi. They were friends for life.

For those on Eugen's wavelength like Orge and Mädi, playing with him was utterly captivating. Cowboys and Indians became a dramatic adaptation of Karl May, anything but milling around making whooping noises. The strategic requirements of chess mimicked the life-and-death struggle of war, another consuming passion. Orge and Mädi were in on Eugen's obsession with war games. This involved much more than the usual fascination of small boys with lining up lead soldiers. Eugen's pre-occupation with death spawned an obsession with great military leaders who controlled the lives of thousands. His hero was Napoleon: 'Enraptured, I had studied his battles and campaigns together with those of Frederick the Great'.[19] Eugen avidly consumed the military historian Karl Bleibtreu's analyses of great leaders' battle plans. Brecht would tell Benjamin of the 'school of strategy' that he had gone through and that, twenty years on, he could still 'probably reconstruct the Battle of Waterloo'.[20]

The little emperor Eugen instructed his friends to bring along their armies, commanding Walter, his cousins Fritz and Richard, Orge, Mädi and Franz Kroher. Franz remembered that under Eugen's direction the toy soldiers were transformed into instruments of military strategy with major destructive potential:

> Eugen made us all take our lead soldiers with us. Then we built little walls of earth and positioned the figures exactly according to Eugen's battle plans. He alone determined the course of the game, one time as Napoleon, another time as

Frederick the Great. We were his generals and did as he ordered. Eugen always dominated the exchanges. He was overbearing and domineering towards his playmates.[21]

Well into adolescence, the war games became ever more elaborate exercises in high strategy. The rich boy Otto Müller joined in; Eugen started calling him Müllereisert because that suited him better. Then Otto began to call himself Müllercisert. The name stuck: he was another life-long friend.

In the afternoons after school, the boys declared war on each other in Eugen's room. Or if the weather was good, in the holidays they would play outside all day on the grass behind Bleichstrasse. The campaigns outside sometimes lasted a whole week. They would crawl around in the undergrowth from morning to night, immersed in hotly contested battles. Orge, Walter and Müllereisert were by now allowed to command armies opposing Eugen's. The Brecht boys wrote their accounts of the battles, Walter emphasising how much his differed from his brother's. The sibling rivalry never ended. In fact, Walter copied much of his brother's account but omitted his conclusion and contested his brother's version of events:

Everyone had an army of tin soldiers of ten to fifteen divisions, forty men strong with artillery. The villages were built of *papier maché*, the rivers marked with twigs. We had fortresses at strategically important points with little ramparts and bastions made of boards from cigarette boxes. [...] There were strict rules. For example, each soldier could only be moved his own length. Only in this way could a commander gain advantage through circumventions and rewards as a result of well thought-through plans. However, they were constantly breaking the rules; then the commanders had to stand up and, upright above their lines of battle, call each other to order by shaking their fists. The artillery pieces were little lead cannons which could be fired with powder crackers. Both sides fired all the artillery pieces at one point on the front at the same time. In that way, the skilful concentration of numbers could decide the battle. If the number of soldiers still standing sank to half that of the enemy, they were surrendered as prisoners. Eugen was always victorious. Things got noisy when one of the other strategists believed that they had achieved a decisive advantage. In the evening, when peace reigned over the battlefield, the room was full of smoke from the powder.[22]

On one occasion, which Walter did not remember but his brother did, Eugen ran into the house with some enemy soldiers, appeared at the toilet window, tore the soldiers' heads off and hurled them down at their owner's feet.[23] Perhaps they were Walter's.

Eugen's imperious manner and obsessive certainty as to what was to be done were, in Walter's eyes, an unacceptable tyranny. He remained bitter decades after his brother's death:

So far as Eugen took any interest in us at all, he treated us young ones no differently from his own contemporaries. He gave himself patronising airs, which must have appeared almost comical, but we did not see it like that. [...] In order to rub in his superiority, he would often treat us as complete fools and hopeless idiots. In some ways we acknowledged his superiority, but we did not acknowledge it with any degree of admiration; on the contrary, his superior stance distanced him from us. We recognised that he was different, we even went so far as to sense his genius. Not that we were familiar with the concept of 'genius', but somehow it had worked its way into our consciousness. So Eugen's airs never seemed particularly excessive, unjustified, or in any way ridiculous, rather they seemed an annoyance, alien, odd, even threatening.[24]

Though physically present in his rather disturbing way, Eugen inhabited a quite different world from Walter. That was his friend Orge's world, too. Although Orge was much older, a mutual fascination drew them to each other in a bond of equals which was rare indeed for Eugen Brecht. Orge was the only one of Brecht's friends who was not from the middle classes: his father, a foreman, died when he was still very young. Orge was a stocky figure with an angular face and dark hair, who endeared himself to Eugen with his love of bizarre songs – he composed some of them himself – and his brilliant skills as a classical pianist. And they shared a macabre fascination with death. One of Brecht's final poems from 1956, 'Orge's List of Wishes', closes the circle on their lives in its concluding lines: 'Of lives, the lucid, / Of deaths, the rapid'.[25]

The younger Walter did not know what to make of Orge, who was bitingly sarcastic and had a strong line in vulgarity, teasing him with his crude talk about sex. Walter could never be comfortable in the presence of this Mephistophelian figure. By contrast, Eugen relished Orge's company and later captured his friend's powerful presence in this portrait: 'His face is pale with strong bones, his forehead curiously widened out, almost brutal and slightly flattened, there's something tough and vicious there; his lips are full and handsome, like a connoisseur's, rather voluptuous; his neck short and powerful. He looks like a prelate'.[26]

Orge and the others were left behind in Augsburg in the summer of 1907. Sophie and Berthold took a four-week holiday on the North Sea coast, spending most of their time on the island of Borkum.[27] They packed off the boys to stay with the forester Knörzinger and his wife in Emmersacker, just outside Augsburg.[28] The Brechts evidently hoped that the boys would benefit from the country life and the fresh air. Walter greatly enjoyed the woodland experience: he played with the hunting dogs, the forester taught him how to smoke a pipe and took him into the forest to hunt for game with his shotgun. Knörzinger had a fine repertoire of scary ballads, the 'Moritaten' which Brecht came to love so much: 'Heinrich slept with his bride, / A rich heiress from the Rhine. / Poisonous snakes tormented him / And wouldn't let him sleep …'. However, life in the countryside with the foresters held little appeal for Eugen. In Walter's view, his brother was already used to the company of friends who looked up to him 'in their fascinated devotion'. Deprived of his audience of admirers, Eugen 'said little, read a lot, in fact always. For all his usual politeness, he remained cool, even if the foresters did everything to make life bearable for the nervous city child'. The Knörzingers could only be at a loss as to what to do with their strange guest.

Eugen's physical condition did not improve and sustained medical intervention was prescribed for the summer of 1908 to combat his heart complaint and the 'nervous twitching of his head'.[29] School records indicate that he missed the final weeks of his primary school because from 11 June to 28 July he had to go with his mother to the children's brine spa at Bad Dürrheim in the Black Forest before he moved up to the more demanding academic environment of the selective Gymnasium. From his sick bed at the sanatorium Eugen wrote postcards to friends and relatives. And Bad Dürrheim was an opportunity to extend his circle of New Year correspondents to include Adolf Kappler from Karlsruhe, with whom he had played the 'robber captain' at the sanatorium.[30] For Brecht, then, from the beginning sickness and writing were closely linked. However, he would quickly learn to deal with sickness in his writing in a manner that was far removed from the popularised Romantic cult of death, which in German culture had become near-synonymous with Richard Wagner's sensationalised treatment of it. While Wagner long held Brecht's older rival Thomas Mann in thrall, intellectually the young Brecht's greater affinity would be with Nietzsche, who in his polemic *The Case of Wagner* of 1888 had famously broken with the 'sickly' composer, whose music, he wrote, was harmful and made him sweat.

The Royal Bavarian Realgymnasium

Eugen Brecht entered Augsburg's Royal Bavarian Realgymnasium in September 1908, having passed an entrance exam in German, Maths and Religion. He would end his schooling there in 1917 with a war-time leaving certificate. Families paid forty-five marks a year for their boys to attend this highly regarded institution. It was a new type of grammar school which had acquired great prestige through its association with Germany's rapid modernisation, fuelled by its burgeoning economic growth. There was a greater emphasis on science and modern languages than in the traditional humanist Gymnasium, which privileged Latin and Ancient Greek. The new approach undoubtedly appealed to Berthold Brecht, whose career at Haindl was rooted in the modern industrial processes. Brecht himself would always emphasise the importance of his scientific education for his art. Along with Maths and Science, German and Religion were cornerstones of the curriculum. Latin was still the first foreign language before the introduction of French and English. When Eugen joined there were 475 pupils at the school. Mädi Hartmann was in the same class, as were a number of boys immortalised in Eugen Brecht's early Augsburg writings: Ernst Bohlig, Fritz Gehweyer and Heinrich Scheuffelhut. There were others in the parallel class: Julius Bingen, Georg Geyer, Rudolf Prestel and Adolf Seitz.

The Realgymnasium was a state school but Religion remained a dominant presence under the clerics' control. Together with the eight other Protestant boys in his class of thirty-one, Eugen attended Pastors Detzer and Krausser's services at school and at the Barefoot Church. The teaching of German and Religion remained synchronised, with the stated aim of ensuring that pupils grew into Christian personalities imbued with the spirit of the Fatherland. In the lower classes, Religion drew on the same material as at primary school. This first phase of the curriculum continued the emphasis on the rote learning of catechisms, culminating in the preparation of pupils for Confirmation. Only in the second phase, from years five to nine, were pupils deemed ready for direct engagement with the Bible. It was presented as the Word of God, as traditionally understood in Protestant theology. The Bible was supplemented by the text of the Augsburg Confession and by material dealing with the Protestant Church in the Kingdom of Bavaria, demonstrating the institutional position of the Church in legal, political and social terms. This approach was liable to re-enforce the embattled consciousness of a Protestant minority in that bastion of the faith, a mindset suggested in Brecht's description of his 'rebellious' Protestant mother. At the same time, they could be secure in the knowledge that, although a minority in the Catholic South, they were part of the majority in the predominantly Lutheran German Empire. In the short term, Eugen Brecht was a conspicuously successful product of this religious indoctrination. Yet the approach left no space for individual interpretation. Avid to discuss texts of all sorts, Brecht could not help but supply his own readings.

In German, too, pupils were entrusted with individual works of literature only in the higher classes. Initially, the teachers presented extracts from texts from the Middle Ages and the Classical and Romantic periods, which underscored official dogma. They treated topics like trust in God and transfiguration through heroic, sacrificial death in war for the Fatherland. Numerous ballads featured from the Wars of Liberation and the Franco-Prussian War, among them verses such as August Kopisch's 'Blücher on the Rhine', in which Blücher surveys the map of France: 'Where's the foe?. – The foe? He's here!. / Where your finger is! We'll slay him! / Where's Paris? – Paris? It's here!. / Where your finger is! We'll take it! / Let's bridge the Rhine!'.

Through the academic year, the boys were treated to an endless round of patriotic celebrations, framed by religious services. The festivities merged seamlessly with the patriotic dogma served up in class. The annual school festival was devoted to a particular patriotic theme every year, celebrating such luminaries as Bismarck, Prince Regent Luitpold of Bavaria, the Kaiser and the King of Bavaria. There would be frequent victory celebrations in the early years of the First World War. The teachers wrote speeches and poems for those occasions and the boys sang patriotic ballads, hymns and choral pieces. Following Luitpold's death, all Bavarian schools introduced a sports day in his memory. Sports were combined with military exercises to promote prowess in war amongst the pupils. The boys received instruction in marching in columns and exercising with staves, which were deployed like bayonets. In addition, the school encouraged boys to join the Wandervogel movement, which promoted the outdoor life, and the Bavarian Wehrkraftverein, or Military League.

The Brecht boys joined the Wehrkraft.[31] It provided pre-military training for some forty or fifty boys from Augsburg's grammar schools. They donned a dark green uniform with a felt hat of the same colour and a leather belt with a heavy metal buckle which emphasised the military style. They reported for duty on Wednesday and Sunday afternoons and on special occasions the retired General von Hößlin would appear on horseback and deliver an address. He was accompanied by the retired but energetic Sergeant Hafner, who enjoyed the boys' company, organising exercises and war games. In the lead-up to war, the Wehrkraft would assume a greater importance still in preparing the boys for military life.

Brecht's father looked on approvingly at his elder son's educational development. Away on business shortly after Eugen had joined the grammar school, he sent a birthday greeting to the 'Gymnasialstudent' Eugen Brecht, in which he gently reminded his son of the responsibilities which he would acquire in his passage towards mature manhood: 'You're getting older and older, and the carefree childhood years that you still have left will soon have passed. So be diligent at school and use your time to become a hard-working man'.[32] What Brecht wrote to Ihering about his grammar school years thirteen years later reads like a conscious riposte with a characteristically Brechtian ironic reversal: 'During my nine years bottled up at an Augsburg Realgymnasium I didn't manage to improve my teachers appreciably. Indefatigably, they promoted my taste for leisure and independence'.[33] In truth, like his father, Eugen Brecht became an extremely hard-working man. He was utterly driven, and was certainly obsessive about his independence, in particular his capacity to determine how to fill his time as he judged necessary. By 1913 Eugen was using the term 'work' in his diary for his writing, the only truly worthwhile work activity.[34] Brecht would work virtually every day of his life to very great effect, deploying his extraordinary talent to fill notebook after notebook with drafts ripe for publication. Time was truly precious: with sickness never far away he knew that he would never have enough time to complete all his urgent tasks. At the end of the first year at the Gymnasium he again spent the summer with his mother at a sanatorium in the Black Forest, this time Königsfeld. Königsfeld is known for its invigorating air and for the hydrotherapeutic Kneipp Cure.[35] Brecht would follow a Kneipp regime as an adult.

At the Gymnasium Eugen initially remained much as he had been at primary school, a quiet, well-behaved pupil, who did not draw particular attention to himself.[36] For the girls he encountered on his way to school every day with Scheuffelhut and Hartmann, he was one of the 'three oddballs'.[37] The oddballs met at a bench by the city moat opposite the Brechts' flat or at the summer house in Hartmann's garden where they did homework together with Adolf Seitz and Josef Schipfel, all the others copying from the one who was best in a particular subject. However, no one copied from Eugen's German because the teachers would immediately recognise it as his work.

His first form teacher was Franz Xaver Herrenreiter, whom Brecht later caricatured as the epitome of a 'monster' teacher.[38] In the first year Eugen performed quite well for Herrenreiter and the other teachers, but after that he no longer excelled academically. He stuffed his satchel full of his own books every day. His performance was always adequate so there was never any real danger of him having to repeat a year, the sanction that hung over all the pupils. In keeping with Brecht's own statements, it has been assumed that the precocious youngster soon saw through the institutional gloss of the school and lost interest in what his teachers were serving up under the guise of knowledge. There is certainly some truth in this but things were happening in the Brecht family which themselves could only contribute to his sense of alienation, confusion and vulnerability.

Sickness and scandal

In 1910, a sequence of events engulfed the Brecht family in a protracted crisis which it could only survive through the tried and tested means of denial. As usual for the Brechts, sickness featured prominently, and as usual it affected Sophie and Eugen. The scandal was the usual stuff about sex. Walter Brecht could not bring himself to write about much of this. Nor would his brother write about it directly, but it gave him a rich store of material for his satires of the cornerstones of middle-class life, the family and business.

Sophie Brecht had been struggling since Walter's birth. One evening, while Walter was sitting with her on the sofa, he was shocked to see the colour drain from her face and the pupils of her eyes disappear, leaving only the whites of her eyes.[39] She lost consciousness for several minutes and came round amidst Walter's cries for help. Sophie Brecht was now in urgent need of support to look after her boys and the household. Berthold Brecht had the answer. In April 1910 he employed the twenty-two-year-old Marie Röcker, taking her into the household as the Hausdame, or housekeeper.[40] Marie Röcker had quite a good level of education, including knowledge of English and French. She had trained as a cook at a large hotel in nearby Ulm. In Walter Brecht's account, Marie Röcker then became a devoted servant of the Brecht family for thirty years.[41] In a sense, that is true.

It was not unusual for the male head of a household to take lovers amongst the domestic employees. Just a month after Marie Röcker had arrived, Sophie Brecht accused her husband of having an affair with her. Unwilling to accept the humiliation of the affair under her own roof, Sophie the rebellious Protestant asserted her strong, independent streak. Marie Röcker promptly left Augsburg. The story, of course, casts in quite a different light Walter Brecht's puzzled account of his father's coldness towards his wife and of his concealment of things. Berthold Brecht's emotional attachment lay elsewhere. Sophie Brecht's humiliation quietly continued: Berthold Brecht kept seeing Marie Röcker after she had been shown the door. Business trips and weekends away were the only cover he needed. In time, Marie Röcker would return to Augsburg and would even re-enter employment in the Brecht household, tending Sophie Brecht until her death. The humiliation was complete. Marie Röcker then lived with Berthold Brecht, ostensibly as his Hausdame, until his death. He left her 12,000 marks in his will.

This episode cannot have escaped the twelve-year-old Eugen's attention and it surely coloured his attitude towards his parents' marriage, towards Marie Röcker and more generally towards the family as an institution shot through with deceit and hypocrisy. The scandal could only bring him and his brother closer to their mother. It impacted on Eugen Brecht personally too. It was at this time that he suffered what he later called a 'cardiac shock'.[42] In the contemporary understanding, a cardiac shock described an enlarged heart failing due to over-exertion.[43] With each over-exertion, the heart muscles become weaker. His condition was deteriorating into chronic heart failure.

The crisis in the Brecht family undoubtedly contributed to the worsening of the boy's condition. The events of 1910 proved too much for Eugen Brecht. His exclusion from activities pursued by other children confirmed his status as strange outsider. At the mercy of his treacherous heart, he would never fully recover his health. By the early 1920s he had, however, adopted a characteristically bravado attitude towards the matter, writing to his friend, the writer Arnolt Bronnen: 'When I was only twelve, I suffered a demonstrable cardiac shock thanks to my daring'.[44] His constitution was hardly robust enough to withstand great stress, be it of an emotional or physical nature. In June he and Walter were again sent to stay in the countryside. However, for some time Eugen Brecht was not allowed to take part in physical activities like cycling or other sports. His recollection of his adolescent condition in 1944 shows that he had become hyper-sensitive, responding to orchestral music like Bach and Beethoven with the fear that it might damage his heart: 'When I heard the *St Matthew Passion* in the Barefoot Church, I decided never to go to a thing like that again, since I abhorred the stupor, the wild coma, into which one became lulled. I also thought it was bad for my heart'.[45] This description of a reduced state of stupefied consciousness, both dulled and feverishly excited, which may be induced by musical performance, is a striking expression of an emotional and physical delicacy, which drew upon a common belief about the deleterious effect of 'pathogenic' music. In later years, Brecht would suggest to his friend, the composer Hanns Eisler, that a critical measure of music was whether it raised the body temperature.[46] The boy would presently grasp how to counter his morbid fear of certain music with his own pleasurable sounds and rhythms.

Hydratopyranthropos

Amidst the turmoil in the Brecht family, the twelve-year-old Eugen had vacated his room for Marie Röcker and moved upstairs to the attic space at the rear of the house. He stayed up there after she left. It was like a studio flat, consisting of a living room with a small bedroom off. It even had a door separate from the family's flat below. Strikingly, the adult Brecht would still seek such arrangements when he shared the same accommodation as his family in the exile years. The boy enjoyed a degree of freedom that was unusual for someone his age. In the years to come, the attic would become a fabled meeting place for the Brecht Circle. For now, it was a place where he could read all he wanted and play with his friends. They witnessed how, as he moved into adolescence, his sharp originality and singularity became something more. The word that his bemused contemporaries most frequently use to describe his manner is: 'idiosyncratic'.[47]

In school, the quiet, withdrawn child began to assert his independent spirit and sheer contrariness. Teachers and classmates looked on in bewilderment as he shifted unsettlingly between extreme forms of behaviour, at one moment elated, at another the withdrawn melancholic. Caspar Neher, who joined the class in 1911, later captured the Brecht he got to know in his picture 'Hydratopyranthropos', the Water-Fire-Man, that is to say a human being constructed out of the most contrary elements imaginable. Neher knew Brecht better than most: he became another life-long friend and, as a stage designer, one of Brecht's most gifted collaborators. And Brecht himself captured his tendency to extreme forms of behaviour in the similarly elemental neologism 'melancholeric'.[48] In the table of humours these two coinages do not match exactly, though the choleric and the fire attributes do. Indeed, these two concepts capture Brecht's susceptibility to the inflammatory effect of fever, from which he frequently suffered. In the quite different context of literary politics in exile in the 1930s, the inflammatory self retained its currency when he came to speak of his very presence as something highly combustible, a 'sort of powder keg, better approached with something cold rather than something warm'.[49]

Eugen Brecht's teachers found him a deeply unnerving presence. A classmate Stephan Bürzle recalls him being both 'rude and reserved at the same time'.[50] The polite and courteous manner of the well-brought-up, middle-class boy was now shot through with an aggressive insolence, which his emphatically slovenly dress and a conspicuous disregard for hygiene only accentuated. Brecht's multiply contradictory, chameleon-like personality, at once beguilingly attractive to some and thoroughly repugnant to others, took to the stage. The other boys looked on as, in the words of another classmate Franz Xaver Schiller, 'Brecht developed very idiosyncratic thoughts, which Professor Ledermann was not inclined to follow. He did not know where to start with Brecht in German'.[51] Although the pupils were still not working with original texts in German and Religion, Eugen Brecht was finding his own way through world literature and forming his own views on the Bible. In German essays, he could get a top mark quite effortlessly. However, he could not resist taking up contrary positions spiced with cheeky humour. For instance, when Ledermann asked them to write on the topic 'What draws us to the mountains?', on the way home with Schiller he said he knew the answer: the ski lift. In four lines of verse he conveyed his view on the Italian-Turkish war in North Africa: 'The Italians are the losers, / That is my conclusion. / The Turks should not give up, / Though Tripoli is lost'. Ledermann's sarcastic response was: 'Look, we have a budding poet amongst us'. The free-thinking boy with the hunger for books was by now avidly composing poems and dramas. Yet Ledermann, the grand-father of another great poet, Hans Magnus Enzensberger, himself occupied the role of school bard with his festive compositions for patriotic celebrations. For Brecht's friend Heinrich Scheuffelhut, Ledermann was typical of the teachers: 'At the Gymnasium most of the teachers were German nationalists. Already at that time Brecht's teachers had no idea what to do with him. These gentlemen did not like the way he treated set topics in History and German'.[52] Depending on how they responded to the boy's 'escapades', in these subjects he would be marked excellent or unsatisfactory, but never anywhere between.[53]

Brecht later suggested to Ihering, quite plausibly in general terms, that he could expect nothing from his teachers and had to become his own teacher. However, this hugely gifted boy did respond to teachers who stimulated him. He was a particularly receptive pupil in Latin, writing in his diary that his Latin teacher Hans Futterknecht was 'very nice. I really like him. He's so sweet. The ideal teacher'.[54] He would be similarly fortunate in his later Latin teacher Friedrich Gebhard, who fostered in him his life-long love of Horace. However, as we shall see, Gebhard, the school's deputy head, would become incensed with his star pupil.

Brecht's exclusion from any strenuous activity meant that, in addition to reading, he focused his energy on games at which he could excel by virtue of his intellect and of an imagination given to the play of powerful contrasts. It was at this time that Eugen Brecht's passion for the theatre was awakened. As with Goethe before him, puppet theatre was the great dramatist's inspiration. Eugen and his friends got hold of a puppet theatre for a mark, which they took on a hand cart to Hartmann's. Eugen was in his element as director and theatre manager, preparing productions with Scheuffelhut,

Hartmann, Walter and Hartmann's cousin, Ernestine Müller. At once, he placed himself at the centre of things in the eminently social setting of the theatre, bringing to life the play of his imagination, which was so suited to the antithetical structure of dramatic action. Brecht explained near the end of his life that his engagement with the theatre began 'when I found other plays wrong' and attempted to show that people behaved differently.[55] It was that simple. He had found his place in the world.

They performed operatic as well as dramatic pieces: Wagner's *Flying Dutchman*; scenes from Weber's *Freischütz* and *Oberon*; Büchner's *Leonce and Lena*; Goethe's *Faust*; Shakespeare's *Hamlet*; and, extracts from the work of a living dramatist of great notoriety, the Munich bohemian Frank Wedekind. In his first venture in the theatre Brecht showed himself to be his father's son: it was a commercial proposition, in which the audience – parents and other people living in the house – had to stump up two marks each. The profits were invested in better puppets and props.

Utterly convinced of his own unique dramatic talent, from the outset the supremely confident Brecht pitted himself against all others: the more illustrious, the better. He attended a performance of Schiller's *Wallenstein's Death* with his school class at the Augsburg Stadttheater. He later claimed that he tried to goad his class mates into behaving badly but did not have much success.[56] The play's setting in the Thirty Years' War was a challenge close to his heart: he was scathing about the 'boring' production, which presented the war in far too cosy a light. What is more, Schiller's *opus magnum* lacked insight into human nature! That said, Brecht would always admire Schiller's dramatic genius, if not his idealism, let alone what directors or teachers made of him. Brecht's singular sensibility fuelled his unerring certainty that other directors were simply wrong. He would lock horns with his teachers over *Wallenstein* again, and in time his certainty would translate into his full frontal assault on the entire western dramatic tradition.

Confirmation, free thinking and pubescence

Eugen's mother, teachers and the clergy urged him to place his hopes for the recovery of his health firmly in the hands of God. Confirmation was a landmark event for the young believer. The course of preparatory instruction began in September 1911 and concluded with the Confirmation service at the Barefoot Church in March 1912. Pastors Detzer and Krausser gave instruction in their homes. The preparation followed the familiar method of imbibing the Bible's lessons for life by learning catechisms off by heart. Hermann Koelle prepared for Confirmation with Brecht: 'It was obvious that Brecht took the Confirmation teaching very seriously. He could recite the assigned Bible texts effortlessly.'[57] Each child also had to recite a short passage from the Bible which had been selected as an especially appropriate maxim. It is likely that Eugen's mother played a role in choosing words from *Epistle to the Hebrews* (13.9) which can also be found in Brahms's *A German Requiem*: 'Do not be turned away by different strange teachings, because it is good for your heart to be made strong by grace, and not by meats, which were of no profit to those who took so much trouble over them'. However easy he found it to learn them, these were challenging words indeed. Try as the young believer might to comply with them, those 'different strange teachings', not to mention the 'meats', pulled him irresistibly toward them. The pubescent Eugen was not just intellectually curious. At a time when girls were still a distant fascination, he had a crush on at least one boy at this time, Emil Enderlin. Eugen went ice-skating with him in the winter of 1911–12 and called him 'le petit'.[58]

Typically, Brecht made poetry out of his mother's disgust with him when he began to masturbate. His body, hitherto a battleground for his physical and psychological complaints, quite suddenly became a pleasure park, too, a source of intense physical delight. Sophie Brecht's strict Christian morality was an irresistible target. His poem 'Confessions from First Communion' contains lines such as 'My mother smelt it on my night shirt' and concludes with the thought that he was 'damned already aged fourteen'.[59] He would capture their angry exchanges over the state of his dirty washing in poems from his early twenties such as 'Outpourings of a Martyr', in which the mother says, 'It's tragic / For a grown-up person to be like this' and, 'You ought to rinse out your mouth; it's a sewer', to which the reply comes, 'I don't put it in my mouth, you know'.[60] All her lessons about the need for cleanliness were in vain. The boy courted the bacteria to which he was so vulnerable.

Shortly after his mother's death Brecht wrote a poem which shows the intimate link in his mind between her and his biblical maxim for Confirmation. First called 'The Bible', then 'Biblical Maxims', before it was published as 'Memories', the poem begins: 'My mother said: Child, the Lord loves the simple hearted. / And always put the Bible on the table for me'.[61] It ends, 'I can still hear her saying my Confirmation piece: / it is good for your heart to be made strong'. Sophie Brecht had the comfort of her faith in the years of her suffering. To the end, she maintained her belief that her ailing and erring son could be similarly comforted if only he would return to the true path. At Confirmation, the deeply serious Eugen was still disposed to believe in God's grace. Yet the free spirit with no interest in repressing his sexual desires could only begin to question the foundations of his faith.

Precocity 1912–14

Banned!

It was not just that Eugen Brecht's pubescent free thinking challenged the dogmatic certainty with which the Church inculcated the Christian message, he was also becoming keenly aware of his own extreme talent. By the age of fourteen he had, in his brother's eyes, embraced his vocation as a poet. And by the following year he was noting in his diary: 'I must always write'.[1] Unlike the parents of many fledgling writers, Berthold and Sophie Brecht supported their boy. For example, they gave him Richard Dehmel's collection of poems *Aber die Liebe* [*But Love*] for Christmas in 1913. Dehmel was a popular Neo-Romantic, who preached free love and championed the organic life of the countryside over the city. These views were typical of the contemporary literary currents that the young Eugen Brecht assimilated before the First World War. The fifty-one-year-old Dehmel, ardently patriotic like almost everyone else in those days, would volunteer for the front line in August 1914.

To the amusement of his friends, Berthold Brecht took to calling his son 'my little poet', while Sophie 'was completely convinced of his calling and felt it to be a blessing that she had borne this difficult son'.[2] She believed, wholly conventionally, that he should now gain access to the courts of kings and princes in the manner of his fellow Augsburg poet, Ludwig Ganghofer.[3] It did not matter to her that Ganghofer peddled chauvinist kitsch. It would matter to her, though, that her son was, in her eyes, a disgusting pornographer. From now on, writing defined Eugen Brecht's existence. Keenly aware of his powers and welling with ambition, he was convinced that fame beckoned. Walking past an open-air orchestral concert at the Augsburg Stadtgarten, the site of the military parades which the boys so admired, he stopped to look at the conductor and exclaimed to his friend Stephan Bürzle: 'I guarantee that one day I'll be standing on a podium like that'.[4] The sickly outsider brought his extreme literary ambition to bear upon every sphere of activity with his friends. It was vital in helping him to overcome his isolation and to achieve the recognition that he craved.

Chess, for example, was an abiding passion which he used to such ends. His range of partners at grammar school had increased to include Heinrich Scheuffelhut, Adolf Seitz, Franz Xaver Schiller, Josef Schipfel, Wilhelm Kölbig, Oskar Sternbacher and Oskar Lettner. Brecht's confidence in his own superiority is apparent in his sheer disbelief at defeat: 'I lost against Kölbig 2:8, an inexplicable matter, since I can play much better than him'.[5] He could console himself with the thought that 'Hartmann stalemated. So I still lead 8:7'. Brecht and his friends founded a chess club at school, Amicitia, which they re-named the Merry Stone Swingers. And Brecht saw to it that they produced two issues of a club magazine, at twenty pfennigs a copy. The commercial dimension was just as much second nature to Eugen as was the writing. He was keen to please Papyrus.

However, one day at school when Ledermann asked Eugen a question in class, a copy of the magazine fell off his knees on to the floor. The officious Ledermann demanded to see the offending material and promptly took it to the headmaster. The outcome was that the Merry Stone Swingers were punished with two hours' detention and the club was dissolved. And so the Merry Stone Swinger Eugen had his first publishing venture banned. It would not be his last to suffer that fate. They had put a joke corner on the back page of their paper: 'What's Professor Tifterling working on now?' – 'He's writing a book about the stomach complaints of meat-eating plants'.[6] Augsburg's Royal Bavarian Realgymnasium was not so far removed from Frank Wedekind's scathing caricature of German school life in *Spring Awakening*. Like the teachers in Wedekind's play, Ledermann and his colleagues were abjectly suspicious of their young charges. How dare they make jokes about teachers! At the start of the school year 1913–14, Eugen's worst fear was to have Ledermann again. In his later portrait of those 'monster' teachers, Brecht would take revenge on their petty bureaucratic mentality and their appetite for stamping on pupils' initiatives, ruining their harmless fun.

Eugen Brecht had discovered the risqué Wedekind, making him his own. The Brechts took the bold step of buying their elder son an edition of Wedekind's poems, songs and dramas. Eugen Brecht had something of Wedekind's Melchior Gabor about him. In adolescence, Eugen became the Melchior of his group, leading the Brecht Circle in sexual exploration and in free thinking, and in so doing, he would come close to sharing the deeply distressed Melchior's fate of expulsion for something he had written.

Lyricism: Rising above the storm

Reflecting on his beginnings, Brecht said: 'In poetry I began with songs to the guitar, sketching out the verses at the same time as the music. The ballad form was as old as the hills, and in my day nobody who took himself at all seriously wrote ballads'.[7] As an adolescent in provincial Augsburg, Brecht had not encountered the latest in contemporary art, Expressionism, which was sweeping through Germany's centres of culture. A major influence upon the Brecht boys was their father's friend Theodor Helm, who visited the musical Brechts, played the lute and sang popular ballads.[8] Brecht would later write scathingly about that 'little philistine rumpot called Helm, an engineer who raves about Goethe and floats his ideals on strings like kites'.[9] However, the Brecht boys took their cue from Helm, picking up the guitar and composing their own texts and tunes. Brecht invented his own simple notation of little crosses with lines below them for the music he wrote.[10] For all the bitter rivalry that marred the boys' relationship, they could find common ground in playing the guitar and singing their songs together.

However, even when it came to music and song, Brecht and Walter were still very different. Walter played and sang very well but was quite conventional in his approach. Eugen, like his hero Wedekind, was never an accomplished player technically but learned to fuse his body, voice and guitar-playing into a beguilingly powerful artistic performance. As we know from our own contemporaries, great guitarist-singers are often like that: we need look no further than Bob Dylan. It is at least of passing interest that Dylan used almost exactly the same words as Brecht to describe his own beginnings and that in the first volume of his autobiography he describes hearing Brecht's songs in Greenwich Village as a life-changing experience.[11] In this way, Brecht had a very specific and profound influence upon the direction of contemporary popular music. We shall pick up on further affinities between these two greats.

Wherever Eugen Brecht heard the authentic rhythms of language and song, he was attracted to them as if by magic. Hearing the cry 'Scooouring sand! Scooouring sand!' ring out along Bleichstrasse, he would come bounding down the stairs and rush outside to see the street seller with his hand cart.[12] It was the same with newspaper sellers and with the travelling show people he encountered at the Augsburg fair, the Plärrer. He became friends with them and learnt the travellers' language. Famously, he would draw on the cries of newspaper street vendors to illustrate his use of rhythm and gesture in his poetry and drama. His views on the innovative potential of popular forms for the art of the new urban age derive from his Augsburg childhood and adolescence. Rhythms could have a vital and energizing effect upon him. He had this to say about the language of Luther's Bible: 'Certain sayings from the Bible are indestructible. They go clean through you. You sit there shaken by shudders that get under your skin and run right down your back as in love'.[13] Affective pleasure in biblical language took hold of his body, arousing intense emotions akin to erotic desire. It would be similar with the soaring rhythms of the swing-boats at the Plärrer. We shall encounter numerous examples of this intense linkage between rhythm and erotic experience, in everyday life as well as in artistic performance.

However, this melancholeric Hydratopyranthropos's magical attraction to the rhythms of language and song could also become bound up with his fears about his debilitating condition. We have seen his account of how Bach's *St Matthew Passion* sent the extremely sensitive boy into a 'stupor', a 'wild coma', fearing for his heart as he struggled to control the effect of musical rhythm upon himself, physically and mentally. And we shall see, too, that he would confide similar alarming responses to music to his close friends Walter Benjamin and Hanns Eisler. Grand orchestral performance, bombast, great piano pieces and also monotonous rhythms could all trigger such responses, with the associated fear of illness and death. Aware that there was a very fine line between life and death, he would write: 'Death is but a half-breath away'.[14] Controlling the impact of musical and linguistic rhythms upon his powerfully lyrical sensibility amidst the 'storm' of his existence could be hugely problematic. The teenage Brecht learned behavioural techniques to alleviate those alarming responses and transform them into pleasurable experience. The supremely gifted Eugen Brecht, then, came to associate poetry with overriding chaotic and life-threatening forces.

Poetic rhythms, in turn, gave his life its significance, transforming abject fear and instability into the dynamic flow of rhythm, of chaos into order, of weakness into strength. Poetry and song could be a strongly life-affirming, physically and aesthetically pleasing act, their very simplicity yielding clarity where there had been the chaos of the storm.

The ever-provocative Brecht would also quickly learn to externalise his fears with displays of ironic distance, teasing contemporaries with shows of the singular sensibility peculiar to artistic genius. A classmate, Rudolf Prestel, who went to the opera with Brecht, witnessed him watching the performance with outstretched fingers. Brecht turned to Prestel and explained that it was given to him to listen to music with his finger tips, as if his fingers were acting like lightning conductors, channelling the charge of the music![15] He maintained to Prestel's brother, Ludwig, that one should play Bach with a changed beat and rhythm, much more simply. In that way, everyone could enjoy the music.

In his search to understand his troubled life, the adolescent Brecht oscillated between a Christian interpretation and one in which the individual will was sovereign. For example, in the short piece *Oratorium*, he identifies the storm as God's work, a test for the wretched artist who doubts God's existence but is swept up in the welling song of transfiguration with which the work ends.[16] By contrast, Eugen Brecht also wrote, in a Promethean manner: 'The storm's still going on but I'll never let myself be dragged down. I'll command my heart. I'll impose a state of siege upon my heart'.[17] At other times, nature emerges as a mediating, transcendent force. Along with the destructive, threatening storm, the tree, that traditional symbol of life, vigour and stability, figures as a key image in the boy's self-understanding, often, however, with a tragic turn. In 'The Burning Tree', the eponymous tree is assailed by flames which are intent on engulfing it. It is about to succumb: 'Yet, still and hugely lighting up the night / Like some historic warrior, tired, dead tired / But kingly yet in his despair / Stood the burning tree'.[18] This is the earliest of several 'tree' poems in which the young Brecht depicted life tragically, engulfed by violence and storms in a dark vision of existence.[19]

The diary of a late Wilhelmine adolescent: Writing, illness, sex

Brecht was by now writing avidly. His earliest known literary work is *Diary N° 10*, which was published for the first time only in 1989. Critics have been slow to exploit the diary, which contributes much to a fresh understanding of Brecht's personal and artistic trajectory before the First World War. He wrote *Diary N° 10* between May and December 1913, just a year after he knew for sure that he was a writer. The title indicates that this diary may well have followed nine others, now lost. Certainly, in it he refers to two earlier diaries. In any case, with the discovery of *Diary N° 10*, from 1913 onwards Brecht's voice becomes a near-constant presence in his biography.

The fifteen-year-old made diary entries almost daily and produced nearly 100 pages of published text. He records literary plans and drafts, life at home and at school, his friendships and sexual interests, his reading and, obsessively, the state of his health: 'During the night I had terrible heart palpitations. [...] The night went on forever!'.[20] As we have seen, fear of death from heart failure torments the sickly, nervous adolescent. This angst-ridden, confessional tone pervades *Diary N° 10*, contrasting starkly with the machismo, sarcasm and cynicism familiar from Brecht's diaries of the early 1920s. And *Diary N° 10* contains a lyrical voice which is at many points manifestly close to autobiographical experience.

This remarkable document takes us right up close to a truly remarkable, late Wilhelmine adolescent, laying bare this troubled, thin-skinned boy's extreme ambition, his hopes and fears at a time when he is struggling to learn how to cope with his violently oscillating feelings. Achieving control over them through ironic stylisation and, later, theoretical elaboration was some way off. The mark of the pre–1914 Brecht is his hyper-sensitivity, apparent in his response to suffering, in the emotional intensity of his lyrical mood and in his highly-strung, frequently disproportionate reactions to events. Against this hyper-sensitivity he was seeking to place an imperious impassivity, which in time would become a cult of coldness and, later still, the carefully controlled channelling of feelings and emotions orchestrated by the master dramatist. The conflict between the play of emotions and their control, between a thin and a thick skin, is integral to the young poet's 'quarrel' with himself, as W. B. Yeats describes the poet's perennial struggle within. At its starkest, suppression of sensitivity can mean the end of creativity, while exposure to it can mean the end of life. Hydratopyranthropos invariably experienced things in such stark contrasts. Finding forms of accommodation was hugely problematic, as the diary shows.

Its eighty poems, interspersed with ambitious plans and drafts for dramas and prose works, reveal a prodigiously productive, compulsive writer, already eyeing greatness. He drew upon traditional forms such as the ballad, though literary trends from around the turn of the century also colour his embryonic taste. The established image of the young Brecht as Bürgerschreck – outspoken, street-wise and relishing polemical exchange – is misplaced at this stage. That captures elements of a self that emerges from his experience of the war on the home front in 1914–16, after which Bert Brecht, as he came to call himself, began to attack the official dogma of God, Kaiser and Fatherland which he had previously revered.

In 1913 Eugen Brecht found the pomp and ceremony of military parades 'really entertaining', like the 'patriotic celebration' which was held in the Stadtgarten on 1 June to commemorate the centenary of the Wars of Liberation.[21] When he attended the school's celebration with Hartmann two weeks later, he found it 'Beautiful – But long'. The patriotic events stimulated Eugen's composition of a number of poems celebrating military prowess and heroic, soldierly death as sacrifice to the German nation, among them 'Banner Song', which begins: 'When the German lion is resting / In the high sheen of glory / We will always maintain / Our manly loyalty to the flag'. It ends: 'You died in the battle and struggle / As a loyal German man'.

Before the war, military parades took place at the Stadtgarten every Sunday. The other boys' displays of emotion were anathema to the deeply serious poet: 'Only Brecht stood to one side [...] very reserved'.[22] He adopted a manner of fastidious contemplation, exercising the strict control of his emotions like the Dichterfürst [poet-prince] Stefan George. Together with Rainer Maria Rilke, George was Germany's foremost living poet, a practitioner of an austere symbolism, whose priestly aura drew prominent artists and intellectuals into the fabled George Circle. In 1913 Eugen Brecht was among the host of George's admirers, announcing in his diary: 'I am converting to Stefan George'.[23] Extraordinary as it now sounds, since George later became one of his pet hates, Eugen Brecht signed up as a disciple in the George cult and penned stern thoughts such as, 'It's not a dishonour to be defeated / But it's a disgrace to admit defeat'. In the sonnet 'Men of Violence' he adopts his most severely militarist position:

> They stride through history
> With an iron, hard visage
> With eyes as hard as stone
> And a brow as fine as marble.
> [...]
> With honour they fight in manly fashion
> And though they crush many with brutal force
> They purify humanity's life.

Their violence is neither gratuitous nor simply for the sake of power but has the noble aim of cleansing humanity. Brecht's trademark dialectical topos of the necessity of violence to transform human life is established: violent sacrifice leads to suffering, which leads to purification. Hence, Eugen understood Napoleon's violence as necessity: 'People call him the greatest mass-murderer in the world. He was not so bad. He saw them all as the masses, the people. He did not kill eight million, rather *had to* kill *one*. But each one in the eight million was for him the only one'. Similarly, the young poet noted thoughts of 'battles, in which thousands perish with pale brows, Caesars who stand there rigid and great and untouched. They regard the people as numbers, as *one* number. And they calculate. They walk stiffly and calmly through rushing time. Only the poet sees the thin, dogged features around their pinched mouths. And he sees their souls'. In 1914 Eugen Brecht would view the Kaiser as the epitome of such a soldier emperor. The monumental resolve of such heroes to purify humanity distances them from the masses, whom they must sacrifice for the cause. In this way, suffering is incorporated within a logic in which its import is negated and explained away. Yet the problem of suffering would not, of course, go away.

On the more mundane level of the boy's everyday cares before the war, the diary reveals a similar anxiety and a desire to establish control when people threatened to escape his sphere of influence. His ill health put him at a distinct disadvantage: 'If only there were hope! If only I could get better. People only value their health when they have lost it! Maybe it will come back! – They're all leaving me, Enderlin, Bingen, Albrecht and even Gehweyer. That's grim. All these "friends" are going'.[24] While he was grounded, they made off in their small groups: 'Bored alone in the afternoon. – Nothing new. My heart's really good. – I'm losing Enderlin, Gehweyer's cycling, Albrecht's playing and swimming, Bingen's doing all three things and Hartmann, who knows? I can't see into him'.

Despite Walter Brecht's view of his elder brother's devoted acolytes, he was not yet – and certainly not yet in his own mind – the undisputed, charismatic centre of attention that he became for the Brecht Circle from the mid–1910s. How could he win the other boys over? He arranged endless one-on-one meetings with them where he could impose himself. He spent a lot of time with Fritz Gehweyer, who would die at the front in the First World War. A talented artist, Gehweyer shared Eugen's enthusiasms. On Sunday 18 May 1913 Brecht noted that the day before they had visited an exhibition at the Augsburg Art Club in the morning and in the afternoon they had enjoyed playing Chopin at Gehweyer's house. It was probably this seemingly innocuous event which Brecht recalled with such trepidation in a conversation with Walter Benjamin in Danish exile in October 1934. Benjamin, who was reading Dostoyevsky's *Crime and Punishment*, was taken aback by Brecht's comments:

> First of all he laid the principal blame for my illness on reading this. And to back up his argument he told me how in his youth the outbreak of a lengthy illness, the seed of which had probably long been present in him, ensued when one afternoon a school friend, against whose intentions he was already too weak to register a protest, played Chopin on the piano. Brecht ascribes particularly malign influences upon one's health to Chopin and Dostoyevsky.[25]

For Benjamin, in their exchanges Brecht was habitually a *provocateur*. However, it so happens that after hearing Chopin Brecht confided to his diary: 'The following night was miserable. Until 11 o'clock I had strong heart palpitations. Then I fell asleep, until 12 o'clock, when I awoke. So strong that I went to Mummy. It was terrifying'.[26] Like Bach and Beethoven, Chopin apparently had an alarmingly deleterious effect upon the boy's fragile organism, triggering the escalation of his chronic heart failure in 1913.

The boy struggled with nightly attacks, while he was seeking popularity in the eyes of Gehweyer and others. Gehweyer's sisters eyed their brother and Eugen, the 'two oddballs', with some amusement as they aped the manners of their male elders:

> After school they often paraded up and down Steingasse. They behaved like two nutty professors. They'd have their hands clasped behind their backs and would talk non-stop. [...] Finally our father asked them if they wanted to have chairs brought outside. A few times Brecht came into our flat too. But he acted in a very self-important way when he saw us. [...] They always had lofty plans.[27]

Girls were still a distant fascination, separated by social convention and adolescent inhibition. For a boy like Eugen in an all-boys' school with a male sibling, intimacy was only to be had with other boys. The budding professor Eugen enjoyed taking his friends to his attic or walking alone with a chosen friend. Never one to underestimate his importance, the teenager acknowledged a rare debt to Aristotle when he stylised himself and his friends as latter-day Peripatetics, whose structured thinking was stimulated by their movement.[28] It is apparent that these one-on-ones were a form of courtship. Again, Eugen Brecht and his friends were following the Peripatetics. He composed the poem 'The Two', in which the love of a couple out walking remains unspoken. It is a half-serious pastiche of Hugo von Hofmannsthal's famous poem of the same title:

> They strolled along together
> And wished to say such loving things
> But found the words far too hard

And uttered their fervent laments
About the weather and the bad times
And nothing about their torrid desire – – –
Many years have passed
But amidst their laments the two
Forgot to speak their love. – [29]

Eugen's ironic treatment of the laments highlights his sense of the futility of diffuse, ill-directed emotion, about which, as we shall see, he was forming the view that it was the mark of a hopeless person.

However, he noted with evident relish Mädi Hartmann's flirtatious comment, '*You*'ve ruined us!' and his own reply, 'I'm *completely* innocent!'. He confides to his diary, 'I really like Hartmann. He's nice – a replacement for le petit? – Hardly! I'll never get over him'. The love-sick Eugen's infatuation with 'le petit', Emil Enderlin, and his crushes on other boys run through the diary in a series of bitchy rivalries in the hot-house atmosphere of the single-sex grammar school. Enderlin was another of Brecht's friends who would die at the front. As we've seen, their relationship went back some two years to the time of Brecht's Confirmation, when they went ice-skating. Now Eugen struggles with a slight from Enderlin: 'I'm not seeing Enderlin any more. The other day he said to me: "You can't go to the military swimming school, you're not in the Wehrkraft anymore!" That hurt me a lot'. Like the other boys, he took some pride in his membership of the Wehrkraft but had been deemed unfit for duty, just as he had been forced to withdraw from other physical activities.

Eugen needed to know that he could 'see into' the others, finding their weak spots to confirm his superiority and thereby dominate sexually as well as intellectually. The ever-shifting kaleidoscope of relationships between the boys was played out in a constant struggle: 'In the afternoon walking with Albrecht. He's a nice boy. Comme ci, comme ça. But naïve as well. The other day he said: "Enderlin's not taking a walk, so I'll go with you!" (Bingen and me!) I got annoyed'. Albrecht did not understand the rules by which Eugen was playing: Enderlin's absence would be an opportunity to court Bingen if he were alone with him. Eugen turned to Hartmann but 'Hartmann felt insulted because he is a blockhead'. When Hartmann fought back, Eugen put him in his place: 'Row with Hartmann. I laughed at him because of his new suit. He bearded me. I dumped him for a week'.

Eugen was 'insouciantly happy' when he heard Weber calling Bingen names. Brecht chose Bingen for a first satirical portrait, in which, again, the Wehrkraft loomed large: 'The core of Mr Bingen's being is the Wehrkraft medal, which he acquired because of his unheard-of snappiness'. He undercut his admiration for Bingen's dashing manner with the suggestion that he wore the treasured medal in bed and in the bath. The rest of the portrait follows the same pattern. Admiration for his appearance – 'very elegant and smart' – is turned on its head with adolescent humour: 'Because of the oppressive and terrible tightness of his trousers the poor boy is forced to keep his hands in his pockets a lot. He does that with a great deal of self-discipline, bravery and stamina'.

But Eugen really liked the look of the witty and entertaining Bingen, who one day 'had a green Wehrkraft hat on. A striking fit. He's nice, upstanding, charming, has no character and is in general a lovely guy. It's just that he makes jokes. I like him. A snob. Ingratiates himself everywhere. He's teased everywhere, but he's taken seriously and is not stupid'. Bingen was usually top of the class. The diarist here uses terms from the boys' group language, an index of their values. 'Snob' is a term of approval, 'upstanding' probably a cipher for the boys' sexual play. Eugen feminises Bingen with 'nice' and 'charming' and gives this a twist with 'has no character', echoing Paul Julius Möbius and Otto Weininger's notorious views on women, with the implication that Bingen was submissive and could easily be won over by a genius male like Eugen Brecht.

On 16 September, the start of the new school year, he appeared to be over his infatuation with Enderlin: 'In the morning saw Enderlin again. Hm! My ardour has disappeared. But I still like him'. The following day he added, 'Enderlin arrived late and looked really pale and bleary-eyed. I'll not call him "petit" any more. No reason to. Unfortunately!'. Gossipy excitement surrounded Eugen's trysts. On that first day back, Oskar Lettner noted in his diary: 'In the last few days Eugen and Pfanzelt have got back together'.[30] Now nearly twenty, Pfanzelt had left school in 1912 to work for the city council. He was on holiday when he met Eugen on the afternoon of the 16th to play chess and to have a long conversation about boys at Eugen's school: 'Pfanzelt talked disparagingly about Honold. Also about Schipfel (+), Hartmann and Schneider'.[31] The following day's diary entry runs a predictable course: 'Walked with Pfanzelt [...] He was a *very* upstanding man. I like him!'. Shortly after, Pfanzelt visited Eugen and, as always, impressed him with his superb piano playing: 'A beautiful scherzo by Schubert and Chopin's glorious funeral march. The wonderful middle piece. It rings out above all the spheres. A gentle, sobbing, fine melody! And yet, beyond everything else, suffering. A pained, tormented soul weeps. And gives comfort'. Pfanzelt was, indeed, a fine musician, whose playing moved his friend deeply. Brecht gave himself to Pfanzelt's Chopin, immersing himself in the Romantic fusion of art and suffering, which he would later mock as pathological.

Pfanzelt's return was not the end of the story with Enderlin: 'In the evening Hartmann was reasonable for the first time since I've known him. Met le petit too. (I cannot write "Enderlin")'. The boy's inability to free himself of his attachment to Enderlin is a familiar scenario throughout Brecht's life: 'Relationship with Enderlin lukewarm. That's the most excruciating thing'. Nor were things easy with Hartmann, who was demonstrating his independence by boasting superior sexual experience: 'In the evening met Bingen. Went walking. Animated discussion. Then called on Hartmann. He and Albrecht are going to the red light area. That's on my agenda too'. As Gehweyer's letters to Brecht from 1915 and 1916 show, things continued much the same after the diary entries break off. Other boys like the blond giant Caspar Neher became close friends and girls would soon start to feature, too. Brecht's relationships with boys in adolescence and early manhood spawned the homoeroticism of early works like *Baal*, *The Life of Edward the Second of England*, 'Bargan Gives Up' and 'Ballad of Friendship'. But from the mid-1920s, when Brecht began to regulate his life on much stricter lines and to tailor his macho public image, it no longer features.

Throughout his courtships, Eugen was contending with his heart and other complaints. However, when he was off school once more, a diagnosis quite different from an enlarged heart was made: 'In the morning the doctor came. A really young one because Müller was away. He examined me precisely: a nervous condition! I should just go back to school. There was absolutely nothing to worry about! Hm! I found that very edifying'.[32] This diagnosis of a nervous complaint clearly riled the boy, whose facial contortions and grimace of childhood settled in adolescence. The young doctor's diagnosis strongly suggested neurotic behaviour and catapulted him right back into the world of his 'nervous' suffering in childhood. However, the young doctor's diagnosis was probably not unwelcome to the boy's parents. They were caring for their teenage son at night as if he were a young child when his mother's health was a major cause for concern in the family and his father had a long-standing gastric complaint, which would soon require surgery.

Two conflicting approaches to medical wisdom clashed in the contrasting diagnoses of Eugen's condition. However imprecise his diagnosis, Müller was satisfied that the boy's complaint was organic, but the young doctor believed that the condition was caused by a nervous complaint, which manifested itself in a heart spasm, in effect a panic attack. Gripped by the abject fear of heart failure, the boy could not, of course, himself distinguish between an organic and a neurotic condition. This only exacerbated his anxiety and confusion. Indeed, until the end of his life Brecht remained distressed by a condition which he knew to be serious but which his doctors could never adequately diagnose. It repeatedly threatened death, only for him to survive. This in turn prompted the abiding fear, fuelled by the stories that children told one another, that after an attack he might be buried alive.[33] That fear, too, remained with Brecht for the rest of his life, prompting him to leave specific instructions for his wife Helene Weigel to deal with his body after his death. Knowing, ironic distance could only take him so far in dealing with his fears.

Therapeutics

On his doctor's instructions – probably Müller's – Eugen regularly attended the Augsburg spa baths for hydrotherapy. But he did so under protest, unconvinced of their capacity to help him. He duly received corroboration of his view: 'At the baths I got a nose-bleed and was afraid'.[34] However, he enjoyed the regular home visits by a physiotherapist, Engelbert Löffler: 'He did gymnastics with me. A very nice, polite and modest man. I really like him'. Brecht appreciated Löffler's efforts to rebuild his motor capacity through behavioural therapy. Such an approach to improving human behaviour through learned techniques would develop into a central tenet of Brecht's philosophical and dramatic thinking. Faced by the continuing failure of conventional bio-scientific medicine, Brecht would experiment with other therapies such as respiratory massage and the Kneipp Cure. Collaborators and lovers from the 1920s to the 1950s, from Elisabeth Hauptmann to Käthe Rülicke, would regularly massage the rheumatic Brecht. And his advice to his sickly lovers Margarete Steffin and Ruth Berlau would be strongly informed by this behavioural thinking.

The state of his health plunged the boy into a bleak assessment of his condition: 'Things are worse again just now with my health. I've got no life apart from school.

It's my only distraction. As long as I can go there, everything will be ok'. On a hiking trip with his classmates to Gablingen, he struggled with his wretched physical state:

> From there to Peterhof, one and a half hours is a long time. Heart palpitations, swift, intermittent. Uphill from Peterhof to Adelsried. Endlessly long. If I'd known in the forest that it was still such a long way, I'd have stopped and lain down. [...] I walked right at the back, with Abenstein and Lemle. Forgot my heart. A fun train journey with Bingen, Neher and Albrecht.

If he could forget his heart, the problem would go away for a while. However, he also knew that this was not always possible: 'State of my heart bad. In the evening my heart was very loud and fast. Fear. No change'. He tended to dramatise other complaints: 'Now and then a bit of headache. *Angst*'. And then: 'I've got catarrh (!) [...] Catarrh awful'. This led to another scene: 'When I tried to turn around on the bench before school started this morning at eight o'clock, there was a stabbing pain in my back. I couldn't even breathe. The pain when I breathed lasted until ten o'clock. Then it got worse. Went home to bed. In the evening I could hardly draw breath anymore'. At the mercy of his catarrh, the bed-bound boy received another visit from the doctor: 'In the morning Dr Müller came. Dry bronchitis. Interesting illness. Anybody can have a cold. But whoever gets bronchitis ... !'. The doctor's knowing gloss on his diagnosis was not lost on the young diarist. As the view gained acceptance in the family that the boy was prone to hypochondria, his kinship of suffering with his mother, hitherto integral to their strong bond, started to break down. Much to his parents' displeasure, the boy continued to stay off school: 'Normally when I'm ill again mummy says: "If only you'd obeyed. I've got it again now". Of course. And this morning she says: "Why aren't you in school?". I'd be afraid to be ill. Daddy's surly and mummy's always moaning about all the work. And so agitated! I'm already worried about the four weeks. Always ranting and raving!'. Sophie Brecht would be supervising her fifteen-year-old during their four weeks together at the sanatorium in Bad Steben. His mother's earlier criticisms of his failure to obey her instructions about cleanliness, which, she claimed, had resulted in him passing sickness on to her, now gave way to the reproach of faking illness. In the face of pressure at home not to be ill anymore and of medical opinion which was ill-informed, conflicting and evidently sceptical towards his claims, the boy could henceforth never be wholly sure whether he was faking it or not and what courses of action lay open to him.

In the summer of 1913 he composed two poems in which he rehearsed contrasting ways to deal with his predicament, signified by the familiar imagery of struggle with a violent storm. The first of the two poems, 'Storm', uses the image in the sense of a military assault, led by a warrior. In the second poem, 'Festive Day', the poet imagines God's protection from the ravages of the world. 'Storm', written in those confusing days before Bad Steben, is a Bonapartist exhortation to realise extreme ambition through ruthless action: 'You must reap the fruits in the very first charge! / Must boldly rise above both peak and vale / And must exploit the happy rapture of that early ardour / In violent charges and endeavour'.[35] Echoing his strategic war games and the language of patriotic verse, the boy adopted what is recognisably the father's way, all militant aggression, violence and the assertion of the individual will, mirroring

Berthold Brecht's attitude towards illness. The military assault must be strategically conceived and rapidly executed. Life is unforgiving to those who do not adopt such an attitude. The overriding imperative is to secure glory through decisive action, which renders all else insignificant.

Brecht's later cultivation of this attitude as the aggressive, macho male has been much remarked upon. The attitude lent itself to Brecht's later adoption of philosophies of will, both individualist, as in Nietzsche, and collectivist, as in Karl Marx. It has not been appreciated how much of what we might call the mother's way survived in the contemplative poet that was always part of Brecht's artistic make-up, too, especially after Brecht's adoption in the late 1920s of the manner of the wisdom writer. The New Testament attitude of non-resistance, embodied by Christ, eventually found expression in the survivalist attitude of Taoist Wu Wei, non-resistance to the flux of things in a dangerously authoritarian world. As we can see, Brecht was no systematic philosophical thinker, rather a highly complex artist, responding to the world experienced through a quite dysfunctional organism, who would famously observe: 'A man with one theory is lost. He needs several of them, four, lots!'.[36] We shall encounter the contemplative manner in 'Festive Day' presently. It was written under his mother's tutelage at Bad Steben, when he returned to her path of Christian rectitude and submissiveness, placing himself in God's hands.

Shortly after arriving at Bad Steben, Eugen captured his first impressions in a poem for the Reitters, showing off his talent to his relatives. He followed up with a letter to Walter in amusing, doggerel French, mimicking Paul Verlaine's *Romances sans Paroles*. The gist of both letters was that it was raining all the time and it was boring, though there were distractions, as he explained to 'Mon cher Gautier' in a French that was fluent but not flawless:

> As-tu déjà un compagnon?
> Moi non!
> Mon ennuie est gros –
> Il y a beaucoup de musique
> Très jolie et chikee
> Et j'attends toujour à une nouveau
> Morçeau![37]

Walter was with his grandma, while Berthold had returned to Borkum for a holiday, this time without the family. Eugen imagined his father 'sitting by the North Sea / sweating in the monstrous heat'.[38] He was probably with Marie Röcker.

Dr Rubner, the house physician at Bad Steben, confirmed the boy's nervous condition on arrival, which Eugen Brecht accepted without demur. He summarised his complaints and his mother's in his diary: 'In the evening we always had headaches. No pains. We tried to keep to the regime. [...] In the second week head better. [...] Thursday mummy vomiting and feeling bad'.[39] Sophie wrote to Walter: 'Eugen finds it so difficult to make friends. He's always busy with his treatment and is not allowed to go on any excursions. After the baths you've got to go to bed for two hours but are not allowed to read'. Tonics like hay flower were used in the baths. He bathed every second day, went on short strolls and drank a beaker of chalybeate water every morning and afternoon, which, as he put it in another letter to the Reitters, 'tastes as sweet as ink'. The house rule forbidding reading in bed after a bath proved particularly difficult for Eugen, fuelling his boredom.

However, life at the sanatorium had its compensations. He attended performances of popular theatre and classical music concerts. Fortified by his treatment, he enthused about Mozart, Wagner, Haydn and Beethoven, taking this 'strong' music in his stride. On arrival his eye had immediately alighted on the reading room, where he spent much time, hatching grand literary plans and noting eleven poems in his diary. For the most part, his compositions were satirical verses about fellow guests and his perennial portrayals of heroic death. He noted with satisfaction the view of his admired Frau Veeh, a fellow patient from Weimar, whom he accompanied on a walk: 'I have the feeling, Eugen, that you will become one of the very greats of our people'.[40] He had evidently left her in no doubt.

'Festive Day' stands out from the other compositions at Bad Steben by virtue of its sustained subjectivity. Its 'inwardness' is the very antithesis of the lyrical persona that Brecht would subsequently adopt, even in contemplative mode. As is well-known, he would later deride the renowned poets of inwardness, Rilke and George. 'Festive Day' invokes the recovery of health and happiness through withdrawal from the stormy world into the immortal soul:

> Once upon a time - - -
> I crept right back inside myself
> And was alone within my soul
> Blissful in the pale half-light.
>
> I espied my heart's pulsing beat
> And felt my red blood racing.
> In my soul there dawned a festive day
> The sun shone pure and good.
>
> And I thought:
> If I could be alone for myself, a being quite alone
> And could hear my soul's secret laughter – - -:
> Rage away, o vale of tears.[41]

Eugen Brecht writes here as the pious son of a devout mother with the devotional attitude encouraged by his Confirmation piece. In its reliance not on the will of the individual but on God's grace for the resolution of his predicament, 'Festive Day' is the antithesis of 'Storm'. The poet conceives of the soul, God's precious gift, as a haven within the self, into which he withdraws. Joyfully, he observes and feels the vigorous working of his heart. Nestled in his soul, he is immune to the ravages of the world around. Christian faith is affirmed in the imaginative projection of a healthy heart and of the soul in harmony with nature.

It is telling that Eugen Brecht confided to his diary that, of all his compositions, he had chosen 'Festive Day' as his first piece to submit for publication to the Munich literary magazine *Jugend* [*Youth*].[42] In the event, he heard nothing back. However, he felt that his heart had improved dramatically at Bad Steben: 'Took fourteen baths.

Drank chalybeate water. Health very good. Heart problems now nearly disappeared'.
However, Bad Steben by no means signalled the end of the matter, despite the boy's
longing to overcome it either by violent action or Christian wisdom. Acutely self-
conscious about his body, he monitored the state of his health daily: 'When I work
in the evening blood rushes to my head at once. That's bad for my sleeping, which is
otherwise good'. And so the health problems recurred through adolescence and into
adulthood, some no doubt imaginary, others very real.

Showcasing extreme talent: *The Harvest*

In his reading and writing Eugen Brecht initially followed Naturalism and the *fin-de-
siècle* aestheticist trends of Symbolism, Neo-Romanticism and *Jugendstil*. He noted
the books he had been reading, sometimes with friends. His parents gave him books
as presents and he bought others himself at Steinicke's bookshop on Ludwigstrasse.
He spent much time in Steinicke's lending library, picking books off the shelves and
reading them at great speed. The girls who worked there were another attraction,
although he was still too shy to speak to them. Among the books that he bought in
1913 were Detlev von Liliencron's graphic poems about the brutality of war, which
were 'very fine ballads!', and an anthology of French poetry with a 'glorious poem by
Verhaeren, "The Rain"', which he bought with five marks from his father.[43] He hoped
to be able to buy a collection of Verhaeren's poems if he could sell some of his own
work. Adding to his collection of Hebbel's *Works*, in June 1913 Sophie Brecht bought
her fifteen-year-old his *Aesthetic Writings*: 'I was really thrilled!'. He was eager to
engage with this famous dramatist's reflections on aesthetics at a time when his own
affective responses to art could only lead him to question Aristotle's *Poetics*, with its
emphasis upon the audience's response to dramatic action through the emotions of
fear and pity. In time, it would be self-evident to Brecht that he must replace this
foundational text of European tragedy with his own quite different dramatic approach.

At school Brecht consumed German classics from the eighteenth and the early
nineteenth centuries and from the medieval period. Latin literature was another
staple. He composed verses in Latin such as the *memento mori* 'Victor Mors', which
begins: 'Omnes victores superat sors; – – / Magnos prosternit/ Neque miseros
spenit – – / Omnes, omnes superat Mors'.*[44] Not only could Eugen assimilate and
re-cast Latin, French and German tropes, his capacity to reflect on his own writing
was already well developed, too. He displayed his ambition to master all the genres
and grand themes, as well as his awareness of his limitations, prefacing his 'Men of
Violence' with the note, 'an attempt to form a sonnet'. He described 'Homeland' as the
'attempt at a ballad. I've not yet mastered the style'. Among other ambitious plans, 'The
Dying Village' aimed to explore what happened when death hit a community: 'Then
characters change, or better, grow more intense. The world changes'. These were the
words of someone sharply aware of the dramatic potential of such extreme situations

---

* The English translation of the title is 'The Victor Death' and of the opening lines: 'Fate conquers all
   victors; – – / It strikes down the great / Nor does it spurn the wretched – – / Death conquers all, all'.

into which people could be plunged and in which intense conflicts were played out, effecting change.

Brecht resembles Schiller and Hebbel in his desire to structure such conflicts with the sharply drawn contrasts at play in his imagination. Yet the young Eugen also acknowledged: 'I don't yet have the strength for dramas. My plans are completely ripe – their elaboration is much, much more difficult'. He told Hartmann about his first drama *Samson* but was later forced to acknowledge: 'I'm not making progress with the drama! It's come to a standstill'. This remained a very real issue for Brecht. He was driven to the dramatically structured representation of conflicts but the execution of the core idea would not come easily to him. Overcoming this difficulty was, of course, absolutely essential if he were to make his mark in the theatre, the sphere of social interaction that was beginning to really matter to him.

He turned to other genres – satire and poetry, – then wrote, 'I'm producing virtually nothing but poetry! – Everything else is dormant!'. He had an extraordinary facility to generate lyrical narratives in ballad form and hoped for a breakthrough with his poetry but maintained a self-critical attitude there too: 'Yesterday sent off a poem "A Hundred Years Ago", which I'd written in the night. Afterwards I saw that various things were missing and that the title was wrong'. The title suggests that the poem was about the Wars of Liberation. It has been assumed that the poem no longer exists. In fact, Brecht followed his own advice and changed the title to the much more evocative '1813', leaving the original title as the opening of the poem: 'A hundred years ago a storm raged / Through German lands from the mountains to the sea'.[45] Later in the year Brecht published the poem as one of an unattributed pair, '1813 1913', in *The Harvest*, the literary magazine which he founded with Gehweyer. These two poems can now be attributed to Brecht. As we shall see, Brecht wrote some 80 per cent of the material published in *The Harvest*, much of which was originally unattributed. The poem '1813' is a celebration of German heroism at the Battle of Leipzig, where Napoleon was defeated. In '1913' the young poet urges his fellow Germans to look to that example of past heroism at a time when 'again a world is standing / Stiffly against us and we are quite alone'. On the eve of the First World War, the young Brecht faithfully represented the patriotic values which he had assimilated.

Yet he remained dissatisfied as he struggled to channel the intensity of his feelings into his art. As we've seen, for a while he believed the way forward to lie with the tightly controlled form and priestly symbolism of Stefan George. Invited in 1928 to comment on George's early influence on him, Brecht, long free of the spell, sidestepped the issue with characteristic ridicule: 'I myself don't object to the fact that George's poetry appears empty: I have nothing against emptiness. But its form is too self-indulgent'.[46] In 1913 George's disciple produced a creditable imitation of the master's form and diction in the heroic military landscape of 'Moon!'.[47] A desolate scene after a battle is depicted through the eyes of the 'blazing stormer', in which smitten heroes are close to death. Yet the austere, Georgean vision gives way in the final stanza to unchecked emotion, the poem ending: 'Moon, oh I really think / You are weeping!'. The self-critical Eugen writes below 'Moon!': 'Final line banal!'. He follows up two days later: 'I understand. It's virtually worthless. All my poetry is a swill of feelings. Without form, style, thoughts. I must change tack. Fine miniatures of poems!'. Georgean diction and form helped to control that swill of feelings in other poems composed at that time. Brecht also evoked a trance-like vision, in which the poet, like the soldier emperor, is distanced from banal, everyday human cares:

> I'm hardly writing. Not a shame. Only occasionally now do I feel in lost hours that I am a poet. Then the worlds sink away. Time stops. And I see people hurrying. Lumbering, grief-stricken figures, reckless adventurers, stray ruminators and thinkers, who remain stuck in their maturation. Workers, who hasten and work and achieve nothing. Battles, in which thousands perish with pale brows, Caesars, who stand there stiffly and great and untouched.[48]

At this juncture when the mastery of feelings was beginning to emerge as a vital issue, Eugen was amply disposed to share George's view of the kinship between poet and soldier emperor. However, Brecht would soon reject artistic immersion in such a trance-like state as pathological, combating it with a vigorous assertion of clarity of artistic vision. Nor was the plight of workers lost on him in his sympathy for human suffering.[49]

Undeterred by the rejection of his poetry and the banning of the Merry Stone Swingers, Eugen Brecht relied on what he could do best as he sought to impress his friends with his talent: he embarked on another publishing venture. He discussed his plans with Gehweyer in August 1913. As with the puppet theatre, hard-nosed business interests figured prominently: 'We discussed a magazine, *The Day*. He asked for one mark to do the writing. I was then supposed to edit, design, hectograph and distribute the magazine. In exchange for a profit of – twenty-five pfennigs! He seems to think I'm stupid'.[50] Gehweyer evidently knew that Eugen really wanted it. They found a way forward, even offering fees to contributors. The plan to publish forty copies fortnightly in an A5 format shows their confidence in the ready supply of material. No prizes for guessing where most of it would come from – and who would pocket the lion's share of the fees. They settled on the title *The Harvest*. Max Hohenester, a talented boy in the parallel class, promised to collaborate. They made a good start with the first issue but by September the picture was mixed: 'We're completing the second number of *The Harvest*. First one sold out! But we'll soon have to stop! Time!!!'.[51] It was the same story in October: 'The magazine's blossoming. Pity we've got to stop soon'. In fact, they pressed on, completing six issues in all in the months until February 1914. The fifth issue, scheduled for completion before Christmas 1913, was in the event pulled, probably because of Brecht's father's serious illness in December.

Like the Merry Stone Swingers' magazine and much work thereafter, *The Harvest* was a collaborative venture, with Eugen Brecht at the forefront as the major creative force. He succeeded in making his world of literature matter so much to his friends that they took part, irrespective of their talent. In addition to Gehweyer and Hohenester, Bingen joined in the editorial work. Max Schneider did some editorial work, too, and had a poem published. Gehweyer was a talented designer who shared Eugen's high ambition for the project, producing multicoloured, filigree illustrations in the art nouveau manner of *Jugendstil*. Eugen was actually the author of nearly all the first issue, though several pieces appeared under the names of others. He drew on his writings in *Diary Nº 10* and experimented by signing his contributions in several ways: Eugen Brecht, E. Brecht, E. B., Bertold Brecht and Bertold Eugen. He settled on Bertold Eugen as his *nom de plume* over the coming two years or so. Pieces from *Diary N° 10* found their way into *The Harvest* under the names of Schipfel, Kölbig and Pfanzelt.[52] Mindful of what had happened to the earlier venture, *The Harvest* had little to do with school. It was conceived as a genuine literary magazine, not a school rag, and was certainly a creative alternative to the drudgery of the boys' education.

Like his other compositions at this time, Eugen's pieces in *The Harvest* do not yet possess the dynamic, musical quality of his work in the war years. He displays his wit and irony in a number of short prose pieces, particularly in the satirical 'Story of Someone who was Never Too Late' with its strong autobiographical echoes of extreme ambition, talent and a fascination with still distant girls.[53] The story was the first piece in *The Harvest* under Brecht's own name. He considered it so important that issue two carried the announcement that it was to appear as a separate publication. All his friends could recognise something of Eugen in the fifteen-year-old in the story, who was 'clever. Very clever. Monstrously clever. He was so clever that in the still of the night he could hear the trees grow and consumptive lizards coughing. Yes – he was even cleverer'. And, as the story goes on to say, he knew it. But his greatest talent was that he was never late. He spends much time thinking how he might use his extraordinary abilities, hovering between a future as a Georgean prince of poets [Dichterfürst] and a Bonapartist soldier emperor. Yet each has its drawback: 'The prince of poets, unfortunately he had to be able to write somewhat. And the soldier emperor has first to find the stupid king to overthrow'. So the boy becomes a sales assistant in a department store with the ambition of becoming the king of the stock exchanges. Then he falls in love, writing a poem to his 'dark-eyed beauty', but he discovers that he had a weakness: he is shy and avoids his future wife whenever he sees her. That is the way things stay until 'one day, when it was raining, he saw her on someone else's arm'. He reflects again and again on his strange predicament: 'How can someone who is *so* clever come too late??????'. The story ends with him going insane thinking about this.

The ironic treatment of the talented but shy youth is already some way removed from the confessional mode of *Diary N° 10* where the boy wrestles earnestly with idealised images of the self and their opposite, feelings of abject emptiness, which feed on his dark anxieties of personal destruction. Irony and self-stylisation, coupled with macho male aggression, would emerge as key literary strategies to drive his anxieties to the margins.

Berthold Brecht's operation: Christian faith and poetic resolve

Berthold Brecht, that arch-enemy of ill-health, was himself laid low with an illness in December 1913 which cut through his son's intense pre-occupation with his own predicament: 'Daddy's hardly allowed to eat anything. Gastric catarrh. We're not used to seeing Daddy at home. He's going to the doctor's tomorrow morning. I'm terribly frightened'.[54] Berthold Brecht had been suffering from stomach ulcers for several years but the boys were shocked to hear the word operation. For them, an operation was not far from death.[55] Eugen was inclined to fear the worst:

Mummy said falteringly: 'Daddy's probably going to Munich next week to see a professor'. I was shocked and saw that Walter was shocked too. His eyes grew really big. O God! (What a comfortable religion Christianity is: One believes firmly in *the* help of God! – And I'm doubting! –) It will surely not be cancer or an ulcer! – – In the evening everyone at home. We're afraid and worried.[56]

This confrontation with his father's mortality became a test of faith, which brought out the radical in the anxious Eugen. He objected to the cosiness of his mother's Christian message with its pat answer that one should trust in God's help. In school, the boy was by now reading the words of the faith directly himself rather than the commentaries which the clerics had previously supplied. His doubt, still that of a believer, was rooted in the evident discrepancy between the theological certainty of his religious education and the profound uncertainties surrounding the human suffering which he witnessed. Essentially the same discrepancy informs his one-act play, *The Bible*, set in the Thirty Years' War. He wrote a draft of the final scene in his diary on 7 December from the perspective of the radical believer testing faith. The play was an implicit challenge, too, to Schiller's idealism in his *Wallenstein* trilogy about the Thirty Years' War.

In his poem 'Care' he captured the foreboding gripping the family:

The day is dead. Grey care
Moves quietly around the quiet house.
It's as if a prayer were searching blindly
Through muggy rooms. And something's there
Outside the door gigantic and silent.[57]

Death enters and two candles for the dead smoulder red in silence amidst prayers and tears.

Deathly quiet pervaded the Brecht household the day before Berthold's departure: 'Daddy's cupping his face in his hands'. Although Berthold had been doing his best to cheer up his son, describing what lay before him in his hearty Badensian dialect, the mood remained sombre: 'Now, 8.30 in the evening. Everyone together in the room. Walter's playing the largo, Daddy's watching by the piano and Mummy's crying. It's so quiet. Unfortunately! – How will things be in a week?'.

Eugen believed that the gravity of his father's illness was being kept from him. He wanted the truth, however unpalatable. Gehweyer's father made light of things: '"Well, what is it now? Don't you think that Daddy will probably have an operation straight away?". I became terribly frightened. It's so muggy. When Uncle Karl came in the evening, Grandma took him off into the kitchen. They're hiding something'. Eugen then wrote a letter to his father which has not survived. In his reply, Berthold urged him as the elder boy to set a good example. He also suggested, unwisely, that a time would perhaps come when the boys would have to do without the support of one or other of their parents. Berthold urged his son not to think of his lines as a farewell letter, which again only prompted Eugen to fear the worst: 'Daddy's having his operation. – Mummy's staying there all the same, despite the fact that he has a carer. Proves the same thing. [...] We're afraid. Everything points to the operation happening tomorrow. God help us!'.

The operation was to be performed by the eminent surgeon and privy councillor Albert Krecke. Eugen noted: 'Aunty travelled to Munich today: More proof. – Horrendous'. Aunt Amalia came by on the Friday evening to let the boys know that the operation had taken place. Eugen wrote: 'He is very weak now. So yesterday was the (serious) operation!'. They told him that his father was making a good recovery and at first he accepted what he was told. But then a conflict erupted when he spotted that the adults were not telling him the whole truth. They evidently believed they should spare the highly-strung boy some of the detail, saying that he could talk to his mother on the phone at his aunt's. However:

> Grandma and Aunty received us ululating. We were sent to the phone. – Mummy said that Daddy's doing well. He's being well looked after. Daddy says hello. – I understood every word. Then my uncle went on the line. 'How is he?' … 'What, still?' … 'The Privy Councillor's coming again today?' … 'Yes. Say hello to Berthold. And get well soon …' Daddy's sicker than we think. A scene. How I hate this harping on about feelings. And all these scenes. Constructed so illogically! […] In the evening I found out that Daddy was better than in the morning. O God. Grandma tells wonderfully sweet stories. Smart woman!

Years later in conversation with Elisabeth Hauptmann, Brecht recalled Grandma Brezing coming in the evening and telling wonderful stories.[58] The boy's pleasure was vitiated by the deeply distasteful sight of his hapless relatives surrendering to their feelings. He did not mention to Hauptmann how his Grandma's stories contrasted with the sheer banality of his other relatives' unstructured display of feelings. This was truly offensive to someone who was discovering how to mediate the acute experience of pain, suffering and emotional turmoil through controlled artistic expression. Unlike his other relatives, Grandma Brezing possessed real artistic understanding. She comforted him again the next evening with 'really lovely' stories 'about lots of people'.[59] This episode shows quite why in later years Brecht recalled his story-telling Grandma Brezing with such admiration.

Eugen was less enamoured with Aunt Amalia, who appeared in the afternoon and started a row: ' "What, you played music yesterday, played the music box? Well, just think what people will say!". Haha! I'm supposed to let myself be bricked in. And wait. Wait!'. At this time of great suffering and anxiety Eugen needed to find ways to express himself: 'I must always write. At this time. Daddy's very seriously ill. "Close to falling asleep" said Grandma. And Aunty: "Daddy … Yesterday was a critical day". And later: "Things aren't better today"'. Like Grandma Brezing, the boy learned to combat illness through a mental and affective concentration upon story-telling. In fact, he began to formulate a 'hard' position towards the expression of feelings and its consequences, which would take on ever greater significance in the years to come: 'One shouldn't offer comfort. Only a warning. No one benefits if we surrender ourselves to these thoughts. We are after all quite young … I can't sit there thinking. I'd rather get a bad name. Anyway … these people. Dumb asses'. If Grandma Brezing is the epitome of female folk wisdom and strength in Brecht's work, Aunt Amalia is the prototype of the stupid bourgeois wife, who mouths conventional morality and muddled feelings, all the while blind to the hypocrisy and corruption within the family, usually represented by an aggressive and rapacious businessman-husband.

Amongst the warnings which Brecht was prompted to compose is 'The Bouquet', his antidote to the 'swill of feelings' amongst his relatives, a miniature of controlled, Georgean artistry. The boy imagines his father's hospital room: 'The tired sun rays / Dance around the room / And the carnation blooms / Must quietly die'. He commented with evident satisfaction: 'Such a little thing, too, is without any verbiage … I am very inclined towards such little poems at the moment. They are dainty and pretty – I think'. Without the subjective religiosity of 'Festive Day', the pared-back objectivity of 'The Bouquet' points the way to other such contemplative verse, culminating in the late 'Buckow Elegies'.

While he dismissed Aunt Amalia, he was more inclined to believe his distressed mother that his father was now getting better. However, her own physical state was worrying: 'In the afternoon we brought Mummy home from the railway station. She was very agitated. Her fingers were moving and twitching all the time'.[60] Sophie Brecht's nervous reaction at this stressful time suggests a condition worryingly similar to both her son's involuntary movement and to Max Hermann's epilepsy. A congenital link between them all may well have existed.

Berthold Brecht's condition improved and his boys visited him on Christmas Day: 'In the morning to Daddy in Munich. Daddy was sitting on the sofa in a little brown jacket. Looked really weak. He was propping his head up with his hand. He raised his head as we went in: Now then! When he looked me in the eye, I saw tears. […] In the evening on the train with Mummy full of joy. She looks really good, truly full of the joys of life. She's doing a lot, a lot more than she should'.[61] Eugen concludes his diary with a re-affirmation of belief: 'Lord God, I thank you! / I cry out from my distress and suffering / And my breast swells with love / Lord God, I thank you!'. However, Berthold Brecht's health problems would not go away. And after he had recovered from his operation, he risked much, both within the family and in public esteem for him as a prominent Augsburg citizen, by bringing his lover Marie Röcker back to Augsburg. It was an open secret that Berthold Brecht was a frequent visitor at her flat on Rosenaustrasse. In fact, as Walter Brecht writes, such was the reputation of his father – and his elder brother – that Haindl's work force later sent a letter to the owners, demanding the dismissal of the 'morally depraved' Berthold Brecht, whose behaviour was as bad as his elder son's.[62]

The relationship between father and elder son was by no means untroubled. The boy's agitated responses during Berthold Brecht's illness had their place in an increasingly turbulent relationship. As can happen when a sensitive adolescent finds that an admired father does not embody every last strength, Eugen projected back on to his father the blame for his own suffering during his father's illness. On that same Christmas Day, Eugen composed 'The Child' and 'The Fathers'.[63] These two ballads treat the murder of boys by three fathers: one recklessly killing his own son; a second with a blood lust fuelled by alcohol; and the third vengeful towards the second, whose son he murders following the murder of his own son by the second. This gruesome slaughter of innocent boys by murderous fathers certainly gives pause for thought. Eugen evidently just had to write in order, through a narcissistic inversion, to deal with the pain and suffering which his father, who had claimed immunity from such pain and suffering, had visited upon him.

Eugen ceased to obey his father and provoked regular altercations.[64] There was equal vehemence on both sides: Berthold had the louder voice but Eugen responded with explosive defiance and scorn. When reports of Eugen's bad behaviour at school reached his father's ears, he insisted that his son should not disrespect his teachers. Walter claims that however angry his father became, he would never beat Eugen. However, Brecht later recalled: 'Whenever my father thrashed me he wailed, though not so truly harrowingly, and then he added that it hurt him more than me'.[65] That sounds more like it.

At times, Eugen's relationship with his mother regained its old intensity. Otherwise it was marked by the self-absorbed adolescent's neglect of anything outside himself and by her own limited horizons: 'Mummy's birthday. I'd completely forgotten. Then I bought *In Tune with the Infinite*. But that didn't really make her happy. Mummy asked where I'd bought it. As if that's what it was about. I'm only glad that I didn't give her the book of poems (mine) after all'.[66] Ralph Waldo Trine's *In Tune with the Infinite*, a cult book amongst the young and non-conformists, was hardly Sophie Brecht's style. Her son was developing a sense of taste, with an associated lifestyle and appearance, which she could only find offensive. His reading included the great French *poètes maudits*, Verlaine and Rimbaud.[67] Their 'wild' writing had not yet left its mark on his compositions but it certainly had on his behaviour. He stank. Like his heroes, he did not change his clothes, rarely washed and did not brush his teeth. After a childhood spent withdrawn because of shame at his fragile condition, this boy with the impeccable manners was going on the offensive, displaying a neglect of personal hygiene, which, as many people attest, remained a life-long habit.

His displays of grossness were in fact also a means to conceal his body's production of unusually rotten smells, particularly bad breath. After listening to his friend Geyer play 'Death in the Forest' from Mozart's 11th piano sonata, Brecht noted on the score: 'He breathed into his hand and / smelled his breath, it / smelled rotten / then he thought: / I'll soon die'.[68] This is Brecht's first use of a motif of gross morbidity which recurs in his writings and is connected with a second motif, appetite. As if his cardiac and motorneural complaints were not enough, Eugen Brecht had developed a renal problem which left him susceptible to, among others things, calcium oxalate kidney stones, which occur when the urine is too alkaline.[69] Halitosis is a frequent side-effect, leaving a metallic taste in the mouth, which impairs the appetite, whatever other impulses and desires the sufferer might have. Brecht's renal condition plagued him for the rest of his life. There is some overlap with the symptoms of carditis – chill, fatigue, dizziness and confusion – which only compounded his predicament. He would later write of his appetite: 'I liked big appetites very much. It seemed to me to be a natural advantage if people could enjoy eating a lot, just if they wished to have a lot, could get a lot out of things etc. My meagre appetite was something I did not like about myself. It is true that I had intense wishes to possess this or that, but they were sudden and irregular instead of constant and reliable'.[70] Weight loss became a perennial problem for Brecht, as it was for his mother. He became a hunger artist of a very specific kind, who wrote of his own lack of appetite and compensated by creating monstrous characters with Gargantuan appetites. And Brecht showed that, for all his impeccable manners, he, like those characters, could behave very badly indeed. He willed himself to become evil, demonic like his club-footed friend Pfanzelt, setting out to seduce boys and, soon, girls, conquering and controlling them, a schoolboy Vautrin or Baal. He was made for the world of the *poètes maudits*.

The Heroism and the Madness of War 1914–16

Our war correspondent on the home front

There was further controversy at school when, in a German class shortly before the outbreak of war, Eugen Brecht sharply attacked Germany's ruling dynasties for their dissolute lives and for keeping their subjects under the lash.[1] The teacher Karl Bernhard was appalled and regretted that a four was the worst mark that he could give. He and his colleagues really had no idea how to deal with this contrary, idiosyncratic pupil. Eugen Brecht's revered soldier emperors like Napoleon and Frederick the Great exemplified the virtues of iron discipline and the utmost dedication to the cause, earning the admiration of their troops, who would – and did, of course – die for them.

The boy's response to the outbreak of war shows that this criticism of aristocratic decadence was quite compatible with ardent support for the patriotic cause. Like his father, Eugen Brecht joined in the general mood of patriotic fervour. Here as elsewhere, he expressed himself in his own particular way, as Walter Brecht points out:

> Daddy was in high spirits, not wildly excited but determined in what he said, emphatically supporting the resolutions of Kaiser, Reich and state. The same held good for Eugen, but he lent what moved him the most distinctive expression. [...] His patriotism went so far that, at the start of the year 1915, he still wrote a poem in homage to Kaiser Wilhelm II on his first birthday in the war.[2]

'The Kaiser' begins with some of Brecht's most cringe-worthy lines:

> Bluff. Loyal. Unbending. Proud. Upright.
> King of the land
> Of Immanuel Kant
> Fighting hard for the most sublime of prizes
> Peace.[3]

Hardly surprisingly, the boy accepted the Kaiser's insistent view that Germany was fighting an essentially defensive war, which had been forced upon it by the other, belligerent nations. This was, of course, a lie. The Reichstag followed dutifully when Wilhelm issued the rallying call: 'I know no parties, I know only Germans'. The call to national unity, which temporarily brought the nation together, would sound hollow in defeat as Germany descended into civil war. However, in 1914 Wilhelm's proclamation had the desired effect of splitting the Left into bitterly opposed reformist and revolutionary factions. Conservatives had always sought to marginalise the Social Democratic Party of Germany (SPD) by denouncing its members as unpatriotic. However, in the 1912 election the SPD had returned the largest number of deputies of any party to the Reichstag. To the astonishment of many, including Lenin, in August 1914 the SPD under Friedrich Ebert was unanimous in following the Kaiser's patriotic call and supporting the decision to fund by domestic credit what everyone thought would be a short war, spurning the New York bond market and placing little emphasis on increased taxation.

Disillusioned with the SPD leadership, the revolutionary socialists Karl Liebknecht and Rosa Luxemburg formed the oppositional Group International, which they later called the Spartacus League. They shared Lenin's view that Ebert and his followers were the dupes of the imperialists and had betrayed the international working class. The SPD leadership's support for additional war credits in 1915 would be the last straw for some other SPD deputies, who broke away to form the Independent Social Democratic Party of Germany (USPD). After initial popular enthusiasm for war bonds, by 1916 domestic investors were diminishing and the authorities had to turn to the banks for short-term loans, which began the fateful, unfunded expansion of the money supply, to which the Bundesrat had agreed in an enabling act on 4 August 1914. This permitted the decree of economic and financial measures for the conduct of war without reference to the Reichstag.[4] While the mark fell steadily against the dollar throughout the war, as did the currencies of other combatants, defeat would trigger economic collapse with hyperinflation, leading to the bankruptcy of the state and many of its citizens. Brecht and his contemporaries witnessed the destruction of the world of 1914.

The huge upsurge in patriotic fervour which gripped Germany in August 1914, matched the mood in the other warring nations. Poets and artists everywhere joined the war effort, articulating an idealistic belief in the necessity of a just war that would swiftly be won in the name of king and country, with God on their side. Among other things, Thomas Mann wrote 'Thoughts in War', which were collected in *Observations of an Unpolitical Man*, and Frank Wedekind wrote his drama *Bismarck*. Eugen Brecht embraced the patriotic mood, discarding his free-thinking *poètes maudits*. His early wartime compositions draw upon 'official' literature like Liliencron's brutally graphic verse and Protestant war theology, which Pastor Detzer propagated in vehemently patriotic sermons at the Barefoot Church.

These compositions, read alongside other sources, show the sensitive, psychologically brittle boy initially devoting himself to the patriotic cause in the name of national purification. He did so by treating suffering as sacrifice – and suffered the consequences in a truly harrowing lesson for life. The assured manner of Brecht's later demolition of discredited patriotic values belies his profound struggle in the years 1914–16, which saw the collapse of his belief in the cause of German Christian nationalism as the reality of suffering left him traumatised, his world shattered. The young Brecht followed a trajectory from idealism to profound disillusion similar to that of the English poet Wilfred Owen, who by 1917 was denouncing Horace's dictum *dulce et decorum est pro patria mori* as 'the old lie'. In Germany, which collapsed in the turmoil of defeat and national humiliation, the denunciation would be all the more bitter.

Before the outbreak of war the Brecht boys were out in uniform on Wednesday and Sunday afternoons in the Wehrkraftverein, Eugen making up for the earlier ignominy that Emil Enderlin had inflicted on him when he had not been allowed to participate.[5] Later, Brecht would claim that he'd always managed to avoid this pre-military training by forging his father's signature.[6] That may well be true of the later stages of the war. However, in the early stages no one wanted to miss out on the action, least of all Eugen Brecht. Teachers and pupils volunteered for the front and numbers in the Wehrkraft soared. The retired generals Rösch and von Hößlin provided leadership. Pupils helped with the harvest and with transportation, others watched out for enemy aircraft.

Johann Grandinger recalls that in August 1914 Eugen Brecht joined the war effort: 'In the first days of the war Brecht had to conduct the nightly watch for aircraft with my father up the Perlach Tower. But in those days enemy aircraft only came as far as Freiburg. At first Eugen also served quite diligently in the Wehrkraftverein. Of course there, too, every free minute was taken up with debate, mostly about literature.'[7] Eugen Brecht immediately wrote in the national cause. His reportage 'Tower Watch' appeared in *Augsburger Neueste Nachrichten* on 8 August 1914, his first mass-circulation publication.[8] He wrote that there were no enemy planes overhead but he could see troop trains leaving the station, carrying soldiers to their 'uncertain fate'. And he could hear the singing of 'The Watch on the Rhine', the anti-French battle song from the Wars of Liberation. The young volunteer's account ends with a call for young people to support the war effort.

How did the sixteen-year-old schoolboy come to appear in the press as the advocate of war only days after its outbreak? Immediately before the war, Eugen Brecht saw his future as a theatre critic in the mould of the famous Berlin critic Alfred Kerr, later an arch-enemy. He introduced himself to Wilhelm Brüstle, the editor of the literary review of *Augsburger Neueste Nachrichten*. In July, Brüstle arranged for Eugen to review a collection of verse by a young poet, Karl Lieblich. Brüstle told Lieblich that he had found a young Augsburg poet, who with this, his first job, would be earning his literary spurs.[9] Eugen had a long conversation with Lieblich as he prepared his review, but the more pressing events of August delayed publication and Eugen made his debut instead as a war correspondent.

Brecht's sympathetic review of Lieblich's poems in September captured the patriotic mood: Lieblich's was a '*German* book'. The review contained quite conventional views on art: Brecht praised Lieblich's affinities with Dehmel and showed his antipathy towards 'super-modernist' aesthetic fashion, particularly the 'city demon' of Expressionism, an allusion to Georg Heym's verse.[10] Brecht expressed similar views on art shortly after in a letter to Caspar Neher, who, like Brecht's other collaborator Fritz Gehweyer, had left the Realgymnasium in 1914 for art college in Munich. Brecht's letter – the first record of his friendship and artistic collaboration with Neher – reveals his extremely high aspirations, which he invested as much in his friend's talents as in his own.[11] He suggested that the figure of Faust in Neher's sketch would be better in profile, perhaps leaning against his writing desk, and that Neher should avoid crude, improbable light effects. He outlined his general aesthetic principles, evidently derived from his reading of Hebbel and the Naturalists, particularly Émile Zola and Gerhart Hauptmann. Citing Hauptmann, he argued that art emerged from a combination of truth after nature with idealism. He also urged Neher to consider that the position of the great Naturalist artist remained vacant. For Eugen, to aspire to anything less was quite pointless.

In his own 'official' war writing, Brecht followed the same precept of combining truth after nature with idealism – until the yawning gap between the two plunged him into a profound artistic and psychological crisis, from which he emerged as if re-born, as the Brecht we know. Well versed in capturing heroic death in the patriotic cause, in August 1914 Eugen Brecht showed Brüstle that he was equipped to support the war effort with his pen. Eugen's next piece appeared on 10 August, in response to the sinking of the German warship Viktoria Luise on 6 August. Eugen conveyed what he had learnt about composure in the face of sacrificial death for the patriotic cause, imputing such composure to the stricken sailors, who 'forgot wife and child, father and mother and went to a certain death for the great cause'.[12] Eugen addressed his fellow citizens as if he were the Kaiser's spokesman: 'Let's show them that we understand their sacrifice and thank them for it!'.

Detzer's patriotic sermons glorifying the Kaiser provided the boy with theological justification of suffering. As a Protestant at war, Detzer evidently felt that he should represent the values of the predominantly Lutheran Reich within the predominantly Catholic South. His sermon at the Barefoot Church on 9 August 1914 made a deep impression on Brecht.[13] The aggressive language fed into 'Thanksgiving Service', a poem which captured the mood of popular euphoria on this first 'Victory Sunday' of the war.[14] It also fed into 'The Sacred Prize', in which, upon hearing the Kaiser's 'thunderous voice', mothers accept the death of their sons without lament as a sacrifice for the 'Great Victory'. 'To be a Mother' conveys a similar message: 'To be a mother / At all times means: suffering'. Sophie Brecht's life was testimony to that. For the deeply religious boy, the model for all suffering mothers is the Virgin Mary and for soldierly sacrifice the suffering of Christ. In time-honoured fashion, religious and secular images of suffering and death as transfiguration merge in the young Brecht's war poetry. As in his pre-war poetry, he is a fervent proponent of the German cause in God's name, which, he believes, can bring national purification for the civilian population as well as the military.

The cleansing power of Detzer's language also colours Eugen Brecht's first 'Augsburg War Letter', one of seven in which he describes the wartime mood on the Augsburg streets for the *München-Augsburger Abendzeitung*.[15] Brecht depicts the patriotic ardour which gripped the departing soldiers and the 1,000s who turned out to cheer them off. He records the unstable, shifting mood of those left behind: on the faces in the streets, euphoria yields to anxiety and torment. Yet such thoughts are held in check by the veneration of the whole population for the Kaiser, who 'has become everyone's hero'. His unifying presence is emphasised in another piece, 'Notes about our Time', which Eugen concluded with Bismarck's famous dictum, 'We Germans fear God and nothing else on earth'.

Eugen Brecht regularly took part in victory celebrations at the Stadtgarten and at school. He celebrated the capture of Liège in an 'Augsburg War Letter' in which 'a wonderfully silent festive joy transfigured everything: nature and people ... Oh, despite all worry and distress, it is, after all, beautiful to be allowed to live at this time, at this time, which, bristling with weapons, purifies people and strengthens them within'. Together with Gehweyer, he produced postcards to support the Red Cross War Aid. Again, Gehweyer was the designer, Eugen the poet. In an 'Augsburg War Letter', he reported upon a benefit event for the Red Cross, a passionate celebration of German grandeur. Once more, the Kaiser's young spokesman urges his fellow Augsburgers on to sacrifice, this time by giving to those whom the war had cast into poverty.

Like the editor of the *München-Augsburger Abendzeitung*, Brüstle saw that Berthold Eugen, as he now signed himself, could quickly deliver the copy that the wartime situation required. Berthold Eugen became a regular freelancer for the two papers and earned recognition – as well as fees – in the first two years of the war. Improbable as it now sounds, Brecht's rise to fame began as a patriotic war correspondent. He met his deadlines for stories, reportage and poems from the Augsburg home front, showing his capacity to intervene rapidly in the affairs of the moment. He would in time develop out of that capacity an instrument for strategic intervention through art. For a while, his ambition to achieve fame through his writing came together with his patriotic fervour in his journalistic adventure. The Brecht family was proud that he was seizing the moment, as he had advocated in 'Storm'. In his brother's estimation, Eugen 'quite certainly felt his vocation confirmed through the esteem which these highly regarded newspapers conferred upon his pieces'.[16] While Eugen was busy with his vital war work, school classes shrank as pupils volunteered or were conscripted. Many died at the front, others returned mutilated.

Insatiably curious, in August 1914 Eugen and Walter walked the streets of Augsburg for hours on end, watching the soldiers on the departing troop trains being showered with flowers by citizens who shared their certainty of victory. Almost immediately, the first French prisoners-of-war arrived at a camp at nearby Lechfeld. Eugen and Walter cycled there with food for the prisoners and talked to one of them in their schoolboy French before Eugen dashed off a piece based on the conversation. The author had mixed feelings toward the prisoner, sympathy for his plight shot through with ridicule for the enemy.[17]

From heroic sacrifice to suffering and madness

For all this, Eugen Brecht can scarcely be viewed as a died-in-the-wool propagandist, unlike Ludwig Ganghofer, who had also attended the Augsburg Realgymnasium and was publishing regular tirades of hate against Germany's enemies in the *München-Augsburger Abendzeitung*. There was a worrying congruence between Hydratopyranthropos's brittle psychological make-up and the febrile wartime mood. Still fervently attached to the story of Christ's Passion, Brecht identified intensely with suffering and death in all their forms despite his efforts to banish them. Artistically, he struggled to grasp the import of events around him and became fixated upon capturing the popular mood, which lurched between euphoria and profound anxiety. In fact, Eugen Brecht emerges as peculiarly vulnerable to the pathological wartime atmosphere, in which the ecstatic celebration of heroic action generally precluded the representation of the gruesome morbidity underlying it.

Alongside the images of military victory and the message of sacrifice for the Fatherland, he produced graphic images of mutilated bodies on the battlefield, which probably draw upon his reading of Liliencron: 'A picture emerges: The last rays of the sun stray over a battlefield strewn with corpses ... Thousands are lying there: dead or with limbs twitching'.[18] A similar pattern informs the next 'Augsburg War Letter', in which, tellingly, wounded French as well as German soldiers are stretchered off a troop train: 'We are sorry for them all. A terrible shudder seizes us when we see these ruins of people'.[19] This show of sympathy for the French is, however, followed by the jarring conclusion: 'In all the sorrow *one* feeling fortifies us, *one* thought makes us almost glad: *German men*. German heroes fighting and suffering!'. He overrode the evident dissonance by cranking up the mythology of nationalist sentiment: 'At this time it's necessary to be strong, as strong as brass, at this time it's necessary to grow with one's higher goals. Sacrifices must be made, even if they are bloody and costly'. Yet the war became a severe psychological trial for the boy, as the clashing images in his mind threatened to overwhelm him. The next 'Augsburg War Letter' reads:

> When we see the tranquil peace around us, silent gardens, grey streets with their busy crowds, we could think of an evil dream, which torments us and casts those gruesome images of death before us. And yet, even if we cannot completely grasp the greatness of our time, because the multitude of images that we are assimilating is too great, we all feel nonetheless the beating of their wings over our heads. We see that everything is transformed. That discord, hatred, pettiness have disappeared. It is as if everything has assumed larger dimensions. From a distance we hear about the heroic deeds of our armies, which storm on from victory to victory for the Fatherland – for us. We feel that new states of being have been created rather than mere deeds, *time* itself rather than mere temporal phenomena. In this way we at home also participate in the fighting, in this way the war also has its purifying effect on us.[20]

The embrace of Detzer's justification of suffering becomes all the more intense as images of suffering assail the boy. Most of the poems which Brecht published from the autumn of 1914 to the summer of 1915 maintain the official stance of sacrifice for the nation. They include 'Hans Lody', whose execution by the British as a German spy led Eugen to produce the poem in his memory and led Gehweyer to illustrate a postcard for a collection at school.[21] However, beginning with 'Modern Legend' of December 1914, some poems tell a different story, in which the impact of suffering, not its theological justification, becomes the harrowing focus of attention. 'Modern Legend' shows people receiving news of defeat with howls from their crazed mouths, which, drunken with madness, cry to the heavens.[22] While the victors experience the ecstasy of release, they nonetheless 'wallow in the old prayer'. The poem ends: 'Only the mothers wept / Over here and over there'. The previously resounding message that suffering is justified is withheld. These mothers no longer possess the iron determination to accept sacrifice in the Christian, patriotic cause. 'Modern Legend' signals a stark shift in perspective, from the poet as the Kaiser's spokesman to his identification with the suffering of ordinary people.

It is, perhaps, surprising that such a message of shared suffering without reference to patriotic sacrifice was published. Eugen Brecht was certainly beginning to exhibit worrying traits for the editors who managed his prolific production. However, amongst his patriotically-minded school friends there was still only one topic: volunteering to serve the Fatherland. Boys disappeared from class from one day to the next. Neher volunteered and was sent to the front in June 1915. He was Brecht's only close friend to spend most of the war in combat. Eugen Brecht, the war's vociferous advocate in August 1914, could not volunteer. He gave his reason why in 'Springtime', a poem not yet treated by critics, which was published in *Augsburger Neueste Nachrichten* on 29 May 1915, just before Neher left for the front. In 'Springtime', Brecht elaborated in devastating fashion upon what he had meant in his musings about the 'tranquil peace around us, silent gardens … then we could think of an evil dream, which torments us and casts those gruesome images of death before us'.

'Springtime' shows the alarming volatility of transfiguration in the hotchpotch of religious and secular dogma. In the play of Eugen Brecht's precariously balanced and gruesomely inclined imagination, a quite different transformation of reality took place from that of national celebration. 'Springtime' captures the boy's abject distress, his psychological torment, his sheer horror and incomprehension at his extraordinary 'visions', in which a scene of civilian peace is transformed into military mayhem. The poem opens with a celebration of spring's magical promise as it blossoms 'in shimmering gardens'.[23] The opening suggests a civic space for parades and celebration like the Stadtgarten. The first dissonance emerges in the lines: 'And yet … we scarcely see it in our servitude / For in our soul only *one* note ever sounds / And our spring visions are dark'. Aspiring to speak for his generation through the use of the first person plural 'we', Brecht writes boldly of our 'servitude'. The dark spring visions cue the entry of cavalry, the Horsemen of the Apocalypse: 'Ringing weapons threaten from gardens and flowers / The blaring of trumpets and stamping of harnessed horses / The whooping thunder of the cavalry charge'. After the charge, 'Bodies lie in flowers / Steaming blood pours / From trembling flower spikes'. The perspective shifts back to the uncomprehending 'we'. In shock, they are gripped by a fearful question: 'Would we be blind for ever / So that with our eyes pained by death / We will no longer see the bright spring smiling?'. The barbarous reality is revealed behind the seemingly ordered and civilised, pre-war military parades and the victory celebrations which followed the outbreak of war. Brecht's was a vision truly blighted by the experience.

However, his appeal to his generation remained unheard: those around him continued to volunteer. Showing great courage in what became his own personal disputation with the official war theology, he published other poems which, like 'Springtime' and 'Modern Legend', capture his abject terror at the war. They do so with an originality in the juxtaposition of imagery, if not yet in musicality, which belies the notion that Brecht overcame a derivative style only in 1916 with 'The Song of the Fort Donald Railroad Gang'. As we shall see, that was a fresh departure in other respects.

'The Officer Cadet' of April 1915 and 'Dance Ballad' of January 1916 articulate shock and horror at the carnage in moving ballads which tell of deeply disturbed individual lives, ruined by war.[24] Any notion of sacrifice for a just and noble cause is abandoned. 'The Officer Cadet' and 'Dance Ballad' draw upon the same setting as 'Springtime', together with the young Brecht's signature image of the storm. The officer cadet, 'strangely agitated' in the days of the spring assaults [Frühjahrsstürme], writes to his mother 'I can't stand it much more', as he hears the hard ringing of the shovels covering his dead friends with earth. Three days later, he leads his company's charge as he

> Slender and pale yet with eyes like sacrificial flames
> … In a drunken rage clouded by blood and steam
> Charged, fought and slaughtered – *five* foes …
> Then, screaming with crazed eyes full of terror, he collapsed and died.

The image of the storm runs as a leitmotif through 'Dance Ballad', which begins with a woman dancing at a fair in the springtime, 'As if the great storm were rocking her soul into the darkness …'. The poem continues: 'Afterwards, some people said / That he had fallen during a great assault / That he stretched out as he died and listened to the spring storm on his death'. The bereaved woman goes insane and dances at fairs for money, looking for him everywhere she goes, but to no avail as in her death dance, 'Crazed, she listened to the autumn storm'. The fruits of victory about which Eugen had written in 'Storm' in 1913 are revealed in 'The Officer Cadet' and 'Dance Ballad' as death and madness.

When Werner Frisch and K. W. Obermeier collected Brecht's wartime writings from the two Augsburg newspapers, they observed that they displayed the 'most profoundly disturbed mental attitude' of their author.[25] It is surprising that critics – and above all Brecht's biographers in thrall to images of Brecht as the ice-cold cynic and political master strategist – have not properly considered Frisch and Obermeier's view. The poems of wartime madness testify to the boy's extreme mental torment, bordering on disintegration. A friend, Max Knoblach, remembers that at this time Eugen Brecht became consumed by an 'intense, vicarious suffering for the misery of others and a pronounced awareness of the sufferings which people impose upon themselves'.[26] Christ's suffering had always been an article of faith for the deeply serious boy, who had embraced its appropriation within war theology. Yet he was now faced with a severe contradiction. How did the extravagantly gifted yet psychologically and physically fragile boy cope with the overwhelming evidence that he and fellow German patriots had been duped into their belief in personal sacrifice?

Zarathustra

In 1914–16, Eugen Brecht came to realise that the German people had a price to pay for the soldier emperor Wilhelm II's pursuit of his grand design to overtake the United Kingdom as the world's leading imperial power. Eugen Brecht had a price to pay, too. He had made a name in Augsburg with his glowing support for the patriotic cause, yet the source of his renown was now a source of torment. His struggle to free himself from the torment induced by his naive belief assumed, as always, a literary form. He began to take his leave of 'official' German literature and to immerse himself once again in the *poètes maudits* and subversives of all hues. As his political awareness grew, he had nothing but scorn and contempt for the catastrophic folly of the German imperial project.

The First World War had a seminal impact upon the writer that Brecht became. Understanding its origins would remain a major pre-occupation. Looking back in exile to the confusions of those wartime days, Brecht produced a magnificent montage of contrasting images and literary allusions, drawn from the official canon and subversive writing. Full of scathing irony, the montage conveys a distance from events and ideas which was not remotely available to the adolescent, caught as he was between his fast-unravelling Christian belief in the national mission and his resurgent admiration for his free-thinking literary heroes:

Zola. Filth. Casanova on account of Bayros's drawings. Maupassant. Nietzsche. Bleibtreu's accounts of battles. Then my Emperor'll be passing right over my grave. In the lending library. And the city library. If you spend the whole day reading you'll be a nervous wreck by the time you're nineteen. But does God exist? You'd be better off playing sport like the others! Either He is good *or* He is all-powerful. That's this modern cynicism. A profession. And thanks to the German way. As long as you're spreading your feet out under your father's table, I refuse to tolerate such views. The world will yet recover. Makes you puke. In corpore sano. Gobineau, the Renaissance. Renaissance men, but the professions are over-populated. Faust. In every German's kit-bag. Singing unto death. The little birds in the wood, they sang so wonderwonderfully. You must never ask me! Is Shakespeare English? We Germans are the most cultivated people. Faust. The German schoolteacher won the war of 1870–1. Gas poisoning and mens sana. As a researcher on the Venusberg. Peace be with his ashes: he hung in there. Bismarck was musical. God is with the righteous, they know not what they do. The stronger battalions help themselves. Artificial honey is more nourishing than bees' honey is too expensive as food for the people. Science has ascertained. Three hostile assertions overcome. The final victory is the best.[27]

The forbidden 'meats' of radical and erotic art were beginning to assert themselves amidst the fragmenting rhetoric of the official literature. Beyond named figures, the montage alludes, in order, to: Heine's 'Two Grenadiers', Brecht's mother, Emanuel Geibel's 'Germany's Calling', Brecht's father, Juvenal's *Satires*, Goethe's 'Wayfarer's Night Song II', Wagner's *Lohengrin* and *Tannhäuser*, Brecht's 'Ballad of the Dead Soldier', the Bible, Frederick the Great's letter to the duchess of Gotha of 8 May 1760, and Nazi propaganda. Apart from the deliberately anachronistic element of Goebbels's infamous 'final victory' harangue, the montage is a wholly plausible rendering of the works and events which populated the adolescent Eugen Brecht's mind.

While in August 1914 Eugen Brecht had taken to the Augsburg streets in the grip of wartime euphoria, in August 1915 he fled Augsburg and its 'stupid claptrap'.[28] The reputation he had acquired in that place had become an embarrassment. He was done with the popular mood. He took to the Austrian Alps with Gehweyer, hiking in the area beyond Bregenz to the south east of Lake Constance and revelling in the solitude. Two postcards have recently turned up which he sent from the Alps to Max Hohenester. Like the letter to Neher and one he sent shortly after to Gehweyer, the cards are full of animated views about his friend's art. Eugen was at the centre of things, prompting the others. He enquired of Hohenester, 'How's your *Dichteritis*?'. This was the condition to which poets (Dichter) like them were susceptible. There is a new tone: 'Gehweyer and I have really got into the habit of not talking to each other. [...] Just now clouds are passing over the mountain again. Where should we go? We have no destination'. He wrote the second card 'on a hot summer Sun-day (sic) on a boat' on Lake Constance. Before his thoughts turned to 'poor Augsburg', he described 'walking at night on the white pier (on paths that are off limits) and seeing the lake glisten as the moon glints in it'. He imagined himself on the swing-boats at the Plärrer, 'soaring up into the heavens, above the angular alleys and Donkey Meadow, and the stupid ape faces gape up in astonishment and I fly away over them all, into the heavens on the great carousel swing! ...!?'.

As he wrote to Gehweyer, he and his friends had been discussing Nietzsche's Zarathustra.[29] Like a whole generation of German artists and intellectuals, Brecht could not resist Nietzsche's extraordinary creation. Like Zarathustra, Brecht loved the solitude of the mountains, and Zarathustra fuelled his disdain for the 'ape faces' in Augsburg. 'Soaring up into the heavens' in the swing-boats at the Augsburg fair became a symbol of life and freedom, as Brecht and his friends sought to escape the ugly reality of wartime Augsburg. The letter to Gehweyer is one of Brecht's rare references to Nietzsche and Zarathustra. They would, however, be of great importance in Brecht's creation of his poetic mythology in the later 1910s. Zarathustra resonated deeply with Eugen Brecht, fuelling his imaginative projections of radical transformation and the sarcastic, scornful mode of theological disputation which presently flowed from his pen.

Brecht complimented Gehweyer on his analysis of Wedekind's *Spring Awakening* and could not resist displaying his artistic authority over his friend – just as he had with Neher – arguing that the play's most beautiful feature was its 'immense verve, the *wonderful harmony of its colours*, especially in the final scene, which is pure Goya'. Brecht displayed his up-to-date knowledge of Wedekind, fearing that his *Bismarck* would be a 'real abomination', which would leave Bismarck unrecognisable. He explained that Bismarck's work in his cabinet was not suited to dramatic treatment. Brecht was not yet in a position to explain how drama itself would have to change. He told Gehweyer to read *Bismarck*, to see Anton Wildgans's new theatrical sensation *Poverty* and to set down his impressions of it 'really nicely' for him as soon as possible. He craved literary exchange about the theatre with his friend at a time when he himself had become an avid theatre-goer. Another school friend, Franz Feuchtmayr, estimated that before he was enlisted in 1916 he went to the theatre with Brecht at least forty times.[30] The theatre mattered hugely to Brecht and his friends, as did now initiating their own performances. They needed more space than his attic or his friends' houses. He explained to Gehweyer:

In the meantime we've carried out an old plan. We (Pfanzelt, Hohenester, Harrer (a fiddler), Ell) are meeting up in a restaurant. It's really lovely. You'll be named an honorary member (external). So write to let us know when you're coming, then maybe we'll change the day! The room's not big, has a high ceiling and a few little tables, a *nice niche, in which a red light glows.* Kreutzer sonata … I sit in a window niche. I see the street in the grey of night through prison bars. Lanterns swing in the tree-lined road. I deliver a monologue in iambics. Hohenester delivers a speech with a flourish. We read *Hamlet* together, a scene. We talk about Zarathustra.

For the first time here the Brecht Circle comes into view. Brecht and his friends had found a space for their theatrical and artistic exchange and experimentation in Augsburg's old town.[31] They met regularly in their room at the restaurant to recite texts and to rehearse scenes from plays. Ell is probably Elisabeth Krause, later Lilly Prem, whom Pfanzelt introduced to Brecht. She is better known as an Augsburg Spartacist in the revolutionary days of 1918–19.

'A schoolboy's mind disturbed by the war'

For the soldiers at the front the euphoria of August 1914 had long since given way to the horrific attrition of trench warfare. There was a huge death toll on both sides. On the Western Front much of Northern France and Belgium was utterly devastated. Europe's politicians and generals were slaughtering a whole generation of young men and destroying the continent's economic fabric, while a few grew fat on the distorted wartime production. Back on the home front in Augsburg, the school authorities persisted in the regular victory celebrations. Now, however, the boys felt them to be hollow and tasteless.[32] They saw their friends' names on the lists of the dead and knew they could be next. With the exception of Brecht they did not remotely begin to formulate any objective analysis of the situation, though in time many of them would come to see their elders as callous monsters who had sent their sons to a certain death.

As Eugen's teachers cast around for suitable material in which to clothe the increasingly threadbare patriotic message, they milked Schiller's pathos and idealism for all it was worth. Since 1914 Eugen Brecht had come to hate precisely those qualities in Schiller, for all his love of Schiller's extraordinary dramatic talent. Having Ledermann as the teacher in 1915–16 when the class read Schiller's *Wallenstein* trilogy only made things worse. Brecht had already made his views about *Wallenstein* known before the war. And in *The Harvest* he had published *The Bible*, with its uncompromising questioning of the Christian message amidst the devastation of the Thirty Years' War. Now he had to write an essay on *Wallenstein's Camp* and argued that, in comparison to the present war, *Wallenstein's Camp* was a beer tent idyll, an 'Oktoberfest with a bock beer bar'.[33] A furious Ledermann read out Brecht's essay to the class and gave it the lowest mark possible, a four. Brecht was so angry that he went to the headmaster, Dr Wilhelm Braun, and complained that the teacher should correct not the author's views, only the style of German essays. Braun did not accept Brecht's argument but, to restore the peace, he prevailed upon Ledermann to give the essay a three.

All this, of course, only exacerbated the animosity between Brecht and Ledermann. In 1915, Ledermann published some war poetry in a supplement to the school magazine:

> Sublime, pure, full of youthful strength and beauty
> Germania stands there loyal, keeping watch,
> Sends her heroic sons as bold as lions
> To the sacred struggle in the battle with Varus.[34]

By 1915 Brecht himself had published poems in which he had exposed the suffering and madness of war. In his eyes, Ledermann and all those like him were unspeakably stupid. In early 1916 Brecht's anguished tone in poems like 'Dance Ballad' gave way in 'Soldier's Grave' – his final war poem published during the First World War and the final piece that he signed Berthold Eugen – to the restrained pathos of the Volkslied form with its echoes of Heinrich Heine:

> My friend is
> Among the soldiers down there.
> I couldn't find him.
> It's all the same.[35]

In the evening, the deeply distressed survivor listens to the wind singing its melody: 'It makes you sad. I don't know why; / It's all the same'. He is a listless counterpoint to the widow left dancing in her madness in 'Dance Ballad'.

However outspoken, Eugen Brecht was an acutely sensitive young man, who was not equipped to withstand the traumas of war. He was on a collision course with authority at home and at school with which he was not at all well suited to cope. So pervasive has the view been hitherto that Brecht could master all such emotional situations that his adolescent crisis in the First World War, let alone its depth, has not been recognised. A chasm opened up between father and elder son over the war. While Berthold Brecht demanded respectable behaviour from his son in public, Eugen showed his contempt for such petty bourgeois values. Not only that. Walter Brecht recalls:

> Eugen represented the interests of the poor, betrayed and oppressed with cutting
> rhetoric and increasingly articulated political opinions. Against the background
> of the apparent failure of the World War his opinions clashed painfully with the
> views of his sternly nationalist and uncompromising father. There were eruptions
> and my father demanded that as long as Eugen sat at his table he should do
> worthwhile things for himself and the community instead of delivering subversive
> speeches.[36]

The war had converted the young Brecht from an ardent supporter of the Kaiser to an increasingly considered and radical opponent of his foreign policy in war. As he articulated the anti-militarist and anti-imperialist convictions which were represented by the Spartacus League and, following its foundation in 1917, by the USPD, it was by no means lost on Brecht that a disproportionate share of misery and suffering fell to the poor in Germany and elsewhere. This perspective was beyond the horizon of his solidly middle-class fellow pupils. In the mid-years of the First World War Brecht's support for positions of the revolutionary Left first emerges.

In January 1916 the school authorities reprimanded him for his behaviour.[37] Then in June 1916, Brecht's Latin class was required to write an essay illustrating the wisdom of Horace's dictum *dulce et decorum est pro patria mori*. Ludwig Wiedemann, a classmate who was called up in 1917, recalls writing passionately about the necessity of heroic death: 'However, Brecht expressed himself quite differently in his essay. We were astonished at his courage. But at the same time we didn't understand what could have moved him to write his essay like that'.[38] Nor could his Latin teacher, the deputy head Friedrich Gebhard, with whom Brecht had an excellent relationship. It was after all Gebhard who had imparted to Brecht his life-long love of Horace and who moreover admired Eugen's gift as a translator of classical texts. He even lent Brecht his own books. Eugen's essay itself has not survived but Müllereisert recalled that it was along the following lines:

> The saying that it is sweet and fitting to die for the Fatherland can only be under-stood as propaganda. To depart this life must always be hard, whether in bed or in battle, and surely all the more so for young men in the blossom of their years. Only simpletons could be so vain as to speak of an easy step through that dark gate – and even then only so long as they think themselves still far removed from their final hour. When the bogeyman does come to fetch them, then they'll take their shields upon their backs and run for it, just like the bloated imperial jester at Philippi, who thought up this adage.[39]

It was not just Brecht's contempt for the patriotic cause which outraged Gebhard. Nor was it simply that the teacher could see himself and his colleagues in the term 'blockheads'. The Latin scholar Gebhard was beside himself because Brecht had called Horace a coward. Gebhard reprimanded Brecht in front of the class, thundering away and threatening expulsion, just as the school had expelled that other poet, Ganghofer.[40] With his head bowed, in the studied silence of the pupil seemingly acknowledging his guilt, Brecht stood there, thin and inconspicuous, and allowed the reprimand to pass over him. His alienation from the institution was complete.

Brecht's expulsion was firmly on the agenda. Biographers have interpreted this whole episode as if the ice-cold, cynical Brecht had emerged fully formed from his mother's womb, much as he suggested in 'Of poor B.B.'. Such an interpretation, as we have already suggested, has no thought for this hyper-sensitive teenager's very brittleness and vulnerability. He had made many enemies among the teachers, who had bitter experience of this 'brash, rude and arrogant fellow', as Ledermann later wrote.[41] Despite the prominence of the boy's father in Augsburg life, Ledermann and his colleagues would have been happy to see the back of him. Conscription would take care of a very necessary lesson in life.

Yet he was saved from this fate by the intervention of an auxiliary teacher, Romuald Sauer. The story has often been repeated how, in the crucial teachers' meeting, Sauer spoke up for Eugen and the expulsion was reduced to a censure. Yet the story, as told, invites the question why so much weight was placed on Sauer's account that his 'vote' proved decisive? Sauer was after all not even a full member of the teaching staff.

He was a Catholic priest, who was helping out at the school during the war. Brecht's previous biographers have never properly considered the import of what Sauer said in Eugen's defence, namely that this 'schoolboy's mind' had been 'disturbed by the war'.[42] Nor has this statement been set alongside the wartime poems, the assessment of them by Frisch and Obermeier, and the accounts of contemporaries such as Max Knoblach.

Brecht's many enemies among the teachers were not disposed to swallow any lies. Why were teachers hostile to Brecht moved by Sauer's statement? The story as it has been passed down explains that Sauer came from the same neighbourhood as the Brechts. He evidently had good reason to use the language of mental disturbance and could produce evidence of the boy's condition to satisfy his listeners, however hostile they were. Indeed, they needed to look no further than those poems of wartime madness, born of the extreme conflict between his ardent belief in soldierly sacrifice for the German imperial mission and the awful reality of the mass butchery of his generation. Walter Brecht has nothing to say about Sauer's assessment of his brother's mental health, but then again Walter has a habit of glossing over difficult issues. Sauer's statement simply underscores what we already know: that Brecht experienced a severe mental conflict. An outright collapse is readily conceivable. His naïve enthusiasm for patriotic sacrifice had crumbled in the face of suffering which, as Knoblach says, he experienced with vicarious intensity. A little later, in December 1917 Brecht himself adumbrated his collapse and recovery in a letter to Neher. In a manner well-nigh unique in the fiercely self-reliant Brecht's writings, he recorded a profound debt of gratitude to Neher for his role in his 'renaissance': 'You summoned up my renaissance and gave me more than any other person. I must write this to you, otherwise I'll forget it and it's so exceedingly important'.[43]

It is clear from Eugen Brecht's wartime writings that he was psychologically quite unsuited for service at the front. That, in effect, is what Sauer was asking the teachers to accept, which they did. And that much was surely obvious to Brecht's parents, too. The enthusiastic Walter Brecht would join the war effort in 1918, to his father's great distress. However, Berthold Brecht would use every last bit of influence that he could muster with Augsburg's great and good to keep his elder son away from the carnage. Eugen Brecht had not yet learned how to deal with the sheer intensity of his feelings: first his identification with the patriotic cause; and then the contrary position of suffering and death. The conflict proved hugely damaging. Until the fighting ended, Brecht wrote just one more poem about the war, 'Mothers of those Missing', which remained unpublished at the time.[44] It depicts mothers whose sons do not come home from the front and who spend their lives unable to free themselves of the thought that they will return. The poem blends sympathy for the suffering mothers with a parody of by now untenable Christian dogma. The mothers pray until one day their prayers are answered in the figure of Christ: 'And they smile as they die transfigured and freed / And pass very lightly into Heaven'. Brecht immersed himself in Spinoza and the Book of Job in 1916 as he sought answers to the problem of suffering, approaching the Bible increasingly as an object of rational enquiry and philosophical disputation, laced with Nietzschean sarcasm, rather than as a source of faith.

Skins thick and thin

The wartime experience of suffering with such a 'thin skin' made the growth of a 'thick' skin to protect his extreme sensitivity an existential necessity. This was an essential lesson of the war. Brecht's recovery from his mental torment was necessarily defined through literature. At the front Neher had learnt how to cope psychologically and artistically with the constant presence of suffering in conditions of extreme hardship and life-threatening danger. In 'Caspar's Song with a Single Strophe' Brecht wrote about the hardness that his artist friend had acquired, a thick skin to hide his sensitivity: 'His fists where we normally have our souls / Are dangerously thick with their sores' and 'Cas has blue eyes like the sky / Fat fists and a great heart'.[45] The motif becomes prominent in Brecht's early work and recurs later. In the 1930s, Brecht would write 'Herr Keuner's Favourite Animal', a poem about an elephant, which has a truly thick skin: 'Knives break within it. But its disposition is tender'.[46] As we have seen, Brecht wrote to his son Stefan in the mid–1940s that he had been thinking about the 'subject of INSENSITIVITY (indestructibility, resilience) which greatly pre-occupied us when we were young'.[47] He told Stefan that his three early plays, *Baal*, *Drums in the Night* and *In the Jungle of Cities*, as well as his first published collection of poems, *Domestic Breviary*, were, he believed, forerunners of the cult of coldness in American literature. Brecht explained that he and his friends

> treated the subject of insensitivity, coming out of a great war, quite personally. How could one become insensitive? The difficulty, not immediately apparent, was that society, awakening in us the wish to be insensitive, simultaneously made productivity (not only in the artistic sphere) dependent on sensitivity, i.e. the productive person had to pay the price of vulnerability. The solution was that insensitivity which is achieved through social sensitivity, through a sort of sensitivity for the collective. In that way, inclemencies become historical, non-private, remediable on a mass basis.

In 1916 Brecht was some way from adopting that position. His views about that German 'tradition' would become ever more scathing as he extricated himself from its pernicious influence. Wedekind was one of the few writers whom he excepted from that critique. Hauptmann's blend of truth after nature and idealism in Naturalism was anachronistic, as was Naturalism in general. In a typical Brechtian reversal, he immersed himself in the literature of the enemy nations, reading much English and American literature in German translation, to add to his beloved French poetry. Brecht adopted the language and themes of writers like Robert Louis Stevenson, Herman Melville and above all that arch-imperialist of the enemy British Empire, Rudyard Kipling. Kipling now became as important to Brecht as Karl May's stories of the Wild West had been. In Kipling, Brecht found a kindred spirit, however improbable Brecht's political development makes this kinship. Brecht was secretly committing a form of literary high treason by turning away from the ballads of Liliencron et al. and towards those of Kipling. There was quite simply no German writer at all comparable to the 1907 Nobel laureate who related his stories and ballads of empire from the perspective of hard-living common soldiers, thick-skinned characters given to the excesses of colonial life, upon whom Kipling refrained from passing judgement. That matched Brecht's needs and allowed him to draw quite different political conclusions from Kipling's own. Kipling told the stories of characters with names like Tom, Larry, Mackie, Jenny, Georgie, Johnny and Jim, who over the years would take on fresh life in Brecht's German songs and ballads. Some would be set to music by Kurt Weill and would achieve enduring international acclaim through their performance by actresses such as Lotte Lenya. In collections like *Barrack Room Ballads* Kipling captured the coarse, direct language of common soldiers and did so with poetic rhythms of great vitality. With Kipling's help, in compositions like 'The Cannon Song' Brecht proceeded to re-fashion the language of German poetry to stunning effect. Then there were the exotic settings of empire with place names like the Punjab, Benares, Mandalay, Burma and Surabaya. These names resonate through Brecht's writing. The harsh conditions and searing heat of these distant outposts of empire and of the jungle become the testing ground for Brecht's characters. In the late 1920s in Berlin critics would write of 'Rudyard' Brecht.

In the mid-1910s Brecht began to write ballads about far-flung adventures involving harsh lessons for hard-living males. In them a young man must acquire a thick skin in the face of death, yet must also retain the receptivity of a thin skin required for artistic creation. In this way, the need for a thick skin, learned from Kipling's writings and Neher's wartime experience, became part of the young Brecht's poetic mythology. When he turned his back on German nationalism, Kipling and Neher became yardsticks for his literary creations. The amoral male adventurers in his early prose, poetry and dramatic works – Baal, Andreas Kragler and Bargan – all have to acquire that thick skin in order to survive. These adventurers are often solitary but are at times in the company of desperate bands of men. Brecht portrayed such a band in 'The Song of the Fort Donald Railroad Gang'. With its publication in *Augsburger Neueste Nachrichten* in July 1916 Brecht marked his renaissance as the English- (or American-) sounding Bert Brecht. His adoption of Bert was of a piece with his espousal of enemy literature, his own personal act of high treason against Wilhelmine Germany. Of course, no one really understood this. Nor was the parallel between the men from the railroad gang and the soldiers at the front made explicit. Brecht was in no doubt that both groups of men were doomed:

> The men of Fort Donald – wowee!
> Made their way upstream where the forests forever soulless stand,
> But one day the rain came down and the forests around them grew into a sea.
> They were standing in water up to the knee.
> And morning's not going to come, they said
> And we'll all drown before dawn, they said
> And dumbly they listened to the Erie wind.[48]

After 'The Song of the Fort Donald Railroad Gang' Brecht published nothing until his obituary for Frank Wedekind in the Augsburg press in March 1918.

Bert Brecht and his Friends 1916–17

Macho man: 'Bonnie Mac Sorel Went Courting'

'Revered Fräulein! Writing this letter is very tricky and difficult. And one has to be very careful if one has, for instance, recently incurred a rather painful threat of expulsion on account of a skittish essay'.[1] Writing his first surviving love letter to Therese Ostheimer in July 1916, Bert Brecht, as he again signed himself, was quite happy to play on his recent local notoriety. He combined that notoriety with the most exquisite literary manner, underscored by his prestigious family background and his reputation as a poet whose 'Song of the Fort Donald Railroad Gang' had just appeared in the Augsburg press. Its cavalier treatment of Christianity in its ironic play on the hymn 'Nearer, my God, to Thee' would hardly have endeared him to the beautiful Therese. She was the devout daughter of a strict Catholic family who would always remain beyond his reach. Nonetheless, he maintained his pursuit for at least three years.

Chasing girls was now a major pre-occupation. From spring 1916 at the latest Brecht invested a huge amount of time and effort in this, initially with strictly limited returns. In time, that would change. Brecht was, as he acknowledged to Therese, hardly an adornment to the streets. Moving between polite reserve and outrageous boldness, the style of Brecht's letter to Therese reveals a play of contradictions reminiscent of the teenager's unnerving behaviour at school. The show of conventional politeness was designed both to impress and to mask his shyness. He always played on his eloquence and developed a manner in his courtships which was simultaneously a show of impeccable manners and of breathtaking audacity. His habitually unkempt appearance added to the beguiling mix. It was accompanied by a complete rejection of the limits that convention placed on sexual relations before marriage. He was gallant, kissing hands with aplomb, but typically single-minded, in no doubt about what he wanted. And just as we have seen in his flirtations with boys, he wanted to control as many partners as possible. The would-be young predator sought to dominate girls with the spell of his language in his network of desire, which he hoped would open the royal road to sex. Sexual activity became a vital part of his construction and assertion of 'selfhood', its importance matched only by writing. The domination that he might achieve by virtue of his intellect could, he was inclined to think, be transferred to sexual domination. For Eugen, for whom walking any distance had been a precarious exercise, sex would become a supremely pleasurable, life-affirming activity. In its vitalist intensity, he could live out his fantasy of overcoming death. It was some time before he got anywhere with girls, but once he had tasted success getting more would become an obsession.

Brecht's adolescent sexual desire has on occasion been flatly equated with sexual success, which has hence been grossly overstated. It is unfortunate that in his study John Fuegi almost invariably takes Brecht's imaginative projections at their word, viewing the inexperienced adolescent as a died-in-the-wool, exploitative sexual demon, who, to the horror of middle-class parents, ruined a whole generation of Augsburg's finest. Gossipy scraps of Brecht's testosterone-charged adolescent world like those below, which he later evoked in *Conversations among Refugees*, have been mistaken for hard facts:

> It's good, unlike the consequences. The period. Little Marie sat on the hillside with its rose bushes, picking blueberries. Cold peasants. She'll let herself be. Taken. The balls. If you're not sixteen it's against the law. Five times. Girls, hold your skirts tight when the winds are blowing, when there's something to be seen. Standing. Didn't watch out. Five marks. In the May devotions. Unchaste. Deadly sin. It's a feeling that goes right through you. She's on fire. A good beating. He gave a false name. Oh, how wonderful it was, on the mouth organ. When her husband was in prison. Deflowered. They were noticed in the city park. At first they don't want to. An ice cream costs five pfennigs. Cinema twenty-five. They like it. Look into my eyes! From behind! Or the French way.[2]

Amongst the other scraps of adolescent 'knowledge' we can read further: 'Sunday afternoon. The brass band from the beer garden. Hot dogs. These girls have got a bad disease. If you go to a woman. Hasengasse 11'.

For a long time girls remained a distant fascination for Brecht. The socialisation of the sexes in the middle classes through radical segregation emphasised that distance, having as a primary function the need to protect girls' virginity from boys' wild behaviour. Eugen's shyness towards girls, presented ironically in the 'Story of Someone Who Never Came Too Late', was an index of his 'successful' socialisation. It was not lost on him that he needed to work on his relations with girls to overcome his debilitating shyness and in order to find an outlet for his pent-up sexual desire. By the spring of 1916 he was going about his pursuit in a concerted way. In fact, he was pursuing at least seven girls with great determination, several of them simultaneously: Therese Ostheimer, Marie Rose Amann and her sister Maria, Lilly Krause, Ernestine Müller, Marietta Neher (Cas Neher's sister) and Paula Banholzer. He maintained his interest in essentially the same group of girls during the coming years. They were all from a similar middle-class background to him, principally schoolgirls whose paths he contrived to cross on their way to school, the English Institute, the Saint Ursula School or the Maria Theresa School. These schools, of course, reinforced the teaching of family and church that girls should only give up their virginity within the sanctity of marriage. German middle-class society rigorously policed its moral code.

While Marietta Neher's initials appear in Brecht's poem 'Memory of a M.N.', the Amann sisters, Marie Rose and Maria, are immortalised, after a fashion, in one of

Brecht's most famous poems 'Remembering Marie A.'.[3] Marie Rose claimed the poem as hers. With its matter-of-fact treatment of the transience of love, signified by the passing cloud, 'Remembering Marie A.' bears the unmistakable signature of the love poetry that Brecht was writing around 1920, when it was composed. However, the poem was then called 'Sentimental Song 1004', an allusion to Don Juan's claim of 1003 conquests in Spain alone.[4] Brecht added a note to the manuscript: 'With a full seminal vesicle a man sees any woman as Aphrodite'. It was simply a celebration of male sexual pleasure. The woman's identity was incidental.

The fifteen-year-old Marie Rose Amann, a pretty girl with dark hair and eyes, first met the young poet at an ice cream parlour in May 1916.[5] She was there with other girls from the English Institute. In her account of their meeting, written as an old lady, she was immediately impressed by his exquisite manners. Unnoticed by her friends, Brecht stole a glance at her with his piercing eyes and had the audacity to slip her a note complimenting her on her long hair and pressing for a meeting. Shortly afterwards he dedicated to her his poem 'Bonnie Mac Sorel Went Courting' with the words 'for my little Rosa Maria A.'.[6] The manuscript turned up at Sotherby's in London in 1988 where it sold for 13,000 marks.[7] 'Bonnie Mac Sorel Went Courting' has not received the critical attention it deserves. It was less a dedication than a warning. As such, it was typical of Brecht's presents to girls, as was his use of the condescending epithet 'little'.

The choice of name in the poem's title testifies to Eugen's reading of 'enemy' literature, here Scottish and Irish ballads.[8] 'Bonnie Mac Sorel Went Courting' is a startlingly assured love poem from one so young and inexperienced. Its composition may well have been prompted by an event which the elderly Marie Rose Amann recalled:

> Near the boating lake by the city moat I quite suddenly received my first kiss from Eugen. I was so shocked and disturbed that I pushed Brecht back. I then said by way of excuse that it was out of fear because I didn't know exactly whether a kiss would have consequences. Then Brecht said: 'My dear child, you must go to your mother and seek enlightenment. That is not for me to do'.[9]

In the poem, the male Bonnie has the choice of three women, Lu, Lee and Maria, the first two forming an obvious pair with similar and contrasting linguistic features in a manner that would become a staple element of Brecht's writing, as he explored his imaginative projections. Bonnie's courtship is not with Maria, who is mentioned just once, and then as less beautiful than Lee. Rather, he courts Lu, who turns her face away from him, and Lee, whom he then marries. Lu lives to regret rejecting him, her hair turning grey. Meanwhile Bonnie, now 'more beautiful than God and his devil' with his young wife Lee, does not recognise Lu any more. In this truly audacious composition, Eugen through Bonnie announced to Marie Rose that she had the choice to be either Lu or Lee, that if she did not take him there were plenty of others who would, including perhaps her sister Maria, and that she would live to regret spurning the opportunity.

However, social convention in middle-class Augsburg placed formidable obstacles in the way of any prospective Bonnie Mac Sorel. Eugen engineered a number of meetings on the street with Marie Rose before he took the bold step of meeting her daily at the school gate. She was promptly summoned to the priest Ignaz Steinhardt, who shared her parents' concern about her meetings with this boy. The elderly Marie Rose enjoyed regaling her listeners with the story which Brecht told her – and which should surely be taken with a very large pinch of salt – that the day after she had been summoned, he went to see the priest himself, impatiently pushing his way into his office and claiming that he wanted to marry the girl. This declaration of undying love evidently drew the priest's response that if that was so, then he personally had no objection. When invited by the schoolboy to take his teachings upon the sanctity of marriage at their word by giving his blessing to Brecht's prospective union with Marie Rose, the cleric had apparently complied. Yet, whatever Marie Rose made of the story at the time, Eugen's victory in this war of words almost certainly took place only in his head.

The cleric had obviously not heard the stories which were circulating about Eugen Brecht amongst Augsburg pupils. Marie Rose later recalled the one in which he was reputed to have burned the Bible and a catechism. She had evidently forgotten his scandalous characterisation of Bonnie Mac Sorel as 'more beautiful than God and his devil'. She recalls that he took her home and introduced her to his ailing mother and that they spent time in his attic. It is not surprising that Marie Rose's parents were completely opposed to the relationship: not only was he claiming that he wanted to marry the fifteen-year-old Marie Rose, he was also trying to court her sister! Maria Amann was twenty-one and worked in her father's shop. Herr Amann, a barber and wig-maker, was so incensed by the ne'er do well Brecht that he banned him from the premises. He was not alone among the solid citizens of Augsburg in his hatred of this slovenly youth and his lunatic behaviour.

However, Herr Amann could not prevent the boy meeting with his younger daughter. Thereafter the relationship with Marie Rose developed in a typical fashion for the young Brecht. It was a far cry from the fantasy world of Bonnie Mac Sorel. He was not handsome, he did not have his pick of women and he could not use the threat of abandoning one for another as a means to secure sex. Yet the obsessively deter-mined Eugen simply did not understand the meaning of the word no. He would not give up until he had overcome the gap between his imagination and reality and had achieved the dominant position he craved. In the prevailing social *mores*, this required great stamina and commitment. Seeking to emulate Bonnie's sexual conquest, his approach was to pursue as many girls as possible and, paying lip-service to prevailing convention, to seek an exclusive relationship with each of them, demanding their fidelity. Meanwhile, he worked on as many other such 'exclusive' relationships as he could. He felt profoundly jealous if they responded at all to the attentions of others. Obsessed with achieving control and sexual satisfaction, he never countenanced the end of a relationship. Whenever he was threatened, he fell back on his extreme eloquence to recover his position, just as that eloquence was his trump card in establishing a position in the first place. In that respect Bonnie was very different from Eugen, though the figure of Bonnie was itself, of course, a product of Eugen's eloquence.

Therese Ostheimer was, like Rose Marie Amann, a pupil at the English Institute.

She was the same age as Brecht and another attractive young woman. He followed Therese home one day and at her gate forced out the words: 'Excuse me, Miss, there's something I want to say to you', to which she responded crisply: 'And I have nothing to say to you'.[10] The Protestant boy began attending services at her Catholic church: he was particularly taken by the May devotions. As an old lady, Therese Ostheimer passed Brecht's love letter on to the Augsburg city library. In it, Brecht mustered all his charm and confidence as a published author to address Therese, whom he knew only by sight. He framed the letter with the conceit that, following preliminaries, the letter proper would begin. He could hence excuse himself for his shyness in not introducing himself to her on the street and engage in a gently ironic demonstration of his exquisite artistic taste, listing his heroes: Shakespeare, Goethe, Verhaeren, Kleist, van Gogh, Marées, Bach, Mozart, (but not Wagner), Hamsun and Strindberg. He wisely omitted riskier names like Wedekind, Rimbaud and Verlaine. His aim was evidently to render everything else about him insignificant through the overwhelming brilliance of his literary style, which would say everything that needed to be said. This paved the way for him to acknowledge that he was not born with looks to 'adorn the streets'. He interpolated compliments to her within his finely wrought sentences, before he requested an 'audience' or else permission to write again, although he assured her that he counted on neither and would be content with any response from her, even 'Go to hell'.

Therese is foremost in Brecht's thoughts in a sequence of diary entries from October 1916.[11] The entries are a revealing, if by now highly stylised commentary on his three principal, closely linked pre-occupations: his continuing ill health and the lessons to be drawn from it; his work and ambitions as a writer; and the prominent place that sexual desire was assuming in his life. Now in his final year at school, he is off again for two weeks with his heart complaint. He is lonely and feeling rather sorry for himself. He views his life as nearly four years of solitude, that is to say, since he was first forced to stay off school frequently on account of his heart and forbidden any strenuous activity with friends. He advances the sort of contradictory responses to his solitude which are so characteristic, born as they are of his oscillation between notions of weakness and strength. On the one hand, he writes, after three years one fears one's own voice and becomes prone to excessive chattering in the company of a good listener. On the other hand, he claims that solitude makes one stronger and that it is best to keep a great distance from other people. Yet when he contemplates a fifth year of solitude, he imagines becoming ill and no longer able to speak.

Common to the three pre-occupations is his construction and projection of a new persona: the macho male adventurer with a thick skin. Yet he himself never loses sight of the profound weakness underlying that projection. Indeed, for Brecht life became a gamble played out between weakness and strength. In that sense, he became a compulsive, Bonapartist gambler, repeatedly staking his life and bluffing others with his highest stake, the strength of his life, which he alone knew could crumble at any minute. He would carry off the spoils that he won with his macho attitude.

The image of the storm remains the crucial point of orientation: 'When a man lives properly he lives as if in a storm, his head in the clouds, his knees wobbling, in the darkness, laughing and fighting, strong and weak, often defeated and never subjugated'. The storm is no longer, as in *Oratorium*, God's test against which the wretched artist measures himself to achieve splendid redemption. Rather, it becomes the hostile, threatening force against which the tough male must measure his existence, fighting fire with fire and deriving life's pleasures from the struggle just as long as they can be had.

A storm rages outside his window for days on end. The self-styled strong male has disobeyed his doctor: 'I'm not going to bed. You fall ill there'. He spends all his time at his writing desk, witnessing the struggle of the trees with the storm, mirroring the storm within, which fills him with 'darkness'. Asserting that he has a real hunger for reality and for work, he sees himself fulfilling the ambitions of the male literary adventurer in the far-off America of his dreams: 'to become rich, to exert influence, to play chess with people. I can write, I can write plays, better than Hebbel, wilder than Wedekind. I'm lazy. I can't become famous. If I do I'll go to America and become a cowboy, ride all day, look at the sky, talk to the bulls and gaze at the grass'. Buoyed by these dreams of adventure and success, his thoughts return to the storm. He now adopts a thoroughly optimistic attitude towards the prospect of recovering his health: 'Now I'm growing healthier. The storm is still going on but I'll never let myself be dragged down. I'll command my heart. I'll impose a state of siege upon my heart. It's beautiful to be alive'. Yet his power to command his heart proves to be more apparent than real. After an awful night, he despairs: 'No. It's absurd to be alive. The heart palpitations last night made me astonished at the first-class work the devil's doing this time'.

However, there is no way back after the assumption of the self-image of the tough male who tests himself against the adversity of a 'very rebellious' heart. The struggle with 'good and evil' continues in philosophical disputation with the books of the Old Testament, Job and Kings, which he reads out aloud in his attic. Sounding as much like Zarathustra as Brecht, he describes the Old Testament as 'incomparably beautiful, strong, but a wicked book'. He feels the challenge to emulate it: 'It's so wicked that one becomes wicked and hard oneself and knows that life's not unjust but just and that that's not pleasant but terrifying'. That macho attitude becomes synonymous with living an authentic life. Brecht increasingly adopts a recognisably existentialist position, which once more reveals the rarely acknowledged influence of Nietzsche.

Brecht enjoys the self-image of vital predator as an antidote to his sickliness. He embellishes the macho image in colourful fashion, goading himself into it: 'I'm wicked and have sat around in desolate pubs, in carts at the Plärrer and with soldiers and know ribald songs and have contempt for all people because they are so corrupt. [...] I'm already somewhat corrupt, wild and hard and domineering'. In the world of the young Brecht's imagination – and not only there – every hard man needs a tender, loving woman. His thoughts return to the 'girl from Gartenstrasse', who has 'tranquil eyes, which are beautiful and intelligent and in which I am a tiger'. Poor Therese! He explains that he needs

> something to keep him on the ground, a lap to lay his tired head in, soft hands, naturalness, lovingness, purity. – I'm often thinking again of little Ostheimer, who looked very sweet when she was talking to the child. [...] Ostheimer has something childlike and something maternal in her face. That's beautiful. She's

straightforward, too, and not as shallow as the others. I'd like to talk to her, nothing else. She's got something wonderfully pure about her.

No doubt, Herr Ostheimer had his own firm views about his daughter's purity – and about Brecht's intentions.

Amongst other Augsburg fathers who had the difficult job of contending with the unrelenting Brecht, the medical doctor Karl Banholzer conducted a lengthy and ultimately unsuccessful struggle over his daughter Paula. Around the time that Brecht met Marie Rose Amann, he also began to chase the fifteen-year-old Paula, who attended the Maria Theresa School. He coined the nicknames Bi, Bittersweet and Paul for her. To her he was Bidi. Bi became his first great love in that highly spirited Augsburg world of the later 1910s, which he first created then destroyed, and along with it his relationship with Bi. Brecht's second wife Helene Weigel, who knew more than most about these things, said much later: 'Brecht had many women but he only loved Bi'.[12] One of his late poems reads:

> Bidi in Beijing
> In the Allgäu Bi
> Good, says he
> Morning, says she.[13]

Brecht could never let go. He told Hermann Gross, whom Bi would later marry: 'I treated her like a princess and I tyrannised her too, but she never noticed'.[14] Like many women at that time, Bi was prepared to put up with a lot if a man held out the prospect of marriage. Bi's own account of their relationship records all that and also the ingenious tenacity of Brecht's pursuit, which lasted some eighteen months before they became a little more intimate in late 1917. His success shows his drive to win out against the odds. The attractive and sporty Paula was never short of admirers. She was no great thinker, nor was she artistic despite Brecht's best efforts to find the actress in her. She embodied a simple fullness of life and beauty which the sickly young intellectual craved. His pursuit was, then, distinctly improbable. To succeed with her was the ultimate affirmation of self-love over self-loathing. That was reason enough to love her like no other. But that love – and the self-love that went with it – was never enough for him.

In the spring of 1916 Paula was being chased by another boy a year older than her, Brecht's friend Otto Müllereisert. When Brecht saw Otto and Paula talking on the other side of the street, he motioned to Otto to come over. After a brief exchange with the older boy Brecht, Otto returned to her, said that he no longer wished to meet with her and disappeared. Brecht later explained to her that he had spelt out to Otto that he must give up any claim on her because she was exactly what he himself was looking for. Müllereisert's friendship with Brecht went from strength to strength.

From that day onwards, Brecht contrived to see Paula daily on her way to school, waiting until she left her house and sauntering along behind her. On other occasions he walked past her or overtook her, raising his trademark sporty cap a little, though he was too shy to speak. Brecht would set his cap askew on his head or pulled it down over his face to conceal any abiding trace of his childhood tic. The cigar would follow.

Paula was quietly amused by his behaviour but did not show it because she did not wish to give him any encouragement to start a conversation. She actually found him quite unattractive and pointedly ignored him. Undeterred, he engaged in what today can only be described as stalking, systematic surveillance of all her movements. He developed a thorough knowledge of all the routes she took, be it to her piano tuition or her dance lessons. When he couldn't track her movements himself, he enlisted friends. She knew before she left her house that her admirer or one of his stooges would be waiting for her outside. For all his tenacity, because of his shyness he could not bring himself to speak to her when he saw other boys showing an interest. Finally, he devised a plan which forced him to do so. Plucking up the courage, he overtook her one day, hesitated and stood in front of her, his face drained of all colour. He then took off his cap, cleared his throat and struggled to form his words. After a few seconds he managed to ask, on behalf of his friend Heiner Hagg, if she would like to take a walk. Now, Hagg was not exactly an adornment of the streets either, so Eugen could expect a resounding no. When that came, he was primed to continue the conversation. He began to speak with such rapidity that she could not get a word in edgeways. She kept on walking and he went on talking. The few words that she did get in were not designed to encourage him. Yet he now felt that he had the right to accompany her wherever she was going. She never arranged to meet him, but when she appeared on the street he always popped up and showed how happy he was to see her. She still gave him no encouragement and tried to avoid him whenever she could.

In Paula's account, that's the way things stayed throughout 1916. Brecht was also finding time to court Lilly Krause and Ernestine Müller as well as Marie Rose and Therese. Lilly wrote to him on 28 December 1916. Hers is the first extant letter from a girl to Brecht. Written in the polite form to 'Herr Brecht', it reads:

> An old proverb says, a long wait is worth it, and you will probably be angry with me. With good reason, I'm bound to say. But I'd like to ask you not to be that way but to think about your little friend sometimes still, even though I, disloyal creature, don't deserve it. Have you recovered your old composure? I wish I could do so too. Unfortunately I can't! At Christmas I did the most disastrous thing that I could ever do in my life. I'd be glad if I could chat with you again for a little while. Maybe I'd take fresh heart. If you do have a little time for me I'd be pleased. There'd be so much to talk about. Sometimes I really think I'm crazy and don't know if I'm coming or going. May I hope for an answer?[15]

There is no record of an answer, which is not to say that the young lover Brecht did not reply. He was also chasing Ernestine Müller. He gave her an anthology of love poems for Christmas and dedicated a number of compositions to her.[16]

The Brecht Circle goes public

By the end of 1916, twenty-one of Brecht's classmates were at war. None of the boys still at school had anything to do with the Wehrkraft or the Wandervogel. There was no let-up in the teachers' inculcation of propaganda, however threadbare it had become. Among the mix of literary and patriotic topics in German lessons was the composition of a volunteer's farewell letter to his relatives: the manner of the leaving had to be absolutely correct.

However, school was a peripheral concern for Brecht. He dreaded the call-up; keeping away from the front was the main thing. In the autumn of 1916, together with his classmates Hartmann and Geyer, Brecht applied to do voluntary service on the home front. The application was approved for a period of one year from 14 October, meaning he could be called up only from October 1917. Brecht, Hartmann and Geyer were also able to take the school leaving certificate, the Abitur, early under less stringent conditions. School would be done with by Easter 1917.

Having secured this stay of execution, Brecht and his friends extracted all the enjoyment they could from life. They chased girls and wrote and performed together. Brecht created an intensity of artistic experience with his own work and with encouragement to others which made this period of youthful precocity and associated megalomania as productive as any in his whole life. He and his friends lived at a permanent artistic fever pitch, devising new texts and melodies and performing them to the guitar.[17] The Brecht Circle now became a public presence or, from another perspective, a public nuisance in Augsburg, with Brecht the ringleader emerging as the Bürgerschreck of legend.

Many people went out of their way to ridicule him, saying he was filthy and gnome-like, his head too big for his body.[18] The officer's son Hanns Otto Münsterer, who would join the Circle in the autumn of 1917, leaves no doubt as to the degree of antagonism, even hatred, which Brecht aroused amongst the closed ranks of Augsburg citizens. Yet that same mix of bashful naivety and outrageous impudence which antagonised teachers and parents was beguilingly attractive to spirited young people like Münsterer, who delighted in the sheer euphoria of the Circle's creativity, driven on by the endlessly inventive Brecht. For Münsterer, the influence of this 'highly important person' was the end of the middle-class assumptions of his upbringing.[19] For Heiner Hagg, Eugen's exuberant, creative presence strengthened the will to live and to enjoy life at a time when the war made so much around them quite meaningless.[20]

Depending upon who was at the front or studying in Munich, half a dozen or so male friends would meet up, and with them a number of girls. The young men might include: Hartmann, Pfanzelt, Hohenester, Gehweyer, Neher, Geyer, Harrer, Hagg, Müllereisert, Lud Prestel, Otto Bezold and Münsterer. In addition to Lilly Krause, Ernestine Müller and Paula Banholzer, the females included the girls from Steinicke's bookshop, Käthe Hupfauer, Ida Grassold and Franziska Lochinger, nicknamed Fannerl, who married Georg Pfanzelt. Nearly all Brecht's male friends played an instrument, some, like Pfanzelt and the guitarist Lud Prestel, extremely well. They performed an endless round of new songs which Brecht made up with his friends. Vitality and instinct were the watch words. Favourites for performance were 'Little Song' about the harmlessness of alcohol and 'Philosophical Dance Song', which ends in typically grim fashion:

We never danced more gracefully
than over the graves of death.

God always pipes most prettily
with our very last breath.[21]

There were parodies of popular hits, filthy four-liners and plenty of insider jokes, such as when Bezold concocted: 'He spied a lass, / his thoughts were not exactly chivalrous / he felt her ass', which Brecht rounded off: 'and now our song is getting frivolous'. This became the standard phrase to bring any risqué conversation to a close.

Brecht's attic was a favourite meeting place. The room had a sloping ceiling, beneath it an iron bedstead with Eugen's guitar hanging from it. The window, giving on to Bleichstrasse, was opposite the inner door. Nailed to the door were Eugen's 'Twelve Suras for my Visitors'. The suras exhorted all those who wished to enter to discard prejudice and parochialism and to bring with them inspiration and talent. They were left in no doubt that they were entering an abode of genius. He gave the abode various names, among them The Wolf's Lair and The Dungeon. Other names like The Kraal would follow. All the props of literary genius were there to see. Every available surface, starting with the floor, was cluttered with books, manuscripts and newspaper cuttings. In one corner there was a music stand with a conductor's baton. For a long time, the score to Wagner's *Tristan and Isolde* was left open. Eugen claimed that he wielded the baton to help calm himself after writing, as if dissipating the charge which had passed through his body. There was a rapid turnover of pictures and drawings that were hung on his walls, displaying his major passions. A portrait of Napoleon was prominent, together with his battle plans. Nietzsche featured for some time, as did Gerhart Hauptmann and Wedekind, together with Neher's charcoal drawings which he sent from the front. In March 1918, following Wedekind's death, Brecht displayed his own mock death-mask, which a local sculptor had moulded from his face. And in the summer of 1918 Brecht put Bezold up to steal two skulls from a charnel house in Franconia.[22] Brecht placed one of them on the Bible, a classic *memento mori* in European painting.[23] In time, pride of place on the attic wall went to Neher's drawing of Baal. It dominated the room, symbolising the Brecht Circle's immersion in the world of that monstrous, demonic creation.

They had a number of places where they met outside in good weather. Like that whole generation, they associated nature with freedom from the oppressive wartime constraints and the deprivations that dominated their lives. Swimming in the Lech with its dilapidated weirs and eddies to the north of the city was a real adventure, which Brecht, becoming physically more robust as he moved through adolescence, was equal to. To get there, they walked up the left bank of the Lech towards Wolfzahnau, leaving behind the industrial area near the Haindl mill. During the day, they sunned themselves on the long, pebble beaches.[24] At night, they stopped at favourite places to play the guitar and sing. With its willows and stony beach, Wolfzahnau was a favourite venue. It gave on to Wolfzahn Island, a nature reserve near the confluence of the Lech and the Wertach. That was a magical place, a mass of green: grass, bushes and trees. On the right bank of the Lech was the Griesle. It was further away, beyond the Lechhausen Bridge. They were particularly fond of it because the swimming was better and the river bank was grassy with willows surrounding it. To the west, in the mid-distance you could see the elegant buildings of Augsburg's old town.

The Brecht Circle became regulars at Gabler's Tavern in the old town. Working men used the main bar, while Brecht and his friends met in the narrow snug off to one side with its simple, painted furniture. As Münsterer recalls, the snug had its quaint side: there were 'two stuffed eels in a glass case, one had lost its head, and a swordfish (or was it a crocodile?) hung from the ceiling'.[25] The Gablers were an elderly couple who enjoyed looking after the youngsters, even though they did not add much to their income. Brecht was a careful, moderate drinker, just as his appetite for food was not great. He came along in the evening to meet the others, armed with his guitar and new lyrics, and they set to work making up tunes for them. Hohenester recalls that Brecht sang 'with an enchanting passion, drunk on his own verses, ideas and creations, just as others get drunk on wine. And he made the others who listened to him drunk as well, as only youth can be'.[26] His voice was in no way conventionally attractive, more like Bob Dylan's 'voice of sand and glue', in David Bowie's memorable words. The Brecht Circle became synonymous with Gabler's Tavern, as did the *Brechtfeste*, the fancy dress parties which the Circle threw there. A recently published photograph shows Brecht dressed as Mozart, Bi as Constanze and two friends as the Munich comedians Karl Valentin and Lisl Karlstadt, later Brecht's friends.[27] In the middle is the Brecht Circle's trademark red Chinese lantern. Gabler's Tavern was the setting for the Brecht Circle's magical counter-culture, a celebration of life in the face of death, which in those years was never far away.

Brecht thought up fun events for the group. His party invitation to Heiner Hagg for the evening of New Year's Day 1917 gives a taste of things. He wrote that they would meet at 6 p.m. in the ice cream parlour for a reunion of the 'New Year spooks'.[28] Hagg was asked to bring along the ingredients for *punsch*, beakers, a sledge, wood in his rucksack, a mouth organ, humour, cigarettes, wellingtons, and a high-spirited, romantic mood. The destination was Nervenheil, a hilly wooded area to the west of Augsburg. Brecht explained to Hagg that they would have a sledging competition under the stars and they would have tea in the forest and duels. Hagg went along with five other male friends and they had their sledging competition before they settled down around a camp fire at midnight to toast each other. With typical bravado Brecht said: 'The fire would be even more beautiful if a naked whore were to jump over it now'.[29]

For Augsburg teenagers the winter meant ice-skating and a chance for boys to hook up with girls to skate in pairs. Or for girls to hook up with boys … Signing herself Rosmarie, at the end of January 1917 Marie Rose Amann wrote a note to Brecht during a free period at school.[30] She invited him to join her and her friends Berta and Anna Beck on a trip out to Stadtbergen. If there was enough snow they could go tobogganing. She asked why he was not skating anymore. It emerges from her note that Brecht had sent her a letter, too, and that their correspondence was punctuated by questions and answers exchanged in code, though he had not answered her question. The use of a secret code must have added a frisson to their interest in each other. She was clearly interested in seeing it develop.

Marie Rose remained on the scene but, to judge from Paula Banholzer's account, Brecht spent the whole of the winter of 1916–17 pursuing Paula on the ice. He tricked the gateman into giving him free entry to the more exclusive part of the rink where

Paula skated. With her superior skills, the sporty Paula easily managed to evade him. Even though he had learned the rudiments of skating, he had, in her view, scarcely mastered the art and had to look on as quicker boys reached her with their invitations to form a pair. Ever resourceful, he took to waiting for her on her way to the rink so that he could claim her as his partner as they entered.

She still did her best to shake him off and the winter passed without Brecht managing to arrange a meeting with her on his own. So he organised his band of dedicated followers to charm her and other Augsburg girls with his talents. The Brecht Circle parading through the streets became a regular sight on Augsburg evenings, featuring Brecht on guitar, Harrer on violin, Pfanzelt directing or playing guitar, and someone or other playing the mouth organ. Hagg, Hartmann or Bezold would hold the red lantern, as they made their way towards some young lady's residence. They would stop in front of the house and launch into their serenades drawn from Brecht's burgeoning repertoire. 'The Song of Complaints' was one. The favourite, though, was 'Serenade' itself, which begins:

> Moon and cat are last awake
> All the people are asleep
> With his lantern Bertie Brecht
> Trots across the street.[31]

The Amann girls were serenaded, as was the Verger's daughter. Brecht knew that she was engaged but could not resist the challenge and she finally appeared at a window – followed by an outraged fiancé who roundly cursed the serenaders below. Several girls have left their accounts of the serenades. Paula Banholzer loved the attention and her parents enjoyed the songs, too, even though they were adamantly opposed to their daughter having anything whatsoever to do with the wild, dishevelled band leader. On one occasion when she failed to appear at her window, Brecht lay down on the pavement in protest and sang.

Still without success in his mission to make Paula his own, Brecht planned a fresh assault. Again he had a cunning plan and again Heiner Hagg was the stalking horse. Heiner himself approached Paula and asked if she would like to meet up with him. She flatly refused, whereupon Heiner asked if she would in that case like to join Brecht for a walk. Taken by surprise, she agreed. That in effect committed her to meeting after meeting with him, mainly for walks through the meadows by the Lech. As always, he did most of the talking: he read from his works, gave her poems or talked about his literary plans. She found herself starting to like him, impressed by his knowledge and talent. His first surviving letter to her is from 17 April 1917.[32] In a short note he excuses himself for having to miss a meeting with her. Demonstrating his thorough knowledge of her daily routine, he suggests that she might be at the Kautzengäßchen at 11.30 a.m. or 1.30 p.m. Failing that, he would wait for her near the Capuchin church at 4.45 p.m.

The Plärrer

Brecht left school at Easter 1917 with his wartime leaving certificate and enlisted for voluntary service on 20 April. He did clerical work for Augsburg City Council, then tended trees for the Häring market garden. Brecht's wartime service has been the subject of much myth-making and ill-founded speculation, some of it fuelled by Brecht's own mischievous account to Sergei Tretiakov. Voluntary service was a perfectly legitimate way to defer conscription. However, the authorities intended that young men should serve on this basis only for a limited period before joining the armed forces. Brecht was summoned to an army medical examination on 8 May. He wrote about it to Walter who was doing service on a farm. Armed with his exemption certificate valid till October, Brecht had only sarcasm for the whole process. He told the doctor: 'I'm sorry. I'd have liked to serve you, sir, but unfortunately that's not possible. Because I've got no time, sir. Maybe another time, in two months or in five months ... Don't worry, sir!'.[33] He suggested to Walter that, given the opportunity, they would have kept him there and buggered him. He added that the small matter of his heart complaint, attested by the family doctor, had also counted in his favour: 'They had a better heart than me. And that's a further reason why they didn't keep me there by force'. He would do anything to avoid the front and, thanks to his father's support, he had further cards to play.

During the in-between time before the dreaded call-up, Brecht indulged his passion for fairs, which brought colour and excitement to the drudgery of wartime life. The Augsburg fair, the Plärrer, was a favourite haunt. Then there was the Friedberger Volksfest, the Lechhauser Kirchweih and the Jakober Kirchweih. The Jakober Kirchweih took place every August barely 500 metres from Brecht's house. He adored fairgrounds, the sounds and smells, the music and the travelling people. He would go a long way for a fair, as far as Munich, where he took in the Auer Dult as well as the Oktoberfest. For a while he was at a fair virtually every day. He wrote his 'Plärrer Song' in the folk-song style, echoing Heine's 'Homecoming':

A child that I saw there
Has hair of shining gold
And eyes that become her
A wonder to behold.

And every roundabout
Is turning in the sun –
And when they come to rest
My head whirls on.[34]

Brecht relished the whirling chaos that accompanied the elation of soaring motion. In this controlled confusion of roundabouts and swings, Brecht, quickly prey to dizziness and disorientation, derived huge pleasure from, in effect, meeting fire with fire. He sent these verses to Neher at the front on 13 April, exclaiming: 'The Plärrer is great [...] The Plärrer is the finest thing there is'.[35]

The very next day Neher had his own moment of disorientation: he was buried alive when a shell exploded near him. He survived but it left him wounded and in shock. Soon after, he was back in Augsburg for extended leave when Brecht found him much changed.[36] Neher was as if back from the dead, the inspiration for Brecht's portrayal of Andreas Kragler in *Drums in the Night*, the soldier returning from the front as if from the grave, at first unable to speak. Neher spent much time at the Plärrer with Brecht, Paula and the gang. Strangely, without referring to the shell-shocked Neher, nor for that matter to his cousin Max Hermann, Walter Brecht writes of the macabre spectacle of a group of wounded soldiers at the Plärrer in 1917.[37] The noise and music were too much for these victims of industrial warfare. First, one of them began to shake, he thrashed around with his arms and face contorted and cried out before he fell to the ground. The other wounded, shell-shocked men followed suit. This scene of ruined humanity stayed with Brecht, who developed a fascination with the capacity of behavioural therapy to mitigate at least some of the damage to the organism. In the early 1930s Brecht would develop an interest in the work of the neuro-psychologist Kurt Goldstein, who in his Frankfurt clinic had developed remarkable new forms of treatment and therapy for brain-damaged soldiers in the First World War.[38]

In Paula's eyes, Brecht was 'strangely attracted' to the exotic fairground world of the Plärrer.[39] He loved listening to the stallholders' cries and would sit watching the shows or wander through the fairground for hours on end. He got to know some of the stallholders and the showmen very well and they liked him too. He was utterly taken by the magical romance attaching to these social outcasts and artistic adventurers whose rough life was very different from his own background. For Brecht in search of the authentic existence about which Zarathustra preached, the fairground performers were people 'without prejudice and without inhibitions, who knew how to live their lives without conventional ties'.[40]

This world gave Brecht a very great deal. The fairground performers drew on traditional ballad forms like the Bänkelsang and the Moritat, the latter ending with a terrifying moral, which was sung to a barrel organ. One of Brecht's most famous lyrics, 'The Ballad of Mac the Knife', was arranged in this way for his recording in 1929. As the fairground balladeers sang their melodramatic tales of gruesome murder, love and retribution, they pointed with sticks to storyboards, narrative sequences of pictures painted on canvas hanging up behind them. Every Augsburger who went to the Plärrer knew the Bänkelsänger from Hamburg with the peg-leg who sang: 'My great wish, my sole desire / Was to see Africa from the oceans. / A prince who came from a foreign land / Bought me and six more Germans'.[41] After every 'land' he spat out a brown mush of chewing tobacco, while his daughter went around with a hat.

These travelling show people embodied the world of adventure that Brecht took from his reading of Kipling, Stevenson, Rimbaud and Verlaine. Hence, the Plärrer was for Brecht *the* 'great cultural event'.[42] He told his friends, 'There you get to know the world as it really is'. Brecht emulated the fairground people with his own melodramatic tales of desperate outsiders couched in vivid imagery like 'The Legend of the Harlot Evlyn Roe' – a name he took from Kipling – and a little later 'Apfelböck, or the Lily of the Field'. Apfelböck was a real-life Munich murderer, whose gruesome tale begins:

'Mild was the light as Jakob Apfelböck / Struck both his father and his mother down / And shut their bodies in the linen press / And hung about the house all on his own'.[43]

It was not just the performers at the Plärrer who captivated Brecht, it was also the fairground rides, particularly the swing-boats. Emphasising as usual that she took the lead in physical exertions, Paula Banholzer says that she persuaded him to join her in a swing-boat but she swung like crazy and Brecht turned white so they had to stop before their time was up.[44] He was so glad to get off the swings but he was 'crazy about them, although he could never really stomach the rocking motion. He always felt sick straight away'.[45] It was like a drug, causing great elation, followed by nausea. But that did nothing to diminish his enthusiasm, which, as so often, proved infectious to his friends, as the diaries of Münsterer and Neher attest. Münsterer wrote:

> As for the girls, he reckoned swinging with them was as good as sleeping with them. For us it became a symbol of life – working your way up until the prow of the swing nudged the canopy – or, if the roof was open, you were hurled out past the flickering lights into the blue night-sky where you could look down on all the glittering splendours of the world below, before that inescapable plunge back down to earth. 'Thus are the damned shown all the bliss of the blessed, before they are cast down into the darkness.' We used to go swinging with Bi, or with the girls from Steinicke's who had their evenings free and were happy to tag along. We were delighted to discover how the same fear which makes men ugly actually makes women more beautiful.[46]

Brecht wrote poems about the swing-boats, among them a memorable prose poem, one of his 'Psalms':

1. You push your knees forward like a royal whore, as if suspended from your knees. Very big. And crimson death-plunges into the naked sky, and you surge upwards, one moment arse-first, face forward the next. We are stark naked, the wind fumbles through our clothes. Thus were we born.
2. The music never stops. Angels blow panpipes in a round dance so that it almost bursts. You soar into the sky, you soar above the earth, sister air, sister! Brother wind! Time passes but the music never.
3. Eleven o'clock at night and the swings close down, so that the Good Lord can carry on swinging.[47]

While God carried on swinging, Brecht and his friends made off into the night, carousing by the Lech till dawn.

Risky relationships

In Paula Banholzer's account, she and Brecht enjoyed a lovely summer in 1917. However, it was not all plain sailing. She was a pretty girl, who attracted the attention of many boys. Though the situation was one which he could not resist, it was not easy for the smitten and acutely jealous Brecht to deal with. He wrote to Hohenester from his Wolf's Lair:

The business with Paula ended ingloriously and absurdly. After I'd given her up, delivered two furious harangues and smilingly flung my blessing at her, [...] that commercial school student stepped in and 'replaced me'. It's a funny feeling when you can't help being ashamed of a ruin that once seemed beautiful – in fact you didn't even know it was a ruin until you got this commercial school student to look at it.[48]

Typically, Brecht's final act in Paula's rejection of him – and it clearly is that – was to deliver speeches. In her account, whenever he was in danger of losing her to some fine fellow he would counter with a speech lasting two or three hours, demonstrating his superior qualities.[49] He later admitted to her that on such occasions he was always trembling inside and would not have known what to do if she had left him. She did not do so, she writes, because she was captivated by his eloquence.

On this particular occasion, the eloquence was to no avail. In his letter to Hohenester he took his revenge. Spurred on by his sheer outrage that a grubby student of commerce had replaced him in Paula's affections, the wounded Brecht told the story of a Zulu tribesman and a wild pig.[50] It is a dazzling display of contrary wit, which shows the young Brecht at his brilliant best. The sardonic tale employs a parodistic inversion of biblical language and a gallows humour born of Brecht's own loss of faith in God, not to mention his loss of Paula – her beauty ruined in his eyes – to depict the tribesman's predicament, in which human appetite and religious belief are reduced to absurdity, as he explodes, having eaten the pig. Brecht thereby demonstrated that he had escaped a fatal trap. Paula would not have forgiven him the analogy with the pig. Brecht commented to Hohenester, who was himself in a wretched situation at the front: 'You see that my life is not terribly amusing. I've come to be as alone as you are unalone'.

Abandoned by Paula and grounded by mysterious stomach pains for two weeks – the two were perhaps connected – Brecht gathered his male friends around him. He went walking with Pfanzelt at Wolfzahn: 'We philosophise about death'.[51] He told Hohenester that he passed his letters to his mother because she understood poetry and him, too. Brecht sent Hohenester three stories by Knut Hamsun and promised him his own *Summer Symphony* when it was finished, assuming that he already knew 'The Song of the Vulture Tree'. This, the latest of his anthropomorphic poems about the destruction of the heroic tree of life, depicts unspeakable violence and suffering in a manner reminiscent of 'Springtime'. The poem begins:

> From the cock's crow to midnight
> The crazed vultures grapple with the lonely tree.
> So many wings darken the sky that for hours on end it sees no light.
> The rushing sound of brazen wings strikes up all around.
> And the lashing wings, whipped out at it,
> Dive down to smash its trembling body, sundering buds and limbs.[52]

After heroic resistance, during which the tree summons all its physical and mental strength, it succumbs to the vultures' horrific assault. It is probably just as well that this scene of carnage did not find its way to Hohenester at the front. It could only have disturbed further the young men who, as had happened to Neher, were taking such a pounding from enemy shells dropping out of the sky.

The convalescing Neher was a frequent visitor, whom Brecht found a great character, ridiculous in his own ingenious way. They spent hours together, cursing women and discussing things like 'two men who know all there is to know about life' and who feel some contempt for it.[53] What grew into the great bond between them was cemented at this time. They worked together on *Summer Symphony*, which remained a fragment, Neher making sketches of Brecht's characters. In a lighter mood, Brecht and Neher visited Augsburg's new Ludwigsbau with Lud Prestel and Pfanzelt, which prompted Brecht's four-liner:

You cannot know
Until you've been,
Ludwig's nicest room
Was his latrine.[54]

Neher had to return to the front in early August and would remain there until the very last day of the fighting. Just what Neher thought of the war emerges from his plan to write a story about his 'three years of imprisonment' in the military, which would include English and French being spoken.[55] He thought of himself as a 'military cow, which was milked and at once produced curd. C-ream, Brecht would say'.

Brecht tried to cheer Neher with joshing missives, calling him 'you big childish cynic' and 'Cyclops with the sinful mind and the virtuous heart'.[56] They had their fallings-out, too. Brecht acknowledged that while he was writing his letters he was, unlike Neher, not in mortal danger, and he explained that he had been trying to keep his friend's spirits up. However, what really got on Neher's nerves in the trenches was Brecht's boasting about girls and his fretting about the exact role he might have to play in the war, pestering Neher with the question whether it would be better to be in the artillery or a medical orderly.[57] Neher suggested that Brecht ask himself which uniform a little girl would like better! For his part, Brecht told Neher that he could not stand the way Neher took refuge in the idea of a harmony informing the affairs of the world, saying that the idea was alien to him. Unlike Brecht, Neher was still religious.

Brecht implored Neher to find a way to escape the front and return home, while Neher sent Brecht his drawings. Brecht commented on them and begged the unforthcoming Neher for his views on the poems he had sent him. Convinced of Neher's great talent, Brecht tried to get his work published in the Munich magazines *Simplicissimus* and *Jugend* or exhibited at the Augsburg Art Club. He captured his feelings about Neher in a number of poems, among them 'About a Painter', drawing upon Kipling's *The Light that Failed*, in which Dick Heldar does his paintings on the interior of a ship taking him from Lima to Auckland.[58] In the poem Brecht also develops a sexual cipher of travel together to exotic places:

Neher Cas rides across the sands of the desert on a dromedary
and paints a green date palm in water-colours
(under heavy machine-gun fire).
It's war. The terrible sky is bluer than usual.[59]

Neher becomes Brecht's artist-soldier-lover in the desert, the image out of which he developed the soldier-adventurer Kragler, who escapes from the searing sun of his captivity in Africa.

In his letters to Neher, Brecht began to oppose the German coalition of wartime interests and to support those who advocated its swift end. He identified the 'diplomats, the military and capitalists' as principal obstacles to peace.[60] There was no doubt where his sympathies now lay. With his first comments on politics and aesthetics, he encouraged Neher to produce 'something political [...] something symbolic à la Goya'. He probably had Goya's gruesome *Disasters of War* in mind. He suggested that such work could be directed against German nationalist forces and the US President Woodrow Wilson, who were opposed to the swift conclusion of peace. Shortly after, he welcomed the Russian Revolution: 'Russia seems to be getting sick and sensible'.

Neher remained Brecht's sounding board for his artistic prospects and his chances with girls, which did not always go down well with Neher whose opportunities were limited to men and prostitutes. When Neher took offence, Brecht replied with typical forthrightness: 'Should I feel sorry for you too? It's better to respect *people*'.[61] Yet Brecht's bad conscience towards his friends emerged after he wrote that he had been ice-skating with Gehweyer and Hohenester who were home on leave: 'Jubilantly greeted by me, they arrived; cautiously avoided by me, they will leave'.[62]

With them and Neher at the front, Brecht cultivated younger friends like Müllereisert and Lud Prestel. At this time, the talented and highly impressionable younger boy, Hanns Otto Münsterer, another budding Augsburg poet, came on the scene, too. Drawing on his diaries, Münsterer wrote a classic account of the Brecht Circle from 1917 until 1921, capturing Brecht's enormous creative vitality, his hunger for experience and his craving for life. In the summer of 1917 Brecht had got to know Otto Bezold, who told Münsterer that he had got to know a 'real poet'.[63] Bezold passed some of Münsterer's poems to Brecht, who asked Münsterer to visit him with some of his work. The customarily dishevelled Brecht's amusement at receiving his guest decked out in all his finery, including grey kid gloves – Münsterer spared Brecht the top hat which would have rounded off the conventional dress code – is captured in the droll portrait, 'Song to Herr Münsterer':

He'd doff for every pretty tree
his (peculiarly scruffy) hat.

The glove he wore of finest grey
was elegantly grand:
Only beasts and beauties – they
Felt his naked hand.[64]

Bi was sitting up in the attic with Brecht when Münsterer arrived. Bi and Bidi were back together. The table was piled high with manuscripts and books and some of Neher's pictures were on the walls. The only lighting was the red Chinese lantern. Brecht was quite taken by Münsterer's reading of his 'The Five Murderers', written in Wedekind's style.[65] He noted Münsterer's verses and passed them to Pfanzelt to set to music. Brecht responded with some of his recent poems and sang others to the guitar, among them 'The Legend of the Harlot Evlyn Roe' and 'Ballad of the Adventurers'. They shared an enthusiasm for Wedekind and Büchner, and Brecht admired Rainer Maria Rilke's *Book of Hours*.[66] He was, though, no longer a disciple of Stefan George. Among German classical dramatists Brecht admired Grabbe, Kleist and Goethe but above all Schiller, 'especially the sinew of the broad dramatic sweep, and the flawless vaulting of his plays and ballads'.[67] These qualities far outweighed what Brecht's teachers had made of Schiller.

Brecht impressed his visitor as a poet, not as a dramatist. Driven by subjective experience, in Münsterer's memory Brecht saw his own life as the subject matter for his art, refracted through multiple prisms of his encounters with other works of art. Brecht's lyrical manner was dominant. The newcomer could only be impressed and not a bit flattered when his host shared with him some of the burgeoning mythology surrounding the Brecht Circle, captured in 'Orge's Reply on being Sent a Soaped Noose':

Once the hatred and venom he'd swallowed
Rose to more than his gullet could take
He would just draw a knife from his pocket
And languidly slit through his neck.[68]

The dandyish Münsterer was utterly seduced by this real poet: 'Soon I succumbed to the spell of this powerful personality and, at least from my side, an intimate friendship developed. I would have gone through fire or to prison for Bert. At the start my love was undoubtedly perversity and only later did it shift from the person to the artist'.[69] In his memoirs, Münsterer describes their relationship as akin to Verlaine and Rimbaud's, a code for homosexual love. Münsterer adds in his diary: 'Both intellectually and physically I have an endless amount to thank Bert Brecht for. He took away from me all vain energy and prompted me to re-build myself completely afresh'.[70] Brecht did for Münsterer what Neher had done in Brecht's own 'renaissance'. In these years of intense creativity Brecht, for his part, not only enjoyed Münsterer's adoration of him but also valued his writing and his views on his own compositions. However, in time Brecht could take or leave Münsterer, to the latter's great distress.

Part Two

Dramatic Iconoclast

To be the Greatest Dramatist 1917–18

Reprieve

There has been a fair amount of speculation why Brecht chose medicine in his programme of study in Munich in the winter semester 1917–18. He said various things at the time, some of those things probably to counter the charge that he was behaving dishonourably in not going to the front. He suggested on one occasion that his mother wanted him to study medicine, in the hope that he could find a cure for her illness. Another view is that he wanted to please Paula Banholzer's father, even that he had thoughts of joining his future father-in-law's practice and eventually taking it over. Over Karl Banholzer's dead body! More pertinently, it is obvious that, by virtue of his own condition, Brecht had more than a passing interest in medicine. In fact, in 1935 Brecht speculated that his scientific education in medicine had 'strongly immunised' him 'against influence from the emotional side'.[1] That's one way of putting it. Medicine was, and remains, the most prestigious profession in Germany, which three of Brecht's friends chose: Müllereisert, Münsterer and Geyer. Two of the foremost writers among Brecht's contemporaries, Alfred Döblin and Gottfried Benn, were also practising doctors. There is an illustrious history of great German dramatists studying medicine, first and foremost Schiller and Büchner. Brecht was alive to such considerations. He was photographed taking Schiller's place on the plinth when Schiller's statue was removed from its prominent position outside the Augsburg theatre during the war.

What can be established is that his registration for medicine deferred the dreaded call-up. Conscription in October 1917 had been looming. However, it was announced on 1 June that the call-up would be deferred for medical students.[2] Brecht again evaded the front. Some of Brecht's contemporaries who had gone to war condemned him for blatant opportunism. Not unduly taxed by his voluntary service, Brecht visited his brother at the isolated farm of Bartlstockschwaige near Donauwörth. Sporting his blue cap, he walked the final six kilometres from the railway station with his rucksack. Walter, eager to please as usual, had quickly become an excellent farm worker, while his brother took walks or sat under the linden trees for hours on end with paper and pencil. Brecht also spent some weeks at the Kopp family's villa by the Tegernsee, a lake just south of Munich where he was a tutor for the Kopps' son Conrad. Brecht would appear in knickerbockers with his cap and glasses, a volume of Schopenhauer tucked under his arm. The knickerbockers were a departure from his accustomed attire. Schopenhauer was a logical step after Nietzsche and Spinoza for a young intellectual concerned about the transformative capacity of the individual will in a world conceived tragically, albeit one tempered by Brecht's sardonic humour. Brecht shared gossip, verses and sketches with Cas Neher in the trenches: 'Dear Cas, You're a great man. But a lieutenant looked at the stars and said to them, "Well, you stars are something and I'm something too. Each in his own way". I'm a tutor'.[3] He told Neher that he rammed things down the boy's throat for three hours every day, and then he was lord of the manor. He spent time in his room, writing, reading Schopenhauer and playing the lute. Or he lay on the grass under the trees, as full of melancholy as a hollow tree is full of honey. He went rowing at night. He said it reminded him of the Plärrer.

Having found his way back into Paula's affections, shortly after his arrival he wrote her a wildly over-the-top letter: 'Beloved Paula! Venerated one! Permit your majesty's most subservient creature to place his most reverent obsequiousness before your tender feet. He has little else to do. Salaam'.[4] The letter continues in the same vein, alternating between the hyperbolic – 'O you sweet gazelle of my dark dreams!' – and the deadpan: 'I've had my hair cut very short. Like Samson. And now I'm waiting for it to grow. After all I've got to have something to do'. Thrilled that the poet had after all won out over the student of commerce, he paraded literary allusions to Heine, Homer and the Old Testament, before concluding: 'You fodder of my run-on sentences, you sphinx of my moonlight-nighttime-boattrip-dream-madness, you sparkling curved mirror of Nirvana, proud, smart pearl fisher in the sea of this nonsense, adorn yourself with the pearls, little Ingeborg Nettle'. After this *tour de force*, he felt entitled to demand a thank-you letter in return. Chastened by the experience of rejection and mindful of the pitfalls of veneration illustrated by the fate of the Zulu tribesman, he was protecting himself from further let-downs by surrounding the object of his desire with bucketloads of irony, confident that it would make her laugh.

However, Karl Banholzer was keen to see his daughter progress to become a PE teacher before she made a good marriage. That ruled out absolutely the ne'er-do-well Brecht. By way of encouragement, Herr Banholzer promised his daughter a horse and a greyhound.[5] Brecht could not resist sending Neher a few choice lines under the title 'Paula!':

> Just do your exercises – and you'll get a horse.
> Your father said so. Sooner not be tied?
> But PT's a fine thing. You must be fit of course
> And, Paul, some women *must* have a horse
> To get a man who'll ride.[6]

Sending these lines to his male friend, with whom he could share real intimacies, enabled Brecht to take revenge for the way she had ditched him. He knew that it was still wishful thinking to see himself as that rider. He acknowledged as much in other lines that he sent to Neher: 'Girls have no use for us poets – We merely *write* / About love, for the fun of it. A scandal … '.[7]

The medical student

In preparation for his first semester, Brecht went to Munich in September. There he met up with Müllereisert, who was also studying medicine before he was called up in 1918. Moving between Munich and his attic in Augsburg, Brecht looked around for lodgings and took a room with Neher's aunt at Maximilianstrasse 43, the first of a bewildering numbers of addresses in the Munich years. On 2 October 1917, Brecht registered at the Ludwig Maximilian University as a student of humanities and medicine.[8] Bemoaning the fact that there was nothing going on, he described a frenetic daily round to Hagg: '8 to 11, 12 to 1; 3 to 6.30; 7 to 10.30 in the lab, at the university, at the theatre. Every day. I gobble up everything within reach and read an incredible amount. I'll digest it in the army'.[9]

Brecht could only expect the call-up to be deferred for a semester. He looked forward to being lazy for a day or so in Augsburg, rather than constantly trying to catch up on himself. At this early stage he took his studies reasonably seriously, though that commitment waned. His courses relating to medicine included one on combating widespread diseases and another on inorganic chemistry, including practical work for students of medicine.[10] Along with a course on literature and philosophy during the Sturm und Drang period of the 1770s, he registered for lectures on the contemporary Scandinavian dramatists Ibsen, Björnson and Strindberg. All enjoyed high esteem in Germany. His reading of Strindberg's *The Conscious Will in World History* continued the thread of Nietzsche and Schopenhauer.[11] He registered for a range of lectures in the humanities in addition to those in medicine. The one on research into the life of Jesus Christ shows his abiding interest in that figure. Others show his interest in subjects of the human sciences such as the history of philosophy, the psychology of religion and anthropology. The course in general anthropology taught by Professor Rudolph Martin dealt with races and peoples of the past and present.

Even though Martin was one of the first anthropologists to use the term 'race' and was a physiological anthropologist, he was not specifically an exponent of racial theory, as expounded by Stewart Houston Chamberlain, Francis Galton and Arthur de Gobineau. The author of the influential *Textbook of Anthropology*, Martin restricted himself to the empirical investigation of inherited features through measurement. Given the general emphasis upon race in the study of anthropology, it is not surprising that the young Brecht initially shared conventionally determinist views. The strongly historicist and determinist approach to academic subjects is also present in other courses which he took, such as the development of animals and plants in geological periods, with particular reference to mollusc fossils.

Munich opened up fresh avenues for Brecht beyond the university. The city was still vying with Berlin to be Germany's leading centre for the arts. During his Munich years Brecht gravitated towards its outstanding artistic personalities, Wedekind, Karl Valentin and Lion Feuchtwanger, though not Thomas Mann – that would never change. However, with his distinctive accent and manner Brecht remained strongly attached to provincial Augsburg, to his friends and to the world of exuberant creativity that they had brought into being. He spent weekends and vacations back home and wrote to Neher that he was not inclined to start friendships with fellow students in Munich: he found them 'terrible windbags in spite of their cultivated manners'.[12]

And there was much unfinished business back home with girls, essentially the same ones he had been chasing since the spring of 1916. Paula Banholzer had now finished school and was less inclined to accept parental authority. She ventured into the attic where she met Brecht's friends and sat while Brecht wrote. He presented Therese Ostheimer and Ernestine Müller with 'Romance', a composition from his stay on the Tegernsee about a ghost ship which arrives on a shore and just as mysteriously disappears.[13] Again, it was not a conventional love poem, more a warning like 'Bonnie Mac Sorel Went Courting'.

Marie Rose Amann was still on the scene in the autumn of 1917. She was not letting Brecht have things his own way and that worried him. In a blend of the serious and of the light-hearted, he begged Neher to intervene with her on his behalf because she did not love him. He should write to her – or better, draw to her – that Brecht was in despair. But Neher should not make him look ridiculous, rather, 'big, eternal, immense, ironic. Etc. But: don't draw me in the nude. Or her either. Or I'll have to wring your neck. Wring. Your neck'.[14] He asked to see the drawing first, but Neher would have to send it 'from the trenches. [...] They're respectable people. Not naked'. Brecht then told Neher that she was seeing someone else. Deeply sarcastic, he produced several variations on: 'I will *not* kiss Rosmarie, since someone else is kissing her', as he paraded his incredulity that he should be denied what he desired. His impulse was to destroy linguistically what he could not have:

> Rosa Maria is not pretty. That was a legend invented by *me*. She is pretty only from a distance or when I ask: "Isn't she pretty?" – Her eyes are dreadfully empty, small, wicked, sucking whirlpools, her nose is turned up and too wide, her mouth too big, red and fat. The line of her neck is not pure, her posture is idiotic, her gait scatterbrained and her belly protuberant. But I'm fond of her. (Though she's not bright and not nice.).

In the ice-cream parlour she let him know: 'In sexual matters I wouldn't be too particular'. He took this to mean that she had a 'dangerous reproductive urge'. He became venomous: 'Doesn't Rosa Maria look sweet in the photos? But she's out for seduction like a bitch on heat. She lay in my arms like gelatin (liquid); she flowed into the creases. Too bad I didn't take her before I thought of it. Would *you* have done? On a bench in the park? "I love you so! Up skirts! Get fucking!" Ugh'. As he acknowledged to Neher, he hadn't actually had sex with her, it was all bravado. But from now on, he wrote about her as if she were a whore.

He was, though, seeing another 'Rosl' from Augsburg. She wrote to him on 27 November 1917 and did so in a hand which is markedly different from Marie Rose Amann's: Brecht was seeing two girls of that name. In fact, Brecht took to mixing up his girlfriends' names. Among other names, including Bittersweet and Paul, Brecht on occasion called Paula Therese, Victoria and Resi, a shortened form of Therese. In her letter, Rosl thanked him for his, explaining that she had not been to Fräulein Gretl's for some days so had got his letter very late.[15] She continued: 'Your wish, which you address to me, will be fulfilled, but only if you definitely want a souvenir from me'. She was expecting to see him the following Sunday. She ended the letter with a kiss. The envelope has a sticker on the back with the words 'with love'. Brecht was achieving a degree of intimacy with numerous girls, using a combination of his impeccable manners and of audacious 'wishes', designed to put the girls on the spot. In April 1918 Brecht let Neher know that Rosl had lost her virginity some time ago: a 'salesman with lecherous fingers' had 'taken her apart'.[16] The Rosl in question appears to be not Marie Rose Amann, but the woman who wrote the letter in November.

Wedekind: The struggle for the succession

The university course into which Brecht channelled much energy but which actually took him away from formal study and towards the theatre was Artur Kutscher's seminar on literary style and criticism. With its emphasis on contemporary theatre, particularly plays that were being performed in Munich, Kutscher's seminar had acquired a legendary status. And Kutscher knew playwrights like Wedekind, who came along and talked about their work. He also had an eye for promoting new talent. Students from all faculties flocked to Kutscher's classes, where there was always lively discussion. The students presented their papers, while Kutscher presided over the exchanges, authoritative in his judgements and enjoying great kudos. The unique Kutscher experience was rounded off by social events and parties, at which Wedekind often sang his songs and played guitar. It was as if tailor-made for Brecht. He revered Wedekind, the epitome of the macho male artist upon whose great personality he modelled himself. That semester Wedekind read from his drama *Heracles* and Brecht wrote of his awe at Wedekind's 'brazen energy. For two and a half hours without a break, without once dropping his voice (and what a strong brazen voice it was), without taking a moment's breather between the acts, bent motionless over the table, partly by heart, he read those verses wrought in brass, looking deep into the eyes of each of us in turn as we listened'.[17]

Brecht saw himself as the next major talent after Wedekind and Kutscher's seminar as the perfect vehicle for its recognition. Brecht compared Kutscher to Neher's portrait 'The Apostle': 'In his classes Kutscher has the same soul – he *is* the apostle'.[18] However, Kutscher was the apostle for another talent. Hedda Kuhn, a medical student with whom Brecht began an intimate relationship, his first of any significance, witnessed events. Late in the winter semester it was Brecht's turn to present a paper. Kutscher had just published a panegyric in the *München-Augsburger Abendzeitung* to the young dramatist and novelist Hanns Johst. The Expressionist Johst was also a guest at Kutscher's seminar. Johst, already displaying völkisch attitudes, later became a prominent Nazi, the President of the Reich Writers' Chamber and the author of *Schlageter*, a play which glorified the life of the eponymous Nazi martyr. Brecht chose to present his paper on Johst's novel *The Beginning*.

Brecht stood up in Kutscher's class, observing everything icily with his piercing eyes in his hard, sharp manner through his metal-rimmed glasses, his hair severely cropped – and proceeded to tear Johst's novel apart in a paper which broke all the rules of academic engagement.[19] The title was a ready target. Brecht compared *The*

Beginning to the situation of a runner who takes an incredibly long run-up but stumbles just before the starting line. The novel was a run-up, nothing more. Brecht's paper was laced with further *bons mots* such as 'This work stinks of stage-fright and stale sweat', 'Johst's novel amounts to a free emancipation from all the problems of form' and, presciently, 'Herr Johst's idealism is not so much sky-blue, it's ultraviolet'. He pronounced it 'uldra-fiolett' in the Augsburg manner. His grating voice matched his idiosyncratic appearance: his articulation was very clear but you could not miss the Augsburg dialect. The expression on his face did not waver, nor did he look at the faces in the audience. As he got into his stride, there was applause, laughter, the shuffling of feet and hissing, but he remained unmoved, utterly self-possessed. The child with the nervous tic had become the consummate, ice-cold performer, who would split any audience right down the middle, many fervent in their adulation, others vehement in their revulsion. That capacity to polarise opinion would be a trademark of his art. Johst's subsequent career, of course, only confirms how right Brecht was to attack him.

There was pandemonium in the lecture theatre. Beside himself, Kutscher threw Brecht out, shouting after him that he was a flagellant and a prole. He would never change his view, which he saw amply confirmed in a letter which he received from Brecht's head teacher in which he warned Kutscher of Brecht's capacity for slander. The standard interpretation of this episode is that it demonstrates how the ice-cool Brecht acted in a wholly calculating way, thriving on the notoriety achieved through his exemplary denunciation of a rival. Exemplary denunciation, yes. Strategic calculation, no. His behaviour exemplified his self-obsessed brinkmanship with little regard for the consequences. He craved Kutscher's recognition that he, not Johst, was Wedekind's heir apparent. As a strategy to gain recognition through the good offices of the apostle Kutscher, Brecht's behaviour was a disaster. He continued to court Kutscher's attention, attending his classes and presently seeking his approval for his poems and for *Baal*. It is said that he visited Johst the day after the denunciation, full of remorse, to confess what he had done. Kutscher would never change his mind.

It is surprising that biographers have not traced in the spat with Kutscher and Johst the thread of Brecht's unadulterated ambition to succeed Wedekind. Exemplary denunciation was the only way the young Brecht knew. With the unstable mix of outspokenness and reserve, Brecht's social interaction at times veered towards self-destruction, unable as the self-absorbed artist was to gauge the dynamics of everyday exchange. Specifically, he failed to deal with the yawning gulf between his self-perception as the greatest talent of the age and the virtually non-existent external recognition of that talent. On this and other occasions, this discrepancy led to major *faux pas* which he subsequently found excruciating when he realised that he had destroyed the very relationships necessary to secure recognition. He saw that the theatre was the institution which could lend him the iconic status he craved, just as it had made Wedekind's fame and that of the greats before him. Yet he could be a liability in that institution, his own worst enemy. This recklessness would take on a particular complexion in his early work in the theatre, where he destroyed relationships left, right and centre – squandering the opportunities afforded by his extravagant talent – until first Lion Feuchtwanger in Munich, then Helene Weigel in Berlin did what they could to take him in hand. And, given his extravagant talent, that would be more than enough. He would then focus his energies upon the destruction of the institution of the theatre itself.

Johst invited Brecht and Hedda Kuhn to his house on Lake Starnberg south of Munich. Johst was enjoying the recognition as a dramatist which Brecht craved: *The Young Man* was premiered at Kutscher's end-of-semester celebration at the Kunstsaal Steinicke where Wedekind was the guest of honour. The premiere of *The Lonely One*, Johst's portrait of the despairing dramatist Christian Dietrich Grabbe, would follow at the Munich Kammerspiele in March 1918. Brecht insisted on visiting Johst alone, warning Kuhn: 'Johst's a völkisch type. Things will get hot. It's nothing for you'.[20] Not that Brecht then broke with Johst. In fact, he actively sought him out in the coming years as a rival against whom to pit himself, rather in the manner of the protagonists Shlink and Garga in his later drama *In the Jungle of Cities*.

The rivalry with Johst smouldered on over the winter. Brecht had long harboured dramatic ambitions and had devised many plans, but after the one-act *The Bible*, had never really moved beyond his acknowledgement in 1913 that he did not yet have the strength to sustain a full-length drama. The public spat with Kutscher and the desire to prove him wrong now spurred him on. Even though everything to date pointed to his talent being as a poet and song-writer, his inspiration remained the multiply-talented Wedekind, poet, singer and dramatist. As always, Brecht would find his own solution: just as his ballads combined narrative, dramatic and lyrical modes, so too would his plays fuse these distinctive elements in a novel theatrical experience.

Shortly after Brecht had heard Wedekind sing at the Munich cabaret Bonbonnière, he wrote in shock to Neher of Wedekind's sudden death. Brecht and Lud Prestel had been singing Wedekind's songs to the guitar down by the Lech one Saturday evening: 'Franziska's Evening Song', 'The Blind Boy', 'Young Blood' and 'Bajazzo'.[21] The day after, 10 March, the paper carried the news of his death. Brecht ended a two-year silence in *Augsburger Neueste Nachrichten* with a fine obituary for Wedekind, whose 'vitality was his finest characteristic'.[22] Brecht wrote that this lent Wedekind an extraordinary presence, whether in a lecture theatre with 100s of students, in a room, or on a stage. Everyone fell silent: 'He filled every corner with his personality. He stood there, ugly, brutal, dangerous, with close-cropped red hair, his hands in his trouser pockets, and one felt that the devil himself couldn't shift him'. His singing voice as he played his guitar was rough, rather monotonous and quite untrained. Brecht wrote: 'No singer ever gave me such a shock, such a thrill. It was the man's intense aliveness, the energy which allowed him to defy sniggering ridicule and proclaim his brazen hymn to humanity that also gave him this personal magic. He seemed indestructible'. The obituary ends: 'Like Tolstoy and Strindberg he was one of the great educators of modern Europe. His greatest work was his own personality'.

That day Brecht published his ballad 'Death in the Forest' in the same paper. It conveys the same incredulity that an individual's enormous vitality and will to live count for nothing in the face of death. Employing the core images from his poetic mythology of the tree and the storm, the poem recounts the final hours of a man in the 'eternal forest', who 'was dying, like an animal dug into the roots / Looking up to the tree tops, where *above* the forest / The storm had been roaring for days above everything'.[23] His friends offer to take him home, but he has nowhere to go and has become 'rotten' through and through, suffering the fate of all organisms. He cries: 'I want to live!', then acknowledges: 'And I must die'. They bury him among its darkest branches. As they ride off they look back at the 'grave-tree': '*And the tree top was full of light.* / And they crossed their young faces'. Transfiguration takes place here in nature, where the young Brecht seeks solace for the fact that death overtakes the vital, creative male. That solace could no longer be found in Christianity. 'Death in the Forest' would be the centre-piece of the final scene of *Baal*, in which Brecht again enacted that same incredulity at the death of a vital, creative man.

In the obituary for Wedekind Brecht wrote that he would not be able to grasp Wedekind's death until he had seen him buried. At the funeral the following Tuesday:

> I saw him in the coffin. One of the greatest surprises I ever had: he looked like a little boy, around his mouth. The sardonic, precious character of his lips, that sated, cynical element all gone! At first you thought he was smiling; but then you saw that he had 'broken the habit' of smiling. [...] Six weeks ago I saw him singing to the guitar in the pub at the end of Kutscher's seminar. He looked as if he could not die.[24]

The funeral was an extraordinary affair. The cortège was disrupted and there were incidents as onlookers, prostitutes, vagabonds and youths joined in. When it finally reached the grave, the crazed poet Heinrich Lautensack fell to the floor and delivered a confused farewell. Brecht then wrote 'On Wedekind's Funeral':

> Baffled, in their black top-hats they stood
> Above the carcass: ravens, strutting round.
> And yet (for all their sweat and tears) they could
> Not put that fairground showman underground.[25]

Brecht struggled to reconcile himself to the brute fact of Wedekind's death. Through his writing and personality Brecht now laid claim to Wedekind's inheritance as that fairground showman.

Baal

Proving himself as a playwright was now Brecht's most urgent task. The outcome at this stage could only be a highly subjective, lyrical work. What Brecht produced was so far removed from acceptable taste that his first play as an adult was simply unstageable in its initial incarnations. Brecht had been moulding his own self-image in the light of his veneration of Wedekind as the consummate artistic personality: vital, cynical and amoral – and of his admiration for similar artistic figures like Verlaine and Rimbaud. He hence saw his own life as the subject matter for his portrayal of a lyrical vitalism which his own physical existence belied. He discovered a further kindred spirit in François Villon – murderer, bandit and ballad singer – in K. L. Ammer's translation of 1907. Brecht was enraptured by Villon's verse, reciting 'Ballade de la grosse Margot' and 'Ballade de merci'.[26] He experimented with the Catholic forms of 'oraison' and 'leçon', so much in evidence in *Domestic Breviary*, his first published collection of verse, and again attended Catholic services with Münsterer, partly to experience the form of the service, partly for the girls, among them the still untouchable Therese Ostheimer. He conjured up Villon's life in his ballad 'Of François Villon':

> God's table was denied to him for life
> So heaven's blessed gifts he could not get.
> His fate it was to stab men with his knife
> And stick his neck into the traps they set.
> So let them kiss his arse while he was trying
> To eat some food that he found satisfying.[27]

In March 1918 he told Neher that he had decided to write a play about Villon. By the spring, the idea had evolved into the first version of *Baal*. It was every bit as feisty as his ballad for Villon. The premiere of Johst's *The Lonely One* in March was a great spur. In fact, the writing of *Baal* became a classic demonstration of the contrary Brecht's assumption of antagonistic positions to existing works. From the assumption of the antagonistic position, that of dramatic denunciation, Brecht worked his way to his own independent creation. Johst's depiction of the wretched dramatist Grabbe larded on the pathos in full-blown Expressionist manner. Grabbe was intended to be the archetypal misunderstood genius. However, Johst asked a lot of his audience: Grabbe deceives his friend Hans Eckardt by seducing his fiancée; he blames his mother for the death of his wife and his child; and, she commits suicide. Dismissed from his job, he takes to drink and dies in penury, bitter and alone, after the good burghers in the town's Ratskeller try to get dirty stories out of him.

Brecht announced in Kutscher's seminar that he was writing a play that was the antithesis of Johst's. The parallels and contrasts with *The Lonely One* are evident in early versions. Baal seduces Johannes's fiancée, he is dismissed from his job, he sings his songs in the pub and he has a confrontation with his mother. However, Brecht does not reproduce the dark mood of Johst's Expressionist play, which is predicated on the tragic disjunction between art and life. On the contrary, Brecht's play overcomes his own Schopenhauerian tendencies in a celebration of the union of art and life. He takes over much local colour from his Augsburg world and describes Baal as not 'handicapped by nature' and 'neither a specially comic character nor a specially tragic one'.[28] In fact, Brecht later recalled a dissolute poet Johann Baal from Pfersee in the mould of the *poètes maudits*, whom Brecht knew from Augsburg pubs.[29] Brecht's Baal is an amoral, vitalist creature of instinct, who entertains his listeners by singing his filthy songs in the pub. For all their differences, he loves his mother. Brecht makes two figures out of Hans Eckardt, the naïve young writer Johannes, whose fiancée Baal seduces, and the musician Ekart, with whom Baal has a homosexual relationship. For Paula Banholzer, Johannes was like the Brecht she knew, while the relationship between Baal and Ekart clearly owes much to the story of Rimbaud and Verlaine.

Brecht was clear in his own mind that what he had produced was the very antithesis of Expressionist fashion. His talent fed on anything at all that resonated with him, be it popular, modern or ancient. His voracious consumption and reproduction of all suitable material set him apart from a self-conscious avant-gardism in which the new was prized as the hallmark of distinction. In a letter to Neher, he set out his trenchant opposition to the most recent art and to Expressionist art in general with a polemical gusto characteristic of his later critical writing:

> This Expressionism is horrible. All feeling for the beautifully rounded or glori-ously hulking body languishes like the hope for peace. The intellect crushes vitality all along the line. Mystical, clever, consumptive, ecstatic pretentiousness runs rampant, and it all stinks of garlic. I shall be banished from the heaven of these noble, intellectual idealists, from these Strindhills and Wedebabies, and then I'll have to write books about your art. All right, I'll stand on my own feet and spit, I'm sick of the new. I'm starting to work with very old material that's been tested a thousand times over, and I'm doing what I want, even if what I want is bad. I'm a materialist and a lout and a proletarian and a conservative anarchist.[30]

The terms of Brecht's contrary position are revealing, starting with the 'gloriously hulk body' and embracing the vital materiality of the life that he sought to champion over the intellect, not to mention the radical and non-conformist jumble of his politics. This approach is the hallmark of the young Brecht. In Baal it yielded a dramatic figure of monstrous proportions, announced in 'Hymn of Baal the Great', in which Baal leaves behind a trail of bodies seduced and spent:

> Baal grew up in the whiteness of the womb
> With the sky already large and pale and calm
> Naked, young, endlessly marvellous
> And Baal loved it when he came to us.
> And that sky remained with him through joy and care
> Even when Baal slept, blissful and unaware.
> Nights meant violet sky and drunken Baal
> Dawns, Baal good, sky apricottish-pale.
>
> So through hospital, cathedral, bar
> Baal trots coolly on, and learns to let them go.
> When Baal's tired, boys, Baal will not fall far:
> Baal will drag his whole sky down below.[31]

Sated, Baal goes to his death.

The speed with which Brecht composed *Baal* established the pattern for many later plays. Equally typical was the fact that Brecht could never leave the work alone, re-writing it again and again in the light of the later positions which he rapidly assumed and then discarded for fresh ones. Work on the first draft of *Baal* consumed Brecht and his friends through the spring of 1918. He was forever reciting new poems, which found their way into the play, among them 'The Song of the Cloud of the Night'. In its simple two-stanza form – 'My heart is dull as the cloud of the night / And homeless, oh my dear!' followed by ''My heart is wild as the cloud of the night / And aching, oh my dear!' – the poem evokes the split between melancholy and creative euphoria within the heart, both the wellspring of Brecht's creativity and a symbol of the suffering from which it emerged.[32] The scene in which Baal's mother enters his room shows Baal the hedonist laid low by his cardiac suffering.

This figure of Gargantuan appetites was a seminal creation of youthful precocity but hugely problematic. Brecht would struggle in his quarrel with himself with that very egotism which was so much part of him, and would later create the reflective, ascetic intellectual Herr Keuner as the counterpoint to the instinctual Baal. Baal embodies, too, the conflict in Brecht between amoral cynicism and a deeply engrained sense of morality, which is closely associated with his sensitivity towards suffering and his mother's influence on him. Baal struggles with this contradiction between moral indifference and an ingrained moral fervour. In the first draft, the way Baal's sensitivity was knocked out of him is a prominent theme. He says that he was beaten until his skin was callused. Behind that hardness, at times he could still, nonetheless, on occasion experience tender feelings.[33] In later versions, as too in the re-working of early ballads for the *Domestic Breviary*, scenes depicting Baal's sensitivity or vulnerability are replaced by episodes emphasizing his brutality.

By the summer, the first version of *Baal – Urbaal* after Goethe's *Urfaust –* was ready. Brecht announced its completion to Neher as *Baal eats! Baal dances!! Baal is transfigured!!! What does Baal do?*[34] Berthold Brecht allowed his son to employ secretaries at the Haindl factory to type up the drafts. They were shocked by what they read. Brecht, ready to be discovered as the leading dramatist of the age, sent the manuscript to the leading German critic of the age, Alfred Kerr, giving him the opportunity to make his greatest discovery. Brecht heard nothing back. He sought the views of the dramatic advisers at Munich's innovative Kammerspiele, Lion Feuchtwanger and Jacob Geis. He also passed the manuscript to Kutscher, who, not remotely inclined to forgive Brecht his gross behaviour, tore the play apart. This left Brecht begging Münsterer to write something to him about this 'Corpse-Kutscher', meaning a coachman of corpses: 'It's enough to make you puke! He's the most shallow individual I've ever come across'.[35] Brecht would not let matters rest.

He would return to *Baal* in 1919, creating a new, fuller draft, richer in its biographical allusions when, as Münsterer put it, the spirit of *Baal* defined their world.[36] Back from the war, Neher produced a marvellous series of Baal sketches. Yet, as we shall see, despite some enthusiastic support, Brecht struggled to get the play staged or published. This wildly extravagant creation was simply too great a challenge to prevailing morality. Further work on *Baal* from late 1919 and 1920 saw much paring back of material from those earlier versions, particularly the strongly biographical relationship between Baal and his mother, as well as elements which Brecht came to feel were too much the product of his confrontation with *The Lonely One*. Yet he could not fail to see that much of the play's vitality had been lost as the amoral hedonist Baal was tamed. The process continued when he returned to the project in the mid–1920s, around 1930, in the late 1930s, and shortly before he died. Brecht's initial instincts had been correct.

The Medical Orderly and the Revolution 1918–19

Another reprieve

Invited on the 10th anniversary of the 1918 November Revolution to describe how he experienced the war's end, Brecht was not inclined to go into detail, writing that he avoided the front line because he was 'favoured by fortune'.[1] How did he do it? In advance of Brecht's medical on 1 May 1918, his brother was examined and selected for the infantry. Walter was delighted when he joined his regiment, Augsburg's Third Bavarian Infantry, in June. The regiment had suffered heavy losses at Verdun and needed fresh recruits. Brecht counted on his bad heart to save him.[2] However, on 1 May he was deemed fit for service in the field as a medical orderly. In response, he produced his famous 'Ballad of the Dead Soldier'. First published in *Drums in the Night*, this poem, perhaps more than anything else, earned Brecht the unrelenting hostility of nationalist circles. In 1935 the poem was cited as a reason for the removal of Brecht's German citizenship. It contains verses such as

> The summer spread over the makeshift graves.
> The soldier lay ignored
> until one night there came an offi-
> cial army medical board.

> The board went out to the cemetery
> with consecrated spade
> and dug up what was left of him
> and put him on parade.[3]

However, Brecht had another shot in his locker. On the day of his medical, his father, by now managing director of Haindl, requested that his son be permitted to continue studying medicine for the current semester.[4] It was very unusual for such a request to be granted. This one was, by Kaspar Deutschenbaur, the civilian chair of the local Augsburg recruitment committee and a future lord mayor. Like Brecht's father, Deutschenbaur was a member of the Augsburg male voice choir.

Around this time the ailing Sophie Brecht was diagnosed with breast cancer, which in 1920 would kill her. She went from operation to operation, staying in hospital for weeks on end, and was confined to bed for virtually the whole time, hardly able to speak. Her pain was dulled by shots of morphine. This was the moment at which, in Walter Brecht's words, 'Marie Röcker's role in the family grew in importance'.[5] Marie Röcker returned to live with the Brechts in June 1918, taking over the running of the household, caring for Sophie and satisfying Director Berthold Brecht's emotional needs.

Brecht wrote a poem for his mother on her birthday, 8 September 1918. In 'The Tree of Brotherhood' he employed his favourite tree imagery to capture the relationship between the two boys as their mother faced the prospect of them both going to war.[6] The poem puts a benign gloss on their relationship, conveying the message of fraternal solidarity in the face of their difficulties. That solidarity would be sorely tested when civil war came to Germany in the autumn of 1918. The terminally ill Sophie could, however, still muster her sense of outrage at her elder son, who remained wholly negligent of personal hygiene, wedded to the most colourful vulgarities and to masturbation. Her vociferous protestations that this would be the death of her prompted him to write 'Outpourings of a Martyr', which begins:

> I, for instance, play billiards in the attic
> Where they hang the washing up to dry and let it piss.
> Day after day my mother says: It's tragic
> For a grown-up person to be like this.
>
> And to say such things, when no normal person would look at things that way.
> Among the washing too ... I call it unhealthy, sheer pornography.
> But how fed up I get with having to watch everything I say
> And I tell my mother: That's what washing's like, why blame me?[7]

The upright Sophie Brecht could not countenance anyone giving way to animal drives when they should be demonstrating that they were fit to take their place in the Christian fellowship. Her son's refusal to bow to her disapproval triggered in Sophie the view that her previously beloved Eugen was only behaving in this way to spite her:

> Then, naturally, she cries and says: But the washing! And that I'd soon have her under the sod at this rate.
> And the day would come when I'd want to claw it up to get her back once more.
> But it would be too late by then, and I'd start finding out
> How much she'd done for me. But I should have thought of that before.

The reproaches came thick and fast, underpinned by the certainty of faith and an accompanying moral stringency, but these things could not touch him any more: 'What business have they got putting that stuff about Truth in the catechism / If one's not allowed to say what is?'. Brecht loved his mother and continued to care for her, introducing his friends to her and wheeling her out into the garden in her bath chair, where he would sit with her. But the old intensity and intimacy in their relationship, grounded in shared suffering, were gone amidst the disapproval and recriminations.

Away from the family, Brecht was living an exciting life. His pursuit of girls on several fronts was beginning to pay dividends. Suddenly, in his letters to Neher all

Brecht's talk was of Paula. In February 1918 he wrote that Paul Bittersweet had finally fallen for him despite her parents' unrelenting attitude. He took the name Bittersweet from Paul Claudel's play *The Exchange*, which he knew in Franz Blei's translation. Louis uses that nickname for the simple, good natured Marthe. Paula was Marthe to a tee. *The Exchange* would become Brecht's favourite present to his women. In 1919 he gave it to Hedda Kuhn and in 1922 to both Marianne Zoff and Paula Banholzer. The exchange in question was partner swapping. Like his compositions 'Bonnie Mac Sorel Went Courting' and 'Romance', this book, ostensibly a present to a girlfriend, was simultaneously a warning. With *The Exchange* as his calling card, Brecht signalled his disregard for the conventions of monogamy governing men's relations with women and of sex restricted to the sanctity of marriage. Paula did not remotely understand what she was letting herself in for. As we shall see, Brecht could behave in a truly appalling way towards her and other lovers, however charming he might also be. Privileged to be in the inner circle of a charismatic genius, they, of course, revered him.

Under the guise of Fritz Bock – the German 'Bock' has the same lascivious connotations as the English 'ram' – Brecht sent a letter to Paula as 'Miss Marie Bock, Cook for Herr Dr Banholzer'.[8] Parodying the Lord's Prayer and the Bible, he confided to 'Saint Cas': 'She's wonderfully soft and spring-like. Day after day, I lead myself into temptation to deliver myself from evil. But I don't want to do what I want to do? But what if *she* does? Write to me, Saint Cas, what will happen then? If someone is better than me, on him will I cast the first stone'.[9] Neher did not reply to this letter, nor to the ones following, in which Brecht added: 'I often meet Bittersweet (Paul) and we go for a stroll in the evening on the grey heath to the right of the Lech. The atmosphere is sensual. But now I've heard what certain people have to say, I'm more or less immune'.[10] This seemingly responsible attitude is at odds with Brecht's later bravado on the subject of sex with a fifteen-year-old.[11] Paula was actually seventeen at the time, still a minor. In March he gave her a ring and told Neher: 'She trembled and kissed me. We didn't say anything. I'm filled with desire to gallop to Asia'.[12] There was a brief setback. On 20 April Brecht told Neher: 'Everybody loves us. And I love everybody – except Bittersweet'.[13]

Things were on again by 1 May when she sent him her first surviving letter. Addressing 'Dearest Bert', Paula wrote with a playful assurance which belies her age, using the same parody of the Lord's Prayer which Brecht had used to Neher:

> Wednesday evening! Thank God the storm's just about died down. My mother was fairly friendly when she spoke to me. Maybe she regretted the fact that she put me in the same category as Marie. She'll still not accept that I went to the theatre alone. Aren't you transported by my diligence? But I was afraid that otherwise you wouldn't get my letter before Saturday. You're not warned against imitating me!! Because you want to hear something loving, exceptionally I'll fulfil your desire and write to you about the most loving thing, namely God! My dear child, just consider that you're alone in this big city, without any human protection to deliver you from evil and always to run after you with the wooden spoon. Take refuge in God, he'll support you, you'll never feel alone and solitary, and never harass other

people to send you material to entertain you that they've cobbled together with drops of sweat and deprivation of their precious sleep.

Go with God, my dear child!

Behave decently like

Your Bittersweet!

You don't need to 'worry' about me. My sadness has flown like ether. (I love you!)[14]

Like the notion of deliverance from evil, the naming of a specific desire was evidently drawn from Brecht's courtship ritual. Despite Paula's words of re-assurance, Brecht remained plagued by jealousy, as he acknowledged in 'Teddy's Song', Teddy being yet another of his nicknames for her:

Teddy says she simply could not ever be so proud,

she'd rather have another kiss if that's allowed.

Gentlemen, there's more to that than meets the eye!

Forget it: no one lets bliss pass them by.[15]

In mid-June Brecht announced to Neher that a catharsis was approaching with Paula, which would most likely have passed by the time Neher had read his letter. Brecht confessed that the matter was churning around deep inside him. He explained that she now seemed to want 'it' and exclaimed: 'May God and I help her!'.[16] By the beginning of July, he was asking Neher what he should do if 'it' had consequences and indeed later in the month he was fretting that her period was three days late. He wrote, presciently, that he would have no idea what to do with a child. He admitted, too, that during the three days that they had recently spent together in the mountains near Lake Starnberg, 'Naturally, I took no precautions, none at all, it would have spoilt our pleasure, it would have been unaesthetic and anyway, I couldn't have. I'm not a tarot player. I can't hold back my trumps'.[17] He did fear for Paula in these circumstances. This time, it turned out to be a false alarm but he would not learn from experience. She would pay the price.

Paula is confident in her own account that when they made love it was the first time for both of them.[18] It seems that Paula was correct in her estimation that she was his first lover of real significance but probably not in her view that he had not slept with a woman before her. Brecht certainly had some sexual experience by this time with Hedda Kuhn and probably with others like Rosl, maybe Marie Rose Amann, too. Brecht was ecstatic after sleeping with Paula. He had spent two years pursuing this beautiful, seemingly unattainable girl and had at last achieved intimacy with her. That had all seemed impossible during his painfully shy adolescence. From now on, he saw himself as the expert sexual operator, finally engaging in a physical activity at which he believed he excelled. He certainly did excel in what he said to her. Then she was his.

All this time, the dreaded call-up hung heavily over Brecht. For someone who took himself and his work so very seriously that he demanded absolute control over every aspect of his existence, the prospect of being stripped of his freedom by the military was tantamount to a death sentence. On 21 July, Berthold Brecht submitted a further request for his elder son's call-up to be deferred.[19] He again based his request on his son's medical studies, arguing this time that if he were permitted to study for a third semester he could be deployed in the army at the first grade for a doctor. However, the submission did not help, nor did the fact that Berthold Brecht pointed out that he had two sons and that the younger one was already serving. In mid-August a letter arrived, rejecting Berthold's application and requiring his son to present himself for duty on 1 October.

Determined to savour his remaining freedom, Brecht exchanged the town for the country once more, taking a holiday in August in the Bavarian Forest with Fritz Gehweyer, who was on leave. They went by train and stayed at the Zwiesler Waldhaus near the Bohemian border. It is well-known today as the oldest inn in that part of Germany, having been built originally to serve the needs of forest workers. Addressing Paula in a letter as 'my dear girl', Brecht played up the rough-hewn manner of their quarters in this 'wooden shack': 'Our room, all wood, is very crude. Two snow-white beds. A wobbly table. In the evening we play the mouth organ'.[20] The place lent itself to the play of his imagination but the lodgings were what young middle-class men would expect, not the primitive world of the forest in which Baal sought a genuine existence. Of course, they cultivated the 'Baal mood', marching through the forest by night and resting in a clearing by day. Revelling in the sunrise like Baal and Zarathustra, Brecht told Bi that he'd played guitar in a forest inn and 'in return they gave us milk and butter, which are *very* rare here. [...] Today we may go as far as the Bohemian Forest. Possibly I'll come home tomorrow. As I choose'. Exactly. In fact, Brecht also sent a love letter from the Bavarian Forest to Ernestine Müller, playing up his vagabond existence with Gehweyer and asking her if she still loved him and was keeping lots of love for him till he came home.[21]

But time was running out. Gehweyer returned to the front and was killed shortly before the armistice. Meanwhile, Brecht wrote to his 'beloved', 'blessed' Cas near the end of August, gripped by ennui:

> I lie on the bed the whole time, thinking of Canada and a roaring blue sky. Aren't you ever coming home? Bittersweet is away and it doesn't matter and I can't work and the sky is a hole I can't spit into, and you aren't saying anything, and German literature is trash, and I'm trash too, and always having to get dressed in the morning and the waiting, and the lousy feeling that nothing matters and that nothing can happen to me except precisely that nothing more can happen to me ... It's enough to make the Devil weep. Where are you staggering around? Accursed Devil! Heavenly Devil! (God puts up with everything! He's in a bad way!) And so is Bert Brecht.[22]

So Brecht did what he always did: he went to the Plärrer where he nearly 'swung himself to death'.[23] He wrote to Münsterer that the summer was too beautiful for him to get any work done, so he was eating ice-cream and playing the guitar, waiting for his death sentence. He had himself photographed with the two skulls which Bezold had stolen for him, one under each arm. And on 3 September Brecht wrote 'Ballad of the Death's Head' for Bezold. As Münsterer writes, the poem records his friends' responses to his acquisitions, beginning with Heigei, his nickname for Müllereisert:

> Heigei says you're just an ageing fossil,
> But then Heigei isn't too polite.

Orge says it takes no mental muscle,
He's guessed your provenance all right.[24]

Bi guesses it is a ship's captain and Cas an innocent girl, while for Brecht himself it is
a poet: 'One whose song poured sweetly forth – like cream, / And who, bathing in a
heavenly aura, / Shot a lantern in his drunken dream'. He concludes: 'Whatsoever was
your fate, it's over: / Now you're just a warning to us all'. Brecht's finest composition in
that final month of freedom is 'Lucifer's Evening Song'. Collected in *Domestic Breviary*
as 'Against Temptation' and used in the first version of *The Rise and Fall of the City of
Mahagonny*, it is a resounding warning not to be seduced by the 'meats' of Christianity
into abandoning life's pleasures:

Do not be led astray
There is no turning back now.
Daybreak will soon be with us
The winds of night are blowing
The morn will dawn no more.

Do not be deluded
That life's of little worth.
Enjoy it to the utmost
It cannot satisfy you
If you must give it up.[25]

On 24 September it was time for Walter to leave for the front. His father was beside
himself –'gaunt and haggard' – when he and Eugen saw Walter off at the station.[26]
Berthold Brecht abandoned his patriotic zeal, cursing the way that children were being
sent to their deaths. Dreading his own call-up on Tuesday 1 October, Brecht sent a
note to Hedda Kuhn: 'I can't come. On Tuesday I'm being buried'.[27]

On the Augsburg front line: From the amputation ward to the clap clinic

Donning his uniform, Brecht took up his duties as a medical orderly in Augsburg.
At this late stage in the war, the square bashing of basic training was dispensed
with. He reported to the field hospital at the Schiller School in Oberhausen, today's
Löweneck School.[28] It was a gruesome place. Directly behind the school was a railway
track, on which trainloads of badly-wounded soldiers were brought directly from
the Alsatian Front for operations and amputations. He later told Sergei Tretiakov
that he treated wounds with iodine and bandaged them, giving patients enemas and
blood transfusions.[29] The scenes which Brecht witnessed would come back to haunt
him. The new recruit put on a brave face in a letter to his brother – Walter was
stationed at Hussigny seven kilometres behind the front at Verdun – claiming that
he was enjoying what he was doing.[30] Brecht sought to reassure his brother that the
war would end in the winter, that he would get back safely and that they could look

forward to going to university together. Shortly after, he was writing that there would be peace by Christmas. The field hospitals were being cleared as fast as possible to deal with the expected mass influx at the war's end. Brecht acknowledged that he had secured a good deal for himself: he was already allowed to sleep at home. He described his duties to his brother. They had their draw-backs: there were always operations to be seen – and heard – and people to be put back together. Trains full of soldiers with Spanish flu had arrived. He advised Walter to get hold of some aspirins if he caught it and to sweat it out. Brecht told his brother, too, that their mother was a little better and 'there is more peace in the house'. Marie Röcker's name remained unmentioned. Despite her abject condition, Sophie Brecht, the Protestant rebel, had clearly not gone down without a fight before 'peace' was restored. Brecht closed his letter with reassuring thoughts. Despite all their scraps, he wrote, they had always stuck together.

After three weeks Brecht was transferred to Ward D at the Elias Holl School, which was reserved for soldiers with sexually transmitted infections.[31] Brecht probably owed this piece of relatively good fortune to another family connection. The head of the field hospital at the Elias Holl School was Dr Julius Raff, an Augsburg skin specialist and family friend. It was said that some of the patients had put a special effort into catching a dose so as to escape the murderous front line. Brecht was tasked with writing up their medical histories. It is a pity that none of Brecht's histories have survived. What we do have, though, is Brecht's 'Song for the Gentlemen-Soldiers of Ward D', with which, as Münsterer recalls, he regaled his patients:

How your loins did burn with fires of passion
in your youth, when you were full of flame.
Wenches are for loving and for thrashing,
that's the way – man's always been the same.[32]

The refrain goes:

These womenfolk! Holy Virgin, Mother of God!
An aching heart is bad, but worse is an aching rod!

Brecht's sardonic humour helped him to make the best of the situation. In fact, he had an abject fear of catching a dose himself. As usual, he coped with his fear by turning it into art. Brecht sang the beginning of each line 'slowly, charged with emotion, before rattling glibly through the rest at an unbelievable pace'.

The posting did nothing to diminish the potential for farce and black humour in Brecht's encounter with the military. Brecht was quick to exploit the fault line between the military proper and the civilian values which Raff represented. Friends who saw Brecht at this time were amazed at his outrageous appearance and behaviour amongst military men.[33] Heiner Hagg admired Brecht's chutzpah. He walked around in yellow half-shoes, without a jacket and any head gear, in a pullover with his hands in his pockets to keep his trousers up. To round off his provocative demeanour, he sometimes carried a riding crop. Prompted by Paula's love of horses, he was taking riding lessons. Brecht told Hagg that his patients showed the true face of society quite openly and without mendacity.

While Brecht entertained his ailing troops, Müllereisert witnessed the outrage of regular soldiers at his behaviour.[34] This was in no way diminished by the fact that Raff so obviously enjoyed Brecht's company, jovially addressing the young medical orderly as 'My dear colleague'. This went to Brecht's head and he began behaving as if he were the Deputy Chief Medical Officer. He arrived wielding a walking cane one day and flouted military rules with a mien of aristocratic nonchalance. Brecht tried the limits of even Raff's patience when he discovered that the family maid had been delivering the young orderly's reports every evening. Nonetheless, when Brecht was discharged his indulgent superior would evaluate his work as 'very good'![35]

Brecht's old classmate Rudolf Prestel, for one, did not admire Brecht's cavalier approach to his duties. Prestel had lost a leg at the front and was awarded the Iron Cross upon discharge. Brecht sent Prestel a poem during his convalescence, designed to raise his morale with the prospect that the war would end soon: 'Wait for a short while / You who are in despair!'.[36] Brecht completely misjudged Prestel's mood. None too enamoured of defeatist sentiments, Prestel bumped into Brecht in Augsburg and challenged him to explain what he was doing at home. When Brecht said he was doing his duty as a medical orderly, Prestel replied: 'Ah, you're emptying the spittoons?'. It is said he then spat in Brecht's face.

Prestel was not alone in his view of Brecht's behaviour. We have seen that Brecht was not always honest with his friends about his motives. He was particularly crass in a letter to his brother of 21 October:

> I don't like it where I am. I think that you above all will understand me when I say that my lot promises to become dreadful: this never-ending, pointless and mind-numbing scribbling, which has absolutely nothing of the romance of greatness, of nemesis, of the idea. Without my hope for a conclusive peace I'd certainly volunteer for active service.[37]

Walter could, no doubt, see through his brother's claim. The utterly self-absorbed Brecht could not conceal that what actually galled him, what he found truly intolerable, was that his precious time for writing was being consumed by petty bureaucratic scribbling.

Walter's account of the suffering that he and his equally patriotically-minded comrades had to endure at Verdun gave Brecht food for thought. He made no secret of his concern at their blind acceptance of the patriotic mission: 'It's the tone, which is so strongly reminiscent of an ancient tragedy, and the most terrifying thing is, I suspect, precisely what gives you heart: this absolute defence of an idea in the most extreme misery'.[38] In fact, the German front was collapsing and the army retreating in disarray after the deadlock of trench warfare had been broken.

Revolution

The end came quickly and with it pandemonium, which Brecht experienced as a heady mix of revolution, artistic activity and procreation. Although he made certain claims to Tretiakov, Brecht generally downplayed his experience of the revolution, out of embarrassment at his political immaturity and the political and artistic choices that he had made. It was, however, one of the most intense periods of his life. In early November the sailors of the imperial fleet mutinied in Kiel, while on the Sunday after All Saints' Brecht and Paula conceived a child.[39] The juxtaposition is not flippant. This conjunction of events left its mark on the play about these days which Brecht wrote in early 1919, first called *Spartacus*, then *Drums in the Night* and dedicated to 'Bie Banholzer 1918'.[40] The pregnancy was confirmed at the turn of the year.

The call for revolution spread like wildfire through Germany. In Bavaria, the USPD's Kurt Eisner led the overthrow of the Wittelsbach monarchy. The King of Bavaria fled and Eisner was elected chair of the revolutionary Workers' and Soldiers' Council. The concept of the council was borrowed from the Russian soviet. Eisner's election was the basis of his legitimacy when he proclaimed the Bavarian Republic, following which he was named Minister President. The following day in Augsburg, Ernst Niekisch, the editor of the *Schwäbische Volkszeitung*, was elected chair of the local Workers' and Soldiers' Council. The red flag was raised over the town hall, and the Workers' and Soldiers' Council took over military and civil powers.

Amidst chaotic scenes in Berlin, on 9 November the House of Hohenzollern collapsed and with it the Wilhelmine Empire as Wilhelm II fled to Holland. The Social Democratic Party (SPD) deputy, Philipp Scheidemann, proclaimed the German Republic from the Reichstag and was followed two hours later by Karl Liebknecht, who proclaimed the Free Socialist Republic of Germany from the Berlin Schloss. The SPD's Friedrich Ebert took over leadership of the government in Scheidemann's German Republic. On 11 November the fighting in the First World War ended on all fronts when the western powers and Germany signed the armistice.

Brecht was busy assembling seven of his favourite compositions in his *Songs for the Guitar by Bert Brecht and his Friends. 1918*. The small collection remained unpublished during his lifetime. With beautiful wit he captured the beguiling contrasts informing his work, describing the collection as 'songs for the guitar of uncommon depth of feeling and of unhealthy crudity'.[41] *Songs for the Guitar* included 'Baal's Song' and 'Song for the Gentleman-Soldiers of Ward D'.

Brecht's wartime duties were not yet done: the clap clinic was needed as much as ever. When Münsterer paid Brecht a visit at work, one of his colleagues showed Münsterer gonorrhoea and other bacteria under the microscope.[42] Münsterer, who himself became a dermatologist, could see that Brecht knew as little about all this as Münsterer himself. However, Sophie Brecht saw her elder son as a budding doctor. Her letter to Walter of 22 November is filled with pride: 'It seems that everybody in the field hospital likes him. They all say to him: he will for sure become a good doctor but would *never* have become a good soldier. But they seem to take him as he is, even his warrant officer, who is otherwise very critical'.[43] No doubt he had good reason to be.

But everything was changing with the collapse of the old order. Walter Brecht was appalled when he returned to his Augsburg garrison and found it in the hands of the Spartacist Workers' and Soldiers' Council.[44] As they demobbed the new arrivals, they treated the old military ways with contempt. And Walter's elder brother became involved with the revolutionaries. On 13 November Kurt Eisner had decreed that Field Hospital Councils should be formed to represent the interests of the wounded.

The decree was implemented in Augsburg on 28 November and Brecht found himself representing his field hospital within the broader structure of the Augsburg Workers' and Soldiers' Council. Brecht's involvement has frequently been confused with the short-lived Bavarian Soviet Republic [Räterepublik] of the following year. What he wrote in 1928 of his activity at the time of the November Revolution is more accurate than things which were later written from a political perspective, most notably by Tretiakov in 1934. In 1928 Brecht wrote:

> At that time I was a soldiers' representative in a field hospital in Augsburg, and in fact I had only taken up this office after several friends had persuaded me insistently to do so, claiming that it would be in their interest. (As it turned out, however, I was unable to change the state in a way which would have helped them.) We all suffered from a lack of political convictions and I myself suffered all the more because of my old inability to be enthusiastic about anything. I was saddled with a great deal of work. [...] Very soon I secured my discharge. In short, I was hardly any different from the overwhelming majority of the other soldiers; of course, they had all had enough of the war, but they were not in a position to think in political terms. I do not particularly like to dwell on it.[45]

This passage confirms that Brecht's involvement stemmed from his service as a medical orderly, not from any overriding political commitment. When his duties came to an end on 9 January 1919, that day simultaneously signalled the end of his Council role. He did not view himself as fulfilling a political brief. As always, he was extremely jealous of his writing time. Hardly surprisingly, he made little impact on the Augsburg Council, whose chair Niekisch later recalled Brecht's membership.[46] Brecht's principal interest was to be demobbed without delay. According to the published plan, that was actually out of the question for people of his age. Again, Brecht was probably able to use his family's connections with Augsburg's great and good, probably Raff, to expedite his release from military service after just three months and nine days.

Meanwhile, at the first conference of the Spartacus League in Berlin on 1 January 1919 Rosa Luxemburg and Karl Liebknecht, together with left-wing socialists from Bremen, founded the Communist Party of Germany (KPD). They followed with a call for resistance against Ebert's SPD-USPD government, which triggered the Spartacus Uprising on 5 January. Their forces occupied the newspaper buildings and seized control of the news media, calling upon the workers to begin the armed struggle against the government. Brecht would use these events as the backcloth for his new play. On 12 January government troops smashed the uprising, then on 15 January, they captured, tortured and murdered Luxemburg and Liebknecht. These events signalled the disintegration of relations between the two principal forces of the German Left. Brecht would return again and again to the grim significance of Luxemburg's murder in the chaotic events surrounding the foundation of the Weimar Republic.

In Augsburg, on 4 January Brecht's friend Lilly Krause, now Lilly Prem after her marriage to her fellow socialist activist Georg Prem, fronted a USPD rally with Kurt Eisner at the Ludwigsbau. The Prems followed the call to join the Spartacists. In the coming weeks, Brecht engaged in intense political debate with them at Gabler's Tavern, where he could be found most weekends. With the Prems, he adopted the position of the 'independent Independent', playing on the term 'independent' in the title USPD, in contrast to their revolutionary party discipline. In a text written in 1935 for use on a visit to Moscow he would claim that he had been a USPD member.[47] There is no evidence to support this. On the contrary, the position of the 'independent Independent' would become a familiar Brechtian position vis-à-vis parties with which the artist shared common ground, similar to the position adopted by that other artistic icon of the revolutionary Left, Pablo Picasso, in his dealings with the French Communist Party. However, unlike Picasso, Brecht never became a party member.

Spartacus/Drums in the Night

Now addressing Paula as Bi, Brecht announced on 29 January 1919 that he was working on a new play.[48] It was already half-complete: he was rising at 6 a.m. and writing until midday. This became Brecht's writing routine. He was working with the recently demobbed Neher. His aim was quite simple: to make money to support Bi and their child. He chose the most topical of subjects, the revolutionary turmoil after the war, and with typical directness he called the play *Spartacus*, finding a place in it for his signature piece, the 'Ballad of the Dead Soldier'. Set in November 1918, the play tells the story of the escaped POW Kragler, parodying the traditional ballad of the dead soldier returning to claim his bride. Kragler returns home from Africa, ghost-like as if from the grave, to find his fiancée about to marry another man, Murk, by whom she is pregnant. Meanwhile, the German revolution rages around them.

Already on 13 February, Neher was noting the completion of the play: 'We embraced and I congratulated him. We smoked a cigarette to our renown'.[49] Like Kragler, Neher himself had, of course, survived near-death when he had been buried at the front. As always, the first draft of the play turned out to be just the first in a tortuous process of writing and re-writing. After completing the first version, Brecht was full of his play and its prospects. He went out to sell it, seeking the advice of the actor Arnold Marlé in Munich's Café Stephanie. Immersed in his newspaper, Marlé said: 'Go to Feuchtwanger'.[50] Lion Feuchtwanger was an established novelist and playwright, who was also a dramatic adviser at the Kammerspiele. Feuchtwanger, who received Brecht at his home, recalled him as 'weedy, badly shaven, scruffily dressed. He clung to the walls, spoke Swabian dialect'. Feuchtwanger was used to writers' lofty claims for their work but Brecht told Feuchtwanger exactly what he had told Bi: that he had written the play purely to make money. By early April Brecht was writing to her: 'A doctor in Munich, who has a lot of clout and himself writes good plays, finds *Spartacus* brilliant. He's going to push it and then we'll get money. It will be published, too'.[51] Feuchtwanger's wife Marta suggested a fresh title, *Drums in the Night*. Shortly after, Brecht was both optimistic and pessimistic as he wrote to Bi of the prospects for *Baal*, too:

> My projects are progressing well, the two dramas will be published come what may, probably performed, too. Now, as it becomes a real prospect, I'm viewing the matter very pessimistically. I'm certain it will fall through. The people are

too enthusiastic for my liking. Today the Hoftheater in Munich asked for the manuscript of *Baal* by telegram. The doctor who 'discovered' me seems to be doing a good job. But I can't really be bothered with that any more. I want to write something new.[52]

In the short term, Brecht's pessimism would be amply borne out.

The original manuscript of *Drums in the Night* has not survived. Brecht worked on the play again in 1920, 1922 and in the early 1950s. Like *Baal*, *Drums in the Night* was never finished to Brecht's satisfaction. Both are typical products of the young Brecht's poetic mythology, extolling the rugged individual, but hugely problematic for the older Brecht. Like Baal, Andreas Kragler is an egotistical anti-hero, both sensitive and brutally amoral with an acquired thick, calloused skin, masking sensitivity. Most shockingly for the later Marxist Brecht, who considered suppressing this play, Kragler places his desire for his own well-being above all other things, most notably the revolution, and his choice is presented in a sympathetic light. At the end of the play, Kragler proclaims: 'The bagpipes play, the poor people are dying around the newspaper buildings, the houses fall on top of them, the dawn breaks, they lie like drowned kittens in the roadway. I'm a swine and the swine's going home'.[53] Kragler chooses in favour of his bed with his fiancée Anna and thus finally returns to life. Despite his best efforts, Brecht could not eradicate what, from a Marxist perspective, could only be viewed as a dangerously counter-revolutionary attitude.

Like Baal, Kragler is a balladesque adventurer, the product of a lyrical imagination attuned to the portrayal of vitalist outcasts, but not yet to sustain the dramatic inter-actions and contrasts of a full-length play. *Drums in the Night* owes much to Brecht's use of key leitmotifs such as the corpse, the ghost, and the red moon, coupled with the raw power of his language. Its earthiness sets it apart from the mannered style of late Expressionism. The play is simultaneously an attack on Expressionist conventions and the beginning of a Brechtian anti-illusionist theatre, drawing upon the style and techniques of fairground performance which he so loved. For example, slogans taken from Kragler's final speech are displayed in the auditorium like story boards. Among them is 'Everybody is Top Man in His Own Skin'.[54] Kragler had grown a 'crocodile skin' in Africa. Another slogan is 'Stop That Romantic Gaping'. In Brecht's particular sense 'romantic' means deluded by idealistic thoughts. These slogans re-enforce Kragler's position at the end when he turns his back on the 'romantic' idea of revolution. By contrast, in his later work Brecht would invite the audience to question such a position through de-familiarising techniques.

Indeed, Brecht did not write *Drums in the Night* as a specifically political play. At the end Kragler is not about to join the German middle-class world. That world is subjected scathing satire in the first half of the play, which culminates in Kragler's challenge to it and his ejection from it by Balicke, Anna's father. Balicke, together with Murk, prospectively Anna's husband as well as her father's business partner, represents the conservative, monarchist position of those in the world of business who made money from the war on the home front. With the onset of peace, Balicke, embodying Brecht's already thoroughly cynical view of business, is shifting production from shell boxes to prams for the expected baby boom. Balicke echoes the conservative press of

1918 in his denunciation of the soldiers who in 1914 had been sent on their way to victory with flowers:

> Now the demobilisation's washing greed, disorder and swinish inhumanity into the still backwaters of peaceful labour. [...] Doubtful characters appearing on the scene, shady gentlemen. The government's being far too soft with those scavengers of the revolution. [...] The masses are all worked up and without any ideals. And worst of all – I can say it here the troops back from the front, shabby, half-savage adventurers who've lost the habit of working and hold nothing sacred.[55]

The heroes of 1914 are the outcasts of 1918, feared and hated by the good citizens at home, who see them as dangerous fomenters of revolution. For Balicke, Kragler must be a Spartacist, a spectre of the revolution. When he first appears and still for a long time afterwards, the deeply disturbed Kragler can barely speak to explain himself and his situation. Murk attempts to buy Kragler's boots off him, an attempt to strip him of the last vestiges of his identity. Balicke and Murk's scornful rejection of Kragler gradually elicits a verbal form of self-defence, which mutates into a verbal struggle between Murk and Kragler over Anna.

Kragler's conflict with Balicke and Murk gives the play real colour and power in its language, while the background threat of revolution adds to the satirical portrayal of the Balickes and Murk in the betrothal scene in the Piccadilly Bar. However, the portrayal of the revolutionaries around the bar-owner Glubb in the second half of the play is less persuasive. In the face of threats from Balicke and Murk, then from the revolutionaries, Kragler succeeds in preserving the identity of the hardened, egotistical adventurer, which he has acquired in the African sun. However, Kragler can achieve nothing more than survival and is without any real prospects for the future. The war in Africa has drained him of any capacity to reintegrate himself within a society itself torn apart by that war.

Bi and Bidi, and Cas

Following Neher's return, his diary, together with Münsterer's, provides a close-up account of activities with Brecht within the revolutionary turmoil of early 1919. It was a time of intense artistic and emotional exchange. Brecht admired Neher's drawings for *Baal* and did his best to promote Neher's work along with his own. Both Neher and Münsterer could lay claim to a relationship with Brecht which was based on shared artistic interests as well as personal attraction. However, Brecht now had sharp criticism for Münsterer's poetry. He pointed out, crushingly, that there was much theory, that there were mistakes and a lack of originality. Münsterer was forced to acknowledge, 'Unfortunately, he's only too right'.[56] For Neher, Münsterer's work was simply a pale imitation of Brecht's.

On the evening of 16 January, three days before the national election, Brecht and Münsterer went round the hustings of the various parties campaigning in Augsburg, ending the evening at the Herrle beer hall listening to Eisner's secretary, Felix Fechenbach of the USPD.[57] On 19 January, the SPD emerged as the strongest party nationally with 37.9 per cent of the vote, the USPD securing only 7.6 per cent. In Bavaria, the situation for the USPD was even worse. It secured just three seats with 2.5 per cent of the vote, compared to 33 per cent for the SPD and 35 per cent for the conservative Bavarian People's Party. The new National Assembly opened in Weimar on 6 February, the SPD heading a coalition government.

That Sunday night of the election there was a *Brechtfest* at Gabler's Tavern to celebrate Brecht's discharge. It followed an evening out with Neher and Müllereisert at a dance bar, The Carp. Münsterer contemplated suicide because his parents would not let him go to the party where Brecht played his *Songs for the Guitar*.[58] Sofie Renner and the Beiacker girls were there, tipsy and dressed as men in uniform.[59] Neher kissed Sofie. Bi stayed away: still a minor, she was pregnant and very angry with Brecht, who had taken to saying to her: 'Let them grow, the little Brechts'.[60] Her life was changing out of all recognition at a bewildering speed. Her parents were furious with Brecht and, deeply ashamed of her, were making decisions over her head. While Brecht delighted in the prospect of being a father, he also experienced the pregnancy as a catastrophe, since it involved a financial commitment which he could realistically only meet if he abandoned his literary ambitions.[61] That, however, was out of the question. Pregnancy as a blessing and a curse becomes a recurrent theme in Brecht's writings as his partners become recurrently pregnant. For those 'little Brechts' he is generally an absent father, doting in his letters and frantically pursuing money-making schemes through writing which for a long time would come to nothing.

Brecht visited Dr Karl Banholzer. He promised to stand by Bi and asked for her hand. Karl Banholzer had never made any secret of his extreme antipathy towards this ne'er-do-well. In a furious confrontation he exploded in an unadulterated expression of sheer hate. It did not help Bi that Brecht did not tell his own family or his close friends that Bi was expecting his child. His concealment of the pregnancy contributed to her enduring sense of bitterness towards him. For all Brecht's trenchant views about bourgeois hypocrisy, he became as much part of the mendacity surrounding the pregnancy as anyone else. He allowed nothing to restrict his freedom of movement and continued to take home other women like Hedda Kuhn and Marie Rose Amann, introducing them to his mother before disappearing to his attic with them.

The Banholzers arranged for their daughter to leave Augsburg at the end of January 1919 and to go and live with the midwife Walburga Frick in Kimratshofen, a village near Kempten in the Allgäu, 120 kilometres from Augsburg. In time-honoured fashion, peasants would be paid to bring up the unwanted child. Meanwhile, the daughter of a good family would bide her time and quietly return to the city as if nothing had happened. Karl Banholzer left Brecht in no doubt that he would have to bear the cost of his daughter's stay at Kimratshofen – four marks per day for her board, plus her other costs – and of the consequences of that stay.[62]

Brecht wrote to Bi during the night after the party at Gabler's.[63] He apologised for losing control, offering the excuse that he had been hurt. He is probably talking about his confrontation with Karl Banholzer. Brecht told Bi that he was going back to Munich the next day for the start of the semester and would not see her for a week. Not able to sleep, he was going to walk down by the Lech. He asked her to come to the station to see him off. She declined that offer and wrote to him, explaining that she would not be writing again. He sent two letters in quick succession on Wednesday and Thursday, protesting that he had had to take that Munich train. He asked why she would not be writing and said that he would be coming home on the Saturday.[64] He then told her that his friends were with him, Neher, Bezold, Geyer, Münsterer – and Hedda Kuhn. He knew full well that the mere mention of Kuhn's name was hurtful to the woman whom he professed he wanted to marry. Bonnie Mac Sorel could not resist turning the screw by parading his desirability for other women.

Back in Augsburg, Brecht met with his friends. On the Saturday he sang for Neher and the following day Neher visited Brecht with Münsterer to hear Brecht and Walter sing ballads by Wedekind.[65] That evening, Brecht put Walter up to phone Bi but he did not do so and Brecht was left to offer his excuses by letter, blaming Walter.[66] Before Brecht went back to Munich, he attended a protest meeting with Münsterer in memory of Rosa Luxemburg, at which Lilly Prem spoke.[67] Shortly after, he attended a similar event in Munich organised by the USPD, at which the anarchist writer Gustav Landauer delivered the address.[68] Brecht composed his 'Ballad of Red Rosa', which begins: 'The red flags of the Revolution / have long ago been swept from the roofs'.[69] Red Rosa is the only one to 'find freedom', as she floats off down the river in the poem's grim conclusion. When Brecht wrote 'Epitaph, 1919' a decade later, he would view politics much more sharply:

> Red Rosa now has vanished too.
> Where she lies is hid from view.
> She told the poor what life is about
> And so the rich have rubbed her out.[70]

On the train to Munich with Neher on 27 January 1919, Brecht announced that he was going to write a novel that would bring in 10,000 marks.[71] Two days later he mentioned the same sum in a letter to Bi. This was his way of showing that he was completely committed to supporting her financially as her father required. Faced by the prospect of fatherhood, his promise to make large sums of money through his writing becomes a constant refrain. He would tell Marianne Zoff essentially the same story of his plans to finance their life together along with their child. He returned to journalism, an earlier source of income, with an enthusiastic review in *Augsburger Neueste Nachrichten* of Hans Karl Müller's recital of German poems. However, Brecht remained financially unsuccessful for several years. Not only that, in his understanding of things, his promise to make large sums freed him to devote himself completely to his writing and associated activities, usually at some distance from his pregnant partner.

Back in Munich he told Bi – about to be marooned for months in Kimratshofen – not to go ice-skating because of her pregnancy. He added that he was learning to dance and could already waltz! He omitted to explain that he was learning with Neher in advance of one of Kutscher's parties, which he was going to attend with Hedda Kuhn.[72] Neher's diary charts Brecht's progress: 'Looked for dance halls and wanted to learn waltzes. By Monday we've both got to be able to'; 'everything is focused on the Kutscher evening. On Monday. Brecht can already dance'; and 'Brecht is dancing'.[73] It was an achievement equal to Baal's. Ostensibly seeking to allay Bi's suspicions but actually adding insult to injury, he wrote of his relationship with Hedda: 'I like her well enough. But you don't need to worry. She's much too bright'.[74]

The only place that Brecht and Bi were going was Kimratshofen and the only thing on her mind was baby clothes. He picked her up the following Saturday and they travelled by train together to Kempten, taking the bus from there. She remembers that he was excessively concerned about her welfare on the journey, given that she was only in her third month.[75] Leaving her in the Fricks' good hands, he resumed his life in Munich and Augsburg. However, that semester he registered for just one course: the human eye, its constitution, functioning and medical care.[76]

After Kutscher's party he wrote to his 'dearest little, angry Bi', claiming: 'Here absolutely nothing is happening, which will be fine by you! Hedda Kuhn has left, having accepted my vow to be faithful. What can I do? Now I've got to be good here!'.[77] Bi had told him that she had an admirer in Kimratshofen. She had also written that she had declined the admirer's invitation to go out, explaining that she had a fiancé. Principal amongst her admirers was Xaver Steinhausen, a law student whose family owned a large estate.[78] He and Bi pursued a lengthy correspondence, while Brecht frequently alludes to Steinhausen in letters, nicknaming him 'Koivi', a Bavarian dialect word meaning clodhopper. All the more so now that she was pregnant and extremely vulnerable, having been cast out of her secure family environment, Bi, it seems, behaved as she had been brought up to, believing in fidelity to the partner to whom one had given oneself.

Brecht certainly expected her to be faithful to him. She, of course, wanted him to be similarly faithful to her, but he shrugged off this attempt 'to make him a better person'. Monogamy was for weaklings, who could not accept life's challenges. In fact, in a notebook Brecht recorded that on 15 February 1919 he had 'put it into Marie'.[79] Had he finally had his way with Marie Rose Amann? Or was it another Marie? 'It feels good, but what of the consequences?'.[80] In a diary fragment from 1919 he writes that by day he studied medicine, by night he 'instructed' Marie.[81] What is more, Brecht extrapolated from his still quite limited sexual experience the idea that all girls should have the same name. After all, he continued, a shirt was simply a shirt. Why should girls have different names, especially if, as proved to be the case, he could never break off from them?

Brecht tried to counter the rumours spreading around Augsburg about Bi's pregnancy. The Hagg family put it about that they were in the know, prompting Brecht's categorical denial.[82] Brecht prevailed upon a friend – almost certainly Ernestine Müller – to write to Therese Ostheimer, who, he had heard, knew of the 'unfortunate' Kimratshofen story.[83] On Brecht's behalf, she begged Therese to 'make no use of your knowledge' and if she had told anyone, to retrieve the situation. It was too late: the cat was out of the bag.

Brecht was together with Neher virtually every day. Neher adored Brecht, noting in his diary on 13 February: 'It's really wonderfully beautiful to be so alone together. He talks of his aesthetics and I challenge him'.[84] They spent the following days in Munich and Augsburg. First, they tried to place Brecht's poem 'Heaven of the Disillusioned' together with one of Neher's drawings with *Simplicissimus*. Over the weekend in Augsburg, they visited Müllereisert and in the discussion of 'Socialism (Spartacism)'

Brecht suggested, rather enigmatically, that 'socialism did not want to bring people's feet to the same level but their heads so that it was vitally necessary to bury their feet'. A somewhat confused Neher crossed out heads and inserted feet at the end of Brecht's *bon mot*. Müllereisert's sympathies lay with the old order: shortly afterwards he joined Franz von Epp's radical right-wing Free Corps, which attracted a number of later Nazis, among them Rudolf Hess.

Brecht and Neher took a late breakfast at Gabler's Tavern that Sunday in mid-February. They drank schnapps and Brecht sang his own songs and one by the notorious Klabund, who in 1917 had been charged with treason after he called for the Kaiser to abdicate. The next day Brecht paid Bi a first visit in Kimratshofen, then returned to Munich where he was in good spirits despite three sleepless nights. However, he suffered the following day with his nerves and was very agitated, overwrought, speaking to Neher shortly after of his problems with his nerves and self-control.

That Friday in Munich the nationalist aristocrat Anton Graf von Arco auf Valley gunned down Kurt Eisner. Although Arco auf Valley was acting alone, the assassination was a turning-point in the political struggle. In time, of course, the forces of the reactionary Right would come together under the banner of National Socialism and Munich would become the principal city of the 'movement'. Eisner had tried to hang on to power following the election defeat in January. He was on his way to tender his resignation when he was shot. After Berlin, it was now the turn of the revolutionaries in Munich. There were more deaths on the streets, huge demonstrations and a protest meeting of the Workers' and Soldiers' Council at the Deutsches Theater. Brecht and Neher attended that meeting and saw a gun shop being looted near the station. The following day they travelled with Elisabeth Geyer to Augsburg where the picture was little different. Three people had been killed and many wounded. Neher joined Brecht and his friends in a procession to mourn Eisner and to oppose reactionary forces. A state of emergency was declared as the Workers' and Soldiers' Council struggled to secure power. There was more gunfire and shops were looted, Neher writing that people just stood there gaping at the revolution, looking dumb.

Life went on for Brecht and Neher, too, pre-occupied as they were as much by their art and their relationships as by politics. Augsburg's 'Revolutionary Sunday' erupted on 23 February when the Workers' and Soldiers' Council seized control. They would hold on to power until 21 April. On that Revolutionary Sunday Brecht and Neher met as usual at Gabler's for a late breakfast. However, they again showed where their sympathies lay when they joined the cortege at Eisner's funeral. Meanwhile, Brecht explained to Neher that he loved Bi but feared the hetaera in her. Truly, he had little to fear from Bi in that respect. Neher, for his part, wrote: 'O Bi, Bert – Bert – Bert, how I envy you Bi'.[85] She went to Munich and stayed with Brecht until the weekend, where they talked to Neher about their plans, drinking tea at Brecht's. Back in Augsburg for the weekend while Bi was stuck in Kimratshofen, Brecht spent Saturday evening by the Lech with his friends, boys and girls, singing and shouting at the tops of their voices. On Sunday afternoon they were joined by a number of girls at Gabler's and in the evening Brecht met Hagg, who organised an outing with some girls. Brecht enjoyed the company so much that he wrote to Hagg from Munich, encouraging him to put on something similar the following weekend.[86] He named the girls he would like to see there: Ida Grassold, Hagg's sister Lotte, perhaps also Bi's sister Blanka! Eager to show off his waltzing prowess, he suggested they go to a place where they could dance.

In fact, they started going to all manner of dives, among them Gambrinus, a cellar bar down on the Judenberg, which, as Brecht's friend Xaver Schaller writes, was frequented by spivs and pimps.[87] There was a police raid one night. Brecht and his friends were arrested and put in cells along with the pimps. On another night, they went to the Seven Bunnies, a brothel where one of the ladies was standing on a table, singing to great applause. Everyone joined in the refrain: 'I've got a tuft of hair on my tummy / Maybe I'm a monkey'. Brecht couldn't resist picking up his guitar and singing Goethe's 'The God and the Dancing Girl', delivering this poem by the great classical author with his rasping voice and idiosyncratic rhythms. The brothel fell silent, everyone was captivated by Brecht's performance. When he finished there was thunderous applause and a man went round with a hat collecting money for the singer, who was not allowed to go until he had given the encore that everyone demanded.

As he would with other women, Brecht now acted as Bi's teacher, asking her how she was getting on with Goethe's *Faust* and promising to bring her other books. And he had convinced himself and her, too, that their child would be a boy: 'My son'. He teased her: 'Please treat the great Brecht's little son with respect!'.[88] Shortly after it was: 'Long live Walter the red-haired one!'.[89] Brecht was trying to arrange for Bi to go with him to the Ammersee, a lake in the foothills of the Alps which was a favourite destination for Augsburgers, but he was encountering resistance from her parents.[90] Elaborating upon his plans, the crass Brecht could not resist telling Bi more details of his life in Munich. He had been to a party at an artists' studio with Neher, hosted by female artists whom Neher knew, Hanne Wenz and H. Eglseder.[91] Brecht told Bi they had made *punsch* and he had played guitar all night while the others paired off. Neher was his witness, Brecht twice wrote, that he had been very good and had drunk only to Bi, saying she was the most beautiful woman in the world. He couldn't resist adding: 'Because I sang so wonderfully and drank, at first I had every chance, every chance with both of them'. Bi did not remotely need to know this but Brecht evidently needed to tell her. He also needed to tell her that Neher wanted to take one of the girls from the party, Trude, to the Ammersee. Brecht asked Bi what she thought about this, explaining that if Neher was with Trude they could be together, too.

If stories of goings-on with art students at parties in Munich were not enough to upset Bi, then a letter to her from her mother was.[92] Frau Banholzer had got wind of Brecht's nights out in Augsburg's dives with Hagg and the gang, among them her elder daughter Blanka. Frau Banholzer made it absolutely clear to Bi that Brecht was the ringleader and a bad influence on the others.[93] People were saying that they had been in a dive by the Lech with a *chambre séparée*. It was not difficult to imagine what they had got up to. Frau Banholzer forbade her daughter to go with him to the Ammersee. There was a frantic round of phone calls and letters. Brecht told Bi how sorry he was that she was suffering so much in this row and told her, too, how offended he was. He composed a letter for Frau Banholzer, which he sent to Bi for her to look at before he sent it. He also asked Bi to send the letter from her mother on to him. Caught between Brecht and her mother, Bi did nothing. They had tense exchanges on the phone and he wrote that he did not want to travel to Kimratshofen any more, suggesting they meet closer to Kempten.[94] He had in any case to pay her living costs for March. Amidst all the antagonism, she depended on him for that.

Despite his constant assurances of his love for her, Bi, of course, feared that she would now lose him. And she could not rid herself of the thought that perhaps her mother was right in condemning him as a thoroughly bad influence on her and the others. He tried to clear the air with a sharp and persuasive letter, pointing out that her mother had been loading the blame entirely on to him and completely exonerating the others: 'But I know the bars and I know the people, I know the usual excuses and the harmless faces. My face is no less harmless and I can only assure you: the worse they make me out to be, the more they must listen to my view'.[95] He continued: 'If a story gets out, it's not a matter of what was done in the bars (*chambre séparée*) or even what was *not* done (a gentlemanly silence is maintained about that), but who was in there, and then suspicions arise, which emerge not from the harmlessness of the gentlemen in question but from the reputation of the bar'.

There is no reason to assume that Brecht and his friends did anything more in the bars and brothels than he and his friend Schaller recounted. Spirited young people have always wanted to see the seamy side of life but not necessarily to participate in the grubby business of bought sex. By the age of twenty-one, Brecht, now sexually experienced, had no need to avail himself of that service. He put much of his energy into maintaining his closest relationships with Bi and Cas, while cultivating others which held out the prospect of sexual pleasure. He continued to pursue Therese Ostheimer, persuading Münsterer, a friend of her brother, to arrange for them to meet at the theatre.[96] Still the resolute Therese remained out of his reach. When they were not at the theatre or at Gabler's, Münsterer and Brecht hung out at Zanantoni's ice cream parlour in the hope of meeting girls.[97] Brecht would chat to Madam Zanantoni or dance with her assistant to guitar music, blustering on to her about the impending publication of a decree to make women commonly-held property. Brecht would perform anywhere, any time. One day he was waiting in a long queue of people at the barber's.[98] Bored, he asked the other customers if they'd like to hear some of his work. He sat on a high stool and read from a notebook. Some listened, open mouthed. When he'd finished he asked them how they'd liked it. Most of the listeners were working men from the Bleich neighbourhood, who did not know too well what to say. All the same, Brecht's performance ended in high spirits.

In early April Brecht and Neher had one of their periodic fallings-out. Brecht had suggested that Neher was still too much of a petty bourgeois in his eagerness to meet his obligations.[99] Then they had agreed they were both geniuses. However, Brecht then became angry with Neher, who wondered whether Brecht was afraid of him. Brecht claimed that all Neher's supposed strength was weakness and Neher wrote: 'Brecht is my enemy'. Each accused the other of egotism. They had a point. They went their separate ways. Although they met again during the momentous events of the coming days, they were still far apart.

The Bavarian Soviet Republic

The revolutionary mood was once more reaching fever pitch. At a mass rally in Augsburg on 3 April, speakers had called for a Soviet-style republic. Over the weekend of 6–7 April in Munich, a left-wing grouping proclaimed the republic, overthrowing the Bavarian government led by the SPD's Johannes Hoffmann, which fled to Bamberg. The grouping was led by Jewish pacifist intellectuals wholly unused to the exercise of power. Among them were the Expressionist dramatist Ernst Toller and the anarchists Gustav Landauer and Erich Mühsam. The leadership collapsed within six days, the KPD figure Eugen Leviné stepping in to replace them. Leviné embarked on radical reforms, expropriating luxurious apartments, giving them to the homeless and placing factories under workers' control. He had plans to abolish paper money and reform the education system.

Leviné refused to collaborate with the regular army of the city and founded his own Red Army under Rudolf Egelhofer. Many unemployed workers volunteered to support the revolutionary government and the ranks of the Red Army soon reached 20,000. In Bamberg Hoffmann gathered an army from remnants of the regular Imperial Army, Free Corps troops of the Ehrhardt Brigade, and followers of Franz von Epp. Georg Prem was the revolutionary commander in Augsburg and Lilly Prem was on the Augsburg Soviet as the leader of the city's revolutionary women.[100] Georg Prem recalled Brecht's great interest in the revolution: 'He was very well disposed to my wife and me despite our tough exchanges. Brecht was also present on several occasions at the meetings of the Workers' and Soldiers' Council, but he was not active'.[101] Just after Leviné had taken over the government, Brecht wrote to Bi that his father had not allowed him to go out because of the unrest.[102] He wrote, too, of those days in Augsburg and of the values which he sought to bring to bear:

> I've completely gone over to Bolshevism. Of course, I'm against all violence, and because I've got influence here I can do some things. Resistance is being organised here with all available means – but if you hear that Augsburg hasn't been fighting and shedding blood, you can be sure that, standing right at the back and nearly invisible, I deserve a lot of credit. The Soviet Republic will win out one day.

Brecht was, perhaps, inclined to overstate his actual influence to Bi but he did have that personal relationship with Georg and Lilly Prem. He got minor things done for friends, like securing permission for Marie Rose Amann to leave Augsburg for her own safety, joining relatives outside the city.[103] And he represented his position, at this stage evidently one of seeking to minimise violence, to the Prems. He added to Bi the following day: 'Perhaps the Soviet Republic won't last much longer. But then it'll come back and it won't be pretty to begin with'.[104] Brecht's statements, of course, reflect debates about revolutionary strategy in Munich and Augsburg rather than those amongst the Bolsheviks in Moscow, whose opposition to the Mensheviks was founded precisely on the Bolsheviks' view that violence was inevitable in revolution. That said, Brecht acknowledged the inevitability of violence when the Soviet Republic returned, which it surely would. When Brecht wrote of resistance, he meant the defence of Augsburg which the Prems were organising in the expectation of attack by counter-revolutionary forces. The very real prospect existed of large-scale bloodshed – he was concerned that this should be avoided – it wasn't.

Brecht's major contribution to the Bavarian Soviet Republic followed the violent suppression of the Augsburg Red Army. Two thousand counter-revolutionary Free Corps troops led by Franz von Epp marched into Augsburg on Easter Sunday, 20 April. Many young Augsburgers who saw themselves defending their middle-class world from the Bolshevik threat joined them for the subsequent attack on Munich, among them recently demobbed soldiers like Walter Brecht and Otto Müllereistert. Neher's parents urged him to join but he declined. Neher wrote: 'The thunder of cannons awoke me. Easter! You could scarcely believe it's Easter. White guards against red guards. Fighting, War between brothers'.[105] How true that was. Close friendships in the Brecht Circle came under great strain and the Brecht brothers found themselves on different sides. Brecht ended a poem to Grandmother Brecht on her 80th birthday with the conciliatory lines:

> [...] in lands grown dark the word from the pulpit and the call of trumpets
> divided the grandsons. But she prayed
> Above the discord for her grandsons on this side and that.
> They, though, in their struggle surely always thought
> Of her in their two camps, and that in the house on the market square
> Rooms were ready for them and the table laid.[106]

Neher noted on 21 April, Easter Monday: 'Spartacus is still fighting in Oberhausen and Lechhausen and holding the line'.[107] But von Epp's forces enjoyed huge superiority over the Augsburg Spartacists, who surrendered that day. Neher added: 'I don't want to write of all the brutality of the government troops that I saw today'. The surviving Spartacists were arrested. Georg Prem was among them but he escaped and went to ground in Brecht's attic. Neher noted, again on Easter Monday: 'Prem changed his clothing today at Bert's and escaped'. Prem recalled that he hid there for two days, then was picked up and taken over the border to Switzerland by an unnamed man who had smuggled deserters over the border during the war.[108] When Münsterer visited Brecht later, neighbours told him the somewhat unlikely story that shots had been fired from Brecht's window.[109] There is no record of the forces of law and order troubling Brecht over the matter.

Neher, working with Brecht on drawings for *Baal*, was visited by Müllereisert, now a civil defence officer, who was 'dead tired and wounded in his left thigh'.[110] He was in a bad way, not least because Brecht had verbally attacked him and said he did not wish to attend his funeral. In the civil war there was a treacherous brutality which was something quite different from the war just ended. The 'war between brothers' tested the closest relationships in a manner which remained all too familiar throughout Brecht's life, leaving deep scars on German society. Müllereisert had in fact enlisted as a spy for von Epp in Munich.[111] Yet, for all their differences, Brecht would not break with Müllereisert and his brother Walter. Equally, until he fled Germany in February 1933, Brecht maintained friendships with people who gravitated to the radical Right like his later friend Arnolt Bronnen. When Brecht returned to Germany from exile, he would resume friendships with figures such as Neher and Herbert Ihering who had stayed in Germany during the Nazi years.

Aftermath

Following the bloody Easter days Brecht and his friends sought refuge, as they had in the war, at the Plärrer, taking to the swing-boats with the girls. Brecht was making a play for Neher's sister, Marietta. Marietta was a keen horse rider, which prompted Brecht to take riding lessons again. He could be seen in the street opposite Bleichstrasse by the city moat, wearing jodphurs and slapping his riding crop against his calf.[112] He would lean against the iron railings, staring into the water for hours on end. He could not, of course, resist the frisson of pleasure at seeing girls' scandalised reaction to him as he recited Nietzsche's infamous dictum: 'When you go to see a woman don't forget your whip'. Brecht got his come-uppance: the horse he was riding fell and he was injured.[113] When Neher visited, Brecht was feeling sorry for himself. He'd escaped with only minor scrapes but described himself in a letter to Jacob Geis as 'half-lame'.[114]

The return of the Plärrer was the perfect opportunity for Brecht to restore his self-esteem. He made bets with girls to see who could soar the highest in the swing-boats.[115] Brecht was there for several evenings in a row with Neher, and they were joined by Marietta over the weekend. For Neher, the experience was 'unbelievably beautiful and full of body, warm and lithe and full of power'. He was elated to be with Brecht who told stories on the way home about his forthcoming wedding and about his friends. Neher felt it was a night in which the sun was in their bodies, a night in which one could do no-one an injustice. However, shortly after Brecht was protesting his innocence to Neher about his relations with Marietta, whom he endowed with similarly 'African' qualities to her brother:

> I was looking forward to the lantern evening and seeing you and Ma and now have to leave. It's shocking and I'm innocent. Your sister never rang. That's a pity. For my mouth was sweeter than honey with wisdom. But your sister, whom I've christened Ma, rides on a grey elephant, lovely and pale and in seven veils, and can't see the beggar sitting in the dust who knows the songs of pure heaven. She's as beautiful as the light in the mornings on the great highways before the dust rises, and she rides like a young panther, but where's she riding to?[116]

Neher knew his friend's ways well enough. Neher was enough the gentleman of his middle-class upbringing to baulk at Brecht's behaviour with his sister: 'What I had suspected has been confirmed. It is that bombshell Bert + Marietta + I exploded. [...] However, thank God everything has been settled amicably'.[117] Neher later crossed out his sister's name. Brecht would capture the strains between Neher and himself in the poetic dialogue of 'Memory of a M.N.'.[118] It is a series of exchanges, which can be read in the numbered sequence as, firstly, one between brother and sister, followed by five between the two friends. A refrain following the first and the sixth verses ends: 'And why not a hundred per cent / But maybe it's good / To know the bitterest thing'. The first verse reads: 'It's like handling rubber / He will be as he is / You cannot mould him / Whoever you may be'. The first exchange between the friends reads: 'Did you find her cheap / Did you say: cotton? / But do not lie now: / Did you have her?'. The final exchange between them ends: 'Don't say she was nothing / Say you saw a better girl'. Neher knew that no one was going to make Brecht a 'better person'. So Neher just had to accept his brilliant friend and collaborator as he was.

Amidst his various liaisons, Brecht also wanted to be together with Bi. He wrote that he imagined her, in her sixth month, as 'a really stout, brown peasant girl'.[119] Whether that pleased her is open to doubt. Again and again, he sought to re-assure her of his love. Yet, as he wrote, part of him knew that their relationship was doomed: 'The days of your bitterness / Will soon be passed, my child / Just as those of undreamt of kisses / Will soon be gone too'.[120] He saw her reverting to the conventional lifestyle of her Catholic, middle-class background, which for him was simply death in life. However, because of her pregnancy outside wedlock, her presence in that world would always be flawed.

Müllereisert and Walter Brecht were with the Free Corps when they moved East from Augsburg for the assault on Munich. They took the city in a bloodbath on 2 May. Walter saw action near Pasing before taking part in the rout of the Spartacists. He witnessed atrocities perpetrated against the Red Army, among them the mutilation of sexual organs. Eight thousand Red Army soldiers were butchered in two days, including the summary execution of Gustav Landauer.[121] The Bavarian revolution was destroyed: Munich would never be the same again. Toller and Mühsam were tried and imprisoned, while the Swiss authorities would return Georg Prem to Bavaria. He surrendered, was tried and imprisoned.

Brecht visited Müllereisert at home on leave and Walter Brecht in the Munich barracks of the Free Corps.[122] For Walter, although Brecht's sympathies lay firmly with the Spartacists, the general excitement left its impression on him. Neher captures something of the confused mood amongst these young men, writing in his diary entry on 19 May of a 'wonderful morning' on the Augsburg-Munich train when he and Brecht listened to Walter's 'very nice' stories about his 'battle with Spartacus'.[123] Neher joined in with his own stories from the front line, mostly, he writes, about schnapps and getting drunk.

In the wake of the political chaos, the University remained closed until mid-June. The authorities urged staff and students to join the Free Corps in the restoration of law and order. Among the students who joined von Epp was Brecht's later friend and doctor, the celebrated Munich personality Johannes Ludwig Schmitt. In due course, Hoffmann's government resumed control but that would not signal the end of the revolutionary turmoil. The counter-revolutionary forces would presently turn on the republican governments in Munich and Berlin.

The 'Lost' Brecht Sons 1919–21

Morbidity and vitality

In the spring of 1919 Brecht's health and state of mind were quite unstable. For Neher, his moods were fluctuating between a profound pessimism and a creative elation, which lifted those round him.[1] However, when he met up with Hedda Kuhn on the weekend of 24–25 May in Ulm, he confided to her that after his wartime service he was afflicted by severe depression. In the grim conditions of post-war Germany, Brecht's condition could only deteriorate. On his next visit to Kimratshofen Brecht took a long walk with Bi. Afterwards, he suddenly took to his bed. In the night she heard him groaning. Frightened, she went to him and saw him lying there covered in sweat, suffering from violent heart spasms. She wrapped him in cold compresses and the spasms abated. They had talked about Brecht's heart complaint before but this was her first experience of it. He told her that he had these attacks quite often and admitted that he had been frightened by the ferocity of this last attack. He acknowledged that it would take some time for him to get over it: 'I've been feeling bad for nearly three weeks now, but today things are better and there is light at the end of the tunnel'.[2] All he really knew was what they had told him as a child: that he had an enlarged heart. But then they had also said that he was faking it. He could never be sure and coped as best he could, as he remained prey to his old complaint and to the terrifying imaginings it triggered, aware that his life might easily be cut short. Such dark thoughts pervade an untitled, nightmarish poem composed at that time. In its bleak imagery, it echoes Nietzsche's 'Grown Lonely', also known as 'The Free Spirit. Goodbye'. Brecht dedicated the poem to Bi, his 'Bittersweet':

> Half asleep in the pallid half light
> By your body, many a night: *the* dream.
> Ghostly highways under very cold skies
> Of pallid evenings. Pallid winds. Crows
> Shrieking for their food, and rain comes at night.
> With the wind and clouds, year after year
> Your face, Bittersweet, grows blurred again
> And in the cold wind I feel trembling
> Gently your body, half asleep, in half light
> A little bitterness still in your mind.[3]

Brecht knew that the hurt and mistrust which Bi felt would never disappear. Despite their intense feelings for each other, that forced them apart. He knew, too, that his behaviour could only contribute to her further hurt and mistrust because he could not stop himself pursuing his affairs.

Other poems from that year cast a morbid shadow, too. Brecht imagined his mother's death, viewing her as the rest of the family did, as someone who 'had given everything and had kept / Nothing for herself'.[4] And he reflected in another poem that year: 'My mother will soon count her fiftieth year / Thirty of which she has spent dying'. Thoughts of the family's record of ill health, early death and the likelihood of his own early death prompted the composition in 1919 of 'The Virginia Smoker', which he later called 'On his Mortality'. It begins:

> Smoke your cigars: that was my doctor's comforting answer!
> With or without them one day we'll end up with the undertaker.
> In the membrane of my eye for example there are signs of cancer
> From which I shall die sooner or later.[5]

This leads Brecht, who had taken a course about the eye, to write in the fifth stanza of an inherited susceptibility to cancer and of the difficulty of diagnosis:

> There are families in which it is hereditary
> But they never admit it nor condemn.
> They can distinguish pineapple from rosemary
> But their cancer may be a hernia to them.

He does not actually write of his mother's cancer. However, the line of inherited family disease which he traces is clearly drawn from her side. He cites the diseased body of his uncle, whom we may take to be Eugen Brezing. As we have seen, he died an alcoholic in 1908. Brecht also refers to the wretched life of his grandfather, who lived a strictly regulated life until he was fifty, then gave up on it. Grandfather Brezing would die in 1922. Brecht notes 'Such a cancer grows subtly; one feels nothing inside', before concluding:

> Our sort know: no point being envious.
> Each man has his cross to bear, I fear.
> Kidney trouble is my particular curse
> I've not had a drink in more than a year.

As we know, the kidney complaint was a very real one. Given his production of oxalate crystals, the condition was probably genetic. The problem may well have emerged again after what Brecht called the 'piss-ups of 1919' at dives like Gambrinus.[6] The escapades are echoed in the prose fragment 'Gossip' where figures in the Cherry Brandy Bar 'did things to their kidneys'. Brecht became susceptible to renal infections and to kidney stones, and the problem had to be managed with great vigilance, including careful control of alcohol consumption. From a present-day perspective it is easy to appreciate that it could conspire with chronic heart failure to dire effect. Brecht, the perennial risk-taker, would neglect his frail body.

However, it is a striking feature of Brecht's personality that his complaints, depressions and pre-occupation with death drove him on in his desire to live life to the full and to capture the moment in what Münsterer calls the 'torrent of dramatic and lyrical inspiration' which flowed from him.[7] In the late 1910s, he and his friends experienced that intensity of life through the immersion of the self in nature which Münsterer recorded in his diary: 'Evening on the banks of the Lech. We sat on the ground, Bert, Otto Müller and I. The sky high, wide and wonderfully blue, fading to orange and finally to violet. Beneath us the crystal, foaming river, and in the distance the black silhouette of the town with its towers and rooftops. The grass was damp with dew. Brecht was singing'.

For Münsterer, 1919 was probably the most intense period of Brecht's creativity. It was certainly the high tide of the young Brecht's lyrical self and the mythology surrounding it. Münsterer describes how 'on hot afternoons we would go swimming in the Hahnreibach, lie naked in the Wolfzahn meadow, or go climbing trees, as Brecht describes in one of the "Gospels" which he read me there on 11 June'. The celebrated verses entitled 'Of Climbing in Trees' evoke those days:

When you come up at evening from the waters
(For you must all be naked, and with tender skin)
Climb then in your great trees still higher
In the light wind. The sky too should be wan.
Seek out great trees that in the evening
Slowly and sombrely rock their topmost boughs.
And wait among their foliage for darkness
With bat and nightmare close about your brows.[8]

Like the swing-boats, rhythmical movement in the trees engendered a mesmeric, poetic mood, which is captured, too, in the equally memorable 'Of Swimming in Lakes and Rivers', a rejoinder to Walt Whitman's rhapsodic 'From Pent-up Aching Rivers' with its swimmer 'motionless on his back lying and floating'. Neher noted: 'I think of Walt Withmann (sic) and hear him talking of swimming in rivers and lying in the hot sand'.[9] Brecht's poem begins:

In the pale summer when the leaves above
Only in great trees' leaves a murmur make
You ought to lie in rivers or in ponds
As do the waterweeds which harbour pike.
The body grows light in the water. When your arm
Falls easily from water into sky
The little wind rocks it absentmindedly
Taking it likely for a brownish bough.[10]

Critics have acknowledged that Brecht captures the sensual pleasure of the body's physical immersion within the organic rhythms of nature and its movement within them in a manner that is new in German poetry. In the Romantic tradition and latterly in Expressionism, the spiritual encounter of the self with nature is enacted. The young Brecht saw his body differently from many other people: he was a creature of the earth, a rock and roller *avant la lettre*. We see in these verses just what his innovative genius was capable of, with its idiosyncratic mix of physiological and psychological sensitivities in conjunction with extraordinary poetic virtuosity. Lines from these poems found their way into the re-working of *Baal*. Yet by 1920 he would be disavowing this mythology of movement in nature, writing in a notebook: 'Man is no swimmer man is not made to fly he is of the species that lies on its back'.[11] After the thrill of rhythmical movement, Brecht would begin to settle into the horizontal mode, conserving his precious energy for his principal activities: writing and sex.

Writing for a wife and child

As always, Brecht spent much time with Neher, whose love life was almost as complex as his own. In addition to middle-class schoolgirls and students, they now eyed up working girls and invited them to their rooms. Neher was thrown out by his landlady because of his antics, while Brecht took an interest in the aphrodisiac johimbin.[12] He put everything else into making his name as a writer to make the sort of money he needed. He was granted permission not to attend lectures and lived in Munich during the week, working with Jacob Geis on what they hoped would be a money-spinning comedy, *Herr Meier and his Son*. However, that came to nothing, nor did the scene of *Herr Makrot* which he wrote shortly afterwards with Geis in Münsterer's garden in Pasing. Brecht worked on a tragedy, *Condel*, which owed much to Georg Büchner, and on two other dramas, *David* and *Summer Symphony*. Again, these projects were not completed.

Brecht and Neher tried without success to get *Baal* published in Munich by Musarion together with Neher's drawings. When they met at the Ungerer open-air swimming pool one beautiful June day, Brecht told Neher that Lion Feuchtwanger had written an awful play, *Thomas Brecht*, using him as the model.[13] Brecht had got to know Feuchtwanger, to whom he had sent *Baal*, but Feuchtwanger was more fascinated by the author than his creation. When they met with Feuchtwanger shortly after at the Orlando Cafe, Neher noted:

> You can see that he hasn't understood *Baal* and you feel he doesn't know what we want or what Bert wants. *Pour tout le monde* for the whole world. Art has got to be for everyone – that's the way things are – not for a small circle of people, who claim to understand it especially well. There has got to be a vigour in it, which grips everyone and unites everyone. Only then are things beautiful and one demonstrably has art. It is undoubtedly wrong to create art only for literary circles and tea clubs. The people do not want philosophy, they want vigour and a quite enormous satiation. And that has certainly been eminently achieved in *Baal*.[14]

Neher's words could almost be a manifesto for the young Brecht proclaiming his *Baal*. Brecht aspired to a new, popular art of the instincts, living the dream of 'vigour and a quite enormous satiation' through *Baal*.

Brecht was Neher's guest at another studio party on 1 July, to which Neher invited Elisabeth Geyer and Berta Schmidt. Neher noted:

The most unbelievable things happened and had to be made good. [...] Schnapps was drunk and there were chaotic scenes. I was especially frolicsome and often didn't know what to do next. At the end Bert sang like crazy, and the light was turned out, and we behaved towards the women in the way that one must behave when the light is turned out, i.e. when it's dark. [...] It was too much, and everything was too crazy. I had completely ruined things with Erta.[15]

Brecht explained to Neher in a lengthy sermon that the affair with Berta Schmidt, like the affair with Trudi Dechant, would lead nowhere because he was not the master of the situation. Brecht made it clear that Neher must listen to his advice if he wished to achieve fame together with Brecht, who certainly was going to achieve fame because he had learned to master situations. Brecht's message to Bi was similar: she must listen to him, not to the priest to whom she had recently been talking, understandably so at a time when the birth of their child was only days away.[16]

However, Bi's ace card in her dealings with Brecht was that she was devastatingly attractive to men – and she knew it. She told Brecht that another beau was on the scene in Kimratshofen, prompting his reply: 'That's a very promising match. You must seize the chance. I'll be the family friend. You'll get a lantern from me for a wedding present'.[17] As we know, a red Chinese lantern was the Brecht Circle's calling card. They introduced some order into their relationship by seeing each other every Sunday, an arrangement which they continued until Bi moved to Munich in the autumn of 1920. This arrangement was supposed to indicate a firm commitment, which would lead to marriage just as soon as Brecht had achieved financial success as a writer. However, as usual it left Brecht free for the rest of the time to do whatever he wanted with whomsoever he wanted. Bi later claimed that she knew nothing about his other relationships until long after Marianne Zoff came on the scene. If so, she was wilfully blind. Elsewhere, her flirtations with other men are part of a picture in which she and Brecht both sought to assert their sexual power through demonstrating their attractiveness to others, Brecht by performing his songs, Bi by being Bi.

She gave birth to Frank Walter Otto on 30 July in Kimratshofen. He was named after, in order, Wedekind, Brecht's brother and Müllereisert. Frank was christened at the village's Catholic church on 2 August. A party followed at the village inn, Zum Fässle. A photograph captures Brecht and Bi, together with Pfanzelt, Blanka's fiancé Georg Wolf, and the godfathers Neher and Müllereisert, the latter still in uniform. There was no one there from Brecht's family. They found out about Frank only in early September, Neher noting: '[Brecht's father] now knows everything about Bi and we are all glad'.[18] On 12 September, Brecht wrote to Bi that their fathers were going to talk: 'Beyond that, I know nothing'.[19] Nothing of significance came of the meeting, beyond the fact that Karl Banholzer put Berthold Brecht in the picture. Brecht would officially recognise Frank the following year, but he would never have regular contact with his first child, let alone a close relationship with him. Nothing could stand in the way of Brecht's struggle for success. It emerged that Frank had been born with a very nasty physical defect, a malformed anus, which meant that he could not retain his faeces.[20] The problem dogged him all his life, impairing his psychological as well as physical development. Frank truly was a lost Brecht son.

Bi was again scarcely replying to Brecht's letters, and when she did it was in the coolest terms. He visited her and Frank in Kimratshofen over the weekend of 16–17 August. However, he took along his cronies Neher, Pfanzelt and Müllereisert. Pfanzelt played the church organ, accompanying Brecht to 'Lucifer's Evening Song' and 'Hymn of Baal the Great'. When Bi and Brecht were alone they quarrelled.[21] He claimed to be trying to find ways for them to be together but everything was on his terms. He wrote that he had met with her parents and they had all agreed that she should stay away from Augsburg over the winter. He told her, too, that her father's view was that she should stay out of the way until she had fully recovered her health and until people had got used to the fact that she was away. Then the matter would be over and done with. Her own view did not count. She was both female and still a minor. It was all agreed over her head, as was the way.

For the Banholzers, there was no question of her keeping Frank, let alone of her bringing him back to Augsburg. Frank was taken into the care of the roadman Xaver Stark, a neighbour of the Fricks. Brecht paid a monthly sum for this service. After three years, Frank was passed on to a peasant farmer in Friedberg near Augsburg. Frank looked a lot like his father and his grandfather Brecht, who was very fond of him and whom Frank liked to visit. Berthold Brecht's fondness would not, though, stretch to him agreeing to his son's later request to take in Frank and bring him up. Frank spent time in Vienna with carers and with the families of Brecht's wives Marianne Zoff and Helene Weigel. Throughout all these years the sickly Frank needed medical attention. He moved to Augsburg in 1935 to be near his mother. However, her husband Hermann Gross would never agree to take him into his home. Frank had dreams of becoming a doctor or an actor but he had neither the intelligence nor the talent. He became a salesman, then a soldier and was killed on the Russian Front in 1943.

Despite Brecht's abysmal relations with Bi's parents, he had still not given up on the idea of marrying her. The frostiness of their exchanges after Frank's birth gave way to a greater sharing of intimacy in his letters to her from late 1919. He advised her, back home in Augsburg earlier than originally planned, how to defend herself against her mother's attempts to make her feel bad about what she had done.[22] He also asked what Frau Banholzer had said about 'Project Munich', by which he meant their plan that Bi should move to Munich so that they could be together, with a view to marrying. The ending of his letter makes clear that the understanding he had reached on that matter with her parents – principally her mother – depended on him achieving the success that he so craved.[23] He took to imagining Bi as a housewife with all the requisite skills and accomplishments, and her mother began to assemble her trousseau. However, Brecht insisted on taking over that responsibility: he was adamant that everything for Bi must be made of silk or batiste.

Entertaining such thoughts of domestic bliss, Brecht re-doubled his efforts to earn money. He was convinced that a breakthrough was imminent. He told Bi that he had attended a recital by the actor Albert Steinrück, who afterward 'saw me in the foyer amongst many fine people and took me by the arm. In a year I'll be taking *him* by the arm.'[24] Brecht had continued to cultivate Hanns Johst, visiting him in September to discuss *Baal*. He wrote a follow-up letter, thanking Johst for the day with him and his wife, promising to send him the new version of his play and inviting

Johst to visit him in Augsburg. Brecht had Feuchtwanger working on his behalf with publishers in Munich and had grounds for guarded optimism when he told Bi: 'I've now agreed a contract with Drei Masken and I'm working on several plays at the same time. Come what may, I want to earn money'. He decided to try his luck with one-act plays, modelling them on Cervantes's interludes, though writing much in the manner of the Munich comedian Karl Valentin. He had seen Valentin's shows and got to know him. Brecht would later write that Valentin had been for him what Arnold Schönberg had been for Brecht's composer friend Hanns Eisler![25] Brecht now went for the serial production of farces with one main gag like Valentin's. He produced six in short order: *The Wedding, The Beggar or The Dead Dog, Driving out a Devil, Lux in Tenebris, The Catch, The Dirty Pig*, as well as *Prairie*, a libretto for a short opera after Knut Hamsun. Despite his prodigious productivity, Brecht's hopes were dashed: Drei Masken withdrew the contract for *Baal* and the short works remained unpublished and unperformed. Only *The Wedding* was performed in Brecht's lifetime.

However, in October 1919 Brecht secured a regular engagement as a theatre and opera reviewer for the newly founded Augsburg USPD newspaper *Der Volkswille*. From 1 December 1920 *Der Volkswille* became the organ of the KPD. The editor, Wendelin Thomas, a USPD Reichstag deputy whom Brecht knew through the Prems, let him attack the city's sleepy municipal theatre. Brecht did so with great gusto. The twenty-seven reviews and polemics published over the coming months certainly stirred things up. In fact, they culminated in a court case against Brecht in early 1921, when the paper was banned for separate, political reasons.

There was by now a real sense of crisis in German theatre, which was rapidly losing its audiences to the cinema and other mass spectacles. In Berlin, Max Reinhardt responded boldly, opening a mass theatre, his 5,000-seat Grosses Schauspielhaus. However, that was the exception. Most municipal theatres like Augsburg's had to be taken into civic ownership in order for them to survive. Brecht's first review set the tone, not just for the coming reviews but also for his sustained attack on the 'bourgeois' institution of the established theatre in the 1920s. He took issue with Hermann Merz's productions of Max Halbe's famous Naturalist work *Youth* and Björnsterne Björnson's *Beyond our Power*.[26] The plot of Halbe's work echoes Brecht and Bi's experience: a young man and woman love each other, the woman becomes pregnant, they are forced apart by social pressures, and made to feel ashamed. The reviewer lambasted Merz's production: the play was 'performed quite wrongly. It was performed for the paying burgher. The burgher believed that it was a sin to love one another without having the money to do so, and for that reason there were theatrical productions in which nothing emerged of the sweetness and ingenuousness of love'. Brecht wrote that Merz's own performance as the priest tended towards the bombastic, like his production in general, which lacked atmosphere and the poetic element. For Brecht, what he called the poetic element was always intimately connected with the proper artistic rendering of emotion, absent from Merz's overblown treatment in Björnson's play. It is revealing that even at this early stage Brecht sought to disarm criticism of his stance by insisting that he was by no means against the display of emotion *per se*. Brecht's sensibility simply required that emotion should be presented in a controlled manner. He reserved some of his barbs for Vera Maria Eberle, who that April had delivered the first professional recital of Brecht's verses, which had not greatly pleased him.[27] Suggesting now that her undulating bosom carried her performance, he mocked her tragic rendering of even the most everyday phrase, inviting readers to imagine how she would deliver 'Pass me the *eau de Cologne*'! Eberle would neither forgive nor forget Brecht's caricature.

In his review of the opera *Don Carlos* Brecht adopted the subjective manner which he admired in Alfred Kerr's reviewing style in order to convey quite a different political message:

> God knows, I've always loved *Don Carlos*. But over the past few days I've been reading Sinclair's *The Jungle*, the story of a worker who's starved to death in the slaughterhouses of Chicago. It's about simple hunger, cold, illness, which push down a man with as much certainty as if they'd been deployed by God. This man has a vision of freedom, then he's floored with rubber truncheons. I know that his freedom hasn't got the slightest in common with Don Carlos's freedom: but I can no longer take Don Carlos's servitude seriously.[28]

Shortly after, Brecht wrote his first piece about Thomas Mann, a review of the latter's reading from *The Magic Mountain* at the Augsburg Börsensaal.[29] Walter Brecht, who went along with his brother, claims that Brecht still approved of Mann at the time.[30] However, the review has a sharply critical edge, beginning with criticism of the organisers' wish to pack in as many prospective season ticket holders as possible, which outweighed consideration of the most suitable venue for such a reading. The acoustics were so bad that those at the back could hear nothing of one of the 'consciously most representative exponents of German literature'. Even at the front, the audience could not hear properly. Brecht described Mann's novel as one which portrays 'a kind of subtle or naive guerrilla war against death, in the careful depiction, never lacking a metaphysical dimension, of the life of a few dozen tubercular patients'. Brecht knew a thing or two about the life of the sick in the sanatorium. Already at this stage, Mann's reflections on sanatorium life left Brecht disinclined to embrace this 'metaphysical dimension'.

Brecht's letter to his father

The sombre certainty in 'The Virginia Smoker' that members of the family could expect only a limited life span spilled over into Brecht's letter to his father on Berthold Brecht's 50th birthday on 6 November 1919. Brecht's letter to his father deserves to be better known, as does his accompanying 'Ode to my Father'. The letter was written within days of that most famous letter to a father in world literature, Franz Kafka's to Hermann Kafka. Unlike Kafka's letter, Brecht's reached its addressee. In stark contrast to Kafka, Brecht praised his father and did so with evident sincerity: 'Mummy was ill a lot and you were ill for many years – but the mental [geistig] atmosphere in which we grew up was healthy. We could above all learn how you *withstand* physical illnesses'.[31] This was, indeed, the crucial lesson to be learned in the Brecht household.

The father had set the example for his children, who could say: 'If nothing becomes of us we ourselves are completely to blame'. Citing Berthold Brecht's favourite analogy of his boys with young stags who should 'break their horns themselves', Brecht wrote: 'Despite all your concern for us we grew up as freely as possible'. In 'Ode to my Father', the son contrasted that freedom with the life that Berthold Brecht had led: 'He who was not always free set his children free'.[32] In Brecht's view, the two Brecht boys were the beneficiaries of the successful struggle which Berthold Brecht's life had been as a self-made businessman. Kafka, of course, decried the self-made businessman Hermann Kafka's crude Social Darwinism. In Hermann Kafka's case, that attitude was bound up with a highly domineering, authoritarian personality much given to threats or shows of violence, which left Franz Kafka feeling utterly crushed. By contrast, Brecht's 'Ode to my Father' ends with a great sense of gratitude, precisely because Berthold Brecht did not habitually use force against his sons:

> He never struggled against what was natural
> But used it for himself and others.
> We all bowed to his influence in silence –
> But he never made us feel his force.

We know, all the same, that Berthold Brecht could, like his son, display a crudely aggressive side. We need only think of his treatment of his wife. In fact, Berthold Brecht's aggression had recently prompted a reader's letter to the *Schwäbische Volkszeitung*, in which 'Director Brecht' was criticised for his coarse language and hostile behaviour towards the firm's union representatives.[33] Brecht's letter and ode were, then, motivated in part by the need to counter, at least in private, this public criticism of his father.

In the letter to his father, the son went on to address the very real political differences that had emerged between them. However, in doing so, Brecht praised his father for the characteristics which he felt he had been fortunate to acquire from him. This again, of course, contrasts with Kafka, who felt that his inheritance from his father was an utter void. Brecht invited Berthold Brecht to consider that the son's political rebellion was grounded in those very characteristics which he had inherited from his father:

> I think that sometimes when we talked about politics you believed that my views were somehow sick or degenerate. That is almost certainly a mistake. It's a healthy sign for young people to go on the offensive rather than to align themselves with those people who have the power and can protect them. What an extraordinary amount I owe you, dear father. How much I've taken over from you in *my* manner will perhaps be said to you on occasion by literary types when they talk about my literary works. I've got to thank you and your love of order for my desire to be clear, your preference for things natural for my appreciation of nature, your straightforward manner for my love of simplicity, your glorious wit for my appreciation of humour. Above all, however, I think of your zest for life, which in difficult times remained indestructible and enabled you to overcome sickness and worry.[34]

Truly, Berthold Brecht allowed nothing to stand in the way of his enjoyment of life. Brecht's words, emphasising his father's zest for life, might well have been construed by the father to mean that the son had at least some understanding of why he had taken up with Marie Röcker while his wife was dying under the same roof. Indeed, Berthold Brecht's sexual habits were another legacy for the son from the father.

Shortly afterwards, Brecht would reflect, in a manner that demonstrates the fluidity of his movement between quite contradictory positions: 'Values are in demand: I've got a sense of values, an inheritance from my father. But I'm also sensitive to the fact that one can completely ignore the concept of value (Baal)'.[35] The hedonistic self-regard which father and son shared inclined them to ignore things that could get in the way of their pleasure, dealing with consequences as and when they arose.

Off to Berlin

Brecht's compositions continued to flow through the winter of 1919–20, not only poems but also early drafts of the homoerotic prose work 'Bargan Gives Up', which Brecht read to Münsterer. Brecht produced short reflections on a variety of topics in literature and theatre, too, which offer early glimpses of later theoretical and polemical positions. Within a general critique of the contemporary avant-garde, he continued his dismissal of Expressionism, charging it with 'crude oversimplification' as a result of its excessive reliance on the 'spirit' and the 'ideal'.[36] Brecht attacked Georg Kaiser as the 'garrulous Wilhelm of German drama', whose plays he found 'very bad' because he lacked the literary power to put flesh on his ideas. He attacked the Dadaists too: 'One of the Dadaists' worst mistakes lies in having their works published, even though they seem to have been produced unmediatedly and for the most immediate present'.

Brecht stylised himself, Zarathustra-like, as a beast of prey, behaving in the theatre as if he were in the jungle: 'I must destroy something, I'm not used to eating plants. [...] I'm calmed by stamping on combatants, who tear each other apart, utter curses which sate me. And the angry little cries of the damned bring me relief'.[37] As so often, Brecht delights in confounding conventional horizons, endowing extreme physical exertion and the inflicting of pain with a calming effect upon himself. Within the self-projection there is therefore the acknowledgement of the pleasure Brecht experienced in causing suffering to others. When he was finally let near a production of his work, he would live the dream, to devastating effect. For the moment, that cruelty found an outlet in attacks on Neher, Brecht announcing that he and Pfanzelt had 'decided to let you go. There's nothing going on with you etc. Someone who can only say five sentences is worth nothing'.[38] A hurt Neher noted their further criticisms: 'There was no prospect of any upswing in my art. I could look around quietly for a job as an art teacher'.

This aggressive self-projection is prominent in Brecht's early pieces on theatre and sport, among them 'The Theatre as a Sporting Institution' – the title a parody of Schiller's 'The Theatre as a Moral Institution' – and 'Theatre as Sport'. The latter was written in response to the challenge posed by the new mass medium of cinema. Typically, the moderniser Brecht stressed that the institution of the theatre must adapt if it were to meet the challenge. He argued that theatre was superior to cinema and that it was wrong to go to the theatre as if it were a church, a courtroom or a school. Rather, the theatre should be viewed like a sporting spectacle. It was, however, not about wrestlers with big biceps. Subtler tussles took place: 'They proceed with words. There are always at least two people on stage, and mostly a struggle is taking place. It is a matter of watching closely who wins'.[39] In its depiction of such struggle, theatre hence captured what for Brecht was the essence of human interaction, as his own early dramas *In the Jungle of Cities* and *The Life of Edward II of England* demonstrate.

For all his energetic self-projections, beyond his reviews Brecht was still bringing in nothing at all to support himself and, prospectively, Bi in Munich, not to mention fetching poor Frank from Kimratshofen. The publication and performance of *Baal* remained a major concern. He saw that play, not *Drums in the Night*, as the work which really showcased his theatrical talent. Brecht began once again to re-work *Baal*, shortening it and excising passages which echoed Johst. Neher felt he had recovered the 'primary effect', which he then sought to emulate in his drawings.[40] Thanks to Feuchtwanger, another Munich publisher, Georg Müller, accepted *Baal*. Brecht still craved Johst's opinion and was relieved to receive a positive answer from his völkisch rival.[41] By then he had completed his revisions, cutting all the scenes with Baal's mother and 'relegating the ghost of *The Lonely One* to the periphery'. The play went to Georg Müller in this truncated form. However, by the summer Brecht had come to realise that he had actually excised vital elements of the play, domesticating what had been a wild, untameable monster, 'which I now realise I completely messed up. Baal has turned to paper, gone academic, smooth, well-shaved, wearing bathing trunks and all that. Instead of becoming more earthy, carefree, outrageous, simple ... In future I shall produce nothing but flaming mud pies made of shit'.[42] Georg Müller typeset *Baal* but in December 1920 would decline to publish it, out of fear of the censor. Only thirty or so copies would be produced for Brecht's private use.

Brecht sought to ingratiate himself further with Johst. After visiting him in Oberallmannshausen he felt they were on such good terms that he asked him to employ Bi in his household![43] When he visited Johst again later in the year he encountered a figure who after the Second World War would play a huge part in spreading his fame, as both friend and publisher, Peter Suhrkamp. Suhrkamp recalled meeting Brecht in late 1919 'at a country inn outside Munich' where Brecht sang a number of ballads to guitar accompaniment, among them 'Baal's Hymn'.[44] For his part, Brecht noted that when he visited Johst in July 1920 he encountered a 'thin-lipped young gent with a coolly ironic look, Suhrkamp, who has what Johst calls a tidy approach to imaginative writing'.[45]

Frustrated by his failure to achieve a breakthrough in Munich, Brecht decided that he had to get himself known in Berlin. The German capital was much more generous in its support for the arts than a now fading Munich and was established as Germany's major theatrical centre. Through Hedda Kuhn he had got to know the young author and journalist Frank Warschauer in Munich. Both were now in Berlin. Kuhn arranged with Warschauer for Brecht to come and stay with him at his flat on Eislebener Strasse, just south of Kurfürstendamm, the fashionable boulevard which was home to some of Berlin's leading theatres.

Following the Greater Berlin Act of 1920, the area of Berlin expanded thirteen-fold and the population doubled to nearly 4 million. Berlin could now do things on a scale that no other German city could countenance. It was about to begin its extraordinary rise to become Europe's leading centre for artistic innovation in the 1920s. Neher was together with Brecht and Bi in the days before Brecht left for Berlin when they attended the premiere of Carl Sternheim's *1913* in Munich.[46] Bi saw Brecht off from Augsburg station early on 21 February 1920. He had procured a seat on the 7.30 a.m. Munich-Berlin express by prevailing upon Neher to take the train from Munich to Augsburg and to whistle to Brecht on arrival so Brecht could take his seat, sparing Brecht a twelve-hour journey standing up. Brecht wrote to 'dearest Cas', 'a good seat is worth a kiss'.[47] Shortly before the train arrived in Berlin, Brecht finished 'Sentimental Song No 1004', which later became 'Remembering Marie A'. Hedda Kuhn was at Berlin's Anhalter Station to welcome Brecht. To Bi he painted a desolate picture of life in the capital: 'You can't get anything done in this city because the distances are too great. If you want to go to a theatre you've got to set off in your youth and you arrive as a grey-beard'. He played the rather dull, responsible husband, who could not really be bothered with Berlin, telling her that he would soon be coming home, probably in a week's time. By 3 March he was fairly certain that he would be coming back the following Monday.

However, he was writing to Jacob Geis: 'The shenanigans in Berlin differ from the shenanigans everywhere else in their shameless magnificence'. And to Neher: 'Berlin is a wonderful thing, can't you steal 500 marks somewhere and come? There is, for instance, the underground and Wegener. Everything is teeming with tastelessness, but on what a scale, my child!'. With his extraordinary features like Verlaine's, the actor Paul Wegener was for the Brecht Circle the perfect Baal. The contrast between shameless, tasteless Berlin and genteel, conservative Munich could hardly have been greater. Brecht would later write that he preferred Berlin to other cities 'because it is constantly changing'.[48] Everywhere he turned there was excitement and opportunity, much of which Brecht, in a state of high arousal, viewed through the prism of sex: 'I've drained the cup. I've been seduced'. And shortly after: 'In the tram a buxom woman was standing with her back to me. I was sitting there, and she often took her weight on her knees, and as she did that I could feel through the soft, matchmaking velvet the soft backs of her knees and the movement towards her thighs and the separation of her legs. I felt that for so long that I became as ravenous as a dog with desire. You longed to separate those full legs. They seemed so yielding and veiled'.

When Brecht finally heard from Bi, he immediately changed his tune, writing on 7 March: 'I can't come home before the middle of next week: it's *not* possible. I still like you a very great deal. There are many more pretty girls here than in Munich, but I've got no great difficulty in being faithful to you (although chances come up everywhere because I'm so "intéressant"!)'. Still he did not come back and the longer he stayed the more he insisted that he was being faithful: 'I'm being indescribably good. Nothing at all's going on in that way. I've got absolutely no time for such things. And I've got no desire either. Warschauer says: You're no poet! A poet and faithful!!! (That's literally true!)'. Brecht laid it on even thicker by describing his daily routine, getting up at eight, reading till ten, on the phone till ten-thirty, going out to the library or a publisher's, lunch from two-thirty until four, mostly at home, then playing music or working, and in the evening theatre. He assured her that his day culminated with his 'major desire' for her before he went to sleep.

Brecht, of course, made no mention to Bi of his frequent meetings with Hedda Kuhn, nor that he had met another woman, Dora Mannheim, at a fancy dress ball in late February. She went as a native African woman with her face painted brown, wearing a black wig and a brown leather skirt. He went as a monk. She was about to go home just after midnight when the monk invited her to dance, warning her that it was a risk: he was not particularly good.[49] After he had trodden on her toes quite a few times, she suggested that they sit down. He then launched into an endless round of stories, stopping only in the early hours when he left her at her flat on Uhlandstrasse, not far from his own place. He visited her the following afternoon and then they met regularly. She took him to places like Trude Hesterberg's cabaret at the Café des Westens on the corner of Kurfürstendamm and Joachimsthaler Strasse. And Hedda Kuhn took him to Liga, a student club in the attic of a fellow student's house on Neue Winterfelder Strasse in Schöneberg, where Klabund was performing his poems and songs.[50] Brecht followed Klabund with his own ballads.

Doubting whether Georg Müller would publish *Baal*, Brecht asked Neher to contact the publisher to make sure that things were proceeding as agreed.[51] In fact, before Brecht's arrival in Berlin, Kuhn had begun negotiations on his behalf with Hermann Kasack of Kiepenheuer. Brecht pressed Kasack to take *Baal* when they met at a café on Potsdamer Platz. Kasack accepted the manuscript, only to decline the work later on 'aesthetic grounds', but that would not be the end of Kiepenheuer's interest. Brecht left a lasting impression on Kasack, who wrote that he had 'hardly ever in his life seen a face with such a variable expression with such capacity to transform itself. There were all the things in it which later surfaced in his works: naivety as well as cynicism, the bad as well as the tender, warmth and brusqueness – and that within an elementary obsessiveness and without any concession to false sentimentality or outdated conventions'.[52] Beyond all this, Kasack noted that Brecht's 'head sometimes twitched nervously': on such a stressful occasion, Brecht struggled to contain the abiding effects of his childhood tic.

While Brecht was pursuing his interests in the theatre and with publishers in the capital, the counter-revolutionary forces, which the government had employed to put down the Spartacists, were now turning on the Weimar Republic and its representatives. The right-wing nationalists heaped blame upon republicans for the 'shame of Versailles'. Rumours of an impending putsch became fact when on Saturday 13 March the leader of the German Fatherland Party Wolfgang Kapp and the army general Walther Freiherr von Lüttwitz joined together to topple the government, which fled to Stuttgart. However, the putsch failed when Berlin workers answered a call for a general strike, paralysing the city. The government was able to return on 20 March.

Brecht took the train to Munich on 14 March to escape the putsch. However, that day General Arnold von Moehl led his own putsch, ushering in a right-wing government for Bavaria under Gustav von Kahr. In contrast to Berlin, in Bavaria reactionary forces now had the upper hand. Before Brecht left Berlin, he rang Dora Mannheim to say that he could not meet her because he wanted to be with his father.[53]

He explained that he himself had always got on well with the workers. However, for Brecht an evening of Karl Valentin's comedy proved a greater attraction. He told Dora Mannheim: 'I ... rolled around laughing. [...] (At that hour you were dancing and did not know my face anymore!)'.[54] Shifting playfully between the polite form and the familiar, he ended his letter: 'And now I'm kissing you on the mouth and asking your forgiveness'. The exchange of photographs was arranged, the putsches were taken as read and Berthold Brecht would surely be fine.

Sophie Brecht's death

The following day Brecht returned to Augsburg, where he met Neher and told him all about Berlin. No doubt Bi got a version of what had happened in boring old Berlin. Brecht and Neher were together for much of the first half of April, working on a project about Charles the Bold and going on the swings at the Plärrer. Neher relished Bi's company: 'I swing with Bie in the boat. It's really beautiful to swing so high with her alone and you feel like a god'.[55] Brecht's diary contains even more musings than usual upon his coming greatness: 'Forty years, and my œuvre is the swan song of the millennium. I love those who are doomed and delight in their demise'.[56] Most memorably, he wrote of the intense, urgent demands that he made upon the world:

> Though I am only 22 and have grown up in the small city of Augsburg on the Lech without having seen more than a fraction of the earth – apart from the meadows, that is, just this city with trees and one or two other cities, though never for long – I am seized with a wish to have the whole world delivered: I wish all things to be handed over to *me*, along with power over all animals; and my grounds for this demand are that I shall exist only *once*.[57]

The urgency of his demand for life had its corollary in his 'black yet lucid' musings on pain and grief:

> Whenever I have seen people wringing their hands or launching accusations as a result of pain and worry they have always struck me as quite failing to appreciate the full seriousness of their situation. For they had completely forgotten that it was all no use; they hadn't yet realised that God had not simply forsaken or offended them, but that there was actually no God whatsoever and that a man who causes a rumpus all by himself on a desert island must be off his head.[58]

Such precepts – recognisably drawn from his father's attitude towards pain and suffering, coupled with the all-pervasive Nietzsche – were put to the test in the most terrifying way when in May the moment arrived which Brecht had dreaded all his life: the cancer which had wracked Sophie Brecht's body overcame her. The expectation of her death did not reduce the shock when it finally happened, at 9 p.m. on the first day of the month. Walter Brecht writes that he, his father and brother were with her: 'Mummy was asleep this evening, and nothing happened, she died in her sleep, quietly, just as she had always been. Later we stood there in the living room. No one spoke.

But the three of us, Daddy, Eugen and I, felt close to one another like never before'.[59] The following morning, a Sunday, Ernestine Müller found Brecht by the iron railings opposite his house, which gave on to the slow-moving water of the city moat.[60] When she asked him what he was doing he explained that his mother had died and he had to write a poem on her death. He then passed Ernestine his 'Song about my Mother', his eighth psalm, a parody of the biblical form which he produced serially that summer:

1 I no longer remember her face as it was before her pain began. Wearily, she pushed the black hair back from her forehead, which was bony, I can still see her hand as she does it.

2 Twenty winters had threatened her, her sufferings were legion, death was ashamed to approach her. Then she died, and they discovered that her body was like a child's.

[...]

4 She died among faces which had looked so long at her dying that they had grown hard.

[...]

6 Oh why do we not say the important things, it would be so easy, and we are damned because we do not. Easy words, they were, pressing against our teeth; they fell out as we laughed, and now they choke us.

7 Now my mother has died, yesterday towards evening, on the first of May. One won't be able to claw her up out again with one's fingernails.[61]

These final words were her perennial reproach for his behaviour, which, she had said, would send her to her grave and which he had reproduced in 'Outpourings of a Martyr'. Among Brecht's numerous meditations on his mother's death, he wrote a prose poem, in which he railed against the God in whom she had believed so ardently. He then reflected: 'My mother has been dead since yesterday evening, her hands gradually grew cold, when she was still wheezing, but she did not say anything more, she just stopped wheezing. My pulse is racing somewhat, I can still see clearly, can walk, in the evening I have'.[62]

The draft breaks off at that point. The reflection on his own physical state is not as strange as it initially appears if one understands just how intertwined Sophie Brecht's ill health and that of her son had always been. Their special bond had been forged in their awareness of the fragility of life, which her death brought home to him with devastating force. The gulf that had opened between them in Brecht's teenage years had meant yawning silences where previously there had been animated exchange. The shock recognition assailed Brecht that the things which had remained unspoken between them could now never be said. He reflected in his diary: 'I loved her in my way, but she wanted to be loved in hers'.[63]

Neher, who had witnessed many deaths at the front, joined his friend by his mother's body and noted: 'I've never seen a woman dead before. It was awful. I drew her and would have liked to draw her for hours on end'.[64] Walter was deeply shocked and offended by his brother's actions the following evening, which Brecht's prose poem above stops short of recounting. He invited his friends round: 'It was as noisy as usual. Who knows what his friends felt watching his extravagant behaviour, this behaviour which contemptuously refused any expression of feeling. Who knows why he did this in his grief. The rest of us who lived in the house were silent in our pain'.[65] This is the way the thin-skinned Brecht dealt with feelings that threatened to assail him, directing them outwards with a narcissistic inversion. This angry and confused young man's behaviour would presently take on distinctly sadistic features, threatening destruction – and self-destruction – until he realised that to survive he must control his behaviour.

He fled Augsburg before his mother's funeral, writing: 'Those were bones which they laid in a sheet. He left before earth had covered her over. Why watch what is self-evident?'.[66] He raged with contempt at the existence which his mother had been forced to endure. Just as during his father's illness in 1913 Brecht had shunned his relatives with their muddled show of feelings and focused his mind on poetry, so too now he fixed his thoughts on his writing in order to capture the momentous import of this event: 'My mother died on the first of May. Spring arose. Shamelessly the heavens grinned'. After the funeral, Brecht visited his mother's grave regularly: 'At home all's quiet. I keep on going to the cemetery, and I like it there'.

Breaking the circle: The serial killer

Sophie Brecht's death left her angry elder son primed to take out his emotional turmoil on those around him. In a thinly veiled self-portrait, he wrote: 'George Beil lost his mother to cancer and had become mistrustful as a result. He had started arguments with some of his friends for ridiculous reasons and had withdrawn completely to his lover, a Jewish medic, at whose place he drank tea around five p.m. nearly every afternoon'.[67] The Jewish medic may be identified as Hedda Kuhn, who was back living in Munich and about whom he had taken to writing that he 'took tea' with her in the afternoon.

Brecht was subject to extreme mood swings and engaged in sadistic displays of aggression. He appeared to Münsterer deeply depressed as he reflected darkly on the times.[68] In Münsterer's view, for most of Brecht's old friends the summer of 1920 signalled the start of a difficult time with him. Brecht began to record his highly combustible, volatile state in a remarkable diary and in a notebook recognises that the silences and resultant lack of trust between friends escalated into lies.[69] He claimed, with contorted logic, that the lies were told in the attempt to retrieve the truth, but the lies came out all the same and friendships broke down. At the end of the summer Brecht acknowledged what he was doing: 'I'm getting on with sawing away the branch I'm sitting on, if only slowly'.[70]

Desperate for success after Berlin, Brecht was, in Münsterer's estimation, mixing almost entirely with journalists and literary types, among them dubious characters like Johst. Münsterer felt marginalised. Brecht sent him his condolences on his father's death but neglected to send off a letter and a card which he had written, before he responded to a letter in May, begging Münsterer's forgiveness for his 'sins'. He admitted that he had not been a good friend and promised to mend his ways, looking forward to meeting up in Munich.[71] Yet when Brecht wrote to Münsterer again shortly afterwards from Augsburg, he adopted the same disingenuous manner of his letters to Bi from

Berlin, claiming that he was alone on his 'island'. Münsterer knew better than most people that a promise from Brecht to mend his ways was worthless. Brecht was driven by self-interest and Münsterer could no longer satisfy that interest. Münsterer had been relegated to an outer circle. Things would never be the same between them again.

Otto Bezold was also studying in Munich, but he was lost from sight too, while Neher and Pfanzelt experienced Brecht's harsh, unforgiving edge.[72] Initially Müllereisert escaped this treatment but their relationship, too, would come under strain. In Brecht's diary, Müllereisert is at first the favoured one as Brecht plays his friends off against each other. However, these strong personalities would not long tolerate such treatment and they would turn the tables on Brecht, to his distress. Pfanzelt could see the change in Brecht, remarking on his vanity and his up-tightness. Neher's adoration for Brecht, however, still knew no bounds: 'Oh, I'd always like to be together with Bert. Always'.[73] They took a studio flat together in Munich in May and Brecht wrote of a trip to Possenhofen on Lake Starnberg with Neher in July: 'It's better with a friend than with a girl. We lay in the water (77° Fahrenheit) and in the forest and then in the boat, then had another swim when night had already fallen. If you lie on your back the stars above move with you, while through you flows the current. At night you tumble into bed like a ripe fruit: voluptuously'.[74] As in 'Of Swimming in Lakes and Rivers', Brecht records here the receptivity of his body to the rhythms of nature, which he took within himself. Shortly after, on 27 July, he wrote 'Ballad of Friendship', the story of two lovers' journey over the oceans through exotic climes:

> Like two pumpkins floating seaward
> Decayed, but on a single stalk
> In yellow rivers, they just drifted
> And played at cards and played at talk
> Shot at yellow moons and loved each other
> Though their love was with averted eye:
>   Remained as one many nights together
>   And also: when the sun was high.[75]

Brecht took a walking holiday with Neher and Müllereisert through villages in Württemberg near his mother's birthplace: 'We bathed every day and didn't do too much walking. Priests gave us bread or five marks, peasants home-made wines. Potatoes we stole'.[76] Unwilling to beg for food and a bed for the night, Neher went home in a huff, ridiculed by Brecht and Müllereisert, while claiming that he was going because he'd lost his watch. Brecht goaded him with their secret code: 'Just as well you didn't lose it in Argentina'. This prompted Neher's reply: 'You don't lose things there anymore'. Brecht countered with: 'It can happen to anybody, even me'. Neher shot back with: 'People like that won't do in Argentina. I'm staying at home'. Brecht had the last word, at least in his diary: 'There are times when he looks like a bumfucker'. They did not see each other for some time. When Otto brought Cas to see Brecht, Brecht was disparaging: 'Not that it was Cas so much as Neher, Rudolf Neher, a school teacher's son'. Brecht captured Neher's demise in a cruel song 'Fat Caspar's Gone and Left Us'.

Brecht was similarly disparaging about Pfanzelt, who was developing worryingly conventional attitudes with Franziska Lochinger, Fannerl, from Steinicke's bookshop.

Brecht contrasted 'Orge' Pfanzelt's swotting as he prepared for his administrative exams with 'Heilgei' Müllereisert's effortless progression as a medical student, for whom life was simply 'sport'.[77] The underlying contrast between the financially independent Müllereisert and the unmonied Pfanzelt remained unspoken. Brecht's situation resembled Müllereisert's more closely than Pfanzelt's financially and also sexually. For Brecht, Pfanzelt acted as the 'protector and spiritual pastor to those young creatures whom Heilgei has been through and is said to curse him like a nigger. (But doesn't screw!)'.[78] Like Brecht, Müllereisert certainly did. At this time Brecht joined Müllereisert in alcoholic binges. Drinking in cheap bars, studio parties, unwanted pregnancies and abortions found their way into many poems at this time as well as into dramatic fragments like *The Brats*, which treated the hotly debated topic of the abortion law.[79] From his own relationships Brecht created roles for Bi, Cas and Marietta Neher, and Marie Rose Amann.

Unlike Müllereisert and Brecht, Neher did not really have his heart in an afternoon with four girls at Müllereisert's flat, which Brecht describes in his diary:

> Nine of us in Otto's flat spent the afternoon slowly filling up with tea and alcohol. Then came jokes, jokes not with the mouth but with the hands. There were four girls there, I sang, but then I chucked the guitar aside, grabbed a girl from Otto (Hansi Haase) and carted her into the Dadaist cabinet. Otto tugged at me, forcing me to fight like a nigger, in the process she hit her head on a chair, bumped it against a cupboard, knocked it against a wooden partition; then on to the ottoman, where I kiss the bruises, it's dark there, she is soft, warm, pretty, we have a wrestling match, but she doesn't want it, people pass through, a girl says 'you've got a face like an orangutan.' I start singing again, just a bit drunk, in a top hat, looking foul, it's a vice den, there's been some filming, then to salvoes from the piano I'm just beginning to scribble a monologue for Malvi on a bit of newspaper, when Cas wrecks my last chance by giving a crude imitation of my recent performance, seizing the girl with his arms like an orangutan, bending her till everything cracks, flinging her against the wall, breaking her bones, in short training her. It doesn't come off, he just makes a mess of things, looks like a flunkey, gloomy, worried, like a pansy, stammers synthetically, acts the simpleton, acts the brute, gnashes his teeth so you can hear it fifteen feet off, grinds his cheek-bones, oozes vitality, but hasn't got his mind on the job. Otto is lying halfdrunk behind the desk with a girl, working away. He has drunk well, filmed well, looks good. The women are stupid, generally speaking no class, a slimy fat Jew is sitting there with his arm round that Müllegger girl whom I'd brought along but didn't address a word to; she'd better watch out what she's letting herself in for. I'm not her nanny. I'll be sorry for her afterwards. But there's nothing I can do about my aversions. Otto's flat is like a junk shop.[80]

At this time, Brecht apparently took pleasure in such sadistic brutality. He had brought Martha Müllegger, and even though he had ignored her, he evidently assumed that his proprietorial right justified his contemptuous remark about the Jew.

Brecht found brutally scathing words for Hedda 'He' Kuhn when their relationship began to fall apart: 'Twenty sins are forgiven, but *one* sin is not forgiven, which is the twenty-first. Go home, adorn your home, He, and say: everything was ok, but he went crazy out in the sun. He [Brecht] said to me: "You have everything that a whore has, just not the body!" '.[81] More was to come in the ninth psalm, 'Of He':

2 [...] she sold her skin for a cup of tea and her self for a whip. She ran among the willows till she was tired out, He did.

3 She offered herself like a fruit, but nobody accepted her. Many had her in their mouths and spat her out again, the good He. He, the sweetheart.

[...]

5 At night she was miserable, blind with vanity, He, and women are night animals, and she was no night animal.

6 She wasn't wise like Bie, the graceful, Bie, the plant, she just kept on running around and her heart was without thought.

7 Therefore she died in the fifth month of the year 1920, a quick death, secretly, when nobody was watching, and she went away like a cloud of which it is said that it never was.[82]

Having taken refuge with Hedda for tea, Brecht takes out his anger on her, demeaning her and contrasting her, the intellectual woman, with the plant-like Bi. The cloud, that recurrent image in the early Brecht for the transience of love, assumes a menacing function, by means of which Brecht 'kills' Hedda, dismissing her from his memory in that same month as his mother's death.

In fact, Brecht continued to drink tea at Hedda's but felt estranged by her passivity.[83] He told her that he loved Bi and Georg, not her. Brecht and Hedda went out to Pöcking on Lake Starnberg for two days with Neher and Edith Blass, where they spent the first day swimming, soaking up the water and the sun, and, as Brecht put it, carrying the smell home. Brecht saw Edith Blass a number of times and compared her and Hedda's false way of talking to Bi's natural simplicity. He had another female visitor: Dora Mannheim stayed over in his room in Munich for two days in July on her way to the Walchensee.[84] They walked by the Isar and lay on the grass while Brecht sang ballads from *Baal*.

Brecht's relationship with Hedda was irreparably damaged when, against his wishes, she decided to stay over at Bleichstrasse in early August. He reduced her to tears with his vicious tongue: 'She begins to look old then: water trickling out of a ruin'.[85] Hedda sent him letters full of reproaches for his bad behaviour, which he accepted quite unmoved, arguing that in those two years since she had started 'making tea' she could have walked away. She then asked why she did not have the strength to tear herself away from a man who did not love her and who was rough and tactless. Brecht acknowledged that he had lied to her and deserved to have mincemeat made of him. However, when things had calmed down, in response to his description of their relationship as a cross between a marriage and an adventure, she began to talk about marriage. Flush with success, Brecht then completely overplayed his hand, giving her a copy of Claudel's *The Exchange*. After this invitation to engage in partner-swapping, there was no way back with a woman like Hedda Kuhn. They met one day in Baden-Baden but it was an unhappy encounter. Their relationship was over. She would free herself of Brecht by marrying a more 'solid' man.

All the while, Bi was in Augsburg, waiting to see Brecht on a Sunday and thinking about their marriage, which, she still believed, would surely follow his artistic break-through. He was outraged to discover that, at a time when her health was bad, her family wanted to send her away into service.[86] Her departure was delayed. They visited Frank in Kimratshofen, went to the Orchid Garden, a wine bar and concert venue, and to Müllereisert's flat. However, the relationship with Bi was never enough for Brecht. He met up with Marie Rose Amann but found her beauty distinctly faded. He could not hide his contempt: she was 'childish, infantile, laughs a lot and in an uneasy kind of way, her laugh is every bit as disconcerting as a haemorrhage'.[87] When he saw her again a few days later he found her a little better:

> We slithered around on a bench, she was pale, childlike, lascivious. The sky was clouded, it swam away over our heads while the wind made a noise among the bushes; groping under their foliage I regret to say. I gave her soft little face a good kissing and squashed her a bit. Apart from that she believes in doing the proper thing in every conceivable situation and has to be home at 9.

He was seeing other women, too, like Hansi Haase, whom he'd been with at Müllereisert's, and Anni Bauer, who visited him in Munich. They drank schnapps and he played the guitar before trying it on. But, he writes, he lost interest and sent her home, fearing that he might otherwise catch gonorrhoea.[88] He had become hard and harsh with others. In his highly promiscuous lifestyle gonorrhoea was a real possibility. Anxiety about sexually transmitted infections dogged him, as did anxiety about pregnancy, prompting the composition of the psalmic parody 'Vision in White' with its two final verses: '5 My sweethearts bring a bit of quicklime with them, in hands which I have kissed. The bill comes for the orange skies, the bodies and the rest. I cannot pay it. 6 Better to die. – I lean back. I close my eyes. The archangels applaud'.[89]

By September Brecht was falling out with Müllereisert. Instead of helping Brecht in the search for accommodation as he had promised, Müllereisert went off with Pfanzelt. Brecht now concluded of Müllereisert, as he had of Neher and Kuhn: 'If he must die, then die he must'.[90] And Brecht could no longer depend on Pfanzelt, whom he had asked to help him re-write the final scene of *Baal*. Pfanzelt went off with Müllereisert, leaving Brecht alone with his bleak thoughts: 'It's ludicrous considering it's all about literature, but I did humiliate myself, and I was powerless. I'm nothing. I feel ashamed'. He withdrew to his attic, where he played billiards alone and confided to his diary: 'I'm very much on my own'.

On the way down

Having driven away his friends, Brecht was forced to confront the stark reality of his situation. For all his talent, charm and sexual successes, he had achieved nothing in the only field of social interaction that really mattered: the theatre. He knew people in Munich like Feuchtwanger, Valentin, Geis and Otto Zarek, another artistic advisor at the Kammerspiele, but these contacts had not enabled him to achieve the success he craved. Brecht's diary becomes a thoroughly depressed rumination upon the whole spectrum of his experience and interests. His admiration for Vincent van Gogh's letters to his brother speaks volumes: 'He has no success but works like a maniac and practically all the time sees the future as blacker than the present, which is too black to start with. There's an enormous amount to be learned from that'.[91] This is the tenor of one of Brecht's starkest poems from this time, 'Born later':

> I admit it: I
> Have no hope.
> The blind talk of a way out. I
> See.
>
> When the errors have been used up
> As our last companion, facing us
> Sits nothingness.

Brecht worried that his art might be 'too primitive and old-fashioned, or else crude and lacking in boldness. I hunt around for new forms and experiment with my feelings just like the very latest writers. But then I keep coming back to the fact that the essence of art is simplicity, grandeur and sensitivity, and that of its form coolness'.

Brecht responded to his turmoil by doing what he always did: 'Berti comes back from the swing-boats strumming through the greensward'.[92] He found the swing-boats at the Plärrer 'utterly satisfying. It's one of the loveliest sports, a profitable way of spending an evening; you go home differently from normal'. In Munich he played the clarinet in Karl Valentin's cabaret spoof of the Oktoberfest alongside Valentin and Liesl Karlstadt. He went to a poetry reading by the Expressionist Else Lasker-Schüler: 'good and bad poems, exaggerated and unhealthy, but extremely beautiful in parts'. But he was disparaging about Lasker-Schüler herself: 'old and worn out, flabby and unappealing'. Brecht was unusually enthusiastic after hearing Johannes R. Becher read his Expressionist verse at Steinicke's. Becher had attempted suicide in 1910 and had made a name for himself as a poet who wavered between Communism and religion. He joined the USPD in 1917, then Spartacists and the KPD but left in 1920 after the failure of the revolution, only to re-join the KPD in 1923. Like Brecht, Becher would gravitate to Berlin, flee into exile from Nazi Germany and after 1945 opt for East Berlin, where he would become the German Democratic Republic's first Minister of Culture.

Brecht's mood did not improve as he reflected on the political situation in Germany. It was now becoming amply clear what it meant for Germany to have lost the war. Brecht did not like what he saw. This angry young man railed against the wretched state of the country as the severe conditions of the Treaty of Versailles began to bite. They, of course, came on top of the grave fiscal risk which Germany had run to finance the war, bankrupting the country. In the Reichstag election of June 1920 support for Ebert's SPD collapsed to just half the previous level. The parties of the extreme Right and Left were the major beneficiaries. At a time when the mark had declined to a tenth of its value against the US dollar in August 1914, German politicians had little interest in pointing to the folly of the wartime printing of money, preferring to place the blame on Versailles. Hyper-inflation was yet to come. Brecht wrote ominously: 'Now they are asking more for the state than ever before. And yet there's no kind of rule people find harder to bear than that of reason. They are prepared to sacrifice everything for spurious grandiose-sounding platitudes'.[93]

The tone was set for the Weimar Republic. In 1920, Brecht admired the conservative-revolutionary views of Oswald Spengler in his 'great work' *The Decline of the West*. Brecht drafted a 'Call for a Strike' of 'twenty-year-olds in a people that is dying', arguing that young people should no longer be prepared to die for an idea and that 'this people will disappear from the face of the earth'. For all his sympathy with the Spartacists, Brecht had no real conception of the proletariat as the rising class. Instead, in the manner of Carl Sternheim's mockery of petty-bourgeois attitudes among the working class in *Tabula rasa*, the satirist in Brecht could not resist depicting a member of the proletariat as enjoying a glass of egg cognac in the morning.

In the poem 'Political Observations', perhaps a rejoinder to Thomas Mann's *Observations of an Unpolitical Man*, Brecht expressed his contempt for his fellow Germans' sheer indifference while their appallingly indebted 'country is groaning beneath the black disgrace': 'For hours on end on the city pond they go boating / Really I'm simply disgusted by what I see / That that's even allowed, when you're up to your neck in debt / In such a political system, boating'.[94] Brecht composed his first poetic address to his country, 'Germany, You Blond Pale Creature', 'the carrion pit of Europe':

> Vultures over you!
> Beasts tear your good body
> The dying smear you with their filth
> And their water
> Wets your fields. [...]
>
> Oh carrion land, misery hole!
> Shame strangles the remembrance of you
> And in the young men whom
> You have not ruined
> America awakens.

Among the victor nations, the USA was emerging for Brecht as for others as the symbol of fresh vitality and strength, with which he realised he would have to contend for the rest of his life. Brecht's 'fad for negroes', in drafts of *Baal*, *Drums in the Night* and several poems, dates from this time.[95] In fact, Brecht became plagued by dire thoughts about the infiltration of his country by foreign bodies out to destroy what was left of it. In his anger and resentment, Brecht demonised the black French soldiers from North Africa, who were among the forces occupying the Rhineland:

> In the Rhineland the niggers are sucking the soil dry. They inseminate the women by squads, get off scot free, laugh when the civil population objects. The behaviour of the German civil population has been exemplary; there have been no reports of murder or manslaughter. These people whose wives have been ruined are miles away from anything resembling lynch law. They gnash their teeth, they go and do

it in the lavatory so nobody can hear. They don't nail those niggers to the door, they don't saw them in two, they clench their fists in a sack and masturbate in the process. They are proving that they are getting their desserts. They are what's left over from the great war, the scum of the population, cut-down loudmouths, dehumanised cattle in the mass, German citizens anno 1920.[96]

It was not just black soldiers whom he saw assailing Germany. He spent time with Warschauer in Baden-Baden, where Warschauer 'sang arias to Zionism': 'this country we live in is finished, is over, going to the bottom; and nothing is better than Zion'.[97] Brecht enjoyed friendships in Munich and Berlin with Jews, among them Feuchtwanger, Warschauer, Kuhn and Mannheim. However, his views on Jews at this time – like his view about the black French soldiers – smack of unreconstructed, provincial attitudes, reinforced by the anthropology student's study of inherited characteristics: 'Oh, this strong, joyous and disreputable people! It covers the surface of the earth like thick plant growth, and how many knives were sharpened against it! They were colder than the North Wind, it froze if it had to go through them. [...] Beneath the kicks of Christian brutes they multiplied like sea urchins, wherever they came to, seas of grain grew, and wherever they left, no grass grew there anymore.'[98] Brecht identified such anti-Semitic attitudes in the Augsburg journalist Wilhelm Brüstle, 'who talked about Jewish girls, being in love with one. He wasn't talking quite like that about Jews the other day, but talk is talk'.[99] Yet Brecht was prepared to excuse Johst's behaviour towards the Jewish Dora Mannheim: 'You shouldn't have allowed yourself to be harangued by him: you've most likely got a false impression of him'.[100] Brecht would learn.

He attended a lecture by Alfons Goldschmidt on the economic situation of Russia but walked out, appalled by the abstract talk about organisations and systems of control: 'At present I am very much against Bolshevism: universal military service, food rationing, controls, conspiracies, economic favouritism. On top of that, at best: equilibrium, standardisation, compromise. I say thanks a lot and may I have a car'.[101] Yet he defended Communism against his father's attacks, which turned into a diatribe against Brecht's own failings:

At lunch Papa was talking nonsense about Communism. Two apples had been stolen from our garden; I stuck up for the thief: trees' products can't be anybody's property. At that Papa started shouting that according to the papers the Allied Commission had instituted closing time at 11 o'clock, that's what Germany has come to thanks to people like us. He'd like to know what I've done for the community so far, absolutely nothing at all. In five years' time I'll still not have my first medical degree. High time I did a proper job of work. My literary achievements in his personal view amount to nothing at all. It all has to be put to the test still. I left quickly. So far I haven't earned anything.[102]

Among the values which Brecht inherited from his father was the firm belief in the importance of earning a crust. From his mother he had acquired a puritanical stringency, and with it a sense of guilt for any failings. Normally so confident in his own gifts, Brecht began to be gripped by a sense of failure, accompanied by feelings of guilt and self-loathing. His inability to complete *Drums in the Night* filled him with shame.

Fevered reflections

Brecht had learned how, in normal circumstances, to will himself to gloss over the huge gulf between his linguistic vitality and his imperfect health. However, his sense of failure began to impact upon him in a wholly deleterious way. Now his underlying physical and psychological frailty manifested itself in weakness and a feverishly vacillating mood, accompanied by the feeling that his body was under attack from within. Just as he had in 1916, he used the figure of the devil to convey his distress: 'I am horribly restless and fidgety. There's a devil in me, it looks as if he's about to start by getting in among the sows. I've been running around like a demented dog and am unable to do anything. Moreover a lot of things are falling apart'.[103] He captured his heart pains and palpitations in lyrical fragments and, turning his thoughts to the theatre, placed himself inside the body of the actor, combining a literary and clinical perspective, and homing in on the heart: 'See what his heart will stand. You must stretch him and then keep an eye on his heart'.[104] Amidst his violent mood swings, Brecht became morbidly pre-occupied by his physical condition: 'On such days your blood never circulates right down to your finger tips, only as far as your wrists, and you'd like to eat your own tongue; except that you have to cart it around with you. On such days people behave so you'd like to let the water out of them. But without water they cannot live. God has diluted them, and there's nothing to be done about it'.[105]

Brecht's mental turmoil fed all manner of reflections, some confused, others lucid, which he committed to his diary in frenetic manner. There are all sorts of beguiling references to what became major aesthetic pre-occupations but the only underlying pattern at this stage is one of highly contradictory, wild swings in Brecht's thought.[106] The corollary of physical strength was powerful art, of physical weakness an impaired literary capacity: 'Perhaps I shall be able to do some powerful art again in the autumn'.[107] He suffered from frequent headaches and speculated upon what it would be like if he could

> only calm down to the great simple rhythm of life, the eating of potatoes, the dances in little plank-lined rooms, the sad sunsets in which the air expands, the unvaried eternal conflicts without distinction or refinement. You rail against the uniformity of all life – the mute, dumb-witted way in which all living creatures refuse to meet their old needs in fresh forms – because you yourself are poor and have no compelling needs.[108]

The rhythms of Brecht's own life were anything but simple. He wondered whether his inclination towards intensity of feeling was a strength or a weakness. After seven thunderstorms one evening he speculated that people were connected electrically with the discharges: 'The lightning gives one courage and tightens the skin on one's face, and the result is clarity. I love thunderstorms'.[109] Achieving clarity of thought through the storm would always be the goal. He contrasted his sensibility born of intensity of feeling – which yielded imaginative constellations of struggle and violent conflict – with his admiration for those whose sovereign detachment meant they could change tack as circumstances dictated without resistance to events. He viewed Jesus Christ as the epitome of that sovereign detachment:

A good man beneath a fig tree, with his heart on his lips, a living impression, a man quite without a navel, a successful creation, aimless, whose back doesn't need any sort of stiffening (fulfilment of obligations or what have you). An invulnerable man, because he puts up no resistance. Wholly prepared to tack, pliable, cloud-like, full of starry skies, gentle showers, wisdom, cheerfulness, trustfulness, possibilities. In short, *the* good man. He cannot be represented dramatically; he doesn't resist.[110]

Brecht encountered such a concept of personality – not resisting and giving oneself to movement and transformation as in the flow of water – in Alfred Döblin's treatment of the Taoist doctrine of Wu Wei in his Chinese novel *The Three Leaps of Wang-lun*, with its idea that 'only one thing helps to counter fate: not resisting'.[111] Döblin's work would inspire Brecht in writing *In the Jungle of Cities*, his depiction of the struggle between two men of contrasting and ever changing dispositions. And Brecht would later write that he had learned more about the epic from Döblin than from anyone else.[112] Around this time too, Warschauer introduced Brecht to the great Taoist philosopher Lao-tsû, who, as Brecht put it, 'agrees with me about so many things that he keeps on being astounded'.[113] Taoist thought would remain a vital point of reference for the eclectic contrarian Brecht, for whom Leninist activism would provide the inspiration for the contrasting concept of interventionist thinking. In this way, the adolescent poet's alternately aggressive and contemplative projections in 'Storm' and 'Festive Day' took on fresh forms in a process of transformation, which continued throughout his life.

Comparing himself to other great German dramatists, Brecht felt that he could never have 'so thoroughly developed a philosophy as Goethe or Hebbel, who must have had memories like tram-conductors [...]. I'm continually forgetting my opinions, can't ever make up my mind to learn them off by heart'.[114] Without any inkling where his ideas and beliefs would lead him, Brecht speculated: 'What shall I do when I'm old, what a miserable existence I'll lead with my decimated past and my battered ideas like so many arrogant cripples'. Turning the comparison with Goethe and Hebbel on its head and typically exaggerating the point, Brecht produced one of his most famous dictums:

A man with one theory is lost. He needs several of them, four, lots! He should stuff them in his pockets like newspapers, hot from the press always, you can live well surrounded by them, there are comfortable lodgings to be found between the theories. If you are to get on you need to know that there are a lot of theories; a tree, too, has several, but only masters one of them, for a while.[115]

The limitations of organic nature had become quite clear.

Brecht formed the view that the conception and representation of theories was an essential adjunct to greatness. From Luther's seminal example, Brecht knew of the extraordinary reputational gain that could accompany new conceptions and knew too of the risks involved in representing them in the face of rigid orthodoxy. Called to Augsburg in 1518, Luther had resisted the attempts of Cardinal Thomas Cajetan to force him to recant his position on indulgences, on justification by faith, and on the authority of the Pope. Cardinal Cajetan's instructions were that if Luther failed to recant, he was to be arrested and sent to Rome. Luther's supporters got wind of this and helped him to escape in the night down the steps leading from Augsburg's old town to the city moat near Brecht's house. Without this act of defiant resistance, the history of Protestantism, which changed the face of Europe, would have looked rather different. Throughout his life, Brecht was captivated by the momentous drama of events surrounding the conception and realisation of a new order. The crucial role of doctrinal theory in the dramatic conflicts of history would never leave him.

For Brecht, German drama was, however, in terminal decline, its place usurped by the cinema. Meanwhile, the rats, whom he named as the great impresario Max Reinhardt and the renowned critic Alfred Kerr, were leaving the sinking ship.[116] Reinhardt had returned to Vienna from Berlin, though that move would prove only temporary. Kerr remained in Germany, becoming Brecht's fiercest critic. Brecht saw himself and like-minded people taking their place to see 'if we can't make her move ahead', even though he only saw himself and the others singing as the ship careered to the bottom of the ocean. He enlarged upon his critique, writing that the theatre's 'evolution has reached its end with nothing but the vanity of the actors satisfying that of an auditorium full of cooks and gastronomic hangers-on'.[117] The culinary imagery to disparage the institution of the theatre given to emotional outpourings, not intellectual reflection, would become a staple in the critical vocabulary which he created in his doctrine to transform the theatre.

. Brecht claimed there was nothing significant to be taken from the rising medium of film. His own film treatments were just as unsuccessful as his plays. The plays remained frustratingly unfinished, unperformed and unpublished. He re-worked *Drums in the Night* for a fourth time but was convinced that it was a bad play. He then worked further on the beginning of the third act and the ending of the fourth, in the hope that the play could be rescued by its 'dynamism and humanity'.[118] The work now had two endings, a comic one and a tragic one. He noted his principal problems:

> It's terribly hard to make this fourth act follow grandly and simply after the first three, at the same time carrying on the external tightening-up of the third, which works pretty well, and bringing the internal transformation (in 15 minutes) forcefully home. What's more, the play's strong, healthy, un-tragic ending, which it had from the outset and for the sake of which it was written, is the only possible ending; anything else is too easy a way out, a feeble concoction, a concession to romanticism. Here is a man apparently at an emotional climax, making a complete volte-face; he tosses all passion aside, tells his followers and admirers to stuff it, then goes home to the woman for whose sake he created the whole mortal fuss. Bed as final curtain. To hell with ideas, to hell with duty!

Yet what Brecht for the first time called the 'gesture' which would enable everything else to fall into place remained frustratingly elusive. The underlying problem is that *Drums in the Night* is a work of balladesque colour, not a play of strongly drawn contrasts sustained to its conclusion. Kragler simply walks away from the conflict.

Slapstick brutality: *Galgei*

By 1920 Kragler's final act of rugged individualism was no longer an option. In August 1918 Brecht had announced to Münsterer his intention to write a play 'for the theatre of the future', *The Fat Man on the Swing-Boat*.[119] Brecht 'evidently wanted to portray the exhilarating liberation of a poor innocent citizen who gets caught up in the hurly-burly of a carnival and the rhythm of the swing-boats'.[120] In the light of Brecht's experience in the wretched post-war years, the story was taking a quite different turn. He channelled dark thoughts of brutality and violence into *Galgei*, initially under the title *Klamauk*, meaning slapstick comedy. The hapless, God-fearing carpenter Joseph Galgei's pleasures and weaknesses are to some extent modelled on what Brecht saw as his own propensities: Galgei is greedy, likes to deceive others and is not honest with himself.[121] He is known to become physically agitated and has a heart complaint.[122] He goes to the Plärrer where, in language redolent of Zarathustran transformation, he describes the effect of the swing-boats: 'When I stood on the swing and gave myself up to the music, I felt that I had overcome all heaviness and was in agreement ['einverstanden'] with moving in a circle, which is what I had done before, but against my wishes'.[123]

However, Brecht's depiction of Galgei is shot through with scathing irony. The hardened, bitter and sadistic Brecht has developed a remorselessly unpitying vision, drawing much from Nietzsche's stark vision of humanity, in a sardonic take on Christian morality in a world dominated by the rapacious business values. The protagonist is no longer the amoral outsider, rather 'citizen Galgei' in a poem of that title, who is set upon by the villains Ligark and Matti.[124] Brecht charted his progress on *Galgei* in a series of diary entries: 'Joseph Galgei fell into the hands of bad men who maltreated him, took away his name and left him lying skinless. Everyone should look to his own skin. [...] The sole problem is: how long can he stand it. [...] They lop off his feet, chuck away his arms, bore a hole in his head till the whole starry heaven is shining into it: is he still Galgei?'.[125] Galgei is transformed into the evil butter dealer, Pick, probably a corrupt form of pig.

However, Brecht was not happy with what he was writing, dismissing *Galgei* as worn out Expressionism.[126] He would resume work on this Brechtian theatre of cruelty in 1921 with the gross thought: 'Perhaps one day I'll do Galgei and have people piss schnapps into his brain and make him a public convenience like all the rest'. However, as he had with *Baal*, Brecht feared that *Galgei* had been over-intellectualised. The project had a long way to run to its conclusion in the mid–1920s as *Man Equals Man*, in which the guileless Galy Gay, a material object in the socio-economic process of business exchange, would be deconstructed and 'rebuilt'.

The ever-supportive Feuchtwanger encouraged Brecht in his work on *Galgei*. For his part, Brecht praised Feuchtwanger as a 'good man and a strong one, extremely clever and decent'.[127] Brecht's father visited Feuchtwanger, his son's most influential advocate, to ask whether his son had the makings of a writer who could live off his work. Feuchtwanger replied that his view was usually that one shouldn't encourage a young person to become a writer. However, if Brecht did not become a writer – he was a genius – then that would be a sin.[128] Berthold Brecht would support his wayward son until 1924 when he could stand on his own feet.

Convicted

At the end of the summer, Brecht noted that 'a lot was started' – usually as he walked along under the chestnut trees near the city moat – but only 'one or two ballads got finished'.[129] By Brecht's standards, that was a mediocre return. He was disturbed by the 'chaos of my papers' and dissatisfied with everything that he had been working on. Thanks to Feuchtwanger, *Baal* was accepted for production by Viktor Schwannecke, Director of the Munich Bavarian state theatres, but Schwannecke's successor Carl Zeiss then turned it down. Brecht lamented that it was goodbye to the winter's great sensation before rejecting this rejection: 'I have no desire not to be performed. I am a very considerable gentleman'.[130] Not only that: 'I am financially dependent on being performed'. However, he did not yet know how to turn things to his advantage.

At long last, 'Project Munich' was about to be realised with Bi. They went there in late September to find rooms. Brecht was pleased to hear from her that Frank had red hair, was cheeky and loved nonsense.[131] However, Brecht was now less than enthusiastic about her, judging that she had grown fat and that the sweetness had left her. Bi lived on Schwanthaler Strasse with her aunt Maria Johanna, a teacher who immediately gave her support to the Nazis when the 'movement' began to emerge as a force. She hated Brecht every bit as much as Karl Banholzer, banning him from her flat. Brecht did as he had done in Augsburg: he appeared on the street and whistled for Bi. She let him in during the morning when her aunt was at work.

In that winter semester 1920–1, Brecht registered for just two courses, one in the history of German literature, the other in preparatory exercises in the laboratory for descriptive anatomy. Bi sometimes went to lectures with him. On one occasion, Brecht and Müllereisert smuggled her into an anatomy class in which an autopsy was being performed.[132] Bi shared something of the life Brecht had been leading in Munich theatre, particularly around Otto Falckenberg's Kammerspiele. Brecht and Bi went out in Schwabing with Valentin, the Feuchtwangers, Elisabeth Bergner, Sybille Binder, Josef Eichheim and Erwin Faber. Normally a great talker, a spellbound Brecht fell silent in Valentin's company. Brecht went with Münsterer to the trial at which Georg Kaiser and his wife were found guilty of theft from a rich benefactor. Kaiser's defence was that his family was hungry. Brecht found that Kaiser 'has been making pretentious speeches and parading like a peacock in the full splendour of his writerdom. Puts forward his entire work as a nervous disease. His wife is marvellous, anxious but calm, treating him like a child. The court amazingly understanding and courteous'.[133] Brecht might have made a similar claim himself. In a short while the opportunity would present itself.

In the autumn of 1920 Brecht's engagement as theatre critic for *Der Volkswille* became an increasingly bitter struggle, in which his powers of denunciation frequently took him way beyond the pale of legitimate criticism of a moribund institution. His review of Goethe's *Torquato Tasso* began with an attack on the proprietor, Carl Häusler, who understood as much about literature 'as a train driver about geography' and 'cobbles together a programme according to the principle: it must cost nothing, it must attract people'.[134] When he called the sentimental *Old Heidelberg* a 'sodding awful play', the theatre withdrew his pass. *Der Volkswille* protested and the mayor intervened, ruling that the reviewer should have his pass restored. In his next review, Brecht observed: 'Despite the touching ministration of the theatre management, which ingeniously chose me a seat so bad that I did not have to see the set, I still saw too much of it'. His review of Gerhart Hauptmann's *Rose Bernd* featured another attack on Häusler, a 'businessman, a former provincial actor, without any intellectual substance', who used the 'stupidity of the public here' as an excuse 'for not fulfilling the most matter-of-fact obligations towards a municipal theatre'. Consequently, the theatre and its audience were wholly unprepared for Hauptmann's 'revolutionary play'. The staff at the theatre wrote to Brecht, rebutting his criticisms, though by now other Augsburg newspapers were also voicing their concerns. Brecht published a reply in *Der Volkswille*, dripping with sarcasm and re-affirming his position. However, Brecht alienated more and more people with his vicious tongue. He dismissed them all as 'dead'. His own isolation increased. As the end of the year approached, he welcomed Dora Mannheim's visit with the words: 'It's good to have someone alive sitting with you if you've got to use all the old and really old ghosts for heating. [...] A lot of things have been broken, even if I'm dwelling quite comfortably amongst the ruins, keeping my body warm with schnapps and curses and reading the paper for intellectual exercise'.[135]

Brecht's bitter struggle with the Augsburg theatre now came to a head with his review of Hebbel's *Judith*. Brecht had left behind his adolescent enthusiasm for Hebbel. The review appeared on 12 January 1921, by chance the day on which *Der Volkswille* was banned for its publication of articles 'endangering the state'. Brecht described *Judith* as 'one of the weakest and most stupid plays in our classical German repertoire. But the same pig who regards Lulu as an insult to women raves about Judith'.[136] He attacked the director, likewise Vera Maria Eberle in the lead role, who was 'diligent and by no means without talent' but who 'lacked [...] the erotic fluidity, the flesh, the obsession and the "pathological element"'. A reader's letter then appeared in *Neue Augsburger Zeitung*, complaining about the 'boorish behaviour' of certain members of the audience, among them the critic of *Der Volkswille*.[137] The critic had laughed repeatedly and disturbed others by leaving his seat after every scene and returning for the next scene several minutes late. The reader suggested that such boors should either be banned from the theatre or shown the door. The council's Theatre Committee proposed that the theatre should withdraw the critic's pass if he repeated his behaviour.

The banning of *Der Volkswille* meant that Brecht had in any case written his final review for the paper. However, things did not end there. It was Vera Maria Eberle who had recently published the article in the *Augsburger Rundschau* which had criticised the figure of Lulu in Wedekind's *Pandora's Box*. She identified herself as the 'pig' in Brecht's review. Supported by her lawyer fiancé, Franz Reisert, Eberle launched a libel action against Brecht. The case was heard in April. Despite a character reference from Feuchtwanger, Brecht was required to pay for the costs of the hearing and for the publication of the court's findings in three Augsburg newspapers. A statement by Eberle's lawyer-fiancé then appeared in the papers on 16 April, giving the assurance of the accused that the words in his review did not relate to Eberle, to whom he apologised. Brecht noted in his diary that this publication prompted 'a great row with Papa, the Eberle woman having published the settlement, which looks disgraceful; I just hadn't paid attention in court, wanting only to win time'.[138]

Brecht's selective perception of reality only made matters worse, as he dug himself into a deeper hole. He published a counter-statement in the same three newspapers on 19 April, in which he stated that he had told Eberle's lawyer that he had no intention of fulfilling the requirement. A counter-counter-statement appeared on 20 April, pointing out that Brecht would have to bear the legal consequences of his action. Brecht was then required to pay 100 marks or spend ten days in prison for his failure to comply with the court's ruling. He was also required to pay 150 marks or to spend fifteen days in prison for libelling Eberle's lawyer. The magistrate was incredulous: 'Does he think he has a puppet theatre in front of him so that he can act as the mood takes him? The settlement was only made with his agreement'. Brecht was spared prison by his father, who made the payment on his behalf. The Eberle affair merely confirmed what many people in Augsburg had long thought: Eugen Brecht was the lost Brecht son.

Brecht in Love 1921

Marianne's toy boy

After alienating his friends and provoking a legal battle which he could not possibly win, Brecht now became entangled in a highly destructive emotional triangle with two figures, Marianne Zoff and Oskar Camillus Recht, every bit as self-obsessed as himself. Over the next year Brecht's life was dominated by his volatile relationship with them. Along with Marianne Zoff's own account and Brecht's letters to her, his diary provides a blow by blow account of one of the most extraordinary periods in Brecht's life. Again, it is as if Brecht was a figure in a Wedekind drama, this time *Earth Spirit*, Brecht playing the young lover Schwarz to Marianne's Lulu and Recht's Schön.

The wannabe diva Marianne Zoff came to Augsburg from Munich in September 1919 following her engagement as a 'special singer' at the Augsburg opera. Their relationship probably started in late 1920 or early 1921, when Brecht's relations with the Augsburg theatre reached their nadir. That may even have spurred Brecht on in his pursuit of Marianne. Critics have generally depicted Marianne Zoff as the diva she aspired to be and as whom Brecht initially saw her, the ideal partner for the brilliant young bohemian dramatist. He admired her 'beautiful, gentle voice' and imagined her playing parts in the plays he was writing.[1] Five years older than Brecht, she was certainly a beautiful woman who knew how to use her physical charms and coquettish manner to attract men. Thanks to her greater maturity, she could not be dominated in the same way as Bi, whom Brecht could always persuade to do his bidding. Brecht found the Jewish Marianne, with her black hair and dark skin, a devastating, exotic beauty. She even looked a little like the famous American diva Geraldine Farrar, whose Carmen was world-renowned. Marianne modelled herself on Farrar and viewed Carmen – the beautiful gypsy girl free with her affections – as her ideal role. Yet she did not remotely possess Farrar's virtuoso talent. After taking acting and singing lessons for her mezzo-soprano voice, she appeared in her first roles in Vienna, including much Mozart and, of course, Carmen. Still in Vienna, she met Oskar Camillus Recht, a businessman and art dealer. He was nine years older. Although Recht was still in his thirties, Brecht would always write of him as if he were an old man. Brecht also characterised Recht as Jewish, using the designation as a term of abuse.[2] Zoff got engaged to Recht in 1915 and lived with him in Munich from 1917. Recht was later an author of detective stories, sometimes under the pseudonym C. Christensen. His business interests included a playing card and book-printing operation at Bad Reichenhall and a Munich publishing house, O. C. Recht Verlag. The publishing house had a serious list in art and literature. The writer Marie Luise Kaschnitz was employed there, as was Hilde Supan. Supan also worked at the Kammerspiele, where Zoff's brother, the novelist and playwright Otto Zoff, was an artistic advisor until in 1920 he became editor of the journal *Wieland*.

Recht lived with Marianne in Augsburg for some months, and then visited her frequently. Neither there nor later in Wiesbaden was Marianne Zoff deemed more than a beginner: she generally occupied minor roles or covered for more established singers.[3] Brecht, however, gushed: 'She acts very beautifully, with calmness and grace, and sings with a slight warble, like a lark'.[4] She was on occasion elevated to bigger roles in Augsburg suited to a mezzo-soprano, including 'trouser' parts playing males, but reviews were, with few exceptions, poor. When she replaced the lead in Bizet's *Carmen*, her performance was criticised severely not only for her acting but also for her singing, which included a serious lapse. Thereafter, her appearances were sporadic. Her Dorabella in Mozart's *Cosí fan tutte* attracted a positive review but another one was more mixed: 'Marianne Zoff endowed Dorabella with the charm of a Rococo figure, without quite being able to overcome in her singing the deficiencies of her training'. Her strength was not in her singing but in her appearance. The reviewer found her acting 'delectable' and could not resist a comment on her breasts.

The failure of her first season prompted her to look for an engagement elsewhere. In September 1920 the Wiesbaden theatre received a recommendation from its resident conductor Carl Schuricht, who had seen her perform in Berlin and described her as a 'musical and thespian thoroughbred', who should be invited to an audition.[5] The artistic director Carl Hagemann wrote after the audition: 'We must keep an eye on this lady. Her voice is not very strong but it's substantial enough'. The next step was to see her perform in Augsburg. The Wiesbaden musical director and pianist Franz Mannstädt formed a favourable impression when he heard her sing Dorabella and she accepted a contract for the 1921–2 season.

During the winter of 1920–1, possessing such a beautiful woman with whom he enjoyed sex as never before became an all-consuming obsession for Brecht. Indulging his usual penchant for pet names, he called her Ma, Mar and Maori Frau. There are various accounts of their first meeting. Marieluse Fleisser writes that Brecht praised her legs more than her voice in a review and when she complained Brecht invited her to meet him.[6] No such review has come to light. Brecht did, however, write: 'She was proud of her legs. / She looked like scorched grass when passionate'. The poem begins:

> On the way from Augsburg to Timbuctoo I saw Marianne Zoff
> Who sang in the opera and looked like a Maori woman
> And was lovely in the grass, also in bed, and looked lovely in her clothes
> And I slept with her too and gave her a child.

As an old lady Marianne Zoff gave her account of their first meeting. Brecht simply came into her dressing room one day and in his thick Swabian accent complimented her on her voice and her performance.[7] She was taken aback by his appearance: he was a little man, as thin as a rake, extremely dishevelled, holding a battered cap in his hand and wearing a shabby leather jacket and scruffy old cord trousers. He sat down and talked non-stop. Part of her wondered why she had not thrown him out at once but another part was fascinated by him: he was like an exotic animal in a zoo. She liked his ascetic skull, he had piercing, dark eyes and slender hands, like a pianist's. His mouth with its slender lips was constantly in motion as he filled her dressing room with smoke from his cheap cigar. After her performance they walked the streets of Augsburg for hours on end until her feet hurt. They then met regularly for walks and he told her everything he knew about the city. It was some time before he made advances but then they got together quickly. She took it upon herself to make sure that the unkempt Brecht was scrubbed clean, which in turn prompted Brecht's poem 'Curtain Lecture' with lines such as 'When do you actually wash your feet?!' and 'You're shaved again as you've never done before / Like a pig with spots!', before it ends: 'And just kiss me again with your tongue!'.[8]

At half past midnight on 13 January 1921, he wrote the poem 'To M.' which begins: 'In that night when you did not come / I could not sleep and walked around outside'.[9] Brecht was love-sick, hooked in a way quite different from his other relationships. Before Marianne, Brecht had been with schoolgirls and students. An opera singer was something else. By now, Brecht's attitude to women was generally what John Willett calls a 'dreadful combination of possessiveness and sense of superiority'.[10] With Marianne Zoff, these attitudes co-exist with a 'totally obsessive physical bond', what in *The Threepenny Opera* he would call 'sexual slavery' [sexuelle Hörigkeit]. Initially, he adopted the conventional attitude of a vulnerable, pining supplicant, subject to romantic self-delusion without parallel in his life. Brecht would remain love-sick for some time but would never succumb to that enfeebled state of mind again. That is not to say that he remained putty in Marianne's hands. The relationship became a highly explosive mix.

In the elderly Marianne's account there is no mention of the other man in her life, Recht, of the combustible triangular relationship or of the money and luxurious presents which Recht showered upon her. She describes Brecht and herself as an impecunious, bohemian couple in love. In addition to the sex, the main ingredients of the remarkable story of Brecht, Recht and Marianne are Marianne's coquettish behaviour towards her two wildly jealous lovers, the constant threat of violence between them and Recht's actual violence towards Marianne as he struggled to control her. Much of Brecht's energy over the coming year was consumed by the illusions which the relationship fostered. Brecht did not register for any university courses in the summer semester 1921 and his matriculation was cancelled later in the year. He went with Marianne to a carnival ball in Schwabing at Steinicke's together with Neher, Müllereisert and the Feuchtwangers. The insanely jealous Brecht was entranced by her beauty. Because of that and because he thought that she might be pregnant with his child, he was prepared to forgive her anything: 'At one point she felt sick, at another she cried because she hasn't had a child, and then she looked marvellous, much should be forgiven her. At the ball she was dressed as a page and was the most beautiful woman there and she handled the men marvellously, all pure and regal and quiet and cheerful and unapproachable yet not proud'.[11]

Back in Augsburg a few days later at the flat of the actors Rudolf and Annie Aicher Brecht encountered Oskar Camillus Recht together with Marianne. Brecht sized up his rival in an encounter of pure theatre: 'I got Recht to act. Richard III. He exhausted all his villainous gestures in no time. I also saw the limits of his temperament. At one point he refused to pick up a knife (I had one too): he's a coward'. Sharing Brecht's bed, Marianne told him all manner of stories about the wretched Recht's wrongdoings, including thefts from her family. He was apparently no less dubious in his business affairs: 'He has been in trouble again somewhere. There was some firm for which he had the right to sign, and he stole money from it, some of it straight out of the till, and now on being threatened with exposure he has threatened to expose the firm for its shady dealings'. Brecht happily noted her claim that Recht disgusted her. But she did not end it with Recht, telling him instead that she did not want to marry before the summer and that in the meantime he had to sleep somewhere else. According to her, Recht agreed to everything – and then went outside and wept. The hard man Brecht noted contemptuously: 'And he loves Machiavelli'. However, in keeping with a pattern that quickly becomes established, she then told Brecht, as he noted: 'After all she let him sleep with her that night, he didn't touch her, and she didn't want to give it to him all at once, he was rather touching'.

Recht took to carrying a swordstick around with him. Brecht's choice of weapon was a revolver. The sheer bizarreness of Brecht's behaviour alienated his friends. Neher looked to reduce his dependence on him: 'I must stop being jealous, that is the first imperative, and put everything into becoming a human being'.[12] However, two days later Neher was drawn back into Brecht's money-making plans in the film industry, working with Brecht on a film script, upon which Brecht pinned his hopes on 'raking up the solid gold'.[13] However, for Brecht, Cas was 'as thick as a plank'. Brecht bitched in his diary about Orge Pfanzelt and Otto Müllereisert, who bitched to Orge about Brecht. Brecht railed:

> Otto, who's unable to get a woman himself (I've spoken to la Reutter and la Günzburger about him) launches a great attack on Marianne, in swinishly crude terms. [...] Orge, the old pedagogue, thinks I've got too many women and feels he's exploited every time one borrows a pin from him. And is jealous of Cas and Otto, in a permanent huff. And the corruption of all those children is to be laid at my door. I'm the politician, the mercenary brute, the shop steward, the reformer.

Brecht, the original genius in the gang, refused to take responsibility for the actions of the others when their behaviour got them into a scrape. Not long after, he wrote that his and Pfanzelt's 'ways have separated'. Brecht had a dream, in which he pushed Otto and others into a car so that he could be alone with Marianne. Otto, unable to bear being alone, made his way to their house and hurled himself down a 'deep dark light-well' to his death. Brecht was 'terribly scared, hugged Marianne and thought "So it has come to this?"'.

Brecht was still making no money. 15,000 marks from the Stuart Webbs film company did not materialise but Brecht stuck to the plan to churn out a few films with roles for Marianne and then quit, well ahead financially so that he could work on *Galgei* and produce 'a few ballads of the old sort, like the Orge songs'. Three of Brecht's film scripts have survived, *The Mystery of the Jamaica Bar*, *The Jewel Eater* and *Three in the Tower*. Brecht passed them to Werner Klette, the Munich critic and agent, but got nowhere. For the first two, he used his favourite genres of detective story and gentleman robber. In the third, *Three in a Tower*, Brecht drew on his life with Zoff and Recht to depict a triangular relationship involving two army officers and a woman. She suffers brutal treatment at the hands of other soldiers.[14]

Brecht was enjoying exhilarating nights of sex with Marianne in his attic, the Kraal, as he'd taken to calling it. On 14 February he wrote:

We spent the whole night together. She has changed. Now there's something childlike about her, something uncertain, small gestures and at moments a breathless little voice. Once I couldn't take her, had to leave her, then she laughed, quite softly and happily, and mocked me. 'That's just what's needed, a good thing that you can't always make it, my stock is going down. That's excellent.'[15]

On the days following he wrote with great pride: '6 p.m. to 9 a.m. Marianne at Kraal'; '10–10 at Kraal'; '7 p.m. to 9 a.m. Marianne at the Kraal'; and 'Ma was here from 8–8 and it's very good. Springtime in the Kraal'. This was a huge physical triumph for Brecht, proof of his masculinity, which he could not demonstrate physically in any other way.

Brecht now needed 'solid gold', not to provide for Frank and Bi but to compete with Recht for Marianne Zoff's affections: 'Marianne [...] goes by car any time she likes. Is prepared to be given fur coats, rings, dresses. For herself. Should one rescue her? I can't pay for her or her things. [...] All that to be chucked down the drain for the sake of a physiological impulse which disappears as soon as it is satisfied!'.[16] In his own estimation, Brecht was merely an 'impertinent, little brat, you can't see my face yet, a certified promise, and what does that bring in?'.[17] But he knew that there was more to his appeal: 'Or is it that I seem all right because I'm always changing? That with me one can have good lighting, theatre, enjoy one's food better, feel music, feel strong, be free to work for something, enjoy esteem, enjoy adventures, do without travels; and on top of that have strength, freshness, novelty, confidence? None of which is certain ....'. Beyond his knowledge of his chameleon-like attractiveness, his other piece of self-knowledge was: 'And I can't get married. I must have elbowroom, be able to spit as I want, to sleep alone, be unscrupulous'. He was sufficiently clear in his self-awareness to act upon this, building his position around it. However, he could not help himself when it came to demonstrating his superiority over Recht by giving Marianne a child.

Brecht's visceral hatred of Recht came out in the apocalyptic, racist language in which he framed his confrontation with him: 'The pogrom is approaching'. This statement of intent followed his reflections upon the place of Jews in history:

One can see where the danger lies: whatever's left over, underdeveloped, undigested, the remnant that one no longer controls. Gradually we clog up with unresolved affairs, half-masticated events. We get poisoned by the unexpected portion. Whatever's been buried sleeps badly. Instead of helping us digest it, the earth spews it out. What the wind failed to dry and the rain to wash away is now growing, and this is poisoning the earth. Corpses are the product of fear. The fear lives on. Why can't the Jews be got out of the way? Because they've been quartered, broken on the wheel, tortured and spat at for the last thousand years. But the spittle gives out before the Jew does. How sad, how devastatingly bitter are those powerful events which we try to resist, liars that we are, by the invention of Tragedy. Every time Reason's mouth has been blocked with earth the stifled outcry has left a gap across the centuries. The cup was refused, and the tragedy never took place (and became necessary).

The tragedy was developing apace. Meanwhile, the story of Brecht, Recht and Marianne continued: 'Marianne's no longer thinking of marrying Recht, she's going to marry me now'. But the toy boy was left hanging around outside her house after attempting to wrest her from Recht:

> Mar and Recht were at the theatre: I went out and met Recht at Maxim. Then he left and went over to the Lamm, asking me to send M. over. When she arrived he was hunching himself into his overcoat. She sat down with Cas and me, he came up: 'You coming? I can't hang about with my coat on'. But she stayed seated. 'I'll come on later'. Exit in a fury. After a bit I asked her to follow him and she said, smiling, but with underlying bitterness, 'Now you're sending me away'. We left together. (I'd suggested we say goodbye before leaving so she could go ahead: she refused.) She then took us along with her to the Lamm, but I didn't want to. (Kept making boobs ...) Subsequently Cas and I followed them and I hung round her house. No light in her window. They must have gone for a long walk. And since she stopped sleeping with him he has carried a swordstick.[18]

Unable to countenance that Marianne was still sleeping with Recht, the love-sick Brecht was struggling, drinking schnapps and taking his revenge on Recht in the savage verses of 'Malchus, the Pig that Fell in Love':

> Here's the story of the goodly pig
> And of his love!
> O, he so wished to be loved
> And got only blows.[19]

During a trip to Munich to meet Klette about *The Mystery of the Jamaica Bar* he even found time to see Bi, who was apparently blissfully unaware of the goings-on in Augsburg. He then encountered Recht and Zoff about to board the Augsburg train. His account of events in his diary is written as if for a film treatment:

> I went up to them, got in, then heard words being bandied: 'Who do you think you are? Is that a way to treat me? I'll slap your face right and left for you. You stay there'. She got in, he tugged her back, she asked would I help her, I helped, saying, 'Stop that. You'd better come along'. He came. She felt sick. Said 'Don't leave me today'. Then he sat beside her with a sinister grin, patting his sword-stick. She raised a smile. I smoked, did my best to restore calm. Suggested she go to the Aichers. We drove there by car. He asked me to keep out. I looked at Marianne and came along too. He was seething. 'So far I've kept my temper. You're not to come along. I won't be responsible for the consequences'. Silent journey. She looked as if she'd been raped. Then Aicher, white as a sheet, eyes popping, trembling, at a loss for words. Recht: 'You go home, don't push me too far. If you want to act as this lady's knight errant you'll have to take the

consequences'. 'I am taking them. What do you intend to do about it?'. Aicher: 'Just go. What am I supposed to do? Just go away'. Recht: 'Come out to the hall'. He shut the door in my face. I pushed him out of the way, fairly sharply. 'Stop that! You're crazy'. I stood in the entrance laughing. Aicher kept begging me to go. Recht shouted agitatedly: 'Keep your nose out of my affairs!'. Marianne said, trembling: 'You go home, I'd like to sleep here, Rudi'. Then on his agreeing: 'You innocent young man'. (She was still play-acting.) I walked off. When I went by later all the staircase windows were lit.[20]

Again, she left her young lover to gaze up at her window from the street. The 'chivalrous' Brecht thought of ways in which he could save her from Recht, even considering that she could go to stay with Hedda Kuhn in Berlin. He really had convinced himself that Marianne did not want Recht's gifts, nor wanted to see him and that she was only doing so because of Recht's threats of violence. When Brecht met her he told her that she should stop accepting Recht's money and call his bluff. In Brecht's view, her mistake was that 'she wants to mollify him, and he knows it'.[21] That was certainly part of her calculation, but only part. Brecht's was that Recht's 'last recourse isn't to his swordstick but to blubbering'. And that, of course, would demonstrate the hard man Brecht's superiority. He had, after all, pushed Recht out of the way! Marianne encouraged Brecht in his belief that he must be prepared to protect her physically, telling him that just the day before Recht had 'started strangling her. He's threatened to murder her again and again'. In his fevered imagination, Brecht concluded that she, too, needed a gun to defend herself: 'If he attacks her she must shoot him down like a mad dog'.

To be a father once more

Brecht began to acquire somewhat greater insight into Marianne's behaviour, but this only prompted him to produce violently abusive comments about her and Recht, along with speculation that 'if the two of them are parted there'll be bloodshed'.[22] Recht was 'this cardboard spewer of monkey's blood, this poor man's Napoleon with the swordstick and self-mutilation'. Marianne was

> the woman, the fetish, who sanctifies his frauds, forgives his murders, lets her mother be abused, sleeps with him, lies to him out of fear, lets herself be strangled, called a whore and kept. He steals, burgles, she asks him for a fur coat even when she's sleeping with me. And at the same time she's childlike enough to want to start a child herself, to weep when it doesn't appear, to kiss me when I look puzzled, to cling to me with a touching impulsiveness.

Brecht claimed that within this emotional maelstrom he was a detached, nonchalant individual: 'I just trot indifferently along, with an unruffled expression, appreciative and irresponsible in bed, deceitful maybe, capable of transcending my own situation, pretty cold'.[23] He was much more bound up emotionally in the deceit than he cared to admit.

In fact, in a moment of insight Brecht recognised what a predicament he was in within the complex struggle that was being played out in his organism between physical weakness and his assertions of strength:

> The organism organises resistance to itself. This is the mirror image of decline, a hair's breadth away from total collapse. There's a galloping reduction of the chances of synthesis, diseases fall on his weakened body, confusing the position. Need for repose, formal cunning, a last remnant of high spirits introducing a risk of extremely subtle devastation into his incredibly high-strung complexities.

There was, however, a simple truth within the emotional complexities and antagonisms of Brecht's relationship with Marianne: Brecht wanted her to have his child. This would bind her to him, not Recht, forcing her to cede her independence to him, while he himself had no intention of ceding his by marrying her. At the same time, he equated the prospect of losing her and his child with death. These were the stakes that Brecht was playing for. It was high-risk stuff.

As usual, Brecht didn't use any protection when they were having sex. And: 'She's missed her period. A child at this point would not be so lovely. And yet I'm pleased at the idea, utter idiot that I am'.[24] When the pregnancy was confirmed, Brecht wrote: 'Now I'm getting a child by black-haired Marianne Zoff of the brown skin who sings in the opera. I kneel on the ground, weep, beat my breast, cross myself a lot of times. The spring wind runs through me as through a paper stomach. I incline myself. A son is going to be born to me. Again'. Once more he savoured the prospect: 'Let them grow, the little Brechts'. However, Brecht of the 'paper stomach' was alarmed for himself. His other women came on the scene again: 'In the evening Bi was at Otto's. We did election speeches in dumb show. [...] Hedda has sent 300 marks for me to go to Berlin with. But what I most long for at present is to learn what I'm to do with Marianne. She is a woman. I've got a woman in Berlin'. It was not at all obvious what he would do with a pregnant Marianne. Berlin was a greater attraction. Marianne was not sure that she wanted anyone's child. She had aborted at least one foetus with Recht. But she made it clear to Brecht that if she did carry a pregnancy through, the child's father must marry her. The net result was, as she put it laconically: 'One way or another, I lost the first child by Brecht'.[25]

First Marianne told Brecht: 'Perhaps I'll go to the doctor because of my job, and I've patched things up with Recht because I'll have to stay with him anyway till June because of the child; told him he's sexually abnormal and will never have anything to offer me'.[26] Proudly, Brecht noted that she'd told him: 'I gave her her first sexual satisfaction'. For Brecht, Marianne looked 'like a Gauguin' and their relationship was 'Tahiti'. He was all the more susceptible to her flattery because he felt himself to be a 'small provisional point, a feeble affair that can't stand much and needs everything to be right for it'. If he recognised that as his physical and psychological condition, he also knew, artistically and selfishly: 'I mustn't let myself get pinned down here by realities. [...] I already have a child who is being brought up among peasants, may it grow fat and wise and not curse me. But now the unborn are competing for me ... To abandon everything gracefully and wander off is all right if there's nothing one wants to do better'.

Marianne announced that she would definitely keep the child – and marry Recht. Brecht knew: 'All I can do is cover paper with writing. [...] I told her "give me three months". She's not giving me them. She's getting a roof over her head with that swine'. Brecht drank alcohol and felt terrible the next morning when Marianne suddenly arrived, fell on him and told him that 'she was through with Recht now, she couldn't go on, she had been picturing how he would be to the child, her child, and she was so appalled she had to throw up and come over'. Brecht convinced himself that he could have his cake and eat it:

> I just can't wait to have children. Timbuctoo is fine, and a child is fine, too; you can have both. It'll be called Peter or Gise, no-one is going to murder her. Right. Then I shall work for Gise as best I can. And that's the best thing for the woman; that swine is no husband for her, and a child is the best thing in the world. I'll help her even if I don't marry her, for I am strictly provisional and need room to take off, I'm still growing.

When Marianne admitted to Recht that she had been with her young lover he became violent: 'He beat her up, dragged her by the hair etc. She had big swellings: was quite confused'. Recht confronted Brecht at Otto Zoff's, making it clear that he would not give up Marianne. Again, Brecht captured the scene like a film treatment:

> Then he started threatening me. I cut him off. 'That's your business. Let's drop it'. He shouted 'Right. Then to put it crudely, I'm supposed to make your bed for you, eh?'. I said, 'No. You're to do nothing at all'. More threats: 'As for what I'm going to do to *you*, that's another matter'. I said, 'Don't let's discuss that. Act'. I said, 'I have my rights. Sit down, I've got something to say to you'. He walked round me, went pale, squinted up at me. Knew what was coming. I said, 'she's going to have a child. She came the night after that scene at the station'. (She had already told him this ...) He flinched, went over to Zoff. 'What do you think of that?'. Zoff remained seated, saying 'All very extraordinary...'. Recht kept on rushing round, gesticulating: 'But it's just not possible. She had her period a week ago. She showed me the bloodstains on her nightdress. We had a quarrel about it'. (He had been unwell, had slept at her flat.)

Brecht maintained a touching faith in what she told him. Sobbing and distressed, Recht appeared to concede defeat: 'It was not granted to me to make this woman happy. It will be your task to do so'. While Recht departed, Marianne lay on the sofa weeping before she went to spend the night with Brecht.

Fresh from his triumph, Brecht told Marianne once more: 'I can't be married'. She again said: 'I can't have the child outside wedlock'. Brecht was critical of her 'mistakes': she took 1,000 marks from Recht, accepted his flowers, thought things over and pledged not to see Brecht for five days. However, happy in the knowledge that the 'child has been saved', Brecht took her to stay for the weekend at Seehof Hotel on Lake Starnberg. Marianne could still not afford to have a child without Recht. She finalised her engagement at the opera in Wiesbaden. Brecht knew as well as she did that her new boss Carl Hagemann would dismiss her if she was pregnant. While Brecht insisted on his own independence, he scoffed cruelly that she was 'hypnotised by her brilliant career like a chicken by a chalk line [...] imagining what it would be like if she visited the doctor'.

Brecht immediately suspected Hagemann as the next sugar daddy. She responded by mocking Brecht: 'You're too young. You go on the swings. You're not someone one can marry'. Brecht still thought he could win: 'I brutally denounced child murder. Little by little she is coming round to the idea of having the child on her own. That's where I want her'. After an afternoon rolling in the grass at the Siebentischwald where 'people could watch us, it really was worth seeing', she let slip some things about Recht:

> On the way back Beelzebub joined us. It emerged that Recht had her once again at the beginning of February, 'a kind of rape', and that at the time she thought for an instant that he might give her a child. Since then she had never been his, but she went on sleeping with him and he still practised perversions on her. That was before her second period, and was 'utterly unimportant'. All the same she was lying that time when she said she had fought him off; in fact, he had been wholly in her and she was disgusted by him.

She might well have thought back in February – and indeed probably also later – that she could be pregnant by either Brecht or Recht.

Never one to miss out on really big complications, Brecht now went about his 'unfinished business with Bi':

> I asked Bi if she would marry me, and she said in three or four years. [...] I told her she didn't love me anymore because nowadays she was always wanting her freedom and not wishing to obey me any longer and I told her all right, I'd let her go. But then she wrote a letter saying she couldn't make the break, she realised that she was not right for me as she was and would like to spend half a year on her own trying to become like she used to be. At that I wrote to her that I loved her and would wait. And she wrote to me that she needed a bit of time and would meanwhile be faithful to me.

Having got that relationship back on track, Brecht went round to Marianne's, 'took her on the sofa and hurried to the station'. But he missed the train and she told him that she'd told Recht that she would marry him if he stopped bothering her, which he had promised to do: 'When I heard this I felt a small thin stiletto pierce my chest'. Brecht left her and went down to the Lech before he went home where he then found her in the Kraal: 'There she was sitting crying and said "Hold me. I can't live without you. Why am I always doing the wrong thing?"'.

The following evening it was Bi's turn for his attentions: 'She was nice, serious and intelligent. I loved her. I kissed her in the bushes. Then I travelled home. (We are going to wait.)'. When Marianne, too, prevaricated, Brecht wrote: 'I'm starting to regard this sort of thing as infantile and told her I won't have it. I laid down what I want'. He had another meeting with Recht, who said that he could not 'lose this woman. He is diabetic, 4.4%, he'll soon be dead, these are his last months, is his corpse then to lie across Marianne's threshold? She is to go off with him somewhere for four weeks. [...] He's clever as only a Jew can be and has the morals of a horse thief'.[27]

Brecht's spies then told him that Bi (together with her sister) had been out in

Augsburg with a musician, the violinist Georg Hupfauer, who paid for drinks and a car. Brecht was beside himself. He now claimed that she was worth more to him than anything. They visited Frank in Kimratshofen. Brecht was entranced by his son. His fears were dispelled that, now nearly two years old, he might look like a peasant: 'The woman brought our little boy. I was profoundly happy. He is slim, with delicate limbs and a fine clear face, curly red hair but smooth in front, he's lively and has big brown eyes. [...] I lent him my hat, then my tie, my watch, ten pfennigs. I shall ask Papa if he can have him to live with him'. And that is what he did:

> I've been on at Father repeatedly about taking in Frank, pointing out the number of empty rooms, just like a hotel, the trees in the garden that nobody climbs, and all that. But he won't bite, and I get depressed, begin to feel ashamed. Marie Röcker's been putting him against it, if only by her expression and her way of coming in whenever I'm talking to Father. I hear all her arguments served up by him. In the old days I always stuck up for her when Mama, Walter and Father too were against her. Now she's dissuading Father from taking in my child because it would be such a nuisance. And Father himself starts saying he's too old and that these women are more than he can cope with and he's no longer all that keen on helping me. Also he's thinking of remarrying and has already started slowly ridding the house of us.

Berthold Brecht obviously wanted something of his life with Marie Röcker. And he surely knew what would be in store for him if he took in the first of the little Brechts that his son seemed bent on introducing to the world as frequently as possible. Brecht concluded with breathtaking unfairness: 'My father invariably abandons me in times of peril'. This of the man who, against his better judgement, had supported his 'lost' son for some years now! Brecht criticised his father who had 'believed a stranger, and wept in front of him and betrayed me'. Berthold Brecht had been talking to Recht. Berthold Brecht declined to visit Frank on the way to Füssen with Brecht and his Aunt Marie, Berthold's sister who was visiting from New York. This prompted Brecht to write: 'One day he won't find it easy to reap what he is now sowing, I reckon. His lack of respect for his own blood makes me begin to lack respect for him. There are signs that the dénouement is approaching. The curtain is about to rise on the fourth Act ...'.

As for the main action in Brecht's soap opera, he knew that he was losing the struggle over the unborn child. Marianne wanted the engagement in Wiesbaden and a roof over her head. Brecht knew that her agent Eugen Frankfurter had told her that the engagement in Wiesbaden would be secure while she was pregnant if she married.[28] However, Brecht's obsessive personality drove him on in his pursuit of his twin goals, the birth of the child and control over its mother, without having to commit to marriage. At this crucial stage in the pregnancy, Marianne again left him for Recht. Defamatory, faecal imagery flowed from Brecht's vicious pen. He imagined her floating away 'festooned with shit and decay so that her face is unrecognisable, it will be a bad summer with her on board'. And he derided her: 'You should be able to rise to the top with *two* children. Why rate yourself so low? Do at least marry a multi-millionaire. But once you're in labour, let me tell you, my hand will mean more to you than all the applause in Wiesbaden'.

Brecht now discovered that, amidst all his own lies and deceit, Bi had been having a life of her own. He was consumed by anger and jealousy: 'Now for retribution and purgatory. Bit by bit I drag a dreadful story out of Bi. She has been corresponding with a café violinist, a slimy fellow, and he kissed her and she visited him and lay in his bed. She never gave herself to him, that's clear from the letters. She's very sorry, but in her view he's an uncorrupted idealist. The days when she's lying are hell'. Brecht couldn't countenance that she had actually slept with Georg Hupfauer. He put his faith in his interpretation of the letters which he had forced out of her. No sooner had he done that than he dreamt about another 'fiancée', Hedda, whom as usual he endowed with grey hair. He was reminded of her when, as he wrote in his diary, 'I found a little lump on my penis which reminded me that she once dreamed I had caught syphilis. Dr. Hirsch at the clinic of course said it was a herpetic blister, nothing special. All the same early in the morning I was worried'. His worries were interrupted when Marianne's sister arrived to tell Brecht that Marianne had

> begun haemorrhaging last night, though she had not yet lost the child. They were unlikely to save it. I was alarmed for her, because it could be her eternal damnation, and I wrote her a line to calm her down. But she didn't want me to come because Recht mightn't like it. Heigei went, we were thinking of an abortion, he suggested E. as a good doctor, she agreed. And on the medicine bottle was written 'Mrs. Recht'. I was appalled at the failure of her theft and that she should abandon my child because her heart was not pure. But I've ceased to love her, am just coldly observing. I have been spending a lot of time with Bi, whose distress has made her thinner so that she has now become childlike and beautiful, and a truth once more: I love and respect her. And I went on the swing-boats with her at the Au fair.[29]

The swing-boats clinched it. Marianne, however, was condemned to 'eternal damnation' because she had killed their unborn child. Brecht met Recht on the street and learnt that

> Marianne had again lost a lot of blood on Saturday and they'd operated on her, also Dr. Wimpfhaimer had been there (who induced her abortion the time before). 'More or less accidentally', said Recht. And I'd not been wanted ... But Recht had spent the whole night by Marianne's bedside. And so the good fairies turned their backs on Marianne Zoff, who started by running around and ended up with a child's little body in the slop-pail. She was not to have a child, the whore; my child went from her because her heart was not pure.

Brecht gave vent to his anger in a vicious diatribe:

> I could strangle that tart. It's the filthiest thing that's ever happened to me. [...] I've never seen the whole swindle of whoredom – romanticism – so nakedly. The pregnant whore unloading. And this is the leaky pot, with every man's discharges trickling into it, that I wanted to install here in my rooms. [...] Pluck her out of me! Out! Out! Now let her be used as a whore, thrown to other men, left for Recht to have.

Brecht slept as if he'd 'committed a murder'. He visited Marianne in her nursing home in Munich and exacted a calculated revenge: 'She wept, I said all I had to say, buttoned up to the neck; she ripped it open, clung to my knees, wept. In two months' time she will come, she wants to be free till then. Cruelly I showed her the photos of Frank, she wept loudly and I pitied her. But then I went away without difficulty, and the days will engulf her'.

These events prompted two savage poems, the 'Ballad of Hannah Cash', who like Marianne does it for money; and 'On the Infanticide Marie Farrar', who shares the name, though only the name, Farrar with Geraldine Farrar, the great Carmen interpreter, upon whom Marianne modelled herself. After failing to abort the foetus, the wretched pauper Marie Farrar murders the boy that she had borne and dies in Meissen prison. The poem acts as a warning to those in a more fortunate position not to abort a foetus. In the opening verse of the 'Ballad of Hannah Cash', Brecht assassinates the dark beauty Marianne's character and talent:

> With her thin cotton shirt and her yellow shawl
> And her eyes twin pools of jet
> And no talent or money, she still had it all
> From her hair like a clear black waterfall
> To her toes that were blacker yet:
>   Yes, that was Hannah Cash, my friend
>   Who made the toffs pay through the nose.
>   With the wind she came and with the wind she went
>   As across the savannahs it blows.[30]

Hannah Cash meets 'Slasher Jack' Kent, recognisably Recht with his swordstick, and they become 'companions for life':

> He may be lame, he may be mad
> He may beat her as he will:
> All that worries Hannah Cash, my lad
> Is – does she love him still?

Brecht's relationship with Marianne, though doomed, still had some way to run. He could never let go.

Struggling for control

Berthold Brecht's unwillingness to accommodate Frank left Brecht 'pregnant with schemes for handing Frank over to Marianne'.[31] She had seen photos of Frank: now she must take him in. Revenge, jealousy and control were now Brecht's guiding principles with her. Marianne visited him, 'swaying, pale as a corpse'. She now understood that Bi was a genuine rival so she told him that she was marrying Recht, while Brecht remained consumed by the struggle for a child with her.

She left Augsburg in May to stay with her family at Bad Reichenhall, where Recht had his interest in the playing-card factory. From there, she intended to go to

Wiesbaden. In a demonstration of his capacity to support her, Brecht came up with 7,000 marks. She claimed that Recht promptly took the money off her.[32] And she wrote to Brecht, suggesting that he should pay her a secret visit. She would bring him his meals every day in his hiding place! Pleading poverty, Brecht protested: 'I'd be put in the linen cupboard'.[33] He suggested that she visit him instead in Munich. They met up in early May when she wept for his 'defunct love' – and returned to Recht.

Not to be with Marianne meant to be with Bi. However, with Bi too, Brecht now saw the limits of his control: 'She lied to me again, went to a café one evening with some clodhopper from Kimratshofen, and I caught her scurrying away unobtrusively, the stupid cow. I told her I had kissed Mar two or three times in the snow in the Siebentischwald one evening; that's as far as I dared go, since she went absolutely white'.[34] Bi, it seemed to Brecht, found out about Marianne now for the first time, however incredible that may sound in a small place like Augsburg.

However, Brecht and Bi continued with their own soap opera, half-believing in the happy ending of marriage. They enjoyed swimming in a lake and he filmed her acting the part of Joan of Arc. They bumped into Münsterer, who wrote: 'We saw each other for scarcely half a minute. You grow so alien to each other after such a long time. Bert mispronounces things, stutters you (in the polite form), turns to Paula. They go off to Otto Müller's, they want me to drop by too, but I don't want to, there's no point'.[35] When they visited Münsterer shortly after all was forgiven: 'Once again, I have seen how much I love him and how remote from the world I am'. Brecht went to the Munich spring fairs with Müllereisert: 'On one occasion Otto hauled me out, filled me with schnapps and dragged me on to a farcical stage where I had to sing the "Sentimental Song". I didn't know it absolutely by heart, and there was a gent by the curtain who kept hissing "Gestures!"; so I broke down and staggered off with a lacerated conscience but with some applause none the less'.[36] And Brecht got together with some of the old Augsburg gang at a Munich inn one night: Münsterer, Neher, Bezold and others. There was chaos and uproar. In fact, their behaviour was so bad that the innkeeper vowed never to give them rooms again.

Brecht still had no luck placing his film scripts and plays so he tried his hand at an advert for cosmetics, while Bi went to Nuremberg in July to take up a job as a governess with a widow, Frau Lessing, and her three children. He caught up with Bi when she went to Utting on holiday with the Lessings, and he spent the first two weeks of August with Marianne in Munich. At one moment, he imagined he could get Marianne to bring up Frank, the next he was writing: 'I must work twice as hard so that I can have him with me'. None of this was remotely realistic, of course, and Brecht now sensed that he was about to lose control of his various women: 'Things are beginning to pile up. [...] There will have to be a final escape, and it will be important not to get the wires crossed'.[37] There were the usual stories and scenes with Marianne, who was with him for a week: 'It started badly, with her saying one night that Recht had tried to rape her; she had been feeble. He had been in her, but she had acted so he couldn't make it. There may have been some untruth in this, but I decided to write it off. We finished up at Possenhofen, where I got a wire from Georg summoning me. It was to do with Bi. By the time I arrived she had gone'. Marianne was about to leave for her engagement in Wiesbaden. The stress Brecht was putting himself under brought on the chorea, which he described as an 'attack of loneliness': 'I'm in my dressing-gown sitting on the sofa with my arms and legs shaking'. He had the consolation that, as Marianne said, she had broken with Recht and would be living off her modest income. However, after she had left he wrote: 'The hunt for her is on once more'. This brought on a wicked headache, which Brecht treated with an anti-inflammatory and a trip to the Plärrer with Münsterer.[38]

He was now stuck in Bavaria while Marianne was off on her own in Wiesbaden. He wanted to know if the 'red-haired gentleman' had appeared on the scene. And he suggested that she should occasionally send him a list of guests from this spa town, marking up the ones who had not fallen in love with her. In a typically contorted Brechtian ploy for control, while he was struggling to keep her apart from Recht, he sought to involve him in a film project with a role for her! This became another trial of strength between the two men, giving rise to yet more accusations of lies and deceit.[39]

Brecht again took his revenge on Marianne in the poem 'Ballad of the Love-Death'. He wrote that it 'signifies a relaxation of my language and a step towards the middle. [...] Cynicism however blasts rocks open'.[40] The verses are a savage parody of Wagner's *Tristan and Isolde*, a pathological take on relations between the sexes in which the male lover murders his 'love':

> Oh, her young pearly body, soft as butter!
> Beaten so raw by wood and love right through
> Dissolves like wood in some old battered cutter
> Beneath a storm. Like grass soggy with dew.

Brecht's struggle with Recht over Marianne, coupled with his own ill health, amounted to a destructive cocktail in his simultaneously morbid and vital view of his life. Unable to free himself from it, he could do no more than cast his own role as a perverse form of heroism: 'The pathological element is the true hero. First on account of its vitality and secondly because it stands out head and shoulders (or possibly a phallus's length) above the crowd'.[41]

Cold Chicago 1921–2

The city, a jungle

'I'm getting so melancholeric', Brecht noted in his diary, pondering the disposition which yielded the troubling extremes of his contrary self.[1] It was much as usual: assertions of vitality alternated with his struggle against morbidity. Brecht's plans for the autumn were to visit Marianne in Wiesbaden and to go on from there to Berlin, the only place to be for any ambitious young playwright. Whilst still in Augsburg, he received more bad news from publishers: 'Already half-rejected by Cassirer, my bundle of manuscripts has now been returned by Kiepenheuer with polite thanks. Very encouraging for me. It's a bad situation. Well, I don't need to make a living out of it. It would be beneath me to strain myself'.

Brecht bolstered his morale by noting several rather self-important statements about literature and drama. The best known – after seeing Georg Kaiser's *From Morn to Midnight* – is: 'I observed that I'm starting to turn classic'. With minor variations, he would repeat this conviction for the rest of his life, to the persistent misunderstanding that it was merely a boast. It was much more: 'People run down the classics for their services to form, and fail to see that it's the form that does the serving. Kaiser and co, with that journalistic (I'd term it) tendency to give every teeny-weeny feeling its own personalised, custom-built, uncompromising formulation only manage to isolate the feeling in question'. For Brecht, form was the vitally important means to channel feelings. A note entitled 'Literature' about how to replace chaotic feelings with clarity and sobriety contains terms which would remain vital points of orientation: 'Simple jocularity. Authenticity. The *spectrum* of feelings: sympathy – indignation. Choice, decision, clarity: *taste*. Buddha. Order without demarcation. Against the fever of sentences. The *chemistry* of the word. Sobriety as the object of art. Inspired everyday life. The ground, materiality, form against chaos, *the soldier against metaphysics!*'.[2] Brecht was writing as much against his own tendency to intensity as against feverish Expressionism. Rimbaud's famous alchemy of the word became his own chemistry of the word. His singular sensibility was rapidly shaping a highly original literary voice. He would attribute his analytical approach to language and form to his 'scientific education', which had led him to the study of medicine. Brecht's knowledge of the human organism, fostered not only by study but also by observation of his own, coloured his vocabulary. The critic Herbert Ihering would immediately identify in

Brecht's stage language a uniquely powerful combination of new forms with an almost palpable bodily materiality. For Brecht, militant opposition to metaphysics was an article of faith. With the term 'sobriety as the object of art', he points the way to *Neue Sachlichkeit*, the New Objectivity of the mid–1920s. With its emphasis on functionality and everyday, mass society, *Neue Sachlichkeit* became the new artistic direction in Germany after Expressionism. It was also a watchword for a measured, progressive attitude to life during those years of relative stability. Typically, by the mid–1920s the restlessly energetic Brecht had identified its limitations.

Among Brecht's musings, two about Berlin stand out. One reads simply: 'Such fear of cold Chicago ... '.[3] That fear sat deeply in his bones. Pitting himself against a city like Berlin was a physical challenge which Brecht knew he might not be equal to but found irresistible. There was an extraordinary symbiosis between the grandeur of his ambition and what Berlin stood for in German life: the capital as a modern, mass city, teeming with opportunities, with a harsh, unforgiving edge and with a dynamism way beyond other German cities, not least in the theatre. Brecht and Berlin would become near-synonymous, defining not just Brecht's own career but also the prevailing image of 1920s Berlin as a site of restless innovation and change, of violence, audacious brinkmanship and unscrupulous dealings. Brecht contributed more than his fair share to that image. In the early 1930s he would also become part of that Berlin which was the principal site in Germany for the class struggle. The SPD and the KPD, together with their associated cultural and paramilitary arms, were major forces in the capital, opposed to the radical right-wing groupings that had come to the fore since 1918. As the 1920s developed, that meant principally Hitler's National Socialist German Workers' Party (NSDAP) and the press magnate Alfred Hugenberg's German National People's Party (DNVP). However, the SPD and the KPD remained bitterly opposed to each other in a way which contributed fatally to the success of the radical Right.

Brecht's musings moved on to the direction that his art must take in the city: 'Wondering what Kipling had done for the nation that "civilised" our world, I made the epoch-making discovery that nobody has yet described the big city as a jungle. Where are its heroes, its colonisers, its victims? The hostility of the big city, its malignant stony consistency, its Babylonian confusion of language – in short its poetry has not yet been created'.[4] Brecht's 'discovery' would indeed prove epoch-making, even though it was not uniquely original. His extraordinary poetic talent would, on the other hand, endow that discovery with a rare originality as he created 'its heroes, its colonisers, its victims' in the forbidding 'jungle' of the modern city, where they struggled with each other and with the city itself. Brecht hatched grand plans for Berlin: an '*Asphalt Jungle* trilogy. Three plays for the Grosses Schauspielhaus: 1. *Mankind in Pursuit of Money*. 2. *Cold Chicago*. 3. *The Forest*. Relevant material: 1. Wu Wei from *Wang-lun*, also *Richard III*. 2. *The Wheel*. 3. The *Malvi* material. Werner Krauss'.

Brecht drew his inspiration for the first play from Shakespeare's villainous king and from Alfred Döblin's *Three Leaps of Wang-lun*. We recall that in Döblin's treatment of the doctrine of Wu Wei 'only one thing helps to counter fate: not resisting'.[5] For *The Forest*, Brecht envisaged the prominent actor Werner Krauss in a re-working of Brecht's *Malvi* draft. Strikingly autobiographical, it is about a man hopelessly in thrall to a high-maintenance lover who dies destitute on Tahiti. For *Cold Chicago*, Brecht was inspired by J. V. Jensen's novel *The Wheel* about the struggle between two immigrants in Chicago. Brecht also knew Upton Sinclair's novel *The Jungle*, again about the struggle of immigrants in Chicago. For Brecht as for others at that time, Chicago and Berlin became interchangeable symbols of the forbidding modern city.

The city as jungle features prominently in numerous drafts with various titles: *The Back of Beyond*, *The Forest*, *Jungle*, *The Antagonists* and *George Garga*. In time, a single play emerged: *In the Jungle*, later *In the Jungle of Cities*. Brecht completed *In the Jungle* in the winter of 1921–2, producing the early dialogue at great speed in Augsburg during walks beneath the chestnut trees by the city moat. A plot outline involving a writer and a businessman shows that Brecht's struggle with Recht was never far away: 'The businessman is an idealist in words, a cynic in actions, the littérateur the reverse'.[6] They pit themselves against each other in a struggle with complex and shifting motivations. He said to Marianne that the play was about 'that black addiction of the brain: winning'. Brecht's initial exhilaration gave way to the lament: 'It's too full of literature'. He had again immersed himself in Verlaine and Rimbaud. The thrill of the urban space would help him recover the excitement: 'One thing is present in *Jungle*: the city. Which has recaptured its wildness, its darkness and its mysteries. Just as *Baal* is a song of the countryside, its swansong. We are on the scent of a mythology here'. How right he was.

Brecht himself was deeply bound up emotionally and psychologically in this lyrical representation of insecure feelings and motivations and had to curb the extraordinary lyrical intensity of his composition:

> There is one common artistic error which I hope I've avoided in *Baal* and *Jungle*, that of trying to carry people away. Instinctively I've kept my distance and ensured that the stage realisation of my (poetical and philosophical) effects remains within bounds. The spectator's 'splendid isolation' is left intact, it is not *sua res quae agitur*, he is not fobbed off with an invitation to feel sympathetically, to fuse with the hero and cut a meaningful and indestructible figure while watching himself in two simultaneous versions. There is a higher type of interest to be got from making comparisons, from whatever is different, amazing, impossible to take in as a whole.[7]

The play was, indeed, well-nigh impossible to take in as a whole. The characters were locked in intense psychological combat in an ingeniously complex, chaotic accumulation of scenes. Like the early *Baal*, *In the Jungle* was scarcely stageable. Brecht would learn to channel his intensity into brilliant stagecraft by developing techniques which became cornerstones of Epic Theatre. He was already embarked on such a path instinctively, fearful of his unfettered emotion.

The play's savage battle is between the Malay Shlink and the French immigrant littérateur Garga. With an eye on leading Berlin actors, Brecht summarised the play:

> The timber dealer Shlink, a Malay (Wegener's type), fights a war of annihilation with the younger George Garga (Granach's type), during the course of which both reveal their most extreme human characteristics. By means of an appearance of passivity the man Shlink slashes through the ties binding young George Garga to

the world round him and makes him fight a desperate war of liberation against
the steadily thickening jungle of Shlink's intrigues against him. Shlink's timber
business and Garga's family are among those annihilated. Increasingly isolated,
more and more tightly entangled, the two go into the woods to fight it out.[8]

In Shlink, the self-made man, Brecht created the great antagonist that his earlier plays
had lacked. He appears to have everything but is suffering from a loss of identity,
his existential angst symbolised by his thick skin which lets nothing through. The
predicament of Garga the littérateur is familiar: to acquire a thick skin to combat
the depredations of modern life means to threaten his artistic sensibility. Locked in
an existential test of wills, each of them struggles to protect his insecure identity, his
'skin', in the face of the other's rapacity. Within the 'steadily thickening jungle', Shlink
seeks the struggle with Garga to combat his own condition, He challenges Garga,
who is employed in a lending library, to, as Shlink puts it, sell him his opinion about
a detective story. For the first time, Brecht here depicts the intellectual in danger
of prostituting himself by selling his thoughts. Shlink knows that Garga would lose
his identity if he sold him his opinion because, as a littérateur, he leads a precarious
existence. Shlink at first has the upper hand but Garga enters Shlink's office with a
revolver and Shlink hands him his business. Now only family duties stand in the way
of Garga's Gauginesque dream of Tahiti. In an act of filial piety, he asks his mother to
go to Tahiti with him! When she refuses he withdraws to Shlink's office, becoming the
businessman he had despised. Shlink usurps Garga's role in his family and the women
are drawn into prostitution. And so it goes on, as they slug it out, each of them at one
moment idealistic, at another utterly mercenary, as carnage is inflicted on the Gargas
in the violent psychological, sexual and economic struggle. Shlink pays the pimp
nicknamed The Baboon twenty pounds to strangle Garga's lover Jane before Shlink
poisons himself. Garga sells the timber business along with his sister and father to the
repulsive Mankyboddle and then sets out for Tahiti.

In the 1923 version Garga, heading south, remains with literature. In his final
words he looks back with regret upon the identity he has lost but with some hope for
the future: 'That was the best time. The chaos is spent. It let me go unblessed. Maybe
work will comfort me. Undoubtedly it is very late. I feel lonely'.[9] In his isolation, Garga
is left rather like Brecht himself, who had 'killed' so many of those around him, as he
struggled with his grief after his mother's death and with the need to destroy everything that he believed was holding him back from literary success. However, Brecht
would discover that the world of the city into which he plunged in pursuit of success
was full of traps, a cold, hostile environment. Astonishingly, he completely excised
the theme of insecure individual psychology from the version of the play published
in 1927 as *In the Jungle of Cities*. In the quarrel with himself about the self and the
world, the great contrarian Brecht would reject the explanatory power of individual
psychology, which failed to take account of truly powerful socio-economic forces. By
1927, the very idea of an individual feeling regret and entertaining hope would sound
ridiculously anachronistic. While he worked on the creation of a protective skin for
himself in the forbidding urban jungle, Brecht eliminated all such sentiment. In 1927,
Garga escapes to the world of new business opportunities in New York and Chicago,

soberly acknowledging his situation in his final words: 'The chaos is spent. That was the best time'.[10]

Decay

The chaos was far from spent. Brecht's neglect of personal hygiene was taking its toll on his frail organism. His mother had warned him that his teeth would rot. Several had to be pulled and replaced with dentures in the autumn of 1921. He celebrated the decay in the self-mocking verses 'Of Bad Teeth':

> I was poor, yet the women were round me like flies
> But since I've had these rotting cavities
> In my mouth, they don't think I'm a chap
> Who can rip his meat up with a savage snap.[11]

He took his mind off the pain by spending time with Georg, Otto and Cas, talking, swimming, playing around and sometimes drinking: 'Shunned by myself, I've seen me fall / An utter victim to alcohol'. He stole from his brother's bottle of schnapps but could not take much. And he could not sustain the self-mockery when confronted with the evidence of his physical decay. In truth, he could not go on much longer as he had been.

He kept up a stream of letters to Marianne but they did not have much to say to each other. Petty jealousies were so much part of their deeply unstable relationship. He dreamt of her body and assured her of his love. She warned him not to drink too much and he warned her off Recht. She begged him to come and be with her, which prompted him to say that the matter was becoming a 'trial of strength'.[12] Her anxieties were well-founded. He was still writing to Hedda Kuhn, who still took herself to be engaged to him. However, the 'Jewess of Berlin', as he had taken to calling her, told him that for the past six months a 'youth' had been courting her: 'But she feels tied; I can't untie her [...] I write her a matter-of-fact letter. Earlier, when in a mess, I had written her a good letter – it was a quiet moment, I was clear-headed – saying "you need good underwear", an act of brutality, a piece of erotic opportunism? There has been no answer. Peccavi'.[13]

Hedda Kuhn really was not his type. Her boyfriend was Ernst Wollheim, a young doctor. She wrote to Brecht again, divulging more: 'If you're coming to Berlin to see me shall I get you a room? As your wife? If so I have been breaking my marriage vows for the past few months'. She had merely been doing as Brecht did and was trying just one last time to secure a commitment from him. His position was: 'I should give her her freedom. It's the only way I can now help her. – I find all the talk depressing, and the evidence of cowardice; but am content with the solution. Have asked her to get me a room'.

Brecht again drank beer, even though he knew that it was not good for him: 'I was rather restless, my hands actually shook, I could only write with reluctance yet didn't want to go to bed'. In the cold light of day Brecht acknowledged the correctness of friends' criticisms: 'True enough, where those related to me are concerned I can be cold and cynical. I drag a lot of things in the dirt, and I make a great many demands. Now and then however I have simply grown sad, not angry or contemptuous or vindictive'. Even the Plärrer lost its magic: 'How boring it all is. What lavatory-tile faces! What voices, like domestic animals! The sideshows add to the romanticism; the people, dumb, sinful and patient, lets itself be titillated. One can't live for ever'. In 'March', Brecht depicts life as an 'alcoholic fog', the final lines betraying his anxiety at his fragility:

> As the sky begins to lower
> To my ravaged heart I cling
> Tenderly. Then I blow over
> Like a snowstorm in the spring.

Brecht embarked on his travels in a precarious physical state. First he went to Nuremberg to see Bi, then travelled overnight to Marianne in Wiesbaden:

> I boarded the train and hunched there eating, sleeping, cursing, dreaming, smoking and boozing for ten hours. By the time we were nearing Höchst I was in a sweat; it's occupied territory there, and I had my revolver with me. In Frankfurt I bought a cigarette box, but the post office was shut and the train had no ornate WC to hide it in. However, no check. At Marianne's I felt immediately at home.[14]

Brecht was, of course, anxious that he might meet Recht with his swordstick. Wiesbaden under French occupation spawned further depressed musings about the humiliation of Germany, which was generating a nationalist backlash: 'This is a tarts' town. Powder, flesh, sensation. Slick pavements, dead straight trees. Chemise-y faces. Frenchmen with nigger bands, dogs, cocottes. Brightly lit cafes, amazing prices, unpleasant looking people'. Like many compatriots, he was full of resentment. He stayed in Wiesbaden for two weeks, witnessing a performance by Marianne amidst poor productions. To make matters worse, Recht arrived and gave her a fur jacket. Helpless, Brecht accepted her claim that she would be giving Recht the money back.

Charlie Chaplin's *The Face on the Bar-Room Floor* was the highlight of the stay. Brecht found it 'the most profoundly moving thing I've ever seen in the cinema: [...] Children and grown-ups laugh at the poor man, and he knows it: this nonstop laughter in the auditorium is an integral part of the film, which is itself deadly earnest and of a quite alarming objectivity and sadness. The film owes (part of) its effectiveness to the brutality of its audience'. In the chemistry between script, actor and audience Chaplin achieved a blend of the comic and the deadly serious that Brecht deeply admired.

The humiliation of Germany was now compounded by the inflation. The devaluation of the mark had left it worth less than one third of a cent. There was worse to come, as hyperinflation rendered financial assets worthless. Through this economic equivalent of an earthquake, the defeated nation wiped out its internal debt but in the process impoverished millions, most notably those conscientious savers who formed the bedrock of middle-class society and who now paid for the folly of the wartime elites. The middle class was ruined. Brecht joined in the chorus of protest, decrying the pernicious effects of the financial markets, according to the workings of which the virtual economy was allowed to suck the marrow out of the real: 'The idiotic and destructive significance of printed paper, one's utter abandonment to infinitesimal differences of calculation, payment, luck, the way a strong, complex and costly organism can be demolished by some barely measurable change in the atmosphere, a trick of the wind, sacrificed without either sacrificer or god'.[15] The economy was as fragile as his own body.

Unsurprisingly, the critique of money was very much in the air at the time. As we have seen, the KPD's Eugen Leviné, the leader of the Bavarian Soviet Republic, had planned to abolish paper money. What all this was about would greatly pre-occupy Brecht, like many others, in the years to come. From the mid–1920s, he would begin to seek out answers from various experts, among them left-wing intellectuals like Karl Korsch and Fritz Sternberg who engaged with Karl Marx's legacy for the contemporary world. Like these figures, Brecht came to adopt ideas around labour theory of value, advocating a system based on the value of production, as opposed to anarchic financial speculation, in which the printing of paper money uncoupled from gold reserves played such a key role. Then as now, such speculation threatened to bring about what Marx had predicted: the self-destruction of capitalism.

Taking up the struggle with Berlin

Brecht took the night train to Berlin on 7–8 November and 'started drinking again, smoked, scarcely slept, staggered out in the rain into the chilly morning with my two suitcases'.[16] His room was on the ground floor of Zietenstrasse 6, 'dark, cold, frightening'. Hedda Kuhn seemed 'pretty sure of herself, alien, remote' and declined Brecht's invitations to meet up with him alone. This prompted him to write that she was 'altogether second-rate'. He saw her with Ernst Wollheim: 'A strong young man with a thick head, rather a brutal face, slow, tough, bourgeois. I've nothing against him. He stood half behind her, half thrusting against her, his hand in his trouser pocket, snorting through his nostrils'. Brecht clearly had just one problem with Wollheim: his existence. Kuhn recalled that Brecht 'could not tolerate another man alongside a woman whom he admired. In Berlin he demanded that I pledge not to marry another man'.[17]

There was a letter waiting from Bi. She was pregnant again. She had, of course, not known that he was stopping off at Marianne's: 'It was a good letter, full of composure and love, without a single murmur of complaint; reading it I loved her very much and was inordinately frightened'.[18] She assured him that everything was all right: 'She has been able to manage on her own. I breathed once more; reverently I read Otto's letter, which I shall always be grateful for, strong, simple, sure'. Müllereisert fixed the abortion. This time, there was no outpouring of bile because a woman had got rid of Brecht's child. Pregnancy was not a necessary element in his control of Bi. Nor was there any question of him going back to Bavaria to be with her. He could take her and leave her.

Recht's manœuvres to regain Marianne were a constant worry. Brecht was also plagued by the fear that she might fall into bed with her new boss Hagemann: 'I don't like the idea of you going to Hagemann's, please decline his invitations. Don't drag it out, rather put an end to it. Tell him clearly: I don't want to and I will stop you falling in love. Or tell him that from me if necessary'.[19] Shortly after: 'I'm glad that you seem to be doing the right thing with Hagemann, you can't give him an inch. Don't allow yourself to be taken in by his tricks'. And Brecht played the big man: 'It's completely out of the question that I would let you go back to Wiesbaden'. As he gained confidence in Berlin – 'my reputation is growing marvellously here' – he dismissed his rival: 'We *laugh* at fellows like Hagemann, my dear. Their sort are legion'. He recommended that Marianne, like Bi, should spend her evenings reading literature, Döblin and Dostoyevsky, and that she should practise being alone, just like him! Fearing Marianne's adeptness at securing film roles via the casting couch, he warned her: 'It's a disgusting business'. His advice was to extricate herself from her engagement in Wiesbaden without putting herself legally in the wrong. He still aimed to make her permanently dependent on him, caring for his children. However, he put it like this: 'We should, I believe, keep an engagement for next year in view. Chase up Frankfurter and maybe travel to Frankfurt yourself. A contract is good, you can always break it'. Quite.

Brecht impressed upon Marianne that in any case Berlin would soon be his. This time he had a calling card: 'Bargan Gives Up', his homoerotic story of brutal, desperate pirates, a 'ship's log of dying men', whose leader Bargan is hopelessly in love with the accursed, arch-cynic Croze.[20] The story had appeared in the September issue of the Munich magazine *Der Neue Merkur*. The editor Efraim Frisch paid Brecht a welcome 300 marks and published 'Of Swimming in Lakes and Rivers' in the December issue, too. People in the know in Berlin took *Der Neue Merkur* and knew the grim message of 'Bargan Gives Up': that whatever people were motivated to do, good or evil, they would fail.

Brecht tried to place a film with Karl Heinz Jarosy and met Kiepenheuer's editor Hermann Kasack. Brecht took in lots of films and theatre: Chaplin's *The Cure* and Leopold Jessner's *Othello* at the Staatstheater. The Social Democrat Jessner's fresh, pared-back interpretations of the classics, beginning with a *William Tell* dedicated to the new Weimar Republic, were hugely controversial with traditional theatre-goers. However, Jessner left Brecht underwhelmed, as did works by contemporary artists on show at the Secession, whom he derided, knowingly, as 'these undernourished specialists in hunger: debilitated figures on the Cross, typical little foetus shapes, "pure spirit", alcohol kept strictly for pickling. [...] This kind of literature results from the blockade. Shortage of raw material all round. No enterprise. Verbal diarrhoea'.[21] He himself, of course, created characters like his pirates, desperate to squeeze every last bit of pleasure out of life. The Secessionists could not see beyond the victim status of their depictions. They presented them bound up in their wretched situation and mired in emotion: 'When does one's body get delivered up to sensation? When it's ill. They abandon themselves to emotion. And yet visions aren't at all the same thing or non-sense-impressions, nor is this cult of sterile idols comparable with the morphia of the word. The healer's art is a cynical one. Dying people are cynics if they have it in them'. With his specialist knowledge of near-death and recovery, Brecht was determined to show he had it in him.

Änne Maenz's bar on Augsburger Strasse was a focal point for the undernourished: young actors, directors, writers and students. Frau Maenz took care of them, feeding them without ration cards. The bar was naturally very popular, attracting figures new to the capital like Brecht and the philosopher Ernst Bloch. Bloch recalled his first meeting with Brecht at Änne Maenz's. Bloch was sitting with a group of film directors, among them Ernst Lubitsch, when his eyes alighted on a young man, shabbily dressed, pale, with lots of stubble and wearing metal-rimmed glasses of the cheapest sort.[22] He was sitting with a beer. One of the group told Bloch: 'The guy sitting there is, I think, called Brecht. He's just moved to Berlin'. Bloch had just read 'Bargan Gives Up' and was mightily impressed by a particular sentence describing how a riverbed which Bargan and his band were following suddenly filled with water: 'The water rose with the solemnity of a phenomenon that understands its business'. Bloch claimed to recognise in Brecht's narrative, saturated with Berlin and Munich street slang, the language of Hegelian phenomenology. Bloch went to sit by Brecht, ordered a beer, raised his glass and said: 'The water rose with the solemnity of a phenomenon that understands its business. Prost!'. Brecht looked up in surprise, turned red and said: "Bargan Gives Up'. We won't give up like that, will we? Bertolt Brecht'.

Brecht's record of his weeks that winter in Berlin shows how close he came to having to give up as he strove to make his mark. One day after lunch, he met with his fellow poet and performer Klabund at the Romanisches Cafe, together with a 'young Hebrew who told me to be at E. Reiss's tomorrow at 12 to discuss an overall contract'.[23] Brecht drank brandy with Klabund before they went to a show, then to Warschauer's for supper. However, the newcomer Brecht felt that he was not receiving the attention he deserved – and badly needed: 'I smoked in the next room or in the lavatory and soon slipped away: I'm still en route for the sun'. At Änne Maenz's he met the actor Alexander Granach, who introduced him to the director Heinz Goldberg from the Tribüne theatre. They arranged some readings. However, 'Half frozen, half feverish, I walked home with a full head, an empty heart, utterly discontented'.

For Marianne, Brecht maintained an optimistic front: 'I'm starting to build the foundations, you'll not have much more to put up with, my dear'.[24] He told Bi that he had the choice of a contract with Reiss or Kiepenheuer.[25] However, Brecht was putting his body through stresses and strains which it simply could not stand. Never far below the surface, Brecht's medical problems burst into the open. He wrote to Marianne: 'I'm on a tram. I spewed up before off the platform, it was snowing in my face; I'm not very well'.[26] On 9 December he wrote in his diary of the ravages of his heart: 'It's always bursting out: the anarchy in the breast, the spasm. Revulsion and despair. It's the coldness you find in your heart. You may laugh and mock at it, but it is present in the laughter and it feeds the mockery'.[27] It fed the coldness and cynicism in the Brechtian sensibility of the 1920s, attracting him, too, to such *bons mots* as Julius Meier-Graefe's characterisation of Delacroix: 'Here was a warm heart beating in a cold person'. Brecht commented presciently: 'And when you come down to it that's a possible recipe for greatness'.

Brecht's suffering is everywhere in his writing. One poem ends with the words: 'A heart is in there, which will soon decay'.[28] Another one about Biti, a pet name for himself, contains the line: 'Biti knows that there are seventy illnesses for a man', followed by: 'Biti knows that there are more illnesses than one can know'. Yet another ends: 'With women's love, calves' tongues / And many a red variety / We did truly not succeed / In shielding the heart from the snow'. He soldiered on, meeting Max Reinhardt and attending rehearsals of Strindberg's *The Dream Play* at the Deutsches Theater. After he had taken tea with Gustav Kiepenheuer, Kiepenheuer and Reiss produced draft contracts, while Walter Feilchenfeldt invited him for talks with Cassirer. However, he over-reached himself once more with drink and women at a wild party where he sang and played guitar:

> One evening a whole lot of us were in a studio. I rapidly got drunk, filled up with brandy, red wine, liqueurs, floated up to the ceiling, couldn't recall a single song. Klabund sang at the piano, soldiers' and whores' songs, danced, worked hard to fend off the women, who were crazy about him, including the one with the black fur trimmings. None of them caused my mouth to water. Esther, the Rose of Sharon, ritually but with a light foot bore her Assyrian head through that smoke-filled dive; a Malay girl danced with me like a whore, we collapsed on the coal box, then she sang French Chansons in a deep smoker's contralto situated around the level of the tip of her heart, music-hall songs accompanied with the bottom; after which H.E. Jacob and I did the dance of the two (cushioned) hunchbacks. At one point Klabund was sitting there in silence listening to me like somebody who has put his coat on, got no itinerary, no money, no use for either, but just listens: here are the first crude barbaric songs of the new age, an age forged in iron. [...] Jacob, that plump-cheeked rubber ball, that trombone-blowing church angel, that squelchy plum jam tart, parodied my rolled Rs and kept telling me: 'They *will* say Becht, it should be Brrrecht, same way as it should be guitarrr and Jarcob'. He had swilled one of his moist eyes in a glass of red wine: there was a red drop dangling from his nose. Around four I was still there in that lurching playbox playing the guitar and singing.[29]

Brecht dragged himself to another rehearsal of *The Dream Play* but then paid the price for the carousing:

> I traipsed home exhausted. Ate and drank and went to bed at 7.30. But they woke me up at 10, and I felt such a pain in me, like a watery jellyfish between the ribs, that I got up. There's no air in this city, you can't live in this place. It had tied a knot in my throat, I got up, fled to a restaurant, fled from the restaurant, tramped around in the icy moonlit night, crawled back here, don't feel like writing, must get back to bed, can't sleep.

He was right back with the heart palpitations and breathlessness of adolescence. Terrifying storms were assailing him from without and within: 'Back to those apoca-lyptic ghostly storms, brushing the roofs with their warm wetness, the influenza weather that poisons one; you lay your eggs in the stove and smoke yourself to death. First thing in the morning you get a heart spasm, then begin prancing around as if made of glass, find you can't work because your room is icy cold'.

Sex would help him overcome his morbid anxiety: 'Tonight Marianne will be here, a barbaric pleasure, then everything will improve and acquire a meaning'. He imagined her arriving and singing her favourite Mahler songs for him. He was all militant aggression in his thoughts of overriding his chronic weakness by drinking schnapps and singing chorales. And then there was Wedekind, whom he described as a great writer for moral improvement: 'him, plus a revolver, plus taste rather than conscience: it's better than getting confirmed. [...] I've a bit of a headache on the left side. Who's that with the headache?'. Who was the angst-ridden weakling, who the great writer-adventurer in the city? However much he willed himself to be the latter, he could still not escape the accursed fate of the former.

Then Brecht's father visited: 'We sat facing one another over a table in a pub, two people who belonged together, a vague relationship but one that says a lot where our sort are concerned. He took a kind of solicitous interest in me, gave me 1,000 marks, talked about his business, never asked how I was getting along with Marianne, told me there'd be ham and duck for Xmas, they'll send me some'. Brecht had the satisfaction that he was making the progress which his father doubted he would ever see. He signed a contract for *Baal* with Erich Reiss on 21 December 1921, giving Reiss the option to publish all his other plays written between 1 January 1920 and 31 December 1924.[30] The contract gave him monthly payments of 750 marks for ballads, stories and *Garga*, with the proviso that if the publisher declined to publish a play which had been accepted for performance the author could turn to another publisher. Hence Brecht felt justified in signing another contract with Kiepenheuer, who would in the event publish *Baal* in 1922. Brecht took pleasure in telling Marianne all about his sharp negotiating skills:

> Reiss offered 750 marks, Kiepenheuer 800. Both want stage rights too. I've already signed up with Reiss, but took the contract back in order to show it to Kasack. I had also to talk to Drei Masken. It seemed a good idea to ask them for 1,000 a month for a year. I also pushed Kiepenheuer up to 1,000. On top of that I got Kiepenheuer to leave Drei Masken the stage rights for my next plays. Drei Masken wavered, offered 500. I hadn't brought my *Garga* with me, as I didn't want to let them have it. But stuck out for the 1,000. Finally they agreed after I had talked them into a stupor.[31]

Supreme confidence in himself as the greatest German dramatist of the age drove Brecht on with escalating demands in an unrelenting verbal assault. After years of frustration, he transformed his finances at a stroke. Acting according to the logic of the market, he extracted as much credit as he could. His burgeoning reputation among the cognoscenti meant, he continued, that Kiepenheuer and Drei Masken, who had earlier rejected his work, were falling over themselves to offer him the best terms. Kiepenheuer agreed to publish *Baal*, *Garga* and a collection of Brecht's ballads. None of these projects would prove straightforward. The ballads would appear only in 1927, *Garga*, as *In the Jungle of Cities*, in the same year.

Among the many social gatherings in Berlin, there was a party at Otto Zarek's parents' villa. Brecht was not the only newcomer there. The young Viennese dramatist Arnolt Bronnen was decked out with his trade-mark monocle and took great care to conceal the war wound in his throat which, however, left him unable to control the pitch of his voice. Bronnen felt that no-one took the slightest bit of notice of him: 'For someone was singing. That someone had put down his little damp cigar, had cradled his guitar in his lap, pressed it against his sunken stomach, and had begun to intone in a rasping, consonantal voice'.[32] Bronnen was swooning like a schoolboy in love: in this 'little, unprepossessing man the heart of this age is beating'. He continued:

> A twenty-four-year-old man, lean and dry, a bristly wan face with piercing button-eyes, an unruly bush of short dark hair with a double crown sprouting obstinate tufts of straggly hair. The second whirl of hair twisted forwards over his narrow forehead so that wisps fell down across his brow. A pair of cheap wire spectacles dangled loosely from his remarkably delicate ears and hung across his narrow pointed nose. His mouth was peculiarly fine, and seemed to hold the dreams which others hold in their eyes.

Much to Bronnen's delight, Brecht was soon spelling his name Bertolt like Arnolt. For Bronnen, Brecht became the 'Animal Tamer', after the role which Wedekind himself played in his *Earth Spirit*, while for Brecht, Bronnen was the 'Black Panther'. Like so many of Brecht's other friends, Bronnen was glad just to have a piece of this genius, however badly he was treated by him. He knew that he was only one of Brecht's many friends, while for Bronnen, Brecht was his only friend. Bronnen captured the essence of their relationship – and not only theirs – in his observation that as a speaker Brecht was always very close, but when spoken to he remained very distant. The homoeroticism of *Baal* and 'Bargan Gives Up' did the rest for Bronnen.

As ruthlessly ambitious young dramatists they had essentially the same attitude: to reject absolutely everything that had gone before in the theatre and to promote themselves indefatigably as the voices of the new age. Unlike Bronnen, Brecht had a very clear idea of how to go about exposing the established, 'culinary' theatre. In his view, it merely pandered to a degenerate bourgeois taste by sating the audience's appetite. Brecht and Bronnen took to attending as many rehearsals as possible, spotting the errors of others and unmasking their inadequacies. They took in afternoon performances on small stages. George Bernhard Shaw was on everywhere, Kaiser and Wedekind were popular, too. Bronnen neglected his day job as a sales clerk at the up-market store Wertheim. Brecht, however, over-estimated Bronnen's capacity to formulate the pithy, sarcastic comments which he himself could produce at will. As so often, Brecht drew on medical vocabulary, this time anaesthesia, to describe how the senses were assailed and thought negated at rehearsals for Strindberg's *Dream Play*:

> Went to the final rehearsal of *The Dream Play* and at last put my finger on the basic flaws that had been tormenting me, only I was numbed by the slickness of the scenes. It isn't a dream. Ought to be crooked, twisted, gnarled, horrible, a nightmare with something delicious about it, a divinity's nightmare. And proves to be something for the right-minded, not a curve in it.[33]

Brecht worked very hard at the rehearsals, honing his dramatic awareness by studying the practice of others, while Bronnen was ecstatic that he could study Brecht.

Marianne had the dubious pleasure of seeing Brecht and Bronnen together when she arrived in Berlin. She managed to prise Brecht away from Bronnen over Christmas when they stayed with the Warschauers, whose hospitality was 'positively Asiatic'. Brecht and Marianne even had their own Christmas tree. Warschauer gave Brecht

Wedekind's *Songs for the Lute*.[34] Marianne gave Brecht Dostoyevsky's *The Idiot*, a tie, a haversack and socks, while he gave her a Turkish cigarette holder, an iron chain, a handwritten ballad and his old favourite, a copy of Claudel's *The Exchange*. Facing the momentous decision to sacrifice her career to be with Brecht, Marianne was not at all enamoured with this last 'present'. Brecht claimed, wholly disingenuously: 'I bought you *The Exchange* without any ulterior motive. I read the play a year ago and was thinking only of its beauty, nothing else. What sort of fiendish intention have you gone and read into it?'.[35] For her part, Marianne let him know what avenues were open to her – and what she was therefore prepared to sacrifice for him:

> Marianne keeps saying how in spite of all she liked Recht after she had left me, that he was tremendously in love. This may be because I'm not getting down to work. She's been going to bars with Hagemann (and others, a married couple), he tried to kiss her in the car, she's written him a fan letter about some production or other. She's had a letter addressed to 'Marianne', a New Year invitation, a party of four, i.e. two couples. She must answer if he is not to make other arrangements. And then (simultaneously) an official letter saying her engagement probably won't be renewed.[36]

Brecht and Marianne spent New Year's Eve with the Warschauers at Reinhardt's last production for the Grosses Schauspielhaus, Offenbach's *Orpheus in the Underworld*. Trusting that her future lay with Brecht, Marianne went back to Wiesbaden to wind things up.

To the Charité

In the New Year Brecht 'plunged back into cold Chicago'.[37] He replied to a letter from Marianne, in which she had set out her 'mistakes', by giving her a dressing-down and warning her to be faithful to him, her 'husband'. He had signed up for a six-day stint for 500 marks to sing 'soldiers' ballads' at Trude Hesterberg's Wilde Bühne. Brecht took to the stage with his guitar and when he struck up 'Apfelböck' and 'Ballad of the Dead Soldier' a riot broke out. Hesterberg had to bring down the curtain. Walter Mehring went on stage and told the audience what a disgrace they were. One day, he said, they would boast that they had been there to hear Brecht sing.

Cold Chicago was proving too much for Brecht. He had been up all hours, eating very little and drinking pretty much anything he was given, even though he knew alcohol would harm his fragile constitution:

> Have suddenly begun pissing blood. I tried to go on living it up, went to the 'Blauer Vogel' with Klabund, Hedda, Bronnen: but thereafter started getting unmistakeable messages from my vital parts. Spent two days by myself lying in my chilly bed, then Hedda and Bronnen turned up. On Monday Frank [Warschauer] took me to the Charité where Hedda had fixed it all with Wollheim. Meanwhile I rang Marianne, who had handed in her notice at Wiesbaden and arrived right away.[38]

Brecht had called Hedda Kuhn in a state of extreme exhaustion. She found him 'seriously ill' in bed and alerted Ernst Wollheim, who admitted Brecht to the Charité on 23 January. Highly suspicious of Brecht's manipulative ways, Wollheim would only admit him after Kuhn had pledged not to visit him on her own.

Brecht was diagnosed with pyelonephritis, inflammation of the renal pelvis, and was kept in hospital for three weeks. In severe cases it can lead to urosepsis, a poisoning of the blood which can spread to the entire body and cause severe complications, at times leading to death. Before treatment with antibiotics was available, people like Brecht without strong natural defences were very prone to the recurrence of the complaint and to complications. Together with his chronic heart failure and Sydenham's chorea, this exacerbation of his renal complaint dogged Brecht all his life. In its milder form, it produces flu-like symptoms, which Brecht would experience periodically, describing them as the flu. In the middle decades of his life, his principal complaint became the renal problem, the cardiac and choric issues settling somewhat, though susceptible to flare up if the renal problem became acute. During the final year of his life Brecht would suffer repeatedly from his renal complaint and its escalating complications.

Brecht was well aware of his propensity to inflammation of various kinds, describing himself later as a 'powder keg, better approached with something cold rather than something warm'.[39] After Brecht's death, Feuchtwanger recalled in a letter to Arnold Zweig: 'He had kidney problems as long as I knew him, and his lifestyle prevented him from keeping to the diet which his doctors had prescribed for him at the start of the 1920s. He could also never have stood for living as quietly and carefully as they had recommended very early on'.[40] In the years to come, Brecht would make major efforts to adjust to a highly regulated diet and lifestyle. His awareness of the biophysical constraints upon his life would inform his thinking and behaviour in a manner which has not yet been appreciated. At the same time, his restless energy would never allow him to settle: he remained Neher's Hydratopyranthropos, the Water-Fire-Man, a bundle of 'melancholeric' contradictions.

From his hospital bed, the former medical student 'cast the occasional very cool glance at the shadowy little vulture overhead, the possibility of TB'.[41] His fevers and breathing difficulties prompted fears of that deadly disease. Those fears were accompanied by others surrounding sexually transmitted infections, which, as he certainly knew, might have had a bearing on his inflamed renal pelvis. While in hospital, Brecht – true to his father's way – never spoke to his visitors about his pain and suffering. Instead, he dealt with them in his verse. Among Brecht's notes from the Charité are verses and prose poetry published as 'Epistles'. The first begins: 'Maybe I came too late. For sure I'll depart too soon. [...] All is fleeting, it won't last long'.[42] This becomes one of Brecht's most insistent refrains, which he broadens from the intensely personal into his view of the transience of modern civilisation. The second epistle begins by echoing the diary entry of 9 December 1921 about his cardiac condition before switching to ironic hyperbole:

> Sick, anarchy in the breast, without the capacity to hate, held prisoner in a musty room, at the same time I put up with being touched by dirty hands. I'm lying there

with dirty underclothes, all they do is sprinkle us with incense, the revolver under the bed only makes me cold! Oh, the athletes who put up with the indifference of the world! Oh, the security of the familiar faces from the Apocalypse, what innocence, how jealous I must be of them! How we despise me, I who am a haze of brandy in my clothes, the lonely dung beetle, the scrounger full of contempt for people!

Like the athletes, Brecht is embarked on an anonymous act of endurance and, like the faces from the Apocalypse, he is thoroughly conversant with death. The imagery of self-loathing in the 'dung beetle, the scrounger' locates the young Brecht once more in striking proximity to the nightmare imaginings of Kafka.[43] Much of Brecht's writing about life in the modern city bears the imprint of events around his stay at the Charité. 'On the Correct Enjoyment of Spirits' describes the impact of alcohol. The heart and the chorea feature, not the kidney problem: 'When I drink the world dies grinning / [...] I like to read the paper, till my hands / Begin to tremble ... / [...] I feel my red heart.'[44] Brecht was in an abject physical state, laid low by Cold Chicago.

Bronnen was at his bedside every day. The state of the ward reminded Bronnen, like Brecht, of the war:

Huge dormitories packed with suffering wretches, foul air, tatty clothing, torn nightshirts and unshaven faces. In one corner Brecht was lying, chuckling away to himself, cocksure and confident: he looked a happy man indeed. Marianne was sitting with him; she had brought him manuscripts, literature and notebooks. A young auxiliary doctor was squatting by his bed. He was so fascinated by his patient that he was at his beck and call at all the hours of the day and night. And so it was that Bronnen was robbed of any opportunity to offer him comfort; instead he was comforted himself. Brecht contended that there was nothing more instructive for a young dramatist than to lie in a big hospital ward – better still: amongst the very poorly. He recommended to his visitor that he take his place in the neighbouring bed; he would not want for an illness.[45]

The prospect was deeply attractive to Bronnen.

Marianne had arrived in Berlin at the end of January and the triangle Brecht-Zoff-Bronnen was formed. She later acknowledged: 'I was jealous of Bronnen. Brecht and Bronnen were very well attuned to each other – and that disturbed me.'[46] On her third day in Berlin matters got much worse when Marianne found Bi's letters in Brecht's room, among them Bi's plea: 'Bert, I don't know where this comes from but I'm always afraid that you're deceiving me. Please write to me.'[46] Marianne took to her bed at Warschauer's with what Brecht took to be a lung complaint. She had poisoned herself. He begged her to stay with him: 'I know that I've not been good, I've lied too and destroyed my face, but I beg you, dear Marianne, to stay with me. I'll act against my laziness and weakness, I've lied a lot too, but you're the only one I love.'[47] When she clearly wanted to end it, it was: 'Dearest, dearest, dearest Marianne, that's crazy, I'll go and look for you, I can't be without you, *dear* Marianne'. She fled Berlin without telling him that she was going to her parents in Pichling, Upper Austria. When he discovered her whereabouts, he could not pursue her because he had no passport. So he stayed in Berlin with Bronnen. At this of all times, he gave Bi, as he had Marianne, Claudel's *The Exchange*. She said she 'liked [it] very much'.⁴⁸ There was a lot that Bi, like Claudel's Marthe, did not understand.

Marianne could hardly bring herself to answer Brecht's letters. They were full of his protestations of love and of his promises not to lie again. He even claimed, wholly implausibly: 'I don't want to have my elbows free'.⁴⁹ When she told him that she was considering an engagement in Vienna, he could only see that as her choosing Recht: 'You're my wife and I beg you not to do anything without me, just as I do nothing of consequence without you'. He asked her to consider the long recovery period that she needed after her illness and that 'neither of us will grow very old'. She would long outlive him. He had been very shaken by his illness, confiding to her that he felt 'weakened by the kidney affair'. His health remained poor. He wrote that he couldn't sleep and was losing more weight in what we know to be a familiar scenario of lack of appetite relating to his kidneys.

Directorial disaster

Even after such a short stay in Berlin, the charismatic Brecht knew everybody, among them stars whom hopefuls like Bronnen could only admire from afar. Brecht was discussing parts in his plays with the most prominent actors, Eugen Klöpfer, Werner Krauss, Paul Wegener and Heinrich George. He knew the most important dramatic advisors, people like Reinhardt's Felix Holländer and Jessner's Heinz Lipmann, as well as critics such as Ludwig Berger and Heinrich Eduard Jacob. All the staff at the publishers Cassirer, Reiss and Kiepenheuer were Brecht fans. No party was complete without him singing his ballads. At Kiepenheuer's carnival party he played the guitar, sang the 'Ballad of the Dead Soldier' and met Oda Weitbrecht, the daughter of a Hamburg bookseller who was on Kiepenheuer's editorial staff.

At this time Brecht also got to know a man who would have a decisive say in his career. As usual without tickets, he and Bronnen wormed their way into Paul Gurk's *Persephone* at the Neues Volkstheater.⁵⁰ Gurk had won the coveted Kleist Prize in 1921. In the interval, Herbert Ihering, the influential young theatre critic of the *Berliner Börsen-Courier*, nodded at Bronnen as he walked past. Brecht insisted that he meet Ihering at once. Bronnen ridiculed the choice of Gurk for the Kleist Prize, prompting Ihering's reply: 'Things will be different this year, I'm awarding the Kleist Prize'. Pointing at Brecht, Bronnen said: 'This is the guy you've got to give it to'.

After the performance they bumped into a crowd of young people. Among them was Moritz Seeler, who was launching the experimental Junge Bühne, a competitor of the Neues Volkstheater with unpaid actors and directors. Seeler announced to Bronnen that he wanted to open with Bronnen's *Parricide*. Convinced that his gruesome tale of murder and incest could never be performed, Bronnen was speechless. Brecht intervened: 'Let him have the play, Arnolt. Just one condition: I'll direct'. It was a done deal. It didn't matter that Seeler had already engaged the three actors – until Brecht got to work.

The list of established names was impressive. Heinrich George was among them. As Bronnen writes, in his mind Brecht could immediately transform the text of a play into a prompt book. However, he did so in keeping with an obsessive vision born of a singular sensibility, which the actors had never encountered. All their training and experience had taught them the importance of carrying an audience with them in a spectacle of emotional identification. That was the measure of success. Brecht lacked any directorial experience which might have enabled him to explain his intentions at the outset. At this stage, they were based on intuitions which he had scarcely begun to articulate beyond the diary entry about not trying to carry the audience away 'with an invitation to feel sympathetically, to fuse with the hero'.[51] In the light of what happened at the Junge Bühne, it's not difficult to see why he felt such a need to enlarge upon these words repeatedly in the years to come. However, where clarification was intended Brecht often succeeded only in compounding confusion.

Preparations began promisingly enough. Brecht told Marianne that he had helped Bronnen to talk through Agnes Straub's part with her and 'she noted everything at once and she implored (implored) me to direct. I was the first (1) person to say such things to her and to get down to things straight away with the actor'.[52] Hans Heinrich von Twardowski and George had the other parts. However, it was not all plain sailing: 'Monday the first stage rehearsal, yesterday and today discussions for hours on end, reading rehearsals, conflicts'. Things rapidly went downhill: 'I'm in a serious conflict with lots of people, a whole gang'. Brecht finally announced: 'After breathtaking rows with Straub I have given up as director! I have fallen out with everybody. They can …'.

In Bronnen's account, Brecht had no time for Straub and Twardowski, while George, a legend in Berlin theatre with his huge stage presence, was not suited to the role of the petty-bourgeois father. Delighting in his control and with typical tenacity and contrariness, the tiny Brecht sought to impose a decidedly understated manner upon the Gargantuan George – and reduced Straub to tears. She and Twardowski meekly accepted Brecht's 'sadistic whipping', but the rows between Brecht and George intensified with each rehearsal.[53] Finally, George shouted down the director, pulled his prompt book out of his Teutonic loden coat, swung it around his head a few times like a tomahawk and hurled it into the auditorium. George stormed out of the theatre, while Straub broke down in a crying fit and had to be helped off stage. Brecht announced: 'The rehearsal will now continue'. Only Twardowski was left on stage, staring blankly ahead, incapable of listening or speaking. Brecht seized the moment. Clearing his throat, he closed his prompt book with a bang, switched off the rehearsal light and said 'Good day!'. He found Bronnen in a state of distress in the back row of the stalls. For Bronnen, in the half light of the theatre Brecht's eyes had a Satanic glow, signalling something approaching a triumph. Brecht said to Bronnen: 'Let me congratulate you. There was nothing to be done with them'.

Seeler engaged Bronnen's fellow Viennese Berthold Viertel, who used his contacts with Felix Holländer at the Deutsches Theater to stage *Parricide*. Starring Alexander Granach and Elisabeth Bergner, it was a spectacular success, catapulting Bronnen to fame. Productions followed in Berlin, Frankfurt and Munich. And news of Brecht's debacle spread like wildfire. He had been trying to persuade Holländer to let him direct at the Deutsches Theater or at the Kammerspiele, but Holländer would not touch him with a barge pole. In time, Brecht's singular vision would, of course, prove to be a huge asset, marking him out as a uniquely talented director. For the moment, what was seen simply as self-obsessed brinkmanship was judged to be extremely dangerous. He had to learn to explain himself and needed people like Feuchtwanger to guide him rather than Bronnen.

Berlin had proved a watershed experience for Brecht. He had tested the limits of his physical endurance and come up alarmingly short. This was surely the 'personal experience' to which Brecht was referring when he talked to Walter Benjamin in 1934 in Danish exile about the 'fear of the inexorable and never-ending growth of big cities', 'the nightmare force with which this idea weighs on mankind'.[54] While the dramatist and poet Brecht extrapolated a general truth about the destructive force of city life in the modern world, which Heiner Müller identified as the seminal Brecht experience, the writer-adventurer's attempt to conquer Berlin had brought him face to face – once more – with his own mortality. This severe jolt forced him to reflect fundamentally upon his approach to life during a protracted period of self-exami-nation and adjustment, which, it must be said, he could never properly complete. As Feuchtwanger observed to Zweig, Brecht was too much a creature of habit. If the assertion of rugged, egotistical individualism led only to further pain and misery, how could Brecht best protect himself whilst not abandoning the risk-taking mentality with which his artistic creativity was so bound up? He had been busy shedding the trappings of his old mythology and the Circle which had supported it, and he had begun to forge a new mythology of the self in the city. However, he had rapidly learned that the city was a very dangerous place.

Brecht began to develop a new 'skin', a fresh 'face', in contrast to the egotistical Baal-like adventurer of Gargantuan appetites. By the end of the decade, that 'face' would begin to resemble that of Herr Keuner, Brecht's creation of the decidedly sceptical, ascetic producer of wisdom who advocated revolutionary change. But that was some way off. For the time being, amidst his capacity to create chaos for everyone wherever he went, while he almost invariably got his own way, Brecht was deeply concerned to protect his body and conserve his energy in order to concentrate as much of it as possible upon his twin obsessions which could be pursued from a reclining position: writing and sex. And he sought tirelessly for ways to overcome the enigmatic and debilitating condition of his body. The search for a solution to his condition would become bound up with the search for ways to overcome the malady besetting Cold Chicago.

The Theatrical Genius 1922–4

The animal tamer loses control

Travelling by train from Berlin to see Marianne in Pichling on 26 April 1922, Brecht wrote the mock confessional 'I, Bertold Brecht'. The verses became famous as 'Of Poor B.B.'. In this brilliant, contrary self-projection, Brecht asserted:

> In the asphalt city I'm at home. From the very start
> Provided with every last sacrament:
> With newspapers. And tobacco. And brandy
> To the end mistrustful, lazy and content.[1]

However, he acknowledged:

> In the grey light before morning the pine trees piss
> And their vermin, the birds, raise their twitter and cheep.
> At that hour in the city I drain my glass, then throw
> The cigar butt away and worriedly go to sleep.

The first version contains lines that Brecht later removed, one of them recalling his hospitalisation for his kidney complaint: 'But I lie there and still feel a stone in my back'. In addition to his 'watery jellyfish' of a heart, the pain of kidney stones would plague Brecht with such 'resolutely physical' reminders of his mortality.[2]

With his health poor and his ego severely bruised, in Pichling Brecht enjoyed the Zoffs' home comforts, writing to his father: 'It's in the middle of the countryside, everything is green, I'm helping a bit with the potatoes, I'm getting brown, eating Bohemian cooking and getting healthier by the hour'.[3] Putting things circumspectly in the light of his strained relations with his father, Brecht asked him if he could pick up a case from the station, explaining his intention to go on to Munich from Augsburg 'if you have no objection'. After the Berlin directorial disaster, withdrawal to Munich made sense. Brecht came to the real point of his letter, which was to ask his father for more money since in the inflation everything was 'so dear, it's all preposterous, everything would be hugely expensive here too if I wasn't a guest'.

For all his problems, in Pichling and elsewhere, Brecht maintained an astonishing literary productivity, asking the now famous Bronnen for progress reports on his Berlin projects and demonstrating that he still dictated the terms of their relationship: 'What about the two films for Kyser? *Garga* and *Parricide*? And what about your latest trip with Stefan Grossmann?'.[4] Brecht and Bronnen had visited Grossmann, a jury member in a competition for the best film exposé run by the director and producer Richard Oswald, who offered the winner a rapidly depreciating 200,000 marks. Grossmann had assured them that he could fix the first prize for them. Brecht and Bronnen submitted their exposé, *Robinson Crusoe on Assuncion*, later changing the title to *The Second Flood*. Brecht was full of his overbearing brinkmanship when he asked Bronnen to make the human events a little more complicated as he typed up their submission and to make it clear to Ihering that when it came to the Kleist Prize, Bronnen himself was 'not satisfied with half the prize. In any case you must tell him that I *definitely* am not, we must each get the *whole* prize successively'. Bronnen duly complied, telling Ihering that Brecht deserved the Kleist Prize more than he did!

Brecht steered his correspondence with Kiepenheuer towards Oda Weitbrecht, his friend from the carnival party, then steered her towards the idea of visiting him in Augsburg. And, fresh from signing a general contract with Rowohlt, Bronnen was expected in Munich for his latest premiere. Suddenly, Brecht withdrew invitations to Weitbrecht and Bronnen to stay with him at Bleichstrasse. He told Weitbrecht: 'I can no longer invite you to live in my father's house since I have completely fallen out with this gentleman'.[5] Weitbrecht delayed her trip but Bronnen could not. In Bronnen's account, Marianne would not let Brecht go from Munich to Augsburg because she feared a female rival might be waiting there for him. As Bronnen knew well enough, in her eyes there were male as well as female rivals. Brecht, who in Bronnen's eyes had lost some of his cocky self-assuredness, wrote to him from Munich:

> I only rolled up here yesterday. I arrived, unannounced, in the middle of the night and saw that machine guns were set up. There's an irritating tone here and I shan't be able to eat and drink here calmly for long. At the moment I'm still engaged in studying the problem of how you could feel comfortable here between two lines of fire. It's fairly humiliating for me, but we'll have to consider where else we can meet. And, by God, I've really been looking forward to seeing you.[6]

Marianne was thoroughly displeased at the prospect of hosting the Animal Tamer and the Black Panther in her flat. Nor did Brecht's father relent. To cap it all, Bi announced that she had got engaged. At once Brecht went to Nuremberg and refused to budge for five days until, with his relentless tirades, he had faced down the challenge from Bi's fiancé. He then went on his way.

The Brecht-Bronnen circus moved on to Munich. Gossip columnists there and in Berlin could not get enough of the Animal Tamer and the Black Panther. Johannes R. Becher was part of their Munich world, as was the novelist Arnold Zweig. The young dramatist Marieluise Fleisser appeared on the scene and fell desperately in love with Brecht. Brecht put Bronnen up with Cas Neher in his tiny room on Türkenstrasse, where, in Bronnen's words, Neher 'was living in the blooming of his sins'.[7] A fresh triangle emerged with Tiger Cas. Flush with success, Bronnen was insufferable. Brecht could now not stomach this 'damned arrogant fellow [...] with an income and big words and a monocle: fully kitted out from a department store – the successful author (*with* monocle 80 marks dearer)'.[8] Not only that, the highly-charged jealousy between Tiger Cas and the Black Panther exploded one evening at Feuchtwanger's when the host stepped in to prevent a drunken Neher clubbing Bronnen over the head with a champagne bottle.

The Jewish Feuchtwanger had dire words of warning for his young friends. He explained that if he had not stopped Neher, he would have soon found himself locked up. Every evening, groups of youths shouted anti-Semitic slogans outside his house and threw sand and stones. Feuchtwanger feared that he and his wife would soon have to leave Munich. He regarded deliberately shocking plays like *Parricide* as an incitement to such behaviour. Brecht sided with Bronnen, viewing self-censorship as capitulation. However, the following day, 24 June 1922, in Berlin a group of right-wing thugs, among them the writer Ernst von Salomon, gunned down the Jewish German Foreign Minister Walter Rathenau. The road to anti-Semitic violence was open. Bronnen himself would join the extreme Right.

Brecht, like Bronnen, was bent upon provocative theatrical innovation. However, publishers were growing wary. There were major setbacks with Kiepenheuer. Inflation was eating into the economic substance of the business so the publisher had to cut production plans. The print-run for *Baal* was reduced from 2,000 to just 800 copies, for the ballads from 2,000 to 1,500, and for *In the Jungle* from 2,000 to 1,500. However, Brecht learned that *Drums in the Night* was to premiere at Munich's Kammerspiele and that, thanks to his friends Erich Engel and Jacob Geis, he could sign a contract for the production of *In the Jungle* at Munich's Residenz-Theater.

With theatrical success beckoning, Brecht was relishing the prospect of seeing Oda Weitbrecht. He teased her that she should not work too hard: nothing was more damaging to the complexion – except chastity.[9] He promised her a kiss and warned her not to be drawn into alcohol and loose living, before repeating his invitation to visit a 'horizontal man in the second storey of a house on Bleichstrasse'. He added: 'I can see your face well, I can talk to you, sometimes you laugh and I take off your glasses'. Brecht could certainly focus sharply upon the face of a woman he desired. The fading memory of someone loved, as in 'Remembering Marie A.', was the corollary. Sexual desire sharpened the focus. The fading memory is all about male desire sated.

A diary entry reveals the male lover's obsessive self-absorption as he looks at his own face in the mirror while eating cherries:

> Those self-contained black bullets disappearing down my throat made it look looser, more lascivious and contradictory than ever. It contains many elements of brutality, calm, slackness, boldness and cowardice, but as elements only, and it is more changeable and characterless than a landscape beneath scurrying clouds. That's why so many people find it impossible to retain ('you've too many of them' says Hedda).[10]

The face, which with its tic had been the mortifying symbol of the nervous boy's wretched weakness, had been transformed into a front of peerless strength, manifest in bewilderingly changeable characteristics, which defied reduction to a single character. Brecht had long since learnt to play on the fact that he could show countless, contradictory faces and that he could rely on the fact that, 'characterless', he could keep all and sundry guessing. In thrall to him, his various sexual partners were exposed to the plethora of 'faces' and associated attitudes, which Brecht switched with such baffling speed as his various intimate relationships lurched from one crisis to another. He protected a vulnerable self by publicly performing a variety of invulnerable selves, displacing emotional involvement through aesthetic self-representation.

Near the end of the summer, Oda Weitbrecht finally made it to Augsburg, but things still did not work out as planned. While she was there, evidently not staying at Bleichstrasse, Brecht sent her a letter: 'This morning I got a letter saying that my child's ill, so I've got to go to the Allgäu. I don't know how long I'll be detained there. It's not pleasant. Maybe you can write me a few lines telling me what you'll do? I've not got a good head today. Forgive me'.[11] In fact, Brecht did not go to see the sick Frank in Kimratshofen. Instead, he prevailed upon Marianne to do so and persuaded her to take Frank back to Munich with her. This left him free to meet Oda Weitbrecht after all. However, Marianne found out. He wrote her a confession of sorts, pleading sickness: 'I know I did wrong. I was very glad that you fetched Frank and that you like him and that he felt that at once. I'm kissing you and kissed you the whole night when you were in Kimratshofen. But I'm ill. Please forgive me, I can't speak well, I easily get in a tangle and a leaf from a tree can knock me over'. The tangle, which Brecht found simply irresistible, had once again proved too much. Taking refuge in physical fragility and psychological instability, he sought to absolve himself of responsibility. He wrote to Marianne again, offering the same excuses and apologising for the hurtful things he had said to her:

> I've got a headache and I'm a little sad that on Friday I didn't control myself. I probably spouted a lot of nonsense at you, but I don't know any more. I'm so glad that you're with Frank and that Frank is with *you*. I'm just not calm because I insulted you. But I love you very much and say that to you every evening. Do you hear me? When I've got some money I'll come for a day or two.

He had evidently made matters much worse with a vitriolic outburst aimed at the woman who was looking after his sick son. He downplayed his loss of self-control, suggesting that she could surely not have taken his 'hysteria' seriously. However, the emotional damage had again been done. It was not just that he had got her exactly where he wanted her, tied to his child while he was elsewhere getting on with his writing and his affairs. Marianne was once again pregnant with his child, whom this time he took to calling 'Peter and Hanne'. However, Marianne was not prepared to keep Frank indefinitely. He stayed with Brecht's father for a while. And Marianne made it abundantly clear that Brecht must marry her if she was to have his child. She used the threat of Recht to get her way. In her memoir Marianne was quite candid: 'The marriage was not important to him. He did not want to marry. The child and I induced him to do so'.[12] It could not last.

Premiere!

Amidst the emotional carnage strewn around Augsburg, Munich, Kimratshofen and Nuremberg, on 29 August 1922 rehearsals began for *Drums in the Night* at Munich's Kammerspiele. Neher was involved in the set design, Otto Falckenberg himself was directing. Brecht could not resist intervening and there were scenes. In fact, as Münsterer recalls, he 'intervened to such an extent that there were several severe disagreements. Falckenberg often got into a temper; half an hour, even a whole hour, might pass in anxious waiting before someone managed to talk him round and calm him down'.[13] Brecht invited a delighted Münsterer to join him in his team. In fact, Münsterer *was* Brecht's team: 'Brecht would constantly solicit suggestions and new ideas – once we had to correct a medical impossibility in the text'. What Falckenberg thought of Münsterer's interventions as fledgling Team Brecht leaves little to the imagination.

Karl Valentin was at the premiere on 29 September, together with the usual Munich and Augsburg crowds, the Feuchtwangers, Geis, Müllereisert and Pfanzelt. Bi and Marianne were both there. Marianne was pregnant by Brecht but the play was dedicated to 'Bie Banholzer 1918' and her pregnancy of November of that year, when the play is set. Bi had returned home from Nuremberg because her father was seriously ill. She attended the premiere with her mother, Brecht's father, Marie Röcker and Walter: 'Brecht was very nervous and infected us at once with his nervousness. Sometimes he shook his head without any reason or made erratic hand movements'.[14] The abiding effects of Sydenham's chorea made themselves felt as Brecht waited nervously for his show to start. Münsterer writes of the premiere:

> The theatre was packed; we were on tenterhooks and running terribly late. Brecht whispered excitedly that the Berlin critics were all there and that, most significantly, Ihering had arrived. [...] At last, with the audience growing restless, the gong rang out three times, the curtains parted – and the catastrophe took its course. Everything that had been meticulously worked out during the rehearsals and had been perfect only that afternoon at the dress rehearsal went horribly awry.[15]

The third act, the best in rehearsals, was a disaster. Nevertheless, thanks to the elemental power of its language, the like of which had not been heard on the German stage for years, *Drums in the Night* was a great success. Herbert Ihering's review in the *Berliner Börsen-Courier* captured this landmark moment for the German stage:

> Anyone who could feel in the air that we must now break out of that barren stagnation, anyone who had already been inspired by Bronnen's creative surge and explosive temperament, must surely be overwhelmed by the sheer transformation which a genius can effect with his very first act. The twenty-four-year-old poet Bert Brecht has, overnight, changed the face of German literature. Bert Brecht has brought to our age a new voice, a new sound, and a new vision.[16]

Ihering set the tone for other critics like Walter Benjamin and Karl Kraus, who would hail Brecht as the voice of a new, post-war consciousness. For Kraus, Brecht was quite simply 'the only German writer worth considering today'.[17] Brecht was Ihering's greatest discovery. Ihering wrote that the 'unparalleled creative force' of Brecht's language conveyed his vision with a 'physical sense of chaos and decay'. Brecht's was a language that 'you can feel on your tongue, in your gums, your ear, your spinal column'. The thin-skinned, sickly Brecht had succeeded in projecting his own physical and existential situation outwards, conveying with a rare linguistic power a general truth about the condition of a sickly Germany, crippled by the war and its aftermath. His peerless artistic strength was intimately linked to his physical weakness. Many of Brecht's fellow Germans were captivated by his vision; many others were utterly repelled by it. It was a recipe for theatrical fame – and notoriety. Ihering's review thrust Brecht into the spotlight as the new icon of the German theatre. The Kleist Prize was in the bag, and with that came the prospect of lots more premieres, publications and publicity. Greatness beckoned. With Ihering's endorsement, it did not matter so much that Germany's leading critic, Alfred Kerr, was at best lukewarm about Brecht's play and his talent. Brecht now had little time for him either. He had after all sent Kerr *Baal* but had received no encouragement whatsoever.

The control which Brecht gradually developed over his material, tempering his intense affective responses with a deliberate, cool intelligence, would make him the prime representative of the 1920s avant-garde, a position which he seized with alacrity and capitalised upon with astonishing skill. Brecht possessed a rare blend of artistic and business acumen, and he had a ravenous eye for publicity. The author of 'Storm', his poem from 1913, knew that it was down to him to seize the pre-eminent position in the German theatre. He noted that he should ask Ihering to arrange for the history of German theatrical successes to be written: 'literature as power'.[18] Brecht appended three exclamation marks. He craved the social power which theatrical success could grant him.

The Munich showdown

Brecht's family and Bi had been expecting him to return to Augsburg with them to celebrate his triumph. However, he made off into the night to celebrate at the Hotel Wolf with his Munich and Berlin cronies. Deeply upset, Bi went back to Augsburg with her mother and Brecht's family. Her father died the following evening. Hearing the news of Karl Banholzer's death, Brecht returned to Augsburg to comfort her. He helped with the preparations for the funeral, composing the death notice. Bi's mother later objected that the notice had been too austere and that people would think that her marriage had been a bad one. Brecht's selection of the site for the grave met with her disapproval, too. She had the grave moved! Brecht had that sort of effect on some people.

Bi had taken an office job in Augsburg. Like millions of others, the Banholzers had lost the value of their savings in the inflation. One morning an unusually agitated Brecht rang her at work, imploring her not to speak to a gentleman who would shortly be calling. The gentleman in question was Oskar Camillus Recht. What Recht had to tell Bi's mother when he turned up at her house confirmed her worst suspicions. She implored Bi to meet Recht. When Bi declined, Recht appeared at her office and introduced himself as Marianne's fiancé. He explained that his bride-to-be was expecting Brecht's child. When Bi had got over the shock, she accompanied Recht to Munich where they met Marianne. The two women tracked Brecht down at the Kammerspiele and invited him to join them at a nearby cafe. The somewhat older Marianne could stand up to him better than Bi, but they could still not get a rise out of him. When Marianne asked him whom he intended to marry, he replied 'rather cynically and utterly amused: "Both of you"'.[19] Brecht would give his gangster Macheath the same line in *The Threepenny Opera*.

Borrowing Brecht's favourite tactic, Marianne engaged in a lengthy diatribe, not letting him get a word in edgeways. With a final flourish, she announced that she was finished with him and left the cafe. Brecht took this as his cue to reach out to Bi but she declined his advance and followed Marianne. The women spent the evening with Recht. Just as Marianne had predicted, Brecht appeared in the corridor as Bi's train left Pasing. He signalled Bi to leave her compartment and join him. She steadfastly ignored him but Brecht would not relent. At Augsburg station he took her by the hand and, despite her protestations, marched her to a cafe. When his avowals of love left her unmoved he changed tack, complaining of his sufferings with Marianne, who was forcing him to marry her, even though he loved only Bi and could only live with her. When Brecht proposed that they marry in the very near future, the infinitely malleable Bi could only say yes.

Consumed by the fear that Marianne might have an abortion Brecht appealed to her to come back: 'I've got to talk to you and will come as often as you wish, until I've talked to you. I've been saying lots of crazy things, just as I was crazy. I've no sense of obligation, I *must* see you'.[20] He followed with: 'I'm crazy, aren't you too? I'll come tomorrow or the day after. I'll definitely come. How's Hannepeter? I saw a child with a sailor suit on, with a woman. That looked good'. Imploring her to 'hang in there', he asked: 'Do you think I'd ever give up Hannepeter? Just be good, dear Marianne! You promised you would not do anything until we'd spoken. [...] You don't have to see me if you don't want to'.

Brecht reflected upon what he'd done with Bi and Marianne, fearing a lengthy punishment for his sinful behaviour. He had 'enjoyed their hearts', he wrote, equating 'enjoyed' with 'conquered'.[21] Switching to the third person as he so frequently did in self-reflection, he acknowledged his betrayal of them as something very real: he had not done the right thing, had behaved in a self-deluding fashion and had betrayed himself.

Capitalising, erratically

Brecht fled to Berlin, where he had serious business. In a piece on *Drums in the Night*, *Baal* and *In the Jungle* in the Berlin magazine *Das Tage-Buch*, Feuchtwanger had proclaimed Brecht Germany's leading young dramatist. Newspapers and magazines began regular publication of his poems and stories. *Das Tage-Buch* announced that Brecht and Bronnen's film treatment was one of four submissions selected to share the prize money in the competition. Brecht and Bronnen received 50,000 marks between them, the equivalent of $729.29 on the day.[22] *The Second Flood* was filmed the following year. And finally *Baal* appeared with Kiepenheuer. On 14 October the *Berliner Börsen-Courier* announced that Brecht had reached agreement with Felix Holländer for the Deutsches Theater to perform *Drums in the Night, Baal* and *In the Jungle*. It was then announced that Brecht had accepted a role as principal artistic advisor and director at the Munich Kammerspiele. Finally, on 15 November in Berlin Brecht received 10,000 marks for the Kleist Prize.

At the Kammerspiele Brecht would begin work with the director Erich Engel, forming another partnership that would last all his life. Brecht had the highest regard for Engel, later describing him to Elisabeth Hauptmann as the prototype of an 'urbane, shrewd director' who combined artistic responsibility with scientific precision in work that paved the way for Epic Theatre.[23] Before Brecht had begun to develop what he meant by this concept, Engel was, like Brecht, promoting intellectual sharpness and reflection in the theatre, as opposed to the prevalence of mood and feeling. Engel and Brecht were made for each other. Brecht later praised the quasi-Epic qualities of Engel's *Coriolanus*: 'He presented the story of Coriolanus in such a way that each scene was self-contained, and only its outcome was used for the whole. In contrast to dramatic theatre, where everything rushes towards a catastrophe and so almost every-thing functions as an introduction, here the totality was present, immobile, in each scene'.[24] When Max Reinhardt engaged Engel at the Deutsches Theater, Engel made it a condition that Brecht, together with Carl Zuckmayer, be offered a contract as a dramatic advisor. This paved the way for Brecht's permanent move to Berlin.

The general public now needed to know more about this exceptional dramatic talent. Brecht sent Ihering a potted biography, shot through with a trademark sardonic irony:

> I first saw the light of the world in 1898. My parents hail from the Black Forest. Elementary school bored me for four years. In the nine years of my pickling at the Augsburg Realgymnasium I made no great contribution to my teachers' advancement. They never wearied of pointing out my penchant for idleness and independence. At the university I read medicine and learned to play the guitar. At secondary school I went in for all kinds of sport and developed a heart condition, which familiarised me with the secrets of metaphysics. During the war, I served as an orderly in a military hospital. After that I wrote a few plays, and in the spring of this year I was taken to the Charité hospital because of undernourishment. Arnolt Bronnen was unable to help me substantially out of his earnings as a sales clerk. After twenty-four years in the light of the world I have grown rather thin.[25]

Brecht was a very thin man, indeed, something of a Kafkaesque hunger artist. Worldly wise, Brecht advised Ihering: 'I am sure that the present Brecht boom, no less than the slump that will follow, is the result of a misunderstanding'. Like all art, Brecht's was and has remained pleasurably subject to multiple misunderstandings.

Back from Berlin, with the usual macho bravado of his letters to Bronnen, Brecht played up the mock-heroics of their dissolute life: 'Those were the days when syphilis swept / Through the cities, apes lost their hair, became a friendly race. / We smoked, read papers, drank brandy, shat, slept / Shut out the heavens and grew commonplace'. However, to Marianne Brecht again offered his state of mind as the excuse for his 'flight' to Berlin, saying, plausibly enough, that he was 'too far gone'.[26] He explained to the pregnant Marianne what he required for his well-being, essentially her devoted understanding for his predicament:

> It's very necessary for us to work out a precise plan for the spring for me to be made sea-worthy again. At this moment of calm I'm alarmed to see how knocked out I am. I think I'll have a lot of work and will need to be fresh. You grasped that my recent paranoia-like break-out, this act in support of my health, was itself a product (and proof) of my illness. I wish I had hung in there until you yourself had regained your full vitality, but at all the pumps now for six months, whistling from all outlets, with all the warning flags on the mast somewhat ridiculous and ungratifying, I am just not particularly far-sighted at the moment.

He could certainly not see beyond his own immediate needs.

As the date of his marriage to Bi grew closer, less and less was said of it. Brecht finally came out with his latest gambit, claiming to her that Marianne would not leave him alone. He had to marry Marianne but really wanted to marry Bi. So he had come up with a plan, which he shared with Bi. He explained that Marianne was only concerned about marriage for the child's sake and he wanted to comply with her wish. So Marianne had to agree to a separation as soon as the child was born. This would leave Brecht free to marry Bi. As usual, with his impeccably contrary logic Brecht managed to talk Bi into this bizarre course of action. Brecht, now a specialist in contracts of all sorts, drew up an agreement to this effect for Marianne and gave Bi a copy. Bi insisted that he should come to her immediately after the marriage ceremony. Brecht said that he would do so, telling her that the ceremony was on 6 November. Brecht duly turned up in Augsburg on that day. Only later did Bi discover that the ceremony had taken place on 3 November and that the newly-weds had enjoyed a short honeymoon! Feuchtwanger who had pressed Brecht to marry Marianne was one witness, Müllereisert the other. Bi writes with some understatement: 'Our relationship clearly suffered because of these events'.[27] Her friends urged her to dump him but even now Bi clung on. However, the separation from Marianne did not happen as agreed, nor, for that matter, did Brecht remotely commit to his wife.

The expert in contracts now considered relationships in terms of unspoken agreements between people. A major problem, he suggested, was that there were two versions of such a contract. In the case of men and women, he mooted, it was the rule that the man could 'demand a huge amount' by virtue of his contract, while the woman had to 'give up a great deal'.[28] She also had to accept some things as unchangeable. However, in Brecht's view that meant women had the consolation that they could fundamentally rely on men! Brecht pleaded with Marianne to come to Berlin. Instead, she went to her parents. Brecht took Dora Mannheim along to the Deutsches Theater for rehearsals of *Drums in the Night*. Otto Falckenberg was again directing and one of the actors was a young Viennese woman, Helene Weigel. Brecht probably saw Weigel there for the first time. She would become his wife and partner of more than thirty years. Weigel certainly saw him. Brecht again intervened massively in the production, to the great annoyance of the actors. He told Marianne that he was having a terrible time, with row upon row with them, above all Alexander Granach, who was playing Kragler, and Blandine Ebinger, who was Anna. The actors went on strike, protesting at their extreme penury in the soaring inflation. There were further disruptions to the rehearsals as the inflation raged on and the crisis gripping German theatres deepened. Many faced closure.

Kiepenheuer and Kasack were not at all pleased with the limited return on their investment in Brecht. They had published *Baal* but had not yet received the ballads, which Brecht had promised in return for their twelve-month retainer. Brecht claimed that he was contractually entitled to the arrangement continuing through 1923. Kasack insisted it was only till the end of 1922. Brecht got his way, noting with satisfaction:

> I've got the best contracts imaginable with distributors, theatres and publishers. I can't complain about the critics nor about the public. If I turn up at the Romanisches Cafe, people raise their voices at lots of tables. But I can't live. I don't drive and don't go to gambling dens. I can't pay my living costs with my income any more. The rent is too high, it consumes the month's income from my Frankfurt production. I assume that the public is too pre-occupied with their own worries about feeding themselves.[29]

While the Berlin production of *Drums in the Night* suffered further setbacks, the Munich Kammerspiele put on a guest performance in Augsburg. The KPD's Alexander Abusch reviewed the production for the *Bayerische Arbeiter-Zeitung*, the successor of *Der Volkswille*. Abusch, who in 1953 in East Berlin would be in the vanguard of Brecht's antagonists, praised the play for its attack on the lower-middle-class mindset of Augsburg's theatre-goers. However, with some justification he objected to the 'purely literary' linkage between the story line and the revolutionary events.[30] The review initiated Brecht's uneasy relationship with official Communism, which remained the way of things all his life.

Drums in the Night finally appeared with Drei Masken and the Berlin premiere took place on 20 December. Amidst the critical acclaim for Brecht's extravagant gifts, in the *Berliner Tageblatt* Alfred Kerr damned him with the faintest of praise. What is more, the cunning Kerr labelled Brecht a practitioner of the very 'culinary' art which Brecht despised: 'In the hands of this talented ragout chef language has been made into a smorgasbord'. The production was not a popular success and closed after just four performances. Brecht fled the scene, back to Marianne in Munich after he had sent her his advance of 30,000 marks, worth just $345.25. They spent Christmas together and moved into a sparsely furnished, two-room flat on Akademiestrasse.

Brecht's hopes of directing in Berlin again were thwarted when Jessner rejected Bronnen's proposal that Brecht should direct his new play *Treachery* [*Verrat*]. For Bronnen, his relationship with Brecht would never again be the same. Brecht was in Berlin briefly to fix further productions of his plays and to offer Ihering poems for publication in the *Berliner Börsen-Courier*. He maintained the usual tone in his letters to Bronnen, inviting him to Munich and writing of 'your friend Bidie on the southern island': 'his kidneys aren't so hot, but his heart is golden' and suggesting that he might travel to Berlin for a fortnight 'once Marianne is delivered'.[31] Thoroughly sick of sharing her husband with Bronnen, Marianne appended her own sarcastic comment: 'Oh, these wonderful letters – please don't throw them away – dear friend, look after them well – I'll make a lot of money out of them again – how are you – I'm longing for you – to curse with you this most vile of all vile people – come soon! Your friend Marianne'. She could not wait.

Brecht and Marianne's daughter Hanne was born on 12 March. He celebrated by re-writing the brothers Grimm's 'The Juniper Tree', a fertility tale which he dedicated 'To Marianne alone'.[32] Brecht would always be much closer to Hanne than to Frank, even if the relationship with her was conducted almost always at a physical distance. As Hanne Hiob she had a successful acting career, including major roles in her father's plays. It was, however, clear to Brecht and Marianne that their relationship was effectively over, though things limped along, Brecht clinging on amidst his many affairs and other interests. When he was at their flat, he was surrounded by cronies like Carl Zuckmayer and Bernhard Reich from the Kammerspiele. Brecht talked, smoked and drank with them until late into the night. Reich later recalled Brecht's disconcertingly categorical manner in their conversations: 'He spoke very quietly, but he made claims, expressing these claims in paradoxical assertions. Absolutely categorical. He did not argue with replies, but swept them aside. He made clear to his partners that he, Brecht, regarded all resistance to him as hopeless, and that he gave them, the partners, the friendly advice not to waste their time and to capitulate right away'.[33] They all wanted a bit of this genius, making life intolerable for Marianne and her child. However, he spent much time away from Akademiestrasse, sometimes in his Augsburg attic, at other times with Bronnen and others in Berlin. In the summer of 1923 Brecht rented a bolthole in Starnberg where he met with Marieluise Fleisser.

Mahagonny on the rise

A fresh crisis gripped Germany after it defaulted on reparations and French and Belgian troops occupied the Ruhr in January 1923. The far Right championed resistance to this 'national humiliation' as a popular cause which resonated with many compatriots. In Munich, Hitler's National Socialists saw their opportunity. Brecht wrote to Bronnen between 'stomach cramps' of 'this cavalcade of sullen dogs! And Hitler on the Monopteros shitting on Moses Iglstein'.[34] The Nazis were becoming a truly menacing public presence with their swastikas, uniforms, banners, provocative marches, political violence and anti-Semitic rabble-rousing.

Before the premiere of *In the Jungle* at the Residenz-Theater, the press reported that right-wing groups intended to disrupt the play. For Brecht, preparations for the premiere meant the usual hectic re-writing, this time together with Feuchtwanger. Erich Engel was directing. Brecht and Jacob Geis joined in. Engel was struck by similarities between Brecht and Garga: 'There is much of Brecht in Garga: the nervous flailing movement of the head, which comes out of his neck at an angle; the grimace as he grins; the tortured animation of his whole body; the hysteria; the strangely graphic mimicry'.[35] No one else recorded with such precision the adult Brecht's tortured condition. For Engel as for those who had witnessed Brecht in childhood, he was a strange phenomenon indeed. His littérateur Garga was a rare challenge for the actor Erwin Faber.

The radical Right decried the play as a glorification of Communism. The ferocity of the dramatic confrontations certainly constituted an all-out assault on cosy middle-class assumptions but it is difficult to find any trace of Communism. That was not yet Brecht's world. However, from now on every Brecht production was steeped in political controversy as he set out to split the audience. The Right identified him as the embodiment of everything they hated. He was out to provoke reactions through his avant-gardist shock tactics, all part of his consuming passion to create a new theatrical spectacle through bold, dramatic innovation suited to mass, urban society. He wrote a programme note for the premiere with headline phrases underlined. Before the performance proper began, young actors dressed as newspaper vendors called out into the audience: 'Jane Garga murder mystery'; 'Sinister affairs in Chinatown'; and, 'Mysterious lynching of the Malay'.[36]

There was much commotion in the auditorium at Brecht's latest offering, which Ihering hailed as 'Brecht's third and richest drama': 'Brecht is not only the strongest visionary power in contemporary German drama but also the greatest master of scenes. With all the conundrums and all the chaos, with all the darkness and all the light of an age that is rotting and is rising again out of the rot – overcoming chaos through composition and form'.[37] At the second performance, Nazis threw gas bombs and the theatre had to be evacuated before the performance could be completed. In a sign of the Munich authorities' supine attitude towards Hitler's thugs, *In the Jungle* was taken off the schedule on account of 'public resistance' to the play and Jacob Geis was dismissed from his post. Thomas Mann wrote in the New York magazine *The Dial*: 'Munich's popular conservatism [...] cannot tolerate Bolshevist art'.[38] Brecht's relations with Mann would never recover.

Brecht went along with Bronnen to see Hitler speak at Munich's Circus Krone. In Brecht's eyes, Hitler was a clown. Brecht and Bronnen talked through the night about their ideas for a mass performance in the circus about hunger, inflation and liberation.[39] In Bronnen's recollection, Brecht for the first time used the term 'Mahagonny' for the naive but extremely dangerous Utopia of the petty bourgeoisie, a dream of undisturbed consumption protected by the forces of law and order. Brecht had probably first come across the term as Mahagonne in O. O. Alberts's 1922 'African' shimmy 'Come to Mahagonne'. The song encourages listeners to forget their wretched daily lives and dream of an imaginary Africa where there are no taxes and sex aplenty, rather like Brecht's Tahiti. His earliest Mahagonny song, the satirical 'Oh, in Mahagonni', plays on the dream of money aplenty: 'Round is the dollar and round is the world / If you have money you need love / If you have no money you need some'.[40]

Germany had none and needed dollars to survive. How it would manage that situation greatly concerned Brecht. For Bronnen, Brecht had seen the 'petty bourgeois brown shirts marching, wooden figures with their wrongly dyed red flag with a hole in it'.[41] The Nazis' position might be threadbare in the eyes of some but its brutal directness attracted many others who sought a simple solution to the national humiliation. Brecht said to Bronnen: 'If Mahagonny comes here, I'm off'. In a letter to Bronnen that summer Brecht wrote of the Nazis' impact: 'Mahagonny has been deporting all Bavarians'.[42] Feuchtwanger's warning about right-wing violence had proved correct. From this point on, talk was not of if, but of how long it would be before they had to flee Germany. In any case, they made plans to get out of Munich. Brecht, like the Feuchtwangers and many others, looked to Berlin.

The threat of violence gripped the streets of Munich after Hitler announced his intention to hold fourteen mass meetings. The Bavarian government declared a state of emergency and put Gustav von Kahr in charge as Bavarian Commissioner, together with the chief of police and the head of the Reichswehr. Things erupted on the evening of 8 November when Hitler and General Erich Ludendorff, supported by armed Nazi militia, took over a meeting which von Kahr was addressing at the Bürgerbräukeller. In what became known as the Beer Hall Putsch, Hitler, seeking to emulate Mussolini's March on Rome, forced von Kahr and the others to pledge that they would join him to topple the government in Berlin. However, von Kahr backtracked. During the night the Nazis drew up a list of Jews for arrest, and the following day Hitler tried to seize control of Munich. However, with their putsch going nowhere, he and Ludendorff marched their militia to the Feldherrnhalle where the authorities confronted them and arrested Hitler. He was charged with high treason and imprisoned at Landsberg am Lech, where he wrote *Mein Kampf*.

Munich had become a very dangerous place for anyone who disagreed with the radical Right. Street fighting between paramilitary organisations formed by the NSDAP and the KPD had become an everyday occurrence. However, following the introduction on 15 November of the temporary currency, the Rentenmark, the government curbed the rampant inflation and much of the associated social unrest. After gold reserves had run out, land and industrial goods were used to guarantee the Rentenmark. One Rentenmark was worth a billion marks. In conjunction with the Dawes Plan, which used American loans to support re-scheduled German reparation payments to European powers, the measure ushered in a desperately needed period of financial stability. In 1924 the Reichsmark was introduced at the same value as the Rentenmark. The stability that was achieved was vital in turning people away from the violence of fringe groups like the Nazis and back towards conventional politics. For a while, the economy boomed and Germany became a site for large-scale investment and technologically driven change. Much of it was centred upon Berlin, which developed at an extraordinary pace as Europe's most 'happening' city. However, Germany was just buying time. Economic stability was maintained only until the next financial crisis, beginning in 1929, severely undermined Weimar democracy. These were seminal years in Brecht's political education.

Helene Weigel

Bronnen was still Brecht's best friend in Berlin. One evening, while Brecht was visiting, Bronnen invited him to take a look at the woman who could be seen in her flat opposite at Spichernstrasse 16. It was the actress Helene Weigel, who had been in *Drums in the Night*. Weigel and Bronnen, both from Vienna, had got to know each other in Berlin. Picking up a blanket from Bronnen's sofa, Brecht went round to introduce himself, saying that he had nowhere to stay.[43] Weigel let him sleep on her couch. After she had retired to her bedroom, Brecht tapped on the door, claiming that the living room was too cold. She clipped him around the ear and gave him a second blanket. Thereafter, he was a regular visitor and they fell deeply in love.

Weigel was different from the women Brecht had known. As the daughter of well situated, assimilated Viennese Jews, she had attended the educational reformer Eugenie Schwarzwald's progressive school. Brought up to be a new woman, Weigel was a figure of brilliance, substance, strength and sexual attraction. Sympathetic to revolutionary politics, she possessed a huge capacity for social solidarity and practical help, which could galvanise those around her. In comparison to Weigel, Marianne was a little girl lost, searching for a man to look after her, which only brought out the worst in Brecht. Professionally successful, Weigel assumed that she would remain financially independent from him and that they would have an open relationship without possessiveness. However, Brecht's behaviour would prompt her to seek an end to the relationship on several occasions. Until Brecht and Weigel fled Germany in 1933, Weigel built a great reputation in the German theatre. She played major roles from the repertoire as well as, finally, the lead in Brecht's adaptation of Maxim Gorky's novel *The Mother*. This cemented their great artistic partnership, which calls to mind the relationship between those two other brilliant artists, Jean-Paul Sartre and Simone de Beauvoir.

In the Berlin years, when Weigel spent much time away from Brecht pursuing her career, they maintained separate apartments. However, in the exile years she would sacrifice her own life to look after her children and Brecht in an almost entirely domestic existence, leaving him free to pursue his plans. Only after they returned to Europe in 1947 could Weigel properly resume her career, confirming her status as an outstanding actress as well as demonstrating her great organisational strength in managing the Berliner Ensemble. Weigel would frequently take the lead in public appearances, protecting an anxious Brecht from situations which he found difficult. And it was Weigel, of course, who after Brecht's death cemented his legacy with the Berliner Ensemble, the establishment of the Bertolt Brecht Archive, and its exploitation in the relationship with his publisher, Suhrkamp.

Brecht needed a personality as big as Weigel from whom to draw strength and against whom to measure himself. With his physical and psychological weaknesses, he was greatly in need of her strength, particularly in social situations where he was quite lost. This dependency was fundamental to Brecht's relationship with Weigel, which endured many trials and tribulations, largely on account of his behaviour with other women, about which she later said: 'All that hurt very, very much'.[44] In US exile, she would re-affirm the principle of openness despite his abuses of it: 'You cannot and do not want to conduct a publicly declared marriage adorned with a stamp. It was never like that either and I have never demanded that'.[45] Weigel demonstrated her own emotional independence early on, leaving him to protest on one occasion that he had not known her address for a week.[46] And in the summer of 1925, when Brecht was planning to see Weigel in Munich on his way to his wife and daughter in Vienna, Weigel was not minded to see him. He was left complaining: 'You wouldn't let me come by way of Munich. You don't even tell me why'. After arriving in Vienna, he asked Weigel: 'Do you miss me??? Are you reserved in your dealings with gentlemen? Do you behave yourself early and late??? I don't wish to be told things'. Hardly. An open relationship with a successful, independent woman might sound wonderful but a deeply jealous Brecht struggled to grant any woman the freedom that he assumed for himself. However, he assured Weigel that she didn't need to have 'any worries about the winter' thanks to his deal with his publisher Ullstein!

It has often been remarked that Brecht did not write love poems for her as he did for other women. He did, however, write poems to Weigel the actress. And, however studiedly minimalist, his shows of affection towards her were consistent. This attitude fitted a relationship that gave his life the strength and stability which he craved but still left him great freedom. Unlike Bi or Marianne, Weigel did not write an account of her life with Brecht and gave few interviews, nor was she any great letter writer. She was certainly highly discreet so we have no information about relationships which she might have had. Again unlike other women in Brecht's life such as Elisabeth Hauptmann, Margarete Steffin and Ruth Berlau, Weigel did not join Brecht in his writing. Nor did she intervene in his directing, preferring to make her points by acting out roles in the evening with him. As a result of these various factors, Weigel, who spent the rest of Brecht's life with him, can easily appear more a background presence in his life than other women. She was certainly a major strength for him throughout all the struggles to come.

Even meeting someone of Weigel's stature was, however, not enough for Brecht. He could not let go of Bi and was always on the lookout for new relationships. Doubting that Brecht would ever divorce Marianne, Bi began to see Hermann Gross, an Augsburg salesman. She informed Brecht that she was intending to marry this 'simpler man'.[47] When Brecht discovered that the Banholzer family accepted Gross as Bi's future husband, he appeared for the usual verbal jousting with his rival. Adopting a manner of calm superiority, he confronted an irascible Gross, who put up a fight for three hours but was always the loser as he struggled to maintain self-control. Gross claimed that he could offer Bi a secure existence, catering for her every need. Brecht simply ignored this, stating categorically: 'Bi knows exactly what decision she must make. She knows that I am divorcing in order to marry her because she is my fiancée. It is Bi's decision. We have to accept what she decides'. Bi chose Brecht. Gross was beside himself. Brecht again went on his way.

Brecht now turned on Marianne, who, despite his warnings, had gone to Vienna: 'Since before your departure for Pichling I said to you as urgently as I could that a journey to Vienna would mean our separation in the sharpest form, it will, I hope, not surprise you that I am now going to instigate a divorce suit against you on the grounds of adultery'.[48] He went on: 'I have, of course, been an idiot. I regret that I've had my time stolen by you. It is significant that the only person whom I have ever trusted apart from my mother turned out to be such a ridiculous, cheap bluff'. He asked her to stop using his name, claiming that he had never wanted them to be apart and that he did not have another relationship. His final words were that he was quite at a loss regarding Hanne, whom he could not let go. Indeed, despite Brecht's stated intention to seek a divorce, the trauma of losing Hanne left him hanging on.

After all the stops and starts, a major theatre was now prepared to go through with a production of *Baal*. In December Brecht travelled to Leipzig where he joined rehearsals at the Altes Theater. Alwin Kronacher was the director. Brecht again overrode the director's authority, taking actors to one side and training them individually in his methods. As usual, this proved highly divisive. Some actors sided with Brecht, others stayed loyal to Kronacher. Lothar Körner, who was playing Baal, was so incensed that he hurled his prompt book at Brecht and locked himself in the toilet. Recalling his Berlin debacle, Brecht mused that the only person missing was Heinrich George.

Leading Berlin critics were present for the premiere. There were tumultuous scenes, with the audience split between adulation and revulsion. The battle lines were drawn amongst the critics, too. Ihering maintained his staunch support for Brecht's talent, while criticising the production as 'inadequate', particularly Körner's performance.[49] Some other critics shared Ihering's reservations. However, Kerr delivered a damning critique: Brecht, a talented poet, was a 'frothing epigone' of a dramatist. The charge would never go away. Ihering was the foremost advocate of Brecht's original genius, Kerr the most vociferous critic of this allegedly derivative dramatist, who should stay with poetry, where his real talent lay. To Brecht's abiding chagrin, other opponents would follow Kerr's line. In a panic, after the premiere the Leipzig authorities had the play removed from the schedule. Ihering protested in vain at the suppression of Brecht's finest early work. Tellingly, when Brecht read *Baal* again in 1938 he commented: 'Pity about it. It was always a torso, and then it was operated on several times, for the (two) book versions and the production. The meaning almost got lost in the process'.[50]

With Brecht away, Bi once more succumbed to Gross. Into the bargain, she found out about Brecht's relationship with Weigel. Tired of waiting for a marriage that even she could see would never happen, Bi wrote to Brecht that she had chosen Gross and that this time it was for keeps. She heard nothing back, which she took to mean that he was prepared to accept her decision. Back in Munich, Brecht wrote two letters to Vienna, the first affectionately to Weigel who had travelled to her parents, the second dismissively to Marianne who had accused him of infidelity.[51] He wanted to know of 'Hellebeast', as he called Weigel, if she was alone, while he wrote to Marianne: 'I've not been together with Bi for four weeks now, haven't seen her any more. She's been engaged for about three weeks. She's getting married in a few weeks. She wasn't the instigator of this, I was'. Bi saw things differently. Brecht had further words for Marianne: 'If I'm correct in what I associate with Vienna, I don't want to see you again nor your child as long as you are with him'. Recht was, of course, the 'him' in question. Brecht rounded things off: 'I feel a great aversion towards you and am deeply ashamed of this time. Your things are ready to be picked up. I'll get rid of the servant. You can go to hell'. Yet as so often with Brecht, what sounded like the end was just another episode.

He joined Weigel in Munich on her trip back from Vienna to Berlin. Asking when he could see her again, he assured her: 'I am permanently devoted towards you,

Madam'.[52] His letters to her generally eschew the rather condescending male attitude towards the supposedly helpless female of his letters to Marianne and Bi. Weigel now provided the most vivid demonstration of her open relationship with him. Two weeks before Bi's wedding to Gross on 1 March, Weigel called her to say that Brecht wanted her in Berlin at once for good.[53] Weigel told Bi that Brecht had found her a job in a bank and a flat for them together. The next day Weigel appeared in Augsburg and visited the Banholzers. Bi, of course, asked why Brecht had not come himself. Weigel could only say that pressing matters had detained him in Berlin. However, Weigel did not have Brecht's power to sway Bi, who opted for solid middle-class life with Gross. That was the end of Bi and Bidi.

Bi's expectations of life with Gross were not fulfilled. She bore him two sons but he refused to take Frank Banholzer into his family on the grounds that he was the son of a man whom he detested. When Brecht died, Gross exclaimed: 'Now he's dead, the dog'. Because of the stigma that she had brought into the marriage, Bi was excluded from family occasions. That exclusion from the German middle-class world, which had begun when Bi became pregnant with Frank, lasted all her life. Meanwhile, by March 1924 Weigel was pregnant with Brecht's third child.

Directorial success

Brecht had agreed to direct Shakespeare's *Macbeth* at the Munich Kammerspiele but felt uneasy and cast around for a replacement. Feuchtwanger came to his rescue, offering to collaborate on an adaptation of Alfred Walter Heymel's German translation of Christopher Marlowe's *Edward the Second*. Unlike Brecht, Feuchtwanger had an excellent command of English. He also had an excellent grasp of history. They chose the title *The Life of Edward the Second of England*. The addition of 'the life of' signals Brecht's growing attraction to dramatised life stories for the form of theatre which he was beginning to develop.

A largely original piece emerged from Brecht's work with Feuchtwanger. For the first time since *Parricide*, Brecht had sole directorial control. Neher designed the set. During rehearsals Brecht made countless changes to the script until the very last moment. This became a hallmark of the Brechtian approach. What Brecht wrote thirty years later about his and Feuchtwanger's intentions rings true: 'We wanted to make possible a production which would break with the Shakespearean tradition common to German theatres: that lumpy monumental style beloved of middle-class philistines'.[54] Only about a sixth of Marlowe's play remained in their adaptation of this history play, in which Brecht's balladesque style was beginning to acquire the episodic measure of his Epic Theatre. He drafted descriptive titles for scenes such as 'Misgovernment under the reign of King Edward in the years 1307–12. A war in Scotland is lost because of the King's indifference'.[55] Following the practice of *In the Jungle*, Brecht had the titles spoken to announce the coming scene, indicating the setting, too, be it London or elsewhere. These titles framed events on stage. Spectators were invited to reflect that they were watching a play, not a slice of life in the Naturalist manner.

The subject matter, typically provocative, was close to Brecht's heart: a study in obsessively masochistic adherence to a course of action that can only bring ruin. King Edward is quite indifferent towards the affairs of state because he is consumed by his homosexual love for the butcher's son Gaveston. Equally indifferent, too, to the despair of his queen and the outrage of the nobility, Edward brings his kingdom to the brink of civil war. The peers of the realm finally declare war on their own king in order to banish Gaveston. As had happened in the German civil war of 1918–19, 'Brother butchers brother'.[56] Edward is finally imprisoned in the Tower of London and smothered to death.

The Latvian actress and director Asja Lacis witnessed Brecht as a 'strange director':

> He worked unusually precisely. He would repeat endlessly a tone of voice or a movement that seemed important to him. He always remained polite and patient, was never abusive towards minor actors. He wanted the whole character to be expressed in every movement. He shaped dialogue and verse differently than actors were used to. He wanted to break their habit of fuzzy, nebulous, general expression. That was the beginning of *gestural speech*.[57]

At this stage the intention was indeed to capture the whole character in every movement. Brecht's uncompromising ambition demanded that interpretative perfection. He was exceptionally sensitive to language and movement, and to the relationship between the two. The director Brecht translated the language and rhythms of the dramatic poet Brecht into consummately choreographed theatre. He would later replace what he came to view as the outmoded notion of individualised character with the hugely ambitious aim to capture within gestures the social conditions informing behaviour. In conversation with Elisabeth Hauptmann, Brecht would be typically categorical about the linkage between language and gesture: 'I only say what I have in my head quite clearly and I only write what I say. [...] For me, everything is a matter of gesture. For that reason language must be clear'.[58] Looking back, Brecht viewed the production of *Edward* as the founding moment of Epic Theatre. And he recalled the solution that he and his collaborators found to the problem of how to present soldiers during the battle scene. Karl Valentin said: 'Soldiers are scared, they're pale'. Brecht responded by coating their faces with white chalk, creating the starkest of gestures.

Once again, talented actors of repute engaged for *Edward* like Erwin Faber (Edward) and Oskar Homolka (Mortimer) had great difficulty adjusting to Brecht. He was reduced to complaining to Ihering:

> I'm in the midst of rehearsals, but it's easier to cut paving stones with one's teeth than to do this kind of thing. These people have no basic feeling for the theatre. These actors have imagination in any number of fields, but in the theatre, no. The fantastic, incredible fact that people with painted faces and speeches learnt by heart should appear on a platform and re-enact scenes from human life amid the inexplicable silence of a crowd of people is lost to this generation, which has invented the dilettante as functionary.[59]

It was not easy for actors trained to please the audience by carrying it with them to understand that Brecht had his own very specific understanding of theatre. His understanding contained truly revolutionary potential for the stage, giving a particular Brechtian shape and direction to many ideas that were in the air at that time of crisis. Brecht was equipped like no one else to exploit the opportunities that it spawned.

It did not help that at the premiere of *Edward* on 18 March 1924, Homolka was visibly drunk and could not remember his lines. Brecht explained to him that actors got drunk after the performance, not before. Reviewers, led by Ihering, praised Brecht's dramatic and directorial gifts in presenting the lyrical scenes with such clarity, stripped of the monumental pretention normally associated with productions of the classics. Brecht's episodic re-working of Marlowe was different again from Jessner's re-interpretation of the classics. Despite the continuing sniping from Kerr after the play's Berlin premiere later in 1924, the production paved the way for Brecht's acceptance as a director in Berlin. A guest performance by the Kammerspiele in Augsburg was a great personal triumph. When Brecht looked through the play thirty years later, unusually he opted to reprint it without any changes. He commented: 'The reader may find something to interest him in the narrative methods and in the emergence of a new stage language'.[60] *Edward* was the culmination of Brecht's work in Munich and the platform for his return to Berlin.

At the Watershed 1924–7

The circus moves to Berlin

Thanks to Erich Engel, Berlin was now established as Brecht's direction of travel. From the autumn, he would be working there as a director in Max Reinhardt's theatre empire. He paid a brief visit to the pregnant Weigel in Berlin before he took a long holiday from April to mid-June on Capri and the Amalfi Coast, using the money from the premiere of *Edward*. He went not with Weigel but with his wife and child. Marianne evidently believed that things were on again, inviting Bronnen to join them on the Baltic that summer.[1] However, Brecht explained to Weigel that Marianne would be returning to her mother's with her daughter for the summer. He told Weigel how much he was looking forward to Berlin and pleaded with her not to have an abortion: '*Don't* be silly. No reason!!!'.

The Italian holiday turned into a general excursion for the Brecht circus. He invited Bronnen to join him and met up in Florence with Weigel, who decided to keep their child. A newly-wed Neher was in Positano with his wife Erika Tornquist. Brecht fled Positano with Neher to explore Naples where, as he wrote with relish, 'there are drinks, music and syphilis'. Such a world of risk and adventure, which he would evoke with typical ambivalence in his Mahagonny songs and opera, was more to his taste than the luxuriant beauty of the Amalfi coast. Asja Lacis was on Capri with Bernhard Reich. There Lacis met Walter Benjamin, whose interest in Communism she had awakened during their affair. Benjamin asked her to introduce him to Brecht but at this stage Brecht was not interested. The meeting of the 'greatest living German poet' with the 'most important critic of the time', as Hannah Arendt later described them, had to wait.[2] Prompted by Benjamin, Lacis would again take steps to bring them together later that year but they still found no common ground.

That summer Brecht worked in Berlin for two weeks with Kasack, who was determined to see Brecht's ballads through to production. However, Brecht left for Augsburg, still clutching his manuscript. He probably suspected that when he finally released it, there would be problems. He spent most of the summer working with Neher on a range of dramatic projects in Augsburg where Marianne joined him in July, unaware of Weigel's pregnancy. It was Weigel Brecht wanted to see, carrying his child 'Peter'. She visited him while she was holidaying on Lake Constance.[3] As they walked down the street one day in Munich, Marianne passed by with Hanne in her pram.

Brecht said a warm hello and walked on. He met up with Bi who told him she was very unhappy. He lamented her loss in two poems, 'About a Love of my Youth' and 'What Happens to a Man'.[4] Brecht asked Weigel to look around for an office job or domestic post for Bi in Berlin or Potsdam. Not only that, Marianne was trying to find a flat in Berlin for Brecht, herself and Hanne. There was briefly a chance that Bi, Marianne and Weigel would all be living in Berlin and that in time Frank could join his mother and the other children in Brecht's polygamous world. The chaos that would surely ensue was another matter. In the event, Marianne and Bi stayed in the South, while Brecht exchanged Munich for Berlin for good on 1 September 1924. He reflected: 'Even the woman I loved in my youth, to whom I was very attached and who slipped from my grasp on account of a strange indifference on my part, appears to me in my memory today like the figure in a book I've read'. It was not so much his defective memory: fresh waves of desire repeatedly captivated Brecht, relegating Bi to a marginal position in his chequered emotional life.

This time nearly everything was in place for Brecht's conquest of Berlin, the city with which his name is always associated. Berlin had by now spawned an exhilarating artistic and intellectual life, fostering new forms of aesthetic experimentation and political attitudes. A widely discussed new work was Georg Lukács's *History and Class Consciousness*, which analysed the fresh form of alienation experienced by industrial workers in the light of revolutionary methods of mass production. In the 1920s Henry Ford's production line would come to symbolise that development, which required fresh modes of intellectual and artistic understanding. Brecht would become the prime representative of Berlin's 1920s avant-garde engaging with the new reality.

In that highly unstable world where everything was up for grabs after the war and the great inflation, Brecht had a ravenous hunger for success which impelled him to go out and grab the most. With his cropped hair under his trademark cap and the perennial cigar to accompany his idiosyncratic, aggressive literary and directorial style, the macho Brecht would rapidly achieve the theatrical fame he had always craved. Berlin was the platform for his huge international success with *The Threepenny Opera* in 1928. With his macabre sarcasm and relish for a polemical fight, his name immediately conjured up notoriety. He would not have wanted it any other way. However, while he careered triumphantly through his decade in Berlin, leaving a trail of destruction behind him, he was aware of the huge gulf between that rapacious macho attitude and the stark reality of his sickly body. All the time that he was generating his magnificent artistic creations, he was plagued by anxiety that his body could not stand the punishment he was meting out to it. His works chart the anxiety as well as the exhilaration of those years.

Brecht's director's contract with Reinhardt was prestigious and he was gaining recognition in Berlin theatrical life for his rare talent. However, he was also a notoriously disruptive presence who had a track record of wrecking productions. He immediately tried to implement his wish for the auditorium to be transformed into a place where people could smoke and drink while thinking about the performance on the stage. This did not go down well. He had an agreement with Reinhardt to direct *In the Jungle*, but in the event Engel did it. An agreement with Jessner for Brecht to direct *Edward* at the Staatliches Schauspielhaus fell apart amidst conflicts over the directorial approach. When Brecht declined to direct a Pirandello play for Reinhardt, the writing was on the wall: his contract would not be renewed.

Wherever Brecht was, controversy was never far away. Herwarth Walden, the editor of the journal *Der Sturm*, accused him of plagiarising Rimbaud's *Une saison en enfer* for *In the Jungle*. Ihering defended Brecht, claiming that Walden had only read the stage copy of the play, not the final printed version, and was making something out of nothing. Brecht maintained that in the published version the borrowings were marked as quotations but quotation marks were not, of course, visible in a text spoken on stage. He skated over the fact that there was no acknowledgement of sources. The controversy escalated into a very personal battle of the critics, led by Ihering and Kerr. Along with Kerr's earlier accusation that Brecht was a 'frothing epigone', the charge of plagiarism would never go away. Nor would Ihering's unstinting support prevent Brecht from criticising him for reviews in which he had, as Brecht put it, shown his support for the 'theatre of the older generation'.[5] Ihering had committed an act of treachery.

Elisabeth Hauptmann

In Berlin, as in Munich and Augsburg, dramatic composition was an eminently social activity for Brecht. Neher had long been important, Feuchtwanger too. As we've seen, the lyrical and balladesque came readily to Brecht but dramatic composition required more than Brecht at this stage could generally supply on his own. With the right collaborators to bounce ideas off, his dramatic work, and it was principally his work, was brilliant. However, without the right people in Berlin he was initially lost. Brecht also had his own special requirements when it came to the custom of writers employing a secretary to organise their professional lives and to deal with such matters as routine correspondence. With Brecht, this function became a particular kind of multi-tasking, involving his physical and sexual as well as professional needs.

On the look-out for new collaborators, he found an outstanding literary secretary in Elisabeth Hauptmann. He would henceforth never be without female support. From this time, too, he began to create strong female roles. Hauptmann's name is closely associated with much of Brecht's most brilliant work from the Berlin years. Her contribution is certainly much greater than was ever known publicly at the time. She herself, however, always acknowledged that Brecht was the presiding genius in the partnership. Hauptmann had come to Berlin in 1922, escaping the career of a teacher which her father had mapped out for her. In those days that career required celibacy of women. That was out of the question for Hauptmann, who shared with Weigel the values of a new woman finding her way in Berlin's literary and theatrical world. As new women, they were both very much Brecht's type, rather like Brecht's later lovers Margarete Steffin and Ruth Berlau. Hauptmann would never achieve the acclaim which the robustly independent Weigel enjoyed. Her position always remained precarious even though she possessed coveted talents and skills. Her American mother had taught her English as a child and had nurtured her love of English and American literature. In Berlin she worked for a writer who was attempting to re-establish book distribution between Germany and the English-speaking world and just before she met Brecht she published a piece of her own work in a magazine. Like Steffin and Berlau after her, but unlike Brecht, Hauptmann joined the KPD. Weigel may have briefly been a member in 1929.[6]

Brecht got to know his 'Chief Girl' Bess, as he called Hauptmann, in the autumn of 1924 through Dora Mannheim. As usual with new female friends, Brecht took Hauptmann for a long walk. She quickly realised that her role was to listen and show her understanding of what he said, responding with her own views. Brecht prized her excellent knowledge of English and American literature and her capacity to produce translations in a fine literary German which approximated to his stylistic requirements, rather like a ghost writer. Hauptmann could even mimic Brecht's mock-Lutheran tones. Only Margarete Steffin would be her equal.

Like Steffin, Hauptmann was an attractive young woman. Her collaboration with Brecht soon involved a sexual dimension. Initially Hauptmann had no idea that Brecht was in a relationship with Weigel, who gave birth to Brecht's second son on 3 November. Brecht offered baby Stefan stern words of advice: 'What is crucial is not how often you achieve success but how many defeats you can endure.'[7] Weigel took a flat with Stefan on Babelsberger Strasse, leaving Spichernstrasse to Brecht for his sole use from February 1925. Hauptmann joined Brecht's growing band of helpers and hangers-on there. All was revealed one day when Brecht and Weigel turned up together with Stefan.

Among other things, Hauptmann translated Kipling's verse for Brecht. He read *Barrack Room Ballads* and *Soldiers Three* in German. At a time when Kiepenheuer was still looking to prise two plays and the ballads out of him, the publisher made plans for Brecht to edit a German edition of Kipling's poems. Kipling was his inspiration in a wholesale re-casting of *Galgei*. The setting became the British Raj and the title *Galy Gay*, the name of the main character, an Irish stevedore. Explaining to Hauptmann that he found it boring to work alone, he introduced her to the project, telling her the plot and where he had got stuck. Hauptmann confessed that she could never get her head round the play with its chaotic sequence of confusing scenes. They would work on the material for more than a year, re-casting it under its final title *Man Equals Man*.

Brecht was so taken by Hauptmann that he persuaded Kiepenheuer to employ her as his personal editor to ensure completion of *Galy Gay*, *In the Jungle* and the ballads. Kiepenheuer would go to almost any lengths for Brecht. Because of such indulgence, Kiepenheuer got into financial difficulties and had to cancel virtually all such arrangements. However, an exception was made for Brecht, and Hauptmann continued to be paid by Kiepenheuer to support Brecht throughout 1925. However, Brecht now entered into negotiations with Ullstein, with whom he signed a contract on 21 July 1925 with provision for the ballads.[8]

Brecht was also in at the start of the new age of radio. The producer Alfred Braun describes Brecht's interactions with Hauptmann as they adapted *Macbeth* for broadcast:

> There was a lady sitting at a typewriter, who was helping. First she put on a record and made music. Brecht raced up and down in the room and ideas sparked

off him. For example, he wanted to give *Macbeth* the form of a Moritat and to introduce every scene with a razor-sharp line. [...] Unfortunately – the secretary did not find that good and said no, and that was it. The secretary's contribution to how the adaptation came about was essential. Brecht really listened to her.[9]

Hauptmann did all manner of work for him. She took care of his correspondence with publishers, attempted to persuade car dealers to give him a vehicle as an advertising ploy and dealt with the tax authorities. Despite his prolific output, in 1927 Brecht claimed to the local tax office that he should be classified as tax-exempt: 'I write plays, and, apart from a few poorly paid incidental jobs, live exclusively on publishers' advances, which are paid to me in the form of loans. Since *for the present* I earn next to nothing with my plays, I am up to my ears in debt to my publishers'.[10] There is no indication that Brecht handed back an advance which he had mistaken for a loan. The letter reveals much about Brecht's economy. He had no regular salary, of course, living off the advances which, according to the logic of the market, publishers deemed that his talent and plans merited. It could be feast or famine. The precarious nature of the writer's existence would be laid bare in exile.

Meeting Brecht launched Hauptmann on an incomparable adventure, which was, however, a well-nigh impossible emotional undertaking. She soon discovered that being Brecht's 'Chief Girl' brought no guarantees. Brecht had ambitions to write a money-making serial novel with illustrations for a mass-circulation magazine and Hauptmann was expected to do much of the work. He told her to be at Spichernstrasse ready for work but suddenly he was nowhere to be seen.[11] He was, of course, in great demand, among other things sitting for a portrait by the Dutch painter Ernst van Leyden, now lost, and another by Rudolf Schlichter with Brecht in a leather waistcoat and a cigar in hand which has become iconic. Hauptmann became angry and distressed when Brecht took to criticising her work and accusing her of laziness. And he offended her with his displays of indifference and 'impoliteness', such as inviting women to the flat where she was waiting, ready to work.

Hauptmann retaliated by taking lovers in the Brecht entourage like the writer and boxer Emil Hesse-Burri. Such arrangements show the sexual openness of the New Women in Brecht's world, correcting the picture which John Fuegi draws of Brecht and his 'harem', in which Hauptmann, Weigel and Brecht's other women struggle in their competition for Brecht's sexual favours.[12] One cannot, however, ignore the hurt which Weigel and Hauptmann – like all Brecht's other women – felt when he broke promises to them, as he often did. He appealed for their understanding by claiming his special needs and by downplaying any emotional chemistry in sexual relations. However, Brecht's polygamous ways, born of his intense, fluctuating desires, involved him in near-constant subterfuges and ruses. He concealed aspects of his relationship with Hauptmann from Weigel; and the shock of Brecht's marriage to Weigel would prompt Hauptmann's attempted suicide in 1929. However, despite many severe tests Hauptmann would remain devotedly loyal to this delicate specimen of extraordinary artistic talent and macho bravado.

Hanging on to wife and child

Marianne took Hanne to stay with Brecht in Berlin but they left in a hurry when Marianne found Brecht and Weigel together. In fact, Marianne had met the actor Theo Lingen, whom she would marry and who would star in Brecht's plays. Marianne later claimed there was another woman in Berlin with two children by Brecht, though she did not name the woman, who died soon afterwards. Marianne believed that Brecht would not initially agree to a divorce because he would then have to marry that woman, even though he saw his future with Weigel. However, Brecht insisted to Marianne that he had no intention of giving up his marriage: again he claimed there was no other woman in his life, that Marianne was his wife and would continue to be his.[13] He warned her that if she should forget these things, 'You will have the hardest struggle of your life in front of you over *our* Hanne'.

Marianne now announced that she knew all about his child with Weigel. Brecht responded with one of his most breathtaking denials: 'I've not grown used to any other child but Hanne and will not do so, never!!! As I've always said to you, *I can't give her up*, there would be vicious fights, *I can't give you up either!* You're wrong about my stance towards Weigel. I'm not on a good footing with her and whatever you do, she will never be my wife'.[14] However much Brecht's relentlessly promiscuous behaviour clashed with his need to preserve existing relationships, the prospect of giving up Marianne and Hanne was truly traumatic. He pleaded with Marianne not to leave him and urged her to follow his example: he claimed that he scarcely left his room, apart from the occasional evening with Oskar Homolka and the odd afternoon at Feuchtwanger's! When Marianne accepted a contract in Münster for the season 1925–6, Brecht displayed the incomprehension of someone who believed he was doing everything humanly possible to support her. To Weigel, he was incredulous that anyone could offer Marianne such a contract.[15]

Brecht was left holding the baby when Weigel starred as Marie at the Munich Kammerspiele in Georg Büchner's *Woyzeck*. With his usual affection when writing about children, he told her that Stefan was doing well: 'He looks content and fat but never smiles. He's very stern but just. He's helping his teeth to push up with whatever he can lay his hands on. He yells terribly and is an unspeakably greedy piglet'.[16] However, it hurt Brecht that Weigel was outdoing him. He had not shone with Reinhardt and needed to step up the publication of poems and stories. He drew up a list of things to learn to do: drive; modern iambics; write a play; photography; ski; sail; ride; English and other languages; finance; technology; anatomy; and Jiu-Jitsu.[17] He would make progress in some areas like driving. That became a passion after Müllereisert taught him to drive in the summer of 1925 and he got a car the following spring. Georg Grosz recalls that Brecht was a brilliant driver, one of the fastest and most reckless he knew![18] Müllereisert bought that first car for Brecht in Weigel's name: she had stumped up the money. It was a 1921 Daimler, parked up in Wittenberg in need of repair. Brecht did not like the car, decided to sell it on and complained to Müllereisert, who defended what he had done on the grounds that the final decision had been Weigel's. Brecht sharply rebuked his friend and claimed that Müllereisert's life was becoming more 'precarious and fraudulent'.[19] Brecht's accusation angered Müllereisert. He paid for the repairs with a loan and told Brecht that as far as he was concerned their friendship was over. Brecht bought himself a big new Opel with an open top, which he enjoyed driving through the countryside out to the west of Berlin to Brandenburg, before cruising back through Berlin in the evening. Like the swing-boats, driving cars was a source of great pleasure as Brecht enjoyed the thrill of speed and control. He had himself photographed with his cap on in his new toy, a trademark Brecht pose.

He made little progress with the physical accomplishments on the list. They were beyond his frail body. Understanding anatomy was, though, an obvious challenge, in terms of how his own enigmatic organism worked and to inform his choreographic work in the theatre. Brecht's fascination with technology and finance came to permeate his writing from the mid–1920s, as he sought to grasp what was driving modern socio-economic behaviour, particularly phenomena such as inflation and the rise of the USA. Learning English and how to really go about writing a play were closely associated for Brecht with these questions. However, in the mid–1920s Brecht's English was quite basic and would remain so until he had spent time in London and New York in the mid–1930s. Refining his writings skills was another matter.

Aided by 'much nicotine', as he put it to Weigel – also a heavy smoker – Brecht began to write sonnets, a number of which he collected as the 'Augsburg Sonnets'.[20] Brecht mastered the sonnet form with aplomb. One of them, 'Discovery about a Young Woman', is amongst his finest poems from the 1920s. It is said that a fleeting encounter in Hamburg with Ernestine Costa, an actress at the Thalia Theatre, prompted the composition, in which sexual desire mingles with thoughts of death, leading to an affirmation of life:

> Next day's subdued farewell: she standing there
> Cool on the threshold, coolly looked at too
> When I observed a grey strand in her hair
> And found I could not bring myself to go.[21]

Another sonnet – it is surely about the black-haired Marianne – ends with a classic Brechtian dismissal of a lover:

> They say one soon forgets her face once out of sight
> Because it seems like a transparent screen
> Through which nothing but emptiness is seen.
>
> They also said her features were not bright
> She knew she'd fade from people's memories
> Nor would she see herself when reading this.

It is true that Marianne was not the sharpest, if not so lacking in self-awareness as Brecht suggested.

Shortly after, Marianne told him that she was pregnant again and asked him what he thought she should do. He knew exactly what he wanted her to do but replied that if she wanted the child she should go ahead, adding that he wanted as many children as possible with her.[22] However, he also advised her that it might be wiser to wait before having another child so as not to jeopardise her stage career. He consulted Müllereisert and sent her ten tablets of sulphate of quinine, explaining that she should tell the chemist that they were for malaria. They might cause some tinnitus but should do the trick! One way or another, Marianne terminated the pregnancy.

They continued to bicker, Brecht complaining that she was always so demanding and dissatisfied. He told Marianne that for years he had feared receiving every one of her letters. As if to emphasise the point, he composed another sonnet, which he later called 'Sonnet of the Bad Life'.[23] It's all about his morbidity. He re-worked the old lines about his halitosis, using the first rather than the third person. He also composed new verses about the wretched affliction that was his body, which his meagre appetite could scarcely keep going:

Oh I'm sick
Of saving my scabby body from misery
Of eating meat so as not to die
From day to day
It's too much trouble
For too little gain
Not to have pegged out by the evening
Is not enough.[24]

For this hunger artist, eating was a chore with little reward. He was becoming skeletal. Hauptmann for one was greatly concerned about his emaciated state: 'He must become *heavier*'.[25]

Marianne now told him of her relationship with Theo Lingen and Brecht replied with the obsessive certainty that Lingen was sexually abusing his daughter: 'I am completely beside myself. I shall do *everything* to protect the child from this fellow. Three months ago the child had pure, clear eyes but now looks gloomy and distraught. Your crime is monstrous. You are what I called you! And now you've lost your head as well! I shall move heaven and earth to get the child'.[26] He begged Marianne to give up Hanne and send her to Berlin, Augsburg or Vienna, anywhere to get her out of Lingen's clutches! Brecht did not have the slightest grounds for his abject suspicions, which did not prevent him from making further allegations along the same lines, ordering Marianne to remove Hanne from Münster. Although he told Hauptmann that he wanted a divorce, he continued to claim to Marianne that he had 'no attachment to another woman', that he was 'devastated' and was about to leave Germany. Hauptmann noted: 'He looks wretched'.[27] Having seen his 'contract' with Marianne break down, in April Brecht submitted divorce papers, citing her cohabitation with Lingen. Marianne retaliated by citing Brecht's relationship with Weigel and their son Stefan. The divorce would be concluded on 22 November 1927. Costs were shared.

Brecht was left to reflect upon his inability to end relationships: he was too weak, avoiding decisions, especially ones which involved an outcome unknown rather than a clear one; he was incapable of breaking off relationships himself; he didn't understand why he always wasted time on people; he was obsessed by meeting people, taking no notice of anything else. Indeed, he had spent so much of his life becoming embroiled in impossibly tangled relationships, which took away so much of the energy that he needed for writing. All this had to change. He concluded: 'Animals certainly don't have

1. Brecht on his first day at school, 1904.
Photographer: not known. BBA FA 01/003.

2. Brecht, his brother Walter, his father Berthold and
his mother Sophie, 1908. Photographer: not known.
BBA FA/06/008.

3. Brecht, playing the guitar, 1916. Photographer: Friedrich Fohrer. BBA FA 01/019.

4. Brecht, with a skull under each arm, 1917. Photographer: Friedrich Fohrer. BBA FA 01/022.

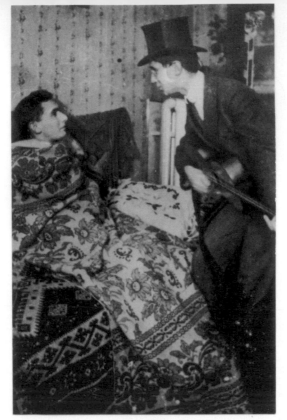

5. Brecht and Georg Pfanzelt, around 1917.
Photographer: not known. BBA FA 06/025.

6. Brecht, Otto Müllereisert, Georg Pfanzelt (standing) and Otto Bezold, 1917. Photographer: not known.
BBA FA 06/026.

7. Brecht and Paula Banholzer, 1918. Photographer: not known. BBA FA 06/035.

8. Brecht (second from left) alongside Karl Valentin and, in the foreground, Liesl Karlstadt in a spoof the Oktoberfest, Munich, around 1920. Photographer: not known. BBA FA 06/040.

9. Brecht and Marianne Zoff, Starnberg, 1923. Photographer: not known. BBA FA 06/050.

10. Brecht (standing), Paul Samson-Körner, Edmund Meisel, Hermann Borchardt, Hannes Küpper and Elisabeth Hauptmann, Berlin, Spichernstraße 16, 1927. Photograph: ullstein bild – Zander & Labisch, Berlin. BBA FA 06/071.

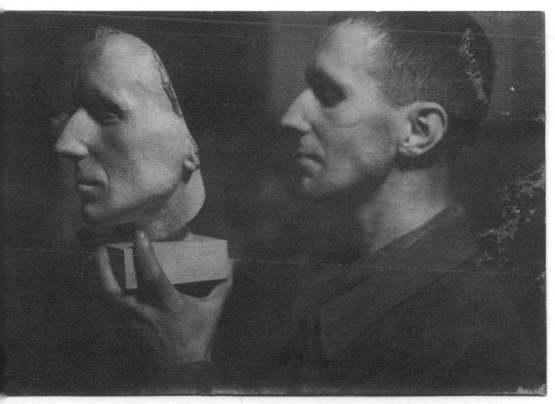

1. Brecht, with his own death mask, 1931. Photographer: Paul Hamann. BBA FA 01/067.

12. Brecht and Bernard von Brentano, Le Lavandou, France, in front of the Hôtel Provence, May/June 1931
Photographer: Margot von Brentano. BBA FA 01/120.

13. Brecht, around 1931. Photographer: not known. BBA FA 01/123.

this interest in others of their species, and I want to fight against it in myself. For, in addition to that, I have no special esteem for people'.[28]

The regulation of appetites: Brecht's programme

During the summer of 1925, which the emaciated Brecht spent in Austria and Augsburg, he took stock of his life at what proved to be a watershed. He had led the life of a young man, testing the limits of the organism while given to the play of instinct and vitalist excess. Just twenty-seven, but frail in the extreme, he had come to understand that he must learn to live within self-imposed restrictions like an older man, taking care to preserve his body and cultivate the intellect, not wild and dangerous instinct. Without any understanding of Brecht's troubled organism, critics and biographers have not identified this crucial juncture in his life. Nor have they therefore grasped its ramifications when addressing a cardinal question in Brecht research: what are the underlying issues which unite the seemingly radically different younger and older Brecht? Questions surrounding Brecht's adoption of Marxism, important as they are, have taken precedence over the investigation of Brecht's fraught relationship with his body and its ramifications for his intellectual and artistic development, as well as his relations with others. Brecht's relationship with his body was reaching a critical point.

In a dialogic 'address' and 'answer' in the latest stage of his quarrel with himself, which Brecht wrote one night in July 1925 at Baden near Vienna, he mused upon everything that he had been able to achieve, including all his 'skulduggery': 'Yet you are not satisfied, Bidi'.[29] He responded: 'I'm not satisfied; for that reason I'm not satisfied'. Moving on to Kochel in Upper Bavaria, he considered his writings. He felt that he had produced them without really trying. If he truly wished to emulate the great classical dramatists, now was the time to concentrate his energy, to make a 'vice out of his excesses', as he put it:

I should draw up a plan and execute it to give my work tradition. Inspiration through manual habit and the pleasure of working something through. I should make an effort to choose a style which permits me to formulate what has to be developed in the most convenient fashion for myself. My appetites should be regulated so that wild turns might be eradicated and long-term interests made tractable. So that, for example, I could write plays very quickly.

As so often, Brecht used the imagery of appetites to consider human motivation, proceeding from his own. By appetites, he meant both his desires, which were huge and impulsive, and his hunger, which on account of his renal condition was meagre. Hence for Brecht appetites could always only be 'too big or too small'. His control over his oscillating impulses was limited, leaving him with 'sudden and irregular', 'intense wishes', which drove him on in his literary and sexual quests. He recognised that some control and regulation of his appetites was necessary in order to eradicate those 'wild turns' in his behaviour if he were to achieve not only his artistic ambitions but also some degree of well-being personally and in his relations with others. Unable to cope any more with the extraordinary emotional and physical chaos and upheaval into which he repeatedly plunged himself, Brecht knew that he had to change his life. However, even from the reclining position in which he indulged his literary and sexual desires, regulating his life would never be easy for a man so driven in his artistic and personal dealings.

Brecht's appetite would continue to pre-occupy him. In 1927 he wrote in his notebook: 'I can't sit comfortably on my backside: it's too gaunt! [...] My appetite is too weak. I get full at once!!'.[30] In May 1928, as he often did, he drew up a list of contrasting pairs to clarify his tastes. With one exception, they confirm his abiding macho self-projection:

Not for conviviality	but for conversations with men
Not for love	but for lust
Not for eating well	but for staying one's appetite
Not for playing	but for working
Not for leisure	but for laziness
Not for girls	but for women

The pair 'Not for eating well but for staying one's appetite' does not fit at all with the macho man's otherwise predictable tastes – until one considers Brecht's condition: that metallic taste in his mouth, which put him off his food and left him always susceptible to weight loss. The regulation of his appetite was, of course, vital for him to maintain his energy levels. A little later Brecht amplified upon his attitude towards appetites in a manner which we noted briefly earlier:

I liked big appetites very much. It seemed to me to be a natural advantage if people could enjoy eating a lot, just if they wished to have a lot, could get a lot out of things etc. My meagre appetite was something I did not like about myself. It is true that I had intense wishes to possess this or that, but they were sudden and irregular instead of constant and reliable, as I would have liked. And above all: if I had what I'd wished for myself, I was quickly sated; so that I felt discomfort in front of a plate with food that I desired because I might not be able to eat it since my stomach was too small. The question was therefore: how might I acquire large and constant appetites?

Brecht was deeply envious of people with large appetites and to compensate for his own lack he created outlandish figures with truly huge appetites. Though 'quickly sated', his compulsion to pursue his desires led to extraordinary and frequently destructive scenes with all manner of people – from friends and lovers through to actors, directors and fellow writers – which could run him into the ground. The question 'How might I acquire large and constant appetites?' was born of a search for normality which was never remotely attainable for the singularly gifted and afflicted Brecht.

However, he realised that he must lend his life a stronger framework, through a regular routine. He established such a routine, interrupting it only when illness forced him to take to his bed.[31] Elisabeth Hauptmann was a key supporting figure in a daily round which began early, at 6 or 7 a.m. Armed with a cup of tea or coffee, Brecht at once went to his desk to write. He took a light breakfast at 8.30, then continued working, usually alone, until 1 p.m. After lunch, he always lay down for 20 minutes. He could relax best when he lay on his back with his arms by his side and his hands beneath his buttocks. The mode of work then changed for the afternoon when his collaborators joined him to discuss what he had done in the morning. He greatly enjoyed these exchanges and noted suggestions. He then took his evening meal and again lay down for 20 minutes before receiving guests for more general conversation. Brecht usually went to bed early, around 9 p.m. He maintained this routine, with minor variations, for the rest of his life.

Amidst this search for normality, Brecht's hugely fertile, febrile mind was firing off new ideas all the time, as he developed his positions with alacrity over that summer of 1925. In the notes from Kochel, he set down an idea which would become a hallmark of his work: the 'training of the audience' in the 'massive social struggles' of the age.[32] The audience's education became a major pre-occupation. Brecht would rarely leave them alone. As he began to assume the mantle of the teacher, a function of the cerebral and sceptical figure of Herr Keuner which he created in 1927, Brecht sought to develop a critical attitude towards the vitalist outsider, embodied first in Baal and presently in Fatzer. The quarrel with himself was truly under way.

The social situation in which individuals found themselves and how they might improve it by learned behaviour to control destructive instinct now became a major concern. In the mid–1920s Brecht was drawn to behaviourist notions, which were very much in the air. In the emphasis upon exercises designed to improve behaviour, they were reminiscent of the behavioural therapy which he had practised in adolescence with his physiotherapist Herr Löffler. Johannes Ludwig Schmitt, the Munich specialist in respiratory massage, herbal and homeopathic remedies, who became a life-long friend and physician, would offer a similar approach to the problems of the organism. Brecht benefited from the techniques employed by both therapists.

In these years Brecht habitually uses medical imagery of illness and recuperation to describe those massive social struggles of the age. He would later argue that all illnesses, including his own, were social in origin. He would come thereby to subsume the chaos of the storm within him within a greater chaos, a narrative of those massive social struggles, to the understanding – and ultimately control – of which he committed his energies. This provided a desperately-needed anchorage for his own life and a framework for the analysis of ills which were, he could argue, not just his own but common to all in contemporary urban life. Even though Brecht would never get to the bottom of his own condition, he could take some comfort from the belief that it was socially derived. He made a leap of faith that his situation, like that of others, could be improved in a major way by the transformative application of modern socio-economic thought and associated therapies in an emerging new age, which he presently began to proclaim.

In his consideration of those social struggles, Brecht identified his programme, at this stage thematically, for his life's work. Dramaturgical considerations would follow. Remarkably clear-sighted, he estimated that he had enough material to write as many as forty or so plays. And, expanding upon the theme of the city as jungle, he had a vision like no one else of what that material would be. The city was his 'heroic landscape', 'relativity' the perspective upon the entry of humanity into the cities at the start of the third millennium.[33] By relativity, Brecht was coming to understand the particular perspective and interests which informed an individual's behaviour. Quite how his protagonists would differ from his earlier hedonistic outsiders, their behaviour intimately linked to the state of their organism, remained to be seen. He estimated a minimum of eight plays drawing on American history and a similar number about the First World War. He saw the German classics, which had been so disfigured by his teachers' wartime propaganda, as a source of comic adaptations, from *Faust* to the *Song of the Nibelungs*. Much of the comedy would derive from the ironic disjunctions between the age of composition and the new age. Comic adaptations of German classics would be integral to his programme with the Berliner Ensemble from 1949, too, when he embarked upon the exploration of what Marx and Engels called the German Misere, Germany's wretched historical development, which reached its nadir in Nazism. Viewing himself as a writer of history plays in the tradition of Shakespeare and Schiller, Brecht pointed forward with his programme to his greatest plays, *Life of Galileo* and *Mother Courage and her Children*, the finest creations of his long years of exile. However, with the rise to power of Fascism and Communism amongst those nations which emerged badly fractured after defeat in the First World War, history was already manufacturing fresh challenges with which this writer of a new type of history play would have to engage. Indeed, all Brecht's plans from the late 1920s onwards would be viewed in the light of these momentous developments since 1918. He had known since the collapse of Wilhelmine Germany that the middle-class world of his upbringing was forever gone. His encounter with Nazism in Munich had prompted him to coin the term Mahagonny, signifying the dangerous, authoritarian illusion that a nostalgically-viewed lost world could be recovered through the re-imposition of law and order. By contrast, Brecht would come to see in the revolutionary politics of working class victory the genuine prospect of shaping the emerging new age.

By the mid-1920s, Brecht had formed the view that innovative technological and financial instruments were generating fresh forms of struggle and shaping human behaviour in momentous and unprecedented ways. He told Hauptmann, with self-important avant-gardist bluster, that he embraced the new age and was probably the only person to recognise it.[34] He claimed that imperialism, together with many other old ideas, was being discarded and that it was only in such new ages that people like him, by which he meant truly important people, became pre-occupied with history. The incorporation of history within plot yielded Brecht's master narratives. All his character types, he said, represented the new type of human being emerging from momentous technological and financial upheaval.

Brecht suggested to Hauptmann that there was a general anxiety during the emergence of a new age, which produced its heroes like Lenin. They were schooled in the old ways but initiated the new. A new age had particular characteristics: borders collapsed; races mixed; and the notion of possessions was lost. Brecht amplified upon his remarks about possessions in conversation with Hannes Küpper, explaining that possessions were being replaced by goods, which could be exchanged. The permanence of ownership had indeed been eroded in the era of mass-produced goods. To explain what he meant by figures representative of the new thinking, Brecht tellingly referred to the way the famous Reformation figures Ulrich von Hutten and Martin Luther had embraced the onset of a new age. The import of Brecht's Protestant upbringing should never be underestimated. It left him with a mindset receptive to the possibility that radical change on a grand scale could be both conceived and implemented. For Brecht, Luther's importance for the church in the Reformation was matched by his own for the theatre at the present critical juncture.

As his intention to write a minimum of eight plays drawing upon American history indicates, at this time Brecht was much more fixed upon the USA, the vanguard power of capitalism, as a laboratory of the new age than upon the USSR. The USA had rapidly overtaken a Germany broken by war and mired in debt to the victor power for decades to come. Walter Brecht had recently gone to live with relatives in Brooklyn, while he learned the latest techniques of paper production. Walter described New York to his brother in glowing terms, wondering at this technologically advanced world and encouraging Brecht to come and see it for himself.[35] Brecht's rather curt, sarcastic reply betrays his jealousy. He asserted his own position in the following lines:

I can hear you saying:
He talks of America
He understands nothing about it
He has never been there.
But believe you me
You understand me perfectly well when I talk of America
And the best thing about America is:
That we understand it.[36]

Brecht certainly tried hard to understand it. While the sheer dynamism of a relentlessly innovative USA strongly appealed to him, he was appalled by the destructive potential of unchecked capitalist innovation. It was not so much the awesome and dangerous factory machines that disturbed him. Like many people before and since, Brecht was worried by the unchecked commodity and financial markets and realised that modern capitalism could only be understood if the markets driving it were the object of enquiry. In the inflation he had seen what a devastating impact they could have. Events in Germany after October 1929 would only reinforce that insight in his increasingly trenchant critique of capitalism.

In August 1925 Brecht asked Walter to send him anything he could about speculation on the Chicago wheat exchange for his play *Jae Fleischhacker in Chicago*. In the months through to the following summer in Vienna when the writer and journalist Egon Erwin Kisch put him in touch with the economist August Singer, Brecht struggled to understand the wheat exchange and the ruthless competition between entrepreneurs for supremacy in the markets. Hauptmann fed Brecht's ravenous appetite for American material of all kinds: from biographies of entrepreneurs like the fabulously rich Vanderbilts and the notorious manipulator of stock prices, Daniel Drew, to tracts about financial speculation, boom and bust, and corruption. With Hauptmann, Brecht embarked on a series of dramatic projects directly or indirectly about the USA which were thematically related to *Jae Fleischhacker in Chicago*: *Man from Manhattan*, *Dan Drew* and *Mahagonny*. Brecht's struggle for a proper understanding of business and finance and for the artistic control of material towards which he was highly ambivalent – attracted as he was to the creative energy of entrepreneurs but aware, too, of the destructive potential of their behaviour – crystallised first in *Mahagonny*. He would return to the material in the early 1930s when he wrote *Saint Joan of the Stockyards*.

In the mid–1920s, Brecht evoked the USA in poems like 'Ane Smith Tells of the Conquest of America' with its ironic perspective upon the achievements of the white man in subjugating native Americans.[37] In his search for an understanding of US social and economic history, Brecht had left behind the romanticised world of Karl May. And in verses such as 'Bidi's View of the Cities' Brecht catastrophised the ultra-modern US cities with their grand skyscrapers, invoking their impending destruction after their seemingly inexorable rise.

Epic dramaturgy: The Brecht entourage at work and play

Brecht returned to Berlin in the autumn of 1925 with completed drafts of the plays and ballads for Kiepenheuer. However, as he had feared, Kiepenheuer did not commit to the publication of the ballads and in 1926 would produce just twenty-five unbound copies for Brecht's private use under the title *Pocket Breviary*. The ballads would be published in 1927 as *Domestic Breviary* in the Ullstein imprint Propyläen. Between Christmas 1925 and New Year Brecht gave Hauptmann a compilation of all the manuscripts they had produced for *Galy Gay*, soon to be *Man Equals Man*. However, the play was still far from finished. Brecht's dedication to Hauptmann includes the observation that she had worked for him all year without any payment. In order to counter persistent misunderstanding, she herself explained that all that year her payment had come from Kiepenheuer. However, that arrangement ended at the start of 1926. She then stepped up translation work to earn her living.

Hauptmann kept a diary for 1926, in which she recorded her work with Brecht, his plans and ideas, as well as her feelings and emotions during this intense period of her life. Brecht's flat at Spichernstrasse was simultaneously his office, where publishers, theatre managers and actors came and went while Hauptmann, Hesse-Burri and others worked with him. Hauptmann's diary of Monday, 4 January 1926 captures a day at the office:

> Wanted to work in the morning – but people from the Munich Kammerspiele were here on account of the production of *Galgei*. They won't give permission for Homolka to be in it. – Afterwards discussed a new play (*Young People Today* – Mentscher) and wrote some things down. Then cinema: *The Sailor* at UFA Zoo. With Buster Keaton. Beforehand Liszt's rhapsody (later in the prelude the same rhapsody as jazz). Glorious film – never boring. Small, sweeping mimicry. Wonderful as a diver repairing ships! Brecht afterwards Café Nürnberg. – Küpper and Homolka. Brecht's purchases are taking giant steps forward. From Christmas: Brown leisure suit, elegant slippers. – Then in the sale yesterday shoes, suit for 120 marks. Tie for 90 groschen.[38]

Like Marianne before her, Hauptmann took it upon herself to dress Brecht, who responded by wearing a 'Manchester workers' suit'. A boiler suit was Brecht's attire for the new age.

Together with Hauptmann, Hesse-Burri and others in the entourage, Brecht started going to boxing matches, the latest fashion in Berlin's artistic circles. Hesse-Burri, who himself boxed, was well in with the boxing crowd and introduced Brecht to the German light-heavyweight champion Paul Samson-Körner. There is a photograph of the Brecht entourage at Spichernstrasse, with Samson-Körner on the piano.

On 6 January Hauptmann noted: 'In the morning Seeler here. Discussion of *Baal*. – 2 o'clock. Then Sybille Binder. Me in the afternoon to Ullstein. In the evening Samson-Körner tells stories. Brecht farces afterwards. Brecht appears in the magazine today – "Hook to the Chin".'[39] Brecht's story was one of several pieces about boxing which he worked on with Hauptmann and Hesse-Burri at a time when he was trying out the short story form from the US. And he accessed mass-circulation magazines and newspapers for his poems and short stories, many written with Hauptmann, both for greater financial gain and to spread his writings more widely. The most ambitious piece was the unfinished 'Life Story of the Boxer Samson-Körner'. The writing of life histories, albeit with maximum freedom for invention, was Brecht's thing.

He took the same approach in yet another re-writing of *Baal* as a 'dramatic biography' with the title *The Life Story of the Man Baal*. Brecht, who directed its production at the Junge Bühne of the Deutsches Theater, later claimed that it was his first drama constructed explicitly as Epic Theatre.[40] *The Life Story of the Man Baal* is much shorter than earlier versions, with only thirteen scenes. Each scene is given an explanatory title such as 'Baal Abuses his Power over a Woman'. Teasingly asserting the material's historical authenticity, Brecht made the palpably false claim that his play was based on a real man, a mechanic with the unlikely name of Josef K. Kafka's *The Trial* had appeared the previous year with its central character of the same name. He set the story in early twentieth-century Augsburg, beginning in 1904, when the poet Baal first entered the company of civilised people, and ending with his death in 1912. Brecht now presents him as a 'passive genius', an 'abnormal' figure, signalling a decidedly critical attitude towards the hedonistic individual, the anachronistic product of an old, bourgeois world.

The representation of passive types, who adapt as best they can to the bewilderingly changing circumstances of the modern world becomes a major pre-occupation in *Man Equals Man*. Galy Gay is such a figure. However, the Baal material, dominated by the larger-than-life Baal, was quite resistant to such transformation. The premiere on 14 February 1926 triggered the usual chaotic audience scenes with shouting, jeering, whistling and clapping. The tumult was followed by another battle of the critics, Ihering and Kerr lining up against each other with their barbs. Brecht hailed the play a success to his brother but most critics came out against the production.

Brecht expounded to Hauptmann his rapidly developing ideas about Epic Theatre. The term already enjoyed some currency in Berlin theatre. For example, in 1924 Alfons Paquet described his play *Flags* as an 'epic drama' on account of the episodic succession of short scenes.[41] Brecht now explained to Hauptmann that his formula for Epic Theatre was to 'act from memory'.[42] Contemporary dramatists, he said, mixed up all the threads of the action with great artistry. However, this meant that actors could not act from memory. What he called the 'quotable gestures which could be cited' – a favourite phrase which indicates Brecht's deep attachment to the poetic density and resonance of language – were missing. Acting from the memory of such quotable gestures was the way to create what he called 'showing scenes'. In this way, the poetry of Brecht's dramas could be translated into precisely choreographed movement, demonstrating meaning. Epic Theatre was an assemblage of such showing scenes. These comments, like his earlier comments about emotion and reason, demonstrate further how much the origins of Brecht's Epic Theatre are to be found not in sophisticated theoretical considerations but in a highly creative, idiosyncratic sensibility. To take the theory most frequently discussed in the context of Epic Theatre: Brecht's interpretation of Marxism would enrich Epic Theatre but Epic Theatre did not itself derive from Brecht's Marxism, as has at times been claimed.

Brecht first used the term Epic Theatre in public in an interview in the summer of 1926, during which he announced: 'I'm for the Epic Theatre!'.[43] He explained that his poetry had a more private character, while his dramas were an 'objective view' of things. To explain what he meant, he employed the language of his sensibility. Rather than actors playing 'to the audience's hearts', he explained, figures should be portrayed 'quite coldly, classically and objectively': 'For they are not matter for empathy; they are there to be understood. Feelings are private and limited. Against that, reason is fairly comprehensive and to be relied on'. The production had to bring out the 'material incidents' in a 'perfectly sober and matter-of-fact way'. Brecht however, had to concede that his plays were 'usually performed all wrong. People perform the poet they imagine me to be'.

Brecht wrote poetry virtually every day, generally a solitary activity when he felt a poem 'coming on'. His verse remained quite un-theorised, while his dramatic writing was already associated with a narrative of rescuing the institution of theatre from the grips of a bourgeois society in terminal decline. For those looking to attack Brecht, the disjunction between lyrical and dramatic production, between the 'subjective' and the 'objective' Brecht, was a ready target. Critics have played on the disjunction to this day. The misunderstandings would persist, to Brecht's great frustration as hostile critics played off Brecht the poet against Brecht the dramatist. In a new edition of his *Anarchy in Drama*, the influential Bernhard Diebold of *Frankfurter Zeitung* would go so far as to claim, employing Brecht's terminology, that his material was not 'suitable for the stage' and his ideas 'not utilisable for the drama'. This would prompt Brecht to write to Döblin about an invitation to read his poems in the Herrenhaus:

> I have serious misgivings, because my poems have so much to answer for that for some time now every rhyme has stuck in my craw. The trouble is that my poetry is the most telling argument against my plays. The reader heaves a sigh of relief and says my father should have brought me up to be a poet and not a dramatist. As though my singular distaste for the existing 'drama' didn't argue in my favour. After all, I'm only trying to develop a form that will make it possible to accomplish on the stage what distinguishes your novels from Thomas Mann's. In view of the extremely recalcitrant nature of the dramatic medium, I don't know whether this

endeavour comes through clearly enough; more often than not the audience's reaction is one of abject fear.[44]

Brecht's final insight was wholly correct. Often an antagonistic pedagogue, he pitted himself against the audience and critics – and himself too –, challenging them to overcome the limitations and weaknesses he identified in existing positions. And Brecht could be frank with Döblin, a hugely gifted novelist who was not a direct competitor. Döblin was virtually the only contemporary to whom Brecht would grant equal status. The pressure which Brecht felt surely now contributed to his imposition of constraints upon himself in writing poetry, in which conventionally understood subjectivity was 'liquidated', in the interest of an objectivity which was conveyed in a restrained, matter-of-fact tone. On the question of subjectivity, Brecht's poetry began to develop with the same logic as his drama.

Man Equals Man

Brecht had sent his brother *Man Equals Man* in February 1926, telling him that he should imagine it as a 'Chaplin comedy, the act of transformation with a jazz band, every number individual and, while they deconstruct their man and their cantonment, all the time they sing the *Man Equals Man* song as they tap-dance'.[45] Brecht had produced a farce for the functionalist age of *Neue Sachlichkeit*, adapting the silent movie genre which Chaplin had perfected. Apart from the slapstick brutality of clown-like figures, the play was virtually unrecognisable from the original Augsburg *Galgei* drafts. Brecht had worked very hard to create something that had always eluded him: the deftest of plots. Unsurprisingly Walter, the student of modern methods of paper production, did not like the macabre comedy, with its vision of a humanity reduced to survival through behaviourist mimicry of capitalist production. Brecht told the press: 'The continuous self is a myth. Human beings are atoms constantly disintegrating and reconstituting themselves'.[46] As he always did anyway, Brecht set about re-writing. Hauptmann estimated this was the seventh re-write and that some scenes had been re-drafted more often still. As so often, he would return to the material repeatedly throughout his life, re-interpreting it in the light of his changing views.

Man Equals Man was premiered simultaneously in the autumn of 1926 in Darmstadt and Düsseldorf. Propyläen would publish the play in 1927. Brecht went to Darmstadt for rehearsals in mid-September where his friend Jacob Geis was directing, while Neher designed the set. For the first time, Neher deployed a half-curtain, which enabled the audience to follow the changes of scenery. The play now bore the sub-title, typical of the historical narrative of Epic Theatre, *The transformation of the porter Galy Gay in the military cantonment of Kilkoa during the year nineteen hundred and twenty five*. As Lyon shows, Brecht had appropriated much material from Kipling's exotic Indian world inhabited by the common soldiers serving in the British Army: Uria, Jesse and Jip are from *Soldiers Three*; Jip's imprisonment in a palanquin in the Pagoda of the Yellow God draws on 'The Incarnation of Krishna Mulvaney'; the break-in at the temple is in the ballad 'Loot'; the elephant imagery is to be found in the story 'Moti Guj

– Mutineer'; and finally, the motif of the three friends who bury a fourth friend occurs in the novel *The Light that Failed*. All this makes for a very strange setting indeed. Brecht employed it in his first parable play with Epic features, such as commentary on events by figures who step out of their roles and the interpolation of poems and songs.

In the Irish stevedore Galy Gay, formerly Galgei, Brecht creates a protagonist wholly at odds with his earlier hedonistic 'Old Adams', the vitalists Baal and Kragler. A simple, passive soul, Galy Gay becomes caught up in events way beyond his control, as he is commandeered to replace a soldier, Jeraiah Jip, lost to his comrades during their illegal entry to the Pagoda of the Yellow God. Brecht used the term 'montage' to describe the technological, composite nature of the change whereby Galy Gay becomes a 'human fighting machine'. To become a 'human fighting machine' may be viewed positively in the sense that Galy Gay thereby realises his own vitality. However, given the depiction of the British Army at the very outset as brutalised and brutalising, his transformation into one of them is morally questionable.[47] Brecht agonised over whether Galy Gay's transformation was to be evaluated positively or negatively. He explored the negative option in 1929 and after the Nazis came to power Brecht definitively regarded Galy Gay's integration into the collective as negative. However, the play was originally a farce about the functionality and exchangeability of human identity, which simply made a mockery of the individual's capacity to assert his will. The audience witnesses characters who are caught up in the advance of British imperialism and whose actions, in a series of ironic reversals, lead them only to lose control of their lives. Satisfaction of basic physical needs is the most that individuals can hope for, as they struggle to adapt to a hostile environment. Such a sardonic take on the human condition is typical of the early Brecht. However, only in later versions would a political Brecht become concerned about the moral implications of Galy Gay's transformation.

The presentation of the characters in the premiere was radically anti-empathetic. Brecht was not interested in any authentic representation of individual psychology, rather in the behavioural phenomenon of the man who accepts his change in the new, collective age. The individual only acquires his identity behaviourally, by virtue of his flexibility in his relationships with others in business exchange, since business deals characterise relations between all the characters. However, in keeping with Brecht's thoroughly cynical view of business, those relations are so much smoke and mirrors, shot through with deceit, as in the sale of a pretend elephant to the hapless Galy Gay. Galy Gay's vitality is at least consonant with his new identity. Renunciation of individualism appears to be the price that has to be paid for survival in the modern world. By contrast, in that world the identity of the 'Old Adam' Sergeant Fairchild, 'Bloody Five', a bastion of the British Army, is in conflict with his sensual nature. In a shocking scene which moves the play beyond farce, he is finally driven to castrate himself. Only Widow Begbick, Brecht's first major female figure, maintains the same identity throughout. This is down to her capacity as a profit-oriented businesswoman to adapt as her situation requires.

Most of the critics gravitated to the Darmstadt production. Reviews were mixed but the play would go on to enjoy great critical acclaim in Berlin and other cities as Brecht explored negative interpretations of Galy Gay's transformation in the collective, which, in Brecht's developing understanding, carried ever more political connotations.

Reading Marx

During a trip to Moscow in 1935 Brecht reflected upon his earlier investigations into the Chicago wheat exchange for the aborted *Jae Fleischhacker in Chicago*:

> I gained the impression that the dealings were downright inexplicable, that is, not accessible to rational understanding, in other words plainly irrational. The manner in which the world's wheat was distributed was utterly incomprehensible, from any angle, apart from that of a handful of speculators, the market in wheat was one huge swamp. The projected drama was never written. Instead I began to read Marx, and it was then, and only then that I did read Marx. And for the first time, my own scattered personal experiences and impressions really came to life.[48]

There is no doubting the seminal importance for Brecht of his reading of Marx. This retrospective view, however, collapses a lengthy and complex process into a quite simple narrative of his excited adoption of Marx. In similar vein, Brecht also later claimed: 'When I read Marx's *Das Kapital* I understood my plays'.[49] However, he offered the important qualification: 'Of course, I didn't discover that I'd written a whole pile of Marxist plays'. At the same time, by the mid–1920s Brecht had certainly formed the view that established drama was unsuited to the depiction of modern industrial processes like the production and distribution of the world's wheat. The episodic and historicising structure of Epic Theatre was emerging as Brecht's response.

Brecht produced his first statements about revolutionary socialism and art in 1926, the year when he also became acquainted with Lenin's *State and Revolution*. It is unlikely that Brecht read this work or Marx's *Das Kapital* from cover to cover. He was never a methodical reader, nor, for that matter, a systematic thinker. In 'On Art and Socialism', designed as a prologue for *Man Equals Man*, he explains that it was in socialism, 'here, amidst *these* oppositions, that I felt at home. It is not permitted to the *art* of this (so costly) period of transition to do more than adopt the "point of view" that it is *here* that the fruitful oppositions lie'.[50] He concludes: 'There can be no doubt that socialism, and by that I mean revolutionary socialism, will transform the face of our land in our own lifetime. Our lives will be dominated by struggles of this kind. As far as the artists are concerned, I reckon they would be best advised to take no heed and do whatever turns them on: otherwise they will be unable to produce good work'. *Man Equals Man* shows that Brecht was far from adopting the party discipline of revolutionary socialism, not to mention integrating it within his artistic practice. He did, however, believe that if he wanted to understand the age he needed to read more Marx. In October Hauptmann noted that Brecht was trying to establish which foundational texts of socialism and Marxism he should read first.[51] Shortly after, he was writing to her that he was immersed in *Das Kapital* and that he had to gain exact knowledge about it. Among his books of the year in 1926 Brecht listed Henri Guilbeaux's *Vladimir Illyich Lenin* and René Fülöp-Miller's *The Mind and Face of Bolshevism*. However, another piece from 1926, 'On Socialism', again shows that he is far from embracing a Marxist position. As Tom Kuhn and Steve Giles observe, Brecht had a 'distaste at the thought of surrendering the individual life in the name of equality' reminiscent of Heinrich Heine.[52] Despite the boiler suit, Brecht would not succumb to the illusion that he could morph his middle-class values and identity into those of workers. Brecht wonders how people might live in a society after a socialist revolution and is troubled by the prospect of being deprived of bourgeois comforts. He finds the uniformity of it all distasteful: 'Are they supposed to crouch in their freshly painted identical huts between gramophones and tins of mince-meat, with their fixed-price women and their identical pipes? That isn't happiness, all opportunity and risk are missing. Opportunity and risk, the greatest and most moral things of all'.[53] Brecht was far too impulsively creative to countenance dispensing with opportunity and risk, those crucial challenges in life.

Marxism interested Brecht as a branch of sociology, yielding historical and theoretical insights which had inspired Lenin and his fellow Bolsheviks. Reading Marx undoubtedly transformed Brecht's understanding of the nature of socio-economic change and of concepts that could be employed for the analysis of art and the theatre in the emerging new age. In response to the question how to perform the classics he first used the term 'material value'.[54] Suggesting that in future the appreciation of art would rely on concepts drawn from labour theory of value, he juxtaposed 'material value' with what he regarded as the outmoded, fraudulent notion of aesthetic value. In a polemic against Leopold Jessner, he dismissed the existing theatre's capacity to make anything of the classics, whereas he claimed that the small group of young practitioners to which he belonged could offer the necessary fresh perspectives, among them political, which the harsh demands of an impatient age required.

Brecht sought to enlist a somewhat reluctant Ihering, that earlier 'traitor' to the cause, as his mouthpiece in the struggle. It was open to question, Brecht wrote, whether his contemporaries had real talent. He had no doubt that they lacked direction. Brecht cut to the chase:

> And even if you believed that the one and only attempt to frame a theory of the theatre, i.e., Jessner's, may lead to something in the nature of a new theatre adequate to the cities of our century, you would have to pay for this opinion by renouncing the creation of new plays: for up until now this style has impoverished (not changed) older works beyond recognition and made new ones look as old as the hills.[55]

Seeking to stiffen Ihering's resolve, Brecht suggested, breathtakingly, to his most loyal and effective publicist: 'There has been something of a vacuum around my affairs these last few years'! Brecht continued in best contrarian mode: 'There is nothing to save in the present-day theatre and the relatively better it functions the more absolutely it must be combated'. The relentlessly iconoclastic Brecht was leaving Ihering far behind.

Monumental Success 1927–8

Out with the old

Brecht was adamant that his generation must present itself in the sharpest of contrasts to the old, which was wedded to a dying 'bourgeois' institution of literature. He had long ago abandoned his adolescent regard for poets like Rilke and George, whom he lumped together with Thomas Mann and other 'bourgeois' writers. Brecht would have none of their cult of the 'spirit'. For him, their aestheticist polarisation of art and life had driven literature to the brink. Rilke was a favourite target. When he died Brecht wrote: 'In several of his poems there is mention of God. I draw your attention to the fact that whenever Rilke is dealing with God, he expresses himself in an utterly camp fashion. Nobody who has ever noticed this can ever again read a line of these verses without a disfiguring smirk.'[1]

Brecht used Willy Haas's Berlin weekly *Die Literarische Welt* as a platform to launch multiple polemics against the established literary world and its theatre. He attacked the 'cheap irony' of Mann's *The Magic Mountain*, recommending detective novels instead. When Mann suggested that the difference between Brecht and himself was not so great, Brecht, who called Mann 'that sort story writer', responded that in a dispute between a carriage and a motor car it would certainly be the carriage that found the difference minimal! Brecht's reverential words for the recently deceased Franz Kafka were simultaneously a display of contempt for the contemporary scene: 'If it is permissible to speak at all about a truly serious figure like Franz Kafka in a literary environment which simply does not deserve any kind of serious treatment, [...] then to do so at least requires an apology. To the credit of the present, it has to be said that it admits quite frankly that it is not for phenomena like Kafka'. Brecht would be as consistent in his admiration of Kafka as he would be in his contempt for the phoney mysticism of fashionable Kafka aficionados – until, reviewing his own procedure in exile under the pressures of combating Fascist Germany, he took issue with Kafka's style in his famous exchanges with Walter Benjamin.

Brecht encouraged young writers to distance themselves from Rilkean nonsense. He set an example with his cycle 'Reader for City Dwellers'. ['Aus dem Lesebuch für Städtebewohner'] In a matter-of-fact tone he pointed out that toughness and resilience were needed in the strange, fleeting and hostile environment of modern urban life, which threatened the identity of the self:

The linen hanging out to dry in the yard
Is my linen; I know it well.
Looking closer however I see
Darns in it and extra patches.
It seems
I have moved out. Someone else
Is living here now and
Doing so in
My linen.[2]

In early 1927 Brecht delivered his most notorious attack on 'bourgeois' literature. Invited to judge a poetry competition for *Die Literarische Welt*, Brecht produced a 'Short Report on 400 (Four Hundred) Young Poets'. He prefaced his comments with lines from his 'Mandalay Song' about Mother Goddam's whore house before caricaturing contemporary German verse as 'pretty pictures and aromatic words'.[3] Brecht dismissed Germany's leading poets whom the young poets had imitated: 'I don't think much of the poetry of Rilke (an otherwise really good man), Stefan George or Werfel'. As for the young poets themselves, Brecht wrote: 'I got to know a sort of youth whose acquaintance I could have done so much better without'. Claiming that he had 'never been particularly interested in poetry', Brecht suggested that it 'must surely be something that one can investigate for its use value'.

In similar vein to Brecht's reference to 'material value', 'use value' meant that, as Tom Kuhn and Steve Giles explain, literature must not only have and express a social base, but literary value itself could only be understood in terms of social function.[4] Brecht's employment of use value as, in effect, an aesthetic category had huge consequences, not least for his own output. If poetry had a future, Brecht maintained, it was in conjunction with ideas drawn from economists' theories of value, including labour theory of value, and from sociology rather than traditional aesthetics. Brecht awarded the poetry prize not to any of the competitors but to Hannes Küpper, whose 'He! He! The Iron Man' celebrated the Australian cycling champion Reggie Mac Namara. Poets and critics were outraged. Together with Willi Fehse, Klaus Mann, son of Thomas, published an anthology of new poetry specifically to rebut Brecht's attack. Brecht was in his element. 'What do you think the public wants from you?', he was asked and gave the crisp reply: 'I think they want to see a bit of life from me for their money'.[5]

Brecht's strategy remained brutally simple: exemplary denunciation of existing artistic practice and relentless promotion of his own work. He could be starkly instrumental in his treatment of other young writers and directors. How far he identified with them depended on how strong he judged his own position, how great their talent and whether they accepted that they were part of his project. Engel, Hesse-Burri and Neher were his. He could take or leave Bronnen. He used his influence with Moritz Seeler to persuade him to put on Marieluise Fleisser's comedy *Purgatory in Ingolstadt*, using the production to showcase his own directorial talent. Brecht rapidly gained recognition as the leading spokesman of the young generation, whose views were eagerly sought. The *Berliner Illustrierte* produced a collage of young writers with Brecht in the middle. One day he felt that Hesse-Burri, Döblin and Gottfried Benn belonged up there with him, on another he could brook no competition: he was disgusted that everyone was writing with such deadly seriousness and he was negative even about Döblin.[6]

Political Theatre, Epic Theatre and the revolutionary cultural scene

The Volksbühne was the traditional home of Berlin's radical theatre. Originally a product of Naturalism in the 1890s, it had, however, become an established institution which would not accept the politicisation that young dramatists were promoting. In March 1927, the Volksbühne took a stand against the foremost representative of the new Political Theatre, Erwin Piscator. With his proletarian Volksbühne, Piscator, a KPD member, was at the height of his fame. Piscator's Political Theatre discouraged the audience from identifying with the characters on stage. Piscator employed film projections, photos and banners with slogans but did not break with established forms as radically as Brecht was now beginning to envisage. Piscator split from the Volksbühne and, with Ludwig Katzenellenbogen's financial backing, founded his own theatre, the Theater am Nollendorfplatz, together with a Dramaturgical Collective comprising several left-wing dramatists. Brecht was one of them for about a year but was never properly on board. His only collaboration to bear fruit with Piscator was the adaptation of Jaroslav Hašek's picaresque novel *The Good Soldier Schweyk*, though the extent of Brecht's involvement remains unclear. Brecht would return to *Schweyk* in exile. In fact, in 'The Theatre Communist' Brecht satirised Communism as the latest fashion to sweep through the modish world of Berlin's Kurfürstendamm, spawning opportunities for self-styled Communist directors on the make:

> For 3000 marks a month
> He is prepared
> To put on the misery of the masses
> For 100 marks a day
> He displays
> The injustice of the world.[7]

It is true that Piscator himself enjoyed the material trappings of success. Brecht recognised Piscator's originality as a director and over the years they talked again and again about collaborative projects but few came to fruition. These highly competitive individuals who occupied rival theatrical positions could never have an easy relationship.

In March 1927 Brecht bracketed Piscator's work with the Epic Theatre which he and like-minded dramatists were producing. And in his next attempt to summarise what constituted Epic Theatre, Brecht wrote of the incorporation of film in 'The Piscator Experiment'.[8] He explained that film was employed to present those parts of the dramatic action that contained no essential dramatic conflict, so as to take the strain off the spoken word, which became absolutely decisive when used. The spectator could witness and judge processes in which protagonists made their decisions, without having to view those processes through the protagonists' eyes. However, Brecht also pointed out Piscator's deficiencies, in contrast to Epic Theatre: what Brecht called the unexploited transition from word to image and Piscator's reliance upon a supposedly over-emotional, 'operatic' style.

Brecht offered Piscator his public support but was, of course, ambitious to promote his own work. Indeed, the Collective proved a bone of contention. As Brecht developed his ideas about Epic Theatre, he had damning things to say about Piscator: 'People tend to see Piscator's attempt to renew theatre as revolutionary. But it is revolutionary neither in terms of production nor in terms of politics, but only in terms of theatre'. When another member of the Collective, Felix Gasbarra, published a piece which appeared to describe himself as its artistic director, Brecht took exception, writing to Piscator: 'I am not prepared to work under Gasbarra's *literary* direction, but under his political leadership I would be. I may be your comrade, but I am definitely not your dramaturg'.[9] Brecht was not actually his comrade. He proposed to Piscator, apparently in all seriousness: 'You abandon the literary character of the collective and make it political, start a "Red Club" (R. C.) and call the theatre R. C. T. ("Red Club Theatre").)'. Brecht suggested that the club 'would use the theatre only for political purposes'. It could 'really play a political role, issue political pamphlets, etc'. Piscator recalled Brecht pacing around the theatre during their altercations, calling out again and again: 'My name is my trademark, and anybody who uses it must pay for it'.[10] The intensely competitive Brecht was convinced that he was greater than the rest of the Collective put together. These exchanges took place before Piscator's new theatre at the Nollendorfplatz had even opened its doors. It did so in September 1927 but was bankrupt by the end of the season with debts of nearly a million marks, half of which was owed to Katzenellenbogen.

Brecht was not part of the working-class revolutionary cultural scene, in which Piscator was a key figure. The scene involved another figure new to Berlin, the Viennese composer Hanns Eisler. Eisler was a pupil of Arnold Schönberg, with whom he had broken politically. He was the brother of Ruth Eisler (later Fischer) and of Gerhart Eisler. Both were influential figures in the Communist International, also known as the Comintern or Third International, the organisation which Lenin established in 1919 to spearhead the triumph of World Communism. Brecht's links with the Comintern would come through the Eislers. By virtue of their political as well as artistic affinities, Brecht's working relationship with Hanns Eisler would become very special and endure to the end of Brecht's life. Like other left-wing artists, they would place work with the organs of the vast media empire which, with the support of the Comintern, Willi Münzenberg established in Germany. When Münzenberg fled into exile in Paris he would salvage as much as he could for the anti-Fascist struggle.

In Berlin Eisler joined with the actor-singer Ernst Busch in composing words and music for workers' choirs at mass events at venues such as the Sportpalast. The Sportpalast, later the venue for Goebbels's notorious 'Total War' harangue, could hold as many as 20,000 people. Mass working-class cultural spectacles using agitprop techniques in support of revolutionary socialism enjoyed a high profile at a time when TV did not exist and radio did not broadcast such material. The Eisler-Busch partnership became famous throughout the German-speaking world with songs like 'Red Wedding'. The district of Wedding was a KPD stronghold in the north of Berlin. All the girls fell in love with the handsome Busch, including the young worker Margarete Steffin, later Brecht's collaborator and lover. With his conviction about the need for theatre to emulate mass sporting events, Brecht could only be impressed by artists like Busch and Eisler. In the early 1930s Brecht would gravitate to that world.

Hitherto anti-bourgeois and anti-capitalist in attitude, Brecht took steps to sharpen his political awareness as he elaborated upon the revolutionary potential of Epic Theatre. In early 1927 he got to know the heretical Marxist sociologist Fritz Sternberg, the author of the well-known book *Imperialism*. They met at Brecht's favourite restaurant, Schlichter's, on Martin-Luther-Strasse in Schöneberg. That was where, as Elias Canetti puts it, 'intellectual Berlin hung out'.[11] It was run by Max Schlichter, brother of the prominent *neusachlich* painter and KPD member Rudolf, who had portrayed Brecht. Schlichter's paintings and Georg Grosz's, too, hung on the walls for sale. Heinrich George, Theo Lingen, Egon Erwin Kisch, Kurt Tucholsky, Alfred Döblin, John Heartfield and Bronnen were regular customers, as were Joseph Goebbels and Albert Speer. Shortly after, Rudolf Schlichter would, like Bronnen, move tables to join Goebbels and his friends on the nationalist Right.

Brecht and Sternberg met at least once a week and Brecht attended some of Sternberg's classes on Marxism. He dedicated a copy of *Man Equals Man* to him as 'my first teacher'.[12] Sternberg found Brecht a highly speculative, impulsive thinker who made great associative leaps, which no one else would remotely consider. This was characteristic of Brecht in intellectual exchange, a Bonapartism quite at odds with a cool rationalism, which prompted him to override considerations that would inhibit others. Brecht and Sternberg wrote two polemical pieces about the crisis in the theatre, which appeared in Ihering's *Berliner Börsen-Courier*. Sternberg went first with an anonymous 'Letter to a Dramatist from Mr X'.[13] Adopting a sweepingly provocative manner, Sternberg judged the decline of the drama a 'historical necessity' because the 'individual with all its conflicts by virtue of its individuality, indivisibility, impermutability' was in the process of disappearing. All drama to date, he asserted, was based on the Shakespearean model of great individuals, which had run its course as the new collective age was emerging out of the decline of capitalism. Sternberg proposed that drama should therefore be liquidated. Brecht responded with 'Shouldn't we Abolish Aesthetics?'.[14] He agreed with Sternberg to the extent that 'old' drama should indeed be liquidated. Building upon his championing of material value and use value, Brecht argued that the sociological rather than the aesthetic perspective was appropriate for a new form of drama, which rejected all that had gone before it: 'The works now being written are coming more and more to lead towards that great Epic Theatre which corresponds to the sociological situation; neither their content nor their form can be understood except by the minority that understands this. They are not going to satisfy the old aesthetics; they are going to destroy it'. A note from Sternberg followed: 'It wasn't Marx who led you to speak of the decline of the drama and to talk of the Epic Theatre. It was you yourself. For, to put it gently, "Epic Theatre" – that's you, Mr Brecht'. Sternberg rightly highlighted Brecht's original genius. Brecht now consistently promoted the sociological, hence scientific, position over the aesthetic, if not any consistently articulated Marxist stance, suggesting in another piece: 'Instead of taking the aesthetic, culinary position criticism should take the sociological, scientific position'.[15]

In the polemical flow promoting Epic Theatre, Brecht produced a piece which has frequently been taken to be part of a clearly formulated theory rather than as one of many pieces dashed off in the cut and thrust of polemical exchange. The scale of Brecht's avant-gardist ambition is apparent in his contention that the '*radical transformation of the theatre*' has to 'correspond to the radical transformation of the mentality of our time':

> The symptoms of this transformation are familiar enough, and so far they have been seen as symptoms of disease. There is some justification for this, for of course what one sees first of all are the signs of decline in whatever is *old*. But it would be wrong to see these phenomena, so-called *Amerikanismus* for instance, as something different from those unhealthy changes stimulated by the operation of really new mental influences on our culture's aged body. And it would be wrong too to treat these new ideas as if they were not ideas and not *mental* phenomena at all, and to try to build up the theatre against them as a kind of bastion of the mind. On the contrary, it is precisely theatre, art and literature which have to form the 'ideological superstructure' for a solid, practical rearrangement of our age's way of life.[16]

With the term 'ideological superstructure' Brecht introduces specifically Marxist terminology to his critical vocabulary for the first time. He explains that it would not be possible to 'expound the principles of the Epic Theatre in a few catch-phrases' since they 'still mostly needed to be worked out in detail'. He offers the following as a principle, perhaps the 'essential point', which has all to do with his sensibility and not with Marxism: 'It appeals less to the feelings than to the spectator's reason. Instead of sharing an experience the spectator must come to grips with things. At the same time it would be quite wrong to try and deny emotion to this kind of theatre. It would be much the same thing as trying to deny emotion to modern science'.

Brecht took care not to use absolute oppositions between emotional engagement and critical distance, something often forgotten in discussion of Brechtian theory. As we know, it was his hyper-sensitivity towards the capacity of art to damage him emotionally and even physically that led him to emphasise control of emotional responses through intellectual distance and analysis. However elaborate his theoretical writings became, this would remain their cornerstone. Tellingly, in the coming months, Brecht broke off several drafts in frustration at his attempts to elucidate further principles of Epic Theatre, which had always to remain work in progress as Brecht struggled to formulate a rational exposition of what were in essence intuitions.

Brecht meets Weill: *Mahagonny*

In April 1927 Brecht's ballads, *Domestic Breviary,* at last appeared with Propyläen. The title parodies Protestant books of religious reflection like Luther's breviaries, which Brecht knew so well. In a somewhat tongue-in-cheek demonstration of his new aesthetic, loosely based on socio-economic thinking, he appended instructions for the use of the collection. The volume also contained Neher's drawing of Hydratopyranthropos, the water-fire-man, Neher's marvellous take on his friend's erratic subjectivity. At the back, Brecht added music for a number of the ballads, among them 'Apfelböck' and 'Ballad of the Dead Soldier'. Brecht, who had previously written his own music, collaborated on these pieces with the young composer Franz S. Bruinier. The collection comprises ballads written between 1916 and 1925, many of which we have discussed. It was divided into a sequence of lessons. Much of the earlier verse now seemed to belong to another age, which Brecht had left behind in his grittily realist poetry like 'Reader for City Dwellers'. That left many critics who did not know his early work confused. However, Kurt Tucholsky produced the boldly prophetic judgement that Brecht, together with Gottfried Benn, was Germany's greatest lyrical talent. In *Vossische Zeitung* Brecht's friend Otto Zarek praised *Domestic Breviary* as the 'most substantial volume of poems for years'.[17] Meanwhile, Alexander Abusch continued his critique of Brecht from a KPD position. Many KPD figures shared Abusch's view that Brecht could not yet relate to the struggle of the proletariat. Abusch argued that while Brecht was anti-bourgeois and attacked the stagnation of that class, his work relied too much on individualistic glorification of alcoholic sensations. That was certainly part of their attraction. When Brecht picked up the collection again in exile in 1940 he observed, cleverly modulating Abusch's earlier view:

> This is where literature attains the stage of dehumanisation which Marx observed in the proletariat, along with the desperation which inspires the proletariat's hopes. The bulk of the poems deal with decline, and the poems follow our crumbling society all the way down. Beauty founded on wrecks, rags becoming a delicacy. Nobility wallows in the dust, meaninglessness is welcomed as a means of liberation. The poet no longer has any sense of solidarity, not even with himself. Risus mortis. But it doesn't lack power.[18]

That deathly laughter was very powerful indeed. By 1940 Brecht did not care to reflect long on the poet's lack of solidarity at that time of decay and decline, which had threatened to envelop him, too.

Domestic Breviary contained Brecht's Mahagonny songs about the gross imaginary city of that name. The Mahagonny songs caught the eye of the young composer Kurt Weill, who suggested to Brecht that he set them to music for the Baden-Baden Festival of German Chamber Music. A pupil of Engelbert Humperdinck and Ferruccio Busoni, Weill had a marvellous musical pedigree and had been making a name for himself, working with Georg Kaiser to renew musical drama. Weill had just written an enthusiastic review of the Berlin radio production of *Man Equals Man*, describing it as the most innovative and best play of the time. He praised Brecht as a 'writer, a real writer', who had resolved at a stroke and with a 'wonderful sensibility' many of the problems associated with writing for the new medium.[19]

Brecht, then, had good reason to be well-disposed to Weill when they met at Schlichter's. Like Brecht, Weill was determined to sweep away hoary old theatrical traditions and to create new forms appropriate to contemporary needs. In Brecht's modern texts Weill saw a spirit at work similar to his own. They immediately agreed to work together and rapidly formed one of the great poet-composer partnerships. Artistic collaboration was their sole common ground. That made things quite different from Brecht's later partnership with Hanns Eisler, which rested on their shared political and aesthetic agendas.

Weill composed the music for the Mahagonny songs in the spring and early summer of 1927. Brecht met Weill in July for rehearsals, having driven down to Augsburg, then to Baden-Baden. Neher designed the stage as a boxing ring, with a wall for the projection of images. In the programme notes Brecht and Weill wrote: 'The little epic play *Mahagonny* simply draws consequences from the unstoppable decay of the existing social strata. It is already addressing a public that demands enjoyment in the theatre in a naive way'.[20] The 'little epic play' for a mass audience was broadcast on the radio. As Jennie, Weill's wife Lotte Lenya sang the 'Alabama Song', which was written in English, launching herself as the great interpreter of Brecht-Weill songs:

> Oh, Moon of Alabama
> We now must say good-bye.
> We've lost our good old mama
> And must have whisky
> Oh, you know why.[21]

On their way to Mahagonny, Jim, Jake, Bill and Joe boast:

> Underneath our shirts we've got
> Money and we've got a lot
> That should smear some smile across
> Your big and stupid face.

This set the tone for what Brecht hailed to Weigel as a 'great directorial success! A fifteen-minute scandal!'.[22] Weill's music earned Heinrich Stroebel's praise in the *Berliner Börsen-Courier* for its original 'blending of jazz, cabaret songs and lyric elements'.[23] The famous Brecht-Weill sound was born. However, the festival audience of middle-class avant-gardists was divided over the lyrics. A majority vehemently rejected the caricature of a middle-class world populated by crooks and whores, and the audience was scandalised when the performers paraded anti-capitalist slogans in the finale. However, a minority ardently supported the production with its cutting-edge social and political message, seeing it as a highly innovative satire upon the grossness of the contemporary western world.

This was enough to prompt Brecht and Weill to develop the material into a full-length opera, *The Rise and Fall of the City of Mahagonny*, a work on the lines of a contemporary Sodom and Gomorrah. Weill's Viennese publisher Emil Hertzka of Universal-Edition urged him to 'exercise the greatest caution' because he feared that Brecht would produce lyrics which were quite unacceptable for a major opera house.[24] Weill responded quite firmly: 'The reason I am drawn to Brecht is, first of all, the strong interaction of my music with his poetry, which surprised all those in Baden-Baden who were competent to judge. But further I am convinced that the close collaboration of two equally productive individuals can lead to something fundamentally new'. Weill was every bit as convinced as Brecht that he was equipped to produce exemplary work for the new age: 'The task is to create the new genre which gives appropriate expression to the completely transformed manifestation of life in our time'. Weill conveyed his excitement that they would produce a 'completely new form of stage work', which would impact upon the stagnant operatic form. Brecht found the opportunity irresistible to create a genuinely popular alternative to an elitist form so remote from ordinary people, which epitomised the 'culinary' theatre he so despised.

After Baden-Baden, Brecht retired to his attic in Augsburg where from August until October he worked on the *Mahagonny* opera and resumed his study of Marxism. He asked Weigel to send him 'all the Marxist literature you can lay your hands on' and told her: 'I'm feeling very well here and am reading the classics (Engels and Marx)'.[25] However, medical matters loomed large in Brecht's letters to Weigel that summer. She and Stefan were on holiday in Vienna with her family, who were looking after Frank. Brecht asked her to consult with Frank's doctor about what medical support he needed – and what would be the most suitable career for his eight-year-old son! While Frank's distressing condition required regular attention, Brecht arranged a consultation for Weigel with his Munich friend and physician Johannes Ludwig Schmitt. Brecht was concerned about his own condition, too. He told Weigel that Heinrich Gottron, a specialist in sexually transmitted diseases at the Charité, 'hasn't found anything more'.[26] However, shortly after he wrote: 'One more thing, Helli: I've had some discharge, little and I'm sure it's only catarrh, because I have catarrh in any case, but go to Gottron come what may!'. The chances of Brecht's discharge being catarrh were probably not great. Brecht befriended Schmitt and Gottron and maintained friendships with these distinguished specialists until the end of his life.

That summer in Augsburg, Brecht began a new drama on which he worked until 1930, *The Downfall of the Egotist Johann Fatzer*. Set near the end of the First World War and depicting a group of four deserters intending to join the revolt against the existing order, *Fatzer* deals with the painful transformation of the individual at the dawn of the new age. Presenting the urban collective and the interests of solidarity for the first time, the work was intended as a decisive shift in Brecht's attitude concerning the individual in society. In similar vein to his adaptation of the Baal material in *The Life Story of the Man Baal*, in *Fatzer* Brecht attempts the critical depiction of the hedonistic vitalist. Seeking to overcome his earlier fascination with this type, not least because he had become aware of the destructiveness of his own impulsive hedonism, in the *Fatzer* project Brecht took a further step, creating a counterweight to the hedonist in the character of Herr Keuner. Keuner epitomises the ascetic, sceptical revolutionary thinker and teacher, as which Brecht was beginning to conceive of himself after the summer of 1925. Keuner condemns Fatzer, taking the lead in the liquidation of this anarchist when Fatzer distances himself from his comrades and endangers the revolution. However, Keuner fails in his request that the vitalist Fatzer declare his agreement [Einverständnis] with his own execution. Fatzer is interested neither in self-renunciation nor in acceptance that the collective view is correct. Despite the fact that Brecht worked on *Fatzer* until 1930, producing a huge volume of material, it is telling that the play remained a fragment, by far the most extensive amongst all his papers, as Brecht struggled with the liquidation of Fatzer, whose character contained so much of his own. Heiner Müller later recognised in his adaptation that the fragment was very important indeed. Fatzer remains a potent symbol in Brecht's work for the hedonistic individual, both vitally creative and unmanageably destructive for the collective.

Back in Berlin that autumn, a struggling Brecht was forced to take to his bed for some weeks because of illness.[27] However, he and Weill made progress on the *Mahagonny* libretto. In November 1927 Weill claimed to an anxious Hertzka that the libretto was being 'shaped entirely according to my instructions', with the music enjoying precedence. Weill sent his publisher a first draft with eighteen scenes on 8 December. However, Hertzka objected that it lacked plot, contained too much 'Wild West realism', not enough symbolism, and requested a 'dose of positive, human qualities'. Around Christmas, Weill explained to Hertzka that he had worked with Brecht to achieve the 'most logical, straightforward and easily comprehensible plot possible', adding: 'In the operatic style I am establishing here, music has a much more fundamental role than in the purely story-line opera, since I am replacing the earlier bravura aria with a new kind of popular song'. In March 1928 Weill told him that they hoped to finish the composition by May. However, another project intervened, which changed their lives.

The Threepenny Opera: A new musical theatre

Elisabeth Hauptmann had been translating John Gay's satirical ballad opera of 1728, *The Beggar's Opera*, a parody of Italian opera style. She told Brecht of the huge success of the revival at London's Lyric Theatre where it had run since 1920 for an astonishing 1,463 performances. Instead of the usual grand music and themes of opera, Gay's work relied on everyday tunes and characters. Some songs by composers like Handel were used, but only the most popular. The audience could sing along to the music and enjoy the characters in this satire about corruption at all levels of society.

The Beggar's Opera had nothing remotely to do with the programme that Brecht had formulated in 1925. He had scarcely touched the material when one day at Schlichter's in the spring of 1928, Ernst Josef Aufricht asked him if he had a new play for the re-opening of the Theater am Schiffbauerdamm, which Aufricht was planning for his birthday, 31 August 1928. Brecht quickly convinced him that his adaptation of the *Beggar's Opera* was the very thing: 'This story smacked of theatre'.[28] Brecht, Weill and Hauptmann signed a contract for the playbook with the theatrical agency and publisher Felix Bloch Erben. Brecht was due 62.5 per cent of the royalties, Weill 25 per cent and Hauptmann 12.5 per cent. Aufricht was by no means sure of the 'atonal' avant-gardist Weill and engaged his own musical director Theo Mackeben, together with the seven-piece Lewis Ruth Band.

The material was right up Brecht and Weill's street. However, it would have to be re-cast substantially to make it work as a satire of modern society. On the other hand, it was a lighter work than German writers were used to. For both Weill and Brecht, it was therefore an opportunity to break down barriers between elite and popular art. Gay's text invited that very approach to satire, revelling in egotistical cynicism and hedonistic energy, which Brecht was actually trying to overcome: an invitation to all to participate in a glorious celebration of pleasure and pain. In Gay's gangster Macheath,

Brecht encountered an irresistible, hedonistic outsider in the same mould as his great early creations. Of course, when Brecht wrote about the project for German critics in January 1929 he pointed to the serious underlying message: 'Just like two hundred years ago we have a social order in which virtually all levels, albeit in a wide variety of ways, pay respect to moral principles not by leading a moral life but by living off morality'.[29] The character of Peachum provides the principal focus for Brecht's critique in a work designed to reveal the true, unacceptable face of capitalism, in which criminals who are simultaneously bourgeois set the tone for business. However, although Brecht endowed Macheath with certain petty bourgeois manners, his fascination with the amoral outsider produced a gangster whose courage and magnetic attraction outweighed the anti-capitalist message. Brecht knew exactly how to make him part of an unforgettable theatrical experience. He would never again allow his audience to enjoy themselves in such an unfettered way.

Brecht, Hauptmann and Weill worked at a prodigious pace. They maintained the three-act structure together with interpolated songs and ballads. They shifted the setting to Victorian London, the epoch of burgeoning capitalism in the archetypal imperial city. Characters are no longer Gay's satires of recognisable national figures but types. The gangster Macheath and the police chief Brown become partners in crime. The action involving Macheath and his cronies is greatly expanded, as are Peachum's unscrupulous business dealings.

Brecht's Peachum acts upon his basic insight as a businessman into how to extract people's money by playing on their sympathies. He disguises healthy individuals as cripples, explaining the basic types of misery, which are: 'Those most likely to touch the human heart. The sight of such types puts a man into the unnatural state where he is willing to part with money'.[30] In Brecht's 'First Threepenny Finale' Peachum proclaims with hand-wringing cynicism:

Let's practise goodness: who would disagree?
But sadly on this planet while we're waiting
The means are meagre and the morals low.
To get one's record straight would be elating
But our condition's such it can't be so.

Despite Brecht's anti-capitalist intentions, many spectators were more than happy to be carried along by Peachum's view that nothing could be changed. Brecht had altered Gay's text substantially and used some Marxist concepts as well as Epic techniques, but, in truth, he had no great interest in preventing a repetition in Berlin of the glorious culinary spectacle at London's Lyric Theatre. And the established tone prevailed even when Brecht later introduced further lines of trenchant social criticism.

Most of the songs that Brecht and Hauptmann introduced to replace Gay's were quite consistent with the original tone. They drew extensively on Kipling's rugged verses, which Hauptmann had translated. For example, Kipling's 'Screw Guns' became Brecht's 'Cannon Song' and Polly's love song draws on Kipling's ballad 'Mary, Pity Women'. The same goes for Brecht's own recent compositions such as 'What keeps Mankind Alive?', sung by Macheath and Jenny as the 'Second Threepenny Finale': 'However much you twist, whatever lies you tell / Food is the first thing. Morals follow on'.[31] The audience would shrug their shoulders along with the actors. Another of Brecht's own compositions, 'Pirate Jenny', is, as Ernst Bloch immediately recognised, the one piece in the play in which there is an outright call for insurrection.

Brecht and Hauptmann made rapid progress on the text and Weill began composing the music in April 1928. Brecht and Hauptmann had a first draft ready for the playbook by early May. Weill's playful, quirky tunes were the perfect foil for the savage lyrics. Weill imbued the form of the ballad opera with his contemporary style, drawing on jazz and dance music. On 10 May Brecht set off from Berlin in his car to work with Weill for a month at Saint Cyr in the South of France. Lotte Lenya, who was with Weill, recalls: 'The two men wrote and rewrote furiously, night and day, with only hurried swims in between'.[32] They were producing the first great modern musical. On 4 June Weill told his publisher: 'I'm working at a high tempo on the composition of the *Beggar's Opera*, which I am finding very enjoyable. It's been written in a style that is very easy to sing because it will be performed by actors. I hope to have it finished by the end of June, and then to complete *Mahagonny* in one go'.[33] Brecht drove back to Augsburg, then briefly to Utting on the Ammersee where Weigel and Zoff were on holiday with Brecht's children, before he went on to Berlin. There, with Weill and Hauptmann he put the finishing touches to *The Threepenny Opera*, as the work was called, thanks to Feuchtwanger. Erich Engel was engaged to direct and Neher to design the set. Brecht got parts for Weigel and Carola Neher, Weill a part for Lotte Lenya.

Rehearsals began on 10 August for a production which is surrounded by legends, many of them spun by those involved. Lenya claimed that Brecht only wrote the 'Ballad of Mac the Knife' with its brilliant opening because Harald Paulsen, an operetta star with a sinister edge, demanded a more striking entrance as Macheath. When Paulsen insisted on a made-to-measure suit with a blue bow tie, Brecht and Weill retaliated with the lurid lines enumerating his infamous deeds. One way or another, the iconic song was born. Brecht now rarely performed but one of the two surviving sound recordings of him singing his own songs has him, in 1929, performing the 'Ballad of Mac the Knife' to the accompaniment of a barrel organ.[34] It was a Moritat, a scary ballad, in the manner of the singers at Augsburg's Plärrer.

Weill was upbeat to his publisher about the prospects for popular success. However, Weigel and Carola Neher had to withdraw, Weigel because of appendicitis and Neher to be with her dying husband, the poet Klabund. She returned after his death but withdrew again, prompting Brecht's mock funeral oration.[35] After the usual cuts, re-writing and all manner of other problems, the dress rehearsal on 30 August lasted until 5 a.m. on the morning of the premiere. Everyone was shattered. Brecht, Weill, Neher and Aufricht then cut the play by three quarters of an hour and called another rehearsal. Everyone was too tired to mount major protests. Weill, however, voiced his outrage when he discovered that Lenya's name had been missed off the cast list.

Everything pointed to the usual scandalous Brecht premiere. Of course, the Nazis and nationalists opposed the work. However, the audience was caught up in a unique theatrical spectacle, which became the most vivid symbol of 1920s Berlin. In Lenya's account, from the moment the 'Cannon Song' began, the audience roared their appreciation as it rolled them along:

John was all present and Jim was all there
And Georgie was up for promotion.
Not that the army gave a bugger who they were
When confronting some heathen commotion.[36]

In a performance steeped in adrenaline, the audience heard in such lines as much a Kiplingesque affirmation of empire as a Brechtian critique of imperialism.

In the world of *The Threepenny Opera*, back on civvy street those rough squaddies like John and Jim could join the constabulary, the gangsters or the army of beggars. The audience witnessed not just their ensnarement in corrupt business practice but also the demise of Macheath, the sex addict. Brecht understood Macheath's predicament and inserted the 'Ballad of Sexual Slavery': 'Who does him down, that's done the lot? The women. / Want it or not, he can't ignore that call. / Sexual slavery has him in its thrall'.[37] Macheath is trapped because of his addiction. However, Brecht, who had performed his own great escapes, grants Macheath a final reprieve and the play ends in farce.

Elements of embryonic Epic Theatre were used, such as the half curtain, the projection screen and putting the orchestra on the stage. Music critics were clear that they had witnessed ground-breaking musical theatre. Theatre critics were less sure about its qualities. Even a supporter like Ihering, while recognising that the play was a breakthrough to popular theatre, described it as a 'light ancillary work'.[38] The critic from the KPD's *Rote Fahne* [*Red Flag*] was in no doubt that the work contained 'not a trace of modern social or political satire'. However, in no time everyone was singing the songs – and they do, of course, contain social and political satire, though not a consistent message of insurrection.

Nor were all the songs Brecht's own. Without acknowledging his sources, he had replaced some of Gay's songs with K. L. Ammer's translations of ballads by Villon. Once again, Alfred Kerr accused Brecht of plagiarism, citing Ammer's translation of Villon's verse and identifying unattributed verses by other authors. Brecht replied: 'An explanation has been asked for. I truthfully explain that I unfortunately forgot to mention Ammer's name. That, in turn, I explain by my fundamental laxness in questions of intellectual property'.[39] Karl Kraus rushed to Brecht's defence as the scandal was played out in the press. Brecht agreed to pay Ammer some royalties, which Ammer passed on to a charity for writers who had fallen on hard times. Meanwhile, Ammer's publisher prepared a new edition of the Villon translation, for which Brecht wrote a foreword! In the event, Kiepenheuer published the book. In his notebook, Brecht reflected that plagiarism was a form of art and that every Golden Age of art was characterised by the energy and innocence of its plagiarism. As so often, Brecht cited Shakespeare in his defence of genius – even though, of course, hardly anything can be reliably said about Shakespeare's own practices.[40] Kurt Tucholsky took to referring to 'Rudyard' Brecht and Tucholsky's cabaret skit did the rounds, in which someone asks: 'Who is the play by?'. The reply is: 'Brecht'. This prompts the first person to ask: 'Then who's the play by?'.[41]

The Threepenny Opera was performed at the Theater am Schiffbauerdamm for the whole of the 1928–9 season and enjoyed phenomenal success throughout Germany.

By January 1929 there were productions at nineteen German theatres, as well as in Prague, Budapest and Vienna. In all, there were 4,200 performances in 1928–9. The text and the music were published and between 1929 and 1931 twenty-one records of the music came out on the German market. *The Threepenny Opera* rapidly became an international success. However, Brecht did not yet conquer America. Despite the fact that Lotte Lenya was Jenny and Louis Armstrong was the Ballad Singer for the premiere at New York's Empire Theatre in 1933, hopes that the show would replicate the German success were dashed: the translation was not good and the show folded after only twelve performances. Success in the USA would have to wait until the famous production in Marc Blitzstein's translation which ran at New York's Theater de Lys from 1954 to 1961. However, from 1929 until Hitler came to power in January 1933, *The Threepenny Opera* was translated into eighteen languages and there were more than 10,000 performances in Europe, with particular success in France and Czechoslovakia. Rich and famous, Brecht set up a Swiss bank account to receive the royalties.[42] Weill became equally famous, while malicious tongues took to calling Hauptmann 'Royalties Saidie'. Today *The Threepenny Opera* remains one of the world's most performed musical dramas.

Part Three

Marxist Heretic

To be a True Comrade: Surviving the Storm as the Smallest Magnitude 1928–9

Berlin portraits

In the autumn of 1928 Brecht, now a Berlin celebrity, moved to a flat at Hardenbergstrasse 1a on the fashionable Charlottenburg 'Knee', the triangle formed by Hardenbergstrasse, Joachimsthaler Strasse and Kurfürstendamm. Mari Hold, who had been a Brecht family servant since she was thirteen, came to Berlin from Augsburg to look after his household. When she married in 1934 Brecht thanked her in a poem for her meticulous work in meeting all his household needs from morning to night:

> The day began early
> When you brought the papers
> To the little bedroom, opening the curtains:
> The stove was warm; the tea was brewed
> When I went to my study
> The oat flakes were ready too.[1]

The ascetic side of Brecht, more pronounced following his monumental success, manifested itself in his mixed feelings about his newly acquired affluence:

> In my bedroom, which is small, I have two tables, one big and one small, an old wooden bed, which is not longer than me but a bit wider even though it's not wider than most other beds, two low Norman chairs with straw seats, two Chinese bedside rugs and a large wooden trunk with canvas straps for manuscripts. On it I've got a film projector, a projection lamp and an electric bowl fire as well as a *plaster cast of my face*. My clothes, linen and shoes are in two built-in wardrobes. My linen includes shirts, bedding to make the bed, seven suits, eight pairs of shoes. There's a lamp hanging from the ceiling and a second one on the table by the bed. I like the room and most of these things, but I am embarrassed about the whole thing because it is too much.[2]

For many people Brecht himself was too much. His notoriety went before him in the cafes and theatres of Kurfürstendamm. At one of Piscator's parties he met Harry Graf Kessler, the aristocratic Anglo-German patron of the arts. Kessler saw in Brecht 'a strikingly decadent head, an almost criminal physiognomy, very dark, black hair, black eyes, dark skin, a strange, furtive facial expression, almost the typical hoodlum. But when you talk to him, he thaws out, becomes almost naive.[3] Kessler concluded: 'He is in any case an "intellect", at least on the exterior, and not unsympathetic'.

However, it did not escape perceptive observers that things were not quite as they seemed behind Brecht's macho and proletarian poses. Elias Canetti got to know him in his 'proletarian disguise' through Karl Kraus at Schlichter's. Canetti did not like Brecht, not least because Kraus, whom Canetti revered, 'treated Brecht with love, as though Brecht were his son, the young genius – his *chosen* son'.[4] Kraus had lauded Brecht as the only living German writer of any consequence. Canetti, who unlike Brecht went on to win the Nobel Prize, produced a portrait of his rival which strongly suggests his suspicion that something beyond mere under-nourishment was wrong with Brecht:

> He was very emaciated. He had a hungry face, which looked askew because of his cap. His words came out wooden and choppy. [...] It seemed incredible that he was only thirty. He did not look as if he had aged prematurely, but as if he had always been old. [...] One of the contradictions about Brecht was that his outer appearance had something ascetic to it. Hunger could also seem like fasting, as though he were deliberately forgoing the object of his greed.[5]

Brecht's premature ageing was, as we know, partly the result of his lack of appetite on account of his renal condition. Brecht was a hunger artist of a very particular kind, a contrarian full of contradiction and paradox, which not even the most perceptive observer could properly fathom. What Canetti witnessed at Schlichter's was that the culinarily fastidious Brecht had a compulsive, ravenous hunger, which drove him on to consume everyone around him artistically and sexually. Elisabeth Hauptmann understood better than most just how much his public manner was 'willed' in a very deliberate, superior style:

> The seated posture – at least as far as I now see it – is not congenial to him. The horizontal position is definitely the only correct one for him. He walks with a very light step – like someone who is in better shape than anyone else and for whom many things are easier. He speaks very quietly but clearly and sometimes he says something that's very crude but sounds very polite. His temples are concave and very thin; thin to the point of bursting; worryingly. Actually, everything about him is very fixed. Alongside inherited traits, things willed, a wish to be a guy – leather cap, tilted forward over his face, half-length leather coat.[6]

Some of this we already know. In order to conserve energy for writing and sex, Brecht walked as little as possible and reclined whenever he could. He had developed that unnerving manner of speech during adolescence, combining the exceedingly polite and outright rude. It remained as disarming now as it had been for his teachers. Hauptmann had a keen eye for other telling details of Brecht's appearance. Her focus upon temples so fragile that they appeared about to burst recalls George Grosz's portrait of another Berlin writer, the emaciated dwarf Max Hermann-Neisse, whose veins Grosz paints protruding alarmingly from his gaunt skull around his delicate temples. Brecht's 'willed' and therefore fixed macho elements were the principal features of his disguise, concealing much of a face that, as we have seen, could be anything but fixed. The cigar did the rest.

The popular author and the revolutionary Left

Brecht had achieved notoriety by attacking all and sundry with gusto but he was now vulnerable to attack himself, not just by the usual suspects like Alfred Kerr but also by those, mainly on the Left, suspicious of popular success. *The Threepenny Opera* confirmed what many on the revolutionary Left thought: Brecht was on a trajectory far removed from their own. Piscator told Brecht that he saw him as a poet despite *The Threepenny Opera*.[7] Although Brecht knew that his future lay with work that would fulfil his programme of 1925, he stood his ground: 'I hope the *3-Penny Opera* doesn't sound too provocative at a distance. She hasn't an ounce of falsehood in her, she's a good honest soul. Her success is most gratifying. It refutes the widespread view that the public is incapable of being satisfied – which comes as something of a disappointment to me.'[8] Brecht, of course, usually worked against the grain of what the public wanted. He had been positioning himself to extract the social power which he craved as a dramatist from his diagnosis of the huge social struggles at the dawn of the new age.

Brecht's in-fighting with figures on the revolutionary Left now began as he engaged more explicitly with their agenda. From the perspective of class struggle, the proletariat was – in theory at least – the major force in the brokerage of social power in the new age. What Brecht knew about working-class politics came not through the KPD or the SPD but through the theatre and through intellectuals such as Sternberg. Brecht boasted to Piscator that while Hermann Ungar's revolutionary drama *The Red General* was being performed, 'catcalls (that no one wanted to acknowledge) were heard from Brecht's box, where a young Marxist by the name of Sternberg is thought to have been sitting'.[9] Ever impatient with mere reform, Brecht was scathing about Berlin's intellectual revolutionaries, comparing them to the Roman reformers, the Gracchi: 'These revolutionaries have never gone beyond the Marxism of the Gracchi and now there will be long years of waiting'.

While he would never have any time for the reformist Social Democrats of the SPD, Brecht was outraged to discover in October 1928 that a number of Berlin writers in the KPD were joining together in a new organisation, the League of Proletarian-Revolutionary Writers (BPRS). BPRS members included several writers who would remain prominent in the cultural politics of German Marxism, among them Becher, Piscator and the proletarian Willi Bredel. Going on the offensive, Brecht decried intellectuals of bourgeois origin who argued that it was 'necessary to submerge oneself in the proletariat'.[10] For Brecht, this attitude was 'counter-revolutionary', a view he shared with Walter Benjamin. Brecht would consistently deviate from the BPRS/KPD line on this question as well as, from the early 1930s, on related aesthetic issues. Brecht understood well enough that his sensibility had been shaped by his middle-class upbringing. Its idiosyncrasies contributed hugely to his dramatic and lyrical power. In 1940 he noted in his journal: 'People often hesitate to call artists like Hašek, Silone [...]

and myself bourgeois writers, but this is quite wrong. [...] The safest thing is to present us and use us as the dialecticians among the bourgeois artists'.[11] Brecht's insistence on this distinction and upon observing the intuitions of his aesthetic sensibility in conjunction with Marxist dialectical materialism would trigger quarrels with the custodians of an official Communist position which never went away.

Brecht asked his friend Bernard von Brentano for his views on what he called the 'congress of proletarian literature proprietors'.[12] Brentano was the Berlin correspondent of the *Frankfurter Zeitung* and a KPD member, who contributed to the BPRS journal *Die Linkskurve*. Revealing his own anxieties, Brecht suggested to Brentano that the BPRS hoped 'with the help of their congress to corner the proletarian market'. Brecht wanted his share of that market. He asked Brentano to compile for him a 'short syllabus for use by an intellectual wishing to learn the fundamentals of dialectical materialism'.

As an agile and avid innovator Brecht became interested in dialectical materialism as a tool of inquiry applicable in historical and contemporary settings. Guided by the teachings of another non-conformist Marxist social scientist, Karl Korsch, Brecht would call dialectical materialism the Great Method, with which, in fulfilment of his programme of 1925, he could analyse the violent dynamic of conflicting class interests in the history of human socio-economic development. Using the Great Method, Brecht would explore the contradictions which, like Marx, he believed would lead to the self-destruction of capitalism in an age of unprecedented violence and upheaval. With much less certainty, he would posit the emergence of a new age out of the ruins of the old, in which the interests of the working class would supplant those of the bourgeoisie. The deeply pessimistic Brecht's hopes that in that new age the cycle of bloody conflict might be broken waxed and waned in the 'dark times' through which he lived.

In a letter to Döblin, whose great experimental novel *Berlin Alexanderplatz* would be attacked relentlessly by KPD and BPRS critics, Brecht dismissed the 'vulgar' Marxist aesthetics emanating from those quarters: 'I have always known that your kind of writing can express our new picture of the world, but now it has also become clear to me that it fills the gap which, precisely, has been opened up by the current Marxist view of art'.[13] Brecht himself would be attacked in *Die Linkskurve* in 1932 by Georg Lukács and Andor Gábor, both representatives of a, by then, dominant traditionalist aesthetic in the journal, which took its lead from retrenchment in Moscow as Stalin consolidated his power. Brecht would not publish a word in *Die Linkskurve*, and in exile his differences with the dangerous Moscow 'camarilla', as he would call the group around Lukács, would only grow. However, already in 1928 Brecht was at pains not to divulge differences in public which the real political enemy could exploit. To the frustration of those many enemies, throughout his life Brecht would make every effort to maintain a loyal front with his political allies despite their differences. Hence Brecht wrote to Ihering, urging him to persuade Piscator to stage *Drums in the Night*: 'At the present time, the mere fact of our collaboration would have an important effect on the public'.[14] Nothing came of the plan.

Brecht now got to know Karl Korsch, whose importance for Brecht would soon eclipse Sternberg's. From the autumn of 1928, Brecht attended Korsch's lectures on

'Scientific Socialism' at Berlin's Academic Beer Halls. Korsch, a Communist intellectual and Reichstag deputy, was, like Sternberg, an uncomfortable bedfellow for the KPD. A more complex thinker than Sternberg, Korsch had been expelled from the KPD because of his critique of leading Communist thinkers in his study *Marxism and Philosophy*. Much to the displeasure of the KPD, Korsch had analysed the ideological weaknesses of Marxism, regarding them as the only credible explanation for the failure of the German Revolution after the First World War. Korsch insisted on the analysis of the specific historical situation, rather than any given ideology, in order to understand afresh what Marxism could offer. Korsch's stance appealed to the insatiably curious dissenter in Brecht, as did Korsch's attempt to oppose the 'vulgarisation' of Marxism by re-affirming the historical relationship between the Hegelian and Marxist dialectic. Korsch was hence an important source for the better understanding of dialectical materialism which Brecht had been seeking.

That autumn of 1928 Brecht affirmed the potential of 'Marxist perspectives' to achieve necessary socio-economic change in Germany: 'For its future Germany requires nothing different from other countries: the most skilful application possible of Marxist perspectives upon its society and economy. It would then of course have the chance, like other countries, to emerge from its cultural morass'.[15] Using Korsch's teaching of dialectical materialism, Brecht would move further away from conventional theatrical and aesthetic categories and would incorporate more Marxist concepts in his expanding critical vocabulary.

Theatrical success, however, remained Brecht's consuming passion. In a clear demonstration of his market position, in the spring of 1929 Brecht signed a lucrative contract with Felix Bloch Erben, which guaranteed him an income of 1,000 gold marks (i.e. marks pegged against the value of gold in August 1914, rather than paper marks, which he evidently did not trust to maintain their value) per month until 1 June 1936 in exchange for performance rights for at least three full-length plays. Brecht held on to other rights. Felix Bloch Erben evidently believed there were more blockbusters in the pipeline.

With his star firmly in the ascendant, Brecht attracted some of Berlin's most talented young artists. Building upon a meeting with Hanns Eisler in Baden-Baden, Brecht spent much time with him in Berlin. Their first major theatrical collaboration came with *The Measures Taken* in 1930. Much more would follow. While adapting Hašek's *Schweyk* with Piscator, Brecht made friends with Georg Grosz who was designing the set. Grosz would illustrate Brecht's children's book *The Three Soldiers* in 1932 and they maintained contact during the exile years even though they grew apart politically.

Rather improbably on the face of things, Brecht and Weigel married in a quiet civil ceremony on 10 April 1929. While Brecht's family was immediately welcoming, some of Brecht's old Augsburg friends, fearing another of Brecht's mistakes with women, needed more time. In some ways, marriage did not change much for Brecht and Weigel. However, their second child Barbara would be born on 28 October 1930 and at that point Weigel ended her engagement at the Staatstheater. While Weigel now became financially dependent on Brecht, he gained emotionally. Moreover, he needed her strength of purpose if he were to establish himself beyond dispute as the greatest dramatist of the age. And her ties with the KPD would in time bring him closer to working-class politics.

Brecht's three other women at the time, Elisabeth Hauptmann, Marieluise Fleisser and Carola Neher, were shocked by Brecht's marriage. Hauptmann and Fleisser made suicide attempts. As for Neher, immediately after the wedding ceremony Brecht went to meet her off a train, armed with a bouquet of flowers, and explained to her that the marriage did not mean a thing. Neher saw things differently: she threw the flowers on the floor at his feet. With Hauptmann things were different. Her contribution to Brecht's work and general well-being was substantial. Brecht depended on her writing, editorial and translation skills. Needing to mend the relationship, Brecht wrote a poem for her in which he begged for her understanding.[16] Quite typically, he wrote unflattering things about her in it, too, which she, quite typically, accepted.

Dr Schmitt's prescriptions and Herr Keuner's teachings

On the surface, Brecht's personal situation could not have contrasted more starkly with the grim reality which was beginning to grip Germany. It was apparent that the country could not meet the huge reparation payments required over an indefinite period in the Dawes Plan. Foreign loans, principally from the USA, had enabled Germany to recover a degree of prosperity. That finance vanished and millions of people became impoverished. As always the poor were hardest hit but the impoverishment again affected the middle classes, too. The Weimar Republic was lurching towards renewed crisis and the state was once more becoming vulnerable to revolution.

The Nazis were hell bent on making political capital out of this latest episode in the 'national humiliation', which for them was the Weimar state. A ban on Hitler speaking in Prussia had been lifted the previous autumn when, surrounded by Nazi thugs, he addressed a mass rally at Berlin's Sportpalast. In fact, all the major popular parties had formed paramilitaries. The KPD had its Rotfrontkämpferbund (Red Front Fighters' League), the far right had the Stahlhelm Bund Deutscher Frontsoldaten (Steel Helmet League of German Front-line Soldiers) and the Sturmabteilung, the SA (Stormtroopers). The SPD formed its Reichsbanner Schwarz-Rot-Gold (Black-Red-Gold Banner of the Reich.) There were violent clashes on the streets and further deaths to add to the escalating total of politically motivated murders. The Berlin Police President Karl Zörgiebel of the SPD banned all open-air public meetings.

While Brecht believed that only radical change, informed by 'Marxist perspectives', could lift Germany out of the mire, the chaos which threatened to envelop the country evoked in him huge anxieties which threatened his precarious health. The macho manner barely concealed his vulnerability. He had learnt from the bitter experience of the early 1920s that he must protect himself physically against dangerous excesses and had accepted the need for the disciplined regulation of his everyday life to curb his erratic, self-destructive egotism. It was only consistent with his intellectual development, which stressed the determining force of socio-economic circumstances, that Brecht should now come to view his own personal well-being – and threats to it – as intimately bound up with conditions in the state and society surrounding him.

At this time Elisabeth Hauptmann, together with Mari Hold, gave Brecht much of the devoted care he needed. With their help, Brecht sought to regulate his body on a daily basis. As Feuchtwanger wrote to Zweig after Brecht's death, Brecht's doctors had provided him with dietary advice to combat his kidney condition for as long as he had known him. Food and respiration are constant topics in Brecht's notebooks around this time. Notes survive from 1929–30 in which Brecht and Hauptmann set down a dietary regime and related prescriptions. They include intensive contrast bath therapy, a more sophisticated version of the hydrotherapy at the Augsburg baths which Brecht had so detested as an adolescent. Hauptmann set out a daily regime in a notebook, some or all of which applies to Brecht:

Sunday	bay leaf tea for three days […]
Monday	St Benedict's herb
Tuesday	2 hipbaths, / healing earth around the neck
	contrast bath for the feet
Wednesday	2 hipbaths
Thursday	alternate douche, hot compress around the body.
	(hay flower Joh. Schaf)
	Rubdown with arnica
	Raw vegetables red cabbage, semolina, spinach bake
	+ mushroom flummeries
Friday 28.2.	(compress affusion)
	alternate douche hot compress
	[…]
Monday	hipbath B
	blue light treatment ¾ hour
	porridge / Leipzig vegetable plate + dumpling /
	dried fruit / semolina […] + salad pineapple
Tuesday	whole body acupuncture, brushed with French brandy,
	beaten with cold towels, oiled.
	hipbath B.
	full bath.[17]

And so it went on for weeks on end – or at least that was the intention. As we have seen, Feuchtwanger said that Brecht could never adhere to his doctor's prescriptions for long.

As Peter Villwock and Martin Kölbel point out, the prescriptions, which end with 'respiratory massage', bear the stamp of Johannes Ludwig Schmitt, the Munich specialist in respiratory massage, homeopathy and herbal remedies.[18] The medicines which Schmitt prescribed have their place in herbal and homeopathic medicine. They enable us to extrapolate the symptoms which Brecht had described to his doctor. Bay leaf, healing earth, hay flowers and arnica can, like contrast bath therapy, be used to combat inflammation and rheumatic complaints. Acupuncture can perform a similar function. St Benedict's herb combats catarrh. Juniper can be used against urinary tract infections. Elemental sulphur can be used in creams to treat skin conditions. Althaea can be used for gargling and treating sore throats, blue light treatment for skin complaints and inflammation.

Schmitt later summarised his approach in *Atemheilkunst* [*The Art of Respiratory Healing*]. He recommended that the body should be brushed when dry, oiled, scraped, gripped and treated in segments, especially by means of massage and the use of needles. Hydrotherapeutic treatment entailed: full baths or hipbaths with and without tonics, underwater massage and brushing, rubdowns and beatings with a wet towel, as well as alternately warm and cold Kneipp affusions. An entry in Brecht's notebook captures such treatment: 'hot wash / cold / brush / oil/ brush / 7 minutes hipbath / really hot / then cold wash / or shower / oil / plenty of butter / not too salty / herbal salt / add the salt when it / comes away from the fire'.[19] Another of Brecht's notes, also probably deriving from Schmitt because the sentiment is hardly Brechtian, reads: 'man is not helped through the intestine but through the purity of his heart. And the heart becomes pure through massage, through breathing etc'.[20] Schmitt emphasised the intimate connection between smooth respiration and natural, biological nourishment. He claimed that his respiratory regime could achieve the following: increased blood flow and lymphatic circulation, with the aim of heightened egestive and regenerative activity; removal of metabolic blockages; a general 'tightening up' of the organism; and the normalisation and improved quality of tissues and their functioning, including the nervous and vascular systems. Schmitt's therapy helped the melancholeric Hydratopyranthropos to calm his agitated organism, which he would later compare to a 'powder keg'.[21]

Brecht's embrace of complementary medicine may surprise readers used to his self-image as a rationalist of the modern, scientific age. Indeed, he had recently discovered logical empiricism and its strict rejection of non-verifiable claims to truth. However, conventional bio-scientific medicine had only ever been able to help Brecht in a limited way. And in Germany the division between bio-scientific and complementary medicine has in any case never been so strict. Brecht embraced complementary medicine for the duration of his life. Indeed, when Brecht died he had a classic German herbal and homeopathic work in the bookcase next to his bed and other classic works in his library.[22] From a present-day diagnostic perspective, it can be said that the combination of therapies which Schmitt prescribed could have had the palliative effect of reducing Brecht's symptoms without addressing his underlying conditions.

Although Brecht swore by Schmitt's treatments, the rationalist in him could never be satisfied by his approach. Brecht used his recent creation, Herr Keuner, to give voice to his concerns in one of his earliest, miniature parables, 'Herr Keuner and the Doctor'. A first version in Brecht's notebook, in which the doctor is actually called Schmitt and Herr Keuner represents the standpoint of logical empiricism, reads:

> Affronted, Dr Schmitt said to Herr Keuner: 'I have talked about so much that was unknown. And I have not only talked, I have also been a healer'. 'Are they well known now, the things you treated?' asked Herr Keuner. Schmitt said: 'No'. 'It is

better,' said Herr Keuner quickly, 'for the unknown to remain unknown than for the number of secrets to be increased'.[23]

The logical empiricist's insistence upon speaking only about what is verifiable and otherwise remaining silent is developed in the second version of the tale. It places Herr Keuner's illness in a social context and contrasts the doctor's religious belief with a system of knowledge based on scientific method:

> Herr Keuner lived in keeping with his times and so he fell ill. Thus, he found a doctor, who helped him in some ways; but to his great distress this help came about through the inexplicable gift of an adept gaze and instinctive movements of the hand, rather than through a transferable and controlling system. Therefore Herr Keuner constantly pressed the doctor to write down everything that he knew so that others could follow suit. Then one day Herr Keuner discovered that the doctor was religious and believed in 'something beyond the world of objects'. From this moment on, he stopped pressing the man for he now knew that he did not know what he was doing. Why else, Herr Keuner said, would he have needed to invent a god?[24]

Brecht continued to seek out the religious Schmitt all the same on the grounds which, near the end of his life, he explained to his friend Peter Suhrkamp: 'His views and his therapies are unconventional and where conventional medicine cannot go further, one should absolutely listen to him. I have had first-class treatments with him'.[25] In fact, on the day Brecht died in East Berlin he was planning to leave his doctors there for Schmitt's Munich sanatorium.

While this second Keuner story begins with Brecht making explicit the link between ill health and the age a man lives in, the connection is more pronounced still in another Keuner tale. It includes a telling reference to Brecht's own principal complaints, to the state and to the disturbing phenomenon of the modern city:

> 'Why are you ill?' people asked Herr Keuner. 'Because the state is not right', he replied. 'That's why the way I live is not right and something is going wrong with my kidneys, my muscles and my heart. When I enter cities, everything is either faster or slower than I am. I speak only to those who are speaking and listen only when everyone is listening'.[26]

In Herr Keuner's striking linkage between ill health and the condition of the state, Brecht draws upon a traditional assumption in Chinese social thought, to be found in the work of Me-ti which Brecht knew well, that good government is a pre-condition for a good life. Herr Keuner's story shows something that critics have not always appreciated: although Brecht came to be deeply suspicious of mere individual experience, he was at this stage no different from many other artists in conflating the realms of personal experience and of broader social conditions. The join between the private and the public is very apparent here.

As we have seen, Herr Keuner is to some extent a cipher for Brecht himself, particularly for Brecht's exploration of philosophical attitudes appropriate for the re-orientation of his life. Logical empiricism would play an important role in the coming decade, influencing Brecht's analytical attitude towards Marxism, while Chinese thought would become prominent in Brecht's writing from the late 1930s. Not only did Brecht wish to slough off the 'skin' of egotistical individualism and adopt that of the self-effacing, ascetic teacher; he was also coming to see any recovery of his health within a context of coming revolutionary upheaval, which would fundamentally alter the social conditions for the recovering self. However, Brecht could not paint a rosy picture of the revolution. When he came to see Germany entering a pre-revolutionary situation his anxieties could only grow, spawning disturbing images of violence and destruction, which he sought to rationalise with thoughts of necessary liquidation in the revolutionary cause.

Brecht would write Keuner stories intermittently for the rest of his life. He endowed his creation with attitudes and concerns characteristic of the later Brecht, by which I mean the Brecht whom we encounter from the late 1920s onwards. Herr Keuner is a sceptic whose favourite animal is the elephant, the creature with the thickest skin. He is the purveyor of the same parabolic story form which had appealed to Brecht since Grandma Brezing's biblical parables had given coherence and shape to the boy's confused feelings. As for the name Keuner, it can be read as a corrupt form of the German 'keiner', suggesting 'no one'. Brecht also pointed to the association with the Greek homophone 'koiné', a common or communal thing.[27] Taking those two senses together, Keuner is a self-effacing, ascetic figure looking towards the new collectivist age. Moreover, his blend of logical empiricism with the dialectical approach equips him to ask searching questions about the transition to that age.

Intriguingly, for Hanns Eisler, Keuner was actually a 'Chinese character'.[28] As we have seen, Brecht had a long-standing affinity with Chinese philosophy, particularly Taoism. He admired Me-ti and Confucius, whose teachings Me-ti had challenged. For Eisler, Brecht himself developed a 'Chinese politeness' similar to Herr Keuner's. From this 'Chinese' perspective, Eisler suggests, Brecht embraced calm reason and reflection in contrast to 'western' egotistical assertiveness, which had proved so highly destructive. Brecht would develop other 'Chinese' literary forms, particularly the aphoristic pieces modelled on Me-ti's style in his *Book of Twists and Turns*. Ruth Berlau later observed of that work: 'When Brecht came on a problem, he would write a little story about it'.[29]

In *Fatzer*, Brecht presents Herr Keuner as a figure who demonstrates the importance of learning forms of agreement [Einverständnis] for the reconstitution of the bourgeois individual in a new collective identity, which involves self-renunciation and acceptance of the collective view. Herr Keuner subsequently appears in several other drafts, among them the short, didactic plays *The Measures Taken* and *He Who Says Yes*, seeking with his parabolic commentaries on events to persuade others to agree to revolutionary requirements entailing the liquidation of the old self. Brecht's source for the term 'Einverständnis' remains uncertain. It has no status in western Marxism. He may have found it in works about modern Chinese philosophy. After the Boxer Rebellion of 1898–1901 Chinese intellectuals translated many western works, including Communist classics. Amongst the new Chinese terms to be coined was 'tongyi' [同一性], a compound of two concepts, 'similar' and 'will', to denote 'comrade'.[30] Tongyi was used by the protesters in the May Fourth Movement of

1919, which paved the way for the foundation of the Chinese Communist Party in 1921. The May Fourth Movement, which itself grew out of agitation for intellectual revolution and socio-political reform, was triggered by anger among Chinese students at the Treaty of Versailles, which allocated former German concessions in Shandong to Japan. It is quite conceivable that Brecht found reference to the term tongyi in a German text in the 1920s and was attracted to it because, a hybrid of western and Chinese Communist thought, it captured the essence of what it meant to be a true comrade. That entailed developing a consciousness of 'similar will' to other comrades. In 1929–30 the term 'Einverständnis' acquires great significance in Brecht's work; not, however, in Epic Theatre but in the new Brechtian form of didactic play, the Lehrstück.

Through the attitudes struck by Herr Keuner, Brecht was in any case trying out a new 'skin', a new 'face', and leaving behind some of the trappings of the old. Brecht would henceforth live the life of the wisdom writer he aspired to be. He presented that wisdom as deriving from a modern, scientific world-view appropriate to the emerging new age, although it drew upon an eclectic mix, including logical empiricism, Chinese philosophy, dissident Marxism and his own idiosyncratic temperament. The self-absorbed artist Brecht could, of course, never simply cast off all the trappings of the old. While he willed change and proclaimed its ubiquity, the underlying problems of his condition never went away, nor did his fundamental drives or temperament, with all their contradictions and shifts of emphasis, ever change.

While Brecht perceived the concerns of the individual as increasingly subsumed within collective solutions, his problems with his own self returned to plague him. At the same time, by seeking to override those personal problems, particularly the suffering of the sickly self, with the conviction that that suffering was principally societal in origin, Brecht overcame the agony of his search for an understanding of his condition in purely personal terms. Convinced that he shared his condition with his contemporaries, Brecht's own condition became a touchstone for the sickliness of the modern world, which he would strive to cure through revolutionary change.

Berlin's Bloody May Day

On May Day 1929 the Berlin SPD Police President Zörgiebel mobilised 13,000 police to enforce a ban on all open-air meetings. This was no easy matter. The KPD insisted that its Rotfrontkämpferbund would take to the streets to combat the far Right's Stahlhelm and SA, not to mention the SPD's Reichsbanner. The bitter divisions between the revolutionary KPD and the reformist SPD had been further exacerbated when at its Sixth Congress in 1928 the Comintern had embraced the view that Social Democracy was the principal obstacle to Communism seizing power at a time when the capitalist system was entering its period of final collapse. Despite internal opposition from the Conciliator Faction led by Karl Volk, the KPD followed the Comintern in adopting the theory of Social Fascism, whereby Social Democracy was labelled an outgrowth of Fascism. By the same token, for the SPD it became an article of faith that dictatorial Communist red equalled dictatorial Nazi brown. This sealed the fatal division of the German Left, which the Nazis exploited during the final phase of the Weimar Republic.

On May Day Brecht witnessed a bloodbath from the window of Fritz Sternberg's flat near KPD headquarters. The first person whom the police killed was an SPD member but the day turned into a murderous attack on KPD demonstrators. In all, the police killed thirty-three people. Sternberg was standing with Brecht by the window:

> As far as we could tell these people were not armed. The police opened fire several times. At first we thought that they were warning shots. Then we saw a number of demonstrators collapsing and being carried away later on stretchers. [...] When Brecht heard the shots and saw that people were being hit, he turned white in the face in a way that I'd never seen him before in my life. I think it was not least this experience that drove him ever more strongly towards the Communists.[31]

In protest at police brutality, the KPD called for more demonstrations. However, the police swept through KPD strongholds and there were further shootings and arrests. The SPD and the KPD traded insults in the Reichstag, while Zörgiebel imposed emergency measures. By 6 May calm had returned to the streets. Thereafter, repressive legislation against the KPD fuelled further claims that the SPD represented Social Fascism.

As Sternberg writes, after the shock of witnessing those deaths Brecht's support for the revolutionary Left began to crystallise. There was surprise in KPD circles. They had never viewed Brecht as a comrade, nor would he ever join the KPD, and in private he would be scathing about the KPD's ham-fisted leadership and about organisations like the BPRS. However, from the summer of 1930 he lent his public support to the KPD as the only grouping capable of achieving revolutionary change. This is not, of course, to say that Brecht swallowed whole the Comintern thesis of Social Fascism. Indeed, Brecht's relationship with official Communism is marked by a deep ambivalence on both sides, which will be a major issue for exploration in the rest of this study. Sternberg recalls Brecht's belief that the KPD was capable of correcting its mistakes. After committing himself to the cause in 1930, Brecht would never abandon his public support for the revolutionary Communist movement despite the severe tests to come: the Moscow show trials; the Hitler-Stalin pact; the East German workers' uprising of 17 June 1953; and Khrushchev's exposure of Stalin's crimes. These events drove away millions who like Brecht had embraced the Communist movement during the crisis years of the late 1920s. To the end of his life, Brecht remained unswerving in his belief that as a result of the massive social struggles of the age, power would shift to the working class in a new socio-economic settlement. The productive capacity of labour, the working class's principal source of power, would emerge as the key form of exchange, replacing the destructive force of stock markets, which had spawned the parasitic *rentier* mentality of the declining bourgeoisie. However, in his final years Brecht would form the view that European Communism, its working class devastated in the struggle to the death with Fascism, could no longer act as the vehicle for change. Brecht would look to China for fresh revolutionary energy, possibly, too, as a refuge from a new European war.

Epic Theatre, popular success, pedagogic exercises

Mindful of his reputation as a serious dramatist in the light of his popular success, Brecht proclaimed that the future of the theatre was 'philosophical'. Epic Theatre remained Brecht's major project for the long term. He set down his latest reflections on Epic Theatre in 'A Dialogue about Acting'. As he would so often, he derived theoretical insights from practical work, on this occasion working with Weigel on her role as the maidservant in *Oedipus*. Brecht recommended, in one of his brilliant obiter dicta: 'Spectator and actor ought not to approach one another but to move apart. Each ought to move away from himself. Otherwise the element of shock necessary to all recognition is lacking.'[32] He wrote of Weigel's performance:

> She announced the death of her mistress by calling out her 'dead, dead' in a wholly unemotional and penetrating voice, her 'Jocasta has died' without any sorrow but so firmly and definitely that the bare fact of her mistress's death carried more weight at that precise moment than could have been generated by any grief of her own. She did not abandon her voice to horror, but perhaps her face, for she used white make-up to show the impact which a death makes on all who are present at it. Her announcement that the suicide had collapsed as if before a beater was made up less of pity for this collapse than of pride in the beater's achievement, so that it became plain to even the most emotionally punch-drunk spectator that here a decision had been carried out which called for his agreement.[33]

The key insight for Brecht was that Weigel's controlled acting style promoted the spectator's distanced intellectual appreciation of the reason for the suicide, resulting not in the transfer of grief via Weigel's maidservant but in agreement [Einverständnis]. Brecht reflected upon how to empower spectators, whose active intellectual engagement enabled them to achieve revolutionary consciousness through agreement. That consciousness could, however, only be imparted via an actor like Weigel who herself embodied a higher consciousness in sovereign performance. Like no one else, she came to represent Brechtian Epic Theatre.

As Brecht determined his strategic direction, Epic Theatre was one of three routes open to him. Capitalising on *The Threepenny Opera* with another Berlin blockbuster was a second possibility. Hauptmann took the lead in developing a sequel to *The Threepenny Opera*. It was surely because Brecht envisaged a different direction for himself that he encouraged Hauptmann in this money-spinning project: 'I'd give you a plot, etc. And you'd hammer out a little play, something very loose and sloppy, you could do it piecemeal if you like. Something heartrending and at the same time funny, for about 10,000 marks. You'd have to put your name to it, but it would do you a lot of good.'[34] Brecht suggested the outline of a plot to her: 'Setting: Salvation Army and gangsters' dive. Content: Battle between good and evil. Moral: Good triumphs'. Brecht was not being serious.

Keen to assert her independence, Hauptmann set to work on the play, the ironically titled *Happy End*, and engaged Brecht for the songs. They would trump the play. The 'Bilbao Song', the 'Song of Mandalay' and 'Surabaya Johnny', all of which Hauptmann had a hand in, became as famous as the songs of *The Threepenny Opera*. The idea was that *Happy End* would come together in a similar way. Aufricht was, of course, keen to stage another great box office hit at the Theater am Schiffbauerdamm. Hauptmann signed a contract with an equally eager Felix Bloch Erben, who gave her an advance of 5,000 marks and committed her to sharing a third of her author's income with Brecht. She created the fiction that the new play was based on the work of an American, Dorothy Lane. That suggested a parallel with the adaptation of Gay's *Beggar's Opera*. It was shaping up as an escapist romp.

However, only two of three acts were ever finished.[35] Aufricht and the director Erich Engel looked to Brecht for the third, but Brecht claimed two were enough and set about carving up the text in rehearsals. When Engel refused to accept his constant changes Brecht accused him of considering changes only if they wouldn't cost money. Claiming that Engel could only make 'old theatre' out of *Happy End*, Brecht declared their collaboration over.[36] Engel warned Aufricht that he would walk out if there was 'further unbearable aggressive behaviour' from Brecht. The aggression continued, Engel resigned, and Brecht directed. He had a dazzling cast: Weigel, Peter Lorre, Carola Neher, Oskar Homolka, Kurt Gerron and Theo Lingen. The first two acts were a great success. However, when the third act began, it quickly became obvious that the actors had no finished stage text. To cap it all, Weigel took to the stage with a sheet of paper and read out lines, later incorporated in *The Threepenny Opera*: 'What's a jemmy compared with a share certificate? What's breaking into a bank compared with founding a bank?'.[37] Portraits of Henry Ford and John D. Rockefeller within mock stained-glass windows were lowered onto the stage. The audience was outraged and critics panned the production. Unwilling to countenance that Hauptmann had written the play, they suggested that Brecht was behind it and that with the attribution to Dorothy Lane he had as usual been laying false trails. Aufricht lost 130,000 marks.

Brecht now stressed all the more the seriousness of his plans after *The Threepenny Opera*, emphasising their pedagogic and reformist as well as philosophical dimensions:

> Today the stage is the forum for the education of the general public. It is unfortunately being used too little in this manner. I believe that in my last work I did enough in the field of the song for me now to deal with the task that I set myself as my main priority. It is to present a type of Lehrstück and to philosophise and reform things from the stage. However, I imagine this task to be exceedingly difficult since drama must not lose anything of its vivid clarity.[38]

Brecht's *Life of Galileo* and *Mother Courage and her Children* would be a dazzling fulfilment of that final requirement. However, in 1930 Brecht employed the term Lehrstück for a number of short didactic plays, six in all, which he would write between 1929 and 1935, whose origins lie as much in the development of New Music as in his reflections upon Epic Theatre. In fact, after the success of *The Threepenny Opera* Brecht turned away from mainstream, professional theatre to the world of New Music and amateur theatre groups. Materially secure, he sought to develop new responses to the deepening economic and political crisis by devoting himself to experimentation with short pieces in his new didactic form. Leaving the mainstream was vital in order to demonstrate that he could thrive outside that existing institutional framework. He would be all the stronger in demanding changes in the mainstream theatre when he returned to it. He could not have imagined that it would be two decades before he could implement what he learned in a concerted fashion.

The Baden-Baden didactic experiments

Under the leadership of the composer Paul Hindemith the annual Baden-Baden Chamber Music Festival was attracting attention as the principal forum for experimentation in New Music. The festival audience was much more attuned to novelty in music than to new theatrical forms. Watchwords associated with the festival were Gebrauchsmusik, or Applied Music, and Gemeinschaftsmusik, or Community Music. The anti-Romantic, utilitarian orientation of the New Music paralleled Brecht's avant-gardist efforts in the theatre. It had, however, not yet reached a wider public. Brecht's collaboration with Weill on the Mahagonny songs and *The Threepenny Opera* demonstrated their capacity to do so.

In 1929 the Baden-Baden Festival was devoted to work for film and radio 'for the masses in the technological age'.[39] Weill was invited to contribute. In search of original material, he approached Brecht, who came up with the idea of a piece based on *WE*, the American Charles Lindbergh's account of his first crossing of the Atlantic by airplane. This became *Lindbergh's Flight*, which later came to be viewed as Brecht's first Lehrstück.[40] *Lindbergh's Flight* was one of two contrasting pieces which Brecht wrote for Baden-Baden in 1929. The second, an improvised piece to which he initially gave the title *Lehrstück*, indicating that the play was itself about a lesson to be learnt, was later called *The Baden-Baden Lesson on Agreement*.[41] Learning how to agree was the lesson. Brecht returned to the same issue of agreement in the further didactic pieces which he wrote in the coming years. In particular, his exploration of agreement to self-sacrifice through death for the revolutionary cause would stir huge controversy. Taking death as the measure of things was obvious to Brecht, as it had been since his first play *The Bible*. His early poems had rehearsed how to die through an emotional sacrifice to the patriotic cause. He now posed the question of how to die with an intellectual agreement to self-sacrifice for the revolutionary cause. With minor variations, in one Lehrstück after another Brecht's protagonists are called upon by the group to consent to self-destruction. The plays demonstrate that there are no easy ways to deal with the conflict between the individual and broader social interests. Amidst the outrage, few people saw what an important question Brecht was posing. It has by no means gone away.

Lindbergh's Flight and *Lehrstück* form the first classic Brechtian pair of counter-plays in his Lehrstück production. Lindbergh's successful Atlantic crossing contrasts with the failure in *Lehrstück* of the French pilot Charles Nungesser, who set off on an Atlantic flight from East to West five days before Lindbergh and was never seen again. While the Epic Theatre aspired to blend pleasure and instruction, Brecht captured an essential element of Lehrstück production when he explained after the performance that *Lindbergh's Flight* was '*not a means of pleasure but of instruction*'.[42] It had 'no value if it does not train. It has no artistic value that would justify a performance not intended for this training'. At a time of deepening crisis, which demanded urgent action, Brecht aimed to create a didactic theatre to train all involved, including the radio listener. Similarly, Brecht emphasised that the piece was 'not intended to be of use to the present-day radio but to *change* it': 'The increasing concentration of mechanical means and the increasingly specialised education – trends that should be accelerated – call for a kind of *rebellion* by the listener, for his mobilisation and redeployment as producer'.

Intending to work on *Lindbergh's Flight*, *Mahagonny* and other projects with Weill in the South of France, Brecht set out for Saint Cyr again from Berlin in a new car, a Steyr. However, an oncoming car which was overtaking a lorry forced him off the road near Fulda. The Steyr crashed into a tree and was a write-off. Brecht was taken back to Berlin with a broken knee cap and a gash on his face, which left a scar. Hauptmann got him a new Steyr by making an agreement that Brecht would do more advertising for the company. As Brecht had told Piscator, his name was his trademark. The Berlin magazine *Uhu* reconstructed the crash in a sequence of pictures, demonstrating how Brecht, described as an expert driver, had avoided a serious accident by managing to swerve out of the way.

After recovering, at the end of June Brecht drove to Unterschondorf in the foothills of the Alps by one of the Bavarian lakes, the Ammersee, south of Augsburg. Unterschondorf became the regular summer destination for Brecht and Weigel until 1933. The Weills, Hauptmann and Erich Engel joined them there that summer. Brecht could be seen in a white suit with white shoes and peaked flat cap, with his son Stefan in tow.[43] Weigel recalls that during the holidays Brecht really never stopped working and would often turn up for a Saturday and Sunday, find everything terribly boring and then go on his way again.[44] Weigel soon realised that if she wanted to see more of Brecht she had to create a work space for him wherever they were staying.

In late July Brecht and Weill drove to Baden-Baden. They were welcomed by Hindemith, who had worked with Weill on the music for *Lindbergh's Flight* and with Brecht on *Lehrstück*. On 25 July a public dress rehearsal of *Lindbergh's Flight* was broadcast on the radio. Brecht had sent the director Ernst Hardt his idea that the rehearsal 'could be used for an experiment, a way of showing, at least visually, how listener participation in the art of radio could be made possible. (I regard such participation as necessary if the radio play is to become an "art")'.[45] Brecht, a man with many theories, was intent on setting the agenda for the new medium. The play became a Lehrstück about the use of radio in the scientific age. Brecht presented Hardt with a 'statement of principles concerning the use of radio' which should be 'projected on a large canvas' for Hardt to read out before the show started. The 'principles' are in fact a classic Brechtian statement about the need for the listener not to be distracted by feelings:

> The enjoyment of music demands that there should be no possibility of distraction. Free-roaming feelings aroused by music, special inconsequential thoughts such as may be entertained when listening to music, physical exhaustion such as easily arises from merely listening to music are distractions from music and take away from its enjoyment. To avoid these distractions the thinking man shares in the music, thus obeying the principle that doing is better than feeling, by humming

the missing parts and following the music with his eyes as printed, or joining others in singing aloud.[46]

Brecht elaborated with his meticulous eye for telling behavioural detail:

> On one side of the stage (with the screen behind them) are the broadcasting apparatus, the singers, musicians, speakers, etc.; on the other side, screened off so as to suggest a room, a man sits at a desk in his shirt sleeves with a musical score and hums, plays and sings the part of Lindbergh. *This is the listener.* Since quite a few specialists will be present, it will probably be necessary to have on one side a sign saying 'The Radio' and on the other a sign saying 'Listener'.[47]

As Marc Silberman writes, Brecht's conception was that the speaker and the listener (playing Lindbergh) should enter into a conversation for the radio audience: 'In other words, the fictional listeners were modelled as active participants by demonstrating how they should listen to the radio. He was not only thematising the radio in broadcast presentation but suggesting how the medium itself can transform social communication through its technological advantage: the ear is to become a voice'.[48]

The voice of the radio conveyed the threat to Lindbergh posed by, in turn, fog, snow and sleep, all of which he overcomes. Brecht initially presented the event as an individual's triumph over nature by harnessing technology, in which luck played a part, too. Only in the version in 1930 would Brecht present it as the achievement of a collective rather than the triumph of an individual, heroic adventurer. In the 1929 version, Lindbergh asserts himself, in response to the optimistic expectations of America and to the pessimism of Europe: 'Two continents, two continents / Are expecting me! I / Must get there'.[49] Lindbergh encourages his engine: 'Now it's not all that far. The time / Has come to pull ourselves together / We two'. After he has landed in France, Lindbergh reflects on the modern, technological age, 'when humanity / Began to know itself', which led to the invention of airplanes, and concludes:

> Near the end of the third millennium, as we reckon time
> Our artless invention took wing
> Pointing out the possible
> While not letting us forget:
> *The unattainable.*

This note, on which the play ended, was on the face of it quite un-Brechtian. Indeed, that version was subsequently little performed. In 1930 Brecht added a new central section, 'Ideology', which bears the stamp of Brecht's adoption of Leninism that year.[50] Lindbergh would evoke the struggle to establish the new age, with its new buildings and with people migrating to the cities:

> Yet it is a battle against what is backward
> And a strenuous effort to improve the planet
> Like dialectical economics
> Which will change the world from the bottom up.[51]

For Brecht, the application of dialectical materialism to economics became an essential

tool in re-grounding the economic system away from capital accumulation and speculation on the basis of labour theory of value in production. The section concludes with
the atheist Lindbergh's call to arms to sweep away the old ways:

> Thus there may still remain
> In our improved cities confusion
> Which comes from lack of knowledge and resembles God.
> But the machines and the workers
> Will battle against it, and you too
> Take part in it
> The battle against what is backward.

The day after *Lindbergh's Flight*, Brecht's counter-play *Lehrstück* was performed to
Hindemith's music. Again, it was broadcast on the radio. Brecht and Hindemith
shared the view that art must have a use value and appeal to a broad community. The
relationship of the individual to the community becomes the focus of interest, the play
attacking bland notions of community current in New Music on the grounds that they
obscure political interests in the emerging collective age. Brecht emphasised use value
in the theatre programme: 'The *Lehrstück*, product of various theories of a musical,
dramatic and political nature aiming at the collective practice of the arts, is performed
for the self-orientation of the authors and of those actively participating, and is not
meant to be an experience for all and sundry. It is not even finished'.[52] Although, as
Brecht claimed, this unfinished work was not ready for the very audience participation
which he was otherwise promoting, it is an extraordinary piece of writing, a cascade
of imagery and philosophical reflections drawn from Brecht's most personal concerns,
interweaved with the story of Nungesser's failure. The work captures the quarrel which
Brecht was conducting with himself about the precariousness of the bodily existence,
indeed of existence in general, during a period of traumatic socio-economic upheaval.

    The reportage of *Lindbergh's Flight* contrasts with the philosophical reflections in
Lehrstück upon the limits of the individual's capacity to master nature. Picking up
on the initially puzzling conclusion of the first piece concerning the '*unattainable*',
Lehrstück asks burning questions: what social value does technological progress
have and what is the value of individual achievement for the community? A chorus
represents the interests of the community in dialogue with the stricken pilot, who
acknowledges his purely egotistical ambition:

> I had been seized with the fever
> Of building cities, and of oil.
> And all my thoughts were of machines and the
> Attainment of ever greater speed.
> I forgot in my exertions
> My own name and identity
> And in the urgency of my searching
> Forgot the final goal I sought.[53]

An inquiry follows into the key question: 'Do men help each other?'. The leader of
the chorus proclaims various achievements of modern civilisation, but each example

is followed by the choral refrain: 'Bread did not get cheaper'. Twenty photographs are projected, 'showing how human beings slaughter one another in our times'. The answer to the question, 'Do men help each other?' can only be a resounding: 'No man helps another'.

Brecht's vision of a cruel society was already too much for some Baden-Baden aficionados, who were demanding that the performance end. There was consternation at the next scene featuring three clowns. Two of the clowns, in bourgeois clothing, saw off the limbs of the third, the petty-bourgeois giant Mr Smith (Herr Schmitt in the German original) in response to his complaints that his limbs hurt. A music critic sitting next to Hanns Eisler fainted at the sight of the clowns sawing through Mr Smith's enormous feet in the graphic demonstration: 'No man helps another'. In the scene 'Instruction' one of the airmen acknowledges:

What I have done was wrong.
Now I learn to see that a man
Must lie prostrate and not strive
For heights, nor depths, nor yet velocity.

The Speaker then reads out the following story:

When the thinking man was overtaken by a great storm, he was seated in a large carriage, taking up much room. The first thing that he did was to descend from his carriage. The second thing was to take off his cloak. The third thing was that he laid himself down on the ground. Thus he conquered the storm in his smallest magnitude. [...] In his smallest magnitude he outlasted the storm.[54]

The thinking man is a Keuner-like counterpoint to the gigantic Mr Smith, who cannot adapt and is destroyed. Indeed, a Keuner story almost identical to the story of the storm features in *Fatzer*, too.[55] As we know, the storm is a Brechtian *Urszene*, a primal scene, in which the individual must withstand the violent forces assailing him from without and within. The self-effacing thinking man who conquers the storm by reducing himself to his smallest magnitude contrasts starkly with the tragic heroism of anthropomorphised figures in Brecht's early poems such as 'The Burning Tree' and 'The Song of the Vulture Tree'. Brecht's perennial experience of his body as a battleground in the storm is now assimilated within an eschatological vision of the comminution [Zertrümmerung, a scientific term used in medicine for the shattering of a bone, in nuclear physics for atomic fragmentation] and reconstitution of the thinker as he passes through the storm, the crucible through which the individual must travel to become the new self in the collective age. The Speaker concludes: 'When the thinking man conquered the storm, he did so because he recognised the storm and agreed to it. Thus, if you wish to conquer death, you may conquer it by recognising death and agreeing to it'.[56]

However, the Crashed Airman Nungesser re-asserts his egotistical self-belief:

But I with my flight
Reached my greatest magnitude.
However high I flew, none flew
Higher.

The Crashed Airman fails to understand that he faces inevitable death. The Chorus describes him as follows:

> He has been branded overnight and
> Since this morning has his breath been stinking.
> See how his flesh decays, and his face which
> Once we knew, is now strange to us.

The recurrent Brechtian motif of bad breath heralds the morbidity of this egotistical individual's body. The Chorus concludes the play with the scene 'Agreement', by which is meant agreement upon the necessity of revolution to address pervasive socio-economic malaise.

As Anthony Tatlow observes, the problem of change which Brecht himself faced was 'not the problem of the proletariat'.[57] With his big car and cigars, Brecht was the bourgeois individual who must change. Survival depended on stripping away the trappings of bourgeois egotism and constructing a different type of human being for the new collective age. At this time Brecht repeatedly takes up the theme of the comminution and reconstitution of the individual.[58] Furthermore, images familiar from Brecht's medical condition, in particular the loss and recovery of breath, come to the fore. In another draft for *Fatzer* Herr Keuner exclaims: 'We are / too chastened, living below the ground / off scraps of meat, breathing laboriously / so inhuman, that cannot go on'.[59] The loss and recovery of breath is a key image in an extraordinary passage which describes the reconstitution of the divided and sickly individual after a time of 'monstrous illness' as the 'dividual', another Brechtian coinage:

> In the growing collectives the comminution of the individual takes place. The speculations of ancient philosophers about man's division are being realised: in the form of a monstrous illness, thought and being are divided in the individual. It falls into pieces, it loses [...] its breath, it passes over into something else, it is nameless, it doesn't hear any call any more, it flees from its expanse into its smallest magnitude, from its indispensability into nothingness – but in its smallest magnitude it recognises, having passed through and breathing deeply, its new and actual indispensability in the whole.[60]

Villwock and Kölbel see Brecht here drawing on a heady mix of Christ's Passion, modern physics, Schmitt's teaching and revolutionary Marxist belief in qualitative transformation through violent revolution. At the same time, Brecht's emphasis upon the biophysical realm is intimately connected to his troubled relationship with his own organism. With such an eschatological vision at this time of acute crisis, Brecht places himself in the company of other artists and intellectuals, among them unlikely bedfellows like Ernst Jünger and Gottfried Benn, who in the terminal crisis of the Weimar Republic developed their visions of radical transformation in bodily terms.[61] While Benn imagined impending biological mutation and in 1933 viewed the National Socialists as the quasi-mythical embodiment of that mutation, Brecht, drawing upon an eclectic range of thought and intuitions, believed that the age of the bourgeois individual would be replaced by the new collective age of the dividual, who had passed through the crucible of socio-economic crisis.

How was *Lehrstück* received? Critics who supported New Music heaped super-
latives upon it. However, there was general incomprehension at Brecht's text. His
depiction of cruelty outraged many people and the local authority withdrew funding.
That spelt the end of the festival in Baden-Baden – it would move to Berlin. Brecht
was assailed by drastically conflicting impulses. On the one hand, he was in the grip
of huge anxiety manifest in a quasi-mystical belief that modern, mass society in its
acute crisis was entering a period of intense, violent transformation. On the other,
he believed in the need for exhaustive, detailed analysis of socio-economic questions
according to the requirements of logical empiricism and the dialectical method. In
1930 Brecht came to see Lenin's doctrine of the necessity of violence in the revolution
as the means to overcome such conflicting impulses, accommodating profound
anxiety within a comprehensible system of thought. At the same time, the complexities and eclecticism of Brecht's responses placed him at a remove from the KPD's
understanding of Marxism-Leninism. A chillingly austere vision of illness and socio-
economic mutation in situations of extreme impoverishment and death was coming
to inform Brecht's work, as he struggled to overcome his earlier, deeply engrained
fascination with larger-than-life, dangerous, egotistical figures like Baal and Fatzer.
Survival appeared possible only under extremely reduced conditions of existence.

Government by Emergency Decree 1929–31

Wall Street hits Berlin: *The Rise and Fall of the City of Mahagonny*

On Friday 25 October 1929 the speculative bubble which had been building for years in the New York financial markets burst, as bubbles must. In his classic study *The Great Crash*, John Kenneth Galbraith writes that the 'faith of Americans in quick, effortless enrichment in the stock market', which had become 'every day more evident', was suddenly dashed to pieces.[1] That would not be the last time that political elites encouraged belief in the capacity of capitalism to deliver effortless enrichment. Nor would it be the last time that speculators and bankers would be allowed to do much as they pleased before governments and peoples were left to clean up the mess. New York's Black Friday signalled the start of the world economic crisis, leading to the Great Depression in the USA and leaving the fragile German economy exposed to the worst of the crisis on account of its dependence on US finance to service its debts. The final consequences of Germany's failure to deal with the crisis would far exceed anyone's worst expectations.

Brecht had seen enough since 1914 to have no faith in the capacity of the political establishment to reform capitalism in the people's interest. He had witnessed the collapse of the German economy after the First World War and had studied the workings of the US financial and commodities markets on which Germany depended. He was keenly aware that the vagaries of the 'virtual' economy could have a devastating effect on the real economy, since speculators' appetite for profits could destroy the livelihood of millions at a stroke. As Brecht had seen graphically on May Day, the state would then use whatever force was necessary to protect law and order.

Because Germany had not been able to meet the conditions of the Dawes Plan, the Allied Reparations Committee had appointed another group, chaired by Owen D. Young. In the spring of 1929 the recommendation of the Young Committee had been approved that Germany should repay 112 billion gold marks over fifty-nine years, consisting of a third payable annually and two-thirds postponable. However, the Young Plan was still-born. After Black Friday the American banks recalled money from Europe and cancelled the credits required for the Plan. The Weimar Republic was reduced to economic and political chaos. Already in January 1930 an NSDAP member, Wilhelm Frick, was named the Interior Minister of Thuringia. Frick was in the vanguard of the cultural backlash in that state, along with the militantly anti-modernist architect Paul Schultze-Naumburg.

In Berlin the coalition government led by the SPD's Hermann Müller collapsed and in March 1930 President Hindenburg appointed Heinrich Brüning from the Catholic Centre Party as Chancellor. His wartime service as an officer made him acceptable to Hindenburg. Brüning's credibility as a politician rested principally upon his financial and economic acumen. When the Reichstag rejected Brüning's proposals, Hindenburg saw this as the 'failure of parliament' and called a general election on 14 September 1930. Disastrously, the election brought a massive upsurge in support for the NSDAP. The Nazis increased their vote from just under a million to over 6.5 million and their seats in the Reichstag from just 12 to 107. Overnight the Nazis became the second largest party after the SPD. The third largest was the KPD, which increased its seats from 23 to 77. Dictatorship was increasingly attractive to many who associated democracy with weak leadership unable to deliver decisive change. There was, of course, no possibility of the SPD and KPD uniting against the Nazis, given the prevailing KPD doctrine of Social Fascism. That failure was compounded by a dogmatic unwillingness on the Left to acknowledge that 'their' working-class voters had opted for the NSDAP. The Left's fetishisation of the working class and, indeed, of the lower-middle class drastically impaired its capacity to analyse the appeal of Fascism. Without any prospect of forging a coalition, Brüning ruled by presidential emergency decree. His cuts in welfare and reductions in wages, combined with rising prices and taxes, increased the misery among working people and the unemployed. Moreover, his deflationary policies guaranteed that unemployment would continue to rise and the crisis to deepen.

For Brecht, these developments demonstrated the dangerous failure of capitalism, susceptible to mutate into its most brutal form, Fascism. As the crisis unfolded, Brecht and Weill put the finishing touches to their opera *The Rise and Fall of the City of Mahagonny*, an imaginary city of excess, an alternative to failing capitalism for the discontented seeking to live out their fantasies of unlimited pleasure. In March 1930 Brecht followed Weill to Leipzig for the dress rehearsal and Weill introduced the 'epic opera' on the radio. Experimental and critical in its trajectory, the work embodied much that the nationalist Right hated. Weill's score broke with the convention of opera by presenting not a composition united by techniques such as leitmotifs but a sequence of self-contained musical settings. Brecht's text matched this approach. Alongside the Mahagonny songs he selected a number of poems, among them 'Tahiti'. He drew upon 'American' imagery such as the hurricane scene, a variation on his *Urszene* of the storm. And then there were Brecht's usual biblical parodies, above all the analogy of Jimmy Mahoney's fate with Christ's Passion. In the hedonist Jimmy, Brecht once more created a vitalist protagonist at odds with his age. Despite all his later efforts to change the conclusion, as in *The Threepenny Opera* Brecht's pre-occupation with bodily appetites produced a work which could never match orthodox Marxist understanding.

Mahagonny caricatures the notion that freedom is available for all by presenting a world in which everyone can do just what they want – provided that they have the money to pay. The City of Mahagonny, founded by three criminals on the run,

Ladybird Begbick, Trinity Moses and Fatty the Bookie, draws upon the popular image of the United States at the time of the gold rush. It attracts adventurers and desperados, brothel madams, pimps and prostitutes. Jimmy is one of a group of four lumberjacks from Alaska who are drawn to Mahagonny. Begbick, a madam, invents the name, meaning city of nets, designed, as she explains, to ensnare people in Suckerville:

> Everywhere men must labour and sorrow
> Only here is it fun.
> For the deepest craving of man is
> Not to suffer but do as he pleases.
> That is our golden secret.[2]

They open the As-You-Like-it-Tavern. Fattie and Moses explain why, in a lawless world, Mahagonny is needed:

> Because this world is a foul one
> With neither charity
> Nor peace nor concord
> Because there's nothing
> To build any trust upon.

The fool's paradise of Mahagonny attracts girls who sing the 'Alabama Song'. Jimmy and his friends Jake, Bill and Joe respond with:

> Off to Mahagonny
> On swift and even keel
> Where civ-civ-il-i-sation
> Will lose its scab and heal.

The English translation does not quite get the German pun on 'syphilisation', a favourite in Brecht's verse since the 1910s, warning of the dire hazards of modern civilisation, where pleasure and excess yield disease and death. Following the success of the songs from *The Threepenny Opera* and *Happy End*, record companies were eager to market the songs from the opera. Lotte Lenya's fame rose to fresh heights.

Even though Jimmy and his friends see disillusioned people leaving Mahagonny in their droves, he mistakenly believes that he can live the dream that he can do whatever he wants there. His friend Jake indulges his culinary fantasy – until he eats himself to death. Jimmy would like a fuck fest with Jenny and bets all his money on Joe winning a prize fight, but Trinity Moses kills Joe. Jimmy then goes on a drinking binge and commits the only unforgivable crime in Mahagonny: he can't pay. He is sentenced to death on the electric chair. In the first versions of 1927 and 1929, which are very different from the version published in late 1930 in Kiepenheuer's new Brecht series *Versuche* [*Experiments*], Jimmy refuses to repent, encourages everyone to continue to indulge their appetites, whatever the cost, and defiantly sings 'Against Temptation', Brecht's resounding warning not to be seduced into abandoning life's pleasures, which he had written immediately before conscription in 1918. The play ends with mass demonstrations against huge inflation, the demonstrators carrying Jimmy's corpse. The spirit of Baal is still alive and kicking as Mahagonny descends into chaos, visited by catastrophe and conflagration, like the biblical Sodom and Gomorrah. The demonstrators' slogans reveal the gross contradictions of capitalism:

FOR THE NATURAL ORDER OF THINGS
FOR THE NATURAL DISORDER OF THINGS
FOR THE FREEDOM OF THE RICH
FOR THE FREEDOM OF ALL
FOR THE UNJUST DIVISION OF EARTHLY GOODS
FOR THE JUST DIVISION OF SPIRITUAL GOODS[3]

A proclamation follows: 'FOR THE CONTINUATION OF THE GOLDEN AGE'. Unable to help the dead Jimmy, all conclude: 'Can't help ourselves and you and no one'.

The Leipzig production triggered one of the biggest scandals in the theatre of the Weimar Republic. Pandemonium broke out amongst members of the audience, who came to blows amidst the whistling, booing and the tumultuous applause, which finally drowned out the opposition. Unlike the Baden-Baden production of the Mahagonny songs, this time the scandal was political. German nationalists and Nazis denounced the play as the embodiment of the 'Jewish-Bolshevik threat'.[4] Fritz Stege, the Nazi editor of *Zeitschrift für Musik*, warned Brecht and Weill that their days were numbered. Leipzig remained firm in rejecting nationalist calls for the play to be removed from its programme but Essen, Oldenburg and Dortmund abandoned productions. *Mahagonny* was a great success in Frankfurt but no Berlin theatre would touch it until Aufricht hired the Theater am Kurfürstendamm in late 1931. Meanwhile, Hitler's close ally Alfred Rosenberg proclaimed in the *Nationalsozialistische Monatshefte* that 'Brecht's texts and Weill's music are never to be regarded as German art'. The scandal would not be forgotten. In the late 1930s the Nazi exhibitions Degenerate Art and Degenerate Music displayed records of *Mahagonny* and *The Threepenny Opera* to warn against Weimar culture. The political controversy obscured serious discussion of the opera in the press. Moreover, Brecht was accused of another act of plagiarism, this time by the relatively unknown Walter Gilbricht who claimed that Brecht had stolen from his play *The City with one Inhabitant*. This time, Brecht could show he had submitted his work before Gilbricht's had found its way to Piscator, where, Gilbricht alleged, Brecht had plundered it. Brecht replied crisply: 'Gilbricht's words cannot be plagiarised'.[5]

Some music critics like Hans Heinz Stuckenschmidt were unstinting in their praise of the work's innovation as a music drama that lent credibility to the new theatre and demonstrated the potential of contemporary opera. Others saw *Mahagonny* as a symbolic representation of capitalism comparable to Wagner's *Ring*. Brecht set down his thoughts about *Mahagonny* in his notes on the opera, his first major theoretical statement about Epic Theatre to be informed by Marxist concepts. Later given the title 'The Modern Theatre is the Epic Theatre', the notes have gone down as a uniquely canonical – and misunderstood – piece. Brecht presented a table of antithetical concepts under two principal headings, 'Dramatic Theatre' and 'Epic Theatre', which have encouraged readers to see absolute antitheses between, for example, acting and narrating, suggestion and argument, and feeling and reason, even though, as Brecht explained in a footnote: 'This table does not show absolute antitheses but mere shifts of accent'.[6] Unfortunately, neither in this piece nor later was Brecht sufficiently clear in his expression to dispel the impression that readers were being presented with such antitheses.

With a side-swipe at Weill – their partnership would not last – Brecht maintained that the analytical separation of elements in Epic Theatre rendered old operatic debates about the primacy of word, music or action redundant. Brecht attacked the naivety of avant-gardists like Weill, arguing that these impoverished practitioners were in thrall to prevailing economic interests. They did not recognise their dependence in a situation in which art had taken on the form of a commodity within the apparatus of the culinary entertainment industry, which Brecht was determined to expose through parody. He asked: 'Why is *Mahagonny* an opera?', then provided the answer: 'Because its basic attitude is that of an opera: that is to say, culinary. Does *Mahagonny* adopt a hedonistic approach? It does. Is *Mahagonny* an experience? It is an experience. For ... *Mahagonny* is a piece of fun'.[7] Brecht derived his own pleasure from parodying the established opera form and adding his own innovations. Speculating that this might lead not to the renewal of the genre but to its destruction, he made his key point:

> Perhaps *Mahagonny* is as culinary as ever – just as culinary as an opera ought to be – but one of its functions is to change society; it brings the culinary principle under discussion, it attacks the society that needs operas of such a sort; it still perches happily on the old bough, perhaps, but at least it has started (out of absent-mindedness or bad conscience) to saw it through ... And here you have the effect of the innovations and the song they sing. Real innovations attack the base.[8]

Brecht explained that he aimed 'to develop the means of pleasure into an object of instruction, and to convert certain institutions from places of entertainment into organs of mass communication'.[9] He would never be satisfied with anything less than institutional transformation on a grand scale.

Didactic experiments in Berlin: Brecht adopts Leninism

Over the winter of 1929 through to the spring of 1930 Brecht worked with Weill and Eisler on a number of Lehrstück pieces for the Berlin Festival of New Music. Elisabeth Hauptmann had been reading Arthur Waley's *The Noh Plays of Japan* and his translation of the Japanese Noh drama *Taniko: The Valley-Hurling*, which she translated into German. Hauptmann rightly saw parallels between Noh and Epic Theatre. In fact, Noh was as if made for Brecht as he sought forms to counter the emotional confusion he experienced in western theatre. Others like W. B. Yeats were attracted to Noh in their critique of naturalistic European realism. Noh combined aesthetics and didactics in word, music and dance in a strict, formal composition with few characters, a choir, narrative exposition, dignified, symbolic representation and the depiction of types, not psychologically rounded characters. Brecht proclaimed that acting should be 'Witty. Ceremonious. Ritual'.[10] He provided his own particular emphasis, seeking to tear off the false facade of Naturalism to reveal underlying causalities in social and economic processes in what he insisted was a genuine form of realism.

Weill shared Brecht's enthusiasm for *Taniko*, which they decided to adapt as an opera for schools, *He Who Says Yes*. Brecht took over 90 per cent of Hauptmann's translation but made some alterations to the story. In the original, the boy was simply thrown to his death in the valley according to ancient religious custom. Brecht and Weill saw that some other motivation was required. Meanwhile, Brecht began work with Eisler on *The Measures Taken*, a second piece for the Festival, which drew on *He Who Says Yes*. They also worked on *The Exception and the Rule*, another short piece adapted from Hauptmann's reading, this time a French translation of a Chinese play, *Ho-Han-Chan, ou La tunique confrontée*. *The Exception and the Rule* is a quite conventional Marxist representation of the master-servant relationship, which shows the paranoia of the ruling class and the support which it receives from the judiciary. The piece ends with the actors urging: 'Even when quite normal, it must astound you / Even when the rule, recognise it as an abuse / And wherever you have recognised abuse / Put it right!'.[11]

Brecht's writing for these projects between the spring and the autumn 1930 takes a decisive turn as they become informed by the Leninist belief in the necessity of revolutionary violence to establish and maintain a dictatorship of the proletariat.[12] This, of course, provided common ground between Brecht and the KPD, which Brecht sought to maintain throughout his many disagreements with Communist figures, including the waxing and waning of his Leninism itself and the inherent impurity of his Marxism in the eyes of its custodians. However, from 1930 we encounter a rather different literary figure in Bertolt Brecht. The relationship of the self to power became a determining factor in Brecht's life, which he lived henceforth as a consciously revolutionary artist. Alongside the German and Soviet Communist parties, the major political forces with which he contended were, of course, Nazism and, in time, the Western Alliance. Within the bleak economic and political situation which endured for the rest of his life, Brecht imposed quite deliberate constraints upon himself in his support of the German and Soviet Communist parties. They included a striking degree of self-censorship in the interest of the revolutionary movement, particularly in his public loyalty towards the Soviet Union as the embodiment of the revolution.

At times he is outspokenly confident in representing the revolutionary cause, at others frustratingly muted and enigmatic in his attitude towards its criminal excesses. At other times still, he succeeds in articulating his acute dilemmas in magnificently drawn, deeply flawed characters such as Galileo. Like Brecht's other great male protagonists, Galileo is characterised by his appetites and desires. This distinguishes them from the sociological analysis of the individual's relationship to society in Marx's classic definition in his 'Sixth Thesis on Feuerbach', according to which the human essence must be construed as the 'ensemble of all social relations'. As Steve Giles observes, Brecht quotes this passage approvingly in his 'Notes to *The Threepenny Opera*' of 1930, only in his very next sentence to qualify the sociological perspective as follows: 'Even human beings, that is human beings of flesh and blood, can only be understood in terms of the processes in and through which they are constituted'.[13] Brecht's work is unthinkable without this biophysical dimension, born of a sensibility acutely aware of the determining power of the body in human life. Indeed, he links it directly with Epic Theatre, arguing that it is the art form appropriate to materialism, a materialism, as Giles puts it, 'grounded ultimately in human physicality'. This sets Brecht perennially at odds with Marxist-Leninist orthodoxy. Brecht the Marxist heretic was born.

At the same time, Brecht's Leninism impacted upon the revolutionary thrust of *The Measures Taken*, taking Brecht and Eisler decisively beyond the ethos of New Music, which fostered the idea of community amongst amateur performers and the audience. When Brecht submitted a draft of *The Measures Taken*, the Festival organisers, among them Paul Hindemith, requested the full text before they would accept the project. Brecht suspected that they were planning to censor his work. A public row broke out and Brecht and Eisler withdrew. Weill withdrew *He Who Says Yes* out of solidarity with them. School children performed it in June under the auspices of the Berlin Central Institute for Teaching and Education. It was broadcast to great acclaim on the radio, the much imitated music being hailed for its renewal of school opera. The play explores the message delivered by the Full Chorus at the start that, for a group, learning to agree is a difficult matter:

> Nothing is more important to learn than agreement
> Many can say yes; at the same time there is no agreement.
> Many are not even asked, and many
> May be agreeing to error. Therefore:
> Nothing is more important to learn than agreement.[14]

Being a good comrade is not easy. The Boy receives permission to accompany his Teacher on a journey across the mountains to a town where he hopes famous doctors will give him medicine for his sickly mother. The report of the Full Chorus echoes Brecht's own boyhood situation: 'The boy was not fit for the exertions of the journey: / He overstrained his heart / Which longed for the order to turn back homeward'. The three other Students remind the Teacher that the ancient custom is that anyone who fails the climb should be hurled into the valley. Not to do so would endanger the whole enterprise. When asked if he is prepared to relinquish his life in accordance with the ancient custom, the Boy agrees and, sacrificing himself for the common good, plunges to his death.

Brecht did not intend the process of learning to be construed as so simplistic as many took it to be. As the Full Chorus had stressed, learning how to agree on such a course of action was an extremely difficult undertaking which required understanding and insight shared amongst the group. The play was construed as an opportunity for the actors and audience to participate in such discussion. As such, it was an encouragement to the KPD to promote discussion of means to achieve ends. However, the boy's self-sacrifice provoked outrage, not just from predictable quarters but also from Brecht's friends. Eisler was appalled by its 'feudalism', while Warschauer wrote in *Die Weltbühne*: 'You see, these people who say yes are strikingly reminiscent of those who said yes during the war'.[15]

Their criticisms and suggestions of the school children prompted Brecht to re-cast *He Who Says Yes* and to write a counter-play, *He Who Says No*. In the brief text of *He Who Says No*, the Boy explains why he does not give his consent: 'As for the ancient custom I see no sense in it. What I need far more is a new great custom, which we should bring in at once, the custom of thinking things out anew in every new situation'.[16] The intention was that the two pieces should be performed together in order to stimulate further discussion. However, no music was written for *He Who Says No*, so the two plays could only be put on together without music.

The Measures Taken was performed later in the year with Slatan Dudow as director. The production involved amateur musicians and workers' choirs, who rehearsed at night after their shifts. The set designer Teo Otto, a friend of Weigel's, joined with Brecht in this venture, which premiered in a night-time production at the Berlin Philharmonic on 13–14 December. The measures of the title concern the Four Agitators' judgement that the Young Comrade must die since his Communist belief is rooted only in his feelings, not grounded intellectually. The Four Agitators explain their decision:

> [...] *It is*
> *A terrible thing to kill.*
> But not only others would we kill, but ourselves too if need be
> Since only force can alter this
> Murderous world, as
> Every living creature knows.
> It is still, we said
> Not given to us not to kill. Only on our
> Indomitable will to alter the world could we base
> This decision.[17]

Brecht himself explained that the play aimed to show 'politically incorrect behaviour and thereby to teach correct behaviour'. The production was praised, particularly the music and the workers' choirs. However, in the conservative and nationalist press the text was viewed a 'dangerous contamination of our cultural values'. The production prompted the Berlin police to open a file on each of Brecht's plays, while critics from the revolutionary Left engaged in extensive debate. Most were disinclined to take lessons in party discipline from a figure who was not even a KPD member. The view that Brecht promoted dangerously autonomous proletkult tendencies would not go away. In *Die Linkskurve*, Otto Biha commented that Brecht, hitherto not known as a comrade, had suddenly exceeded all expectations, even though he unfortunately knew little about the KPD.[18] Alfred Kurella, writing in the Moscow publication *Literature of the World Revolution*, questioned Brecht's distillation of problems within an 'artificial model', rather than representing reality mimetically, as Georg Lukács proposed. Like others before and after him, Kurella criticised Brecht's play for showing his 'idealistic', that is to say merely intellectual, appropriation of Marxism without the experience of the revolutionary struggle. Kurella objected, too, to the unrealistic plot in which an experienced revolutionary required an inexperienced young comrade to undertake ever more difficult illegal acts. Kurella's damning, summative judgment was that Brecht displayed remnants of petty bourgeois thinking. Brecht was so incensed by Kurella's criticism that he phoned him and said, in his thickest Bavarian accent: 'You're not my friend any more'.[19]

Nowadays such position-taking will sound arcane to many, but the in-fighting was intense. Like Abusch and Lukács, Kurella would police Brecht's work for the rest of his life, leaving him at times feeling personally threatened. In 1930 Lukács and Kurella were in the vanguard of attempts to secure agreement for a mimetic aesthetic at a time when there was no generally accepted contemporary Marxist position on literary theory. In particular, Brecht's deeply held views about the necessity of formal innovation were anathema to them. For Lukács, the defence of established form was integral to the defence of culture against the depredations of capitalism. Brecht defended himself in a number of theoretical pieces about the genre of the Lehrstück, arguing that he had achieved a fundamental communicative shift by removing the distinction between actor and audience. He maintained that, in contrast to established culinary theatre, all participants were engaged in a process of learning and of translating what had been learned into real-life action. Brecht's intellectual and artistic dispositions attracted him more readily to heretics like Korsch, who emphasised historical contingency of forms, and to individualists like Benjamin, with whom, as we shall see presently, Brecht had been developing the concept of 'interventionist thinking'. In the new collective age, it was the corollary to the concept of agreement.

Saint Joan of the Stockyards

After his earlier attempts to depict the financial and commodity markets in drafts treating the Chicago stockyards and exchanges, the Wall Street Crash prompted Brecht to return to the subject. With a nod to George Bernard Shaw's *Major Barbara* and *Saint Joan*, over a two-year period Brecht worked on *Saint Joan of the Stockyards* with Hauptmann, Hesse-Burri, Dudow and the young author Hermann Borchardt, producing a first piece of full-length Epic Theatre for mainstream theatre from a Marxist perspective. It is one of the plays for which Hauptmann came to feel she had not been given sufficient credit, artistically and financially.[20] *Saint Joan of the Stockyards* analyses the conflict between labour and capital, depicting the rapacious, inherently self-destructive nature of capitalist production and the weaknesses of the labour movement. The play is about that, not centrally about the rise of Fascism. In Pierpont Mauler the energetic, manipulative dissembler, who has little desire to enjoy material success, Brecht created a character more complex and contradictory than the conventional, exploitative capitalist. Like Shlink of *In the Jungle of Cities*, Mauler is driven by the thrill of the struggle for power. Brecht had not yet forgotten his reading of Nietzsche. With an egotism that knows no bounds, Mauler takes his place amongst Brecht's dramatic creations, from Baal to Fatzer and Jimmy Mahoney. Mauler draws on insider knowledge from Wall Street to destroy his competitors in the meat trade by cornering the market, one day forcing prices up artificially to make a killing, on another deflating them in order to win out once again. Labour is shed and hired, only to be shed once more. When workers protest against the bosses' brutal practices by staging a general strike, the police and army smash them.

As a counterpoint to Mauler, Brecht developed the Salvation Army girl Joan, a character type first used in *Happy End*, as an anglicised Joan of Arc character, Joan Dark. While the ending parodies Schiller's *Maid of Orleans*, Joan Dark is much more than a travesty of Schiller's Joan. Through melodramatic exchanges with Mauler and others presented in a rapid sequence of scenes, Joan undergoes a learning process, if one that remains significantly incomplete, concerning the question of how to control the Maulers of this world. She announces at the outset that in this time of confusion and turmoil: 'We propose to bring back God'.[21] Her belief that the workers need 'God's word', a 'higher, finer, more spiritual joy' is, however, shaken as, ever curious, she examines the confrontation between labour and capital. She challenges the view of the rich that the poor are simply morally depraved, asking in a more pointed way the question that is posed in *The Threepenny Opera*: 'Where are these people's morals to come from when they have nothing else? Where are they going to get morals without stealing them?'. For a while, Joan, in an allusion to the reformist approach of the SPD to labour-capital relations, believes that with Mauler's support she can reform the conditions of workers. That support does not, however, materialise. Joan recognises Mauler's culpability and pledges to stay in the stockyards until the workers' grievances have been addressed. Mauler himself fears a bloody Communist insurrection. However, Joan, abhorring violence, leaves the stockyards and fails thereby to complete her mission on the workers' behalf. The self-destructiveness of the capitalist system becomes manifest in the mass collapse of banks. Brecht shows this in a montage of newspaper headlines about the crash, contrasting it with other headlines about the success of the USSR's five-year plan. At the end Mauler, alluding to the Fascist rapprochement of industry and the state, seeks to rescue the system through corporatism, while Joan collapses and dies, renouncing God and acknowledging her failure to change a system in which the 'baseness of those on top is beyond measure'. In the parodic ending, the rich victors in the struggle between capital and labour canonise Joan 'in the service of God, warrior and martyr'.

Brecht achieved what he set out to accomplish: a piece of Epic Theatre for the mainstream about the clash between labour and capital, underpinned by Marxist analysis. *Saint Joan of the Stockyards* subsequently acquired an almost mythical status as the fulfilment of Brecht's Marxist project for the Theatre. However, it was performed just once during Brecht's lifetime, in 1932 on the radio. After Hitler came to power, theatres shelved productions; among them one planned by Gustaf Gründgens whose dazzling stage career in Nazi Germany was the butt of Klaus Mann's satire in his novel *Mephisto*. The sheer scale of Brecht's piece militated against performance under the difficult circumstances of exile.

When he returned to Germany after the Second World War, *Saint Joan of the Stockyards* did not feature in the repertoire of the Berliner Ensemble. It received its world premiere only in 1959 at the Deutsches Schauspielhaus in Hamburg where Brecht's daughter Hanne Hiob starred as Joan in a production directed by Gründgens. Brecht had written to Gründgens in 1949: 'You asked me in 1932 for permission to produce *Saint Joan of the Stockyards*. My answer is yes'.[22] Other productions followed but, as John Willett remarks, none of them 'securely established the play in the world repertoire'.[23] However, as Loren Kruger shows, recent revivals demonstrate that the play has lost none of its relevance in a world repeatedly damaged by the dubious practices of the financial markets.[24]

Filming *The Threepenny Opera*

Brecht's publisher, Felix Bloch Erben, were looking to make a killing out of the film rights for *The Threepenny Opera*. The prospects were good for such a stage and recording sensation. Bloch Erben secured Brecht's agreement for a deal with Nero Film, as did Weill's publisher Universal with him. Yet there were major disagreements amidst increasingly bad-tempered exchanges. As Steve Giles shows, the contract allowed the authors co-determination on the screenplay adaptation but not on the film itself.[25] Nero later contended that Brecht sought sole determination. Brecht not only found it impossible to relinquish claims upon work he had produced; he was also determined to expose the commodity status of art by producing a script which, unlike the play, had an explicit Marxist message. The director G. W. Pabst, the scriptwriter Leo Lania and Nero's lawyer went to see Brecht at Le Lavandou in the South of France but could not reach an agreement with him. Brecht returned to South Germany in early July and worked on the script with Lania, Caspar Neher, Dudow and Weill.[26] He agreed with Nero in early August that he would write a treatment, *The Bruise*, and could request changes as long as they did not affect the essentials of the script. Brecht and Lania then worked in Unterschondorf as the disputes continued. On 18 August Nero banned Brecht from working on the script and on 23 August the firm terminated its agreement with him and offered him compensation. Lania was sacked and Béla Balázs engaged as a replacement. However, Brecht continued work on *The Bruise*, an altogether uncompromising picture of gang warfare and corruption in high places which went wholly without legal redress. He returned to Berlin with *The Bruise* completed in early September.

When Nero began shooting the film without consulting Brecht, Weill walked out in protest, and Brecht and Weill each launched legal action against Nero to prevent the company from making and distributing the film. In a war of words which continued in the press while the court case opened on 17 October, Nero objected to the 'political tendency' of *The Bruise*. On 4 November Brecht's case was dismissed on the grounds that any cinematic re-working of a play required extensive changes to the author's work. This was a ground-breaking ruling against the author in favour of the commercial interests of the film industry. Brecht was ordered to pay costs. He lodged an appeal but before the appeal was heard he reached a settlement with Nero, who agreed to pay Brecht a fee and to release the rights after a number of years for Brecht to make his own film of the work. The Nero film finally premiered in February 1931, featuring Carola Neher, Lotte Lenya, Rudolf Forster and Ernst Busch. It was a great popular success despite the usual Nazi protests and the fact that it was banned in Baden, Brunswick and Thuringia.

Meanwhile, Brecht began work on the *Threepenny Lawsuit*, his 'sociological experiment', analysing his experience of Nero and the court case, which had afforded Brecht 'new insight into the structure of cultural production in contemporary capitalist society'.[27] Conceiving works of art as commodities, Brecht reflected on the conditions which made such a case with such an outcome possible. With a confidence that he maintained until 1933, Brecht argued that the outcome was part of a progressive process, the next stage of which was the destruction of bourgeois ideology through the self-destructive forces of capitalist production. That was, he argued, the final sense of the trial, a sociological experiment which laid bare how culture functioned in capitalism.

Brecht and Benjamin, *Krise und Kritik* and the failure of intellectuals

Since the spring of 1929 Brecht had been meeting with Walter Benjamin, who told his friend Gershom Scholem of his 'very friendly relationship' with Brecht, explaining that it was based 'less upon what he has produced (I know only *The Threepenny Opera* and his ballads), than on the well-founded interest one must take in his present plans'.[28] Brecht's relationship with Benjamin developed into an intense exchange of ideas. Benjamin took Brecht along to meetings of Berlin's Philosophical Group, a high-powered, private grouping of scholars and intellectuals. Figures in the Group like Korsch and Döblin were more to Brecht's taste than its leader, the speculative Jewish thinker Oskar Goldberg. When Brecht burst out laughing during a lecture, the speaker replied: 'At this time we've got to learn new ways of doing things, you too Brecht, even if you are the great Brecht!'.[29] Werner Kraft could not fathom what Brecht was doing there, while Scholem could not imagine what the philosophical Benjamin might see in Brecht. For Benjamin, Brecht was quite simply a phenomenon: he hailed him as the best singer-songwriter since Wedekind. Benjamin now tied his intellectual fortunes closely to Brecht's, seeing his own interests represented by the 'small circle around Brecht'.[30] In the spring of 1930 Benjamin worked on a 'Commentary on Poems by Brecht', the first major outcome of their 'very interesting dealings', as he put it to Scholem.[31] With a firm eye on exerting public influence, Benjamin and Brecht considered leading a reading group that summer to 'annihilate Heidegger'.[32]

However, Benjamin explained to Scholem that Brecht was in 'quite a bad way' and was intending to go away. In late May 1930 Brecht set off for Le Lavandou in his Steyr. On the way, he sought treatment from Schmitt to supplement his dietary and physiotherapeutic regime. Brecht also stopped off in Geneva where he met his oldest Augsburg friends Pfanzelt and Hartmann. From Le Lavandou he announced to Eisler that he had 'survived Schmitt'.[33] Brecht had noted down Schmitt's dietary prescriptions: 'Meat apart from pork / As much butter as possible / Cook with butter / Mashed potato rice / Beans but / Few pulses / Savoy / Black salsifies / No cauliflower or sprouts/ Horseradish, parsley / Cocoa, oat cakes / cocoa with oats / Or tea / Lemonade'.[34] Brecht noted that he should drink two cups of teas with honey and should take two baths a week, including one with malt in it. He also jotted down comfrey, an anti-inflammatory herb for skin treatment, and althaea, which can be used for gargling and treating sore throats.

A recuperating Brecht could celebrate the appearance of the first volume in the series, *Versuche*. The volumes were presented in the new form which Brecht had proposed: paper-bound with a cover of a grey cardboard and uncut. The first volume included *Lindbergh's Flight*, extracts from *Fatzer* and the first batch of Keuner stories.

The second volume would come out near the end of the year, containing *Mahagonny* and Brecht's notes on the opera, *The Baden-Baden Lesson on Agreement* and extracts from the cycle 'Reader for City Dwellers'. Brecht had been writing his city poems since 1921 as he developed his major theme of the entry of humanity into the jungle of the modern city. The city was above all a hostile place in which people were exposed to the damaging effects of modern technological society, driven by the obscure workings of finance. Brecht's cold, inhumane, poetic language captured that reality in warnings such as:

> See when you come to think of dying
> That no gravestone stands and betrays where you lie
> With a clear inscription to denounce you
> And the year of your death to give you away.
> Once again:
> Cover your tracks.[35]

The political climate only added to the sense of danger. Feuchtwanger invoked a mood of impending 'extermination' for artists and intellectuals, who by now faced the very real prospect of a Third Reich: 'When one moves amongst Berlin's intellectuals one has the impression that Berlin is a city made up of nothing but future emigrants'.[36] Unlike Feuchtwanger, up to January 1933 Brecht downplayed the Nazis' prospects, maintaining that the Left would eventually win out. That, however, pre-supposed a capacity to co-operate and compromise which simply did not exist, not least amongst the Berlin intellectual elite.

The 'Chinese' Brecht adopted a striking form of exchange with Benjamin, which Benjamin's cousin Günther Anders captures as follows: 'At times there were conversations (for example with Benjamin), even conversations with explosive content, from which the uninitiated involuntary witnesses could only receive the impression that two gentlemen were conducting a Confucian ritual'.[37] Anders continues: 'I do remember that *Benjamin understood Brecht far better than Brecht understood Benjamin*. Benjamin was used to interpreting literature; Brecht, although bubbling over with enthusiasm, was not used to the complexities of the brooding WB. Their "*friendship*" was therefore probably, as one might say, *asymmetrical*'. Benjamin was fascinated by the revolutionary Brecht's capacity to override conventional intellectual inhibitions with Bonapartist decisiveness of thought, which in turn fed his contempt for the vacillations of intellectuals, or 'Tuis' as he called them. However, as their friendship developed in exile, Benjamin and Brecht, as Wizisla shows, emerge as intellectual equals, sharing much common ground and respecting differences in method and evaluation.

The leadership role of intellectuals in the crisis played a prominent part in Brecht's exchanges with Benjamin. They developed the partisan concept of 'interventionist thinking' to challenge Karl Mannheim's position in his influential new book, *Ideology and Utopia*.[38] Mannheim had borrowed Alfred Weber's notion of the socially unattached intelligentsia to argue that the intelligentsia was suited to provide leadership by virtue of its 'free-floating' position as a social stratum to a large degree unattached to any social class. By contrast, Brecht and Benjamin were in no doubt that material interest decisively shaped the behaviour of the intelligentsia. And they followed Marx in the belief that philosophers should no longer merely interpret the world but intervene to change it. That followed from their understanding of their material interests. At this juncture Brecht and Benjamin came to agree that dialectical materialism was the means to achieve that understanding and Leninism, buttressed by interventionist thinking, the means to act upon that understanding.

From the autumn of 1930, Brecht and Benjamin's critique of Mannheim's free-floating intellectuals gained expression in plans for a journal, *Krise und Kritik*, which would debate the leadership role of the bourgeois intellectual in the deepening crisis. It was necessary to challenge the threat of Nazi organisations such as the Kampfbund für deutsche Kultur [Militant Association for German Culture], not to mention the assumption of the KPD and BPRS that bourgeois intellectuals would somehow metamorphose into working-class intellectuals. Brecht discussed *Krise und Kritik* with Benjamin, Ihering, Brentano, Bloch, the art critic Gustav Glück, Siegfried Kracauer and the publisher Ernst Rowohlt. Although the plan was not realised, Wizisla's recon-struction of the discussions and preparations for publication until the summer of 1931, when the project collapsed, reveals much about the ambitions and divisions among Berlin's left-wing intellectuals.

Brecht and his friends shared a conviction that a state ruled by emergency decree demanded of them a commitment to Leninist revolution. Benjamin described *Krise und Kritik* as a journal 'in which the bourgeois intelligentsia can account for itself in regard to positions and challenges which uniquely – in current circumstances – permit it an active, interventionist role, with tangible consequences, as opposed to its usual ineffective arbitrariness'.[39] Ihering was to be the principal editor and Benjamin, Brecht and Brentano co-editors. The others would be advisors. The first issue was planned for April 1931. However, through the autumn of 1930 there were differences at editorial meetings, and *Frankfurter Zeitung* blocked the involvement of its own people, Brentano and Kracauer. After a meeting on 26 November Bloch and Kracauer had grave doubts about the project, not least because, as Kracauer put it in a letter to Theodor Adorno, who at this time was close to both Benjamin and Brecht, the meeting had been 'so amateurishly conducted'. Bloch commented to his future wife Karola Piotrkowska: 'Through Benjamin and Brecht the thing has – apart from its obvious importance – something unnecessarily offbeat, even cliquey. [...] Besides, the alliance of the pure man of genius, Benjamin, with the unwashed genius Brecht is exceedingly curious'.

The project limped on through the winter. By February 1931 the editors had received essays by Brentano, Georgi Plekhanov and Alfred Kurella. At this point Benjamin withdrew because none of the essays matched the agreed principles or could 'claim to have been written by an expert authority'.[40] While all agreed upon the centrality of dialectical materialism and upon the concept of interventionist thinking, they differed vastly upon how the concept should be applied, not least because Kurella followed the KPD/BPRS line. The relationship between content and formal innovation in art, so important for Brecht and Benjamin, was a source of great antagonism. As Brecht had done since the mid–1920s, he supported the experimental novelists Joyce and Döblin, and decried Thomas Mann's 'closed' conventionality. Benjamin saw

Brecht as the figure supremely capable of combining advanced aesthetic techniques with political commitment. These two were light years away from Kurella, who had recently written the stinging review of *The Measures Taken*. He represented the Comintern line on Social Fascism as well as the need for bourgeois intellectuals to submerge themselves in the proletarian struggle, foregoing formal 'niceties' in the interest of maximum clarity in the presentation of content. The writing was on the wall. Wizisla puts it as follows:

> There opened exactly the same abysses that divided other left-wing intellectuals at the close of the Weimar Republic. The ability to compromise was limited. It totally failed when individual interests broke up intended alliances with such vehemence that one wonders if the participants realised the significance of the political force-field in which they were operating.[41]

Brecht was not alone in underestimating the Nazi threat. In behaviour reminiscent of his approaches to his rival Johst in the theatre, Brecht now tried to recruit Lukács as a contributor. However, he succeeded only in exacerbating existing divisions. Lukács, who championed Thomas Mann's 'critical realism' within his mimetic theory, had recently returned to Berlin from Moscow, working as a functionary on behalf of Moscow's International League of Revolutionary Writers (ILRW). His brief was to overcome the 'polarising tendency' amongst the German intelligentsia, with a view to consolidating support for the Comintern position. Like Kurella, Lukács could only envisage *Krise und Kritik* resembling a Party organ. Lukács already regarded Brecht as a 'deviationist', a judgement tantamount to the charge of Trotskyism.[42] The judgement would be dangerously damaging to Brecht in Party circles until the end of his life. A letter from Brecht to Lukács from the summer of 1931 – it was not in the event sent – reveals the great differences between them:

> Brentano and I have been sceptical from the start about the propaganda *methods* you propose, and are also opposed to your over-abstract definition of 'intellectual'. [...] It seemed to us that a magazine in the form you recently proposed would be ineffectual and even harmful. A purely didactic approach, putting too much stress on our superiority, is ill advised, even if we know that thanks to the disruption of their economic foundations some intellectuals are now open to discussion. It is undoubtedly a mistake to suppose that because intellectuals have been jolted by the crisis the slightest push will send them toppling like ripe pears into the lap of Communism.[43]

Brecht added: 'Dear Lukács, you have made even us, Brentano and myself as well, only too well aware of your superiority, and Brentano's outburst, when he insisted on your listening to his arguments, has shown you how far one can go in dictating to him'. The differences between Brecht and representatives of the emerging KPD position in Marxist aesthetics culminated in the Weimar Republic in Lukács's polemic in *Die Linkskurve*, in which he argued that Brecht's juxtaposition of 'interpret' and 'change', deriving from Marx's final thesis on Feuerbach was mechanical and falsified Marx.[44] For good measure, Andor Gábor weighed in criticism of Brecht's 'idealism'.

Ihering's withdrawal from the editorship, Rowohlt's financial collapse and an emergency decree of press restrictions put final nails in the coffin of *Krise und Kritik*. Brecht and Brentano joined the 'Fighting Committee for the Freedom of Literature' against censorship. The KPD paper *Rote Fahne* [Red Flag] reported a rally, at which Brecht described the interests of creative intellectuals as '*inseparably* linked with those of the proletariat'.[45] From this time on, and especially after what Brecht could only construe as the colossal defeat of January 1933, his treatment of the intelligentsia in works like the unfinished 'Chinese' *Tui* novel and the fragmentary *Book of Twists and Turns* would frequently be laced with irony and sarcasm.

Meanwhile, there were tumultuous scenes at the Berlin production of a re-written *Man Equals Man* in February 1931, which Brecht himself directed. The play was removed from the programme after just four performances and Brecht came under sustained attack in the press. Supported by Hesse-Burri, Brecht had forced reluctant actors to adopt his vision of Epic Theatre, which he had expounded in his *Mahagonny* notes. Brecht noted also: 'Actors must alienate characters and events for the spectator so that they strike him'.[46] The production entailed the transformation of the soldiers into monsters on stilts and wires with half-masks and gigantic hands. All the actors were required to speak gestically and demonstrate distance from the character they were playing.

Bernhard Diebold and Alfred Kerr attacked Brecht's theory and practice, and even Ihering queried the application of Epic techniques. The left-wing Béla Balázs and Ludwig Marcuse joined in. Replying to his critics in *Berliner Börsen-Courier*, Brecht published 'The Question of Criteria for Judging Acting', citing Peter Lorre's exemplary style. Karl Kraus defended Brecht and in a letter to Scholem Benjamin expressed his solidarity with Brecht and his 'small but most important avant-garde group'.[47] Benjamin's essay 'What is Epic Theatre?' was accepted by *Frankfurter Zeitung*, only for Diebold to intervene. Acceptance of Benjamin's piece, which argued that Epic Theatre changed the function of that institution from entertainment to the generation of knowledge, became rejection. Brecht's opponents in editorial offices were gaining the upper hand. This only added to the pressure from Nazis and other nationalists. From now, theatres were increasingly reluctant to stage Brecht, fearing that mayhem would ensue.

Benjamin's diary of Le Lavandou

In May 1931 Brecht once again drove down to the South of France in the Steyr. He stopped off in Augsburg to visit his father who had been ill but who was, Brecht told Weigel, astonishingly well.[48] He met up with the Brentanos in Lausanne, driving with them to Marseilles and from there to Le Lavandou. He omitted to tell Weigel that Hauptmann was with him. After he arrived in Le Lavandou on 15 May he wrote to Weigel that he had joined the Weills in Hotel Provence and that Hauptmann and Hesse-Burri were staying in a guest house nearby. Brecht added for Weigel's benefit: 'I don't think there can be any such gossip'. In fact, Brecht was staying with Hauptmann and the Brentanos in Villa Mar Belo. When Hauptmann left on 27 May, Carola Neher arrived from Nice to take her place. Weigel stopped writing to Brecht.

At the end of May Benjamin joined Brecht and the others in Le Lavandou. Benjamin reflected on his difficulties in communicating with Brecht and on the 'difficulty inherent in working with him. I, of course, assume that I am the one who will be able to deal with that if anyone can'.[49] Benjamin kept a diary of their six weeks together. Their conversations meandered through many topics, among them court cases against Schiller and Proust, an idea for a detective drama, and the idea, probably deriving from Lenin, of an International Society of Materialist Friends of the Hegelian Dialectic. One evening in the Café du Centre Brecht told Benjamin, Brentano and Hesse-Burri that there were 'good reasons for thinking that Trotsky was the greatest living European writer'.[50] Although Brecht had taken Stalin's part against Trotsky one evening in 1927, his admiration for Trotsky's writings, if not the political strategies of this banished revolutionary, remained: in 1942 Brecht would read Trotsky's book on Lenin 'with great pleasure'.

At Le Lavandou Brecht, as Benjamin wrote to Scholem, 'seemed to devour' Kafka's posthumous volume, *The Great Wall of China*, which Benjamin had given him.[51] Benjamin was surprised by Brecht's 'thoroughly positive attitude to Kafka's work'. As we know, in 1925 Brecht had described Kafka as a 'truly serious figure', a 'prophetic writer' whom he knew like the back of his hand. Kafka had just one subject, the 'astonishment of a man who feels that huge shifts are in the offing in every aspect of life, without being able to find a niche for himself in the new order of things'. Brecht added that when working with Piscator he had compared Kafka and the figure of K. with Schweyk: 'the man who is astonished by everything with the one who is astonished by nothing'. Brecht and Benjamin would resume their reflections in exile.

Brecht was 'greatly exasperated' by the news from Berlin.[52] After the Viennese Credit Anstalt Bank collapsed in May 1931, Brüning had maintained a brutal deficit-reduction strategy, sucking demand out of the system in a deflationary downward spiral. He had issued another emergency decree on 5 June, cutting salaries and benefits, which only exacerbated the crisis. There were violent clashes between demonstrators and the police, and street fighting between Nazis and Communists. Brecht revised his earlier belief that it would be years before a pre-revolutionary situation materialised in Germany. He now believed that radical change could happen quickly. He offered Benjamin his views about the masses, namely that in contrast to intellectuals the 'proletariat's sense of reality is incorruptible'.[53] Brecht hoped that the crisis would unite the proletariat. However, Brecht proposed things which for Benjamin contained decidedly 'outlandish features': 'If he were sitting on the Berlin executive committee, he would devise a five-day plan, according to which at least 200,000 Berliners would be eliminated within that period. Simply because this would ensure that "people get involved". "If this were done, I know that at least 50,000 proletarians would have been made to participate actively"'.[54]

However shocking, such a train of thought was by no means foreign to the habitually radical Brecht. His draft 'Defence of the Lyric Poet Gottfried Benn' reads: 'The revolutionary intellect differs from the reactionary intellect in that it is a dynamic and, politically speaking, liquidating intellect'.[55] We have seen similar themes of alienation, extinction and killing in 'Reader for City Dwellers', *He Who Says Yes / He Who Says No* and *The Measures Taken*. We are reminded, too, of the adolescent Brecht's justification of Napoleon's mass killing. There is no doubt that, however troubling Brecht found death personally, he saw himself living in an age where socio-economic conflicts were on such a severe scale that mass killing must be accepted as inevitable. Brecht's adoption of Leninism, of course, strengthened his conviction that murder was justified, as did his reflections on agreement to self-sacrifice. As Wizisla points out, in 1931 Brecht was invoking 'counter-violence' to a coercive system of rule by emergency decree.[56] In his eyes, the state had thereby forfeited its credibility. Brecht was quite prepared to countenance violent dictatorship as an alternative because, selectively, the ends justify the means.

Despite Brecht's activist insistence upon interventionist thinking, he was, as Bloch and Kracauer suggest, a creative genius not given to organisational tasks, who was routinely highly speculative and other-worldly in his conversational exchanges. They often yielded remarkable results but were not easily reproduced by others, let alone by an organisation like the KPD striving for clarity of purpose within hierarchies of communication. Brecht wrote that he 'thought in the heads of others, and others also thought in his head.'[57] For Benjamin, Brecht habitually performed 'provocative tricks'. Sternberg recalls that Brecht demonstrated extraordinary dramatic talent in conversation with figures like Döblin and Piscator when Brecht voiced very pointed views, very sharp, aggressive aphorisms:

> On such occasions his manner of speaking was often very different from that in other conversations we had in private. When I asked Brecht about this, he maintained that what he said in discussion of this kind, where between four and ten men were present, did not need to be his own opinion, any more than what he put in the mouth of a character in one of his plays. He said that he made some of these pointed remarks in order to provoke people, to draw them out, to make the situation more dramatic. And in fact he often succeeded in this. After such discussions we knew a great deal more about some people than before.

As these bourgeois intellectuals sought new ways to organise themselves, Brecht and his friends promoted an alternative public sphere distinct from both the mainstream and from the KPD's own organisations. The International Society of Materialist Friends of the Hegelian Dialectic was one such organisation. Brecht wrote a number of texts about the Society and drafted statutes. The first reads that the Society was to learn and teach 'interventionist thinking [...] leading to world revolution.'[58] The fourth statute required that members of the Society should represent theses which had been approved by a majority, externally and without any critique. Brecht did not see the KPD as the vehicle to represent the Society. Far from it: 'The organisation of the dialecticians takes place outside the Communist workers' party and achieves its conclusion in the organisational unification with it'. An approach both sectarian and conspiratorial was the way to destroy bourgeois society. Members were to maintain their bourgeois occupations and activities unless otherwise instructed by the Society. Yet Brecht actually had little faith in the capacity of intellectuals to act effectively as dialecticians. He told Benjamin that different intellectuals were needed from the present ones, who would die out not a day too soon. Brecht needed some genuine working-class intellectuals.

Solidarity with the Working Class 1931–3

Kuhle Wampe

As Chancellor Brüning persisted with his deflationary policies the economic and political situation in Germany continued to deteriorate. Unemployment rose beyond five million and would reach six million by early 1932. Brüning was Foreign Minister as well as Chancellor in a cabinet which acted in an advisory and executive capacity for President Hindenburg. In the autumn of 1931 at Bad Harzburg the press magnate Alfred Hugenberg challenged Brüning's position with the formation of the right-wing Harzburg Front. The Front comprised conservative nationalist elements, Hitler and leading industrialists, including the former President of the Reichsbank, Hjalmar Schacht. Hugenberg aimed to exploit Nazi successes at the polls for his own political ends by persuading Hindenburg to remove the Brüning government. However, Hugenberg proved unable to manipulate the Nazis. On the contrary: large donations from German industrialists boosted the NSDAP substantially.

While this grim scenario was unfolding, in the summer of 1931 Brecht worked at Unterschondorf with his collaborators Ernst Ottwalt, Eisler and Dudow on a new film project, *Kuhle Wampe*. The title was taken from the weekend campsite of the same name outside Berlin on the Müggelsee, which like other such lakeside sites had become a semi-permanent residence for unemployed, homeless people. Brecht and the others signed a contract with the Comintern-sponsored film company Prometheus and Brecht joined in the filming in the Berlin area in September. Prometheus was one of the numerous KPD-aligned ventures run by Willi Münzenberg, who led Comintern propaganda efforts in Western Europe semi-independently. However, the company went bankrupt. The film was completed by the Swiss company, Praesens, after Brecht and the others had secured financial support from an entrepreneur who, it is said, insisted that his car should be shown in the film.

Kuhle Wampe opens with an unemployed young man throwing himself out of a window in sheer despair. His family is ejected from its flat and moves to Kuhle Wampe. The daughter Anni, the only member of the family in work, becomes pregnant by her boyfriend Fritz. On the evening that they become engaged, Fritz claims that the pregnancy has forced him into marriage. Anni leaves him, moving in with her friend Gerda. However, she gets back together with the now unemployed Fritz at a workers' sports event. Brecht's climax of the film shows Anni, Fritz and their friends returning home by train, arguing with rich, middle-class passengers about the economic crisis. When one of the workers says that the rich will not change the world, one of the rich asks: 'Who else can change the world?'. Gerda's reply is: 'Those who don't like it'. The film's ending with Brecht and Eisler's 'Solidarity Song' is a ringing call for revolutionary change:

> Workers of the world, uniting
> That's the way to lose your chains.
> Mighty regiments now are fighting
> That no tyranny remains![1]

The authorities banned *Kuhle Wampe*: its Communist message was deemed liable to undermine the 'republican-democratic constitution'. The ban triggered protests in the liberal and left-wing press, and Praesens lodged a protest but the ban was upheld. Harry Graf Kessler, whom Praesens called as an expert witness, wrote in his diary that the film should surely not be banned on account of its politics. That would make the Weimar Republic more reactionary than the Wilhelmine Empire. There were public demonstrations and press protests, while a world premiere was planned for Moscow. Praesens cut some offending material and, on re-submission, the censor approved the film for release in Germany. The bans and public protests generated great interest in the Berlin premiere which finally took place in late May 1932. As many as 14,000 people saw it in its first week and the 'Solidarity Song' was published in a print-run of nearly 20,000. It rapidly became famous as a workers' anthem.

Brecht and young Berlin radicals: Margarete Steffin

As we know, in 1918–19 Brecht's sympathies had lain with Spartacus and the USPD rather than with the reformist SPD, which came to be closely identified with the Weimar Republic. Nothing had happened during the intervening years of Brecht's political education to alter his dissatisfaction with Social Democracy. Brecht attacked the Weimar constitution in a number of poems, mocking the discrepancy between formal democratic provision and actual practice, particularly in the field of justice and property law. He joined protests against the sentencing of the pacifist Carl von Ossietzky and his collaborator Walter Kreiser to eighteen months' imprisonment in November 1931 for high treason and espionage. In 1929 they had revealed in *Die Weltbühne* – Ossietzky was the editor – secret plans in contravention of the Treaty of Versailles for the re-armament of the Luftwaffe and for training pilots in the Soviet Union. The Ossietzky case became notorious. Brecht was in no doubt what it meant: 'The judgement by the Imperial Court against Carl v. Ossietzky shows how the German bourgeoisie is arming itself in every respect for the final struggle. Now it is starting to lock up its pacifists'.[2] Ossietzky would be released in the Christmas amnesty of 1932 but the Nazis incarcerated him in a concentration camp after the Reichstag fire. Ossietzky received the Nobel Peace Prize in 1935 and died in custody in 1938.

Among those for whom in 1931 the Ossietzky scandal became a rallying point was a young, working-class group from Treptow. They performed around Berlin with their choir, led by the KPD member Margarete Steffin, and appeared in cabaret and agitprop pieces. In her early twenties, the clerical worker Steffin was a highly principled, disciplined and self-confident woman, who was always prepared to defend her opinions. As a child and teenager, this daughter of a building worker and seamstress had been deeply serious about her pietistic religion. That same deep seriousness was manifest in her political activism. However, in the mid–1920s she contracted tuberculosis, which afflicted her for the rest of her short life.

Steffin and her friends took courses at Berlin's Marxist Workers' School. They included classes in speech and breathing techniques taught by Weigel, who took the young performers under her wing. She decided that Eisler and Brecht, whom they knew as the author of hit songs, would have to meet them. Brecht, however, showed no interest. So Weigel took the initiative and invited them to Brecht's flat but even then they found Brecht a remote figure whose art was not really their sort. Seeing the premiere of Brecht's Lehrstück *The Measures Taken* had not changed their mind. In fact, they found *The Measures Taken* so strange that they parodied it, much to Steffin's amusement, as she noted in her diary: 'It's a pity that Brecht doesn't want to know anything at all about the KPD. The unclear elements of *The Measures Taken* derive from his ignorance of the working class. In this way he can never really create anything for us. If he'd not had Eisler by his side he would have been finished right away'.[3] The criticisms were essentially the same as the official KPD criticism of *The Measures Taken*. Brecht himself expected that, once people understood him properly, they would accept his views.

Brecht expected, too, that the social power which he craved through the theatre would then accrue to him. However, Piscator's theatre was more to the taste of the youngsters from Treptow. They joined the group of amateur and professional actors at the Junge Volksbühne who worked with Piscator at various theatres and performed with Münzenberg's Red Aid as well as with the KPD. Steffin had a small part in the stage adaptation of Theodor Plivier's novel *The Emperor's Coolies* at the Lessing Theatre and in Friedrich Wolf's *Tai Yang Awakes* at the Wallner Theatre. There has been speculation that Steffin had a part in crowd scenes in *Kuhle Wampe*. Steffin certainly knew that world of tent dwellers but she was not involved, unlike her friend Richard Müller, who joined a group by the lakes near Körbiskrug and took part in the film.[4] However, Steffin did participate in 'We Are Sooo Content', a cabaret production of the Junge Volksbühne's Red Revue for which Erich Weinert, Günther Weisenborn, Brentano, Ottwalt and Brecht supplied texts. There was music by a number of composers, among them Weill and Eisler.

However, cracks had started to appear in the Brecht-Weill partnership. During rehearsals for *Mahagonny* in Berlin in late 1931, their differences came to a head in a classic argument between writer and composer over whether the words or the music should enjoy precedence. In his memoirs Aufricht claims that during their altercation Brecht knocked a camera out of the hand of a photographer who had just taken a shot of Brecht and Weill, and shouted after the hastily departing Weill: 'I'm chucking this fake Richard Strauss down the stairs with all his war paint on'.[5] Weill and Brecht now vied with each other over their collaborator Neher. In Weill's view, Brecht was 'employing every possible means to get him away from me'. Weill told Lenya of the scheming, controlling Brecht's ruses, Brecht's mockery of Weill's work and Brecht and Eisler's attempts to upstage him. Eisler now became Brecht's regular musical collaborator.

Brecht's compositions for the Red Revue included 'Song of the SA Man', who responds to the call 'Germany awake' and follows the marching orders of his Chief of Staff:

> I thought that the left road led forward
> He told me that I was wrong.
> I went the way that he ordered
> And blindly tagged along.
> [...]
> They told me which enemy to shoot at
> So I took their gun and aimed
> And, when I had shot, saw my brother
> Was the enemy they had named.[6]

The abiding trauma of civil war in which brother fought brother assumed a fresh reality in the paramilitary street fighting. Brecht's SA man knows that if his brother is defeated, 'I shall be lost as well'. However, the sheer oppression of the Nazi terror machine meant that in the civil war which the Nazi state fought against its own people such an insight could not always change minds.

In the Red Revue there was a mix of professional actors, like Weigel, Ernst Busch and Valeska Gert, and amateurs, among them Steffin and Herwart Grosse. For a while, Steffin was in love with the handsome singer Busch. However, in October she was invited to a rehearsal for 'We Are Sooo Content' at Weigel's flat where she met Brecht properly for the first time. She wrote that he 'looked very tired and weary' and soon took his leave.[7] Brecht was very taken with Steffin. Herwart Grosse remembers rehearsing with Brecht at his flat and then being told by the others that there was something between Brecht and Steffin. The premiere of 'We Are Sooo Content' took place in front of 1,200 people on 18 November 1931 at the Bachsaal. Because of the emergency decrees, the performance was only permitted under police supervision. There were three further performances at other venues around the city, again under police supervision.

Brecht's relationship with Steffin inspired him to write love poetry of a tenderness that is without parallel in his œuvre. Steffin responded with a greater tenderness still and a longing which became ever more desperate as her health deteriorated and Brecht declined to be exclusively hers. Brecht used familiar strategies to maintain his emotional distance, calling Steffin 'my soldier of the revolution' and giving her the nickname Muck, alluding to Little Muck from the fairytale of the same name by Wilhelm Hauff. At the start of the relationship Brecht wrote a sequence of sonnets for her, beginning with the following lines:

> When one day we broke up into YOU and ME
> And our beds were HERE and THERE
> We assigned an unobtrusive word

Which was meant to say: I'm touching you.
[...]
And when we were with people we didn't know
We used this word in a familiar way
And knew at once: we were devoted to each other.[8]

The word in question was 'Grüss Gott', a South German greeting on the lines of 'God bless you'. Steffin responded with her own sonnet for Brecht:

I've been bound to you, quite devoted
Since I discovered the will to say 'you'.
What's wrong with me must get better
If only I do not lose your love.

The seriously ill Steffin was deeply in love. However, Brecht would not leave his wife and children for a new lover. His marriage to Weigel was quite different from his relationship with Marianne Zoff. Steffin would have to accommodate herself to that reality.

The Mother

In the autumn of 1931 Brecht began work on the stage adaptation of Maxim Gorky's classic novel of the Russian revolutionary movement, *The Mother*. For once Brecht was treating material with a positive trajectory: the life and struggles of Russian workers, beginning in 1904–5, the first stage of the revolution, and leading to October 1917. The mother in question, Pelagea Vlassova, has until 1904–5 led a wretched life, beaten and humiliated by her drunken, now dead husband and resigned to her fate, placing her trust in God. Initially hostile to revolutionary politics, Vlassova gets to know revolutionary workers through her son Pavel, a metal-worker. She distributes leaflets to help him avoid arrest. Vlassova takes part in a demonstration on May Day 1905 in which police shoot on peaceful demonstrators, echoing events in St Petersburg on that day as well as, for Brecht, in Berlin on May Day 1929. At the demonstration Pavel is arrested and sent to Siberia. Increasingly determined, his mother then learns to read, helps striking peasants and runs an illegal press in her home. When Pavel escapes from Siberia and is shot, she continues the struggle alone, rising from her sickbed to protest against the First World War in defiance of the beatings she receives. The play ends with her in an anti-war demonstration, carrying a red flag in support of the Bolsheviks, confident that victory will be theirs.

Günther Weisenborn and Günther Stark had produced a first adaptation. However, conversations with Brecht about the situation in Germany and about Brecht's Epic Theatre persuaded Weisenborn to continue the project with him as a Lehrstück with a strong agitprop element, showing the path to revolution. Hauptmann, Dudow and Eisler joined Brecht and Weisenborn at Brecht's flat every morning from 9 a.m. till 1 p.m. Brecht's aim was to bring out the relevance of Gorky's story for the pre-revolutionary situation in Germany. Hence he emphasised the growing political consciousness of the revolutionary collective and of Pelagea Vlassova.

Again, under the auspices of the Junge Volksbühne a group of young amateur actors came together with professionals like Weigel and Busch for rehearsals of *The Mother*, which began in December. Brecht offered Steffin the small part of the maidservant. Weigel felt that taking the lead as Pelagea Vlassova was a risk because, as she put it, at first Brecht did not have 'such a high opinion of her as an actor'.[9] However, Weigel's performance as Pelagea Vlassova would change all that. That and Mother Courage would be the roles of her life. The great artistic symbiosis between Brecht and Weigel was established with the Epic style.

The first performances of *The Mother* from 12 January 1932 were closed ones for workers at the Wallner Theatre. The play transferred to the Komödienhaus am Schiffbauerdamm, where it premiered on 17 January. From there it went to the Lustspielhaus on Friedrichstrasse until early February. Heinz Lüdecke attended a rehearsal and reported in the *Illustrierte Rote Post*: 'Something is being created here which demands positive evaluation' and Ihering praised Weigel's performance, arguing that the style of the production liberated her talent.[10] In the mainstream press only Kurt Pinthus shared their enthusiasm. Other reviewers showed their contempt for Brecht's politicised theatre. Brecht himself explained that *The Mother* was conceived as a different type of Lehrstück:

> Written in the style of the didactic pieces, but requiring actors, *The Mother* is a piece of anti-metaphysical, materialistic, non-Aristotelian drama. This makes nothing like such a free use as does the Aristotelian of the passive empathy of the spectator; it also relates differently to certain psychological effects, such as catharsis. Just as it refrains from handing its hero over to the world as if it were his inescapable fate, so it would not dream of handing the spectator over to an inspiring theatrical experience. Anxious to teach the spectator a quite definite practical attitude, directed towards changing the world, it must begin by making him adopt in the theatre a quite different attitude from what he is used to.[11]

'Practicability' of revolutionary action had emerged as a key term for Brecht as he used the theatre to demonstrate the growth of Pelagea Vlassova's revolutionary consciousness. The character has great potential for emotional identification, which, as Laura Bradley shows, Brecht employs selectively alongside Epic techniques.[12] Pelagea Vlassova's revolutionary consciousness is expressed in the verses 'Praise of the Third Thing', which she recites:

> People keep telling you how
> A son is soon lost to his mother. Not to me:
> I kept in touch with mine. D'you want to know how? Through
> The third thing.[13]

The relationship between mother and son is cemented through the third thing, revolutionary activism. The first and second things are therefore the people in the relationship which belief in and work for Communism enables. In this way, Brecht demonstrated the congruence between his own trajectory and revolutionary practice and invoked the third thing in his relationships with women who shared his beliefs.

Steffin's tuberculosis had re-surfaced during rehearsals. She received treatment at the sanatorium in Hohen-Lychen near Fürstenberg north of Berlin. In January 1932 Brecht invited Steffin to live in his flat rather than return to her parents' damp ground-floor dwelling at Lasdehner Strasse 5.[14] Steffin found herself in a new world. Brecht's flat was a meeting place for his literary and political collaborators and for the group which began to meet there with Korsch – and continued to do so until 1933 – after Korsch's second lecture to the Society for Empirical Philosophy, 'The Empiricism of Hegel's Philosophy'. Like Brecht, Korsch was exploring links between logical empiricism, Hegel and Marx. Döblin, Brentano, Dudow, Hauptmann, Heinz Lagerhans, Paul Partos, Herbert Levy and Horst Horster belonged to the group. In November 1932 Korsch would continue his searching critique of Marxism in his lecture series 'Things Alive and Things Dead in Marxism', which he delivered at the Study Circle on Critical Marxism at the Karl Marx School in Neukölln. Korsch wrote to Sydney Hook on 26 December that at the seminar at Brecht's they were exploring the practice of dialectical thinking from a pragmatic point-of-view in order to mould it into a 'genuinely practicable, empirical, concrete and revolutionary mode of thought'.[15]

Steffin and her friends, whose principal point of reference was the KPD, remained politically unsure of Brecht and heretics like Korsch. When Richard Müller visited her at Brecht's flat and saw the volumes of Marx and Lenin, Steffin commented: 'Yes, good old Brecht, he sees that if he wants to write plays according to our understanding he must also know our classics'.[16] A shared passion for revolutionary literature and theatre bridged the gulf between the successful middle-class writer and the young working-class woman. The assumption was that Steffin would follow an acting career. However, like Elisabeth Hauptmann, Steffin placed her literary and theatrical talent in the service of Brecht's genius. She displaced Hauptmann as Brecht's closest collaborator. Steffin could express herself with simplicity and precision and could constantly surprise and challenge Brecht with well-founded opinions. Organisationally, Steffin was superb, undertaking editorial and secretarial work with energy and meticulous commitment, thereby maintaining Brecht's flow of publications and his correspondence with fellow writers. Brecht, who enjoyed the role of the teacher, came to enjoy being Steffin's pupil. Hauptmann struggled to come to terms with her relegation to an outer circle, while Steffin herself struggled from operation to operation, rather like Brecht's mother, never sure how long her life would last. Brecht must have been keenly aware of the parallel. Steffin stayed at Brecht's flat initially until March 1932 when her condition deteriorated and she suffered attacks of fever. In the past she had received only the most basic treatment that standard health insurance could cover. Now Brecht arranged for her to be treated at the Charité's prestigious Hermannsdorf Clinic by the famous surgeon Ferdinand Sauerbruch. Steffin remained in hospital for two months while Sauerbruch temporarily closed down a lung to give it the chance to recover.[17]

Brecht's devotion to Steffin was hugely problematic for Weigel. She had accepted his many lovers but only if he kept things at a discreet distance and did not house them in his flat. She was also deeply worried that Steffin could pass her contagious disease on to her children. Around March 1932 Weigel resolved to leave Brecht.[18] He asked her not to:

> There's no reason why we should unnecessarily widen an unnecessary rift. And I've told you in all sincerity, putting up Grete was a purely practical matter. Not for a moment was I concerned with having her near me, but only with putting her up. I'd have very much preferred it, and it would have been much more practical if you had put her up somewhere. It isn't as though her sickness were contagious. But even now I must ask you not to find fault with me for putting her up in Hardenbergstrasse, but to help me if it should again become necessary to put her up somewhere. She is now at the Charité, and then she's going to Russia, to the Crimea. She can't go back to Hardenbergstrasse, because it would be unhealthy for her and dangerous for me, but as you know, I'd like to help her (as long as it doesn't cost too much). And in between the Charité and the Crimea she may have to stay somewhere. Where? Dear Helli, you mustn't make a big thing of this. I can't bear to let myself be influenced by gossip or having to make allowances for the fantasies of a few old maids, you know that. But I am fond of you as ever.[19]

As usual, Brecht wanted to maintain an existing relationship while pursuing a new one. However, despite his best efforts he could not change Weigel's mind. She did, however, act upon Brecht's request to find Steffin somewhere to live. On 1 April Weigel and the children moved out to the western suburb of Zehlendorf and let Steffin use her old flat. Weigel then rented a flat for Steffin near her in Zehlendorf. Showing her characteristic human solidarity, Weigel cared for Steffin, cooking her hearty meals to aid her recovery. The next stage in her convalescence was a stay at a sanatorium in the Crimea, which was organised through the KPD. Steffin left Berlin for Moscow on 13 May, by which time Brecht was in Moscow too.

Moscow

The Soviet League for Magazines and Newspapers had invited Brecht and Dudow to the Moscow world premiere of *Kuhle Wampe*. They set off on the sleeper from Berlin on 7 May 1932 for a two-week visit, accompanied by the famous Soviet film director Sergei Eisenstein, who was on his way back from Mexico. Soviet comrades caused Brecht and Dudow some embarrassment, as Brecht saw it, when they asked them how they felt when they crossed the border.[20] Brecht later wrote:

> Crossing the border of the Union
> The land of working-class reason
> Above the tracks we saw
> A sign with the inscription:
> Welcome workers!
> But returning to the land of chaos and crimes
> Our homeland
> For trains travelling west we saw

A sign with the inscription:
The revolution
Breaches all borders.[21]

Brecht had understood the Soviet comrades' question. He noted that the sleeper was roomier than in the West, with sumptuous old coaches kept running in a makeshift fashion.[22]

Brecht and Dudow were greeted in Moscow by a group led by the dramatist and translator, Sergei Tretiakov, the head of the Foreign Section of the Soviet Writers' Union, whom Brecht had got to know in Berlin in 1931. During Brecht's visit the Soviet secret police, the NKVD, opened a file on Brecht.[23] Tretiakov's avant-gardist position on art and aesthetics was much closer to Brecht, Benjamin and Brentano than to the Soviet orthodoxy emerging under Stalin's rule or, for that matter, to KPD figures like Johannes R. Becher and Georg Lukács, both of whom had criticised Tretiakov after his Berlin visit. Tretiakov promoted Brecht in the USSR, publishing Russian translations of his work. However, in 1937 Tretiakov would be murdered in the Great Terror, one of an alarming number of Brecht's Moscow friends who suffered that fate.

Old Berlin friends were at the station to greet Brecht: Bernhard Reich, Asja Lacis and Erwin Piscator. Reich, who held a professorship at a drama school, invited Brecht to his place that evening. In keeping with the usual living arrangements, which, Brecht suggested, reminded him of Munich's bohemian quarter Schwabing, Reich had a room divided in two which Brecht found 'quite pleasant'. They drank tea and ate caviar with eggs and bread and butter. The next day Brecht met Piscator, who was in Moscow making preparations to film Anna Seghers's novella *The Revolt of the Fishermen of St Barbara*. Brecht found Piscator very grumpy despite his claims that he was being well cared for. Brecht felt that Piscator was right to complain about a 'lack of order' but that he himself was doing little to change things. Piscator went off to Odessa while Brecht noted his impressions: the workers on the streets looked 'strikingly well, free', different from the way they were depicted in the West, 'not at all starving'. Tretiakov gave Brecht a tour of the city in his car. They visited a secret print works and Lenin's mausoleum. Brecht spent the afternoon with the writer Ossip Brik at his well appointed flat. Brik had worked closely with Mayakovsky before the poet's suicide in 1930. Brik evidently treated Brecht as an insider: they talked about the problem of people out to wreck the system. That evening Brecht was taken to Academic Artists' Theatre for the 1,000th performance of Carlo Gozzi's tragi-comic fairytale play *Turandot*, which would inspire Brecht's own play of that name.

In advance of the world premiere of *Kuhle Wampe* on 14 May, Brecht gave interviews and Tretiakov publicised his work in the press. While the film had generated great notoriety in Berlin, it met with blank incomprehension among Moscow filmgoers, who could not understand how unemployed people could own wrist watches, bicycles and motor cycles. One reviewer wrote:

The impact of *Kuhle Wampe* is impaired by the fact that the action of the film only takes place though dialogue, through conversation. German proletarians do not just conduct nice conversations on the underground. On the contrary, they are conducting a struggle against Hitlerism and Social-Fascist reaction. This struggle is presented in the film through allusions. And even these allusions cannot be detected in the scenes in which the colony of the unemployed is shown. – Brecht is a great revolutionary artist but we cannot acknowledge his first film as a complete success.[24]

Steffin joined Brecht in Moscow in mid-May, accompanying him through the rest of his visit as his translator. On 21 May she travelled to the Crimea, while Brecht flew from Moscow to Kaunas in Lithuania and took the train from there to Berlin. His final experience of Moscow was not good. At the airport, the authorities confiscated manuscripts and two albums with photos of productions of *Man Equals Man* and *The Mother*.[25] Brecht had to ask Steffin to retrieve the items from the airport before she left Moscow.

Abiding illusions: The house by the lake

In June 1932 Hindenburg appointed a new government under Franz von Papen. Unemployment benefit was promptly cut by a further 23 per cent and the ban on the SA and the SS lifted. Street violence rose to new levels. Papen used Hindenburg's emergency powers to dismiss the Prussian government under the SPD's Otto Braun and, declaring a state of emergency in Berlin and Brandenburg, appointed himself Reichskommissar. In a general election held on 31 July 1932 the NSDAP emerged as the largest party with 37.4 per cent of the vote. However, Hindenburg did not accede to Hitler's demand that he be named Chancellor and that the Nazis should have the office of Prussian Minister-President and a number of ministries in their gift.

As usual, Brecht spent the summer in Bavaria. Steffin joined him at Unterschondorf after Weigel and the children had left. He took Steffin to the Tegernsee and to Munich where they saw a show by Valentin and Karlstadt. In late July Steffin announced to her sister a double 'sensation': she might be cured and she might be pregnant. In a sonnet imbued with that singular Brechtian emotional distance, Brecht signalled to Steffin his agreement that she should have his child, whilst reminding her of the abiding tubercular problem.[26] He worked with Steffin on an adaptation of Shakespeare's *Measure for Measure*, which would in time become *Round Heads and Pointed Heads*. He had begun the adaptation in November 1931 with the director Ludwig Berger for the Young Actors' Group at the Volksbühne. Brecht would later write that *Measure for Measure* was Shakespeare's 'most progressive' work, demanding of people in positions of authority that they 'shouldn't measure others by standards different from those by which they themselves would be judged'.[27] Although the adaptation was not originally about Nazism at all, it would become Brecht's first anti-Fascist play, one of the few which Brecht directed during his years of exile. However, as Tom Kuhn and John Willett write, 'the bones of Shakespeare could not provide a very satisfactory framework for a parable on Fascism'. An enormous amount of work went into *Round Heads and Pointed Heads*, but it proved to be a long and complex work which was never a stage success. Brecht underestimated the centrality of race in Nazi ideology. However, the play is, as Kuhn and Willett argue, more than a botched satire on

Nazism. In particular, 'the use of racist politics, or even war, as a calculated distraction from social and economic problems is depressingly familiar'. *Round Heads and Pointed Heads* would become a lightning rod in the literary politics of exile in Moscow. After that, Brecht would never return to the play.

Brecht now took a step which, retrospectively, seems quite bizarre at a time when the Nazis had become the biggest political grouping in the Reichstag: borrowing money from his father to buy a country house. The property was at Utting on the Ammersee near Unterschondorf. Believing that the German proletariat would prove the decisive force in the struggle with Fascism, Brecht engaged in the wishful thinking that the KPD's call would succeed for a united anti-Fascist front at the grassroots level with SPD supporters, bypassing the SPD leadership:

> In Berlin's eastern districts Social Democrats called
> 'Red Front!' in greeting, and even wore the badge
> Of the anti-Fascist movement. The pubs
> Were full to bursting on discussion nights
> And from that moment no Nazi
> Dared walk the streets on his own
> For the streets at least remain ours
> Even if the houses are theirs.[28]

Brecht himself became a property owner on 8 August 1932. His father met the price of 11,400 marks and Brecht signed a contract for the purchase from the retired policeman, Josef Ritter von Reis. Brecht signed an agreement with his father to re-pay the sum in blocks of 2,000 marks together with interest of 5 per cent, while his father took out a mortgage on the property of 7,500 marks.

Brecht moved in on 11 August together with Steffin and Dudow. He invited Eisler and Brentano to join them, asking Eisler if he would like to come and look into Steffin's blue eyes.[29] He encouraged Brentano to come and look at the houses in the area, assuring him: 'It's very nice living here'. Brecht was so taken by the property that he wrote three pieces about it. The first is a piece of descriptive prose about the garden and trees. In the second, a poem written in Danish exile, he reflected:

> For seven weeks of my life I was rich.
> With my earnings from a play I bought
> A house in a large garden. I had been
> Looking over it for more weeks than I lived in it.[30]

In a further poem he acknowledged:

> The joy of proprietorship was strong in me, and I am glad
> To have felt it. To walk through my garden, to have guests
> To discuss plans for building, like others of my profession before me
> This pleased me, I admit it. But now seven weeks seems enough.

In fact, during the seven weeks in which Brecht was savouring the joy of proprietorship the Munich police were reporting to the Berlin police on his holiday arrangements. Brecht was described as a convinced Communist writer, active on behalf of the KPD even though he had not yet proclaimed that publicly. He was said to earn a very great deal of money from his writing, which was of the lowest moral standing.

Brecht and Steffin travelled back to Berlin on 20 September. He now employed her as his secretary, paid her a salary and rented a room for her at Pension Dittmann, Hardenbergstrasse 37, close to his own flat. On 6 October Brecht and Weigel signed a rental contract for a large flat in Charlottenburg at Leibnizstrasse 108. Weigel moved in with Stefan and Barbara but Brecht did not. Instead, he remained at Hardenbergstrasse with Steffin close by. He again wrote to Weigel, trying to save their marriage:

> I'm writing instead of talking, because it's easier. I have such a distaste for talking that it's always a struggle. This is how it usually is with us: small psychic upsets, which can have many causes and are largely inexplicable, sometimes brought on by misunderstandings and sometimes by the fatigue or irritability that comes of work, in other words by external causes, give rise to big, impenetrable upsets.[31]

Brecht acknowledged that when that happened he could not 'repress a disagreeable and undoubtedly wounding tone'. He added: 'And you make forbidding or tragic faces', then reflected: 'One should try not to attune the body to the mind, since the body supplies more naive and more carefree reconciliations. And indeed it is always a mistake to blame the body (when something goes wrong)'. He asked Weigel not to forget that 'at present (and as a rule) I am doing difficult work and if only for that reason unable to express myself mimetically etc., and that I dread private conflicts, scenes etc., which wear me out'. He claimed that he was not leading a 'dissolute life. Nothing of the kind'. Brecht's appeal to reason and dialogue, of course, masked his expectation that Weigel should accept the behaviour of the genius. He was telling Weigel much the same as he had told Zoff ten years earlier. This time, though, the physical side of the relationship was suffering.

Steffin's condition now deteriorated badly and Sauerbruch had to operate again. She chose that course despite considerable risks because the prognosis was bleak. Brecht sought to reassure Weigel: 'You don't need to worry any longer about Grete. She's at the Charité for observation'.[32] Deeply distressed, Steffin underwent operations to combat her tuberculosis and to terminate her pregnancy with Brecht's child. Brecht wrote to her after a visit early in the New Year, maintaining that Sauerbruch was very optimistic.[33] Brecht's old Augsburg friend Müllereisert was equally pleased. Brecht ended his letter: 'In my pocket I've got three little rings for you to choose from, maybe I can show you them tomorrow'. Brecht was showing his commitment to Steffin, even though what he meant by commitment could never be enough for her.

Yet another election was called on 6 November 1932 and the Nazis lost two million votes. Some saw this as a turning-point: Brecht celebrated with the satirical 'The Führer Said' to the tune of 'It's a long way to Tipperary'.[34] However, the Führer was far from finished. Brecht spent his final New Year in Germany before exile in interesting company. Sternberg writes of Brecht's links with the 'idealistic young Nazi students', who visited Brecht to discuss the political crisis. As he had with Johst, Brecht needed to test himself against his rivals. Sternberg was among the guests at Brecht's New Year's Eve party, to which he invited his old friends Bronnen and Rudolf Schlichter, together with their radical right-wing accomplices, among them Ernst von Salomon, one of assassins of the Foreign Minister Walter Rathenau. Some of these friendships may have come about through Johannes Ludwig Schmitt. Schmitt was by now a prominent member of Schwarze Front [Black Front], the nationalist and socialist splinter group of the NSDAP led by Otto Strasser. In any case, those assembled drank a toast to a 'successful, bloodless right-wing putsch'.[35] Brecht most likely believed that any putsch from the Right would be followed by revolution from the Left.

Aware that time was short, Brecht was implementing a plan to publish as much of his work as possible in the *Versuche* series. Following the publication of the third volume in January 1932, he had been pursuing plans for five more volumes to appear during that year, bringing together his writings for the stage, radio, opera, film and theory, with a view to combining them in what he called a 'collective pedagogy'.[36] However, Kiepenheuer, anticipating that Hindenburg would capitulate to Hitler's relentless pressure to name him Chancellor, hesitated to put volumes four to six on the market. Four and five did finally appear at the end of the year, without any fanfare and without any reviews. Volume five featured *Saint Joan of the Stockyards*. Volume six, with *The Exception and the Rule*, did not get past proofs. In early January Kiepenheuer produced volume seven, which included *The Mother*. Volume eight, featuring *Round Heads and Pointed Heads*, was destroyed at the proof stage.

Brecht had given *Round Heads and Pointed Heads* to Weill, who found it 'in part [...] very beautiful'.[37] However, Weill told Lenya on 9 January 1933 that Brecht had been pestering Aufricht to bring the two of them together and that when they met, 'I was quite cool and restrained, while he was sedulous, submissive, shit-friendly'. Brecht claimed he had a great role for Lenya in a shorter play, a supplement to *Mahagonny*. However, when Brecht rang at 2 a.m. he explained to Weill that he wanted to 'dramatise' *Lindbergh's Flight*. Weill exclaimed to Lenya: 'Isn't that insane? Now he's calling me all the time; I should meet with him, but I don't want to yet. This time he will hear things from me that so far no one has ever told him'. Unprecedented things were, indeed, about to happen, on a scale that no one could begin to imagine.

Into Exile from Nazi Germany 1933

Flight

On 30 January 1933 Hindenburg finally accepted what his advisers, principally Franz von Papen, were telling him and named Hitler the German Chancellor. Like many in the German elites, von Papen believed that once in government Hitler could be controlled. That naive misjudgement ushered in a shocking sequence of events which represented an 'appalling fracture in the social, cultural and political life of Germany'.[1] As Nazi Germany pursued its geopolitical and racial obsessions, much of Europe and the countries beyond were devastated.

Even after 30 January, Brecht and Weigel underestimated the situation, believing that it would not be necessary to emigrate, rather that they might need to go to ground for a while in Bavaria.[2] However, Brecht's life as a professional writer in Germany unravelled at great speed with violent disruption to his intellectual and artistic development. Brecht had always lived an extraordinary, borderline life of brinkmanship, struggling to maintain control over the various strands: literary and business matters; political interests, which were now defined primarily by anti-Fascism and support for the Soviet Union; and the controlled chaos of his personal life in its sexual, domestic and medical dimensions. At times, we shall now see the narrative focus upon Brecht's life and work shifting rapidly between these strands as we follow him – beset by anxiety and from 1935 officially stateless – into exile. More than ever, Brecht relied on writing as an activity to control his anxieties, generally maintaining a facade of strength. However, he struggled to deal with ever greater complexity, risk and danger, as the restrictive conditions of exile rendered a lifestyle such as his, pursued within an organism such as his, precarious in the extreme.

Looking back in 1938 upon what the Nazi regime had done to him, Brecht told Benjamin: 'They have proletarianised me, too. Not only have they robbed me of my house, my fishpond, and my car, but they've also stolen my stage and my audience'.[3] At stake was not just Brecht's dependence as a dramatist upon the German language – in 1933 he had just a smattering of English and the most rudimentary French – but the symbiosis between his theatrical style and Berlin theatre life. He would have to adjust his compass to a highly unstable international environment full of national variations about which he understood too little and where opportunities for the performance of his works were at a premium. Characteristically, Brecht met the fresh challenges with all his reserves of talent, charisma, sharp intelligence and agility, skulduggery and Bonapartist desire. However, he would quickly discover that even all that was not enough and he experienced bitter defeat, humiliation and deepening isolation. The explosive contrarian re-doubled his efforts, adopting striking new modes of behaviour in an exile existence on the margins of legality. Meanwhile, as ever he pursued greatness with a rare tenacity, born of an unshakeable belief in his genius.

All these developments, of course, directly affected Brecht's family and those close to him like Steffin. After her latest operation, she was to go to a branch of the famous German Sanatorium Davos at Agra above Lake Lugano in Switzerland. She was briefly arrested before she travelled south and would never set foot in Germany again. Already on 4 February 1933 Hitler had granted himself emergency powers to 'protect the German people' by acting against any forces opposing him, in the press and at political meetings. After Weigel had performed Brecht's 'Lullabies', she, too, was arrested and held for several hours.[4] On 12 February Brentano called together fellow left-wing writers – among them Brecht, Döblin, Lukács, Leonhard Frank, Theodor Plivier and Hermann Kesten – to discuss action to oppose Hitler.[5] Frank said playfully to Brecht: 'I thought the idea here was to start a revolution', to which Brecht replied: 'Then you'll be pleasantly disappointed'. Citing his receipt of letters threatening a visit from five SA men, Brecht mooted the establishment of a bodyguard for threatened writers.

Brecht then underwent a hernia operation at Dr Mayer's private clinic on Augsburger Strasse where he remained until late February. Brecht was planning a trip to Vienna in mid-March at Richard Lanyi's invitation to read from his works. The reading was probably no more than a pretext and Brecht was in any case unsure if he would be allowed to cross the Austrian border. He told Lanyi that because of the political situation he had to speed up the publication of his works, which he viewed as his one weapon against Hitler.[6] However, Kiepenheuer was forced into administration and published volumes of *Versuche* were remaindered in Vienna.

At the end of January Brecht had assured Fritz Wreede, the owner of the publishing house Felix Bloch Erben, that he would soon have proposals for new plays.[7] However, citing the political situation, Wreede declined a request to perform *Saint Joan of the Stockyards* in Prague, while those organising a performance of *The Measures Taken* in Erfurt were accused of high treason. Brecht had hardly proved the blockbusting best-seller Wreede believed he had signed. On 27 February Wreede pointed out that Brecht had delivered *Saint Joan of the Stockyards* late and there were few opportunities for performance. Wreede added that rather than adapting Shakespeare's *Measure for Measure* as agreed, Brecht had written his own play, *Round Heads and Pointed Heads*. The limited chances the play had were now gone and Brecht had not come up with the proposals which he had promised in January. Wreede cut to the chase: the payment to Brecht of 1,000 gold marks per month could no longer be justified. In the coming months Wreede would decline all Brecht's attempts to reach an understanding.

Mid-evening on that same 27 February the Nazis, it seems, set fire to the Reichstag and blamed it on the Communists. The next day Hitler declared a state of emergency to 'protect the people and the state' against high treason. Shortly after, the Nazis pushed through legislation which authorised the government to rule for four years without consulting the Reichstag. Sternberg suggests that Brecht would not have been compelled to leave after the Reichstag fire.[8] However, Walter Mehring had tipped Brecht off, having been warned by a friend in the Foreign Ministry that he should leave Germany. Brecht and Weigel had made preparations to flee. Hauptmann would look after the children, who would follow later. On the last photo taken in Berlin Brecht wrote: 'The cases are packed'. On 27 February he was still at the clinic on Augsburger Strasse. He had left boxes of manuscripts with Hauptmann and others. Brecht and Weigel took refuge with their friend Peter Suhrkamp, staying the night of 27 February with him. Suhrkamp gave Brecht and Weigel money and Müllereisert drove them to the station the next morning where they boarded the train to Prague. At the border crossing, Brecht used the papers issued for his reading in Vienna. His flat was searched that same day. In Prague Brecht and Weigel met the publisher Wieland Herzfelde, who would be very important for Brecht in exile, and on 3 March they travelled on to Vienna, where Karl Kraus greeted them with the words 'The rats are boarding the sinking ship'. They stayed with Weigel's family, who like Brecht's own, would help them financially in the exile years. Stefan took a flight to Prague and joined his parents in Vienna, while Hauptmann took Barbara to Brecht's father in Augsburg. She was there for some time before Mari Hold took her to her parents. Weigel then arranged for Barbara to be smuggled out of Germany by an English Quaker, Irene Grant, who took Barbara to Basel and passed her on to Mari Hold. From there, Mari Hold and Barbara travelled to Vienna.

Struggling with the KPD in the anti-Fascist struggle

Brecht was now without any established literary scene, without its familiar structures and demands. In exile, theatres and audiences, publishers and other networks were improvised, fragmented and amateurish in comparison with the intense and highly organised cultural life of Berlin where Brecht could always share his ideas with supportive collaborators. Brecht writes of the situation in exile: 'Teaching without pupils / Writing without fame / Are difficult', before identifying the 'man to whom no one is listening': 'He speaks too loud / He repeats himself / He says things that are wrong: / He goes uncorrected'.[9] To have no listeners around him was a profoundly disorienting experience for Brecht. To make his living he was condemned to a peripatetic existence, chasing such royalties as he could accumulate that were lodged with publishers and banks in various countries.

The two main working-class parties established organisations in exile, the SPD in Prague and the KPD in Moscow. The Socialist Workers' Party (SAP) established an office in Paris with Fritz Sternberg and the union official Jacob Walcher, whom Brecht greatly admired. Walcher and Sternberg both met Trotsky in France shortly after going into exile. The SPD's focus in its regular reports was upon political analysis of events in Germany, while the KPD, with the backing of the Comintern, developed cultural as well as political activity. Although Brecht read SPD reports, his sympathies lay with the KPD, which he understood he could not ignore if he wished to maintain some semblance of a literary career. However, Brecht knew, too, that as a writer of bourgeois origin he could not rely upon the KPD, the BPRS and the Comintern to represent his interests. He would always maintain his independence from the KPD.

In Vienna, Brecht met with other émigrés, among them Eisler, Sternberg, Brentano, Oskar Maria Graf and the influential KPD/BPRS figure Johannes R. Becher. Becher was doing the rounds of western European capitals to gauge the mood on behalf of Moscow's ILRW, within which the BPRS was subsumed. Discussion centred on how writers might organise professionally and politically. At this stage, Becher indicated his support for a western European secretariat for exiled writers in Paris and then went on his way.

Meanwhile, Weigel faced an uphill struggle to re-establish her acting career in exile and, with that, her financial independence so that she and the children could leave Brecht. That would prove beyond her. For virtually all the exile years Weigel was reduced to the role of mother and housewife, caring for Stefan, Barbara and Brecht himself when he was there, and at times for his lovers, too. In the coming years, Brecht would spend much time far away from his wife and children, partly out of necessity and partly following his own desires, as he pursued his literary projects, anti-Fascist activity and affairs. In Vienna, Weigel met her former teacher Eugenie Schwarzwald and her school friend Maria Lazar. They all knew the famous Danish writer, Karin Michaelis, to whom Lazar wrote on 10 March, asking what it would cost for her and her daughter, together with Weigel, Brecht and their children, to rent one of her houses on the Danish island of Thurø near Svendborg.[10] Michaelis would let them use her villa Torelore for free over the summer months.

Before arrangements had been finalised with Michaelis, Brecht and Weigel explored other options. He went to look for a place to live in Switzerland, because he expected that friends such as Feuchtwanger and Döblin would settle there and that Weigel might be able to work at the theatre in Zurich. Steffin was, of course, in Switzerland, too. When Brecht arrived in Zurich on 13 March there was a letter waiting for him from a distressed Steffin, who was quite uncomfortable in the luxurious surroundings of Agra.[11] Brecht's reply reveals that Steffin was deeply unhappy at the way her fellow patients were treating her and that after the Reichstag fire most of them either acquiesced in Nazi terror or actively supported it. In fact, in 1933 the sanatorium became a base for the Lugano branch of the NSDAP and in 1937 the doctor in charge, Hanns Alexander, would found an Agra branch of the NSDAP.[12] The swastika was hoisted over the sanatorium and Jews banned from the premises. Brecht praised Steffin, 'my little wife', for her calm and courageous struggle against her illness.[13] He gave vent to his anger, saying that she did not belong in such an environment of slackers and pensioners at a time when German workers had been taken completely unawares and were without funds and leadership. Brecht wrote six 'Rules for M. S.', instructing her how to combat her illness.[14] The rules are essentially what Brecht had learned from his father: 'Fight against illness not as an invalid but as a healthy person. Fighting against illness is a healthy thing'. Brecht also wrote a scathing attack on the medical profession, 'Do Doctors Want To Cure Patients?', which was undoubtedly informed by his knowledge of Steffin's medical history and of her treatment at Agra. Brecht's view was that profit was doctors' prime motive, not improving patients' health.

On his way to Lugano Brecht met Feuchtwanger in St Anton. Brecht had also met a number of Berlin friends in Zurich: Döblin, Anna Seghers and Kurt Kläber. Kläber, an influential figure in the BPRS who had been detained after the Reichstag fire, told Brecht of his house in the mountain village of Carona on the Italian border near Lugano. Brecht wrote to Weigel that he and his friends had decided to find somewhere to live by Lake Lugano and suggested that she come along. Meanwhile, he paid the first of several visits to Steffin and wrote eight sonnets for her during her time at Agra. She responded with her own. On his visits he brought her little toy elephants which he collected on his travels. Encouraged by Brecht, Steffin performed poetry recitations and plays at the sanatorium and began to gather newspaper articles about Nazi Germany, creating an archive which he would use in his work. With Kläber and Brentano, Steffin and Brecht visited Hermann Hesse in nearby Montagnola. Brentano began to write for the quality Swiss German press, *Neue Zürcher Zeitung* and *Die Weltwoche*, not only distancing himself from Marxism but in time embracing a German nationalist position and even trying to return to Nazi Germany in 1940. Brecht's association with this 'renegade' and others like the journalist Armin Kesser would only give further credibility to the view of Lukács and others in KPD circles that Brecht was a 'deviationist'. In Lugano Brecht met Kesser, who noted their discussion of whether it was 'advantageous' for a writer to 'align himself with his personality, the work of his experience', or the opposite, the 'elimination of the individual'.[15] Brecht claimed that he was inclined to the latter, that one had to eliminate 'oneself'. However, he acknowledged that it was a big topic. It remained *the* big topic.

When Weigel visited Carona with Stefan and Barbara in early April, she knew that Brecht was continuing his relationship with Steffin. Weigel continued to think of separation. However, Brecht, seemingly confident that he and Weigel had agreed to settle near Lugano, wrote to Steffin: 'I'll always be able to see you'.[16] Not only that, he was committing to a future with her, saying that he viewed the success of her treatment as the 'basis for everything else'. Weigel, however, was by now set on Denmark. When Brecht visited Steffin again near the end of her treatment, Alexander claimed that a further operation had improved her condition but another one would be necessary.[17] A deeply unhappy Steffin told Brecht that she could not face another operation and had decided to rely on other means, even though that meant that she also had to give up hope of having children. She had regarded the recovery of her health and the birth of Brecht's child as the means to win him for herself. That was a remote possibility.

In April Brecht took a short trip to Paris where he met Benjamin, Eisler and Seghers. He wrote to Weigel, wondering whether Paris might be a suitable place to settle.[18] It was after all a city and it was not expensive. Despite their earlier falling-out, Weill had arranged for Brecht to work with him in Paris on the libretto of the ballet *The Seven Deadly Sins of the Petty Bourgeoisie*. Edward James, an English patron of the arts, was arranging for his wife, the German dancer Tilly Losch, to perform it along with Lotte Lenya. However, Brecht fell very ill in Paris, confined to bed with his kidney complaint, which would dog him during the exile years, leaving him susceptible to the renal and cardiac complications against which he sought to inure himself through his strict regime. In that age without antibiotics, rest in bed was prescribed.[19] Brecht still dashed off the libretto. Arguably his slightest work, it employs his device of splitting a person into two characters in order to depict the contradictions in an individual life. The piece features two sisters, Annie I, the manager, and Annie II, the artiste. Annie I launches her sister within a constantly fluctuating market in which she achieves success. After avoiding the deadly sins for seven years, they earn enough money to buy a house for themselves and their family.

Brecht would return to Paris for rehearsals where Steffin joined him shortly before the premiere on 7 June. Cas Neher was involved, in his last production with Brecht until 1947. And it would be Brecht's last ever production with Weill, for whom Brecht was, as he put it to Lenya, 'that swine'.[20] Walter Mehring, who reviewed the premiere, celebrated it as a great evening for the best of the German theatre but others were less enthusiastic.[21] It was little more than a compilation of songs for Lenya to sing in the popular 'American' style. The play then transferred to London's Savoy Theatre. Brecht would never return to the work.

Back in Carona, Brecht and Kläber put out feelers to Thomas Mann, who was living nearby, with a view to arranging a meeting. Brecht had recently written an exceptionally polite letter to Mann, full of praise for Mann's public statement in support of socialist humanism:

> Permit me to inform you of the profound and sincere respect with which your statement in favour of the German working class has been received by friends I have spoken to in Berlin, Prague, Vienna and Zurich. I am writing you this because, as is widely known, your statement, which has preserved the good name of German literature, has brought you numerous enemies and no doubt endangered you as well, and because, what with the total intimidation of the progressive bourgeoisie, I assume that you cannot have heard much about the effect you have produced by coming out in support of the oppressed majority of our people.[22]

Mann, however, kept his distance, going out of his way to avoid Brecht and his left-wing friends.

Brecht and other émigrés looked on while in Berlin the Nazis fuelled a student campaign against the 'un-German spirit', demanding the removal from bookshops of works which represented that spirit. On 8 May Max Liebermann resigned as President of the Prussian Academy of Arts and virtually all remaining members followed him. Many had, in any case, fled into exile. Hanns Johst and his Nazi cronies took their place in the Academy and on 10 May 1,000s of books embodying the 'un-German spirit', among them works by Brecht, were burned on the square outside the opera house on Unter den Linden. The Propaganda Minister Joseph Goebbels presided. While Goebbels demanded the support of German writers for the new regime, Brecht wrote a fictive interview in which he answered the question why his books were entered on a black list as 'un-German' if he was not a Jew: 'The National Socialists regard only a part of all Germans as German. They regard anybody indiscriminately as un-German who has a different view of the social question than Herr Hitler. And just like many millions of Germans I have a different view of the social question than Herr Hitler'.[23] That distinction remained crucial for Brecht, not the Nazis' racial obsession.

Gottfried Benn, whom Kurt Tucholsky had described as the greatest living German poet alongside Brecht, scandalised émigrés when he lent the Nazis his public support.

Having taken Heinrich Mann's place as chair of the Literature Section in the Prussian Academy, he delivered a radio broadcast 'The New State and the Intellectuals', in which he described the Nazi movement as embodying a 'new vision for the birth of humanity' and as the 'last great conception of the white race'. When Klaus Mann protested, Benn warned him in his 'Answer to Literary Émigrés' that a new biological type was emerging. He mocked writers who had gone into exile and were sunning themselves on the French Riviera whilst Germany was being transformed by such momentous events. For Brecht, Benn was simply a 'slime ball'.[24]

In the press and on the radio Brecht followed the visit to London of Alfred Rosenberg, Hitler's foreign policy expert, who was seeking support for the regime. The visit was a PR disaster. *The Times* reported on 15 May that Rosenberg had little understanding of Britain and of British ways and no grasp of the English language. Brecht mocked Rosenberg in his 'Ballad of Foreign Policy':

> He could speak no English
> It's a thing he hadn't learned
> For four days he didn't get the Brits
> And at long last he returned.

> And he said to his friend Hitler:
> Isn't it a total farce
> That you must speak English
> To lick an English arse?[25]

This coarse tone can be frequently heard in Brecht's anti-Fascist satires from the early period of Nazi rule.

The Nazis again targeted Brecht's flat, which Hauptmann was looking after. Brecht told Margot von Brentano that they had mostly taken books, probably his collection of books about war.[26] He encouraged Brentano himself to come to Carona 'especially as Kläber, who has full powers to act on behalf of the firm, is already here'. By the 'firm', Brecht meant the KPD in exile, which, as we know, Brecht could not afford to ignore. As if to underline the point, Brecht's fraught relations with Fritz Wreede at Bloch Erben further deteriorated when Brecht explained that a performance of *The Threepenny Opera* was being planned in Paris for the Committee of German Émigré Jews.[27] Wreede replied that nothing was known about the plan in Berlin and that 'in such delicate circumstances and with such a delicate aim' Wreede reserved the right to 'block such a performance'. Brecht proposed a compromise for the payments set out in his contract, which Bloch's legal department dismissed as unacceptable. Brecht threatened legal action but was powerless. Wreede relished kicking Brecht when he was down: 'You have permitted yourself a very luxurious literary life at our expense. I have always experienced the burden that this represented as pressure upon us and invited you to see that perhaps too tactfully, as month after month passed without your dramatic works bringing us earnings of even one single mark'. Brecht proposed a meeting to settle their differences but Wreede was not interested. He demanded repayment of the money that Brecht had received and offered to return the stage manuscripts of *Saint Joan of the Stockyards* and *Round Heads and Pointed Heads*, provided the authorities would permit them to leave Germany! Meanwhile, through Benjamin Brecht got to know the Basel theologian Fritz Lieb in Paris and gave him the authority to look after his royalties and other funds in his account with Crédit Suisse in Zurich gathered through the Société des Auteurs et Compositeurs.[28]

Weigel travelled from Switzerland to Denmark via France with Mari Hold, Stefan and Barbara. They did not stop off to see Brecht in Paris. Karin Michaelis was accommodating a small colony of German exiles in her summer houses on Thurø, among them presently Brecht's collaborator Ernst Ottwalt and his wife Waltraut Nicolas, whom Weigel helped to leave Germany.[29] Weigel, Stefan and Barbara, together with Maria Lazar and her daughter, made themselves at home in Michaelis's attractive stone house, Torelore, which gave on to the water. When Brecht told Steffin that he was going to live with his wife and family she was devastated. He sought to soften the blow by describing Denmark as a temporary arrangement and asked Steffin to find a house for Weigel and him in Paris, and a flat for herself. Recalling what Weigel had said to her in Berlin, 'I'm sorry for you, my dear child', Steffin considered just walking away.[30]

However, Brecht won her over to continue their literary and sexual relationship. At Brecht's behest, she stayed in Paris to set up a German Writers' Service to promote German writers' works with the press. This was Brecht's version of the secretariat he had discussed with Becher in Vienna. Brecht was concerned to have a vehicle over which he, not the KPD or any other organisation, had control. In that way, through a network of collaborators he could promote his own interests and Steffin could generate an income. Steffin asked a number of prominent left-wing writers for their work and received material from Brentano, Kläber and Seghers. Steffin told Brecht that she would not be taken for granted: 'I'm representing you with your friends, admirers, enemies, comrades, but not with your women'.[31] She told him, too, that dreams of him with other women tormented her at night: 'I see you with some women or other, get very agitated, wake up repeatedly, always such a stupid palaver'. Such a dream found its way into a sonnet in which she imagines Brecht's women arriving by his bed all together: 'Those you once chose for your fun / Have their evil way with you'. Steffin would mark every day of her separation from Brecht in her diary until they met again in Paris in the autumn.

Brecht set off for Denmark on 20 June together with Willi Münzenberg. Münzenberg had transferred his publishing empire to Paris where he also established a secretariat for his high-profile World Relief Committee for the Victims of German Fascism. Münzenberg had contracted Otto Katz to write the famous anti-Fascist *Brown Book* about the Reichstag fire and the trial which followed. Brecht did some editorial work on the project. Parting from Münzenberg, he travelled on to Thurø where, for the first time, he was going to live together under one roof with Weigel and their children. Weigel's condition for staying with him was that the affairs must end.[32] Guided by earlier experience when they had holidayed together, Weigel prepared a study for him where the children could not disturb him. It had to be a fairly large room because Brecht needed space for up to three tables to accommodate material from current projects and to pace around in thought.

Brecht arrived in Denmark to the news that the Nazis had impounded his car on the grounds that it was Communist property and hence illegal since the promulgation of the law to protect the German people and the state. In November another law was passed, permitting the Gestapo to freeze the bank accounts of fourty-four exile writers, among them Brecht, and to impound their assets. Brecht and Weigel were very fortunate indeed that the wealthy Michaelis was prepared to support them. She would do so generously for several years, writing off a substantial debt in May 1940.[33] One of Michaelis's guests, Johanna Mockrauer, wrote to relatives about the Brecht clan: 'Bert Brecht is living here with his family. She is an actress. Two children: a slender boy, Steffi, is like a little street urchin and a three-year-old girl Barbara, very intelligent, very cute. [...] Brecht always goes around in a sort of blue boiler suit with a cap and really closely shaven head. His appearance is very pointedly proletarian but he is a nice, amiable man of good family'.[34] Weigel shared his proletarian appearance. The Communist writer Alfred Ostermoor was another guest, who was always welcome for lunch and conversation. Weigel was an outstanding and enthusiastic cook, who at Torelore assumed the role which she would fulfil throughout the exile years of feeding and entertaining guests daily as a distraction for herself and for Brecht from his work.

Brecht registered with the authorities on 20 July 1933. He was accompanied by Karin Michaelis, who vouched for the truth of his statements.[35] Brecht inquired whether he could expect his residence permit, initially valid for six months, to be extended, because he was looking to buy a house for his family near Svendborg. If the permit could not be extended he would settle with his family in Paris. Brecht stressed that he was financially secure so that he and his family had no need to find work in Denmark. He explained that his wife was Jewish and that the family therefore needed a place of refuge. After this meeting, Brecht and his family were always classified in Denmark as racially persecuted, never as Communists nor even as opponents of Nazism. He assured the authorities that he was interested purely in pursuing his career as a dramatist, that he was in no way politically active and that he would not combat the German government nor involve himself in German politics.

The residence permit would be extended every six months, and Brecht and Weigel would buy a waterside house on the western edge of Svendborg, a fisherman's cottage at Skovsbostrand 8. It had a thatched roof supported by wooden staves, which for Brecht looked like a rudder to guide the passage of its inhabitants.[36] With its sloping, grassed garden, the house looked directly on to Svendborg Sound, a busy channel with ferries, fishing boats and other traffic. German cities like Flensburg and Kiel were only a hundred or so kilometres to the west and the south. Brecht would complete the purchase of the house on 9 August for 7,000 kroner. Weigel's and Brecht's fathers are said to have put in money and Brecht formally acknowledged that Michaelis had provided funding for the house, which was refurbished in the autumn and was ready for them to move in just before Christmas.[37] Brecht himself put in royalties from his Swiss bank account from *The Threepenny Opera* and from his adaptation of *The Threepenny Opera* as *The Threepenny Novel*, or *A Penny for the Poor* as the first English translation was called of the 500-page novel which he began that summer and completed in a year. In recognition of his drastically reduced opportunities and of the fact that novelists like Feuchtwanger and Thomas Mann would have greater economic potential than a dramatist, both in German and in translation, Brecht, a practised short story writer, embarked on this novel, his choice of material clearly born of his desire to exploit his huge success with *The Threepenny Opera* – and, as we shall see, to outmanœuvre the publisher Felix Bloch Erben.

Brecht countered the problems of isolation and of neglect of his work through extensive correspondence with publishers and fellow writers. Weigel began to type for him but damaged her wrists in the process. Hauptmann was still in Berlin and Steffin kept him informed of events in Paris. Brecht drafted a series of 'unpolitical letters', satirical accounts of the émigrés he had encountered in the Viennese coffee houses, who remained helplessly mired in their illusory bourgeois ideology in the face of Nazism:

> There was a consensus that a new age of barbarism was approaching. The horrors were the consequences of a despicable warlike spirit which had, in some myste-rious way, achieved the upper hand. It was a natural catastrophe, comparable with an earthquake. Some nineteen years previously something similar had occurred, another natural catastrophe; the whole world, at least insofar as it was civilised, had attempted for four long years, not without some success, to butcher one another, following yet again some dark, barbaric urge.[38]

The corollary was the certainty amongst such émigrés that the humanist spirit would win out: 'People were generally still convinced that now, as in the great war nineteen years ago, a few lone voices of reason in the coffee houses would prevail, the mild, the sublime, the incorruptible voices of humanity. These voices, it was said, could never be fully silenced, not by any earthly power'. Brecht commented:

> What I objected to in their ideas was, briefly, the lack of prospects. The images these good folk made of reality were perhaps authentic, but they were no help. One might well describe the appearance of these new masters as barbaric, and call that which drove them a dark urge, but what was gained by such explanations? These explanations sufficed perhaps to induce a certain melancholy, but were hardly designed to teach how we might overcome the situation.

Like most German émigrés, Brecht argued for a united front against Nazism. How that might be achieved politically by the warring KPD, SPD and SAP was another matter. Brecht described the situation in exile to Tretiakov, his closest Moscow ally:

> Among the comrades, I've found considerable confusion everywhere; after so short a time we have friction, distrust, scepticism or illusions. Almost all the professional revolutionaries seem to have stayed in Germany, but there is very little communication with them; up until now the existence of the Party seems to have impaired rather than fostered cohesion among the refugees; they're waiting for directives, Party lines, arbitrations etc. Everything is centralised, and the centre doesn't answer.[39]

It was too much to expect that the cumbersome KPD would transform itself into an effective umbrella organisation for refugees scattered to the four winds. And Brecht, the great artistic individual not given to organisation, had never been within KPD lines of communication, however justified his complaint about its centralising tendency.

Brecht wrote similarly to Becher about strategy and 'extreme discouragement and confusion'.[40] Again adopting the shared perspective of a comrade, Brecht proposed to Becher an 'authorised conference among a few colleagues at which we would arrive at a definite decision concerning the scope and methods of our future work'. Brecht claimed there was a window of opportunity to win over non-aligned left-wing writers to the KPD position. Among the important Soviet figures for such a conference he named Tretiakov, Karl Radek of the Comintern, and the influential *Pravda* journalist and Kremlin insider Mikhail Koltsov, who had responsibility for German exiles in the USSR and Western Europe. Tretiakov, Radek and Koltsov would all be executed in the Great Terror. In fact, of those Soviet comrades whom Brecht named, only one, S. S. Dinamov, survived.

Brecht sent Tretiakov *Round Heads and Pointed Heads*, and Tretiakov told Brecht of his progress with translations of *The Measures Taken*, *The Mother* and *Saint Joan of the Stockyards*. They appeared together in 1934 as *Epic Dramas*, introduced by Tretiakov, who dedicated a copy to Brecht, 'the great heretic'.[41] Brecht recommended Carola Neher as Joan for Tretiakov's planned production of *Saint Joan of the Stockyards* but that did not come off. However, recognising Moscow's importance as one of the few places where he might see his work published and performed, Brecht told Tretiakov that he would be 'glad to work in Russia for a while some time in the autumn'.

Through the editor Hermann Kesten, Brecht interested the Amsterdam publishing house Allert de Lange in *The Threepenny Novel*. It would remain his one substantial work of novelistic fiction, a success for which he secured a high advance of 3,000 guilders. Though Brecht briefly saw an opportunity to bring together a number of his works with de Lange, the only project he realised was *The Threepenny Novel*. Illustrating the peculiar pressures of publishing in exile, Brecht had to resist when Gérard de Lange informed him that 'as a matter of principle we publish no novels or books which agitate against the present regime in Germany or in which there is even any talk about the present situation in Germany'.[42] Brecht replied to de Lange: 'Obviously I cannot accept such a right to censor the philosophical and political content of my work. [...] My work on the novel is going well and I hope to deliver it well before the agreed deadline'.

Amongst Brecht's correspondents, Brentano, though still a KPD member, was increasingly critical of the Party's acceptance of Moscow's directives. He sent Brecht two letters, alerting him to actions by the KPD within Germany and in exile, which he attributed to Stalin's leadership.[43] On 18 July Brentano wrote that the regional leadership in Frankfurt had agreed to report to the police all Trotskyists and members of other groupings, particularly the SAP. In the first round of denunciations four workers had lost their lives. Brentano's view was that class solidarity should transcend party loyalty. In his second letter of 23 July, Brentano told Brecht that Becher had just performed a u-turn over the question of the Parisian secretariat when they met in Zurich on 20 July, following the earlier agreement in Vienna: 'He calls the impulse to common sense, which had befallen him in Vienna, a shameful time, which he does not want to be reminded of'. Brentano regarded Becher's attitude as 'completely in line' with Stalin's policies promulgated through the Comintern, about which at this stage Brecht apparently had 'no illusions'.[44] The Comintern maintained the Social Fascism line, the absurdity of which was manifest in the Nazis' banning of the SPD. Becher now rejected a 'western European secretariat' for exile writers, suggesting that they should concentrate on literary matters! In his report to the ILRW, Becher described the situation amongst writers in Swiss exile as 'extremely involved and confused'.[45] Becher identified Brentano's disruptive role in adamantly propagating the theory of a petty bourgeois victory in Germany, which was 'upsetting' some and convincing other 'proletarian comrades'. Trotsky was identified as the instigator of that theory. Brentano was, Becher claimed, too close to the Social Democrats and to the Italian anti-Fascist author Ignazio Silone, whom many in Moscow, though not Becher, viewed as the mastermind behind the rampant Trotskyism in Switzerland.

Expecting Becher to visit Brecht in Denmark, Brentano advised him: 'Stay tough. Don't go along with this irresponsible policy'.[46] Brentano urged Brecht to insist on the western European secretariat, taking advantage of opposition to the Comintern line. In the event, Otto Biha was sent to see Brecht, who heeded Brentano's warnings. Meanwhile, the KPD member Steffin had written Brecht several letters, outlining her difficulties with the German Writers' Service. She was dissatisfied with the material writers were giving her and sought Brecht's guidance on how to proceed, particularly whether to bring on board Alfred Kurella, 'who could be very helpful in various ways'.[47] Brecht knew that Kurella meant a struggle for Party control. She told Brecht that similar agencies were being developed in Prague and Paris. After Biha's visit Brecht wrote a firm letter to Becher, beginning with the German Writers' Service: 'Comrade Grete, who looks after my affairs in Paris, writes that the business of the proposed agency for placing stories and articles in newspapers, so as to make some money and get the pot boiling again, has given rise to all sorts of malicious gossip. Please do what you can to stop it'.[48] Brecht invited Becher to contribute, explaining, 'Anyone who is against Fascism and wants to sell articles can participate', and suggesting that if the 'club', by which he meant the Party, 'goes in for something of the same sort, we can work together'. Brecht continued: 'There seems to have been all sorts of gossip about the plan we made in Vienna for a permanent meeting place in Paris, but I think B[iha] realises that they will have to supply us systematically with material, advice and collaboration from over there'. By 'over there', Brecht meant Moscow. He complained to Becher of the 'ghastly atmosphere of distrust and slipshodness that keeps taking over. Why must that be? You, too, must do something to stop it'. There was no prospect of that: Becher was entwined in the paranoid world of Stalinist bureaucracy in a way that Brecht would never be. Becher would later perform another u-turn, embracing the secretariat as a vehicle for the ILRW to organise authors in the united anti-Fascist front which it began to proclaim in 1934.

Brecht had few illusions about Becher. Speaking to Benjamin about Becher's poem 'I Say Quite Openly ...' Brecht suggested: 'When Becher says "I", he regards himself (since he's President of the League of Proletarian-Revolutionary Writers of Germany) as exemplary. The only thing is that no one wants to emulate him. They simply conclude that he's pleased with himself'.[49] Indeed, the Vienna meeting would prove damaging to Brecht and his 'deviationist' friends. When the German Commission of the Soviet Writers' Union met in closed session after the first Moscow show trial in 1936, the Hungarian dramatist Julius Hay denounced the 'most miserable defeatism' of the 'Brecht Circle' which he had witnessed in Vienna.[50] In 1933 Brecht certainly came to see Hitler's appointment as Chancellor as a massive defeat for the Left and opposed the KPD position represented by Fritz Heckert, a member of the Politburo and the Executive of the Comintern, who in his pamphlet *Why Hitler in Germany?* denied any crisis in the working-class movement and demanded swift and firm action against any defeatists.[51] Hay would later seek to blacken Brecht's name in *Das Wort*, the Moscow journal of which Brecht was an editor.

Brecht's letter to Becher did nothing to dispel the gossip about Steffin's agency nor to reduce pressure on her to make it a Party instrument. Using the same arguments as in his letter to Becher, Brecht urged her to resist this pressure: the agency was a private undertaking; it was not a Party matter and should not be subject to its control; and if the Party established a similar agency, they could work together.[52] Still the intimidation did not stop, and Brecht urged her: 'Treat all matters with the club as things to be deferred and don't get upset'. There was little more to be said. The German Writers' Service died a death.

Brecht told Steffin of another visitor from Moscow, Béla Illés, Secretary General of the ILRW. Illés had invited Brecht to a conference in Moscow, to which Brecht had encouraged Illés to send Steffin an invitation, too. Brecht told Steffin: 'I don't know if I'll go. Illés invited Helli as well to give talks for a month on Moscow radio. In short, I haven't made up my mind whether to go …'.[53] A few days later he told Steffin that Weigel was definitely going to Moscow in mid-September so Steffin could come to Denmark to see him. He had been regularly sending her drafts of *The Threepenny Novel* for comment. It was now two-thirds ready.

Brecht received visits from two other women who played major roles in his life. In August Elisabeth Hauptmann visited Thurø from Berlin. There had been several searches of her flat and Brecht's. However, working with Brecht's father, she had managed to rescue manuscripts and books. She brought manuscripts with her and a pearl necklace belonging to Weigel.[54] Brecht pleaded with her not to return to Berlin. However, Hauptmann, like Steffin and Weigel, was dedicated to the 'third thing', the revolution. Hauptmann went back, intending to rescue more of Brecht's material. Hauptmann's visit was followed by that of the Danish Communist Party member Ruth Berlau, who had made headlines with her trip to Moscow on a bicycle. Berlau, an actress at Copenhagen's Royal Theatre, had gone to Torelore to ask Michaelis to address a group of drama students in Copenhagen in September. Weigel invited the small party to stay for a meal. Berlau was very taken with her hosts: she found Weigel deeply impressive and Brecht very humorous. Berlau won Weigel to sing Brecht's four 'Lullabies' at the students' evening, Berlau driving them to Copenhagen for the event where they got to know Berlau's husband, the well-known doctor Robert Lund. They all became good friends. Berlau, however, was smitten by Brecht.

France with Steffin

In late August Brecht announced to Steffin that he would be visiting her in Paris: 'I'll stay for at least three months and we can give thought to what to do after that. Maybe Mecca'.[55] Weigel had followed Illés's invitation to 'Mecca' but could not fulfil her programme because she required emergency treatment to terminate an ectopic pregnancy with Brecht's child. Steffin, for her part, was desperate to see Brecht after a separation of eighty days: 'Is he coming? Alone? To me?'. Brecht arrived on 10 September and stayed with Steffin in Paris for a week, working to secure theatre and film contracts for *Round Heads and Pointed Heads*. He got a translation started and worked with Eisler on a collection of songs written between 1918 and 1933. Steffin had been organising the material. Brecht and Eisler looked through the collection which they entitled *Songs, Poems, Choruses* (*Lieder, Gedichte, Chöre*) in preparation for publication in Paris by Münzenberg's anti-Fascist Éditions du Carrefour.

Brecht and Steffin travelled to the South of France to see the Feuchtwangers at Sanary-sur-Mer where there was a colony of exile writers, among them Alfred Kerr, Ernst Toller, Franz Werfel, Friedrich Wolf, Heinrich Mann and Arnold Zweig. Staying with Steffin at the Hotel de la Plage while he worked on his novel, Brecht wrote to Weigel: 'It's boring here on the Mediterranean'.[56] He suggested that he probably wouldn't be away for long. The five weeks in Sanary were happy times for Brecht and Steffin. Brecht brought along a concertina, which Steffin played while the others sang. However, Brecht was scathing to Weigel about his fellow émigrés' political delusions:

> The refugees here are not a very pleasant sight. Döblin horrified me in Paris by proclaiming a Jewish state with its own homeland, donated by Wall Street. Out of fear for their sons, they are all (including Zweig here) relying on the Zion Real Estate speculation. So Hitler has turned not only the Germans into Fascists but the Jews as well. No one here cares about what's really going on in Germany. Heinrich Mann is imitating Victor Hugo and dreaming of a second Weimar Republic.[57]

For Brecht, the very idea of a return to a system like the Weimar Republic was ludicrous. In this letter Brecht was, of course, addressing his Jewish wife, albeit Weigel had left the Judaic religion. As Marxists, they shared the view that religion and race were obsolete categories, designed to deflect class interests. For Brecht, in reviving Theodor Herzl's efforts to create a Jewish state in Palestine, Döblin and Zweig were prey to similar obfuscatory thinking to the Nazis.

In early October, Brentano updated Brecht on the KPD in Germany. The Party was working in some places 'with great courage but their politics are so stupid that no one knows what to do with them'.[58] In Switzerland, the Party had 'sidelined' Kläber. This was evidently a consequence of Becher's fact-finding trip. Brentano told Brecht provocatively that Kläber had 'as a matter of fact your stay in Carona to thank for that. These little fellows took exception to it'. Even though they could never deny the value of his extreme talent in the anti-Fascist struggle, influential figures in the KPD would never trust Brecht. Meanwhile, Tretiakov, who helped to look after Weigel in Moscow, wondered why Brecht was not playing a more prominent part in anti-Fascist action. Brecht explained his position: 'The time for spectacular proclamations, protests etc. is over for the moment. What is needed now is patient, persistent, painstaking educational work as well as study. Among other things, we (Kläber, myself and a few others) have tried to set up an archive for the study of Fascism. Of course it's all very difficult. I keep hearing that I've become a Fascist or Trotskyist or Buddhist or God knows what'.[59]

Brecht had hardly withdrawn from public view. In truth, he was more comfortable working through figures like Münzenberg than Becher. He was planning to publish his songs and had been publishing anti-Fascist poems in newspapers in Paris and Prague. They included 'Awaiting the Second Plan', in which he contrasted the dangerous racist claims of the Führer with the measured five-year plan of the Soviet Union, designed to alleviate hunger and exploitation. The plan is: 'Realisable by any people of any race / Based on plain considerations such as can occur to anyone / Who is neither an exploiter nor an oppressor /'.[60] With its autarkic economic system, the USSR had protected itself from the collapse of economic activity in the Great Depression, but the Soviet system had its own severe limitations and reactionary characteristics which were becoming glaringly obvious.

Brecht would publish 'In Praise of Communism' in Münzenberg's *Gegenangriff* and 'Address to Comrade Dimitrov, when he Fought in Leipzig before the Fascist Court' in Münzenberg's Parisian *Unsere Zeit*. The heroic Dimitrov was convicted in the Leipzig Reichstag trial and deported to Moscow where he became Secretary General of the Comintern. Dimitrov's secretary was Alfred Kurella. Numbers two and four of Brecht's 'Hitler Chorales' appeared in Prague in Wieland Herzfelde's *Neue Deutsche Blätter*. They parodied Protestant hymns, among them Julie Hausmann's 'O take my hand, dear Father' which Brecht's mother had sung to him as a child. Brecht satirised his own side, too, in a poem, unpublished at the time, in which he mocked Kurella's officious, bureaucratic manner – as well as his stutter – in the lines, 'A glass of water for Comrade Alfred! / Let him know the truth! / Be careful with Comrade Alfred! / Don't be too hard on dear Comrade Alfred! / In the Party for seventeen years!'.[61]

In mid-October Brecht returned with Steffin and Arnold Zweig from the South of France via Avignon to Paris, where he met with Benjamin daily. After Paris, Brecht and Benjamin would cement their working relationship in three summers spent together at Svendborg in 1934, 1936 and 1938.

Meanwhile, in Berlin Hauptmann was trying desperately hard to rescue Brecht's remaining papers. There was a case full of manuscripts in Berlin to be moved from Pension Savigny. However, on the night of 15–16 November the place was searched and material in the case examined 'page by page', as Hauptmann wrote to Brecht's father on 10 December.[62] Miraculously, none of the material was removed. However, Hauptmann was arrested and a woman who was due to take the case on 16 November could no longer do so. Hauptmann's relatives in the USA intervened on her behalf, she was released at the start of December and fled to Paris. From there she would go on to the USA. Hauptmann wrote her letter to Brecht's father from Paris, urging him to try to get hold of the case. However, in a passage in which the KPD member Hauptmann reveals how she attempted to camouflage her working relationship with Brecht, she wrote to Brecht's father about the Berlin police: 'For the people there *I* have fallen ill in Paris and can hardly leave my hotel room. I have, also for those people (= the police), fallen out with your son'.[63] Amidst Hauptmann's attempts to disguise her interactions with Brecht, they did actually fall out.

In the tangled web of his sexual and literary affairs, exacerbated by exile, another moment had arrived when Brecht lost control. He was terrified that Hauptmann, like Steffin, was intending to come to Svendborg at a time when he had promised to Weigel there would be no more affairs. Brecht behaved very badly towards Hauptmann, provoking a severe conflict by accusing her of not doing enough to keep his manuscripts out of the clutches of the Gestapo. Losing them was wholly unacceptable: they were not just his writings but works born of the absolute necessity to combat Fascism. Hauptmann collapsed.[64] When she had recovered, she gave him a copy of the letter she had sent to his father. Brecht then wrote her a letter, which has not survived, in which he declared their relationship definitively over. In her reply, imitating his extremely cool style, Hauptmann said that his letter had been written as if to a 'convict'. She continued that she was not interested in Parisian intrigues and wanted the relationship to end completely. In saying this, she spelt out how unsatisfactory a relationship with Brecht was for a partner exposed to his emotional austerity:

> You are apparently happy. With a *complete* break from you I too, you can believe me, will find what I want: a great, natural and very tender relationship with a person in my work, too. Our relationship was somewhat austere, ungainly and not tender, but it was the *greatest* working friendship that you will ever have and which I will ever have. I will have a *good* heart again and perhaps we'll see each other again some time.

Brecht wrote to Weigel from Paris in mid-December that his return had been delayed for a few days because, as he put it, employing camouflage of his own: 'Walter's father had someone phone that he would meet me in Strasbourg, so now I'm sitting in the train to Strasbourg'.[65] In a letter to Korsch shortly afterwards Brecht writes openly of 'my father's wish that I should go to Strasbourg'. Brecht met with his father to discuss what could be done about the manuscripts. Hauptmann had, in any case, managed to dispatch a 'shipment of dishes', which contained some manuscripts. She confided to Benjamin: 'Br. claims that now the papers are lost he has nothing that we could talk about'.

However, Brecht did receive the manuscripts, as a later letter from him to Hauptmann reveals. What is more, Hauptmann worked with Benjamin on Brecht's collection of songs and Brecht arranged for Hauptmann to stay with his relatives when she reached New York. After a while, the old, familiar tone returned to their correspondence. Later that year, Hauptmann wrote from St Louis, praising the publisher Wieland Herzfelde's efforts on Brecht's behalf throughout the world.[66] Herzfelde and Brecht had begun to discuss a major undertaking, the publication of Brecht's collected works in Herzfelde's Comintern-sponsored Malik Verlag. Hauptmann predicted that within five years Brecht would be in the United States: Europe could not offer sanctuary from Nazism much longer and Brecht could thrive in the USA. Indeed, Benjamin passed on to Brecht Hauptmann's view that Brecht could quickly achieve a breakthrough in the USA. Hauptmann was glad to help Brecht: 'If you come, you can find no one better than me to guide you and to access things for you. And quite privately too I would be very pleased if you were to come'.

Svendborg 1933–4

Welcome to Danish Siberia

Brecht and Steffin left Paris on 19 December for Dunkirk where they took a ferry to Esbjerg. While Brecht went to Svendborg, Steffin travelled on to Copenhagen where she took a room at the Hotel Nordland, which was much frequented by Comintern agents. Feeling lonely, the following day Steffin asked Benjamin to come to Copenhagen. Brecht, however, contacted Berlau, asking her to take care of Steffin, and Berlau took Steffin to her flat. Weigel, Stefan and Barbara had just moved into Skovsbostrand 8. Hauptmann and other Berlin friends had sent on furniture, books and manuscripts to various Danish addresses. With limited funds, Weigel created an attractive interior where she and Brecht entertained guests most evenings, as they would throughout the exile years.

Brecht would immortalise Skovsbostrand 8 in the motto to his *Svendborg Poems*, which captures not domestic comfort but the deep anxiety which beset the author in a perilous exile:

Refuged beneath this Danish thatched roof, friends
I follow your struggle. I send to you now
As from time to time in the past, a few words, startled into flight
By deadly visions across Sound and foliage.[1]

If they went out in a boat into the Sound, German vessels patrolling the waters would come up close. Life beneath the Danish thatched roof would last for six years of ever deadlier visions as the German navy's guns thundered away during manœuvres.

Brecht urged Benjamin to come to Svendborg where Benjamin's books would be arriving from Berlin: 'It is pleasant here, not cold at all, much warmer than in Paris. Helli thinks you could manage here on 100 Kr (60 RM, 360 francs). Moreover the Svendborg library will get you *any* book. We have radio, newspapers, playing cards, your books soon, stoves, small cafés and an uncommonly easy language, and the world is expiring *more quietly* here'.[2] Like most foreigners, Brecht struggled with Danish pronunciation. Benjamin told Brecht that he was still submitting work to German newspapers but it was mostly not being published. However, Benjamin managed to place a number of pieces in *Vossiche Zeitung* and *Frankfurter Zeitung* in 1933 and 1934, some under pseudonyms. When Benjamin sought Brecht's advice about whether he should join the recently established Reich Writers' Chamber, Brecht suggested: 'You should always insist that you're a bibliographer, i.e. a scholar and ask if there isn't some organisation you can join. [...] There is no real reason why you shouldn't join an obligatory organisation'.

Brecht talked political theory and strategy with Korsch, reflecting in a long letter of 25 January 1934 upon the attempts of the Austrian Social Democratic leaders Otto Bauer and Karl Kautsky to restore democracy.[3] In March 1933 the Christian Social Chancellor Engelbert Dollfuss had suspended parliament over a trivial matter and then ruled by emergency decree, abolishing civil liberties and sidelining the Social Democrats. Recalling Korsch's critique of Kautsky, Brecht mocked Kautsky and Bauer's reformist agenda: 'Democracy through socialisation, socialisation as a means of promoting democracy! What can one say to that?'. When Austrian workers launched the Austrian Civil War with an armed revolt against Dollfuss on 12 February 1934, the Social Democrat leaders hesitated before supporting the call for a general strike. After four days of bloodshed Dollfuss put down the revolt. The Social Democratic Party was banned, its leaders executed and members put in concentration camps. Karl Kraus publicly supported Dollfuss, Otto Bauer fled the country, Austro-Fascism was born, and the road would open to Hitler's annexation of his country of birth.

Another of Brecht's principal correspondents, the increasingly disillusioned Brentano, pointedly asked Brecht whether a revolutionary Communist attitude like Brecht's own could serve the cause or whether it was only serving the Party apparatus.[4] Preserving that apparatus with its present personnel and theoretical position was not, in Brentano's view, serving the cause. Brentano added that he had never regarded German Communists as Bolsheviks, merely as discontented Social Democrats, hyper-reformists. Brecht responded with his firm view that one could only help matters by pushing through socialism, not by simply promising it, and socialism could only be pushed through by means of dictatorship. He recommended that Brentano write about the inability of the bourgeoisie and petty bourgeoisie to administer the state competently. Socialism could deliver what was required, a system built upon production, not the financial markets. Brentano could not allow Brecht's views on dictatorship to pass without comment. Brentano was also for the dictatorship of a class 'but not for that of the clique', by which he meant the Stalinist leadership of the KPD.

In the New Year Brecht urged several friends, among them Korsch, Döblin, Benjamin, Brentano, Eisler and Kläber, to come and stay in 'Danish Siberia', as he described his new home to Brentano.[5] He added: 'In May, when the trees blossom, I'll be going over there to have a serious word with Uncle Joe under 150,000,000 eyes. In the name of the League of Clergymen in Distress'. Brecht highlighted to Korsch the revolutionary transformation of material production as the central political and economic question:

Nothing, it seems to me, has ever brought out more clearly the profound wisdom of the [Marxist] classics in leading the proletariat to see revolution as the means of transforming material production. Material production is not only the historical basis of state systems, [...] it is itself the goal. That is the crux. Everything else is secondary, derivative and free to take its own form. The state form resulting from such a genuine, basic, radical transformation may be democracy – provided the word continues to be used after the content has undergone a complete change. Then the struggle for democracy becomes a mere matter of tactics: people fight for it because they expect it to bring about the transformation of material production; in which case democracy becomes the 'lever'.[6]

In truth, such a system would rapidly collapse if everything else was allowed to assume its own form, particularly the markets. It is not simply that Brecht's talent was not in organisational questions: Brecht the dialectician and logical empiricist never thought through what the transformation of material production actually meant for the political economy.

Turning to the second big question, European Fascism, Brecht rejected the view that 'leading' nations were entering a 'completely Fascist phase': 'There are compelling reasons for German Fascism, which do not apply to other countries'. As so often, Brecht identified the First World War as a crucial issue for analysis: 'We still haven't the faintest idea of the significance of the World War. Its origins remain shrouded in dense fog'. He urged the 'strictly concrete study of our situation', using the tools of dialectics, as Korsch had taught him. A little later Brecht spelt out what he meant, alluding to Korsch's major work *Marxism and Philosophy* and in the process demonstrating the distinction which he, like Korsch, made in Marxism-Leninism between ideology and analytical enquiry: 'What Marxist-Leninist methods and constructions seem to you to have taken on an ideological character, i.e. to have detracted from the solution of certain questions and the launching of certain operations, and which methods and constructions have (to the detriment of the revolutionary movement) been discontinued? (Including of course all methods of struggle, party forms etc.)'. Brecht followed with the related question: 'What has been the experience of the working class in its attempts to make political use of its place in the productive process (strikes, union contracts, sabotage, etc.)?'. For good measure, Brecht invited Korsch to consider writing a critique of Stalin's *Problems of Leninism*.

Steffin joins Weigel and Brecht

Weigel had no idea that Steffin was in Denmark, let alone that she would presently be arriving on her doorstep as a permanent fixture in their lives. Steffin had left Berlau's flat after some three weeks to stay at Westergaard guesthouse. Brecht wrote to Steffin: 'Unfortunately Eisler hasn't replied when he's coming. You ought to turn up about the same time'.[7] Brecht visited Steffin in Copenhagen on 18 January 1934 and stayed with her until the end of the month. They finalised the collection of songs and worked on the final chapter of *The Threepenny Novel*, which he completed shortly after and sent to de Lange. Steffin had intended to return briefly to Berlin but abandoned the plan when she heard how people returning from abroad were being interrogated.

When Brecht returned to Copenhagen in early February, he celebrated his birthday with Steffin in style at the Grand Hotel. She was working on his behalf with Copenhagen publishing houses and with Otto Gelsted, who was translating *Round*

Heads and Pointed Heads. Brecht was attempting to secure a premiere at Copenhagen's Dagmar Theatre. However, Steffin had a major concern. Using prophetic words, she warned him about the intrigue, distortions and story-telling emanating from Berlau: 'If a beautiful girl should ring you up, you must consider the consequences, from gossip to having children. It's no concern of mine anymore. You're in the dark'.[8] Brecht had been warned: Berlau had him in her sights.

In late February Eisler and his partner Lou Jolesch arrived in Svendborg. They stayed near Brecht at Stella Maris guesthouse. Steffin appeared, too, as planned, at first taking a room at Stella Maris. Despite her deteriorating health, Steffin joined Brecht and Eisler every day to work on *Round Heads and Pointed Heads* for the Copenhagen premiere. However, Eisler returned to Paris with Lou Jolesch, claiming that he felt too drawn into work on the text to the detriment of the music. He promised to return in a while. However, in a letter to Korsch Brecht suggested that Jolesch had been behind their 'flight' and Steffin wrote to Benjamin that Brecht had made no secret of his dislike of Jolesch.[9] Much to Brecht's annoyance, it would be some time before Eisler returned.

In April Brecht and Eisler's *Songs, Poems, Choruses* appeared with Münzenberg's Éditions du Carrefour in a print run of 3,000. Brecht and Eisler were frustrated in their attempts to smuggle the book into Germany. Eisler was, however, pleased with the 700 orders placed before publication.[10] *Songs, Poems, Choruses* is in two principal sections, '1918–1933' and '1933', and two supplementary sections, including songs from *The Mother* and *The Measures Taken*. We have examined a good number of the individual pieces. The collection opens with 'Ballad of the Dead Soldier' and closes with a new composition 'Germany', which begins with the famous lines:

> O Germany, pale mother
> How you sit defiled
> Among the peoples!
> Among the besmirched
> You stand out.[11]

The poem tells the story of her sons' brutal violence, of oppression and of vicious exploitation. It ends:

> O Germany, pale mother
> What have your sons done to you
> That you sit among the peoples
> A mockery or a threat!

In keeping with Brecht's programme of 1925, the songs show Germany's path from the First World War. In Brecht's understanding, the pernicious continuity of the Prussian militarist tradition and of class differences in the enduring crisis of capitalism had culminated in the mutation of the Weimar Republic into Nazi lawlessness and violence. 'To the Fighters in the Concentration Camps' describes brutal persecution in Germany – and highlights resistance to it:

> Little as we hear about you, we still hear you are incorrigible.
> Unteachable, they say, in your commitment to the proletarian cause

Unshakably persuaded that there are still in Germany
Two kinds of people, exploiters and exploited
And that the class struggle alone
Can liberate the masses in cities and countryside from their misery.[12]

For the promotion of the collection Brecht selected a long poem not ostensibly about Germany, 'Late Lamented Fame of the Giant City of New York', written in the wake of the Wall Street crash.[13] In this way, he drew attention to the underlying linkage between the German and US economic crises, the most severe in the world as trade between nations shrank by two-thirds. Brecht used his favourite image of the skyscraper to represent US ambitions – and to show the world's leading capitalist power on its last legs:

Today, when the word has gone round
That these people are bankrupt
We on the other continents (which are indeed bankrupt as well)
See many things differently and, so we think, more clearly.

What of the skyscrapers?
We observe them more coolly.
What contemptible hovels skyscrapers are when they no longer yield rents!
Rising so high, full of poverty? Touching the clouds, full of debt?

The USA had lost the lustre it had enjoyed in Brecht's imagination in the 1920s. Now, however, was the time of Roosevelt's New Deal and of the Glass-Steagall banking regulations, which were designed to combat the causes of the Great Depression, particularly the speculative bubble of the 'roaring' 1920s, by separating retail and investment banking. Roosevelt's approach to socio-economic problems redoubled the efforts of his predecessor Herbert Hoover. The efforts of both contrasted sharply with the deflationary economic policies in Germany which had fuelled the socio-economic turmoil that had helped to usher in Nazism. When George Grosz read Brecht's poem in US exile, he wrote to him that his depiction of the USA was 'somewhat wide of the mark'.[14] He contrasted the 'great life' available in the USA with 'angst-filled Europe'. Grosz, now far removed from earlier Communist sympathies, said that life in the USA was like European life before the war and suggested that the USA showed similarities to the USSR! For Grosz, the USA was 'socialist' in comparison with the 'feudal European countries and provinces'. Suggesting that Brecht's image of a USA on its last legs was 'Marxist wishful thinking', Grosz concluded: 'No Bert, you've got to see it for yourself'.

After the publication of *Songs, Poems, Choruses* Eisler noted with satisfaction: 'The book is being received favourably everywhere'.[15] Klaus Mann reviewed the work anonymously in *Die Sammlung*, Werner Türk in *Die Neue Weltbühne* in Prague and Arnold Zweig in Prague's *Neue Deutsche Blätter*. Mann and Zweig praised Brecht's gift for blending the poetic and the political in poems of great clarity and simplicity. Mann highlighted Brecht's 'Germany', together with his uncle Heinrich Mann's essays as the most powerful statements of opposition to Nazism. Zweig bracketed Brecht with Heinrich Heine as the most accomplished exponents of a combative, activist style, which was 'far superior' to the work of Rilke and Hofmannsthal. Zweig told Brecht that he had a small but important group of supporters in Haifa, who were reading his verses with a 'deep sense of joy and gratitude': 'You are the most important new writer since the war. Your tone of voice and what you produce are as inimitable as Georg Büchner's, and fortunately you have lived longer than him and you must first of all catch up with me and then Feuchtwanger before you are allowed to think seriously about gall stones'.[16]

The KPD's Türk praised Eisler and Brecht's political commitment and the combativeness of their songs, emphasising their value in the anti-Fascist struggle. Brecht was without doubt the greatest anti-Fascist lyrical talent available to the KPD. However, figures like Türk now had an aesthetic orthodoxy to observe: Socialist Realism, which owed much to Lukács's theoretical statements and to the belief that art must inspire the masses with uplifting images of society in its revolutionary development. From this position, Türk criticised the pessimism of Brecht's treatment of social and political issues. Brecht's 'negativity' would be held against him for the rest of his life and criticism would take on a sinister edge as the Party imposed the Socialist Realist 'method' on artists.

The promulgation of Socialist Realism formed the centrepiece at the infamous 1934 Soviet Writers' Congress. Brecht had received an invitation from Béla Illés, Secretary General of the ILRW, but excused himself on health grounds. Following Gorky's address, Andrei Zhdanov, Karl Radek and others championed Socialist Realism and denounced Modernism and its leading representatives such as James Joyce. Zhdanov took up Stalin's description of the writer as the 'engineer of the human soul' in order, like Türk, to invoke the need for a 'Revolutionary Romanticism' on a materialist basis. Tretiakov himself had spoken at the Congress about tactics to attract prominent writers like Heinrich Mann and Lion Feuchtwanger to a united anti-Fascist front, who did not want to be viewed as fellow travellers of an ILRW. Tretiakov was keen to discuss the theoretical ramifications of these issues with Brecht, who responded with the short piece, 'On the Term Revolutionary Realism', in which he argued, against Zhdanov et al., that writing opposed to Fascism was necessarily revolutionary and realistic.[17] Brecht understood the importance, in a debate amongst Marxists, of taking his stand on the terrain of realism. He argued, quite pointedly, that writers really only needed encouragement from politicians to speak the truth: 'A country that can cast off illusions and has a use for every kind of truth, turns to the realism of its working masses! Construction is accomplished on the basis of simple, useful thoughts; whoever has understood is in agreement. The enthusiast does not lose his view of reality, the sober-minded does not lose impetus'. Brecht had already developed a sophisticated aesthetic position without Zhdanov's questionable intervention or Türk's advice. As we know from as early as *Drums in the Night*, Brecht had harboured profound suspicions about the claims of 'Romanticism', which he equated with the 'illusions' to which he refers above. Brecht would never budge on this issue, nor indeed could he, given the origin of his aesthetic position within a deep existential need for clarity and sobriety.

Chess with Benjamin

Despite Svendborg's remoteness from major centres of German exile Brecht praised Weigel's choice in a letter to Grosz:

> The island of Fyn is known as the garden of Denmark. As far as the eye can see, everything is green and, more important, these people have good commercial contracts with England. The branches of the fruit trees have to be propped, the fishermen thrust spears into the waters of the Sound and a few hours later pull out dozens of eels. I live well, I've written a 500-page novel, and what's more, I have a good commercial contract with a Dutch publishing house.[18]

Brecht's father and his childhood friends Hartmann, Pfanzelt and Müllereisert all visited, as did his 'teachers' Sternberg and Korsch. In 1936 Marianne Zoff and Hanne would come to stay, while in the summer of 1934 Brecht had Walter Benjamin's visit to look forward to.

Benjamin's friends Adorno and Scholem remained concerned about Benjamin's relationship with Brecht. Gretel Karplus, who would marry Adorno, wrote to Benjamin, warning that Brecht was a 'great danger' for him.[19] Benjamin explained to her that the 'rewards of these connections, whose dangers are obvious, will become clear'. Indeed, in Hannah Arendt's estimation, Brecht became for Benjamin probably 'the most important person in the last decade of his life, above all during his period of emigration'. While Brecht simply overwhelmed many people as he brooked no opposition, Benjamin's formidable mind was equal to the encounter. His intellectual range, spanning dialectical materialism and Jewish mysticism, challenged Brecht's integration of dialectical materialism within an aesthetic sensibility which demanded the transformation of obscurity into clarity. There was ample scope for agreement and disagreement in the exchanges between Germany's foremost poet and foremost critic.

Before Benjamin's visit Brecht's health was not good. On 2 June Benjamin wrote to Steffin, expressing the hope that the 'novelist' had fully recovered.[20] The author of *The Threepenny Novel* was suffering from kidney pains and had to reduce his workload before, in mid-June, he was admitted to Svendborg hospital. From there, he wrote to Feuchtwanger of his 'little urethral calculus made of pretty oxalate crystals'. Passing kidney stones through the urethra was excruciating. The penis, the source of such immense pleasure, was also a site of extreme pain as his malfunctioning organism generated the crystals. For Brecht, there was always a price to pay. Typically downplaying the complaint while quite pre-occupied by his body and its prospects of recovery, Brecht worked and corresponded with friends from his hospital bed as he convalesced over the next month. It is likely that the urethral calculus contributed to the urethral stricture which plagued Brecht during his later years, triggering complications which in turn contributed to his death.

He remained driven by an intense wish to put behind him the barely diagnosed cardiac and motorneural problems as well as his renal condition. These things left him susceptible to inflammation, fever and complaints such as catarrh, with the prospect of serious complications if he did not rest. Having considered his health problems in

the light of the revolutionary transformation of social conditions, Brecht now speculated about the body's own capacity to overcome deep-seated medical problems. In
conversation with Günther Anders, Brecht would extrapolate this capacity from the
alleged fact that 'people renew their physical body of cells totally every seven years'.[21]
In a piece about the self-healing potential of the body, 'Kin-jeh's Medical Theory', an
early draft for the *Book of Twists and Turns* in the style of the Chinese philosopher
Me-ti, Brecht speculated upon the combination of the Great Method of dialectical
materialism with homeopathy, an element of Schmitt's therapy. Brecht used the name
Kin-jeh as a cipher for himself:

> Me-ti said: Kin-jeh once studied medicine. He said that he can imagine the
> following on the basis of the Great Method: experiments have been done which
> show that particular pathological phenomena in bodies can be cured by agents
> which produce similar phenomena in healthy people. In this way, febrile disorders
> can be cured by agents which likewise cause fever. One can view the sickly body
> as self-healing.[22]

On the manuscript Brecht added: 'Body does not wish to remain the same but
to change'. Brecht yearned for that revolutionary transformation and, for once an
optimist, in the guise of Kin-jeh viewed the play of contradictions in the complementary dialectical and homeopathic processes as a good way of thinking about
revolution. Otherwise, clearly suffering in the extreme conditions of exile, Brecht
became chronically pre-occupied by how to cope with the propensity of his organism
to inflammation, which he understood both physically and temperamentally, affecting
his artistic responses.

Benjamin arrived on 20 June. He took up residence at Stella Maris and visited
Brecht in hospital. During his stay Benjamin detected Brecht's greater propensity to
agitated, hustling behaviour: 'Whether he sometimes feels especially challenged by
me, or whether such behavior comes more easily to him now than it used to, what
he himself thinks of as the inflammatory side of his thought [die hetzerische Haltung
seines Denkens] comes to the fore in discussion much more often now than it did
formerly'.[23] Benjamin noted that Brecht adopted a 'special vocabulary', essentially that
of polemical dismissal, when his 'inflammatory' side predominated. Favourite terms
were 'Würstchen' [little sausage] to indicate a writer's insignificance and 'Klump'
[junk] to describe any works that 'lack an enlightened tendency, or whose enlightened
tendency he denies'. Controlling his propensity towards such polemical attitudes,
which, as we can see, coloured his aesthetic tastes, would become a major challenge
for Brecht as, in the coming years, he coped with extreme pressure.

Brecht was disarmingly clear about the source of the problem. Benjamin was taken
aback when an 'inflammatory' Brecht identified Benjamin's reading of Dostoyevsky's
Crime and Punishment as the 'main cause' of Benjamin's own illness: 'And by way of
proof he told me how, when he was young, a chronic illness whose germ had been
latent in him for a long time broke out one afternoon when a school friend played
Chopin on the piano, at a time when Brecht was already too enfeebled to protest. He
ascribes to Chopin and Dostoyevsky particularly dire effects on health'.[24] Brecht noted
in his diary on 18 May 1913 that he had played Chopin with his friend Fritz Gehweyer,

after which: 'The following night was miserable. Until 11 o'clock I had strong heart palpitations. Then I fell asleep, until 12 o'clock, when I awoke. So strong that I went to Mummy. It was terrifying'. The anxiety-laden memory of his ill-understood, chronic condition had never left him. Emotion-laden art could do that sort of thing to him. For the 'inflammatory' Brecht, Chopin was on a par with the 'Würstchen' Dostoyevsky. Neither was far off being a 'Klump'. The normal body temperature was the measure of 'good' art, controlling emotion with appropriate aesthetic form. However, for an agitated Brecht, susceptible to fever during his convalescence, such a state was difficult to achieve

In Svendborg hospital Brecht read Benjamin's latest essay, 'The Author as Producer', which prompted Brecht's response that his social position was that of an upper-middle-class writer.[25] That was not apparent in many aspects of his lifestyle. Before Benjamin's visit, Brecht had acquired an old Ford for 350 kroners. They enjoyed amusing exchanges about it, like Benjamin's comment: 'How is the car? If necessary, please lay a floral tribute on its cold engine on my behalf'.[26] Brecht's study better reflected his socio-economic status. It encompassed the width of the house at its far end, with two windows looking on to the Svendborg Sound, giving him ample room to pace up and down in thought. Benjamin records two personal touches: 'On a horizontal beam supporting the roof of Brecht's study, there is a painted inscription: "The truth is concrete". On a window ledge stands a little wooden donkey that can nod its head. Brecht has hung a little notice around its neck with the words: "I, too, must understand it"'. Weigel had given Brecht the donkey for his birthday. Friends listening to Brecht's texts tapped the donkey's head to alert him to difficult passages requiring simplification.

Brecht, Steffin and Weigel had developed a form of accommodation at Skovsbostrand but arrangements were not without their tensions. In particular, the tubercular Steffin had her own eating arrangements separate from the others because Weigel rightly feared her children could be infected. Benjamin remarked to his Dutch painter friend Anna Maria Blaupot den Cate: 'That the closeness of Steffin sometimes makes the atmosphere in B's house oppressive, you will in any case easily be able to imagine. Besides, she is kept in such seclusion that days often go by without my seeing her'.[27] Out of a mix of jealousy and concern for her children, Weigel insisted that Steffin move out. She took two rooms in the thatched cottage opposite Skovsbostrand 8. On several occasions Steffin had to deny to the Danish police that she was working as Brecht's secretary, claiming that she was there to convalesce. She would later enter into a pro-forma marriage with fellow Communist Svend Jensen Juul to get a Danish passport, putting an end to the police interrogations.

Brecht was furious with Eisler for not returning to Svendborg to complete *Round Heads and Pointed Heads*, for which Per Knutzon had been identified as the director: 'I can't see why you now withdraw your firm undertaking to come at once and not spend more than a week in Paris. The whole future of our work together may depend on it. Anyway, it's the eleventh hour for us and we know it. It's essential that they should hear the music. I am obliged to hold you wholly responsible if it all falls through'.[28] Eisler and Lou Jolesch returned in early July, Jolesch recalling their stay with a fisherman's widow near Skovsbostrand 8:

The rented piano from Svendborg took up almost the whole space of one room, despite which Eisler played and sang his compositions for *Round Heads and Pointed Heads*, as they became ready, to the Brechts, Grete Steffin, Karl Korsch and Walter Benjamin, who were just able to squeeze in, pressed closely together, with the door open, mostly by the light of the smoking paraffin lamps, for there was no electric light in this shack.

However, Knutzon now wanted to direct *The Mother* rather than *Round Heads and Pointed Heads*. He told Brecht that Jørgen Rothenburg, the lawyer advising the investors in the production, feared that the censor or, in effect, the German embassy would want to ban the play.[29] Furthermore, for Rothenburg the play not only lampooned Hitler too obviously but also treated the 'Jewish question' in a way which Jewish patrons would disapprove. That is to say, Brecht treated the question merely as a deliberate political distraction from the key question of class interest. Brecht argued:

> I can't imagine how he can be so wrong about the effect of the play. It certainly does not tend to provoke a discussion of the Jewish question. It would do so only if it depicted the unjustified sufferings of the Jews. What it does show is that the 'Jewish factor' plays no part in the way National Socialism (and other reactionary systems e.g. Zsarism, Pilsudskyism, etc.) exploit the racial question politically.[30]

Treating anti-Semitism as just another political question in the practice of reactionary systems, Brecht failed to grasp how deeply rooted the Nazis' racial obsession with Jews and other 'inferior' races was and therefore how extremely dangerous this defining characteristic of German Fascism was too. While Brecht recognised that Nazi racism distinguished German from Italian Fascism, like many other people he underestimated the Nazis' obsession.[31] *Round Heads and Pointed Heads* would receive its Copenhagen premiere two years later in still more disturbing circumstances.

Visitors to Skovsbostrand 8 were invited to play board games and cards and to follow political developments on the radio. Brecht and Benjamin played chess in silence every day after lunch. Three out of four surviving photographs are of them playing chess in the garden. As Wizisla writes, the game provided a background for a jokey, friendly rivalry. Brecht wrote to Steffin: 'I have had a beautiful chess set made here for ten kroner, finer and just as big as Benjamin's'.[32] When Benjamin took a trip north, Brecht wrote to him: 'The chess board lies orphaned; every half hour a tremor of remembrance runs through it; that was when you made your moves'. However, looking to the future Brecht wrote: 'I doubt if we'll be able to play chess under the apple trees for many more summers'. After Brecht had fled Denmark in 1939, Benjamin wrote to Steffin in Sweden: 'The chess games in the garden are now over too'. Finally, Brecht's poem 'To Walter Benjamin Who Killed Himself Fleeing From Hitler' recalls a scene at the chess table 'in the pear tree's shade'.

The news from Germany during Benjamin's visit was Hitler's murder of the SA leader Ernst Röhm and his associates. With its mix of penetrating insight and wishful thinking, in a letter to Brentano Brecht treated Hitler and his cronies with humorous condescension:

> He has plenty of moves left, he can still make himself useful to the dominant

clique in a number of ways; still, his possibilities are limited; the revolutionary demands of the SA probably boiled down mostly to *paid* holidays, and when they get them they'll have nothing to wear but their uniforms. To forbid the wearing of the uniform under these circumstances amounts to nudism.[33]

Brecht questioned the reality of the regime's apparent strength:

On the whole the ruling apparatus is consolidating itself, growing stronger but more isolated, losing its metastases in the 'people', becoming something more and more extraneous, a foreign body. Undoubtedly this is a good thing. And the process is a rapid one. The regime is indeed growing stronger, but regardless of how it solves the unemployment problem, it is drawing on the budget of the future.

Like many compatriots then and now across the political spectrum, following the hyper-inflation Brecht had no faith in counter-cyclical Keynesianism to deal with deep-seated economic crisis. However, under the economic management of Hjalmar Schacht the Nazis now embarked on their own brand of a New Deal for Germany, with the construction of motorways and other public works, not to mention their use of political prisoners as forced labour, which would become industrial-scale slavery and murder. Brentano, for his part, voiced his profound shock at the brutal reality of Nazism: 'How in all the world is it that this lunatic is murdering my best friends?'.[34] The terror would only intensify after Hindenburg died in August and Hitler received 89.9 per cent of the votes to confirm him as President.

Satire and parable: Brecht, Benjamin and Kafka

Brecht and Benjamin considered the techniques required of art in response to the new forms of terror manifest in the contemporary world. Brecht had just finished *The Threepenny Novel*, his satirical account of financial skulduggery in the City of London. He vehemently rejected all forms of obscurantism, metaphysics and prophetic vision, since they were ultimately grist to the Fascist mill, distracting from the necessity of political action against Fascism.

As we have seen, in 1931 Benjamin had given Brecht Kafka's *The Great Wall of China*, which Brecht, viewing Kafka as a 'prophetic writer', had 'devoured'. The collection includes 'The Silence of the Sirens', Kafka's re-writing of a famous episode in Homer's *Odyssey*. In Homer, the cunning Odysseus avoids the terrible fate of all other mortals, surviving the Sirens' song by binding himself to his mast and stopping his rowers' ears with wax. Kafka introduces his re-writing as 'proof that inadequate, even childish measures may serve to rescue one from peril'.[35] In Kafka's story, Odysseus – travelling alone, his ears stopped by wax and bound to his mast – would, in his innocent elation, still have perished if the Sirens had only sung. However, they had a more fatal weapon still: they remained silent. At the same time, Odysseus did not 'hear their silence', believing that they were singing and that he alone did not hear them. All they wanted was to see the radiance of Odysseus's great eyes. He escapes them.

Kafka's story ends with the narrator conceding that the cunning Odysseus might have noticed the Sirens' silence and have held up to them and the gods his pretence merely as a sort of shield.

Brecht, who had been developing a prose technique of pared-back clarity and simplicity, at times in conjunction with outspoken, decidedly provocative narrators, had written his own 'Odysseus and the Sirens' in 1933 as one of his 'corrections of ancient myths'. He appended the following: 'One finds a correction for this story in Franz Kafka, too, which does not in truth really seem credible latterly!'.[36] The first half of Brecht's piece recapitulates Homer's myth, concluding: 'The whole of antiquity believed in the success of the sly one's cunning'. This leads in the second half to a punchy, authorial commentary:

> Are we saying that I am the first to register concerns? I said to myself: all well and good, but who – apart from Odysseus – says that the Sirens really sang, at the sight of the bound man? Are we saying that these powerful and adroit women really squandered their art on people who possessed no freedom of movement? Is that the essence of art? My preference is to assume that that the distended throats seen by the rowers were cursing the damned wary provincial with all their might, and our hero performed his (equally attested) contortions because he was in the final analysis embarrassed!

Brecht's attack upon the 'damned wary provincial' can be read on two levels. As in Brecht's other corrections of myths, there is a challenge to prudery and a mockery of those whose sexual inhibitions prevent their exploitation of beauty. Brecht's narrator suggests that both Homer's and Kafka's Odysseus belong in that category. On the second level, Homer's Odysseus symbolises the suffering of all Greeks as he leads them home, rescuing them from peril. Brecht insists, in contrast to the petty-bourgeois mentality of the 'damned wary provincial' that things always remain the same, on a form of encounter with art which retains its 'freedom of movement' to change the wretched situation of those exiled from their homeland.

Brecht deployed the same combination of pellucid clarity and provocative narrative voice, satirising the petty bourgeois mentality, in other prose compositions. However, during Benjamin's stay, Brecht explained that he felt a 'strange indecisiveness' about his literary plans.[37] Brecht mentioned to Benjamin two satirical prose projects, the larger one the *Tui* novel, which was 'intended to provide an encyclopaedic survey of the follies of the Tellectuall-Ins' but which remained incomplete. The smaller one was the story 'Few Know Today', about the 'fate' of Giacomo Ui, which Brecht later developed into the play *The Resistible Rise of Arturo Ui*.[38] For the story, he borrowed Benjamin's copy of Machiavelli's *History of Florence*, which again combines a sober, factual style with the narrator's strongly subjective interventions. As in the earlier prose work 'Death of Cesare Malatesta' and in the later *Business Affairs of Mr Julius Caesar*, Brecht employed this technique in an exposure of conventional accounts of historical events, pointing up factual and interpretative discrepancies. Through satirical counter-pointing of historical parallels in a parabolic form, Brecht sought to provoke his readers into grasping fatal continuities which must be broken. His principal area of concern remained Germany from the First World War to Hitler's rise to power.

Brecht had established anti-Fascist satire as his strong suit, but the bourgeois artist he took himself to be wondered aloud to Benjamin how effective his satires really were in reaching their intended readership, the proletariat. He worried, too, that his self-imposed, rationalist austerity in the anti-Fascist struggle was squeezing the life out of his art. As Benjamin noted, Brecht had

> misgivings that concern his satirical and especially his ironic stance as such – the more so, the closer Brecht's involvement with the problems and methods of prole-tarian class struggle becomes. Such misgivings – which are essentially practical in nature – might be comprehensible, but not if they are identified with other, deeper-lying doubts. These deeper-lying reservations concern the artistic and playful aspect of art – above all, those impulses that from time to time make art resistant to reason. Brecht's sustained efforts to legitimate art vis-à-vis rationality have driven him again and again to the parable, a form in which artistic mastery is demonstrated by the fact that, in the end, the artistic elements cancel one another out.[39]

Benjamin believed that Brecht was less worried about legitimacy *per se* than about the efficacy of his methods. Living in remote Svendborg, Brecht certainly had good reason to ponder how effective a weapon his writings against Hitler's dictatorship might be. Moreover, he told Benjamin: 'I often imagine being interrogated by a tribunal: "Tell us the truth. Are you in earnest?". I would have to confess that I am not completely in earnest. I think too much about artistic matters, about what might work on the stage, for me to be completely serious. But having uttered this disclaimer, I would go on to add an even more important claim – namely, that my behavior is *legitimate*'.[40]

Brecht wondered whether only those whom he called 'substance writers' and whom he viewed as entirely serious, like Lenin, Confucius and Gerhart Hauptmann, really achieved anything. While Confucius's parables were appropriate to Confucius, a work such as a tragedy by Euripides would not be. Nor would a political novel be appropriate to Lenin, since it would diminish him in our eyes. Brecht summarised: 'All this amounts to a distinction between two types of writers: the visionary, who is in earnest, and the reflective writer, who is not quite serious'.[41] With good reason, Brecht had always placed himself in the latter category. However, he found himself by force of circumstances pushed more and more in the direction of the serious visionary, a position he was reluctant to assume, even though he was aware that the price for not doing so might constitute failure.

It is against this background that Brecht's famous exchanges with Benjamin about Kafka took place. Brecht explained that, on the basis above, Kafka, though a great writer like the dramatists Heinrich von Kleist, Christian Dietrich Grabbe and Georg Büchner, was indeed a failure. Kafka's starting point was the parable:

> But Kafka then develops the parable. It grows up into a novel. And a closer look reveals that it has contained the seed of the novel from the outset. It was never completely transparent. Furthermore, Brecht is convinced that Kafka would never have discovered his own proper form without Dostoevsky's Grand Inquisitor and that other parabolic passage in *The Brothers Karamazov*, where the corpse of the

holy Staretz begins to stink. In Kafka, then, the parable is in conflict with the visionary.[42]

As a philosopher of Jewish thought interested in mysticism, Benjamin must have felt that this last criticism and that of a lack of transparency were directed as much at him personally as at Kafka. Brecht went further: 'As a visionary, Kafka saw what was to come, without seeing what exists now'. Benjamin noted:

> Brecht emphasises the prophetic element in Kafka's works, as he did earlier, in Le Lavandou, and even more explicitly to me. Kafka had only one problem, that of organisation. What gripped his imagination was his fear of a society of ants: the way in which people become alienated from each other by the forms of their life together. And he foresaw certain forms of this alienation – such as the methods of the Russian Secret Police. But he did not find any solution and has never awoken from his nightmare. Brecht added that Kafka's precision was the precision of an imprecise man, a dreamer.

Dismissing Kafka's narrative approach in this way, Brecht saw himself by contrast as a reflective writer employing reason to generate an understanding of 'what exists now', the dynamic complexity of which it was his task to reveal as clearly as possible in the anti-Fascist struggle.

Shortly after, Benjamin passed to Brecht his essay about Kafka, which he had written for *Jüdische Rundschau* on the 10th anniversary of Kafka's death. Over the coming three weeks Brecht twice responded evasively when Benjamin mentioned the essay, so Benjamin took his work back, only for Brecht to broach the matter abruptly on the evening of 4 August. Citing the Kafka essay, Brecht told Benjamin that Benjamin 'could not entirely escape the charge of writing in diary form, in the style of Nietzsche': 'It was interested in Kafka only as a phenomenon: looked on the work as if it – and likewise the author – were a product of nature and isolated it from every possible context, even the author's life'.[43] Brecht claimed that Benjamin 'was always interested exclusively in the question of *essence*'. Now well into his stride, Brecht launched a trademark polemic, arguing first that the correct approach was to ask what Kafka did, how he behaved. He told the great critic Benjamin that he should start with the general rather than the particular! Brecht was then sarcastic about the company Kafka kept, in effect damned wary provincials:

> He lived, in Prague, in an unfortunate milieu of journalists and self-important literati. In that milieu, literature was the principal reality, if not the only one. And this view of things was inseparable from Kafka's own strengths and weaknesses – his artistic value, but also his uselessness in many respects. He was a Jewboy (you could also coin the term Aryan-boy) – a feeble, unattractive figure, a bubble on the iridescent surface of the swamp of Prague's cultural life, and nothing more.

From Berlin days, Brecht knew some of those journalist types whom Kafka had known in Prague, figures like Max Brod and Willy Haas. Brecht had formed a thoroughly negative view of them and their milieu, with which, for Brecht, Kafka and his works were inextricably linked. As editor of *Die Literarische Welt*, Haas had abandoned the revolutionary Left in 1929–30 for the new conservatism sweeping the continent.

Brecht was now unstoppable, taunting Benjamin with an imagined dialogue between Lao-tsû, whom Benjamin mentions in his essay, and his disciple Kafka:

Lao-tsû: Very well, then, Disciple Kafka, is it true that the organisations, the legal and economic institutions, around you have begun to give you the creeps?

Kafka: Yes.

Lao-tsû: You cannot find your way around them anymore?

Kafka: No.

Lao-tsû: A stock certificate terrifies you?

Kafka: Yes.

Lao-tsû: And now you are longing for a leader you can rely on, Disciple Kafka.

Beyond the point of no return, Brecht announced: 'I reject Kafka. [...] The images are good. But the rest is obscurantism. It is sheer mischief. You have to ignore it. Depth takes you no further. Depth is a dimension of its own, just depth – which is why nothing comes to light in it'. Again, Benjamin the scholar of Jewish philosophy could not miss that this was equally aimed at him. While conceding that his essay was a 'diary-like set of notes' with echoes of Nietzsche and that Kafka 'contained a lot of debris and rubbish and detritus – a lot of real mystery-mongering', Benjamin defended his method: 'descending into the depths is my way of journeying to the antipodes'.

The battle between the writer and the critic returned to Benjamin's essay. Brecht's antagonism burst into the open with his assertion that the essay 'promoted Jewish Fascism' and 'increased and spread confusion' about Kafka 'instead of dissipating it'.[44] In the wake of the Holocaust, Brecht's charge of Jewish Fascism will look hideous to many people. The term had, however, been current since the late 1920s as a label for fanatical supporters of a Zionist state. However, even if we allow that Brecht was simply not attuned to elements of Benjamin's Jewish thought, his reproach, as Wizisla writes, still went beyond what was acceptable.[45] For Brecht, Benjamin's 'obscurantism' negated the key category of class in social analysis. What really mattered for Brecht was to shed light on Kafka, 'formulating the practical proposals that could be distilled from his stories'.[46] Brecht saw *The Trial* as a 'prophetic' work: 'You can see from the Gestapo what can become of the Cheka'. Again, Brecht was not blind to the potential for escalating terror in the Soviet Union. For Brecht, in *The Trial* Kafka captured the 'fear of the inexorable and never-ending growth of big cities'. Brecht acknowledged from his own 'intimate experience [...] the nightmare force with which this idea weighs on mankind'. It spawned a complex urban world, which left many people, particularly among the petit bourgeoisie, longing for a strong 'leader'. Even though Brecht excluded Kafka personally from that charge, he left Benjamin in no doubt about his view that Kafka's work depicted the world as a baffling, therefore unchangeable phenomenon from the perspective of the petit bourgeois. For Brecht, Kafka remained the 'damned wary provincial' of 'Odysseus and the Sirens'.

Brecht's exchanges with Benjamin are rightly regarded as amongst the most significant between German émigré writers. Clearly, Brecht's attacks on Kafka were intimately bound up with his frustrating situation as a political artist in exile. Despite the harshness of Brecht's assertions during this agonising ordeal for Benjamin, their relationship survived the exchanges. Benjamin remained until the autumn and wrote a complimentary review of *The Threepenny Novel*. Brecht, for his part, wrote an essay about modern Czech literature, in which he acknowledged the importance of depth and expressed his great admiration for Kafka, while pointing out weaknesses.

During Benjamin's stay, a polio epidemic broke out in nearby Fåborg and from late August until the end of October Weigel took Stefan and Barbara to the seaside village of Dragør just to the south of Copenhagen. Brecht and Weigel had old Berlin friends living there, Horst and Ange Horster, who had set up a puppet theatre. Brecht joined them there on 8 September for the month while Steffin travelled to Moscow, staying with Asja Lacis, before going to a sanatorium in the Caucasus. Benjamin visited Brecht at Dragør for a few days in late September. However, upon arrival Brecht had been struck down by a cold with 'horrid catarrh'.[47] As he later told Steffin, he was so concerned that he sought out Copenhagen's best specialist, who told him that his doctor in Svendborg was an ass and that his catarrh came from his medicine. That autumn Brecht had further tests, reporting to Weigel in October that the ethmoid bone, separating the nasal cavity from the brain, was fine.[48]

In Dragør Brecht received a visit from Wieland Herzfelde, who had travelled from Prague to discuss the publication of Brecht's *Collected Works* in Herzfelde's Malik Verlag. The success of *Songs, Poems, Choruses* had strengthened Brecht's market position. He concluded a contract with Herzfelde to publish, initially, several dramas from the late 1920s and early 1930s. The first two volumes of this flagship project of German anti-Fascist literature would appear in 1938.

London, Moscow and New York: Stanislavsky's Pre-Eminence 1934–6

Lunch at the Savoy

Brecht went to London on 3 October 1934, hoping to do deals for films and translations of his plays. Among other things, Brecht made an agreement with an agent for
W. H. Auden to choose two of Brecht plays for translation. Brecht was soon telling
Weigel what a wretched place London was: there was no proper food and 'the theatres
are antediluvian'.[1] Eisler was in London, too. He and Brecht wrote 'Saarland Song',
supporting the Saarland's existing neutral status in advance of the plebiscite on 13
January 1935. Willi Münzenberg distributed 10,000 copies in the Saarland but the
Saarlanders would opt for Nazi Germany. In London Brecht lived below Karl Korsch
for two-and-a-half months in Herbert Levy's house, 24 Calthorpe Street off Gray's Inn
Road. Brecht found Korsch much changed, profoundly depressed and disillusioned
with the Communist movement. When Steffin, by now in the Soviet sanatorium, asked
Brecht if he was travelling alone, he sent her two new sonnets and told her: 'I'm living
with the professor but he's no substitute for you'.[2] Brecht discussed Korsch's biography
of Karl Marx with him, advising against any heroic portrait. Korsch would presently
join the small Brecht circle in Svendborg, staying there on and off until October 1936
while he worked on Marx.

Despite all the chasing around, the desolate interludes and the sheer effort entailed
in using the underground and buses, Brecht found London 'better than Paris, bigger
and greyer, so better'.[3] However, he complained to Steffin: 'I'm freezing. They only have
open fireplaces here. Mine's a coal fire; above me Korsch has a gas fire in his fireplace.
He's freezing too. The English eat leather and grass'. Plagued by stomach pains, Brecht
lamented: 'The English cuisine is life-threatening'. He grumbled about the difficulty
of prising any money out of the English: 'It's a very old, hardy, seasoned form of
capitalism'. Reminded of his difficult, early days in Berlin, he turned his hand to writing
stories for the booming British film industry, again without success. There was better
news on the theatre front when he attended Rupert Doone's production of T. S. Eliot's
Sweeney Agonistes at the new Group Theatre. W. B. Yeats was in the audience too. Yeats
like Brecht was perhaps attracted by the affinity between Eliot's short, stylised play and
Noh drama. As Willett writes, Brecht told Doone that 'it was the best thing he had seen
for a long time and by far the best thing in London'.[4] Brecht was, of course, not alone in

praising oriental forms in the attack on conventional European realism. For example, in his *Le Théâtre et son double* Antonin Artaud praised Balinese dancers for a physical, non-verbal theatre of gesture as opposed to an intellectual-psychological form. While Artaud's emphasis is different, the critique of realism is similar.

The Threepenny Novel, set in Victorian London, now appeared to generally positive reviews. Brecht's Marxist satire upon a corrupt capitalist society integrated realistic detail within a parabolic 'model' of such a world. Leo Lania's review in *Pariser Tageblatt* compared Brecht to Swift, while in Prague's *Europäische Hefte* Wilhelm Schlamm suggested that the novel should be mandatory reading for German students of history, economics, sociology and psychology, since it was 'probably the safest prophylactic for the occupational disease of intellectuals today, namely Fascist infection'.[5] Werner Türk in *Die Neue Weltbühne* hailed Brecht's novel as his 'most important and mature' work. However, a forthright Feuchtwanger told Brecht that London's rich and incorruptible civil servants behaved differently from the way he portrayed them, nor was Peachum's beggar business possible in London.[6] Feuchtwanger added soon after that the novel was an 'excellent caricature of an extreme doctrinaire Marxist's world-view'. Inviting Brecht to stay at Sanary-sur-Mer, Feuchtwanger teased him further: 'You know, Brecht, how much interest I take in whatever form your Marxism assumes at any given time'.

The only hostile review was by Alfred Kantorowicz, who delivered a Marxist kiss of death in *Unsere Zeit*: it was an 'idealistic book', not a work of realism.[7] Kantorowicz was not just anyone. A KPD member, he was Becher's secretary in Paris. Brecht wrote to Becher, defending his novel as a realist work and pointing out that Kantorowicz's position lent the attack, 'lethal among Marxists', an 'official note'.[8] Becher denied that Kantorowicz was writing in an official capacity, agreed with Brecht's criticism of the review and arranged for two positive reviews to appear in *Unsere Zeit*. In this first serious difference of opinion in exile about realism, Becher ensured that the troublesome but supremely gifted Brecht should be both criticised and fulsomely praised. The episode captures Becher's habitual equivocation as well as Brecht's ambivalent relations with the KPD.

On the look-out for funds to support anti-Fascist activity, Brecht arranged to meet Elizabeth Princess Bibesco, daughter of the British Prime Minister Herbert Asquith and wife of the Romanian diplomat, Prince Antoine Bibesco. The Princess was herself a writer associated with the Bloomsbury Circle. She invited Brecht to lunch at the Savoy but he failed to appear. Shortly afterwards he explained to the princess quite why: he had been refused entry by a man of 'ministerial rank' – the doorman – who, judging Brecht by his appearance, took him for a 'dangerous individual'.[9] Brecht's attempt to enter by another door was thwarted: 'It was clear to me that without the help of at least fifty heavily armed dockers I could not hope to extract you from that building'. The custodians of London's rigid social code treated Brecht as the proletarian he appeared to be. Brecht told Margot von Brentano: 'London is a wicked hard-bitten town. The natives here are among the most vicious in Europe. There is a high culture of corruption'. He told Steffin: 'Everything is tough here, life puritanical, believe me, Muck'. Despite the fact that he had offers to translate his novel into Czech, Polish, Danish and French, Brecht felt that he had forgotten how to do deals. He had been told, too, that the prospects for an English translation of *The Threepenny Novel* were not good, because English readers would not understand the work even though the setting was London. To illustrate his point, Brecht told Steffin that the unemployed had just sent wedding presents for the marriage of the Duke of Kent to Princess Marina of Greece. London's deferential public sphere would not be receptive to Brecht's socio-economic critique.

However, Brecht still believed that he could make money in London from films and translations. On Kortner and Eisler's recommendation, the film producer Max Schach engaged him for the script of *The Bajazzo* after Ruggiero Leoncavallo's opera *Pagliacci*. Brecht now stayed on Abbey Road with André and Jean van Gyseghem of the Unity Theatre.[10] He visited Rupert Doone and probably met Auden. Even though Brecht, unlike Eisler, took his work on the script quite seriously, it would be the usual story: Brecht could not deliver commercial material and was paid off.

Shortly before Brecht returned to Svendborg on 20 December 1934, in *Pariser Tageblatt* he published the first version of the piece he later called 'Five Difficulties in Writing the Truth', his celebrated rallying cry to anti-Fascist writers inside and outside Germany seeking to impact upon German public opinion. He initially identified three difficulties: anti-Fascists must be prepared to resist those in power in order to tell the truth; they must be capable of recognising the truth, which required knowledge of economics, history and materialist dialectics; and, they must possess cunning in proclaiming the truth to people who themselves adopted cunning as they listened.[11] For Brecht, the underlying, economic truth was clear: some of the world had descended into Fascist barbarism because capital had resorted to extreme violence to maintain its ownership of the means of production. In the much longer, definitive text Brecht summarised the five difficulties as: 'the *courage* to write the truth, even though it is suppressed everywhere; the *cleverness* to recognise it, even though it is disguised everywhere; the *skill* to make it fit for use as a weapon; the *judgment* to select those in whose hands it will become effective; the *cunning* to spread it amongst them'.[12] He devoted the most space to cunning. However, he began with the necessity of a critique of Nazi language: 'Anyone in our times who says *population instead of 'Volk'* and *land ownership instead of 'soil'* is already denying his support to many lies. He divests the words of their lazy mysticism'. Inside Germany Victor Klemperer was doing precisely this, compiling his *The Language of the Third Reich: A Philologist's Notebook*. As fine examples of cunning in smuggling in the truth, Brecht cited the 'substance writers' Confucius and Lenin, ancient and modern classics such as Lucretius and Shakespeare, as well as the great satirists Thomas More, Voltaire and Jonathan Swift. Through a mixture of ironic and direct statements readers would be encouraged to change their views. For Brecht, the ultimate aim was to develop in readers in Germany a revolutionary consciousness which would lead them to overthrow Nazism.

It is, of course, impossible to assess what impact Brecht's tract had in Germany. However, it was adopted as an unofficial manifesto by émigrés in many countries and its precepts inform Brecht's own anti-Fascist writing. What is more, he conveyed his ramified message with a simplicity and clarity unparalleled in the anti-Fascist movement. The Communist cause had no one else like him. At once Münzenberg recognised the propaganda value of the piece, smuggling it into Germany disguised as a first-aid manual and passing it to, among others, André Gide, André Malraux, Thomas and Heinrich Mann, and Feuchtwanger. Becher distributed Brecht's 'excellent article' in a circular to fellow writers and wrote to Brecht that it was one of his best 'theoretical' pieces.[13] Becher sent it to Moscow for further use. At the landmark 7th Comintern Congress in August 1935 the Comintern's General Secretary Georgi Dimitrov would echo the Brechtian strategy, proposing a 'Trojan Horse' approach to infiltrating Nazi Germany. Becher now drew Brecht into strategic discussions about plans for a Comintern-led Writers' Congress in Paris on 10 May 1935, the anniversary of the Nazi burning of books. However, Brecht responded cautiously, doubting the value of mere get-togethers. Always keen to urge concerted action through interventionist thinking, Brecht proposed the compilation of an encyclopaedia exposing the mendacity of Fascist slogans.[14] He urged others to promote the idea and began to draft entries. However, the idea was not taken up.

Consulting Brecht was all the more important for Becher since the KPD had now lost Brecht's friend Brentano. Brentano had taken to equating Stalin's totalitarian dictatorship with Hitler's. Brecht countered by reminding Brentano that the Russian proletariat was isolated in its efforts to revolutionise the production process.[15] That, Brecht claimed, was the crucial pre-condition for individual freedom. Accepting the necessity of dictatorship and of violent repression, Brecht challenged Brentano: 'How can you call the Bolsheviks Fascists? Do Fascists abolish the private ownership of the means of production? Do Fascists establish and maintain the dictatorship of the proletariat?'. For Brecht, it would remain an article of faith that revolutionising the means of production by abolishing surplus value and the profit margin would yield individual freedom. Although in private Brecht came to acknowledge the autocratic Stalin's role in the Great Terror, he would never give anti-Communists like Brentano the opportunity to claim that he was against the Soviet Union. Indeed, in deliberate contrast to the growing Stalin cult, in his new, aphoristic *Book of Twists and Turns*, for which he wrote occasional pieces until the end of his life, Brecht described Stalin as the 'useful one'.[16] Brecht simply did not wish to recognise the dangerous form of charismatic leadership that, for all their differences, Stalin, like Hitler, was exercising.

Mei Lan-fang: The Peking Opera in Moscow

In January 1935 Brecht received an invitation from Piscator, in his capacity as President of the International League of Revolutionary Theatre, to what Piscator called a 'constructive discussion' at a conference of producers in Moscow.[17] Aware of the attacks on modernism and the avant-garde at the 1934 Soviet Writers' Congress, Brecht nonetheless drew on his *Mahagonny* notes for a landmark theoretical piece about Epic Theatre, 'Theatre for Pleasure or Theatre for Instruction?'. He took it to Moscow for Tretiakov to arrange publication. The notes had been written for a work designed for mainstream theatre. To return to them was an indication that Brecht, his theatrical ambition crippled by exile, was seeking to re-enter that world with fully developed pieces of Epic Theatre. Arguing first that epic techniques equipped the theatre to become a forum for instruction in a manner that was closed to Aristotelian theatre, Brecht insisted, too, that in Epic Theatre instruction could accommodate pleasure. Brecht was concerned to downplay the dichotomy between emotion and reason which he himself had, of course, encouraged. As John White observes, 'His interest is now more decidedly in highlighting the enjoyment that comes with learning'.[18] This shift instigated a process of change which would have a great impact upon Brecht's dramatic production, sanctioning the co-presence of didacticism and pleasurable artistry and leading in time to a fresh exploration of individual desire. What is more, in 'Theatre for Pleasure or Theatre for Instruction?' Brecht now described as 'alienation' his technique of making the familiar strange on stage in order to stimulate critical thinking.[19] However, at this point he still did not use 'Verfremdung', the term which he would make famous, rather the Hegelian concept 'Entfremdung', which he had used already in 1930. Nor does Brecht expand upon his use of the term. He went on to argue that not every country had a theatrical culture in which new drama could be performed. It required a certain technological level and a 'powerful movement in society which is interested to see vital questions freely aired with a view to their solution'. Brecht maintained that, for a variety of reasons, Epic Theatre could not be performed in Germany, Paris, Tokyo, Rome and London. Nor would the USA prove receptive to Epic Theatre. And Brecht would eventually have to add Moscow to his list. After *The Threepenny Opera* in 1930, there was no production of a full-length Brecht play in Moscow during his lifetime.

Brecht set off for Moscow on 12 March via Stockholm and Helsinki. Steffin met him in Leningrad and travelled with him to Moscow where he stayed at Novaya Moskovskaya Hotel. Tretiakov and Piscator looked after him and he lunched at the Russian Writers' Club. He met the influential *Pravda* journalist and publisher Mikhail Koltsov and his partner Maria Osten. Brecht would work with them in the coming years. Within the Soviet command structure Koltsov had particular responsibility for German émigrés in the USSR and Western Europe. However, Steffin wrote to Benjamin that on Brecht's arrival in Leningrad he was 'at once ill for four weeks, flu with especially unpleasant headaches'.[20] Brecht told Weigel that he was suffering from a 'rheumatic headache' at the back of his head on the left, which meant that his head hurt every time he moved. Shortly after, he wrote: 'I'm still in bed with a thick head and fever'. By April he was reporting to Weigel that he had had a bout of 'stupid flu, mainly headache, from the neck up to the temple', but it was now better. He later wrote that he had had to take to his bed with flu for more than a fortnight 'for fear of complications' but assured her he was now all right apart from occasional residual headaches.

Brecht raised himself from his sickbed for a major dramatic experience, his first encounter with Chinese theatre. He shared this with a number of other prominent literary and theatre personalities invited to Moscow, including Edward Gordon Craig, André Malraux, Harold Clurman, Joseph Losey and Lee Strasberg. The famous Chinese actor Mei Lan-fang was in Moscow for a series of guest performances with his ensemble from the Peking Opera. Tretiakov, who was behind Mei Lan-fang's visit, invited Brecht and Steffin to performances and meetings with the Chinese actors. Steffin wrote to Benjamin of their 'great enthusiasm' for Mein Lan-fang.[21] After a private performance at the Chinese embassy on 19 March, there was a special performance for leading figures in Moscow theatre. Mei Lan-fang's ensemble then performed *The Drunken Beauty* and *The Fisherman's Revenge* in Moscow and St Petersburg. Brecht saw these plays and attended a final discussion on 14 April together with the cream of Soviet theatre, except Constantin Stanislavsky, which the great avant-gardist Vsevolod Meyerhold introduced.[22] Tretiakov, who had been a regular at the Peking Opera during his years in Beijing, spoke with enthusiasm. He was followed by Meyerhold, who welcomed this stimulus for the new theatre in Moscow. Eisenstein, who saw affinities with Meyerhold's theatre, felt Mei Lan-fang's rich formal artistry gave fresh impetus to the cinema when, as he put it, such qualities had atrophied in the struggle for Socialist Realism.

Brecht would not have dissented from these views. Steffin wrote to Benjamin of the 'banquets and evenings for Brecht, at which much from his recent works was discussed and shown'.[23] However, Brecht's work was also the subject of decidedly critical discussion. In an essay in *Internationale Literatur* Peter Merin followed a similar line to another piece by A. Brustov, generally praising Brecht's works but criticising his theoretical interest in experimentation and formal innovation at the expense of progressive content. Brecht was expected to take note. For all the interest in Mei Lan-fang's visit, no one in Moscow could ignore emerging divisions. The Party was lionising Stanislavsky's great Moscow Art Theatre as the model for Socialist Realist drama. Established during the Czarist era, Stanislavsky's system of empathetic Naturalism cultivated the actor's psychological identification with his role. The Party contrasted the Stanislavskian system with the 'Formalism' of 1920s avant-gardists like Meyerhold and Tretiakov, whose work would be associated with the proletkult claim of artistic independence and labelled the pernicious aesthetic equivalent of Trotskyism. Stanislavsky's system became a norm for drama, equivalent to Lukács's theories for the novel.

Rather than giving Tretiakov 'Theatre for Pleasure or Theatre for Instruction?' in order to influence debate, Brecht returned to Berlin with it in his suitcase.[24] Brecht was clearly reluctant to engage with political forces from his own side, which were being mustered against avant-gardists like himself. In later searing exchanges with his own side Brecht would again withhold his views from publication, adopting an approach in the literary struggle in which cunning took precedence over courage. Brecht was under no illusion that there was in any case always a price to pay.

The Chinese dramatic manner fascinated Brecht. In it he saw vivid parallels to the challenge he was mounting to the western 'Aristotelian' theatrical tradition, embodied for him by Stanislavsky. In 'Observations about the Art of Chinese Acting' Brecht noted affinities between Chinese acting and Epic Theatre.[25] The essay also acted as a foil to initiate his sustained critique of Stanislavsky, much of which served as unpublished self-orientation while he refined his own position, not as intervention in debate. Brecht identified in the highly conscious attitude of the Chinese actor the awareness that he was performing a role, not embodying it, and that his intention to appear strange, indeed disconcerting to the audience, lent his presentation of everyday actions a truly arresting impact. Brecht cited a scene from *The Fisherman's Revenge*, in which a girl rows an imaginary boat, steering it through a difficult stretch of water in such a way that a whole series of images is conveyed to the audience, who are witnesses to her adventure. Brecht observed that, in contrast to the general western view that Chinese actors were cold and lacked feeling, he admired the capacity of Chinese theatre to represent moments of great passion without over-excitement. In other words, Chinese theatre passed the Brechtian test of not affecting the normal body temperature, at which maximum cerebral clarity could be achieved. For Brecht, western art, by contrast, not least Stanislavskian theatre, remained beholden to the sanctimonious, corrupting influence of metaphysical beliefs, conveyed on stage through a form of hypnotic mimicry. In Brechtian terms, this was akin to falling into a feverish stupor. In his critique of Stanislavsky Brecht used the imagery of the organism inflamed and out of conscious control which he reserved for perniciously bad art. Brecht's extreme rejection of Stanislavsky was, it should be stressed, unwarranted by the standards of fellow dramatists, including those opposed to conventional realism, who admired Stanislavsky for his great achievement with the Moscow Art Theatre.[26]

Before Brecht and Steffin left Moscow, they got precious tickets for the May Day parade on Red Square. He recorded his impressions in an interview with the Moscow *Deutsche Zentral-Zeitung*, above all his sense of the city's triumph over adversity in constructing a new world.[27] The paper published his eulogy to Soviet planning and construction undertaken by the proletariat, 'The Moscow Workers Take Possession of the Great Metro on April 27, 1935', which presents the metro as the realisation of socialist production: 'Now that the railway was built in accordance with the most perfect plans / And the owners came to view it and / To ride on it, they were the selfsame people / Who had built it'.[28] Like Brecht's 'The Carpet Weavers of Kuyan-Bulak Honour Lenin', who decide on a modest plaque on a wall for Lenin rather than erecting yet another monument to their leaders, this poem praises the achievements of Soviet workers themselves.

Brecht talked on Moscow radio about German revolutionary theatre after the First World War, and an evening dedicated to his work took place on 12 May at the Foreign Writers' Publishing House. The tiny auditorium was packed with prominent German émigrés: Wilhelm and Arthur Pieck, Fritz Heckert, Friedrich Wolf and Becher. Wieland Herzfelde spoke about Brecht's works. Brecht described his first reading of Marx and read some of his anti-Fascist poems, while Carola Neher and Hanni Rodenberg sang his songs, and Alexander Granach presented two scenes from *Round Heads and Pointed Heads*. Two members of the Comintern Executive, Béla Kun and Vilis Knorin, were present. Kun was fascinated by Brecht and encouraged him to write short sketches about life in Nazi Germany, an idea that he would embrace in a more direct approach to anti-Fascist theatre. This encouragement equally implies criticism of *Round Heads and Pointed Heads*, which other figures in Moscow found too remotely intellectual. At a subsequent meeting Knorin emphasised that the task of the anti-Fascist writer was to warn of the Fascist threat of war.[29] Brecht took these messages to heart and over the next two years viewed himself as fulfilling a Comintern brief in his anti-Fascist writing. He would later regard the Hungarian Kun as a supporter of his work. However, in the power struggle in the Comintern played out around the show trials, Dimitrov, with Stalin's encouragement, would dispose of Kun and Knorin. While in Moscow, Brecht had a disagreement with the film director Gustav von Wangenheim over a role for Weigel, which, unbeknown to Brecht, would be held against him at that perilous time.

On the way back to Denmark a second Brecht evening took place in Leningrad, at which Steffin recited 'Children's Songs for Proletarian Mothers'.[30] Constantin Fedin and Theodor Plivier spoke, Brecht read his poems and a recording was played of Carola Neher singing Brecht's songs. Brecht returned to Svendborg and thanked Koltsov for the trip, which was 'refreshing in every respect'. Steffin returned to Moscow. From there she would tell Brecht in early1936 that while *The Threepenny Novel* was about to come out there in German and Russian editions, there was now uncertainty over Moscow and Leningrad productions of *Round Heads and Pointed Heads*.[31] Nikolai Okhlopkov had been due to direct in Moscow but in the light of the 'great discussion about Formalism' he observed jokingly that it was 'unacceptable'. It would prove to be no joke. Valentin Stenitsch also advised Steffin 'privately' that there was 'not much point' in Brecht coming to Moscow. A number of Steffin's initiatives on Brecht's behalf did not now materialise. For example, she mediated offers of work on films of *Schweyk* and about the Nazi 'martyr' Horst Wessel but Piscator advised against them and urged Brecht to join him instead in Engels, the capital of the Volga German Republic, to establish a theatre and a film production company.[32] Brecht and Weigel were both desperate to work regularly in the theatre again, and he suggested that she might go to look around to see if the place would be suitable for their children. It would be their good fortune that nothing came of this.

Family matters

Brecht returned to Svendborg on 21 May 1935, while Steffin initially stayed in Copenhagen. The family servant Mari Hold had exchanged the Brecht household for marriage to a local butcher, Jørgen Henrik Ohm. She was replaced by Mie Andersen. Back in Germany, Bi had been taking steps to bring Frank, now fifteen, to Augsburg from Vienna where Weigel's sister had been looking after him. Bi wrote to Brecht, asking for financial support so that Frank could train to be a dentist but Brecht baulked at the cost.[33] In a letter to Weigel, Brecht's father urged realism about Frank's abilities. Berthold Brecht also made wholly unguarded comments about the desperate state of Germany under the Nazis: 'We live in a coercive state, worse than the Middle Ages. You have no idea about the wholly new kind of psychosis of our German people'.

Bi, dropping dentistry for acting, carried out the plan to bring Frank to Augsburg, though not directly into her home with Hermann Gross. Frank was delighted to be living with his grandmother and to be finally near his mother, whom Weigel advised against an acting career for Frank on account of his health and recommended a practical profession instead.[34] Berthold Brecht committed himself to helping Bi take care of Frank and gave him a monthly allowance of 25 marks, while Brecht, for whom it was important that Frank should learn a trade and earn money, committed 50 marks per month for a year, funding permitting.[35] Funds were a real concern for Brecht. By March 1936 he was writing to Karin Michaelis that he and his family owed her an 'awful lot of money', some 41,500 kroner, and that it was well-nigh impossible to earn money in the film industry.[36]

Bi told Brecht that Frank was going to become an apprentice salesman, even though he had got the worst mark in the aptitude test.[37] He could not learn a craft because he was 'terribly unpractical, boring, lazy and sickly as well. In this hot weather he can't leave the house at all. He can't stand the sun and gets headaches at once'. Frank's apprenticeship was in nearby Friedberg with Kelpan, a firm owned by Hugo Maria Kellner, which made light filters for photography. Brecht's father had, it seems, asked a favour of his friend Kellner. The hapless Frank made a poor impression upon some colleagues at Kelpan, who found him messy and careless, although others found him kind and considerate, if withdrawn. Frank, meanwhile, told his father proudly that he had bought a suit with the fifty marks he had sent him.[38]

On 8 June it was announced that Brecht had been stripped of his German citizenship. He reflected in a manner typical of his approach to exile, seeking to override anxieties by objectifying his situation: 'The plight of those who had fled seemed no worse to me than / The plight of those who had stayed'.[39] For the moment his passport remained valid. In the hope of preventing any reprisals against his family in Germany, Brecht drafted a bogus letter to his father in the third person, which he may or may not have sent:

> Since you refuse to correspond with Herr Bert Brecht, I have the honour to inform you of the following at his behest. Though Herr Bert Brecht would have preferred to spare your feelings, he could not possibly have abstained from making public statements against the National Socialist regime. As you know, he has never shared your political opinions. He could not possibly have kept silent. It would have meant abstaining from all literary work. It has come to his ears that you threatened some time ago to disinherit him, if you have not already done so. He has asked me to tell you that it would take more than this to deter him from expressing his convictions.[40]

Brecht ended his letter to his father on a familiar note of filial affection: 'In conclusion he wishes to assure you that his feelings of gratitude towards you and his love for you are unchanged'.

Defending culture

It was two years since Brecht had seen one of his plays on the stage. The premiere of *Saint Joan of the Stockyards* was planned for September in Copenhagen. However, the director Thorkild Roose withdrew and the production collapsed. For some time, Brecht had been meeting with Ruth Berlau to discuss a translation of *The Mother*, on which she had been working with Otto Gelsted for the amateur Revolutionary Theatre. The premiere of scenes from *The Mother* took place while he was still in Moscow. Work on the play continued after his return. Unusually, on his trips to Copenhagen Brecht had not been visiting Steffin. When Brecht wrote to her on 5 June it was to say that he was glad that she had called him and that she should not believe all the gossip.[41] He excused himself by saying that he had arranged for her to go and live nearby on Thurø with Karin Michaelis. That meant he would be able to visit her by car and they could be together. However, Steffin's suspicions were not unfounded. She knew of Berlau's designs on Brecht, and he now wrote to Steffin cruelly: 'Ruth has arrived, unfortunately only by bike. She intends to go back on Saturday'. Brecht's meetings with Berlau were becoming intimate, a fateful turn of events for them both.

The officially stateless Brecht travelled to Paris with Karin Michaelis on 15 June for the first International Writers' Congress for the Defence of Culture, which took place at the Mutualité from 21–25 June. Benjamin met Brecht and Michaelis at the Gare du Nord and they stayed at a modest hotel in the Latin Quarter. Michaelis found Brecht a wonderful travelling companion, extremely polite and respectful towards her, even though he was the centre of attention 'for the most famous artists and the most beautiful women'.[42] Following the example of French workers, who in February 1934 ignored ideological barriers and united against the Fascist threat in Paris, preparing the way for Léon Blum's Popular Front government, the Comintern's Georgi Dimitrov buried the policy of Social Fascism and proclaimed a united, anti-Fascist front. Building upon the Parisian groundswell, the Comintern planned a new base in Paris to replace the ILRW. Unbeknown to Münzenberg, the Comintern intended to integrate his semi-independent organisation within the new structure. The official strategy for the Congress was to downplay the leading role of Soviet Communism and to attract prominent fellow travellers by stressing shared humanist values such as the cultural heritage, the nation and culture, and, of course, the defence of culture. Two-hundred-and-fifty writers from twenty-seven countries, among them André Gide, Henri Barbusse, E. M. Forster and Robert Musil, came together to hear their peers deliver eighty-nine speeches about Fascism, the world economic crisis and the USSR's Five-Year Plan. Gide offered his most ringing endorsement of the Soviet Union. In what was deemed a spectacularly successful event, those assembled founded the International Writers' League for the Defence of Culture. Brecht, however, adamantly opposed to fudging such issues, began his address, 'A Necessary Observation on the Struggle against Barbarism', by highlighting the following: 'In order to achieve profits, in our times cereal crops and cattle are destroyed. The destruction of culture has no other purpose'.[43] Lauding the Soviet example of collectivisation, Brecht proclaimed: 'Comrades, let us talk about the conditions of property ownership!'. His call fell on deaf ears. Brecht's partisan analysis of Fascism as the continuation of capitalism by more brutal means alienated both liberals and the proponents of the Comintern policy of a united front, who were at pains to downplay their Marxism.

On his return to Denmark Brecht wrote to Korsch that the conference, though an opportunity lost, had been rich in satirical material. Since the failure of the journal *Krise und Kritik* he had only scorn for the, in his eyes, mercenary attitudes struck by reformist and liberal intellectuals: 'I've been at the Writers' Congress where I collected quite a lot of material for my *Tui* novel. Heinrich Mann, for instance, submitted his paper on "Human Dignity and Freedom of the Spirit" to the Sûreté before delivering it'.[44] Brecht produced a draft in which he had his Tuis 'rescue culture' and announced to Georg Grosz, who visited Svendborg shortly after: 'We have just rescued culture. It took 4 (four) days, and then we decided that we would sooner sacrifice all else than let culture perish. If necessary, we'll sacrifice ten to twenty million people. [...] Fascism was condemned. What for? For its *unnecessary* cruelties'. Brecht collected vast amounts of material satirising the follies of intellectuals but his *Tui* novel remained frustratingly unfinished. He would find a suitable form for the material only after 17 June 1953 in his final drama, the burlesque *Turandot or The Whitewashers' Congress*.

Münzenberg followed up in Paris with meetings through 1936 and into 1937 at the Lutetia Hotel hosted by Heinrich Mann, aiming to develop a broad anti-Fascist Popular Front. The Lutetia Circle, or Popular Front Committee, attracted a number of prominent figures, among them Feuchtwanger, Albert Grzesinski, the former Berlin SPD Police President and Prussian Interior Minister, Jacob Walcher, and Willy Brandt, then of the SAP, as well as members of the KPD's Politburo, which suspected that Münzenberg intended to establish a German government in exile, bypassing KPD control.[45] Walter Ulbricht was dispatched from Moscow to impose Party discipline. He denounced the SAP as Trotskyist, sidelined Münzenberg with accusations of links with reactionaries and halted the work of the Circle. The KPD began to investigate Münzenberg and in May 1938 would strip him of his membership. The Lutetia Circle was doomed, as was an openly anti-Stalinist Münzenberg.[46]

Demonstrating his own approach to the defence of culture, between late August and early October 1935 Brecht worked with Steffin on his final Lehrstück, *The Horatians and Curiatians*, a play for schools. He had expected Eisler to collaborate, but, much to Brecht's annoyance, that again did not materialise. In late August, Brecht complained to Eisler that he had only begun *The Horatians and Curiatians* because Eisler had been asked to produce the work for the Red Army and because he was expecting Eisler's input for the music.[47] Busy with his own schedule, Eisler once more gave Brecht no encouragement. Brecht tried again in early September but by then Eisler was about to take up a short-term professorship at the New School for Social Research in New York. Brecht and Steffin were left to complete the work, which appeared in January 1936 in *Internationale Literatur*.

Brecht drew on a story from ancient Rome by Livy about a conflict between Rome and Alba Longa, famously treated by Pierre Corneille in his play *Horace* and by David in his painting 'The Oath of the Horatii'. In Livy, Rome and Alba Longa agree to settle their conflict through duels. In Brecht's version, the Curiatians of Alba Longa are the aggressors, relying on a war of conquest to alleviate internal social conflict. Three Horatian generals of Rome and three Curiatian generals of Alba Longa debate their tactics, accompanied by a chorus. At first the Roman Horatians fare badly and two Horatians are killed. The surviving Horatian knows that he is not equal to the three Curiatians together but has the beating of them individually. So he flees, in the expectation that he will be able to separate them as they pursue him. He manages to do this and defeats all three. This story was, of course, intended to resonate with fellow émigrés, encouraging them in their belief that by deploying similarly cunning tactics they could contribute to the defeat of Nazi Germany. However, readers in Moscow like Bernhard Reich did not like the work at all.[48] It was, arguably, more Taoist than Marxist. There was no enthusiasm for a production.

Debacle in New York: *The Mother*

Eisler worked on Brecht's behalf in New York to arrange a production of *The Mother* with the Theatre Union, well-known as a non-aligned theatre of the Left. After the failure of *The Threepenny Opera* in 1933, Brecht was determined to achieve the break-through of Epic Theatre in the USA which he craved. However, from the outset there were fundamental differences between Brecht and figures in the Theatre Union. Brecht wrote to the play's translator Paul Peters and to Victor Jerry Jerome, the Head of the US Communist Party's agitprop department, that he saw no prospect of a production because the translation had transformed *The Mother* into an anachronistic piece of Naturalism. Brecht wrongly assumed that Jerome could simply determine what went on at the Theatre Union. However, Jerome regarded Brecht as the great hope of prole-tarian theatre and would use all his influence to support him and promote his work in the USA. Jerome would take Brecht to parties and introduce him to prominent figures on the American Left such as the composer Marc Blitzstein and his wife Eva Goldbeck and to other influential people in American cultural life like Archibald MacLeish and John Houseman. Blitzstein would dedicate his musical *The Cradle Will Rock* to Brecht and translate *The Threepenny Opera* for the acclaimed New York production in the 1950s.

Brecht explained to Jerome that he could not countenance differences in style leading to another failure like *The Threepenny Opera*. So he offered to direct *The Mother* himself. The situation was not so different from Brecht's first directorial effort in Berlin with Bronnen's *Parricide* when the actors were quite unprepared for his theatrical vision. This time, Brecht tried to forewarn his hosts, writing to Jerome: 'It has never been easy to teach actors this style, but it has always worked out in the end'.[49] In New York, Eisler supported Brecht in his negotiations with the Theatre Union, suggesting that once in the city Brecht could get things done 'like a knife through butter'.

Manuel Gomez of the Theatre Union visited Brecht in Svendborg in early October. They agreed upon a performance version of *The Mother* and made verbal agreements which Brecht later referred to as a contract. Brecht wrote to Peters again with a list of his requirements for the production, including the translation of at least the first five chapters of his notes about the play for the director and stage designer.[50] He explained: 'In Berlin we got a strong and pure effect with a stage set consisting entirely of canvas. We used lots of light, which made the figures, surrounded by graffiti and projected photographs, stand out clearly'. And Brecht told Peters that he had 'great hopes for our work together'. However, Brecht would presently discover, to his great consternation, how much America's progressive theatre, grounded in Naturalism and psychological realism, had embraced his *bête noire* Stanislavsky.

Brecht embarked on his first journey to the USA on 7 October 1935, travelling to New York by boat, his trip financed by Karin Michaelis. He arrived on 15 October and stayed at 104 East 9th Street, in the same building as Eisler, Elisabeth Bergner and her husband Paul Czinner. Brecht told Weigel that he found his small flat 'not too expensive. Food is cheap. [...] We could manage here'.[51] Elisabeth Hauptmann joined Brecht from St Louis for the duration of his stay. The premiere of *The Mother* was scheduled for the Civil Repertory Theatre with its capacity of 1,100. Brecht was invited to attend rehearsals where the inexperienced Victor Wolfson was directing. As we know, Brecht felt that he could only bring his singular theatrical vision to bear through sustained involvement in rehearsals. As soon as they began, Brecht was at loggerheads with Wolfson, whom Eisler described as a 'seventeenth-rate disciple of the great Stanislavsky minus his talent'.[52] The clash of styles brought out the worst in Brecht. Wolfson and the others could not bear Brecht's arrogance, which they felt was born of the Marxist's belief in his superior knowledge. The only person who had an inkling of what Brecht was about was the set designer Max (Mordecai) Gorelik, who remained one of Brecht's staunchest allies in US theatre. The dramatist Albert Maltz, a founding member of the Theatre Union who was on its executive board, recalls Brecht's behaviour towards Wolfson. Brecht thundered out, 'This is shit', in a voice that would have 'humiliated the fight announcer at Madison Square Garden'.[53] Maltz continued: 'We had in our midst a screaming banshee [...] I can still hear [...] his Prussian drill master's call, *Sitzung*, i.e. meeting. We often had several a day'. Maltz and others had a ready comparison: Hitler.

Brecht was banned from rehearsals. He tried to influence things by presenting his theory of Epic Theatre to the board of the Theatre Union and Eisler joined Brecht in protesting about the quality of the music. Brecht also protested about the fact that 'I have been unable to set foot in your theatre since a pianist with your connivance threatened me with violence'.[54] The pianist had threatened to 'break every bone in his body'. Brecht complained about cuts made contrary to the contract and about not being able to give the director contractually agreed instructions. He threatened: 'If you should really see no possibility of granting me a few last *undisturbed* rehearsals, I shall feel obliged to oppose the performance of the play. And you force me to take the same step if you cannot give Eisler the assurance he demands'.[55] Brecht and Eisler turned to Jerome, who reached an agreement with the Theatre Union to perform the play without cuts. There were, however, further cuts. Following a full dress rehearsal in front of an audience of workers Brecht fired off a plea on 15 November that he be allowed to 'straighten out the production'.

Brecht and Eisler made suggestions which were largely ignored. They were then banned from the premiere of their own play! Elisabeth Hauptmann and Lou Jolesch witnessed the debacle. In the *New York Times* Brooks Atkinson described the production as an 'animated lecture on the theme of revolution, which may have educational value, but which is desultory theatre'.[56] Other reviewers panned the production, too. Brecht and Eisler pleaded once more for the opportunity to put the play into a 'politically and artistically acceptable form'. Performed thirty-six times, *The Mother* was a financial disaster for the Theatre Union from which it would never recover. And Brecht's hopes that he would achieve his breakthrough in the USA were dashed. He was left to reflect on his impotence to avert disaster in the following lines:

> The repute of his power went before him, not of his successes. Now
> It follows him. Powerless. Stranded, he sits
> On a foreign chair, a beginner
> Who is already finished. His hubris

Comes from things past. Useful
He was. Dangerous
He is no more.[57]

In the deepening storm of the 1930s, the *enfant terrible* of the 1920s would look for
ways to mitigate his 'powder-keg' self's capacity for controversy.

During the time remaining in New York Brecht made every effort to communicate
his position. In his 'Criticism of the New York Production of *The Mother*', intended
for publication in *New Masses*, he explained that the unfamiliar type of non-Aristotelian theatre developed in Germany since 1918 required directorially 'special kinds
of political knowledge and artistic capacity', which had not been employed in the
production.[58] Brecht wrote angrily to Piscator about the 'badly butchered' production:
'stupid mutilations, political ignorance, backwardness of all kinds'. He presented his
theory of a non-Aristotelian theatre in 'The German Drama: pre-Hitler' in the *New
York Times*, which was reprinted in London's *Left Review*. This was the only work with
which Brecht reached a wider audience. He proclaimed that a generation of young
actors had been trained in Berlin's theatres in the new style of Epic Theatre and of the
Lehrstück, the objective of which was to 'show the world as it changes (and also how
it may be changed)'. As Brecht's confidence in the Soviet experiment diminished, his
evolving aesthetic would place the question of 'how' increasingly in the audience's
court.

With business still to do in New York, including negotiations for the publication of
The Threepenny Novel and *Round Heads and Pointed Heads*, Brecht could not get back
home for Christmas. He told Weigel that Christmas was 'horrible': 'Eisler and I spent
the evening with people who had no children, and somebody went on and on singing
Scottish ballads. I'd have liked to put you to bed, Helli, the same as other years'.[59]
Steffin had been feeling neglected and isolated that autumn. Brecht sent her Christmas
presents but she had already set off for a clinic in Moscow before they arrived. In the
event, Brecht and Steffin did not meet between October 1935 and May 1936.

Brecht told Steffin that he was not comfortable in New York and was whiling away
his time with Eisler at the cinema. They went to lots of gangster movies and Brecht
collected newspapers articles about gangland murders, particularly the rise and fall
of the gangster boss Dutch Schultz, which would feed into *The Resistible Rise of
Arturo UI*. Brecht joked to Eisler that although he didn't normally drink he couldn't
bear New York without whisky.[60] However, all was not doom and gloom. Brecht saw
George Gershwin's *Porgy and Bess* and Marc Connelly's acclaimed *Green Pastures*.
He was taken by the ideas of the director Joseph Losey, whom he had got to know
in Moscow and who after the war would direct stage and screen versions of *Life of
Galileo*. They identified similarities between their approaches and Losey later tried to
interest people in Brecht's plays. Brecht saw the New York Group Theatre's production
of Clifford Odets's *Paradise Lost* at Longacre Theatre and scenes from Odets's *Waiting
for Lefty* at Madison Square Garden. Brecht seemingly found a congenial figure in Lee
Strasberg, who had also been in Moscow and who led the Group Theatre. Like other
theatrical progressives, Strasberg was steeped in Stanislavsky. Strasberg channelled his
expertise into the highly influential school of Method Acting. Eisler had interested

Strasberg in a production of the Lehrstück *The Measures Taken*. Strasberg and Brecht began rehearsals in January 1936 but stopped after about two weeks. Before Brecht left New York he wrote to Strasberg enthusiastically about the rehearsals, which they had had to end for unspecified 'political reasons'.[61] Brecht told Strasberg that he saw mainstream theatre as a 'bourgeois drug traffic and emotions racket' but added: 'The few rehearsals with you and your group have at least shown me that a revolutionary pedagogic theatre is possible here too'. It was, indeed, important for the revolutionary artist Brecht to take away that message from a place which he might need as a refuge.

Although Brecht had been stripped of German citizenship, the German Consulate General in New York extended his passport's validity until 26 January 1941. This was probably not administrative incompetence, rather a ploy designed not to alarm other governments. Brecht left New York on 5 February 1936 and arrived in Svendborg on 16 February after four-and-a-half months away. He thanked Hauptmann in a letter for looking after him and in a poem for the 'unforgettable night'.[62] After Berlau had visited him in February Brecht wrote the lines: 'Once above the pillow / He saw this peach-like face / Saw it with the feeling: / Don't go there again'. Brecht did not heed his own warning. In Berlau he encountered a lover whose borderline personality and sexual needs closely resembled his own. There was strong sexual chemistry between them. However, Brecht had learned to control his self-destructive tendencies much more successfully than Berlau. She became addicted to alcohol, which drastically reduced her threshold of inhibition. However diligently Brecht played the therapist as well as the lover, instructing her upon how to control her behaviour, the two roles would prove fundamentally irreconcilable.

Re-thinking, re-branding: The Alienation Effect

Brecht's visits to two major international centres for the theatre, Moscow and New York, had confronted him with a stark awareness of the uphill struggle he faced to gain acceptance for his work. Across the political spectrum, many dismissed his approach as at best eccentrically opposed to the core theatrical experience of empathy, at worst perniciously so. If little else, Moscow and New York had in common an enduring legacy of Naturalism mediated by Stanislavsky, which for Brecht, if not for many others, was simply anachronistic. He was hardly well placed to influence things from Svendborg. Gorelik sent him two issues of *Theatre Workshop* in which Stanislavsky's work was discussed. Brecht adopted his best polemical tone to comment on the arrival of this 'first wave of Russian theatre', which he found 'pretty muddy. [...] Not a word about classes, not a word about society, not a word about economics, and the revolution just hasn't happened'.[63] Brecht conceded that Stanislavsky's system was progress of a sort, if only because it was a system. He contrasted starkly the 'mystical, cultish character' of Stanislavskian method – a 'high point of bourgeois theatre' – with Epic Theatre, arguing that Stanislavsky's production of 'total empathy' was an act of violence. For Brecht, it was no accident that left-wing theatre people in the USA were starting to discuss Stanislavsky: 'this way of acting appears to grant them an unprecedented empathy with proletarian people'. Gorelik published a piece about *The*

Threepenny Opera and Epic Theatre in *Theatre Workshop*. Seeking to capitalise, Brecht drafted a lengthy letter to *Theatre Workshop*, praising the journal for what it had done in introducing Stanislavsky and other 'great Russians', subjecting them to searching criticism and presenting Epic Theatre. However, both John Howard Lawson and Edmund Fuller attacked Brecht's whole approach. Ernst Toller, whose Expressionist pathos Brecht had ridiculed since the early 1920s, repaid Brecht with an attack on Epic Theatre in New York's *Sunday Times*, where Gorelik leapt to Brecht's defence.

Walter Benjamin arrived in Svendborg in early August 1936 and stayed until mid-September. There is no diary of this stay. That summer Brecht was also meeting daily with Korsch to comment on his biography of Marx, which appeared in English in 1938. Striving to understand and thereby surpass Stanislavsky's success, Brecht asked Steffin to get him an English edition of Stanislavsky's *My Life in Art*.[64] After his stays in London and New York Brecht could now read English much more easily. Shortly after, he told Piscator that he had read *My Life in Art* with 'envy and anxiety': 'The man put order into his system and the consequence is that the Stanislavsky school has swept Paris and New York. Must that be? We are really unworldly dreamers'. Brecht was determined to show he was anything but. He suggested that Piscator visit him in Svendborg to discuss how they could spread their ideas about the theatre. He had always understood the need to propagate a distinctive doctrine if he were to achieve true greatness. The Brecht brand, which had brought such success in Berlin, had not captured the imagination in his various international engagements since 1933. He saw that, in step with his developing views upon the interplay of pleasure and instruction in the theatre, he must refine his theatrical doctrine if he were to achieve the international recognition he craved.

Brecht did that against a reading of Stanislavsky, in a sustained meditation which would culminate in the sprawling mass of material in the marvellous, unfinished *Messingkauf Dialogues*. As White notes, Brecht's working hypothesis was that Stanislavskian empathy was 'ill-equipped to deliver political insights'.[65] Brecht's aesthetic instinct, from which Epic Theatre had emerged, had always been to create intellectual distance from events on the stage by rendering the familiar strange. To describe this in terms of an acting technique to be employed at specific junctures to highlight the approach of Epic Theatre he now coined the term 'Verfremdung' – a variant upon his earlier use of 'Entfremdung' which concerned more the cognitive process in the audience.[66] He used the new concept in the expression 'Verfremdungseffekt', in abbreviated form 'V-Effekt', which would prove spectacularly marketable in the decades to come. The term is generally known in English as the 'Alienation Effect' or 'A-effect'. We will adopt that usage, even though the sense is better rendered by 'estrangement' or 'defamiliarisation'.

For his first substantial articulation of the concept Brecht again drew upon his experience of Chinese theatre. 'Alienation Effects in Chinese Acting' appeared in 1936 in *Life and Letters* but only in 1949 in German. Written for the English-speaking world where he increasingly saw his future, the piece differs from all Brecht's aesthetic statements since 1930 in dispensing with Marxist concepts altogether, substituting purely historical and social categories. The restrictions upon émigrés in various countries had no doubt impressed this expediency upon Brecht. He drew on his encounter with Mei

Lan-fang to claim that traditional Chinese theatre excmplified the use of the A-effect, which his Epic Theatre had developed independently.[67] Again, Chinese theatre is a foil for Brecht to define his position vis-à-vis Stanislavsky. Hence, Brecht explains that in Chinese theatre the artist's objective is to appear strange and even surprising to the audience, something which the actor achieves by looking strangely at himself and his work, not by embodying the character he is representing.

Mindful of the grounds he himself gave for the polarised interpretation of his statements, Brecht noted that the apparent coldness of Chinese performance did not mean that Chinese theatre rejected all representation of feelings:

> The performer portrays incidents of utmost passion, but without his delivery becoming heated. At those points where the character portrayed is deeply excited the performer takes a lock of hair between his lips and chews it. But this is like a ritual, there is nothing eruptive about it. It is quite clearly somebody else's repetition of the incident: a representation, even though an artistic one.

Brecht contrasted this approach with traditional western drama, empathy-laden and appealing to the subconscious, its endpoint reached in Stanislavsky's system, which was designed to manufacture what Brecht calls, rather contemptuously, a 'creative mood'. Instead of forming the illusion of a timeless, universal human condition, the aim of Epic Theatre was to historicise events. Brecht claimed that in any case the demands which Stanislavsky's system made upon actors left them 'exhausted' and hence only able to copy behaviour! Brecht would make contrasting claims for the 'lightness' of actors in Epic Theatre. 'Alienation Effects in Chinese Acting' concludes with a ringing endorsement of Brecht's theatre of social change:

> In setting up new artistic principles and working out new methods of representation we must start with the compelling demands of a changing epoch; the necessity and the possibility of remodelling society loom ahead. All incidents between men must be noted, and everything must be seen from a social point of view. Among other effects that a new theatre will need for its social criticism and its historical reporting of completed transformations is the A-effect.

Armed with the A-effect, Brechtian, not Stanislavkian, theatre pointed the way.

Attempting to gather forces sympathetic to his ideas and critical of Stanislavsky's, Brecht proposed a discussion forum about dramatic issues. He gave it the name Diderot Society after Denis Diderot, the materialist thinker and dramatist of the French Enlightenment, whose *Paradoxe sur le comédien* is an assault on the fusion of the person and part in the actor.[68] Diderot shared with his contemporaries a concern about the relationship between pleasure and instruction on the stage. After visiting Brecht in Svendborg, Gorelik began parallel planning for a Society for Inductive Theatre, for which Brecht was to write words of introduction. In surviving drafts Brecht uses the term 'inductive' for his theatrical practice, in the sense of an understanding derived from observed behaviour on stage. Brecht and Gorelik compiled an impressive list of members, among them Benjamin, Eisler, Piscator, Jean Renoir, Frantisek Burian, Léon Moussignac, Per Knudzon, Nordahl Grieg, Per Lindberg, W. H. Auden, Christopher Isherwood, Rupert Doone, Archibald

MacLeish, Eisenstein and Tretiakov. Brecht proposed that members should contribute to journals, which would present new ideas systematically and create a new terminology for a theatre concerned to represent both the socio-economic conditions of contemporary society and how they might be changed. What is more, the Society would act as a forum for the critical discussion of Stanislavsky's work. As prospective members were, no doubt, aware, all this was Brecht's own agenda. He proposed to Gorelik a piece about Piscator's experiments, Bernhard Reich's study of Shakespeare and Benjamin's essay on the effect of technical reproducibility on the arts. Brecht promised Gorelik a piece on stage construction and sent Slatan Dudow an invitation to join: 'We must do something to ensure that something comes of the avant-garde. Otherwise it will become a derrière-garde'.[69] Dudow accepted but nothing came of the plan. While Brecht would never abandon the spirit of experimentation, the forces of reaction which were tightening their hold on culture and politics would affect him, too. When Stanislavsky died in 1938, Brecht had only contempt for his influence, writing of the 'hypocrisy of the Stanislavsky school' and his 'cult' as a 'catchment area for everything that is sanctimonious in theatre arts'.[70] However, Brecht had been quietly learning a good deal by measuring himself against a figure whom he envied deeply.

Round Heads and Pointed Heads was again scheduled for performance in Copenhagen in the autumn of 1936. It was Brecht's first opportunity to test the A-effect. Per Knutzon was engaged to direct the play in Danish translation at Frederiksberg's intimate Riddersalen. The well-known cabaret star Lulu Ziegler was to play Nanna. However, when Danish Nazis, like the German embassy, protested and there were calls from conservative groups for the play to be banned, the price Brecht paid for the premiere to go ahead was that there should be no allusion whatsoever to the Nazis' treatment of Jews.[71] Brecht's aim was in any case more general. Weigel, however, asked the Jewish Maria Lazar not to attend and when Lazar realised why after the premiere, she confronted Weigel and received confirmation of her suspicions. However, anti-Nazis greeted the premiere with great applause and the attacks continued all the same upon this 'camouflaged' version, as Brecht described it to Becher.[72] In fact, the Danish Right called for Brecht's deportation. However, reviews were poor, as were the audiences, and the play soon closed. All this was very sobering. The actors thanked Brecht and Weigel for the privilege of performing the play but the simple fact was that in 1936 there was no real audience for a full-length Brecht play in a European capital like Copenhagen.

Determined to learn from precious stage experience, Brecht produced notes on the production. He was pleased that the spectators were allowed to smoke and drink in the auditorium. What he had tried to achieve in Berlin in 1924 to stimulate the audience's reflective capacity was possible in Copenhagen. He described the play as the 'parable type of non-Aristotelian drama', in which the 'modes of behaviour shown by the actors had transparent motives of a social-historical sort'. This approach was intended to have a 'decisive influence on the spectator's own social behaviour'. Again, these terms were employed without any explicit references to Marxism. As usual, Brecht had to tackle the issue of audience emotion and the critical approach which he was seeking to inculcate. He explained that he had brought the issue into focus with the A-effect:

The meeting of the two de Guzmans in the eighth scene (a street in the old town) was based on Claudio's conversation with Isabella in Shakespeare's *Measure for Measure*. The scene has to be played with complete seriousness in the heightened and impassioned style of the Elizabethan theatre. The Copenhagen production alienated this style by having it rain during the scene and giving umbrellas to all appearing in it. In this way the heightened style of playing was artistically alienated.[73]

Drawing attention in this rather contrived, 'Formalist', anti-illusionist manner to the outmoded conduct of the upper classes was not the most promising introduction of the A-effect. In time, a more subtly dissonant A-effect would become the headline concept within the acting style of the Epic Theatre. What did the A-effect amount to at this stage? Steffin told Brecht that he had not adequately explained the term.[74] Brecht accepted Steffin's challenge, concentrating greater attention upon the actor in essays and, where possible, in productions of what in the late 1930s he would quite pointedly call his 'experimental theatre'.

Anti-Fascism and the Show Trials 1936–8

Das Wort

Following the New York debacle, in March 1936 Brecht had entered into an agreement in Moscow to co-edit a new monthly journal, *Das Wort*. It was his first major commitment in Moscow and it would be his last. The association caused him major reputational damage. *Das Wort* had been conceived as a flagship for the Comintern's anti-Fascist Popular Front. Becher was the driving force, together with the prominent publisher and *Pravda* journalist Mikhail Koltsov. After Thomas and Heinrich Mann had declined Becher's invitation to assume the editorship, Willi Bredel, a KPD writer in Moscow, and Feuchtwanger in Sanary-sur-Mer joined Brecht as editors. Bredel carried the major editorial burden until he went to fight in the Spanish Civil War. The editorial staff included Fritz Erpenbeck, Franz Leschnitzer and Heinrich Meyer. Alfred Kurella, Dimitrov's secretary, was invited to all editorial meetings. Wieland Herzfelde supported Bredel during the launch phase. Brecht and Feuchtwanger accepted their roles on the condition that they each received a typescript of every issue and that publication was subject to their approval or disapproval. Their link with Moscow was Maria Osten, Koltsov's partner who had worked with Herzfelde in Prague. Given the distances, timescales and the personnel involved, this agreement was always open to abuse. Brecht and Feuchtwanger had accepted a poisoned chalice.

Brecht was in London that spring to work with Eisler on the film script for *The Bajazzo*. He was joined there by Steffin, who wrote to Benjamin that Brecht had also been writing 'wonderful new things', by which she probably meant the cycles 'German War Primer' and 'German Satires', which he would begin publishing soon after.[1] Brecht spent time with Osten, who wrote to a Moscow friend: 'I am staying with Brecht [...], who is constantly trying to abduct me to Denmark'.[2] She apparently stayed with Brecht for some weeks, preparing for the first issue of *Das Wort*, before she joined Koltsov in Spain. After many delays, the first issue appeared in July 1936. Bredel complained bitterly to Osten and others about Brecht's categorical 'directives'. Brecht changed his ways, making regular suggestions to Bredel and submitting his own work.[3] After 'Song of the Animating Effect of Money' in the first issue, the second contained Brecht's famous 'Questions from a Worker who Reads', which begins: 'Who built Thebes of the seven gates? / In the books you will find the names of kings. / Did the kings haul up the lumps of rock?'.[4] Brecht's correction of conventional historical narrative highlights the role of workers themselves rather than of leaders, whose role a more conventional narrative would highlight. Brecht, moreover, maintained the perspective of an alternative history in the face of the Stalin personality cult. Brecht would also come to see how, in a highly personalised form of Muscovite monarchy, Stalin was removing many co-workers from the pages of history whom he saw as a threat to his power, among them military leaders, Bolsheviks who had fought with Lenin and avant-gardists with similar ideas to Brecht. In the Great Terror unleashed against the Soviet people, the NKVD, the secret police, smashed the Comintern, arresting some 70 per cent of German exiles working in the cultural sphere. Many would never be seen again. In 1937 Heinrich Meyer of *Das Wort* would be arrested, sentenced to death and shot. The Soviet command economy preparing for a coming European war required the destruction of culture, too.

Arrests were already part of everyday life in Moscow. They intensified in March 1936, and on 9 August an article appeared in *Deutsche Zentral-Zeitung*, arguing that the German exile community was at particular risk from Trotskyists, Zinovievists and Fascists. On 21 August Bredel informed a general assembly of Moscow writers: 'We are posing this question within our number and are checking out each one of us'.[5] That month the actress Carola Neher, Brecht's lover from Berlin days, was arrested and accused with her husband Anatol Bekker of carrying messages from Prague for the Trotskyist Erich Wollenberg. In the first Moscow show trial, which ended on 24 August 1936, all sixteen accused of building an anti-Soviet Trotskyist-Zinovievist Centre were sentenced to death and executed. In the Basel *Arbeiter-Zeitung* Ignazio Silone published a sharply-worded letter of protest to *Das Wort*, describing precisely what was happening in Moscow, including the use of torture. Despite their bewilderment at events, many western supporters of the Soviet Union defended the trials. The editors of *Das Wort* maintained a deafening silence. From its inception this anti-Fascist flagship was fatally undermined.

Shortly after the first trial, from 4–8 September the German Commission of the Soviet Writers' Union convened a series of nightly closed meetings, at which German exile writers, among them Bredel, began purging themselves. Under the watchful eye of Koltsov's subordinate, Mikhail Apletin, Deputy Chair of the Writers' Union and Secretary of its Foreign Commission, they dutifully engaged in self-criticism and settled old scores. It was a grotesque realisation of Brecht's exercises in 'agreement' amongst comrades in the practice of the Lehrstück. All major KPD figures in cultural life abased themselves. Becher and Lukács set the tone, speaking in defence of their own actions and incriminating others. Before leaving early – which was held against him – the habitually lachrymose Becher talked of his deep anguish at not being able to cross the border back into Germany in 1933. Kurella, Hugo Huppert, Gustav Regler, Erich Weinert and Friedrich Wolf all contributed as required.

Brecht's name emerged a number of times in the speakers' trawl through their past lives for links which might save or damn them. Whilst Ernst Ottwalt described Brecht as a '100% honest anti-Fascist', he distanced himself from his involvement in *Kuhle Wampe*, the film he had made with Brecht. The Hungarian dramatist Julius Hay denounced the 'most miserable defeatism' of the 'Brecht Circle', among them Brentano and Weigel, which he had witnessed in 1933 in Vienna.[6] We have seen that, unlike the KPD's Fritz Heckert, Brecht recognised that in January 1933 the revolutionary Left had suffered a massive defeat. Gustav von Wangenheim followed Hay in attacking Brecht. Wangenheim told of his conversations with Steffin, Piscator and Brecht in Moscow in 1935 concerning Wangenheim's preference for Lotte Loebinger over Weigel for the film *The Fighters*. Wangenheim said that Piscator had rung him about the role, asking whether Weigel was 'too Jewish' and he had answered: 'That may be'. Wangenheim continued: 'Out of this story Brecht made a diabolical story by declaring that I promoted the view that Jews were not allowed to perform in Moscow. Steffin declared in front of Party comrades and non-aligned people: That must be printed in foreign newspapers. Wangenheim must be expelled from the Party'. Ottwalt now joined Wangenheim, recalling Brecht saying: 'What if I write to my friend Feuchtwanger that she can't act in Berlin because she's a Communist and can't act in Moscow because she's a Jew?'. Brecht's letter to Joris Ivens of 19 May 1935 confirms that Brecht did indeed believe Wangenheim had rejected Weigel on account of her 'Jewish appearance'.[7]

In November 1936 the large-scale round-up of German exile intellectuals began. Ottwalt and Waltraut Nicolas were arrested, as was the actor Alexander Granach. Bernhard Reich and Asja Lacis were later detained, and the exile community in Engels, which Brecht, Weigel and Piscator had considered joining, was destroyed. In early October the KPD Chair Wilhelm Pieck advised Piscator, who had worked closely with Pieck's son Arthur, to stay in Paris.[8] Wilhelm Pieck had just reported to the KPD Piscator's 'very questionable political stance, which brings him very close to Trotskyists'.[9] In October *Das Wort* launched a series of essays by Georg Lukács, a first step in the doctrinal purge of German exile intellectuals, in which he asserted intellectual leadership under the orthodoxy of Socialist Realism. In his discussion of Naturalism and Formalism, Lukács sharply criticised modernist experimentation as 'Formalist', that is to say interested in formal experimentation for its own sake rather than in content, which should convey a work's uplifting revolutionary message for the masses. Brecht asked Piscator to write something for the journal 'to make it a little better. It stinks'.[10] Brecht submitted Benjamin's essay 'The Work of Art in the Age of its Technological Reproducibility', but the Moscow editors rejected it. By now, Feuchtwanger viewed himself and Brecht as mere figureheads.

A second show trial against alleged Trotskyists ended on 30 January 1937 with thirteen death sentences and lengthy periods of incarceration. A third would follow in March 1938 when, among other leading Bolsheviks, Nikolai Bukharin, the Politburo member and Chair of the Comintern, whom Stalin had out-manœuvred but who had recently criticised Stalin's leadership, was sentenced to death and executed. For many western supporters of the USSR that was the final straw. *Das Wort* broke its silence after the second trial, publishing pieces supporting the trials by Brecht's Danish friend Martin Andersen Nexø, Feuchtwanger and Bredel. Brecht collected newspaper articles about the trials and sought to develop a position. That was no easy matter. After the third trial he would produce a draft 'On the Moscow Trials' in the form of a letter to an unnamed recipient, which was first published in 1993. Brecht effectively bypassed the issue itself, summarising his attitude towards the Soviet Union principally in terms of a critique of those on the Left, including Trotskyists, whose opposition to Stalin played into the hands of those clamouring for war against the USSR: 'To adopt an attitude in opposition to the government of the Union, which is staging these trials, would be quite wrong – since this would automatically, and in no time at all, be transformed into an attitude of opposition to the Russian proletariat, which stands under the threat of war from global Fascism, and to the process of the construction of Russian socialism'.[11] Brecht, then, accepted the official view that the trials demonstrated that an international conspiracy was out to destroy the Soviet Union. The trials therefore had substance and Brecht supported them as a necessity. He cast doubt on stories of forced confessions since he could not countenance such a 'gulf between the regime and the masses'. Furthermore, he argued that people on the Left should not allow their judgement to be clouded by the Stalin cult. The text breaks off at that point. Brecht chose not to consider how much the cult of the dictator was the product of Stalin's own brand of charismatic rule, just as Brecht's socio-economic analysis precluded consideration of that factor in Hitler's hold over the German people.

An agitated Brentano sent Brecht two letters about rumours in the western press which implicated Brentano in the arrest of their mutual friend, Ottwalt. The papers were reporting allegations that Ottwalt had written pro-Hitler letters to Brentano, who had passed them to the Soviet authorities. Brecht stonewalled: 'I've received your letter, but I don't understand it ("don't understand" shouldn't be taken to mean anything diplomatic)'.[12] Brecht twice cast doubt on the veracity of reports which had appeared in 'bourgeois' newspapers before stating: 'I still believe that the Bolshevik party is deeply rooted in the Russian proletariat and that the Russian economy is engaged in a great revolutionary process'. Brecht suggested waiting until 'authentic' information was available. Meanwhile, Ottwalt was stripped of his KPD membership and in 1939 sentenced to five years in a Siberian camp, where he died in 1943. In what was becoming a routine procedure, the Soviet authorities deported Waltraut Nicolas to Germany, handing her over to the Gestapo.

Amidst these grim developments, Brecht and Feuchtwanger continued to place their own work in *Das Wort*. In publications from 'German War Primer' and 'German Satires' Brecht conveyed his message with the clarity and simplicity for which *Songs, Poems, Choruses* had been praised. Moreover, he demonstrated a mastery of his poetic idiom of exile, epigrammatic in form, lapidary in style, which quite simply redefined German poetry:

> The war which is coming
> Is not the first one. There were
> Others before it.
> When the last one came to an end
> There were conquerors and conquered.
> Among the conquered people
> Starved. Among the conquerors
> The common people starved too.[13]

Brecht was absolutely clear that Hitler meant war. But that was not all: as in all wars, it was the poor on all sides who would pay. Brecht urged his readers not to participate in preparations for war or in war itself:

General, your tank is a powerful vehicle
It smashes down forests and crushes a hundred men.
But it has one defect:
It needs a driver.
[...]
General, man is very useful.
He can fly and he can kill.
But he has one defect:
He can think.

This challenge to people to take their lives into their own hands in both thought and deed has its corollary in 'German Satires' in the exposure of the deceit routinely practised by the Nazi leadership:

The famous remark of General Goering
That guns should come before butter
Is correct inasmuch as the less butter it has
The more guns the government needs
For the less butter it has
The more enemies.[14]

For his 'German Satires' Brecht drew extensively upon newspaper and radio reports, integrating the material with characteristically simple diction arranged in sharp, ironic juxtapositions. With the satires Brecht was pursuing Dimitrov's 'Trojan Horse' strategy in exemplary fashion. He was smuggling his message into Nazi Germany by having the Comintern broadcast them into the country on its short-wave German Freedom Station, which during the Spanish Civil War was based at Pozuelo del Rey near Madrid. Brecht's verses contributed to the 'truly sensational' and abiding impact of the German Freedom Station in Germany, which the exile SPD's *Report from Germany* attested in April 1937.[15] Listeners could hear Brecht's 'Difficulty of Governing':

Ministers are always telling the people
How difficult it is to govern. Without the ministers
Corn would grow into the ground, not upward.
Not a lump of coal would leave the mine if
The Chancellor weren't so clever. Without the Minister of Propaganda
No girl would ever agree to get pregnant. Without the Minister of War
There'd never be a war. Indeed, whether the sun would rise in the morning
Without the Führer's permission
Is very doubtful, and if it did, it would be
In the wrong place.[16]

Brecht's great artistry rendered the complex simple, capturing the tone of direct and spontaneous speech which won over listeners who thought they had no ear for the complexities of modern verse.

Das Wort published Feuchtwanger's attack on André Gide's account of his trip to Moscow, *Retour de l'URSS*, in which the previously supportive Gide had expressed his disappointment at the Soviet experiment. For Feuchtwanger, Gide had struck a blow not just against socialism but against progress. Feuchtwanger undertook his own fact-finding trip to the Soviet Union in early 1937. His visit included attendance at the second show trial, a meeting with Stalin and interviews with the press. Brecht sent a letter to Feuchtwanger in Moscow via Maria Osten, asking him to approach Stalin's secretary for information about Carola Neher.[17] Not wishing to criticise the Soviet Union, Brecht suggested that a mistake might have been made amidst the 'only too well justified countermeasures against Goebbels's networks in the USSR'. This was, however, sufficient to renew the NKVD's suspicions about Brecht.[18] Brecht sent Feuchtwanger further requests to help Neher in the coming months. Feuchtwanger replied on 30 May 1937 that he had not received Brecht's letter while he had been in Moscow.[19] While there he had nonetheless been aware that Neher was in prison. According to the German actor Hermann Greid, who visited Brecht that summer, Brecht could not contain his anger at Neher's treatment.[20] Brecht wrote 'Washing C.N.', recalling how he had shown her how to wash her face in the morning with ice in the water to sharpen her mental awareness as she learnt difficult lines. He then addresses her in the present, acknowledging his helplessness while hoping she can help herself:

> Now I hear that you are said to be in prison.
> The letters I wrote on your behalf
> Remained unanswered. The friends I approached for you
> Are silent. I can do nothing for you. What
> Will your morning bring? Will you still do something for yourself?
> Hopeful and responsible
> With good movements, exemplary?[21]

In 1937 Neher received a ten-year jail sentence and died in prison in 1942.

Feuchtwanger returned to France and published *Moscow 1937*. Citing his conversations with Stalin, he treated thorny issues such as dictatorship, the relationship between Stalin and Trotsky, and the trials. In a display of his even-handedness, he acknowledged the USSR's deficiencies but gave the benefit of the doubt to this progressive experiment in constructing a rational system. He argued that the trials should be seen against the background of Stalin's struggle with the brilliant but deeply flawed Trotsky, who was driven by a desperate need to undermine his rival's rule. Brecht praised *Moscow 1937* as the best account of the USSR in European literature.[22] Steffin, however, asked Benjamin: 'Have you read Feuchtwanger's great words? Will the wise Feuchtwanger never regret that they had to drag these words out of him?'. In November Brecht would again ask Feuchtwanger what could be done for 'poor' Neher, adding: 'If she has been convicted, I'm sure it hasn't been without ample evidence but over there they don't operate on the "one pound of crime one pound of punishment" theory, they only want to protect the Soviet Union'.

Brecht wrote more letters on behalf of other victims of this 'rough' Soviet justice. He appealed to the banker Max Warburg and to Jewish help groups to come to the rescue of his friend Hermann Borchardt, who had been teaching history and philosophy in Minsk.[23] Borchardt's methods were severely criticised and he was 'repatriated' to Buchenwald in complete mental disarray, where he lost his fingers and his hearing in the brutal abuse. Borchardt desperately needed confirmation of employment or an invitation from another country, so Brecht asked Grosz if people in New York like Felix Weil or Friedrich Pollock could help, maybe Arnold Zweig in Palestine or Otto Rühle in Mexico. Brecht also contacted people in Scandinavia and England in the hope of finding a teaching post for Borchardt. When Borchardt finally made it to the USA, Brecht wrote to him: 'I wish I were in the USA'.

In the Moscow terror, the gulf widened between western émigrés like Brecht and Eisler Eisler was in Svendborg for much of 1937 before leaving for the USA – however loyally they behaved towards the USSR, and KPD figures in Moscow, who were required to demonstrate their vigilance and indispensability. Wilhelm Pieck noted that Becher was an 'organisational and political failure' with *Internationale Literatur* and that Brecht was 'greatly hampering' the work of *Das Wort*.[24] Steffin witnessed Brecht's anger at an essay which Julius Hay had submitted. The journal had published an extract from *Round Heads and Pointed Heads* and Bernhard Reich's essay praising Brecht's work and critical of Hay's dramas. Hay's latest work was *Have*, a popular comedy or Volksstück about greed in village life which for Brecht stopped short of Marxist analysis. Hay's response to Reich was to criticise Epic Theatre as a degenerate form of bourgeois theatre and to attack Brecht's *Round Heads and Pointed Heads*, arguing that identifying the physical features of particular groups was grist to the Fascists' racist mill.

Brecht wrote to Piscator in Paris of the 'disgusting little article by Hay, containing violent attacks on Reich, me and you'.[25] Brecht put much effort into blocking publication of Hay's piece. Hay responded to a first letter from Brecht that his criticism was not about formal issues but about profoundly political matters: Brecht had produced a wrong-headed theory of race and an incorrect representation of Fascism. We have seen the limitations of Brecht's classically Marxist analysis of racism as a function of the capitalist political economy, as well as his acceptance that his play be performed without allusion to the Nazis' treatment of the Jews. However, we have seen, too, that, within that 'camouflage', audience and press reactions demonstrated that everyone, Nazis and anti-Nazis, grasped his more general point. Brecht told Hay: 'When "for the deepest political reasons" you attack the use of the "Trojan Horse" technique in the theatre, you had better be very careful. For even the Communist members of the editorial board are bound to wonder whether this particular question should be fully aired'.[26] Aligning his practice with Dimitrov's Comintern strategy, Brecht warned Hay: 'I advise you not to publish this particular article: it does not serve our common cause'. Hay's article did not appear.

Hay had, in fact, written that his opinion was 'shared by all the comrades' he had consulted. This set the alarm bells ringing. Brecht asked Becher whether Hay had spoken to him and asserted: 'The article is an attack on all camouflage in the theatre; he just won't let Dimitrov's Trojan Horse appear on the stage'. A seriously concerned Brecht urged Becher: 'We must do everything in our power to prevent a public quarrel about literary form, which, as Hay's article shows, would undoubtedly become most acrimonious, and must stop him from denouncing and sabotaging literary attempts to smuggle in the truth about the enemy in camouflaged form'. Becher had, of course, praised Brecht's 'Five Difficulties in Writing the Truth' and had disseminated it widely in recognition of Brecht's unsurpassed gift in providing literary leadership in the anti-Fascist struggle.

After the New York debacle, Brecht was anxious about the damaging effect of a concerted assault upon Epic Theatre from his own side. Far from relishing the prospect of polemic, for which he was, of course, renowned, in March the self-avowedly 'inflammable' Brecht memorably described himself to Steffin as a 'sort of powder keg, better approached with something cold rather than something warm'.[27] Cold presses were needed, not torches. He was after all still Neher's Hydratopyranthropos, The Water-Fire-Man. In April he advised caution to Dudow about the latter's draft essay containing passages about Epic Theatre, writing that a 'really moderate' tone was needed after he had rejected Hay's essay and echoes of the 'Formalism' debate could 'still be heard beneath the surface'.[28] To underline his point, Brecht cited the subtle, circumspect manner in which British academics such as the philosopher Bertrand Russell articulated their differences with others. Brecht realised that he required a very different strategy from his explosive polemics of the Weimar Republic and that in particular he needed to adopt something like the covert strategy of the Trojan Horse towards his own political side. In what was increasingly a struggle for survival, cunning was beginning to eclipse courage amongst the five difficulties in telling the truth.

Brecht's women: Rallying to Republican Spain, rebelling against Brecht

In Denmark, Brecht was spending time with Berlau at the house just outside Copenhagen in Vallensbaek which she had bought for them to be together. Berlau recalls driving Brecht there through the snow on the back of her motorbike, while he puffed away on his perennial cigar – and continued puffing while she made the fire.[29] They were working on a farce, *Everyone Knows Everything*, about the legendary Danish burglar Storm Nielsen, who lived very modestly and whom Karin Michaelis had taken in at Torelore. The great cartoonist Storm Petersen produced illustrations. However, a marginalised Steffin claimed that Brecht had surrendered his artistic integrity by ignoring their cardinal principle that a political contradiction must be embedded in all works. In the complex web of intensely lived artistic, political and personal selves, the sharp ends of divergent interests were exposed. The domestic atmosphere at Skovsbostrand now changed. Weigel and Steffin had devised a form of accommodation which Berlau's presence disrupted. Steffin, now living in Svendborg town, ceased to wear the ring which Brecht had given her and Weigel, trapped for so long in her domestic existence, again began looking for a way to escape Brecht with her children. She received an invitation from the Catalonian Socialist Party to work in Barcelona. When Piscator advised against the project, Weigel's deep frustration welled up: 'I've had it right up to here with my idiotic existence. I was and still am a useful person. My hibernation has been going on too long'.[30]

In July 1937 Brecht travelled to Paris with Karin Michaelis and Berlau for the final session of the Second International Writers' Congress for the Defence of Culture. The focus of attention for anti-Fascists had switched to the Spanish Civil War. Brecht spoke out against the Nazi bombardment of Republican Spain, an extension of the Fascist terror in Germany:

> The monstrous events in Spain, the bombardment of defenceless towns and villages, the slaughter of whole populations, are now opening the eyes of more and more people to the fundamentally no less momentous, but simply less dramatic, events which happened in my own and other countries, where Fascism fought victoriously for power. They can now discover the terrible common cause of the destruction of Guernica and the occupation of the German Trades Union buildings in May 1933.[31]

While Stalin was avenging himself on real and imagined opponents in Moscow, the Comintern had mobilised anti-Fascist forces in a rainbow alliance of international brigades for the great campaign of the Popular Front, the defence of the Spanish Republic against General Franco's Falangist putsch. There were trade unionists and reformist and revolutionary socialists, among them Trotskyists and anarchists as well as card-carrying Communists. Much pathos attaches to accounts of this last attempt by a Popular Front to defeat Fascism before Nazi Germany plunged Europe into war. While, for Italy and Germany, Spain was about achieving Fascist domination in Europe, the officially neutral UK and France – under huge pressure from the UK – pursued appeasement of Fascism by imposing an arms embargo on the Republic. Indeed, an MI6 officer flew Franco from the Canaries to Spanish Morocco, triggering the start of the war. For the USSR, Spain was about both the anti-Fascist struggle and preventing Trotskyists and other deviants from seizing power. The Soviet purge of the Trotskyists proved more successful than the campaign against Fascism. Indeed, as the European war approached, for Stalin domestic security came to far outweigh internationalism.

Brecht's friend and Maria Osten's partner Mikhail Koltsov was in Paris for the congress. It is said that in addition to his job as *Pravda*'s chief reporter Koltsov was a Soviet political commissar in Spain, though this was, of course, never publicly acknowledged. Koltsov was Ernest Hemingway's Karkov in *For Whom the Bell Tolls*. When Koltsov flew back to Madrid, Berlau went with him, staying in Spain for several months. Brecht retaliated in verse: 'When she drinks, she falls into any bed'.[32] Since Marianne, he had not been abandoned by a woman in this way and found the experience deeply distressing. Steffin was very worried by Brecht's 'clearly discernible unease'.[33] Once more, at a time of stress the chorea returned. Attempting to deal with his distress, in his *Book of Twists and Turns* he adopted the guises of Kien-leh and of the Chinese philosopher Me-ti, writing pieces about his 'sister' and 'pupil' Lai-tu. Despite the ciphers and the formal restraint, Brecht's aggression toward Berlau bursts into the open as he 'kills' her in his writing:

> When Me-ti's favourite pupil Tu had fallen in the civil war because he (sic), although he had a particular assignment and was prepared for others, had taken up weapons, Me-ti refused to describe him as a good revolutionary. He gave no

adequate reason why he should exchange one assignment for another. He believed
that war only took place where there was shooting; he could see no further than
50 metres and in actual fact died like a hoodlum.[34]

In some pieces Brecht described his abandonment by Lai-tu, in others he wrote that
he had sent her away. Brecht's women, however, were not disposed to accept every last
element of his control.

After Brecht had returned from Paris to Denmark with Michaelis, he confirmed
in writing to her on 22 July 1937 that he now owed her 52,000 kroner: 'I received this
sum of money from her in the past four years for the purchase of a house, a trip to
America and for the maintenance of my family'.[35] That same day he urged Michaelis to
present the letter to the Société des Auteurs to claim royalties, which, he hoped, would
accrue from Ernst Josef Aufricht's forthcoming production of *The Threepenny Opera*
in Paris. Brecht himself could not get a penny from Germany. As we know, Brecht had
authorised Fritz Lieb, a Basel professor of theology close to Benjamin, to deposit any
royalties gathered by the Société des Auteurs in an account with the Zurich Crédit
Suisse. Brecht was by now looking to the USA for support from the American Guild
for German Cultural Freedom so that he could continue as an independent author.
Brecht wrote: 'I derive next to no income from my writings'.[36] He was awarded a grant
in the spring of 1938, which was extended that autumn.

In similar vein to Béla Kun in Moscow, Slatan Dudow had been encouraging Brecht
to produce short anti-Fascist works for his exile theatre in Paris.[37] Brecht responded
with a piece for the struggle in Spain, *Señora Carrar's Rifles*, on which he worked
with Steffin, completing it by August. For this one-act play, designed to slot into an
evening's anti-Fascist programme, Brecht and Steffin drew upon J. M. Synge's *Riders to
the Sea*. In Synge's play the mother has lost five sons and dreads losing her sixth, while
in Brecht's Señora Carrar loses her husband but is determined to keep her sons from
the war – until her elder son Juan is brought home dead. Carrar, releasing the rifles
her husband had kept, joins her younger son José and his comrades in the struggle for
the Republic against the Falangists.

Brecht persuaded Dudow to put on *Señora Carrar's Rifles* in Paris that autumn
around the same time as Aufricht was scheduling *The Threepenny Opera*. In that way,
he could come to Paris just once, saving money because, as he put it, he was no longer
so rich.[38] Aufricht paid for Brecht and Weigel to travel to Paris on 12 September for a
month. Brecht was also attempting to prevent Felix Bloch Erben taking royalties from
productions of *The Threepenny Opera* in Copenhagen and Stockholm. Brecht wrote
to Bloch Erben on 19 October, demanding that the contract be dissolved. However,
Bloch Erben continued to take their cut. Indeed, in Copenhagen Per Knutzon did not
keep an agreement with Brecht, who was furious when he discovered that Knutzon
had passed the royalties to Bloch Erben. Brecht complained to the Chair of the Danish
Communist Party, Aksel Larsen, who censured Knutzon. Brecht would have nothing
more to do with him.

In Paris Benjamin joined Brecht at rehearsals for *The Threepenny Opera*. Brecht
was working with prominent French actors but had little French. The premiere took
place at the Théâtre de l'Étoile on 28 September but the play was not the hoped-for,

money-spinning success and closed after fifty performances. *Señora Carrar's Rifles* was to be performed in German at the Salle Adyar. Weigel rehearsed with Dudow and old Berlin friends like Steffi Spira, while Brecht visited Feuchtwanger in Sanary-sur-Mer with Maria Osten, staying there until 9 October.[39] Brecht and Feuchtwanger were exasperated by their treatment in Moscow and told Osten that they would only continue with *Das Wort* if an office was established in Paris to facilitate contributions from western émigrés and the timely payment of fees. Osten took their demands back to Moscow while they followed up with a letter which remained unanswered for some time. Agreement upon the office was reached in early 1938 but it would be established only much later that year.[40]

Brecht returned to Paris in time for the premiere of *Señora Carrar's Rifles* on 16 October. It was a great success among the German exile community. The novelist Anna Seghers praised Weigel's Carrar, while Brecht wrote to Korsch: 'Helli was better than ever, she lost nothing by the interruption, and she was glad of that. Her acting was the best and purest that has been seen in the Epic Theatre anywhere. She plays the part of an Andalusian fisherman's wife, and it was interesting to see how she was able to negate the usual contradictions between a realistic and a cultivated style of acting'.[41] The play, devised with the direct appeal of agitprop, is constructed in conventional 'Aristotelian' manner in terms of the unities and in the sense that the audience identifies with Señora Carrar's dilemma and that she breaks the suspense only at the last moment, encouraging others to join the anti-Fascist struggle. With this combination of theatrically pleasurable and instructive elements Brecht was developing a popular realism closer to the practice of mainstream theatre. At the same time, Weigel, trained in the Epic Theatre, could step outside the character, demonstrating, rather like Mei Lan-fang, the attitudes and motivations of the character for the public to consider, rather than simply embodying the character 'hypnotically'. In the late 1930s, this highly stageable play would enjoy success in several countries. Berlau directed an amateur production in Copenhagen, which her Swedish friend, the MP Georg Branting, saw and he arranged a production in Stockholm in 1938, directed by Hermann Greid with advice from Brecht. A production in Prague met with an enthusiastic audience response, Martin Andersen Nexø's essay about the play appeared in *Das Wort* and Ernestine Evans's translation, designed to stimulate interest in the US, in *Theatre Workshop*. Thanking Dudow for his production, Brecht acknowledged: 'Actually almost my entire contribution in exile is concentrated upon your activity in Paris'.[42] Considering Brecht's experience in Moscow, New York and Copenhagen, that was certainly true.

On Brecht's return to Skovsbostrand, Steffin, who was ill and desperately in love, made a stand. Steffin and Brecht were alone in the house because the children were staying with a neighbour while Weigel was away. As usual, Brecht refused to be drawn by a display of emotion and defended his relationship with Berlau. Steffin backed down and remained in the house until Weigel returned. Weigel would have liked to stay in Paris that autumn. The German actors in the cabaret La Laterne invited her to join them. They could not, however, live off their earnings, while Dudow was frustrated that the cabaret was not allowed to present anything critical of German and Italian Fascism. Rather than returning to Denmark, Weigel travelled to Vienna, hoping to perform *Señora Carrar's Rifles* there and then in Prague. Brecht wrote to her in late October, asking when she'd be back and saying that he'd like to see her again 'some time'.[43] She had told him that she would not be back before early December. He then wrote: 'Watch your morals. I think fondly of Paris and am most devoted to you'. However, he then changed tack, enlisting his son and sending Weigel a 'Resolution', which reads: 'Dear Comrade, the Council of Husbands and Sons has resolved to demand of you that after completion of your obligations you return *without delay* and resume your activities here. You are required to report to those named below as soon as possible. With revolutionary greetings Steff bidi'. Weigel responded that she would be returning only around Christmas! Brecht now sent her a poem dedicated to her, 'The Actress in Exile', in which he celebrated her performance as Señora Carrar, carefully recording her preparations:

> Now she makes up. In the white cubicle
> She sits forward, on the edge of the makeshift stool
> Putting on her greasepaint before the mirror
> With easy gestures.
> Carefully she rids her face of
> Everything remarkable: it will reflect
> The quietest reaction. Now and then
> She lets her fine supple shoulders
> Fall forward, as do those who
> Work hard.[44]

For good measure, Brecht placed the poem with *Pariser Tageszeitung*. In her search for work and a place to live for her and her children, Weigel went to Zurich. She let Benjamin know that she would be in Paris from 12 November.[45] Her intention to return to Prague for a production of *Señora Carrar's Rifles* did not materialise and, having explored her options, in November she was forced to return to her quite unsatisfactory domestic existence at Skovsbostrand.

After Berlau's return from Spain, Brecht joined her in Copenhagen where she was directing *Señora Carrar's Rifles*. Steffin wrote of Berlau in her diary: 'I very much wish that she would snuff it. I would buy her a beautiful wreath'.[46] When Steffin began to take other lovers, Brecht was brutally dismissive in his verse, expressing his disgust in 'Last Love Poem' with its imagery of 'pus'. 'On the Unfaithfulness of Women' begins with the poet considering that he might 'allow' her to lie with other men, before reflecting: 'If only each hug of the five-minute husbands / did not change her at once so much!'.[47] Brecht could not bear the change which took place in his mind with the awareness that she had gained sexual pleasure with another man. His domestic arrangements, which lent his difficult life comforts and an agreeable regularity, if by no means bourgeois normality, were threatening to unravel.

Brecht directed his anger at Berlau when she could not answer his questions about the Spanish Civil War.[48] She seemingly had no understanding why no united anti-Fascist front had been established amongst Anarchists, Communists and Trotskyists. Brecht had pleaded for such a front in a letter to the exile German Writers' Association, albeit with a clear bias towards the Communists, namely: 'The Communists among us have always made the greatest sacrifices in support of a united struggle for freedom and democracy in Germany'.[49] While that might please friends in Moscow, others would beg to differ. Koltsov could have told him a thing or two about Stalin's approach to the Anarchists and Trotskyists in Spain and how Stalin's emissary Walter Ulbricht had sidelined German 'deviationists'.

The Moscow camarilla moves against Brecht

'I can't go to the USSR!!!!', an alarmed Steffin wrote in her diary in September 1937.[50] Although Steffin gave no reason, she suddenly abandoned her plan to go to a Soviet sanatorium. A trip which Brecht was planning also did not happen. News may just have arrived of Tretiakov's arrest in July as a German and Japanese spy, which prompted Brecht to tell Korsch that his literary contacts in the USSR had become 'very thin'. Tretiakov would be found guilty and executed in 1939. What is more, in September 1937 Alfred Kurella, using the pseudonym Bernhard Ziegler, launched a new front in *Das Wort* in the doctrinal struggle against Formalism which sent a chill through anti-Fascist artists. A helpless Brecht found his own journal being used as a platform to attack him and his friends. A little later Brecht observed to Benjamin that he had inherited his 'profound hatred of clerics' from his grandmother and remarked of Kurella, Lukács et al.: 'Those who have appropriated and used Marx's theoretical doctrines will always form a clerical camarilla. Marxism does after all lend itself all too easily to "interpretation"'.[51] History has borne out Brecht's identification of the Soviet system as a quasi-theocracy. In *Life of Galileo* he would explore what that meant for innovators like himself whom the camarilla branded heretics.

Kurella's starting point was Klaus Mann's essay about the Expressionist poet Gottfried Benn, who had declared his support for Nazism in 1933. Kurella also picked up on Lukács's earlier attacks on Expressionism to argue – with breath-taking over-simplification – that Expressionism, which he used as a proxy for modernism and avant-gardism, had found a home in Fascism and that Expressionism was therefore alien to anti-Fascists.[52] A whole generation of German writers in exile had committed the sins of their youth in the excesses of the 'Expressionist decade' of the 1910s. It was an obvious focus for the doctrinal purge. The Moscow editors of *Das Wort* invited discussion of Kurella's piece, expecting loud protests from western émigrés, which the Muscovites could then quash in a demonstration of the western émigrés' Trotskyist deviance. However, Ernst Bloch inquired sarcastically whether 'Ziegler' – also the name of a Nazi ideologue – had written his piece before or after the Nazis had denounced Expressionism as 'degenerate art'.[53] The notorious Munich exhibition of so-called degenerate works had just opened. Together with Hanns Eisler, Bloch replied to Kurella/Ziegler with two pieces, advising the 'theoretician' to be more measured in his advice to modern artists. The pieces appeared not in *Das Wort* but in *Die Neue Weltbühne*.

Between December 1937 and June 1938, with Bredel in Spain, *Das Wort* published twelve essays in its Expressionism Debate, which culminated in Lukács's final essay 'Realism is at Stake'. Brecht was again being kept out of the loop. In March 1938, for example, he wrote to his 'dear friends' in the editorial office that he had not yet received the material for the latest issue even though the deadline for his response had passed.[54] On 2 May he wrote to Erpenbeck, from whom he had received proofs for the final round in the Debate:

> It is not my impression that we have conducted our business particularly well, the business of realism in literature. The weaknesses of the principal Expressionist works have not been demonstrated through reference to realists: the concept of realism has appeared very narrow, one almost has the impression that we are dealing with a literary fashion with rules that are being derived from a few arbitrarily chosen works. [..] We are surely in a position to present a much more broadminded, productive, intelligent concept of realism.[55]

Erpenbeck wrote to Bredel on 20 July 1938 about the evidence of 'sectarianism' and of efforts to make Brecht repent.[56] Erpenbeck argued that the Popular Front was at stake, the campaign to win over the masses: 'To give an example, it is more important to persuade Brecht – who is a highly talented dog – to write *Señora Carrar's Rifles* and 'The Judicial Process' and not the *Round Heads and Pointed Heads* and other Lehrstücke. Let him get angry about Lukács's theories, as long as he follows them in his practice (despite his inner resistance).' In fact, in his journal Brecht attributed Lukács's significance purely to the fact that 'he writes from Moscow' and wrote of Lukács's views on the realist novel: 'such obtuseness is monumental'.[57] Erpenbeck was underestimating how much he and the other Muscovites were bending to demands for doctrinal purity and overestimating how far Brecht was responding specifically to their threats. His recent theatrical works were rather the result of longer-term adjustments, which he had undertaken in response to the exile situation, the establishment of the Popular Front and the definition of his position vis-à-vis Stanislavsky. As we shall see, Brecht's problems with his own side prompted further adjustments which hardly signalled a rapprochement with the Muscovites, whom he took to calling 'Murxists', 'Murks' in German meaning a botch. Most importantly, Brecht continued along the path of literary and theatrical innovation which had defined his life's work.

In his letter to Erpenbeck of 2 May Brecht rejected the proofs for the latest issue of *Das Wort*, containing Kurella's concluding comments in the Expressionism Debate. Brecht wrote: 'Your position, that of Ziegler and of Lukács, is absolutely not that of the editors'.[58] Kurella was delighted to receive Brecht's protest, exclaiming to Erpenbeck: 'Now the cat's sticking his head out of the bag'.[59] That this was a co-ordinated political campaign against Brecht, Eisler and their friends emerges clearly when Kurella adds:

> I'll give a copy of the letter to Walter and will also speak with him and see how we should react. The crux of the matter is: at any rate he is now so 'stimulated' that he will write for sure. And that is a gain however you look at it. How nicely the links we have long suspected in that theatre wing are revealing themselves. Of course the Bloch-Eisler campaign (which is what it was, after all) did not spring from their empty bellies.

· 'The Judicial Process' is a scene from *Fear and Misery of the Third Reich*.

Walter is Walter Ulbricht, the most powerful KPD politician in Moscow and in post-war East Germany.

In his concluding essay Lukács cited Hans Jakob Christoffel von Grimmelshausen's *Simplicissimus* as a fine example of realist, plebeian literature in the German tradition, which had no need of Formalist ploys like montage: 'It can be left to the Eislers to appraise the montage value of the battered pieces of this masterwork – for a living German literature, it will continue to exist ... as a vital and typical totality in all its greatness'.[60] Brecht, of course, saw that Lukács's attack on 'the Eislers' – together with a conciliatory gesture towards Brecht that was in fact designed to drive a wedge between Brecht and Eisler – was directed equally at him. The Muscovites had been trying to engage Brecht in debate all along but, as we have seen in the exchanges with Hay, the convert to a 'more moderate' tone had been unwilling to participate in a public exchange damaging to anti-Fascists. These matters were no arcane, merely literary musings, but could, rather, assume life-and-death significance. Lukács, Kurella and Hay were all driven by the imperatives of the Great Terror, which required a doctrinal purge of those same anti-Fascists. Knowing Brecht from Berlin days, Kurella believed that he was 'so "stimulated" that he will write for sure'.

However, under the treacherous conditions of exile Brecht had been disciplining his inflammable self, adopting a strategy of covert behaviour towards his own side, thereby protecting himself from the wild unpredictability of polemical exchange. Wary of his propensity to spark controversy, in a remarkable letter to Dudow Brecht enlarged upon what he had said to Steffin in March 1937. Describing himself once more as a 'sort of powder keg, better approached with something cold rather than something warm', Brecht again asked Dudow that, if he should write about him, he should do so in terms as cool as possible.[61] Not only that, he believed that his theoretical positions, which, of course, related to his highly combustible sensibility, greatly exacerbated his propensity to spark controversy. He explained to Dudow that for this reason he had not published hundreds of pages of theoretical writings. What he had published were pure commentaries on current literary and theoretical works. Moreover, Brecht believed that if he published reasonably general theoretical works, that would hamper his practical work. As always, measuring himself against the greatest, he felt in any case that at that moment in time his theory 'lacked the practical impulse, which classical authors seek in theory: the vivid, real, palpable'. As a result, his theoretical works had something about them, which was 'without proof, dogmatic, merely interested in concepts'.

The letter to Dudow provides an illuminating commentary upon Benjamin's note of his conversation with Brecht shortly after: 'The writings of Lukács, Kurella, and others disturb Brecht. He thinks, though, that one should not oppose them on theoretical grounds'.[62] Brecht's instinct to seek further practical experience on the anti-Fascist stage with Dudow was surely correct. His instinct, too, was to employ cunning in evading the trap set by his opponents from his own side. However, just as there was a price to pay for his silence about the Great Terror, so too would Brecht have to deal with the consequences of not confronting his Moscow adversaries with his general theoretical pieces. Certainly, such a confrontation would have been explosive and would have further damaged the anti-Fascist movement. However, it would have served to clarify positions at a time when the principal interest in Moscow was internal security and when a waning Soviet commitment to anti-Fascism, which was not lost on Brecht, would presently go into precipitous decline.

Brecht sent Kurella a restrained response to Lukács, 'Minor Correction'. The closest it comes to polemic is: 'In my opinion Lukács should refrain from using such a plural form as long as there is only one Eisler amongst our musicians'.[63] Lukács had used the pejorative term 'the Eislers'. However, Brecht's response was not accepted, nor did *Das Wort* publish another piece in which Brecht praised Eisler's combination of artistic mastery with popular appeal. Brecht had proposed it as the first in a series of short biographies about prominent German artists and intellectuals in exile, the intention being to demonstrate the range of realist writing by using specific examples, not general theoretical statements. Brecht actually promised Kurella a theoretical essay 'The Popular and the Realistic', but an unpublished letter to Erpenbeck of 7 September 1938 shows that Brecht then declined to send it: 'You continue to remind me about the essay on the popular. I had already written it, but now I cannot rid myself of the impression that whenever I write about realism I only become entangled in squabbles – given the way my production is treated'.[64] Brecht described Lukács's publications to Erpenbeck as 'rigid, one-sided, intransigent, emphatically very formal dogmatism'. 'The Popular and the Realistic' was published only posthumously. Brecht wrote: 'Reality alters; to represent it the means of representation must alter too', before countering Lukács's view that Balzac's work was a model for the contemporary novel: 'The criteria for the popular and the realistic need to be chosen not only with great care but also with an open mind. They must not be deduced from existing realist works and existing popular works, as is often the case. Such an approach would lead to purely formalistic criteria'.[65]

It was an 'inflammatory' Brecht who, in three letters to his publisher Wieland Herzfelde in Prague from mid-March, 31 May and 7 June 1938, formulated his alternative strategy to a damaging confrontation with the camarilla on theoretical grounds. Highly agitated, Brecht spelt out to Herzfelde, with the hyperbolic bluster of Bonapartist interventionism, the immense importance he attached to the immediate publication of his latest work, which would demonstrate his literary pre-eminence amongst anti-Fascists:

> By intervening in debate, you can now procure for me the decisive position in exile literature, which I haven't enjoyed up to now. And simultaneously you can make the publishing house the dominant one at a time of the greatest difficulties. [...] In this way, we shall, for example, practically decide the whole Formalism dispute, which will otherwise cripple and sideline twenty years of work. My most recent works are the first non-controversial ones whatsoever! That view is held by colleagues (from Toller, Regler, Erpenbeck, indeed even Lukács to Feuchtwanger and Döblin) as well as our friends.[66]

Brecht saw correctly at this terrifying juncture in the literary politics of the German Left that if he did not recant, the Muscovites would stop at nothing to expose and destroy the heretic they had identified years before in Berlin. He would be excluded from the Comintern-led anti-Fascism and branded a Trotskyist like his murdered friends. Brecht's unbridled ego rose to the challenge, as he spurred himself on with the hyperbole. Posterity's judgement would be that it was not misplaced. In a display of his literary greatness he would sweep aside all opposition and 'practically decide the whole Formalism dispute, which will otherwise cripple and sideline twenty years of work'. Brecht would use this latter phrase several times to indicate that his whole literary career was at stake. We shall see him reflecting on his work of those twenty years again and again. To highlight the critical moment, Brecht proposed to Herzfelde that the publication be called *1938*.

What were the recent, 'non-controversial' works with which Brecht, in demonstrating his literary pre-eminence, could also show that he was no longer the deviant sectarian that Erpenbeck, Lukács and others took him to be? Brecht urged Herzfelde to proceed with the immediate publication – as an advance publication from volumes three and four of his *Collected Works* – of a new drama *Fear and Misery of the Third Reich*, his *Poems from Exile* (which he later named *Svendborg Poems*) and, perhaps, three essays. By three essays he did not mean theoretical responses in the Expressionism Debate, rather, as he explained to Herzfelde in March, 'Five Difficulties in Writing the Truth' and his two addresses to the writers' congresses for the defence of culture.[67] Brecht intended to present his anti-Fascist literary practice as the embodiment of the Comintern 'Trojan Horse' strategy. As we shall see, he would do that and much more besides as he proceeded with his great exile works. Brecht also adopted other literary practices strikingly different from the prescriptions of the camarilla. He composed a number of brilliantly irreverent 'Studies', critical re-readings of German classics in sonnet form, and with Steffin produced German translations of six Chinese poems by Po Chu-i from Arthur Waley's English translation from the Chinese.[68] Like the Taoist Lao-tsû, Po Chu-i, who twice went into exile, considers appropriate forms of social behaviour, combining observation and reflection with a sharp eye for social injustice and paradox.

In May volumes one and two of Brecht's *Collected Works* in German appeared with Herzfelde's Malik, incorporating all the dramas since *Man Equals Man*. Ernst Bloch's review in *Die Neue Weltbühne* with its pointed title 'A Leninist of the Stage' led the praise for Brecht's great dramatic achievement. Volume three would comprise the early plays, together with *Fear and Misery of the Third Reich*, while volume four would contain Brecht's collected poems, from *Domestic Breviary* to the most recent, *Svendborg Poems*. In Prague Herzfelde accommodated Brecht's insistence on the advance publication. However, Herzfelde could only move as quickly as the publishing process permitted. Events of world-historical import were unfolding around him, which the British Prime Minister Neville Chamberlain shamefully described as a 'quarrel in a far-away country between people of whom we know nothing'.

Fear and Misery of the Third Reich

'Probably the most representative thing that I can publish since we have been outside Germany', Brecht commented to Herzfelde about his new play *Fear and Misery of the Third Reich*.[69] Brecht was investing heavily in the prospects for his latest anti-Fascist

satire, stressing to his publisher that it 'must for political reasons come out this year'.
Brecht toyed with a number of titles, among them *The Spiritual Upsurge of the German
People under the Nazi Regime* and *Germany: A Fairy Tale of Horrors*, alluding to that
earlier exile Heinrich Heine's *Germany: A Wintry Fairy Tale*. Brecht described the
project to Dudow, who had encouraged Brecht to write it for his theatre, as 'a series
of short plays (10 minutes)' rather than as a single play, and to Piscator as 'short and
very short plays that I've grouped together under the title *Fear and Misery of the Third
Reich*'.[70] Continuing the direct engagement with Fascism in *Señora Carrar's Rifles*, it
was precisely the sort of realistic depiction of everyday life in Nazi Germany which
he had discussed with Béla Kun. The montage technique of short tableaux meant
that directors could select scenes for production as circumstances required. Brecht
worked with Steffin, whose parents, visiting from Berlin, praised the authenticity of
the material.

Brecht's own high estimation of *Fear and Misery* is shared by John and Ann White,
who describe the play as 'Brecht's most impressive anti-Fascist work'.[71] However, the
difficult production history of a variable text has hampered that recognition, and other
plays have eclipsed it. Its short tableaux showing the wretched existence of a terrorised
population are a devastating indictment of the Nazi dictatorship. As the Whites show,
the play 'occupies a unique position among Brecht's anti-Fascist works by virtue of its
ingenious combination of documented source-material, a series of fictive, yet plausibly
realistic, incidents, and a framework designed to deploy both Epic and Aristotelian
elements'.[72] For his depiction of the daily social reality of the Third Reich, Brecht drew
upon the newspaper archive of life in Nazi Germany which he had been compiling
with Steffin. The SPD's regular *Report from Germany*, which had featured the impact of
the German Freedom Station, was another important source. In the later *Messingkauf
Dialogues* Brecht described the scenes as follows:

> You saw people of pretty well all classes, and how they resisted or knuckled under.
> You saw the fear of the oppressed and the fear of the oppressors. It was like a
> great collection of gestures, observed with artistry: the quarry looking back over
> his shoulder (and the pursuer's look too); the sudden silences; the hand that flies
> to one's own mouth when one is about to say too much, and the hand that falls
> on the wanted man's shoulder; the extorted lie, the whispered truth, the mutual
> distrust of lovers.[73]

Like other works from the time such as his 'Speech on the Power of Resistance of
Reason' the play is informed by a progressive view that discontent with the regime
would lead to resistance and to its overthrow as the German people overcame the
fear which Nazi terror had instilled. Hence, alongside the depiction of conformity the
scenes reveal signs of opposition, many of them covert, in isolated acts, ranging from
insubordination and dissent to resistance. Opposition to the regime, would, of course,
never acquire the dynamic of mass resistance which Brecht and others hoped for.

Brecht told Dudow proudly: 'Now that the thing is finished, it's really representative of exile literature. Technically interesting as well'.[74] He published seven
scenes in *Das Wort*, beginning with 'The Spy' in March 1937. In the closing essay
in the Expressionism Debate, Lukács's praised 'The Spy', suggesting that Brecht had

abandoned Epic Theatre for a form of realism, if not directly Socialist Realism. Brecht observed scornfully that Lukács was treating him like a sinner returning to the bosom of the Salvation Army. As usual, Lukács's judgement was as much a threat as praise: indeed, he later 'corrected' it.[75] Lukács had overlooked the fact that, as Brecht put it triumphantly, the play was a montage of scenes in a 'table of gestures', rather like the fairground storyboards depicting grim events, to which the barkers pointed with their sticks: 'the gesture of keeping your mouth shut, the gesture of looking about you, the gesture of sudden fear etc. The pattern of gestures in a dictatorship. Now Epic Theatre can show that both "intérieurs" and almost naturalistic elements are within its range.'[76] Brecht's mastery of dramatic technique permitted that opening to a greater range of styles in the exploration of elements of social behaviour than had been possible in a framework emphasising didacticism. As the Whites show, the multiple ironies in the citizens' covert behaviour could be rendered most tellingly by a subtly understated A-effect, in which, for example, hints of dissent are embedded in everyday behaviour.

Brecht told Piscator, who in the spring of 1938 was about to leave Paris to set up a drama workshop in New York, that it might be just the thing for an American audience: 'Everybody is wondering how long a war Hitler could fight. And the so-called democracies are very much interested in knowing how the Nazi dictatorship affects the various social groupings'.[77] Brecht suggested that a production might draw on the style of his old favourite, Goya's *Disasters of War*. However, Piscator did not pursue the project and Brecht looked to Dudow in Paris, countering Dudow's concern that the new play might simply be too depressing: 'It shows how fragile the Third Reich is in all its parts and aspects, that it is held together by violence alone. [...] On the whole I don't think the production will depress people. No more, actually less, than a Brueghel painting or a set of Daumier drawings'.[78] The analogy with painting, of course, stressed the visual quality of his 'table of gestures'. Dudow's decision to stage the play in the spring initially alarmed Brecht, who was writing further scenes, making twenty-five in all. He added 'Plebiscite' after the Nazi occupation of Austria in March 1938, following which more than 99 per cent of votes cast supported Hitler's 're-unification' of Austria with Germany. There was a strong family interest in this particular matter: Weigel tried to persuade her father to join them in Denmark from Vienna. He declined the offer and Nazis beat him in the street before in 1941 he was deported to the Lodz ghetto.

In May Weigel went to Paris for rehearsals. Benjamin greeted her with carnations. Telling Brecht 'I would need you in all circumstances, for all things and at all times', Weigel complained to Brecht about the quality of her fellow actors and about Dudow's directing, particularly his refusal to allow Benjamin and Piscator to attend rehearsals.[79] Eight scenes were selected for the premiere, which took place at the Salle d'Iéna under the title *99%. Scenes from the Third Reich*. Paul Dessau wrote the score, initiating another of Brecht's distinguished musical-dramatic partnerships. Weigel earned great praise for her performance in three roles, particularly that of the Jewish wife Judith Keith, who resolves to leave her 'Aryan' husband and go into exile, ostensibly in order not to affect his career as a doctor but actually in the knowledge that he will disown her. A matter-of-factly determined Judith Keith first makes phone calls to friends, explaining that she is 'going away for a bit', then rehearses various versions of what she might say to her husband, before their short, final exchange when he bluntly states that things have to be this way. It is spring but she is taking her fur coat, and the scene concludes with his pathetic, hypocritical words: 'After all it's only for two or three weeks'.[80] As the Whites show, 'almost everything that is said or done in the final minutes of this scene has in some way been prepared – and estranged in one sense or another – by the wife's dummy runs. For this reason the audience is able to tap into the complex subtext of the short, concluding dialogue with a heightened – and extremely partisan – awareness'.[81] In this scene and in others the 'more moderate' Brecht eschews ostentatious anti-illusionist devices and deploys 'covert alienation devices' to devastating effect. In his review for *Die Neue Weltbühne* Benjamin explained how each scene exposed the great lie which was the Nazi regime's reign of terror. Greatly pleased, Brecht later wrote:

> What was so unusual was that the players never performed these ghastly episodes in such a way that the spectators were tempted to call out 'Stop'. The spectators didn't seem in any way to share the horror of those on the stage, and as a result there was repeatedly laughter among the audience without doing any damage to the profoundly serious character of the performance. For this laughter seemed to apply to the stupidity that found itself having to make use of force, and to the helplessness that took the shape of brutality. Bullies were seen as men tripping over, criminals as men who have made a mistake or allowed themselves to be taken in. The spectators' laughter was finely graduated.[82]

The play was a triumph for Epic Theatre, subtly enriched by the A-effect and more conventional 'Aristotelian' elements, which encouraged the audience's analytical appreciation.

Fear and Misery of the Third Reich is the first of Brecht's brilliant dramas of survival in dark times from the final years of Brecht's Scandinavian exile, in which, as he put it in 1941, the 'plays tend to fly apart like constellations in the new physics, as though here too some kind of dramaturgical core had exploded'.[83] The Brechtian planetarium of explosive dramatic energy was harnessed to stunning effect in a magnificent riposte to his Muscovite opponents of aesthetic and intellectual innovation. Imbued with a fresh sense of urgency, he observed: 'The overall production plan is, however, constantly getting broader. And single works only have a chance within such a plan. [...] Thirty years would not be too much for what has to be done. For there is also a lot of topical stuff to do'.[84] Delighted by his collaboration with Dudow, Brecht ridiculed exile theatre in the Muscovite seat of power: 'So the proletarian theatre in exile is keeping the theatre alive, while in Moscow Maxim Vallentin, the one-time director of a Berlin agitprop group, has gone over to bourgeois theatre and announced that in art an appeal has to be made to the emotions, which can only mean that reason has to be switched off'. Brecht was outflanking his opponents, embedding the exploration of emotion and interior spaces within Epic Theatre's framework of intellectual reflection and encouragement to anti-Fascist action.

Part Four

Chastened Survivor

Survival in an Age of Reaction 1938–9

A last summer with Benjamin

In late June 1938 Benjamin joined Brecht at Skovsbostrand, staying until mid-October. Benjamin again kept a diary of their exchanges. He was working on 'Commentary on Poems by Brecht' and 'Paris of the Second Empire in Baudelaire'. Brecht was scathing about Baudelaire and was struggling with *The Business Affairs of Mr Julius Caesar*. He had embarked on the project in 1937, first as a play about the dictator, then as a novel. He told Korsch that he intended to present Caesar 'hovering above classes', while doing the business of a privileged class, and to show that wars were undertaken ultimately to exploit one's own people.[1] However, the attempts of Caesar, the imperialist businessman, to stay ahead of his creditors ultimately prove vain. Brecht did extensive work on his novel, developing a complex narrative but it remained incomplete. Benjamin was pre-occupied by his own projects and explained to Gretel Adorno: 'I have not even read his new, half-finished novel yet. Naturally, I have neither the time nor the opportunity to get involved in something alien to my own work'.[2]

During Benjamin's stay Brecht began to keep his journal on a regular basis. When he read it through in 1942 he noted: 'Naturally it is quite distorted, for fear of unwelcome readers, and I will have difficulty following its guidelines one day. It stays within certain bounds'.[3] Brecht, of course, lived with the very real fear that his writings might be confiscated and used against him, particularly that any criticism of the USSR could see him branded a Trotskyist. He reflected, too, that the journal contained 'so little that is personal' and accounted for that in part because he himself was 'not very interested in personal matters (and don't really have at my disposal a satisfactory mode of presenting them)'. Since the late1920s he had developed a literary procedure which relegated to the margin those personal and domestic issues which are so prominent in his early writing. The journal must be read with care, in conjunction with other material. For the summer of 1938, Benjamin's diary is therefore a vital source.

Standing in the garden overlooking the Svendborg Sound with Benjamin one July evening, Brecht reflected on how the Nazis had 'proletarianized' him: 'Not only have they robbed me of my house, my fishpond, and my car, but they've also stolen my stage and my audience'.[4] He continued: 'I cannot acknowledge that Shakespeare was fundamentally a greater talent. But he could no more have written merely to stockpile than I can'. Characteristically, Brecht spurred himself on by pitting himself against the greatest. He talked to Benjamin with disarming candour about his extreme personality, measuring himself against the most extreme: 'I know that when people talk about me they'll say: "He was a maniac". If accounts of these times are handed down, an understanding of my mania will be handed down as well. The times will be the backdrop for my mania. But what I actually want is for them to say: "He was a *middling* sort of maniac".'[5] Brecht recognised a real maniac when he saw one.

When Benjamin suggested that Brecht should exclude his children's verses from his *Svendborg Poems* because they would disrupt the contrast between the private and the public, Brecht strongly disagreed: children were the hope for a different future, especially at the onset of an age dominated by Fascism, in which life would continue in an 'epoch without history'. He saw his role as keeping alive the idea of change in history. Hearing Brecht speak, Benjamin experienced something quite unprecedented: 'I felt moved by a power that was equal to that of Fascism – one that is no less deeply rooted in the depths of history than Fascism's power'. Brecht now spoke 'with rare forcefulness': 'It is vital that nothing be overlooked. They don't think small. They plan thirty thousand years ahead. Horrendous things. Horrendous crimes. They will stop at nothing. They will attack anything. Every cell convulses under their blows'. Brecht understood the genocidal mania which gripped the Nazis, which entailed destruction of the foetus: 'They are planning immense devastation'.

Throughout the 1930s, that age of deepening reaction and extreme violence, Brecht and Benjamin derived great strength from their friendship. As Wizisla observes, these two hugely gifted and remarkably driven individuals 'handled differences impressively; each knew the arguments of the other, and there was nothing that they had to prove to each other': 'The closeness, indeed the affection that had grown between Benjamin and Brecht was expressed in a great measure of agreement on questions concerning work, and in the remarkable frankness with which judgements were pronounced whose transmission to the "outside world" was fraught with the utmost danger'.[6] Brecht read to Benjamin some of his unpublished responses to Lukács, which Benjamin termed 'disguised yet vehement attacks'.[7] And Brecht showed Benjamin Kurella's vicious attack in *Internationale Literatur*, in which Kurella associated Benjamin with the Nazi Heidegger. Benjamin commented to Gretel Adorno: 'This publication is quite wretched'. Echoing his stark comment to Herzfelde, Brecht described the Muscovite line to Benjamin as a 'catastrophe for everything we've committed ourselves to for 20 years'.

When conversation turned to the fate of Moscow friends, Benjamin noted: 'I receive very sceptical replies every time I touch on the conditions in Russia. When, the other day, I asked if Ottwalt was still doing time, the answer was: "If he can still do anything, he is". Yesterday Steffin said that Tretiakov was probably no longer alive'.[8] Béla Kun of the Comintern, whom Brecht described as his 'greatest admirer in Russia', would also soon be killed. In the 1990s, it emerged that Stalin had denounced Kun to Georgi Dimitrov: 'Kun has acted with the Trotskyites against the Party. In all likelihood he is also mixed up in espionage'.[9] Like his secretary Kurella, Dimitrov survived by sacrificing others. Brecht told Benjamin that while Lukács was held in high esteem in Moscow, he himself had 'no friends there at all': 'And the Muscovites themselves don't have any either – like the dead'.[10] In his comments on the Soviet political economy gearing up for war, Brecht echoed Trotsky's criticisms of Stalin's strategy, which had eschewed world revolution, while his rule had reverted to a grotesque form of monarchy:

> The socialist economy doesn't need war, and that's why it can't stand war. The 'love of peace' felt by the 'Russian people' expresses this, and only this. There can be no socialist economy in any single country. The Russian proletariat was, by necessity, dealt a severe setback by rearmament – and, what's more, was thrown back to long-superseded stages of historical development. Monarchy, among others. In Russia personal authority reigns supreme. Obviously, only idiots could deny this.

For Brecht, the partisan supporter, not only had the USSR lost the revolutionary dynamic of a new society marching towards Communism but it had also assumed a reactionary form. Brecht had only sarcasm for Marx's prophecy that the state would wither away: ' "The state must vanish." Who says this? The state'. Benjamin added: 'Brecht, looking cunning and shifty, steps in front of the armchair I'm sitting in and, pretending to be "the state", says, with a sideways leer at an imaginary client: "I know – I'm *supposed to* vanish" '. In a separate note Brecht reflected on his own relationship with the state: 'I, for example, want to live with little politics. In other words, I don't want to be a political subject. But that's not supposed to mean that I want to be the object of a lot of politics. [...] With this stage of affairs it is quite likely that I must spend my whole life in political activity and that I will even lose it in the process'.[11] When Benjamin suggested of Lukács, Kurella et al., 'One can't form a state with these people', Brecht replied: 'Or one could form *merely* a state, but no community. They are, after all, enemies of production. They're afraid of production. You can't trust it. It's unpredictable. You never know what will come out of it. And they themselves do not want to produce. They want to play apparatchik and control others. Each of their reviews contains a threat'.

Brecht showed Benjamin his new 'Stalin poem', 'The Peasant's Address to his Ox', after an Egyptian peasant song from 1400 BC. It is a Brechtian *Animal Farm*, satirising a reactionary Soviet monarchy of workers and peasants:

O ox, our godly puller of the plough
Please humour us by pulling straight, and kindly
Do not get the furrows crossed.
Lead the way, o leader, gee-up!
We stooped for days on end to harvest your fodder.
Allow yourself to try just a little, dearest provider.
While you are eating, do not fret about the furrows: eat!
For your stall, o protector of the family
We carried the tons of timber by hand. We
Sleep in the damp, you in the dry. Yesterday
You had a cough, beloved pacemaker.
We were beside ourselves. You won't
Peg out before the sowing, will you, you dog?[12]

Benjamin comments: 'At first, I didn't get it. On a second reading, when the thought of Stalin crossed my mind, I didn't dare take it seriously'. Stalin was, indeed, the ox.

The poem is an acid take on Brecht's observation: 'It's already considered an inten-
tional omission if the name Stalin doesn't appear in a poem'. Brecht told Benjamin
that he had expected his response and went on to stress 'among other things, the
positive aspects of the poem', hovering as it does between satire and affirmation: 'It
was indeed a tribute to Stalin – who in his opinion had made immense contributions'.
Brecht explained that because Stalin was not yet dead he could not offer a 'different,
more enthusiastic tribute'! Satirised as the powerful, stolid beast, Stalin is the object of
the resentful peasant's excessive dependence as he treats him like a god, in a manner
reminiscent of Brecht's early parable of the Zulu tribesman and his pig. Written from
the peasant's perspective, the poem emphasises his illusions and his role in the cult
of Stalin. What is conspicuously absent from the poem – and, we can infer, from the
Soviet Union – is the intelligence of the thinker, unlike the poem we shall encounter
shortly, 'Legend of the Origin of the *Book of Tao-tê-ching* on Lao-tsû's Road into Exile',
in which Lao-tsû alights from his ox to write his book.

In a piece for his *Book of Twists and Turns* Brecht, employing the cipher To-tsi,
considered Trotsky's writings about Stalin's rule, noting the narrow base of its support
and observing grimly: 'Twenty years after the club had assumed power the prisons
were still overflowing and there were death sentences and trials everywhere, in which
even old members of the club were implicated. Great wars with bourgeois countries
were imminent'.[13] Using the cipher of Ni-en for Stalin, Brecht wrote other pieces about
his rule. In 'Ni-en's Trials', Brecht under the guise of Me-ti insists that guilt must be
proven and that he cannot believe something that is unproven. That damages the
people. In 'Ni-en's Constitution' Me-ti says of the Soviet Union:

> The new system, the most progressive in world history, is still working very
> badly and hardly organically and needs so much effort and the use of so
> much force that the freedoms of individuals are very slight. Since the system
> is enforced by very small units of people, there is compulsion everywhere and
> no real popular rule. The lack of freedom of opinion, of freedom to form coali-
> tions, the paying of lip-service, the powers of magistrates, prove that by a long
> way all the fundamental elements of the Great Order have not been developed,
> nor are they being.

In 'Ni-en's Autocracy' Brecht contrasts Lenin, the theoretician of the revolution, with
Stalin: 'Ni-en plays the part of the emperor'. What is more: 'As the struggle intensified
the state apparatus separated from the working class and assumed a reactionary
form. Ni-en became an emperor for the peasants when he was still a secretary for the
workers. Then he became an emperor for the workers, too'. Assuming such a form, in
which the revolutionary energy of the working class is suppressed by the reactionary
force of the state bureaucracy, the USSR under Stalin's rule had become a negative
force in world politics. It was not simply the extreme reactionary power of Fascism
to which Brecht attributed the advent of 'dark times'. The Bolshevik movement had
mutated into a repressive bureaucracy, another grotesque manifestation of the Tuism,
the sale of ideas, for which Brecht satirised intellectuals. Heralding a major re-orientation in his thinking, Brecht now withdrew from the position of Leninist partisanship
which he had adopted in 1930, accepting that the completion of the revolution had

been deferred indefinitely and that in those dark times the principal issue had become survival.

As we shall see, Brecht's analysis of the East German popular uprising of 17 June 1953 would similarly identify the separation of the SED leadership and the state bureaucracy from the workers and peasants. However, he would resist the conclusion that the Marxist-Leninist state could only ever reproduce itself on the basis of a repressive bureaucracy. While Brecht saw himself as reliant upon the Red Army to end his exile, he acknowledged that there were grounds for 'justified suspicion' about Russian affairs and that 'if eventually it proved correct, one would have to fight the regime – and *publicly*, to be sure'.[14] A little later, Brecht adopted a somewhat more positive stance: 'In Russia, a dictatorship rules *over* the proletariat. So long as this dictatorship is still bringing practical benefits to the proletariat [...] we should not give up on it'. With the Soviet economy on a war footing, Brecht had no means of knowing whether such benefits were accruing. In effect, Brecht was deferring a judgement on the present state of the USSR indefinitely, just as he had come to accept the indefinite deferral of the completion of the revolution. The remaining basis for his support was the bare fact of the October Revolution, which, in his estimation, epitomised the achievements of the Russian proletariat and placed the USSR on a quite different footing from Fascist and liberal democratic states. Aided by the Hegelian dialectic, Brecht could argue that its assumption of a reactionary form was merely a temporary phenomenon, not a permanent state of affairs. Where would fresh revolutionary energy come from and with it possibly the return to Leninist partisanship? Brecht speculated on the Red Army in the coming struggle with Nazism.

Hearing Brecht's talk of a 'workers' monarchy', Benjamin 'drew an analogy between such an organism and the grotesque freaks of nature which, in the shape of horned fish or other monsters, are brought to light from out of the deep sea'.[15] Events in Moscow, not least his doctrinal struggle with the camarilla, had changed a great deal for Brecht, too. He suggested to Benjamin with a serious undertone: '"We are fortunate when we hold an extreme position and a reactionary age catches up with us. We then wind up at a moderate standpoint". This was, he claimed, what had happened to him: he had become mellow'.[16] It was not only that Fascism was in the ascendant, seemingly remorselessly so. Brecht's identification of the USSR as a reactionary system in a reactionary age, relying upon coercion, not upon its founding principle of reason, was a major factor in Brecht's 'mellowing'. However, Brecht maintained his Marxist mode of analysis. His self-image as 'mellow' is both relative and of a piece with other elements of behaviour which Brecht had recently adopted, which he had captured in the image of a powder keg best kept cool. While he adopted more covert strategies in his work, it retained its explosive potential.

Benjamin remarked to Adorno that his exchanges with Brecht had been 'much less problematical than what I had been used to'.[17] When their conversation turned to the 'old topic' of logical empiricism, Benjamin was 'fairly intransigent' and the conversation threatened to take an 'unpleasant turn'. That was averted when Brecht, for the first time, acknowledged the 'superficiality of his formulations'. He did so with the rather enigmatic formulation: 'To the deepest need there corresponds a superficial approach'. Following his recognition of the grim political reality and in acknowledgement of personal failure in the struggle for survival, a transformation in Brecht's philosophical attitudes was now well under way, accompanied by a re-ordering and re-weighting of the contradictions in his patterns of behaviour.

Brecht was, of course, concerned about the reputational damage which he and Benjamin were incurring on account of the 'internal regressions' in the USSR: 'We've paid for our positions; we're covered with scars. It's only natural that we should be especially sensitive'.[18] Before he left Svendborg Benjamin attempted to break down the mistrust towards Brecht amongst the Marxists of the Institute for Social Research, the Frankfurt School, now at the New York Institute for Social Research. In his search for common ground, Benjamin took great trouble to describe both Brecht's critique of and his abiding support for the Soviet Union, which Benjamin himself shared, and repeated for Gretel Adorno Brecht's fears about the attacks of Lukács et al.: 'As for Brecht, he is trying his best to make sense of what is behind Russian cultural politics by speculating on what the politics of nationality in Russia requires. But this obviously does not prevent him from recognising that the theoretical line being taken is catastrophic for everything we have championed for twenty years'.[19] When Horkheimer asked about Brecht's political position, Benjamin responded: 'It was clear to me that the difficulties encountered by our side in any debate with the Soviet Union would be particularly great for Brecht, whose audience included parts of the Moscow working class'. Benjamin explained to Horkheimer that he and Brecht still regarded the Soviet Union as a 'power whose foreign policy was not determined by imperialistic interests, and therefore as an anti-imperialistic one':

> That we still do this, at any rate at present, and that therefore, if even with the most weighty reservations, we still see the Soviet Union as an agent of our interests in a future war as well as in the delaying of this one, could also accord with your way of thinking. That this agent is the most costly imaginable, since we have to repay it with sacrifices which quite particularly diminish our own obvious interests as producers, is something which it would not enter Brecht's head to dispute, since he realises that the present Soviet regime is a personal one with all its terrors.[20]

Benjamin's efforts on Brecht's behalf came to nothing. Gershom Scholem told Benjamin that Horkheimer and the others were all 'keen and very outspoken anti-Stalinists', among whom there was 'not a good word to be heard' about Brecht.[21] Indeed, they viewed Brecht as a 'petit-bourgeois *poseur* and an apologist for Stalin'.[22] Writing to a sceptical Adorno, Benjamin ascribed Brecht's intellectual isolation principally to his loyalty to the Soviet Union: 'Given the conditions under which he currently lives, he will be challenged, head-on so to speak, by this isolation during a Svendborg winter'.[23] That winter Brecht would respond with some of his greatest writing.

The perils of the autumn

Brecht made representations about his treatment in Moscow, turning first to Bredel as a fellow editor of *Das Wort* and then to Becher as editor of *Internationale Literatur*.

Brecht was quite frank to Bredel, who had personal experience of the vicious Lukács from the days of *Die Linkskurve*:

> Unfortunately my collaboration on *Das Wort* is becoming increasingly problematic. More and more it seems to be taking a peculiar line, turning into the organ of a strange alliance dominated by a small clique, apparently led by Lukács and Hay and committed to a very definite ideal of literary form, which leads them to combat everything that doesn't fit in with this formal ideal derived from the bourgeois novelists of the past century.[24]

Brecht told Bredel of his great concern that Lukács, in his recent essay in *Internationale Literatur* 'Marx and the Problem of Ideological Decline', 'actually strikes out at me, lumping me together with bourgeois decadence, and this at a time when God knows that questions of form should be the least of our worries'. Lukács had accused Brecht of 'abstraction' in class analysis in the manner of writers who capitulated in the face of the capitalist world! Brecht complained to Bredel that Erpenbeck occasionally invited him to participate in debates which he found 'extremely harmful and confusing', not least because they invariably ended with 'good old Lukács's opinion being vaunted (at least by Lukács himself) as the one and only Marxist view'. Brecht warned Bredel that his treatment by *Das Wort* 'can't go on much longer'.

Brecht had had enough of Becher's *Internationale Literatur*. He had sent Becher 'Legend of the Origin of the *Book of Tao-tê-ching* on Lao-tsû's Road into Exile', his homage to Taoist philosophy, with which, we may recall, he had first recognised his close affinity some twenty years earlier. Brecht protested about Lukács placing him 'in the drawer of bourgeois decadence' and declared that he had no desire to engage in such exchanges, especially with a war threatening.[25] He declined to collaborate with the journal until a more serious and more productive approach to literature had replaced this 'criticising of Formalism'. Citing the extraordinarily narrow definition of the term Socialist Realism in Becher's journal, Brecht asked him not to publish his poem. Becher published it anyway in January 1939.

Did Becher understand it? In this great poem Brecht reflected upon his predicament in the light of the Taoist doctrine of Wu Wei with its paradox of non-action and action. The centrepiece of the poem is the famous exchange between the customs man and the boy concerning the elderly philosopher Lao-tsû's teachings. In response to the custom man's question: 'How did he make out, pray?', the boy, paraphrasing the *Book of Tao-tê-ching*, replies: 'He learnt how quite soft water, by attrition / Over the years will grind strong rocks away. / In other words, that hardness must lose the day'.[26] Bidden by the customs man, Lao-tsû alights from the ox which is carrying him into exile and composes the eighty-one sayings in the *Book of Tao-tê-ching*, which, as Antony Tatlow writes, 'teaches survival in a dangerous age, triumphant subservience'.[27] In the dark times of the late 1930s, Brecht's Leninist partisanship gives way to a Taoist attitude of survival through submission to the endless flux of things, the means by which the weak may evade the plans of the strong and, in the longer term, prevail by aligning themselves with the 'quite soft water'. This lends them the confidence to adopt a stance of composure in the face of adversity and profound uncertainty, which closely resembles the ataraxia propounded by the Greek sceptics, by the Epicurean Lucretius and later by Montaigne, then Hegel. Brecht now cultivated this stance, taught by these great writers. The poem initiates a strand of Taoist survivalist thinking in Brecht's work, employed partly heuristically, partly confessionally, partly in an exculpatory way and partly critically towards the Taoist paradox itself, which we can trace through his major compositions of the late 1930s and early 1940s. Shortly after, 'Legend of the Origin of the *Book of Tao-tê-ching* on Lao-tsû's Road into Exile' appeared in the Swiss anti-Fascist newspaper *Schweizer Zeitung am Sonntag*, together with a commentary by Benjamin. Benjamin and Heinrich Blücher later distributed the poem in the French internment camps for German émigrés in France, where it had a remarkable, galvanising effect upon its anti-Fascist readers.

Like Lao-tsû, in the face of severe adversity Brecht remained on the path to greatness. However, the congruence between his trajectory as a revolutionary artist and the Soviet Union as the embodiment of the revolution was fragmenting, while Fascism was in the ascendant. The next crisis to be triggered by Hitler's territorial claims was imminent in the Sudetenland, which had been assigned to Czechoslovakia in the Treaty of Versailles. Hitler provoked border incidents and sought the assent of the western powers to his demands. After Britain's Prime Minister Neville Chamberlain had met with Hitler at Bad Godesberg, the appeaser Chamberlain accepted the Nazi position. Brecht sat over the radio with another visitor Fritz Sternberg as Hitler threatened war if other western leaders did not join negotiations. On 20 September Brecht sent the Czech President Edvard Beneš a telegram: 'Fight and those who are vacillating will close ranks with you'.[28] However, France's Edouard Daladier capitulated to Hitler's demands in Munich. Brecht commented: 'Very worth noting for *Caesar* the French ruling class's about-turn in the face of Hitler's threat of war, the breach of treaty Czechoslovakia wiped off the map, France's position as a great power destroyed. They only wage wars of conquest, they only defend their own conquests. At any time they will sacrifice political power for business reasons'.[29] The path was open for Hitler to occupy the Sudetenland in early October. Brecht, the student of military strategy, correctly observed that the Sudetenland was a springboard for Hitler's 'wars of conquest' in the East. He had no doubt that the destruction of the USSR was Hitler's final target. However, Brecht had studied Napoleon's campaigns and was in no doubt that Hitler would fail and would do so at horrific cost.

Preparations for the advance publication of *Fear and Misery of the Third Reich*, *Svendborg Poems* and the three essays, as well as of the two final volumes of the *Collected Works*, were nearing completion in a by now hopelessly compromised Prague. Playing on the German saying from the First World War, 'May God punish England', Brecht commented to Martin Andersen Nexø: 'My publisher Herzfelde is in Czechoslovakia, which England doesn't want to defend, even though he is bringing out an edition of my collected plays. God is punishing him'.[30] With the Nazi occupation of Prague imminent, in November Herzfelde fled to Geneva and from there to London. The window of opportunity which Brecht had seen to settle the Expressionism Debate through a demonstration of his peerless anti-Fascist literary credentials had slammed shut. The grim events which engulfed the publisher ruled out productions of *Fear and Misery of the Third Reich* across virtually the whole European continent. Brecht was gripped by the fear that his own reputational and, indeed, physical destruction was imminent.

Svendborg Poems: 'Words startled into flight'[31]

Herzfelde hoped to recover material he had abandoned in Prague, among other things proofs of Brecht's poems. However, they were destroyed in January 1939, in advance of the German occupation of Czechoslovakia. Malik's volumes three and four of Brecht's *Collected Works* were lost forever. Anxious to save *Svendborg Poems* from that fate, Brecht urged Berlau to 'learn his poems by heart'.[32] Berlau did more than that. Using a copy of the Prague proofs still in Svendborg and drawing on Steffin's editorial expertise, Berlau organised and financed their publication in Copenhagen. In June 1939 a thousand copies of *Svendborg Poems* would appear with the Universal printing press under the auspices of the American Guild for Cultural Freedom and the Diderot Society. The collection bore London rather than Copenhagen as its place of publication. Brecht signed a hundred copies which were sold for ten kroner each rather than the usual three. Some went to friends. Thanking Brecht for the poems, Feuchtwanger told him in his usual, forthright manner that he had read them several times: 'Some of them are glorious and will certainly endure, some others are rather too cheap and I would not have collected them'.[33]

As Ronald Speirs writes, there is an alternation through much of the collection between the depiction of the sheer wretchedness of this reactionary age and consideration of how resistance, underpinned by reason and class solidarity, can bring about change through a 'process of teaching and learning'.[34] For example, the fourth section includes a number of poems for Steffin, reflecting upon the social origins of illnesses like hers in poverty and poor housing, highlighting the need for radical social change. The children's poems in section two, which Benjamin feared could disturb the contrast between the private and the public, include 'The Tailor of Ulm (Ulm 1592)'. The tailor claims to the bishop that he can fly but plunges to his death from the church roof. The poem ends with the invitation to readers to consider the bishop's re-affirmation of the Church's teaching that man must not presume: 'Let the church bells ring / It was nothing but a lie / A man is not a bird / No man will ever fly'.[35] In Brecht's age of aviation, children might recognise the cleric's absurd dogma and work towards a fresh age of reason.

The collection exemplifies what Brecht stresses elsewhere in his exile poetry: that it was simply impossible for him to write verse in the traditional manner. In 'Solely Because of the Increasing Disorder' he describes his self-imposed restrictions, writing that 'some of us' had decided, 'To speak in future only about the disorder / And so become one-sided, reduced, enmeshed in the business / Of politics and the dry, indecorous vocabulary / Of dialectical economics'.[36] In the anti-Fascist struggle, Brecht and like-minded men had resolved, 'To speak no more of cities by the sea, snow on roofs, women / The smell of ripe apples in cellars, the senses of the flesh, all / That makes a man round and human'. Political reality had determined that in the quarrel between didacticism and artistry the former had to be privileged to the detriment of the latter and that mankind could no longer experience a wholeness deemed essential for proper human life. Similarly, 'Bad Time for Poetry', one of Brecht's most celebrated poems, concludes:

In my poetry a rhyme
Would seem to me almost insolent.

Inside me contend
Delight at the apple tree in blossom
And horror at the house-painter's speeches.
But only the second
Drives me to my desk.[37]

For Brecht, the articulation of the truth to challenge the 'house-painter' Hitler required that poems assume the character of documents for the reader's use. The isolated émigré eschewed the complexity of refined metaphorical expression that had become synonymous with a modern sensibility. He combined a subjective perspective with comment upon political events in a strikingly lapidary style, conveying complex situations in language of great simplicity. Brecht's language matched his view of a humanity reduced by the politics of the age. Modulating his production between ballads and epigrams, Brecht re-fashioned the idiom of German poetry.

Brecht viewed his new poetry not only in the light of Hitler's speeches but also of Lukács's vicious charge of bourgeois decadence. This prompted Brecht to survey his poetry over twenty years and to reflect on similarities and differences between *Svendborg Poems* and *Domestic Breviary*. He wrote that *Domestic Breviary* was 'undoubtedly branded with the decadence of the bourgeois class'.[38] He viewed *Svendborg Poems* dialectically as 'both a withdrawal and an advance':

> From the bourgeois point of view there has been a staggering impoverishment. Isn't it all a great deal more one-sided, less 'organic', cooler, more 'self-conscious' (in a bad sense)? Let's hope my comrades-in-arms will not let that go by default. They will say the *Svendborg Poems* are less decadent than *Domestic Breviary*. However I think it is important that they should realise what the advance, such as it is, has cost. Capitalism has forced us to take up arms. It has laid waste our surroundings. I no longer go off to 'commune with nature in the woods', but accompanied by two policemen.

Albeit it in somewhat attenuated form, the charge of decadence issued by those 'comrades-in-arms' remained. Brecht was aware that, viewed strictly on the Moscow camarilla's own very narrow terms, the charge contained some truth, just as there was more than a grain of truth in pointing to Brecht's great pre-occupation with form. For all that 'staggering impoverishment', traces of so-called bourgeois individualism could, in fact, still – and resurgently – be detected in Brecht's poetry. Brecht was only too aware that in the policing of culture, the NKVD and the Gestapo were pursuing a similar brief to eradicate decadence.

In fact, everywhere Brecht went from 1939 until the end of his life, be it the Communist world or the USA, surveillance of this bourgeois exponent of political art was the norm. Finding ways to deal with the associated anxieties and threats became essential to his survival. In his plight as a stateless and isolated intellectual, Brecht saw himself doubly assailed by forces which he ascribed to those 'dark times', as he put it in the central motif of *Svendborg Poems*. Among the three mottos in the collection are the following defiant lines: 'In the dark times / Will there also be singing? Yes, there will also be singing / About the dark times'.[39] That assertion of life through song was vital. He evaluated the forces assailing him quite differently, of course. Nonetheless, the realisation that he was under mortal threat from his own as well as from the Fascist side had profound consequences. While Brecht's anti-Fascist message is maintained with an exemplary clarity and suggestive force, the other profound dangers associated with the dark times are conveyed in conspiratorially allusive imagery. Teasing out the anxious Brecht's covert messages is not always easy.

We have already examined a good number of the anti-Fascist verses in *Svendborg Poems*, principally those from 'German War Primer' and 'German Satires'. These verses are in the first and fifth sections of *Svendborg Poems*, which follows the structure of *Domestic Breviary* in its division into six sections. Brecht's treatment of the Soviet Union is initiated by 'The Carpet Weavers of Kuyan-Bulak Honour Lenin'. The carpet weavers' decision to honour Lenin with their practical work and a wall plaque rather than a monument sets the tone. The poems which celebrate the October Revolution and subsequent achievements like the Moscow metro consistently foreground the role of the workers, adopting the same proletarian perspective as 'Questions from a Worker Who Reads' and withholding the officially required praise of Stalin. The 'deviationist' Brecht knew the dangers of not participating in the cult of leadership. While Brecht's Soviet poems affirm his bedrock Marxist position that the Revolution distinguishes the USSR from other states, he treats his distance from the USSR under Stalin covertly in the fourth section in 'The Farmer and his Ox'.

The corollary of Brecht's isolation from the USSR and his persecution by his own country is the re-emergence in *Svendborg Poems* of an existential tone of anxiety and fear of death, which is so prominent in *Domestic Breviary*. Assailed from two sides, Brecht is beset by doubt, impotence and failure, and struggles to recover his composure.[40] As so often, Brecht's own problems as an artist and intellectual were not those of the proletariat. They were no less real for that. In *Domestic Breviary* the existential tone of the young poet had been laced with sarcasm and an amoral irony, at times displaying a cruel disregard for human life. The sarcasm and amoral irony vanish in the chill recognition of human life threatened in the *Svendborg Poems* where we witness the meditations of an older voice chastened, if not yet crushed, by experience, particularly in the third and sixth sections.

The motto opening section six reads: 'You who sit in the prow of the boat / See the leak at the bottom end / Take care not to avert your gaze / For you are not out of the eye of death'.[41] Constant vigilance in the face of dire threats is required in the struggle for survival. The third section is entitled 'Chronicles', like the section in *Domestic Breviary* which contains ballads of desperate adventurers, pirates and Wild West pioneers who perish. In *Svendborg Poems* 'Chronicles' opens with the already mentioned 'Questions from a Worker Who Reads', and the second half of the section records the achievements of the proletariat, not only Soviet workers but also US comrades in 'Coal for Mike' and in 'How the Ship "Oskawa" was Broken up by her own Crew'. The crew gradually destroy the ship in protest against poor pay as it crosses the Atlantic. Alongside these workers' tales, 'Chronicles' contains a sequence of ballads about thinkers and teachers in history and legend like Lao-tsû, their achievements and their failures, which capture elements of Brecht's own plight. As Anthony Phelan points out, 'The Shoe of Empedocles' offers a 'dangerous parallel' to Brecht's situation: 'Empedocles was a teacher, orator, scientist and supporter of popular causes, but one who nevertheless lost the favour of the people and died in exile in the Peloponnese. Brecht's exile from the full brunt of political struggle, and the accompanying possibility of *failure* as teacher or orator offering to serve a popular cause, are at issue here'.[42]

The sixth section of *Svendborg Poems* is a sustained meditation upon the poet's plight in the long present of exile. Brentano singled out 'Thoughts about the Duration of Exile' for praise, adding provocatively that he had heard that Brecht's relations with Moscow were no longer so intimate.[43] The first part of the poem rehearses a number of optimistic scenarios, unlike the second:

> Look at the nail you knocked into the wall:
> When do you think you will go back?
> Do you want to know what your heart of hearts is saying?
> Day after day you work for the liberation.
> You sit in your room, writing.
> Do you want to know what you think of your work?
> Look at the little chestnut tree in the corner of the yard –
> You carried a full can of water to it.[44]

Again, the poem records Brecht's profound fear that his life's work might be dismissed and forgotten. The poet who would speak for the oppressed reflects that he has been reduced to cultivating his own garden.

The collection ends with Brecht's most famous meditation upon exile, 'To Those Born Later'.[45] This moving work of restrained pathos is a great confession of weakness and failure, but also a plea for understanding about the predicament which the poet shared with a generation of émigrés. Originally three separate pieces now arranged in a long, triptych-like poem, which moves from the present to the past and back to the future, this wonderfully quotable narrative verse places the story of failure directly within the context of the central motif of the collection: 'Truly, I live in dark times!'. In those times, 'The man who laughs / Has simply not yet had / The terrible news'. As in 'Bad Time for Poetry', Brecht considers the austere poetic imperative of anti-Fascist resistance: 'What kind of times are they, when / Talk about trees is almost a crime / Because it implies silence about so many horrors?'. He describes the guilt associated with maintaining a precarious material existence:

> It is true I still earn my keep
> But, believe me, that is only an accident. Nothing
> I do gives me the right to eat my fill.
> By chance I've been spared. (If my luck breaks, I am lost.)

Brecht aspires to the wisdom of the 'old books' about how to lead a good life, recognising the inadequacy of his own, but also of the old wisdom itself in the 'dark times' of 'strife', 'fear' and 'violence'. Unable to deny his appetites, he pursues his 'desires', whilst recognising the weakness that signifies. Like the great character he would presently create, Galileo Galilei, Brecht saw the price to be paid in that brutal age for dependence on the creature comforts of life. He was no hero.

The second part recounts the life of the political subject, again echoing Brecht's own: 'I came to the cities in a time of disorder'. As so often, Brecht's point of departure is the end of the First World War and the hunger and revolution which followed, in which: 'I rebelled with them'. This stanza, like each of the six in the second part, ends with the refrain, 'So passed my time / Which had been given to me on earth'. Brecht acknowledges the limits of his literary opposition to the ruling 'murderers': 'My tongue betrayed me to the butchers. / There was little I could do. But those in power / Sat safer without me: that was my hope'. Hope gives way to a further acknowledgement of weakness, as the second part concludes on a wistful note of resignation, recognising that the 'goal' of revolution now 'Lay far in the distance': 'It was clearly visible, though I myself / Was unlikely to reach it'.

In the third section, the poetic voice shifts to the 'we' of his generation and begins with a grand address to

You who will emerge from the flood
In which we have gone under
Remember
When you speak of our failings
The dark times too
Which you have escaped.

Brecht evokes the arduous generational experience of revolutionary émigrés with a harrowing poignancy: 'For we went, changing countries oftener than our shoes / Through the wars of the classes, despairing / when there was injustice only, and no rebellion'. Their fundamental failing lies in their inability to create a properly humane order, since survival had become the single imperative: 'Oh, we / Who wanted to prepare the ground for friendliness / could not ourselves be friendly'. The poem closes with his address to those 'born later', in which he allows himself to anticipate an age when such a humane order has been established:

But you, when the time comes at last
And man is a helper to man
Think of us
With forbearance.

This appeal to humane values, articulated in the light of acknowledged failure and defeat, marks out 'To Those Born Later', together with 'Legend of the Origin of the *Book of Tao-tê-ching* on Lao-tsû's Road into Exile', as seminal pieces in *Svendborg Poems*, setting the tone for Brecht's late work. In 1930 Brecht had endorsed the necessity of violence against the bourgeois individual in the Leninist revolution. He had seen the consequences and recoiled. From now on, Brecht's work contains a markedly humanist dimension, in the specific sense of an appeal to mankind's innate goodness, which he asserts in opposition to deepening barbarism. Brecht's humanism employs a vocabulary of social interaction recognisably Chinese in origin, stressing politeness, kindness, composure and friendliness, as well as goodness.[46] Moreover, the appeal to humane values informs Brecht's development of ethical categories in his theoretical statements about the theatre as much as in the imagery of his poetry. As we shall see, Brecht's notion of ethics is anything but quiescent. With the 'claw' as well as the 'elegance' of Chinese art, as Brecht put it in his poem 'On a Chinese Carving of a Lion', he challenges prevailing western ethical norms, sharply focused upon the non-negotiable category of individual responsibility, which Brecht had assimilated during his stern South German Protestant upbringing.[47]

Life of Galileo: The fragmenting wisdom of the unheroic heretic

'Not only do you seem to me to have captured profoundly Galileo's personality, but also the importance of his presence in the development of intellectual history and with that in history in general,' Albert Einstein wrote to Brecht on 4 May 1939, praising his new play *Life of Galileo*.[48] Einstein continued: 'You have understood how to create a dramatic framework which is uncommonly captivating and which must especially interest us too on account of the strong links to the problems of the present time'. Brecht had sent his play to Einstein and to others who might influence its dissemination when, after Herzfelde's flight, any possibility of publication by Malik had disappeared. Recipients included Eisler, Piscator and Fritz Lang in the USA, his translator Desmond Vesey in London, German-language theatres in Basel and Zurich, and Benjamin and Pierre Abraham in Paris.

Brecht had long been interested in the philosophical and social ramifications of modern physics, from the role of the Italian mathematician and astronomer Galileo Galilei to that of Einstein in recent revolutionary developments. Brecht had been doing preparatory work for his play since the spring of 1938, initially calling it *The Earth Moves*. He read Galileo's *Discourses* and writings by two of his contemporaries, Francis Bacon's *Novum Organum* and Michel de Montaigne's aphorisms. Brecht also consulted Emil Wohlwill's *Galileo and his Battle for the Copernican System* and Leonardo Olschki's *Galileo and his Age*. Contemporary material included the protocols of the Moscow show trials, particularly Bukharin's self-criticism and defence.[49] Brecht's preparatory reading would resonate through his later work.

Brecht was not alone in recognising that the age of religious wars which had convulsed Europe in the sixteenth and seventeenth centuries offered telling parallels to the ideologically saturated struggle over knowledge and power between Fascist, Communist and liberal-democratic states. Brecht presents Galileo's life story in fourteen scenes covering nearly thirty years during the Counter-Reformation, which Brecht clearly understood as an age of reaction like his own. He emphasised that Galileo, who sets out to spread fresh knowledge for a new age, does not at the outset assume a position of opposition to the authority of the church. Rather, that authority's exclusive claim to truth forces him into the role of the heretic. Indeed, for Brecht the church's role in the play was precisely to represent authority:

The play shows the contemporary victory of authority, not the victory of the priesthood. It corresponds to the historical truth in that the Galileo of the play never turns directly against the church. [...] Casting the church as the embodiment of authority in this theatrical trial of the persecutors of the champions of free research certainly does not help to get the church acquitted. But it would be highly dangerous, particularly nowadays, to treat the matter like Galileo's fight for freedom of research as a religious one; for thereby attention would be most unhappily deflected from present-day reactionary authorities of a totally unecclesiastical kind.[50]

If the secular dimensions of the authority of the Church are emphasised, by the same token, Brecht had told Benjamin that summer what, in his view, distinguished the atheistic USSR from other political systems: 'Those who have appropriated and used Marx's theoretical doctrines will always form a clerical camarilla. Marxism does after all lend itself all too easily to "interpretation".'[51] The atheistic Soviet Union under Stalin had become a quasi-theological system, a reactionary authority hostile to new thinking, which resembled the Catholic Church in the Counter-Reformation. *Life of Galileo* explores the clash between a 'clerical camarilla' and a heretic espousing new thinking. The parallels between the heretics Galileo and Brecht in the 1938 'Danish' version of the play are very striking indeed, particularly concerning Brecht's public diminution as the heretical editor of *Das Wort*: he had failed to defend himself publicly against the *ad hominem* attacks of the camarilla and to speak out against the murder of his friends in the Great Terror. Like Galileo, he feared that his reputation would now be destroyed.

However, the subsequent course of wartime politics and of Brecht's own situation conspired to obscure the close parallel between Brecht's own predicament and Galileo's. Brecht's re-writing of *Life of Galileo* began in the USA in 1944 during the wartime alliance of the USSR and the western powers against Germany and Japan. The work assumed a huge urgency after the USA had dropped the atomic bomb. The incorporation of this factor lent the play a quite different trajectory in the discussion of scientific responsibility, eclipsing the original context of composition in 1938. In the very different world after 1945, critical reception followed this new trajectory, in which, among other things, it was axiomatic that *Life of Galileo* was an anti-Fascist play. Nor did Brecht have any interest in re-visiting the traumas of his relationship with Moscow. The 'Danish' *Galileo* was largely forgotten. It was published authoritatively only in 1988 and has been viewed only as an appendage to the later, canonical English and German versions. However, as we shall now see, the 'Danish' *Galileo* is the most crucial work in Brecht's intellectual biography. Not only is it, behind the mask of Galileo, his most personal play; the philosophical and dramatic problems which Brecht addresses are of fundamental importance for our understanding of his life's work

The 'Danish' *Galileo* is an anti-Fascist play only in terms of incidental detail such as Galileo's warning to Andrea: 'Look out for yourself when you travel through Germany with the truth under your coat'.[52] When Karl Korsch, himself no stranger to charges of heresy in the Communist movement, read *Life of Galileo* he was in no doubt that Brecht's treatment of the subject was all to do with his relations with Moscow and the show trials. In June 1939 Korsch wrote to Paul Partos: 'Although people seldom organise their private lives according to the principles of their general convictions, after this depiction of Galileo I cannot think that Brecht will continue to be so faithful to the line'.[53]

Brecht wrote the play at great speed, noting on 23 November 1938 that he had finished *Life of Galileo* in just three weeks.[54] He would refine the play with Steffin over the winter, when he also sought out scientists from Niels Bohr's team in Copenhagen. That winter it was announced, too, that Otto Hahn and Fritz Strassmann had split the uranium atom in Berlin. During the autumn in Copenhagen Brecht met Ferdinand Reyher, who worked in the Hollywood film industry. Brecht had known Reyher since 1927 and now encouraged him to promote his new work in the US.[55] Unsurprisingly, Reyher considered a film treatment most appropriate. However, Brecht produced Epic Theatre, telling Reyher: 'Instead of a film treatment I'm sending you a play. It contains a gigantic role, and if we approached a big, influential actor with it, perhaps he would help bring about a production'. Brecht had his sights set on Broadway. In the logic of his dramatic imagination, after his withdrawal from disciplined, Leninist partisanship the Baal-like 'gloriously hulking body' with huge and unpredictable appetites returned. Writing that same day to Herbert Levy that he had 'once more succumbed to the temptation to try to achieve contact with the theatre', Brecht wondered if Charles Laughton, an actor who could truly embody such a character, might be interested in the role.[56] Laughton would, of course, later play Galileo with distinction after co-writing the English version with Brecht.

Galileo is the first of a series of brilliant dramatic creations from the late 1930s and early 1940s about which Brecht would remark:

> It is a matter of creating rich, complex, developing figures – without introspective psychology. The normal behaviouristic images are very flat and blurred. [...] The comminution, fragmentation, atomisation of the individual psyche is a fact, i.e. if one identifies this peculiar lack of a centre in individuals, it is not a result of faulty habits of observation. It is just that one is facing new configurations which have to be mapped out afresh. Even dissolution does not result in nothing. In addition to which the frontiers of the individual psyche are still clearly visible. Even the new configuration reacts *and acts* individually, uniquely, 'unschematically'.[57]

What were these new configurations? How did Brecht go about mapping them out afresh? And what therefore becomes of Galileo in this ominous process of dissolution?

Like the theatrical revolutionary Brecht, Galileo is an exceptionally innovative intellectual, aspiring to knowledge which will usher in a new age. Brecht places him at centre stage throughout. The 'gloriously hulking body' enters as a 'powerful physicist with a tummy on him, a face like Socrates, a vociferous, full-blooded man with a sense of humour'.[58] He epitomises the hedonistic individual in the physical terms that Brecht had always desired for himself. Projecting onto this character, too, a number of his psychological traits, Brecht draws a magnificent character on a Shakespearean or, perhaps better, Jonsonian scale, deeply imperilled in treacherous times, who is all the more vulnerable on account of his wholly contradictory impulses. Enormously egotistical, the great innovator Galileo is driven on as much in his research as in his private life by fickle appetites, which both compete with and complement his other lodestar, reason. As we know from 'To Those Born Later' and elsewhere in Brecht's work, appetites are both a strength, encouraging ever more vital activity, and a weakness, since a dependence on them makes one extremely vulnerable to threats of their curtailment. So it is with Galileo. Typically, Brecht would not be able to leave him alone, re-working his creation repeatedly for the rest of his life.

The play opens with Galileo seeking to demonstrate that, in contrast to officially sanctioned Ptolemaic cosmology, which teaches that the sun goes around the earth, Copernican theory correctly states that the earth goes around the sun. However, as Galileo heralds the onset of a new age of scientific inquiry and social justice, he displays a naive belief in the power of reason. He chooses to leave the relative safety of Padua for the prestigious centre of power, Florence, where he aims to further his career. His friend Sagredo warns him not to go, reminding him of the fate of the monk and astronomer Giordano Bruno, who was burned at the stake after the Inquisition found him guilty of heresy. Galileo believes that he will avoid such a fate because he has proof, whereas Bruno merely had a hypothesis: 'I believe in the gentle power of reason over people. Over time they cannot resist it'.[59] However, after Galileo has encountered the power of the Church in Florence, particularly the representatives of the Roman Inquisition, he exclaims: 'The only truth that gets through will be what we force through: the victory of reason will be the victory of people who are prepared to reason, nothing else'.[60]

Galileo now tells his pupils a story about the Cretan philosopher Keonos – a reprise of a Keuner story from 1929, 'Measures Against Power' – that is emblematic of events to follow. Much admired for his love of freedom, Keonos is visited one day during the time of dictatorship by an agent, who shows him a certificate issued by the city's rulers. It states that any abode he sets foot in should become his and he should be given everything he wants. He asks Keonos if he will serve him, and Keonos does so for seven years without speaking a word: 'When the seven years were over and the agent had become fat from all the food, sleep and giving orders, the agent died. Keonos wrapped him in the putrid sheet, dragged him out of the house, washed the bed, painted the walls, took a deep breath and answered: no'.[61] While everyone else laughs at the story, Galileo's faithful pupil Andrea shakes his head.

As Heinrich Detering has shown, in the Keonos story Brecht enacts the Taoist doctrine of Wu Wei with its paradox of non-action and action.[62] The thinker survives by evading a confrontation with the powerful agent, whom he cunningly overcomes by pampering him to death, whereupon the thinker is free to speak once more. As the play continues, the Inquisition brands Galileo a heretic and places his work on the Index of Forbidden Books. Andrea is adamant that Galileo will be prepared to die for his beliefs, but Galileo recants, leaving Andrea, unable to look at an almost unrecognisable Galileo, to proclaim: 'Unhappy the land that has no heroes!'.[63] Galileo responds: 'No. Unhappy the land where heroes are needed'. The liquidation of such a contrary and 'defeatist' figure as a danger to the revolutionary collective, as in *Fatzer*, was by now an unthinkable scenario. Galileo spends the years from 1633 until his death in 1642 under house arrest.

The survivor Galileo accepts that there is a price to pay for survival. How could this be represented dramatically? After completing the play, Brecht noted: 'The only difficulties arose with the last scene. Just as in the case of St Joan, I needed a neat stroke at the end to ensure that the audience had the necessary detachment, even somebody empathising without thinking must now feel the A-effect when he empathises with Galileo. With rigid epic presentation an acceptable empathy occurs'.[64] In that highly contradictory scene, in fact the penultimate scene, Galileo becomes the object of the audience's alternation between empathy and critical distance, as they participate emotionally and intellectually in the fate of the great researcher, who is diminished – and recognises his diminution – in the brutal subjugation of reason to power.

Critics have puzzled over the ultimate import of that scene. Under house arrest, the compulsive researcher continues his work and conspires with a stove-fitter to smuggle out the *Dialogues* to Holland. Is Galileo after all a hero of the resistance? He receives a first visit after many years from Andrea, who, unaware of Galileo's covert actions, remarks upon Galileo's 'utter capitulation', a view with which Galileo concurs: 'The depth of my repentance has earned me enough credit with my superiors to be permitted to conduct scientific studies on a modest scale under clerical supervision'.[65] When the discussion moves on to the significance of Galileo's recantation for the scientific community, which has been cowed by the event, Galileo echoes the severely self-critical attitude struck by Bukharin at his trial, which for Brecht clearly provided a key analogy with Galileo's predicament and his own. Galileo comments:

> Shortly after my trial various people who had known me earlier were good enough to credit me with all kinds of noble intentions. I wouldn't have this. To me it simply signified a decline of the critical faculties, brought about by the fact that they found drastic physical changes in me. After carefully considering all the circumstances, extenuating and otherwise, it is impossible to conclude that a man could arrive at this state of – call it obedience, from any other motive than an undue fear of death.[66]

Galileo remarks upon what the scientific community must think of him: 'Science has no use for people who fail to stick up for reason. It must expel them in ignominy, because, however many truths science knows, it could have no future in a world of lies. If the hand that feeds it occasionally seizes it unpredictably by the throat then humanity will have to chop it off. That is why science cannot tolerate a person like me in its ranks'.

Galileo admits to Andrea that he has had 'relapses'. However, he claims that he has only been writing for himself and that his protectors have been locking his work away securely. In front of a sobbing Andrea, Galileo then represents the epitome of cunning ambiguity, describing his 'fear' that his writings, concealed in his globe, could, nonetheless, fall into the wrong hands and be taken abroad. In any case, he continues, there is nothing left of himself, since 'I have destroyed myself. [...] At one time the author's name had some significance in the scientific world. But he has revealed himself to be a liar'.[67] Maintaining this categorical moral stance, Galileo insists that inaction leads to moral compromise. He therefore insists, too, that the writings must be subjected to the most rigorous scrutiny and that he himself should not be regarded as a role model. The egotistical self-image of the great man of science who would change the world has been shattered. He is a shell of his former self, a picaresque survivor among the wreckage, diminished in his own eyes as well as in those of the rest of the world.

At the heart of this extraordinary scene, there is a yawning gap between, on the one hand, a fragmenting Galileo's actions of surrender and cunning dissent and, on the other, his self-lacerating evaluation of them. Wu Wei provides the structuring principle for survivalist behaviour underlying his actions. In expounding the story of Keunos, Galileo has demonstrated his understanding that, in order to live through the appalling trials of the age, different modes of behaviour are necessary, as is a re-evaluation of the egotistical individual. However, Galileo tears himself apart as he struggles with the implications of his contradictory survivalist behaviour. Even as he continues to act according to the logic of Wu Wei, he engages in the severest self-stricture, condemning his actions because they betray the bulwark of western ethical standards, non-negotiable individual responsibility, with its expectation of heroic self-sacrifice. The man who heralds the new age with his scientific discoveries lives ethically in the world of the old.

Nothing could demonstrate more vividly Brecht's view – drawing upon Einstein, he would expand upon it in his *Short Organum for the Theatre* – that ethical norms lag behind a social reality shaped by new forces of the scientific age to which man typically responds with muddled emotions:

> Mankind today, living in a rapidly changing world and rapidly changing himself, has no image of this world which is accurate and on the basis of which he could act with the prospect of success. His ideas about man's communal life are asymmetric, imprecise and contradictory, his picture of it is what one might call impracticable, i.e. with his picture of the world, the world of man, before his eyes man cannot master this world.[68]

In his wretched plight Galileo is, however, not yet finished. Among his final meditations is a wonderfully idiosyncratic, Brechtian juxtaposition of reason and egotism:

> You have had experiences which could have given you a quite wrong view of what we've always termed the future of reason. But of course, no single man could either bring it to pass or discredit it. It is too big an affair even to be contained inside a single head. Reason is something people can be divided into. It can be described as the egotism of all humanity. Such egotism is not strong enough.[69]

The egotism of reason is both necessary and insufficient, just as are the dividuals – as we must describe them, using Brecht's earlier neologism – who embody its particles. What further source of strength is there? Brecht has no crisp Marxist-Leninist response. Finding an answer is left to the audience. Can these dividualised egos learn to take control of their lives through a new social ethic based on the recognition of shared interests and responsibilities, which gains expression in good governance? At the very end of the play, Galileo affirms a discernibly Taoist belief in reason and human progress within the flux of things beyond the present age of reaction:

> Even a person like myself can still see that reason is not coming to an end but

beginning. And I still believe that this is a new age. It may look like a blood-stained old harridan, but if so that must be the way new ages look. When light breaks in it does so in the uttermost darkness. While a few places are the scene of the most immense discoveries, which must contribute immeasurably to human-ity's resources for happiness, great areas of this world still lie entirely in the dark. In fact the blackness has actually deepened there.

From a Marxist-Leninist perspective, such an ending was preposterous. Korsch could not resist teasing Brecht about his great drama, particularly the ending, his observa-tions beautifully poised between deep admiration and wicked irony:[70]

I find it strong and good – perhaps too heavy intellectually to stir – as 'play' – impressions, experiences, shocks and catharses, which in any case are not wanted by you, on the in any case non-existent stage. But between ourselves, in the terrible sadness of the ending something like 'catharsis' did appear or occur. Such a colossal figure constructed purely from the intellect is a fine achievement of historical materialism.[71]

Thematically and formally, *Life of Galileo* signals Brecht's withdrawal from immediate revolutionary positions. He was, of course, uncomfortable about this. Typically, he considered re-casting this psychological study along more didactic lines because he felt it to be 'technically a great step backwards' and suspected it to be an 'opportunistic', 'empathy' drama along the lines of *Señora Carrar's Rifles*.[72] The ghost of the Lehrstück stalked his thoughts. He had, however, left that dramatic position behind. He had written *Fear and Misery of the Third Reich* in a more fluid, hybrid mode, enriching the dramatic trajectory of *Carrar*. The 'Danish' *Galileo* stands out as a landmark achievement in Brecht's dramatic œuvre, a brilliant meditation upon his own plight, which reverberates throughout his work.

Moscow or the USA?

In December 1938 Brecht received news from Maria Osten in Paris which 'horrified' him.[73] A rumour had reached her that Mikhail Koltsov had been arrested. The arrest had taken place on 12 December. Brecht wrote to Osten: 'I've always seen him working indefatigably for the Soviet Union. Have you any idea what he's been accused of?'. Koltsov was accused of spying for the UK. Koltsov's arrest speeded the closure of *Das Wort* well in advance of the Hitler-Stalin pact. Brecht was quite candid to Osten: 'The magazine is getting steadily more vapid and formless. It's an outrage what they've done to a good idea'. At the point of its demise, Brecht the heretic had his say with the publication in the journal's final issue of his essay 'On Rhymeless Verse with Irregular Rhythms'. Again, Brecht did not submit a work about general theory but about his practice as a realist poet, specifically how he conveyed particular gestures by using formal innovations which contravened 19th-century norms. The publication was in fact fortuitous, Erpenbeck writing to Brecht that he had been able to slip it in at the last moment because another piece had been removed![74]

Erpenbeck left Brecht and Feuchtwanger largely in the dark and unpaid for their work. Brecht complained about their treatment in three letters to Becher before telling Erpenbeck that it was 'just about the shabbiest treatment I've had from any publication'.[75] He summarised the situation after Koltsov's arrest: 'My last connection there. Nobody knows anything about Tretiakov, who is supposed to have been a "Japanese spy". Nobody knows anything about [Carola] Neher who is supposed to have done some business for the Trotskyists in Prague on her husband's instructions. Reich and Asja Lacis don't write to me any more'.[76] Brecht observed bitterly: 'Marxists outside Russia find themselves in the position Marx adopted towards Social Democracy. One of positive criticism'. When he heard of Tretiakov's death, he wrote 'Are the People Infallible?':

> My teacher
> Tall and kindly
> Has been shot, condemned by a people's court
> As a spy. His name is damned.
> His books are destroyed. Talk about him
> Is suspect and suppressed.[77]

The refrain, 'Suppose he is innocent?', runs through the seven sections of the poem, which remained unpublished in Brecht's lifetime.

Against his better judgement, Feuchtwanger, hoping to leave France for the USA, supported Maria Osten's return to Moscow to help Koltsov. However, in Moscow in July 1939 the KPD's Walter Ulbricht, Philipp Dengel and Kurt Funk (i.e. the post-war SPD politician Herbert Wehner) would sign a document, accusing Osten of consorting with the circle around the Malik publishing house in Prague, particularly the Conciliators who met at Café Volk, including Kurt Volk, Arthur Ewert, Lex Ende and John Heartfield, Wieland Herzfelde's brother.[78] Unforgivably, the Conciliators had advocated co-operation with other left-wing parties before the KPD had adopted that policy. Because of this and her links with Ernst Ottwalt and Carola Neher, Osten was suspended from the Party pending the outcome of investigations into her relationship with Koltsov.

Brecht noted that Steffin now never heard from acquaintances in the Caucasus or Leningrad, that Béla Kun, the only politician he knew, was under arrest, that Meyerhold had lost his theatre, and that literature, art and political theory were all shot: 'What is left is a thin, bloodless, proletarian humanism propagated by officialdom'.[79] Kafka's nightmare vision of a 'society of ants' had come true. It was not lost on Brecht and Weigel that it was only a matter of time before Germany occupied Denmark and that Hitler's alternation between non-aggression pacts and threats of belligerence could only lead to a new European war. Nothing could persuade Brecht to take refuge in Moscow. Nor does Brecht appear to have considered Great Britain as a refuge. Despite the fact that he was opposed to the USA politically, it was his best option outside Europe. He had contacts there and a chance of making a living as an independent author. He remained driven by the ambition to conquer the American stage even though its entertainment industry had shown little interest in his Epic Theatre and class-conscious writing. In February 1939 Brecht suggested to Korsch, who had gone to the East coast of the USA in 1936, that he and his family would come over if they could get US immigration papers.[80] Aware that the annual German quota was vastly oversubscribed and tightly administered, he asked Korsch if he knew how he could expedite matters with an 'official teaching appointment'. Steffin described Brecht's strategy to Benjamin: 'Brecht has decided to try through friends to be treated as an exceptional case (for people who have close relatives over there or people who, for example, get a teaching contract) or to wait and see whether he earns money there, possibly through *Galileo*, otherwise to stay as long as possible on this gradually darkening green island'.[81]

Brecht put out feelers to other friends in the USA. Their responses were contradictory. While Eisler suggested that left-wing theatre was all the rage, Piscator, chastened by his own failures, warned Brecht that political art was now impossible.[82] Brecht hoped that he might re-launch his partnership with Kurt Weill, now a Broadway success. Weill was trying, unsuccessfully, to sever their contracts with Felix Bloch Erben in Berlin and Universal Edition in Vienna. Brecht contacted Weill about a Parisian plan for a film of *Mahagonny* and asked him about the prospects for *The Threepenny Opera* in the USA. Given its earlier failure, Weill was cautious about its chances: 'One could risk it, of course, only with a completely new adaptation (which must be done by someone first-class) and with one of the best Broadway producers'.[83] In this and other exchanges, the old rivalry between the poet and the composer was never far below the surface: Weill, whose success gave him the whip hand, knew that Brecht would never be content to be his librettist.

Pondering the ethics of survival in the clash between conventional western morality and Taoist thought, Brecht began work on a new play, *The Good Person of Szechwan*: 'It is a bit of a charade, what with the costume switches and the changes in make-up. But I can use it to develop the epic technique and get back up to standard again'.[84] He took up drafts from 1927 and 1930 under the headings *Fanny Kress or The Whores' Only Friend* and *Love Is the Goods*. Both present whores swapping between female and male identities in the struggle for material and sexual dominance. In the meantime, Brecht's interest had shifted from the exposure of the rapacity of human behaviour in the capitalist struggle, an issue of economics rather than morality, to the question of what conditions would permit a life of dignity for the mass of people, who survived at mere subsistence level. As he struggled with the material over the coming two years, he would discover how resistant it was to being re-cast in the fresh mould.

Aware that with any new work he would most likely be seeking outlets in the USA, Brecht's thoughts turned to contemporary American literature. His deep suspicions about its dependence on the Hollywood film industry emerge in a letter to Elisabeth Hauptmann and in a note: 'Interesting, the new "realistic" American literature (Cain, Coy, Hemingway). These people protest against the prevailing descriptions of certain milieux, bank heavily on the novelty of "unbiased" description. It all remains within the domain of the formal. At its inception stands the experience of film (and at the end stands Hollywood)'.[85] For Brecht, these authors, together with their tough, romantic male heroes, were in thrall to the 'great emotions racket' of the US entertainment industry. Later, when he saw the film of John Steinbeck's *Grapes of Wrath* he commented: 'You can still see that it must be a great book, and the entrepreneurs probably did not want to "take all the strength out of it". So they stew the subject in tears till it is tender. Where "suggestive" acting does not predominate, there are powerful effects'. The only way Brecht could succeed in the USA was if the whole entertainment industry was transformed in his own image. He would never give up.

Flight Eastward to the West 1939–41

Lidingø

Nazi Germany now proceeded upon its aggressive expansion, occupying Prague and the rest of Czechoslovakia in March 1939. Despite his misgivings, Brecht joined the quota queue for the USA, submitting an application for entry visas for himself, Weigel and their children. Because of her tuberculosis, Steffin could only qualify for a visitor's visa. As a fallback, they also submitted applications for Mexican visas. It would take more than two years for the matter to be resolved, and then, as Brecht expected, by other means. All the while, the situation would become more precarious and, as James K. Lyon remarks, 'Brecht found America's golden door opened to him through the exertions and largesse of kind friends and generous strangers, not to mention a substantial portion of good luck'.[1] Elisabeth Hauptmann worked on Brecht's behalf and the émigré film director Fritz Lang collected funds to support him and his family in his first six months in the USA. Fritz Kortner, Weill, Piscator, Eisler, Oskar Homolka, Bruno Frank and, when he reached the USA, Feuchtwanger all contributed, as did Dorothy Thompson, the prominent journalist close to the White House. However, in order to circumvent the quota Brecht needed a written job offer from the USA. There was no sign of that.

With Denmark under threat, the Brechts had to find another asylum in Europe. In the face of Sweden's restrictive asylum policy, particularly towards Communists, influential Swedish friends Georg Branting and Henry Peter Matthis secured an invitation for Brecht to enter the country to pursue a socially useful activity. In conjunction with the Swedish Amateur Theatre Association, they arranged for Brecht to deliver a number of lectures. Matthis formally invited Brecht to Stockholm and helped with visas. Thanking Matthis in April, Brecht told him that he and Weigel had been 'extremely depressed and worried for some weeks. According to the newspapers, Berlin has denied that German troops were being concentrated on the Danish border'.[2] Everyone knew what was coming. Brecht and Weigel asked the actress Naima Wifstrand, who had translated *Señora Carrar's Rifles* and taken the lead in the Swedish production, to look for a flat for them in Stockholm. Weigel arranged the sale of their house and prepared their departure. On 22 April they took the evening ferry from Copenhagen to Malmø with Berlau, who had good connections in Sweden, and from there the train to Stockholm, while Steffin remained in Copenhagen to look after the children until their visas arrived.

After a few days at Stockholm's Hotel Pallas, Brecht and Weigel rented a house owned by the sculptor Ninnan Santesson at Lövstigan 1 on the island of Lidingø, just to the east of Stockholm. Maria Lazar and her daughter followed. Steffin, Stefan and Barbara arrived on 7 May, and Steffin took a room in a bungalow nearby. It was just as well that the rent for the house was minimal: Brecht was earning next to nothing. For him, the place was 'ideal': 'with firs running right up to it on two sides [...] the study, previously a sculptor's studio, is 7 metres long, 5 metres wide. So I have many tables'.[3] Brecht spread out his many projects on the tables. Weigel took care of the rest. Seeking to persuade Benjamin to join them, she told him of the fine libraries in nearby Stockholm and of the good-quality food.[4] That enabled her to provide well for the small Brecht Circle at their house in the evenings. Brecht's grant from the American Guild for German Cultural Freedom was raised to $60 and extended for six months. This was very welcome since Brecht and Weigel ran out of money in Sweden after spending the proceeds from the sale of their house and after Weigel had sold her jewellery. It made little sense trying to settle: the intention was to leave for the USA as soon as visas arrived. Securing visas as known Communists would, however, prove a long-drawn-out, deeply unsettling experience for Brecht and his family.

Meanwhile, back in Germany, on 20 May 1939 the sixty-nine-year-old Berthold Brecht died in hospital in Darmstadt, following a bizarre accident. He had driven to Darmstadt in extreme distress to be with his son Walter, having run over and killed his dear friend Franz Xaver Schirmböck as he was backing his car to leave his house. Berthold Brecht was admitted to hospital suffering from bilious attacks, to which he succumbed. His employers, the Haindl family, lavished praise upon their loyal servant of forty-six years, who left 12,000 marks to Marie Röcker and the rest to Walter: a stately 77,559.78 marks. To avoid any confusion, he had declared Walter his sole heir. Stripped of German citizenship, Brecht was forbidden any inheritance in any case but his daughter Hanne was entitled to claim the house in Utting. There was still a mortgage on the property: Brecht had not amortised his father's loan. In order to secure the property from the reach of the state, Walter drew the attention of the Augsburg administrative court to Hanne's right to it. Theo Lingen completed the acquisition on her behalf, fulfilling Brecht's wish that she should assume ownership and that it should be available for him on his return. Finally, Frank Banholzer received a regular income from Berthold Brecht's legacy. All this became known to Brecht only after his family had traced him to Sweden where Walter visited him in August 1939.[5]

While Brecht resumed his work routine on Lidingø, Weigel ensured there were guests for conversation in the evening, among them Naima Wifstrand and Ninnan Santesson. The exile scene in Stockholm was a different world from the seclusion of Skovsbostrand. Brecht had regular discussions with their neighbour, the German émigré actor and director Hermann Greid, who had visited them at Skovsbostrand and directed the Stockholm production of *Señora Carrar's Rifles*. They discussed Marxist ethics, which Greid was writing about. However, Brecht, his Marxism enriched by Taoist paradox in his *Book of Twists and Turns*, found Greid's views 'utterly amateurish' and satirised his idealism: 'He is still totally taken up with the question of how men would have to change in order to change the world, so that they could change themselves'.[6] In Stockholm, Brecht and Weigel were involved in the celebrations of the Danish working-class author Martin Andersen Nexø's 70th birthday. Brecht had worked with Steffin on the translation of Nexø's memoirs and dedicated to Nexø the poem 'How Future Ages Will Judge our Writers'. At Nexø's birthday party, Brecht met Hans Tombrock, a vagabond German working-class artist who had recently made his way to Sweden. Brecht and Tombrock became close friends. Encouraged by Brecht, who was always on the lookout for someone to replace Caspar Neher, Tombrock produced a sequence of engravings for *Life of Galileo*. However, Brecht, as always a stern taskmaster, was unhappy with Tombrock's inability to 'sustain a consistent style'.[7]

Brecht hosted meetings with August Enderle, the SAP leader in Stockholm, and with Paul Verner and Herbert Warnke, defenders of the Spanish republic who had fled after Franco's triumphant entry into Madrid. Brecht began to receive monthly financial help from his US support group, led by Fritz Lang, who assured Brecht that he had many friends committed to helping him maintain his independent production.[8] Brecht thanked Lang for the second money order of $80: 'It really helps me to work on in independence'.[9] Brecht cultivated other US contacts, principally Piscator and Gorelik, in the attempt to secure productions of *Fear and Misery of the Third Reich* and *Life of Galileo*. He also signed a five-year contract for the two plays with the Basel publisher Kurt Reiss, who took over responsibility for Brecht's account with Crédit Suisse in Zurich.[10] The links with Reiss and with the Zurich Schauspielhaus would make German-speaking, neutral Switzerland a very important place for Brecht in the remaining years of exile and beyond.

Dramatic experiments: Epic Theatre as grand synthesis

As envisaged, Brecht embarked on his socially useful activity. This meant that some fortunate Stockholm students and amateur actors got to hear the world's leading theatrical innovator at the height of his powers, when he was evolving his theoretical positions in concert with great dramatic compositions. Brecht's students could have little inkling about all this. In his lecture 'On Experimental Theatre' Brecht suggested the new drama's affinity with scientific method as well as with his own *Versuche*, explaining that for at least two generations European theatre had been engaged in a period of experimentation, which was still going on.[11] He surveyed major innovators, grouping their work in his two familiar categories, entertainment and didacticism, which, he added, frequently overlapped. Praising Piscator's political theatre, he introduced the proposition that theatre had entered a new crisis with the 'growth of political reaction'. A crisis was, of course, always an opportunity: what applied in Brecht's theoretical reflections upon the theatre also applied, as we have seen, in his poetic and dramatic practice.

Brecht expounded how the crisis had developed in aesthetic terms, writing that with Piscator 'aesthetic considerations were entirely subject to political' ones as they strove towards a 'new social function for the theatre'. Brecht cited *The Threepenny Opera* to demonstrate that entertainment and didacticism could no longer simply co-exist loosely in a shared theatrical experience; rather they 'openly conflict', splitting the audience into 'at least two mutually hostile social groups'. Brecht, who had come to see that 'enjoyment of learning depends on the class situation', was the past master of revealing the conflicts between entertainment and didacticism, forcing the two apart. He summarised the impasse that established theatre reached: 'The more we induced the audience to identify its own experiences and feelings with the production, the less it learned; and the more there was to learn, the less the artistic enjoyment'. In order to move beyond the impasse, it was necessary to consider how the two could be fused on a fresh basis in a theatre showing 'models of men's life together such as could help the spectator to understand his social environment and to master it both rationally and emotionally'. This brought the story right up to date with Brecht's invitation to the audience to consider the implications of Galileo's plight.

In the same vein, again drawing upon Einstein, Brecht identified the problem of an increasing gulf between man's scientific discoveries on the one hand and the incapacity to organise human life in a constructive and productive manner on the other. Alluding to the latest discoveries in uranium fission, he suggested that they led only to imprecise emotional responses of fear and trauma. This acted as a bridge to his fundamental point that traditional theatre based on empathy did not equip the audience to think clearly and objectively about core dilemmas, and thereupon to intervene and change the situation. Techniques such as the A-effect, designed specifically to stimulate such thought and action, had, he claimed, been employed with actors in Epic Theatre at the Schiffbauerdamm. By the same token, Brecht argued that because the purging of the emotions of fear and pity in Aristotelian catharsis was essentially passive, it should be replaced by an active audience attitude towards events on stage. Engendering in the audience a desire for knowledge and a willingness to help others was paramount. This fresh emphasis upon an inquiring and co-operative attitude of mind within Brecht's Marxist analysis points the way beyond Galileo's plight and that of Brecht's generation in 'To Those Born Later'. These reflections, in turn, pave the way for Brecht's treatment of ethical questions in his later parables. Reformulating Immanuel Kant's reflection upon the question *What is Enlightenment?*, Brecht concluded his lecture with his challenging to contemporary theatre: 'How can the unfree, ignorant man of our century, with his thirst for freedom and his hunger for knowledge; how can the tortured and heroic, abused and ingenious, changeable and world-changing man of this great and ghastly century obtain his own theatre which will help him to master the world and himself?'.

The students sought out Brecht afterwards, as did a group of actors who wanted to hear about the A-effect. Brecht had a further opportunity to develop his ideas when Naima Wifstrand opened an acting school in Stockholm and engaged Weigel as a practical teacher. Weigel relished this rare opportunity to work. Brecht went along, too, and worked alongside his wife on scenes and exercises, frequently using Shakespeare. This work stimulated 'Exercises for Actors' and 'Short Description of a New Acting Technique, which Produces an Alienation Effect' as well as feeding into Brecht's sprawling, performative presentation of his theoretical ideas in the fragmentary *Messingkauf Dialogues*, a work which captures the great artistic symbiosis between Brecht and Weigel.

Brecht had begun *The Messingkauf Dialogues* in the winter of 1938–9 during revisions of *Life of Galileo*. The dialogue form echoes Galileo's *Discourses*. Brecht had chosen the dialogue form in order to leave space for the reader to adopt their own point-of-view, thereby disarming dogmatic critics. It became another of those projects on which Brecht worked on and off until the end of his life. He incorporated material from it in 1948 in the better-known, concise summary of his theories in *Small Organum for the Theatre*. The eminently readable *Messingkauf Dialogues* take place between an Actor, an Actress, a Dramaturg, a Stagehand and a Philosopher, who meet on the stage over four nights after a performance to discuss a new way of making theatre. Other characters put in an appearance, principally the Augsburger, whose views, like the philosopher's, reflect aspects of Brecht's, while those of the Actress reflect aspects of Weigel's.

We have discussed Brecht's dramaturgical positions as they have developed, charting the opposition of Epic Theatre to conventional European realism and to the Stanislavskian method. The Philosopher leads the discussion about a theatre appropriate to the age of scientific experimentation and innovation. He himself uses the term 'Messingkauf'. 'Messing' is the German for brass, 'Kauf' for purchase. The Philosopher, who feels himself an 'intruder and an outsider', explains what he means:

> I can only compare myself with a man, say, who deals in scrap metal and goes up to a brass band to buy, not a trumpet, let's say, but simply brass. The trumpeter's trumpet is made of brass, but he'll hardly want to sell it as such, by its value as brass, as so many ounces of brass. All the same, that's how I ransack your theatre for events between people, such as you do more or less imitate even if your imitations are for a very different purpose than my satisfaction. To put it in a nutshell: I'm looking for a way of getting incidents between people imitated for certain purposes; I've heard that you supply such imitations; and now I hope to find out if they are the kind of imitations I can use.[12]

Like Brecht, the Philosopher has a radically utilitarian temperament, questioning the assumptions upon which the whole institutional apparatus of the theatre is built. However, Brecht's reflections on the Fourth Night of *The Messingkauf Dialogues* show how far he had travelled since his polemical attacks on the established theatre in the 1920s, when, in discussion with Sternberg, he had advocated the liquidation of aesthetics and their replacement by sociological categories. His work on *Fear and Misery* and *Galileo* had encouraged him in fresh, synthesising ambitions, carried by his confidence in accomplished actors' capacity to convey didactic questions through the aesthetic 'lightness' with which he had equipped Epic Theatre by means of the A-effect. A series of journal notes amplifies upon *The Messingkauf Dialogues*: 'In the aesthetic sphere, which, incidentally, is on no account to be seen as being "above" the sphere of the dogmatic, the question of what is didactic becomes a purely aesthetic question, to be answered as it were autarchically. The utilitarian disappears in a peculiar fashion in this case: it only surfaces, say, in expressions like "the useful is beautiful".'[13] Brecht summarised: 'The philosopher's plan to use art for didactic purposes merges with the artists' plan to invest their knowledge, experience and social curiosity in art'. He glossed his refinement of the A-effect, contrasting it with the attitude of empathy and stressing that the A-effect was no 'Formalist' gimmick but embedded in real-life situations, designed to highlight underlying causalities. All this lent the dramatist a level of subtle control over performance, guiding audience response, too, which enabled Brecht to claim: 'This type of art also generates emotions; such performances facilitate the mastering of reality; and this it is that moves the spectator'.[14]

That 'mastering of reality' through sophisticated aesthetic control had its own exhilarating effect, driving Brecht on in his dissemination of his highly original dramaturgy with its in-built challenge to the audience's horizons. Brecht now went further in reconciling the false dichotomies which he had often encouraged, combining *ratio* and *emotio* in a manner bordering on the promiscuous, as he considered Stanislavsky alongside fairground shows and accommodated the affective factor:

> On the one hand the *act of empathy* occurs in conjunction with rational elements, on the other hand the A-effect can be used in a purely emotional way. Stanislavsky uses long analyses to achieve empathy, and in the panorama pictures in fairgrounds ('Nero Watches Rome Burning', 'The Shooting of the Anarchist Ferrer', 'The Lisbon Earthquake') the A-effect is pure feeling. In the Aristotelian theatre the empathy is also intellectual, and the non-Aristotelian theatre employs emotional criticism.[15]

At the same time, Brecht's fundamental dramaturgical drive towards narrative clarity, in the interest of revealing underlying causalities, ensured that all this did not mean a return to conventional realism. Brecht continued his synthesising reflections on the theatre during his flight through Scandinavia: 'It becomes clear to me that the antagonistic configuration "reason in this corner – emotion in that" has to go. The relationship of *ratio* and *emotio*, with all its contradictions, has to be examined minutely, and opponents cannot be allowed simply to present Epic Theatre as rational and counter-emotional'.[16] He had earlier staked all on resolving his artistic and personal dilemmas through didacticism in the service of the revolution. In the 'dark times', which saw the return of the 'gloriously hulking body', he devised a workable accommodation of conflicting forces, regulated by the broadened Epic approach, which depended heavily for its realisation in production on the consciousness and accomplishment of actors and directors. In the never-ending struggle for artistic pre-eminence, tactical considerations could not be neatly separated from theoretical positions, despite his avowal that non-Aristotelian theatre was just one possible approach without 'usurpatory aspirations towards theatre in general'!'[17] Brecht's 'mellowing' was a decidedly relative notion. After his depiction of *Galileo*, the intellectual survivor, Brecht would produce a series of outstanding dramas in quick succession, offering further perspectives upon the predicament of survivors in those 'dark times'.

The Hitler–Stalin pact

The Brechts monitored political developments nervously on the radio, extremely worried that they would soon be forced to continue their flight. Brecht's radio became one of his most treasured possessions. He even dedicated a poem to it. 'To a Portable Radio' begins: 'You little box I carried on that trip / Concerned to save your works from getting broken / Fleeing from house to train, from train to ship / So I might hear the hated jargon spoken'.[18] On 2 June 1939 Scandinavian foreign ministers discussed Germany's offer of a non-aggression pact but failed to reach agreement. The matter was left to individual governments. Sweden opted for neutrality, leaving it free to continue supplying Germany with iron ore and other materials for the Nazi armaments industry. This display of business as usual prompted Brecht to write the one-act play *How Much Is Your Iron?*, concealing his authorship under the name John Kent. Amateur actors performed the play at Tollare College in August in a knock-about, clown-like style, directed by Berlau, who visited that summer. Its message was that economic dependence made neutrality a delusion. Brecht spoke out publicly against Swedish neutrality, arguing in a newspaper interview that the position led to decline and subjugation, delivering people up to the dictators' stooges.[19]

Brecht's loyalty to the USSR was now tested to the very point of destruction by the announcement on 23 August that Germany and the USSR had concluded a non-aggression pact. Neither would join a third power in attacking the other. Notoriously, Germany and the USSR also signed a secret protocol dividing Northern and Eastern Europe into German and Soviet spheres of influence. The pact followed the USSR's failure to forge an alliance against Germany with the UK, France, Poland and Romania. Fearing Soviet imperialist ambitions, Poland and Romania had refused to grant the USSR transit rights within a collective security agreement. News of the pact caused consternation among German émigrés. Those loyal to Moscow found their position hopelessly compromised. Münzenberg denounced Stalin as a traitor who had betrayed socialist ideals. Heinrich Mann locked himself in his study for two days and spoke to no one, while Thomas Mann, no Moscow loyalist himself, saw a great chasm open which swallowed all hope in one merciless gulp; at that moment the past was cut off from the future.[20] On 1 September Brecht noted: 'At 8.45 in the morning Germany warns all neutrals against flying over Polish territory. Hitler addresses the Wehrmacht. In between, the melancholy marches with which German militarists like introducing their bloodbaths'.[21] Brecht was visibly shaken by events. Steffin told their Danish friend and translator Fredrik Martner that he was 'not quite fit and well'.[22]

While the USSR's critics argued that its actions had exposed its naked imperialist ambitions, supporters like Brecht fell back on the notion that the USSR needed a buffer against incursions and, more plausibly, that it was buying time to strengthen its defensive military capability before the inevitable Nazi onslaught. Brecht found Hitler's speech on 1 September 'strikingly insecure ("I am determined to show determination"). The loudest applause when he says that traitors have nothing to expect but death. This is the clique, the gang, the foreign body that begins a war minus God and plus bread coupons'.[23] On that same 1 September Brecht was invited to a lunch in Thomas Mann's honour at the Stockholm city hall. Mann was in town for a meeting of the German Writers' Association in Exile. Brecht noted: 'Mann is opposed to the USSR's support for Hitler. Erika Mann, his daughter, finds the pact logical and comprehensible, but is against the view that it helps the cause of peace'.

On 3 September Britain and France declared war on Germany when Hitler ignored the joint British–French ultimatum to cease hostilities against Poland. Brecht wrote: 'Only in the evening did the terrible truth dawn on everybody'. He expanded the following day: 'I was pretty convinced the English would draw back at the last minute.

But Churchill seems to have pulled it off. The question now is whether they will actually fight a war. The machinery will probably be very hard to set in motion. Hitler will soon have achieved a *fait accompli* in the East, at which point they may negotiate after all'. Germany took the West of Poland in what Hitler termed a Blitzkrieg, a war of lightning speed. Brecht observed: 'For the USSR it would only be possible to enter the war on the western side'. He recognised Nazi aggression against Poland as nothing less than a 'war of annihilation'. Germany occupied Warsaw within days without any western response, established its General Government of the West of Poland and Danzig, and then went about the gruesome destruction of this 'inferior' Slavic people, including its military and intellectual elite and its sizeable minorities, principally Jews and gypsies. Brecht resisted the commonsense interpretation of Soviet strategy: 'The Germans' statements that the Russians are reaching military agreements with them grow more and more definite. This nonsense is gladly disseminated'. Much of it was true. On 9 September Brecht had to acknowledge a terrible truth: 'The Union will in the eyes of the proletariat of the world bear the terrible stigma of aiding and abetting Fascism, the wildest element in capitalism and the most hostile to the workers. I don't think more can be said than that the Union saved its skin at the cost of leaving the proletariat of the world without solutions, hopes or help'. Unlike many others, Brecht was still prepared to maintain his support for the USSR.

There was worse to come. The Red Army occupied Eastern Poland and the Soviet Foreign Minister Molotov invoked blood ties between the Poles, Ukrainians and Byelorussians to justify the fourth partition of the Polish state. Brecht acknowledged that 'every ideological veil' had been 'torn to shreds': 'The abandonment of the slogan "the USSR needs no foot of foreign soil", the appropriation of the Fascist hypocrisies about "blood-brotherhood", the liberation of "brothers" (of Slav descent), all the terminology of nationalism. This is addressed to the German Fascists, but at the same time to the Soviet troops'. Brecht conceded the USSR's 'grave political errors' and once more acknowledged the nature of Stalin's rule: 'Stalin finds it impossible to start a war in a revolutionary manner, as a people's war'. The emperor Stalin had embarked on his own expansionist dreams, creating an empire which would last just fifty years.

Epic Theatre against war: *Mother Courage* and *Lucullus*

In early September Brecht was struggling with *The Good Person of Szechwan*: 'Bogged down in the work on the parable. It doesn't flow properly. Much of it is too contrived, the whole is still just so many parts'.[24] On 27 September 1939, the day Poland surrendered to Nazi Germany, he again dropped the project and began a new work, his great anti-war play *Mother Courage and Her Children: A Chronicle of the Thirty Years War*. Since his Augsburg adolescence, when he had treated the Thirty Years' War in *The Bible*, challenging Schiller's idealism in *Wallenstein*, Brecht had been equipping himself to write a historical parable about the folly of war. In order to reflect on the dark times of his new age, he again positioned himself in that earlier dark age of Counter-Reformation Europe and, following the rapid composition of *Life of Galileo*, he produced another masterpiece at breakneck speed. A first draft of *Mother Courage* was finished by 3 November, by which time Germany and the USSR had completed their dismantling of Poland.

There are few traces of preparatory work. In Sweden, Brecht found himself in the territory of the Swedish general from the Thirty Years' War, Count Oxenstierna. He and the Swedish King Gustav Adolphus had had a close relationship with their Lutheran peers in Germany. As Brecht had written in *How Much Is Your Iron?*, that same territory was now yielding its materials in exchange for a dubious prospect of survival. Brecht asked Naima Wifstrand to tell him about a famous Swedish survivor from the Russian–Swedish war, the canteen woman Lotta Svård. Wifstrand gave him a translation of Johan Ludvig Runeberg's *Tales of a Subaltern*, which includes ballads about Svård. Brecht created his own canteen woman, Anna Fierling, whose bravery earns her the nickname Mother Courage. For that nickname, Brecht drew on Grimmelshausen's picaresque novel, *Trutz-Simplex*, with its figure of Courasche, the arch-swindler and troublemaker. Envisaging a production in Sweden, Brecht wrote the part for Wifstrand and for Weigel the role of her mute daughter Kattrin.

Fierling's resourcefulness and wit are subjected to the severest test in the sequence of twelve scenes, each announced in the Epic manner by a description of events to follow, rather like the chapter headings in a picaresque novel. The opening scene is introduced as follows: 'Spring 1624. The Swedish Commander-in-Chief Count Oxenstiernia is raising troops in Dalecarlia for the Polish campaign. The canteen woman Anna Fierling, known under the name of Mother Courage, loses one son'.[25] The contemporary dismantling of Poland by the German and Soviet armies is never far below the surface in this play, beginning with the campaign on Polish territory fought by the Protestant and Catholic armies. Brecht presents the unfolding seventeenth-century wartime situation from the perspective of the common people caught up in it. In the German text, they all speak a rough-hewn, south German dialect that Brecht adapted from 'Hašek's way of speaking in *Schweyk*'.[26]

War is exposed as a rapacious act of economic exploitation, the reality of which is glossed over by the rhetoric of glory and honour proclaimed by the rulers and their lackeys, not least religious orders who support war in God's name. For Oxenstierna's recruiters, war is the natural order of things, which peace threatens to disrupt, with damaging consequences for a morality based on order and discipline. War also offers the opportunity of profit which people become so hooked on that they dread peace, which would shatter their livelihood. Anna Fierling is one such person. She follows the armies around on her canteen wagon with Kattrin and her two sons, Eilif and Swiss Cheese. Eilif is bright and brave, Swiss Cheese simple but honest. Kattrin is a quite selfless soul, who emerges as the first in a series of female figures who in Brecht's late ethical dramas carry the burden of representing innate human goodness by virtue of their maternal instinct. Señora Carrar's motivation earlier had been somewhat different. The arc of Brecht's creativity connects, too, with his grieving mothers from the First World War. Anna Fierling, her own maternal instinct competing with her business sense, announces herself on stage with her song, offering her wares to the soldiers while they take a break from battle. She has no illusions about the gruesome reality of war for them: 'Captains, your men don't look so well. / So feed them up and let them follow / While you command them into hell'.[27] She follows with the grim refrain with which she also ends the play:

The new year's come. The watchmen shout.
The thaw sets in. The dead remain.
Wherever life has not died out
It staggers to its feet again.

Courage and others like her do not expect more from life. Their view is that nothing will change. Like Galileo, she is a survivor, but the mentality of the business woman is diametrically opposed to the intellectual's belief that all is subject to change and that life can be improved: 'You can say victory and defeat both come expensive to us ordinary folk. Best thing for us is when politics get bogged down solid'. The exploration of such contrasts and oppositions runs through the roll of Brecht's 'great' survivors. The nickname Courage, she proclaims, 'Is the name they gave me because I was scared of going broke, sergeant, so I drove me cart right through the bombardment of Riga with thirty loaves of bread aboard. They were going mouldy, it was high time, they hadn't any choice really'. She identifies the threat of economic loss as the driving force in her brave action, not any altruistic conviction. In her recognition that courage can be a quite misplaced virtue in war, especially for soldiers with a 'rotten general', she is the vehicle for a Brechtian critique of conventional virtue, drawing again on the *Book of Tao-tê-ching*: 'Because he's got to have men of courage, that's why. If he knew how to plan a proper campaign what would he be needing men of courage for? Ordinary ones would do. It's always the same; whenever there's a load of special virtues around it means that something stinks'.[28] Her amplification, 'In decent countries folk don't have to have virtues', glosses the Chinese philosopher Me-ti's belief that good government is a pre-requisite for good behaviour. In a later speech, she picks up the same strand of thought, integrated within a Brechtian picaresque scenario, in which the common people undermine the ambitions of the masters of war by evading the life-threatening tasks which the masters set them in the interest of their own glory:

Can't help feeling sorry for those general and emperors, there they are maybe thinking they're doing something extra special what folk'll talk about in years to come, and earning a public monument, like conquering the world for instance, that's a fine ambition for a general, how's he to know any better? I mean, he plagues hisself to death, then it all breaks down on account of ordinary folk that just wants their beer and a bit of chat, nowt higher. Finest plans get bollixed up by the pettiness of them as should be carrying them out, because emperors can't do nowt themselves, they just counts on soldiers and people to back 'em up whatever happens, am I right?[29]

With cunning, the weak may survive, while the glory which the masters of war crave eludes them. However, there are severe limitations to Courage's own cunning. Her knowledge about the turn of events is a long way behind the leaders'. And, for all her bravery and her understanding of war, Fierling fails to learn that she cannot combine war-profiteering and motherhood, even when, in the first scene, each of her children draws the black cross signifying impending death, and the sergeant comments: 'Want to live off war, but keep yourself and family out of it, eh?'. She maintains:

> Poor folk got to have courage. Why, they're lost. Simply getting up in the morning takes some doing in their situation. Or ploughing a field, and in a war at that. Mere fact they bring kids into the world shows they got courage, cause there's no hope for them. They have to hang one another and slaughter one another, so just looking each other in the face must call for courage. Being able to put up with emperor and pope shows supernatural courage, cause those two cost 'em their lives.

Accepting her plight with a willed blindness within her courageous attitude, this 'great' survivor lives off the war and loses her children one after another, each ironically on account of the principal virtue that they embody, which is revealed as their greatest weakness. What is more, when faced by the unenviable choice of losing her livelihood or a child, she makes a business calculation, through which in practice she opts for her livelihood and reveals herself to be, in the words of the Chaplain, a 'hyena of the battlefield'. Unable to reconcile the contradictions in her life, Courage is reduced to a classic Brechtian didivual. Her inhumanity contrasts with the noble self-sacrifice of Kattrin, who is shot while beating the drum to save the Protestant town of Halle from Catholic attack – and to save her mother who is in the town. The situation is similar to that in Brecht's first play, *The Bible*. The state in which Brecht leaves Fierling at the end of the *Mother Courage* echoes the madness of women grieving the dead in Brecht's poignant ballads of the First World War. Courage believes that she can sing to Kattrin while she's 'going to sleep':

> Lullaby baby
> What's that in the hay?
> Neighbours' kids grizzle
> But my kids are gay.
> [...]
> Lullaby baby
> What's that in the hay?
> The one lies in Poland
> The other – who can say?

The nickname Courage has, of course, acquired a deadly ironic ring: for people caught up in war, courage is not sufficient to ensure survival. On the contrary, it may precipitate death. Brecht, the author of 'Five Difficulties in Writing the Truth' had learnt that courage was an over-rated and much-abused virtue. It is left to the audience to consider the implications. Do the common people possess the cunning and collective will to extricate themselves from war by declaring it inimical to humanity and insisting on the pursuit of socially useful activity?

Brecht followed up shortly after in November with the composition in a week of a complementary anti-war piece in fourteen short scenes, the radio play *The Trial of Lucullus*. Drawing on a story from Roman history about the victories and conquests of one of its most successful generals, the play inquires how Lucullus's achievements are to be evaluated. Brecht noted: 'It more or less reaches the limit of what can still be said'.[30] Hilding Rosenberg was to compose the music for the play, which was to be broadcast on Swedish radio.

During the pomp and ceremony of Lucullus's funeral procession, onlookers are divided: on the one hand there is the merchant's admiration for the fortunes which have accrued and, on the other, women's anger at the price they have had to pay with the death of their sons. The Children's Chorus shows that, like the enthusiastic young Brecht before 1914, they have been groomed in the imperialist ideology at school:

> In the schoolbooks
> Are written the names of great generals.
> Whoever wants to emulate them
> Learns their battles by heart
> Studies their wonderful lives.[31]

In the dramatic situation of a trial, which Brecht increasingly employed, the Gatekeeper from the Realm of Shadows is joined by a Jury of the Dead, comprising everyday people: the Teacher (who was a slave), the Baker, the Fishwife, the Farmer and the Courtesan, all sitting in judgement upon this master of war to determine whether he will go to Hades or the Elysian Fields. The trial is the setting for a demonstration of Brechtian Taoist ethics, applied not to a survivor of the misdeeds of the masters of war but this time to such a master himself. Lucullus stands out from the others awaiting their fate through his sheer arrogance. The principal criterion for the Jury's approval is a person's usefulness and for the Jury's rejection, if the person has murdered: 'You must account for your life among men. / Whether you have served them or harmed them'. The figures from the frieze depicting Lucullus's achievements speak out, among them the conquered, who tell of Lucullus's acts of pillage and destruction, which he proudly acknowledges. An exasperated Judge of the Dead exclaims:

> Anger us no more with your triumphs!
> Have you no witnesses
> To any of your weaknesses, mortal?
> Your business goes badly. Your virtues
> Seem to be of little use.

Lucullus's Cook, supported by his Baker, who is also on the frieze, has warm words for his master's Epicurean taste and his delight in trying new recipes with the Cook: 'He ranked me next to the kings / And gave my art recognition. / That's why I call him human'. In that familiar Brechtian topos, appetites define properly human behaviour in terms of a capacity for pleasure and, at the same time, an exposure to vulnerability. In a further testimony to Lucullus's weaknesses, inverting the ethical norm, it emerges that he had prevented his soldiers from destroying works of art and books, and his conquering army had brought a cherry tree back from Asia, planting it in the Apennines. The Farmer congratulates Lucullus:

> [...] When all the booty of conquest
> From both Asias has long mouldered away

> The finest of all your trophies
> Renewed each year for the living
> Shall in spring flutter its white-flowered branches
> In the wind from the hills.

Working with the grain of elegant, fertile nature to extract its ever-renewing vitality for the benefit of human life is a further item in Lucullus's favour as, at the close of the play, the court withdraws for consultation. It is left to listeners to determine their judgement of the case.

However, the Swedish broadcaster withdrew from the project. Brecht had, it seems, exceeded the limit of what could be said. With support from Jewish émigrés, Hermann Greid performed *The Trial of Lucullus* as a shadow play with a group of young people. Brecht's Swiss publisher Kurt Reiss arranged for the work to be broadcast on 12 May 1940 by the Berne studio of Radio Beromünster. However, with plays like this and *Mother Courage* Brecht was storing up trouble for himself from his own side, who saw in them a pacifism which had nothing in common with Leninist partisanship. Brecht could point to his Marxist analysis of socio-economic relations, but for KPD members that made Brecht just half a Marxist, as they had always believed him, at best, to be.

Skirting the theatre of war: On to Finland

On 30 November 1939 the Soviet Union embarked on the next phase of the secret protocol. After Finland had rejected the Soviet request to establish military bases on its soil, the Red Army marched into Finland without any declaration of war. However, the Soviets met with stiff resistance in the Winter War, which saw the USSR expelled from the League of Nations. By January 1940 Brecht was contemplating the impossible: 'The world situation is getting more and more confused. [...] The USSR could find itself in the position of having to support the Nazi regime, and how is that to be done even using furnace tongs?'.[32] The Swedish press was strongly behind Finland, celebrating stories of Finnish resistance to vastly superior Soviet numbers. Brecht wrote a satirical riposte to the general euphoria, 'The Finnish Miracle', which appeared in Swedish in the Communist newspaper *Ny Dag* under the pseudonym Sherwood Paw. Allegedly a re-print from the US *Shrewd Man's Review*, the piece mocked the claims of extraordinary Finnish military feats and of a defence of civilisation and democracy. Brecht pointed out that the Finnish commander-in-chief Carl Gustav von Mannerheim was the same man who had suppressed the Social Democrats in the civil war of 1917–18. Brecht saw the alternative for Finland as lying between Fascism and Communism. The notion of national, let alone regional, self-determination had become a fiction, in which Finland was just another Scandinavian pawn in the broader strategic and ideological struggle. However, in mocking stereotypical depictions in the Swedish press of the Soviet 'terror regime' and the Russian people's 'total enslavement', Brecht was trivialising what he knew of Stalin's Russia. The Winter War ended in March 1940 when the USSR and Finland signed a peace treaty, in which Finland relinquished eleven per cent of its territory and thirty per cent of its economic capacity. The USSR had, however, failed in its objective to conquer the whole country. In June 1940 the USSR would embark upon the next phase of the secret protocol, the occupation of the Baltic states.

Since the outbreak of war the Swedish secret service had been taking a greater interest in German émigrés. Figures like Paul Verner and Herbert Warnke, who had discussed the defeat of the Spanish republic at Brecht's house, were interned. Brecht was concerned for his own safety and that of those around him. Police questioned people crossing the bridge between Stockholm and Lidingø, among them a friend of Brecht's son who was asked about visitors to Brecht's house. A warrant was issued for Steffin's arrest while she was back in Copenhagen receiving medical treatment. While Brecht resumed work on *The Good Person of Szechwan* and the *Caesar* novel in March, his own health was suffering in a familiar way: 'Bedridden three weeks with influenza. I am helpless against the clutches of that kind of thing when I have no major work on the go. In addition to which I cannot work with a temperature'.[33] For visitors, Brecht became visibly more and more nervous and very restless but, as Johannes Edfelt saw it, adopted a cynical mask to appear tough.[34] However practised, this required a great effort of will. Brecht's Swedish residence permit was not extended and on 8 April he visited the Czech émigré actor Valter Taub, who recalled: 'A great restlessness had seized him. He said that the occupation of Norway and Denmark was to be expected in the coming days. It was becoming advisable to leave Sweden without delay'. Similarly, Lucie Taubova recalled Brecht saying: 'I'm not playing the hero. I'm going. It's better to have a Brecht on the outside rather than in a concentration camp'.

He combated extreme anxiety with thoughts of a 'little epic work', 'The Fears of Mr Keuner', about a picaresque figure in the manner of Candide or Gulliver: 'Herr Keuner is afraid that the earth may become uninhabitable if too great crimes, or too great virtues become necessary before a man can make enough to live on. Thus Herr Keuner flees from country to country, since too much is asked of him everywhere, be it self-sacrifice, or bravery, or cleverness, or desire for freedom or thirst for justice, or cruelty, or deceit etc. All these lands are uninhabitable'.[35] Brecht had learnt from Taoist philosophy that conventional western virtues were no guide to survival. Good government was nowhere to be found.

On 9 April 1940, the German army occupied Denmark and attacked Norway, concluding another victorious Blitzkrieg campaign in June. Sweden re-affirmed its neutrality, at the same time allowing Germany transit routes for the Norwegian campaign. On that same 9 April the police summoned Ninnan Santesson and searched Brecht's house for political publications. Santesson found Brecht in a very agitated state, convinced that they must flee Sweden immediately.[36] Branting and others agreed. In just a few days they would be gone, this time with few possessions. In addition to a few items of furniture, manuscripts and minor items like a silver whisky flask and two Bavarian hunting knives, Brecht listed objects from which he drew strength in his struggle for survival: the two volumes of Brueghel's pictures and some books; the Chinese picture scroll 'The Doubter'; three Japanese masks; and, two little Chinese carpets.[37]

Finland was the only possible direction of travel. Branting's Finnish friend Mary Pekkala put him in touch with her sister-in-law, the writer and public personality

Hella Wuolijoki. Brecht wrote to Wuolijoki: 'It seems possible that we won't be able to stay here much longer. If we can show an invitation from you, we might get Finnish visas on the strength of it. Could you send us one?'.[38] After Karin Michaelis and Ninnan Santesson, in Wuolijoki a third Scandinavian female artist of means came to Brecht's rescue, using her contacts to smooth the passage to Helsinki. Meanwhile, Brecht contacted Berlau in Copenhagen, allaying her fears by telling her that he would '*always* organise your journey with ours'.[39] He outlined the plan to go to Finland and from there to try to get to the USA. He urged her to apply for a US visa as soon as possible. Having divorced the wealthy Robert Lund, Berlau made her life dependent upon Brecht's and from now on experienced great anxiety at the prospect of separation. She would engage in public protestations of her love, which Brecht and others, not least Weigel and Steffin, found distasteful. This would lead to more exaggerated behaviour, Berlau's anxieties increasingly fuelled by drugs and alcohol. It was a recipe for a ruined life.

On 17 April 1940 a distressed Brecht assembled with Weigel, Stefan and Barbara, together with Steffin, Hermann Greid and other refugees, at the Skeppsbron quayside in Stockholm. Matthis, Santesson and Lazar saw them off as they boarded their ship to the Finnish port of Turku. Peter Weiss ends the second volume of his magisterial novel, *The Aesthetics of Resistance*, with a scene based on Matthis's description of events, in which 'Brecht, making his way across the gangplank, – the swastikas were waving to his left on Blasieholmen from the building of the German embassy and to his right on Stadsgard Wharf from the German freighters – collapsed and had to be supported, almost carried on board'.[40] From there, Brecht witnessed the struggle of another survivor: 'The young widow for whom the ship stops, so that she can clamber aboard up a ladder from an ice-floe'.[41] Arriving at Turku the following day, they took the train to Helsinki where they rented rooms in the Hospiz guesthouse at Vuorikatu 17 near the main station. Shortly after, Karin Michaelis formally declared that Brecht and Weigel no longer owed her money.[42] Michaelis had spent much of her fortune supporting them and others, but she herself now had to flee from the Nazis to the United States.

Brecht was well known in Finland after productions of his works and was soon discussing projects with writers and theatre people. He conducted two interviews on arrival, expressing the hope that *Mother Courage* would soon be performed in Stockholm and Zurich. However, official Finnish artistic organisations were reluctant to make a lot of the refugee, who had after all mocked the Finns in the Winter War. On 22 April Brecht and Weigel moved into a flat at Linnankoskenkatu 20A in the Helsinki district of Töölö. Weigel drove around in a truck, picking up furniture donated by, among others, Mary Pekkala, the composer Simon Parmet, Hella Wuolijoki, and the writer Elmer Diktonius. Stefan and Barbara shared a room, Brecht had a bedroom-study and Weigel slept in the kitchen. Re-establishing a work routine in a calm environment with stimulating conversation in the evening was essential for Brecht to recover his composure. Weigel once more created that environment, deploying her culinary skills as she entertained her dinner guests: Wuolijoki, Diktonius and other writers, Erkki Vala, Arvo Turtiainen, Hagar Olsson and Eric Olsoni, as well as Hermann Greid and Arnold Ljungdal, also a refugee from Stockholm. Those who met

Brecht in Helsinki were struck by his unassuming manner.[43] Adopting the wisdom writer's attitude of imperturbability, in his everyday interactions Brecht managed to hide the anxieties which threatened to overwhelm him.

Thanks to Piscator, Brecht secured the offer of a post in the USA. Piscator was directing the Dramatic Workshop at the New School for Social Research in New York, where Eisler, too, was now based. The School's President Alvin S. Johnson intervened on Brecht's behalf, as he did on behalf of so many from his 'University in Exile', telegraphing Brecht the offer of a teaching post in literature, which was available from May 1940 until January 1941. As Lyon writes, the offer, which was later extended to September 1941, probably saved Brecht's life.[44] On 2 May 1940 Johnson urged the American consul in Helsinki to grant the visa without delay. Brecht estimated that they would have to wait in Helsinki for at least a month, maybe longer. A month would turn into a year.

Having received the letter from Johnson, Brecht was now obliged to lodge a formal application with the US consulate in Helsinki for a visa outside the quota system. Brecht did not, however, follow the correct bureaucratic procedure. In a questionnaire for the US authorities he later wrote that in May 1940 he had asked the American consul in Helsinki, verbally, 'not in writing', 'for tourist visas because I was afraid we should not get the immigration papers without delay'.[45] He also tried to apply pressure through friends in New York and Helsinki. In his 'Ode to a High Dignitary' Brecht suggests that he presented himself to the vice-consul responsible, Lawrence von Hellens, four times: 'Twice I have had my hair cut for your sake / Never / Did I go to you hatless, my shabby cap / I always hid from you'.[46] However, Brecht's attempt to override the bureaucracy failed: 'This last application was refused'. Steffin told Eisler that the consul's view was that at such times the chance offer of a job did not justify a tourist visa.

It was not lost on Johnson that Brecht's association with Communism was a key issue. In the cases of Eisler and Piscator, Johnson had managed to get round the question and he had categorised Brecht, whom he regarded as a 'great man', merely as a sympathiser.[47] However, immigration was now being policed more rigorously. When Archibald MacLeish was asked to comment on Brecht's politics, he responded: 'I met him on several occasions in New York three or four years ago. Although I do not know him well, I believed at that time that he was a Communist. Whether he still is a Communist I have no means of knowing. If I had to guess, I should guess that he is at least a "fellow traveller" '. This reasonable assessment was on the file, together with Brecht's signed statement that he was not a member of the Communist Party. Meanwhile, other people in the USA intervened on Brecht's behalf, principally his translator Ernestine Evans, who was shown a letter from the US consul in Helsinki Harold Schantz, which said that Brecht was 'not inadmissible'. However, nothing more happened until the autumn.

Hoping that their visas would come through quickly, Weigel made reservations on a US cargo boat leaving for the US on 5 August 1940 from Petsamo (from 1944 the Russian Pechengsky District), Finland's sole ice-free harbour giving on to the Barents Sea and the western passage to the USA. Brecht wrote: 'Curiously, I examine the map of the continent. / High up in Lapland, / Towards the Arctic Ocean / I still see a small door'.[48] The boat left Petsamo twice a month and had room for fourteen passengers. In mid-May Berlau arrived in Helsinki where she took a room in a guesthouse. Brecht asked her to book her berth individually but she reacted to his request with consternation. For Weigel, Berlau's arrival was a gross intrusion as she struggled with an already precarious situation. Brecht had gone too far.

While German troops continued their advance through Norway, on 10 May the German occupation of Holland and Belgium began, opening the way for the attack on France. By 3 June German troops were approaching Dunkirk, having cut off French troops from Belgian and Allied forces. After the Allied evacuation of Dunkirk, German troops moved quickly through France. These events were painful listening for Brecht: 'Now that the news has turned so bad I am even considering switching off the early morning wireless. The little box sits by my bed and my last move at night is to turn it off, my first in the morning to put it on'.[49] Brecht tried to find out from Fritz Lieb in Basel what had become of Benjamin. By the time Lieb could forward Brecht's letter, Benjamin had left Paris with his sister Dora in advance of the Nazi occupation of the French capital on 14 June. 'Hitler Dances: Führer does Jig for Victory' is the title of a bizarre photographic sequence in the US magazine *Life*, which Brecht pasted in his journal together with his comment: 'The French generals end the war as tamely, incompetently and treacherously as the French politicians began it. And England! Judas has been betrayed! But think what the peoples are having to suffer'.[50] Brecht added: 'Fall of France, collapse of a world empire in three weeks'. Another empire, he pointed out, had been 'rocked to the foundations': 'A ring of iron is closing round Britain'. Brecht feared for Feuchtwanger, who had been interned in France, but in August he heard that Feuchtwanger had made it to Lisbon on his way to the USA. Heinrich and Nelly Mann accompanied Lion and Marta Feuchtwanger on their hazardous journey across the Pyrenees.

With studied under-statement Brecht wrote to Arnold Ljungdal in June 1940: 'Our trip to America isn't getting ahead very well'.[51] The Nazi occupation of northern Norway had all but closed the western passage to the USA from Finland. There remained only the arduous and expensive land and sea route to Los Angeles, which they had understandably wanted to avoid, since it took them through dangerous terrain: Moscow, Vladivostok and Yokohama. Germany concluded a trade agreement with Finland, Brecht noting ominously: 'Over Europe falls the shadow of a gigantic famine that is approaching. There is no more coffee here, sugar is scarce, cigars (for me part of my means of production) are getting prohibitive. Everything shows the growing might of the Third Reich'.[52]

Marlebäck: *Mr Puntila and His Man Matti*

Faced with a longer stay in Finland, Brecht and Weigel accepted Wuolijoki's invitation to spend the summer on her estate, Marlebäck, four hours by train from Helsinki. Wuolijoki, who was much more than just a writer, had bought Marlebäck in 1920 and had exploited its timber resources. Formerly married to a Social Democrat politician, she remained active in left-wing politics. Though not overtly Communist, she had strong links with Moscow and had, in fact, brokered peace negotiations with the USSR to end the Winter War. When hostilities between Finland and the USSR resumed in June 1941 with Finland now supporting Nazi Germany, she was arrested and in 1943 sentenced to life imprisonment for hiding a Soviet paratrooper-spy. Brecht and Weigel sent statements in support of Wuolijoki, but they counted for nothing. She was, however, released after the ceasefire in 1944 and resumed her influential role in Finnish life.

The Brechts moved to Marlebäck in early July. Initially, Steffin and Berlau lived in Wuolijoki's manor house, while Brecht, Weigel and the children lived in a 'villa surrounded by lovely birch trees' close by.[53] Fourteen Karelian refugees from the Soviet aggression were housed on the estate. The manor house was also a summer salon, where politicians, journalists, artists and diplomats met. The Soviet ambassador was a frequent guest. It emerges from Brecht's letter to Berlau in August 1945 that in the summer of 1940 Wuolijoki's Soviet guests offered Brecht their support, should he wish to return to Berlin after the defeat of Nazism in the war with the Soviet Union which they all knew was coming.[54] Brecht, of course, understood that international prestige could open doors but also that domestic politics, not least in the Soviet Union, often followed quite a different logic, deeply hostile to diplomatic privilege.

Every day in the late afternoon at Marlebäck, Brecht and the other residents used the sauna in a wooden hut down by the river. Brecht described the experience in some detail:

> You go through the changing room into a small dark room dominated by a huge stone stove. You take off the wooden lid and pour hot water from an iron pot that stands beside the stove on round stones the size of your fist stacked directly over the fire. Then you climb up a few steps to a wooden platform and lie down. When you begin to break sweat you whip the open pores with birch twigs, then you go out and plunge into the river. When you emerge – the cool water does not seem cold – you leave a trail of birch leaves behind you. At night too, you find some in bed. 'You sleep with the birch', says H.W. Finnish soldiers built saunas even in the most advanced positions.[55]

Afterwards everyone came together in the manor house for coffee and conversation about political developments. Wuolijoki recalls:

> Brecht huddled up in an armchair by the veranda door, dark and without a collar, smoking a cigar as usual, Helene with her noble profile and her slender fingers operated our silver Viennese coffee machine ..., carefully, she measured the exquisite, fragrant powder. [...] The great actress's fingers were hopelessly rough and reddened from peeling potatoes and washing the dishes for her refugee family, and her hair grey from the worry, but her eyes radiated humour and joie de vivre.[56]

Meanwhile, Berlau sat there 'as beautiful as a flower, laying her mysterious Mona Lisa smile at Brecht's feet'. Of Steffin Wuolijoki writes: 'Poor Grete with her big, loyal eyes, always smiling and fun-loving – with a sunny calm she bore the stamp of death on her face'. Steffin sat in a corner, noting down Wuolijoki's endless round of stories, which engrossed Brecht: 'What a gripping epic storyteller she is, sitting on her wooden stool and making coffee! It all comes out biblically simple and biblically complex'.[57] She was rather like Grandma Brezing, only hilariously funny. He added: 'She looks wise and lovely as she tells of the ruses of simple people and the stupidity of the upper crust, shaking with perpetual laughter and now and again looking at you with sly winks, as she accompanies the various personages' words with epic, flowing movements of her lovely fat hands'. Stimulated by Wuolijoki at Marlebäck, Brecht revealed a side which he reserved for a select few, entertaining everyone with a one-man-show, imitating the greats of Berlin theatre and Hollywood, climbing on the table to deliver a speech and crawling around on his stomach on the floor.

Berlau angered the other women with her lovesick behaviour. On one occasion, she made coffee after dinner and poured it for everyone but added cream and sugar only for Brecht.[58] She felt alone when apart from Brecht and consoled herself with the plentiful supply of fruit schnapps. Her behaviour proved too much for Wuolijoki, who insisted that she leave her house. Berlau's behaviour now began to anger Brecht, too. He sent her the first letter of a type which continued for the rest of his life, in which he sought both to excuse his own behaviour and to calm her: 'I am very depressed that I was so vehement and coarse but there are two difficulties. The first is that it makes me very anxious to know that you are waiting for me and need me; and the second is that at times when I am immersed in work I become completely unsensual and the most harmless observations of an erotic nature become almost unbearable for me'.[59] Brecht asked Berlau to believe that this really was so.

Though financially independent, psychologically Berlau was wholly dependent on Brecht. He still believed that he could teach her to control her behaviour, advising her shortly afterwards: 'Ruth, please don't take any more powders'. However, his absence caused her to panic and to behave in an erratic, self-destructive manner. He wrote her a longer letter, in which he spelt out what had become of their relationship, now that she was convinced that he enjoyed treating her badly: 'For you a kind of servitude has now probably grown out of that and I've become a tyrant for you. But that is bad instruction and a bad dialogue'. He saw writing together as a form of therapy. 'Kin-jeh's Shadow' in the *Book of Twists and Turns* ends with the following: 'It took some time before I learnt that it takes two people to be close to one another. When I went away from Kin-jeh, did not need him or was not useful to him, I was away from him, not nearby'.[60] After a while, Berlau was allowed to move back into the manor house but from this time onwards she was prey to dark thoughts and outbursts of uncontrolled aggression.

Brecht found the light summer nights at Marlebäck 'very beautiful': 'I got up at three o'clock because of the flies, and went out. Cocks were crowing, but it had not been dark. I like to relieve myself in the open air. Funnily enough I never think about work at such a time. These are not working hours'.[61] He began *Conversations among Refugees* at Marlebäck as a light-hearted distraction. The setting is the restaurant at Helsinki station where two exiles, Ziffel, the physicist, and Kalle, the worker, while away their time in meandering exchanges. They encompass memories of childhood and school years as well as of exile, some of which, as we have seen, are recognisable as Brecht's own. However, the phenomenally productive Brecht briefly experienced something all too familiar to many writers, a moment of 'blockage', which he took to calling this 'in-between time'.[62] He was unable to conclude *The Good Person of Szechwan*, the *Caesar* novel and *The Messingkauf Dialogues*. He reflected: 'It is impossible to finish a play properly without a stage. The proof of the pudding ...'.[63]

The blockage in fact prefigured the release of a fresh wave of creative energy as he broke through the shell of the refugee's intellectual isolation. The first products of this fresh creative surge are 'Finnish Epigrams', in the style of Greek epigrams, which he would assemble in the 'Steffin Collection'. They include two poems which describe, quite unexpectedly, the glorious intensity of his senses that summer, which Brecht found 'so very rich and varied on such a grand scale'.[64] 'Larder on a Finnish Estate, 1940' reads:

> O shady store! The scent of dark green firs
> Comes nightly swirling in to blend itself
> With that of sweet milk from enormous churns
> And smoky bacon on its cold stone shelf.
>
> Beer, goats' milk cheese, new bread and berries
> Picked from grey undergrowth heavy with dew ...
> To those fighting the war on empty bellies
> Far to the south: I wish it were for you.

'Finnish Landscape' begins:

> Those fish-stocked waters! Lovely trees as well!
> Such scents of berries and of birches there!
> Thick-corded winds that softly cradle air
> As mild as though the clanking iron churns
> Trundled from the white farmhouse were all left open!
> Dizzy with sight and sound and thought and smell
> The refugee beneath the alders turns
> To his laborious job: continued hoping.

Brecht had not written poetry like this since his early twenties. As in *Svendborg Poems*, the arc of creativity connects him back to the verses of *Domestic Breviary*. The fresh opening to nature signals a dramatic shift from the austere, disciplined self of his 'one-sided' poems towards the hedonistic creature of the senses which he always was, too. The body with its vital, unpredictable appetites has returned in Brecht's poetry as in his drama. The exile's political consciousness is by no means effaced by this receptivity to nature, which the partisan Leninist Brecht had initially forbidden himself in the Comintern's anti-Fascist struggle. His anti-Fascism is, however, now a struggle for survival, in which each and every trace of life is precious.

Brecht's journal contains similar passages to his verses: 'The lakes with their plenitude of fish, the woods with their beautiful trees and the scent of berries and birches. The tremendous summers which burst out overnight after the interminable winters, great heat after great cold. And as the day disappears in winter, so the night disappears in summer. And then the air is so powerful and tastes so good that it almost satisfies your appetite unaided'.[65] The remarkable quality of the air – for Brecht an index of well-being – was quite unprecedented. In California he would find the air difficult to breathe, exacerbating his physical problems. In the beneficent environment of Marlebäck, the delicate Brecht could feel something like vigour.

The compositions from a Finnish summer do not, of course, reveal Brecht's belated assumption of a Romantic sensibility, the pitfalls of which he could simply not countenance. As Hans Peter Neureuter shows, Brecht's Finnish poems celebrate his observation and enjoyment of the objects he encounters on the estate, mediated by the senses in the manner of the poetry he was reading. Brecht comments: 'The mood of these Greek epigrams is set by their marvellous concreteness, together with their sense of how a specific wind (evening wind, dawn wind, April wind, wind off the snows) will stir the leaves and fruit on a given tree'.[66] In the manner of the classical Greek 'mood' – a term long banished from Brecht's critical vocabulary – his Finnish epigrams convey an opening of the senses upon which he reflects repeatedly in his journal from August, as he considers, too, Goethe's poetry and affirms that 'art *is* an autonomous sphere, though by no means an autarchic one. [...] Possible criterion for a work of art: does it enrich the individual's capacity for experience?'.

As always happened when Brecht met a talented person, he was inspired to work with Wuolijoki. Together they wrote a drama, *Mr Puntila and His Man Matti*, for a Finnish competition, based on her hilarious stories of her relative Roope Juntula, who emerges as a classic Brechtian contradictory character, flitting back and forth between one behavioural pole and another: 'Adventures of a Finnish landowner and his chauffeur. He is only human when he is drunk, since that is when he forgets his own interests'.[67] Much of the colour of life at Marlebäck which Brecht captured in poems and his journal finds its way into his earthy adaptation, from the smells of the countryside and farm to the sauna, the milkmaids, and the pleasure of relieving oneself at night in the open. Diplomats are there, too, the butt of Brecht's satirical gifts with their mealy-mouthed forms of words. *Puntila* was the first of two comic interludes in Finland between the more arduous works of survival.

While Brecht greatly admired Wuolijoki, he believed that their collaboration was 'hampered by her conventional dramatic technique'. He put his own stamp on the material: 'What I have to do is bring out the underlying farce, dismantle the psychological discussions so as to make room for tales from Finnish popular life or statements of opinion, find a theatrical form for the master/man contradiction, and give the theme back its poetics and comic aspects'. It was as easy as that. Brecht found *Puntila* 'sheer relaxation' after the travails of *The Good Person of Szechwan*. The play was finished by 19 September: 'The work went very smoothly once I had a few linguistic models, each of about 20 lines (the Puntila tone, the Kalle tone, the judge's tone.) [...] It is a little fatted calf of a play. More landscape than in any other play of mine, expect perhaps *Baal*. The tone is not original, it is Hašek's way of speaking in *Schweyk*, as already used by me in *Courage*'.

Like his mentor Karl Valentin, Brecht's comedy derives from the ingenious manipulation of one core gag, in this case the burlesque inversion of normal behaviour in the person of the estate owner Puntila. He is another of Brecht's monster egos with enormous appetites, who can delude himself that he belongs to another age when class differences did not matter. He explains that when he is drunk he is friendly and generous towards his fellow human beings: 'In full possession of my faculties, master of my feelings'.[68] However, he is subject to 'attacks': 'When I get these attacks of total senseless sobriety I sink to the level of beasts. I have absolutely no inhibitions'. Managing Puntila with his violent moods swings in the farcical sequence of twelve scenes falls to his quick-witted chauffeur Matti, another exemplar of the Taoist attitude of triumphant subservience, who adjusts his responses in keeping with Puntila's moods. At times, Matti is reminiscent of Georg Büchner's Woyzeck as well as Hašek's Schweyk, simply parroting back what he knows Puntila wants to hear. At other times, he knows he can trade insults with impunity. Above all, however, Matti insists on his integrity: 'I'm not going to be treated like one of your cattle'. While Puntila oscillates wildly in his behaviour, achieving nothing because his contradictory actions cancel themselves out, the subtly ironic Matti becomes indispensable to him and engineers the opportunity to marry Puntila's daughter, Eva. However, Matti sets Eva tests which she fails, demonstrating that her privileged upbringing has left her ill-equipped to perform the traditional duties of a working man's wife. He turns his back on a privileged life and at the end calls for all servants to take their lives in their own hands:

> And if it's sad to find out in the end
> That oil and water cannot ever blend
> Let's waste no tears, there's nothing we can do:
> It's time your servants turned their backs on you.
> They'll find they have a master really cares
> Once they're the masters of their own affairs.

When Wuolijoki translated the play she initially had great trouble with Brecht's creative vision and dramatic technique, which made for playwriting so different from her own. They submitted the play under the name of Ursus. Soon after, she altered her view of the play, saying it 'is very rich' and that Puntila had become a 'national figure'.[69] She was delighted that the critic Olavi Paavolainen had declared *Puntila* a 'classic Finnish national comedy. He knows of no work where so much is said in such a concentrated fashion about Finland'. Brecht observed wryly: 'So now I know that the *Edda* was written by a Jew, and *Isaiah* by a Babylonian'. However, they did not win the competition, which Brecht, knowledgeable in such matters, said was because Wuolijoki had not lobbied the jury. It would be staged only after the war.

Stranded in Helsinki: *The Good Person of Szechwan* and *Arturo Ui*

Following the trade agreement between Finland and Germany, in the late summer of 1940 Finland allowed German divisions transit rights to northern Norway. In fact, significant numbers of German troops remained in northern Finland, in position to launch an attack on the Soviet Union. German could now frequently be heard on the streets of Helsinki. On 5 October the Brechts returned to the capital. In a state of high anxiety, they no longer answered to their names in public. Brecht and Weigel found a flat with two rooms and a kitchen at Köydenpunojankatu 13A near the port. Brecht wrote: 'I look out on sky, a bit of harbour with little steamers and the wooden sheds of a box factory. The house is modern, the rooms whitewashed'.[70] However, space was at a premium. Steffin lived nearby with Wuolijoki, and Berlau took a room at a guesthouse. As usual, Brecht rose early and wrote on his own in the morning, Steffin then joined him to discuss his drafts and after lunch he visited Berlau, before spending the evening with his family and friends.

As Brecht had feared, in the winter of 1940 there were extreme food shortages. Everyone was suffering. Barbara also contracted tuberculosis, which remained undiagnosed until it was treated successfully in the USA. The normally robust and cheerful Weigel became quite emaciated, stressed and depressed.[71] With his usual understatement Brecht noted of himself: 'Slight attack of sciatica, unpleasant enough to hinder my working. On such occasions I register just how much good health means to my writing, I write from the top looking down'.[72] The image of writing 'from the top looking down' meant for Brecht enjoying a vantage point, from which he could maintain mental control and clarity of thought, beyond the reach of physical frailty. Steffin's condition worsened. She had been losing weight for months. In mid-November she went down with flu and at the start of December she collapsed in a fever, as the tuberculosis burst into the open once more. Her doctor instructed her to cease all work. She did that for a while but Brecht urged her to follow the 'drug of work' which, he claimed, would help her. This time she could not regain her strength.

The latest news about their visa applications probably contributed to her collapse. On 29 November Brecht heard that, apart from Steffin, they had been granted Mexican visas. Steffin told Elisabeth Hauptmann that if Brecht got the chance to leave he must take it, irrespective of her own situation.[73] Feuchtwanger urged Brecht to do the same. However, Brecht was prepared to risk everything to ensure Steffin could go with them. They pursued a fallback position, in which Steffin would initially go to Haiti, for which visas could be secured more easily, and join them later in Mexico. However, their hopes of reaching the USA rose when near the end of November the consul declared that there was no obstacle to their application being approved, provided they could supply a financial guarantor. Only now did they scramble to put arrangements in place. Bureaucratic procedure was not their strong card. Feuchtwanger co-ordinated things in the US, ensuring that by late February 1941 four affidavits were in place. Hoffmann Hays signed one, as did the Hollywood director William Dieterle, guaranteeing Brecht and Weigel $200 per month until Brecht could support himself and his family.[74] With no English, Weigel had few expectations of work as an actress in the US.

Over the winter, despite 'long reluctance and Grete's illness' Brecht finally completed the ethical parable *The Good Person of Szechwan*, which he had been working on intermittently with Steffin and Berlau since March 1939.[75] Brecht hoped that verses and songs 'may make it lighter and more entertaining' but remained concerned about its length. The play's message is strikingly simple: given the state of modern society, it is impossible to be good and stay good if you want to survive. The play, essentially a critique of conventional western morality from the perspective of Chinese ethics, shows how far Brecht had travelled from Leninist partisanship. Western ethics, represented by the gods and their representatives of business and property on earth, stress individual responsibility irrespective of broader social conditions. We are reminded here again of the ethics of the Protestant religion in which Brecht was brought up. The assumption in the writings of Me-ti is, by contrast, that morality is a matter of good government. The weight of personal responsibility in western morality becomes too much for a mere individual to bear. In the conditions of what Brecht described as planned scarcity under capitalism, in the play the poor are excluded from the credit available to property and business owners, living an itinerant life of casual work and petty criminality. In a re-working of the destruction of Sodom and Gomorrha, Brecht inserts the three gods into this scenario. They seek exemplars of a good life, as under-stood by the gods' 'commandments', recognisably biblical prescriptions for a virtuous, godly life. Brecht then drew upon the stock situation in Chinese drama of a virtuous character struggling to survive in the face of cruel behaviour, modifying it to represent the contradictory forces of bourgeois capitalist behaviour within a single figure, who responds to those forces by adopting correspondingly contradictory social selves. Drawing inspiration from earlier creations like Pierpont Mauler and Puntila, Brecht constructs his ethical parable around the figure of Shen Te, the naive and sentimental good prostitute, who has to adopt the guise of her ruthlessly exploitative 'cousin' Shui Ta in order to survive. Shui Ta rescues Shen Te's business, a gift of the gods, from wrack and ruin after she has absent-mindedly given chunks of it away to the poor. Critics have objected that Shen Te lacks credible human motivation in a drama where the schematism of an original idea dominates character portrayal and interaction. While there is something in this, *The Good Person of Schechwan* has its place amongst Brecht's canonical dramas of the exile years, standing out in its treatment of ethical questions during the dark years at the turn of the 1940s through the highly innovative blend of Marxist analysis and Chinese social philosophy. Brecht sent the play to a number of friends but heard nothing back and by 20 April 1941 was noting despondently: 'The tanks of the victors of 1940 have buried *The Good Person of Szechwan* beneath them. With every report of Hitler's victories my significance as a writer diminishes'.[76]

Given the presence of German troops in northern Finland, the overland route via Moscow was now the only viable option for Brecht and Weigel, albeit a terrifying one. However, Brecht secured the protection of one of his last Moscow contacts, Mikhail Apletin of the Soviet Writers' Union, formerly Koltsov's deputy. Brecht sought Apletin's help in procuring tickets from Leningrad to Vladivostok, asking Apletin to use his Moscow royalties and to make available 750 roubles worth of convertible currency in dollars to fund the rest of the trip.[77] Feuchtwanger put his Moscow account at Brecht's disposal for the trip and Dieterle guaranteed any funds still required. When by early March the entry visas for the USA had still not arrived, they decided to embark on the trip as far as Mexico and, in the cases of Steffin and Berlau, Haiti. Brecht again wrote to Apletin, asking for 1,500 roubles to be left for him at the Finnish-Soviet border and for funds to be available in Moscow to buy the tickets to Mexico.[78] However, in late March a US entry visa came through for Berlau. Shortly after, an alarmed Brecht wrote to Wuolijoki that the Japanese were ceasing to issue transit visas: 'Please try your best to find out if it's possible to get a passage on a freighter from Murmansk or Odessa or Vladivostok. It's getting *extremely urgent*'.[79]

Amidst all the commotion, in March 1941 Brecht drew upon his tale of Giacomo Ui and dashed off *The Resistible Rise of Arturo Ui*. Ui/Hitler, oscillating between indolence and brutal anger, is one of Brecht's great satirical creations, a delight for any actor equipped to exploit the great parodist Brecht's dramatic gift. There are echoes of Shakespeare's *Richard III* and *Julius Caesar*, and of Goethe's *Faust*, as well as of Charlie Chaplin's *Great Dictator*. Brecht's use of roughly hewn blank verse in the grand style of the verse drama brilliantly counterpoints the sordid content of the dialogue. This made for a second element of parodistic alienation. Brecht's second comic interlude immediately before leaving Europe, is distinctly more sinister than the first, *Puntila*, and distantly echoes *The Threepenny Opera*. He shifted his focus of attention from what might make a good society in *The Good Person of Szechwan* to the rise of Hitler and of Fascism more generally, which, the Announcer tells us, 'is known to our whole continent'.[80] Brecht reflected: 'In *Ui* the problem was on the one hand to let the historical events show through, and on the other to give the "masking" (which is an unmasking) some life of its own, i.e. it must – theoretically speaking – also work independently of its topical references'.[81] The historical events in this darkly satirical parable play concern the years of Hitler's rise to power, from his relationships with Hindenburg (Dogsborough), Goering (Giri), Givola (Goebbels), through the Reichstag fire and on to the murders in 1934 of Ernst Röhm (Ernesto Roma) in a St Valentine's Day massacre and of the Austrian dictator Engelbert Dollfuss (Dullfeet). The events culminate in Germany's annexation of Austria. The play exploits quite brilliantly the analogy between Fascists and hoodlums, which remains compellingly relevant today. For his 'gangster play' about 'the gangster play we know', as Brecht put it, he used the newspaper cuttings about the mobs, particularly the rise and fall of the gangster boss Dutch Schultz, which he had collected in New York in the winter of 1935–6, as well as his extensive knowledge of gangster movies and detective stories.[82] The play demonstrates graphically to the audience how the Fascists – Ui like Hitler rises from a modest background – use violent intimidation through 'protection' to take advantage of the climate of weakness and insecurity in all social classes, not least traditional land-owning and business elites, engendered by a crisis in the capitalist cycle. With the aim of squeezing out further profits, they seize control of the sources of financial, business and political power, particularly the corporate Cauliflower Trust, the city council and the judiciary. Using the threat of their bodyguards and machine-gun-toting cronies, they bribe and blackmail key individuals, infiltrate and corrupt civic and business institutions, and destroy organised labour, reducing workers to consumers with values no different from the hopelessly corrupted lower middle classes. All this, Brecht's title reminds us, can be prevented. The play's final line 'The bitch that bore him is in heat again', offers a further chilling reminder of what may be in store.[83]

Brecht wrote *Arturo Ui* for the American theatre. However, when he arrived no US theatre would touch a work which exposed the country's social and economic life as latently Fascist, susceptible to the same collapse into lawlessness as Europe. Nor would lampooning Hitler be acceptable in Germany in the decades after the Holocaust. There was no publication or production of the play in Brecht's lifetime. However, it was published in the special issue of the journal *Sinn und Form* compiled after Brecht's death. After the premiere in Stuttgart, a clowning Ekkehard Schall put his stamp on the role of Ui with the Berliner Ensemble in a production lauded in Paris and London as well as Berlin. Thereafter a number of leading actors played the role, Christopher Plummer and Al Pacino in the USA, Leonard Rossiter in London and Jean Vilar in Paris. Nowadays the play is enjoying renewed currency with its stark warning against the resurgence of Fascism. *Arturo Ui* and *Fear and Misery* remain powerful anti-Fascist weapons.

While they waited in Helsinki, the Zurich Schauspielhaus was preparing for the premiere of *Mother Courage and her Children* on 19 April. The Schauspielhaus was the last major European theatre that was prepared to perform a Brecht play. Even then, the Swiss police noted their concerns about Brecht despite the fact that they had approved the play.[84] The cast included Wolfgang Langhoff and Wolfgang Heinz, with Brecht and Weigel's friend Therese Giehse in the title role. Leopold Lindtberg directed and Teo Otto designed the set. Brecht wrote: 'It is courageous of this theatre which is mainly composed of refugees to put on something of mine. No Scandinavian stage had the guts to do it'.[85] The production was a great success with the audience and with critics but Brecht believed that his intentions had been misconstrued. Above all Giehse portrayed Courage quite uncritically as an overwhelmingly sympathetic character, a great survivor struggling against the odds to save her children. Brecht insisted that she be viewed critically as a figure who did not learn the lessons of life, and he re-worked the play in 1948 to ensure that it reflected his intentions.

Finally, on 3 May the US entry visas arrived for Brecht, Weigel and the children. Steffin's visitor's visa also arrived, describing her as Wuolijoki's secretary. Meanwhile, as Brecht noted, 'German motorised divisions were multiplying in the land, Helsinki was full of German "travellers", the tensions between Germany and the USSR were growing'.[86] There was no time to lose. At their farewell dinner on 12 May at the prestigious Hotel Torni the news came through that Rudolf Hess had undertaken his bizarre flight to Scotland, prompting Brecht's comment: 'Hitler predicts the annihilation of the island, his second-in-command flees there to safety. Very Epic Drama that ...'.[87]

To the Finland Station, and onward to LA

The Brechts left Helsinki by train for Leningrad on 16 May 1941 with their remaining possessions packed in twenty-four boxes and cases. It was Brecht's first trip to the Soviet Union since 1935. If all went well they would be in California by late July. Later that day, they arrived at Leningrad's Finland Station, where on 3 April 1917 Lenin had alighted to take charge of the Russian Revolution. They continued their journey by train to Moscow the next day. Apletin, now Alexander Fadeyev's deputy in the Soviet Writers' Union, led a small reception committee of friends, which included Maria Osten, still suspended from the Party and isolated in her campaign for Koltsov's release. Koltsov had been sentenced to death in February 1940.[88] What Brecht and Osten said to each other about her own case and Koltsov's is not known. She would be arrested in June 1941 and executed the following year. Her NKVD file actually contains a reference to Brecht as a 'Trotskyist'.[89] He knew that he was in great danger and could not be sure whether his status as a prestigious supporter of the Soviet Union hosted by Apletin would protect him. Apletin later said that he had offered Brecht money as the USSR could use a friend like him in the USA.[90] Brecht declined but agreed never to speak against the USSR. That required no change in his behaviour. He arranged with Apletin that he would correspond with him under the pseudonym Karl Kinner or K. K.[91]

The Brechts occupied an apartment at the Metropol Hotel while they arranged their onward journey. Weigel bought tickets for the Trans-Siberian Express to Vladivostok and for the boat to Los Angeles. Together with Osten, Apletin's secretary Lydia Gerassimova looked after their daily needs. Brecht was 'assisted' by the Austrian writer Hugo Huppert, a dubious figure in the Muscovite Terror and no friend of Brecht's. Huppert recalls Brecht as 'tormented by nervous anxiety', 'taciturn, palpably enervated and disgruntled'.[92] Fearful of arrest, the agitated Brecht drove around Moscow with Huppert quite aimlessly in a taxi. Describing Lukács during the taxi ride as the 'old vicar', Brecht showed no interest in the sights: 'I'm not a tourist here, never have been. I know this city anyway. Like any refugee I'm tired'.

Brecht had no reason to trust Huppert or anyone else. He had few friends among the surviving Moscow émigrés. He talked to writers and to editors of exile journals, which continued their pale existence during the Hitler-Stalin pact. Bernhard Reich, who had been released from prison, while Asja Lacis remained behind bars, visited him at the Metropol Hotel.[93] Brecht promised to intervene on her behalf with a Soviet diplomat but could achieve nothing because it transpired that the diplomat had himself been arrested. There was a party at the Writers' Club to celebrate Johannes R. Becher's 50th birthday. There Brecht talked to the Berlin working-class poet Erich Weinert, Becher's sworn enemy, and discussed Herwarth Walden's recent arrest with Huppert, to whom Brecht described Walden as 'one of the most flawless characters he had ever known'. It was Walden, we may recall, who had accused Brecht of plagiarism in Berlin in 1924. Brecht also saw Lukács, who had now been on the receiving end of attacks and was seemingly prepared to accept these, Brecht's conciliatory words: 'There are some people who are trying to influence you against me. Let us make an agreement not to be provoked by either into quarrelling'.[94]

Brecht's aim was simply to leave Moscow as quickly as possible. At first Steffin acted as the party's interpreter but her rapidly deteriorating health forced her to withdraw to a separate room where she received treatment. On the morning of 29 May Brecht and Weigel were doing Steffin's packing when Brecht realised she was so weak that 'moving her could be fatal': 'At midday I went with her in a little ambulance to the "High Mountain" sanatorium in Moscow. She had several times to be given oxygen, she looked very changed and tired and often said "write to me".[95] That day tickets came through for a Swedish boat departing from Vladivostok. Brecht tried to change them for a later boat but that was impossible. Theirs was the only ship scheduled for June and there were no flights in and out of Vladivostok at a time when Brecht wrote that the US's entry into the war was imminent. When he visited Steffin at midday on 30 May he explained to her that she would be able to get a ticket for a later boat. He brought a little toy elephant to add to her collection, before departing at 5 p.m. on the

Trans-Siberian railway. Brecht left copies of manuscripts with Steffin: 'She sensed how serious her condition was, but I blamed it all on her heart, and she believed me'. The treacherous heart!

Before they left, Brecht formally thanked Apletin and the Writers' Union for helping them during their stay and for looking after Steffin.[96] Johannes R. Becher and his wife Lilly saw them off at the station. The train journey across the Eurasian land mass with other German, Austrian and Czech refugees took ten days. In Moscow, Maria Osten visited Steffin, recording their conversations in a diary, and Brecht and Steffin exchanged telegrams. On 4 June Steffin woke early for breakfast, read Brecht's latest telegram and at 8.30 a.m. asked for a glass of champagne. Her condition deteriorated rapidly and she died at 8.55 a.m. She was thirty-three. Brecht was just east of Lake Baikal at Ulan-Ude when at 10 p.m. that evening he received a telegram with the dire news from Apletin and Fadeyev. Osten captured Steffin's last moments in a telegram to Brecht the following day: 'She repeated the word "doctor" three times. Died peacefully. At the post-mortem the doctor found both lungs in their final stages. Huge cavities, heart and liver much enlarged. A death mask was taken for you'.[97] Huppert attended the cremation on 6 June. For months, Brecht was utterly disconsolate. Nothing since his mother's death had hit him so hard. He wrote several poems for Steffin, among them 'After the Death of my Collaborator M.S.': 'My general has fallen / My soldier has fallen / My pupil has gone away / My teacher has gone away / My nurse has gone / My nursling has gone'.[98] She had meant so much to him. In the final section he writes: 'I walk around restlessly, unseeing / In a grey world, stunned'.

The Brechts arrived in Vladivostok on 10 June. They spent three days there, awaiting the departure of the cargo boat S.S. Annie Johnson, a small freighter with room for a number of passengers. Its Swedish owners had switched it from the dangerous North Atlantic to the Pacific, moving between Russia and the USA under a neutral flag. On 13 June the five-week voyage began with fifty-one passengers on board. They had got out just in time. On 22 June Germany launched Operation Barbarossa, with massed troops crossing the border into the Soviet Union, and that same month the USA stopped issuing visas to anyone with close relations in Germany.

On the boat Brecht got to know the young Austrian émigré Egon Breiner, whom he would continue to see in California, where Breiner worked as a fitter for Southern Railway. During the voyage Brecht telegraphed Elisabeth Hauptmann, once to say they were on their way to the US, once more from Honolulu, before he sent a letter stressing their need for accommodation. At the end of June the ship docked to load copra at Manila where it was delayed for five days until a typhoon had passed. Brecht wrote verses in which passengers speculate upon reasons for the delay: 'Some said it was because of a typhoon raging to the north / Others feared it was German raiders. / All / Preferred the typhoon to the Germans'.[99] In 'Landscape of Exile' Brecht stylised the voyage as a last peacetime crossing of the Pacific: 'But even I, on the last boat / Saw the gaiety of the dawn in the rigging / And the greyish bodies of dolphins emerge / From the Japanese Sea'.

Disgust 1941–2

A hunger artist in Hollywood

'The oil derricks and the thirsty gardens of Los Angeles / And the ravines of California at evening and the fruit market / Did not leave the messenger of misfortune unmoved', Brecht wrote in 'Landscape of Exile' of the S.S. Annie Johnson's approach to Los Angeles on 21 July 1941 and of his first impressions of the city.[1] Telling Breiner, 'I don't want any trouble with the US authorities', before the ship docked Brecht threw overboard the German editions of Lenin's works which he had bought in Vladivostok. He was entering a different world. After the extreme pressures and extraordinary achievements of the later Scandinavian years, exile in the USA was not just a great anti-climax. As James K. Lyon remarks, in the USA Brecht 'suffered more financial deprivation, greater intellectual and emotional isolation, and more resounding failure and indifference towards his genius than he had known for years, or would know again in his lifetime'. Brecht's Californian exile was a thoroughly disturbing experience, which drastically impaired his creative capacity and elicited a flow of vituperation in his journal and in letters to close friends unparalleled since the early 1920s. He wrote to Berlau: 'That in running away from Hitler we've had to hide in this shithouse – must mean something'.[2] And he told Korsch: 'My intellectual isolation here is horrendous; compared to Hollywood, Svendborg was a metropolis. You must have been in situations where you put off the most vital calls because your trousers need mending'. Brecht, in fact, took to putting off most communication with the outside world, hardly ever replying to letters. His journal assumed a 'safety-valve' function in the USA. Brecht confided to it views and feelings of conflict with others which he concealed in public. As far as he was able, the 'inflammable' Brecht cultivated a 'Chinese' politeness, a public inscrutability.

Marta Feuchtwanger, together with the actor Alexander Granach, now in the USA after imprisonment in Moscow, met Brecht, Weigel and the children off the boat at San Pedro harbour. William Dieterle paid their rent on an apartment at 1954 Argyle Avenue, Hollywood. The following day Brecht visited Feuchtwanger in Pacific Palisades. Brecht found his old friend had aged but was otherwise the same. Feuchtwanger advised Brecht to stay in California: the cost of living was lower than in New York and there were opportunities to work in the Hollywood film industry. Brecht would join the large number of German émigrés looking to make quick money from scriptwriting.

The USA had, we know, long had a special place in Brecht's mind, initially as a source of fresh vitality in contrast to a Europe exhausted by war, later as the epitome of the rampant growth and inevitable self-destruction of high capitalism. Hollywood was that in spades, a magnet for footloose finance in a popular entertainment industry on a quite unprecedented scale. For Brecht, Hollywood contained all the reasons why the USA was bound for destruction. An opulent microcosm of US society, it exuded a belief that the buoyancy of a credit-driven economy like its own would enable the country to escape the scarcity which continued to blight Europe. Brecht had, of course, devoted his life to combating capitalism as the source of planned scarcity. The US solution was, by contrast, more capitalism.

Brecht's antipathy towards the Hollywood 'dream factory' was, however, not just the result of intellectual differences. It was grounded as much in an instinctual, emotional response born of a sensibility which spawned extremely pronounced aesthetic oppositions, according to which the Hollywood artistic 'narcotics industry' was decidedly the very antithesis of genuine art. Brecht's whole aesthetic position was opposed to everything Hollywood represented. Compromise did not come into it. What is more, despite his love of the cinema, Brecht had never developed any real creative affinity with the industry. That could not change in Hollywood where Brecht lived on the breadline for much of the time. His contempt for the film industry pours out as he responds to the movie men's taunt in the poem 'Deliver the Goods': 'When I see their rotting faces / My hunger goes away'.[3] Hollywood brought out the austere ascetic in Brecht, who could find few outlets for his appetites and lived like a hunger artist in the midst of an opulence which he denounced. As Lyon observes, Brecht came out of necessity and stayed only as long as necessary.

Brecht found an attic room for Berlau with the Dutch painter Ernst van Leyden, an old Berlin friend who had portrayed Brecht in the mid–1920s and would paint Brecht and Weigel broadcasting to Germany in 1944. Berlau, Brecht's remaining collaborator, could, however, never replace Steffin's literary and organisational gifts, nor could she remotely attain her goal of prising Brecht away from Weigel. He told Berlau that he had left Germany with a Jewish woman and he would return with one. Weigel, for her part, again found herself reduced to looking after the household and the children and to hosting dinner parties for entertainment and conversation. Typically, she threw herself into this activity. However, in six years in the USA she had just one acting role, a walk-on part in the film of Anna Seghers's novel *The Seventh Cross*, starring Spencer Tracy. She trained her body every day but had few opportunities even to give acting lessons. Weigel therefore became almost completely dependent on Brecht materially. Barbara went to high school after recovering from the tuberculosis contracted in Finland. Stefan would join the army, take out US citizenship and stay in the country.

Brecht and Weigel found a wooden house to rent for $48.50 a month at 817 25th Street in Santa Monica, only a short distance from the Pacific Ocean. With support of $120 a month from friends for their first year via the European Film Fund, they could just about keep their heads above water. The income was that of an unskilled worker in California and half that of a skilled craftsman. For furniture they looked to the Salvation Army: Brecht had become a character in his own satire of charity in capitalism. They received free medical help from fellow refugees. A car was out of the question but Brecht had his own study space. On the day they moved in, 1 August, he observed:

> Almost nowhere has my life ever been harder than here in this mausoleum of easy going. The house is too pretty, and here my profession is gold-digging, the lucky ones pan big nuggets the size of your fist out of the mud and people talk about them for a while; when I walk, I walk on clouds like a polio victim. And I miss Grete, here especially. It is as if they had taken away my guide as soon as I entered the desert.[4]

As he had in his wartime letters to Neher and in *Mahagonny*, Brecht repeatedly used the name Tahiti for a place which he regarded as a fool's paradise. Brecht believed that he had arrived in a country where people had simply not realised they were as doomed as the Europe he had fled with his feelings of guilt, failure and defeat. He remarked upon his profound sense of dislocation:

> I feel as if I had been exiled from our era, this is Tahiti in the form of a big city; at this very moment I am looking out on to a little garden with a lawn, shrubs with red blossoms, a palm tree and white garden furniture, and a male voice is singing something sentimental to piano accompaniment – it's not a wireless. They have nature here, indeed, since everything is so artificial, they even have an exaggerated feeling for nature, which becomes alienated.

The view of the San Fernando Valley from Dieterle's house exemplified California's falsity: 'An incessant, brilliantly illuminated stream of cars thunders through nature; but they tell you that all the greenery is wrested from the desert by irrigation systems. Scratch the surface a little and the desert shows through: stop paying the water bills and everything stops blooming'.

He saw only tasteless artificiality and reacted with disgust and not a little self-loathing, giving full vent to his feelings in his journal. His tiny study had pink doors: 'I can only take three paces when I am working. There is something indescribably cute and ignoble about the place'.[5] The clean lines of classical modern design in Scandinavia had suited Brecht but he now saw a demeaning gaudiness everywhere:

> Remarkable how in this place a universally depraving, cheap prettiness prevents people from living in a halfway cultivated fashion, i.e. living with dignity. [...] Here you feel like Francis of Assisi in an aquarium, Lenin in the Prater (or at the Munich Oktoberfest), a chrysanthemum in a coalmine or a sausage in a greenhouse. [...] Mercantilism produces everything, but in the form of saleable goods, so here art is ashamed of its usefulness, but not of its exchange value.

Landing in this ultimate realisation of culinary art, whose exchange value bore on its capacity to foster illusions, was for Brecht a truly grotesque irony. He would later write of the debilitating effect of the place upon his art: 'Everything here is pervaded by the indescribable ugliness of the lie traffic. Even the fig trees sometimes look as if they had just told and sold some contemptible lies. The early morning hours are almost the only time when I can write anything halfway decent'.

For the anti-Fascist émigré, the USA's continuing neutrality in the war was deeply frustrating. He could not forget that the 'butchery 15,000 kilometres away, which is deciding our fate right across Europe at its broadest point, is only an echo in the hubbub of the art-market here'.[6] At a time when Nazi Germany was destroying Europe, Brecht, his status diminished to picaresque survivor, had become a bit-player in the capitalist swindle. Brecht concluded a letter to his translator Hoffman Hays: 'The worst of it is that everybody here is trying to convert himself and everybody else into a hundred per cent American in record time, it makes me feel rather seasick'. Brecht was himself congenitally incapable of the rapid assimilation that was so much part of the US success story. He observes: 'Odd, I can't breathe in this climate. The air is totally odourless, morning and evening, in both house and garden. There are no seasons here. It has been part of my morning routine to lean out of the window and breathe in fresh air; I have cut this out of my routine here. There is neither smoke nor the smell of grass to be had'. After the splendid richness of the air at Marlebäck, Brecht recoiled from the garish excesses of Hollywood, amusing himself by looking for price tags on trees and hills: 'You are constantly either a buyer or a seller, you sell your piss, as it were, to the urinal. Opportunism is regarded as the greatest virtue, politeness becomes cowardice'. In a 'state set up directly by the bourgeoisie, which is not for one moment ashamed of being bourgeois', Brecht had recourse, as we have suggested, to the restrained public manner of a 'Chinese' politeness.

He recorded his life as a jobbing scriptwriter in the cycle, 'Hollywood Elegies', a typically ironic and laconic take on a genre normally associated with rueful responses to loss. The elegy became a staple. The most famous piece in the cycle is 'Hollywood': 'Every day, to earn my daily bread / I go to the market where lies are bought / In hope / I take up my place among the sellers'.[7] For Brecht, everything in California had been commodified, any sense of history and culture lost in a society where only the market, lubricated by credit, counted. Brecht reflected upon Shelley's words about the City of London: 'I / Who live in Los Angeles and not in London / Find, on thinking about Hell, that it must be / Still more like Los Angeles'.[8] When he showed the elegies to his friend Hans Winge, an Austrian writer who worked in an underwear factory, Winge remarked: 'It's as if they'd been written from Mars'. Brecht and Winge formed the view that this 'detachment' was not a 'peculiarity of the writer's, but a product of this town'. It was the product of Brecht's sharp perspective upon an extraordinary place: 'These houses don't become someone's property by being lived in, but by means of a cheque, the owner doesn't so much live in them as have them at his disposal. The houses are extensions of garages'. The US attitude to money revealed for Brecht a mentality of 'colonial capitalism': 'You get the impression that everybody here is where he is just to get away. They are only in the USA to make money. It is nomadic theatre, by people on the move for people who are lost. Time is money, prefabricated types are assembled, rehearsals are a matter of patching things together. Nobody lives in the colonies'.

Brecht, too, needed to make money in his colonial existence. He told Piscator that he remained interested in the teaching job at the New School in New York and suggested that he might conduct a dramatic workshop.[9] He explained that if he did not take the post, his plan was – much as Feuchtwanger had advised him – first to earn money in Los Angeles which would finance a stay in New York, where he hoped to stage a recent work. Many people divided their time between Hollywood and Broadway in this way. Brecht would do so, too, seeing Hollywood as a stepping stone to address his only real ambition for the US, Broadway success. He suggested to Hays that *Fear and Misery of the Third Reich* might work best. However, he did not expect much: 'Of course I have few illusions, I know New York from 1935'.[10] Hays, for his part, praised Brecht to James Laughlin, the publisher of New Directions: 'He is, I think, the only poet to really absorb Marxism and use it creatively in the theatre'. Brecht wrote to Weill and Piscator about the prospects for *The Good Person of Szechwan* and encouraged Piscator to read *The Resistible Rise of Arturo Ui*. Piscator liked Brecht's Fascist-gangster play, as did Berthold Viertel, but nothing came of it. Weigel tried to interest Elisabeth Bergner in *The Good Person of Szechwan* but she was 'very disappointed on reading it and found it "as boring as it is grandiose"'.

On the lookout for work in Hollywood, Brecht accepted invitations from film people, among them Fritz Lang. After his enormous success in Germany as the director of the Expressionist films *Metropolis* and *M*, Lang had made a big name in Hollywood. His parties were opportunities for German scriptwriters to make contacts. As a group they were held in high esteem. One of them was Brecht's friend Ferdinand Reyher. Never short of ideas for film treatments, Brecht told Reyher of his old project *Jae Fleischhacker in Chicago* and they developed a film story, *The Bread-King Learns to Bake Bread*. It is informed by Brecht's analysis of the capitalist market and by his view that Americans were nomads, who didn't know anything about eating and couldn't make bread: 'There is no proper bread in the States and I like my bread. My main meal in the evening is bread and butter'.[11] Brecht would often voice his disapproval of US food with the words, 'We didn't have that in Augsburg'. Nothing came of *The Bread-King*. Berlau assisted Brecht on another film treatment *The Snowman*, and on *Bermuda Troubles* with the German actor Robert Thoeren, who had become a successful scriptwriter, owning a 'luxury villa and a chicken farm as a hobby'. *Bermuda Troubles* was based on a story in *Life* magazine about illegal exports from the island. Brecht quickly tired of Thoeren, who 'rambles on without a pause, without any plan, carefully avoiding actual thinking'. The project fell apart. Brecht worked with Peter Lorre on *Rich Man's Friend*. *Valse Triste* was the title of another treatment. None of them amounted to anything. However, Brecht's work was good enough to be plagiarised. Brecht identified Elisabeth Bergner and Arch Oboler as the culprits, passing off as Oboler's own a radio play which Berlau had given them about the Norwegian anti-Fascist struggle.[12] Brecht found more evidence of Bergner's nefarious doings, this time together with her husband, the producer Paul Czinner, who had passed on to Billy Wilder a script written with Brecht. A friend of Wilder's subsequently sold the script for $35,000 – Brecht did not see a penny.

Brecht found it deeply frustrating that proven talent counted for nothing in the Hollywood lottery and that mediocrity often brought huge rewards. Salka Viertel was one of the successes in the émigré scriptwriting world, working with Greta Garbo. Brecht and Weigel were close to Viertel and her husband the theatre director Berthold Viertel, whom they knew from Berlin days. At the Viertels', Brecht would meet personalities like Aldous Huxley, Christopher Isherwood, W. H. Auden, John Houseman, Charlie Chaplin, Igor Stravinsky and Charles Laughton. Salka Viertel recounted for

Brecht the tale of how 'in a film that was to present the life of Madame Curie, what was originally to be the main scene was cut. In it the Curies reject a huge American offer for their method of producing radium, since they, as scientists, cannot turn inventions into monopoly products. The industry didn't want to shoot it, though they had at first been very keen on it. It is immoral to do something for nothing'.[13]

In all, Brecht wrote some fifty film treatments in Hollywood. As he later wrote to Weill, the consequence was that he didn't 'get around to any proper work anymore, an unbearable situation, as you can imagine'.[14] Brecht's output was reduced to a trickle: there is little in the way of theoretical reflection, no significant prose work and he even wrote poetry only occasionally. When he could free himself from scriptwriting he concentrated his efforts on plays but would never regain the sustained excellence of the late Scandinavian years.

At the scriptwriter Hermann Manckiewicz's, Ben Hecht confirmed Brecht's worst fears about New York theatre: 'Nobody is writing serious plays any more'.[15] Broadway was going through a lean period. Brecht commented: 'The effect of the crisis in 29 and the New Deal seems exhausted, it was too weak to put the drama on its feet. Broadway triumphed and demonstrated that it has a stomach like Mithridates for minor poisons. The muckrakers have turned into gold-diggers'.[16] Among other things, the New Deal's Federal Theatre Project, which provided jobs for aspiring young playwrights like Arthur Miller, was closed in 1939 amidst congressional fears about Communist infiltration. Miller, like other social dramatists, struggled with the culture of the commercial theatre. Brecht reflected further on Hecht's words: 'Horrifying as it is, this system might function if the political situation were different (maybe the situation at the cradle of capitalism, in Elizabethan times, wasn't very different from what it is now, at its grave). But you need the great tabula rasa to play on, the sense of beginning, and the audience that is productively concerned about public affairs, about res publica'.[17]

Brecht was describing the type of situation which he had exploited so successfully in German theatre after the First World War. For all the contrasts, the world as he saw it in Hollywood recalled his brutally satirical creations from the mid- to late 1920s such as *Man Equals Man* and *The Baden-Baden Lesson on Agreement*, depicting humanity reduced to mimicry of capitalist production. Of course, for many Americans proud of the USA's status as a great power, underpinned by the enormous vitality of business, finance and technological development, Brecht's view was simply insulting. Brecht, for his part, felt that the USA 'blows my *Tui* novel to smithereens. It is impossible to show up the sale of opinions here, where it is nakedly practised'. Acknowledging the pervasive belief in the markets, he ruefully conceded: 'All that only applies to Europe'.[18]

Amongst the survivors, mourning the dead

Shortly after arriving in Santa Monica Brecht met Walter Benjamin's cousin, Günther Stern (Günther Anders), who told Brecht of Benjamin's suicide: 'Walter Benjamin has poisoned himself in some little Spanish border town. The *Guardia Civil* had stopped the little group he belonged to. When the others went to tell him the next morning that they were being allowed to carry on, they found him dead'.[19] Walter Benjamin took his life at Port Bou during the night of 26–27 September 1940 with an overdose of morphine. According to Hannah Arendt, Brecht responded to the news by saying that 'this was the first real loss that Hitler had caused German literature'. From Stern and Arendt, Brecht gained the impression that Benjamin's friends in the USA could have done more to get him out of Europe.

Brecht wrote four poems about Benjamin's death. Two are epitaphs, 'Casualty List' and 'To Walter Benjamin Who Killed Himself Fleeing From Hitler'. Another, 'On the Suicide of W. B.', begins:

> I'm told you raised your hand against yourself
> Anticipating the butcher.
> After eight years in exile, observing the rise of the enemy
> Then at last, brought up against an impassable frontier
> You passed, they say, a passable one.
>
> Empires collapse. Gang leaders
> Are strutting about like statesmen. The peoples
> Can no longer be seen under all those armaments.
> So the future lies in darkness and the forces of right
> Are weak. All this was plain to you
> When you destroyed a torturable body.[20]

Brecht understood the choice his friend had made. The fourth poem, 'Where is Benjamin, the Critic?' becomes a lament for other friends lost in Europe, too:

> Where is Benjamin, the critic?
> Where is Warschauer, the radio broadcaster?
> Where is Steffin, the teacher?
> Benjamin is buried on the Spanish border.
> Warschauer is buried in Holland.
> Steffin is buried in Moscow.
> I drive along the bomber-hangars of Los Angeles.[21]

Preparations for more killing were being made. Brecht's poetic responses to the shattering news are exemplary demonstrations of the sensibility of restrained emotion, which we have witnessed at other times of distress. Lyon observes: 'By refusing to express grief, these poems, like scenes in some of his plays, become that much more powerful through their control of undeniable emotion'.[22]

Brecht recorded his thoughts of Steffin, too: 'I often see Grete with the belongings which she was always packing into her suitcase. The piece of silk with the portrait painted by Cas; the little wooden and ivory elephants from various towns I had been in; the Chinese nightgown; the manuscripts; the photo of Lenin; the dictionaries. She understood beautiful things, just as she understood beauty in language'.[23] Steffin was, indeed, a gifted woman. He reflected a while later upon the effect of her loss upon him:

> For nearly a year I have been feeling deeply depressed as a result of the death of my comrade and collaborator Steffin. Up to now I have avoided thinking at all deeply about it. I'm not frightened so much of feeling pain, it's more that I'm ashamed of

it. But above all I have too few thoughts about it. I know that no pain can offset this loss, that all I can do is close my eyes to it. Now and again I have even drunk a tot of whisky when her image rose before me. Since I seldom do this even one tot affects me strongly. In my view such methods are just as acceptable as others that are better thought of. They are only external, but this is a problem which I don't see how to resolve internally. Death is no good for anything.

So the depression continued:

I have done nothing and will do nothing to 'get over' the death of Grete. What good does it do, reconciling yourself to things that have happened? There are still many ends to this rope, waiting for things to be attached to them. Hitler and hunger killed her. Hitler is still alive, and hunger rules the world. My efforts to save her were defeated. And I was not able to make it easy for her. You should forget your successes, but not your failures.

An overwhelming sense of failure, guilt and self-loathing gripped the survivor, who had lost his most valued collaborators Steffin and Benjamin, as he re-lived the pain of their deaths in 'I the Survivor': 'I know of course: it's simply luck / That I've survived so many friends. But last night in a dream / I heard those friends say of me: "Survival of the fittest" / And I hated myself'.[24]

'And now to the survivors!', begins Brecht's caustic journal entry immediately after his recording of Benjamin's death. If Brecht could not become reconciled to the loss of Steffin and Benjamin, he could equally not become reconciled to the company of his fellow survivors. As always with Brecht, someone had to pay. His response to Korsch's inquiry about his relations with Thomas Mann is legendary: 'I meet Thomas Mann only casually and when that happens 3000 years look down on me'.[25] It happened far too often for Brecht's liking. Brecht and Mann were invited to the endless round of parties in the German exile community, grim encounters between damaged egos upon which Brecht exercised his sardonic wit.

Just about everyone apart from Brecht and Hanns Eisler was a voluble anti-Stalinist. Not only had Thomas Mann washed up there; the Marxist intellectuals from the Institute for Social Research were in the vicinity, too. At the journalist Rolf Nürnberg's garden party Brecht met the 'twin clowns Horkheimer and Pollock, two Tuis from the Frankfurt Sociological Institute'.[26] The Institute, established in Frankfurt in 1923 with private funds, had transferred to the USA from Paris in 1939. For Brecht, it was a bourgeois sleight of hand to believe, as the Marxists of the Frankfurt School did, that the revolution did not depend on insurrection by the working class. In Brecht's eyes, the sociologist Max Horkheimer and the economist Friedrich Pollock were intellectual frauds, who had survived while two true Marxist intellectuals, Steffin and Benjamin, had perished, the latter as a direct result of the Tuis' inaction. The bile poured out of Brecht:

Horkheimer is a millionaire, Pollock merely from a well-off background, which means Horkheimer can buy himself a university chair 'as a front for the Institute's revolutionary activities' wherever he happens to be staying, which for the moment is at Columbia, though, since the rounding up of the Reds has started on a grand scale, Horkheimer has lost the urge 'to sell his soul, which is more or less what you always have to do at universities', and has gone West, where paradise awaits.

The quotations are apparently the words of the 'twin clowns' themselves. For Brecht, who had investigated the workings of the Chicago wheat exchange, the notion that the Institute was intellectually independent because it was financially independent was grotesque: the funds were provided by the Argentine wheat exporter Felix Weil. Horkheimer and Pollock, Brecht continued, 'keep about a dozen intellectuals' heads above water with their money, and these in turn have to contribute all their work to the journal without any guarantee that it will ever be printed. This enables them to maintain that "saving the Institute's money has been their principal revolutionary duty all these years"'. The implication is shocking: Benjamin had received a small stipend from the Institute, had published in their journal, had his work turned down and had taken his own life in penury.

Brecht was not alone in questioning the Institute's leadership. Korsch, whose head they also kept above water, wondered to Herbert Levy about the people whom Brecht was now physically close to in Hollywood, 'last but perhaps least fortunately to Horkheimer, Marcuse and the other lights of the "Institute", which seems to consider a further retreat West for a small but select elite while the remainder may be thrown overboard'.[27] Writing to Korsch, Brecht was scornful of Horkheimer, Pollock and Herbert Marcuse: 'A film about Lourdes is being made soon; I imagine they have their eyes on the clerical roles'. After Brecht and Eisler had lunched at Horkheimer's, Eisler suggested a plot for the *Tui* novel, the story of the Institute: 'A rich old man (Weil, the speculator in wheat) dies, disturbed at the poverty in the world. In his will he leaves a large sum to set up an institute which will do research on the source of this poverty. Which is of course, himself'.

Before Suhrkamp published Brecht's journal in 1973, Siegfried Unseld invited Horkheimer to comment on the charges. Horkheimer wrote that Brecht had frequently invited him to his house to discuss important issues and had behaved as if he were well-disposed towards him.[28] Horkheimer explained that he was not a millionaire at that time and had held a professorial title only in Frankfurt. When the Institute moved from Paris, Columbia University provided a building on its campus free of charge. This enabled collaborators to flee Europe for the USA. Horkheimer confirmed the normal editorial practice of work being returned to contributors if it was not selected for publication. The Institute had funds in the USA because, anticipating that the Nazis would come to power, it had deposited money provided by the Weils in a Dutch bank. Finally, the decision to leave New York for California had nothing to do with any 'rounding up of the Reds' at Columbia: the Institute was independent of Columbia.

Brecht could have found out any of this if he had wished. His anger at their treatment of Benjamin, their, as he saw it, fraudulent claims of intellectual independence and, finally, his own difficulties came together in his vicious caricature of the 'Frankfurturists', as he took to calling them. In Berlin before 1933 he had been at the very least their equal, both intellectually and materially. The linkage between the Institute and the wheat exporter was one thing, the prudence shown by the Institute before January 1933 another. Brecht had seen his own early fortune disappear, having invested in the house at Utting just before the Nazis came to power. His material situation was now precarious. Moreover, in the USA he was extremely vulnerable to accusations of Stalinism and was rightly fearful of a witch-hunt. He knew that the anti-Stalinist Marxists of the Institute had nothing to fear.

For the Frankfurt Marxists, Brecht was an anti-intellectual apologist of Stalinism, wedded to an illusion of working-class victory, which they had overcome. As Horkheimer notes, despite Brecht's savage words he continued to see people from the Institute. Brecht and Weigel were, in fact, very close to Theodor and Gretel Adorno, as Adorno's letters to his parents show: 'For the rest, the only people we see quite a lot are the Brechts, with whom we get on very well'.[29] Weigel invited the Adornos to dinner regularly, while Brecht retained the firm conviction of his superior talent: 'Adorno here. He has grown round and fat and brings an essay on Richard Wagner, not uninteresting but restricted to grubbing around for complexes, inhibitions, suppressions in the consciousness of the old mythmaker, in the manner of Lukács, Bloch, Stern, all of whom are merely suppressing an ancient form of psychoanalysis'.[30] A struggling Brecht would nonetheless ask Adorno to intervene on his behalf with Weill over a production of *The Threepenny Opera*.

The US enters the war

On 7 December 1941, while Brecht was working on a film script with Fritz Kortner, *Days on Fire*, the Japanese attacked the US fleet moored at Hawaii's Pearl Harbour: 'It became clear to us that we were "in the world" again. A giant nation was rising, still half-asleep, to go to war'.[31] While Brecht now had some prospect of acquiring a *raison d'être* in the USA, the USA's entry into the war changed many other things. The sizeable Japanese community on the West coast was interned. Brecht and his fellow German émigrés feared the same treatment. In the event, the US government decided against the mass internment of German émigrés on the grounds that they had fled their country as opponents of the US's Nazi enemy. However, the US reserved the right to intern people deemed hostile to its values. Brecht attempted pre-emptive action. Two days after Pearl Harbour he wrote to Archibald MacLeish, one of his few links with the Washington establishment: 'I am most anxious to do my bit fighting the Nazis, the world's scourge'.[32] Brecht volunteered his services to 'broadcast right from here into Germany the truth which might easily act as an incentive to revolt'. According to an FBI report, Brecht also declared his intention to become a US citizen. He requested first papers but did not pursue the matter. He was now required to register as an enemy alien who could be drafted into the armed forces because he was under forty-five. The lottery system used for conscription meant that he might well be called upon to serve.

On Christmas Day Brecht listened to Churchill's address to the US Senate, while he and Weigel entertained the Feuchtwangers, Bergner, Czinner, Granach and Lang with a German Christmas. Brecht was always extremely sceptical about Britain's war aims, particularly the 'Tory' claims about the imminence of a second front in the West to divert German forces from the struggle against the Soviet Union. In the summer of 1942, for example, he recorded reports that 'London circles see the Serbian insurgent army, now that they have been "recognised" by the 15-year-old King Peter in exile, as the second front'.[33] Shortly after, Brecht noted: 'It is not true that the Tories do not want to distinguish between Hitler and the German people. Only that when they say the German people they mean the industrialists and generals'. Brecht clearly feared that behind the demand for unconditional surrender lay ingrained British imperialist attitudes, which would result in decades of exploitation of the German people.

The next day Homolka came round and played chess with Brecht. Perhaps prompted by thoughts of Homolka's suitability to play the lead in *Life of Galileo*, Brecht wrote of the play: 'It is as if I were remembering a strange, sunken theatre in ancient times on a submerged continent – here all they are concerned about is selling an evening's entertainment. [...] The idea that matters of concern to the nation might be treated on the stage is utterly fanciful, since nothing of the kind happens anywhere else in the entertainment business'.[34] Clearly, things of the kind were happening and the frustrated Brecht knew about them. In discussion with visitors the next day, Brecht defended the stylistic innovations and social comment in the new Orson Welles film *Citizen Kane*. While his own talent remained completely unrecognised, Brecht consoled himself with the thought: 'Of course the soil here is not conducive to developing talent'. Soon after, he had similar thoughts about his verse: 'To write poetry, even topical poetry here amounts to withdrawing into an ivory tower. It is like plying the art of the goldsmith. There is something quaint, something oddball, something limited about it. It is like putting a message in a bottle, the battle for Smolensk is a battle for poetry too'. Poetry was part of a civilised world.

Brecht sent his poem 'To the German Soldiers in the East' to the Mexican exile journal *Free Germany*. The poem was also broadcast on Moscow radio. Unbeknown to Brecht, his son Frank Banholzer was among the soldiers in the East:

Brothers, if I were with you –
Were one of you out there in the eastern snowfields
One of the thousands of you amid the iron chariots –
I would say as you say: Surely
There must be a road leading home.[35]

Brecht warns the soldiers trapped in those snowfields that the road back to Smolensk is 'too far'. The German armies would have to endure another Russian winter while they besieged Stalingrad, until in February 1943 the 6th Army was cut off and destroyed in this definitive turning point in the war after El Alamein. Frank Banholzer would later perish on the Eastern Front, killed in November 1943 in an explosion at his barracks.

In advance of a similar move in Moscow, in February 1942 the KPD's Ludwig Renn issued a call in Mexico's *Free Germany* for a broadly based 'Free Germany' movement, in effect a renewal of the Popular Front, for a post-Nazi Germany. In March Brecht joined with Heinrich Mann and Feuchtwanger to issue a call to their fellow Germans via the New York *Intercontinent News* to 'end the most pernicious and senseless of wars [...] Overpower your Führer, who is leading you, laden with hatred and ignominy, to ruin'. Brecht remained in no doubt that Hitler could not win the war. The call for the German people to rise up against Hitler became a regular refrain for Brecht and his fellow émigrés. Insurrection would legitimise post-war German self-determination, meaning that the German people would not be treated as the objects of Allied policy in the wake of the unconditional surrender which the Allies were demanding. The activities of Brecht and his fellow émigrés prompted concerns in US government and security circles, which stepped up surveillance. Meanwhile, in April 1942 the 'Free Germany' policy was approved in Moscow and implemented in German prisoner-of-war camps over the following year, leading in July 1943 to the establishment of the National Committee for a Free Germany (NCFD). Brecht would join an émigré pressure group with similar interests to the Mexican and Moscow initiatives, which would only add to US security concerns.

Mixed fortunes among the great

The struggling Brecht resumed contact with Weill in March 1942, asking him about the prospects for a production of The Threepenny Opera by a black troupe led by Clarence Muse.[36] In a conventionally polite reply, the successful Weill sympathised with Brecht's need to make quick money and, claiming that he wished Brecht had contacted him earlier, pointed out the problems that he himself had encountered in considering such a project. When Brecht heard that Weill was openly expressing his doubts, he begged him to understand his plight: 'I have no sources of income and have constantly to chance my arm drafting these film stories'. Adorno now wrote on Brecht's behalf to Weill, who paraphrased Adorno's 'completely idiotic letter' for Lenya, which sought to explain why the play, which had earlier failed in the USA, could now succeed: 'The ideological situation in America could not be compared to the German one of 1929; America was not yet ready to accept the authentic Threepenny Opera, which is so inseparably tied to a climate of crisis'. Weill was, moreover, angered by the fact that Brecht had disclosed to Muse the contents of their mutual correspondence: 'The good old swinish Brecht method'. Weill presented his conditions, principally that production rights were valid only for California.[37] For Brecht it was

> a nasty letter full of attacks on me and praise of Broadway, which will put on anything if it is good, and has been developing the experiments Europe pioneered. The last play he did the music for ran 14 months. It was called Lady in the Dark. (They say it's an amusing potboiler.) The letter begins with the fact that he is writing the letter in English. 'It's easier for me and I like it better'.

For Brecht, that said it all. Lenya gave Weill every encouragement to make Brecht squirm: 'The whole Brecht schit (sic) – is just too funny for words. "Could you come to Hollywood". Good God! Sounds like the good old days when he tried to keep your name off the program'.

Brecht wrote to Weill once more in April, suggesting that they put to one side 'all the misunderstandings and boring half-rifts', which, he claimed, were so much a product of the times.[38] He reminded Weill of all the fun they'd had and what they'd achieved, adding pointedly that he had never lost any of his friends. Weill forwarded the letter to Lenya: 'It sounds very pitiful and I feel sorry for him. Maybe we are a little unjust towards him. He probably went through so much that his nicer side is on the surface again. I just hate to triumph over somebody who is down on the floor'. Weill considered sending Brecht some money but Lenya dissuaded him, arguing that Brecht was selfish and would never change. Weill received a contract for *The Threepenny Opera* from Brecht's agent George Marton, which was 'So incredible I don't believe my eyes. They disregard completely my demands and the whole thing is as crooked and exploitative as only contracts with Communists can be'. Weill did not pull his punches with Marton: 'This is the most shameful proposition that ever has been made to me. My agent and my publisher did not find one paragraph in this document that would serve as a basis for discussion'. Weill told Brecht that he could not waste any more time on 'this ridiculous affair', lectured him on the complexities of the US theatrical system and extricated himself by politely echoing Brecht's offer to collaborate again. Brecht had the consolation that Berthold Viertel was about to produce scenes from *Fear and Misery of the Third Reich* in New York.

Brecht turned to his old friend Feuchtwanger and did the Hollywood rounds with him. They visited Max Reinhardt and his wife Helene Thimig for lunch: 'He resides in a big villa by the sea, stuffed with his Berlin furniture and *objets d'art*. The old magician, small, standing firmly on his feet, pale as an ink-drawing that has been treated with blotting paper, with the slow, impressive movements, the deep voice, the tongue still in the cheek with all the old relish'.[39] Brecht visited Alfred Döblin and found him unemployed: 'He has nothing and has nowhere to go'. Brecht saw that he was not alone in failing to adjust while mediocre talents enjoyed huge rewards. Döblin, who like Heinrich Mann had earlier been hired on a short-term scriptwriting contract by Warner Brothers, speculated: 'It might be possible to screw something out of the film industry if you could set up a brothel for elderly ladies, for that would help tame the censorship which is largely in the hands of these ladies'. Brecht met Heinrich Mann at Feuchtwanger's and found the elder of the Mann brothers quite pitiful: 'Each week he goes to pick up his unemployment benefit of $18.50 since his contract with the film company, like Döblin's, has run out. He is over 70. His brother Thomas is in the process of building a huge villa'. Brecht added later that Heinrich Mann 'has no money to call a doctor, and his heart is worn out. His brother in that house he built, with 4–5 cars, literally lets him starve. Nelly, just 45, vulgar and with a coarse prettiness, worked in a laundry, has taken to drink. The two of them sit, among cheap furniture and the few books Mann managed to salvage, in a stuffy little Hollywood villa'. Thomas Mann did actually help his brother financially. Nelly committed suicide.

In this claustrophobic émigré world, encounters between Brecht and Thomas Mann were inevitable. They met following the death of Max Reinhardt and at the 65th birthday party for Alfred Döblin. Weigel organised the party with Elisabeth Reichenbach at the Playhouse on Montana Avenue. Speakers included Heinrich Mann and Weigel. She read Brecht's words about his great debt to Döblin, who had 'taught him more than anyone else about the nature of the epic'.[40] When Döblin replied, he appalled all those present with an attack on moral relativism and a plea for firm religious values. Brecht acknowledged that Döblin had been 'dealt some very severe blows, the loss of two sons in France, a 2,400-page epic that no publisher will print, angina pectoris (that great saver of souls) and life at the side of an incredibly stupid and philistine woman'. Döblin had allowed the Christian Right to get at him.

Brecht observed: 'An awkward sensation came over the more rational of his listeners, something like the sympathetic horror felt when a fellow prisoner succumbs to torture and talks'. Brecht later used proceeds from his work on *Hangmen Also Die* to provide Döblin with financial support.[41]

The émigré community was inward-looking, riven and unpleasantly acrimonious. Again at Feuchtwanger's, Brecht met the 'world-famous historian of the Weimar Republic' Emil Ludwig.[42] Ludwig subscribed to the position articulated most recently by the British diplomat Sir Robert Vansittart in *Black Record: Germans Past and Present* (1941) that the Nazis were simply the latest incarnation of the bellicose German character, a 'butcher-bird' out to attack its neighbours. The Vansittartist position buttressed the demand for unconditional surrender and plans to ensure that Germany could never rise as a military power again. Thomas Mann more than flirted with this position, helping it to gain acceptance amongst US elites for decades to come in a vast, muddled literature about the German 'spirit'. Ludwig proclaimed: 'People expect a forecast from me. Fine, I'll make a forecast. I can do it with quite different prospects from an astrologer. I predict that Hitler this year will be assassinated by his generals. I say this year, but it can just as well be the spring of next year, that I can't know, but it will be soon'. Brecht noted that Ludwig, whose biography of Hindenburg he had read while writing *Arturo Ui*, had attributed the First World War to the Kaiser's inferiority complex, caused by his short left arm, and that Ludwig was a 'very inhibited, slightly inebriated, not very self-confident person, but one who has the "spark", absolutely devoid of personal philosophy, unoriginal, but wholly in thrall to originality, stupid, but full of respect for wisdom'. Brecht knew Ludwig to be the uncle of his dead friend Frank Warschauer, whom he had remembered in 'Where is Benjamin, the Critic?'. 'Abruptly, with annoyance', Ludwig said of Warschauer: 'A nephew of mine who has never done anything, insignificant, could never see anything in him. I hear he committed suicide in Holland when Hitler marched in, so I mustn't say anything against him'. Warschauer was, Brecht observed, 'immeasurably superior to him in human terms'. He noted what Ludwig did next: 'He took his glass and with an "if I may, dear lady" carefully splashed some red wine on the parquet floor, a drawing-room libation. Marta Feuchtwanger afterwards wiped it up with a rag, so that it would not be trodden into the carpet'.

Brecht told Korsch of his unedifying encounters: 'Even in the backwoods of Finland I never felt so out of the world as here. Enmities thrive here like oranges and are just as seedless. Jews accuse one another of anti-Semitism, the Aryan Germans accuse one another of Germanophobia'.[43] Brecht told Curt Riess, Secretary General of the German-American Writers' Association, that he was not about to start an argument with anyone. Determined to avoid destructive controversy, he was maintaining a front of politeness, confiding his cutting opinions to his journal and to close friends like Korsch and Eisler.

Like many others in the émigré community, Brecht viewed with suspicion those who made significant efforts to integrate:

It is difficult for refugees to avoid either indulging in wild abuse of the 'Americans', or 'talking with their pay-checks in their mouths' as Kortner puts it when he is having a go at those who earn well and talk well of the USA. In general their criticism is directed at certain highly capitalistic features, like the very advanced commercialisation of art, the smugness of the middle classes, the treatment of culture as a commodity rather than a utility, the formalistic character of democracy (the economic basis for which – namely competition between independent producers – has got lost somewhere). So Homolka throws out Bruno Frank because he gets to his feet and shouts, 'I will not permit the President to be criticised here', Kortner shows up Lang as the source of an anti-Semitic remark, Nürnberg hates Lorre etc.[44]

When Brecht's actor friend Fritz Kortner used the phrase 'talking with their pay-checks in their mouths', he was referring to Fritz Lang. Apparently because of this, Lang later denied Kortner a role in *Hangmen Also Die*. Brecht was decidedly cool about Lang's enthusiasm for the USA: 'He again praises Atlantis to the ersatz skies. He sees a special lifestyle where I only see high capitalism: possible that I can't see the "real" Atlantis for the high capitalism; but he just obscures it. Here you have the unadulterated version before you; development, without anything actually developing'. For Brecht, Kortner was 'quite exemplary in his ability to resist assimilation. He even denounces the climate'. Brecht did much the same.

Brecht was suspicious of the upper-class British authors in Hollywood. While he tried to secure W. H. Auden as a translator, he was sarcastic about Auden's poetry, which he lumped together with Eliot's: 'Thumbed through volumes of poetry by Eliot and Auden. Veritable poetic prophecy. Catholicism (or Marxism) plus intimate revelations. They observe the flight of the birds – in the dusk – and pick bad omens for the rulers out of the entrails of their sacrifices. Otherwise, they only consort with their peers, yet they do not smile when they meet'.[45] Christopher Isherwood came to dinner: 'small, gentle, tough, patient, and trying'.[46] Brecht wanted him to translate *The Good Person of Szechwan* but Isherwood was not taken by it. When the conversation turned to Isherwood's Buddhist belief – he was living in a Buddhist retreat – Brecht told him bluntly that he had been 'bought': 'He looks at his watch and stands up. One doesn't talk about that kind of thing, waiter, bill please! I have the feeling a surgeon would have if the patient stood up during an operation and walked away: all he has received is a wound'. Brecht drafted two letters to Isherwood to explain his behaviour and later tried to win him for the translation of *The Caucasian Chalk Circle* but, in this case too, Isherwood declined.

Brecht was irritated by the left-wing US dramatist Clifford Odets, author of *Waiting for Lefty*, who had left the American Communist Party in 1936. Eisler brought Odets to meet Brecht and they discussed a film version of *Fear and Misery of the Third Reich*. Odets produced an outline, injecting a psychological realism which Brecht flatly rejected. When Eisler sang Brecht's Finnish poems to his musical settings, Odets apparently responded: 'That's the kind of thing you can only do when you're poor'.[47] Brecht later met Odets at a party and praised Spencer Tracy's acting in *The Seventh Cross* 'for a few almost sublime expressions which are otherwise thin on the ground here'. Brecht noted: 'Odets hadn't noticed and was annoyed when I advised him to see the film again. He kept clutching his chest and insisting that he hadn't noticed anything. For him the cinema is a kind of electric-shock machine and he just registers its discharges'.

The exile community at least showed its appreciation of Brecht's work. One evening in a Jewish club, probably the Soto Jewish Center in East Los Angeles's Boyle Heights, Kortner read from Brecht's 'German War Primer' with its stark message that the poor always pay most dearly in wars: 'The effect is surprisingly powerful. (The audience consists of Jewish refugees, mostly well-off.) Kortner does not read them as single poems but makes a rhapsody of the whole thing, reading quietly, musically, a little sadly at first, then ending aggressively, a masterly performance'.[48] Kortner understood how to convey the controlled aggression of Brecht's anti-Nazi work. Jewish refugees, well-off and not so well-off, welcomed a work that was both anti-Nazi and anti-war. Yet, as Brecht and Eisler reflected, Kortner, an actor versed in the Epic style, could get no roles: 'Real acting is frowned upon here and only accepted from negroes. Stars don't act parts, they step into "situations". Their films form sort of comics (a novel of adventure in instalments), which show a fellow in tight corners'.

Brecht's correspondence with Korsch was a life-line. As usual, they swapped observations about contemporary politics. Brecht took issue with Korsch's critique of the Soviet Union, arguing that the dialectical method could put Stalin's rule in proper historical perspective. Their disagreement over the Soviet Union made no difference to their strong relationship, Brecht writing: 'I regard you as my teacher, your work and your personal friendship mean a great deal to me'.[49] Brecht noted that Korsch 'gives a short survey of the state of monopolisation in the USA, in the light of which it seems that democratic principles can in fact no longer have any function'. Similarly, Brecht noted Kortner's scepticism when the documentary maker Herbert Kline suggested that a 'certain resistance to Fascism can be expected from the Americans' sense of democracy'.

Brecht reflected on European politics in his journal in a manner that he would never articulate in public: 'In a certain sense the similarities of the two great movements, Fascism and Bolshevism, which have created the new state forms in accordance with their joint tendency toward planned economies, emerge more clearly than their dissimilarities'.[50] He enumerated the similarities: 'all-powerful parties, working both in parliament and with para-military formations, the revolutionary forms, the hierarchies, the police systems, the five-year plans, the propaganda methods, the militarisation of youth, the myths, the controlled prices, the waves of terror etc etc'. Where did this leave reason, the founding principle of the USSR? The common features of Fascism and Bolshevism, of course, provided the basis for the theory of totalitarianism, which Brecht would oppose during the Cold War. Brecht claimed that there was a key difference: 'There are also quite different classes at whose behest this centralisation (which is costing these various classes a great deal) is being implemented'. By cost, Brecht meant not least human life. Brecht's reading of Boris Souvarine's *Stalin: A Critical Survey of Bolshevism* prompted further thoughts. He found Souvarine's account of the transformation of the Bolsheviks from professional revolutionaries into bureaucrats and officials a depressing read, confirming much of what he knew. He reflected that the rise of Fascism had shown the matter in a fresh light because 'in its attempts to create state capitalism the German petty bourgeoisie

has borrowed certain institutions (plus ideological material) from the Russian proletariat which is endeavouring to create state socialism. In Fascism socialism is
confronted with a distorted mirror-image of itself. With none of its virtues and all
of its vices.[51] Brecht could still muster arguments to justify bureaucratic socialism.
However, fundamental questions such as the organisation of economic activity and
the withering-away of the state remained unresolved.

Hanns Eisler: Encounters with music and critical theory

'When I see Eisler it is a bit as if I had been stumbling confusedly around in some
crowd of people and suddenly heard myself called by my old name', Brecht wrote when
his friend arrived from New York in April 1942.[52] Brecht saw how badly he himself
had lost his way: 'Actually there are many things since June 41 that I have not really
come to terms with, such as the loss of Grete, the new environment, even the mild
climate here. And then the roulette-like gamble with the stories, the confrontations
with the successful and the unsuccessful, the lack of money'. All this had taken a heavy
toll on his productivity: 'For the first time in 10 years, I am not working seriously on
anything, with the results one might expect. I don't remember a single breath of fresh
air in all these months. It is as though I were sitting one kilometre below ground,
unwashed and unshaven, waiting for the outcome of the battle for Smolensk'. Eisler
was aware what all this meant for Brecht: 'Boredom made him physically sick. [...] He
either had to create something or read or speak'.

Brecht took interest in Eisler's work on '14 Ways of Describing Rain', a project
funded by the Rockefeller Foundation, which at this time of war aroused Brecht's
suspicions about 'Tuistic' sponsorship. Eisler explained that the project was about
different ways of mourning. Brecht listened to Eisler's 'records with the rain poems'
at Adorno's and found them 'very beautiful, remind you of a Chinese ink drawing'.[53]
During his conversations with Eisler Brecht made notes about what was required for
musical composition and appreciation, which betray Brecht's life-long anxiety about
the damage which his combustible organism, particularly his heart, might suffer in the
face of intense musical rhythm. He explained: 'One of the most important instruments
for judging music is a clinical thermometer. The normal temperature of the human
body is about 37 degrees. After passionate, fiery or merely intense music one needs to
check whether this temperature has remained constant. In the case of Bach, even with
the most passionate works, it does'. Brecht then speculated: 'We could try to write new
folk-songs, composed in the new manner. Why should the people not sing like that,
with their temperature at 37 degrees, of course?'. We may recall that the adolescent
Brecht had speculated on the possibility of re writing Bach in a simpler fashion so as
to reach more people.

Critics have had little to say about such seemingly un-Brechtian statements,
which appear to be a world apart from the rationalist image which Brecht generally
presented. They are, however, of a piece with it: the common denominator is the
recipient's capacity to regulate artistic impressions, whether by physical or mental
means. As we know, Brecht had not always been able to listen to Bach's work without

experiencing a rise in his body temperature but now he could do so. Eisler, clearly aware of his friend's views, comments on the matter at some length at the beginning of his conversations about Brecht with Hans Bunge:

> Whether or not the normal body temperature stays at 37 degrees when you listen to Bach … I doubt that. First of all, I just have to think of the expression on Brecht's face to see how moved he was when I played Bach to him. It seemed to me that his temperature was significantly higher. Take, for example, the *St Matthew Passion* (the great E Minor section at the beginning, 'Come you daughters, help me mourn') or the first twenty pages of the *St John Passion*. I don't want to cast doubt on my late friend, but I'm convinced his temperature rose alarmingly, especially because he so admired Bach for his great ability to compose narrative.[54]

Eisler concluded: 'What Brecht loved in music was clarity and the avoidance of feverish excitement'. We have seen how he equated that with 'confused emotions'. A letter from Brecht to his son Stefan shows that the matter was discussed as a real problem within the family.[55] Brecht sought to alleviate his son's fears that they had not allowed him to have music tuition because he was 'too ill', explaining that they had simply not wanted to increase his sensitivity. In this view of things, there is a fine line between sensitivity and illness. Eisler placed Brecht's statements in a shared context with another literary great:

> Brecht's remark about the increase in temperature through listening to music and the possibility of assessing music by this means is typical Brecht – and it is a very clever remark. Indeed, you can already find something similar in Goethe. Everyone knows about Goethe's dislike of Beethoven (maybe dislike is too strong a word, rather a lack of understanding). Because Goethe spoke of emotional confusion when listening to Beethoven's music. That meant it made him hot and bothered but with nowhere to go. It's like excitement *pour* excitement. If you can have *l'art pour l'art*, so you can also have fever *pour* fever. And that made a clever man like Goethe very irritable. The same applies to Brecht.[56]

Brecht and Goethe were not alone amongst great German writers in complaining about the debilitating physical effect of music. In *The Case of Wagner* Nietzsche describes himself as sweating when he listens to the harmful work of the decadent composer and in *The Gay Science* he similarly writes of the stupor which Wagner induced. Schiller, meanwhile, describes music as an intrusion. All these great German exponents of poetic rhythm record the deleterious impact of great composers' musical rhythms as something experienced physically. The poets' irritability recalls the perennial struggle for pre-eminence between composer and librettist, which Brecht and Weill played out. Brecht could, of course, play ironically upon his affinity with great literary antecedents, not least parodying Romantic associations between art and illness. However, we have seen how, in numerous statements throughout his life, not least in his letter to his son advising him on his health, he highlighted the potentially damaging effect of music upon the organism. As we saw at the start of this study and shall see in greater detail presently in a journal note following a piano recital by Eduard Steuermann, Brecht was quite explicit that his anxiety had its origin in the damage that music could do to his heart. Like Goethe, Brecht sought to 'look after himself', behaving in such a way as to counter the feverish excitement which music could induce in him. As always when dealing with personal problems, Brecht adopted ironic distance as a protective mask, which lent him latitude for the simultaneous concealment and display of an essential truth.

Eisler was working with Adorno on a book about music in film.[57] Through Adorno, Eisler received invitations to the seminars of the Institute for Social Research and, as Erdmut Wizisla shows, Brecht accompanied him on at least two occasions in the summer of 1942.[58] Aldous Huxley's *Brave New World* was among the reading matter for discussion. Horkheimer, Pollock, Herbert Marcuse, Stern, Hans Reichenbach and Eduard Steuermann attended the first seminar at Adorno's, dealing with the relationship between needs and culture. Brecht and Eisler took issue with the thesis that unleashing productive forces would lead to the elimination of crises, material deprivation – and also culture. Brecht said: 'I believe that socialism has never thought of satisfying material needs. Socialism sees itself confronted by planned scarcity, which it wishes to eliminate. Where is there today a genuine movement to actually satisfy needs in a broad sense?'. The discussion at the second seminar, introduced by Stern, explored Reichenbach's question whether a society could be conceived in which cultural values could be created that would not be misused as instruments of the ruling class. Wizisla points out that in his response Brecht alluded to Benjamin's seventh thesis in 'On The Concept of History', in which the triumphant rulers carry off cultural artefacts as booty, before he asked the question: 'Are you not afraid that the needs of the ruling groupings alone always underlie culture, that these cultural values can each be expressed in terms of quite specific profits?'.

In his journal Brecht adopted a quite different, ad personam tone, amplifying sarcastically upon Huxley's link between suffering and culture: 'He establishes a certain lowering of cultural needs. The more iceboxes, the less Huxley. When physical needs have been satiated (Vice-President Wallace has already held out the prospect of a glass of milk a day for all mankind) spiritual needs suffer. Suffering has been created by culture; so is barbarism likely to ensue if they put a stop to suffering?'.[59] Brecht added: 'Reichenbach is concerned like all Social Democrats with preserving the "tradition" undamaged in a classless society. Saving the nation's works of art keeps him awake at night, whereas it puts me to sleep. In vain we explain to him that art-works have assumed the same character as artefacts in general, namely they have become commercial commodities'. Brecht concluded: 'Only those arts which make a contribution to saving mankind will be saved. Culture must lose the character of a commodity in order to become culture again'.

There was, it seems, no meeting of minds. Brecht noted that 'Dr Pollock, the economist', 'formerly Frankfurt, now Hollywood, is convinced that capitalism can rid itself of crises simply by means of public works. Marx could not predict that governments would one day just build roads'.[60] Germany had, of course, prepared for war on the same basis. However, counter-cyclical Keynesianism could be employed in other ways. Brecht and Eisler apparently lost patience with all this talk and decided to 'get across everyone'.

In the company of Adorno and other 'Frankfurturists', Brecht felt obliged to attack one of their heroes, Arnold Schönberg, 'just to shock them'.[61] Schönberg was, of course, Eisler's teacher and the figure upon whom Thomas Mann modelled the composer Adrian Leverkühn in his novel *Doctor Faustus*, which he wrote with the benefit of discussions with Adorno. Later, Brecht would enjoy a lecture by Schönberg and found that he had 'great charm'. Schönberg was full of colourful stories but what really attracted Brecht was that Schönberg 'sees himself as an historical phenomenon': 'I liked the old man a lot'. Schönberg, like Brecht, was aware of his importance in world history. However, at Adorno's Brecht went on the attack:

> When I poured scorn on the unnatural declamation of texts by the School of Schönberg, Adorno defended them as being brought about by the 'development of music', which required large and abrupt intervals. So it is exclusively construc-
> tional, almost mathematical considerations and postulates of pure logic in the assembly of tonal material that force musicians to whinny like dying warhorses ...

Brecht later suggested that Schönberg was 'saving classical music to destruction': 'There is something circular about this music, the movement isn't going anywhere, the logic only satisfies itself'. However, when Brecht and Weigel were invited to dinner at Schönberg's together with Dessau and the Eislers, Brecht was again taken by the 'astonishingly lively, Gandhi-like Schönberg in his blue Californian silk jacket, a mixture of genius and craziness'. Brecht added: 'A string in me "vibrates sympatheti-cally" when he complains that in music there is no purely musical conceptual material. Form, as an example, he defines as follows: it is the repose between two forces acting on one another. (Seemingly a field concept.)'. Like Schönberg, Brecht understood the secret power of form, a little like the eye of the storm.

The roulette winner: *Hangmen Also Die*

Brecht's ambition remained to conquer Broadway, while Berlau continued her vain quest to prise him away from his family. Frustrated by her life in California, in May 1942 Berlau addressed a conference on equal rights for women in Washington and accepted an invitation from the Danish Department of the Office of War Information in New York to speak about the women's conference. Berlau then announced to Brecht that she was staying in New York. Her female friend Ida Bachmann, the Head of the Danish Department, had arranged a job for her as an announcer. That was timely as her financial reserves had nearly run out, and her relationship with Brecht remained unsatisfactory. She also discovered that she was entitled to $75 per month from her divorced husband Robert Lund. From June, Berlau and Bachmann shared a top-floor apartment at 124 East 57th Street in Manhattan.

While Berlau encouraged Brecht to come to New York, his aim remained first to earn money in California. He also entertained thoughts of a defence-related job so that he would be allowed to travel without the usual restrictions on enemy aliens.[62] Neither was very likely. All the same, Brecht asked Berlau to look around for a place for him to live with his family in New York where Weigel hoped there would be acting opportunities. However, Brecht was exasperated when Berlau did not write about the New York German-language premiere of Viertel's scenes from *Fear and Misery of the Third Reich*, staged to raise funds for anti-Nazi refugees. He reminded her that it was his first production since arriving in the USA.[63] Hermann Kesten's review in New York's *Aufbau* celebrated the production's great success with the predominantly German and Austrian audience, which donated $400 to help refugees escape from France.[64] The scenes were repeated in June.

Berlau now attempted to force the issue with Brecht. It became obvious to him that she had taken a lover: 'I don't know who you are with and working with. Maybe you have no time'.[65] Berlau was seeing a younger colleague, Bernard Frizell. In the expectation that their relationship was over, Brecht considered – in a passage which reveals the mental processes by which he sought to objectify a situation and maintain control over his life's work – how he might put distance between himself and her without offending her:

When this woman began to threaten my capacity for work with her egocentricity, I decided to remove myself from her influence. I made the decision as casually as possible, without, as it were, noting it myself, and filed thoughts about her among the questions which are by nature insoluble. I was careful, however, not to think badly of her, on the contrary, I forced myself to think well of her, albeit in an objective and therefore strange fashion, the way you think of people who are not close to you. Instead of nursing anger at her fickleness, I found that I could approve of her sporadic friendliness, instead of being pleased at her affection I applauded her independence etc. Nothing is harder than to give up somebody without devaluing them, yet that is the only right thing to do.[66]

Sympathetic attachment, however, proved stronger than willed indifference. Brecht sent her the poem 'The Mask of Evil':

On my wall hangs a Japanese carving
The mask of an evil demon, decorated with gold lacquer.
Sympathetically I observe
The swollen veins of the forehead, indicating
What a strain it is to be evil.[67]

Despite Brecht's urgings to 'smooth' her brow, the anger would never leave her. Brecht, however, had no real desire to end the relationship, rather to maintain it in a way that it did not damage his family. Precisely that, however, Berlau found unacceptable.

On 28 May 1942 Brecht met Fritz Lang and talked on the beach about a 'hostage film'.[68] The previous day, the reign of terror presided over by the Deputy Protector of Bohemia and Moravia Reinhard Heydrich had been interrupted when he was fatally wounded in an attack in Prague by a team of Czech and Slovak soldiers dispatched by the Czech government-in-exile in London. Assuming that the assassination was the work of the Czech resistance, Brecht and Lang quickly put together an outline which they called *Silent City*. Although Brecht found the pitch 'pure Monte Carlo', it would become the anti-Fascist classic *Hangmen Also Die*, Brecht's only complete Hollywood film project. After Lang had received a promising response from a producer, he and

Brecht worked full-time on the script from 9 a.m. to 7 p.m. Brecht complained: 'How I hate these little heatwaves that beset everybody as soon as money is in the offing (win time to work, better house, music lessons for Steff, no further need for charity)'. Commercial imperatives always overrode aesthetic precepts: 'There is a remarkable term that always crops up whenever the logic of events or of the continuity cries out to be discussed: "The public will accept that"'. For Brecht, who had spent his career challenging his audience to learn from events on the stage, this dictum signified a gross abdication of artistic responsibility in a mindless entertainment industry. Brecht, who thought he knew a thing or two about contracts, witnessed Lang's negotiations with the 'money men': 'The figures and the agonised screams can be heard below, like in a propaganda film, "$30,00" – "8%" – "I can't do it". I go out into the garden with the secretary. Gunfire out at sea …'. The film was contracted to United Artists. Brecht signed up for $5,000, with $3,000 to follow, and worked at the studio full-time on what he described as an 'infinitely dismal fabrication' in 'hot office rooms' together with the writer John Wexley. Brecht saw himself in 'dire straits', 'dropped at the very centre of world drug-trafficking, amidst the ultimate Tuis of that trade'. As he had in London in 1936, for a short while in LA Brecht became a regular office worker. He took sandwiches from home for lunch, with which he drank a little Californian white wine, but he developed abscesses in his gums and had to have three teeth pulled.[69] He reflected: 'I was already clearly aware how badly my brain was functioning, how quickly I tired, how low one's vitality gets, and so on. Five days of taking vitamin pills and I was fit again. What striking proof of the social origins of the proletarian "inability to think"'.

Writing to Korsch, Brecht was quite upbeat about the project: 'The script at least is nothing to be ashamed of'. However, Brecht suspected the motives of Wexley, who earned $1,500 a month and was

> supposed to be very left and decent. I first go through a sequence with him, and he dictates it to the secretary. She makes four copies, and when I ask for one he makes childish excuses. At the top of the page stands 'John Wexley' and the date, and there is no name against the individual suggestions. In one scene he needs a German translation; so he puts handwritten additions on one copy and hands it to me. I take the sheet with me. Then there is some phoning around, he says I took a sheet he needs, he can't get on with his work. It would seem that these tricks are highly paid.[70]

Brecht persuaded Wexley to write a completely different 'ideal' script at Brecht's in the evening to be shown to Lang later: 'I have naturally laid the main emphasis on the scenes with the people'. However, when the writing reached the critical phase, 'Lang hauled poor Wexley into his office and screamed at him behind closed doors that he wants to make a Hollywoodpicture (sic), and shits on scenes that show the people'. Brecht remarked how the prospect of $700,000 had changed Lang: 'He sits with all the airs of a dictator and old movie hand behind his boss desk'. It is said that when Lang removed the part of Mrs Dvorak which Brecht had written for Weigel, Brecht refused to enter his studio again.[71]

When the work was over, Brecht reflected upon his employment in much the same way as in 1936: 'I feel the disappointment and terror of the intellectual worker who sees the product of his labours snatched away and mutilated'.[72] The alienation he experienced was very real: 'Interesting how a person falls apart if one function is closed down. The ego becomes formless if it is no longer addressed, approached, ordered around. Alienation of the self sets in'. Brecht reflected how he had worked to 'avoid getting involved in their grubby little problems, like finding those slick, smart "lines" and the transition from one pointless situation to another, and writing gush in general, all of which I left to others. That kind of thing can seriously damage your handwriting'. He was left feeling that the work on the film had 'almost made me ill'. It had made him ill.

The production of the film did nothing to improve matters. Brecht attended the shooting and found further serious grounds for complaint. Heydrich was played by Hans Heinrich von Twardowski, whom, we remember, Brecht had traumatised in Bronnen's *Parricide* in Berlin in 1922. What is more, the producer Arnold Pressburger planned to name Wexley as the sole scriptwriter, undermining Brecht's chances of further employment.[73] Brecht took the matter to the Screenwriters' Guild. Lang and Eisler, who had written the musical score, supported Brecht. However, Wexley denied Brecht's substantial involvement and the Guild found against Brecht, who wrote: 'The sight of intellectual mutilation makes me physically ill. It is scarcely possible to stand being in the same room with these intellectual cripples and moral invalids'.[74] When the film was released the following March, Wexley was named as the scriptwriter after an original manuscript by Lang and Brecht. The film was a critical and box-office success. For all the shenanigans, *Hangmen Also Die* changed things for Brecht, bringing in around $10,000, enough money to afford a better house and to devote himself to his own writing again. When Weill met Brecht in Hollywood he wrote to Lenya: 'I think I will do a show with Brecht *for you*. He has enough money now for two years and could come to N.Y.'.[75]

4. Brecht and Walter Benjamin, playing chess, Skovsbostrand 8, Denmark, 1934. Photographer: not known. BBA FA 07/026.

. Brecht, Henry Peter Matthis, Margarete Steffin and Stefan Brecht, Lidingö, Sweden, 1939. Photographer: enry Peter Matthis. BBA FA 07/151.

16. Ruth Berlau, Lidingö, Sweden, 1939. Photographer: not known. BBA FA 07/116.

17. Brecht and Helene Weigel, Santa Monica, around 1943. Photograph: Hollywood, Hobby. BBA FA 08/144.

18. Brecht and Charles Laughton, Santa Monica, 1945. Photographer: Ruth Berlau. BBA FA 08/077b.

19. Brecht, New York, 1946. Photographer: Ruth Berlau. BBA FA 03/087b.

SMOKE SCREEN is thrown up by cigar of German-born Writer Berthold Brecht, an acquaintance of Communist Gerhard Eisler. His thick accent mystified the committee, which excused him after he denied being a party member.

20. Brecht before the House Un-American Activities Committee, 30 October 1947. Photographer: not known. BBA FA 03/122b.

21. Brecht and Caspar Neher, Zurich, 1948. Photographer: Ruth Berlau. BBA FA 08/204c.

22. Brecht, Helene Weigel, Erwin Geschonneck and Angelika Hurwitz during rehearsals for *Mother Courage and her Children*, Berliner Ensemble, 1951. Photographer: Hainer Hill. BBA FA 12/007.1.

23. Brecht, Weissensee, Berlin, 1953. Photographer: Gerda Goedhart. BBA FA 04/081-ÜG.

24. Brecht and Helene Weigel, Berlin, 1 May 1954. Photograph: ADN-ZB/Sturm. BBA FA 09/138.

25. Harry Buckwitz, Peter Suhrkamp and Brecht, during rehearsals for *The Caucasian Chalk Circle*, Frankfurt am Main, 1955. Photographer: not known. BBA FA 09/180.

26. Brecht in his flat at Chausseestrasse 125, Berlin, 1955. Photographer: Gerda Goedhart. BBA FA 05/126.

Ever the Enemy Alien 1942–5

Writing for Broadway

With his earnings from *Hangmen Also Die*, in the summer of 1942 Brecht and Weigel acquired a house, which she had found, on the rent payment system in Santa Monica at 1063 26th Street. They also acquired a car, a second-hand Buick. Weigel trawled second-hand shops, selecting furniture out of which she conjured a stylish interior in which her family could begin to settle for the first time since Skovsbostrand. Brecht told Berlau with a certain satisfaction, which she surely did not want to hear, that the house was 'old, forty years old, built in the days when Hollywood didn't exist'.[1] He amplified in his journal: 'California clapboard, whitewashed, with an upper floor with 4 bedrooms. I have a long workroom (almost 7 metres), which we immediately whitewashed and equipped with 4 tables. There are old trees in the garden (a pepper-tree and a fig-tree)'.

Owning a property which suited his needs was important to Brecht: 'For the first time, I actually feel halfway all right here. I am alone downstairs, it is one-thirty in the morning. I can even go into the garden without going through anybody's room. From my desk I can see automobiles going down the street'.[2] Shortly after, he added something that he had thought impossible in California: 'The house is very beautiful. In this garden it becomes possible to read Lucretius once more'. The Epicurean Lucretius's *De rerum natura*, his meditation upon how to overcome the fear of death and to achieve a state of ataraxia, that imperturbability which Brecht sought in philosophers from ancient China to modern Europe, had a place in Hollywood after all. Typically, however, in 'Summer 1942' he juxtaposes his fresh sense of well-being with the harsh economic and political reality:

> Day after day
> I see the fig trees in the garden
> The rosy faces of the dealers who buy lies
> The chessmen on the corner table
> And the newspapers with their reports
> Of bloodbaths in the Soviet Union.[3]

Financial security meant that Brecht could resume his own playwriting. Over the coming years he wrote three new plays and a new version of *Life of Galileo*, all intended for mainstream Broadway theatre. However, only one of the new plays matched the standard of the later Scandinavian work and none achieved the breakthrough he craved. In November 1942 he enlisted Feuchtwanger's help for *The Visions of Simone Machard*, a play about the fall of France in June 1940, which he had begun in the autumn of 1941. He had first called the play *Voices*, noting that the voices were those of the people and that 'our social circumstances are such that in wartime not only the ruled but also the rulers of the two hostile countries have common interests. The owners and the robbers stand shoulder to shoulder against those who do not recognise property – the patriots'.[4] Brecht's premise that only those without property could be unimpeachable patriots was provocatively partisan.

Brecht and Feuchtwanger settled into a regular routine from 11 a.m. to 2 p.m. at Feuchtwanger's palatial mansion, Villa Aurora, off Sunset Boulevard. Brecht found Feuchtwanger's politics suspect: he accepted Marx's 'laws of the class struggle' only for classes, not for individuals. They worked 'exclusively on the structure, for which Feuchtwanger's dogged defence of naturalistic probability is very useful. His outmoded "biological" psychology holds up a little'.[5] The play's eight scenes tell the story of the servant girl Simone, who is inspired in her dreams of saving her country from the invading Germans by a book about Joan of Arc. Like Kattrin in *Mother Courage*, she beats a drum as she invokes the spirit of French unity but discovers that her homeland is bitterly divided. The officers reveal their Fascist attitudes as they turn tail, while the owning classes hoard their assets rather than deploying them to help their compatriots, many of whom are now refugees. In Simone's dream sequences, the play moves between June 1940 and the France of Joan of Arc, the latter time acting as a foil for critical comment on a dramatically alienated present.

Within Brecht's compositional programme *The Visions of Simone Machard* is a complementary work to *Arturo Ui*, showing the process of Fascist infiltration of a conquered country. Having protected their assets rather than their compatriots, the owning classes pursue business as usual in their deals with the conquerors. Simone follows the instruction of the Angel in her dream to 'Go forth now and ravage' in order to destroy material goods owned by the French such as petrol, which the conquering army needs for its tanks.[6] The honest and upright Simone readily admits her crime of arson to the owners of those goods. In a travesty of a trial in a French ecclesiastical court, which shows Catholic France set on a course of clerico-Fascism like Austria and Italy, she is banished to the infamous Disciplinary Order of Saint Ursula. As she is taken away, the Angel re-appears with a message of hope, which is echoed in a further act of arsonist resistance committed by the refugees.

Brecht enjoyed working with Feuchtwanger despite their differences, which Feuchtwanger was not inclined to press. Brecht wrote that Feuchtwanger had a 'feeling for structure and appreciates linguistic refinements, is also capable of making poetic and dramaturgical suggestions, knows a lot about literature, pays attention to arguments and is pleasant to deal with, a good friend'.[7] William Dieterle admired the 'wonderful dynamism of the action'. Feuchtwanger then produced a rough English translation, with a view to securing a production. The hope was that his famous name could help them where Brecht's could not. In fact, Brecht would never pay much attention to the play again.

Brecht's name still counted for something in one part of distant, war-torn Europe. There were more productions of his latest works in that last continental outpost of German anti-Fascist theatre, the Zurich Schauspielhaus, where *The Good Person of Szechwan* premiered in early February 1943. Leonard Steckel directed and Teo Otto again designed the set. Maria Becker took the lead as Shen Te/Shui Ta, Karl Paryla was Yang Sun and Therese Giehse Mi Tzu. There was much critical praise, together with some misunderstandings. The reviewer in *Die Weltwoche* wrote of Brecht's 'phenomenal journey of inner maturation ... from activist nihilism to an affirmation of humanity' before concluding: 'The Communist Brecht reveals himself to be an apologist of bourgeois capitalism'.[8] Even allowing for the ambiguities of Brecht's works, that was stretching things. The premiere of *Life of Galileo* would follow in Zurich in September 1943, the only production of the original *Galileo* in Brecht's lifetime. Again Steckel directed and Otto designed the set. Steckel himself took the lead, emphasising the philosophical dimensions of the torn Galileo's struggle for the truth. The production was an enormous success: the audience applauded after each scene and demanded curtain call after curtain call.[9] Critics and audience alike understood that the chilling tale of the great researcher's predicament at the hands of the Inquisition was urgently relevant in the dark times of a Europe dominated by reactionary forces. The 'Danish' *Galileo* still awaits re-discovery for the world stage.

Momentous events were unfolding in the European war. The Battle of Stalingrad reached its conclusion on 2 February with the Red Army's destruction of the German 6th Army. The Soviets now drove back German forces relentlessly. Brecht knew what lay ahead, writing in 'Homecoming':

My native city, however shall I find her?
Following the swarms of bombers
I come home.
Well, where is she? Where the colossal
Mountains of smoke stand.[10]

As thoughts among the émigrés turned to the politics of German re-construction after the defeat of Nazism, the US authorities stepped up surveillance of these enemy aliens, particularly the large communities in Los Angeles and New York. Like the other allies, the USA, of course, had an interest in determining not only the outcome of the war but also its aftermath. During Brecht's remaining five years in the USA, the FBI subjected him to close surveillance. At times, agents from the Office of Strategic Services (OSS), a forerunner of the CIA, intervened, too. Neighbours acted as informants, convinced that Brecht and Weigel were spies.[11] Other information came from within the émigré community. While the experience of surveillance did nothing to improve Brecht's view of the USA, this practised survivor complied meticulously with requirements. The FBI noted that Brecht was 5' 8", 130 pounds, with brown eyes. Normally wearing a grey flannel shirt or mufti and baggy trousers, he and William Dieterle had been to the Filmarte Theatre, which had previously shown Russian films. That was sufficient grounds for suspicion. Brecht told Berlau that a man – he meant an FBI agent – had been asking about her and that he had told him that she had worked on a film with Elisabeth Bergner and for the radio.[12] When asked what she lived off, Brecht had replied that Berlau had brought some money to the USA and had links with the Danish envoy in Washington.

Planning his trip to New York, Brecht used an invitation from Piscator to secure permission to travel. He left Santa Monica for New York at 5 p.m. on Monday 8 February 1943, travelling via Chicago. His train was 'full of soldiers, mostly other ranks, really nice boys with very good manners, playing cards, drinking beer and lemonade, listening to the radio. They turned off the radio instantly whenever a news bulletin started'.[13] Brecht recorded his impressions of America, 'Arizona and Texas remind you very much of Siberia, seen from the train. The grey two-storey wooden farms and the people look very poor'. He reached New York on the Friday morning for what became a three-month stay. He elected to arrive in the theatrical capital of the US generally unannounced. However, the FBI was on his case, noting that he went directly from the station to Berlau's apartment at 124 East 57th Street. During his stay Berlau's telephone was bugged and conversations with friends were recorded.[14]

124 East 57th Street is the scene of the famous photo of Brecht smoking his cigar with measured satisfaction on the balcony with the Manhattan skyline in the background. Shortly after arriving, he saw Elisabeth Bergner and met with Korsch and all manner of old friends and acquaintances, learning of their mixed fortunes in New York. Brecht's publisher Herzfelde was running a stamp shop. Brecht noted that his fellow Bavarian Oskar Maria Graf had 'not learnt a single word of English'.[15] The impresario Aufricht was in New York, too, having fled Paris. He took Brecht to a Chinese theatre in a big, old building on a side-street near the Bowery where the audience, mostly Chinese, came and went during five-hour performances by the Cantonese Players. For a while, Brecht went along nearly every day, captivated by the spectacle, and took along friends, among them the composer Paul Dessau and a Chinese man, who acted as Brecht's translator. Whenever he returned to New York, Brecht would visit the Chinese theatre, while back in Los Angeles Brecht would cultivate a friendship with the Chinese Communist writer and actor H. T. Tsiang.

Brecht met Sternberg in New York but they argued, Brecht erupting with anger when Sternberg suggested that he was only emphasising the positive elements of Soviet policy and the negative ones of the Western Allies.[16] After so long on the defensive, Brecht could now go on the front foot over the Soviet contribution to defeating Fascism. He had discussions with other émigrés, who were generally more political than their counterparts in California: Karl August Wittfogel, Heinz Lagerhans, Maximilian Scheer, Hermann Budzislavsky, Jacob Walcher and Eisler's brother Gerhart, a long-standing Comintern figure working for US Left-wing publications whom the FBI kept under close surveillance. Elisabeth Hauptmann was living in New York with Horst Baerensprung, a lawyer and formerly the Social Democrat Police President of Magdeburg. Hauptmann and Brecht visited George Grosz on Long Island after viewing an exhibition of his work. Brecht felt that, in contrast to the mid–1930s, Grosz was 'rather disappointed with America'.[17] He later helped Grosz to get an exhibition in California. Hauptmann met publishers about English editions of Brecht's work, for which the theatre critic Eric Bentley, who was teaching English at UCLA, was envisaged as the general editor. Bentley had earlier approached Brecht, asking if he could translate some of his works, and Brecht had readily agreed. This is how a relationship began which was of great importance for the dissemination of Brecht's work in the USA. With Hauptmann and Hoffman Hays, Brecht began an adaptation of John Webster's *Duchess of Malfi* for Elisabeth Bergner. It seems that this was her way of making amends for earlier misappropriations of Brecht's work. Writing for a star such as Bergner was an opportunity to make money. However, progress was sluggish, not least because of Bergner's interventions, and the project dragged on until 1946.

Bergner, Piscator and Peter Lorre were behind an evening of Brecht's anti-Nazi poems and songs on 6 March at the studio theatre of the New School for Social Research, which was organised by the New York Tribune for Free German Literature and Arts in America. Herzfelde introduced the show, Lorre and Bergner performed Brecht's works, as did Paul Dessau to one of his own musical settings. Brecht found that Bergner and Lorre had 'forgotten nothing, their techniques have remained completely fresh' and encouraged Dessau to follow him to California, where they collaborated while Dessau worked as a gardener.[18] Henry Marx wrote an enthusiastic review of the Brecht evening for the *New Yorker Staatszeitung und Herold*, featuring an interview in which Brecht regretted that he would never be able to write in English and saw 'no possibility for the performance of his plays, which, with all their revolutionary innovations, arose in the soil of a tradition that simply does not exist here'.[19]

However, another Brecht evening was held in April at the Heckscher Theatre on East 104th Street, when Herbert Berghof read from Brecht's *Contemporary Picturebook*, accompanied by projections.[20] Brecht had been developing this combination of text and images from the war in the emblematic quatrains of the photo-epigrams which he collected in the *War Primer*, a 'radically probing version of documentary'.[21] One of the photos shows a city street reduced to rubble by bombing and an epigram reading:

Here are the cities in which once our 'Heils!'
Acclaimed our war machine as it paraded.
But these are nothing to the thousand miles
Of foreign cities that it devastated.[22]

Brecht's work also featured at the anti-Nazi rally *We Fight Back*, which took place at Hunter College in Manhattan. Again, Lorre and Bergner performed Brecht's work, together with Lenya, accompanied by Weill. At Aufricht's instigation, Brecht and Weill came together, signing an agreement for an adaptation of *The Good Person of Szechwan*. In early May Brecht spent a week working on a draft with Weill at his house in New City.

Like Bergner, Peter Lorre was hugely successful in the USA. Brecht had great affection for him and later tried to help him overcome his drug habit. Brecht and Lorre worked on a film script, *The Crouching Venus*, at Arrowhead, a 'playground of the rich', of which Brecht wrote:

There's an artificial mountain lake with pine trees and oaks, the whole thing fenced off, because it's owned by a private company. It's as quiet as living in a forest between two sawmills, because speedboats are always thundering across the lake. Lorre is living with a millionairess, the daughter of a Chicago meat king, the children bite mummy's pearls to see if they're real or prove to the guests they are.

A little girl asked me when I arrived if I was a chauffeur, then if I was an actor, then a writer. Already her instinct is infallible. I was obviously a menial.[23]

Lorre, however, looked after Brecht: 'Lorre rides, swims, drives a speedboat, shoots clay pipes and is generally nice, somewhere between my patron and my student'. Thanks to Brecht, they even worked: 'We discuss the story in the morning, that's a concession to me; otherwise it's not normal to work if one goes out to work. I don't feel a single cubic metre of ground under my feet, merely Lorre's bank balance, in this polluted continent in a lost century'. Brecht could at least have an intelligent conversation with Lorre. Later, in January 1947, Brecht would write to Lorre's psychiatrist Max Gruenthal about Lorre's drug addiction, explaining that few people could 'remain sober in an industry which only produces narcotics in the mind'.[24] However, Brecht explained that he would be needing Lorre fit and well in Berlin. After his return to Berlin Brecht composed the poem 'To the Actor P. L. in Exile', whom, he wrote, he needed in a country destroyed. To Brecht's mind, Hollywood had destroyed Lorre.

At the Office of War Information in New York, Lenya recorded Brecht's 'Song of a German Mother' with music by Dessau in a series by John Houseman, the head of the Radio Program Division of Overseas Broadcast. However, Brecht noted: 'The German desk sabotages it'.[25] Houseman abandoned the project when the State Department's German desk and British intelligence objected that broadcasts by émigrés 'created hostility in their German listeners'. What is more, in late March R. B. Hood, the Special Agent in Charge of the FBI's Los Angeles office, wrote about Brecht to his boss J. Edgar Hoover, inquiring whether the US Attorney 'will authorise the arrest of Subject as an enemy alien with a view to his internment?'.[26] Evidence against Brecht as a Communist and an enemy of capitalism had been compiled from two principal sources, Mr and Mrs Fritz Nuernberger and T. W. Baumfeld of Arnold Productions. Friedrich Torberg would also act as an informant, citing Brecht's Lehrstück *The Measures Taken*. Hoover submitted an application for Brecht's internment to the US Attorney's office. The surveillance intensified.

Brecht returned to Los Angeles by train in late May. It was not lost on the Brechts that the FBI was bugging their phone. Trying to make light of the intrusion into their privacy, which at this stage remained unauthorised, Weigel and Marta Feuchtwanger took to reading out recipes to each other down the phone from cookbooks in Polish.[27] Regular reports were logged on Brecht's visitors. The FBI noted that Brecht had gone to an event with a young Soviet journalist, with whom he had also spoken at William Dieterle's house together with other German émigrés.[28] Franz Werfel and Douglas Sirk joined the émigré informants. However, the FBI's plan to intern Brecht was thwarted when on 26 June 1943 the Justice Department declined to issue a presidential warrant for Brecht's arrest 'at this time'.[29] The FBI would maintain its interest, resuming intensive surveillance from the summer of 1944 until the autumn of 1946 and again during the autumn of 1947.

In July 1943 Berlau was sacked from her job with the Office of War Information because she was a member of the Danish Communist Party.[30] She took a factory job for a short while. In his letters, Brecht sought to allay her fear that he did not want her in Los Angeles. However, Berlau's patience snapped when Karin Michaelis, now in New

York, was planning a visit to Brecht and Weigel, and Brecht told Berlau that he did not want her to accompany Michaelis. In a stay which lasted eight months Michaelis became part of the lively social circle around the Brechts. Berlau, however, became very angry, taunting Brecht that he was living a petit bourgeois idyll.[31] Brecht replied: 'Your tone is hateful and ironic. [...] I no longer know what to do or what advice to give you, Ruth, for I do know what your shift from love to hate, from friendship to enmity, has already cost us'. Brecht, so needful of calm and composure, was trying to settle into something resembling a regular existence in Santa Monica with Weigel, Stefan and Barbara. To their great amusement Brecht, who was no gardener, reflected that, among the simple pleasures which the new house afforded, 'What I enjoy doing is sprinkling the garden'.[32] That August he wrote:

> O sprinkling the garden, to enliven the green!
> Watering the thirsty trees. Give them more than enough
> And do not forget the shrubs
> Even those without berries, the exhausted
> Niggardly ones. And do not neglect
> The weeds growing between the flowers, they too
> Are thirsty. Nor water only
> The fresh grass or only the scorched.
> Even the naked soil you must refresh.

Brecht felt that the poem displayed an innovative quality which distinguished it from his other work. What did he mean? He had found himself no longer writing the poetry of survival in war. Rather, this poem was a celebration of undisturbed growth through the gardener's careful cultivation of a variety of vegetation. In Lyon's estimation, the poem presents a reverse Social Darwinism in the cultivation of all the vegetation rather than select plants, for each according to its needs.[33] The gardener's beneficent activity remained a live thought for Brecht, who would presently employ the motif of watering the garden on a much larger scale in the Prologue to *The Caucasian Chalk Circle*. There, after the expulsion of the Nazis the Agronomist explains to the villagers the benefits of irrigation for the growth of fruit and vines.

The poem triggered Brecht's reflection that a lyrical œuvre 'must have an (inner) history', which might echo or be in contrast to external history.[34] Here Brecht draws upon the instinctive dialectic which informs his creative rhythm. Come what may, poetry without an external history had become unthinkable. His poetry all had the 'character of experiments', which were 'ordered in a certain relationship to one another'. He compared its inner history to Picasso's 'periods'. Picasso was becoming a measure of artistic accomplishment as Brecht embarked on a fresh period in his work, dramatic as well as lyrical. He included 'Of Sprinkling the Garden' in a collection of ten poems he had written in the US. When he later compiled his *Poems in Exile* he wrote, 'The poems are written in a kind of "basic German". This in no sense corresponds to a theory, reading through such a collection I'm conscious of the lack of expressiveness and rhythm, yet when I am writing (and correcting) every uncommon word sticks in my craw. Poems like "Landscape of Exile" I'm not putting in, they are already too rich'.[35] Just as he reflected with some satisfaction upon his lyrical œuvre, so too Brecht took heart from what he had achieved in writing ten plays in exile: 'not a bad repertoire for a defeated class', even though 'every time a work has been finished in these last years there has been a soul-destroying interlude to be endured as it lay in an unnatural state of non-use'. He had compiled a dazzling repertoire and there was more to come.

At Weill's house, Brecht had written an outline plot for *Schweyk in the Second World War*, envisaging a Broadway musical. He had always loved Hašek's novel, which he had re-read on the train from New York to Los Angeles. He now resumed work on this third play about a 'great' survivor after Galileo and Mother Courage, consulting with his son, who doubted whether the plot could stand the shift from the Habsburg Empire to the Nazi occupation, and with Lorre, whom he earmarked for the lead.[36] Brecht outlined what he intended for Schweyk:

> Under no circumstances must Schweyk become a cunning, underhand saboteur. He is just an opportunist specialising in exploiting the little opportunities that remain open to him. Inasmuch as he approves of any kind of order, he honestly approves of the existing order, destructive as its consequences are for him, even a nationalist order which he only experiences as a form of oppression. His wisdom is devastating. His indestructibility makes him the inexhaustible object of maltreatment and at the same time fertile ground for liberation.[37]

By 24 June Brecht was writing: '*Schweyk* largely finished. A counter-play to *Mother Courage*. In contrast to the *Schweyk* which I wrote for Piscator in about 27 – a straight montage from the novel – the present one (in the Second World War) is considerably sharper, corresponding to the change from the established tyranny of the Habsburgs to the Nazi invasion'. As we know, the extent of Brecht's involvement in Piscator's adaptation remains open to doubt. Brecht sent the new play to Weill piecemeal as drafts became ready, asking for improvements. After Weill visited Brecht in Santa Monica in late June Brecht noted: 'His judgement in dramatic matters is good. e.g. he misses the survival element in *Schweyk*, which I had included in the short outline'. Brecht did more work on the survivor Schweyk, whose portrayal comes to include elements of the previously rejected 'cunning, underhand saboteur', but Brecht never settled on a single, final draft.

While *Schweyk in the Second World War* displays trademark Brechtian dramatic brilliance, it does at points strain credibility despite Brecht's best efforts to fashion a plot from Hašek's work suited to the Nazi occupation. Like *Hangmen Also Die*, *Schweyk* is set in Prague. It depicts the interaction of the SS and Gestapo with the local population within the framing device of a 'Prologue in the Higher Regions' – which features Hitler, Himmler, Goering, Goebbels and von Bock – and an 'Epilogue', in which Schweyk and Hitler meet on the never-ending road to Stalingrad. Schweyk sings to Hitler as the Führer attempts to escape in a wild dance: 'The east wind is far too cold, and hellfire is far too hot / So they've left it to me now to say whether or not / I should heap you with shit or riddle you with shot'.[38]

Brecht had taken the decisive turn in the war on the Eastern Front as the signal to go one step further than Arturo Ui in a comic portrayal of Hitler which some critics have found distasteful. Brecht puts Hitler centre stage in a satirical unmasking of the

Führer, of his economic motives in war and of his dependence upon the support of the 'Little Man', be he German, Austrian or Czech.[39] In this portrayal, then, Brecht maintains his Marxist interpretation of Nazi expansionism, in which racism is a by-product of economic aggression. Brecht was perhaps less shocked than many others as the scale of Nazi genocidal atrocities became known because, as his conversations with Benjamin demonstrate, he had fully expected them as a consequence of Fascist rule.

The 'Little Man' in question, in the shape of the dog dealer Schweyk and his photographer friend Baloun, meets with the SS and Gestapo at Anna Kopecka's Chalice Tavern. Baloun's craving for food leaves him vulnerable to them in exchanges characterised by the vicious arrogance of the occupiers, and the locals' blend of resigned acquiescence and covert dissent. As in *Fear and Misery of the Third Reich*, there are tell-tale cracks in the facade of Nazi power and evidence that order and discipline are beginning to fragment. The servant girl Anna, for example, says: 'I'm told we were very rash to go into the Moldau gardens. It's dangerous because of the German deserters who set on you'.[40] There is also evidence of resistance when Anna's friend Kati remarks: 'The SS are jumpy too because yesterday they pulled another SS man out of the Moldau with a hole in his left side'. At the same time, critics have rightly pointed out that the plot depends on a rather strained portrayal of the SS as the dupes of the amiable, indestructible trickster Schweyk.

The dramatic potential of Schweyk had long fascinated Brecht. Unlike Galileo and Courage with their egotistical and material needs in those dark dramas, the unassuming, picaresque Schweyk does not experience his plight as the division of his own nature. Even though he will never lead the way, the quick-witted picaro Schweyk, without the 'bourgeois' baggage of Galileo and Courage, is able, like the unencumbered intellectual Keuner, to pass through the crucible separating the dark times from those beyond. Schweyk's survival instinct enables him to evade traps, his manner contrasting with the viciously acquisitive, if militarily and ideologically blinkered, attitudes of the SS and Gestapo surrounding him. While this survivor's nature is uncomplicated, his picaresque behaviour can acquire intricacy: he evades the soldiers' grasp with a brand of truth-telling in which the naive and the cunning are virtually indistinguishable within a behavioural pattern informed by the familiar paradox of non-action/action of Wu Wei. He sees the chasm which divides those in the 'Higher Regions', with their aspirations to accumulate power, from the interests of the Little Man, whom the powerful would deploy as their instruments: 'The common herd's a thorn in the flesh of any great man, it's like Baloun with his appetite getting half a Frankfurter for his supper, it's no good at all'.[41] The plans of the 'great' cannot be implemented by the likes of Baloun, never mind by the 'great' themselves.

What is more, the play's interpolated songs underscore the message that there are forces greater than the Hitlers of this world, as in 'Song of the Gentle Breeze' with its celebration of nature: 'They fear the whirlwind's terrible strength / And long for the gentle breeze'. At the play's conclusion, the 'Song of the Moldau', performed by all the actors, is a resounding affirmation that, in the flux of things, there will be change and that the days of the great are numbered:

For times have to change. All the boundless ambitions
Of those now in power will soon have been spent.
Like bloodspattered cocks they defend their position
But times have to change – which no force can prevent.

The stones of the Moldau are stirring and shifting
In Prague lie three emperors turning to clay.
The great shall not stay great, the darkness is lifting.
The night has twelve hours, but at last comes the day.[42]

Hence, the play begins to look beyond the dark times of the tyrants, articulating the potential for the victory of the common people in a manner which would later inspire Bob Dylan's composition of 'The Times They Are A-Changin'' with its resounding conclusion, 'The first one now will later be last'.[43]

Brecht turned his attention to securing a contract for a production of *Schweyk* with Weill. In the USA, Weill always had the upper hand. However, Brecht insisted on an equal standing rather than being merely Weill's librettist.[44] While Weill wanted a big-name translator, Brecht engaged the poet Alfred Kreymborg. However, this deeply antagonised Piscator, who had the rights to *Schweyk* in the USA and in any case wanted Kreymborg to translate his own version for the Theater Guild. Although Kreymborg did the work quickly as expected, Brecht was disappointed with the outcome. Weill then backtracked, telling Brecht that 'some American writers had told him the play was too un-American for Broadway'. Despite the fact that Brecht persuaded Eisler to do the music, the play would never reach the US stage. It would be premiered only after Brecht's death.

The struggle for a new Germany begins

A key Allied war aim was to destroy German military capacity for ever. What would become of the German nation as a whole after the unconditional surrender which the Allies were demanding was another matter. There was significant support for the Vansittartist position that all Germans had incurred guilt collectively for Nazi crimes and should be punished accordingly. It followed that no significant democratic forces existed which might represent another Germany. Deeply mistrustful of British imperialist and US capitalist interests, Brecht was fundamentally opposed to the Vansittartist position.

At Brecht's instigation, prominent German émigrés in Los Angeles met on 1 August 1943 at the Viertels' to work on a public declaration of support for the National Committee for a Free Germany (NCFD), founded in July 1943 by Moscow émigrés in conjunction with German soldiers in Soviet POW camps. Erich Weinert was the chair, flanked by senior army officers from the camps. The Mann brothers were at the Viertels', as were Feuchtwanger, Bruno Frank, Ludwig Marcuse and Hans Reichenbach. Thomas Mann had recently submitted a piece to the Mexican *Freies Deutschland*, in which he expressed his agreement with the goals of the NCFD.[45]

For the FBI, the venue at the Viertels' could not have been better. Salka Viertel's secretary Marion Bach was an FBI informant, as was Ludwig Marcuse's wife.[46] After four hours of discussion the émigrés agreed on the following:

> At this moment, when the victory of the Allied nations is approaching, we the undersigned writers, scientists and artists of German extraction deem it their duty to declare openly: We welcome the declaration of the prisoners-of-war and exiles in the Soviet Union, calling upon the German people to force its oppressors into unconditional surrender and to fight for a strong democracy in Germany. We too deem it necessary to distinguish clearly between the Hitler regime and the classes linked to it on the one hand and the German people on the other. We are convinced there can be no lasting world peace without a strong democracy in Germany.[47]

Quite what they all understood by democracy was another matter. Brecht recorded the role played in the discussion by Thomas Mann, who saw himself – and was seen by US elites – as the leading light amongst German émigrés in the West:

> Thomas Mann wrote the first sentence. He had reservations about the mention of the Soviet Union. The last time I saw him, in February, he said, as he juggled with a plate of sandwiches, 'I should like the Russians to be in Berlin before the Allies'. Afterwards I discovered that on that afternoon he had recorded a speech of congratulations for the Red Army at the Russian Consulate and had then been wined and dined. Now Bruno Frank persuaded him that not to mention the Moscow committee would just be odd, and the discussion turned to the notion of 'classes linked to it', for which Thomas suggested 'guilty by association' and Heinrich 'trusts'. In the end everybody agreed to the above formula and Thomas went down and read it to the women with visible satisfaction.

However, the next morning Thomas Mann, in Brecht's words, 'calls Feuchtwanger: he is withdrawing his signature because he is "feeling low", we are making a "patriotic declaration", which amounts to a "stab in the back" for the Allies, and he would be unable to call it unfair if the "Allies were to punish Germany harshly for ten or twenty years"'. Why had Mann changed his mind? Sources do not shed on this episode beyond the known fact that Mann held deeply ambivalent views, that his political naivety left him open to manipulation from all sides and that he was anxious not to upset the US authorities because he had an application pending to become a US citizen. As we shall see presently, sources do shed further light upon a similar episode shortly after, when a confused Mann again abandoned his fellow émigrés.

Following Mann's first retraction, Brecht deplored the 'single-minded cringeing' of these 'pillars of culture', suggesting that if the Hearst press took up Goebbels's words that Hitler and Germany were one and the same, Mann and others would accept them.[48] Brecht viewed Mann's action as treason against the German people, for which he should be punished: 'For a moment even I considered how "the German people" might live down having tolerated not only the crimes of the Hitler regime but also the novels of Herr Mann, specially when you think that the latter don't have the support of 20–30 armoured divisions behind them'. On 9 August Brecht recalled the previous

Sunday when Mann 'leant back and said, "Yes, they are going to have to kill half a million in Germany". It sounded absolutely bestial. It was a stuffed shirt speaking'.

Mann noted in his diary shortly after that he had received a 'lengthy visit from two FBI gentlemen about the group in Mexico, Katz, B. Brecht'.[49] Mann, in fact, talked to the FBI quite regularly, sometimes about his application for US citizenship, at others about fellow German émigrés. He was not alone in doing so: émigrés were in a vulnerable position. We have seen that Brecht divulged things to an agent about Berlau. What did Thomas Mann tell the agents? We don't have his exact words but Brecht noted, perhaps with some licence:

> Thomas Mann, so first-hand reports tell me, is going around saying 'those lefties like Brecht' are carrying out orders from Moscow in trying to get him to make declarations about the need to distinguish between Hitler and Germany. That reptile cannot imagine anyone doing something for Germany (and against Hitler) without orders from anywhere, and spontaneously regarding Germany as something other than a lucrative audience. The perfidiousness with which the Manns – his wife is very active in this area – spread these slurs, which they know full well can do a great deal of harm, is striking.[50]

Brecht was also concerned about the harm that was being done to the German civilian population by Allied bombing. Following the decisive turn in the desert and in the East, Brecht regularly records the destruction of German cities in his journal, accompanied by graphic photos: 'The heart stands still when one reads about the air-raids on Berlin. Since they are not linked to military operations one can see no end to the war, just the end of Germany'. Brecht told Berlau how proud he was of the Danes taking up arms against their oppressors: 'Even in Svendborg there's been fighting'. He mused that the name on 'our little book' of *Svendborg Poems* 'has very much gained in value' and that 'those friendly people have opened their little Second Front. I only hope they're not expecting help … '. The Nazis responded to the Danish general strike with a murderous wave of terror. At this juncture, Brecht criticised the Allies for not opening the second front in the West, which the Soviets had been demanding. Brecht repeats the criticism in his journal until the Normandy landings.

If the direction of the war gave Brecht and his friends fresh hope and yielded a redoubling of support for the Soviet Union, they were appalled by the position which Johannes R. Becher – the dubious leader of German culture in Moscow – had adopted with the publication of his 'German Doctrine'. Brecht wrote that it 'stinks of nationalism. Again Hitler's nationalism is quite naively accepted; Hitler just had the wrong brand whereas Becher has the right one'.[51] Becher, of course, took his cue from the Soviet war propaganda of a country united behind its avuncular leader. For Brecht, Becher's position that nationalism could overcome the weaknesses of Left-wing literature was 'appalling, opportunistic drivel'. Brecht acknowledged the importance of a 'national front for peace and freedom against Hitler' but wondered: 'Is this gigantic, philistine superstructure necessary?'. He quoted Becher: 'We must show German figures that embody everything we conceive of as representative of the new German man. [...] It is a new sense of community that is being formed, in order that Germany's will be done, and that we should be the agents of this, and it is the highest thing of all that guards over such a common weal, the genius of an eternal Germany'. Brecht commented crisply: 'Pass the sickbag, Alice!'.

Becher was setting the tone for cultural policy in a post-Nazi socialist Germany, where Brecht, like Becher, saw his future. After reading an account of the German extermination of Jews in Poland, Brecht observed: 'I really wish no more would be said or written about "German man" (pronounced cherman), so as to save us from having to ascribe these qualities to every one of us. All these expressions coined by smart salesmen that peddle "German scholarship", "German spirit", "German culture" lead inexorably to "German atrocities"'.[52] He continued: 'Germany must emancipate itself not as a nation but as a people, more precisely as a working class. It is not a case of "never having been a nation", it was a nation, i.e. it played the nation game for a stake in world power and developed a stinking brand of nationalism'.

Around this time, Brecht's relations with the representatives of the Soviet Union in Los Angeles intensified. It can be reasonably assumed that Brecht received briefings from them on evolving Soviet policy for a post-war Germany. The FBI noted that Brecht, Weigel, Eisler and the Kortners had attended a reception at the Soviet Consulate to celebrate the October Revolution, when they were 'very much encouraged and reassured'.[53] It was of interest to the FBI that the Soviet Vice-Consul – and principal KGB agent in Los Angeles – Gregory Kheifetz, visited Brecht in late October. Kheifetz was, of course, channelling reports back to Moscow. Documents secured in the Venona project include his report of 31 October 1943 under the guise of KhARON following a conversation with Heinrich Mann, in which Mann is said to have told him that discussions about a future German government were taking place at Carthage, Washington DC.[54] The former Berlin SPD Police President and Prussian Interior Minister Albert Grzesinski was chairing meetings, which envisaged a broadly based government to include Heinrich Brüning, Social Democrats and Thomas Mann. Heinrich Mann disclosed that his brother was in Carthage during a trip to the East coast.

In fact, Grzesinski was working together with the émigré Protestant theologian and existentialist philosopher Paul Tillich to establish not a government in exile but a pressure group in which Brecht became involved, The Council for a Democratic Germany. Tillich had been dismissed from his professorship at Frankfurt in 1933 and had gone to New York's Union Theological Seminary. The Council sought to encourage the German people to rise up against Hitler and demonstrate thereby that German democracy had popular legitimacy. During the autumn of 1943 a leading role in the Council was earmarked for Thomas Mann. Brecht travelled to the East coast on 15–19 November to join discussions with Tillich's group, which embraced a wide spectrum of political and theological views. A number of the founding members of the Council had been involved in Heinrich Mann's Lutetia Circle in Paris. It was hence somewhat different from the Moscow-inspired NCFD. However, the FBI at once associated the Council with the NCFD and viewed it as Communist-inspired.[55]

Brecht had been following Tillich's statements with interest for some months, noting in his journal: 'It is almost only in a religious context that one finds any parallel to these social struggles in the bourgeois camp. You just have to compare Thomas Mann with Tillich. Something like religious socialism exists, and exerts itself against clerico-fascism'.[56] The Council, however, wanted the prestige which went with Thomas Mann's name. On 27 October Mann agreed to assume the leadership of the Council and on 4 November, while Brecht was still in California, discussed the role with Tillich, Carl Zuckmayer, Karl Frank, Siegfried Aufhäuser, Paul Hertz and other Council members.[57] Zuckmayer, Frank and Aufhäuser were all talking to the OSS. For good measure, Mann invited another OSS informer, the Catholic journalist Werner Thormann, to the meeting. At first, Mann felt he would not be able to see it through, 'but then persevered to the dubious outcomes'.[58] Mann's heart was not really in representing the case for German democracy.

The OSS, under its Director, General William 'Wild Bill' Donovan, rode to his rescue. As Alexander Stephan shows, DeWitt Poole of the OSS's Foreign Nationalities Branch guided Adolf Berle, Assistant Secretary of State, as he steered Mann away from involvement in the Council.[59] 'Mann overboard!', was the cry from Council members after Mann announced his withdrawal at a meeting in his hotel room on 26 November which Brecht attended. Mann noted in his diary: 'Searing matter/, declining and consoling them'.[60] They were left 'speechless and shocked', not least by Mann's claims about his conversation with Berle, namely that Germany would be occupied for a minimum of fifty years and all children would be quarantined from the children of Allies for thirty years. Tillich told Mann that he had 'pronounced a death sentence upon Germany'.[61] OSS observers believed Mann to be repeating as much what his daughter Erika, herself an FBI informant, was saying as what he might have heard from Berle. Mann's muddled views were rapidly transformed into a dogmatic position about Germany and the Germans which was the reverse of his unpleasant chauvinism in the First World War. Like his daughter, Thomas Mann now forcefully proclaimed a German collective guilt and set the seal on his break with his fellow émigrés in a reader's letter to the *New York Times*, published on 29 November, in which he denied that the State Department had 'invited him to join or preside over a Free German Committee, nor do I consider the moment opportune for the formation of such a body'.[62] Travelling back to the West coast, Mann recalled Brecht's 'tauntingly embittered face' and feared that the 'Party liner' Brecht, 'will do wicked things to me' 'when the Russians help him into power in Germany'.[63] It is likely that Mann had heard Brecht's view that he should be punished. Mann had betrayed his fellow émigrés twice in a matter of months, helping to destroy the prospects for a broadly based coalition of German interests in the USA committed to the construction of a democratic Germany. Mann simply did not believe that such democratic forces existed. He asked himself not what he had done but 'How did I let it be noticed, this disbelief ?'.[64]

How serious were Mann's betrayals? Brecht wrote what Lyon calls 'one of the bitterest poems of his life', 'Upon the Nobel Prize Winner Thomas Mann's Authorising the Americans and the English to Punish the German People Ten Full Years for the Crimes of the Hitler Regime':

> With his hands in his barren lap
> The refugee demands the death of half a million people.
> For their victims he demands

Ten years of punishment. The sufferers
Must be chastised.[65]

Thomas Mann cannot, of course, be accused of starting the Cold War single-handedly. However, his vain and gullible acquiescence in the manoeuvrings of the OSS certainly contributed to the politics of division, which the OSS, like Kheifetz and the KGB, was already practising.

On 1 December Brecht wrote to Mann: 'I feel obliged to tell you of the consternation you aroused in all the people I spoke to after the meeting by saying quite plainly that you doubted whether there is any appreciable difference between the Hitler regime and its following on the one hand and the democratic elements in Germany on the other'.[66] Brecht referred Mann to the grouping around Tillich and the 'old working-class parties', before citing the hundreds of thousands of Germans who had sacrificed their lives or were incarcerated on account of their resistance to Hitler. Brecht continued: 'Accordingly, esteemed Mr Mann, all our friends are sincerely afraid that you, who more than any of us have the ear of the American people, may cause them to doubt the existence of democratic forces in Germany more than they do already'. Brecht invited Mann to 'reassure our friends as to your attitude in this most important of all questions'. Mann recorded his receipt of Brecht's 'severe letter' 'on account of my lack of belief in German democracy'.[67] In his reply Mann referred Brecht to his lecture 'The New Humanism' at Columbia University on 16 November, which in fact pre-dated his most recent démarche, when, hardly surprisingly, he had used some of the same arguments as the Committee.[68] Mann claimed erroneously that none of the 'gentlemen' from the Committee had attended the lecture and explained that although he assumed a collective guilt of the German people, he differentiated between degrees of guilt. The principal guilt lay with the powerful cartel of Junkers, the military and industrialists, who had been responsible for two world wars. At the same time, he continued, he had warned against the creation of such a group as the Committee which might be seen as an attempt to shield Germany from the enormity of Nazi crimes against humanity. Mann urged Brecht and his friends to take no initiative until the military defeat of Nazi Germany when the world could see that Germany's 'unrevolutionary people' had 'purified itself'. In early December Council members, including Brecht, met at Tillich's home and agreed to press ahead without Mann.

Brecht was again staying with Berlau on East 57th Street, this time until 22 March 1944. The debacle with Mann took its toll. Brecht succumbed to 'flu', writing to his wife in mid-December: 'I've just put eight days of flu behind me, on the first days I had a fever at 39°. [...] I wanted to call you but then I thought you'd just be afraid'.[69] Shortly after, he wrote: 'Today, Monday, I'm up for the first time properly after the flu, without fever since the day before yesterday, but somewhat unsteady after the ten days (and before that I didn't feel especially well)'. Among other things, on 22 December, along with Jacob Walcher, Albert Norden, Albert Schreiner and Gerhart Eisler, Brecht had attended an anti-Fascist rally of 3,000 people at Carnegie Hall on the tenth anniversary of the Reichstag Fire Trial. Paul Robeson had invited Brecht to contribute, the only German refugee to take to the platform. In the wake of the Mann fiasco, Brecht delivered a text firmly directed against Vansittartism: 'Everyone who will, can see that

German enemies of Hitler, especially the German workers, are naturally aligned with the Allied peoples in the struggle against Hitler and those who commission him'.[70]

Brecht wrote a number of similar texts at this time for the Council and participated in the seven recorded meetings of the nascent organisation which he attended between 11 January and 11 March 1944. In particular, he argued that the old differences between the working-class parties must be overcome and that they must work together with parties representing middle-class interests. He insisted, too, that the Council should include the Communists Albert Schreiner and Felix Boenheim. Brecht denied to Weigel that his trip was 'pleasurable': he was working hard but deriving little satisfaction.[71] Things were moving forward very slowly, there were many opportunities, but again and again they came to nothing. He was looking forward to coming home: 'It's difficult here and I miss you'. And, for all the undemonstrative manner of their relationship, he showed his affection for her in another letter: 'I am kissing you carefully and carelessly, thoroughly and fleetingly, quickly and slowly, Heli'.[72]

The FBI was maintaining its keen interest in Brecht, intercepting a letter from Korsch and registering Gerhart Eisler among Brecht's visitors.[73] Eisler was suspected of espionage on behalf of the Soviet Union. On 19 January Brecht was placed on the FBI's national surveillance list and his name was added to the local list when he returned to Los Angeles. At Aufricht's behest, Eisler's sister Ruth Fischer visited Brecht that month. Aufricht was trying to place *Schweyk* on Broadway and had heard that Fischer was planning to expose Brecht's whole œuvre as a subtle act of support for Stalin.[74] Aufricht hoped that a meeting with Brecht might dissuade her. Fischer had been a radically independent leader of the KPD in 1924–5 before Ernst Thälmann steered the party towards a strongly pro-Moscow stance. She had, however, denounced Trotsky at the Comintern's Fifth Conference, contributing to Stalin's rise to power. In the meantime, she had become an agent for the US intelligence organisation The Pond, another forerunner of the CIA. Unsurprisingly, Aufricht's plan for a rapprochement between Brecht and Fischer backfired: they spent the evening cursing each other as heretics. In April 1944 Fischer would denounce Brecht as a 'Minstrel of the GPU'.[75]

Pursuing his literary interests during his remaining weeks in New York, Brecht suddenly felt, after such a long run of disappointment and frustration, that famine might turn into feast. He persuaded Auden, who lived close by on 57th Street, to collaborate on the English adaptation of *The Duchess of Malfi*. Brecht enjoyed working with him on the iambics. Elisabeth Bergner had input, too. He recorded other developments: 'Negotiated with Harris about *Galileo*, came to an agreement with Weill for the *Szechwan* play as a semi-opera. Contract with Broadway for a *Chalk Circle*, fixed up by Luise Rainer. Began the play. – In the meantime Feuchtwanger has signed for a film of *Simone* (I'm on to get $20,000). Buy new trousers'.[76] Harris was the director Jed Harris, whose production of Thornton Wilder's *Our Town* Brecht saw in New York. The Austrian film star Luise Rainer was at the height of her fame. Like Bergner, Rainer was a glamorous woman keen to help the impecunious Brecht. He had spoken to her about the *Chalk Circle* in October and had begun work on a draft, while she introduced the project to the New York backer Jules Leventhal, who wanted her on Broadway.[77] A contract was agreed with Leventhal and Robert Reud, while Rainer persuaded Leventhal to give Brecht an advance of $800.

Feuchtwanger had signed for them both with MGM for *The Visions of Simone Machard* and had immediately given money to the impoverished Weigel. Brecht told Korsch: 'I had money trouble for a good six months (now I've drawn a number in the Hollywood lottery that should last me about two years) and am trying my hand at commissioned adaptations'.[78] It mattered little that the film of *The Visions of Simone Machard* would never be made: Brecht had his new trousers and employed Berlau to promote his interests in New York before returning to LA in late March. She acted tirelessly in her utterly partisan promotion of his work, treating it rather like a cult and exasperating many negotiating partners in the process. Brecht left New York in the knowledge that Berlau was pregnant. He was caught between the hope that the pregnancy would help to stabilise her psychological state and the fear that her expectations, which he could not meet, would exacerbate problems. He wrote to her, encouraging her to work, 'Otherwise Simone will become lazy'.[79] As usual, he played with a number of names: Maria and Susanne were other ones for a girl, Michel for a boy. He would use Michel, in English Michael, as the name for the child in *The Caucasian Chalk Circle*.

Brecht pursued Council business in Los Angeles. Aware that his mail was being monitored, he explained to Korsch that the Council 'owes its existence to mild alarm over certain imperialistic tendencies and has no connection with the committees in Mexico, London and Moscow'.[80] He added: 'It's against either eastern or western orientation of a democratic Germany, against partitioning, against intervention in the event that Germany liberates itself from Hitler and the classes behind him and against Pan-Germanism'. The letter concludes with Brecht's belief that the working-class parties had a natural majority in Germany. As he had argued at Council meetings, the lesson for the German Left was unity.

Brecht enlisted several émigré friends for the Council, particularly on the West Coast. He invited Heinrich Mann to join the committee, suggesting erroneously that the US State Department, initially cool towards the project, 'has now become quite friendly'.[81] He reported to Tillich upon acceptances from Heinrich Mann, Kortner, Feuchtwanger, Bergner, Czinner, Jessner and Berthold Viertel. Further discussion was needed with Döblin, Horkheimer and Lang. In the event, Döblin declined, citing Thomas Mann's position and suggesting the absurdity of participating in an organisation which from the outset the USA did not support. Brecht urged Tillich to proceed with the speedy establishment of the Council, which, Brecht added, should supply German POWs with anti-Nazi literature and consider broadcasting to Germany.

The Council for a Democratic Germany was launched in May 1944. It was, however, not wanted by the State Department, which viewed it as, in its inimitable phrase, 'prematurely anti-Fascist'. The press weighed in with attacks on the Council and the US authorities would not permit it to work in POW camps. Concerned about Brecht's links with the Mexican and Soviet sister organisations of the Council, in the spring of 1944 the FBI re-graded him from G = German to R = Radical.[82] An informant cited Tillich as saying: 'We have two and a half Communist representatives in the Council. Brecht is the half'.[83] The FBI's scrutiny of Brecht's post included a letter from Anna Seghers, who was described correctly as close to the Mexican Free Germany organisation, which the FBI was monitoring with the approval of the Mexican government.

Among Brecht's visitors the FBI noted Gregory Kheifetz and recorded Brecht's other contacts with the Soviet consulate: he attended a farewell party for the film director Mikhail Kalatosov and met the Vice-Consul Mikhail Vavilov at Heinrich Mann's. When an FBI officer engaged Brecht in conversation, he denied links with the Free Germany committees in Mexico and the Soviet Union, explaining that the Council for a Democratic Germany was not the same as Free Germany and that there was no such movement in Los Angeles. He knew nothing of meetings at which there had been discussions about a post-war German government. When asked if he would take on a government role in Germany, he said he would not: he simply wishes to return to work in the German theatre. Brecht's life was the theatre, not public administration. Nonetheless, the FBI took to calling him one of the 'leading Communist Party functionaries'. They learned that he and Hanns Eisler, fearing internment at the end of the war to prevent their involvement in German re-construction, had met with the Czech consul in Los Angeles, the nephew of Edvard Beneš, to discuss the possibility of acquiring Czech papers to facilitate an early return to Europe.[84] Brecht had said he wanted to leave the USA 'as soon as possible'. The Czech papers would materialise, though not the early return.

The prospect of leaving moved a little closer when on 6 June Brecht was playing chess with Eisler and they heard on the radio that Allied troops had landed on the Normandy coast. At last, the second front had become a reality: eye-witness reports were already coming in. With hugely superior numbers amassed against Germany in the East, West and South, defeat was only a matter of time. Shortly after, on 20 July the officer Count von Stauffenberg failed in the attempt to assassinate Hitler at his East Prussian headquarters. Hitler took bloody revenge. Deeply cynical about the motives of the military, Brecht wrote: 'When snatches of information about the gory goings-on between Hitler and the Junker generals trickled through, there was a moment when I had my fingers crossed for Hitler; for who, if not he, is going to wipe out this band of criminals for us?'.[85] Brecht had no idea that the resistance group involved civilians as well as army officers.

Brecht, the student of military strategy, plotted the course of battles on a map on the wall of his study: 'The conquests of the Nazis stand out in lobster-red. Now this army is going down like ninepins. The generals are deserting, abandoning their war to its own devices with the cry that the corporal has bungled it. What a rabble! The fact is simple: they have lost it comprehensively'. Brecht was left to ponder the deeply uncomfortable question of why the German people continued to fight for the Nazis. His answer was: 'The Germans are still fighting because the ruling classes are still ruling'. While Romania collapsed and Paris fell shortly after, the Nazi elite followed Hitler on his lunatic path of victory or destruction, maintaining their grip over the German people to the very end with an escalating regime of brutal terror in which willing executioners eliminated any sign of dissent.[86]

The Caucasian Chalk Circle

During the spring and summer of 1944 Brecht worked on *The Caucasian Chalk Circle*, embarking on a work of reconstruction after his plays of survival. He was uneasy about the Broadway contract: 'Interesting how much is destroyed when you are squeezed between "commission" and "art". I dramatise unenthusiastically in this empty, aimless space'.[87] Rebellion against commercial constraints brought out the best in him. He quickly wrote a first version of a great, sophisticated piece of Epic Theatre – and fell out with Luise Rainer in the process. She withdrew but he continued to act as if she would take part. Working with a commercial contract confirmed Brecht's belief that the USA was barren terrain for theatrical innovation: it had been like 'writing a play for the tundra'. His old supporter Max Gorelik visited him with an American producer-writer from Republic Pictures, George Auerbach. They asked Brecht what the play meant: 'And then they set out to criticise the structure. Where is the conflict, the suspense, the flesh and blood etc? I try to expound the complex and audacious structure of *Hamlet*. So what, so Hamlet ain't builded'. As they were leaving they apparently said: 'He'll never be a success. He can't create emotions, he can't even get identification, so he goes and makes up a theory, he is crazy and he's getting worse'. Brecht had only contempt for them: 'The prostitution of these "artists" is total'.

In *The Caucasian Chalk Circle* Brecht addressed the pressing question of how a society might re-constitute itself after throwing off the Nazi yoke and its racist ideology of blood and soil. Brecht's setting for the Prologue was not by chance Georgia, the homeland of the Soviet leader which the Nazis had so coveted for its oil reserves. The Prologue – to which he added the title 'The Struggle for the Valley' shortly before his death in order to accentuate its importance – is a somewhat uneasy mix of politically strategic and deeply personal projections. After Stalingrad, the Red Army had driven German troops back from the Caucasus, the first region to be liberated by the Soviet people. However, as we have seen, from the Soviet occupation of Poland through to Becher's recent 'German Doctrine', Brecht's own political side had been engaging in its own form of nationalist discourse, which Brecht deplored almost as much as the Nazis'. Brecht's choice of Georgia for a demonstration of an enlightened attitude towards disputation of the ownership of land and, in the main body of the play, of kinship was strategically very pointed indeed. The exchanges and resolutions in the play could offer a stimulus to thoughts about the construction of a post-war Europe free of racist nationalism and in which productive forces could be cultivated on the rational basis upon which the USSR itself had been founded.

As the above already suggests, Brecht's motivation was, equally, deeply personal. Through the darkest times of the late 1930s and early 1940s, he had consoled himself with the thought that fresh revolutionary energy could emerge amongst Soviet workers in the light of the Red Army's ultimately successful struggle against Nazism. There was by now absolutely no doubt in Brecht's mind that the Soviet Union would play a major role in determining the future of a post-Nazi Germany. In the 'Struggle for the Valley' between the goat-breeding Galinsk kolchos and the fruit-growing Rosa Luxemburg kolchos, there is the sense of the spirit of a new age born out of the struggle against Fascism. The Comrade Agronomist, in military uniform, secures the agreement of the two opposing factions by invoking that spirit:

> Last winter, comrades, while we were fighting here in these hills as partisans, we discussed how after the expulsion of the Germans we could increase our orchards to ten times their former size. I have prepared a plan for an irrigation project. With the help of a dam on our mountain lake, three hundred hectares of unfertile land can be irrigated. Our kolchos could then grow not only more fruit, but wine as well. The project, however, would pay only if the disputed valley of the Galinsk kolchos could also be included.[88]

Her words receive a ringing endorsement from the peasants. The previously obstructive Old Man exclaims: 'Our thanks to the comrades of the Rosa Luxemburg kolchos and to all those who defended our country'. The Peasant Woman adds: 'Our thoughts were that our soldiers – both your men and our men – should return to a still more fertile homeland', and the Girl Tractor Driver concludes: 'As the poet Mayakovsky said: "The home of the Soviet people shall also be the home of Reason!"'. Brecht was, of course, equally aware that conflict resolution in the Soviet Union could be conducted on a basis far removed from reason, as he had shown in the plight of the isolated intellectual Galileo, echoing the fate of Bukharin and other Bolsheviks in the Great Terror.

A decade would pass before – with the Cold War at its deepest – *The Caucasian Chalk Circle* reached the German stage in productions by the Berliner Ensemble in East Berlin in 1954 and the following year in Frankfurt, West Germany by Harry Buckwitz. By then, particularly in the West, Brecht's depiction of the 'Struggle for the Valley' had simply become unstageable because it would be taken for Soviet propaganda of the crudest sort and confirmation of the worst suspicions about Brecht in the West, where it was rumoured that the Prologue had been written in 1954. Already in May that year Peter Suhrkamp had asked Brecht to remove the Prologue for publication because it could be an 'embarrassment'.[89] Brecht declined Suhrkamp's request:

> I don't quite understand your objection to the Prologue, that was the part of the play I wrote first, in the States. The problem of the parable-like play has to be derived from the needs of a real situation, and I think this is done in a light, amusing way. Without the Prologue there's no way of knowing why the play is no longer 'the Chinese Chalk Circle' (with the old verdict) or why it's called 'Caucasian'. I started by writing the short story [...] first. But for purposes of dramatisation, it needs an explanatory historical background.[90]

The real situation of 1944, of course, differed hugely from 1954. In fact, Buckwitz obtained Brecht's permission to omit the Prologue from the Frankfurt premiere, establishing a West German version of the play clearly at variance with Brecht's artistic intentions.

The short story to which Brecht refers is the 'Augsburg Chalk Circle' which he had written in Sweden, drawing upon the Chinese story 'The Chalk Circle', with its strong resemblance to the biblical Judgment of Solomon. Brecht had first encountered the Chinese tale in 1925 in Berlin in his friend Klabund's dramatisation. Brecht's 'Augsburg Chalk Circle' includes two principal elements which he develops in his

Caucasian Chalk Circle: the story of a maidservant Anna who rescues a child forgotten by its mother as she flees the army of invading Catholics in the Thirty Years War; and, the story of an unconventional judge, Ignaz Dollinger, who has the maidservant and mother perform the test of the chalk circle. The child stands in the circle while the women pull him towards themselves. When the maidservant lets go, the judge awards her the child on the grounds that the mother would 'tear him cold-bloodedly in two'.[91]

Brecht re-worked these two strands in the historical context of medieval Georgia with the interlinked stories of the Maidservant Grusha and the Judge Azdak. Scenes two to four tell Grusha's story, five and six that of the Judge. The three elements of the play are bound together in Epic style by the Singer, who appears near the end of the Prologue to introduce the scenes that follow. The Governor is murdered by the insurrectionist Ironshirts, while his wife is so concerned to save her dresses that she forgets her son Michael as she flees. Grusha rescues Michael from the pursuing Ironshirts.

Brecht spent much time deliberating upon the character traits of Grusha. The initial portrayal suffered from the dramatically unconvincing characteristic of excessive goodness. Feuchtwanger told Brecht: 'Grusha is too saintly' and Brecht responded: 'It does in fact seem to me a mistake to isolate her good deed as an accident. For F. it derives quite simply from a quality of "goodness". I am re-writing'.[92] A dissatisfied Brecht had already been looking to Pieter Brueghel the Elder for guidance, pasting a photograph of his 'Mad Meg' in his draft and writing of Grusha:

> She should be simple and look like Brueghel's Mad Meg, a beast of burden. She should be stubborn and not rebellious, submissive and not good, long-suffering and not incorruptible etc etc. This simplicity must in no way be equated with 'wisdom' (the well-known stereotype), but it is quite consonant with a practical bent, and even with a certain cunning and an eye for human qualities. – Grusha ought, by wearing the backwardness of her class openly like a badge, to permit less identification and thus stand objectively as, in a certain sense, a tragic figure ('the salt of the earth').[93]

Brueghel's extraordinary creation leaves its mark on the Grusha that emerges from Brecht's revisions. She becomes an unsentimental character of substance who overcomes internal and external conflicts in a war-torn world out of joint. In the light of dangers and hardships shared with the child, when she shows great bravery, she gradually accepts her role as Michael's mother, even though, as she acknowledges, it involves her in an ever worsening personal plight: 'Terrible is the temptation to do good!'.[94] She has the wit to impersonate a rich woman to protect the child, but when she is spurned by the rich, she castigates them in the name of insurrection: 'You monsters! And they're already nailing your heads to the wall!'.

Grusha enters into a marriage of convenience with a peasant However, the war ends and the Grand Duke returns together with his soldiers, among them Grusha's fiancé Simon. This heralds the arrival, too, of the extraordinary Judge Azdak, formerly a village clerk and another Brechtian creature of hedonistic appetites, 'certainly Brecht's most scurrilous and original figure'.[95] Brecht spent two weeks struggling with the character of Azdak, until he saw the 'social reason for his behaviour'. He needed to show how with a truly careless, ignorant, downright bad judge, things can turn out all right for those who are actually in need of justice. That is why Azdak had to have those selfish, amoral, parasitic features, and be the lowest and most decrepit of judges. But I was still lacking some basic cause of a social kind. And I found it in his disappointment that the fall of the old rulers did not bring about a new age, but just an age of new rulers, as a consequence of which he continues to dispense bourgeois justice, but in a degenerate, subversive fashion, serving the absolute self-interest of the judge.

The self-interest of the disappointed revolutionary does, in fact, serve the interests of the poor against the rich. Like Schweyk, Azdak is a disarmingly frank truth-teller: 'War lost, but not for Princes. Princes have won *their* war. Got themselves paid 3,863,000 piastres for horses not delivered!'.[96] Azdak proclaims: 'Gone is the era of confusion and disorder, and the great times which I found described in the Song of Chaos have not yet come':

> Sister, hide your face; brother, take your knife, the times are out of joint.
> The noblemen are full of complaints, the simple folk full of joy.
> The city says: let us drive the strong ones out of our midst.
> Storm the government buildings, destroy the lists of the serfs.
> Now the masters' noses are put to the grindstone.

Azdak's allegiance to the cause of the poor determines the struggle between Grusha and the returning Governor's wife, who depends on the legal recognition of Michael as her son in order to access her husband's legacy. She, of course, expects her blood bond to be re-affirmed in the Judge's pronouncement. Asked by Azdak, 'What's your answer to all this and anything else the lawyer might have to say?', Grusha answers: 'He's mine'.[97] Azdak further warms to her when she attacks him as a 'bribe-taker!'. He instructs the two women to take the test of the chalk circle, announcing: 'The true mother is she who has the strength to pull the child out of the circle, towards herself'. Twice the Governor's Wife pulls the child out of the circle after Grusha has let go and cried in despair: 'Am I to tear him to pieces? I can't do it!'. Confounding his own rules by awarding the child to Grusha, Azdak also claims the governor's estates for the city. The play ends with a dance during which Azdak is lost in the throng, never to be seen again, while the Singer comments, 'His time of Judgment as a brief / Golden Age was almost just', before turning to the audience:

> But you, who have listened to the story of the Chalk Circle
> Take note of the meaning of the ancient song:
> That what there is shall belong to those who are good for it, thus
> The children to the maternal, that they thrive;
> The carriages to good drivers, that they are driven well;
> And the valley to the waterers, that it shall bear fruit.[98]

The singer invites the audience to reflect upon the Prologue in the search for solutions to social conflicts which might enable society finally to move into a new age, beyond the crass inequality and injustice that have marked the dark times. The glimpse of a new age of justice in the final scene and the Prologue is that and only that. The task of constructing a just society remains to be undertaken and, in Brecht's understanding conveyed through Grusha and Azdak, requires a human solidarity and co-operation latently present in humans, which the maternal instinct quintessentially represents.

Despite his compositional choices and the break-down in relations with Rainer, Brecht still hoped for a Broadway production. He tried without success to enlist Christopher Isherwood to translate and was angered when Isherwood offered him some money to help him out. Leventhal and Reud employed James and Tania Stern to do a rough translation and Auden to polish it for the stage.[99] They worked together and Auden delivered the manuscript to Leventhal. However, Brecht tried to prevail upon Auden to revise the whole thing, believing that he had only translated the songs. He wrote to Stern, thanking him for his translation but telling him that he now had a new version, which he was sending, and asking for Auden's address: 'I'd much rather have an imaginative free adaptation by him than a Broadway production'.[100] Brecht followed with a letter to Auden in English: 'I am very pleased to have your collaboration for *The Circle of Chalk* (by the way, do You think the title reads well in English?), and I am eager to read Your adaptation. If You do (or have done?), the lyrics first, Eisler would like to get them as soon as possible. Perhaps Mr Stern told You that I made some changes – I send them to you'. This episode, it seems, contributed to Brecht's strained relationship with Auden and to Auden's view that Brecht had 'poor manners'. Berlau maintained contact with Auden over the coming months, sending Brecht the latest version in the spring of 1945. He replied: 'The poetry hasn't all been done with the same care, and worse, Auden hasn't changed one word of the prose. I don't think it will do'. The prospects for a Broadway production disappeared.

A world fragmenting: The death of a child

In the fifth month of her pregnancy Berlau encountered a severe problem, a tumour in the womb which should have been removed immediately. A hysterectomy would, however, have meant the termination of the pregnancy. Berlau travelled to Los Angeles with a key to Peter Lorre's apartment. Brecht joined her there but she soon left and took a room at the Chalet Motor Hotel in Santa Monica. FBI informants noted that a man they identified as Brecht carried her luggage to the hotel and paid her bills in cash.[101] She told a hotel employee that she had fled to the US after her Danish husband had been taken prisoner in Norway. The operation was deferred until the seventh month to give the child a chance to survive. An extremely agitated Berlau was prey to panic attacks, while Brecht was in a state of high anxiety, recording what it meant for him to experience the fragmentation of his mental world:

In distraught moments the components of the mind break up like parts of a mortally stricken empire. Communication between parts ceases (it suddenly becomes apparent that the whole thing consists of separate parts), they now only have the meaning they have for themselves, which is not much. It can happen that all of a sudden I can see no sense in institutions like music or politics, see my nearest and dearest as strangers etc. Health consists of equilibrium.[102]

Brecht knew that maintaining equilibrium in such circumstances was well-nigh impossible and that the stress which he experienced left him susceptible to physical complications which he feared greatly. He tried to make light of things, noting the following day: 'Remarkable how worry and nervousness make your shoulders fall forward. What keeps them back in normal times?'. In the midst of this distress, on 16 August 1944 Brecht attended a private piano recital by Eduard Steuermann, who played a Mozart rondo, one of Bach's English suites, some Schubert variations and Beethoven's Hammerklavier Sonata. It was this recital which at this critical juncture prompted one of Brecht's most striking meditations upon his response to music:

> Even as a boy when I heard the *St Matthew Passion* in the Barefoot Church, I decided never to go to a thing like that again, since I abhorred the stupor, the wild coma, into which one became lulled, in addition to which I thought it was bad for my heart (which had been enlarged by cycling and swimming). I can now listen to Bach, I believe, with impunity, but I still don't like Beethoven, that surge to the sub- and supernatural with all its (for me) attendant kitschy effects and 'confused emotions'.[103]

Brecht was indeed struggling with his 'confused emotions'. On 3 September he noted laconically: 'Ruth has an operation in Cedars of Lebanon'.[104] Cedars of Lebanon was a Jewish hospital on Los Angeles's Fountain Avenue. Berlau gave birth prematurely to a boy, Michel. She gave the father's name as Michel Berlau, a 39-year-old Dane. The doctor Gordon Rosenblum, whom Lorre engaged, performed a Caesarean section in the attempt both to deliver the baby and to perform the operation on the tumour. Dressed in a white surgical apron and hat, Brecht saw Berlau afterwards in an iron lung. She was scarcely aware of what was happening and believed she was about to die. Michel, who carried all her hopes for a life with Brecht, lived for only one day.[105] Brecht later told Berlau that he had seen him in the ward for premature births.

In the days following, Eisler witnessed a Brecht who was distraught in a way he had never seen him.[106] Brecht could only tell his friend that it was a private matter. In his journal he recorded his daily routine, which was much as usual but clearly required great effort to sustain: 'Plan for the day: get up at 7. Radio. Make coffee in the little copper pot. Morning: work. Light lunch about twelve. Rest with a crime novel. Afternoon: work or pay visits. Evening meal at 7. Guests after. At night half a page of Shakespeare or Waley's Chinese poems. Radio, crime novel'.[107] He visited Berlau every day but soon removed her from the expensive hospital and took her to stay with Salka and Bertold Viertel, where, supported by the Eislers, she gradually recovered in a room which Brecht rented from them. Berlau had failed in her attempt to secure at least parity with Weigel through the birth of Brecht's child. The attempt could never be repeated and Berlau became consumed by extreme jealousy and more prone to aggression, reproaching Brecht for his petit bourgeois idyll with wife, family and mistress, especially as, she claimed, he made no secret that he wished her to return to New York. She would do so only at the end of March 1945.

It was probably around this time that Weigel began a letter to Brecht about their relationship which may or may not have been sent.[108] It is the only written testimony that we have from Weigel in which she explains something of her perspective upon their marriage and its difficulties for her. She reflected that she felt foolish in rebutting his physical advances but confessed astonishment at what she described as his immediate re-kindling of interest. In her understanding of things: 'You cannot and do not want to conduct a publicly declared marriage adorned with a stamp. It was never like that either and I have never demanded that'. She explained that she did not demand that because she assumed that it would not work for him: 'However, I suddenly find that you are conceding such expectations to another woman. Your response to that is that you completely disappear. Silent for three weeks, you introduce a complete change. That is a kick in the teeth of especial vehemence. I am not insensitive. If you want to change your life in this way, I cannot'. The text breaks off at that point. Weigel had reached the limit of her tolerance of Brecht's behaviour.

Under extreme psychological pressure, Brecht found himself assailed by familiar symptoms, stopped in his tracks by what he described as the 'old Russian headache', the severe 'rheumatic headache' which had kept him bed-ridden during his Moscow visit in 1935. He noted:

It is about eleven o'clock at night. I am sitting with a whisky. (I don't often) and reading Gide's *Journal 1940*. It is quiet and it is pleasant to sit isolated like this, but then I can't resist switching on the radio for the news although there won't be anything new in it – I listened at half past nine and half past ten. The fact is that there is no reasonable rest except what our surroundings (in the broadest sense) offer. To cut yourself off from the world is to immerse yourself in the raging torrent of the void. So I am writing this now as I listen to the radio and then I shall carry on reading Gide as I listen.[109]

As the carefully orchestrated chaos of his domestic life once again unravelled, Brecht found himself exposed to that 'torrent', much as he had been in his many crises since the storms of childhood. Seeking to immerse himself instead in reading and writing, Brecht felt capable only of 'doing a little translating'. He was composing more German versions of Waley's English translation of Chinese poems. Brecht reflected:

Astonishing what an ass this excellent sinologist Waley is! He cannot grasp that for Po Chu-i there is no difference between didacticism and amusement. No wonder we find that learning, practised as the quick purchase of knowledge for resale purposes, arouses displeasure, in happier times learning meant a pleasurable absorption in the arts (in the Baconian sense). Literature, in didactic as in other works, manages to enhance our enjoyment of life. It sharpens the senses and transforms even pain into pleasure.

Brecht would never put more clearly the therapeutic effect of literature upon him. By concentrating upon reading and composition he could override the 'torrent of the void'. 'Confused emotions' then gave way to clarity, suffering to enjoyment, as he kept the outside world at bay. Brecht alighted upon Waley's translation of Po Chu-i's

'Resignation', adding two lines of his own at the end, which imply that the 'mood of despair will pass'.[110]

Continuing work as Brecht's assistant, Berlau assembled a photographic archive of his work. This was the origin of the famous 'model' books, charting productions through rehearsals to stage performance. Berlau had taken a three-month course with the photographer Joseph Breitenbach in the spring of 1944 when she also learnt to store data on microfilm. Over time, she would generate a huge body of material. The FBI's suspicions were aroused not only by the microfilms but also when the physicist Hans Reichenbach, who had knowledge of the atomic bomb programme, helped Berlau to develop a technique to photocopy typescripts. The FBI became convinced they had found evidence of espionage. This is just part of the picture of the greater intensity of FBI surveillance of Berlau and Brecht towards the end of the war.

Amongst other anxieties, Brecht could not be sure what lay in store for his son Stefan, who in September 1944 learned that he was to join the US 26th Army for basic training later in the month. Stefan decided to see some of the USA first, travelling to San Francisco, Saint Louis and New Orleans. After basic training, Stefan was sent to the University of Chicago to learn Japanese. Stefan suffered health problems and, aware of his father's susceptibility to uncontrolled movements, evidently feared there might be a propensity towards epilepsy in the family. Brecht advised his son to go to a doctor and dismissed the 'old family talk' that his uncle Eugen's illness could have been that condition. He suggested to his son that his problems were psychological and quite understandable in the light of the constant upheavals of exile, with the sudden travel and all the talk of the Gestapo.[111] As we may recall, the alcoholic Eugen Brezing's son Max Hermann was epileptic. It remains unclear whether Eugen Brezing was, too.

Tracking the war's end, working with Laughton

In the autumn of 1944 Eric Bentley's translation of *Fear and Misery of the Third Reich*, done under Brecht's close supervision, appeared with James Laughlin's New Directions under the title *The Private Life of the Master Race*. Bentley's accompanying portrait of Brecht describes a 'face no longer young' which 'bears the imprint of suffering': 'He can be quiet, embarrassed, somber, but suddenly the dark eyes flash, he jumps up from the chair and paces the room waving his cheap cigar. At such times he talks in tirades. Metaphors and anecdotes of Brechtian concreteness flow freely from his lips. His laugh is sharp and staccato. His slight body and gnome head become important'.[112] Reviews of *The Private Life of the Master Race* were generally favourable, one going so far as to suggest that this 'original documentary play offers plausible hints of the resuscitation of Broadway'.[113] Berthold Viertel worked on a production plan for *The Private Life of the Master Race*, in which American troops guard the exits and German POWs, drawn from the professional groups represented in the play, are interrogated. Brecht wrote to Viertel: 'I'm still racking my brains trying to decide whether a production now would really be a good thing. Any reference to the "sound core" of the German people, who are still displaying a very crude shell, takes on a very special meaning in the USA'.[114] As

Brecht acknowledged to Viertel, his work with the Council for a Democratic Germany had heightened his sensitivity towards this matter. However, his active participation in that organisation, 'inhibited in its activity, ignored, unpopular as it may be', had, as Brecht conceded to Tillich, waned.

In the Los Angeles émigré community Weigel vied with Lou Eisler to put on the best dinner parties. While the Eislers laid claim to Charlie Chaplin, the Brechts could point to Charles Laughton as 'theirs'. Brecht and Weigel had got to know Hollywood greats like them and Groucho Marx at the Viertels. They spent an evening with them all in November at the film producer Ernest Pascal's.[115] There Chaplin joined Brecht and Weigel in listening to the latest developments in the war on the radio. Like the great Munich comedian Karl Valentin, Chaplin was one of the few figures to whom Brecht deferred, sitting spellbound by his conversation. Brecht met Chaplin again at the Eislers when Chaplin did a 'wonderful impression of a Chopin film', *A Song to Remember* with Paul Muni as the professor.[116] Chaplin told them about a Bluebeard film he was planning, *Monsieur Verdoux*, and about his intention to 'abandon the Charlie of the classic films'. In Eisler's account, Chaplin later invited 200 friends and acquaintances to a private showing of *Monsieur Verdoux*:

> Among them were very wealthy people – the whole great film industry – and there were some bohemian friends, to whom Brecht and I must have belonged, since we had nothing to do with the film industry. In certain scenes – for instance when the bankers jump out of the window and shoot themselves during the economic crisis (there is a short sequence in this movie) – you could hear two people sitting a long way from each other laughing very loudly. That was Brecht and me. Everyone else kept silent because there were bankers in the audience watching the film too.[117]

Eisler recalls: 'Chaplin didn't know what to make of Brecht, who he thought was a highly interesting man. Chaplin didn't speak German and Brecht's plays weren't translated into English'.

As we know, Brecht had long admired Charles Laughton. Laughton had enjoyed Hollywood success since the early 1930s but retained theatrical ambitions. He read Brecht's *Schweyk* with great enthusiasm, Brecht noting that Laughton had read two acts to Eisler, Winge and him: 'We laughed like mad, he understood *all* the *jokes*! See?'.[118] Refreshingly for Brecht, Laughton was neither upper-class English nor a German émigré pretending to be an American. Rather, this son of a Scarborough hotelier was the sort of big theatrical personality in a hulking body that Brecht found irresistible. He loved his anecdotes: 'A Bond Street tailor only agreed to make suits for the international film star if he kept it secret since otherwise his Tory customers would stay away'.[119] He delighted in Laughton's company: 'He reads *Measure for Measure* for us at our place, and *The Tempest* at his place. He sits cross-legged on a white sofa in front of a magnificent Bavarian Baroque long-case clock so that all you can see is his Buddha-like belly, and he reads the play from a little book, partly like an actor, laughing at the jokes and excusing himself here and there for not getting a scene quite right'. Laughton fired Brecht's visual imagination: 'His reading leads me to see Prospero like that remarkable portrait of Napoleon on St Helena, wearing a straw hat, with a yellow complexion and looking like a Dutch planter. He reads Caliban with pity'. Brecht had in mind Paul Delaroche's painting of a podgy, seedy Napoleon, far removed in its realism from the image of the glorious emperor.

It is no accident that Brecht's encounter with Laughton prompted not just thoughts about Napoleon, the hero of his youth, but also further reflection upon one of his greatest creations, the character of Galileo, which Harris was interested in putting on the stage. When he had written the play in 1938, Brecht had asked Herbert Levy if he thought Laughton might be interested in the role, which he had clearly written with him in mind. Brecht now had the chance to win Laughton over in what became Brecht's only really important dramatic encounter in his six years of US exile. Brecht and Laughton began an English version of *Life of Galileo*, which Brecht was convinced would make his name on Broadway. A rough English version already existed, probably thanks to Elisabeth Hauptmann. Laughton engaged two writers from MGM studios, Brainerd Duffield and Emerson Croker, to make the English more idiomatic. Brecht and Laughton worked on their own version that winter, Brecht describing their collaboration as the 'classic one of our profession – playwright and actor'.[120] They complemented each other, Brecht reducing Laughton's elevated language to realistic proportions. They moved quickly through the work, deferring difficult issues and interrupting work when Laughton was away filming, beginning with *Captain Kidd* in early 1945.

Brecht followed the final Soviet offensive on the Eastern Front on his radio. By the end of January 1945 the Soviets had reached Upper Silesia and the River Oder, only 65 miles from Berlin. Stalin could virtually dictate terms at the Yalta Conference in early February. He was deeply anxious that, after a war which cost the USSR 27 million lives, within a generation Germany might be in a position to launch fresh aggression in concert with the Western Allies.[121] He was therefore concerned to bind the Western Allies into a common security system, in which Germany could no longer be the aggressor. Reparations to facilitate the re-construction of a USSR devastated by Nazi aggression were also high on his agenda, in particular access to the heavy industry in the Ruhr. Roosevelt, Churchill and Stalin at least agreed upon the need to dismantle Germany's military potential, to end the quasi-feudalism presided over by Junker landowners in Prussia through land reform and to de-Nazify the country with a programme of anti-Fascist re-education. Brecht noted that there were 'terrible newspaper reports from Germany. Ruins, and no sign of life from the workers'.[122] The absence of any popular uprising against Hitler at this late stage in the war was, Brecht noted, a 'source here of such angry comments'. Brecht still held out the hope to Tillich that German workers would rise: 'Of course German workers can still participate, for a long time still, in the subjugation of Nazism'. He continued: 'I am, of course, far from suggesting remorse as a political stance and, whatever Thomas Mann says, the Germans will be able to show their face when it's right to do so'.

The FBI was monitoring Brecht's moves. They intercepted a letter to him from Paolo Milano, informing Brecht of Ignazio Silone's interest in putting on *The Good Person of Szechwan* in Rome.[123] Brecht was overheard discussing with Billy Wilder the prospects for distributing American films in Germany. Brecht mentioned Herbert Ihering as someone in Germany who enjoyed his complete trust. Conversations with Otto Katz and Robert Riskin of the Office of War Information were overheard in which Brecht inquired about a post which might enable him to get to Europe more easily. The FBI read Brecht's letter written to Anna Seghers, in which he wrote conspiratorially that a closer climate would be better for everyone in the family. When he added that he was looking forward to seeing Seghers again, the FBI reasonably concluded that Brecht was looking to return to Germany soon. Seghers would be one of the first people Brecht met on his return to Europe.

Brecht wanted Berlau to return to New York to work on his behalf. The FBI searched her luggage during her train journey to the East coast, read a letter from Brecht and three more which she wrote to him on the train. Berlau feared that Brecht now wanted to be rid of her for good. He allayed that fear in a letter she opened on the train, in which he explained that he merely wanted to maintain their relationship without affecting his family. Berlau threw herself into her work for him, turning the flat she shared with Ida Bachmann into a photo lab, covering every last space with Brecht's manuscripts and the photocopies she had made. He sent her some photos of himself as a child, suggesting a similarity with Michel.[124] This was Berlau's only means to picture their child.

While the end of the European war approached with the final Soviet offensive on Berlin, the prospects of post-war co-operation among the war-time coalition were severely dented with the death on 12 April of President Roosevelt. Brecht praised Roosevelt as the 'enlightened democrat', noting with concern: 'The leadership of the democracies passes to Churchill'.[125] The UK electorate would presently remove Churchill, leadership of the democracies passing to Roosevelt's quite inexperienced, anti-Communist successor Harry S. Truman. The Red Army had Berlin encircled by 24 April and five days later the first group of German Communist émigrés, led by Walter Ulbricht, flew to the German capital from Moscow. The Ulbricht Group comprised figures selected for political and administrative tasks in the Soviet Zone of Occupation. In step with Stalin's strategic aim to safeguard Soviet interests through agreements with the Western Allies, the Ulbricht Group was under strict instructions not to proceed with the separate 'Sovietisation' of that zone but to stress anti-Fascism and German unity on the basis of a western-style democracy. 'All-German', anti-Fascist institutions should be created accordingly, enabling Germans to complete the 'bourgeois' revolution of 1848. However, schooled in Leninist democratic centralism, neither the Ulbricht Group nor the leading officers in the Soviet Military Administration for Germany (SMAD) were equipped to implement such a policy with any consistency. The disparities between rhetoric and action rapidly compounded the great mistrust towards them amongst the Western Allies and the German population. In May the cynical Ulbricht himself put things as follows: 'Things must look democratic but we must have everything under our control'.[126] However, another member of the Group, Anton Ackermann, would proclaim the 'special German path to socialism', which distinguished Germany from the Soviet Union and the emerging people's democracies in Eastern Europe. The contradictions represented by the positions occupied by Ulbricht and Ackermann would leave SED policy hamstrung until the workers' uprising in East Germany on 17 June 1953.

The Ulbricht Group included some of those who had recently met under Wilhelm Pieck's leadership at Moscow's Hotel Lux to discuss the development of culture in a post-Fascist Germany. Fritz Erpenbeck and Gustav von Wangenheim were present. Becher, Friedrich Wolf, Hans Rodenberg and Maxim Vallentin spoke, Vallentin about Soviet theatre and Stanislavsky's method as the model for German theatre.[127] Vallentin would put that into practice in Weimar, while in Berlin Erpenbeck would have responsibility for the re-construction of theatres. A course was set for post-war culture that could come as no surprise to Brecht: it was merely a continuation of 'bourgeois' theatre imposed in Moscow, coupled with the toxic nationalist message which Becher had been preaching and accompanied by the threat of repression of dissent.

On 8 May Brecht noted: 'Nazi Germany capitulates unconditionally. The President makes a speech on the radio at six in the morning. As I listen I contemplate the Californian garden in bloom'.[128]

Part Five

Contentious Master

After the Dark Times – The Cold War 1945–7

Beyond the terror: Re-writing *Galileo*

With the European war over, in the spring of 1945 the founding congress of the United Nations took place in San Francisco. The establishment of this institution, a legacy of Roosevelt's presidency, was intended to herald a new age of international co-operation after the struggle to defeat Fascism. The programme for UN delegates featured a stark reminder of that age of barbarism, Brecht's *Private Life of the Master Race* in Eric Bentley's translation. The director for the play's English-language premiere, a student production at Berkeley, was Arthur Schnitzler's son Henry, who telegraphed Brecht to report enthusiastically: 'Audience followed every scene with profound attention'.[1]

Bentley had also initiated an off-Broadway production of the play with a young producer Ernest Roberts and his experimental group, The Theatre of All Nations. Piscator was directing. Bentley had, however, not secured Brecht's agreement. Brecht alerted Berlau: 'We can't afford a cheap, slipshod production of *Master Race*. Bentley has the right to refuse his translation; but no one but me can give out production rights'.[2] He had no desire to see his work once more performed by an experimental troupe of students and émigrés. He travelled to New York to oversee the production with Eisler, who was to compose the music. On arrival, Eisler was immediately called back to a Hollywood studio. Brecht, however, insisted that Eisler complete his work before leaving, and he did so 'while waiting for his ticket', composing 'brilliant theatre music'.

However, Brecht found all his worst suspicions about the production confirmed – and proceeded to sabotage his own play, demonstrating all the ruthless vindictiveness of which he was still quite capable. He clashed with Piscator, who in a diplomatically worded letter showed great understanding as he withdrew: 'When I direct, I need the time for myself without your co-directing – and when you direct you need the time without me. For my part, I have conceived a different physical performance from yours, and I have greater difficulties in following your version – enough so that I suggest that you take over the directing'.[3] Brecht's response shows the same desire not to inflame the situation: 'The disgusting part of it is that we just haven't time to think our theoretical differences through. Of course it's quite possible that the present balladesque framework isn't enough by itself. You just have to believe that, even if I were convinced, it's too late for me to make an artistically radical change'. This time there was no bad blood. Piscator allowed Brecht to use actors from his Theatre Workshop and Brecht brought in Berthold Viertel. Three days before the premiere on 11 June, Brecht told Weigel that it was a 'big, bloody mess': 'Of course, I'm in the thick of it from nine in the morning till two a.m.'. In just a few days Brecht butchered his play, insulting actors as he cut their lines and demolishing the great scene 'The Jewish Wife' because he found the actress Vilma Kurer so mediocre.

As Brecht knew it would, the premiere brought another humiliation at the hands of New York critics, who again mercilessly panned a Brecht production. He complained to Weigel that no one understood the elderly Austrian actor Albert Bassermann's English: 'a sort of Turkish with a Saxon accent'.[4] Brecht noted: 'The press attacked the production, spared the play. Nobody discussed the content'. The general view was that, with the European war over, the content was no longer topical. However, another self-styled master race was still to be bombed into submission in East Asia and in the future there would, of course, be no shortage of 'great' leaders ready to step forward.

Brecht stayed with Berlau at 57th Street until 15 July, meeting with left-wing émigrés such as Budzislavsky, Hermann Duncker and Hans Marchwitza and attending a meeting of the Council for a Democratic Germany in Felix Boenheim's flat with Tillich, Scheer, Norden and Walcher. Back in Santa Monica, Brecht noted with approval that the Potsdam Conference had confirmed the Yalta Agreement: Germany was to be treated as a single economic entity, divided into zones of occupation.[5] As we have seen, guided by security and economic considerations, Stalin sought to bind the Western Allies into arrangements treating a demilitarised, denazified Germany as, he claimed, a western-style democracy. This essentially remained the USSR's negotiating position throughout Stalin's remaining years in repeated diplomatic efforts, culminating in Stalin's notes of March and April 1952. On the back foot at Yalta and Potsdam, the Western Allies profoundly distrusted Stalin's motives, overestimating the USSR's capacity to dominate Germany. Never taking Stalin's offers seriously and from 1947 guided by the Truman Doctrine of containment of Soviet expansionism, the Western Allies played the role of principal perpetrators in the division of Germany. Becher and other returning KPD émigrés would counter the politics of division by playing the German nationalist card for all it was worth through new, 'all-German', anti-Fascist institutions. However, the notions of political and economic freedom which the KPD elite shared with the SMAD alienated the vast majority of the German people, who responded much more positively to the Western Allies' practice of liberal democracy during the deepening split of the Cold War.

Brecht's correspondence from the spring of 1945 suggests that he was benefiting from quite optimistic briefings on Soviet policy for Germany at the LA consulate. He wrote to Tillich just after the Potsdam Conference:

It seems to me definitely positive that Germany is going to be treated as an economic unit. Anyway, to have a democratic administration built from the bottom up is better than establishing a central government, which in the present state of things could not accomplish much. Besides, it seems to me that the occupation period has been made surprisingly short. I have the impression that the Allies plan to evacuate Germany some time after 1948 on the condition that democratic, anti-imperialist institutions have developed sufficient strength in the meantime.[6]

However, Brecht predicted that the Potsdam Declaration would trigger a crisis in the Council for a Democratic Germany, which did indeed split into warring factions and was subsequently dissolved.

Between Laughton's film shoots, he and Brecht continued work on *Galileo*, often in Laughton's garden with its pre-Columbian art, at other times at Brecht's where Laughton and Weigel were firm friends. Brecht always worked with Laughton in English, and with this regular practice Brecht now became quite comfortable in the language. They finished a draft on 30 July which they showed to friends.[7] However, Hans Winge felt the play was an inconsequential, minor work, and Brecht, mistrustful of his own creation, felt he could not disagree as far as the form was concerned. Despite his enthusiasm for Laughton, he did not 'defend this play particularly strongly' and acknowledged that Laughton had 'no political thoughts whatsoever'. Brecht continued: 'Alongside the theme that in this form of society a desire for knowledge can be fatal (since society both produces and punishes it) another theme emerges, namely the decisive difference between "scientific progress pure and simple" and science's social and revolutionary progress'. What did Brecht mean by 'this form of society'? We shall see presently. Brecht conceded that his Galileo was 'interesting at least as a contrasting example to the parables. They are the embodiment of ideas, whereas here a subject gives birth to certain ideas'. However, something was clearly missing.

On 6 August the USA acted to end the war with Japan, dropping an atomic bomb which flattened Hiroshima. Two days later another bomb was dropped on Nagasaki. Finally cowed by these terrifying acts of war, on 14 August the Japanese leadership declared its unconditional surrender. The story of the physicist Galileo suddenly appeared in quite a different light. While, as Brecht wrote, Laughton feared 'quite naively' that science might be 'so utterly discredited by it', in Brecht's view, 'The atom bomb has, in fact, made the relationship between society and science into a life-and-death-problem. [...] This superfart is louder than all the victory bells'.[8]

The world had entered a new era, marked by the terrible destructive potential of scientific innovation, which, Brecht knew, the *Galileo* material simply had to be moulded to capture. In a preamble to the US version Brecht wrote: 'The "atomic age" made its debut at Hiroshima in the middle of our work. Overnight the biography of the founder of the new system of physics read differently. The infernal effect of the great bomb placed the conflict between Galileo and the authorities of his day in a new, sharper light. We had to make only a few alterations – not a single one to the structure of the play'.[9] Brecht understates the scale of the changes which he and Laughton made, with help on the way from Hauptmann and Reyher. He describes Laughton's approach:

> Driven on by his theatrical instinct, Laughton plugs away relentlessly at the political elements in *Galileo* too. At his behest I have worked in the new 'Ludovico-line', and the same goes for the reordering of the last Galileo scene (handing over the book first, then the lesson that the book must in no way alter the social condemnation of the author). Laughton is fully prepared to throw his character to the wolves. He has a kind of Lucifer in mind, in whom self-contempt

has turned into a kind of hollow pride – pride in the magnitude of his crime etc. He insists on a full presentation of the degradation that results from the crimes which has unleashed all Galileo's negative features. All that is left is the excellent brain, functioning in the void independently of the control of its owner who is happy to let himself sink.[10]

This characterisation in fact reflects more Brecht's intentions than Laughton's, who would play Galileo with great sympathy for his plight. A play emerged which was quite different from the 'Danish' *Galileo*. The Keonos parable was omitted, its Taoist implications lost from sight, especially as the sequence of events in the penultimate scene yielded a different behavioural logic. The 'Ludovico-line' is all about embedding the *Galileo* material within a recognisably early capitalist setting. This setting, quite undeveloped in the original play, is represented in something of its contradictions by the progressive Ironfounder Matti, later called Vanni, and by Ludovico, the young scholar from a rich, landowning background, who is interested in the applications of new knowledge but not in social justice. In Brecht's understanding, his earlier term 'this form of society' pointed firmly towards a socio-economic parallel with contemporary capitalism. Hence, the ready association of clerical authority with Stalin's quasi-theological USSR in the 1938 *Galileo* becomes in 1945 a representation of the interplay of science and authority in the struggle of early capitalism to emerge from feudal and ecclesiastical authority! The plight of the scientist becomes, in Brecht's view, his abject betrayal of the cause of social justice. If in Brecht's new reading the traumas of the late 1930s were concealed from public view, he himself remained anxious about their likely recurrence.

Berlin hails its distant master

Observing European politics from California, Brecht had 'very mixed feelings' about the Labour Party's victory in the British general election: 'The mass protest against Tory rule will probably lead to a confused tolerance of rule by the social-democratic party machine. The "western bloc" is turning pseudo-progressive.'[11] That is one way of putting the reconciliation of the interests of labour and capital, which was mediated by the state in many European countries, producing a defensible record of economic growth and social stability after the chaos of the preceding decades. Stalin was much more positive about this development than Brecht.[12]

As usual, the FBI was tracking Brecht's movements. There were conversations with a Dr A. J. Cardinal following the latest Soviet news about the growing divisions between the Allies and with the Soviet Vice-Consul Eugen Tumantsev, who had visited Brecht.[13] The FBI noted a meeting of several people at Brecht's house on 15 August 1945, among them Alfred Döblin, who was planning to go to France. On that same day in Berlin there was a premiere at the Hebbel Theatre, *The Threepenny Opera*. The director was Karl-Heinz Martin, a founder member of the Cultural League for Democratic Renewal [Kulturbund], one of the 'all-German', anti-Fascist institutions which the Soviets created in the Soviet Zone. Johannes R. Becher was its President. Through the Kulturbund, SMAD cultural officers launched a charm offensive to win over German artists and intellectuals to promote its 'all-German', anti-Fascist agenda. Many of those won over would not share Becher's nationalist enthusiasms.

Martin took to the stage before the premiere of *The Threepenny Opera* to introduce Brecht and Weill to the German public in their absence. This legendary piece of Berlin theatre, erased from the public imagination since January 1933, returned to the stage to great popular acclaim with all its unpredictable vitality and explosive force. However, Brecht's Muscovite foe Fritz Erpenbeck, a member of the Ulbricht Group, attacked the Hebbel Theatre for putting on a play with such a lumpenproletarian orientation.[14] The KPD politician Hans Jendretzky joined in the criticism. Brecht's work had lost none of its provocative power. Günther Weisenborn, Brecht's collaborator on *The Mother* in 1931, challenged Jendretzky, writing that the production sent out a welcoming signal to the 'strongest dramatic talent of our country over the ocean'.[15] Others would echo Weisenborn's words. However, Brecht himself remained extremely wary of the inflammatory potential of his work:

> We hear that *The Threepenny Opera* has been performed to packed houses in Berlin but then had to be taken off, at the instigation of the Russians. The BBC (London) reported that the ballad 'food is the first thing, morals follow on' was the reason for the protest. Personally, I would not have permitted the production. In the absence of any revolutionary movement, the play's 'message' is pure anarchism.[16]

Brecht wrote to Mikhail Apletin, Erich Weinert and Edward Hogan, a US cultural officer in Berlin, to express his displeasure that *The Threepenny Opera* was being performed. He requested that no further productions of his plays should take place without his express permission, since he needed to make changes in keeping with the new situation. When he heard that the Deutsches Theater was planning a *Life of Galileo* in the Danish version performed in 1943 in Zurich, Brecht wrote to Berlau: 'I'll try to stop that too, until I'm there myself'. That remained his stock response to all requests to stage his works.

Brecht was now targeted in the Soviet charm offensive. He had re-affirmed his loyalty to the Soviet Union in exchanges with Los Angeles consular officials following his conversations with Soviet diplomats in Finland in 1940 and with Apletin in Moscow in 1941. Via the Soviet consulate in Los Angeles, he now received an offer of support if he should choose to return to Berlin. He alluded to the offer in a letter to Berlau in August: 'Do you remember the people we met at Hella Wuolijoki's? They asked me if I intended to go back to Berlin. I said it would probably take some time, but that then I would want to go. They agreed and said they would help me'.[17] Brecht promised Berlau that he would include her in his plans. He also alluded to the offer in a letter to Apletin, in which he said that he was waiting for the time when he and his family could 'see Germany (Berlin) again': 'However, I know that patience is necessary, and it is easier for us with the thought that our friends have not forgotten us'. There was nothing to keep Brecht in the USA. The FBI regarded him as a 'suspected agent of the Soviet government', who might be involved in 'Soviet espionage activities in the

Los Angeles area and Communist infiltration of the movie industry'. In the eyes of the US authorities, these were grave matters.

As the FBI noted, Weigel was devoting her energy to practical help. She sent a huge number of CARE packages to family and friends in Germany, including Herbert Ihering, Peter Suhrkamp and Georg Pfanzelt.[18] In October Brecht replied to a letter from Suhrkamp, the first to reach him from Germany: 'You were one of the last people I saw in Germany – it was from your flat that I went to the station the day after the Reichstag fire; I've never forgotten your help in getting away'.[19] Suhrkamp had led the rump of the S. Fischer publishing house after the Jewish Gottfried Bermann Fischer had fled to Sweden, until Suhrkamp was himself incarcerated in Sachsenhausen. On 8 October 1945 Suhrkamp received the first publisher's licence awarded by the British in Berlin. Brecht looked forward to working with Suhrkamp in the dissemination of his new works and asked him for news about Caspar Neher, whom he needed for his sets, about Herbert Ihering, the actor and director Ernst Legal, Emil Hesse-Burri and Otto Müllereisert. Uppermost in Brecht's thoughts were the people he might need in the theatre. While Brecht tried to find out Neher's address, Ihering, head dramatic advisor at the Deutsches Theater, wrote to Brecht on 24 October. Ihering, another beneficiary of the Soviet charm offensive, had been prompted to contact Brecht by the SMAD cultural officer Ilya Fradkin, who knew Brecht's work in Tretiakov's translations. Ihering told Brecht that the theatre was very interested in staging both *Mother Courage* and *Life of Galileo*, and urged his protégé to return: 'Dear Brecht, we have a great desire to see you and talk to you'.[20]

Berlau's breakdown

Brecht was relying on Berlau to look after his business interests in New York. However, she was frequently not there when he phoned and when she did answer he had the impression that she was not alone. Another crisis was building. She could not get over the trauma of Michel's death and, feeling her life falling apart, began to drink heavily. She took a Danish seaman as a lover and wished to end her relationship with Brecht. Viewing herself as a member of the Danish resistance, she accused him of shying away from the anti-Nazi struggle in Denmark. Brecht could have turned his back on her. Instead, he sent her a poem, 'The Writer Feels Betrayed by his Friend', in which he urged her to stop her sexual adventures because they did nothing to help her.[21] Brecht wrote grimly of his disappointments with her, from which it was 'difficult and dangerous to learn'. Part of him wanted to be rid of her, but the greater part of him still did not want to let go. Echoing an earlier journal entry, he added: 'Bad behaviour makes people worse, good better. Our punishment for those who disappoint us is to diminish what we expect of them. Anger is translated into indifference. Relations are restored on a lower level. The process of disintegration goes on'.

And so it did. She took another Danish seaman lover but he returned to his ship and her condition deteriorated alarmingly. She became confused in her speech and violent towards Ida Bachmann.[22] Finally, on 27 December 1945 Bachmann called Elisabeth Hauptmann and Peter Lorre's psychiatrist Max Gruenthal. Berlau attacked Gruenthal, who fled, returning the following day with Ferdinand Reyher and colleagues from Bellevue mental hospital where Berlau was taken in a straitjacket. With a financial guarantee from Bergner and Czinner, which they would seek to recover through the production of *The Duchess of Malfi*, Berlau was admitted to the private South Oaks Hospital in Amityville on Long Island. Her state of mind oscillated between extreme agitation and the depths of lethargy and despair. Her doctor's view was initially that her situation was not so serious, but knowledge of her sister Edith's similar condition prompted a revision. She was treated with electroconvulsive therapy. Brecht passed letters to her through Reyher. Again, Brecht suffered with familiar symptoms, telling Reyher in January 1946 that he had a 'nasty flu with a pretty high fever'.[23] The corrosive relationship was starting to eat away at him.

As soon as Berlau could do so, Brecht talked to her on the phone, and, having himself recovered, went to see her in New York in early February. He told Weigel that Berlau was suffering from a mental disturbance, which made it difficult for her to maintain any semblance of composure.[24] She saw herself and her fellow patients as comrades in a concentration camp who had to be freed. Brecht speculated that if Berlau could get a little better, it would be best if she went to Denmark with a female friend, an idea that he would return to frequently in the coming years. He believed that exile had exacerbated her alcohol problem and the end of exile would bring alleviation. On 11 February 1946 Brecht began the 'longest letter I have ever written' to Weigel about Berlau's illness.[25] He sent the letter on 16 February, prefacing it with a typically understated expression of his affection for his wife: 'I am learning: to wash glasses and cups, sweep the floor, remove the trash, make scrambled eggs and soups, all self-taught. I feel very attached to you when I wash glasses, something that you have done for so long, among other things'. He described Berlau as unable to receive visitors and feverish, refusing to take food and drink: 'She was completely as if in a dream, erratic, hugely agitated, her expression changing tremendously quickly and extremely theatrical in her gestures'. Viewing her fellow patients as victims, Berlau asked Brecht if he could get them all out. When he said he couldn't, she reached for his jacket and said: 'Then farewell'. Brecht observed that she could no longer reconcile her 'emancipation' with the 'collaboration and involvement in my business and with the cult which she has practised with my works and with me'. Brecht took Berlau back to East 57th Street in late February. At first she could not be left alone but then became very calm, completely exhausted. She remained under observation with major memory loss.

In between looking after Berlau, Brecht was, as usual, meeting with friends like Budzislavsky, Schreiner, Norden and Korsch. He did a radio broadcast to Germany on Heinrich Mann's birthday and met with Karin Michaelis, who was in a wretched financial situation and would die in penury back in Denmark in 1950. He discussed the publication of his collected dramas in English with Reynal and Hitchcock, signed a contract, received an advance of $500 and did planning for the edition with Bentley and Hauptmann, who moved to Santa Monica.[26] In the event, nothing came of the edition, not least because Brecht was so fastidious about the translation of his works. He himself had considered *The Duchess of Malfi* complete in the summer of 1945, when he had written to Berthold Viertel: 'Please don't let E. Bergner draw you into a conversation about the *Duchess*. The slightest hint could lead to a demand for a complete reworking'.[27] Brecht had introduced new motives of greed and jealousy in the adaptation and strengthened social and political comment, including a much greater emphasis upon the conduct of foreign wars. In this way, *Malfi* contains recognisably Brechtian elements but he never properly owned and authorised this commissioned work, unlike other collaborative adaptations. In fact, Bergner informed Brecht that the present version was only the 'basis' for the further work. And so it went on, as Brecht invested more and more in the project. As many as six very different drafts were written between 1943 and 1946, none of which can be identified as a final, authorised version. Brecht wrote to Weigel of his meetings with Auden about the adaptation in February and March 1946: 'Work with Auden is going really well, even though he is difficult, a non-dramatist of the purest sort'.[28] Brecht sent portions of the work to Bergner and reported: 'The discussions are interesting. Auden is very amiable and open. Let me know if you have any objections'. At her behest, Brecht persuaded Auden to include the trial scene from Webster's *White Devil*. Brecht was by now telling Weigel that progress was very slow because Auden was 'very lazy'. However, by early April they had signed off a draft.[29] Brecht told Weigel that he was looking to finalise *Malfi* with Bergner in the days after her arrival on 14 April 1946. They discussed who would direct and who would compose the music, with a view to a production that autumn.

As Brecht's thoughts turned to his return to Santa Monica, it was clear that he could not leave Berlau alone and he explained to Weigel that he could not return to Santa Monica without her.[30] Although Weigel had looked after Steffin, she refused to be drawn into Berlau's circle of carers. She did, however, arrange accommodation for her in Santa Monica with a Norwegian friend, Anna Harrington. Brecht returned to Santa Monica with Berlau in late April.

Planning the return to Europe

For more than a year, from early January 1946 until February 1947, during and after the period he was caring for Berlau and experiencing extreme anxiety himself, Brecht's journal entries cease. Relatively few letters and poems have survived from this period, nor did Brecht do more for the theatre than the *Galileo* and *Malfi* adaptations. Meanwhile, the wartime coalition between the Soviet Union and the Western Allies was beginning to disintegrate: the former coming to dominate Eastern Europe, the latter Western Europe. Stalin's nightmare would come true, in which the heavily industrialised West of Germany was rapidly re-built with US support and joined with the Western Allies in a highly antagonistic stand-off with the USSR. The population in the East of Germany was set to pay the much greater price for Nazism, while those in the West were the recipients of US finance intended to demonstrate the superiority of capitalism in a proxy economic and ideological struggle. A divided Germany would rapidly become precisely what Stalin wished to avoid: a dangerous fault-line within a divided continent, the site of a latent civil war within the Cold War.

A devastated Berlin became a nest of intrigue. After much hesitation, in the Soviet Zone and the Soviet Sector of Berlin the Socialist Unity Party of Germany (SED) was founded on 21 April 1946. Designed to overcome the historical enmity between the working-class parties, it went ahead as a forced merger between the SPD and the KPD. With the support of the Soviet authorities, the SED swept to victory in the 1946 elections for local and regional assemblies held in the Soviet zone. However, the SED got less than half the votes of the SPD in Berlin, where the bulk of the SPD had resisted the merger, following the example of the strongly pro-western SPD leader Kurt Schumacher. The German Left remained fractured after all. In Brecht's view, Schumacher's SPD had once more thrown in their lot with the bourgeoisie rather than supporting their fellow workers. The 'natural' majority of the working-class parties remained an illusion. The USA and the UK took a major step towards the establishment of separate East and West German states when they ignored Soviet diplomatic efforts and, in contravention of the Potsdam Agreement, created a bi-zone on 1 January 1947, which the French subsequently joined. Far from requiring reparations of Germany, the USA, in search of new markets after the war, would presently offer financial assistance in the form of the Marshall Plan to boost economic activity in an exhausted and impoverished Europe.

Brecht's surviving correspondence from 1946–7 sees him pursuing publishing and performance rights for his works in Europe, re-establishing links with friends and making plans for fresh collaboration. He also began to take legal steps to free himself from his contract with Felix Bloch Erben. On 11 January 1946, Brecht had sent Suhrkamp power of attorney to act on his behalf in Germany regarding productions of his works, signalling that he wanted his works to appear with him.[31] He suggested that his first publication could be a collection of songs and poems and enclosed 'The Children's Crusade' as a present. The correspondence marks the beginning of the hugely successful partnership which would bring such prestige and wealth to both parties. Shortly after, Brecht responded to his Swiss publisher Kurt Reiss, who had contacted him already in August 1945 to suggest that they develop their collaboration, offering him the Swiss rights to *Life of Galileo*, *The Good Person of Szechwan* and *Mother Courage* for five years.[32] Brecht and Reiss reached an agreement on these and other works.

Recognition was growing that Brecht's work contained powerful warnings as well as demanding agendas for change in a devastated Europe. The first post-war Austrian production of a Brecht work took place in March 1946 with *The Good Person of Szechwan* at Vienna's Theater in der Josefstadt. The production went ahead in the face of Brecht's opposition. He argued that too little of his theoretical writing was known in Europe and that Paula Wessely did not convince him as the lead.[33] She had actually acted in Nazi films. *Mother Courage* followed shortly after in the same theatre and had an extraordinary impact. Ihering repeated his call for Brecht to return to Berlin a number of times, telling him that everyone had been reading *Mother Courage* with great enthusiasm. Brecht himself saw it as the most suitable play for a Berlin production, with Weigel in the lead, marking her return to the German stage.

Brecht wanted just one Broadway success for all his efforts in the US years. He notes the well-connected Laughton's efforts in the winter of 1945–6 to promote a production of *Life of Galileo*:

Laughton caught up in the machinations of his agent is an instructive performance.

He read the play indefatigably to soldiers, millionaires, agents, friends of the arts. Not a single response, it seems, was negative or even cool. Then the question of a production arises and his agent says, not before the autumn, stressing the danger of the summer break. (He wants to be involved in the financing himself, which takes time.) [Orson] Welles agrees with me that spring would be better politically (interest in the struggle between the scientists and the state, atom bomb etc.); since he couldn't then be the producer (he can't raise the money that quickly), he puts it as follows: he couldn't take the responsibility vis-à-vis the backers if it were to be spring.[34]

The project rapidly acquired a Byzantine complexity, much of it down to Brecht. He and Laughton signed a contract, aiming for a production in the autumn of 1946 by Welles's Mercury Theatre. Despite Laughton's antipathy towards Czinner, Brecht wanted him as co-producer in order to maintain the 'European element'.[35] Czinner also had access to finance. The plan was to rehearse in Hollywood, open in San Francisco and transfer to Broadway. Brecht had a number of difficult meetings with Welles, which led him to doubt Welles's business acumen and integrity, before concluding that he was not really interested in him: he only needed Laughton for Galileo.[36] Welles, for his part, wrote to Laughton: 'Brecht was very, very tiresome today until (I'm sorry to say) I was stern and a trifle shitty. Then he behaved. I hate working like that'. Welles evidently stopped returning Brecht's calls.

Meanwhile, unbeknown to Laughton, Brecht had been re-working the play with Reyher and Hauptmann. That, in turn, would prompt a further re-write by Brecht and Laughton, before Brecht and Reyher undertook more revisions still in the autumn. And, without Welles's knowledge, Brecht and Laughton had been pursuing a separate 'film option' through Laughton's agency, Berg-Allenberg.[37] They signed with Mike Todd, giving him the option of a stage production, too. At this point, Welles and his partner Richard Wilson withdrew, the latter regretting the lost opportunity to deliver 'one of the greatest productions in contemporary theater'. Todd himself then withdrew, leaving Brecht and Laughton without a producer, although they had found a director, Joseph Losey, whom Brecht knew from Moscow and New York in the mid–1930s. Amidst continuing uncertainties, largely centring on Brecht's re-writes, later in the year Laughton would accept a role in the Hitchcock film *The Paradine Case*, which delayed production until 1947. Laughton's agent offered Brecht $5,000 to 'defray part of the cost to you which the possible delay may occasion', prompting Brecht to write to Weigel about Laughton's 'sellout': 'Tell him in any case that I left up to you the decision whether to accept the $5,000 and that you accept it or advise me to accept it'.[38] They were in no position to turn it down.

Brecht re-established contact with his family in Europe and with old Augsburg friends. In the autumn of 1945 he had met Otto Zoff, Marianne Zoff's brother, in New York, who had told him that Marianne and Theo Lingen were in Austria with Brecht's daughter Hanne, a gifted young actress.[39] He sought news from them about Neher, Müllereisert and his brother Walter. He wrote to Marianne and Hanne again in the summer of 1946, encouraging Hanne in her acting ambitions and saying that if he was to return to the theatre in Berlin, he would rely a lot on her step-father Lingen.

Brecht wrote to his brother in May 1946. Without receiving Brecht's letter, Walter wrote to him on 14 June, telling him of Frank Banholzer's death and about the devastation of Augsburg. Pfanzelt was alive but Hartmann had died of a heart condition. Walter asked his brother for a letter confirming their conversation of August 1939, in which Brecht had advised Walter to join the Nazi party to protect himself from any persecution as the expatriated Brecht's brother.[40] Walter thanked Brecht 'with all my heart' for the testimony he sent. Brecht wrote to Pfanzelt in the summer of 1946, too, telling him about his plans and a little later about life in California: 'Here everything can be had except the little dollars without which nothing can be had. Hollywood, now undoubtedly the cultural centre of four-fifths of the world, is only fifteen kilometres away, you can smell it from here'.[41] Looking forward to returning to Europe, Brecht later added: 'I must say you are a prime attraction for me in the old latitudes'.

By now, Brecht was making plans to return, in the first instance, to Switzerland. It transpired that he had accumulated enough royalties with Reiss from the great productions at the Zurich Schauspielhaus to live there for a year.[42] In July 1946 the Praesens film company, which had financed Brecht's film *Kuhle Wampe* in 1931–2, informed the Zurich police that Brecht wished to come to Switzerland with his wife and daughter for a year or so. That month Brecht sent a letter to A. N., probably Albert Norden, who had resumed his political career in Berlin with the SED, telling him of his wishes for Berlin: for Weigel to play Mother Courage and for himself to work in the theatre if Bernhard Reich or Jacob Geis would come to run 'our old Schiffbauerdamm Theatre'. Organisation was not Brecht's thing. Brecht claimed to A. N. that he had heard nothing about any opportunities for him there: 'It would be good, too, if you could arrange for Piscator to be invited. I don't know what's happening with him just now, but you should try everything if you're interested in having political theatre'.

That other very close, old friend Caspar Neher now contacted Brecht, expressing his joy upon reading the lines which Weigel had sent him in which he had received a long hoped-for sign of life: 'I'm hungering after the latest things by you, which I can't get hold of anywhere. [...] If I could I'd get on the next coal train right away and come to see you'.[43] He wrote that he had spent a lot of time listening to Brecht's records with Müllereisert and that he was in need of a long conversation with Brecht himself. Brecht responded: 'The best thing would be if we could start collaborating again as soon as possible. I've received enquiries for plays from Berlin (Deutsches Theater) and Heidelberg (Hartung), and in every case I'm going to insist on your doing the sets'.[44] Neher was delighted at the prospect of working with Brecht again. He read *Mother Courage* and *The Good Person of Szechwan* and told Brecht: 'Both excellent plays, which one would have to talk about, since the forms of performance cannot be found easily'. He told Brecht he was making drawings for his plays: he intended to design the set for *Fear and Misery of the Third Reich* and asked Brecht if they would be going ahead with plans for other plays in Switzerland. Neher urged Brecht to go there. He described a poem that Brecht had sent him as 'amongst the greatest things I've had my hands on for a long time'. 'It would be good', Neher added, 'to build a sort of Brecht Theatre, like the old Globe Theatre in London, but not in Berlin, probably in the most densely populated zone, the British'. Neher and Brecht shared a vision for a theatre but Neher had no desire to work in a world dominated by Soviet Communism.

In October 1946 Brecht wrote of working together in Northern Italy or Switzerland, 'concentrating on theory and occasionally working up a play for Germany'.[45] Alluding to his conversations with the Soviets, Brecht speculated to Neher that in time they might have use of the Theater am Schiffbauerdamm. Brecht always had his eyes firmly on a return to that scene of his great success. Reminding Neher of his drawing of Brecht as Hydratopyranthropos, the Water-Fire-Man, Brecht added: 'I'm convinced that we'll build up a theatre again; really no one but you and I can do it'. When Brecht again mentioned the Theater am Schiffbauerdamm in December 1946, he said he had received offers to use it but that 'must be kept strictly between ourselves'. By this time Brecht was also telling Neher: 'I am working on getting to Switzerland about June'. From there he envisaged performing his plays in Germany with a touring company.

The Brecht-Auden adaptation of Webster's *The Duchess of Malfi* was finally moving forward to production. We have seen that there were differences of opinion between Brecht and Bergner. However, when at the end of August he wrote to her about 'our little bone of contention', expressing the hope that he would be able to help with the production, he did not know the half of it.[46] When Brecht embarked on his sixth trip to New York in mid-September, driving across America with Berlau in Laughton's car, the Brecht-Auden adaptation had already been abandoned. In August Czinner had engaged Auden's friend George Rylands, a director from the old school, who had recently made a success of Webster's play in London. Rylands refused to use the Brecht-Auden version and Bergner – to her 'shame', as she later put it – accepted his demands for the first out-of-town performance which took place at Providence, Rhode Island before Brecht arrived.[47] When it moved on to Boston on 25 September it was still billed as the Brecht-Auden adaptation. Brecht witnessed the deception and wrote to Czinner the following day, insisting that the 'adaptation by Auden and myself must absolutely be re-instated' and that the 'present director' be removed.[48] Brecht requested a response by 30 September. The play moved on to Hartford, New Haven and Princeton, by which time Brecht was considering legal action. He wrote to Weigel: 'Bergner is bad, weak and under fire because of her accent'. He insisted that his name be removed from the billing before the play opened on Broadway in mid-October where it received a bad press. Rylands left after a week and the play was discontinued after four. Brecht telegraphed Weigel: 'As to Bergner I saw what an actress you are'. He added shortly after: 'At a few points one sees with horror that she was once a talent'. Czinner, who had paid Berlau's medical bills during her breakdown, now withheld Brecht's royalties to recover his costs.[49] Brecht returned to Santa Monica.

The Berlin charm offensive continued, with Ihering once again urging Brecht to return and Wolfgang Langhoff inviting Weigel to play Mother Courage at the Deutsches Theater.[50] Langhoff, who had acted in Brecht's plays in Zurich and had taken over as artistic director of the Deutsches Theater, followed with a lengthy letter and two telegrams in December 1946, formally inviting Brecht and Weigel to return. Langhoff wrote that, faced with the pessimism of the French existentialists, the German public was crying out for Brecht but he remained silent. Langhoff asked for Brecht's permission to put on *Schweyk* but Brecht declined. Instead, he identified *Fear and Misery of the Third Reich* as a possibility for the Deutsches Theater and asked Langhoff whether the Theater am Schiffbauerdamm could be appended to that theatre. Brecht had his sights set firmly on the Theater am Schiffbauerdamm. When Langhoff pressed to perform *Schweyk*, Brecht again turned him down, explaining that in his revisions few of the songs had been written and none of the music. For that reason, he added, he had proposed *Fear and Misery*: 'My plays written in exile, all written for a future German theatre, could, I think, become really good little artistic and political capital if we fully exploit them'. Langhoff would follow up with a contract offer to Weigel in May 1947 for a guest engagement at the Deutsches Theater and its Kammerspiele from 16–31 August 1948. Langhoff directed *Fear and Misery* in January 1948, prompting the philosopher and critic Wolfgang Harich to describe Brecht in *Tägliche Rundschau* as the 'most powerful German dramatist of our epoch'.[51]

Late in his stay in the USA, Brecht had a great musical experience, belatedly discovering folk music, a strand of US popular culture which, through Brecht's impact upon Bob Dylan, would later come to bear Brecht's own imprint. When Brecht heard Burl Ives perform folk songs at a friend's house, another guest Riki Riker was startled by Brecht's powerful endorsement of Ives as a 'great man'.[52] Brecht then went around telling people that he had discovered a new American idiom. He responded similarly when Naomi Replansky played a record with the great blues guitarist Huddie Ledbetter, known as Lead Belly, performing 'The Gray Goose'. Brecht was inspired to produce his own German version of the lyrics.[53] With so little of his work in print – though that would begin to change with the publication of Hoffman Hays's bilingual *Selected Poems* in 1947 – few people knew of Brecht's own beginnings in folk music and ballads, which shared such a close affinity with the popular radicalism of US folk music. Dylan, who in the first volume of his autobiography describes the life-changing experience of hearing Brecht's songs in Greenwich Village, fully recognised that affinity in works that fused Brecht with the American folk music in Dylan's own powerful new idiom.[54]

The plan for the return to Europe took firm shape when in March 1947 Brecht, Weigel and Barbara had their application accepted for US exit and re-entry visas for Switzerland. The plan was to sail from New York to Europe and to make first for Zurich and to live in Northern Italy or Italian-speaking Switzerland near Lugano, the area Brecht had explored back in 1933.[55] Stefan Brecht was now a US citizen, studying at Harvard. Differences between son and father are apparent in their exchange of letters over the poem 'Freedom and Democracy'. Stefan complained about the poem's 'sluttishness' before rejecting his father's adherence to a Leninist notion of freedom 'which has come to nothing'.[56] Brecht in turn expressed his annoyance with his son's 'schoolmasterly' manner. Soon the Atlantic would separate them.

Brecht remained cautious about the offer of a theatre for the 1947–8 season, which he clearly understood to be the Theater am Schiffbauerdamm, and was firmly opposed to returning immediately to Germany.[57] Reports of the scale of devastation evoked great anxiety in him, strengthening his resolve to live initially outside Germany and to establish whether there was a suitable place to perform his new repertoire of the exile years in his own style. Karl-Heinz Martin followed Langhoff's invitation with another letter in January 1947, urging Brecht to return.[58] Brecht replied that he wished to do so but lacked knowledge about the German situation and Weigel added that she was waiting for an opportunity to work again. Martin took this as his cue to urge Weigel to return so that they could learn from her and place her 'in the most important and significant position'. Martin was not alone in recognising Weigel's importance for the re-construction of German theatre, not only as an actress but also on account of her organisational talent. Brecht and Weigel were a formidable combination.

For the moment, Switzerland remained the major centre for the production of Brecht's plays. *Fear and Misery of the Third Reich* premiered at Basel's Stadttheater in January 1947. In an elegant review for *Schweizer Annalen* the dramatist and novelist Max Frisch observed:

> It is certainly a good and important thing that this play is being staged, and whoever calls it a revue should call it a revue for the memory. Perhaps that is why it is so unpleasant. If mankind possessed a memory, would not some things be better? One would put a bullet in one's temple or change. Brecht hopes for the latter. That's why he speaks to us so soberly, without noise or any escape into the past which often regards itself as poetry; his poetry is his seriousness, his love of humanity. And his beauty, it seems to me, resides in the dignity of his concern.[59]

Frisch intimates that for him and for others Brecht was defining an agenda for change just as Brecht had after the First World War. This time it was based on a decidedly sober appraisal of the situation in a Europe devastated by Fascism.

Brecht's agenda contrasts starkly with the shamelessly opportunistic, nationalist message which Becher was conveying after his return to Berlin. Brecht's journal entries resume on 20 February 1947 with a sardonic comment on the publication of Becher's 'Death and Resurrection' in the Berlin weekly *Sonntag*: 'The Pied Piper of Hamelin must at least have known how to whistle'.[60] Brecht knew what to expect from his Communist peers in Berlin. He noted the latest attack by Andrei Zhdanov, the Soviet Politburo member responsible for culture, on literature in the Soviet Union, which, in a predictable pattern, Zhdanov followed in 1948 with a renewed attack on Formalism. This threatened to undermine completely the SMAD's charm offensive, as many prominent artists turned their backs on East Berlin. Brecht, however, seemingly believed that the Soviets would treat Germany differently. There would be some truth in this until 1951.

Seeking to protect himself against the return of repression in the arts, Brecht emphasises repeatedly in his correspondence the importance of assembling a strong team for the theatre which he wished to create, including stalwarts whose judgement in organisational as well as artistic matters he could trust implicitly in the face of intrigue and pressure. In the Danish *Life of Galileo* and in the *Svendborg Poems* Brecht had captured the plight of the isolated intellectual in dark times. From now on, his actions were guided by the conviction he must surround himself with like-minded people if he were to return and, amidst the coming struggles, exercise the power and influence he had always craved in the creation of a new theatre for a new society. He identified Neher and Weigel, Geis, Lorre, Kortner and Homolka and saw Piscator as an important ally in such an undertaking. However, Piscator resisted all approaches and stayed in New York until 1951 when he returned to the Federal Republic of Germany.

Galileo reaches thc US stage, Brecht performs for the House Un-American Activities Committee

From mid-April to early August 1947 Brecht was immersed in work on the US premiere of *Life of Galileo*. Laughton and T. Edward Hambleton each put up $25,000 and acted as co-producers for the opening at the Coronet Theatre in Hollywood. The aim was to transfer to New York. Joseph Losey came to California to direct. Loscy and Brecht got on well: they fell out only twice. Recalling that at this time Brecht was always accompanied by two or three women, Losey famously said of him: 'He ate very little, drank very little, and fornicated a great deal'.[61]

Laughton's return to the stage after thirteen years was a Hollywood society event. The whole run of seventeen performances sold out in advance, with some 4,500 people seeing the play. The audience at the premiere on 24 July included Charlie Chaplin, Ingrid Bergmann, Anthony Quinn, Gene Kelly, Sam Wanamaker and Frank Lloyd Wright. Brecht's disagreement with Laughton over the evaluation of Galileo's behaviour remained unresolved, Laughton depicting Galileo's plight sympathetically, while Brecht wanted to see his condemnation as an opportunist. Predictably, many reviewers found the play too heavy intellectually, but that did nothing to dim Brecht's sense of triumph at his first US production on his own terms.

By the time *Life of Galileo* opened in New York on 7 December Brecht was already in Switzerland. Alerted to Brecht's plans, the FBI's R. B. Hood made one last attempt to apprehend him, contacting J. Edgar Hoover on 8 August.[62] Hood proposed that Brecht should be deported – that happened to Hanns Eisler – and that a stop notice be placed on Brecht's file so that he would be monitored if he attempted to re-enter the USA. Despite the fact that Hoover supported Hood, the FBI's plan went awry. Brecht and Weigel sold their house and were preparing to leave the USA in mid-October when on 19 September Brecht received a summons to appear before the House Un-American Activities Committee (HUAC) as one of the 'Hollywood Nineteen'. Already in May, when Hanns Eisler had appeared before HUAC, Hood had transferred information gathered by the FBI to Robert E. Stripling, HUAC's Chief Investigator.[63] This material formed the basis for HUAC's questioning of Brecht, too, in its attempt to determine Communist influence on the Hollywood film industry. Hoover postponed plans for the FBI to apprehend Brecht until he had appeared before HUAC. Brecht set off for New York by train with Weigel and Barbara on 16 October. There Brecht, the aficionado of Schweykian triumphant subservience, rehearsed for his coming performance with Budzislavsky. On 26 October Brecht travelled to Washington with Joseph Losey and T. Edward Hambleton. Hambleton had booked a flight for Brecht to Paris in his name for the day after the hearing on 30 October, in case there was any attempt to detain Brecht. For good measure, Brecht was carrying Czech papers.

The footage of Brecht's HUAC appearance shows him with apparently very little command of English, finding it hard to follow Stripling. While others in the 'Nineteen' declared that the question whether they were members of the Communist Party was unconstitutional, Brecht, 'as had been agreed with the other 18 and their lawyers [...], as a foreigner, answer[ed] the question with "no", which also happens to be the truth'.[64]

Some of the 'Nineteen' later disputed Brecht's account. John Howard Lawson, Albert Maltz and others from the New York debacle of *The Mother* were, however, no friends of Brecht. Brecht explained to Stripling that he was an independent writer who wanted to remain independent and not belong to any party. Stripling read from *The Measures Taken* and requested that Brecht summarise the plot. Brecht's repeated pretence that he did not understand prompted Stripling to read out more and more of the English translation, and Brecht in turn described the passages as inaccurate translations. It became hilarious comedy, worthy of Karl Valentin. Brecht summarised in his journal: 'I refer them to the Japanese model, define its content as dedication to an idea, and reject the interpretation that the subject is disciplinary murder by pointing out that it is a question of self-extinction. I admit that the basis of my plays is Marxist and state that plays, especially with an historical content, cannot be written intelligently in any other framework'. Brecht speculated that it benefited him that he had 'almost nothing to do with Hollywood', had steered clear of US politics and that the others had refused to testify. In fact, HUAC did not seem too interested in pursuing Brecht with more searching questions, even though the US authorities would show their hostility to Brecht when he returned to Europe. Some of the other 'Hollywood Nineteen' would later be blacklisted. Joseph Losey left the USA for the UK where he and Harold Pinter formed a great partnership.

Brecht left Washington immediately with Losey and Hambleton and that evening listened to his hearing on the radio with Weigel and the Budzislavskys. Feuchtwanger congratulated Brecht on his performance, which, he said, had brought Brecht lots of good publicity. When Brecht met Laughton in his 'Galileo beard' the following morning, Laughton was 'pleased that it isn't going to take any special courage to play Galileo'.[65] Brecht made his way to the airport and took the flight to Paris that afternoon. Weigel and Barbara followed by boat.

Hydratopyranthropos Surveys the Wreckage 1947–9

Brecht ante portas

On arriving at the airport in Paris on Saturday 1 November, Brecht bumped into his Hollywood acquaintances the film director Donald Ogden Stewart and his wife, the journalist Ella Winter. They got him a room in a hotel near theirs and stood him some meals. They had been neighbours of the Viertels until HUAC took an interest in them and they left for England. They introduced Brecht to Joe Forster, the editor of *New Masses*, who was in Paris looking to interview Pablo Picasso. Brecht found Paris 'shabby, impoverished, one big black market'.[1] He took in Gide's adaptation of Kafka's *The Trial* at Jean-Louis Barrault's Théâtre de Marigny but found it a 'flashy production, lots of tricks, instead of a representation of confusion just a confused representation; an attempt to convey fear to the audience. De Gaulle ante portas'. He encouraged Weigel to take their daughter to see Picasso's *Guernica* at the Musée d'Art Moderne when they passed through.

Anna Seghers, a KPD member who had returned to Germany from Mexican exile, was about to arrive from Berlin, so Brecht delayed his onward journey to Switzerland, asking Neher to make arrangements for his arrival in Zurich on the Wednesday. A concerned Neher had sent a letter to Santa Monica, saying they would have to discuss whether their theatrical plans could be realised in the devastated German capital.[2] Seghers, who was living in the American Sector of Berlin, had written to Weigel quite frankly about the difficulties of working but not living in the East of the city amidst the fear and intrigue: 'It will strike you when you're here that it is very difficult to find people with whom one [...] can speak normally about work'.[3] People working in the cultural sphere were drawn into the intrigue as they were co-opted to one side or another. To work with one of the Western Allies was to court the suspicions of the Soviets, and vice versa. Many friendships broke down as the Cold War deepened.

Brecht stayed up half the night talking to Seghers, 'white-haired, but her beautiful face fresh', from whom he learnt about life in the German capital:

> Berlin is a Witches' Sabbath where they don't even have broom-handles. [...] In order to safeguard her Mexican passport she is not living in the Russian Sector, so she does not get the privileges without which it is impossible to work. She wants

her books to be read in the non-Russian zones too. She seems to be perturbed by the intrigues, suspicion and spying.[4]

Nonetheless, Seghers did what was expected and moved to East Berlin. What she and others had to say confirmed Brecht in his very cautious attitude towards his return. His friend Jacob Walcher, back in Berlin from New York, described the 'quite extraordinary' difficulties' in the city.[5] Brecht arranged for Walcher to receive royalties from the Berlin production of *The Threepenny Opera*. He remarked to Eisler, 'Berlin seems to be getting like Shanghai', and told Berlau, 'Definitely, one must have a place to live outside Germany'.[6] On the train to Zurich the following day Brecht was pre-occupied by Berlin, writing to a fragile Berlau in New York: 'I gather from what Anna Seghers told me that it's very important for us to build up a strong group. It's impossible to exist there alone or practically alone'.[7]

Zurich, *Antigone*

Brecht took a room in Zurich's old town at the Hotel Zum Storchen where he and Neher saw each other for the first time since 1933. For Brecht, he was still the same old Neher, 'even if physically reduced'.[8] Neher noted that Brecht had put on weight, was 'more manly, more reserved and his tenderness was directed more outwards. [...] His front of hardness had completely fallen away. His inherent goodness came to the fore'.[9] The real Brecht whom he had known since adolescence, before the brutalisation of war and social struggle, was visible once more for Neher after long and painful years apart. Brecht was, however, reluctant to reveal this self to other people. Max Frisch, who got to know Brecht well in Zurich, recalls that he behaved differently with Neher: 'Relaxed, almost comfortable, different from usual; Brecht was jolly'.[10] This 'mellow' self was reserved for family and those closest to him. Brecht and Neher met daily to work on a German translation of the 'American' *Life of Galileo*. Hans Curjel, who witnessed them working together, described Neher as Brecht's 'second self'.[11] Neher had been designing sets at the Schauspielhaus for Carl Zuckmayer's *The Captain of Köpenick*. Brecht's old friend Zuckmayer, recently back from exile and now a US cultural attaché, was enjoying great success with that play and *The Devil's General*. As we know, the Zurich Schauspielhaus had acquired a very special importance indeed for Brecht. There alone in continental Europe his great works of exile had been premiered during the war. Otherwise, little of Brecht's work was known in Europe. Nothing new had been published since 1938 and almost everything had been destroyed or was out of print.

Neher introduced Brecht to the people at the Schauspielhaus, with whom he at once began to discuss projects: the artistic director Oskar Wälterlin, the dramatic advisor Kurt Hirschfeld and his colleague Uz Oettinger. Brecht was given use of a studio flat attached to the theatre. At Hirschfeld's he met Max Frisch and the young director Benno Besson, who would join him in Berlin. Brecht and Neher met Fritz Kortner, freshly returned from the USA, and Teo Otto, the stage designer at the Schauspielhaus. Otto had worked with Brecht in Berlin in 1930 on *The Measures Taken* and on Zurich's *Mother Courage* in 1941. Within days of arriving, on 9 November Brecht did precisely what the FBI had wanted to stop him doing. Greatly exercised by the prospect of another war, this time fought with nuclear weapons, Brecht met with other writers in Zurich to draft an appeal for peace addressed to writers of all nations. In addition to Frisch and Zuckmayer, Brecht's co-signatories included somewhat unlikely allies, now united against war: Horst Lange, Erich Kästner, Alexander Lernet-Holenia and Werner Bergengruen. Brecht sent the appeal to fellow writers, among them Feuchtwanger in the USA, whom he told that reports from Germany were 'dark'.[12] Meanwhile in Washington, on 12 November J. Edgar Hoover, quite unaware of Brecht's Swiss peace initiative, wired his Special Agent in Charge of the FBI's New York office, instructing him to 'interview subject without undue delay'.[13] Agents entered the Maxine Elliott Theatre on West 39th Street to arrest Brecht during rehearsals for *Life of Galileo*. Brecht had left the room.

Rehearsals had resumed in New York with Laughton as Galileo and with Losey directing. The aim was to transfer to Broadway with commercial backing after a successful opening at Maxine Elliott's. Hans Sahl wrote an enthusiastic review for *Neue Zürcher Zeitung* and Piscator sent his congratulations. However, fearing the worst, Brecht asked Berlau from Switzerland how the premiere had been received: 'Was it a failure? Then one can't put on theatre in New York – very possible'.[14] After receiving the New York reviews, which highlighted Laughton's excellence, Brecht all but gave up on Broadway, not least because of Brooks Atkinson's 'nasty' review in the *New York Times*, essentially a repetition of his annihilation of *The Mother* twelve years earlier. His self-belief nonetheless quite intact, Brecht consoled himself with the thought that 'after this demonstration of the new theatre to the specialists I doubt if the serious drama in the States will ever be the same again'.[15] He repeated the sentiment in a letter to Laughton, which ends: 'I can hardly express how proud I am of our collaboration'.[16]

Brecht's reflections upon the reviews initiate a sustained critique of bourgeois culture in his journal: 'The disgruntled New York press complains at being required to think about *Galileo*, since it is quite incapable of responding. The bourgeoisie is no longer prepared to indulge in the kind of general, unspecialised thinking which plays about itself demand'.[17] He parodied the US mentality: 'Thinking doesn't get you anywhere; what is the point of all this drivel from existentially worse-placed nations about "decisions that have to be taken" – what could it be other than Fascism, which, it cannot be denied, was an unmitigated disaster'. Having fled the unashamedly bourgeois USA and arrived in Switzerland, continental Europe's sole 'intact' bourgeois society at a time when he saw Germany divided between bourgeois and proletarian interests, Brecht was insistent that the structures and forms of bourgeois society must be swept aside.

His appeal for peace reached Lieutenant-Colonel Alexander Dimshitz, Head of the SMAD's Cultural Department in Berlin, a German-speaking Mayakovsky expert. This prominent figure in the Soviet charm offensive wrote a letter to Brecht, which Frisch took to Zurich: 'I hear you intend to come to Berlin shortly to arrange the performance of your works, which the German stage has been so missing. In case you need our help in any respect during the realisation of your Berlin plans, we are most sincerely ready to smooth the path to the success of your work'.[18] It appears that

Brecht left this and other letters from the SMAD unanswered. Meanwhile, Curt Riess, an acquaintance from the USA now with the US press camp in Berlin, wrote that he was authorised to tell Brecht that if he wished to return to Germany it would probably be best to do so through the Americans, otherwise things might look a little strange, especially after what had happened in Washington.[19] Brecht was not inclined to let considerations such as HUAC, nor this implicit threat, guide his behaviour. In the event, his US re-entry permit would not be extended and, after putting out feelers to the Americans in Berlin through Kurt Hirschfeld, he would not receive permission to enter Germany through the US Zone.[20]

In his first interview since his return to Europe with his Los Angeles friend Hans Winge, which appeared in Zurich's *Die Tat* on 15 November, Brecht explained his intention to stay in Europe for a year, travelling in Germany. Beyond that, he did not have specific plans. He said he did not know which zone he would initially live in and distanced himself from disputes and political debates: he had come 'as a writer to develop a picture of the intellectual, artistic and technical situation of German theatres and to take a view later'.[21] Similarly, Brecht advised his US collaborators Elisabeth Hauptmann and her then partner, the composer Paul Dessau, not to think of returning to Europe before the following autumn. Until Hauptmann reminded him that he had forgotten to ask the question, Brecht simply assumed she would work for him.[22]

Brecht arranged for his actress daughter Hanne to visit Zurich for a few weeks, using discussions at the theatre as a pretext. Hanne would stay in Zurich until late February. In typical Brecht manner, she at first omitted to tell her father that she had married the doctor Joachim Hiob-Sproesser. Meanwhile, Weigel and Barbara arrived in Zurich on 19 November. Hans-Walter and Renate Mertens let the Brechts use the upstairs flat of their house at Bünishoferstrasse 14 in Feldmeilen, just outside Zurich. What is more, Brecht and Neher had recently met with Hans Curjel of Chur's Stadttheater, who had worked with Brecht in the late 1920s. Curjel's stage was the town's old cinema. Among other ideas, Curjel suggested a production of Sophocles's *Antigone*. With Antigone's challenge to Creon's bloody rule, the play was highly topical: Jean Anouilh's *Antigone* had premiered in Paris in February 1944 under the German occupation as, for some, an allegory of resistance.

Brecht saw *Antigone* as an opportunity to 'do preparatory work on *Courage* with Weigel and Cas for Berlin'.[23] Brecht was planning to put on *Mother Courage* in April at the Deutsches Theater or the Theater am Schiffbauerdamm. Adapting Sophocles's work as Epic Theatre was an attractive proposition. The *Antigone* project rapidly turned into a Brecht-Neher adaptation of Friedrich Hölderlin's extraordinary translation. Discovering an 'astounding radicalism' in Hölderlin's language, Brecht noted: 'On Cas's advice I am using the Hölderlin translation, which is seldom or never performed because it is considered too obscure. I come across Swabian accents and grammar-school Latin constructions and feel quite at home. And there is some Hegel in there, it is presumably the return to the German-speaking world which is forcing me into this enterprise'.[24] As David Constantine and Tom Kuhn write, Hölderlin's 'linguistic strangeness' captivated Brecht, who took over about half of Hölderlin's text and, without any hint of Brechtian parody, 'homogenised his own language with that highly idiosyncratic base'.[25] Constantine's translation conveys the strangeness of

Hölderlin's work in lines such as Antigone's comparison of her impending death with Danaë's: 'On Sipylus' peaks / She is crouched and shrunk / To a slow stone, they put her in chains / Of ivy and winter is with her'.[26]

Brecht and Neher had completed a draft by mid-December but returned to it later in the month. Neher, who probably understood Brecht better than anyone, delighted in his friend's extraordinary compositional capacity: 'It is always a great pleasure to watch how he rejigs the acts without forgetting what has been said. He retains two or three drafts in his head alongside each other and so can jump easily from the first to the third, from the third to the second'.[27] Brecht described his approach to the play as a rationalisation: ' "Fate" eliminates itself all along the line of its own accord. Of the gods only the local popular deity, the god of joy, remains. Gradually, as the adaptation of the scenes progresses, the highly realistic popular legend emerges from the ideological fog'.[28]

Rehearsals had begun in Zurich with Weigel as Antigone and Hans Gaugler as Creon when Berlau arrived on 10 January, hoping to find Brecht living in his studio, not with Weigel and Barbara in Feldmeilen. Deeply affronted, she took a hotel room where he visited her, followed soon after by Neher, Brecht's co-director. When Brecht suggested that she should photograph and document *Antigone*, Berlau, consumed by jealousy, wrote him a 'last' private letter, stating that she should be directing and that photography was demeaning: she would not spend the rest of her life in a dark room.[29] Brecht responded with an emphatic clarification of living arrangements: 'For *many* years now I would have liked to have for myself again what I actually always used to have, a retreat (a room) for myself. That is because I can work well there and keep myself fresh. [...] However, you should not insist that I have promised that to *you*, I have promised it to *myself*'.[30] He reminded Berlau that he still did not have any money to speak of. She stayed briefly at the studio before taking a room at Dufourstrasse 32. While Brecht, Neher and Weigel travelled to Chur for rehearsals on 16 January, Berlau initially stayed in Zurich but joined them on 4 February. Her photographs would form the basis for the first model book, documenting a production through rehearsals to performance, which became a staple in Brecht's late work.

Brecht's *Antigone* begins with a Prelude, set in Berlin in April 1945, which shows two sisters cowed by the collapsing regime's reign of terror as their deserter brother is hanged by the SS. Brecht then presents Sophocles's compliant Ismene, who counsels her sister Antigone to forget the horror of Creon's murder of their brother, the deserter Polynices, during the Theban attack on the city of Argos. However, Antigone defies Creon's order to leave their brother's corpse to rot in the sun and, when she is arrested, attacks Creon: 'Screaming for unity you live on discord'.[31] In her uncompromising truth-telling, Antigone is reminiscent of Brecht's Simone Machard. However, Brecht is torn between his desire to present a character taking a stand against tyranny and his intention not to lionise Antigone as an allegory of German resistance. Brecht attempted to counter this inherent ambiguity, emphasising that her challenge to Creon's rule comes from within the ruling caste of Thebes. Indeed, Brecht was concerned to avoid a moral message whatsoever:

> The moral decline derives from an enterprise for which the state is not yet strong
> enough. It could be poor weaponry, or a bottleneck in food supplies caused by too

small a fleet of vehicles, or strategic errors that provide the immediate grounds for the descent into brutality; mishandling of the economy is also adduced as a reason for taking the war option; but that too amounts to feebleness.[32]

Within a materialist framework, Brecht foregrounds the brutal terror of Creon's dictatorship as the 'remarkable element in this Antigone play – the role of force in the collapse of the head of the state'.[33] Creon plunges the city state of Thebes into an orgy of violence, which he justifies by claims of victory. Departing from Sophocles, Brecht presents not a war won by Creon's Thebes, but by Argos which, like the Soviets' Stalingrad, withstands the aggressor and turns the tables. Faced by overwhelming defeat, the monstrous Creon, who has condemned both Antigone and his son Haemon, her betrothed, seeks to recall Haemon: 'Come and be a help now in the great collapse. / Forget the things I said for when I was master / I was not master of my senses'. Haemon has already taken his life. Antigone is dead, too. Hitler-like, Creon utters his final words: 'So now Thebes falls. / And let it fall, let it with me, let it be finished / And there for the vultures. That is my wish now'.

After many hitches, during which Brecht's nerves became very frayed, the premiere of *Antigone* took place on 15 February. Neher populated the stage with totem poles to represent the primitive nature of Creon's rule. The audience was swelled by friends who had travelled from Zurich and Basel. Critics had warm words for a great theatrical event, Weigel's return to the stage, but the play went down badly with the Chur public, who stayed away from the two remaining performances of this experimental production. A single matinee performance followed in Zurich. There would be just one small-scale revival in Brecht's lifetime in the East German town of Greiz.

Berating the bourgeoisie

Brecht reflected that no real critique of Nazism was taking place in Germany because it was deemed 'beneath criticism'.[34] His own views were based squarely on the classic Marxist analysis that Nazism was a reactionary movement of the petty bourgeoisie, which was threatened by the rise of the working class: 'National Socialism must be regarded as the socialism of the petty bourgeoisie, a crippled, neurasthenic, perverted popular movement which produced or promised to produce a surrogate for what was being demanded from lower down the social order, one which would not be too unacceptable to the ruling class'. Brecht told Neher: 'I have never regarded Nazism as an excrescence but always as a consequence of perfectly normal development'.[35] In Zurich, he embarked on discussions with intellectuals who had a strong, if not uncritical, allegiance to the Swiss bourgeois world, among them Max Frisch and the German art critic Armin Kesser, whom Brecht knew from Berlin days. Both left diaries of their exchanges with Brecht, whose experience of Switzerland prompted the parting remark: 'The effect of bourgeois propaganda is overpowering here. [...] If you appeal to objectivity they suspect you of being an agent of Stalin'.[36]

Kesser paid Brecht a visit at Feldmeilen, finding him 'fairly unchanged':

Blue worker's top, strikingly clean, open shirt, unshaven, his hair like a closely cut felt cap. At the ends of his overalls you could see his woollen underclothes. Black glasses, felt slippers. His face has lost something of its sharpness. His lower cheek is quite mildly bloated, which gives his appearance something sensitively father-like. His upper dentures form a semicircle corroded black, the consequence of smoking his Virginias; his fingernails not cleaned. The whole thing an act, a costume. Brecht said that he could not imagine a more stupid bourgeoisie than the Germans. They had started two world wars and gained nothing, so they would now probably wage a third.[37]

Was Brecht, as Kesser suggests, merely a petit-bourgeois *poseur*, whose act he could see through? When Kesser objected that the blame did not lie with the bourgeoisie alone, Brecht acknowledged that was a simplification: they had fought the first war alongside the Social Democrats, the second alongside the Nazis. Kesser wondered how far Brecht still really believed such things and reflected how German his attitude was, romanticising the dethroned theory of the class struggle, as Kesser put it. For him, Brecht epitomised 'German self-banishment; proletarian-romantic apostleship; sectarianism out of unconscious religiosity; poisoning oneself; a celebration of suicide'. After the conversation, Brecht re-affirmed his belief that 'to denazify the German bourgeoisie is to debourgeoisify it'.[38] His reading of Friedrich Meinecke's *The German Catastrophe* – for Brecht the 'liberal-bourgeois standpoint' on Nazism – elicited the comment: 'The gas chambers of IG-FARBEN trust are monuments of bourgeois culture'.[39] Similarly, after reading Eugen Kogon's *The SS State* and Goebbels's diaries, he launched into a lengthy exposition upon recent German history as a catalogue of the crimes and follies of the bourgeoisie.

Kesser's next meeting with Brecht prompted the observation that the terrifying Brecht should be with the Gorgons:

> Making oneself hateful, poisoning oneself – just so as not to be confused with this (bourgeois), not to be 'healthy' in this company. I view him from the perspective of a German cultural physiognomy. – His 'dialectics' and Marxist dogma, all a German abstraction, romantic post-religiosity. But how fraternally close to one's own opportunities. – He is at a turning point. His inner and outer experience is beyond the doctrine, and yet it holds him, as a template for a role.[40]

The poison had always been in Brecht. Already in adolescence he had turned its debilitating effects outwards in a display of willed hatefulness. The teeth had become blacker while he had sought remedies for the diseases which, as he saw it, afflicted him and the society around him. His extreme experience of that dire German trajectory had taken him through a searing ordeal, leaving him, still Neher's Hydratopyranthropos, the Water-Fire-Man, scarred and diminished. The Leninist vanguardism had returned, somewhat weaker after the Great Terror, but Brecht remained convinced that Marxist analysis, combined with resolute dictatorship, showed the way to drain the poison from the unhealthy body which he shared with his fellow countrymen.

Kesser noted that while Brecht was lecturing him on Marxism 'he scarcely raised his gaze from the table'. Kesser was convinced that Brecht was 'dreaming deeply': 'I observed his sunken eye lids, the theological fire of his eyes turned inwards and was shocked: this is a doctrinaire dreamer'. They were in different worlds. Brecht returned to his journal, lambasting the mendacity and venality of bourgeois intellectuals, who, with the time-honoured opportunism which he satirised in his *Tui* drafts, had taken to promoting the theory of totalitarianism: 'The bourgeoisie is now staging a worldwide mobilisation of intellectuals for a crusade for "western civilisation". [...] The intellectuals cast a veil over the dictatorial character of bourgeois democracy not least by presenting democracy as the absolute opposite of Fascism, not as just another natural phase of it where the bourgeois dictatorship is revealed in a more open form'.[41] For Brecht, the achievements of liberal democracy – for example, civil rights and the rule of law – were enjoyed by those with financial and political power but remained on a purely formal level for ordinary citizens.

In Brecht's estimation, the time had come for the application of economic principles to transform the lives of the workers in Europe. He now re-affirmed a vision of the revolution through which 'the proletariat liberates itself as the greatest productive force. In one huge mass process the masses achieve freedom through production'. Brecht's language here echoes Marx and Engels's majestic vision of workers overcoming their alienation from the means of production. However, Brecht's idealist rhetoric is no more than an echo down the ages of Marx and Engels's own Utopianism. There is still no indication how, following the abolition of rentier interests, the economy would be organised without markets to generate such dynamically liberating production. Brecht was aware of the coercive role of the bureaucracy and the police in the economic life of the Soviet Union. However, part of him, invoking the goodness of enlightened producers, apparently believed that a Marxist state could run its economy without brute force. It must be said that when the opportunity arose Brecht did all he could to empower employees in his theatre.[42] However, another part of him, still invoking Leninism, was prepared to justify such force on the grounds that residual bourgeois elements must be eradicated by the state. How the state bureaucracy would then wither away remained the open question which it had been for Brecht in the late 1930s.

Brecht spent much time in Zurich with Max Frisch, whose view of bourgeois Switzerland was by no means uncritical. Although Frisch, like Kesser, was not taken by Brecht's Marxist dialectics, he produced a sharply insightful and sympathetic portrait of him. Frisch ascribed his fascination with Brecht, whom he regarded as the greatest living writer in the German language, to the fact that he genuinely lived the life of the mind, quite without vanity. Brecht's expectation of any conversation was a challenging exchange of contrary positions in order to establish how things might be changed. Where Kesser saw only a dreaming *poseur*, Frisch recognised Brecht's extraordinary intellectual commitment to change. He lived his life on the edge 'with regard to an imagined world, which does not yet exist anywhere within time, visible only in his behaviour, which is a lived contradiction, inexorable and never worn down through decades of hardships as an outsider'.[43] Brecht's asceticism, Frisch wrote, was akin to a priestly attitude, which was, however, devoted to the earthly rather than the divine.

Frisch spent time with Brecht in his study, which reminded him of a workshop, cluttered as it was with Brecht's papers, his typewriter, scissors, glue and photos. However, he had the impression that this modest, retiring refugee could pack it all up and leave within 48 hours. Brecht never talked to Frisch about personal experience, nor at all directly about himself. The perceptive Frisch understood better than most Brecht's 'Chinese' imperturbability in his interactions with others, finding in him a 'rare sort of unmoody politeness, akin to a ritual but sincere'.[44] Frisch sent Brecht his pen portrait and he replied: 'I read with amusement your charming and friendly sketch of the strange bird of passage – a man with whom I myself am slightly acquainted'.[45]

In April 1948 Frisch introduced a Brecht evening in the cellar of the Volkshaus bookshop, at which Brecht quietly read his poem 'To Those Born Later', then ceded the floor for recitations by Weigel and Giehse. Frisch, a practising architect, took Brecht to see new estates built for Zurich workers. Brecht was at first surprised by such comfort but became angry that the workers had fallen for this swindle: 'Huge blocks of three- and four-room flats. the house-fronts face the sun and there is a little greenery between the houses; inside "mod cons" (bath, electric cookers), but all very tiny, these are prison cells, little rooms where the commodity called "labour" can recover its strength, upgraded slums'.[46] When he was shown a new municipal swimming pool, he observed: 'these giant pools for thousands make the poem [...] "Of Swimming in Lakes and Rivers" a recollection from history'.

Brecht had sought to keep open a route back to the USA. That was blocked when the State Department declined to renew his re-entry permit. However, the American Academy of Arts and Letters, together with the National Institute of Arts and Letters, awarded Brecht a prize of $1,000 and invited him to receive it on 21 May. Graciously accepting the award, Brecht added: 'Unfortunately, I will be unable to attend the annual ceremonial as I am at present living in Switzerland'.[47] Brecht was granted a four-month extension of his Swiss residence permit, but by now the Swiss police were making 'urgent', 'discreet' inquiries about him.[48] In the light of the decision by the US State Department, Brecht requested a Swiss identity pass for six months which would enable him to travel. The police indicated a willingness to grant the pass but in May the Swiss Federal Attorney wrote to the Police Department in Berne: 'It is in our interest on political-policing grounds that Brecht should leave Switzerland as soon as possible. We request that you therefore do not issue him with a pass'.[49] Meilen council established that Brecht had moved there without permission and he was asked to sign a declaration that he would 'never claim nor occupy another lodging in Meilen'.

So, in the spring of 1948 Brecht found himself in a difficult position. Unable to return to the USA and having problems in Switzerland, he was unwilling to commit himself to permanent residence in Germany. He wrote to Reyher that he was considering settling in the Salzburg area. Weigel had been an Austrian citizen and there was some prospect of an engagement for Brecht at the Salzburg Festival. In Zurich Neher had introduced Brecht to the composer Gottfried von Einem, the recently appointed Festival Director. He was keen to engage Brecht and initiated the process, while Brecht confirmed his interest.

Meanwhile, Kurt Hirschfeld from the Zurich Schauspielhaus travelled to Berlin on Brecht's behalf. The purpose of Hirschfeld's trip was, however, not to talk to the Soviets but to the US cultural officer responsible for theatres, Benno Frank.[50] Hirschfeld informed Frank that Brecht did not wish to live in Germany under military occupation, whatever the zone. He was therefore not disinclined to stay in Switzerland but the authorities were making things difficult for him. Hirschfeld disclosed to a surprised Frank that Brecht had left letters from the Soviets unanswered concerning arrangements for his return. Hirschfeld explained that Brecht had seen how wretched conditions were when he had travelled through the USSR in 1941 and had no intention of subjecting himself to surveillance or censorship in the Soviet Zone.

Hirschfeld divulged to Frank that before Brecht had left the USA he had received an offer to work as a dramatic advisor with Erich Engel at his old haunt, Munich's Kammerspiele. Hirschfeld asked Frank if Brecht might receive permission to enter the US Zone. Munich is, of course, only a train ride from Salzburg and Zurich. Because Brecht was so prominent, Frank had to refer the issue to Robert Murphy, the US Political Advisor on German Affairs. Then, understanding that the matter had been agreed and merely awaited confirmation, Frank met with Brecht and Weigel in Zurich. Brecht was, it seems, enthusiastic, Weigel less so. However, shortly after Frank was informed that the US Secretary of State had intervened to declare Brecht's application null and void. Brecht was banned from entering the US Zone. But for the Secretary of State's intervention, Brecht's great theatrical experiment might have been launched in Munich rather than Berlin. Theatre history would have looked a little different. In the event, Erich Engel would join Brecht in Berlin.

Over the coming months Berlin would crystallise as Brecht's only real option in the struggle to realise his theatrical ambitions. He would have to reconcile himself to living in an occupied, divided country and to the prospect of surveillance and censorship, well aware of the reputational damage which might ensue. Along the way, he might well need to adopt the survival mode of exile. The thought of a second exile from a deeply unstable Germany would never leave him. Indeed, the clearest signal that divisions between the occupying forces were now unbridgeable came on 20 June 1948 when the Western Allies, in further contravention of the Potsdam Agreement, introduced a currency reform in the western zones and four days later in West Berlin. Shop windows filled with goods at affordable prices and, as economic growth gathered pace, drawing upon Marshall Aid and marginalising the black economy, little more rationing was required. The import of the currency reform, which signalled the start of the Economic Miracle, was not lost on Brecht. It confirmed his view of a Germany divided into a bourgeois West and a proletarian East, locked antagonistically in an undeclared civil war. The Soviets countered the western currency reform with their own on 23 June and the following day the Soviet blockade of Berlin began. The USA and UK launched an airlift to supply West Berlin. It continued for nearly a year until agreement was reached to convene a conference between the foreign ministers of the four powers to discuss Germany's future. In the propaganda war the Western Allies were lauded as the saviours, the Soviets and their supporters in the SED as the villains. Without popular legitimacy, the SED leadership, weak and paranoid, would never escape this tarnished image.

Guided by his strong instinct for power, if not by any order from Stalin, in the summer of 1948 Walter Ulbricht took the currency reform as his cue to stage a power grab in the name of revolutionary socialism. With the support of the SMAD's Colonel Sergei Tulpanov, Ulbricht began to amass dictatorial powers at great speed, overriding the SED's Central Secretariat with a small Secretariat of the Politburo. He began to purge institutions, groups and individuals representing bourgeois interests, as he steered the Soviet Zone and East Berlin towards the establishment of a separate German socialist state. This state, so the argument went, effectively turning Stalin's strategy on its head, would act as a magnet for the population in the West, which would seek to join a unified, socialist Germany. However, Stalin would summon Ulbricht, Pieck and Otto Grotewohl to Moscow in December 1948 and re-affirm his strategy, after which Pieck noted: 'Path to socialism in a zig-zag'.[51] Politics and culture in East Germany would remain deeply unstable for the foreseeable future, shot through with dangerous contradictions born of the weakness of the Soviet and SED positions.

Brecht witnessed the political drama of the summer of 1948 from Feldmeilen where he enjoyed his 'first European spring for 8 years. The colours of the plant world so much fresher and less crude than in California. [...] The proliferation of wild flowers on the old civilised continent astonishes us'.[52] Unable to pursue invitations outside Switzerland, Brecht co-directed *Mr Puntila and his Man Matti* at the Zurich Schauspielhaus, though he could not be named, since he was not permitted to work. Leonard Steckel was Puntila and Teo Otto designed the set. There were enthusiastic reviews of this Brechtian comedy, which was described in the programme as Brecht's 'after stories by Hella Wuolijoki'. However, in Munich there were at once allegations of plagiarism against Brecht over this work jointly written with Wuolijoki. Some things never changed. The day after the premiere he wrote to her, asking what he should do with her portion of the royalties.[53] She replied: 'I think that at present you certainly need it more than I do – pay me some time when things are going well for you in your kingdom'. Brecht commented on the affair to Neher: 'I'm always moved if the papers don't scream for the police'.[54]

In Zurich Brecht had seen the German film idol Hans Albers in Franz Molnár's *Liliom*, describing him in his journal as a 'tall elegant fellow with a certain vulgar charm, not without a hint of violence'.[55] Brecht could use him. He and Albers reached an agreement that Albers would star as Macheath in *The Threepenny Opera* in Munich. However, during discussions with Albers that summer Brecht was not well and again succumbed to his renal problem, with it a propensity to inflammation. He was treated by the urologist Artur Schweizer. Brecht wrote to Albers: 'I am still in hospital with pyelonephritis, but I am considerably better'.[56] As we shall see, recurrence of the urological condition was becoming frequent, together with an increasing suscepti-bility to complications.

Brecht had recovered sufficiently by August to enter Germany again for the first time, travelling with Frisch and Hirschfeld to see a performance of Frisch's play *Santa Cruz* directed by Heinz Hilpert at an undestroyed Konstanz in the French Zone.[57] Thanks to the efforts of Hirschfeld, Brecht had received confirmation that he would after all receive a Swiss identity pass. Presumably, he was allowed to enter Germany for the day on that basis. Frisch describes their border crossing and their walk into the town. On the way Brecht stopped to light his cigar and, gazing upwards, observed: 'The sky is no different here!'.[58] This statement was, Frisch notes, 'accompanied by that involuntary gesture that occurred quite often: he moved his gaunt neck backwards and forwards in his collar, in a nervous twitch which relaxed him'. After the performance Brecht remained silent until they had crossed the border. He then exploded, raging at the thoughtless repetition of old ways, 'as if only their houses were destroyed, their artlessness, their rash conclusion of peace with their own country. All that worse than feared'.[59] To Frisch it sounded like a declaration of war. Brecht concluded: 'You've got to start right back at the beginning here'.

Brecht directed some of his anger at Curt Riess, who had requested of Brecht a positive assessment of his biography of Goebbels. Riess evidently had no idea that Brecht had produced his own portrait of Goebbels as Givola in *The Resistible Rise of Arturo Ui*. Divulging through wicked irony that he had not properly read Riess's book, Brecht explained that he missed

> that principal point which would immediately enthuse me to offer loud public praise, namely that G. was a bourgeois politician (i.e. the 'gifted' functionary of an especially rotten bourgeoisie). At the end, which one of course necessarily reads last, he is not in your account, say, the cornered rat, but a gangster on account of whose heroism one forgets that he is a gangster. The Lethe potion is definitely one of the things which should not be offered to the Germans.[60]

When Hilpert asked Brecht for a play of his to perform, Brecht had no hesitation in recommending *Arturo Ui*: 'The right place for it is a German stage'.[61]

While Brecht remained trapped in Switzerland, he was attracting great interest from actors and directors wishing to work with him on his new repertoire, as well as from publishers eager to have a slice of coming success. The entrepreneurial Brecht set in motion a chaotic auction of his works reminiscent of what he had done in Berlin in 1921: reach agreements with several publishers simultaneously, play them off against each other, drive up the price and close a deal on the best possible terms. In addition to Kurt Reiss in Basel, the Munich book and theatre publisher Kurt Desch joined in, as did Peter Suhrkamp, who had visited Brecht in February 1948 to discuss collaboration. Anticipating forthcoming productions, Suhrkamp lost no time in printing Brecht's plays. In the summer of 1948 an angry Suhrkamp alerted Brecht to the fact that in the Soviet Sector of Berlin Aufbau was claiming that it had been granted the rights to his works published by Wieland Herzfelde's Malik and Aurora, not just for the Soviet Zone but for the whole of Germany. Both Suhrkamp and Reiss urged Brecht to clarify the situation with a binding decision.

Unable to travel to Munich, Brecht sent Berlau there to work with his old friend Jacob Geis in negotiation with Desch. In a typical Brecht ploy, Berlau put it to Desch that he should buy a car for Brecht and charge it to his account, to be offset by royalties from production rights for *Galileo*, *Puntila* and *Schweyk*. Brecht had in mind a Steyr convertible like the one from his Berlin days. An eager Desch confirmed this arrangement to Brecht and also his agreement with Herzfelde concerning the distribution of Brecht's Malik and Aurora texts in the western zones! Meanwhile, Brecht wrote to Suhrkamp, who was due to meet Reiss in Basel, asking him to discuss with Reiss a regular payment to Brecht so that he had a secure income. Brecht made a similar request to Desch. He encouraged Herzfelde, still in the USA, to continue with the production of his collected works. Mentioning a possible partnership with Desch, he wrote to Herzfelde of his discussions with another publisher, E. Oprecht, about the resumption of the *Versuche* series. He then encouraged Suhrkamp to publish *Versuche*, telling him of his discussions with Oprecht! The chaos was almost complete. However, Suhrkamp would finally have none of it, insisting on sole rights for Germany. Suhrkamp knew when to be firm with Brecht. He held out for that position and won, publishing Brecht's collected works and *Versuche*. Aufbau would publish them under licence in the East. Berlau returned to Zurich without the Steyr.

Brecht had other unfinished business with publishers. He employed a lawyer to work with Kurt Weill's lawyer on the dissolution of Felix Bloch Erben's contract for *The Threepenny Opera*. Jacob Geis informed Bloch Erben on Brecht's behalf that at the latest since his expatriation from Germany Brecht had regarded his contract with Bloch as invalid. On the grounds that Allert de Lange had done nothing to promote *The Threepenny Novel*, Brecht sought to place that work with Desch. A legal dispute ensued, which would drag on acrimoniously and at some cost to Desch until after Brecht's death.

On 30 August Brecht received the extension of his Swiss identity pass, valid until the end of February 1949. Despite his difficulties with the authorities, Brecht continued to entertain thoughts of Switzerland as his principal domicile. However, the authorities were continuing their 'discreet' inquiries. On 7 September the Federal Attorney's office noted that 'at times persons unknown met' at Brecht's flat.[62] Noises reported by a neighbour suggested that a transmitter was being used and monitoring was ordered. Now able to leave and re-enter Switzerland until February, Brecht and Weigel, a year later than originally envisaged, planned their trip to Berlin. He alerted Hauptmann and, conceiving a similar arrangement to the earlier one with Kiepenheuer, encouraged her to write to Suhrkamp about their plans for Berlin. Barbara would remain in Zurich to continue her education, to which Brecht would make his own contribution on his return, taking her to the carnival in Basel.

New theatre, new age? *Short Organum for the Theatre*

Brecht and Weigel already had in place the essential ingredient for a triumphant return to Berlin: Weigel taking the lead in *Mother Courage* at the Deutsches Theater with Brecht directing. However, their visit was about much more, namely whether behind the flattering invitations there was substance which matched their own aspirations. For Weigel, that meant the chance to re-establish herself as one of the leading actresses on the German stage and very likely to use her formidable organisational skills to manage a theatre, which, she would later remark, Brecht had long admired.[63] It seems that he earmarked her for such a role in 'his' theatre. Weigel, not Brecht, was the organisational talent. Brecht's goal remained quite simply the realisation of his life's work through the establishment of a new theatre for a new age of reason, with his own works at the core of a repertoire performed in a new style of Brechtian realism.

Brecht's vanguardist aspirations remained a challenge to any theatrical culture. His project assumed greater urgency still, as his ill health reminded him that his life would not be long. Was a devastated Berlin – recently emerged from the depredations of Nazism and its future quite unclear under highly antagonistic military occupation – really the place for him? Brecht's political allies working in the Soviet Sector with the SED and SMAD, many of them returning émigrés like him, were negotiating the minefield of cultural politics between the unstable poles of democratic anti-Fascism and revolutionary socialism at a time when their political capital had already been much diminished in the struggle with the West. In Zurich Brecht could not properly grasp what that meant. Certainly, Ihering, who had encouraged Brecht's return, would support him, as would others, but Brecht had bitter experience of political allies who were fiercely opposed to his aesthetic experimentation. And what of the proven propensity of revolutionary socialism to engage in the authoritarian repression of the arts? At such a time of upheaval in such a place as Berlin, his project was fraught with danger. While supremely confident in his artistic ability, Brecht understood his limitations in such an environment. In the 'Danish' *Life of Galileo* he had provided the classic depiction of the unheroic intellectual, diminished in the struggle with repressive authority. Would he expose himself to such a fate in Berlin?

Following Weigel's promptings, in the summer of 1948 Brecht prepared his defences for Berlin, returning to the theoretical justification of Epic Theatre. The matter had been on his mind already in the autumn of 1946 when he re-established contact with Neher. While Brecht was still in the USA, Bentley had urged him to marshal his theoretical writings, articulated in the sprawling mass of the *Messingkauf Dialogues* and the occasional notes and pieces which had followed. It could not have been lost on Brecht that in 1945 in 'German Literature in the Age of Imperialism' Lukács had re-stated his criticism that Brecht's formal experimentations led him to miss the social point of art. Brecht had also read Ottofritz Gaillard's *The German Stanislavsky Book*. It was introduced by Maxim Vallentin and contained an appendix on amateur acting by Otto Lang, which had been published as a guide to Socialist Realism in the German theatre. Much as Vallentin had envisaged at the KPD meeting at Moscow's Hotel Lux in early 1945, following his return to Germany Vallentin founded a new acting school in Weimar with Gaillard and Lang: The Institute for the Methodical Renewal of the German Theatre.

Brecht could hardly be surprised at what his adversaries were doing, as he composed his *Short Organum for the Theatre*, passing it to Frisch for comment. A principal aim was to explain to his Muscovite opponents now in Berlin that they had nothing to fear from his theatre: it was not narrowly didactic but combined learning with pleasure in the interest of revolutionary transformation. On 18 August 1948 he noted:

> Main thesis: that a certain form of learning is the most important pleasure of our age, so that it has to occupy an important place in our theatre. This way I was able to treat the theatre as an aesthetic enterprise, which makes it easier to describe the various innovations. This means that the critical attitude to the social world no longer suffers from the blemish of being unsensual, negative, inartistic, as the ruling aesthetic would have it.[64]

By the 'ruling aesthetic', Brecht probably meant any place where the theatre of empathy dominated, i.e. virtually everywhere between New York and Moscow. The *Short Organum* is more than just a re-statement of *The Messingkauf Dialogues*. There the dialogic, open form invited further exchange about what the new theatre might look like. The *Short Organum* – the Greek organon means an instrument, tool or organ – goes further. Brecht's title alludes to Francis Bacon's attempt in his *Novum Organum* to establish his scientific method of inductive reasoning from experience in contrast to Aristotle's syllogistic system in his *Organon*. What Bacon had done for modern science, Brecht proposed to do for aesthetics, extrapolating general truths from practical experience. The *Short Organum* is simultaneously a defence of Brecht's aesthetics and an indication of experimental applications. Very deliberately mixing the language of science and aesthetics in a Baconian, aphoristic style, Brecht constructs his argument in seventy-seven numbered clauses, presenting the key elements of his experimental theatre in a framework of aesthetic theory around his main thesis: 'that a certain form of learning is the most important pleasure of our age'. The aphoristic style enables Brecht to adopt a highly promiscuous approach to logical exposition. Like other great German aphorists, Georg Christoph Lichtenberg and Friedrich Nietzsche, Brecht delights in paradox and in mixing the abstract and the material, the serious and the humorous, the cerebral and the carnal in a manner reminiscent of Galileo's pleasure in learning and appetite. Indeed, Brecht cites *Life of Galileo* repeatedly. Brecht's meditation upon that other great pioneer of the empirical method for a new age emerges as the second presiding spirit of the *Short Organum*.

Emphasising the centrality of plot in composition and staging, to some extent Brecht presents issues familiar from his earlier theoretical writings such as the channelling of emotion within distanced forms of representation, employing the A-effect, the means to reveal social causation beneath surface appearances. However, drawing upon his Marxist economic Utopianism, Brecht discusses at some length how the theatre might represent the socialist aspiration for workers to achieve genuine productivity by overcoming alienation from the means of production. The pleasure of learning in the new theatre, designed to foster critical intelligence, is equated with the pleasure of learning in a non-alienated place of work. Can the vanguardist theatre act as a microcosm, pointing the way for industrial production, just as it might act as the forum for the treatment of conflict resolution in *The Caucasian Chalk Circle*? Could freshly empowered workers seize possession of the means of production and transform the workplace into a laboratory for the new society? Alluding to Schiller's essay 'The Theatre as a Moral Institution', Brecht noted that learning was to his aesthetics what morality was to Schiller's. Alleviating that huge burden placed upon learning was a principal task in his theatrical experiment. And could workers be empowered in this way?

Brecht appended a Prologue to the *Short Organum*, a teasingly ironic composition, signalling to his old adversaries the tentatively experimental nature of his undertaking, which should not be taken as dogma, nor interpreted in the light of dogma. Referring to himself in the third person and alluding to the controversies around the *Mahagonny* opera, Brecht offered a potted history of his theatre, from its relative neglect of aesthetics in favour of social function and its denunciation of a decadent mainstream culture, the 'bourgeois narcotics trade'.[65] It was, he writes, the misrepresentation of social life in the mainstream theatre which prompted his call for precise aesthetic representation for a new scientific age of learning and his threat to 'emigrate from the realm of what is pleasing', the traditional ground of aesthetics. While during exile there had been few opportunities to test his innovations on the stage, the opportunity was now there. Citing the reflections of the great scientific pioneers Galileo, Einstein and Oppenheimer upon the relationship between scientific and aesthetic innovation, Brecht, in a delicious stroke of irony, reminded his adversaries of what was at stake by introducing his own Galileo moment: 'Let us recant, no doubt to general dismay, our intention to emigrate from the realm of what is pleasing, and let us profess, to still more general dismay, the intention to settle in this realm. Let us treat the theatre as a place of entertainment, as behoves an aesthetic, and let us investigate what sort of entertainment appeals to us!'. Let the experiment begin!

Using a Czech transit visa and a Soviet permit for Berlin, Brecht and Weigel travelled to Berlin by train. They set off on 17 October for Salzburg, which for Brecht had a 'clapped-out, exhausted feel'.[66] They met Gottfried von Einem for discussions about a contribution to the Salzburg Festival. Muscovite ghosts from the mid-1930s stalked their exchanges as they discussed the 'Russian anti-Formalist campaign'. Before his recent death, Andrei Zhdanov had initiated a fresh purge of the arts in the USSR with a renewed Campaign against Formalism. Max Frisch had told Brecht that the Campaign had been an issue at the Rally for Peace which he had attended in Wroclaw in August. There, Brecht noted approvingly, Picasso had declared that 'he too was against Formalism, the other side's Formalism'.[67] For Zhdanov's supporters and their victims it was no laughing matter.

Brecht and Weigel now entered the Eastern Bloc, travelling to Prague, where they met with Hanns and Louise Eisler. They visited Kafka's birthplace and the Jewish cemetery, Brecht noting: 'Of 37,000 Jews 800 came back after the Hitler occupation'.[68] Brecht viewed Prague, where the Czech Communists had recently staged a coup to consolidate power, differently from Salzburg: 'No exhaustion here, but that condition which looks like poverty and is usual after upheavals. Society is compelled for the first time to put its productive elements on the table for all to see and it turns out to be too little'.

Brecht, Weigel and the Eislers continued their journey by car, reaching the German border around noon on 22 October. The Kulturbund, together with the SED and representatives of the theatre, hosted a reception in Dresden. Later, Alexander Abusch appeared with two cars at the zonal border outside Berlin to take them to the Kulturbund in the Soviet Sector, where Becher, Ihering and Dudow welcomed them. As he had in Dresden, Brecht declined to speak to the press. Brecht and Weigel took rooms with other returning émigrés, among them Arnold Zweig, in the domestic wing of the grand, burnt-out Adlon Hotel near the Brandenburg Gate. From the Adlon, Brecht could just make out the ruins of Friedrichstrasse in the darkness, writing that Berlin was 'an etching by Churchill after an idea by Hitler', 'the heap of rubble outside Potsdam'.[69] Rising early the following morning, he made his way down Wilhelmstrasse to the Reich Chancellery at 6 a.m. 'to smoke a cigar down there, so to speak'.[70] He encountered 'a few workers and rubble women':

> The rubble bothers me less than the thought of what people must have gone through while the city was being reduced to this rubble. A worker shows me the way. 'How long before this looks like something again?'. 'There will be a few grey hairs before that. If we had some financiers it would be different, but we don't

have any financiers any more. So? ... good morning'. To me these ruins are a clear indication of the former presence of financiers.

The ruins of the Reich Chancellery were the ultimate representation of Brecht's vision of the modern city, destroyed by the contradictions of the economic system which had created it.

He was down to business at once, meeting Gebrüder Weiss about the publication of the model book of *Antigone* and *Tales from the Calendar*, a compilation of stories and poems. He discussed the continuation of *Versuche* with Suhrkamp's Hermann Kasack. Kasack, who had worked with Brecht for Kiepenheuer in the 1920s, found him terrific company after so many years. On the first afternoon there was a reception at the Kulturbund, at which Dimshitz welcomed Brecht on behalf of the SMAD, followed by Langhoff and Ihering on behalf of the Deutsches Theater. Brecht again remained silent: 'I've decided to find my feet and not make public appearances'.[71] He was, in fact, inhibited by the state of his teeth and took drastic action: 'Had eleven teeth pulled to make tabula rasa for dentures since I have been too much hampered in speaking lately'.[72] He met up with his old friends Walcher and Müllereisert. Müllereisert had stayed in Berlin and looked 'worn out by the apocalyptic years'.

Following up his agreement with Albers to play Macheath in Munich, Brecht explained to Weill that he had produced a new, legally distinct version of the play to circumvent Felix Bloch Erben and had arranged for Albers to tour West Germany in the spring of 1949. However, Weill responded that Brecht's changes to *The Threepenny Opera* had weakened the original and asked whether they were just for Munich. In a conciliatory letter Brecht re-assured Weill about the play and about their dispute with Bloch Erben: 'For a final settlement we shall just have to get together. Believe me that I shall do nothing contrary to your interests, nothing whatsoever, and shall always ask your opinion, not least because I'm still hoping for further collaboration with you'.[73] The Munich production would go ahead. Jacob Geis then told Brecht that Bloch Erben were asserting their rights, Brecht could either come to an agreement with the publisher or go to court. Brecht again tried to circumvent Bloch Erben, lining up Suhrkamp as a replacement and requesting the Munich Kammerspiele to pass on royalties to Geis, not to Bloch. Brecht then entered into negotiations directly with Bloch Erben, who finally accepted the dissolution of both the contract to distribute *The Threepenny Opera* of April 1928 and the general contract of May 1929.

Brecht began preparations for *Mother Courage* at the Deutsches Theater, working with a greatly aged Erich Engel. It so happened that Brecht's old Moscow adversary Julius Hay's *Have* was premiering in that theatre. *Have* was generally well received, if not by Brecht: 'Appalling performance, hysterical and stilted, totally unrealistic'.[74] Brecht and Engel altered the first scene of *Mother Courage* to prevent a repetition of the Zurich production when the audience had sympathised with the plight of the 'eternal mother creature', which was 'not really the point'.[75] Brecht began 'cautiously introducing the Epic mode in rehearsals. The scenes begin to fall into place of their own accord once the fulcrums become visible'.[76] He added: 'We really need four months of rehearsals. In these circumstances it isn't possible to make it Epic', before concluding with delightful paradox: 'You cannot burden the actors with the process of lightening everything in so short a time'.[77] Brecht noted: 'I put in ten minutes Epic rehearsal for the first time in the eleventh scene. Gerda Müller and Dunskus as peasants are deciding that they cannot do anything against the Catholics. I ask them to add "said the man", "said the woman" after each speech. Suddenly the scene became clear and Müller found a realistic attitude'.[78] By demonstrating the defeatist attitude rather than embodying it, actors in Epic Theatre invited the audience to consider alternatives without any dogmatic intervention. When Müller nonetheless complained about the Epic exercise, Brecht dismissed her in his journal as a 'crater exhausted by an excess of eruptions'.

Talking about an ensemble, taking Berlin by storm

Between rehearsals, that autumn Brecht began serious discussions with Dimshitz and other Soviet theatre officers. The SMAD, not the SED, led the initiative, supported by Becher at the Kulturbund. However, the senior SED politician Wilhelm Pieck invited Brecht, Weigel and Langhoff to his flat on 6 November, together with the leading SMAD cultural officer, Sergei Tulpanov. Key SED politicians were present, too: Walter Ulbricht, Otto Grotewohl, Anton Ackermann, who had ministerial responsibility for culture, and Paul Wandel, Head of the German Administration for Public Education. Becher attended, as did another KPD Moscow émigré, Hans Rodenberg. This turn-out could be mistaken for a serious declaration of united intent. Brecht and Weigel were not so easily taken in. The SED leadership would give initial support and Brecht's fellow poet Becher fully recognised his enormous talent, though he would tack to the SED leadership's demands. As we shall see, Langhoff had his own agenda and Ulbricht had no patience with the arts if they did not conform to the Party's agenda. Mediocre SED bureaucrats and journalists like Rodenberg, Erpenbeck and Abusch would seek to ingratiate themselves with their leader by exposing Brecht's decadent deviance, albeit in the mistaken belief, which they shared with Lukács, that Brecht was susceptible to correction over matters of literary form.

However, in the autumn of 1948 the efforts of the SMAD and the SED were directed towards wooing the master of the German stage to return to Berlin. Invited to submit his ideas, Brecht discussed with Langhoff, an unlikely ally given his more conventional aesthetic approach,

> [a] project for a *studio theatre* to be attached to the Deutsches Theater. First year: involvement of top émigré actors through short guest appearances (Giehse, Steckel, Lorre, Homolka, Bois, Gold), build up a company in conjunction with them. Three or four plays, say *Galileo* (with Kortner) or *Schweyk* (with Lorre); *Zheleznova* (Gorky) with Giehse and Steckel; a Lorca or an O'Casey. Development of Epic acting through demonstrative children's theatre.[79]

Brecht submitted his plan entitled 'Theatre Project B', 'B' probably standing for Berlin. In addition to the specific reference to Gorky's *Vassa Zheleznova*, the plan contained acknowledgement of the importance of Russian, Czech and Polish drama and reference to political education. Above all, the plan was conceived to achieve the international impact which Brecht and his sponsors craved.

At Becher's instigation, Brecht also signed an agreement with *Sinn und Form* for a special Brecht issue in a print-run of 8,000. *Sinn und Form*, edited by the poet Peter Huchel, was the new, 'all-German' journal of the Kulturbund, which would presently become the flagship of the German Academy of Arts. In the legendary special issue, which appeared in early 1949, German readers were introduced to the Brecht of the exile years through the first publication of *The Caucasian Chalk Circle*, *Short Organum for the Theatre* and an extract from *The Business Affairs of Mr Julius Caesar*. There were essays by Ihering, Ernst Niekisch and the émigré Hans Mayer, who had returned to a chair in Leipzig. Brecht talked through with Mayer line by line his essay on the plebeian tradition in Brecht's work and thanked Huchel for his efforts: 'It's really the first publication that brings me together with the Germans, apart from my own efforts. A kind of petition for entry into literature'.[80] It was the start of a highly productive relationship with the journal, which became Brecht's principal literary platform in the GDR, a key element in the defence and presentation of his aesthetic position, where he could publish when other avenues were closed.

As he reflected upon what he had witnessed in the city, where he saw contrasting approaches to its future in the western and eastern sectors, Brecht's satirical eye alighted upon the officer class at the British Club in Berlin: 'The ballroom is empty, with an old-fashioned string trio playing waltzes. A few officers and ladies are clustered round the bar. They stand stiffly, very drunk, conversing. Each guest an empire unto himself'.[81] Brecht was frustrated that the Western Allies were blocking progressive Soviet initiatives and thereby simply redirecting Fascist attitudes:

> Everywhere in this great city, where everything is always in flux, no matter how little and how provisional that 'everything' happens at the moment to be, the new German Misere is apparent, which is that nothing has been eliminated even when almost everything has been destroyed. Powerful impulses are coming from the Russians, but the Germans elect to frolic in the backwash which arises when other occupying powers try to stem this movement. The Germans are rebelling against the order to rebel against Nazism; only a few hold the view that an imposed socialism is better than none at all.[82]

Brecht was one of the few, despite the fact that he had identified the separation of the bureaucracy from the working class as a major reason for the reactionary turn of the USSR in the 1930s. His bedrock position remained that revolutionary socialism was superior to liberal democracy and that the rest was detail, which could be dealt with later, however painful the consequences.

Looking beyond Europe, Brecht considered that the revolution which was sweeping Mao Zedong to power in China was destroying old imperialist assumptions: 'In Asia huge developments are impending which the Americans simply haven't noticed'.[83] He observed, more plausibly, the 'victory of the Chinese Communists which will change the face of the world' and produced a German version of Mao's poem, 'Thoughts While Flying over the Great Wall'.[84] Mao's dialectical thought appealed to Brecht. He would presently hail China as the symbol of hope for working-class victory, contrasting that country with an exhausted Europe, where the working class had been devastated in the struggle with Fascism. However, in China as in the Soviet Union and the Eastern Bloc, bureaucratic directives and repression would in coming decades supplant revolutionary energy as the driving force in a socialist economy.

Brecht now experienced the thin end of that wedge, the first in an unending round of officious, censorious interventions by SED politicians and bureaucrats, who saw it as their responsibility to police a cultural sphere, created under the auspices of the SMAD, which enjoyed generous subsidies with lavish individual contracts for prominent figures. Quite simply, the Party expected the subsidised arts to buttress its fragile leadership. Erich Honecker, leader of the Free German Youth (FDJ) and in 1971 Ulbricht's successor as SED General Secretary, complained to Brecht about his 'Construction Song for the FDJ' with its line 'No Führer can lead us out of the mess'.[85] In Honecker's view, no one wanted to hear about Hitler and the lines could be construed as a rejection of the SED's leadership! Brecht was indeed urging people to take responsibility themselves. The SED's paranoia would only grow, as, in the eyes of a weak leadership isolated from the population, Brecht became identified with dangerously independent proletkult experimentation, which in the USSR Socialist Realism had supplanted. Brecht's struggle with the SED leadership would crystallise around the question of authority and leadership in the arts. For the dictatorial Ulbricht and his allies that was irreducibly a question of the political leadership which they, not Brecht, exercised.

On 6 January 1949 Brecht was summoned from rehearsals to discuss 'Theatre Project B' with the Mayor of East Berlin, the SED's Friedrich Ebert, the son of the SPD Reich President of the same name from the 1920s. The meeting was attended by Anton Ackermann and Hans Jendretzky, Wolfgang Langhoff, Fritz Wisten, the artistic director of the Volksbühne, and Kurt Bork, an official responsible for theatre who had worked with Brecht and Weigel during the Weimar Republic. Wisten, a Jewish survivor, had been freed from a concentration camp in 1945 and had led acclaimed productions at the Theater am Schiffbauerdamm. He was using that theatre until the Volksbühne was ready for use again.

Brecht's paper was on the same lines as his note of discussions with Langhoff.[86] It highlighted the role that an ensemble could play in 'again making Berlin Germany's cultural centre'. For a season, guest performances by foreign theatres and by great émigré actors would take place. A permanent ensemble of around twenty-five actors was needed, including a number from the USA and Switzerland. There was apparently nothing to be learnt from actors who had emigrated to Moscow. The ensemble would develop a 'realistic new performance style on the basis of modern plays', creating model productions for tours through Germany. Administratively, the ensemble would initially be attached to a large theatre like the Deutsches Theater.

The meeting which promised so much was a harrowing, hugely disappointing encounter for Brecht. Ebert was not only reluctant to support Brecht's proposal; he was very rude to him. For Brecht's part, since he had told Neher of the offers to use the Theater am Schiffbauerdamm, he had come to assume that it would be his. For Brecht, to return to Berlin meant returning to the scene of his greatest triumph. However, none of those present acknowledged any awareness of the offers. He records the discussion as follows:

The mayor said neither hail nor farewell, didn't address me once and uttered only one sceptical sentence about dodgy projects which destroy things that are already in place. The representatives of the SED (Ackermann, Jendretzky, Bork) suggested the Kammerspiele for the project, along with guest appearances at the Deutsches Theater or in Wisten's theatre. There was also talk of economies and of the need to find a home for the Volksbühne until its own theatre is restored. (This social-democratic petty bourgeois enterprise, 'every little man in his private box', has been relaunched and is churning out ham performances.) For the first time I am conscious of the foetid breath of provincialism here.[87]

Brecht had reacted very badly when told that he could not have the Theater am Schiffbauerdamm because Wisten was using it. An initial diplomatic silence about Wisten became in Brecht's journal the sarcastic dismissal of a rival. Brecht told Engel of his anger. Like everyone else, Engel knew that, in the extremely difficult circumstances of post-war Berlin, the offer was actually a very good one. Brecht had once again badly miscalculated in a stressful social situation, when his imperious attitude towards securing his interests left him blind to the virtues of compromise. The inflammatory Brecht was in need of cold presses. Bork described events in a letter to the city councillor Max Kreuziger. Whilst not concealing the scepticism of many people and the high costs involved, Bork wrote that Brecht's presence in East Berlin theatre would counteract the departure of so many prominent figures to the West.

The premiere of *Mother Courage and her Children* on 11 January demonstrated just what a force Brecht and Weigel could be. The public and critics alike greeted the production with adulation. Brecht's great anti-war statement and Weigel's stunning lead performance were the stuff of legend, the foundation of Brecht's world-wide post-war fame. The play held up a mirror to an audience who had gone to war for Hitler and supported him to the bitter end. After a first closed performance before trade unionists, Brecht recorded his pleasure at his discussions with them. In the wake of this enormous triumph, Brecht's supporters rallied to rescue the theatre project. Leading East Berlin critics Paul Rilla, Max Schroeder, Wolfgang Heise, Ihering and Wolfgang Harich hailed Brecht's success. The Soviets offered Brecht strong backing, principally Dimshitz.

However, Brecht had powerful enemies in East Berlin, too, mainly from the old Moscow camarilla, who would never accept his aesthetic experimentation. On 17 January, Erpenbeck, editor of the monthly *Theater der Zeit*, launched a broadside, not against *Mother Courage*, which he found 'glorious', but against Brecht's whole dramatic method in *Short Organum for the Theatre*. Erpenbeck argued that, in less talented hands, the approach would lead to the death of theatre. He amplified the following day in *Die Weltbühne*, where he immediately played his most lethal card, suggesting that Brecht's approach was the 'path to a decadence alien to the people'.

However, what counted in Zhdanovite Moscow did not necessarily hold in East Berlin in 1949. With Dimshitz's express consent, that same day Harich, Engel and Rilla called a meeting of Brecht's supporters. Weigel, Huchel, Langhoff, Ernst Busch, Dudow, Ihering, Legal, Dessau, Eisler, Bork and Stefan Heymann, an official in the SED Central Committee's Cultural Department, all joined Harich's 'little plot', founding a group called Friends of Bertolt Brecht. Harich fired off a ten-page missive to Ackermann, explaining, among other things, that technically and architecturally, in Brecht's eyes, the Kammerspiele were inappropriate, unlike the Theater am Schiffbauerdamm.[88] Angelika Hurwitz, who was playing Kattrin in *Mother Courage*, joined Harich in *Die Weltbühne*, rebuffing Erpenbeck's charges. However, on 12 March a Soviet intervention in *Tägliche Rundschau* under the pseudonym Susanne Altermann took things further, criticising Erpenbeck's superficiality and Harich's impetuosity, but defending Erpenbeck in so far as the contradictions in Brecht's work must be investigated. On the one hand he 'tore off the mask of war', on the other he depicted the 'drama of the people's great capitulation, which subjugated itself without a struggle to its seemingly inexorable historical fate'. The author underlined the fundamental importance of the discussion to come. Although Brecht would have dismissed the idea that his works presented an inexorable fate, he was certainly alert to their inherent contradictions, noting, 'how deeply my plays' susceptibility to misunderstanding is rooted in the plays themselves'.[89] He remained quite open to advice on that matter.

As always, Brecht was prepared for debate. His fellow playwright Friedrich Wolf, a staunch believer in the centrality of the positive hero in Socialist Realist drama, asked why there was no character in *Mother Courage* who found the answer to the problem. FDJ members asked similar questions. Brecht replied that it was not necessary to put a bellwether on stage! He noted with satisfaction that 'from the written utterances of Wolf and Erpenbeck which attempt to toe the line, it emerges that our moves against empathy, precisely because they have worked so well with a workers' audience, have caused a degree of panic'.[90] With his wonderful production Brecht had won the first round in his struggle with the custodians of Socialist Realism.

By the same token, Brecht's view had rapidly been proved correct that he needed a strong team around him. No sooner was he back in Berlin than he was in the fight he had worked so hard to avoid with the Muscovites in *Das Wort*. Prominent individuals across the range of cultural life, influential writers and directors as well as actors and critics, had come out in numbers to support him. Brecht certainly needed to see this show of support to confirm that he could embark upon the new struggle from a position of relative strength. He had seen that Berlin could be different from Moscow. However, how long would one be able to say that? The prospect of securing his own ensemble was irresistible but Brecht remained by no means convinced that he should settle in this nest of intrigue.

Nonetheless, confident that with SMAD support his proposal would be accepted, Brecht issued invitations to actors and directors to work with him in Berlin. Emphasising to Neher that for *Courage* the 'West sectors gave us as good a press as the East sector. In theatre it's still possible to work both in the East sector and the West', Brecht urged him to keep his diary free for the next season: 'Thanks to the many privileges enjoyed by artists, life here is almost normal, and the cultural climate is incomparable'.[91] He encouraged Leonard Steckel to join the project as a director: 'The audience, especially the working-class audience (we work in close collaboration with the unions and the Youth Organisation), is magnificent, as the reception of *Courage* shows. This is a place where the tradition of the Zurich exiles can really be carried on'.[92] Brecht told Kurt Weill that Lenya would be needed in Berlin. However, Weill and Lenya stayed in New York, where Weill died the following year. Brecht travelled to Leipzig to discuss his approach with Hans Mayer's working-class students in a university 'transformed'.[93] When a student asked why it was necessary to deal with old stories again and again, Brecht replied that it was to make sure such questions wouldn't have to be asked again and again.

On 30 January the SED Central Committee reached a preliminary conclusion about 'Theatre Project B': that, pending the return to the Volksbühne, Wisten would remain in charge of the Theater am Schiffbauerdamm but that theatre should be available for Brecht and Weigel's use. Seemingly reconciled, Brecht encouraged Piscator, still in New York, to join him in Berlin: 'We'll take the best of what is here, which isn't bad. (All, it goes without saying, miles above the New York level)'.[94] He explained that he was going back to Zurich to renew his papers before returning to Berlin. However, the project briefly stalled in February because, as David Barnett shows, Brecht and Wisten could not agree upon the sharing of space. Although Bork asked the Deutsches Theater to cancel all contracts in Brecht's name, he continued to work on Brecht and Weigel's behalf.[95] He briefed Kreuziger and Ebert on the Central Committee's stance in advance of a meeting with Pieck on 14 February and provided a paper for the meeting, addressing the remaining issues between Brecht and Wisten, having agreed the paper with Dimshitz. The following day Weigel talked with Langhoff and the administrative director of the Deutsches Theater. The day after, the Cultural Department of the Central Committee discussed the incorporation within the Deutsches Theater of an ensemble led by Helene Weigel. The intention was to place the ensemble within the purview of the municipality, which would provide the funds. Weigel then submitted costings to the Cultural Department so that a budget could be secured, while Brecht thanked Becher as President of the Kulturbund, without whose 'unstinting support the field of activity' that is now being created in the theatre could not have been created'.[96] In good spirits, he observed: 'Have got into the habit of leaning out of the window in the morning; the air here is so powerful. And I have almost abandoned another habit, that of reading crime stories before I go to sleep. I have hardly finished 2 or 3 in all the time here. Helli starts preparing for the theatre project'.[97] As we know from Finland and California, as well as much earlier in Berlin, the quality of the air was an index of Brecht's well-being. He noted too: 'Motto for a volume of *New Poems*: the excitement of the mountains lies behind us, before us the excitement of the plains'.[98] Tellingly, when these lines were later published, they read much more soberly: 'The travails of the mountains lie behind us. / Before us lie the travails of the plains'.[99]

Before Brecht left Berlin on 22 February, he finalised the contract with Suhrkamp and Erich Wendt for Aufbau to publish his works in the East under licence. Hauptmann had just arrived to do editorial work. In July 1949 Brecht and Suhrkamp would agree terms for Suhrkamp to employ her. However, in the event, until 1951 Hauptmann would be attached to DEFA, the East Berlin film studio located in Babelsberg. There, among other things, she represented Brecht's interests in abortive film projects, first *Eulenspiegel*, then *Mother Courage*.[100]

While Weigel stayed in Berlin, playing Courage and conducting negotiations for the ensemble, Brecht returned to Switzerland with Berlau via Prague. From Zurich Brecht wrote to Weigel: 'The *Courage* production has caused a sensation even here, where most people have read only the West Zone papers. Everyone says your success has been enormous. People are taking a real interest in the new company, all the more so as the theatre here is falling apart'.[101] He sent Weigel details of his recruitment efforts and drew up a timetable for the coming season. The ensemble would be launched with Margarete Steffin's translation of the anti-Fascist Nordahl Grieg's play about the Paris Commune, *The Defeat*. Brecht was attracted to the play by more than sentimental reasons. In Karl Marx's estimation, the workers of the Paris Commune had staged the first properly proletarian revolution, defying their own bourgeoisie as well as the occupying Prussian forces. For Brecht, who did not yet actually know Grieg's play, there was surely much to learn from this story.

While Brecht advised Weigel to take it easy with her acting and business commitments, he urged her: 'Hurry up and get a car'. He wanted that Steyr. It was a blow that he failed to secure for Berlin the services of his best male leads, Lorre, Homolka and Kortner. At first, Viertel backed off, too, but agreed after Brecht, stressing the urgent importance of the project, pleaded with him: 'Rifts are deepening, scepticism is turning to suspicion, prejudices are crystallising; mediocrities getting big jobs and forming tenacious cliques. [...] Believe me, it's really important to build up a production group. We must show that such a project can be realised. And time is running out'.[102] Vigilant following the attacks upon him, in his strategic conception for the ensemble Brecht saw a particular role for Viertel as a more conventional director steeped in psychological realism, who could be a foil for Brecht's own approach.

Weigel's work in Berlin was bearing fruit. On 23 March the Secretariat of the SED Central Committee proposed the establishment of the ensemble to the Politburo and on 1 April the Politburo adopted a resolution to proceed, thereby guaranteeing the finance. However, neither Ebert nor Kreuziger would accept responsibility on behalf of the municipality and Bork was required to return to the Secretariat. Finally, on 29 April Ulbricht signed off the foundation of the 'Helene Weigel Ensemble' with a budget for its first season of 1,125,000 marks, 340,000 marks for start-up costs and $10,000 in fees for actors from abroad. Having secured political approval from the SMAD, Ulbricht, as Barnett shows, urgently appealed to Heinrich Rau, the chairman of the German Economic Commission, to reach a decision on funding, which was now to include an annual sum of $10,000 to pay for guest actors from the West, adding that 'the political dimension of the matter' had been cleared with the Soviets.[103] On 18 May Bork sent an 'attestation' to Brecht and Weigel, confirming that Ebert and Kreuziger's refusal to accommodate the project had been circumvented:

> The Berliner Ensemble, Head Helene Weigel, is an institution of the German Administration for Public Education in the Soviet Zone of Occupation. Since the German Administration for Public Education is the legal repository of this institution, it does not need special approval by the municipality of Greater Berlin. Frau Helene Weigel is empowered immediately by the German Administration for Public Education with the establishment of the Ensemble.[104]

The Ensemble, which Brecht and Weigel at first called the New Berliner Ensemble, was placed within the purview of the supportive Wandel's education bureaucracy. Weigel signed a contract for a year in the first instance. The Berliner Ensemble was a provisional entity without the theatre which Brecht craved.

Bork addressed the issue of accommodation for Brecht and Weigel, working in tandem with his wife, Elfriede 'Blacky' Bork, whom Weigel recruited as her head of administration. Weigel rejected a flat in Berlin-Johannisthal before accepting a villa in its own grounds in Berlin-Weissensee, Berliner Allee 119, formerly a doctor's residence under the control of the Soviet Headquarters Command. Brecht advised Weigel to speak to Suhrkamp and Wendt about it: 'If we can raise the money it would be good to buy the house. *Courage* itself should bring in enough, plus the other plays. Somebody will just have to advance the money'.[105] As always, Brecht's instinct was to achieve independence and security through property, using his publishers' confidence in his extreme talent as the basis to cover costs through advances. Weigel made arrangements for their belongings to be sent to Berlin from Stockholm, Moscow and Zurich. Their Swiss friend Victor Cohen helped in Zurich and would in future act as a conduit for Brecht and Weigel to move money and goods between Zurich and West Berlin.

Suppressing the revolution: *The Days of the Commune*

Lodged at the Zurich guest house Au Bien Être, Hottingerstrasse 25, Brecht maintained his usual routine, rising early and working over coffee. As well as Berlau, Neher was there to assist him. Hauptmann would help in Berlin. Having finally read Grieg's *The Defeat*, Brecht told Weigel: 'Don't show it to anyone else, it's astonishingly bad, but I think it can be changed, I've taken lots of notes. Anyway, I now understand Engel's horror. Still the play has good roles and they could be made better. I'll cut out the petit-bourgeois nonsense and put some life into it, while sticking to the historical facts'.[106] Engel had refused to direct it, nor could Brecht tempt Piscator. In case his adaptation, *The Days of the Commune*, should not be ready, Brecht was considering launching the Berliner Ensemble with Georg Büchner's *Danton's Death*. The two works have in common not only the subject matter of what could be learnt from the failure of revolution but also an approach based on documentary montage. In Brecht's adaptation Grieg's work became little more than a point of reference for his own historical drama of the Commune. It has a special place in Brecht's work, akin to the 'Danish' *Life of Galileo*. Again, Brecht allowed himself to be guided by historical sources. The Paris Commune had become a classic subject of study in Marxist historiography. Brecht drew on accounts by Marx, Lenin, Prosper Lissagaray, Sergei Akhrem and Hermann Duncker, as well as the protocols of the meetings of the Commune and maps of the Paris area. Historians' critical analysis of events provided Brecht with the vantage point for their Epic representation.

The parallel with the 'Danish' *Life of Galileo* holds good, too, for a difficult production history that has obscured the qualities of *The Days of the Commune*. When Brecht wrote to Weigel about the nearly completed play on 23 April something had happened – probably concerns in East Berlin about the subject matter – to upset their plan to launch the Berliner Ensemble with it. In fact, as Barnett shows, the

SED leadership would remain exercised by the work, decreeing in mid–1951 that it required a 'fundamental review'.[107] Brecht suggested they begin with neither *The Days of the Commune* nor *Danton's Death* but with *Mr Puntila and his Man Matti*, 'which is much less controversial; besides the Commune play is an enormous production and if we put it in third place, we could work on it all through the season'.[108] *Puntila* was, of course, fresh in his mind from the Zurich production. The sheer scale of *The Days of the Commune* with more than forty roles clearly made it a daunting task. However, he added the following: 'I've stuck scrupulously to the truth, which as we know is not to everyone's liking'.

Faithfulness to Marxist sources counted for nothing when political interests were at stake. It was perhaps not just the reluctance of the SED leadership, like the KPD before it, to reflect critically and openly upon the failures of the revolutionary Left. Other objections could be raised, not least along the lines of Honecker's recent intervention over 'Construction Song for the FDJ': a work showing the proletariat without strong, unified leadership might undermine the SED's own. Another possible angle was that the SED's promotion of itself as the champion of peace and German unity precluded the representation on the Berlin stage of irreconcilable differences in a civil war between a revolutionary Left and a reactionary Right, supported by an occupying power. The analogy could be readily drawn with the deepening split between the proletarian East of Germany and the bourgeois West. According to that logic, the Western Allies occupied the role of Bismarck and his Prussian forces in cahoots with the bourgeoisie, the Soviets that of the International.

In *The Visions of Simone Machard* Brecht had, of course, already represented the Marxist position that in order to secure its material interests the bourgeoisie would be prepared to sacrifice its unpropertied compatriots by cutting a deal with the occupying forces of a bourgeois power. According to that view, essentially the same scenario was being enacted in a divided Germany where there was an acute danger of a latent civil war escalating within the broader East-West confrontation. In 1918–19, following German defeat, Brecht had, of course, witnessed the civil war between the revolutionary Left and government forces. Undoubtedly, he saw parallels in the present situation. To revisit the Paris Commune was an opportunity to learn lessons for an effective defence of revolutionary achievements. Analysis of the failings of the Communards could assist the proletarian East in resisting the power of a resurgent bourgeois West.

The principal failings of the Communards in Brecht's dramatic documentary are their inability to secure control of the Bank of France and their reluctance, on humanitarian grounds, to attack the bourgeois enemy of the government forces and officials who have retreated to Versailles. Instead, the Communards spend their time debating how a truly democratic state might look on the threshold of a new age. The key figure in Brecht's dramatisation is Pierre Langevin, who recognises these mistakes and criticises the Communards' naive notion of freedom from a Leninist perspective: 'We should have been prepared [...] to forgo personal freedom until the freedom of all had been achieved'.[109] He does not enlarge upon how the freedom of all could be achieved. As we know, Brecht's answer elsewhere was through socialist productivity. While the Commune prevaricates, the government forces re-group, using funds from the Bank to pay Bismarck in exchange for the return of 200,000 French prisoners-of-war, who are used to smash the Commune. The play ends with the bourgeoisie on the walls of Versailles, watching the slaughter through opera glasses.

Brecht's message for the present day would have been loud and clear: a highly inflammatory call to Leninist-Spartacist insurrection in a divided Berlin. Political events would, of course, unfold over the coming forty years in which the bourgeois West would defeat the proletarian East in a proxy economic war. However, by late April 1949 Brecht was aware of the play's unacceptability, even if he did not yet properly grasp the highly defensive mind-set of the SED leadership. Brecht the anxious, covert operator now took over. After delaying its production once more, he would claim to Bentley: 'I've made no attempt to bring out parallels between Paris in 1871 and Berlin in 1949, even where that would have greatly simplified the play'.[110] Now quite uncertain, Brecht sent *The Days of the Commune* for comment to his historian friends Albert Schreiner and Hermann Duncker, writing to the latter: 'There are probably terrible errors. It was very difficult to present simultaneously the errors and the greatness of the Commune. I am very much in need of your advice'.[111] The comedy *Puntila* would prove a much safer production with which to launch the Berliner Ensemble as Brecht attempted to adjust his ambitions to the political reality. The revolutionary attitudes which he had been honing in Zurich in 1948 were not wanted in Berlin in 1949. *The Days of the Commune*, controversial in the best Brechtian manner, remained quite unknown during his lifetime.

Brecht's efforts to renew his Swiss papers in Zurich failed. With that, any thought of establishing Switzerland as his principal domicile had to be abandoned. Brecht again turned to Gottfried von Einem, with whom he was corresponding about a piece for the Salzburg Festival, *Salzburg Dance of Death*. Brecht suggested that much better than an advance for that work, which in fact never materialised, would be an Austrian passport, which did. He explained that Weigel, born in Vienna, might be repatriated and wondered whether he could get an Austrian passport as her husband. Furthermore, 'I can't settle in one part of Germany and be dead for the other part'.[112] As Brecht explained to Weigel, an Austrian passport would enable them to keep links to as many German theatres as they needed: 'Then we could work wherever we pleased'.[113] Equally, Brecht was not prepared to grant production rights if he could not enter a particular zone to supervise difficult works. Von Einem pursued the matter and by 20 April Brecht was writing to the authorities in Salzburg to request papers, indicating that he intended to regard himself as an Austrian citizen and to make Austria, specifically Salzburg, his permanent place of residence. He laid it on thick, attending the Austrian consulate in Zurich wearing a strange blue hat and a tie and telling the authorities that in Austria he could find an atmosphere conducive to his work, particularly at the Salzburg Festival and Vienna's Burgtheater. When references were requested, Brecht named Kurt Horwitz of the Basel Stadttheater, Oskar Wälterlin of the Zurich Schauspielhaus and Albert Einstein of Princeton.

These names did the trick. Brecht left Zurich on 24 May, travelling with his daughter Barbara to Salzburg. At the border he received an Austrian residence permit and registered with the authorities, using von Einem's address, Mönchberg 17. In his future correspondence with the authorities, Brecht gave von Einem's address as his permanent Austrian residence. The matter of citizenship would be decided in Brecht and Weigel's favour in April 1950, despite a hostile press campaign. The press then turned on von Einem, their vicious denunciation leading to his dismissal from his post.

Brecht and Barbara left Salzburg for Prague, and after three days in Prague they took the train to Jütebog. Weigel collected them and drove them to Berlin. Dimshitz and other first-wave SMAD cultural officers were gone, summoned back to Moscow. When he learned of Dimshitz's departure, Brecht asked Weigel: 'Who's going to help us now?'.[114] He opted for papers as a stateless person.[115]

The Quest for Acclaim: Issues of Authority 1949–51

Domicile Berlin

Children's voices, radio music, rustling leaves, trams, twittering of birds. The packing cases arrived from Stockholm, not much of the furniture, most of the books. From Moscow the manuscripts Grete left. The luggage from Switzerland is still on the way. *Courage* is still a sell-out at the Deutsches Theater. Helli has office space at the Möwe, an ensemble has been put together.[1]

Brecht conveyed his upbeat mood to his journal after just a few days back in Berlin. He and Weigel had been re-building a life there at great speed, hand-picking a group of talented and loyal people in their quest to re-establish Berlin as the leading German centre for the theatre. The Berliner Ensemble was Brechtian collaboration on a grand scale, some sixty people, giving undreamt-of opportunities to artists, particularly young talent, emerging from the war and burnt-out cities. They would quickly become aware that they were involved in something very special indeed.

However, part of Brecht remained firmly anchored in the world of the refugee. He hung his 'No masks and picture scroll representing the Doubter' in his house in Weissensee, which he viewed through mistrustful eyes: 'Even now / On top of the cupboard containing my manuscripts / My suitcase lies.'[2] Such feelings would never leave him. Four years after the defeat of Nazism, Germany remained a sinister place, where everyday life could yield up terrifying reminders of the horror. For Brecht and other refugees of the German Left, it was not just the legacy of Nazism but also that of vicious in-fighting which had plumbed the depths in the Great Terror, when betrayal had been the price of survival. Brecht now learned that survivors of the Terror in the SED elite wished to award him a National Prize along with Johannes R. Becher and Heinrich Mann. However, whilst theirs would be first class, his would be second. He let it be known through Weigel that he would have to reject a second-class prize: 'I would consider that kind of classification harmful.'[3]

Brecht's health remained poor, the urological condition by now a persistent problem. He had an appointment on 22 June at St. Hedwig's Hospital, a Catholic foundation on Grosse Hamburger Strasse. As always, he sought out a top consultant, Germany's leading urologist Ferdinand Hüdepohl, who also held a teaching appointment at

the Charité. It seems Brecht did not know that in the Germany of the Third Reich
Hüdepohl had from 1934 been a member of the SS and that in 1939 he had replaced
his Jewish boss at St. Hedwig's, Alexander von Lichtenberg, who had made the
Urological Department the biggest and most modern in Europe.[4] It could have been
a scene from *Fear and Misery of the Third Reich*. It is an extraordinary thought that
only days after his return from exile Brecht unwittingly entrusted his sickly body to
this former SS man. Always anxious about resurgent Nazism, Brecht would later write
verses such as 'The One-Armed Man in the Undergrowth': 'He straightens himself,
holds up his hand to feel / If it's raining. Hand upraised / The dreaded SS man'.[5]
Hüdepohl became Brecht's trusted physician for the next seven years when Brecht
worked hard to secure his future in East Berlin. In 1953, he supported Hüdepohl's
nomination as Doctor of the People of Outstanding Merit and in 1955 he proposed to
Grotewohl that Hüdepohl be awarded a coveted individual contract. In fact, Hüdepohl
had no intention of moving to East Berlin from West Berlin where he had a private
practice and, from 1956, an appointment at the Franziskus Hospital.

Upon his first examination of Brecht Hüdepohl reported that the urological
condition was serious, a complication arising from Brecht's susceptibility to pyelonephritis and kidney stones. Brecht was suffering from a urethral stricture with
pronounced inflammation of the prostate gland. Such a stricture is normally due to
scar tissue, which narrows the urethra. In turn, the narrowing causes a build-up of
urine in the prostate, which could trigger prostatitis. It is likely that Brecht's urethral
calculus of 1934 contributed to the scar tissue. Hüdepohl recommended that Brecht
should only be treated in hospital and explained that he had refrained from a further
examination out of fear of infection. He admitted Brecht to St. Hedwig's for three
weeks to address the stricture and related issues.

The procedure to deal with a stricture is to widen the urethra either by passing a
bougie into it or by performing an urethrotomy, a surgical operation. Yet even with
surgery, a stricture tends to recur and treatment has to be repeated periodically. As we
shall see, the complaint persisted, with inflammation of the prostate and also of the
renal pelvis, which plagued Brecht during his remaining years, triggering complications, which finally contributed to the steep deterioration of his health and his death.
Brecht consulted Hüdepohl regularly during these years. There is no indication that
the specialist urologist Hüdepohl was aware of Brecht's cardiac problem, which from
May 1951 would be on record at the Charité.

As he had in 1948 in Zurich, Brecht spent the summer recuperating. Feuchtwanger,
a fellow sufferer with whom Brecht had corresponded about his complaint in 1934,
heard from Zweig of Brecht's problem and wrote to console him.[6] By late August he
was well enough to drive to South Germany with Berlau. It was his first opportunity
to return to Bavaria, just days after the first general election in the western zones
when the Rhinelander Konrad Adenauer's Christian Democratic Union (CDU), in
conjunction with its Bavarian sister party, the Christian Social Union (CSU), emerged
ahead of Kurt Schumacher's SPD as the leading grouping in a coalition government in
the Bundestag with the liberal Free Democratic Party (FDP). Already seventy-three,
Adenauer would remain in office until 1963, an extremely effective Chancellor who
established the political culture of what became a respected liberal-democratic state.

While the Bundestag began its work in Bonn, the SMAD and the SED responded with the foundation of the German Democratic Republic (GDR) in October 1949. Elections would take place in 1950, restricted to a carefully controlled list of candidates in a National Front of 'block' parties led by the SED. As General Secretary of the SED Central Committee and Chair of the Secretariat of the Politburo, Ulbricht was confirmed as the major power-broker. Otto Grotewohl became the Minister President and Chair of the Council of Ministers, while Wilhelm Pieck was the state President. Brecht congratulated Pieck, sending him a 'little poem, which might far more aptly be spoken by you than by its author'.[7] Brecht's title 'To my Countrymen', plays on Pieck's habit of opening his speeches with the words 'My countrymen'. The poem is a plea to fellow Germans to reject war and embrace peace:

You men, reach for the spade and not the knife.
You'd sit in safety under roofs today
Had you not used the knife to make your way
And under roofs one lives a better life.
I beg you, take the spade and not the knife.

On the trip south, Brecht's first destination was Salzburg where he met von Einem and dealt with passport formalities. He then drove to Munich to meet Geis, Desch, Giehse and Kortner, before visiting Albers at Lake Starnberg. The Munich production of *The Threepenny Opera* had taken place in April with Albers as Macheath. They discussed the touring production but could not agree and that fell through. Augsburg was the next stop. There Brecht was united with Pfanzelt, who was 'still the same'. Brecht viewed the ruined city from the Perlach Tower where he had served as a schoolboy in 1914.[8] Augsburg, which Brecht had described to Benjamin in exile as 'that shithole', was 'somewhat damaged, strange, leaves me cold'. On a postcard to Giehse he described the city as 'unchanged by bombardment'.

Launching the Berliner Ensemble

While the Deutsches Theater mounted guest performances of *Mother Courage* in the West German cities of Braunschweig and Cologne, Brecht returned to Berlin to lead his new team at the Berliner Ensemble. In mid-September he began rehearsals with Erich Engel for *Mr Puntila and his Man Matti*. Neher joined them shortly after. Leonard Steckel was Puntila and Erwin Geschonneck Matti. Heinz Kuckhahn and Benno Besson were Brecht's assistants, while Dessau supplied the music. For this inaugural production of the Berliner Ensemble on 12 November 1949, Picasso's 'Dove of Peace', which Picasso had drawn that year for the Paris International Peace Conference, was sewn on the curtain. Brecht wrote: 'The Berliner Ensemble has taken Picasso's valiant 'Dove of Peace' as its emblem: the site of knowledge of human nature, of social impulses and of entertainment'.[9] It remains the emblem of the Ensemble today. *Puntila* was very well received: there were many curtain calls and the play was hailed for its renewal of German comedy. Brecht noted that members of the government 'joined in the laughter and applause' and Brecht praised Weigel's achievement as 'an indescribable effort in this city of ruins'.[10] Brecht's co-author Hella Wuolijoki saw the production and stayed with Brecht and Weigel. Meanwhile, Viertel led rehearsals for Gorky's *Vassa Zheleznova*, which premiered on 23 December, again to great acclaim. Whilst acknowledging Brecht's successful opening, in the official SED newspaper, *Neues Deutschland*, Erpenbeck enquired sarcastically where the Epic Theatre was. Brecht wrote in his journal: 'It is of course only as Epic as they can take (and we can offer) today. [...] But when will the real, radical Epic Theatre come into being?'.[11] Erpenbeck probably knew as well as Brecht that the Epic Theatre of *The Days of the Commune* was in Brecht's drawer.

For the moment, Brecht accepted that his efforts to create a new theatre had to proceed differently from the experimentation proposed in *Short Organum*, practised in *Antigone* and envisaged for *The Days of the Commune*:

> The *Short Organum* comes at a time when theatres in progressive countries are being mobilised for the production of qualities needed by the state. The act of empathy is centred on the hero of labour etc. His primitiveness is what recommends him: but in fact he also makes the whole enterprise primitive. This means the choice of genre is now important. Most subjects of a state-building nature tend to fall under the heading of comedy.

Brecht certainly took into account the needs of the state at this time of upheaval. However, he could not be so primitive: his efforts to depict a hero of labour, Hans Garbe, would fail. After the debate over *Mother Courage* and the deferral of *The Days of the Commune*, Brecht was aware that the state builders would rather not see the enactment of potentially tragic conflict affecting the new society. Comedy, which could reconcile the sharp ends of conflict, was the safer choice, which, he thought, would enable him to sidestep the controversy surrounding his depiction of 'negative' characters. He would devote much energy to the comic but would often stray from safer modes as his gift for parody and satire took over.

As his first half-year back in Berlin ended, Brecht passed a hand-written note to Weigel: 'Thank you for a good year, about which you were the greatest thing'.[12] That autumn Brecht had finally bought his Steyr convertible, the Ministry for Public Education had confirmed that it wished the Berliner Ensemble to continue the following season, and Erpenbeck had given Brecht a collection of his essays and reviews with the dedication: 'Despite everything – most sincerely and with true esteem'.[13] That would not be his last word. What is more, an openly hostile Langhoff refused to extend the Berliner Ensemble's use of the Deutsches Theater, jeopardising its future. Bork was left to find an alternative, initially mooting the Comic Opera where Walter Felsenstein was the artistic director. Brecht and Weigel rejected the SED Central Committee's proposal that the Berliner Ensemble should rehearse in the House of the Culture of the Soviet Union and perform in a range of theatres. Pieck then informed Weigel that the arrangement with Langhoff would continue, together with more guest performances. However, Weigel responded that this was a much worse prospect for the year to come and Brecht drafted a letter of protest.[14] As Barnett shows, the dispute rumbled on, Langhoff writing to Wandel in March 1950 to justify his position and to offer his resignation, which was not accepted.[15] Meanwhile, Weigel approached Pieck and Wandel, whom she told of Brecht's refusal to put in any more effort when the prospect was of closure.[16]

At this stage, Brecht and Weigel were able to draw upon sufficient support at the highest level to avert the threat. The Central Committee granted the Berliner Ensemble use of the Kammerspiele and funds to build a rehearsal stage. The understanding was that things would stay that way until Wisten moved to the Volksbühne. However, relations with Langhoff did not settle. Brecht and Weigel were probably unaware of Langhoff's own weak position. An SED member, he was suspected of links during his Swiss exile to Noel Field, the US citizen and Soviet spy whom the Hungarians detained in 1949, claiming that he had run a ring of anti-Soviet agents during and after the war. Following Field's arrest, the first post-war show trials took place in Budapest and Prague, triggering panic as the spectre of the Great Terror stalked the Eastern Bloc. However, Langhoff retained his position and continued to disrupt the work of the Berliner Ensemble. After a conversation with him, Weigel left Stefan Heymann of the SED's Central Committee in no doubt about the 'difficult situation' for the Berliner Ensemble: she could give no guarantees about three forthcoming productions at the Kammerspiele, given the limited rehearsal times available.[17] Weigel took the matter to Ulbricht, explaining that rehearsal times were being cut at the Deutsches Theater before the new rehearsal stage was ready. Following Ulbricht's intervention, the rehearsal stage was ready for the autumn of 1950.

Brecht had his own worries. Despite the clamour from many quarters, he would not permit unrestricted productions of *Mother Courage*. He was anxious to avoid misunderstandings about his approach in a Germany where, he believed, the theatres were still so much under Nazi influence and where his theatre must be distinguished from otherwise dominant 'empathy' theatre and the Stanislavskian method. His insistence upon control extended to the requirement that a model book should be used as guidance in productions of his works and that his assistants should attend rehearsals. He sent Berlau to direct *The Mother* in Leipzig where he joined her for final rehearsals before the premiere on 15 January 1950, the anniversary of Rosa Luxemburg's murder. As Laura Bradley points out, this was no coincidence: the programme contained Brecht's poem to Luxemburg and Karl Liebknecht, together with an essay by Hans Mayer, 'Karl and Rosa'.[18] In the attempt to revive audience interest in the revolutionary tradition, the production replicated agitprop elements from 1932. While there was much critical praise, one reviewer contended that Brecht's 'Marxist advocacy of self-reliance filled spectators with dread'.[19] What is more, the SED official Hans Kaufmann took Brecht aside to warn him of the Party's difficulties with the play's avant-gardism and sectarianism. Far from seeking to revive popular interest in the revolutionary tradition, the SED leadership wished to overcome citizens' hostility to its rule by highlighting its capacity to create German unity and by presenting the Russian people in a benign light in a work by a Russian author. The SED had a mountain to climb. The legacy of Nazi propaganda against Bolshevism remained strong, compounded by the Red Army's orgy of rape and destruction on its march through Germany to Berlin.

When Berlau's Leipzig model transferred to Schwerin, where Hanns Anselm Perten directed, Brecht reflected in early April, 'how difficult it is to transfer humour and grace. Her model is like a straitjacket, which of course greatly hinders its appeal to the public'.[20] Brecht negotiated the minefield of East German cultural politics by highlighting humour and grace rather than agitprop. What is more, the prescription of a Brechtian model caused anger and resentment in many quarters. A West German press campaign began against Brecht the theatre 'dictator'. In time, the call would go out for a boycott of Brecht's works on account of his alleged justification of Stalin's crimes in his support for the Soviet Union. The campaign was no less astonishing than the one which would presently be launched against him in the East.

Berlau, charged with creating a model book for the production of each work, had moved into a generously sized flat in a central location, Charitéstrasse 3. She was, however, consumed by jealousy that not she but Weigel was sharing the limelight with Brecht. Not only that, he was, of course, the centre of attention for other women in Berlin theatre. She began to abuse him verbally. He at first deflected the attacks, suggesting that they forget the very nasty things she had said and apologising for making her work so hard. She then launched a venomous attack on Weigel, telling her that in the exile years she had pitied her but not now: 'You are playing (although not epically but dramatically) the lead in *Courage*. You are leading Brecht's theatre, you have a house, a car'.[21] Requesting money in return for her expenditure on Brecht and his daughter Barbara, Berlau demanded that Weigel keep Brecht out of their altercation: 'Leave him in peace, he's got to get better'. She added that Brecht was under-nourished and that *she* would cook for him. This sorry tale continued with Brecht sending a messenger to Berlau with the request that she return his daughter's red shoes and Berlau replying that she had given the shoes to the poor but would retrieve them.[22]

He declined to visit her in her hostile and agitated state. She requested a contract as the head of the literary and photographic archive at the Berliner Ensemble and another for the production of the model books. Her psychological state declined and on 2 March Brecht accompanied her to the Charité where she spent three weeks in the Neurological Department. She claimed that she had become agitated because he had not wanted her at rehearsals, adding that she felt she was five years too old for him. In fact, she had disrupted rehearsals in a drunken state and had been ejected. Brecht could do no more than appeal to her sense of the '*third thing*', 'the personal and the private recede into the background. The *third thing* is socialism', adding, 'Let's pretend we have only just met and try to be nice to each other'.[23] This emancipated woman working for the revolution would just have to get used to not always being centrally involved in his daily life. Weigel and Brecht met Berlau's contractual demands. However, she would not be able to live on her income from these sources, even though it was more than adequate by East Berlin standards. Brecht and Weigel would have to pick up the tab.

Institution-building: The Academy of Arts

Notoriously the great iconoclast, Brecht was putting much energy into the creation of elite cultural institutions in East Berlin alongside the Berliner Ensemble. He put relatively little, by contrast, into mass organisations like the Kulturbund and the Writers' Union. He was already developing a productive relationship with *Sinn und Form*, whose editor Peter Huchel later recalled Brecht saying that the Berliner Ensemble and *Sinn und Form* were the GDR's 'best visiting cards'.[24] Brecht recognised, too, the opportunity afforded by the plan to replace the discredited Prussian Academy of Arts with a German Academy of Arts, the title of which stressed the 'all-German' character of the mooted institution. When told of the plans, Brecht had remarked to Arnold Zweig, who became the inaugural President after the death of the President-designate Heinrich Mann: 'This Academy, I hear, will pay salaries, procure flats, and even enable certain members to obtain grants for young artists and writers, and I've been hearing a good deal lately about real need among young people. So there would really be some point in this Academy'.[25] The prospect of a working institution with funds rather than a representative showcase appealed to Brecht, who added pointedly: 'We should get the most modern people for the modern arts'. Brecht understood that, if structured and financed appropriately and populated with the 'most modern people', the Academy could exert influence in a difficult environment in which the SED's cultural nationalism was scarcely attuned to modernist attitudes. The ageing Brecht clearly envisaged that the Academy could contribute to his legacy if young artists and writers could work with him, just as he was cultivating new talent at the Berliner Ensemble. In addition to his assistants at the Berliner Ensemble, he would assemble a small group of Meisterschüler [pupils of the master], drawing on state support. Brecht attended preparatory meetings with other founding members of the Academy including Eisler, Weigel, Ernst Legal, Langhoff, the painter Otto Nagel and the composer Ernst Hermann Meyer. There was no built-in SED majority at the outset in this institution founded on the basis of artistic excellence. A number of the 'most modern people' became academicians and Brecht's close allies. A member of the Literature Section, Brecht also attended the Section for Performing Arts and joined the group charged with drafting statutes. The 'all-German' *Sinn und Form* was adopted as the Academy's journal. These were major cultural resources alongside the Berliner Ensemble. Brecht sought to promote them through the suggestions which in the poem 'I Need No Gravestone' he had long seen as integral to his legacy:

> I need no gravestone, but
> If you need one for me
> I would like it to bear these words:
> He made suggestions. We
> Carried them out.
> Such an inscription would
> Honour us all.[26]

The Minister President Otto Grotewohl delivered the Academy's inaugural address in March 1950, proclaiming it as the 'supreme institution of the German Democratic Republic in the field of the arts'.[27] This statement would come back to haunt Grotewohl when Brecht and his supporters took him at his word. Turning to the principal political issue at stake, Grotewohl warned that the Academy's efforts should be directed against Formalism and Cosmopolitanism, the decadent, modernist art of the imperialist West. As the Academy's administrative director Rudolf Engel later acknowledged, none of the founding members remotely shared Grotewohl's Zhdanovite view. However, his words also conveyed a naked threat to the GDR's own artistic elite, with discernible anti-Semitic undertones, in the climate of intrigue and denunciation sweeping the Eastern Bloc. Under the Jewish Arnold Zweig's leadership, the Academy would, as far as possible, ignore the SED's anti-Formalist agenda. To the Party's annoyance, it operated more as a representative body than as a working institution. Brecht would, in fact, not condone Zweig's politically ineffectual leadership. Already at its Third Party Conference in 1950, the SED's frustration with 'its' artists and intellectuals came to the fore when the SED leadership, in strikingly rebarbative language, accused them of failing to recognise that the 'construction of a progressive German culture could only be undertaken in a relentless struggle against the theories of Cosmopolitanism hostile to the people, against bourgeois objectivism and against American cultural barbarism'.[28] In time-honoured fashion, the struggle would presently be directed not only against the enemy in the West but also against the insidious enemy within, whose alien form only the most vigilant could discern. The SED bureaucracy was spawning a network of agencies to supervise culture. 'Prussian' socialism knew no other way.

Already in March 1950 Brecht found his work the subject of censorship when a body called the Cultural Advisory Board for Publishing forbade the publication of his *War Primer*, arguing that, in its generalised pacifist stance, it did not have enough to say against imperialist warmongers. Grotewohl endorsed the ban. This bureaucratic approach was different from the public debate surrounding the anti-war *Mother Courage*. The authorities were also examining another of Brecht's anti-war pieces, *The Trial of Lucullus*, which he had written in 1939 and recast as an opera with music by Dessau. On 25 March Bork recommended the work to the Cultural Department of the SED's Central Committee. At this stage, no objection was made to Brecht's text but Dessau's music was still to be examined by 'reliable comrades'.[29] Permission was granted to perform *The Trial of Lucullus* at the State Opera in the coming season.

The government now decreed that the Cultural Commission from the Ministry of Public Education should join the Academy in its work. Brecht questioned this decree and presented a paper to the Literature Section, proposing that the state should invest the Academy with the power to adjudicate upon questions of aesthetics and impact concerning decisions to ban publications, performances or exhibitions of works of art. The Literature Section re-affirmed that the Academy was, as Grotewohl had put it, the GDR's supreme institution in the field of the arts. As a member of the group charged to write the statutes of the Academy, Brecht ensured that these words were enshrined in the draft which was presented to the government. Ratification of the statutes would become a source of bitter dispute, dragging on for years. The struggle over the statutes exemplifies the broader struggle over cultural policy, in which Brecht would use the Academy as an instrument to defend and promote his artistic interests and those of fellow academicians in the face of attacks from the SED leadership and its officials.

Only a year after returning to Berlin, Brecht was, just as he had feared, exercised by bureaucratic interference in artistic production. That process, he noted, required sensitive treatment:

> When it comes to planning in the arts, you have to proceed very carefully. The
> techniques – and one needs techniques – cannot just be separated from the social

functions which they have. And you rarely get masterpieces from people who are keeping their heads down – yet masterpieces are what is needed. [...] On the whole the less said about stylistic matters the better. And, if the artists are to be won over, it is better to show that you do not understand them (even if you are prepared to learn), than to attack them. In the arts as in sleeping together, need is the seducer, but, just as when you are sleeping with someone, there must be no hard words.[30]

There would be many hard words and relationships of all sorts would be damaged by petty officials who had little time for such subtleties.

Brecht recognised that the Academy's bureaucratic arm was the route to engage the state bureaucracy in pursuit of his interests. In the struggle with Langhoff, the administrative director Rudolf Engel sent a letter to the Minister of Public Education, describing the achievements of the Berliner Ensemble and presenting the proposal of the Academy that the Ensemble should be permitted to use the Deutsches Theater and the Kammerspiele.[31] The Academy invited consideration that the Ensemble might be given the re-built Lessing Theatre. Brecht went on the offensive in the Academy, too, arguing that Vallentin's Stanislavskian Theatre Institute in Weimar should be subjected to a close inspection because its graduates did not possess necessary expertise.[32]

Charting realism with the Berliner Ensemble

Brecht greatly enjoyed the first May Day parade in Germany's new socialist state:

> Glorious day. Watch the demonstration at the Lustgarten from the stands. At the front the Free German Youth with blue shirts and flags, and companies of the people's police. Then an hour-long procession of machines, wagons, exhibitions of clothes etc on lorries, pictures and banners. The demonstrators amble along, as if they were going for a walk and stop briefly in front of the stands. As the Chinese participant is speaking doves are released. (Not far away an American helicopter circles over the counter-demonstration beyond the Brandenburg Gate.) An astonishingly large number of districts of West Berlin are represented, in spite of the pressure from over there. The BE rolls by on its lorry, Barbara sitting in Courage's wagon and waving a red flag. Helli is greeted in every street, women hold up their children. 'That's Mother Courage!'.[33]

Brecht was moved to write the lines:

> The theatre of the new age
> Was opened, when onto the stage
> Of a destroyed Berlin
> Courage's wagon rolled
> And six months later
> In the demonstration of 1 May
> Mothers showed Weigel
> To their children and
> Praised peace.[34]

German mothers should never again allow politicians to take their children to make war.

Max Frisch was staying with Brecht and Weigel that May Day. He felt out of place as a westerner at a reception hosted by the Berliner Ensemble, unable to respond to a rather forced demonstration of eastern largesse. Frisch felt that he and Brecht were living in different worlds. However, when Frisch saw Brecht's adaptation of J. M. R. Lenz's *The Tutor or The Benefits of Private Education* that evening, 'It was a shock. For the first time I see what theatre is'.[35] After deferring *The Days of the Commune* for the second time, Brecht had chosen historical material which, if less obviously so, contained great explosive force. He rapidly produced his adaptation of Lenz's macabre tragi-comedy of 1774, with few additions of his own but many cuts and alterations. With *The Tutor*, Brecht embarked upon his first production for the Berliner Ensemble of a work from the German classical era. However, his choice of *The Tutor* was quite deliberately at variance with the official view of that era. Lenz was a peripheral, tragic figure in an age in which Goethe and Schiller became pre-eminent, idealised as the epitome of a humanist culture. Aiming rather to uncover the roots of realism in the German theatre, which provided the inspiration for his own work, Brecht had returned to what he saw as its Shakespearean beginnings in the Sturm und Drang, the iconoclastic artistic movement of the 1770s when this brilliant, young generation of dramatists transformed the German theatre in an Age of Genius,. He saw Lenz's little-performed play as leading back 'in a direct line to the German classics, which derive from Shakespeare, and can therefore be used as a preliminary study for a new way of doing Shakespeare's plays'.[36] Shakespeare remained for Brecht the measure of peerless dramatic excellence, the great forerunner of Epic Theatre.

Brecht had had the play 'at the back of my mind for a long time'.[37] In an essay on realism in 1940 he had described Lenz's pitiful tutor Läuffer as a tragic figure. However, in the same year he had re-written *The Tutor* as a sonnet, one of a number of brilliantly irreverent, satirical 'Studies', in which Brecht concludes of Läuffer, a 'trans-Rhenanian Figaro': 'His gut may rumble, but he knows his station. / He cries, groans, curses, opts for self-castration'.[38] While Beaumarchais's Figaro, like Brecht's servant Matti in *Puntila*, is a master of triumphant subservience, Läuffer is an abject lackey, a victim of German Absolutism. Noting that 'the grand style has come down to us only in connection with idealistic themes', Brecht drew Hans Mayer into the discussion of the play's historical importance: 'The play is a true *comedy*, and it is characteristic that the classical authors totally neglected this realistic genre. (*The Broken Jug* may be an exception, but it is also Kleist's most realistic work and interestingly enough it too, like *The Tutor* is a parable.)'.[39] Kleist's *The Broken Jug* would follow.

Rather than employing the interpretative prism of classical humanism promoted by the SED, in his quest for realism Brecht highlighted an alternative reading of German history, what Marx and Engels had called the German Misere. By this, they meant the wretched course of German history in which the German people had failed to complete their historic, revolutionary mission, be it through the Peasants' War of 1524–6 or the 1848 Revolution. Brecht noted of *The Tutor*: 'It is to my knowledge the earliest depiction of the German Misere, and very sharp at that. [...] Here a man, in order to remain socially acceptable, has to be physically emasculated'.[40] Läuffer castrates himself after seducing his charge, Major von Berg's daughter Gustchen.[41] With its drastic symbolism, *The Tutor* initiated Brecht's critical interrogation of the German Misere, which, for Brecht, had reached its nadir in Nazism. In approaching the roots of realism on the German stage in this way, Brecht was challenging the custodians of Socialist Realism such as Erpenbeck and Wolf. In their grossly simplified understanding, deriving from Lukács's writings, German Classicism was the antecedent of Socialist Realism, the cultural high point of an inviolable humanist heritage. Furthermore, in the strange world of the SED's cultural nationalism, German Classicism was heralded for its power to unite all Germans in the face of division driven by the West.

Benno Besson, Egon Monk, and Peter Palitzsch did preliminary work on the production with Brecht, who was pleased with the choice of the play 'for the actors to practise the realistic, and simultaneously the grand style. This is the way to Shakespeare, the way back to him; this much of him was understood in Germany'.[42] Brecht was a master manipulator of those styles. Many changes were made to the text during rehearsal. Brecht again had the actors speak their lines in the third person, 'with descriptive insertions': 'As they read they then do the moves and the main gestures. This clarifies the content and gait of the scene, and Geschonneck, who is so excellent in the naturalistic mode, gets a feeling for the Epic style for the first time and becomes "transparent"'.[43] The premiere was another huge success, enjoying undivided critical esteem. Again Erpenbeck joined in, 'dazzled' and not at all 'alienated' by this realistic theatre with its climaxes of hot emotion, as he put it in his review in *Neues Deutschland*.[44] Brecht would, no doubt, have said that Erpenbeck had not appreciated the Epic style. In any case, Erpenbeck remained relaxed at the Berliner Ensemble's approach to this peripheral work.

With the stunning success of *Puntila* and *The Tutor* the Berliner Ensemble had rapidly established itself as the hottest ticket in Berlin. Over the summer of 1950 guest performances by the Berliner Ensemble in West German cities drew a mix of rave notices and abject warnings of SED propaganda. Meanwhile, Brecht repaired to Ahrenshoop on the Baltic coast. The SMAD had granted members of the Kulturbund use of the resort. Stefan Brecht joined his family there for a month. Brecht noted:

> Drive to Ahrenshoop, Helli with the children, Ruth and I in the Steyr. There are a few old fishermen's houses, which look good, even when painted dark blue, or dilapidated or even renovated for the tourist trade. [...] It is pure Nazi territory and, until now, nothing much has happened, nothing could happen; there are too few places where you could make a start. Little tourist entrepreneurs feel hampered everywhere by measures against the black market, and being peasants they have to hand over their produce etc. Since the area is under the Kulturbund, it is visited in the summer by people who belong pretty directly to the new government.[45]

How, beyond the imposition of restrictions, would the new economy work for the citizens of Ahrenshoop? Would it encourage them to abandon old allegiances? No one really knew.

While the altercations with Langhoff continued, Brecht, still without the prospect of a theatre of his own, took a second trip to Munich in early September for the production of *Mother Courage*, staying there quite demonstratively for all of six weeks at the start of the season. He had no formal contract at the Berliner Ensemble and could always find work at the Kammerspiele. He drove to Bavaria with Berlau in his Steyr, stopping overnight in Upper Franconian Pegnitz: 'The view from the Weisses Lamm inn on the market place in the early morning light is like a delicately, powerfully coloured Brueghel and is equal in beauty to the view from a flea-ridden hotel on the old harbour in Marseilles'.[46]

In Munich he met up for rehearsals with Giehse. They were supported by a growing crew of assistants and visitors eager to learn from the master: Monk, Rainer Wolffhardt and Eric Bentley, as well as Harald Benesch and Wolfgang Heinz from Vienna's New Scala. Brecht met with the brilliant Austrian critic Ernst Fischer and with the young English director Peter Brook, lauded for his productions of Shakespeare. Brook was interested in producing *Mother Courage* at London's Embassy Theatre. Always concerned that a production should match his own aspirations, Brecht suggested to the theatre agent Jan van Loewen that Bentley might co-produce or advise. After an evening with his publisher Desch, Ernst Schumacher, who was writing a doctorate on Brecht for Hans Mayer, and a number of young authors, Brecht noted: 'No knowledge of the GDR. Tell of land distribution, workers' and peasants' universities. The FDJ's Whitsun meeting, and explain why socialism is for peace, capitalism for war: that their existence depends on the SED's difficult struggle in the East. They listen politely'.[47] In the land reform of 1945–6 the SMAD had expropriated landowners with more than a hundred hectares and handed the land to the peasantry. Brecht viewed the West of the country, by contrast, repeating a failed economic and social model, re-floated with US finance, which bred an aggressive Fascist mentality. Brecht, Berlau and Bentley visited the Oktoberfest but young men began to sing an anti-Semitic song and Brecht erupted with anger, tipping over the benches as he walked out. Such experiences drove Brecht on in his strong support for the GDR's campaign for peace and unity at a time when the Federal Republic was moving towards the ratification of the General Treaty with the Western Allies, which would entail the remilitarisation of the Federal Republic. Brecht and other members of the Academy's Literature Section would issue a call for German writers to unite on the questions of peace and unity.[48]

Brecht invited Marieluise Fleisser to the Kammerspiele and introduced her to Giehse. Münsterer, whom he also invited to rehearsals, wrote of seeing Brecht:

> One often reads about the reunion of friends after a long separation – Lotte and Goethe, Verlaine and Rimbaud. Such meetings can be cold and distant. I was apprehensive. It is a symptom of Brecht's singular human qualities in later years that, when we did meet, it took just a few short minutes to rediscover the genuine warmth of our long gone youth. Day after day, or at least as often as my professional commitments would permit, I attended the rehearsals of *Mother Courage* and was once more together with Brecht. One of my last great joys, and indeed a particular honour, was the brief hour that the poet spent with me on the very day of the premiere.[49]

That evening of 8 October Brecht sat nervously in a little inn on Hildegardstrasse, waiting for Monk's reports from the premiere at the Kammerspiele on the nearby

Maximilianstrasse.[50] The production was another enormous success, which Brecht recorded with pleasure: 'The moves based on the model are triumphant. Giehse, Domin, Blech, Wilhelmi, Lühr, Lieffen, quite different from Berlin and excellent. During the entire rehearsals not one dispute. Giehse is quite admirable in the way she completely revamps the moves she had used with such success in Zurich and Vienna.'[51]

Upon returning to Berlin, Brecht tested what support he could muster by proposing at an Academy Plenary on 6 November that a number of Meisterschüler should be funded by the Academy and trained at the Berliner Ensemble in dramaturgy and directing. Engel referred the proposal to Wandel and also to Egon Rentzsch, Head of the Cultural Department of the SED Central Committee. Rentzsch responded tartly that the first condition which Brecht needed to fulfil for a Marxist training of the students was his own partisanship.[52] Despite this intervention, Brecht gained support for the initiative, resisting efforts to impose a prescribed curriculum and exam regulations and appointing Horst Bienek, Wera Skupin and Claus Küchenmeister. Brecht explained to the Academy's Performing Arts Section that he could only train Meisterschüler in his method, arguing, too, that theatres led by strong personalities like himself and Felsenstein should be treated individually and left alone by the authorities.

At the Berliner Ensemble Brecht began preparations for *The Mother*, which replaced *Life of Galileo* in the schedule because Leonard Steckel, who had played Galileo with such distinction in Zurich, was not available.[53] Brecht's old friend Jacob Walcher, whom the SED would presently denounce as a member of criminal factions, delivered a series of talks to the Ensemble about the Russian Revolution. Brecht's intention was to present the Russian Revolution in *The Mother* as the achievement of an established socialist society.

After reading a dissertation about Gorky and Brecht by a working-class student for Hans Mayer in Leipzig, Brecht lamented there was ideology everywhere: 'The first thing we have to do is institute exhibitions and courses to develop taste, i.e. for the enjoyment of life'.[54] The student was the twenty-eight year old Käthe Rülicke, whom he invited to Berlin. He sang the praises of the hedonistic life of art and science, explaining that dialectics were all about wit: if you could not tell a joke you could never be a dialectician. He added in a thick Bavarian accent: 'If professors lived sensibly and practically and had a sensible sex life, they would have a sensible body of knowledge'.[55] He appears to have been joking that the homosexual Mayer's sex life was the reason for his student's lack of taste. Having imparted his wisdom to the attractive Rülicke, Brecht employed her as an assistant. She became a stalwart of Brecht's productions, an assiduous note-taker who produced a vast amount of material, recording many of Brecht's casual observations. Brecht wrote love poetry for her:

> Seven roses on the bush
> Six belong to the wind
> One will stay there, so there's just
> One for me to find.
>
> Seven times I'll summon you
> Six times stay away

But the seventh, promise me
Come without delay.[56]

As we know, Weigel had accepted Brecht's relationships from the start, aware of the strength of the bond that united them. Even though Rülicke's sexual relationship with Brecht did not last, her arrival in Brecht's life, followed by Käthe Reichel and Isot Kilian, both actresses at the Berliner Ensemble, would trigger further crises for Berlau. Like Hauptmann, who was now separated from Dessau and deeply depressed, Berlau would see herself as relegated to the margins, toiling for Brecht far away from the limelight and with little of the old intimacy. She responded with anger and aggression. Remarkably, Brecht continued to take her with him on trips, encouraging her in her work to aid the recovery of her health.

Brecht now engaged the talented, though untrained Reichel, whom he took under his wing. He was soon writing love poetry for her and employing her in 'Steffin's role', the maid servant in *The Mother*. Berlau reacted very badly to Reichel's arrival, making scenes and haranguing Brecht in public. Deeply embarrassed, he let her know how angry he was. However, he remained wedded to his belief that productive activity could overcome all manner of problems, suggesting to Hella Wuolijoki that Berlau might direct his works in Scandinavia. He also supported the initiative of Berlau's friend, the Dutch photographer Gerda Goedhart, who arranged for her to direct *Mother Courage* at Rotterdam's Toneel Theatre. Berlau's trip to Rotterdam proved traumatic. She returned to Berlin in a precarious state and lost all control at a rehearsal for *The Mother* on 4 January 1951 when she slapped Brecht in the face. Müllereisert sedated Berlau and took her to the closed psychiatric unit at the Charité.[57]

Berlau begged Brecht to visit her in hospital but he himself was far from well. His letters to her, first in Rotterdam, then in Berlin, chart the recurrence of his renal condition, including bacterial infection, which left him exhausted. Quite typically he deflected his own problems, writing of Neher's illness and claiming that he himself was just a bit tired.[58] However, he then wrote that he had contracted a fever and was staying at home, where he had slept the whole day. He rose from his bed to declare himself quite satisfied with the first, closed performance of *The Mother* on 10 January. Neher's set design met with 'general approval' and Weigel's Vlassova 'couldn't be bettered': 'The audience, which is average Volksbühne, takes it in its stride. About forty curtain calls, several times with the safety curtain. Our more relaxed handling of the old model which Berlau reproduced excellently (and strictly) in Leipzig just last year seems successful.'[59]

The 'old model' of 1932 had used Neher's spare set with strong agitprop features designed to urge revolutionary activism. Neher alluded to that set for the new production but Pelagea Vlassova's story was presented within the context of a family history in an established, post-revolutionary society. The set as well the costumes displayed rich historical authenticity, complementing the representation of characters and their interaction which emphasised nuance and humour as they proceed confidently and determinedly to fulfil their historic mission. All this was, as Brecht noted, designed to increase the appeal of the Soviet Union to a distinctly sceptical German public. Weigel commented that she played the lead both more gently and more obstinately than in the past. The agitprop features of the 1932 production were restricted to the role of the choir as Brecht made a great effort to integrate his work within the emerging East Berlin theatre culture. He was rewarded with great critical acclaim for the premiere on 12 January.

However, by this time Brecht was far from well. On the day of the premiere, he had to explain to Berlau that he was too weak to help her and asked her to moderate her tone.[60] She was discharged from the Charité and wrote to Suhrkamp: 'To the people here I'm just Brecht's lady friend, who was once beautiful, but Brecht is now out for younger blood'. She added: 'He has always treated me like dirt – but unfortunately I love him'. The day after the premiere Brecht admitted defeat, placing himself in Hüdepohl's care, who hospitalised him on 15 January. Hüdepohl had access to the best medication available: at latest during this stay at St. Hedwig's, Brecht was treated with the new wonder drug, the antibiotic penicillin. Berlau went to convalesce at the idyllic Schloss Wiepersdorf south of Berlin, a writers' retreat with a special place in German literature as the home of the Romantic poets Achim von Arnim and Bettina Brentano. Brecht would visit her there but not alone.

The Trial of Lucullus: From subservience to sovereignty

While Brecht was contending with Berlau during his recovery in hospital, on the weekend of 20–21 January 1951 the SED leadership and SMAD launched a broadside against modernist art with the publication in the SMAD's *Tägliche Rundschau* of 'The Ways and Wrong Ways of Modernism'. The piece bore the same pseudonym, N. Orlov, as others of similar character published around that time.[61] In this opening salvo in the Campaign against Formalism, terminology which had been tainted by Nazism was used quite shamelessly: 'Art which takes decadence and subversion as its model is pathological and anti-aesthetic'. Invoking Stalin's leadership, the article affirmed: 'The struggle against all influence of western decadence and the cult of the ugly in the art of the GDR is an important social task'. Shortly after, Hans Lauter described Formalism in terms typical of the SED's nationalist rhetoric:

> The most important characteristic of Formalism is the endeavour, on the pretext or in the mistaken intention of developing something 'completely new', to achieve a complete break with the classical cultural heritage. That leads to the rootlesness of national culture, the destruction of national consciousness, promotes cosmo-politanism and means thereby direct support for the American imperialist policy of war.[62]

The message was that cultural life in East Berlin now had to play by the same rules as the rest of the Eastern Bloc. The appeal to German unity had to proceed from a clear distinction between a healthy culture in the East and the decadence of the West. What the SED would now regularly describe as Brecht's 'proletkult' aesthetics, typical of 1920s avant-gardism, had, they claimed, long been dead in the USSR where Socialist Realism was pre-eminent. On 23 January the SED's Politburo instructed that a conversation should take place with Brecht about 'corrections' to *The Mother*. Egon Rentzsch requested that seats should be available for the play at short notice 'when the Politburo is about to reach decisions on theatre matters'.[63] These moves mark the beginning of the concerted campaign to undermine Brecht's aesthetic stance. That Brecht was hospitalised with a serious complaint at the very time when this public attack was launched upon him and his collaborators cannot have been lost on his opponents, who were content to proceed against him. After two weeks at St. Hedwig's, Brecht was discharged on 27 January with a course of penicillin.

In addition to *The Mother* there was another issue at stake: the production at the State Opera of Brecht and Dessau's *The Trial of Lucullus*. Opera was, of course, one of the sacred cows of the cultural heritage, which the SED leadership was bound to defend in its established form on the grounds of national unity. As Brecht had acknowledged in his prologue to his *Short Organum*, for some he had remained the dramatic iconoclast who had declared war on the opera form in the 1920s. The SED bureaucracy had been monitoring plans for the production after N. Orlov had violently attacked Ernst Legal in *Tägliche Rundschau* following the premiere of Glinka's *Ruslan and Ludmilla*. Orlov had called for action against the management for the reprehensible treatment of a Soviet work in the western, decadent style. When Legal sought approval for the production of *The Trial of Lucullus*, Maria Rentmeister at the Ministry of Public Education asked to see the score. The Ministry repeated its request on 9 January 1951 and warned Legal that his request to transfer an advance to the conductor Hermann Scherchen had been blocked. It appears that the score was still not submitted.

By now, rehearsals had begun but Dessau, unlike Brecht a Party member, was prepared to withdraw the anti-war work. However, at a time when the US general Douglas MacArthur had been amassing his troops on the border of South Korea with China, Brecht was opposed:

> The subject is important just at this moment, when the Americans are issuing such hysterical threats. Dessau is naturally afraid of attacks on the form, but even these, if that is what they really intend, will be less drastic if the content is so important. In the end both Dessau and I are convinced that the form of the opera is its content. In addition to this you must never be afraid of criticism; you either refute it or you put it to constructive use, that's all. Why should we assume that the situation will be more favourable in the autumn if we haven't made the effort in the spring?[64]

Brecht and Dessau were aware that the latter's music – 'an eclectic distinctive musical ensemble by operatic standards and a consistently dissonant musical language' – left them vulnerable.[65] However, as Scherchen acknowledged, the score was merely an accompaniment to a great literary work. Brecht knew that the SED leadership was actually concerned about the content of the text and had no real understanding of its form. What exercised the leadership was the text's seemingly pacifist message and its criticism of a 'great' leader in war. A covert critique of Stalin's dictatorship was too close for comfort. The bureaucracy identified pacifism as a major problem in the DEFA film script for *Mother Courage*, too.

For the defence of his interests, the physically frail Brecht fell back on the behavioural pattern of the practised survivor, tailoring the Wu Wei doctrine of non-action and action, of compliance and self-assertion, in his improvised engagement with the SED leadership. As in the earlier struggle with the Moscow camarilla, for his own guidance he produced a series of statements about Formalism, which remained unpublished at the time.[66] An extraordinary sequence of events now unfolded. On 14 February Ulbricht formally requested that Brecht's fellow academician, the composer Ernst Hermann Meyer should, together with Rentzsch, provide an assessment of the text and music. Meanwhile, the Ministry for State Security (Stasi) had a seat reserved at the State Opera for the forthcoming performances of the work.[67] Then, on 8 March sixteen comrades from the Cultural Department and from the Ministry of Public Education, together with several composers and critics, including Ernst Hermann Meyer, Georg Knepler, Harry Goldschmidt and Nathan Notowicz, entered the theatre unannounced during a rehearsal. The conductor Scherchen initially declined to continue in front of these people and the following day four 'music experts' failed to gain entry. An official from the Ministry of Public Education invited Ernst Legal to consider what might be performed instead of *Lucullus*.

Meanwhile, Brecht commented to Käthe Rülicke that the Campaign against Formalism was a 'gross political mistake, because it intensified divisions'.[68] By this Brecht meant divisions between Germans in East and West. Reflecting that only he and Becher were truly for the GDR, he suggested that, at this time in an unhealthy age, a transitional dictatorship with all its severity and injustice was necessary to ensure survival: the arts had to take a back seat. He concluded: 'Our age still lacks "great art" – apart from Brecht, who was, however, a "burgher in opposition"'. Shortly after, he added that the dictatorship of the proletariat was an unpropitious time for the arts: 'Politics is in the foreground, social tendencies are often even inimical to art, restrict (because of the necessity of dictatorship) free development, including art'.[69] The dialectical imagination could justify all manner of things as the dark times continued under a different guise.

Claiming the support of Knepler, Notowicz, Goldschmidt and Eisler, who agreed to discuss the music with Dessau, Meyer reported that Dessau's music contained 'all the elements of Formalism'.[70] On 12 March the SED banned the public performance of *The Trial of Lucullus* and decreed that after a rehearsal on 13 March Erpenbeck would chair a discussion, involving comrades and artists as well as officials, members of the Academy and of the Kulturbund. At this point, Brecht, demonstrating that he in no way saw himself as an opponent of the Party, appealed to Ulbricht for help. He pointed out the relevance of *Lucullus* in the light of a revanchist West German military and argued: 'In my opinion we should let ourselves be guided by *content* until the difficult problems of form have been solved'.[71] For Brecht, the essential point was that *Lucullus* condemned wars of conquest. He had always sought to maintain as a point of principle that this differentiated the USSR from rapacious, imperialist powers. However, as SED leaders were aware, the USSR's wartime and post-war actions rendered such a distinction unsustainable.

The Central Committee mustered 150 people to attend the rehearsal on 13 March. Meyer opened the ensuing discussion with a quotation from Stalin. Only Scherchen, Goldschmidt and Zweig defended the opera against the many voices ranged against it. The discussion resumed in the evening. Having dissuaded Scherchen from leaving the city, Brecht and Dessau secured agreement for them to complete rehearsals in advance of a 'rehearsal performance' behind closed doors on 17 March. That same day, at the 5th Conference of the SED Central Committee *Lucullus* and *The Mother* were held up as prime examples of Formalism. Rodenberg attacked *The Mother* because its didacticism was 'an end in itself and that is Formalism', while the SED's strategist Fred Oelssner described it as 'somehow a hybrid of Meyerhold and proletkult'.[72] Weigel spoke in the play's defence, while Becher entered a plea, in Party jargon, to moderate, but by no means abandon, the attack on Brecht: 'Of course, we need to give Brecht more time than we, let's say, could give me. At the moment Brecht is using up his old baggage. [...] We must not stop criticising him, but must criticise him as wisely as he too is wise'.[73]

The Ministry of Public Education secured all the tickets for the closed 'rehearsal performance' that evening and distributed them free of charge to the Central Committee and the Ministry (500 tickets), the Free German Youth (300 tickets) and the Free German Union Congress (300 tickets). The remaining tickets were given to the Academy, the Music Conservatory and other institutions. The Berliner Ensemble received all of twelve tickets. However, Brecht, Dessau, Scherchen and Legal fought to secure some 200 tickets for people sympathetic to the work, among them western journalists.

Anticipating a scandal, many people gathered in front of the theatre and were handed tickets by people who didn't want to be forced to watch an opera. Following a short speech by Legal, the show began. The critic of the West Berlin paper *Der Abend* witnessed events: 'After the first scenes there were still whistles and boos. However, the applause began, which rose to a hurricane of acclaim at the end. Author and composer kissed in front of the curtain. The pre-ordained debacle did not happen. Ernst Legal stood next to Brecht, too. Wilhelm Pieck and Walter Ulbricht had left the house immediately after the first applause'.[74] Another eyewitness wrote: 'After each scene the applause welled up, and after the last curtain the audience was going wild. The people were not just standing up to applaud; they were getting on their seats and applauding in ecstasy. Brecht, the composer and the director were summoned, the people were cheering them, they were shouting, it was an orgy of applause'. It was like the old days, only now Brecht's opponents were from his own political side – and he had trounced them. Brecht, Dessau and Legal had received a huge demonstration of support from the audience, as they spectacularly turned the tables on the Party dogmatists. Scherchen declared it was his greatest ever success with a modern work. The West Berlin theatre agent Hermann Gail congratulated Legal on the 'sensational success'.[75] While much was made in the western press of the censorship of a great work, there was a stony silence in East Berlin. The *Lucullus* affair was an early landmark in what became a familiar scenario around 'dissident' art as the work of Eastern Bloc artists, suppressed in the East, was lauded in the West. The issue was particularly acute on the German-German border and SED politicians typically reacted in a highly defensive way. When *The Trial of Lucullus* was finally reviewed in *Neues Deutschland*, the pretence was maintained that the production had been a failure.

It had, however, been an unnerving experience for a deeply unpopular SED elite paranoid about the usurpation of their claim to leadership. The ban was re-affirmed.

Brecht responded with letters to Wandel and Ulbricht in which he adopted an attitude of conspicuous respectfulness, whilst arguing that there were important pointers for the future in a production involving the 'most progressive' elements in the GDR. He wrote to Wandel: 'We are deeply grateful to you for [authorising] the performance of *Lucullus* before an audience of the most progressive elements of our young republic. Such performances can indeed help to clarify the problems of a new art'.[76] Brecht suggested to Ulbricht that he had 'demonstrated the republic's great comradely under-standing for the difficulties besetting artists in the present phase of reconstruction. A production of this kind shows artists – and the most progressive element in the public – the way that art and the public should take'. Brecht thereby invited the SED leadership to enter into a dialogue with him as the representative of those 'most progressive elements'. They had to do so if they were to regain control of the situation. Wilhelm Pieck invited Brecht and Dessau to visit him at home on 24 March, where they were joined by Wandel, Ackermann and Hans Lauter. Always open to advice about content, Brecht agreed to alterations to the text, particularly the ending and the title, now *The Condemnation of Lucullus*. The following day, Rülicke noted Brecht as saying: 'A bad time for art. One can surely not take as a yardstick the bad taste of the proletariat, imposed by the bourgeoisie. An obstructive cultural policy'.[77] On a more conciliatory note he added in his journal: 'It is evident that during upheavals of these dimensions the arts will run into trouble even where they help to show the way ahead'.[78] In a further note of the meeting with Pieck Rülicke added: 'It was agreed that it would be announced that the revised version of *Lucullus* would be prepared for production for the coming season in order to unite the factions which had arisen amongst creative artists as a result of this discussion'.[79] The 'most progressive elements' had been heard.

Brecht shared his changes to his text with, among others, Ackermann, to whom he wrote that he had 'begun to rework the text in such a way as to render even a *mistaken* opinion that the work embodies pacifist tendencies impossible. Indeed, I owe you thanks for insisting that *activity* must be mobilised against wars of conquest'.[80] He challenged Ackermann over the official criticism of Dessau's music: 'You do not put forward any arguments as you do in connection with the text, but merely express a general condemnation which gives the composer nothing to go by'. Finally, he defended Dessau's music, explaining to Ackermann that Dessau himself was against Formalism and concluding: 'The main thing is that our artists are prepared to make changes and that they support you wholeheartedly'. Pieck called interested parties together again in early May when the changes were agreed. The Politburo later confirmed that, with changes to the music, the work could be performed in the coming season. No appre-ciable changes would be made but the production would still go ahead.

In reflections which contrast starkly with his initial view that the arts had to take a back seat in such an age, Brecht now told Rülicke that art needed a 'sovereign attitude', which was not possible 'if people were always squinting at the most recent guidelines of the Central Committee'.[81] Rülicke noted: 'Brecht does not want to learn how to write from Ulbricht, how to translate his thoughts, expressed by someone from the Free German Youth. On the contrary, politicians should learn from poets, who represent the whole of society (example Lenin – Gorky)'. However, Brecht would never allow himself such triumphalism in public. On the contrary, following a speech in Leipzig on 16 May at a congress convened to discuss the 'Indivisibility of German Culture', Brecht told journalists: 'There is no intervention on the side of the authorities. Such reports in the western press are ill-informed'.[82] He followed up by telling Viertel, as he did others, that the dispute had been 'refreshing and instructive'.[83]

Brecht was considering how to assert the sovereignty of the arts and use the Academy as a platform to go on the offensive through institutional channels. In a draft for the Performing Arts Section he wrote that, following the 'suppression' of the opera in what appeared to be a 'dictatorial administrative act', productions of *Lucullus* should be approved throughout the GDR.[84] However, he opted to apply more subtle pressure, informing Pieck that Dessau had rejected a request to perform the piece at the Cologne opera festival in June 'because there was reason to suspect that the Cologne people could misguidedly make so hasty a production the occasion for a demonstration'.[85] The premiere of *The Condemnation of Lucullus* was set for October at the State Opera and Brecht would authorise other productions in the West.

He had demonstrated rare qualities, refusing to be backed into a corner, seeking out the opinions of his critics and incorporating them in his work. The SED leaders had become his latest collaborators. By engaging with senior SED figures, Brecht hoped not only to convince them about individual works but also that modernist artists could make the case for socialism themselves without the ugly trappings of German cultural nationalism. However, Brecht had also won a remarkable, popular victory, which terrified the SED. The SED hierarchy was now full of spite towards the ailing Brecht, not a Party member but dictating Party policy, and was determined to take him down.

Leadership Struggles: Correcting the Heretic? 1951–3

Attrition

The SED leadership took steps to ensure that there would be no repeat of its humili-ation in the western press over *Lucullus*. On 2 May 1951 the Politburo created the State Commission for Artistic Affairs to formulate, implement and police cultural policy. Within its all-encompassing brief, the 'Arts Commission' was to assume responsibility for the Berliner Ensemble and the Academy of Arts. That summer also saw the creation of an Office for Literature to supervise writing, which, again, was a direct challenge to the Academy. Helmut Holtzhauer, a KPD member incarcerated throughout the Nazi years, was appointed chair of the Arts Commission. His team included Maria Rentmeister, Hans Rodenberg, Erpenbeck and Wilhelm Girnus. This body was resolutely committed to the implementation of Socialist Realism as the state's approved artistic method. What is more, for all these people Brecht epitomised the GDR's problems with the arts.

While the attacks upon Brecht continued in the Campaign against Formalism, at the same meeting on 2 May the Politburo directed Girnus to act as Brecht's very own cultural policeman. Girnus was instructed to 'undertake regular political work with Bert Brecht and to provide him with help'.[1] Brecht's ruminations in Skovsbostrand about surveillance during the decay of capitalism held good, too, for East Berlin. It was not quite the same as Galileo's house arrest, more a way of 'helping' Brecht direct his energies along the SED's lines. Senior politicians could thereby be relieved of their very time-consuming engagement with this idiosyncratic genius. Girnus, the arts editor of *Neues Deutschland*, was one of the most forceful, feared and dogmatic SED cultural officials of the early 1950s. A member of the KPD resistance, he had emerged from Nazi incarceration, including Sachsenhausen and Flossenbürg, espousing the Leninist equivalent of the Vansittartist view that the German people could only be saved from themselves by drastic, corrective measures. Brecht required correction, too, on account of his supposed proletkult indiscipline and other delinquencies. Girnus provided Ulbricht with regular reports upon his discussions with Brecht, who could be in no doubt what Girnus's attentions meant. Much later, in a letter to senior SED figures in 1978, another low point in the Party's relationship with writers and artists, a mellower Girnus reflected:

Of course, we shall still have problems with literature in a hundred years [...] just as Marx and Engels had with, among others, Heinrich Heine and F. Freiligrath, Lenin with Gorky and Mayakovsky, and we with Brecht (at present we are behaving as if there had never been such issues with Brecht, but one only needs to read his diary entries to see in black and white that something else is happening, and from my personal dealings with him I could say a thing or two.).[2]

Girnus presented himself to Brecht, who was outside the Party's channels of communication, as an advisor on cultural politics. He sought thereby to make himself the conduit and filter for Brecht's public statements. On occasion, Brecht would work with Girnus on texts about cultural politics for publication in *Neues Deutschland*. However, the control would not always work smoothly by any means.

It cannot have been lost on Girnus and the Party leadership that the *Lucullus* Affair had taken its toll on Brecht and that he had been unable to recuperate amidst the attritional pressure. He would, in fact, never properly recover. Brecht's decision to return to Berlin was proving costly but that cost had to be set against the opportunity to realise his theatrical ambitions while contributing to the idea of a socialist Germany. Moreover, as he acknowledged to von Einem: 'Trying to build up a new theatre leaves me with no time to write for it'.[3] Brecht underwent an examination at the Charité, which included x-rays of his lungs and his heart. The report upon the x-rays of 25 May 1951 confirms things we know from Brecht's childhood illnesses: Brecht's heart was somewhat enlarged to the left with a protruding aortic knob.[4] The report also indicates alarming deterioration. There was hardly any contraction of the retrocardial space. While the heart beat could be discerned on the left contour of the heart, pulsation could scarcely be detected on the right. In radioscopy from a transverse angle, the barium passage of the oesophagus showed hardly any pulsation from behind the heart. Only after deep inhalation could stronger heart movements be discerned. These details of the ill-functioning, diseased heart show how serious Brecht's chronic heart failure had become. He was, moreover, highly susceptible to bacterial infections of the heart, spreading from the kidney and prostate to inflame the already diseased organ, causing endocarditis, and, finally, cardiac failure. However, neither Brecht himself nor the doctors who treated him during the last year of his life would reveal any awareness of these findings in their communications. There is no indication in Brecht's frequent statements about his heart in 1955–6 that they were communicated to him. It appears that Theodor Brugsch, the senior physician who cared for Brecht at the Charité in the spring of 1956, opted to spare him the news of this incurable condition.

In June the Cultural Department of the Central Committee was asked to assess the ideological situation in the Academy, on the understanding that the problems with Brecht were bound up with the more general problem of that institution.[5] The report revealed what everyone knew: that the state had founded an elite institution for the arts which, like the state itself, was hamstrung by contradictory and, as was increasingly obvious, irreconcilable policy objectives: on the one hand, the pursuit of German unity through an 'all-German' approach to politics and culture; and on the other, the partisan agenda of the separate socialist state, including the propagation of the official cultural policy of Socialist Realism. If the latter objective were now prioritised, the former must be subordinated. Initial elections to the Academy had been decided on the basis of artistic excellence, with partisanship understood only in the general sense of anti-Fascism. As we have mentioned, the balance of the membership reflected the fundamental contradiction. Brecht and his supporters – for the Cultural Department, not only Eisler, Zweig, Huchel, Ihering and Weigel but also Becher – were in a slender majority, viewing the institution as a representative bridge-building organ for German cultural unity, which should therefore have nothing to do with the partisan Campaign against Formalism. Indeed, for the authors of the report Formalists and Formalism enjoyed ascendancy in the Academy! Noting that the Brechtian mode of theatre with its proletkult tendencies was dominant, the Cultural Department concluded that although Brecht was good his methods must not be allowed to gain popularity. Therefore, the Performing Arts Section needed new, Marxist blood.[6] For the Cultural Department, Brecht was not a real Marxist. Reliable Marxists were required to develop a stronger ideological line in the Academy where Becher should finally take a lead.

While these initial steps were being taken to curb Brecht's influence and to re-position the Academy, Brecht again spent the summer at Ahrenshoop. He noted: 'Still exhausted, I nevertheless work at the typewriter in the cool of the morning.'[7] Typically, he sought to turn debilitating fatigue into freshness and strength. He took along material for a play about the bricklayer Hans Garbe, whom the government was feting as a new, class-conscious worker after his heroic efforts to repair a Hoffmann kiln. Garbe met Brecht three times to talk about his life and work. Brecht, too, saw Garbe as a new worker, describing him to the French press as someone who possessed a 'new consciousness and sees the world with fresh eyes'.[8] Brecht speculated that his Garbe project 'would be the same type of play as the histories, i.e. it would not start from an idea'. In fact, it did start from an idea, the grand vision of non-alienated labour, which Brecht attempted to embed within recent events: 'The worker gets on his feet by producing. Need to examine what exactly changes in him and for him if instead of being shaped by history he begins to shape it himself – the condition being that this is not a purely personal process, since it concerns a class.'[9] What had changed for the working class six years after the defeat of Nazi Germany and two years after the establishment of the GDR? Brecht envisaged the work as a 'fragment in huge, rough-hewn blocks', an imperfect realisation of an awesome vision. The Garbe material would never match the vision, nor add up to a drama.

For all Brecht's best efforts to contribute artistically to socialist construction with his own brand of socialist realism, the Party's abject fear that star artists might usurp their authority through the cult of personality re-surfaced when Erich Honecker once more intervened in Brecht's work. This time he requested the removal of Ernst Busch's name from Brecht's 'Herrnburg Report', a piece of verse reportage set to music by Dessau about an incident on the German-German border. Ten thousand young people had been detained when seeking to re-enter the West German state after taking part in the Whitsuntide meeting of the FDJ in Berlin. Brecht had written the piece for the World Festival of Youth in East Berlin in the summer of 1951. Addressing Honecker as Erich Honegger, as if Honecker's views might be mistaken for those of the Swiss composer Arthur Honegger, Brecht declined the request to remove Busch's name. However, Honecker repeated the request with great tenacity over the coming weeks.

Honecker and Margot Feist, his later wife and Education Minister, attended the two rehearsals with Rentzsch. In Ahrenshoop, Brecht then met Rentzsch, who claimed that a sense of proportion was the only consideration: Busch was the only person in the text to be mentioned by name, not Ulbricht or Pieck. Although Brecht removed the reference to Busch, after the premiere the work was, as Brecht put it, 'suppressed, and finally taken off the repertoire by decree'.[10]

Brecht returned to Berlin in mid-August and asked Wilhelm Pieck 'if he would mind listening to it'. As a result, 'Herrnburg Report' was performed the following morning, not to its intended audience but to members of the government! Afterwards, Brecht was informed that they were 'satisfied' but that Grotewohl found there was 'something academic' about it: 'Presumably he feels that formal elements are always taking the songs out of immediate reach'. Brecht noted that the leaders simply wanted people to write 'from the heart'. He then contacted the choir master Hans Sandig, who told him of his astonishment at the 'evidently conscious neglect' of 'Herrnburg Report'.[11] Originally, Honecker had attached great importance to the work but had then told the organisers that they should not present it 'too often'. They had then compounded Honecker's own excess of zeal. Brecht dedicated 'Herrnburg Report' to Busch in its published form.

Struggling for peace

A concerned Rülicke noted that Brecht had not recuperated at all during his holiday: he was really worn out, in a virtually permanent state of exhaustion.[12] Brecht now learned that he was to be awarded the GDR National Prize, First Class, a handsome 100,000 marks. Brecht invested in property outside Berlin where he could go to rest at weekends. An estate agent drew his attention to a property for sale in Buckow, 65 kilometres east of Berlin in the Märkische Schweiz [Switzerland of the Marches], a little piece of the sub-Alpine world embedded in the North German Plain, rather like the terrain south of Augsburg around the Ammersee. The area derives its name from the, for the state of Brandenburg, unusual geography of hills and lakes, stretching for some 30 kilometres and two to six kilometres in width, which was formed in the Ice Age. Buckow had a name as an artists' retreat: friends like Egon Erwin Kisch and John Heartfield had lived there. What is more, Buckow is a spa, practising the Kneipp Cure, which Schmitt had recommended to Brecht more than twenty years earlier.

Brecht told Rülicke that the property, a tower near the station at Hauptstrasse 42, was the 'realisation of a dream': he 'walked through the whole garden and called me as his witness that he had truly once walked through it'.[13] Brecht said to Rülicke that he would not swap it for Goethe's garden house in Weimar. Later, Brecht and Weigel looked at other houses in Buckow, among them Seestrasse 29: 'An old, not ignobly built little house with another more spacious but equally simple house attached, about fifty paces away, on a beautiful site on the edge of the Scharmützelsee under big old trees. Something like this would be affordable, even with the upkeep. You could invite people to stay in the bigger house'.[14] It had been an artist's studio, with a glorious window giving on to the lake. A stream from the Scharmützelsee skirted the property on its way to the Buckowsee. Brecht could take the waters in his own garden. In 'The Flower Garden' he would write of the property and the beneficent effect he hoped for from it:

By the lake, deep amid fir and silver poplar
Sheltered by wall and hedge, a garden
So wisely plotted with monthly flowers
That it blossoms from March until October.

Here, in the morning, not too frequently, I sit
And wish I too might always
In all weathers, good or bad
Show one pleasant aspect or another.[15]

Brecht now demonstrated much greater ambition for Buckow than merely a weekend retreat for himself. He agreed contracts to buy or lease three properties in the village: Hauptstrasse 42, Seestrasse 29 and a piece of land with a garden house by the promenade on the Buckowsee for Käthe Reichel to use. The tower was available for Berlau and other visitors, while Brecht himself would be able to deliver master classes at Seestrasse 29. Some outside the magic circle at the Berliner Ensemble looked on askance.

Meanwhile, Brecht developed a peace initiative with a profile only he could muster, supporting Grotewohl's call for German re-unification with full sovereignty as the Federal Republic pursued its highly controversial path towards re-armament through the General Treaty. Advised by Girnus, Brecht composed his 'Open Letter to German Artists and Writers', in which he asked stark questions of his fellow Germans: 'Will there be war? The answer: if we arm for war, we will have war. Will Germans shoot at Germans? The answer: if they do not talk to each other, they will shoot at each other'.[16] Famously, Brecht's appeal, with its pointed reference to the Punic Wars between Rome and Carthage, ends: 'Great Carthage waged three wars. It was still powerful after the first, still inhabitable after the second. It was no longer to be found after the third'. Brecht's words were greeted with euphoria in some quarters, particularly in the East, but treated with scorn in influential circles in the West.

Stalin would try one last time to engage the West in his policy for Germany, issuing his notes of March and April 1952 to the western powers, proposing a peace treaty with Germany, the withdrawal of all foreign military personnel and the introduction of the normal components of western democracy. Brecht would join other members of the Academy's Presidium in signing a manifesto in support of the Soviet initiative. However, the western powers insisted on the involvement of a United Nations commission, aware that the USSR regarded the UN as a US instrument. The Soviet Union and the GDR responded with a blockade of movement between East and West. The integration of the Federal Republic within the Western Alliance would be completed in October 1954 when, in the face of great opposition in the West as well as the East, it joined NATO. In East Berlin the Adenauer government's action was denounced as treasonable: Germans could indeed be ordered to fire on Germans. The

Western Alliance was, however, playing a long game. Before his death, Stalin had to accept the status quo of German division and the need to incorporate the GDR within security arrangements for Eastern Europe. East Germans fired on East Germans seeking to escape to the West.

Before the ceremony for the National Prize on 7 October 1951, Brecht was, according to Rülicke, in a state of 'great agitation', 'anxious about people not known to him'.[17] Public occasions were always a strain but his ill health exacerbated the nervous tension, leaving him susceptible to his old complaints. With a knowing allusion to Brecht's essay 'On Rhymeless Verse with Irregular Rhythms', the poet Günter Kunert who encountered Brecht at the time wrote of the 'unrhythmic, irregular movements of his round head'.[18] As Rülicke notes, Brecht tried to externalise his problems, but this time he could not: 'Brecht is complaining about a general state of weakness. He says that he feels like the only one who's sober among a lot of drunks; that he scarcely has the strength for rehearsals, by midday he's completely exhausted; that he's depressed and is living on a single track, very isolated; but that he's afraid of disrupting his rhythm through distractions'.[19] By his rhythm he meant his work rhythm, which he was maintaining by a sheer act of will. Through the mix of political pressure and failing health Brecht was being forced into a place where he did not want to be. He attended the award ceremony with Weigel and Hauptmann. The laudation honoured Brecht the poet, not the dramatist. He sat with Arnold Zweig at the state banquet that evening where they were joined by Becher. Brecht then succumbed to a fever, which prevented him from attending the premiere of *The Condemnation of Lucullus*. Some reviews praised the opera while Girnus criticised its 'dangerous proximity to symbolism'.[20]

The fever lingered on, with familiar bacterial infections, which by now probably included urosepsis as well as the cardiac and renal complaints, leaving Brecht exhausted and depressed. He spent the autumn in this reduced state when there were sinister developments in the Eastern Bloc. The leading Jewish politician Rudolf Slánský and associates were arrested in Prague and accused of belonging to an international conspiracy. Brecht's Meisterschüler Horst Bienek was arrested, too, and sentenced to twenty-five years' hard labour in Siberia. The terror gripping Eastern Europe was coming chillingly close.

On New Year's Day 1952 Rülicke itemised Brecht's daily routine to help him concentrate on his work, emphasising his need to focus on his own writing between 7 and 8.45 a.m.[21] He would then deal with current issues and correspondence, working with his collaborators in the afternoon. However, his routine was immediately disrupted when the SED opened a new front in the Campaign against Formalism with vicious attacks by Kurt Magritz and Girnus on the Academy's exhibition of sculptures by the Expressionist Ernst Barlach. After visiting the exhibition, Brecht struck an unusually resigned, weary note: 'The Barlach exhibition in the Academy of Arts was attacked so violently in the *Tägliche Rundschau* and *Neues Deutschland* that the few surviving artists were cast into lethargy. I made notes, bringing out the positive values and the exemplary quality of the work, defending it against their completely abstract demolition using social-critical weapons'.[22] As he went on to note, he was by no means against social-critical arguments per se: 'I established how right, i.e.

pointing in the right direction, social critical arguments are, even in the weakest and most incompetent hands, and I made my notes accordingly'. In his defence of the progressive moment in art, Brecht's 'Notes on the Barlach Exhibition' as usual avoid general theoretical pronouncements, remaining on the ground of practical criticism, informed by a social-critical perspective. He sought thereby to demonstrate a balanced approach, which was missing in the abstract condemnation of Girnus and Magritz. His notes conclude: 'Abstract criticism does not lead to realistic art'.[23] Brecht submitted them to Girnus at *Neues Deutschland* but he rejected them, so Brecht turned to Huchel at *Sinn und Form*, who published and was damned. Huchel recalled: 'At that time in the GDR the word was: whoever is for Barlach is supporting American imperialism. So I was summoned to Becher who berated me'.[24] The rhetoric hardened, the SED's Cultural Department commissioning an 'exposé about the Formalist Brecht Circle'.[25] *Theaterarbeit*, a fine collaborative work charting the first six productions of the Berliner Ensemble with beautiful texts, photos and illustrations, was to be subjected to particular scrutiny and official press reviews were to be prepared. As the President of the 'Formalist' Academy, Arnold Zweig was singled out. A film of his novel *The Axe of Wandsbek* was banned on the grounds of Formalism.

Brecht had put off the distressing medical procedure with Hüdepohl even though the corollary was by now near-permanent exhaustion. On a visit to Warsaw and Krakow with Weigel in late February he had to severely curtail his programme.[26] They still saw a number of plays and photographs of the 1929 production of *The Threepenny Opera* at Teatr Polski, visited Chopin's birthplace and discussed a guest performance in Poland, which evolved into a major tour, the Berliner Ensemble's first outside the German-speaking world. Back in Berlin in early March, Brecht finally responded to Rülicke's urgings to go to Hüdepohl's clinic.[27]

Tackling the roots of realism, treating contemporary transformations ·

Encouraged by the response to the Berliner Ensemble's adaptations of Lenz's *The Tutor* – Kleist's *The Broken Jug* would follow in January 1952 – Brecht began to approach Shakespeare. With his assistants he translated and adapted *The Tragedy of Coriolanus*, which had interested him since Erich Engel's production in the 1920s. Brecht saw *Coriolanus* as 'probably the only Shakespeare of any topicality which we can halfway cast'.[28] Brecht highlighted the clash between the egotistical individual and society:

> The tragedy of the individual man naturally interests us less than the one the individual man brings on the community. We must at the same time stay close to Shakespeare if we are not to mobilise all his outstanding qualities against ourselves. So we think it is best to turn the hurt pride of Shakespeare's Coriolanus into another significant attitude not too remote from Shakespeare, namely Coriolanus's belief in his indispensability. This is what brings about his ruin and robs the common weal of a valuable man.

Brecht completed the adaptation over the coming two years. However, the Party leadership decreed it artistically unacceptable to caricature classical works and opposed a production of *Coriolanus*.[29] Brecht's adaptation was not performed in his lifetime but has generated much interest since.

Brecht now undertook a bold investigation of realism, returning to the Sturm und Drang and the young Goethe's *Urfaust*. This early fragment of Goethe's *Faust*, which in its final form came to be regarded as the German national epic, was, however, a different proposition from the obscure *Tutor*. The dynamic, striving Faust embodied the SED's faith in the German people to fulfil its historic mission in the first German socialist state. Brecht's friend Hanns Eisler was also attracted to the *Faust* material, drawing on the chapbook legend for what he envisaged as a new national opera, *Johann Faustus*. Brecht and Eisler shared the view that *Faust*, like *The Tutor*, should be re-interpreted through the prism of the German Misere. From the outset, they were on a collision course with the SED.

Brecht discussed *Urfaust* with Neher and his assistants, Kurt Palm, Hainer Hill and Egon Monk, developing a bold, contrastive conception: 'Dürer's Middle Ages, so that the devil, the magic and the whole business of the old puppet play can be presented naively, while Goethe's "modern" bits, the Gretchen tragedy and the students in Auerbach's Cellar appear alienated'.[30] He imagined the 'Earth Spirit as a croaking, crouching animal à la Bosch and the Devil as a popular devil with horns and a club-foot'. The material brought out the irreverent mischief-maker in Brecht. The idea was to depict a Faust of great contradictions, not simply a figure striving for knowledge, but a charlatan and a seducer.

Rehearsals began in February for an experimental production at Potsdam's Brandenburgisches Landestheater, at a remove from East Berlin critics. Brecht hoped to gauge reaction there before bringing the play to the Deutsches Theater. He entrusted the production to the young Egon Monk. Youth would be the hallmark of the production. Goethe's *Urfaust* was not remotely the work of the mature Goethe that the SED had in mind, that is to say the epitome of German classical humanism. Brecht took great delight in rehearsals, writing that *Urfaust* was 'written in the manner of a cabaret. It has "numbers" that can be divided off individually. *Urfaust* is a truly Epic play'.[31] The SED leadership would not understand the enduring iconoclasm of the contentious master, seeing only caricature and heresy where Brecht saw exuberant dramatic pleasure: '*Urfaust* with the young people is fun from the start. A beautiful realistic poem! Of course, done as naively as this, it may cause annoyance. Our public's schoolmasters feel they are being talked down to if they are given the chance to be entertained'.[32] Brecht again engaged Dessau for the music and reflected upon the recalcitrant spirit which *Urfaust* brought out in him: 'I am by nature a difficult person to control. I reject angrily authority that exists without my respect, and I can only regard laws, regulating people's lives together, as provisional proposals constantly to be changed'.[33]

Reflecting, 'When I analyse a work critically, that means that I bring it to a point of crisis', Brecht concluded, 'We have been taking it too naively, Goethe is not naive, but has the taste for the naive you get in those born late. The Earth Spirit for instance is a flash of light on the wall of the hermit's cell, and the sentimental verse fits this. So oil has to be poured on the water in the well once more'.[34] He changed the sequence of scenes so that the tragedy could 'come to life', adding: 'When Eisler saw the scene in which Faust goes into Gretchen's room, he couldn't stop shaking with happy laughter, since, in spite of his pleasure in the poem, he also saw the element of depravity clearly expressed. This is an intruder taking irresponsible pleasures, for he even turns his awareness of his own baseness into pleasure'. Eisler recalled: 'Well, if you haven't seen Brecht during the rehearsals for *Urfaust* you have seen nothing. How the infuriated Brecht cut those parts of Goethe's text which he thought were rubbish! Really, only someone like Brecht can get away with that'.[35] Could he?

Urfaust premiered on 23 April with Johannes Schmidt as Faust and Käthe Reichel as Gretchen. Most reviews were enthusiastic but the critic of East Berlin's *Neue Zeit* warned of the danger of such a 'Formalistic experiment' and suggested that by taking the production to Potsdam a prickly, defensive Brecht had adopted a 'hedgehog position towards the press'.[36] Three weeks later, a letter appeared in the *Märkische Volksstimme*, in which the SED's Party Organisation for Brandenburg Theatres attacked Monk's 'Formalist' production with its 'decadent' Faust and its 'falsification of the classics', a 'dangerous experiment' for theatre history, in which Monk's Faust was simply a charlatan. The Party Organisation provoked severe altercations in the theatre and the production was discontinued. Weigel applied to the Arts Commission for *Urfaust* to transfer to the Theater am Schiffbauerdamm in the next season but the application was rejected. She and Brecht would, however, not give up and secured permission for the play to transfer to the Kammerspiele at the Deutsches Theater.

Amidst the attacks on *Urfaust*, in early May Brecht had to visit the Charité for an exploratory investigation of his stomach. Rülicke wrote that she had never seen Brecht, still in pain, so nervous, bitter, and unfair towards others. She and others saw that Brecht, who had set out to empower his employees, was favouring Reichel: 'Brecht has invested daily work in Reichel during the last quarter, often individual rehearsals in the afternoon as well – the others have been badly neglected'.[37] Rülicke, who had become Brecht's nurse, carrying medicines around for him, sought to understand: 'Of course, he is working far too much, burdening himself with all manner of things'.

After the Garbe project had stalled, Brecht attempted to tackle the transformations taking place in the countryside. A young writer, Erwin Strittmatter, was composing a work about the revolutionary changes in agriculture in the wake of the land reform of 1945–6 when the property of large landowners and Nazis had been handed to peasants. In fact, the SED would presently collectivise the peasants' land. Brecht contacted Strittmatter and began work with him on his comedy of rural life, *Katzgraben*, hoping to stage a dramatic work which dealt with the reform from a strongly supportive position.[38] In the depiction of individualised characters contributing to these historic changes Brecht drew upon Stanislavsky. Brecht had been reviewing the value of Stanislavsky in notes addressing the question of 'What, among other Things, Can be Learnt from Stanislavsky's Theatre'.[39] We shall see presently what this meant in practice.

Strittmatter stayed with Brecht in Buckow where Brecht spent much time from late June to early September. Brecht noted with pleasure: 'Outside my door is a corner formed by a demolished greenhouse and another wall. There are grass and pines, wild roses climb the walls. I have managed to find a thin café-table and a bench, with iron legs and the remains of white paint, very elegant'.[40] Stefan visited from the USA and Brecht worked with Strittmatter on *Katzgraben*, initially mustering fresh energy. He rose at 6 a.m. and worked from 8 a.m. to 2 p.m., then again in the evening for two to three hours. However, four years to the day before Brecht died, Rülicke noted: 'Sometimes I am frightened how grey and broken-down Brecht looks in the morning. It has only become clear to me here that Brecht is growing old – prematurely in fact'.[41] Brecht himself reflected: 'I, Bertolt Brecht, the son of bourgeois parents / Have leafed through my conscience this summer / With the feeling that time is short'.[42] The SED's pressure upon him since his hospitalisation in January 1951 had undoubtedly accelerated the ageing process. He also had petty harassment to contend with. Driving between Berlin and Buckow with his portable typewriter and his case containing his manuscripts, Brecht was repeatedly detained at the Hoppegarten control point between Berlin and the GDR, even though he received a special permit.

On his strolls with Rülicke at Buckow, which Brecht took with a walking stick, a recurrent topic was the exile which he felt would be necessary to escape the coming European war. Brecht wondered whether, as in Utting, he would have just one summer in his house. With the prospect of a European conflagration, Brecht said: 'Now only China remains for emigration'.[43] Amongst the visitors that summer were Neher, Eisler, Lukács, Dessau, Walcher and Girnus. With Walcher, Brecht discussed a play about Rosa Luxemburg, in which Weigel would take the lead. With Eisler Brecht discussed Eisler's *Johann Faustus*. They enjoyed cooking and playing chess, too. They talked to Girnus about artists' support for peace in advance of the SED's Second Party Conference. Brecht and Eisler co-signed a text, 'Cultural Support', which appeared in *Neues Deutschland* on 4 July. Acknowledging that 'the intensifying imperialist threats of war necessitate additional work by artists and writers for peace', they proposed the creation of artistic focal points in large factories where writers and artists would support theatre and opera performances designed for workers: 'The cultural focal points should equally be treated as political focal points, in which the most important politicians and officials systematically undertake educational work'.[44] The aim was to strengthen the cadre of workers supportive of the socialist project of the GDR. However, their proposal was misunderstood by the Siemens-Plania factory as an offer to train young amateur actors. There was further scope for misunderstanding when Girnus told Ulbricht that Brecht and Eisler would value support for their work through briefings from leading comrades like Pieck, Grotewohl and Ulbricht himself. Girnus suggested to Ulbricht that the Party could thereby exercise a 'more decisive influence' upon GDR artists.[45] The nature of that influence would presently become graphically clear.

Ulbricht's revolution

At its Second Party Conference in July the SED leadership responded to the western rejection of Stalin's notes by announcing its intention to proceed with the Construction of the Foundations of Socialism. Finally, Ulbricht's stalled revolution of

1948 could be completed. The leadership signalled an end to the compromises with bourgeois democracy which had, in their view, bedevilled the fledgling socialist state. Brecht, too, was impatient to see socialism implemented with alacrity and accepted that there would be casualties on the way. He believed that the German people would rally to genuine socialism when they could see the benefits deriving from a dictatorship exercised in the interest of the working class. However, there is little evidence that Brecht believed that the right people were in power to implement this huge agenda in the conditions of a territory impoverished by war and competing with a western German state buoyed up by US capital. The SED leadership utterly misjudged the situation, proceeding with structural reform at breakneck speed and imposing demands upon the economy which the population was not equipped to meet. In the arts, the Party pursued its anti-Formalist agenda with vehement dogmatism, scapegoating Brecht and his supporters – no enemies of the government – who were themselves casualties of the Ulbricht revolution. Here as elsewhere, the SED wildly overestimated its capacity to implement policies which demanded rapid restructuring, coupled with drastic savings targets.

The Arts Commission was in the vanguard, engineering the removal of Ernst Legal from the State Opera and of Ernst Busch from his own publishing house, which was nationalised. The popular Busch was accused of sectarian, proletkult tendencies and right-wing opportunism. Legal resigned from the Academy and Hans Rodenberg of the Arts Commission replaced him despite opposition from academicians, including Weigel, Busch and Brecht. Brecht observed that he was not alone in not being aware of any artistic achievement by Rodenberg which he could describe as even average.[46] Rodenberg's 'election' initiated the long-term strategy to shift the balance in the Academy towards SED members. The institution was infiltrated by mediocre bureaucrats who seriously damaged its standing.

The ailing Brecht was alive to this challenge. At a Plenary in September he affirmed the Academy's supreme status in the arts as an advisory body to the government: 'We must be able to intervene at the highest level in the difficult situations in the various artistic fields that constantly arise during the great upheavals that are taking place. If, say, the Arts Commission makes one of its numerous errors, the Section that is affected must be in a position to intervene at a higher level about the Arts Commission.'[47] The Academy President Arnold Zweig protested to Holtzhauer about the Arts Commission's treatment of Legal but Holtzhauer simply dismissed Zweig, rebuking the Academy for its critical attitude towards the GDR government and telling him that he did not understand! Zweig, not an SED member, could, indeed, not fully grasp what the Party was doing. During the Barlach Affair, the indolent Becher had finally accepted that, as the Academy's Vice-President, he should act to protect the institution that he had helped to establish, which was in danger of becoming the creature of the Arts Commission.[48] He positioned himself to replace Zweig and received backing from the Politburo. Unlike Weigel, Brecht would support Becher's appointment on the grounds that the Academy must assert its leadership in cultural policy. However, events were set in train from the summer of 1952, driven by the Arts Commission, that were designed to transform the Academy into a fully functioning instrument of SED cultural policy, eradicating Formalism and promoting

Socialist Realism, in a manner which left the vacillating Becher utterly compromised. Alexander Abusch, like Rodenberg a Party hack, was levered into the Academy and, with Becher's connivance amidst bitter opposition from Zweig, into the key position of Secretary of the Literature Section. Abusch, recruited by the Stasi as the 'unofficial collaborator' 'Ernst' to combat residues of Trotskyism, would wreak havoc in the Academy.[49]

Brecht submitted a still incomplete *Katzgraben* to the Arts Commission. Holtzhauer would reply that the play lacked a genuine conflict. Not without conflict, the play represents the change of consciousness in GDR citizens under conditions of non-alienated labour. Brecht struggled to identify a powerful dramatic moment noting with concern: 'It became apparent that the small peasant who was originally intended to be the hero has been supplanted by the Party Secretary, since he was the only one capable of taking a passionate attitude. This would seem to indicate that the only group in which more profound movements of the soul are to be found are the political initiators.'[50]

In mid-November Brecht travelled to Frankfurt for the final rehearsals of *The Good Person of Szechwan*, directed by Harry Buckwitz. Buckwitz had seen Brecht's *Mother Courage* in Munich and resisted huge pressure from the Frankfurt CDU to abandon his production. In his few days in Frankfurt, Brecht tried to 'give the production a little clarity and lightness' and spent time with the set designer Teo Otto, carefully selecting a pub each evening after work.[51] It had to be a little place with Munich beer. Brecht left Frankfurt just before the acclaimed premiere, Buckwitz describing the production to him as the 'most important and greatest theatrical experience in recent years'.[52] Brecht had valuable allies in Frankfurt and Munich.

Back in Berlin, he saw Weigel in *Señora Carrar's Rifles*, directed by Monk. Brecht remained in Berlin while eighty-three members of the Ensemble spent nearly all of December in Poland. After he had averted the Arts Commission's attempt to have *The Mother* banned there, performances of that play, of *Mother Courage* and of Kleist's *The Broken Jug* took place in Warsaw, Lodz and Krakow. There was a Brecht evening in each of these cities, too. Amidst the positive reviews, *Mother Courage* was criticised officially on the familiar grounds of its pacifism. Meanwhile, in Berlin Brecht further curtailed his activities, writing to the organisers of the Peoples' Congress for the Protection of Peace in Vienna that he could not attend because his doctor forbade it. For the time being, Brecht struggled on, noting in his journal how the act of writing had become second nature in enabling him to override his physical distress:

> I have, as far as I can recollect, never written a single line when I wasn't feeling well, physically. Only this feeling of well-being can give you the sense of being on top of things which you need if you are to write. You have to write from the top downwards, you have to sit above your subject. Of course, conversely, this kind of well-being more or less sets in when I sit down at the table with the typewriter.[53]

Brecht was now highly dependent upon such behavioural techniques to maintain his regular round of work. Mental strength was what he had left.

He mustered that strength to challenge staff at the Berliner Ensemble to improve their work, displaying a notice, 'About the work of the Dramatic Advisors, Directors, Assistants and Pupils of the Berliner Ensemble'.[54] Brecht had, of course, set out to establish a working environment which would liberate creative energies. After succinctly listing achievements, he was uncompromising towards weaknesses, principally that staff were not seizing the opportunity to learn so that the 'management feels tempted to introduce bureaucratic measures (with regulated working hours, insistence on deadlines etc.)'. He complained about the poor quality of directors working in the evening, about the failure to study model books and the shameful level of discussion about the *Katzgraben* adaptation: 'Political interests were as weak as artistic ones'. Monk and Palitzsch had, however, raised legitimate concerns about the dramatic potential of that project. Finally, Brecht requested an uncompromising critique of his own failings and suggestions for improvements.

At an Academy Plenary in January 1953, Brecht maintained his fierce criticism of the Arts Commission: young writers were receiving lessons in literary style from Party bureaucrats![55] A report upon the mood of academicians written for Grotewohl highlighted Brecht's anger at the artistic and political censorship exercised by the Arts Commission. However, Becher was allowing Abusch free rein in the Academy where, in conjunction with the Arts Commission, he was planning a series of events designed to impose official cultural policy upon academicians. The topics chosen for 'discussion' brought into a single focus the related problems of the Academy, *Sinn und Form* and its editor, and Brecht and the Berliner Ensemble.

On 15 January Huchel was reprimanded at the Academy's Presidium for publishing Eisler's *Johann Faustus* and Ernst Fischer's laudatory essay 'Doctor Faustus and the German Peasants' War'. Eisler's depiction of the failure of German intellectuals to support the peasant uprisings was clearly intended as a critique of those intellectuals, principally in the West, who opposed the GDR's progressive national mission. However, the Party was deeply opposed to the interpretation of the canonical Faust figure through the prism of the German Misere. Abusch seized upon the publications to demonstrate Huchel's severe lack of editorial judgement and the false conception of German Misere shared by Eisler and Fischer. It was well-known that Brecht shared that conception, too, and that Eisler had consulted his friend in the composition of his text. Abusch now engineered a situation in which *Sinn und Form* was to act as a forum for the repudiation of *Johann Faustus*, led by Abusch's own piece concerning the appropriation of the classical heritage, as represented by Goethe's *Faust*.

Towards the Galileo moment

In January, it was announced that the Academy would be the venue for the First German Stanislavsky Conference, which would take place in April under the aegis not of the Academy but of the Arts Commission. The conference was to be dedicated to the question 'How Can We Appropriate Stanislavsky's Method?'. The Arts Commission was in no doubt that everyone had to appropriate it, the Academy in particular. It was an open secret that the conference was to be a reckoning with Brecht's theatre. At a meeting of the Performing Arts Section in January, Brecht explained that he 'had to strictly reject the elevation of Stanislavsky's way of working into a dogma, a rigid law. If, on the other hand, a blend with other ways of working (systems) is possible, he would find this way of learning and application good'.[56] That was precisely what Brecht intended with *Katzgraben*.

While Hüdepohl once more admitted Brecht to St. Hedwig's from 29 January to 9 February, in the wake of the Slánský trial an atmosphere of totalitarian terror was taking hold of East Berlin. Indeed, 'the campaign of vilification in the build-up to the [Stanislavsky] conference [...] risked becoming theater's equivalent of a show trial'.[57] On the defensive, Brecht reflected that the Potsdam *Urfaust* had emphasised only negative features of Faust and that the positive should be developed in Berlin. Again, Monk would direct. Brecht wrote notes for the production but attended few rehearsals because from late February until late May he was pre-occupied with *Katzgraben*. Assailed on two fronts in his theatre, he only had the energy to cover one. Working closely with Strittmatter, he put his defences in place in advance of the Stanislavsky Conference, producing a series of texts for his own guidance.[58] Brecht clearly made some use of Stanislavsky in his efforts to create rich, rounded characters, who had emerged from the radical transition to conditions of non-alienated labour. However, as Barnett shows, rehearsal notes indicate that, for tactical reasons, Brecht's statements designed for publication tend to exaggerate the importance of Stanislavsky. Rehearsals remained much the same as for other projects of the Berliner Ensemble, enriched by such Stanislavskian elements as Strittmatter's character biographies for the three main characters. Brecht explained to a Chilean visitor: 'We shall try to use whatever in Stanislavsky can help us in our tasks, and whatever does not help us we will develop further ourselves. We shall not simply take over this method'.[59] Brecht built his position for the Stanislavsky Conference upon similarities and differences. However, such distinctions were too subtle for the Party bent on radical re-structuring at breakneck speed.

Indeed, the SED's programme was putting a severe strain on the GDR economy, exacerbating hostility towards the government amongst the population. Increasingly desperate, the SED leadership repeatedly begged Moscow for credits but was rebuffed on each occasion. On top of everything else, Stalin's death was announced on 5 March, adding to the turmoil in the Eastern Bloc. Like other prominent artists and intellectuals, Brecht joined in the mourning with the publication of a statement which reads: 'The oppressed people of five continents, those who have already liberated themselves, and all those who are fighting for world peace, must have felt their hearts miss a beat when they heard that Stalin was dead. He was the embodiment of their hopes. But the intellectual and material weapons which he produced remain, and with them the method to produce new ones'.[60] He also wrote a brief note, 'Stalin': 'I praise him for many reasons. Mostly, however, because under his leadership the robbers were defeated. The robbers, my countrymen'. After Stalin's funeral, the SED leadership again requested credits but the Soviets explained that they were planning a New Course, designed to improve living standards, and urged the SED to do the same. Instead, the SED imposed further drastic savings: ration cards were withdrawn from two million people, predominantly property owners; and, production norms for workers were raised by at least 10 per cent. Cuts were required of the Berliner Ensemble, too, which were probably intended as a prelude to the withdrawal of all state funding. Meanwhile, a leadership struggle began in Moscow between Lavrentiy

Beria, Nikita Khrushchev and Georgiy Malenkov, during which Beria would take steps to jettison the GDR.

For the moment, events in East Berlin maintained the trajectory established at the Second Party Conference. Shortly before the Berlin premiere of *Urfaust* on 13 March, Brecht struck a weary, wistful note: 'Our performances in Berlin have almost no resonance any more. The press notices appear months after the first night, and there is never anything in them anyway apart from a few pathetic bits of sociological analysis. The public is the petty bourgeois public of the Volksbühne, workers make up scarcely 7%'.[61] What is more, the technical staff at the Deutsches Theater had been disrupting rehearsals, claiming that the comic treatment of two scenes was disrespectful towards Goethe. Officials from the Arts Commission attended rehearsals and Langhoff wrote to Weigel, forbidding evening performances unless they were closed to the public![62] He claimed that otherwise *Urfaust* would clash with his theatre's production of *Faust 1*. The upshot was that *Urfaust* was performed just six times in Berlin. The only review in March spoke of a 'deformation of a great work of the national heritage', a Formalist interpretation drained of its humanist content.[63] After the humiliation of *Lucullus*, the Party, through the Arts Commission and Langhoff, had effectively silenced the Berliner Ensemble. Monk left for the West.

Members of the Berliner Ensemble had good reason to fear for their future. Without their knowledge, in March the Theater am Schiffbauerdamm was earmarked for the Garrisoned People's Police, the forerunner of the GDR army, after Wisten had vacated it, a decision confirmed by the SED Central Committee on 9 April.[64] We know what symbolic value Brecht attached to the return to the scene of his greatest triumph. This calculated insult shows what value the Party now attached to East Berlin's most feted theatre company. In late March another of Brecht's Meisterschüler, Martin Pohl, was arrested. The Stasi extracted a confession of espionage which he later retracted, but he was sentenced to four years' imprisonment. Brecht tried to help Pohl, who left for the West after serving two years.[65] This act of repression has its place amidst many others against non-SED figures as the Party ruthlessly asserted its leading role.[66] As state terror gripped the GDR, citizens fled in their droves, 58,000 in March alone. Many of those who stayed directed their anger at the government, which was fostering the cult of Ulbricht's personality in advance of his 60th birthday.

Erpenbeck chaired the Stanislavsky Conference on 17–19 April. The proceedings were little more than an orchestrated denunciation of Brecht's theatre. Langhoff delivered the keynote lecture, claiming that Stanislavsky had established the 'objective law' inherent to acting.[67] Maximilian Vallentin proclaimed: 'From now on, Stanislavsky is our yardstick'. Deeply unnerved by the occasion, Brecht had Weigel read the text that he had prepared. They countered the unrelenting anti-Brecht tone with conciliatory statements, stressing affinities between Brecht and Stanislavsky. However, in his closing address Langhoff denied such affinities: 'My view is that it would be very wrong to say today that the views which Brecht expresses in his *Short Organum for the Theatre* correspond to or are broadly similar to Stanislavsky's method. On the contrary, I believe that they deviate from this method in many decisive and essential respects'. Brecht and Weigel had already left the building. Brecht wrote 'Some Thoughts about the Stanislavsky Conference', wondering whether 'My friend Langhoff' had not 'created some confusion'.[68] On the contrary, for the SED the Stanislavsky Conference was a key component in the campaign to eradicate Formalism.

The pressure on Brecht and his fellow academicians intensified. Becher abandoned Huchel to the humiliation of ritual self-criticism and dismissal from his post, while Abusch orchestrated the Wednesday Gatherings (*Mittwoch-Gesellschaften*) in the Academy. The Wednesday Gatherings were planned as exchanges about Eisler's *Faustus* between, on the one hand, Eisler, Brecht and their supporters and, on the other, Abusch, Girnus and other Party figures. The intention was clear: to force acceptance of the Party's position. Abusch led the first discussion on 13 May with his paper 'Faust – Hero or Renegade in German National Literature?'. He contested the view that German intellectuals had betrayed progressive national forces and held up Goethe's Faust as a 'great positive hero of the classical national drama', thus as an antecedent of Socialist Realism.[69] For Abusch, Eisler had negated the progressive potential of Goethe's great figure through his misguided focus upon the German Misere. This disqualified him from producing a new national opera treating the figure of Faust. Exercised by the question of national legitimacy, Girnus followed with the charge that the Jewish Eisler was actually mounting an attack on the GDR, adding in nakedly threatening fashion: 'Eisler is expressing a foreignness towards the German people, towards the national traditions of the German people, towards its history'.[70] Others joined in the attack on Eisler's work, leaving him deeply distraught. Brecht played for time.

That same day, Brecht was encouraged to attend a forthcoming meeting with Holtzhauer at the Academy to discuss the 're-organisation of theatres'.[71] However, the meeting did not take place, probably because the ground had not yet been laid sufficiently to inform Brecht that the Theater am Schiffbauerdamm had been allocated to the Garrisoned People's Police and that no provision had been made for the Berliner Ensemble. The dissolution of Brecht's master classes was also on the agenda. The East Berlin rumour mill was full of gossip about the impending demise of the Berliner Ensemble.

Prior to the second Wednesday Gathering, under the intense pressure of events Brecht's relationship with Weigel collapsed. During rehearsals for *Katzgraben* Brecht had lost his self-control and criticised her several times severely in front of others.[72] It was not the first time that Brecht had belittled Weigel's intellectual capacity in public. This time she had had enough. Despite Brecht's protests that she should not have carried over his artistic criticisms into the private realm, she left their house in Weissensee and moved with Barbara to a flat on Reinhardtstrasse near the Deutsches Theater.[73] Following these scenes, on 23 May the premiere of *Katzgraben* took place at a Deutsches Theater resembling a mausoleum. Brecht stayed away, leaving Rülicke to report the debacle: 'House only half full, audience obnoxious. During the first two scenes nothing but dumb faces, nobody dared to laugh, applause for the scenes actually only in the dark. Awful atmosphere, everyone was just waiting for the reaction of the others. I've never seen anything like it in the theatre'.[74] She remarked that people had only come to witness a scandal: 'Someone invests a year's work and waits to see if he will be broken because of it'. *Katzgraben* remained in the repertoire until 1956 but, despite Brecht's hopes, it was never a success and was decried in the West as propaganda.

The second Wednesday Gathering on 27 May saw the pressure on Eisler, Brecht and their supporters intensify while the political crisis deepened. Taking her cue from Abusch's paper, that morning Johanna Rudolph attacked Brecht's *Urfaust* in *Neues Deutschland*.[75] The same day Ulbricht described Brecht and Eisler's depictions of Faust as a 'Formalist disfigurement' of Goethe's great creation. An extremely cautious Brecht presented his 'Theses on the *Faustus* Discussion' in an atmosphere of unremitting hostility.[76] Tempering his support for Eisler's text with some criticism of Eisler and Fischer as well as of Eisler's critics, he again sought to establish common ground. However, there was no prospect of that as long as Brecht and Eisler maintained their critical perspective on the German tradition, which their opponents were by now ritualistically dismissing as treasonable.

Brecht faced the prospect that the third Wednesday Gathering on 10 June would be his Galileo moment. The pressure to recant had become immense. However, the pressure on the SED leadership from other quarters was by now greater still. While public hostility towards Ulbricht's rule was rising to a crescendo in East Berlin, his revolution had already been abandoned in the Kremlin. Desperate to jettison the GDR, on 27 May Beria had returned to Stalin's agenda of seeking a treaty with the western powers for a united Germany. Beria envisaged western economic aid in exchange to rebuild the USSR. Ulbricht, Grotewohl and Oelssner were summoned to Moscow on 2 June to hear Beria demand 'swift and vigorous corrections' of the mistaken policy for the Construction of the Foundations of Socialism as well as Malenkov's warning: 'If we do not correct now, there will be a catastrophe'.[77] Averting the catastrophe through the New Course became the imperative. The senior Soviet diplomat Vladimir Semyenov attended a meeting of the SED Politburo on 6 June to underscore the policy, the goal of which, he stressed, was German unification. At that meeting, Oelssner was joined by Wilhelm Zaisser, Beria's counterpart as the Minister of State Security, in urging a policy review in the light of 'Ulbricht's dictatorship'. Semyenov urged the formation of a collective leadership and on 9 June the SED Politburo hurriedly announced its New Course. This volte-face caused consternation among Party workers, who had been battling to implement the Ulbricht revolution. The Soviets approached figures like Zaisser and Rudolf Herrnstadt, the editor-in-chief of *Neues Deutschland*, encouraging them to tell Ulbricht to step down. His birthday celebrations were off the agenda.

The impact of the New Course was apparent at the third Wednesday Gathering the next day. Non-SED academicians like Zweig rallied around Brecht, finding their voices, while Brecht himself assumed a central role, presenting his revised 'Theses' and challenging the crude assertions of his opponents, whose certainties began to crumble. As the SED group lost ground, Becher in the chair finally offered some protection to Eisler, criticising Girnus, where previously he had lent him support. The position that Abusch had been building in the Academy since the autumn of 1952 was rapidly unravelling.

Catastrophe: Rescuing culture

Brecht retired to Buckow. Emboldened by the announcement of the New Course, on 12 June he protested against the dissolution of his master classes and on 15 June told Grotewohl: 'Helene Weigel and I find it increasingly distressing that the Ensemble should be regarded as an economic luxury'.[78] He reminded Grotewohl of the agreement that the Ensemble should move to the Theater am Schiffbauerdamm once the Volksbühne was ready for Wisten, then entered high-risk territory, issuing an oblique threat to abandon the GDR if he was not granted his theatre. Referring to the 'wild rumours' in the West about 'friction' between him and the government, he stated: 'If the Berliner Ensemble, which is known far beyond the borders of Germany, were to take over the Theater am Schiffbauerdamm, my solidarity with our republic would be evident to all'.

This, for a member of the nomenklatura, well-nigh treasonable statement boomeranged alarmingly upon Brecht when the Republic was plunged into a crisis threatening its very existence. On 16 June the West Berlin radio station RIAS began to report demonstrations in the East of the city. Brecht at once returned to Berlin and met with friends. The following morning demonstrators marched on the House of the Ministries, demanding the resignation of the government and free elections. The demonstrations rapidly spread to other East German towns and cities. While the Berliner Ensemble continued rehearsals for the adaptation of Molière's *Don Juan*, Brecht went out on Unter den Linden to gain an impression of events. He would state in his later analysis, which is largely in keeping with the official SED position, that demonstrations by East Berlin workers with legitimate grievances had been infiltrated by dubious elements from the West, among them war-mongering Nazis intent on destroying the GDR. The use of force to suppress the demonstrations was therefore justified.

Having played upon his capacity to do quite well without the GDR, Brecht, faced with this dire threat to the socialist state in which he had a major stake politically and artistically, dispatched letters to Ulbricht, Grotewohl and Semyenov, which underscore his loyalty to the USSR, the GDR and the SED. He wrote to Semyenov: 'May I at this moment express to you my inviolable friendship with the Soviet Union'.[79] He asked Grotewohl: 'What can we at the Academy of Arts and the Berliner Ensemble do? Will you speak on the radio? That would be a good thing. We would be glad to provide songs and recitations by Ernst Busch and other artists'.[80] Brecht concluded his letter: 'With unstinting allegiance to the Socialist Unity Party of Germany'.[81] Brecht wrote the following to Ulbricht: 'History will pay its respects to the revolutionary impatience of the Socialist Unity Party of Germany. The great debate with the masses about the tempo of socialist construction will have the effect of testing and safeguarding the achievements of socialism. At this moment I feel I must assure you of my allegiance to the Socialist Unity Party of Germany'.[82] Brecht's survival instinct briefly met with Ulbricht's as they struggled to save their skins, together with the fledgling German socialist state. Their views diverged drastically upon how that should be done. As everyone knew, a 'great debate' had been the last thing on Ulbricht's agenda in his disastrous revolution. A desperate Ulbricht seized upon Brecht's letter and cynically published just the last sentence in *Neues*

Deutschland. Brecht was left seething, while Ulbricht thanked 'Comrade Brecht' for his support and looked forward their next conversation.[83] Brecht's letter to Ulbricht outraged many people and there were renewed calls for a Brecht boycott in the West. Over the coming weeks Ulbricht recovered his position, ousting his opponents in the Politburo, watering down the New Course and working with the Soviets to discipline the East German population. While Beria was arrested and shot on 26 June, Ulbricht stayed in power until 1971.

On the morning of 17 June Brecht called a staff meeting at the Berliner Ensemble, at which he repeated his view that a 'great debate' with the masses was required. He again attempted to approach East Berlin radio but was spurned. The radio maintained a deafening silence while at 1.30 p.m. the SMAD declared a state of emergency and Soviet tanks took to the streets. That afternoon, Brecht attended an emergency meeting of the Academy's Presidium.[84] Abusch and Engel proposed that the Academy contribute to the re-establishment of order with a manifesto declaring its confidence in the government. Clearly wary of the Academy committing itself thereby to the continuation of existing cultural policy, Brecht countered that such a statement could only be made once the government itself had spoken. In the circumstances, he argued, academicians might voice their support individually on the radio and through similar activity.

With the SED's weakness laid bare, Brecht was immediately alive to the opportunity to cast off the repressive cultural apparatus, summoning energy for the struggle. Alluding to the New Course, Brecht proposed that academicians should address the 're-structuring of cultural life' in the light of an urgent and open discussion of errors in cultural policy and of the damage done by the unprofessional, bureaucratic management of the arts. Over the coming weeks the New Course would remain Brecht's key point of reference and the Academy his principal forum for activity. Lazarus-like, he assumed the leading role in a series of emergency meetings, in which he pressed the case for change. At a Plenary on 18 June he was elected to a group which met on 20 June to discuss what elements of cultural policy had to be altered. On 22 June Holtzhauer attended a special meeting of the Academy to respond to the charge of 'dictatorial, bureaucratic interventions'.[85]

Following the publication of Brecht's mutilated letter to Ulbricht, on 23 June *Neues Deutschland* published Brecht's clarification of his position, 'The Urgent Need for a Great Debate':

> On the morning of 17 June, when it became clear that the workers' demonstrations were being used for the purposes of war-mongering, I expressed my commitment to the Socialist Unity Party. I hope now that the provocateurs are being isolated and their lines of communication cut. At the same time, however, I hope that the workers who demonstrated out of justified dissatisfaction will not be equated with the provocateurs, so that the great debate concerning the mistakes made on all sides, which is so urgently needed, will not be rendered impossible from the outset.[86]

He repeated essentially the same position in a note 'Concerning 17 June 1953' and enlarged upon the threat of war posed by resurgent Fascism in a letter to Peter

Suhrkamp, in which he acknowledged the SED's serious mistakes whilst stressing its historic achievements.

At a Plenary on 26 June Brecht presented proposals for changes in cultural policy, which were adopted as a ten-point 'Declaration by the German Academy of Arts'.[87] The first point aimed directly at the abolition of the Arts Commission and those following at the re-establishment of the principle that artistic and editorial responsibility should rest with artists, editors and their organisations, not with bureaucratic organs. However, Grotewohl banned publication of the document, triggering Brecht and Felsenstein's threat to resign from the Academy and Brecht's shift to outspoken public polemic.[88]

At the same Plenary on 26 June Brecht and Eisler exacted revenge on Abusch and Friedrich Wolf for their sustained assault on Huchel. At a meeting about *Sinn und Form* on 2 July, Brecht mounted a savage attack on Abusch and the Academy's Presidium. He doubted whether the Presidium's actions had reflected academicians' wishes and expressed his profound mistrust of Abusch's actions. Therefore,

> Brecht will propose to the Plenary that, apart from the President, all the permanent secretaries be elected again. He will also explain why he regards the fresh election of secretaries as necessary. The composition of the Presidium does not correspond to the requirements of the present situation. We need someone here who has the trust of the whole section. The election of the Vice-President must be repeated, too![89]

After achieving Huchel's re-instatement, Brecht continued the offensive, galvanising fellow academicians. He mocked Holtzhauer's appearance before them in the poem 'Unidentifiable Errors of the Arts Commission':

> Invited to a session of the Academy of Arts
> The highest officials of the Arts Commission
> Paid their tribute to the noble custom of
> Accusing oneself of certain errors, and
> Muttered that they too accused themselves
> Of certain errors. Asked
> What errors, however, they found it wholly impossible to recall
> Any specific errors.[90]

Previously unthinkable, this poem appeared in *Berliner Zeitung* on 11 July. Four days later, bureaucrats and Party hacks were again the butt of Brecht's satire in the same newspaper in the poem 'The Office for Literature'. On 12 July the 'Declaration by the German Academy of Arts' finally appeared in *Neues Deutschland*. Brecht complained pointedly to Grotewohl the same day: 'Everywhere the New Course is being obstructed by the rigidity of the administration'.[91] Brecht had few illusions about the prospects for a great debate led by the SED, for whom, as he put it, 'again and again decrees took the place of persuasion'.[92] However, after 17 June the badly weakened SED leadership could not afford to lose artists of the calibre of Brecht and Weigel. On 15 July, the Cultural Department of the Central Committee noted that the resolution concerning the use of Berlin's theatres would be changed in the manner suggested by Brecht to

Grotewohl in order to accommodate the Berliner Ensemble.[93] On 22 July Grotewohl's office informed Brecht that he approved Brecht's proposal but a final decision had to await the completion of work on the Volksbühne. The struggle was not over.

Buckow: Literary reflections

From early July to September Brecht spent much time at Buckow, while Weigel and Barbara holidayed on the Baltic island of Rügen. Brecht had been feeling unhappy alone in the house in Weissensee and started to look for a place nearer to the theatre. He quickly found the flat at Chausseestrasse 125 where he would spend his remaining years. He described it to Weigel:

> Block at the back (like the front block very old, two storeys, dates from the eighteen thirties, consequently congenial, modest, built for unpretentious people), one enormous room with a large window, one medium-sized room and one small (not very small) one. Small kitchen, a shower will have to be put in, gas and electricity already installed. Toilet on the stairs. Garage downstairs, goes with the flat. Behind the back block a small garden which, let's hope, belongs to it, with an unimpressive tree. Windows look out on the cemetery, all very green and spacious.[94]

He later added to Suhrkamp that the building was

> next to the 'French' graveyard, where Huguenot generals and Hegel and Fichte are buried; all my windows look out on the cemetery grounds. It's not without its cheerful side. I have three rooms on the first floor of the back building, which like the front building is said to be about a hundred and fifty years old. The rooms are high and so are the windows, which have pleasant proportions.[95]

The graveyard in question was the Dorotheenstadt Cemetery. Brecht had chosen to spend his final years with a vantage point upon the place where he, too, would be buried. Weigel responded from Rügen, showing her side of that understated emotional relationship: 'It's a pity that you didn't come, although the weather was not absolutely beautiful, but it seems to me that I've really picked up, and maybe it would be important for you, too, not only to take a holiday near Berlin but to take in a real change of climate – at least for a short while'.[96] Through such gestures of affection they edged back towards each other.

In Buckow Brecht discussed the dire political and economic situation with a plumber with his own business. He told Brecht some things he wanted to hear and others which he didn't:

> The apparatus of officialdom is inflated, the money goes into unproductive work. The farmers have no workers. A girl gets 400–500 marks in an office. An apprentice whom he sacked for theft and stupidity is now in the People's Police and has applied to go to officers' school. People in town are saying that Nazis condemned to ten years for crimes against 'human rights' are being recruited into

the People's Police. Under Hitler officialdom was also inflated, but there was more money then. The Russians want to impose their Asiatic culture on Europe.[97]

The plumber drank a glass of Brecht's red wine. Before he left he invited Brecht to play chess and said, 'What we need is free elections', to which Brecht responded, 'Then the Nazis would be elected'. However, the plumber disagreed and commented: 'You can't open your mouth, haven't been able to for twenty years'. Brecht's relations with another Buckow tradesman became fractious. He became involved in a dispute over building work with a builder Gustav Günzel, during which, suspecting a political motive, he engaged the GDR's celebrity lawyer Friedrich Karl Kaul. Günzel had been a prominent Nazi and had ceased contact with Brecht after 17 June, 'probably in the hope that the two houses [...] would no longer remain in my possession'.[98] If property lent Brecht a sense of security, the threat of its loss contributed to his great anxiety. Brecht would later remark: 'This country still gives me the creeps'.[99] That anxiety about resurgent Fascism strongly coloured Brecht's attitudes.

Meanwhile, the struggle over cultural policy raged on. Primed to stifle any groupings outside the SED and to safeguard his own position, Girnus reported to Ulbricht his alarm that Wolfgang Harich, who had earlier formed Friends of Bertolt Brecht, might be aligning himself with Brecht's attacks on the bureaucracy and cultural policy in his call for a review of the cultural pages of *Neues Deutschland*.[100] Harich would be arrested shortly after Brecht's death in the crackdown following the Hungarian Uprising and, amidst protests from Weigel, sentenced to ten years after signing a statement of culpability. Girnus also reported to Ulbricht a long conversation with Brecht at Buckow on 25 July.[101] Brecht had utterly condemned SED cultural policy since the Fifth Plenary of January 1951, when the Party had launched the Campaign against Formalism. He had insisted that whatever Zdhanov might have said in the Soviet Union, such views had absolutely no currency in the GDR. Brecht was quite categorical that the struggle against Formalism and decadence was a 'Nazi thing'. The word 'Volk' should not be used at all because it was a Nazi term. It is a measure of the SED's weakness that Girnus recommended to Ulbricht the 'elastic treatment of the whole affair'. Playing Brecht's teacher and displaying his knowledge as a Party insider, Girnus suggested to Ulbricht that giving Brecht the Theater am Schiffbauerdamm could have a 'pedagogical effect' since he would be obliged to win over an audience! Still in control of the cultural pages of *Neues Deutschland*, Girnus promised Ulbricht that he would arrange reviews of Brecht's productions. Girnus would, however, shortly be moved to work with the Committee for German Unity.

On 4 August Weigel met Paul Wandel, now Secretary of the Central Committee, who hoped shortly to confirm the move to the Theater am Schiffbauerdamm.[102] Brecht wrote to Wandel on 4 August, too, citing the concern of academicians that the Arts Commission might not after all be abolished. That would be 'interpreted not as firmness but as obstinacy, an inflexible opposition to reason. Indeed, what point can there be in prolonging a creeping malaise, a feeling, ruinous to all creativeness, of being at the mercy of an all-powerful institution that is unable to make its demands understood?'. Brecht proposed that the Arts Commission 'should be ruthlessly and sweepingly dissolved' and that a Ministry of Culture might assume its responsibilities.

He concluded: 'What we need now is simply to leave artists free to produce; they can do so much if left alone (and intelligently guided)'. He sent Wandel a poem 'The Truth Unites', in which he argued that the truth which workers needed to hear was that they were in mortal danger of being cast into a new war by a resurgent Fascism. They must therefore bring the petty bourgeoisie under their leadership. He warned: 'We have a West of our own over here!'.[103] In similar vein, Brecht noted that the SED must become the 'advocate of the common people, fight for their interests, win their trust, intervene, in contrast to the bureaucracy'. Brecht, however, had long experience of the Communist movement's preference for bureaucratic dictat over dialogue.

Brecht published an article in *Neues Deutschland*, 'Cultural Policy and the Academy of Arts', responding to Walter Besenbruch's polemic against the Academy's 'Declaration'. Besenbruch had accused elements in the Academy of opportunism and the Academy in general of failing to give a Marxist lead. Brecht responded that the Academy was not a Marxist body and protested against the administrative imposition of rules upon artists 'like bad beer'.[104] In case this public statement should leave anyone in the West in doubt over his position, Brecht wrote 'Not What Was Meant', a sharp riposte to western reports that events in the Academy were merely a struggle for freedom of expression.[105] The poem associates such a view with an exploitative ideology of freedom-for-all which would re-instate Fascist barbarism: 'The arsonist with his bottle of petrol / Sneaks up grinning to / The Academy of Arts'. The poem concludes: 'Even the narrowest minds / In which peace is harboured / Are more welcome to the arts than the art lover / Who is also a lover of the art of war'. By that measure, the cultural bureaucrats, who were after all anti-Fascists, were not the real enemy. However, Brecht had denounced their weddedness to Nazi terminology and would presently develop that critique. Meanwhile, the Politburo confirmed that the Berliner Ensemble rather than the Garrisoned People's Police would occupy the Theater am Schiffbauerdamm.[106] Brecht and Weigel would only believe it once they saw it.

On 20 August Brecht began his reflections on the workers' uprising with the arresting statement in his journal, 'Buckow. *Turandot*. Also the 'Buckow Elegies'. 17th June has alienated the whole of existence'.[107] To convey his sense of alienation he used his own term 'verfremdet' and continued with words that convey the very strangeness of his shocking encounter with a fetishised working class:

> Despite their pathetic helplessness and lack of direction, the workers' demonstrations have shown that this is the rising class. It is not the petty bourgeois who are taking action, but the workers. Their slogans are confused and powerless, foisted on them by the class enemy, and there is no strength in their organisation, no councils have been set up, no plan has been formed. And yet here we had the class in front of us, in its most depraved condition, but nevertheless the class. The important thing would have been to use this first encounter to full advantage. This was the point of contact. It came not as an embrace but as a slap in the face.

For Brecht, the big question was what had to be done so that the 'rising class' might be reconciled with the Party which claimed to represent its interests so that the class enemy could be defeated. In Brecht's view, the only alternative to socialism was

Fascism and war. Indeed, the traumatic vision of resurgent Nazism informs much of Brecht's writing from the summer of 1953, questioning the GDR's claim to be the home of anti-Fascism but occluding the equally troubling question of the SED's right to rule. Brecht detected residual Fascism in all areas of German life, most strikingly in the GDR bureaucracy. He wrote a preface to his play *Turandot*, which remained unpublished until the demise of the GDR. It concludes: 'Under the new commanders, the Nazi apparatus once more set itself in motion. Such an apparatus cannot be imbued with a new spirit through control from above; it needs control from below. Unconvinced but cowardly, hostile but cowering, ossified officials began again to govern against the population'.[108]

Many of Brecht's direct opponents in cultural affairs had, of course, spent the Nazi years in exile or in prison. However, Brecht was concerned with Fascism in the everyday life of the regime which the SED's propagation of German cultural nationalism by the likes of Abusch and Girnus had done little to challenge. This is a major theme in the 'Buckow Elegies' which he wrote that summer, picking up on his ironic use of the term in the 'Hollywood Elegies'. He composed twenty-three elegies, most of them miniature aperçus of life in the GDR, but published just six relatively innocuous ones that year, among them 'The One-Armed Man in the Undergrowth' about 'The dreaded SS man'. 'Eight Years Ago' is a similar reflection:

> There was a time
> When all was different here.
> The butcher's wife knows.
> The postman has too erect a gait.
> And what was the electrician?[109]

Others elegies like 'Still At It' and 'Hot Day' record the persistent presence of reaction, while others still like 'Great Times, Wasted' reflect upon opportunities for change squandered by damaging administrative fiat: 'What's the point of cities, built / Without the people's wisdom?'.[110] The polemical Brecht emerges in 'The Solution', his famous satire of the cultural bureaucracy written after Kurt Barthel had openly threatened workers in *Neues Deutschland* on 20 June:

> After the uprising of the 17th June
> The Secretary of the Writers' Union
> Had leaflets distributed in the Stalinallee
> Stating that the people
> Had forfeited the confidence of the government
> And could win it back only
> By redoubled efforts. Would it not be easier
> In that case for the government
> To dissolve the people
> And elect another?

As we have seen, Brecht did not actually believe that the German people were ready to reject Fascism in free elections. In 'Nasty Morning', Brecht guiltily recognises his own privileged distance from workers:

Last night in a dream I saw fingers pointing at me
As at a leper. They were worn with toil and
They were broken.

You don't know! I shrieked
Conscience-stricken.

The public is intertwined with the private in the manner of the *Svendborg Poems*. In 'The Smoke', Brecht follows his polemical interventions within the upheaval with a measured appreciation of the value of everyday human life:

The little house among trees by the lake
From the roof smoke rises.
Without it
How dreary would be
House, trees and lake.[111]

Brecht's thoughts about his ageing emerge in 'Firs' as in the early hours he sees the copper of the fir-trees: 'That's how I saw them / Half a century ago / Two world wars ago / with young eyes'. However, Brecht remained impatient for change to make good opportunities squandered. 'Changing the Wheel' records the poet's frustration: 'I do not like the place I have come from. / I do not like the place I am going to'.[112] The motto of the collection picks up on his favourite motifs of movement and non-resistance in Wu Wei: 'Were a wind to arise / I could put up a sail / Were there no sail / I'd make one of canvas and sticks'. However, the tailwind which would facilitate Brecht's activity remains frustratingly absent. He suggests in 'Reading Horace' that the dark times have not passed, despite the demise of two of the real maniacs of the age, Hitler and Stalin. The 'cryptic anti-Stalinist' poem 'Iron' is an appeal for the flexibility and therefore durability which wood offers over the rigidity of iron – or steel, Stalin meaning Man of Steel – within the 'great storm' of the age.[113] 'The Muses' captures the grotesque spectacle of Stalinist culture which threatened still to engulf Brecht:

When the man of iron beats them
The Muses sing louder.
With blackened eyes
They adore him like bitches.
Their buttocks twitch with pain.
Their thighs with lust.[114]

In *Turandot or The Whitewashers' Congress*, which Brecht composed that summer, the Chinese princess Turandot is the capricious, foolish muse, eager to be seduced by the 'elegant formulation' of the Tuis, fraudulent intellectuals prepared to do the bidding of those in power and hostile to genuine artistic and intellectual production.[115] Brecht remarked to Rülicke upon the back-tracking he was witnessing from the New Course: 'The whitewashing is in full swing. What an opportunity to become a good Communist!'.[116] Brecht's approach, fuelling his confidence in genuine production and his critique of intellectual fraud – a matter which had exercised him since his depiction of the littérateur George Garga in *In the Jungle* – remains recognisably that of the Korschian method, employing the Marxist dialectic as an analytical tool.

Brecht drew upon Carlo Gozzi's sarcastic, tragi-comic operatic treatment of the Turandot legend. Seeing it in Moscow in 1932 had prompted him to assemble his own satirical *Turandot* and *Tui* material in the 1930s and 1940s. *Turandot* is full of Brecht's sardonic jokes born of his intellectual encounters: from the BPRS and the KPD, Goebbels, Rosenberg and the 'Zieglers', the Paris congresses, the Moscow camarilla and the show trials, the Frankfurturists and HUAC, to the SED's Campaign against Formalism. He was struck by the very strangeness of his creation: 'When I look at *Turandot* now – she stands right outside German literature and seems, as single persons often do, shaky on her pins. If I were wholly a comedy writer, which I almost am, but only almost, then such a work would have relatives grouped round it, and the clan would be able to impose itself'.[117]

She was not altogether alone but the undertaking certainly had its risks. Brecht built upon his comic experiments in *The Tutor* and *Urfaust*, branching out into the exuberant popular form of burlesque in a play designed for high-tempo performance and echoing Marx's observation that history repeats itself, first as tragedy, then as farce. Ever probing ironic dissonances between form and content in order to bring out serious underlying issues, Brecht's burlesque highlights the grim repetition of intellectual prostitution, which he had witnessed once more that summer. Undoubtedly, his composition was informed by the view which he had conveyed so forcibly to Girnus that the SED's cultural nationalism exhibited fateful continuities with that of the Nazis. As Brecht knew from bitter experience, the SED was drawing directly upon a reactionary Stalinist cultural nationalism which had strong affinities with the Nazis' own. The German socialist project in the GDR remained mired in the 'dark times' of the 1930s.

From the outset, Brecht's irreverent treatment of an extremely sensitive issue placed *Turandot* well beyond the pale for the SED's cultural policemen. At the same time, Brecht's critique was not confined to the failings of the new socialist state within a divided Germany. He acknowledged: 'As for the "message" of the work, there's nothing simple about it'.[118] Brecht's satire is not a reckoning with the GDR: the play holds up land reform as a policy which wins the peasant Sen's approval, indicating that more, not less, socialism is required. Brecht's *Turandot* is rather a critique of the type of society he had known all his life, which had produced intellectuals as an unremittingly parasitic presence, propagandists either masquerading as academics and professionals or out in the open as PR people and lobbyists. What is more, Brecht the academician was himself no longer an independent producer but belonged to the intellectual elite implicated in his critique.

That critique is embedded in a China of the Turandot legend which bears traits of both the threadbare *ancien régime* of the last Emperor and of Germany during the protracted crisis of the dark times through and beyond the collapse of the House of Hohenzollern. In Brecht's understanding, 'Chima', as he referred to his parabolic creation, had yet to emerge from those dark times, during which Communism struggled to supplant a discredited system buttressed by Fascism. He put it as follows: 'After writing *Life of Galileo*, in which I had portrayed the dawning of an age of reason,

I wanted to portray its evening, the dusk of that variety of reason which, at the end of the sixteenth century, had launched the capitalist age'.[119] As always, Brecht identified the struggle for economic power as the underlying issue during this late time of perverted reason.

Brecht's burlesque has distinct echoes of his classic treatment of Fascist infiltration in *Arturo Ui* and of capitalist exploitation of the commodities market in *Saint Joan of the Stockyards*. *Turandot* exposes a political economy dominated by the financial machinations of the Emperor and his entourage. The Emperor is, however, a weak, anachronistic figurehead, manipulated by his brother and the Tuis of the court. They enjoy the wealth generated by their manipulation of the price of cotton – a staple commodity upon which the people depend – through over-production, destruction and hoarding of the crop. The decrepit system is symbolised by an ancient, patched coat, hanging by a thick rope in a decaying round tower, which the Emperor shows to his daughter: 'My dear Turandot, this is it, the revered tunic. Your ancestor wore it in battle and, being a poor man, he sometimes had to patch the bullet holes himself, as you can see. Every emperor wears this tunic at his coronation, because of the old prophecy associated with it. The confidence of the people in their emperor is indispensable'.[120] The legend has it that 'as long as it hangs there on its cord, the people will be bound to the Emperor'.

The Emperor's rule may be hanging by a thread, albeit a thick one, and he also has to hear the protests of the people's representatives. However, the Tuis from the Union of Clothesmakers and the rival Union of the Clothesless fight amongst themselves over their platitudinous re-cyclings of Marx and finally have to be separated by the Emperor. He concludes: 'The question "Where is the cotton?" should be debated and resolved by the cleverest and most learned men in the land. I proclaim and summon herewith an extraordinary Tui Congress, which will surely be able to explain satisfactorily to the people where it's all gone, all the cotton in China'.[121] The Tui who provides the most convincing account will receive the hand of the Emperor's daughter in marriage. The others will be decapitated, serving as an example to opponents of the system, who include the popular leader in the countryside, Kai Ho, a Mao Zedong-like figure.

We encounter the Tuis at their Academy and their teahouse, where their principal activity is selling opinions at the highest price. Their opinions are all about buttressing the existing order and discrediting Kai Ho. However, those who come forward to address the question 'Where is the cotton?' all fall short. Following a scholastic disquisition on the nature of cotton, Ke Lei claims, wholly implausibly, that the harvest has failed. Xi Wei maintains, again quite implausibly, that the 'disappearance of the cotton on its way from the fields to the cities can be explained by the steady advance of culture through our land: it is being bought by the people themselves!'.[122] The next candidate, the philosopher Munka Du, with some resemblance to Adorno, is vetted for un-Chinese attitudes, including sympathy with radical ideas, while supporters of Kai Ho enter the debating chamber and are forcibly removed. Espousing the cause of freedom of speech, Munka Du explains: 'It's not a question of cotton, it is a question of the freedom of beliefs about cotton, which itself is not at issue, which is not our business here. Here, at this hour, it is not a question of business, but a question of opinions'. While he invokes virtue and inner freedom, there is increasing commotion, during which the bandit Gogher Gogh appears but is dragged away, Kai Ho's supporters re-assert themselves and Munka Du blurts out: 'I'm not concerned with the cotton stashed in the Emperor's warehouses, I am concerned with freedom!'. Like the other Tuis, Munka Du is decapitated and his impaled head is displayed on the city wall.

Gogher Gogh re-appears, offering protection to the state and winning over Turandot as he explains: 'A nation without literature is no proper cultural nation. But it has to be a healthy literature'.[123] The Tui Ka Mü echoes this sentiment: 'And this is new music. It's in trouble because it's not "true to the spirit of the people"'. Gogher Gogh explains to the Emperor: 'The people are a danger and a threat to law and order. [...] The question about the cotton, you mustn't answer it, you must have it outlawed'. Helping the Emperor to hold on to power and admired by Turandot, Gogher Gogh is named Chancellor and has half the cotton burned, which serves as a pretext to round up the unions and remaining Tuis. However, the writings of Kai Ho remain in circulation and the peasant Sen, looking forward to land reform and the end of the Tuis, departs to join his forces with words that echo Brecht's own upon the value of genuine, productive learning: 'Thinking is the most useful and pleasurable of activities'.[124] The play ends with Kai Ho's forces at the city's gates, the ancient tunic gone and a soldier telling the Emperor, Gogher Gogh and their entourage: 'You're finished now!'.

Clearly, any new production would have to take into account China's development into authoritarian capitalism, buttressed by the Communist Party bureaucracy. The corrupt Tuis live on, controlling production. Brecht, of course, knew that 'It will carry on like this for a while, until the intellectuals are no longer outside and in opposition to the rest of the population, and the whole population, on the contrary, has been intellectualised'.[125] As Brecht had acknowledged, his message was by no means simple. He left the play almost complete after further work in 1954 but production plans for the GDR were not realised and the play was not premiered until 1969 in Zurich, directed by Besson. The audience was receptive to *Turandot* but critics could muster little enthusiasm.

The New Age of the Theatre 1953–6

Victory on two fronts

Brecht and his supporters maintained the pressure for change in Berlin. Following a discussion with Girnus about theatre reviews, Brecht suggested a battle of the critics and that young theatre lovers should be invited to review: 'The only important thing is that they are really allowed to give expression to their own opinion and only be advised politically'.[1] In September he complained to the editorial board of *Theater der Zeit* about the magazine's 'superficial', 'hopelessly dilettantish' review of *Katzgraben*, questioning the credentials of the reviewer, Lily Leder. He forwarded his letter to the Academy, with the request that it demand the re-organisation of the magazine, whose editor Erpenbeck, he remarked, had gone to China for three months without naming a deputy.

Broadening the attack, Brecht offered strongly worded advice on reform of the People's Chamber, over which Grotewohl presided.[2] At an Academy Plenary, which was attended by senior people from the state radio station, Brecht launched a swingeing attack, describing their practices as 'dirty tricks', highlighting their unpopularity in comparison to Western stations and criticising them for blocking the Berliner Ensemble's offer to broadcast on 17 June.[3] Academicians' angry rejection of failed cultural policy focused afresh upon Holtzhauer, who was still bent on rooting out Formalism, maintaining that the modern dance taught by the academician Gret Palucca was a deformation of classical ballet. On 1 October, an alarmed Langhoff wrote to 'Hans', probably Johannes R. Becher, that non-SED academicians 'around Brecht' were 'really threatening an open fronde'.[4] Felsenstein had said they should emigrate at once, while Busch was considering returning his National Prize, giving up all public responsibilities and suing Holtzhauer for slander. Academicians would simply not tolerate his bureaucracy.

Amidst the antagonisms, Brecht, Weigel and Busch travelled to Vienna for the latter part of October for the final rehearsals at the New Scala of *The Mother*, which Manfred Wekwerth, one of Brecht's assistants, had been preparing. There were familiar conflicts. Actors trained in 'empathy' drama experienced great difficulty in adjusting to Brecht's approach. Brecht took in Vienna's Brueghels and a Bosch and spent time with Eisler, who had fled to Vienna after the Wednesday Gatherings and whose 'productive crisis continues'.[5] Brecht encouraged his friend to compose an act of his

Faustus, which he promised to stage, while Eisler wrote a letter to the SED Central Committee, regretting a drunken episode when he had been arrested in West Berlin. Eisler explained that 'after the attack on *Faustus* he had 'lost any impulse to compose music' and had suffered the deepest depression.[6] It was some time before Eisler could bring himself to return to East Berlin.

Weigel delivered a dazzling performance as Pelagea Vlassova, while she and Brecht overcame their differences. After he had returned to Berlin, Weigel wrote: 'I wish you were still here. Thank you for the nice weeks'.[7] Brecht travelled back with Vladimir Pozner, whom he had known a little in California and who was in fact a Soviet spy. Brecht engaged Pozner to write the script for the film of *Puntila*.[8] They worked together at Brecht's new flat on Chausseestrasse. Pozner recalls that Brecht's study

> was surrounded by a jumble of curiously shaped and un-matched armchairs, very small tables, a tiny harmonium, a portable typewriter. Half-smoked cigars lay around on pewter plates; on the walls there were an engraving, Chinese masks, and two small old photos, one of Marx when his beard was still black, and the other of a very young Engels. All the horizontal planes disappeared under a chaos of paper: music, manuscripts, letters, posters, books.[9]

When Weigel returned, Brecht visited her at Reinhardtstrasse, armed with a bouquet of violets, and asked her to join him at Chausseestrasse. She did so and brought her taste to bear on the interior, furnishing Brecht's flat and the one she moved into above with Biedermeier furniture. The interior of Chausseestrasse 125 has been preserved in that style. Today it is a museum devoted to Brecht and Weigel and also houses the Brecht Archive. Brecht described his flat to Suhrkamp: 'The largest room is about nine metres square, so I can put in several desks for different jobs. Actually the whole place is well-proportioned, it's really a good idea to live in houses and with furniture that are at least a hundred and twenty years old, let's say, in early capitalist surroundings until later socialist surroundings are available'.[10] Brecht also surrounded himself with East Asian objects, indicating an abiding 'emotional and intellectual engagement of some substance' with this alternative to western individualism. As Tatlow further observes:

> In the library the splendid portrait of Confucius hung beside the scroll of Mao Tse-Tung's poem 'Snow'. On the bookcase opposite stood the picture of the Kabuki actor; above it hung those three Noh theatre masks. The only picture in the privacy of his bedroom was the 'blue-ink' scroll of the Chinese 'philosopher', deep in thought, whom he called the 'doubter'. He carried this talisman and those Noh masks on his journey round the world.[11]

Brecht, who depended upon Weigel to organise his life, now looked to her to organise his death. In November, he wrote her a letter, which was to remain sealed, with instructions about what was to be done in that eventuality.[12] He would issue further instructions in an unsealed letter to the Academy director Rudolf Engel: 'I would like to be buried in the graveyard next to the house where I live, in Chausseestrasse'.[13]

Brecht mustered energy for the production of one of his last great plays of exile to reach the German stage, *The Caucasian Chalk Circle*. Angelika Hurwitz was Grusha and Ernst Busch Azdak. Brecht devoted enormous time and effort to this production, working on the music with Dessau and viewing the play as the culmination of his efforts to create an ensemble versed in the Epic style. He noted:

> Roles like Grusha and Azdak cannot be shaped in our times by the work of the director alone. No less than five years at the Berliner Ensemble were necessary to give Angelika Hurwitz the right foundations. And Busch's whole life, from his proletarian childhood in Hamburg via the struggles in the Weimar Republic and the Spanish Civil War to the bitter experiences after forty-five, was necessary to bring about this Azdak.[14]

Azdak's motivation was, as Brecht had put it in 1944, born of his 'disappointment that the fall of the old rulers did not bring about a new age, but just an age of new rulers, as a consequence of which he continues to dispense bourgeois justice, but in a degenerate, subversive fashion, serving the absolute self-interest of the judge'.[15] Brecht understood that disappointment as well as the adoption of that intensely egotistical mode of behaviour. Like others of his generation, Brecht's horizons were not those of German division.

There would be 125 days of rehearsals and eight rehearsal performances for *The Caucasian Chalk Circle*, during which there was mounting criticism in East Berlin, which would turn into another reckoning with Epic Theatre. Between rehearsals, Brecht maintained the pressure for the abolition of the Arts Commission. In a letter to Ulbricht in December, he cited the importance of the New Course and urged the establishment of the Ministry of Culture.[16] The Arts Commission, he explained, had contributed greatly to the fact that 'we have not been able to win over important artists up to now for Marxism and the GDR'. In fact, Brecht's own work continued to be censored but he now simply rejected the authority of the censor. He railed against the Office for Literature, which had passed his *War Primer* to the Central Committee for its view, having his secretary convey to the Office that 'he was responsible politically for everything he wrote, not the Central Committee'.[17] He informed the publishing house, Eulenspiegel, that he himself had granted permission for the work to be published after explaining to the Office that 'works by members of the Academy of Arts are not subject to the control of this Office'.[18] He kept up the attack at an Academy Plenary at the year's end, arguing that the Office for Literature should not be incorporated within the Ministry of Culture and censorship should be abolished.[19]

Brecht turned his attention to the future of the Berliner Ensemble. Unwilling to countenance further prevarication, he threatened to halt planning for productions in 1954–5 and to wind down his commitment in the present season.[20] His warning that he was struggling to keep talent like Curt Bois from leaving for the West was also a coded threat about himself. At Weigel's request, he spelt out his position in a letter to her of 31 December 1953: 'I myself cannot accept wasting further months in senseless work. [...] I think it is now for the government to inform us when it can create decent working conditions'.[21] It fell to Holtzhauer in one of his final acts with the Arts Commission on 6 January 1954 to sign the paper confirming that the Berliner Ensemble would take over the Theater am Schiffbauerdamm, responsibility for which passed from the East Berlin Council (sic) to the Ministry of Culture.[22] A weak and defensive SED had acceded to the demand of the artistic elite that the Arts

Commission and related elements of its cultural bureaucracy should be replaced by the new Ministry. In the trial of strength between the Academy and the Arts Commission, the Academy, led by Brecht, had quite improbably won out.

Pre-eminence

In January 1954 Becher became Minister of Culture and Brecht joined its Cultural Advisory Board. That year, Brecht was also appointed Vice-President of the Academy. However, the officials whom Brecht so deeply mistrusted were incorporated in the new Ministry. Seeking to imbue it with a fresh spirit, Brecht wrote a piece about issues facing the country's theatres and delivered a short address at the opening ceremony, entitled pointedly 'It Is Now Down to Us':

> I regard the re-organisation of our cultural institutions as a valuable contribution of the government of the German Democratic Republic to the great struggle for a more prosperous and auspicious Germany. The re-organisation – and this is something quite new and exemplary in Germany – is being undertaken by the state in partnership with artists and writers. It is now down to us writers and artists to develop a fresh sense of initiative. That means: boldness, imagination, wisdom and humour.[23]

The artistic elite invested some hope in the new arrangements precisely because, in Brecht and Becher, prominent artists were involved. Brecht had emerged from 17 June with his authority hugely enhanced among fellow artists. During the two remaining years of his life the worst excesses of the Campaign against Formalism were averted but the in-fighting with Erpenbeck et al. continued. After Brecht's death Abusch, who had followed the ailing Becher to the Ministry of Culture, would denounce Becher to Ulbricht and slip into the dying man's shoes.

Between January and March 1954, the Theater am Schiffbauerdamm was modified to meet the needs of the Berliner Ensemble for the opening with an adaptation of Molière's _Don Juan_. Brecht remained concerned that the building work would damage the performance schedule. They not only had the opening to consider but also two guest productions that summer in Paris following an invitation to the First International Festival of Dramatic Art, the Théâtre des Nations. The Berliner Ensemble was struggling with the demanding schedule and, as a last resort, Weigel appealed to Brecht to demand action.[24]

Elisabeth Hauptmann had been deeply involved in the adaptation of _Don Juan_ in addition to her editorial work for Brecht's _Collected Works_, which now began to appear with Suhrkamp and Aufbau. With considerable justification, Hauptmann complained to Brecht about her working conditions, which were so bad that she could not attend rehearsals for _Don Juan_.[25] Since she hardly saw Brecht, she objected ferociously via Käthe Rülicke to her meagre royalty payments for _The Threepenny Opera_: 'You who on the first of every month receive your regular sum and probably don't do without the payment of expenses, behave like pigs'.[26] After threatening to go elsewhere, in the summer Hauptmann would receive a contract as a dramatic advisor.

For the opening on 19 March 1954 the name of the Berliner Ensemble was displayed proudly at the top of the theatre's tower. In addition to Picasso's 'Dove of Peace' on the front curtain, the Ensemble had adapted as a poster the scarf which Picasso had designed for the French delegation at the World Festival of Youth in East Berlin in 1951. It depicts the dove surrounded by four heads representing people from the four corners of the earth. Brecht's verses of peace were displayed in the entrance hall of the theatre:

At first you acted in the ruins. Now
You'll act in this fine house, for something more than fun.
From you and us a peaceful WE must grow
To help this house to last, and many another one. [27]

Benno Besson directed *Don Juan*, Erwin Geschonneck played the lead, Ekkehard Schall was Don Alfonso and Barbara Berg, Brecht's daughter and Schall's future wife, was Angelica. The adaptation, parodying court life and the pretensions of rulers, was both a safe choice and a popular success, seeing eighty performances.

While ill health curtailed activity, Brecht still attended selected events. In April he travelled to Knokke in Belgium for a meeting with other European writers, among them Carlo Levi, Jean-Paul Sartre, Simone de Beauvoir, Anna Seghers and Constantin Fedin. The intention of the organiser, Baron Allard, was to develop a forum like the Paris Congress for the Defence of Culture of 1935. Brecht proposed that a protest against the hydrogen bomb should be included in a communiqué but no agreement could be reached. He continued the theme that the people of the world should be alerted to the extreme dangers of the atomic age in a speech at the World Peace Conference in East Berlin, and in June he travelled to Amsterdam for a meeting of the PEN Club. At the Rijksmuseum the student of the human body asked to be photographed looking at Rembrandt's 'The Anatomy Lesson of Dr Joan Deyman'.

In late June Brecht travelled to Paris for the Festival of Dramatic Art. The premiere of *Mother Courage and Her Children* at the Théâtre Sarah Bernhardt on 29 June was an extraordinary triumph, hailed in the Parisian press by, among others, the young Roland Barthes.[28] Two further performances followed and one of Kleist's *The Broken Jug*. With *Mother Courage* the Berliner Ensemble won first prize for the best play and for the best production. Brecht's Epic Theatre was on everyone's lips as news of the success spread around the globe from the world's foremost centre for artistic innovation. Brecht had broken through the shackles which the East and West German campaigns had imposed upon him. The pre-eminent international status which he had always believed would be his had now been achieved. Amongst the letters of congratulation was one from Feuchtwanger, who told him he had been reading of his success in newspapers from many different countries and how much he missed an 'eloquent debate with you, conducted in Munich Humanist and Augsburg Renaissance German'.[29] In response to the upsurge in demand for his works, Brecht engaged his Swedish publisher Lars Schmidt to deal with distribution to additional countries.[30]

Brecht again retired to Buckow for the summer where he posted a notice on the door of his study, explaining that, in consideration of the fact that he had only a few weeks each year for his own work, he had decided to create a sphere of isolation,

that while working he had to look after his health and that every human voice was a
welcome excuse to interrupt his work.[31] He asked readers of the notice not to regard
this arrangement as too binding. With quiet satisfaction, Brecht listed his achievements in the poem '1954: First Half', which he dedicated to his new lover Isot Kilian,
an actress at the Berliner Ensemble who was married to Wolfgang Harich:

> No serious sickness, no serious enemies.
> Enough work.
> And I got my share of the new potatoes,
> The cucumbers, asparagus, strawberries.
> I saw the lilac in Buckow, the market square in Bruges
> The canals of Amsterdam, the Halles in Paris.
> I enjoyed the kindness of delightful A.T.
> I read Voltaire's letters and Mao's essay on contradiction.
> I put on the *Chalk Circle* at the Berliner Ensemble.[32]

'A.T.' is probably a cipher for Kilian, whom in a note he compared to Bi Banholzer,
writing:

> My present girl-friend, who may be my last, resembles my first. Like her she too
> is light-hearted; as in the former's case, deeper sentiments surprise me. These
> women weep when scolded, whether justly or unjustly, simply because they are
> being scolded. They have a kind of sensuality that needs nobody to arouse it and
> that isn't much good to anyone either. They want to please everybody, but are not
> pleased to accept everybody whom they please. My present girl-friend is, like that
> earlier one, at her most affectionate when she is being pleasured. And I don't know
> whether either of them loves me.[33]

However, after Brecht had found Kilian in the company of a young man on the sofa in
Brecht's study, he commented:

> I find I have lost my respect for her; she seems cheap to me. Not without relief
> I note the total disappearance of love in me. She, however, is still distressed,
> does not defend herself, behaves as if she had just been surprised in a silly and
> unnecessary affair. She can only think of one thing to do: whenever it is at all
> possible she asks my advice. Advice is something I can neither refuse nor keep
> to myself.[34]

The relationship with Kilian continued, while Brecht reflected further: 'Lovers can't
tone down their requirements either, and make do with partners who are less than
was originally assumed'.[35]

In Buckow Brecht struggled to conclude *Turandot* to his final satisfaction. Nor
would the deep anxiety which Brecht had expressed in the 'Foreword to *Turandot*'
leave him: 'Recently when I went out to Buckow with young people from the dramatic
advisors' office, I was sitting in the pavilion while they were working in their rooms
or chatting. It suddenly occurred to me that, had I fallen among them ten years ago,
all three of them, whatever they had read of mine, would instantly have handed me
over to the Gestapo ...'.[36] In fact, the SED was busy developing its own monstrous

successor to the Gestapo, the Stasi, which perpetuated a culture of fear in the GDR, compounding the abject mistrust already present between citizens.

Back in Berlin in October, there was much disquiet among employees of the Berliner Ensemble at the burden which had been placed on them during the move to their new home. The guest performances in Paris had taken their toll and many felt the demands which Brecht had made during rehearsals for *The Caucasian Chalk Circle* to be excessive. Brecht had to pay for his Paris success as the custodians of East Berlin culture demonstrated that the play was emphatically not what was required. His opponents were fighting him every inch of the way as he asserted the pre-eminence of his theatrical style, achieving on stage what he had failed to achieve in print in 1938 when Herzfelde was forced to flee Prague. A fragile Brecht again saw his life threatened: 'That you'll go down if you don't stand up for yourself / Surely you see that'.[37]

The premiere of *The Caucasian Chalk Circle* on 7 October – it had been delayed because the state workshops had not been able to provide the sets and costumes in time – was singled out for the most vehemently hostile criticism of Brecht's East Berlin years. However, the audience was now not afraid to show its appreciation: there was a massive show of support with as many as fifty-six curtains calls at the premiere. The production would be repeated 175 times. While the Party's critics did not doubt the play's technical quality and Angelika Hurwitz earned great praise as Grusha, Jürgen Rühle led the attack on this 'long-winded' play in the SMAD's *Sonntag*, arguing that Brecht was the 'victim of his theory of Epic Theatre' and that he failed to show the necessary dramatic link between the Prologue and the *Chalk Circle*.[38] *Neues Deutschland* demonstratively ignored the play, prompting Brecht to repeat his invitation to Wandel to attend, and Erpenbeck renewed his campaign against Epic Theatre in *Theater der Zeit*, declaring Epic Theatre a dead end and a waste of Brecht's great talent. Hurwitz and Hans Bunge, a recent addition to the Berliner Ensemble, leapt to Brecht's defence in *Theater der Zeit*. Brecht maintained a public silence, noting that a fruitful discussion ought to move beyond purely formal criteria to embrace social questions and asking himself: 'How can a linden tree be expected to conduct a discussion with someone who reproaches it for not being an oak?'.[39] However, with Brecht in attendance, the Performing Arts Section of the Academy resolved that Erpenbeck's one-man editorial board at *Theater der Zeit* should be dissolved.[40]

In the Federal Republic, Brecht's international success could no longer be denied. Sabina Lietzmann commented upon the spectacle in East Berlin for the *Frankfurter Allgemeine Zeitung*, lending Brecht the aura of dissidence:

> The party press continues to ignore Bert Brecht's *Caucasian Chalk Circle*, the most important artistic event in East Berlin in recent months. The discomfort which its most prominent and idiosyncratic artist causes for cultural functionaries is evident not just in this fact; the reviews in other East Berlin newspapers clearly show how difficult they find the evaluation of productions whose artistic quality is obvious but which, in eastern terminology, display undeniably 'Formalist' traits.[41]

The official SED position was again made to look ridiculous on the broader German and international plane. Brecht would never be forgiven in East Berlin, nor would other East German artists be later, for whom praise in the West meant denunciation in the East. Indeed, Brecht was the prototype of those 'critically loyal' GDR artists to whom the West German press lent a dissident aura during the Cold War, only to denounce them in the fiercest terms after German re-unification on account of their undisputed proximity to the regime.

After the extraordinary expenditure of effort and energy amidst the extreme antagonisms and reversals of fortune over the past year, an exhausted Brecht began in the course of 1954 to acknowledge that his artistic and intellectual energy was failing him.[42] His eyesight was now poor and his slight frame had become bloated, as had his face. After struggling with *Büsching*, as the Garbe project was now called, Brecht was forced to concede to Claus Küchenmeister and his wife Wera, both Brecht's Meisterschüler: 'I can't do it anymore. You younger people have got to take things forward'.[43] He noted with a blend of wistfulness and irony: 'Of course I was gifted too, particularly forty years ago, sexually transmitted diseases do that for you'.[44]

Faced by a budget cut when he wanted to expand the Berliner Ensemble to include a film studio to enable actors to work in both fields, an imperious Brecht wrote to the Minister Becher: 'One must treat the important theatres differently from the unimportant ones. That is not difficult: we do not have many important ones'.[45] While the public attacks on Brecht's theatre continued, in the GDR's modestly corrupt economy of scarcity he accepted Becher's offer of one of the three new EMW cabriolets available amongst a batch otherwise produced for export.[46] Moreover, on 18 December it was announced that Brecht was to be awarded the Stalin Prize for Peace. As things turned out, Brecht would be one of its final recipients. The committee, consisting of Alexander Fadeyev, Ilya Ehrenburg, Louis Aragon, Anna Seghers and Pablo Neruda, had initially nominated Thomas Mann, who declined, noting in his diary: 'The things one throws away for love of the "free world". It's around 300,000 francs'.[47] Brecht accepted the Swiss francs and pledged his continuing commitment to the peaceful re-unification of Germany.[48] There were congratulations from friends and tormentors in East Berlin and the usual derision in the West.

The organisers of the International Festival of Dramatic Art invited the Berliner Ensemble to return to Paris in 1955. Brecht could not resist ratcheting up the pressure on his opponents with his choice of *The Caucasian Chalk Circle* for Paris. Meanwhile, as more and more West German theatres challenged the Brecht boycott, *Life of Galileo* received its German premiere in Cologne. Each scene of this, Brecht's last great exile work to be staged in Germany, was greeted with applause in Friedrich Siems's triumphant production. *The Caucasian Chalk Circle*, too, premiered in the West with Harry Buckwitz in Frankfurt. Buckwitz again overcame massive opposition to the production from the city's Christian Democratic Union (CDU). Brecht travelled to Frankfurt for final rehearsals and for discussions with Suhrkamp, whose protégé Siegfried Unseld looked after him. As so often, Brecht left before the premiere, moving on to Munich to discuss the forthcoming *Good Person of Szechwan* with Neher and Hans Schweikart. Brecht's 'premature' departure from Frankfurt, together with his refusal to be interviewed, was seized upon by the press, which was more interested in political scandal than in the production itself. In what became a familiar western journalistic ritual, many critics who could not conceal their admiration for Brecht's play generally covered their backs by denouncing his politics. Brecht told Berlau that the series of productions in the West was 'important, because afterwards, whatever new things are put on, these will leave a memory'.[49]

Brecht set off for Moscow via Warsaw on 17 May with Weigel and Rülicke. In Warsaw they visited the book fair and strolled around the re-built city, the predictably regular design of which disappointed Brecht. The following day they flew to Moscow where, as in May 1941, Mikhail Apletin greeted Brecht. Brecht was shown the city by taxi in somewhat different circumstances from his eerie trip with Huppert in 1941. He took in lots of theatre, enjoying Mayakovsky's *Bathhouse* at the Theatre of Satire and discovering 'alienation effects everywhere, comic pathos'. He found *Much Ado About Nothing* at the Art Theatre disappointing. Directed by a pupil of Stanislavsky, it was '"traditional" (within the bad tradition of the [18]80s), with hollow emotions, petty bourgeois inwardness, garden-gnome comedy'.[50] On the other hand, Ostrovsky's *The Passionate Heart* filled him with 'enormous pleasure. All Stanislavsky's greatness made apparent'.

Despite the publicity surrounding the award ceremony of the Stalin Peace Prize on 25 May, there was still no hint on Moscow's stages of the international acclaim for Brecht's own dramatic greatness. Indeed, as we have seen, the award recognised Brecht's work for the cause of peace. He was accompanied by Nikolai Okhlopkov, who recalled wryly that in 1936 he had been banned from performing Brecht's *Round Heads and Pointed Heads*. At that time, Brecht had also been advised to stay away from Moscow. In his acceptance speech, which Boris Pasternak had translated at Brecht's request, Brecht identified the capitalist perversion of human nature as responsible for two world wars, arguing that socialist society transformed its citizens into peace-loving people. He concluded: 'Now, approaching old age, I know that a monstrous war is being prepared anew. But a quarter of the world has now adopted peace, and in other parts socialist ideas are advancing. [...] Long live your great peaceful state, the state of the workers and peasants'.[51] As we know, the recent incorporation of the Federal Republic into NATO, which prompted the creation of the Warsaw Pact, had confirmed Brecht's worst suspicions about the belligerent West.

Seeking to rectify his absence from the Moscow stage, Brecht wrote to Okhlopkov: 'It really grieves me not to have been able to show my plays in the Soviet Union. [...] It is my greatest wish to bring my theatre – the Berliner Ensemble – to Moscow. Can you help me?'.[52] Brecht fired off letters to actors and directors. Having seen Faia Ranevskaya in Ostrovsky's *Storm*, he invited her to play Mother Courage.[53] A key contact was Ilya Fradkin, who as a SMAD officer had promoted productions of Brecht's works in Berlin and encouraged his return. Fradkin now mediated discussions about a two-volume edition of Brecht's plays in Russian. However, Brecht was later outraged when Rülicke did not receive permission to visit Moscow on his behalf.[54] In no other country, he said, had he been refused the opportunity to influence the publication of his works. He would ask a rehabilitated Bernhard Reich to represent him in discussions with Moscow publishers and to improve the Russian translations of his works. However, Brecht would not live to see the Berliner Ensemble's *Mother Courage* in Leningrad and Moscow in 1957.

Brecht travelled to Paris in mid-June for the staging of *The Caucasian Chalk Circle* at the Théâtre Sarah Bernhardt. Pozner, who acted as Brecht's interpreter and assistant, writes that the play 'struck like lightning' in the five days of its run.[55] As he did so often, throughout the performances Brecht sat in a cafe drinking a beer and smoking cigars. Critics vied with each other in their praise, the reviewer in *L'Express* hailing it as the theatre of the future: 'At last the theatre one dreamt of! A theatre in which one rejects the unnecessary conflicts of conscience in salon theatre and takes the most effective elements from the Elizabethans, the Chinese, the great epic novels, folk poetry'.[56] Kenneth Tynan wrote in *The Observer*: 'Once in a generation the world discovers a new way of telling a story; this generation's pathfinder is Brecht'.[57] Just as Brecht had come to seek lessons from Stanislavsky, now other directors and actors rushed to discover Brecht's secret. Even now, however, the struggle in East Berlin continued unabated. Only after Brecht's promptings would *Neues Deutschland* acknowledge his success, not by publishing its own review but by reprinting reviews from the international press.

Brecht returned to Berlin via Munich in late June, attending final rehearsals for *The Good Person of Szechwan* with Neher and enjoying the Munich speciality of white sausages with him. Brecht again met with Münsterer, telling him that he was 'tired, very tired'.[58] Brecht also attended Johannes Ludwig Schmitt's clinic and received a number of remedies to support his vital organs and circulation, among them hepata, cholestanol and anacardium.[59] As usual, Brecht left Munich before the premiere, returning to Berlin 'exhausted', as he wrote to Berlau, to whom he issued another warning after her drunken behaviour had left a trail of destruction: 'Even if I myself wanted it, the Ensemble will no longer tolerate the way you behave like a camp commander when you are drunk, and you have been drunk for days'.[60] He saw a return to Denmark as her only option, adding: 'Once you were only Shen Te, then sometimes the cousin, now only the cousin exists'. He asked her to calculate how much she would need to live in Denmark, assuming that she had a job, concluding: 'We seem to have to part as enemies, we can see each other as friends again'.

Following 'various inquiries from London', where there was growing curiosity about his work, Brecht had emphasised to his Swedish agent Lars Schmidt:

> In the case of a first production in a foreign country, or of a production in a capital or other major city, the ultimate decision rests with me, and not with, for instance, the translator. In each case of negotiation I have to be informed about the names of the director, main actors, the reputation of the theatre, and if the play has not been translated before in a satisfactory way, of the translator.[61]

Brecht was again contesting Bentley's right to take the lead and was annoyed that Joan Littlewood's Theatre Workshop had announced a production of *Mother Courage* without signing any agreement with him. Littlewood had been at the Paris festival. Brecht asked Schmidt to inform her that he had secured Brecht's agreement for a production of *Mother Courage*, provided that Littlewood played the lead and that one of his assistants, Carl M. Weber, advised during rehearsals. Littlewood accepted the conditions, but directing and playing the lead proved too much for her and Weber phoned Brecht to tell him that her replacement Catherine Parr was not equal to the role.[62] Weber followed with a letter, explaining that he had not been welcome at rehearsals because the troupe had the impression that the Berliner Ensemble was watching over it. Brecht wrote to Littlewood, who played Courage at Devon's Tor and Torridge Festival, but the performance went so badly that the London production was called off.

Brecht now contacted his London agent, Margery Vosper, claiming that Laughton wanted to play Galileo in London – he had not actually approached him – and suggesting they press ahead with a production of *Mother Courage* by Bentley, with Elsa Lanchester, Sybil Thorndike, Beatrix Lehmann or Edith Evans in the lead.[63] In September there was a visit to Berlin by a group from London, which included John Fernald, newly appointed as Principal of the Royal Academy of Dramatic Art, Peggy Ashcroft, John Gielgud and George Devine, who had just been named artistic director for the English Stage Company at the Royal Court Theatre. After seeing the Berliner Ensemble's adaptation of George Farquhar's *The Recruiting Officer* – another directorial success for Besson – the group discussed with Brecht and Weigel a guest performance by the Berliner Ensemble in London. Brecht told Feuchtwanger that, among other things, they were interested in performing *Galileo* and asked him to contact Laughton about a return to the London stage, adding with some satisfaction: 'Since Paris there's no real danger in staging a play of mine in Western Europe'.[64] Brecht had outflanked his enemies in East and West Germany. However, Feuchtwanger informed Brecht that Laughton, while a great devotee of Brecht, would under no circumstances return to London's West End.[65] In October 1956 Peggy Ashcroft would star at the Royal Court in Devine's *The Good Woman of Szechwan*. For good measure, Sam Wanamaker attended a number of performances by the Berliner Ensemble in advance of his London production of *The Threepenny Opera*, for which he engaged Neher to design the set.

Deadly inflammation, severing the link

When Max Frisch visited Brecht in September 1955 he looked 'ill, grey, his movements remained chary'.[66] In August Brecht had consulted Otto Mertens, a specialist in internal medicine from the Westsanatorium, Charlottenburg, who acted as Brecht's principal physician through the early course of his final illness until late March 1956. During that time, Brecht was also treated by Hüdepohl. There is no indication that Mertens or Hüdepohl were aware of the x-ray report upon Brecht's heart condition from May 1951. Isot Kilian recorded the treatment by Hüdepohl and Mertens in a document, 'B's Illness Conduct of the Doctors Treating Him'.[67] On 21 September Mertens undertook a general examination of Brecht and prescribed medication, including cordalin, to ease what Kilian calls 'pressure on the heart'. Throughout the treatment Mertens remained decidedly relaxed. He appears not even to have taken a fresh x-ray. However, repeatedly that autumn Brecht voiced his concern about his heart to friends and to Mertens, consistently describing his illness in those terms, whilst typically downplaying its significance. On 1 October he wrote to Berlau, now in Copenhagen looking for a house: 'I had a bit of fever and my heart is a bit shaky'.[68]

He was, as he wrote to Therese Giehse, alert to the fact that 'several good people of our generation had recently died of heart trouble (Fr. Wolf, Weiskopf) or had fallen gravely ill (Becher, Bredel, Fürnberg, Ackermann)'.[69]

Brecht attempted to maintain a normal schedule. Discussions began at the Berliner Ensemble about the production of *Life of Galileo*. Brecht the contrarian selected the slender Ernst Busch, physically the antithesis of Laughton, for the lead. However, Brecht had been steadfastly ignoring his renal condition until he could do so no longer. On 15 October he consulted Hüdepohl, who, as Kilian writes, performed a 'cleansing of the urethra which should have been undertaken long ago'. This time the procedure proved very painful, leaving Brecht 'extremely exhausted'. Hüdepohl prescribed the antibiotic hostacycline. In extreme pain and still exhausted, Brecht drove to Buckow. From this point in time, Brecht suffered from an undiagnosed, insidious illness, which, according to Kilian, resembled flu. From a present-day perspective, it is not difficult to identify the symptoms as an escalation of his existing propensity to urosepsis, deriving from his renal complaint. At the latest during Hüdepohl's procedure, bacteria entered Brecht's urethra and infected the renal pelvis, the inflammation most likely already affecting Brecht's vulnerable heart. Brecht had only mildly high temperatures, normally not above 37.3 °C. However, he monitored his temperature with concern.[70] During the abiding exhaustion, the flu-like illness came and went, lasting around three days on each occasion. Brecht consulted Mertens every three weeks or so, who prescribed further medication to improve cardiac performance, including digitalis and polyvital, but remained relaxed about Brecht's condition. Mertens should surely have hospitalised Brecht in the autumn of 1955. Instead, he went without hospital treatment until April 1956.

In early December 1955 Rülicke wrote to Walter Nubel: 'At the moment no work is progressing since he does not feel at all well and in the near future must go for a cure. – That is why it is uncertain, too, when he can begin with the production of *Galileo*'.[71] Mertens then said that Brecht's heart condition was improving and Brecht agreed that the pressure on his heart had receded. Mertens had no objection to rehearsals for *Galileo* beginning on 14 December and Brecht told Berlau, 'My heart is starting to get better'.[72] However, after rehearsals, which by now never lasted more than two to three hours, Brecht was very exhausted indeed.[73] On 26 December he went to the cinema with Kilian to see a Karl Valentin film but had to leave because he could get no air.

Brecht resumed rehearsals for *Galileo* on 3 January 1956 and felt well enough to travel to Rostock the following day for rehearsals for *The Good Person of Szechwan*. He then attended a number of sessions of the 4th German Writers' Congress in Berlin from 9 to 14 January and delivered a somewhat improvised speech. However, according to Kilian, from January until the end of March, Brecht had the flu-like illness at least once a month and consulted regularly with Mertens. Nonetheless, he maintained his extensive business correspondence, continued rehearsals for *Galileo* and discussed the forthcoming production of J. M. Synge's *Playboy of the Western World* with his assistants in his flat, taking part in rehearsals, too.

From 7 to 11 February Brecht undertook his last journey abroad, travelling with his daughter Hanne and Elisabeth Hauptmann to see Giorgio Strehler's *The Threepenny Opera* at the Piccolo Teatro in Milan. Brecht attended final rehearsals, admiring Teo

Otto's set. He enjoyed Strehler's company and also attended a reception in his honour hosted by the theatre and his Italian publisher Einaudi. However, Brecht was visibly uncomfortable, taking refuge in a corner and disappearing when it was safe to do so. Teo Otto recalls supporting his friend:

> In poor health, he was hugely allergic towards people and noise. To keep his back free, he stood in a corner. He tugged at my coat when it became too much for him. His weakness left his face covered in sweat. I took him into an adjoining room where he sank down, exhausted. His eyes were like two spots in his white face. His neck was twitching nervously.[74]

As his body failed him, the chorea re-emerged. The following morning, Brecht's 58th birthday, he took breakfast with the German émigré Erwin Leiser, who had been mounting an ultimately unsuccessful campaign for Brecht to receive the Nobel Prize. Leiser recalls: 'The snow storm was drumming against the windows of the Manin Hotel. We were joking gingerly about our shared heart problems, which in my case were only occasional. Suddenly he lowered his voice and said: "One knows that it will in any case be an easy death, a gentle knocking at the window panes"'.[75] Brecht called off a public discussion that afternoon but attended the magnificent premiere that evening, after which he and Strehler received a storm of applause. Brecht told Berlau that the production was 'brilliant in conception and detail and very aggressive'.[76] Praising its 'passion and coolness, ease and precision', Brecht invited Strehler – 'probably the best director in Europe' – and his cast to perform *The Threepenny Opera* at the Theater am Schiffbauerdamm. He added: 'I wish I could let you have all my plays in Europe, one after another'.

Shortly after returning to East Berlin, Brecht read reports in the western press of something he had long known about and initially endorsed without understanding its actual scale, Stalin's murder of millions in the Great Terror. In a closed session of the Soviet Communist Party, the leader Nikita Khrushchev had denounced his predecessor's crimes. Rülicke secured a copy of the speech for Brecht who was 'deeply affected' when he read it.[77] He discussed it with friends such as Strittmatter, Walcher and the Schwerin theologian Karl Kleinschmidt, as well as writing texts which endorse the criticism from a perspective nonetheless supportive of the Marxist project: 'The escape from the barbarism of capitalism may itself still have barbaric features'.[78] As he had earlier, Brecht criticised Stalinism for its 'atrophy of the dialectic' with its reactionary consequences for Soviet society: 'Without knowledge of the dialectic, such transitions as that from Stalin as motor, to Stalin as brake are not comprehensible. Nor is the negation of the Party through the state apparatus'. However, Brecht continued to believe that Marxism-Leninism would not necessarily result in a bureaucratically controlled command economy of scarcity. Characteristically, he turned his text into a call for the achievement of true Communism: 'The liquidation of Stalinism can only succeed if the Party mobilises the wisdom of the masses on a gigantic scale'. Quite what that meant for economic behaviour remained unclear. Brecht composed the following lines about the abiding barbarism of Stalin's rule:

The Czar spoke to them

With rifle and whip
On Bloody Sunday. There
Then spoke to them with rifle and whip
Every day of the week, every working day
The esteemed murderer of the people.[79]

The repression which had triggered the revolution of 1905 remained a fact of life under the mass-murderer Stalin.

Brecht's flu-like symptoms returned and he had to interrupt rehearsals for a week in early March. Later that month he was still hoping that *Galileo* could premiere in May. However, on 28 March Kilian voiced her concerns to Mertens, suggesting that rehearsals might be too demanding for Brecht and that he should convalesce outside Berlin. A still relaxed Mertens responded robustly that there was no reason for her to be concerned. In his view, convalescence outside Berlin was the path of least resistance, which doctors almost invariably chose for their patients, but that was unnecessary for Brecht, who would regain his health.[80] However, that same afternoon, Brecht alerted Kilian to how bad he felt. He had a temperature of 39.05°C. Kilian called Mertens, who was astounded and promised to come. When he had still not turned up after two hours, Brecht's daughter Barbara went to fetch him. Kilian's text breaks off at this point when Mertens's relationship with Brecht, his family and close friends clearly broke down. What for Brecht was an emergency, as he anxiously monitored his body temperature, was for Mertens seemingly something that could wait. Family and friends were rightly concerned about Brecht's condition. A temperature above 40°C can signal life-threatening hyperthermia. Any further details of Mertens's treatment in Kilian's account are lost, not to mention those concerning the doctors who followed him. Brecht's high temperature was soon brought under control. Nevertheless, he was now by no means well. On 31 March he had to ask Erich Engel to lead rehearsals for *Galileo*, which ended on 19 April amidst differences between Engel and Busch.

This time Brecht found it impossible to cope and on 12 April he was admitted to a private ward at the Charité run by the GDR's most distinguished physician, the elderly Professor Theodor Brugsch. Brecht dealt with correspondence and received friends for short visits. Neher and Aufricht were among the first. A few days after his admission, Brecht was already thinking about follow-up treatment in May in Munich with Schmitt, who visited him in hospital. Brugsch's hand-written notes recording his treatment of Brecht have survived.[81] There were two elements to Brugsch's diagnosis: pyelonephritis, inflammation of the renal pelvis; and, bacterial endocarditis, an inflammation of the heart's inner lining or valves. Brecht's aortic valve was affected and E. coli bacteria were identified as the cause of both infections. These were probably the bacteria which had entered Brecht's urethra and affected his renal pelvis as a result of Hüdepohl's procedure. Treatment with antibiotics – streptomycin-pantotenat and chloramphenicol – in conjunction with cortisone and, to support the heart, strophanthin and later digitoxin brought about an improvement but not a definitive cure of the infection in the heart and the renal pelvis.

By the end of April Brecht was writing to Busch that his recovery was dragging on and that he would not be able to resume *Galileo* that spring.[82] He told Rülicke that after *Galileo* he would leave directing to his assistants, while he worked on his theory.[83] He told Berlau, 'The inflammation of the heart valve has settled somewhat', adding to Feuchtwanger, 'It's endocarditis, but benign, and it seems to be subsiding'.[84] Brugsch had, it seems, assured Brecht of the benign nature of his heart condition: the inflammation could be cured. Hauptmann told Suhrkamp essentially the same thing: 'The good news is: Brecht's heart is actually much better than was initially assumed. The bad news is: a heart valve is affected by this wretched infection, which is so difficult to cure'.[85] Brugsch surely knew that Brecht's condition was irreparable, as indicated in the x-ray report of 1951, but sought to spare him the distressing truth.

Brecht himself was preparing for death. In one of his final poems, 'When in My White Room at the Charité', he drew for one last time upon Lucretian natural philosophy to reflect upon acceptance of the finality of death: 'Already for some time / I had lost all fear of death. For nothing / Can be wrong with me if I myself / Am nothing'.[86] However, in his quarrel with himself about the final question Brecht continued to oscillate between acceptance of death and anxiety about what it entailed. Indeed, the ending of the poem contains an acknowledgement of transcendent desire quite foreign to Lucretian philosophy: 'Now / I managed to enjoy / The song of every blackbird after me too'.[87]

Brecht was allowed to leave the Charité on 12 May but was kept under daily medical supervision. Brugsch ordered a diet which included the traditional raw egg in red wine and, dispensing with antibiotics, from mid-May sought to immunise Brecht against his infection by injecting him weekly with ever-increasing doses of E. coli vaccine taken from dead E. coli bacteria. Hans Karl Schulten observes that such a vaccine therapy was already deemed obsolete and concludes that Brugsch's immunisation was 'at best without effect'.[88] Brecht's life could have been prolonged somewhat if he had continued to receive antibiotics but the underlying condition of his heart meant that he could not survive long. However, the official report of Brecht's death, issued by Brugsch's clinic, conflates the two stages of his treatment in a, provisionally, successful outcome: 'The infection, which had already taken hold of the heart, was brought under control successfully through intensive treatment with antibiotics and a vaccine therapy'.[89] The report states that in June and early July Brecht recovered well but that in July he appeared to over-exert himself in preparations for the London productions. In fact, the weekly injections with the dead E. coli bacteria continued through July and from 26 May until 8 August Brecht spent almost all his time in Buckow, receiving visitors, dealing with correspondence and writing when he could. In early August he had a notice posted at the Berliner Ensemble concerning the approach which actors should take to performing in London: 'There is in England a long-standing fear that German art (literature, painting, music) must be terribly heavy, slow, laborious and pedestrian. So our playing needs to be quick, light, strong'.[90] In advance of the London productions of *Mother Courage*, *The Recruiting Officer* and *The Caucasian Chalk Circle*, Brecht received John Willett several times. Brecht and his daughter approved Willett's translation, *The Good Woman of Szechwan*, which George Devine used at the Royal Court, while Elisabeth Hauptmann corresponded with Willett's publisher, Methuen, initiating a relationship which achieved so much for the promotion of Brecht's work in the English-speaking world.[91]

Exceptionally, on 14 June Brecht went to Berlin for a rehearsal and an Academy meeting. He returned to Buckow with the composer Kurt Schwaen, but Schwaen realised that Brecht was very tired and left on 16 June. Another visitor was Brecht's theologian friend Karl Kleinschmidt, to whom Brecht gave his views about an obituary: 'Don't write that you admire me. Write that I was recalcitrant and intend to remain that way after my death. Even then there are still certain opportunities'.[92] Brecht again visited Berlin on 27–28 June and discussed with Hauptmann Suhrkamp's production of volumes five and six of his plays, as well as plans for volumes seven to ten. She told Suhrkamp that Brecht 'looks quite well, but feels like a holiday'.[93] Over the coming weeks, Brecht maintained his dialogue with the GDR political elite. Grotewohl visited with his wife and they discussed the use of the radio and the design of the Buchenwald memorial. Citing the recent refusal of papers for Rülicke to travel to the USSR, he urged the Ministry of Culture to do more to exploit exchanges through cultural agreements with the USSR, China and the people's democracies.[94] Girnus visited and they had a long conversation, mostly about Brecht's work.

In late July Brecht told Suhrkamp that he was feeling better and encouraged him to join him at Schmitt's Munich sanatorium for a month from mid-August: 'His opinions and methods of treatment are unconventional, but I think he should be listened to when conventional medicine has failed'.[95] Hauptmann repeated the invitation to Suhrkamp: 'You know that Brecht thinks a tremendous lot of Schmitt, not least because he has now again at once supplied the correct diagnosis, which was also confirmed after lengthy investigations in the laboratory'.[96] The identification of the E. coli bacteria was one thing, the treatment with the E. coli vaccine was another. Brecht told Kilian: 'I'm lying down a lot, now with the higher dosages I need two and a half days to recover. However, progress is satisfactory'.[97] Shortly after, he added: 'Today is one of the black Saturdays and I'm dragging two million dead coli bacteria around with me as if they weighed two million pounds'.

Brecht's son Stefan arrived and Besson and Wekwerth visited to discuss the production of *Days of the Commune* in Chemnitz. Eisler and Brecht had lengthy conversations, Brecht affirming that *The Measures Taken* was his major play for the theatre of the future.[98] He was drawing upon it for his last dramatic project *The Life of Einstein*, in which, following Einstein's death in 1955, he again intended to treat the dilemmas of the great physicist in the nuclear age. However, Brecht's draft reveals a quite different personal pre-occupation. It begins: 'Then his aorta burst'.[99] Einstein had declined to have an operation on an aneurysm in his main artery, which could have extended his life.

Brecht completed his course of injections and received a visit from Brugsch in early August before he went on holiday. As Brecht finalised his Munich trip, Weigel wrote to Therese Giehse, apparently drawing upon Brugsch, 'The heart valve infection has been cured' but added that Brecht was 'in a state of exhaustion, which is incomprehensible to me and which disturbs him because it makes him unable to work'.[100] She asked Giehse to find another heart specialist in Munich and to urge Brecht to consult him. By now, in fact, Brecht had become extremely irritated by Brugsch's bland assurances about the prospects of his recovery, writing to Paul Dessau on 8 August, the day he returned to Berlin: 'Brugsch was always enthusiastic how healthy I was, but in truth

I could not stand a conversation lasting five minutes'.[101] Brugsch had certainly under-stated the gravity of Brecht's condition to the former medical student, who claimed proficient knowledge. Brecht's final encounter with doctors was engendering the same frustration as the withholding of information during his father's illness in 1913. The next appointment with Brugsch was on 15 August, but in the event Brugsch would not see his patient alive again. Brecht wrote the lines:

> I do not believe, my dear, that the lion is a lamb.
> I do not believe, my dear, that the lamb is a lion.
> I do not believe, my dear, in magic formulae.
> I do not believe in intelligence beneath a glass
> I do, however, believe that the table has four legs.
> I do, however, believe that the fifth is a cramp
> And if the cramp really grows, my dear,
> A man will slowly die of a heart cramp.[102]

Unlike the poorly briefed doctors in Brugsch's team who cared for Brecht during his absence, Brecht knew that he was dying from his heart complaint. Seemingly in order to protect his confidential relationship with his celebrity patient, Brugsch had not divulged to them everything he knew. They paid Brecht home visits but underesti-mated the severity of his condition, not even admitting him to hospital when during the week of Brugsch's absence his health deteriorated sharply. Amidst the panic and confusion of the days immediately before and after Brecht's death, his doctors covered up their omissions and failures in the official report.

When Professor H. H. Hennemann visited Brecht on 9 August, he was aware that Brecht had heart trouble and a history of prostatitis but knew nothing specifi-cally about the endocarditis. Much later, Hennemann recalled that during his first visit Brecht complained about his cardiac condition, which Hennemann, following an initial examination, considered to be angina pectoris.[103] In fact, by now Brecht was probably showing signs of stenosis of the aorta, a narrowing of the aortic valve, a typical complication of endocarditis which created a sound that could be detected with a stethoscope.[104] Pending Brugsch's return, Hennemann recommended only warmth and dietary therapy, including bearberry leaf tea, a traditional herbal remedy with antibacterial properties for cystitis, which Hennemann had also identified.

When Brecht emerged from his flat on 10 August to attend a rehearsal, Rülicke was 'shocked at how ill Brecht looked. He spoke so quietly that his voice could scarcely be heard on stage. He left the rehearsal early – he did not have the strength to see it through'.[105] The official report states that in the days after 10 August Brecht experienced tiredness and exhaustion: 'He could scarcely leave his bed and had no appetite whatsoever'. Quite breathtakingly, the report maintains that in those days 'no symptoms whatsoever showed which pointed to a heart disease'. Brecht now drafted a letter to Brugsch, completed on 13 August with Kilian, but not sent, in which he announced that he was taking his business elsewhere: 'Nothing has been lost from the gains of the treatment, but no recovery has begun'.[106] Brecht planned to travel by sleeper to Munich on 14 August with Stefan and Kilian, while Weigel and Barbara stayed in Berlin preparing for London.

During the night of 13–14 August, Brecht's condition deteriorated alarmingly.[107] He muttered to Hauptmann in the morning: 'This is a joke – or am I seriously ill?'.[108] He roused himself to order his affairs. He directed Hauptmann to transfer 40,000 kroner to Denmark for Berlau to buy the house they had discussed.[109] He specified a number of other things, which he dictated to Otto Müllereisert, who attested that, although physically weak, Brecht was fully conscious and of sound mind: 'My sole heir is my wife, Helene Weigel. She is not only my sole heir, she also has executive power in carrying out my wishes'.[110] She was to continue with the Berliner Ensemble as long as she felt she could 'maintain its style'. Brecht dictated five wishes: that Barbara should receive the tower on Hauptstrasse in Buckow; Stefan the royalties from US productions; Käthe Reichel the house on the Buckow promenade; Isot Kilian the royalties from the songs accruing from her performances as ShenTe/Shui Ta with the Berliner Ensemble; and that Berlau receive the money for the house, which would pass to Weigel after Berlau's death.

When Brecht's family summoned Brugsch on 14 August, he declined to attend.[111] With his body failing him, Brecht drifted in and out of consciousness.[112] The family summoned a heart specialist, Professor Beyer. Around midday Brecht succumbed to a general collapse and his heart began to race. An electrocardiogram was finally brought which showed the heart racing faster through the afternoon. Meanwhile, his blood pressure had fallen so far it could scarcely be measured. Beyer's attempts to resuscitate Brecht's failing heart were abandoned at 11.30 p.m. when Brecht was declared dead. His last words were: 'Leave me in peace'.[113]

The official report identified the cause of death as a heart attack, which had taken place several days earlier, undetected.[114] Almost certainly, heart failure was the cause. The underlying reason for the deterioration of Brecht's condition was the heart disease which Brecht had carried nearly all his life. His heart condition was vulnerable to complications from the urinary tract infections to which he was extremely prone. Further courses of antibiotics, along with the removal of the septic focus, could have given some respite.[115] However, Brecht's condition was irreversible.

Brecht had promised to Kleinschmidt that he would make things difficult for the living. When Helene Weigel opened the envelope which Brecht had given her in November 1953, she found his carefully choreographed instructions for his funeral.[116] Following a lifetime of mis-diagnoses of his condition and of fears that he might be buried alive, Brecht had some reason to mistrust his doctors' capacity to pronounce upon the demise of his organism. He instructed his wife to ensure that he was, indeed, dead. Weigel engaged the pathologist C. W. Büsing, who severed Brecht's left femoral artery, the extension of the descending aorta which carries blood to the legs.[117] On 17 August at 8.45 a.m. Brecht was buried at the Dorotheenstadt Cemetery in a steel coffin with a headstone bearing just one word, Brecht. Only family and close friends attended, no music was played and not a word was spoken.

Notes

Introduction

1 Brecht's undated letter to his son is in BBA 2869.
2 D 126.
3 Peter Thomson, 'Brecht's Lives', in *The Cambridge Companion to Brecht*, Peter Thomson and Glendyr Sacks (eds) (Cambridge: Cambridge University Press, 1994), pp. 22–39 (38).
4 Max Frisch, *Gesammelte Werke in zeitlicher Folge*, Hans Mayer and Walter Schmitz (eds), 12 vols (Frankfurt am Main: Suhrkamp, 1976), vi. 1, p. 33.
5 BFA 28, 58.
6 MAH xxxii.

Prelude

1 FO 39–43.
2 WB 210.

Chapter 1

1 WB 157.
2 Jürgen Hillesheim, 'Zwischen "Frühlingserwachen", Melancholie und kleinbürgerlicher Enge"', BYB, 35 (2010), 241–67 (257).
3 Hillesheim, BYB 35, 245.
4 Hillesheim, BYB 35, 247.
5 Hillesheim, BYB 35, 248.
6 WB 349.
7 P 107. I have preferred 'My mother carried' to the translator's 'My mother moved' for the German 'trug mich'.
8 C 9.
9 See C 12 and BBA E24/035–036, E24/045–046 and E24/069–070.
10 FO 247.
11 FO 31.
12 Helmut Gier, 'Eine Jugend in Augsburg – ein Augsburger in München', in *der junge brecht*, Helmut Gier and Jürgen Hillesheim (eds) (Würzburg: Königshausen & Neumann, 1996), pp. 13–31 (p.19).
13 FO 30.
14 WB 200.
15 In an undated letter to his son Stefan from the mid–1940s, Brecht sought to dismiss the family talk of Eugen Brecht's epilepsy. (BBA 2865)

16   Hansjörg Kammerer, 'Bertolt Brechts Prägung durch schwäbische Frömmigkeit', *Blätter für württembergische Kirchengeschichte*, 98 (1998), 191–201 (195).
17   WB 192.
18   WB 65–6.
19   BBA E 24/107.
20   C 10.
21   WB 156–7.
22   P 272.
23   HOM 8.
24   HOM 8.
25   BFA 18, 219–20.
26   FO 29.
27   WB 54 and 76.

Chapter 2

1   See Eberhard Rohse, *Der frühe Brecht und die Bibel* (Göttingen: Vandenhoeck & Ruprecht, 1983), p. 32. Further details of Brecht's religious education are drawn from Rohse unless otherwise indicated.
2   BFA 27, 353.
3   C 11.
4   BBA E24/031–032.
5   WB 82–3.
6   See Stephen Parker, 'What was the Cause of Brecht's Death? Towards a Medical History', BYB, 35 (2010), 291–307. See also, Thomas Meissner, 'Zu Unrecht zum Neurotiker gestempelt. Wie Brecht ganz echt am Herzen litt', *CME*, 2011.5, 36–7. Meissner's piece is supported by the cardiologist Erland Erdmann's expert opinion.
7   As we shall see, Brecht uses the image of the storm repeatedly in his poetry and in his diary from his teenage years onwards.
8   BFA 28, 177 and J 324.
9   See Ronald Speirs, 'Die Meisterung von Meister Tod', BYB, 32 (2007), 31–56 and M 2, 664.
10 The condition is also known as St Vitus's dance and chorea minor.
11 Ronald Speirs, ' "Kalt oder heiß – Nur nit lau! Schwarz oder weiß – nur nit grau!" Melancholy and Melodrama in Brecht's Early Writings', BYB, 31 (2006), 43–62 (44).
12 WB 53.
13 BFA 13, 131.
14 BFA 26, 14.
15 JH1 116–17.
16 WB 263.
17 *Hebbels Werke in zehn Teilen*, Theodor Poppe (ed.) (Berlin, Leipzig, Vienna, Stuttgart: Deutsches Verlagshaus Bong & Co., 1908) is in Brecht's library in the Brecht Archive in Berlin. Brecht's annotation is in the margin of volume nine, page 115, line 19.
18 BFA 13, 127.
19 BFA 22, 103.

20 BSW 2, 481.
21 FO 44.
22 WB 54–5.
23 BFA 27, 360.
24 WB 209–10. I have used the translation by Tom Kuhn and Karen Leeder in HOM 121–2.
25 P 13.
26 D 19.
27 Ralf Witzler, 'Des "Dichterlings" Direktor. Zur Person des Chronisten Berthold Friedrich Brecht', in *Brecht und Haindl*, Jürgen Schmid (ed.) (Augsburg: Wissner, 1999), pp. 195–217 (p. 203).
28 WB 136–50.
29 FO 47.
30 C 13.
31 WB 277.
32 C 13.
33 BFA 28, 177.
34 BFA 26, 97.
35 The Kneipp Cure is named after its inventor, the Bavarian priest Sebastian Kneipp (1821–97).
36 FO 49.
37 FO 68.
38 BFA 18, 212.
39 WB 69–70.
40 JH1 152.
41 WB 261–2.
42 L 72.
43 Carl Pietzcker, *'Ich kommandiere mein Herz'. Brechts Herzneurose – ein Schlüssel zu seinem Leben und Werk* (Würzburg: Königshausen und Neumann, 1988), p. 14.
44 L 72. I have preferred 'cardiac shock' to the translator's 'heart seizure' for the German 'Herzschock'.
45 J 324.
46 HE 13. See James Kennaway, *Bad Vibrations: The History of the Idea of Music as a Cause of Disease* (Farnham: Ashgate, 2012), particularly pp. 114–15 for a brief discussion of Brecht's theory of drama in the light of the intoxicating power of musical theatre.
47 FO 75.
48 BFA 26, 242.
49 R 267.
50 FO 75.
51 FO 61.
52 FO 69.
53 FO 105.
54 BFA 26, 49.
55 BFA 30, 105.
56 BFA 21, 266.
57 FO 63.
58 BFA 26, 97.
59 BFA 13, 266.

60 P 15–16.
61 BFA 13, 184.

Chapter 3

1   BFA 26, 98.
2   FO 29 and WB 263.
3   HOM 19.
4   FO 76.
5   BFA 26, 12.
6   FO 63.
7   J 11.
8   WB 57.
9   D 85.
10 FO 168.
11 For Bob Dylan on his beginnings, see the interview with him in Martin Scorsese's film, *No Direction Home*. For the impact of Brecht's songs upon Dylan, see Bob Dylan, *Chronicles* (London: Pocket Books, 2005), pp. 272ff.
12 FO 131.
13 D 36.
14 BFA 13, 184.
15 FO 166.
16 BFA 10, 7–10.
17 BFA 26, 108.
18 P 3.
19 See James K. Lyon, ' "Auch der Baum hat mehrere Theorien": Brecht, Trees, and Humans', BYB 31 (2006), 155–70. I should also like to thank Ronald Speirs for sharing with me his unpublished manuscript ' "Ich gedenke einenen ganzen Zyklus 'Leben' zu schreiben". The ambitions of the young Bertolt Brecht'.
20 BFA 26, 14.
21 BFA 26, 24, 35 and 34.
22 FO 76.
23 BFA 26, 75, 19, 12, 65 and 80.
24 BFA 26, 9 and 24.
25 BSW 2, 789.
26 BFA 26, 9.
27 FO 91–2.
28 FO 130.
29 BFA 26, 28, 9, 25, 19, 49, 42, 45, 25, 21, 51 and 77.
30 CE 11.
31 BFA 26, 77, 79 and 88.
32 BFA 26, 14.
33 M 2, 664.
34 BFA 26, 15, 79, 30, 35, 40–1, 46, 50 and 51–2.
35 BFA 26, 43.
36 D 42.
37 BFA 13, 36.

38 BFA 28, 11–12.
39 BFA 26, 55, BFA 28, 10 and 12.
40 BFA 26, 67.
41 BFA 26, 65.
42 BFA 26, 67 and 97.
43 BFA 26, 15, 52 and 25.
44 BFA 26, 29, 12, 14, 49, 18, 19, 30 and 71.
45 E 111, 74 and 112.
46 BFA 21, 247.
47 BFA 26, 75.
48 BFA 26, 79–80.
49 BFA 26, 15–17.
50 BFA 26, 69.
51 BFA 26, 79 and 85.
52 JH2 43.
53 BFA 19, 10–12.
54 BFA 26, 89.
55 WB 68.
56 BFA 26, 90.
57 BFA 26, 90, 91, 92, 94, 494, 95, 96 and 97.
58 KH 56.
59 BFA 26, 99, 98 and 99.
60 BFA 26, 100.
61 BFA 26, 101–3.
62 WB 155.
63 BFA 26, 101–3.
64 WB 64–5.
65 BFA 28, 153.
66 BFA 26, 75.
67 FO 75.
68 FO 168.
69 BFA 28, 424.
70 BFA 26, 292.

Chapter 4

1 FO 75.
2 WB 216–7.
3 BFA 13, 76.
4 Gerald Feldman, *The Great Disorder: Politics, Economics and Society in the German Inflation, 1914–1924* (New York and Oxford: Oxford University Press, 1993), p. 26.
5 FO 85.
6 HOM 14.
7 FO 85.
8 BFA 21, 7–8.
9 BFA 21, 597.
10 BFA 21, 23–5.

11   BFA 28, 15.
12   BFA 21, 8- 9.
13   BFA 21, 593–4.
14   BFA 13, 71 and 72.
15   BFA 21, 10–12, 12–13, 16 and 28.
16   WB 218.
17   See Jürgen Hillesheim, ' "Spottlust und vielleicht ehrliches Mitleid": Bertolt Brechts "Ah … nous pauvres" ', *German Life and Letters*, 61 (2008), 311–23.
18   BFA 21, 15. I should like to thank Ronald Speirs for pointing out the relevance of Liliencron's work at this juncture.
19   BFA 21, 17–18.
20   BFA 21, 18–19.
21   C 35.
22   BFA 13, 73–4.
23   BFA 13, 82.
24   BFA 13, 80–1 and BFA 13, 87.
25   FO 88.
26   FO 103.
27   BFA 18, 221–2.
28   Eugen Brecht wrote this and the other things summarised below in his postcards to Max Hohenester of 7 August 1915 and 26 August 1915, published in BYB 26 (2001), [x]–2.
29   BFA 28, 18–19.
30   FO 105.
31   See also Jürgen Hillesheim, ' "Frauen des Proletariats! …". Neues über Lilly und Georg Prem', BYB 31 (2006), 31–42 (35).
32   FO 106.
33   FO 100.
34   FO 76.
35   BFA 13, 89.
36   WB 64–5.
37   Jürgen Hillesheim, 'Homoerotische Dimension. Fritz Gehweyer war ein Vertrauter BBs. Dokumente einer Freundschaft', *Augsburger Allgemeine*, 2 February 2013.
38   FO 110.
39   HOM 139.
40   FO 111.
41   FO 100.
42   FO 112.
43   BFA 28, 41.
44   BFA 13, 92–3.
45   BFA 13, 99.
46   BFA 14, 317. I should like to thanks Ronald Speirs for drawing this poem to my attention.
47   Brecht's undated letter to his son is in BBA 2869.
48   P 3–4.

Chapter 5

1 BFA 28, 20–2. An earlier letter from Brecht to Therese Ostheimer was intercepted by her father and destroyed. See Helmut Gier, 'Der Gymnasiast Brecht und seine erste Liebe', *Sinn und Form* 40 (1988.1), 8–15 (10).
2 BFA 18, 221 and 220.
3 JH2 261.
4 BFA 11, 318–19.
5 FO 114–15.
6 BFA 13, 89–90 and 432.
7 JH1 28.
8 The name MacSorley occurs in that tradition. I should like to thank Murray Pittock (University of Glasgow) and Katherine Campbell (University of Edinburgh) for this information.
9 FO 116.
10 HOM 70.
11 BFA 26, 107–9.
12 PB 123.
13 BFA 15, 274.
14 PB 116.
15 Jürgen Hillesheim and Stephen Parker, '"Ebenso hieß das Mädchen nicht andauernd Marie"', *German Life and Letters*, 64 (2011), 536–51 (537).
16 FO 123.
17 WB 236.
18 HOM 16–17.
19 N1 453.
20 FO 133.
21 HOM 43 and 44.
22 HOM 52.
23 I should like to thank Henry Phillips for drawing this to my attention.
24 WB 235–6.
25 HOM 64.
26 FO 135.
27 See Jürgen Hillesheim, 'Fotografiertes "episches Theater": Bertolt Brecht wird zu Mozart', *Acta Mozartiana*, 57 (2010), 167–73.
28 BFA 28, 23.
29 FO 126.
30 Hillesheim/Parker, 537–8.
31 BFA 13, 93.
32 BFA 28, 23–4.
33 BFA 28, 24.
34 P 10–11.
35 BFA 28, 48.
36 BFA 28, 26.
37 WB 24.
38 BBA 461/85–6.
39 PB 139.
40 FO 212.

41   FO 214.
42   FO 212.
43   P 24.
44   PB 139.
45   FO 214.
46   HOM 68–9.
47   P 39.
48   L 22.
49   PB 41–2.
50   L 23–4.
51   L 23.
52   BFA 13, 95.
53   L 22.
54   HOM 44.
55   N1 423.
56   L 26–7.
57   BFA 28, 51 and 54.
58   James K. Lyon, *Bertolt Brecht und Rudyard Kipling* (Frankfurt am Main: Suhrkamp, 1976), p. 26.
59   P 11.
60   L 33, 28 and 31.
61   L 30.
62   L 34.
63   HOM 6. After the Second World War Bezold would become the Bavarian Interior Minister.
64   HOM 7.
65   N1 453.
66   HOM 28.
67   HOM 30.
68   P 13–14.
69   N1 453.
70   N1 453.

Chapter 6

1   J 4.
2   FO 146, 143 and 144.
3   L 24.
4   BFA 28, 27–8.
5   PB 44.
6   L 25.
7   L 24.
8   C 49.
9   L 31.
10   FO 146–7.
11   C 49.
12   L 31.

13 FO 125.
14 L 29, 32, 35 and 39–40.
15 Hillesheim/Parker, 548.
16 L 40.
17 BOT 3.
18 L 30.
19 FO 151–2.
20 FO 151.
21 BFA 21, 35.
22 BOT 3.
23 BFA 11, 307–8.
24 BFA 28, 45.
25 HOM 158.
26 HOM 28.
27 P 17.
28 CP 1, 367.
29 JH2 235–6.
30 L 48. I have preferred 'gloriously hulking body' to the translator's 'splendidly crude human body' for the German 'prächtig ungeschlachten Leib'. Brecht's 'Strindhills' and 'Wedebabies' are plays on the names Strindberg and Wedekind.
31 CP 1, 3.
32 P 15.
33 BFA 1, 55.
34 L 49.
35 L 55. The translator omits the phrase 'It's enough to make you puke!' for the German 'Zum Speien!'.
36 HOM 63.

Chapter 7

1 BAP 52.
2 BFA 28, 47.
3 CP 1, 391.
4 FO 172.
5 WB 262.
6 BFA 13, 118.
7 P 15–16. I have preferred 'outpourings' to the translator's 'utterances' in the title of the poem for the German 'Auslassungen'.
8 BFA 28, 584.
9 L 36.
10 L 36.
11 HOM 36 and 133.
12 L 38. In exchanges with Neher, the image of travel to an exotic place is a cipher for love-making.
13 L 40.
14 Hillesheim/Parker, 538–9.
15 HOM 35.

16   L 49.
17   L 51.
18   PB 38.
19   FO 173.
20   L 52–4.
21   BFA Registerband, 742.
22   L 54.
23   BFA 28, 66.
24   HOM 52–3.
25   MAH 28–9.
26   WB 286.
27   BFA 28, 66.
28   For details of Brecht's service at the Schiller School, see Jürgen Hillesheim, 'Dem Elend der Front so nah', *Augsburger Allgemeine*, 7 December 2012.
29   HW 71 and FO 198.
30   BFA 28, 67 and 68.
31   FO 174.
32   HOM 55, FO 198 and HOM 55.
33   FO 176.
34   FO 177.
35   FO 174.
36   BFA 13, 116, FO 179 and E 33.
37   BFA 28, 69.
38   BFA 28, 68.
39   BFA 28, 75.
40   BFA 1, 176.
41   BFA 28, 44.
42   HOM 54.
43   C 61.
44   WB 309.
45   BAP 52.
46   FO 180–2.
47   J 4.
48   BFA 28, 71.
49   N1 425.
50   FO 189.
51   BFA 28, 77.
52   BFA 28, 81.
53   CP 1, 115.
54   CP 1, 114–15.
55   CP 1, 70–1.
56   N1 458.
57   N1 455.
58   N1 455–6.
59   N1 424.
60   PB 43.
61   KH 69.
62   PB 50.
63   BFA 28, 70.

64 BFA 28, 70.
65 N1 455.
66 BFA 28, 71.
67 HOM 58–9.
68 FO 186.
69 HOM 59.
70 P 176.
71 BFA 28, 592.
72 FO 186.
73 N1 425.
74 BFA 28, 71.
75 PB 46.
76 FO 186.
77 BFA 28, 72.
78 See 'Meine Mutter verlor zeit ihres Lebens kein schlechtes Wort über Brecht. Nina Kuhnert im Gespräch mit Gerhard Gross', *Dreigroschenheft*, 2009.4, 22–6 (24).
79 BBA 437/06.
80 BFA 18, 221.
81 BFA 26, 113.
82 FO 220.
83 The letter from Frl. Müller to Therese Ostheimer is in SBA, Nachlass Therese Ostheimer.
84 .N1 425, 426 and 426–7.
85 N1 428.
86 BFA 28, 74.
87 FO 192–3.
88 BFA 28, 81.
89 BFA 28, 85.
90 BFA 28, 75.
91 N1 431.
92 The letter to Bi from her mother is discussed by Brecht in his letter to Bi of 29 March 1919 (BFA 28, 76).
93 BFA 28, 78.
94 BFA 28, 77.
95 BFA 28, 79.
96 IIOM 70.
97 HOM 61.
98 FO 194.
99 N1 429–31.
100 FO 202.
101 FO 206.
102 BFA 28, 81.
103 FO 203
104 BFA 28, 83.
105 N1 432.
106 BFA 13, 133.
107 N1 432.
108 FO 204–5.
109 N1 458.

110 N1 432.
111 HOM 76.
112 FO 210.
113 N1 433.
114 BFA 28, 83.
115 N1 434.
116 BFA 28, 84.
117 N1 437.
118 BFA 13, 325.
119 BFA 28, 82.
120 BFA 13, 132.
121 WB 324–7.
122 N1 434 and WB 333.
123 N1 435.

Chapter 8

1   N1 438, FO 198 and PB 52.
2   BFA 28, 85.
3   BFA 13, 133.
4   BFA 13, 140 and 144.
5   P 87–8.
6   BFA 26, 125 and BFA 19, 38.
7   HOM 66.
8   P 29.
9   N1 440.
10   P 29.
11   BBA 1504/35.
12   N1 365 and 431.
13   N1 436.
14   N1 437.
15   N1 438 and 440.
16   BFA 28, 85.
17   BFA 28, 85.
18   N1 441.
19   BFA 28, 88.
20   See Karoline Sprenger, ' "Ich war 18 Jahre, Brecht 21½ Jahre alt ...": Paula Banholzer
     über ihren und Brechts Sohn Frank', BYB, 35 (2010), 266–75 (273)
21   BFA 28, 87.
22   BFA 28, 91–2.
23   PB 56–7.
24   BFA 28, 89.
25   BFA 29, 239.
26   BFA 21, 37–9.
27   HOM 61–2.
28   BFA 21, 59.
29   BFA 21, 61.

30 WB 17.
31 BFA 28, 90.
32 BFA 13, 134.
33 FO 28.
34 BFA 28, 90–1.
35 BFA 26, 116.
36 BAP 24–5, BFA 21, 48–9 and BAP 25.
37 BFA 21, 53.
38 N1 442.
39 BFA 21, 57.
40 N1 444.
41 BFA 28, 96.
42 D 11.
43 BFA 28, 99.
44 C 80.
45 D 9.
46 N1 448.
47 BFA 28, 98, 99, 103, 102 and 101.
48 BFA 21, 267, BFA 26, 114–15 and BFA 28, 104–5.
49 Dora Mannheim, 'Aus dem Alltag eines Genies', in *Begegnungen mit Brecht*, Erdmut Wizisla (ed.) (Leipzig: Lehmstedt, 2009), pp. 29–36 (30).
50 FO 243.
51 BFA 28, 101.
52 Hermann Kasack, 'Der Augsburger Bert Brecht', *Schwäbische Landeszeitung*, 3 January 1947.
53 Mannheim, 'Aus dem Alltag eines Genies', p. 31.
54 BFA 28, 106.
55 N1 450.
56 BFA 26, 116.
57 D ix.
58 D xx.
59 WB 348–9.
60 FO 247–8.
61 P 40–1.
62 BFA 13, 169.
63 BFA 26, 117.
64 C 89.
65 WB 350.
66 D xiii and 10.
67 BFA 17, 398.
68 HOM 91ff.
69 BBA 813/43.
70 D 55.
71 BFA 28, 107, 111 and 112.
72 BFA 26, 169, 132 and 137.
73 C 90.
74 D 11.
75 P 52.
76 D 15, 17 and 36 and BFA 13, 178.

77   D 7.
78   D 18. I have preferred 'is said to curse him like a nigger' to the translator's 'is said to have no words too bad for him'. The German is 'und schimpft dort auf ihn anscheinend wie ein Neger'.
79   BFA 10, 143.
80   D 38–9. I have preferred 'nigger' to the translator's 'negro' for the German 'Neger'.
81   BFA 26, 117.
82   P 41–2.
83   D 4, 5 and 10.
84   C 95.
85   D 14 and 28.
86   D 3–5.
87   D 20 and 22.
88   D 4.
89   P 38.
90   D 52, 53 and 54.
91   D 9, P 59 and D 4–5.
92   BFA 26, 118, D 20 and D 4.
93   D 27 and 50, BFA 21, 46–7 and BFA 19, 46.
94   BFA 13, 194 and P 57–8.
95   HOM 83 and BFA 13, 146 and 174.
96   D 54. I have preferred 'niggers' to the translator's 'negroes' for the German 'Neger'.
97   D 50.
98   BFA 21, 44.
99   D 27.
100 BFA 28, 111.
101 D 45. I have preferred 'standardisation' to the translator's 'transformation' for the German 'Uniformierung'.
102 D 49 and 44.
103 D 52.
104 BFA 13, 166 and 177 and BFA 21, 70.
105 D 22.
106 Speirs, BYB, 31, 45.
107 D 10.
108 D 8.
109 D 9.
110 D 36.
111 BFA 26, 580.
112 BFA 23, 23.
113 D 50.
114 D 21.
115 D 42–3.
116 D 52.
117 D 119–20.
118 D 14 and 33–4.
119 BFA 28, 66.
120 HOM 68.
121 BFA 10, 18.
122 BFA 10, 25 and 26.

123 BFA 10, 26. What may be Brecht's earliest use of 'einverstanden', which in the later 1920s became a key term in his thinking about the individual and the collective, is embedded in what is recognisably a variant on the famous Nietzschean paradox of heroic Zarathustran acceptance of the eternal recurrence of the same where the philosophy of will meets the non-resistance of Wu Wei.

124 BFA 13, 157.

125 D 7 and 26.

126 D 8 and 68.

127 D 7.

128 FO 191.

129 D 55 and 47.

130 D 3 and BFA 21, 52.

131 D 42 and 51.

132 PB 59–60.

133 D 60.

134 BFA 21, 76, 77, 84, 79 and 80.

135 BFA 28, 112–3.

136 BFA 21, 97.

137 FO 255 and 256–62.

138 D 87.

Chapter 9

1 BFA 26, 256 and D 62.

2 See Hiltrud Häntzschel, *Brechts Frauen* (Reinbek: Rowohlt, 2002), p. 46.

3 For Zoff's engagement in Augsburg see Karoline Sprenger, 'Der "Bürgerschreck" und die "verkrachte" Opernsängerin', BYB, 34 (2009), 25–42.

4 D 75.

5 For Zoff's engagement in Wiesbaden see Gerhard Müller, 'Bitte, schicke mir die Rezension', *Dreigroschenheft*, 2006.1, 35–45.

6 FO 250 and D 102.

7 PB 157.

8 BFA 13, 180–1.

9 BFA 13, 205.

10 D xiv.

11 D 59–60.

12 C 106.

13 D 61, 65, 63,73, 161 and 65.

14 Brecht is said to have written another script, *Mysteries of a Barber's Shop*, in which Valentin appeared in 1923.

15 D 60 and 60 5.

16 D 61–2.

17 I have preferred 'brat' to the translator's 'packet' for the German 'Knäuel'.

18 D 67.

19 BFA 11, 65.

20 D 68–9.

21 D 69.

22 D 70.
23 D 71.
24 D 72 and 74.
25 PB 165.
26 D 76, 76–7 and 79–85.
27 D 87, 91, 96–7, 111 and 114.
28 D 90, 92, 93 and 94.
29 D 94, 95, 96 and 74.
30 P 69–71.
31 D 97 and 98.
32 D 106.
33 D 106, BFA 28, 118 and D 112.
34 D 96.
35 C 116 and 117, D 105.
36 D 105 and C 120.
37 D 113, 114 and 117.
38 BFA 28, 123.
39 BFA 28, 125 and 132.
40 D 118 and P 72–3.
41 D 131.

Chapter 10

1 D 126, 132 and 113.
2 BFA 21, 99.
3 D 141.
4 D 119 and 147–8.
5 BFA 26, 580.
6 D 101, 133, 135 and 146.
7 D 159.
8 CP 1, 431.
9 BFA 1, 435.
10 CP 1, 178.
11 P 75.
12 BFA 28, 130.
13 D 130 and 133–6.
14 D 137, 137–8 and 140–1.
15 D 142.
16 D 143–4.
17 FO 263.
18 D 143.
19 BFA 28, 136, 139, 138, 145, 140, 141 and 137.
20 BBA 1086/19.
21 D 144.
22 Ernst Bloch, 'In einer Berliner Kutscherkneipe', in *Begegnungen mit Brecht*, p. 38.
23 D 147.
24 BFA 28, 145.

25 L 61–2.
26 BFA 28, 142.
27 D 148 and 98.
28 BFA 13, 229, 237 and 239.
29 D 149, 150, 152 and 150–1.
30 BFA 28, 614 and BFA 26, 582.
31 D 157.
32 HOM 168, AB 14, HOM 169–70 and AB 25.
33 D 150.
34 D 153.
35 BFA 28, 153.
36 D 153.
37 D 157, BFA 28, 153, D 153 and BFA 26, 582.
38 D 157 and FO 263.
39 R 267.
40 Lion Feuchtwanger's letter to Arnold Zweig of 6 May 1958 is in *Lion Feuchtwanger-Arnold Zweig. Briefwechsel 1933–58*, Harold von Hofé (ed.), 2 vols, (Berlin: Aufbau, 1984), ii, p. 387.
41 D 158 and AB 22.
42 BFA 13, 252.
43 In *In the Jungle of Cities* Shlink calls Garga a dung beetle, trying to force him into this role and to dispose of him. I should like to thank Ronald Speirs for this observation.
44 BFA 13, 259.
45 HOM 170–1.
46 PB 166.
47 BBA E 21/102.
48 BFA 28, 154–5 and 155.
49 BFA 26, 563.
50 BFA 28, 158, 159 and 160.
51 AB 36 and 38.
52 D 159.
53 BFA 28, 156, 157 and 159.
54 AB 42 and 43.
55 BSW 2, 787.

Chapter 11

1 P 107 and BFA 13, 242.
2 Ronald Speirs, ' "Of poor B.B." – and others', in *Empedocles' Shoe: Essays on Brecht's Poetry*, Tom Kuhn and Karen Leeder (eds) (London: Methuen, 2002), pp. 41–52 (45).
3 BFA 28, 161.
4 L 65 and AB 50.
5 BFA 28, 164.
6 BFA 28, 164–5.
7 AB 68.
8 BFA 28, 166.

9   BFA 28, 165–6.
10 D 112.
11 BFA 28, 168, 169 and 170.
12 PB 174.
13 HOM 103.
14 PB 75.
15 HOM 104.
16 HOM 166.
17 W 103.
18 BBA 436/41.
19 PB 84.
20 BFA 28, 174 and 176.
21 BBA 436/97–8.
22 C 148.
23 C 181.
24 BAP 65.
25 L 71 and 69.
26 BFA 28, 179.
27 PB 88.
28 BFA 21, 112.
29 BFA 26, 278.
30 BFA 1, 558.
31 L 74 and 76 and BFA 28, 192.
32 BFA 19, 180.
33 W 8.
34 L 76. The Monopteros is a Greek-style temple in the English Garden in Munich.
35 C 156.
36 CP 1, 432.
37 C 157.
38 C 158.
39 AB 141.
40 BFA 13, 273.
41 AB 143 and 144.
42 L 80.
43 KW 41.
44 HHW 54.
45 BWB 194. It is unclear whether Weigel actually sent the letter.
46 BFA 28, 288 and L 99 and 100.
47 PB 93 and 95.
48 BFA 28, 203–4
49 BFA 1, 534.
50 J 17–8.
51 BFA 28, 206–7.
52 L 96.
53 PB 97.
54 CP 1, 454.
55 CP 1, 186.
56 CP 1, 209.
57 C 168.

58 KH 37.
59 L 84–5.
60 CP 1, 454.

Chapter 12

1   BFA 28, 211 and L 97.
2   W 20.
3   KW 42.
4   BFA 28, 216, 13, 294–5 and 26, 288.
5   L 98.
6   KW 68.
7   BFA 13, 285.
8   BFA 28, 647.
9   KH 63–4.
10 L 114.
11 KH 46.
12 KH 74.
13 BFA 28, 220–1.
14 BFA 28, 226.
15 L 100. The translation excludes Brecht's sarcastic 'Monthly salary 550 marks astonishing'.
16 BFA 28, 228.
17 BFA 26, 279.
18 M 1, 498.
19 C 214.
20 L 99.
21 P 114.
22 BFA 28, 232, 234 and 243.
23 BFA 13, 306.
24 BFA 13, 309–10.
25 KH 43.
26 BFA 28, 249 and 251.
27 KH 45.
28 BFA 26, 293.
29 BFA 26, 281–2 and 283.
30 BFA 26, 289, 290 and 292.
31 This section draws on M 1, 494.
32 BFA 26, 283.
33 BFA 26, 282.
34 KH 49.
35 BFA 26, 563–5.
36 P 156.
37 BFA 13, 286–7, 13, 306 and KH 47.
38 KH 35.
39 KH 35.
40 BFA 21, 196 and CP 1, 146 and 140.

41   John Willett, *The Theatre of Erwin Piscator* (New York: Holmes and Meier, 1979), p. 57.
42   KH 50.
43   BOT 14–16.
44   L 122.
45   BFA 28, 249.
46   BFA 26, 682.
47   See RSP 139ff.
48   J 4–5.
49   BFA 21, 256.
50   BAP 35 and 37–8.
51   KH 61 and C 219.
52   BAP 15.
53   BAP 34.
54   BFA 21, 181–2.
55   L 105–6.

Chapter 13

1   BAP 40, 30, 41 and 40.
2   P 143.
3   BAP 47–9.
4   BAP 14.
5   BFA 21, 117.
6   KH 42 and 44.
7   P 113.
8   BAP 64–6.
9   L 110.
10   Erwin Piscator, *The Political Theare*, trans. Hugh Rorrison (London: Methuen, 1980), p. 196.
11   Elias Canetti, *The Torch in My Ear*, trans. Joachim Neugroschel (London: André Deutsch, 1989), p. 272.
12   S 12.
13   BFA 21, 674–5.
14   BOT 20–2.
15   BFA 21, 232.
16   BOT 23.
17   C 228 and BFA 21, 311.
18   J 89.
19   SW 90.
20   BFA 2, 454.
21   CP 2, 175 and 179.
22   BFA 28, 289.
23   SW 99.
24   SW 101.
25   L 111 and BFA 28, 294.
26   L 118 and BFA 28, 311.
27   BFA 28, 296, SW 102, BFA Registerband, 757 and SW 102.

28 A 64.
29 CP 2, 310.
30 CP 2, 98 and 123.
31 CP 2, 145.
32 SW 107.
33 C 247.
34 Brecht recorded the 'Song of the Insufficiency of Human Endeavour' as well as 'Ballad of Mac the Knife' for Orchestrola.
35 BFA 19, 299.
36 CP 2, 113.
37 CP 2, 130. I have preferred 'sexual slavery' to the translator's 'sexual obsession' for 'sexuelle Hörigkeit'.
38 C 251 and 252.
39 BFA 21, 316.
40 C 268–9.
41 Kurt Tucholsky, *Lerne lachen ohne zu weinen* (Berlin: Rowohlt, 1931), p. 346.
42 John Willett, *Brecht in Context* (London: Methuen, 1984), p. 239.

Chapter 14

1 BFA 14, 217.
2 BFA 26, 295.
3 C 255.
4 Canetti, p. 278.
5 Canetti, pp. 272–3.
6 KH 63.
7 C 253.
8 L 120.
9 L 120.
10 BAP 85.
11 J 85.
12 L 119–20.
13 L 122.
14 L 123.
15 BFA 21, 256.
16 BFA 13, 364.
17 BBA 828/02–3. The notes relate to the period from 23 February to early March 1930.
18 N7 464–5.
19 N7 244–7.
20 N7 256.
21 R 267.
22 Eduard Winkler's *Sämmtliche Giftgewächse Deutschlands* (Berlin, 1832) was in his bookcase next to his bed, while his library contains other classic texts, Christoph Wilhelm Hufeland's *Die Kunst das menschliche Leben zu verlängern*, 2 vols (Jena, 1798) and a 1943 edition, *Aus dem Kräuterbuch des Dodonaeus*. (BBB 551 and 431)
23 BBA 363/81 and K 77. In Chalmers's translation, which I use, Schmitt's name is abbreviated as S. Chalmers has Mr Keuner, whereas I use Herr Keuner.

24   BFA 18, 29.
25   BFA 30, 471.
26   K 83.
27   BFA 18, 461.
28   HE 140.
29   RB 51.
30   I should like to thank Dr Zheng Yangwen of the University of Manchester for drawing the term 'tongyi' to my attention.
31   S 25.
32   BOT 26. I have preferred 'shock' to the translator's 'terror' for the German 'Schrecken'. I should like to thank Steve Giles for this suggestion.
33   BOT 28. I have preferred 'agreement' to the translator's 'acquiescence' for the German 'Einverständnis'.
34   L 123 and 123–4.
35   A 97–101.
36   BFA 28, 324 and C 274. Brecht later mended his relationship with Engel.
37   CP 2, 166.
38   BFA 21, 342–3.
39   BFA 3, 401.
40   After Lindbergh had begun to support the Nazis and to oppose US involvement in the war in 1941, Brecht removed his name from the title of the play, which was henceforth known as *The Ocean Flight*.
41   I have preferred 'agreement' to 'consent' in the title for the German 'Einverständnis'.
42   BFR 38–41.
43   C 271.
44   KW 56.
45   L 125.
46   CP 3, 317.
47   L 125.
48   BFR 41.
49   CP 3, 14, 15 and 19.
50   See W 16.
51   CP 3, 10 and 12.
52   CP 3, 325.
53   CP 3, 24, 25, 26, 27 and 34.
54   In the interest of consistency and accuracy, I have preferred 'smallest magnitude' to 'smallest dimension' for the translation of the German 'kleinste Größe' in various texts by Brecht from this time.
55   BFA 10, 518 and 18, 28.
56   CP 3, 35, 38 and 41.
57   T 459–60.
58   N7 500–1.
59   BFA 10, 475. In my choice of 'ground' I follow Villwock and Kölbel, who have 'boden' instead of 'Baum'.
60   BFA 21, 320. In my choice of 'call' I have followed Villwock and Kölbel's 'anrufen' (N7 376), which corrects 'Vorwurf'.
61   See David Roberts, 'Individuum und Kollektiv: Jünger und Brecht zu Ausgang der Weimarer Republik', *Orbis Litterarum*, 41 (1986), 157–75.

Chapter 15

1   John Kenneth Galbraith, *The Great Crash 1929* (Harmondsworth: Penguin, 1960), p. 35.
2   CP 2, 174, 175 and 179.
3   BFA 2, 391 and 392.
4   BFA 2, 465 and 468.
5   BFA 21, 399.
6   BOT 37.
7   BOT 35.
8   BOT 41. I have preferred the Marxist 'base' to the translator's 'roots' for the German 'Basis'.
9   BOT 42.
10   BOT 26.
11   CP 3, 176.
12   W 16.
13   MAH xxxii and BOT 46.
14   CP 3, 47 and 51.
15   CP 3, xiii and C 288.
16   CP 3, 59.
17   CP 3, 87, BFA 24, 96 and BFA 3, 441.
18   C 302.
19   M 1, 362.
20   See Willett, *Brecht in Context*, p. 242.
21   CP 3, 207, 210, 238, 306 and 310.
22   L 453.
23   CP 3, xxv.
24   Loren Kruger, 'Reviving *Saint Joan of the Stockyards*', in *Brecht and the GDR*, Laura Bradley and Karen Leeder (eds) (Rochester, NY: Camden House: 2011), pp. 223–41.
25   Steve Giles, *Bertolt Brecht and Critical Theory: Marxism, Modernity and the Threepenny Lawsuit* (Berne: Lang, 1997), p. 15.
26   CE 22.
27   Giles, p. 13
28   W 1.
29   C 269.
30   W 2.
31   C 284.
32   BC 365.
33   BFA 28, 330.
34   N 7, 332 and 336.
35   P 132.
36   C 303.
37   W 19.
38   W 83–4.
39   W 66 and 90.
40   BC 371.
41   W 91.
42   Georg Lukács, *Record of a Life* (London: Verso, 1983), pp. 91–2.

43   L 127–8. Wizisla dates the letter to the summer of 1931 rather than the autumn of 1930. (W 212)
44   C 338.
45   W 72 and 86.
46   BFA 21, 396. Brecht did not use his later term 'Verfremdung' for alienation, rather 'Entfremdung', the term used by Hegel, who wrote that the familiar was not recognised because it was familiar.
47   BC 377 and W 112–13.
48   BFA 28, 335, L 128 and W 35.
49   BC 368.
50   BSW 2, 477, W 28–30 and J 273.
51   BC 383–4 and BSW 2, 477 and 478.
52   W 36–7.
53   BSW 2, 482.
54   W 36.
55   BAP 85.
56   W 38.
57   BFA 21, 420, W 39 and S 36.
58   BFA 21, 528 and 526, and C 309–10.

Chapter 16

1   P 186 and C 322–3.
2   C 314.
3   R 141.
4   R 130.
5   A 126 and LW 68 and 69.
6   P 191–2.
7   R 143 and 135.
8   BFA 11, 185, BFA 28, 361 and BFA 11, 361.
9   KW 80.
10   C 317.
11   CP 3, 352.
12   Laura Bradley, *Brecht and Political Theatre: The Mother on Stage* (Oxford: Clarendon Press, 2006), p. 40.
13   CP 3, 137.
14   R 145.
15   KKB1 416.
16   R 146.
17   R 147.
18   M 1, 487.
19   L 131–2. Reiber dates the letter dates from at latest March 1932 rather than December 1932, (R 151).
20   BFA 26, 297.
21   BFA 14, 150.
22   BFA 26, 297.
23   See Sabine Koller's review of V. F. Koljazin, *Tairov, Mejerchol'd i Germanija. Piskator,*

Brecht i Rossija (Moscow: Izdatel'stvo 'Gitis', 1998) in *Balagan*, 6, 2000.1, 126–32 (131).
24   C 328.
25   BFA 28, 340.
26   BFA 11, 185.
27   CP 4, ix, x and xi.
28   P 206.
29   BFA 28, 341.
30   P 220 and 221 and C 334.
31   L 130.
32   L 131.
33   BFA 28, 345.
34   BFA 14, 151 and S 36.
35   S 37.
36   C 319.
37   LW 73, 72 and 73.

Chapter 17

1   BAP 117.
2   KW 96.
3   BSW 3, 340.
4   KW 89.
5   AK 743 and 744.
6   BFA 28, 346.
7   C 343 and 345–6.
8   S 38, M 1, 463, C 344, CE 69 and AK 750.
9   P 255–6.
10   KW 97.
11   R 166 and 170.
12   WW1 34.
13   BFA 28, 348–9.
14   BFA 22, 7 and 8.
15   AK 745.
16   BFA 28, 354.
17   C 362 and R 179–80.
18   L 135.
19   A 140.
20   LW 166.
21   C 363.
22   L 132 and C 356.
23   BFA 26, 299.
24   BFA 22, 9.
25   BFA 14, 166.
26   L 134.
27   C 361, C 357, C 361–2, L 137–9 and C 390.
28   WW1 164. Brecht later set up a bank account in Zurich with the Union Bank

of Switzerland under the name of his Stockholm publisher, Lars Schmidt.
(WW1 165)

29 KW 102.
30 SB 68 and R 181.
31 C 369 and 370–1.
32 KW 111.
33 CE 37.
34 C 372–3.
35 C 372.
36 BFA 14, 219.
37 CE 28.
38 BAP 127–9.
39 L 135.
40 L 136.
41 CE 26 and L 141 and 140.
42 BFA 28, 706 and L 147.
43 BFA 28, 702–3 and C 374.
44 See W 59 for Wilhelm Speyer's letter to Benjamin of 29 May 1933 in which Speyer reports Brecht's view.
45 DP 93 and RM 176–7.
46 C 374.
47 SB 70–1 and 94.
48 L 143–4.
49 BSW 2, 784.
50 RM 431.
51 BFA 22, 19.
52 BFA 28, 377 and 383.
53 BFA 28, 375 and 376.
54 KH 162–4.
55 BFA 28, 383, KW 111 and C 380.
56 L 145.
57 I have preferred 'turned into Fascists' to the translator's 'fascised' for the German 'faschisiert'.
58 BFA 28, 706 and C 381.
59 L 152.
60 P 204.
61 BFA 14, 310.
62 C 383.
63 C 385, KW 112.
64 KH 169 and 170.
65 L 149–50, BFA 28, 396, KH 169 and CE 26.
66 C 415 and 394.

Chapter 18

1 P 320. I use Anthony Phelan's translation 'a few words, startled into flight' for 'ein paar Worte, aufgescheucht'. See Phelan's 'Figures of Memory in the "Chroniken"'

in *Brecht's Poetry of Political Exile*, Ronald Speirs (ed.) (Cambridge: Cambridge University Press, 2010), pp. 172–89 (189).

2   L 152–3 and 169.
3   L 165–7.
4   BFA 28, 709 and 397 and C 390.
5   L 167–8.
6   L 165–6 and 170.
7   BFA 28, 402 and SB 107.
8   SB 115.
9   L 170 and SB 119.
10 BFA 11, 371.
11 P 218–20.
12 P 217–8.
13 P 167–74.
14 BFA 11, 382, BFA 28, 730 and C 407.
15 BFA 11, 371 and 372.
16 C 406.
17 BFA 22, 39.
18 L 184.
19 W 9–10 and 55.
20 C 400 and BFA 28, 424.
21 Günther Anders, 'Bertolt Brecht. Geschichten vom Herrn Keuner', *Merkur*, 33 (1979.9), 882–92 (885).
22 BFA 18, 60 and 500.
23 BSW 2, 789 and 790.
24 BSW 2, 789 and BFA 26, 9.
25 BSW 2, 783.
26 W 57 and BSW 2, 785.
27 W 35.
28 L 172 and W 56.
29 BFA 28, 719.
30 L 172.
31 BFA 29, 19.
32 W 59, L 238, L 230, W 59 and BFA 15, 41.
33 L 177.
34 BFA 28, 726.
35 Franz Kafka, 'The Silence of the Sirens', in F. K., *The Complete Short Stories*, Nahum N. Glatzer (ed.) (London: Minerva, 1992), pp. 430–2 (430).
36 BFA 19, 338.
37 BSW 2, 788.
38 BFA 19, 367–75 and BFA 28, 439.
39 BSW 2, 789.
40 BSW 2, 784.
41 BSW 2, 784.
42 BSW 2, 785.
43 BSW 2, 786.
44 BSW 2, 787.
45 W 166.
46 BSW 2, 786 and 787.

47   BFA 28, 439.
48   L 186. I have preferred 'ethmoid bone' to the translator's 'septum' for the German 'Siebbein'.

Chapter 19

1   L 186.
2   BFA 28, 448.
3   BFA 28, 449, 454, 458 and 459.
4   Willett, *Brecht in Context*, p. 61. I should like to thank Henry Phillips for the observation about Artaud.
5   C 416.
6   BFA 28, 451 and FB 1, 28 and 32.
7   C 416.
8   L 192.
9   L 188 and 189 and BFA 28, 464 and 465.
10   Willett, *Brecht in Context*, p. 62.
11   BFA 22, 71–4.
12   BAP 141–2 and 149.
13   Johannes R. Becher, *Briefe 1909–1958*, Rolf Harder (ed.) (Berlin: Aufbau, 1993), p. 194.
14   L 189 and BAP 131–3.
15   L 193 and 194.
16   BFA 18, 66.
17   BOT 76.
18   JW 70.
19   BOT 71 and 76.
20   SB 134–5, L 201, BFA 28, 496 and 497, and L 202.
21   SB 137.
22   See Lars Kleberg, 'Lebendige Impulse für die Kunst', *Balagan. Slavisches Drama, Theater und Kino*, 2 (1996.2), 85–100.
23   SB 135.
24   BFA 22, 915.
25   BFA 22, 151–5.
26   I should like to thank Henry Phillips for this observation.
27   BFA 22, 929.
28   P 249.
29   BR 372.
30   C 444 and L 204.
31   SB 181 and 182.
32   C 477 and L 232.
33   BFA 28, 452–3. Berthold Brecht's letter to Weigel of 16 December 1934 is quoted by Erich Unglaub, 'Topographie und Biographie: Frank Banholzer', in *Brechts Söhne: Topographie, Biographie, Werk*, Wolfgang Conrad et al. (eds) (Frankfurt am Main: Lang, 2008), pp. 11–60 (28–30).
34   Frank Banholzer's letter of 1935 to Weigel is in BBA 0654/139 and Weigel's to Paula Gross of 7 May 1935 in BBA 0654/140.

35 L 203.
36 CE 27.
37 Unglaub, p. 30 and pp. 32–3.
38 BBA 654/145.
39 P 251.
40 L 207.
41 BFA 28, 505 and 506.
42 C 449.
43 BAP 157 and 162.
44 L 206 and 208.
45 DP 186ff.
46 After Münzenberg had publicly opposed Stalinism, he was murdered in a French forest in the autumn of 1940.
47 L 211–12 and BFA 28, 769.
48 SB 172.
49 L 217 and C 459.
50 L 217–19.
51 L 219.
52 HE 102.
53 JKL 8–9.
54 L 220 and JKL 9.
55 L 221 and 222.
56 JKL 9.
57 BFA 14, 312.
58 CE 30.
59 BOT 81, L 223 and BOT 77–81.
60 L 227 and BFA 28, 542.
61 C 471.
62 L 228.
63 BFA 14, 320 and 321.
64 L 242, BFA 22, 280–1 and 285, BFA 29, 39–41, JKL 14 and C 499.
65 BFA 28, 548 and L 233.
66 JW 86.
67 BHB 4, 180.
68 BOT 91–9.
69 I should like to thank Henry Phillips for this observation about Diderot's work.
70 CE 27–8.
71 J 18.
72 KW 119–20.
73 L 247.
74 BOT 101–2.
75 SB 218.

Chapter 20

1 SB 202.
2 David Pike, *Lukács und Brecht* (Tübingen: Niemeyer, 1986), p. 214.

3   DP 211.
4   P 252.
5   DP 311.
6   RM 291, 432 and 416.
7   BFA 28, 501.
8   Willett, *The Theatre of Erwin Piscator*, p. 143.
9   RM 567.
10 L 235.
11 BAP 184 and 185.
12 L 239 and 240.
13 P 288 and 289.
14 P 300. I have changed the translator's order of phrases in the final four lines. I should like to thank Peter Thomson for this suggestion.
15 BFA 12, 377.
16 P 295–6.
17 L 255.
18 Koller, 131.
19 FB 1, 38.
20 C 511.
21 P 290.
22 L 261, SB 227 and L 270.
23 BFA 29, 16, L 241, JKL 255, and L 240 and 257.
24 RH 16 and R 271.
25 L 248 and BFA 29, 583.
26 L 246–7 and 247–8.
27 R 267.
28 BBA 2600, CE 29 and BFA 29, 37.
29 RB 53.
30 C 497.
31 BAP 169–70.
32 BFA 14, 351.
33 Klaus Völker, *Brecht-Chronik* (Munich: dtv, 1984), p. 83.
34 BFA 18, 163–4 and 165.
35 CE 28.
36 L 292.
37 BFA 4 509.
38 L 258, A 150, C 518–9, C 523, BFA 29 and 69ff., and L 277 and 287.
39 CE 29, DP 220 and BFA 29, 64.
40 In an unpublished letter to Erpenbeck of 7 September 1938, Brecht complained that he and Feuchtwanger had not even had an answer to their letter. (BBA 4007)
41 L 271.
42 CE 30.
43 L 264 and 265, and BFA 29, 56.
44 BTP 76–7.
45 BWB 168.
46 R 277 and 279.
47 BFA 14, 383–4.
48 RB 50.
49 L 263.

50 R 275 and BFA 29, 50 and 58.
51 BSW 3, 336.
52 C 521.
53 DP 287.
54 BFA 29, 79.
55 BFA 22, 1038.
56 BFA 22, 1039.
57 J 14 and 15.
58 CE 32.
59 DP 293.
60 DP 292.
61 CE 30.
62 BSW 3, 337.
63 BFA 22, 402 and 403.
64 BBA 4007. Brecht produced other pieces critical of the Moscow camarilla which remained unpublished at the time. See BAP 213–14.
65 BOT 110 and 112.
66 BFA 29, 96.
67 BFA 29, 79.
68 BFA 11, 257ff.
69 BFA 29, 79.
70 L 258 and 280.
71 JAW 7.
72 JAW 1.
73 MD 67.
74 L 286. I have preferred 'exile' to the translator's 'refugee' for the German 'der Emigration'.
75 JAW 183.
76 J 13. I have preferred 'gesture' to the translator's 'gest' for the German 'Geste'.
77 L 280.
78 L 281–2.
79 BWB 173–4. Dudow explained to Brecht in a letter of 6 July 1938 that he refused to discuss Weigel's performance with him because of the way she had bad-mouthed him as director to the other actors. (BBA 2586)
80 CP 4, 161 and 166.
81 JAW 208 and 189.
82 MD 67–8.
83 J 145.
84 J 14.

Chapter 21

1 L 171.
2 BC 571.
3 J 193–4 and 143.
4 BSW 3, 340.

5   BSW 3, 339–40. I have preferred 'if' to the translator's 'when' for the German 'wenn'
     and have re-instated the italics of the German original in 'middling'.
6   W 61.
7   BSW 3, 339, BC 572 and W xx.
8   BSW 3, 337 and 338.
9   See Kevin McDermott and Jeremy Agnew, *The Comintern* (Basingstoke: Macmillan,
     1996), p. 148.
10   BSW 3, 339, 337 and 336.
11   BFA 22, 304 and BSW 3, 338.
12   P 313 and BSW 3, 338 and 336.
13   BFA 18, 173, 169, 170 and 171.
14   BSW 3, 338 and 340.
15   BSW 3, 340.
16   BSW 3, 337.
17   BC 576 and BSW 3, 337.
18   BSW 3, 338.
19   BC 572 and W 63.
20   W 63–4.
21   W xxi.
22   Martin Jay, *The Dialectical Imagination* (Heinemann: London, 1973), p. 202.
23   BC 576.
24   L 290.
25   BFA 29, 109.
26   P 315.
27   T 452.
28   L 291.
29   J 18 and BFA 22, 471.
30   L 279.
31   See Phelan, 'Figures of Memory in the "Chroniken"', in *Brecht's Poetry of Political
     Exile*, pp. 172–89 (189). My section on *Svendborg Poems* is informed by a reading of
     this collection of essays.
32   RB 231.
33   CE 34.
34   Ronald Speirs, 'Introduction', in *Brecht's Poetry of Political Exile*, pp. 1–15 (2).
35   P 244.
36   P 225.
37   P 331.
38   J 16–7.
39   P 320.
40   See the essays in *Brecht's Poetry of Political Exile* by Elizabeth Boa, 'Assuaging the
     Anxiety of Impotence', and Ronald Speirs, 'The Poet in Time'.
41   BFA 12, 81.
42   Phelan, 'Figures of Memory in the "Chroniken"', p. 179.
43   C 585.
44   P 302.
45   P 318–20.
46   T 369ff.
47   P 431.
48   CE 34.

49   M 1, 652.
50   CP 5, 192–3.
51   BSW 3, 336.
52   CP 5, 262.
53   KKB1, 752.
54   J 19.
55   L 294.
56   BFA 29, 121.
57   J 143.
58   CP 5, 193.
59   BFA 5, 31.
60   CP 5, 63.
61   BFA 5, 72–3.
62   Heinrich Detering, *Bertolt Brecht und Laotse* (Göttingen: Wallstein, 2008), p. 57.
63   CP 5, 91.
64   J 19.
65   CP 5, 95.
66   CP 5, 259–60 and 261.
67   BFA 5, 105.
68   BFA 22, 548.
69   CP 5, 262.
70   For this observation, see Hans-Harald Müller, 'Brechts Leben des Galilei: Eine Interpretation zweier Dramen' in *Verwisch die Spuren! A Re-assessment of Bertolt Brecht's Work and Legacy,* Robert Gillett and Godela Weiss-Sussex (eds) (Amsterdam and Atlanta: Rodopi, 2008), pp. 227–38 (235).
71   KKB1 780.
72   J 23.
73   L 295.
74   Erpenbeck's letter to Brecht of 1 April 1939 is in BBA 1396/88.
75   L 315.
76   J 20.
77   P 331.
78   RM 570–1.
79   J 20.
80   L 297.
81   SB 298–9.
82   SB 276, BFA 29, 134 and 145.
83   LW 306.
84   J 25.
85   J 24 and J 128–9.

Chapter 22

1   JKL 23.
2   L 300.
3   J 31.
4   KW 161, C 573 and KW 170.

5   After Berthold Brecht's death, his sister Fanny Fränkel in New York wrote to Kurt
    Weill, asking if he could help in locating Brecht. (BBA 2973)
6   J 43.
7   J 102.
8   CE 35
9   AS 196. Brecht's letter to Lang of 27 August 1939 was intercepted by the FBI. It is not
    in the editions of Brecht's letters.
10 CE 35 and WW1 164.
11 BOT 130–5.
12 MD 6.
13 J 135.
14 J 81–2.
15 J 110.
16 J 135.
17 J 125.
18 P 351.
19 C 583.
20 Evelyn Juers, *House of Exile* (London: Allen Lane, 2008), p. 262.
21 J 31.
22 C 589.
23 J 32, 33, 34, 35, 36, 43 and 37.
24 J 35.
25 CP 5, 109.
26 J 98.
27 CP 5, 111, 135 and 11.
28 T 451–2.
29 CP 5, 154, 118, 157, 165 and 185.
30 J 37.
31 CP 4, 274, 280, 291–2, 293 and 294.
32 J 46.
33 J 48.
34 HPN 291, C 602 and R 309.
35 J 48.
36 C 603.
37 J 40–1.
38 L 321.
39 BFA 29 163.
40 Peter Weiss, *Die Ästhetik des Widerstands*, 3 vols (Frankfurt am Main: Suhrkamp,
    1983), ii, p. 326.
41 J 54.
42 CE 37.
43 HPN 80.
44 JKL 23 and L 322.
45 BBA 3390.
46 P 357, BBA 3390 and HPN 298.
47 C 617 and HPN 301 and 300.
48 JKL 27.
49 J 57.
50 J 70, 71, 86 and 91.

51 L 327.
52 J 71.
53 J 77.
54 L 397.
55 J 88.
56 KW 172–3.
57 J 95 and 80 and HPN 99.
58 KB 137.
59 BFA 29, 186–7, 192 and 194.
60 BFA 18, 187.
61 J 78.
62 J 80, 86 and 89.
63 J 73.
64 J 79 and P 352 and 353.
65 J 79.
66 J 80 and 91.
67 J 93, 95, 97 and 98.
68 CP 6, 221, 220 and 307.
69 J 103, 110 and 129.
70 J 103.
71 C 625.
72 J 110 and 114.
73 C 627.
74 CE 37.
75 J 129.
76 J 142–3.
77 L 330 and C 628.
78 BFA 29, 199.
79 L 333.
80 CP 6, 119.
81 J 137.
82 J 136.
83 I have preferred George Tabori's much cited translation here to Ralph Manheim's 'The womb he crawled from still is going strong'. (CP 6, 211)
84 CE 37.
85 J 143.
86 J 150.
87 J 149.
88 In the official account he was executed the following day, in some others in 1942.
89 Reinhardt Müller, *Menschenfalle Moskau* (Hamburg: Hamburger Edition, 2001), p. 265.
90 KB 149.
91 L 335. No such letters appear to have survived.
92 Hugo Huppert, *Schach dem Doppelganger* (Halle and Leipzig: Mitteldeutscher Verlag, 1979), pp. 29–31.
93 BR 376–9.
94 Lukács, *Record of a Life*, pp. 178–9.
95 J 149, 151, 150 and 151.
96 L 333.
97 J 151.

98   P 364 and 366.
99   P 363.

Chapter 23

1   P 364, JKL 314 and JKL 1.
2   L 366 and 351.
3   JKL 53.
4   J 157 and 159.
5   J 248, 210 and 366.
6   J 159, L 336, J 193 and 198.
7   P 382. I have preferred 'in hope' to the translator's 'hopefully' for the German 'hoffnungvoll'.
8   P 367 and J 257 and 166.
9   L 337 and L 340–1.
10   L 336, JKL 44, L 344 and J 173.
11   J 161 and 174.
12   J 215 and 220.
13   J 168.
14   BFA 29, 223.
15   J 165.
16   Mithridates VI of Pontus regularly took small amounts of poison, thus developing immunity.
17   J 166.
18   J 222.
19   J 159 and W 180–1.
20   P 363.
21   W 183.
22   JKL 37.
23   J 207, 216 and 243–4.
24   P 392 and J 160.
25   L 338. Brecht's comment both echoes Napoleon's as he stood in front of the Egyptian pyramids and alludes to Mann's almost completed tetralogy *Joseph and his Brothers*, part of which is set in ancient Egypt. I would like to thank Ronald Speirs for drawing the latter point to my attention.
26   J 160.
27   KKB1 997, L 339 and J 23.
28   BFA 27, 377.
29   See Erdmut Wizisla, 'Originalität vs. Tuismus. Brechts Verhältnis zu Walter Benjamin und zur Kritischen Theorie', in *Der Philosoph Bertolt Brecht*, Matthias Mayer (ed.) (Würzburg: Königshausen und Neumann, 2011), pp. 199–226 (205).
30   J 192–3 and 220.
31   J 177.
32   L 345, C 663, C 669 and J 209.
33   J 246 and 247.
34   J 185, 186 and 218.

35   P 373.

36   BFA 29, 221, LW 307, BFA 29, 223, and LW 318 and 320.

37   C 675, J 221–2 and LW 322.

38   BFA 29, 227 and LW 328, 329, 332 and 331.

39   J 231, 166, 175 and 307.

40   BFA 23, 23 and J 292.

41   JKL 209.

42   J 195, 194 and 195.

43   L 339 and BFA 29, 216.

44   J 170, 260, 193 and 171.

45   J 239.

46   J 298, CE 42 and C 734.

47   J 243 and J 332.

48   J 171 and J 247.

49   L 352 and J 167 and 197.

50   J 167.

51   J 285.

52   J 223 and HE 71.

53   J 224.

54   HE 14.

55   The undated letter is in BBA 2865.

56   HE 14 and 301.

57   *Composing for the Films* was published by Oxford University Press in 1947 under Eisler's sole authorship.

58   Wizisla, 'Originalität vs. Tuismus', pp. 217–19. The further course of my argument here draws upon Wizisla's findings. Wizisla's principal source is Horkheimer's *Gesammelte Schriften*.

59   J 252 and 255.

60   J 252 and L 338

61   J 250, 251, 229, 331–2 and 333.

62   BFA 29, 229.

63   L 350.

64   C 683.

65   BFA 29, 244 and KB 170.

66   J 241.

67   P 383.

68   J 235, 238, 241, 243, 246, 248–9 and 249.

69   J 253, BFA 29, 249–50, J 272 and L 351.

70   J 251, 257 and 259.

71   KB 171.

72   J 259 and 261.

73   C 700.

74   J 274. I have preferred 'intellectual' to the translator's 'spiritual' for the German 'geistig' and have included 'physically' ['physisch'], which the translator omits.

75   LW 367.

Chapter 24

1   L 366 and J 252.
2   J 253.
3   BTP 101.
4   J 183.
5   J 270 and 279.
6   CP 7, 37.
7   J 273 and C 702.
8   BFA 6, 442.
9   BFA 5, 373.
10 P 392.
11 JKL 36 and 35 and C 700.
12 BFA 29, 257 and C 700.
13 J 276.
14 C 706.
15 J 278 and A 260.
16 S 45.
17 J 278 and JKL 256.
18 J 278.
19 C 702 and JKL 99.
20 WP xi.
21 Tom Kuhn, 'Poetry and Photography: Mastering Reality in the *Kriegsfibel*', in *'Verwisch die Spuren!': Bertolt Brecht's Work and Legacy*, pp. 169–89 (189).
22 WP 75.
23 L 360, J 283 and L 360.
24 BFA 29, 409 and P 418.
25 J 278 and JKL 274.
26 AS 208–10.
27 C 707. The FBI only received permission to monitor the phone in February 1945. (AS 212–13)
28 C 713 and Juers, p. 337.
29 AS 210.
30 KB 183 and C 714.
31 L 367–8.
32 J 261 and P 382.
33 JKL 208.
34 J 291.
35 J 339–40 and 286.
36 C 707.
37 J 279 and 280, L 360 and J 282.
38 CP 7, 138.
39 CP 7, 87.
40 CP 7, 107 and 115.
41 CP 7, 78 and 87.
42 CP 7, 138.
43 Esther Harcourt identified this link. See Jason Zinoman, 'When Bobby Met Bertolt, Times Changed', *New York Times*, 8 October 2006.

44   L 356 and 364.
45   Mann's statement, dated 26 July 1943, appeared in *Freies Deutschland* on
     6 August.
46   Juers, p. 337.
47   J 288 and 288–9.
48   J 290 and 291.
49   Thomas Mann, *Tagebücher 1940–1943*, Peter de Mendelssohn (ed.) (Frankfurt am
     Main: Fischer, 1982), p. 614.
50   J 298 and 294 and L 366.
51   J 306.
52   J 307.
53   C 723.
54   The document is among the Venona papers available on line at http://archive.
     org/stream/1943_31oct_new_german_gov#page/n0/mode/1up (last accessed 25
     September 2012).
55   C 726.
56   J 300.
57   AS 102.
58   Mann, *Tagebücher 1940–1943*, p. 646.
59   AS 103ff.
60   Mann, *Tagebücher 1940–1943*, p. 651 and AS 111.
61   Mann conveyed this in a letter to Agnes E. Meyer of 5 December 1943, which is in
     Thomas Mann, Agnes E. Meyer, *Briefwechsel 1937–1955*, Hans Rudolf Vaget (ed.)
     (Frankfurt am Main: Fischer, 1992), p. 524.
62   AS 112.
63   Mann to Meyer, 5 December 1943 in Thomas Mann, Agnes E. Meyer, *Briefwechsel
     1937–1955*, p. 524.
64   Thomas Mann, *Die Entstehung des Doktor Faustus*, in T. M., *Gesammelte Werke*,
     Hans Bürgin and Peter de Mendelssohn (eds), 12 vols, (Frankfurt am Main: Fischer,
     1960), xi, p. 188.
65   JKL 270.
66   L 374.
67   Mann, *Tagebücher 1940–1943*, p. 655.
68   Thomas Mann, *Briefe 1937–1947*, Erika Mann (ed.) (Frankfurt am Main: Fischer,
     1963), pp. 339–41.
69   BWB 191 and 192.
70   BFA 23, 31.
71   BWB 193.
72   BWB 222.
73   C 727–8 and 734.
74   A 258–9.
75   Ruth Fischer, 'Bert Brecht: Minstrel of the GPU', *Politics*, April 1944, 88–9.
76   J 308.
77   CE 44.
78   L 377 and BFA 29, 329.
79   BFA 29, 326.
80   L 377 and 378.
81   L 377 and C 734–5.
82   AS 196.

83   C 733, 736, 741–2 and 740–1.
84   AS 200–1.
85   J 321 and 324.
86   See Ian Kershaw, *The End: Germany 1944–1945* (London: Penguin Books, 2012).
87   J 309, 311 and 312.
88   CP 7, 146
89   BFA 30, 581.
90   L 530.
91   SS 200.
92   J 322.
93   J 319.
94   CP 7, 165 and 171.
95   T 293 and J 311.
96   CP 7, 212 and 221.
97   CP 7, 228, 232, 234 and 235.
98   CP 7, 236–7.
99   JKL 128.
100 L 384, 385, JKL 238 and L 391.
101 AS 219.
102 J 326.
103 J 324–5.
104 J 327.
105 A funeral director's receipt for $31.50 indicates that Brecht bore the cost of the funeral. (BBA 3044)
106 RB 159.
107 J 327.
108 BWB 194.
109 J 334–5, 336 and 335.
110 T 142.
111 BBA 2865.
112 JKL 95.
113 JKL 133.
114 L 387 and CE 46.
115 J 334.
116 J 344.
117 HE 18–19.
118 L 381.
119 J 309.
120 J 358–9.
121 See Wilfried Loth, *Stalins ungeliebtes Kind: oder warum Moskau die DDR nicht wollte* (Berlin: Rowohlt, 1994).
122 J 345 and 344 and CE 50.
123 C 749.
124 BFA 29, 379. Kebir suggests that the letter is from April 1945, not April 1946. (KB 225)
125 J 347.
126 Loth, p. 42.
127 CE 47.
128 J 348.

Chapter 25

1 JKL 140.
2 L 391 and J 349.
3 JKL 135, L 393, BWB 197 and JKL 136.
4 BWB 200 and J 349.
5 C 760.
6 L 396.
7 C 760 and J 350.
8 J 355.
9 CP 5, 199.
10 J 356.
11 J 355.
12 Loth, pp. 32–3.
13 C 760–2.
14 C 763.
15 C 762.
16 J 355, CE 52–3 and L 398.
17 L 397, CE 52 and AS 228.
18 C 764.
19 L 398.
20 C 765.
21 BFA 15, 160 and J 359.
22 KB 206–8.
23 BFA 29, 375.
24 BWB 203 and 204.
25 BWB 207–9 and 213.
26 BWB 206.
27 L 394 and BFA 29, 359.
28 BWB 206 and JKL 142.
29 BWB 218, JKL 142 and BWB 226.
30 KB 210.
31 L 400 and CE 53.
32 WW1 303 and BFA 29, 374.
33 C 773.
34 J 360–1 and JKL 178.
35 BWB 204.
36 BWB 225 and JKL 179.
37 JKL 180 and 179.
38 JKL 183 and BWB 232.
39 CE 55, BFA 29, 369, CE 60–1 and C 776.
40 C 776 and CE 60.
41 L 413, 424 and 428.
42 CE 63 and CE 61.
43 CE 56.
44 L 403–4 and CE 59, 62 and 63.
45 L 417, 418 and 420.
46 CE 61.

47   JKL 145.
48   L 415 and BWB 228, 229 and 232.
49   JKL 148.
50   C 781, 783 and 784, and CE 64 and 65.
51   C 811.
52   JKL 246.
53   BFA 15, 178.
54   Bob Dylan, *Chronicles*, pp. 272ff.
55   L 426.
56   BFA 29, 725 and BFA 29, 416–17.
57   BFA 29, 409.
58   CE 64 and 65 and C 790.
59   C 785–6.
60   J 362 and 364.
61   JKL 221.
62   AS 206.
63   AS 228.
64   J 372.
65   J 372.

Chapter 26

1   J 272–3.
2   WW1 535.
3   CE 67.
4   J 373.
5   C 802.
6   L 441 and L 440.
7   L 440.
8   BFA 29, 428.
9   WW2 13.
10   Max Frisch, *Tagebuch 1968–1975*, in M. F., *Gesammelte Werke in zeitlicher Folge*, Hans Mayer and Walter Schmitz (eds), 12 vols (Frankfurt am Main: Suhrkamp, 1976), iv, 1, pp. 23.
11   Hans Curjel in *Gespräch auf der Probe*, Clemens Witt (ed.) (Zurich: Sanssouci, 1961), p. 11.
12   BFA 29, 429.
13   AS 206.
14   BFA 29, 437.
15   L 442.
16   CE 72.
17   J 379.
18   CE 70.
19   BBA 3179.
20   WW2 99–101.
21   C 801.
22   CE 73.

23   J 377.

24   J 380 and 377.

25   CP 8, 221.

26   CP 8, 35.

27   CE 79.

28   J 377.

29   CE 75.

30   BFA 29, 452. Kebir reasonably concludes that this letter was written in January 1948, not in the spring or summer. (KB 255)

31   CP 8, 23.

32   J 379.

33   CP 8, 204, 47 and 50.

34   J 379–80.

35   L 419.

36   J 392.

37   AK 750–1.

38   J 382.

39   J 389.

40   AK 752.

41   J 387.

42   See David Barnett, 'Undogmatic Marxism: Brecht Rehearses at the Berliner Ensemble', in *Brecht and the GDR*, Laura Bradley and Karen Leeder (eds) (Rochester: Camden House, 2011), pp. 25–44 (26).

43   Max Frisch, *Tagebuch 1946–1949*, in M. F., *Gesammelte Werke in zeitlicher Folge*, ii, 2, pp. 595.

44   Frisch, *Gesammelte Werke in zeitlicher Folge*, ii, 2, p. 599.

45   L 488.

46   Frisch, *Gesammelte Werke in zeitlicher Folge*, vi, 1, p. 23 and J 391.

47   L 445.

48   CE 74.

49   CE 79.

50   Information at this point is taken from David Bronsen, 'Brechts Rückkehr', *Die Zeit*, 8 November 1968.

51   Loth, p. 147.

52   J 388 and 391.

53   CE 81.

54   BFA 29, 458.

55   J 387.

56   BBA 507/81. The letter is unpublished and undated but is probably from that summer. On 10 August 1948 Berthold Viertel drafted a letter to Brecht, writing that Teo Otto had told him Brecht was better again. Viertel inquired what was wrong with Brecht's kidneys but struck out the question in the next draft. DLA Viertel 69.2031/1.

57   The trip took place before Frisch travelled to Prague on 23 August.

58   Frisch, *Gesammelte Werke in zeitlicher Folge*, vi, 1, pp. 30–1.

59   Frisch, *Gesammelte Werke in zeitlicher Folge*, vi, 1, p. 31.

60   CE 83–4.

61   CE 83.

62   CE 84.

63 HHW 32.
64 J 392.
65 BFA 23, 65–6.
66 J 394.
67 J 401.
68 J 395.
69 J 401.
70 J 399.
71 J 400.
72 J 403.
73 L 457. I have preferred 'not least' to the translator's 'if only because' for the German 'schon da'.
74 J 399–400.
75 J 404.
76 J 409.
77 J 411.
78 J 405.
79 J 409.
80 L 477.
81 J 410.
82 J 404–5.
83 J 412.
84 J 417.
85 BFA 15, 197.
86 CE 85–6.
87 J 415–16.
88 Wolfgang Harich, 'Brief an Anton Ackermann', *Sinn und Form*, 50 (1998.6), 894–90.
89 J 384.
90 J 418.
91 L 455 and 452 .
92 L 454.
93 J 417.
94 L 457–8.
95 Bork, 'Betrifft: a) Volksbühne Berlin b) Projekt "B" (Brecht)', February 1949, LAB C Rep 120 1529.
96 L 459.
97 J 419.
98 J 418.
99 P 415–6.
100 Hauptmann and her old friend Emil Hesse-Burri collaborated on the script for *Mother Courage*, which, because of political and artistic reasons, failed to bear fruit in Brecht's lifetime. It would be a similar story with a film of *Puntila*.
101 L 460.
102 L 466 and BFA 29, 529.
103 Walter Ulbricht's letter to Heinrich Rau of 29 April 1949 is in HWA 161.
104 C 869.
105 L 470.
106 L 459.

107 Barnett cites Trautzsch, 'Protokoll Nr. 91 der Sitzung des Sekretariats des ZK am 2. August 1951', SAPMO BArch DY 30/J IV 2/3/220.

108 L 468–9.

109 CP 8, 111.

110 L 482. I have preferred 'even where' to the translator's 'not those' for the German 'selbst wo'. I have included 'greatly' for 'sehr', which is omitted by the translator.

111 BFA 29, 559.

112 L 473.

113 L 468.

114 L 463.

115 Brecht and Weigel were later required to take German papers as a condition of their membership of the German Academy of Arts.

Chapter 27

1 J 419.

2 P 416.

3 J 421.

4 For details of Hüdepohl's career, see Slatomir Joachim Wenske, *Die Herausbildung urologischer Kliniken in Berlin. Ein Beitrag zur Berliner Medizingeschichte* (PhD, Charité-Universitätsmedizin Berlin, 2008), p. 132.

5 P 443.

6 FB 1, 80.

7 L 483 and P 417.

8 J 422, BSW 3, 339 and BFA 29, 550.

9 BAP 307.

10 J 424.

11 J 424.

12 BFA 29, 570.

13 C 905.

14 BFA Registerband, 740–1.

15 Langhoff's letter to Wandel of 15 March 1950 is in BArch DR 2/8237.

16 Weigel's letter to Wandel of 22 May 1950 is in BArch DR 2/8237.

17 CE 98.

18 Bradley, *Brecht and Political Theatre*, p. 63.

19 Bradley, *Brecht and Political Theatre*, p. 63.

20 J 426.

21 C 907.

22 C 910.

23 L 490–1.

24 See Stephen Parker and Matthew Philpotts, *Sinn und Form: The Anatomy of a Literary Journal* (Berlin and New York: de Gruyter, 2009), p. 30.

25 L 477–8.

26 P 218.

27 Matthias Braun, *Kulturinsel und Machtinstrument: Die Akademie der Künste, die Partei und die Staatssicherheit* (Göttingen: Vandenhoeck und Ruprecht, 2007), p. 35.

28   C 929.

29   C 917.

30   J 428.

31   CE 96.

32   CE 95–6.

33   J 427.

34   BFA 15, 226.

35   Frisch, *Gesammelte Werke in zeitlicher Folge*, vi, 1, p. 34.

36   J 425.

37   J 425.

38   P 312.

39   L 491–2.

40   J 425.

41   Brecht, who called the German teacher 'that most sexless of creatures', had used the castration motif in *Man Equals Man*. (J 419)

42   J 425.

43   J 426.

44   C 918.

45   J 430.

46   J 430.

47   J 431.

48   CE 100.

49   HOM 111.

50   KB 272.

51   J 431.

52   '*Die Regierung ruft die Künstler*', Petra Uhlmann and Sabine Wolf (eds) (Berlin: Henschel, 1993), p. 147.

53   Bradley, *Brecht and Political Theatre*, p. 63.

54   J 429.

55   C 926.

56   P 430.

57   KB 280–1.

58   BFA 30, 47.

59   J 432.

60   BFA 30, 52, RB 219 and BFA 30, 54.

61   It has been claimed that the senior Soviet diplomat Vladimir Semyonov was the author of this and other pieces but this remains unproven.

62   Hans Lauter, 'Der Kampf gegen den Formalismus in der Kunst und Literatur, für eine fortschrittliche deutsche Kultur', in *Die dopplelte Staatsgründung*, Christoph Kleßmann (ed.) (Göttingen: Vandenhoeck & Ruprecht 1986), pp. 527–31 (529).

63   Barnett cites Egon Rentzsch's letter to Walter Kohls of 14 February 1951 in SAPMO BArch DY 30/IV 2/9.06/188.

64   J 433.

65   Joy Calico, *Brecht at the Opera* (Berkeley, Los Angeles and London: University of California Press, 2008), p. 115.

66   BAP 309–17.

67   VO 66–7.

68   C 952.

69 VO 178.
70 VO 80.
71 L 498.
72 VO 173.
73 CE 101.
74 C 955.
75 VO 179.
76 L 499.
77 VO 196.
78 J 433.
79 VO 200.
80 L 500–1.
81 C 960.
82 Calico, p. 127.
83 BFA 30, 75.
84 BFA 23, 138.
85 L 501.

Chapter 28

1   VO 220–1.
2   SAPMO BArch DY 30/IV B 2/2.024/113. Girnus sent his letter of 22 February 1978 to Erich Honecker and Kurt Hager.
3   L 498.
4   BBA 509/70.
5   DD 33–8.
6   'Die Regierung ruft die Künstler', p. 171.
7   J 439.
8   BFA 10, 1279.
9   J 438.
10 J 439.
11 C 977–8.
12 C 978.
13 C 985.
14 J 442.
15 P 439.
16 BAP 317–18.
17 C 983.
18 HW 189.
19 BFA 27, 568.
20 C 985.
21 C 992.
22 J 441.
23 BAP 324.
24 Peter Huchel, *Gesammelte Werke*, Axel Vieregg (ed.), 2 vols (Frankfurt am Main: Suhrkamp, 1984), ii, p. 374.
25 VO 278.

26 BFA 30, 115.

27 Rülicke's letter to Brecht of 21 March 1952 is in BBA 972/113.

28 J 434–5.

29 Barnett cites Trautzsch, 'Protokoll Nr. 91 der Sitzung des Sekretariats des ZK am 2. August 1951', SAPMO BArch DY 30/J IV 2/3/220.

30 J 441–2.

31 BFA 23, 192.

32 J 442.

33 BFA 27, 361 and BFA 23, 192.

34 J 443–4.

35 HE 57.

36 See Deborah Vietor-Engländer, *Faust in der DDR* (Frankfurt am Main: Lang, 1987), p. 141 and p. 142.

37 C 1014 and 1015.

38 Strittmatter was concealing elements of his life in the Third Reich. Strittmatter's wartime service in the 'Ordnungspolizei', which was assigned to the SS, was only discovered in 2008. Strittmatter had applied to join the Waffen SS but had been rejected. See Werner Liersch, 'Erwin Strittmatters unbekannter Krieg', *Frankfurter Allgemeine Sonntagszeitung*, 8 June 2008.

39 BFA 23, 167–8.

40 J 445.

41 C 1025.

42 BFA 15, 263.

43 C 1021 and 1023.

44 BFA 23, 208–9.

45 CE 111.

46 CE 113.

47 CE 114.

48 Braun, *Kulturinsel und Machtinstrument*, pp. 55–7 and 62–3.

49 *Wer war wer in der DDR*, Bernd-Rainer Barth et al. (eds) (Frankfurt am Main: Fischer, 1995), p. 13.

50 J 446.

51 J 446.

52 C 1042.

53 J 452. I have preferred 'I wasn't feeling well' to the translator's 'I wasn't well' for the German 'ich mich nicht wohl befand' and 'Only this feeling of well-being can give you the sense of being on top of things' to the translator's 'all this healthiness gives you a sense of being on top of things' for the German 'Allein dieses Wohlbefinden verleiht die Souveränität'.

54 BFA 23, 220–1.

55 CE 116 and 117.

56 CE 116.

57 JW 2–3.

58 BFA 23, 224–36.

59 C 1047.

60 BAP 324 and BFA 23, 226.

61 J 454.

62 Barnett cites Langhoff 's letter to Weigel of 10 March 1953 in BBA uncatalogued file 'Aktuelles'.

63   C 1049.
64   CE 118. Barnett cites Martin Helas's letter to Egon Rentzsch of 23 March 1953 in SAPMO BArch DY 30/IV 2/9.06/188.
65   For example, on 1 July 1953 Brecht wrote to the Minister of Justice, seeking an explanation for the arrest. (BFA 30, 182)
66   Loth, p. 195.
67   Jochen Staadt, 'Brecht, Weigel und die Staatliche Kunstkommission', in *Die Eroberung der Kultur beginnt*, Jochen Staadt (ed.) (Frankfurt am Main: Lang, 2011), pp. 371–2.
68   BFA 23, 236.
69   JF 53.
70   JF 71.
71   Staadt, p. 375, DD 70 and BFA Registerband, 750.
72   C 1060–1.
73   BWB 283.
74   C 1059.
75   Johanna Rudolph, 'Weitere Bemerkungen zum "Faust"-Problem', *Neues Deutschland* 27 May 1953. Details of Ulbricht's speech are given in Vietor-Engländer, p. 154.
76   BAP 327–31.
77   Loth, p. 203.
78   BFA Registerband, 750 and L 515.
79   BFA 30, 178.
80   L 516.
81   BFA 30, 179. The English translation does not include this ending of Brecht's letter.
82   L 515–16. I have preferred 'impatience' to the translator's 'patience' for the German 'Ungeduld'.
83   BFA 30, 549.
84   DD 78–9 and 79–80.
85   C 1065.
86   BAP 332.
87   BAP 333–4.
88   CE 123.
89   AKB ZAA 323.
90   P 436.
91   L 518–19.
92   BAP 336.
93   CE 122 and BFA 30, 549.
94   L 519.
95   L 528.
96   BWB 296.
97   J 455.
98   BFA 30, 415.
99   J 458.
100 CE 124.
101 C 1070.
102 BWB 299 and L 520–1.
103 BFA 30, 191 and C 1075.
104 BOT 266.
105 P 437–8.

106 CE 122.
107 J 454.
108 BAP 336.
109 P 443.
110 P 440.
111 P 442.
112 P 439.
113 P 442 and T 467.
114 P 445.
115 CP 8, 133.
116 BFA 30, 180.
117 J 455.
118 J 456.
119 CP 8, 248.
120 CP 8, 142 and 138.
121 CP 8, 141.
122 CP 8, 157, 163 and 164.
123 CP 8, 167, 184 and 171.
124 CP 8, 189 and 193.
125 J 456.

Chapter 29

1   BFA 30, 196 and 205.
2   C 1118.
3   CE 125.
4   CE 126.
5   J 456.
6   JF 263.
7   BWB 307.
8   C 1084. The *Puntila* film was completed in Vienna but could not be shown publicly because of contractual disputes.
9   HW 180.
10 L 528.
11 T 3.
12 BWB 311.
13 L 541.
14 J 457–8.
15 J 311.
16 BFA 30, 224.
17 CE 134.
18 BFA 30, 294.
19 CE 128.
20 BWB 312.
21 BWB 315.
22 CE 128.
23 BFA 23, 271 and 272.

24 BWB 320.
25 C 1091.
26 C 1106 and 1122.
27 P 446.
28 Roland Barthes, 'Théâtre Capital', *Observateur*, 8 July 1954.
29 FB 1, 88–9.
30 C 1118 and 1124.
31 BFA 27, 363.
32 P 447.
33 J 457.
34 J 457.
35 J 458.
36 J 458.
37 P 452.
38 BFA 8, 470.
39 BFA 23, 314.
40 CE 138.
41 C 1127.
42 BFA 27, 362.
43 C 1117.
44 BFA 27, 363.
45 BFA 30, 304.
46 C 1131.
47 Thomas Mann, *Tagebücher 1953–1955*, Inge Jens (ed.) (Frankfurt am Main: Fischer, 1995), p. 295.
48 BFA 23, 320. Brecht asked for half the prize to be paid into his Swiss bank account and for the other half in East German marks. (CE 139)
49 L 541.
50 J 460.
51 BAP 340.
52 L 542.
53 BFA 30, 345.
54 BFA 30, 457.
55 HW 170.
56 C 1171.
57 Kenneth Tynan, 'Some Stars from the East', *The Observer*, 26 June 1955.
58 HOM 112.
59 BBA 975/69.
60 BFA 30, 351–2.
61 BFA 30, 316.
62 BFA 30, 618.
63 BFA 30, 349.
64 L 549.
65 FB 1, 94.
66 Frisch, *Gesammelte Werke in zeitlicher Folge*, vi, 1, p. 37.
67 BBA 1826/01–02. In the form in which it has been preserved, Kilian's statement deals only with treatment from August 1955 until 28 March 1956 and breaks off in mid-sentence at the foot of its second page without discussion of treatment from April onwards.

68 BFA 30, 379.

69 L 550.

70 Temperature charts are in BBA 1826/06–07, BBA 2044/11–12 and BBA 0975/89–94.

71 BFA 10, 1295.

72 BFA 30, 408.

73 BBA 1826/02.

74 C 1209.

75 C 1209.

76 L 556 and 557 and BFA 30, 428.

77 C 1227.

78 BAP 341.

79 BFA 15, 300.

80 BBA 1826/02.

81 BBA 1852/28–33.

82 BFA 30, 449.

83 C 1227.

84 BFA 30, 450 and 451.

85 C 1228.

86 P 452. The allusions to Lucretius's *De rerum natura* are explained in BFA 15, 498.

87 Speirs, 'Die Meisterung von Meister Tod', p. 32.

88 Hans Karl Schulten, 'Überlegungen eines Arztes zum Tod von Bertolt Brecht. War die Diagnose Herzinfarkt richtig?', *Dreigroschenheft*, 2000.1, 5–8 (6).

89 SAPMO-BArch, DY 30/IV 2/11/v 43. In addition to the official report, which was signed by Professor Brugsch, Professor Beyer and Dr Krocker, a shorter report was signed by them and Dr Otto Müllereisert. It was published in *Neues Deutschland*.

90 BOT 283.

91 C 1238.

92 C 1242.

93 C 1240.

94 BFA 30, 468.

95 L 561.

96 C 1246.

97 BFA 30, 473.

98 C 1248.

99 BFA 10, 984.

100 C 1250.

101 BFA 30, 476.

102 BFA 15, 306.

103 BBA Z30/139.

104 Schulten, 7.

105 C 1251.

106 BFA 30, 478.

107 SAPMO-BArch, DY 30/IV 2/11/v 43.

108 Hauptmann reported Brecht's words to Suhrkamp, who reported them to Neher in a letter of 21 August 1956. See Wizisla (ed.), *Begegnungen mit Brecht*, p. 374.

109 After Brecht's death Berlau chose to use the money differently. (C 1252)

110 C 1252.

111 BBA Z52/25.

112 SAPMO-BArch, DY 30/IV 2/11/v 43.

113 C 1253.

114 Awareness of the cover-up probably prompted Erich Mielke's hint to his fellow Stasi officers that he knew that the cause of Brecht's death was not a heart attack. See Peter von Becker, 'Erich Mielke und des Dichters Herzschlag', *Der Tagesspiegel*, 15 August 2006.

115 Schulten, 8.

116 BWB 311.

117 BBA 890/56. For the pathologist the left femoral artery also provided ease of access.

Abbreviations

Full bibliographic details are provided in the Bibliography.

A   Ernst Josef Aufricht, *Erzähle, damit du dein Recht erweist*

AB   Arnolt Bronnen, *Tage mit Bertolt Brecht*

ABC   Theodor W. Adorno and Walter Benjamin, *The Complete Correspondence*

AK   Armin Kesser, 'Tagebuchaufzeichnungen über Brecht 1930–1963', *Sinn und Form*

AKB   Akademie der Künste, Berlin

AS   Alexander Stephan, *Im Visier des FBI*

BArch   Bundesarchiv

BAP   Bertolt Brecht, *Brecht on Art and Politics*

BBA   Bertolt-Brecht-Archiv

BBB   *Die Bibliothek Bertolt Brechts*

BC   *The Correspondence of Walter Benjamin*

BFA   Bertolt Brecht, *Werke: Große kommentierte Berliner und Frankfurter Ausgabe*

BFR   Bertolt Brecht, *Brecht on Film and Radio*

BHB   *Brecht Handbuch*

BM   Eric Bentley, *The Brecht Memoir*

BOT   Bertolt Brecht, *Brecht on Theatre*

BR   Bernhard Reich, *Im Wettlauf mit der Zeit*

BSW   Walter Benjamin, *Selected Writings*

DTP   Bertolt Brecht, *Bad Time for Poetry*

BYB   *Brecht Yearbook*

BWB   *'ich lerne: gläser + tassen spülen': Bertolt Brecht-Helene Weigel Briefe*

C   Werner Hecht, *Brecht Chronik 1898–1956*

CE   Werner Hecht, *Brecht Chronik: Ergänzungen*

CP	Bertolt Brecht, *Collected Plays*
D	Bertolt Brecht, *Diaries*
DD	*Zwischen Diskussion und Disziplin: Dokumente zur Geschichte der Akademie der Künste (Ost)*
DLA	Deutsches Literaturarchiv
DP	David Pike, *German Writers in Soviet Exile*
E	*Bertolt Brechts Die Ernte*
FB	Lion Feuchtwanger, *Briefwechsel mit Freunden*
FO	Werner Frisch and K.W. Obermeier, *Brecht in Augsburg*
HE	Hanns Eisler, *Fragen Sie mehr über Brecht*
HHW	Werner Hecht, *Helene Weigel*
HOM	Hanns Otto Münsterer, *The Young Brecht*
HPN	Hans Peter Neureuter, *Brecht in Finnland*
HW	*Brecht As They Knew Him*
HWA	Helene-Weigel-Archiv, Berlin
J	Bertolt Brecht, *Journals*
JAW	John and Ann White, *Bertolt Brecht's Furcht und Elend des Dritten Reiches*
JF	*Die Debatte um Hanns Eislers Johann Faustus*
JH1	Jürgen Hillesheim, *Augsburger Brecht-Lexikon*
JH2	Jürgen Hillesheim, *'Ich muß immer dichten': Zur Ästhetik des jungen Brecht*
JKL	James K. Lyon, *Bertolt Brecht in America*
JW	John White, *Bertolt Brecht's Dramatic Theory*
K	Bertolt Brecht, *Stories of Mr Keuner*
KB	Sabine Kebir, *'Mein Herz liegt neben der Schreibmaschine': Ruth Berlaus Leben*
KH	Sabine Kebir, *'Ich fragte nicht nach meinem Anteil': Elisabeth Hauptmanns Arbeit mit Bertolt Brecht*
KKB1	Karl Korsch, *Briefe 1908–1939*
KKB2	Karl Korsch, *Briefe 1940–1958*
KW	Sabine Kebir, *Helene Weigel: Abstieg in den Ruhm*
LAB	Landesarchiv, Berlin

LW	*Speak Low (When You Speak Love): The Letters of Kurt Weill and Lotte Lenya*
M	Werner Mittenzwei, *Das Leben des Bertolt Brecht*
MAH	Bertolt Brecht, *Rise and Fall of the City of Mahagonny*
MD	Bertolt Brecht, *The Messingkauf Dialogues*
N	Hans Christian Nørregaard, 'Bertolt Brecht und Dänemark', in *Exil in Dänemark*
N1	Bertolt Brecht, *Notizbücher, 1 bis 3*
N7	Bertolt Brecht, *Notizbücher, 24 und 25*
P	Bertolt Brecht, *Poems*
PB	Paula Banholzer, *So viel wie eine Liebe: Der unbekannte Brecht*
R	Hartmut Reiber, *Grüß den Brecht. Das Leben der Margarete Steffin*
RB	*Living for Brecht: The Memoirs of Ruth Berlau*
RM	Reinhard Müller, *Die Säuberung: Moskau 1936*
RSP	Ronald Speirs, *Brecht's Early Plays*
S	Fritz Sternberg, *Der Dichter und die Ratio*
SAPMO BArch	Stiftung Archiv der Parteien und Massenorganisationen der DDR im Bundesarchiv
SB	Margarete Steffin, *Briefe an berühmte Männer*
SBA	Bertolt-Brecht-Forschungsstätte, Staats- und Stadtbibliothek, Augsburg
SS	Bertolt Brecht, *Short Stories*
SW	Jürgen Schebera, *Kurt Weill: An Illustrated Life*
T	Antony Tatlow, *The Mask of Evil*
VO	*Das Verhör in der Oper*
W	Erdmut Wizisla, *Walter Benjamin and Bertolt Brecht*
WB	Walter Brecht, *Unser Leben in Augsburg, damals*
WP	Bertolt Brecht, *War Primer*
WW1	Werner Wüthrich, *Brecht und die Schweiz*
WW2	Werner Wüthrich, *1948: Brechts Zürcher Schicksalsjahr*

Bibliography

Archives

Akademie der Künste, Berlin.
Bertolt-Brecht-Archiv, Berlin.
Bertolt-Brecht-Forschungsstätte, Staats- und Stadtbibliothek, Augsburg.
Bundesarchiv, Berlin.
Deutsches Literaturarchiv, Marbach am Neckar.
Helene-Weigel-Archiv, Berlin.
Landesarchiv, Berlin.
Stiftung Archiv der Parteien und Massenorganisationen der DDR im Bundesarchiv, Berlin.

Brecht's works in German

Brecht, Bertolt, *Werke: Große kommentierte Berliner und Frankfurter Ausgabe*, edited by Werner Hecht, Jan Knopf, Werner Mittenzwei and Klaus-Detlef Müller, 30 vols and Registerband (Berlin and Frankfurt am Main: Aufbau and Suhrkamp, 1988–2000).
—'Postkarten an Max Hohenester: 7. und 26. August 1915', *Brecht Yearbook*, 26 (2001), [x]–2.
—*Notizbücher, 24 und 25, 1927–1930*, edited by Martin Kölbel and Peter Villwock, vol. 7 (Berlin: Suhrkamp, 2010).
—*Notizbücher, 1 bis 3, 1918–1920*, edited by Martin Kölbel and Peter Villwock, vol. 1 (Berlin: Suhrkamp, 2012).
—'*ich lerne: gläser + tassen spülen*': *Bertolt Brecht-Helene Weigel Briefe 1923–1956*, edited by Erdmut Wizisla (Berlin: Suhrkamp, 2012).

Brecht's works in English

Brecht, Bertolt, *Brecht on Theatre*, edited by John Willett (London: Methuen, 1964).
—*The Messingkauf Dialogues*, edited by John Willett (London: Methuen, 1965).
—*Collected Plays*, edited by John Willett, Ralph Manheim and Tom Kuhn, 8 vols (London: Methuen, 1970–).
—*Diaries 1920–22*, translated by John Willett (London: Methuen, 1979).
—*Poems 1913–1956*, edited by John Willett, Ralph Manheim and Erich Fried (London: Eyre Methuen, 1981).
—*Short Stories 1921–1946*, edited by John Willett and Ralph Manheim (London and New York: Methuen, 1983).

—*Bad Time for Poetry: 152 Poems and Songs*, edited by John Willett (London: Methuen, 1991).

—*Journals 1934–1955*, translated by Hugh Rorrison (New York and London: Routledge, 1996).

—*War Primer*, edited by John Willett (London: Libris, 1998).

—*Brecht on Film and Radio*, edited by Marc Silberman (London: Methuen, 2001).

—*Stories of Mr Keuner*, translated by Martin Chalmers (San Francisco: City Light Books, 2001).

—*Brecht on Art and Politics*, edited by Tom Kuhn and Steve Giles (London: Methuen, 2003).

—*Rise and Fall of the City of Mahagonny*, edited by Steve Giles (London: Methuen, 2007).

Works of reference

Adorno, Theodor W. and Walter Benjamin, *The Complete Correspondence 1928–1940*, edited by Henri Lonitz and translated by Nicholas Walker (Cambridge: Polity Press, 1999).

Anders, Günther, 'Bertolt Brecht. Geschichten vom Herrn Keuner', *Merkur*, 33 (1979. 9), 882–92 (885).

Aufricht, Ernst Josef, *Erzähle, damit du dein Recht erweist* (Berlin: Propyläen, 1966).

Banholzer, Paula, *So viel wie eine Liebe: Der unbekannte Brecht* (Munich: Universitas, 1981).

Barnett, David, *A History of The Berliner Ensemble* (Cambridge: Cambridge University Press, 2014, forthcoming).

—'Undogmatic Marxism: Brecht Rehearses at the Berliner Ensemble', in Bradley and Leeder (eds), *Brecht and the GDR*, pp. 25–44.

Barth, Bernd-Rainer, et al. (eds), *Wer war wer in der DDR* (Frankfurt am Main: Fischer, 1995).

Barthes, Roland, 'Théâtre Capital', *Observateur*, 8 July 1954.

Becher, Johannes R., *Briefe 1909–1958*, edited by Rolf Harder (Berlin: Aufbau, 1993).

Becker, Peter von, 'Erich Mielke und des Dichters Herzschlag', *Der Tagesspiegel*, 15 August 2006.

Benjamin, Walter, *Selected Writings*, edited by Michael W. Jennings et al. and translated by Rodney Livingstone et al., 4 vols (Cambridge, MA and London: Belknap Press, 1999).

Bentley, Eric, *The Brecht Memoir* (Manchester: Carcanet, 1989).

Bloch, Ernst, 'In einer Berliner Kutscherkneipe', in Wizisla (ed.), *Begegnungen mit Brecht*, pp. 37–8.

Boa, Elizabeth, 'Assuaging the Anxiety of Impotence', in Speirs (ed.), *Brecht's Poetry of Political Exile*, pp. 153–71.

Bradley, Laura, *Brecht and Political Theatre: The Mother on Stage* (Oxford: Clarendon Press, 2006).

—and Karen Leeder (eds), *Brecht and the GDR* (Rochester: Camden House, 2011).

Braun, Matthias, *Kulturinsel und Machtinstrument: Die Akademie der Künste, die Partei und die Staatssicherheit* (Göttingen: Vandenhoeck und Ruprecht, 2007).

Brecht, Walter, *Unser Leben in Augsburg, damals* (Frankfurt am Main: Insel, 1985).

Bronnen, Arnolt, *Tage mit Bertolt Brecht* (Vienna, Munich and Basel: Desch, 1960).

Bronsen, David, 'Brechts Rückkehr', *Die Zeit*, 8 November 1968.

Bunge, Hanns (ed.), *Die Debatte um Hanns Eislers Johann Faustus* (Berlin: BasisDruck, 1991).

—(ed.), *Living for Brecht: The Memoirs of Ruth Berlau*, translated by Geoffrey Skelton (New York: Fromm, 1987).

Calico, Joy, *Brecht at the Opera* (Berkeley, Los Angeles and London: University of California Press, 2008).

Canetti, Elias, *The Torch in My Ear*, translated by Joachim Neugroschel (London: André Deutsch, 1989).

Detering, Heinrich, *Bertolt Brecht und Laotse* (Göttingen: Wallstein, 2008).

Dieckmann, Friedrich, 'Platz dem Wünschelrutengänger! Harichs Theaterbrief und die Gründung des Berliner Ensembles', *Sinn und Form*, 50 (1998.6), 904–11.

Dietzel, Ulrich, et al. (eds), *Zwischen Diskussion und Disziplin: Dokumente zur Geschichte der Akademie der Künste (Ost) 1945/1950–1993* (Berlin: Henschell, 1997).

Dylan, Bob, *Chronicles* (London: Pocket Books, 2005).

Eisler, Hanns, *Fragen Sie mehr über Brecht: Gespräche mit Hans Bunge* (Darmstadt: Luchterhand, 1986). [Forthcoming as *Ask me more about Brecht: Hanns Eisler in Conversation with Hans Bunge*, edited and translated by Sabine Berendse and Paul Clements.]

Esslin, Martin, *Brecht: A Choice of Evils* (London: Methuen, 1984).

Feldman, Gerald, *The Great Disorder: Politics, Economics and Society in the German Inflation, 1914–1924* (New York and Oxford: Oxford University Press, 1993).

Feuchtwanger, Lion, *Briefwechsel mit Freunden 1933–1958*, edited by Harold von Hofé and Sigrid Washburn, 2 vols (Berlin: Aufbau, 1991).

Fischer, Ruth, 'Bert Brecht: Minstrel of the GPU', *Politics*, April 1944, 88–9.

Frisch, Max, *Gesammelte Werke in zeitlicher Folge*, edited by Hans Mayer and Walter Schmitz, 12 vols (Frankfurt am Main: Suhrkamp, 1976).

Frisch, Werner and K. W. Obermeier, *Brecht in Augsburg* (Berlin and Weimar: Aufbau, 1998).

Fuegi, John, *The Life and Lies of Bertolt Brecht* (London: Harper Collins, 1994).

Galbraith, John Kenneth, *The Great Crash 1929* (Harmondsworth: Penguin, 1960).

Gier, Helmut, 'Der Gymnasiast Brecht und seine erste Liebe', *Sinn und Form*, 40 (1988.1), 8–15.

—'Eine Jugend in Augsburg – ein Augsburger in München', in *der junge brecht*, edited by Helmut Gier and Jürgen Hillesheim (Würzburg: Königshausen & Neumann, 1996), pp. 13–31.

Giles, Steve, *Bertolt Brecht and Critical Theory: Marxism, Modernity and the Threepenny Lawsuit* (Berne: Lang, 1997).

Gillett, Robert and Godela Weiss-Sussex (eds), *Verwisch die Spuren! A Re-assessment of Bertolt Brecht's Work and Legacy* (Amsterdam and Atlanta: Rodopi, 2008).

Häntzschel, Hiltrud, *Brechts Frauen* (Reinbek: Rowohlt, 2002).

Harich, Wolfgang, 'Brief an Anton Ackermann', *Sinn und Form*, 50 (1998.6), 894–90.

Hayman, Ronald, *Brecht: A Biography* (New York: Oxford University Press, 1983).

Hebbel, Friedrich, *Werke in zehn Teilen*, edited by Theodor Poppe (Berlin, Leipzig, Vienna and Stuttgart: Deutsches Verlagshaus Bong & Co, 1908).

Hecht, Werner, *Brecht Chronik 1898–1956* (Frankfurt am Main: Suhrkamp, 1998).

—*Brecht Chronik: Ergänzungen* (Frankfurt am Main: Suhrkamp, 2007).

—*Helene Weigel* (Frankfurt am Main: Suhrkamp, 2000).

Hillesheim, Jürgen and Ute Wolf (eds), *Bertolt Brechts Die Ernte: Die Augsburger Schülerzeitschrift und ihr wichtigster Autor* (Augsburg: Maro Verlag, 1997).

—*Augsburger Brecht-Lexikon* (Würzburg: Königshausen & Neumann, 2000).

—'*Ich muß immer dichten*': *Zur Ästhetik des jungen Brecht* (Würzburg: Königshausen & Neumann, 2005).

—'"Frauen des Proletariats! …"'. Neues über Lilly und Georg Prem', *Brecht Yearbook*, 31 (2006), 31–42.

—'"Spottlust und vielleicht ehrliches Mitleid": Bertolt Brechts "Ah … nous pauvres"', *German Life and Letters*, 61 (2008), 311–23.

—'Zwischen "Frühlingserwachen", Melancholie und kleinbürgerlicher Enge"', *Brecht Yearbook*, 35 (2010), 241–67.

—'Fotografiertes "episches Theater": Bertolt Brecht wird zu Mozart', *Acta Mozartiana*, 57 (2010), 167–73.

—'*Instinktiv lasse ich hier Abstände …*': *Bertolt Brechts vormarxistisches Episches Theater* (Würzburg: Königshausen & Neumann, 2011).

—'Dem Elend der Front so nah', *Augsburger Allgemeine*, 7 December 2012.

—'Homoerotische Dimension. Fritz Gehweyer war ein Vertrauter BBs. Dokumente einer Freundschaft', *Augsburger Allgemeine*, 2 February 2013.

—and Stephen Parker, '"Ebenso hieß das Mädchen nicht andauernd Marie"', *German Life and Letters*, 64 (2011), 536–51.

Hofé, Harold von (ed.), *Lion Feuchtwanger-Arnold Zweig. Briefwechsel 1933–58*, 2 vols (Berlin: Aufbau, 1984).

Huchel, Peter, *Gesammelte Werke*, edited by Axel Vieregg, 2 vols (Frankfurt am Main: Suhrkamp, 1984).

Huppert, Hugo, *Schach dem Doppelgänger* (Halle and Leipzig: Mitteldeutscher Verlag, 1979).

Jacobs, Nicholas and Prudence Ohlsen (eds), *Bertolt Brecht in Great Britain* (London: Irat Services, 1977).

Jay, Martin, *The Dialectical Imagination* (London: Heinemann, 1973).

Juers, Evelyn, *House of Exile* (London: Allen Lane, 2008).

Kafka, Franz, *The Complete Short Stories*, edited by Nahum N. Glatzer (London: Minerva, 1992).

Kammerer, Hansjörg, 'Bertolt Brechts Prägung durch schwäbische Frömmigkeit', *Blätter für württembergische Kirchengeschichte*, 98 (1998), 191–201.

Kasack, Hermann, 'Der Augsburger Bert Brecht', *Schwäbische Landeszeitung*, 3 January 1947.

Kebir, Sabine, '*Ich fragte nicht nach meinem Anteil*': *Elisabeth Hauptmanns Arbeit mit Bertolt Brecht* (Berlin: Aufbau, 2006).

—*Helene Weigel: Abstieg in den Ruhm* (Berlin: Aufbau, 2002).

—'*Mein Herz liegt neben der Schreibmaschine*': *Ruth Berlaus Leben vor, mit und nach Bertolt Brecht* (Algiers: Editions Lalla Moulati, 2006).

Kennaway, James, *Bad Vibrations: The History of the Idea of Music as a Cause of Disease* (Farnham: Ashgate, 2012).

Kershaw, Ian, *The End: Germany 1944–1945* (London: Penguin Books, 2012).

Kesser, Armin, 'Tagebuchaufzeichnungen über Brecht 1930–1963', *Sinn und Form*, 56 (2004.6), 738–59.

Kleberg, Lars, 'Lebendige Impulse für die Kunst', *Balagan. Slavisches Drama, Theater und Kino*, 2 (1996.2), 85–100.

Knopf, Jan, *Bertolt Brecht* (Munich: Hanser, 2012).

—(ed.), *Brecht Handbuch*, 5 vols (Stuttgart: Metzler, 2001).

Koller, Sabine, 'V.F. Koljazin, *Tairov, Mejerchol'd i Germanija. Piskator, Brecht i Rossija*', *Balagan*, 6 (2001.1), 126–32.

Korsch, Karl, *Briefe 1908–1939*, edited by Michael Buckmiller et al. (Amsterdam: Stichting beheer IISG, 2001).

—*Briefe 1940–1958*, edited by Michael Buckmiller et al. (Amsterdam: Stichting beheer IISG, 2001).

Kruger, Loren, 'Reviving *Saint Joan of the Stockyards*', in Bradley and Leeder (eds), *Brecht and the GDR*, pp. 223–41.

Kuhn, Tom, 'Poetry and Photography: Mastering Reality in the *Kriegsfibel*', in Gillett and Weiss-Sussex (eds), *Verwisch die Spuren!*, pp. 169–89.

Kuhn, Tom and Karen Leeder (eds), *Empedocles' Shoe: Essays on Brecht's Poetry* (London: Methuen, 2002).

Kuhnert, Nina, 'Meine Mutter verlor zeit ihres Lebens kein schlechtes Wort über Brecht. Nina Kuhnert im Gespräch mit Gerhard Gross', *Dreigroschenheft*, (2009.4), 22–6.

Lauter, Hans, 'Der Kampf gegen den Formalismus in der Kunst und Literatur, für eine fortschrittliche deutsche Kultur', in *Die dopplelte Staatsgründung*, edited by Christoph Kleßmann (Göttingen: Vandenhoeck & Ruprecht, 1986), pp. 527–31.

Liersch, Werner, 'Erwin Strittmatters unbekannter Krieg', *Frankfurter Allgemeine Sonntagszeitung*, 8 June 2008.

Loth, Wilfried, *Stalins ungeliebtes Kind: oder warum Moskau die DDR nicht wollte* (Berlin: Rowohlt, 1994).

Lucchesi, Joachim (ed.), *Das Verhör in der Oper* (Berlin: BasisDruck, 1993).

Lukács, Georg, *Record of a Life* (London: Verso, 1983).

Lyon, James K., *Bertolt Brecht und Rudyard Kipling* (Frankfurt am Main: Suhrkamp, 1976).

—*Bertolt Brecht in America* (New Jersey: Princeton University Press, 1980).

—'"Auch der Baum hat mehrere Theorien": Brecht, Trees, and Humans', *Brecht Yearbook*, 31 (2006), 155–70.

Lyon, James K. and Agnes E. Meyer, *Briefwechsel 1937–1955*, edited by Hans Rudolf Vaget (Frankfurt am Main: Fischer, 1992).

Mann, Thomas, *Briefe 1937–1947*, edited by Erika Mann (Frankfurt am Main: Fischer, 1963).

—*Gesammelte Werke*, edited by Hans Bürgin and Peter de Mendelssohn, 12 vols (Frankfurt am Main: Fischer, 1960).

—*Tagebücher 1940–1943*, edited by Peter de Mendelssohn (Frankfurt am Main: Fischer, 1982).

—*Tagebücher 1953–1955*, edited by Inge Jens (Frankfurt am Main: Fischer, 1995).

Mannheim, Dora, 'Aus dem Alltag eines Genies', in Wizisla (ed.), *Begegnungen mit Brecht*, pp. 29–36.

McDermott, Kevin and Jeremy Agnew, *The Comintern* (Basingstoke: Macmillan, 1996).

Meissner, Thomas, 'Zu Unrecht zum Neurotiker gestempelt. Wie Brecht ganz echt am Herzen litt', *CME*, (2011.5), 36–7.

Mittenzwei, Werner, *Das Leben des Bertolt Brecht*, 2 vols (Berlin and Weimar: Aufbau, 1988).

Müller, Gerhard, 'Bitte, schicke mir die Rezension', *Dreigroschenheft*, 2006.1, 35–45.

Müller, Hans-Harald, 'Brechts Leben des Galilei: Eine Interpretation zweier Dramen', in Gillett and Weiss-Sussex (eds), *Verwisch die Spuren!*, pp. 227–38.

Müller, Reinhard (ed.), *Die Säuberung: Moskau 1936: Stenogramm einer geschlossenen Parteiversammlung* (Reinbek: Rowohlt, 1991).

—*Menschenfalle Moskau* (Hamburg: Hamburger Edition, 2001).

Münsterer, Hanns Otto, *The Young Brecht*, edited and translated by Tom Kuhn and Karen Leeder (London: Libris, 1992).

Neureuter, Hans Peter, *Brecht in Finnland* (Frankfurt am Main: Suhrkamp, 2007).

Nørregaard, Hans Christian, 'Bertolt Brecht und Dänemark', in *Exil in Dänemark*, edited by Willy Dähnhardt and Birgit S. Nielsen (Boyens & Co: Heide, 1987).

Parker, Stephen, 'What was the Cause of Brecht's Death? Towards a Medical History', *Brecht Yearbook*, 35 (2010), 291–307.

Parker, Stephen and Matthew Philpotts, *Sinn und Form. The Anatomy of a Literary Journal* (Berlin and New York: de Gruyter, 2009).

Phelan, Anthony, 'Figures of Memory in the "Chroniken"' in Speirs (ed.), *Brecht's Poetry of Political Exile*, pp. 172–89.

Pietzcker, Carl, *'Ich kommandiere mein Herz'. Brechts Herzneurose – ein Schlüssel zu seinem Leben und Werk* (Würzburg: Königshausen und Neumann, 1988).

Pike, David, *German Writers in Soviet Exile 1933–1945* (Chapel Hill: The University of North Carolina Press, 1982).

—*Lukács und Brecht* (Tübingen: Niemeyer, 1986).

Piscator, Erwin, *The Political Theare*, translated by Hugh Rorrison (London: Methuen, 1980).

Reiber, Hartmut, *Grüß den Brecht: Das Leben der Margarete Steffin* (Berlin: Eulenspiegel, 2008).

Reich, Bernhard, *Im Wettlauf mit der Zeit* (Berlin: Henschel, 1970).

Roberts, David, 'Individuum und Kollektiv: Jünger und Brecht zu Ausgang der Weimarer Republik', *Orbis Litterarum*, 41 (1986), 157–75.

Rohse, Eberhard, *Der frühe Brecht und die Bibel* (Göttingen: Vandenhoeck & Ruprecht, 1983).

Rudolph, Johanna, 'Weitere Bemerkungen zum "Faust"-Problem', *Neues Deutschland* 27 May 1953.

Schebera, Jürgen, *Hanns Eisler* (Mainz: Schott, 1998).

—*Kurt Weill*, translated by Caroline Murphy (New Haven and London: Yale University Press, 1995).

Scholem, Gershom and Theodor W. Adorno (eds), *The Correspondence of Walter Benjamin 1910–1940*, translated by Manfred R. and Evelyn M. Jacobson (Chicago and London: University of Chicago Press, 1994).

Schulten, Hans Karl, 'Überlegungen eines Arztes zum Tod von Bertolt Brecht. War die Diagnose Herzinfarkt richtig?', *Dreigroschenheft*, 2000.1, 5–8.

Speirs, Ronald, *Brecht's Early Plays* (London: Macmillan, 1982).

—'"Of poor B.B." – and others', in Kuhn and Leeder (eds), *Empedocles' Shoe*, pp. 41–52.

—'"Kalt oder heiß – Nur nit lau! Schwarz oder weiß – nur nit grau!" Melancholy and Melodrama in Brecht's Early Writings', *Brecht Yearbook*, 31 (2006), 43–62.

—'Die Meisterung von Meister Tod', *Brecht Yearbook*, 32 (2007), 31–56.

—(ed.), *Brecht's Poetry of Political Exile* (Cambridge: Cambridge University Press, 2010).

—'The Poet in Time', in Speirs (ed.), *Brecht's Poetry of Political Exile*, pp. 190–210.

Sprenger, Karoline, 'Der "Bürgerschreck" und die "verkrachte" Opernsängerin', *Brecht Yearbook*, 34 (2009), 25–42.

—'"Ich war 18 Jahre, Brecht 21½ Jahre alt ...": Paula Banholzer über ihren und Brechts Sohn Frank', *Brecht Yearbook*, 35 (2010), 266–75.

Staadt, Jochen (ed.), *Die Eroberung der Kultur beginnt* (Frankfurt am Main: Lang, 2011).

Steffin, Margarete, *Briefe an berühmte Männer*, edited by Stefan Hauck (Hamburg: Europäische Verlagsanstalt, 1999).

Stephan, Alexander, *Im Visier des FBI* (Stuttgart: Metzler, 1995).

Sternberg, Fritz, *Der Dichter und die Ratio: Erinnerungen an Bertolt Brecht* (Göttingen: Sachse und Pohl, 1963).

Symonette, Lynne and Kim H. Kowalke (eds), *Speak Low (When You Speak Love): The Letters of Kurt Weill and Lotte Lenya* (London: Hamish Hamilton, 1996).

Tatlow, Antony, *The Mask of Evil* (Berne: Peter Lang, 1977).

Thomsen, Frank, et al., *Ungeheuer Brecht* (Göttingen: Vandenhoeck & Ruprecht, 2006).

Thomson, Peter and Glendyr Sacks (eds), *The Cambridge Companion to Brecht* (Cambridge: Cambridge University Press, 1994).

Tucholsky, Kurt, *Lerne lachen ohne zu weinen* (Berlin: Rowohlt, 1931).

Tynan, Kenneth, 'Some Stars from the East', *The Observer*, 26 June 1955.

Uhlmann, Petra and Sabine Wolf (eds), *'Die Regierung ruft die Künstler'* (Berlin: Henschel, 1993).

Unglaub, Erich, 'Topographie und Biographie: Frank Banholzer', in *Brechts Söhne: Topographie, Biographie, Werk*, edited by Wolfgang Conrad et al. (Frankfurt am Main: Lang, 2008), pp. 11–60.

Vietor-Engländer, Deborah, *Faust in der DDR* (Frankfurt am Main: Lang, 1987).

Völker, Klaus, *Brecht: A Biography* (London: Boyars, 1979).

—*Brecht-Chronik* (Munich: dtv, 1984).

Weiss, Peter, *Die Ästhetik des Widerstands*, 3 vols (Frankfurt am Main: Suhrkamp, 1983).

Wenske, Slatomir Joachim, *Die Herausbildung urologischer Kliniken in Berlin. Ein Beitrag zur Berliner Medizingeschichte* (PhD, Charité-Universitätsmedizin Berlin, 2008).

White, John, *Bertolt Brecht's Dramatic Theory* (Rochester: Camden House, 2004).

White, John and Ann White, *Bertolt Brecht's Furcht und Elend des Dritten Reiches* (Rochester: Camden House, 2010).

Willett, John, *The Theatre of Erwin Piscator* (New York: Holmes and Meier, 1979).

—*Brecht in Context* (London: Methuen, 1984).

Witt, Clemens (ed.), *Gespräch auf der Probe* (Zurich: Sanssouci, 1961).

Witt, Hubert (ed.), *Brecht As They Knew Him*, translated by John Peet (London: Lawrence and Wishart, 1980).

Witzler, Ralf, 'Des "Dichterlings" Direktor. Zur Person des Chronisten Berthold Friedrich Brecht', in *Brecht und Haindl*, edited by Jürgen Schmid (Augsburg: Wissner, 1999), pp. 195–217.

Wizisla, Erdmut (ed.), *Die Bibliothek Bertolt Brechts* (Frankfurt am Main: Suhrkamp, 2007).

—*Walter Benjamin and Bertolt Brecht: The Story of a Friendship*, translated by Christine Shuttleworth (London: Libris, 2009).

—(ed.), *Begegnungen mit Brecht* (Leipzig: Lehmstedt, 2009).

—'Originalität vs. Tuismus. Brechts Verhältnis zu Walter Benjamin und zur Kritischen Theorie', in *Der Philosoph Bertolt Brecht*, edited by Matthias Mayer (Würzburg: Königshausen und Neumann, 2011), pp. 199–226.

Wüthrich, Werner, *Brecht und die Schweiz* (Zurich: Chronos, 2003).

—*1948: Brechts Zürcher Schicksalsjahr* (Zurich: Chronos, 2006).

Zinoman, Jason, 'When Bobby Met Bertolt, Times Changed', *New York Times*, 8 October 2006.

Index